CW00494941

8TH EDITION

WISDEN

CRICKETERS' ALMANACK

AUSTRALIA

—— 2005-06 ——

8TH EDITION

WISDEN

CRICKETERS' ALMANACK

AUSTRALIA

—— 2005-06 ——

Hardie Grant Books

Published in 2005 by
Hardie Grant Books
85 High Street, Prahran, Victoria 3181, Australia
www.hardiegrant.com.au

The Australian edition of the *Wisden Cricketers' Almanack*
published by Hardie Grant Books under licence from
John Wisden & Co Ltd.

Cased edition ISBN 1 74066 327 6
Leather bound edition ISBN 1 74066 381 0
(Limited edition of 100)
ISSN 1441-1725

Typeset by
Prowling Tiger Press
Printed in Australia by Ligare Book Printer

Preface

When we say that *Wisden Australia 2005-06* came together, we mean it literally. John Harms filed his piece on the changing face of Australian cricket grounds from a B&B in rustic Roma in the Queensland outback, Gideon Haigh sent his coverage of the Ashes bits at a time from backpackers' hostels in England. Sambit Bal pushed aside the piles of paperwork in the Cricinfo Asia office in Mumbai to put the finishing touches to his coverage of Australia's groundbreaking tour of India last year.

Matt Price, we like to imagine, filed his reflections on Twenty20 cricket from the parliamentary press gallery in Canberra, or perhaps from the back of press box somewhere as Fremantle lost another game it should have won. Mike Coward's piece arrived from one sweep of the NSW coast, Phil Wilkins' from another, Ken Casellas' wrap of Western Australia's season from among sheafs of football statistics in the ABC box at Subiaco Oval, and Nabila Ahmed put the finishing touches to her pen pictures of the Victorian players while bunking down at an aunt's place in London. Ah, the wonders of technology.

But Jack Brown, secretary of Wallsend Cricket Club and *Wisden*'s man in Newcastle, was taking no chances; he hand-wrote his report and hand-delivered it to the *Wisden Australia* office, making his first visit to Melbourne in 33 years.

The Editor's Notes were largely written in the blear of several long Ashes nights. It was the single major happening in world cricket in the last 12 months, and so forms the heart of this year's publication. *Wisden*'s publishers held its presses for longer than any other publisher would have dared to make sure that our coverage was up to date, comprehensive and meaningful in the best *Wisden* tradition. Gideon Haigh did not miss a minute or an idea.

When it came to putting the rest together, we found ourselves blessed as ever. Charles Davis had trawled exhaustively through the careers of Shane Warne and Muttiah Muralidaran and culled out the best bits for us. Price was titillated by Twenty20, Tim Lane turned on by the role of television in cricket in the new century. Belinda Clark managed to find a little time between a World Cup, an Ashes tour and her new post at the Centre of Excellence to take us into the dressing-room on the day of the World Cup final. John Benaud objected to charges of parochialism among selectors.

Benaud also refers to the fine line selectors must walk, always conscious of the difference between stability and stagnation. *Wisden Australia* walks the same line. Last year, *Wisden* got an exciting makeover. This year, we have consolidated and fortified the strength of the publication. The statistics section has been tightened. The names of all Australian women cricketers have been added to the Births and Deaths section. We flatter ourselves to think that the mix now is pretty damned good.

I am indebted to many people. In no order, they include: Sandy Grant and Mary Small at Hardie Grant, immediate past editor Chris Ryan, *Wisden* UK editor Matthew Engel and his deputy, Hugh Chevallier, *Wisden* jack-of-all-trades Peter English, the copyeditors, the proofreaders, typesetter Lynne Hamilton, master statistician Ross Dundas, long-time friend Tony Heselev, colleagues and honourable rivals Malcolm Conn, Robert Craddock and Martin Blake. All have prodded, encouraged, reproved, suggested, tut-tutted, soothed and saved many days before publication day, but above all inspired at the right moments. Finally, a big thank you to Jasmin Chua who, like me, made her debut at the *Wisden* desk this year, and sailed along with me turning a venture into adventure, and to my sons Nick, Josh and Max, who must have wondered many times who was that grumpy old man locked up in the study again, but were generous enough never to say so.

GREG BAUM
Editor

Contents

1 Comment

2 The Players

3 Records

4 International Summer

5 The Domestic Scene

6 Australians Abroad

7 History and Law

8 The Wisden Review

A STAR IS BORN: Michael Clarke rejoices in his
stunning debut century in Bangalore.
Picture by Hamish Blair, Getty Images.

1

Comment

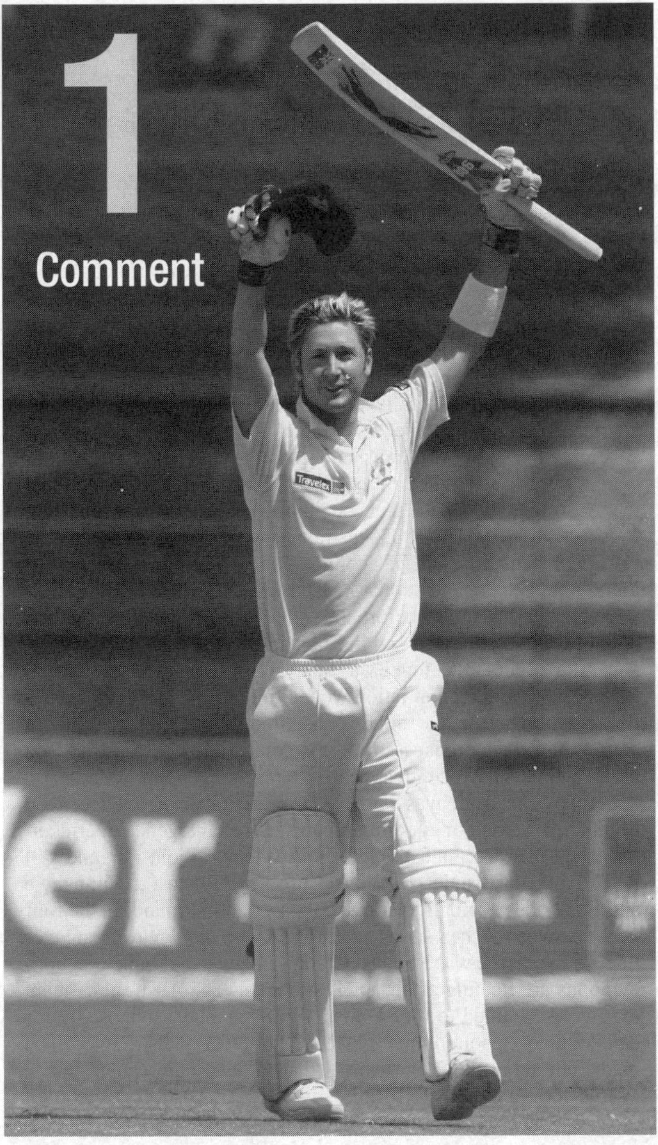

Notes by the Editor

The Australian dynasty, like all empires, has seemed so invulnerable for so long that the idea it might be at an end comes as a shock. Although it took England until the last day of the last Ashes Test to prise Australia's last finger-hold from the urn, the moral margin between the sides was wide. The English in their thousands danced and sang in Trafalgar Square as if this was a kind of liberation. It was at least a watershed. Australia's era of absolute rule was over; the cricket world would be a different place henceforth.

Trends in sport generally are at work months and sometimes years before they become discernible. So it was that defeats for Australia in a series of minor matches at the start of the Ashes tour were written down as aberrations. Looking back, it can be seen that the Australian tide had been beginning to ebb for a while, and England's to flow. The 2005 Australians were conspicuously old by historical standards. Old has connotations of set ways and unwillingness to change, and sooner or later must also mean brittle. Few were prepared to say so before the series, in Australia because they did not want to believe it and in England because they did not dare. Australia's standard defence was that in this highly professional era, fitness, work and rehabilitation were as much a part of a cricketer's living as playing, so age and responsibilities would not weary them as they did their predecessors. This could only ever be true to a point, and Glenn McGrath appeared to reach that point in England.

Perhaps the truth was darker, too dark to acknowledge. Rod Marsh had warned of a looming hiatus in the emergence of cricketing talent in Australia as he left the Academy to join England's in 2002. At the last Under-19 World Cup, Australia lost to Zimbabwe and Bangladesh, and did not make it past the first round. In the four years between Ashes series in England, the only player younger than 25 to emerge was Michael Clarke, and even he found that honeymoons are fleeting affairs in Test cricket. The Australia A team that was scheduled to tour Pakistan in September, supposedly for development, featured three players 30 or older and struggled. The bald truth about the 2005 team is that the two oldest men, Shane Warne and McGrath, are still the two best. As Australia teetered in

England, Marsh criticised the selectors, saying they had not been proactive enough. This was seemingly a contradiction of himself, for how could the selectors have picked boldly from a bare cupboard? But perhaps he was saying that when the time comes to take the plunge, Australia have until recently preferred the darkness of the future, scary but exciting, to the greyness of the past.

Critics began to pop up. Steve Waugh was one, saying Australia appeared to lack their characteristic hunger. Ian Chappell was another saying Australia had been overrated. The identity of the critics was as instructive as the criticisms. Before the series, it had been Englishmen doubting England, or Australians full of hubris. Now it was Australians despairing of Australia, or otherwise wiping egg from their faces.

The world and the tide had turned. In a series played in Homeric temper, England outdid Australia in all facets, batting, bowling, fielding and, uncharacteristically, thinking. They ambushed Australia with reverse-swing, the critical element of surprise. They set unorthodox fields, goading Matthew Hayden at Edgbaston into hitting a first-ball catch to a fieldsman who should not have been there. As a psychological point, this was reminiscent of Merv Hughes' seemingly daft slower ball that skittled Chris Broad, previously a scourge to Australia, at Headingley in 1989 when this journey began. It seemed to say that the old rules no longer applied. England demonstrated a hard-headed preparedness to stretch laws to their limits; this was once Australia's preserve. The run-out of Ricky Ponting at Trent Bridge, pivotal to the series, was effected by a super-sub fieldsman who could not command a regular game for his county. You could even argue that England took the initiative two years previously when they pioneered and began to popularise Twenty20 cricket. They were on the front foot throughout.

England bowled to carefully hatched plans and batted with intent. Australia, excepting Warne and McGrath when he played, bowled an assortment of lines and lengths and batted naively. Suddenly, it was clear how many times in the previous 12 months Gilchrist had spared Australia's blushes with a bit of lower-order swashbuckling. In England, he could not. Ponting's captaincy at times was listless, prompting widespread criticism. But any captain is only as good as his team. When Australia took all before them in the 2003 World Cup under Ponting's still young leadership, he was acclaimed as near to a genius. Now Michael Vaughan had the team, and the player, Andrew Flintoff, about whom Marsh said midway through the Trent Bridge Test: "He's just too good for Australia." In ten years, that had been said only of Lara, Tendulkar and, briefly, Dravid. Flintoff is arguably a greater nemesis than any of them, because he can bowl.

Australia were unlucky with two untimely injuries to McGrath, with a string of doubtful decisions, and to be deceived at the toss at Edgbaston. But they were culpable in the bowling of no-balls – several of which cost wickets – and the dropping of catches, elementary disciplines in which Australia once prided themselves. England were unlucky, too, and on a grander scale; except for a day's rain at Old Trafford, they would have won back the Ashes long before the last Test. Besides, when injuries beset England in Australia on their last tour, this country's judgment was not that they were unlucky, but soft. We cannot have it both ways.

England did hesitate when on historic thresholds. They nearly gave away winning positions at Edgbaston and Trent Bridge, and failed to consummate one at Old Trafford (but the point should not be lost that they had the running of all three matches). It was as if they dared not pinch themselves. Indeed, the whole series was played in an attitude of suspended belief in both hemispheres. In England, commentators called 7 for 450 a "fairly strong position", betraying fears that Australia were giants that must awaken, sooner or later. In Australia, the sentiment was the same. Even as the series slipped away, the consensus of thoughtful people was that England had blown their chances and would soon falter, and the real Australia would assert themselves. It didn't happen. It couldn't happen. Yes, England twice seized up instead of seizing the day, but so did Australia when they came at last within grasping distance of victory over the mighty West Indies in 1992-93. So often, the last step to the overthrow of tyranny is the hardest. When Australia did at last take that step, it did not look back for ten years.

The Ashes series was celebration of cricket. Yearning and anticipation sold out the first four days of every match, England's jubilant emergence sold out the fifth, and the vibrant style even when Australia were on top meant that no one was the least inclined to go home. Cricket has too many endemic problems to herald this as another Golden Age, but at least the game's oldest rivalry had been reborn. The Ashes have their meaning back. The gauntlet is now at Australia's feet. Under Leigh Matthews, the Brisbane Lions won three successive Australian rules premierships, but tumbled down the ladder this year. When asked after a good win if the Lions were back, he replied: "Let me say this; we will never be back." He meant that the only way for a fallen mighty was forward, with a new team, new ideas and new ways. So it is for Australian cricket. The challenge is to rise again immediately. Sixteen years without is at least a baker's dozen too many; ask England.

A fill of the kill

Early this year, I had the parent's unique privilege of watching my teenage son make his first competitive run, scored from a snick to third man, and to witness the joy that lit his face when he realised it was there for the taking. When I asked him later if his hours of practice had prepared him for his moment of truth in the middle, he replied: "No, because out there, I knew I was on nought!" Nought is where everything begins, all of cricket's endlessly renewable dreams, and often enough where they end, too, as he quickly discovered. But that streaky single and all the possibilities that flowed from it affirmed for me that this was a game whose faith was worth keeping.

Whether the rest of the country felt the same was problematic. Soon afterwards, I was at dinner with a group of friends, educated, erudite men who prided themselves on their love and knowledge of sport. This night, over an agreeable red, they debated the relevance of cricket in the contemporary sporting landscape. All professed themselves to be enthusiasts still, but when I asked if anyone had heard the stumps score from the Test in New Zealand, none even had remembered that Australia were playing. Earlier in the summer, Cricket Australia had made plain its concerns about a flattening of interest, particularly marked in one-day cricket, as measured by attendances and television ratings. The aggregate crowd for the two finals of the VB Series was barely 65,000; once, the Melbourne game would have drawn more by itself. The only match that necessitated locking the gates was the Australian debut of Twenty20 in Perth, featuring two state teams in a hastily arranged exhibition. CA was sufficiently taken to move immediately to wedge a mini-series into this summer's program, a haste that was itself an announcement of anxiety about the health of cricket in its more usual forms.

There is some mitigation for the slackening in patronage. Since the summer's cricket schedule was rearranged into blocks, the one-day finals have fallen outside the school holidays, alienating some of the game's natural audience (this is under review). In Melbourne, the spectacularly successful makeover of the Australian Open tennis tournament has piped some of the crowds away across the footbridge to Melbourne Park. In Melbourne and Brisbane, ground reconstruction has temporarily reduced capacity, and made something of a mess of aesthetics. It is possible even that the break-neck speed at which Test cricket is now played has made the limited-overs game redundant (Addressing this in negotiating the new seven-year television rights deal with Kerry Packer's Channel Nine, CA for the first time allowed for live, all-day telecasts into the host city henceforth.)

But it was difficult to shake a sense that an even more fundamental force was at work, and that Australian cricket had become a victim of its own supremacy. Sad to say, even in the finest of games, virtuosity, if it is sustained for too long, grows humdrum, even tedious. *The Age*'s Jonathan Green, a wry observer, wrote that cricket in Australia had become like a series of public executions, and that cricketers in Australia conducted themselves with the grim demeanour of executioners. Meanwhile, Gideon Haigh, author and former editor of *Wisden Australia*, addressing the Como Writers' Festival, observed a growing disconnection between the Test team and the rest of the cricket-loving population. He spoke poignantly of how play had stopped in his park game on the Saturday afternoon when Steve Waugh played his last innings for Australia, and that when he was finally out, a round of applause broke out spontaneously to harmonise with the applause crackling from car radios. But he said it had become harder to feel that this affection was appreciated or reciprocated. To watch Australia now, he said, was to have a sense of watching a club, a damned good club, but as removed and remote from his as one in the next suburb.

Too great expectations

This Australian team, who could at last be said to be all-conquering after winning in India last spring, seem destined to leave a complex legacy. The record will stand for itself; it is comprehensive. They upped the ante in all parts of the game, slathering runs at an unprecedented rate, skittling opponents in a session or two when bowling, marauding in the field. They redefined the roles of opening batsman and wicket-keeper, and had the luxury of reviving lost arts: left-arm wrist-spin, for instance. About the suspicion that they happened to play in an era of overwhelming mediocrity elsewhere in the world, they need neither blush nor apologise, for a team can play only in their own time. But latter-day Australia is also the most exposed team in cricket history, because of exploitative mass media, certainly, but also because of their own eagerness to exploit media in all its forms. Champions and teams of the past were known only by their deed on the field, one dimension of many. Roland Perry's new biography of Keith Miller, *Miller's Luck*, explores some of his all-too-human vices, about which a tactful silence was kept in his time, indeed his lifetime. Shane Warne would not be spared now; the modern star comes to us in blotchy, warty, nose-picking close-up. This familiarity has bred a level of contempt that quickly hardened into schadenfreude when the good times stopped rolling, even momentarily. The Australians have done their own reputation a disservice with periodic episodes of obstreperous behaviour and poor grace; assuredly, that was not Miller's way.

But the modern invincibles leave another problem, created not only out of the best of intentions, but their summary execution. Warne, for instance, has set a new standard for spin bowling, thrilling one generation, but slowly disillusioning the next as they try to reach that mark, inevitably fail and are looked upon askance for it. Stuart MacGill is by any previous estimation a great leg-spinner, yet some regard him sniffily. For the promise he showed as a schoolboy leggie, Cameron White was catapulted into the Victorian captaincy at the age of 21, putting him sometimes in charge of Warne, an absurdity. Unreasonable expectations cut both ways. White made the tour of India last year, said he was happy for the learning experience, but reportedly was disgusted when Nathan Hauritz was preferred to him as the injured Warne's replacement for the last Test. State coaches have told of young players who set out to perform like Gilchrist, only for their games to fall apart when they fail, as they must. Gilchrist, they ought to be reminded, once made a double-century on a Perth pitch that was reported as unfit and dangerous. Gilchrist is like Warne, a freak in his times. It is not that they have left big boots to fill, but that they are several sizes too big and the wrong shape for any successor. Henceforth, Australia's victories will be harder won by merer mortals. It took England 20 years and half a dozen next Bothams to find one. Australia, of course, continues to anoint new Bradmans every decade or so.

Reality bites

The Ashes became the bend in the road of history at which it was
possible to look back and see these things clearly, and look forward,
too. Three features stood out. The first was the lead-up, which was
hopelessly unbalanced, but did include a party-like Twenty20 international in Southampton, from which the whole series seemed to
take its cue. Seemingly, this was the spark that when lit touched not
upon damp and dead wood, as expected, but tinder. Perhaps
Twenty20 will, after all, have a longer life than the yo-yo and
Rubik's cube. Secondly, the Ashes games were keenly and closely
contested, a latter-day novelty. Because human nature is perverse,
the more vulnerable Australians were more appealing, too, even in
their own country. Victory snatched from the jaws of defeat is
always more satisfying than victory by annihilation. (By series'
end, though, Australia's followers might have concluded that while
a little fallibility is an endearing thing, virtuosity still has much to
recommend it.) In Australia, sensible people sat before their television sets through the dead of the night, bleary-eyed and transfixed.
Not only did my blase friends mentioned above now know the
score, but so did a few who historically were unfussed by cricket.
SBS gained record ratings (though we must be wary of the publi-
cists' guiles, for doubtlessly cricket was still well beaten by sundry
American police dramas and *Big Brother*, the most witless television ever made in Australia). In 1987, when a mediocre Australian
team clung by their fingernails to a draw with New Zealand at the
MCG, so to register a rare series win, people clustered around television sets all over the country and cheered to the echo. In 2005, as
Australia crushed New Zealand in two series, few in *The Age* sports
department cared to look up even for a moment from their turf
guides and football previews.

By July, though, the antennae were quivering, the Ashes series was
a long time coming, around two-and-a-half years, in which time anticipation had built up to a feverish pitch. This surely was one of the
keys to its runaway box-office success, at a time of indifference and
apathy. Amid the dross of endless one-day tournaments and mis-
named Test series against minnows that are no test at all, the Ashes
stood out as something worth the wait. It was absence that made all
hearts fonder, and harder; England played as if all of their cricket existence had been a preparation for this moment, giving weight to the
idea that the game runs the risk of going rotten from over playing. The

ICC's answer to every problem is ever more cricket. The latest gimmick is the Super Series, Australia versus The World, which was set down for Sydney and Melbourne in October. Hopefully, it will have lived up to its welter of pre-publicity. We knew that it would be a big event because an endless stream of media releases told us so, in the same way that Melbourne's Commonwealth Games will be a big event and that is official. At the naming of the teams in August, the CA chief executive James Sutherland said this series was "much anticipated". This was between the third and fourth Tests in England, when Australian followers had a mind for only one contest, and it was not the Johnnie Walker Super Series. Perverse as only cricket can be, the Ashes militated against the credibility of the Johnnie Walker series, for by the time it began, Australia was no longer number 1 in the world on any scale except the mathematical. Previously, Rest of the World series were played in fallow summers or in emergencies. This was not one. The moral of the last year of cricket surely is that despite the doomsday prophecies, there is nothing wrong with the game as long as the contest is fair dinkum, the prize is real and the people are not made to feel that they are being kidded. At the time of writing, the Johnnie Walker series promised to be about as real as reality TV.

England's ambush marketing

When England last won the Ashes before their long drought began, they succeeded by Trojan horse theory. England arrived in Australia in the summer of 1986-87 with a team of such benign appearance and so unthreatening in their early endeavours that they were made welcome here. Then, when Australia were least expecting it, England burst out from behind their camouflage of mediocrity and laid waste to the country. For the next decade and a half, England's mediocrity proved to be no disguise, though Australia remained on guard.

But is it possible that this year Australia were ambushed by a kind of reverse Trojan horse? For some time, England have been inviting Australia's warriors into the counties and shires, not singly as was once the case, but two and three at a time. They have made them convivially welcome and pacified and softened and mollycoddled them with easy runs, cheap wickets and fat chéques. Meantime, the English were toughening up their own finest with a regime modelled on the Australian blueprint. Part of it is the less-is-more principle. England put players on central contracts and kept them out of all but a bare minimum of county games to reduce a workload that might blunt their skills and dull their appetites. Australians rushed in to take up the slack.

So was this year's Ashes series the springing of a trap? How was it, for instance, that no one among the Australians appeared to know and anticipate England's newfound facility with reverse-swing? Were they too intent on second helpings? Probably not. Conspiracies are notoriously difficult to orchestrate. County clubs are not known for their appreciation of the bigger picture. They wanted the best players, and if England's were not available, Australians would more than do. But it had the effect of a trap.

Some questions remain. Why were some Australian players allowed to take up county contracts while awaiting the Ashes to begin? Part of the secret of Australia's success in 1989 was the captain Allan Border's calculated decision to put a distance between himself and some in the England team to whom he had been close. Cricket is not war, but it is best played on a war footing. For months before the Ashes began, the papers were full of how Hampshire team-mates Shane Warne and Kevin Pietersen had become bosom buddies. Warne was Australia's best player in the Ashes series, so no one would suggest that he was ever confused about which side he was on. But what about the rest?

It would not be unreasonable now for CA to review the annual migration and set limits. When the West Indians were staffing county clubs, it was said to be no good for English cricket, but it proved fatal for the West Indies, too, in the long run. It will be hard for Australia to argue for a loosening of ties, for the money is extravagantly good, the time is spare and the players are adamant about their rights. None the less, it would not hurt to re-examine the lines.

The toy of six

At times during the Ashes series, cricket looked to be a game that had outgrown its old environs. When Andrew Flintoff was in full flight at the crease, he looked outsized, like a modern man in the doorway of a 17th century English pub or a tourist coach wedged between the hedgerows of a country lane. At Edgbaston, Flintoff hit seven sixes, more in one match than any previous man in Ashes Tests (later matched by Kevin Pietersen at The Oval). He hit them high and low, straight and square, with his eyes open and once with his eyes shut. He was not alone. All summer long, the ball flew to and over the boundary in an endless stream. The aggregate was 682 fours and 50 sixes. For comparison, Sir Donald Bradman hit six sixes in his entire Test career. Bill Ponsford did not hit one, and Keith Miller was not once hit for six, and it was not as if he bowled to contain. This modern fetish for boundaries has had a pronounced effect on scoring rates. A team that does not score at four an over now is stonewalling. On the first day of the Edgbaston Test, England rattled along at five, a headlong charge. Charles Davis, cricket aficionado and statistician, says that the incidence of boundary hitting is at an historical high.

The reasons for this outbreak of gigantism are obvious enough. Already small grounds have been made smaller by the use of boundary ropes, introduced as a safety measure, commandeered now as an advertising vehicle. Better drainage has made for quicker outfields. Pitches generally are better, too. Bats are more powerful, and so are batsmen, since they have been spending their downtime in the gym and the nutritionist's clinic instead of the bar. Improved protective equipment, especially helmets, has emboldened hitters. The effect has been to enlarge batsmen and shrink grounds.

Much has been gained, but something has been lost. Threes, for one thing. The judgment batsmen needed to run them, for another. The element of dare, for a third. Davis noted that batsmen of, say, the Chappell era, appeared to be putting much more effort into their strokeplay for much more meagre result. Batsmen heaved with all their full-blooded might, but only sometimes reached the boundary. It was all some could manage to clear the infielders, let alone the distant fence. Sixes still thrill, but they no longer connote risk. A batsman needs only to hit the ball cleanly to know that it will go all the way. Sometimes he needs only to block it with the full face of his bat to watch it rebound as if spring-loaded down the ground for four. Some, Hayden for instance, can and have mishit balls for six forward of the wicket. Timing helps, but is no longer at the heart of the craft. Commentators used to speculate on a ball in flight and whether or not it had the carry. It was a delicious part of the game. Now, a commentator is likely to find himself wondering how the batsman's mere tap had somehow flown the boundary rope.

Golf has had a long-running debate about technology and tennis has one periodically, but cricket has never opened one. There was the comical contretemps when Dennis Lillee tried to use a custom-made aluminium bat in Tests, and a flare-up when Dean Jones questioned the width of the West Indian Keith Arthurton's bat, which was subsequently found to exceed regulations. These were fleeting moments. There were stirrings of an issue developing before the Ashes series this year when Lord's demanded to see Ponting's extravagantly made-up bat, but concluded that its carbon backing broke no rules.

Cricket now needs this debate. You cannot outlaw technology, as golf has found; too many have too much invested in it. Nor can you deny progress. No one is advocating a return to the matchsticks of the Bradman era. But cricket is obliged to maintain the delicate balance between bat and ball. Here is one idea to explore: Dispense with boundary ropes. If safety is the issue, pad the fences. Allow fieldsmen to take catches while leaning on or holding onto a fence. Batsmen must not be deterred from taking on the boundaries, but they must be made to take their chances.

Heavy losses lead to new directions

After a year of crossroads for Australian cricket, a new map is in order. The men's team won in India, ticking off the final box on the chart of world dominance, but a year later came to their Waterloo in – of course – England. Likewise, the women's team won the World Cup, but in this same calendar year surrendered their Ashes. These were big, hard falls. In the domestic season, Tasmania won a title, a rare feat put in sombre perspective soon afterwards when Scott Mason, an opener and popular squad member, died suddenly of a heart attack. The lesson, I suppose, is to know and cherish what you have while you have it.

The television contract with Nine was renewed, and so was the memorandum of understanding with the Australian Cricketers' Association. Neither was straightforward. Nine seized on a lull in ratings and attendances to advance and win an argument to put on live telecasts in host cities, which was previously out of the question. The negotiations with the players' association were even more fraught. CA argued for the abandonment of the principle whereby the players received a percentage of all cricket income, and offered a flat amount instead. The cricketers objected. Tensions ran high for a time, though not as publicly as when the ACA was first formed in 1997. But when the dust cleared, the players had kept their hard-won percentage. This was a parting gift from Tim May, the one-time Test bowler, who is off to the United States with his family but will maintain his post with FICA, the international players' body. May made a distinct place for himself in Australian cricket history, as an aggressive and aggrieved off-spinner, as the man who with Craig McDermott took Australia to within a single run of a series victory over the then invincible West Indies in Adelaide in 1993, and finally as a pioneer of the rights of players. One of my favourite memories of May says much about him. It was on a plane returning to Australia after a Pakistan tour in 1994. Mid-flight and unannounced, May bailed up Trent Bouts, then cricket writer for The Australian with this greeting: "I'm going to play cricketer for a moment." He then tore strips off Bouts for having written unflatter-ingly of May's efficacy in the field. When finished, he said: "Now I'm taking off my cricketer's hat. How did you enjoy the tour?" There was a sequel. After a slipshod performance in the field one day during that Australian summer, he crossed paths with Bouts and muttered: "You were right!" May's approach to cricket and life was angry, combative and run with a sense of the injustice of it all, but it was also tempered by dry humour, rough grace and an obvious pas-sion for what he was doing, and by this alchemy he made a vital and lasting contribution.

Football mad, cricket sad

Cricket's biggest fight ought not to be with itself, but against the ogres of winter. Football is threatening to monster the game, stealing seasons, players and grounds. I have heard tales from all over, but know Melbourne best. It is possible to name a full XI of cricketers who were picked for Victoria's Under-17 team and were thought good enough at least to have a chance of state selection, but who were spirited away by Australian football instead, and will never play cricket again; their football clubs will not let them. Not least among them are Jonathon Brown, Luke Hodge, Jimmy Bartel, Luke Ball and Brett Deledio, all well known to football fans, and it is said that Nathan Ablett, the diffident younger son of the great Gary, was also a sublime cricketer.

The battle for hearts and minds is unequal. Football offers the multi-gifted youth four or five times as many professional places, and up to ten times the earning capacity. Once it was possible to play both, but the seasons overlap now by months, the commitment to either is heavy and the football clubs like to wrap their stars in cotton wool between winters. Of course, Australian football cannot offer international representation, and rugby league can only in mock form. But only one or two of each new wave of cricketers stands to have a lasting career in the Test team anyway; the odds are formidable. Besides, money is an end in itself, now that it is so lavishly available. Athletics and other worthy so-called minor sports suffer from the same suffocating syndrome. But Australians ought to beware mono-culture. Perhaps its legacy is already upon us. As noted above, Marsh warned years ago that the coming generation was thinner for talent than the last, and the Ashes series seemed to bear him out. Perhaps football mad has become cricket sad.

Simultaneously, cricket is disappearing from inner suburban grounds. Five in the Melbourne club competition have had to move to more outer suburbs and a sixth, Prahran, is under immense pressure to vacate their Toorak Park ground after 126 years. At least two sub-district clubs, Coburg and Box Hill, are also in the gun.

Several imperatives are driving this sporting variation on the property market and urban sprawl. One is financial; these are amateur clubs of limited means. Another is the creeping evil of user-pays, an article of faith for some governments and councils, leaving one to wonder why they collect taxes and rates in the first instance. But football is playing its dastardly part. Three of the evacuees have yielded their grounds to once-brotherly football clubs who wanted the facilities year-round. The same dynamic is weighing on Coburg and Box Hill. Because it suits them, football clubs and councils portray cricketers as a rich and privileged elite who are unfairly occupying the playgrounds of the masses. It is an absurdity, of course; football has the money and the pull now; it is why it attracts the players and wants the grounds as exclusive domains. A variation on the theme emerged late in the winter at the Gabba when the Brisbane Lions, nouveau rich Johnnys-come-lately, demanded that the permanent wicket block be replaced by drop-in pitches. Apparently, they wanted to save their soles. Cricket must fight this piracy.

The worst of times

It was in many ways a wretchedly sad year. The collapse of the Zimbabwe team was not cricket's fault, but was a legacy of the collapse of the country. None the less, the ICC did no one a favour by insisting that other countries fulfil their contractual obligations to play there. Politically and morally, this was doubtful. Practically, it vas disastrous as a series of notoriously one-sided matches and eries ensued. One day in Harare, New Zealand bowled out Zimbabwe twice. This so-called Test coincided with the second of he Ashes series, at Edgbaston, the epic England won by two runs and dubbed immediately (if too breathlessly) "The Greatest Test". It made for a sorry contrast. *Wisden Australia* joins with others in demanding that the ICC suspend Zimbabwe until further notice. Once, we thought it was important for Zimbabwe to continue to play, as a show of solidarity with the cricket-playing rump. Now it is clear that sanctioned internationals are self-defeating. The international cricket community can and must continue to support Zimbabwean cricket, but in a lower key. Humiliation might be the path to redemption in the Bible, but not in Matebeleland.

There were other sadnesses. The death of David Hookes continued to hang like a pall as the awful events of that night in early 2004 were very publicly revisited at a committal hearing in November and a trial nine months later. Darren Lehmann's face in both courts was taut, but blank. He said at the trial that the 18 months after Hookes' death had been the worst of his life. He had retired from international cricket, and it was clear that some of his old, blithe self had gone forever, too. So had a part of everyone who knew Hookes.

In Asia, a tsunami wreaked unspeakable havoc, and in London, so did bombs. Neither directly affected Australian cricket, but both were confronting to cricketing sensibilities. The tsunami struck on Boxing Day, the biggest day in Australian cricket, and the bombs coincided with the start of the Ashes, the biggest series. Cricket had to think about its place in the scheme of things. Its response to the tsunami was straightforward. The destructive wave had washed away the ground at Galle where Shane Warne had made his triumphant return to Test cricket earlier in the year. Warne patched up his differences with Muttiah Muralidaran, Muralidaran patched up his differences with Australia and in January both played in an inspiring exhibition match at the MCG that raised nearly $15 million. All involved can be proud of their efforts.

The bombing of London was a more delicate matter. Most of the Australian players had wives and families with them, and some suddenly felt small and vulnerable. Jason Gillespie said that if there was another attack, he would have to think about abandoning the tour. Regrettably, this brought out the sabre-rattlers in Australia who condemned Gillespie for timidity and said what a poor companion he would make in the trenches. We for our part applaud Gillespie for putting family before all, even career. We wonder at the mentality that appears to hold that until a man has been torn apart by shrapnel, he has not proved himself. Gillespie proved man enough a few weeks later when, even as his bowling career was slipping away, he and his few batting skills stood between a phalanx of England bowlers and his wicket for hours, playing his part in the fable of the Edgbaston Test. He wasn't AWOL at Old Trafford, either. Australians should be encouraged that at least some leading sportsmen have cricket and life in perspective. Ponting missed a Test in 2004 because of the death of an aunt, and a Pura Cup match at the start of last summer to be at his wife's university graduation. Good for him on both accounts; we cricket fans have certain rights to him, but his family have more and greater.

Wonderful Warne or Shane shame?

What to make of a man who regained the world this year, but lost his wife and kids? This much, to begin: we must be fair and stringent in our reviews, but not sanctimonious. Shane Warne, Simone and their three children must first of all have sympathy, for the road ahead will be stressful. It was Warne, the peerless and controversial cricketer who took his 600th wicket at Old Trafford, but it was Warne, the father with an aching heart, who then kissed the wrist-band given to him by his daughter, by then far away back in Australia. Warne had also been on Ashes tour when she was born in 1997. He celebrated then with champagne and cigars in Oxford, but it was somehow a muted affair. The life of the sporting international is luxurious for individuals, but remains tough on families, and not all are able to bear it.

Warne was again the overarching figure in Australian cricket in the last year. He took wickets at his usual prodigious rate. When he reached 300 in 1997, this writer and others speculated on his chances of going on to 600, and concluded that the notion was fanciful. As it happened, he flew from 500 to 600 wickets in fewer Tests than between almost any other milestones. He was named *Wisden*'s Leading Player of the Year. He took 40 wickets in England and batted courageously in the already legendary Tests at Edgbaston, Old Trafford and Trent Bridge. There were times during the Ashes series when he seemed to be the only Australian up for the fight.

Plainly, he had to close his mind to the emotional turmoil, or else he could not have played such cricket. Once, such a feat of mental discipline would have been thought inspiring. Now, some wondered if it indicated a heart hardened to a disturbing degree. When his name popped up in a conversation one day around this time with a pillar of Melbourne society, a cricket enthusiast, my interlocutor was scathing. "The man's a twit, isn't he?" he said. Nine came to the same conclusion more formally, judging a clutch of revelations in English newspapers to be the straw that broke the camel's back, cancelling his lucrative contract. Whichever side of the Warne divide you stand, the fact is once that whereas a cricketer of his stature and achievement would once have enjoyed the unconditional support of the whole country, it is now conditional, and in some places does not exist at all.

This is a problem. Media prurience certainly plays its part, for it is not as if Warne's antics actually shock anyone any more. Still, somehow, we feel let down. Men are uncomfortable because they feel cricket is too good a game to be held up to ridicule in this way. Women react archly because they see in Warne all that is coarse and destructive about sport. They find it impossible to watch the sublime cricketer without an awareness of the vulgar man. "For a while, it seemed, we all tried to pretend that the bloke was just a bit of a dill, that he'd come to his senses and learn to keep his pants on. And for a while, I tried with everyone else to separate his on-field prowess with what he was doing off it," wrote author and broadcaster Tracee Hutchinson in *The Age*. "But it's a bit like trying not to notice the elephant sitting in the lounge room."

The English make a distinction between the two Warnes easily, but not us Australians. They accept him in his halves, we fight unavailingly to reconcile them. We romanticise our sporting heroes. Indians deify theirs. The English, seemingly, go along with theirs. This helps to explain a riddle. At the start of the year (while he was on tour with Australia in New Zealand), Warne announced that he and his family were about to move to England. This apparently was news to Simone and – it can be seen now – an insight into the state of their marriage. But Warne dumbfounded listeners when he said he wanted to get away for a while from Australia and its antagonistic media. The British tabloids are infamously voracious, and have a particular appetite for the sort of scandal in which Warne was constantly embroiled. How could this be?

But Warne was speaking only his truth. The tabloid exposes are irritating, but not nearly as irritating as the character assassinations here. In a column in *The Times*, Warne made no effort to justify his escapades, saying only that what happened between people in private should stay that way. A television advertisement for hair replacement therapy in which he appeared soon after his marriage break-up also included a joke about text messaging. Concerning anyone else, this would have been thought brazen, akin to Bill Clinton cracking a gag about dry-cleaning and Monica Lewinsky's dress. But scarcely an eyelid was batted.

However, Australian allegations that some in the dressing-room had grown tired of his antics and were annoyed at how they reflected on the team were to his mind more damning than any tabloid mischief-making; they went to his standing as a cricketer. The truth is that after all these years, the English dote on him more than his countryfolk do. "Our expectations of Warne are probably less grand than yours," a female English friend wrote. We grew up with George Best and Ian Botham. Their flaws endear us to them and sustain them in our affections. To my knowledge, there has never been any confusion over whether they were sporting heroes or role models so I'm not sure where the grey area came in or how Warne commandeered it."

The English are puzzled by Australia's bipolarity about Warne. To me, it is like the difference between family and friends. You can secretly love the roguish genius in another family, but you fret about the one in your own. The fact is that, for better and worse, England can never own Warne, and Australia can never disown him. In the Ashes series, we were glad of that.

A Special Broadcasting Service

The carnival screened by SBS night after night in the latter part of the winter was typical of the network's fare. It was long-winded, in an unintelligible language, with sub-titles that were scarcely illuminating. There was some elaborate costumery, much ceremony, occasional wanton violence and a touch of pathos, but not as much sex as usual, except in the sub-text. The endings didn't always makes sense ...

These notes would not be complete without a dipping of our lid to SBS's work on the Ashes. None of the major networks was prepared to cover the Ashes (although Seven came in for the preceding one-day series, already long forgotten), so the alternative stepped in. The coverage was a revelation. Channel 4's camerawork was the equal of Nine's here, and some of its effects were better. Simon Hughes' instant analyses of developments in the game were among them. Not for the only time this year, the English led the way.In the SBS studio, Simon Hill became the unexpectedly authoritative voice, and Dean Jones and Greg Matthews managed to be at once lively and relevant, a trick that is beginning to elude some at Nine. Importantly, the series passed blessedly without viewers having some monstrous artefact of memorabilia shoved down their late-night throats. The cricket proved a ratings winner for SBS. In keeping with the theme of the series, the underdog won the day.

Warne and the wrong'un

by CHARLES DAVIS

Wisden assembled 100 distinguished judges for its 2000 edition and asked them to settle on five "Cricketers of the Century". Shane Warne was on that exalted list. The accolade effectively named Warne as the greatest bowler of the century and probably of all time.

Five years on and Warne stands as the all-time leading wicket-taker in Tests, with more than Lillee and Thomson combined. In 2005 *Wisden* called him the leading cricketer in the world. Yet there are doubts. Warne is hardly a bowling, or even a spinning, equivalent of Sir Donald Bradman. The Sri Lankan Muttiah Muralidaran has been relentlessly gaining statistical ground on Warne to the extent that judging the greater bowler is a matter for genuine debate.

Warne and Muralidaran made their debuts within eight months of one another in 1992, and have enjoyed long, eventful, contemporaneous careers. Those journeys – both controversial – have sparked debate and analysis that is often passionate and sometimes vindictive. For many, positions were entrenched long ago. These pages will attempt to be dispassionate, asking only what we can learn about these great bowlers simply through their Test statistics. It will not be concerned with other sensibilities, and will conclude by ranking them among all bowlers.

The taking of more than 500 Test wickets is a grand achievement, but if we are really to evaluate careers of modern players against one another, and especially against their predecessors, it is not a fair measure. Traditionally, the primary measure of a bowler has been his average. Since part-timers occasionally do well in this category, a second figure – the average number of wickets per match – should always supplement this. Many other statistics are available; the resource grows vaster by the year. With ever-growing computer power, there is a temptation to slice and dice the numbers over and over until coming up with the answer you want. This article will do some of that, but the reader should try to keep in view the bigger picture. There is no single "killer stat" buried in the data, but each one tells a bit of the story.

William West/AFP/Getty Images

Arch-rivals, but both on the side of cricket: Shane Warne and Muttiah Muralidaran in companionable mood at the tsunami relief match at the MCG.

A problem with comparing careers in broad terms is that cricket is a team game played around the world. Murali and Warne have bowled against different opponents under a mix of conditions. If judging a player means judging their performance in a variety of venues, then listing averages in each country should be instructive.

Leading Bowling Averages

Wickets per match

	Warne	Muralidaran	Warne	Muralidaran
Australia	25.0	116.0	4.78	1.50
England	22.9	21.5	5.24	8.00
India	43.1	48.7	3.78	3.00
New Zealand	21.3	29.4	5.44	3.25
Pakistan	28.0	21.5	6.00	7.00
South Africa	23.0	26.0	5.11	5.83
Sri Lanka	21.5	20.6	4.63	6.45
West Indies	39.6	18.2	2.43	6.25
Zimbabwe	22.8	27.5	6.00	3.71

While Murali enjoys a superior career bowling average of 22.7 to Warne's 25.0, he is not as adaptable as the Australian. Looking at performance across all countries, Warne has a better mark in five out of nine: in wickets per match he leads in four. Let's call this one a draw. Even when examining a 90-Test career, such results can be unreliable. In 13 years, Muralidaran has played only two Tests in Australia and three in England, while the most recent of his five in India was in 1997. Warne has bowled 17 times in England, not including 2005. Before the West Indies series in July, Muralidaran had played more Tests in Colombo (27) than he had outside the sub-continent (19), and seven of those were in Zimbabwe.

There is a paradox in the averages. For Tests in Sri Lanka Murali has a better mark than Warne by about one run. For matches away from there Warne leads by a similarly small amount. Yet if the figures are combined, Murali's lead is substantial. The explanation lies in the fact that Muralidaran has played so much more in Sri Lanka, where both bowlers have excelled. This weighting is a critical factor. Ultimately, it would be unfair to discount Murali's success at home too much – he can't help it that he plays there so often – but respect for his figures may well come down to a value judgment as to the importance of matches in Sri Lanka. This leads to the question of whether Muralidaran benefits from home-ground help.

Warne bowls: who'd be a batsman?

The issue of advantageous conditions in certain countries is complex. It seems obvious from the home-and-away figures that Sri Lanka favours Murali's bowling, but finger-spinners as a group do not fare especially well there, averaging about 38 runs per wicket over the last 20 years – little different to their numbers elsewhere. However, it has been a graveyard for leg-spinners, with Warne an extraordinary exception: bowlers of this type other than Warne have averaged 45.

In Australia, some of Warne's figures go against conventional wisdom. Although the SCG has long been regarded as the best turning wicket, and the place where the Australian selectors are inclined to let loose two leg-spinners, Warne's average there (27.5) is inferior to his record at Melbourne (24.7) and Brisbane (20.1). He has collected only 20% of his home wickets at the SCG, whereas Stuart MacGill has taken 37%.

Curiously, when MacGill and Warne have played together in nine Tests it is MacGill who emerges with the better record, averaging 24 to Warne's 32. However, it is important to remember that MacGill tends to be selected more often when conditions suit leg-spinners; Warne does the better of the two under less favourable settings. Warne's ability to keep matters under control, or even to excel, when pitches do not suit him, sets these two bowlers apart.

> "Murali's lead in wickets per match is aided by the fact he has fewer elite bowling colleagues competing for wickets. But Murali does not enjoy as much synergy from his team"

Murali's lead in wickets per match, it can be argued, is aided by the reality that he has fewer elite bowling colleagues competing for wickets. Up to a point it is true, but Murali does not enjoy as much synergy from his team, and he must often act as main strike weapon even when he is off form or conditions do not suit him. This can adversely affect a bowling average.

On the negative side of Warne's ledger is the unavoidable fact that he has never bowled to the dominant team of his time, simply because he plays for them. Murali has had to deliver against the Australians in ten Tests, but this component is rather cancelled out by his 14 against Zimbabwe – more than any other player except his team-mate Chaminda Vaas – in which he has invariably returned figures that have boosted his statistical coffers.

Warne does rely on fieldsmen and umpires a little more than Muralidaran. Catches form 59% of Warne's haul compared with 55% for the Sri Lankan. Warne takes 20% of his wickets lbw to Murali's 16%. Murali gets more catches through close-in fieldsmen – predominantly on the off side whereas Warne's victims fall to the leg-side trap – but Warne gets a lot more from the wicket-keeper, about one-tenth of his dismissals.

The researcher Ross Smith has reported that Warne and Muralidaran have conceded more sixes than any other bowlers in Tests. Warne has given up more than three times as many as MacGill, the nearest Australian, but it is not surprising the pair that has done more bowling than any other should have conceded the most sixes. While Warne leads that list, Smith notes that the data for the 1990s is sometimes incomplete or unobtainable. It is likely that the full totals for sixes off the two bowlers are similar, at around 140 to 150 each.

A statistic common to spin bowlers is that a relatively high proportion of their wickets are tail-enders. About 37% of Warne's victims bat from Nos. 8 to 11, an exceptionally high proportion – Glenn McGrath's mark is 25% while Muralidaran's is 31% – but there are qualifying factors at work. Playing in a team of exceptional pace bowlers, Warne sometimes does not get much of a look in when early wickets fall quickly. Australia also bowl their opponents out more often than other teams, so there are extra lower-order scalps available. Adjusting for this, Warne takes about 3% more of his wickets as available tail-enders than Murali, which is not a huge difference.

Which batsmen do best against Warne and Muralidaran? The question can be answered in detail for Tests since 1999, as ball-by-ball data is almost complete. It produces a few surprises, reminding us that while there are more matches than ever, opponents do not necessarily come head-to-head more often. Warne has not played against West Indies since 1999, and he has not dismissed Brian Lara in a Test since 1997. The Indian foursome of V.S.S. Laxman, Sachin Tendulkar, Rahul Ganguly and Sourav Dravid has scored almost 700 runs off Warne since 1999, at an overall average of more than 56. Jacques Kallis and Stephen Fleming also have strong records.

Murali bowls: who'd be a batsman?

Muralidaran, for his part, has not bowled to Tendulkar in a Test for eight years. But he has had his fill of Lara, who has 372 runs against him for only three dismissals since 1999. Inzamam-ul-Haq (253 runs at 84) and Andy Flower (165 runs at 82.5) have also played Murali especially well. The overall records of the two bowlers against elite batsmen – those who average over 45 – are similar. They average about 50 against Warne and Murali, a fairly typical result for today's leading bowlers. Interestingly, McGrath is a major exception; he averages only 25 against the elite opponents, far better than any other present-day player.

So where do the two heroes stand among the ranks of the great bowlers? Is the question answerable? Many have said that comparing the cricketers of different eras is a fool's game. Many others cannot resist, and there are ways of treating the statistics that iron out the anomalies between the eras. The use of standard statistical tools and the calculation of appropriate adjustment factors according to the strength of the game at different periods can produce adjusted averages that are statistically rigorous. I have written a book on this theme, *The Best of the Best*, but space prohibits a full explanation of the methods. Suffice it to say that due consideration can be given to the following factors:

> "On the negative side of Warne's ledger is the unavoidable fact that he has never bowled to the dominant outfit of his time, simply because he plays for it"

- standard of opposition faced by players on a Test-by-Test basis
- differences between countries in which performances were recorded
- changes in run-scoring standards over cricket history
- changes in the number of elite-level players over time
- length of players' careers.

The ranked statistical list that follows has been updated to include results over the last five years. It gives equal weight to bowling average and wickets per match, with adjustment factors applied. Rankings of current players are not absolute in that their performances could change in the future.

THE BEST OF THE BEST

	Tests	Bowling Average	Multi-factor Adjusted Bowling	Adjusted Wkt/Match	Bowling Rating
1 S. F. Barnes (England) 1901–1913	27	16.4	21.4	6.30	5.66
2 M. Muralidaran (Sri Lanka) 1992–	**92**	**22.7**	**22.0**	**5.86**	**5.47**
3 W. J. O'Reilly (Australia) 1931–1945	27	22.6	21.5	5.23	4.87
4 R. J. Hadlee (New Zealand) 1972–1990	86	22.3	21.2	5.01	4.79
5 C. V. Grimmett (Australia) 1924–1935	37	24.2	24.7	5.72	4.56
6 D. K. Lillee (Australia 1970–1983	70	23.9	23.1	5.07	4.42
7 M. D. Marshall (West Indies) 1978–1991	81	20.9	20.3	4.64	4.39
8 G. D. McGrath (Australia) 1993–	109	21.3	21.5	4.60	4.35
9 G. A. Lohmann (England) 1886–1896	18	10.8	23.2	5.29	4.31
10 S. K. Warne (Australia) 1992–	**123**	**25.4**	**24.6**	**4.78**	**4.13**
11 A. Kumble (India) 1990–	92	28.2	26.5	5.01	4.06
12 F. S. Trueman (England) 1952–1965	67	21.6	22.9	4.49	3.93
13 J. Garner (West Indies) 1976–1986	58	20.98	21.06	4.47	3.87
14 C. E. L. Ambrose (West Indies) 1988–2000	98	20.99	20.11	4.13	3.85
15 A. A. Donald (Sth Africa) 1992–2002	72	22.25	22.45	4.58	3.82
16 H. Ironmonger (Australia) 1928–1932	14	17.97	19.55	5.18	3.80
17 Imran Khan (Pakistan) 1971–1991	88	22.81	22.38	4.11	3.79
18 Waqar Younis (Pakistan) 1989–2003	86	23.56	24.71	4.34	3.66
19 C. T. B. Turner (Australia) 1886–1894	17	16.53	25.23	5.05	3.65
20 S. M. Pollock (Sth Africa) 1995–	93	22.09	22.21	4.05	3.63

The process produces quite a diverse list, with a range of historical periods, bowling types, and countries represented. S.F. Barnes, that great, enigmatic medium-pacer of the Golden Age, holds on to the No. 1 ranking he earned in the 2000 analysis, in spite of the fact that his real-life bowling average of 16.4 has been bumped up to 21.4 by the adjustment factors.

The ranked list puts Muralidaran almost at the top of the pantheon, confirming his statistical rarity. Warne, too, is in elite company and, like Muralidaran, has soared up the charts since 2000, moving from 24 to 10. Murali has risen from 13 to 2. If one substitutes the

> "Muralidaran's ability to sustain an extraordinary strike-rate combined with a world-class average is unmatched in living memory"

statistics that are most favourable to Warne, based on the country-by-country analysis, he rises to fifth, with Muralidaran fourth.

So, although we can find statistics that capture the rare range and adaptability of Warne's bowling, the weight of the figures must remain in Muralidaran's favour. His ability to sustain an extra-ordinary strike-rate combined with a world-class average is unmatched in living memory. Warne may be the "Bowler of the Century" when his overall impact on the game is considered. Great player that he is, Warne's numbers come close – but do not quite justify – such a judgment. If the figures are to be trusted, Muralidaran is the greatest bowler of our time.

Charles Davis is a Melbourne-based cricket writer and scientist.

Short-sighted – or visionary?

by MATT PRICE

The scene is a trendy, crowded, late-night bar. In the background, rather incongruously, we spot a selection of bats, pads and other miscellaneous gear. A handsome young bloke, Cricket Guy, wanders in and eyes a couple of attractive maidens. "Hi girls," he chirps suggestively. They ignore him, but a text message arrives on one of their mobiles. It is from Cricket Guy and reads: "stay up late for a quickie?" The women, unsurprisingly offended, smash him in the gob.

Is this a scene from a horribly cheap X-rated video available from under-the-counter retailers in the mean streets of capital cities? Not at all. It was the rudimentary plot for Seven's promotion of the Twenty20 match between England and Australia at the start of the Ashes tour in June. Since the hit-and-whiz game was being screened live from Southampton in the absurdly early hours of the morning, Cricket Guy's text message played on the double entendre ("stay up late for a quickie," geddit?). Seven's less than subtle advertisement of the 20-overs-a-side slashfest ended with a similarly raunchy proclamation: "There is one message we want to send to the Poms and we're going to deliver it ... WITH BALLS!"

Technically, this was a touch misleading; England thrashed Australia by 100 runs. But since the score barely matters in this abridged, eminently disposable form, the unabashed marketing theme – cricket as porn – seemed otherwise perfect. If you are shocked and disgusted that the denizens of the sport have allowed their underpants to be removed and the great game defiled, get over it. A Twenty20 wallop may convert practically all of the virtues of Tests – think patience, guile, gentility, technique, subtlety, politeness, endurance and stamina – into laughable liabilities, but it is here to stay. Returning to Seven's raunchy theme, it's all about bottoms. On seats.

Tony Dodemaide, the man who organised the first Twenty20 match in Australia, was also present at the birth of the monster in

England. A more-than-handy Victorian bowler who played ten Tests and 24 ODIs, Dodemaide headed to the United Kingdom at the end of his playing career to learn cricket administration. He spent five years at Lord's as the MCC's head of cricket, and was its representative when the ECB first gathered to contemplate arranging a modified competition. "Given some of the things that were being planned," Dodemaide recalls, "it was probably wise it sent a youngish Australian to those early meetings, rather than some of the more crusty traditionalists."

The product of ECB marketeers, Twenty20 was squarely aimed at young people with scant knowledge or regard for the game's dearly held traditions. "When you look at the crowds for something like the Lord's Test, which is pretty much a sell-out, you imagine cricket's doing well in England," Dodemaide says. "But that's a one-off game at a relatively small ground that seats about 30,000 in a city of 10 million. Outside that, a lot of the county clubs have been stagnating. What we set out to do was target people not traditionally interested in the game, many of whom, frankly, thought cricket was boring."

> "If you're shocked and disgusted that the denizens of cricket have allowed their underpants to be removed and the great game defiled, get over it"

For years English village and pub teams have been exploiting the long summer days to play 20-over matches, beginning after work and ending around 8.30 p.m. The ECB grabbed hold of this rudimentary concept, dressed it in bras and knickers, and celebrated an astonishing success.

In 2003, the inaugural Twenty20 competition between counties attracted huge crowds. Sanctioned gimmickry extended well beyond the amphetamine-fuelled slash-and-bash rules. At one match four lucky supporters were provided with luxury armchairs outside the boundary, but inside the fence, and served non-stop pizza and beer. At another there was a hot tub. Warwickshire officials lined up members of each sex to participate in a speed-dating scheme, where prospective partners were given until the fall of the next wicket to chat each other up.

"It was a real leap of faith by the ECB, but it worked," Dodemaide says. "At the start of that first competition we had no sponsors. By the end people and corporations were jumping on board and the finals at Trent Bridge were a sell-out." Inspired by this dazzling Twenty20 vision, Dodemaide arrived in Perth at the start of 2004 to become chief executive of the Western Australian Cricket Association. Not long afterwards, the WACA looked to a rather better credentialed Test fast bowler, Dennis Lillee, to fill its presidency. Lillee leapt on Dodemaide's idea of exploring the format as a viable, long-term option.

"I was really excited," Lillee recalls. "I'd heard of its amazing success in England and the thing that appealed to me was, like when 50-overs was first introduced, it was something aimed at the crowd – cricket as entertainment. It's over in two-and-a-half hours and played in late afternoon, early evening, which means you can bring your family along and go out afterwards."

David Williams, the newly appointed WACA chairman, was just as enthusiastic as Lillee and Dodemaide. Even so, all three were bowled over by what transpired. Looking through the domestic calendar, Dodemaide took advantage of a January 2005 Pura Cup fixture at the WACA between Western Australia and Victoria. Knowing the visitors usually travelled to Perth early, Dodemaide suggested the experiment and the Victorians quickly agreed.

"To be honest, we had no idea what to expect," Dodemaide recalls. "We didn't know whether we'd attract 200 people or 2,000." An inspired decision to charge a peppercorn entry fee – $6 for adults, $3 for children – drew an amazing crowd of more than 20,000. It was the first WACA lock-out since the West Indies tour of 1981 and hundreds of people were turned away at the gates. "We were absolutely stunned," Dodemaide says. "We thought it might prove popular, but people really voted with their feet."

Shane Warne's inclusion for Victoria contributed to the marketing masterstroke, but he was walloped for six off his first ball and finished with 1 for 32 from 13 deliveries. Not that he was the least bit perturbed. "It was absolutely fantastic, sensational," Warne oozed afterwards. "The atmosphere was brilliant. It attracts a different crowd, a much broader cross-section than just cricket buffs, and the time-frame and non-stop action makes it a winner."

The result was a resounding eight-wicket victory to the Western Warriors with Luke Ronchi shellacking 67 runs from 24 balls. The following night in Adelaide a similarly huge crowd watched Australia A wallop Pakistan in the same format. A month later,

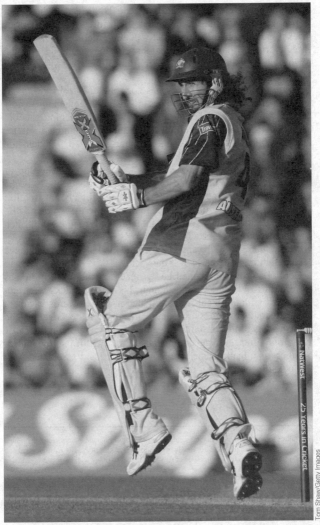

None of the old rules apply in Twenty20. Here, Jason Gillespie plays hard-hitting batsman.

Australia beat New Zealand in front of 30,000 in Auckland in a "retro" game, with players taking the field in early World Series Cricket garb and hairdos, and Ricky Ponting murdering 98 runs in 55 deliveries. "I haven't done that since primary school," was the Australian captain's response to smashing four sixes off a Daryl Tuffey over.

While the lure of the quickie has now proven irresistible to antipodean supporters, administrators in Australia seemed thrown by the mass appeal of cricket porn. After initially preaching caution, Cricket Australia hastily arranged an interstate competition for January 2006. "I don't think this is a short-term fad," Dodemaide says, "it's the future."

Unsurprisingly, the experience isn't everyone's plastic cup of Powerade; traditionalists tend to regard the intrusion the way the Vatican greeted the contraceptive pill. "The officials must realise the harm it will inflict on the game in the long-term," warned Dilip Vengsarkar, the former Test captain, in the *India Times*. "Batsmen who are good sloggers will be preferred over technically correct players ... there won't be any place for the kind of artistes who have been delighting spectators over the years."

Geoff Lawson complained he "grimaces at the head-up hoicks more akin to under-12", and thought his fellow quicks were not impressed with a mutant form weighted heavily towards batsmen. "The diversions of dress and hair did not serve to cover up the inadequacies of this bastardised game," Lawson wrote in the *Daily Telegraph* after the Adelaide match. "Twenty20 it may be called, but there is a bank vault full of short-sightedness associated with this phenomenon. Play it if you will, but it just isn't cricket." When

---

Australia's top-order collapse in the Twenty20 match against England at Southampton on June 13 was actually one of the most extreme in international cricket history. The Australians at one stage were 7 for 31: to find an instance of Australia losing so many wickets for fewer runs, in any full international match, one has to go back to the last day of a Test at the Oval in 1896, when Australia lost 7 for 14 on an unplayable wicket. It is even worse when we consider that Australia at one stage had been 0 for 23, so losing its first 7 wickets in the space of 8 runs and 20 balls. No team, in Test, ODI, or Twenty20, has ever given up its first seven wickets in so short a span. The previous worst was the West Indies, who went from 0/16 to 7/25 in 36 balls in an ODI against Zimbabwe (of all teams) in 2000-01.

it comes to opinions on vision Lawson, a trained optometrist, is certainly qualified.

Yet cricket increasingly dances to a Twenty20 tempo. The recent Ashes series was much more allegro than adagio and surely only a crack forensic scientist could detect any difference in the approaches of Adam Gilchrist in the short and long forms. "I remember it all being said 40 years ago about one-day cricket," chuckles Lillee at the criticism. "It's here to stay. During World Series Cricket, the main people involved discussed taking cricket to the United States and the suggestion back then was they wouldn't go for one-dayers, so we'd have to shorten it to 25-overs a side. It's interesting how history repeats itself."

> "Traditionalists tend to regard the intrusion the way the Vatican greeted the contraceptive pill"

The conventional limited-overs format has already been grappling with the allegedly ever-diminishing attention span of the modern sports fan. Supersubs and convoluted fielding arrangements have been introduced to pep up ODIs, which are under more threat from the explosion of Twenty20 than Tests. Why subscribe to *Playboy* when the porn channel is available 24/7?

Ian Chappell, Lillee's old captain and fellow short-game pioneer, is philosophical about the prospect of the ultra-abbreviation being cemented in the domestic and international calendar. "Limited-overs cricket is always going to live up to its name – it's limited," Chappell told *Wisden*. "The greater the limitations the more predictable it becomes because captains don't have the same opportunities to employ imagination and initiative."

Chappell said the game is like an "in" pub: as soon as a better one comes along people move to it. "It will fill a niche for people who have limited time to watch," he said. "The administrators would have been derelict in their duty if they hadn't programmed matches as the public like it. The real trick would be to ensure that the people the games attract become cricket fans rather than Twenty20 fans, but I am not sure the administrators have the vision or the knowledge to go that far."

The logic of gatekeepers desperately inventing formats to entice the bored fan means our grandchildren will probably be watching Five5 contests in the ad breaks between Big Brother XXIV. Perhaps

Chappell is wrong and administrators are engaged in a brilliant conspiracy, promoting these silly, disposable, meaningless quickies to deepen the public's appreciation for proper cricket. Pornography, after all, is ultimately degrading, unsatisfying and no match for a respectable, faithful and enduring partner.

Matt Price is a journalist in the Canberra press gallery who writes for The Australian.

Andrew Flintoff, England's hero, consoles Brett Lee, almost Australia's, at the end of the epic second Ashes Test at Edgbaston; an image that defined a series.

Shane, 533 wickets and the new world record-holder acknowledges the Chennai crowd's appreciation of his feat. Indian legend Sachin Tendulkar calls him "God's gift to cricket".

Old game, new angles: Brad Haddin, with a free hit in an Australia A vs Pakistan Twenty20 game in Adelaide, lets the ball hit his stumps in order to run byes.

Long shadows make for a pleasing effect as Victorian captain Cameron White bowls at the SCG.

An Australian crowd in typical humour, enjoying the entertainment and making some of their own.
This is the Adelaide Oval during a one-day game.

Hamish Blair/Getty Images

An umbrella field for Darren Lehmann and Michael Clarke as they pause for a drink in Chennai.

CRICKETER OF THE YEAR: Glenn McGrath, poised to deliver.
The batsman knows what is coming, but can he do anything about it?

PURA CUP CRICKETER OF THE YEAR: Michael Bevan lets his inner libertine loose.

The mystery of the missing cycle

by MIKE COWARD

Australian teams of recent years have attained such levels of excellence the notion of cyclical power and influence has almost become a misnomer. The conviction that fertile ground is discovered after fallow periods has long given succour to the nakedly ambitious minnows and the leviathans suffering unforeseen periods of uncertainty or conflict.

For some captains, and even coaches and chief executives, the mystical cycles of success and failure can be a stock justification for immediate predicaments. "It's cyclical," they say off pat. "Fortunes change, the wheel will turn; it always has." Over the past decade the movement has been imperceptible. If not discredited, the cyclical theory is being loudly questioned and if not for the riveting 2005 Ashes series it may already have been dismissed as irrelevant.

Such has been the dominance of the Australian Test and ODI teams that even the most rabid supporters have grown weary at the inevitability of success. Furthermore, a good number of them are willing the opposition to prosper. Anything for a contest is the cry of all but the most chauvinistic and Anglophobic. At best this is cheeky, at worst plain arrogant. But it is a raw fact and the game's governors must confront it. It is only a matter of time before the crowds will decline and, in turn, gate receipts and the bounty from sponsors and television moguls.

Uncompetitive elite-level contests are uninteresting and unsustainable. Test cricket desperately needed the Ashes series to recapture attention and imagination because corresponding events in Sri Lanka and Zimbabwe caused considerable anguish. That England could compete with Australia was a revelation. It had been widely believed for some years that Australia and their crack XIs had raised the bar to an unattainable height, although the argument was refuted outside Australia. However, there can be no doubt that if a system of cycles is still in existence the time between them has increased significantly.

Until England's emergence from the wilderness, India were the only country to seriously question the Australians' right to rule since 1995, when West Indies finally lost grasp of the Frank Worrell Trophy and Mark Taylor held it aloft. Since then Taylor's successors, Steve Waugh and Ricky Ponting, have honed their upper body by lifting every prize on offer to them. While Michael Vaughan and company are chuffed at their improvement they would do well to remember English cricket has had a nasty habit of sitting back after isolated successes. England will only truly regain respect and recognition if success can be sustained.

The enthralling Ashes campaign should not obscure the fact that there has been an alarming decline in overall standards because of an uncompetitive environment. This has been most evident in the Test arena where it is impossible to paper over deficiencies in attitude, temperament and technique. Liberties can be taken in the 50-over game and in the laughing-clowns Twenty20 distraction, but there is no escaping scrutiny through five days where reputations are made and broken.

> "Anything for a contest is the stock cry of all but the most chauvinistic and Anglophobic"

It is an unpalatable truth that there are easy pickings on offer at the start of the 21st century. This is unacceptable. There have been other periods of rich pickings but never a bonanza like this. The painful racial and party politics that have diminished Zimbabwe cricket and the consequences of the inexplicable fast-tracking of Bangladesh to Test status have placed the game in a dreadful bind. Both countries are hopelessly out of their depth. That the governments of Zimbabwe, Bangladesh, Sri Lanka and Pakistan continue to have a direct say on cricket matters in their countries exacerbates the problems confronting the ICC and adds to the despair of legislators unencumbered by party political meddling and the provocative intervention of bureaucrats.

While the total of ICC members is growing the elite group is small and if a one-time powerhouse is rendered impotent for any length the game can quickly lose its appeal. England and West Indies being so inept at the same time caused the game considerable heartache, although it did permit India to challenge Australia and demonstrate they have the playing ability to complement their imposing reputation as the wealthy powerbrokers.

The sphere of influence within the game has changed dramatically since the tumultuous 1970s and 80s and world cricket now looks to Australia instead of England for direction and inspiration. Australia have accepted this heady responsibility with alacrity and considerable energy. Indeed, midway through 2005 five of the ten Test-match countries were coached by Australians and Rod Marsh was still dispensing good advice to the young and ambitious towards the end of his term at the ECB Academy. While it is true Cricket Australia and its key people have grasped and run with the technologies and philosophies, it is the stability and continuity born out of the chaos of the 1970s and 80s that has underpinned the success.

As 2005 marks the centenary of Cricket Australia (previously the Australian Board of Control for International Cricket and the Australian Cricket Board for 30 years from 1973) sporting and social historians have detailed the most telling events in the evolution of the game's national authority. Nothing can compare with the havoc and confusion wrought by the schisms caused by the radical World Series Cricket movement and the unsanctioned teams to South Africa. The mid-1980s was the nadir and not until Allan Border defied considerable odds and led Australia to the World Cup in 1987 was there a sign that they could regain face and credibility. This success did not put an immediate end to the darkest period, but it gave rise to hope of prosperous days. However, not even a

---

TEST-PLAYING COUNTRIES OF THE PAST TEN YEARS

(September 1, 1995 to September 1, 2005)

Team	Tests	Won	Lost	Drawn	%Won
Australia	118	77	23	18	65.25
South Africa	109	52	24	33	47.71
Pakistan	91	37	33	21	40.66
England	120	47	37	36	39.17
Sri Lanka	91	34	31	26	37.36
India	93	29	30	34	31.18
New Zealand	87	26	30	31	29.89
West Indies	103	25	53	25	24.27
Zimbabwe	68	7	41	20	10.29
Bangladesh	38	1	33	4	2.63

Hamish Blair/Getty Images

India conquered at last, and acting captain Adam Gilchrist makes a blood-curdling sight.
Third Test, Nagpur, 2004.

supreme optimist could have forecast the spectacular era that followed Border's '89 Ashes triumph.

Since then Australian cricket has been radically restructured and the vision of key personnel has seen new benchmarks set, attained, re-set and attained. With their standard-bearing Test and ODI teams, they have aggressively pursued perfection and demanded the rest of the world follow. Some countries have invested in the knowledge, imagination and work ethic of Australian coaches – Dav Whatmore guides Bangladesh, Bennett King West Indies, Greg Chappell India and Tom Moody Sri Lanka – while others have shied away from the challenge and been rebuked on occasions for an apparent willingness to accept an inferior station. Of course, Australia have been fortunate that men of exceptional foresight and capacity have provided such stability over a prolonged period. They have had only five Test captains since Border succeeded Kim Hughes in 1984 and that includes Adam Gilchrist, who has filled-in on six occasions. Other countries have appointed as many in a season or two.

> "World cricket now looks to Australia for direction and inspiration. Midway through 2005 five of the ten Test-match countries were coached by Australians"

Away from the middle the Cricket Australia chief executives David Richards and Malcolm Speed gravitated to the top job at the ICC and after a period as Cricket Australia's chairman, Malcolm Gray presided over ICC. The game's new world might now be administered from Dubai in the United Arab Emirates, but to a large extent it revolves around Australia and Australians.

As the acknowledged leader, the country has a responsibility to share values, attitudes and structures just as it does manpower, coaching philosophies and techniques. Learning a great deal from the collapse of the game and its culture in the West Indies, Cricket Australia vigorously maintained standards, actively guarded against complacency, invested heavily in the young and bright-eyed on and off the ground and marketed the game with panache. The result has been a spectacularly sustained period of prosperity. It has taken an eternity, but it is earnestly hoped England, too, have now learned the lesson.

   For some years debate has raged about the greatness of the teams led by Border, Taylor, Waugh, Ponting and Gilchrist. Alongside whom do they sit in the pantheon? Are these indomitable XIs as good as the 1948 Invincibles? Or Joe Darling's men, or Warwick Armstrong's, or Richie Benaud's or those led by the brothers Chappell? Their excellence is undeniable, but the fact they have so rarely played in a consistently competitive environment has, in the minds of some critics and past players of distinction, cruelled their chances of being bracketed with the greatest sides of the past.

   It is harsh to be penalised for ruthless domination at a time of unsettling devaluation of once inviolable records. Australia have taken the game to a level beyond the imagination just a few summers ago. Now they can render world cricket another enormous service by inspiring others to match their standards and ensure the game, especially in its purest form, remains relevant and enthralling well into the 21st century.

Mike Coward is cricket commentator for The Australian.

The trouble with extra cover

by TIM LANE

The relationship between television and sport is an easy target. They are one of those couples – one with wealth, the other with beauty – whose reasons for being together cause talk. But to the surprise and envy of all, they survive. The mutual benefits outweigh the alternative. The doomsayers, meanwhile, go on predicting that implosion is never far away.

It is the impression of unhealthy possessiveness that causes suspicion. There's a sense that TV wants something resembling ownership for its dollar – that each time it opens its cheque-book it wants to buy a little more of its partner's soul.

When in the late 1970s Kerry Packer forced Australian cricket face first over a desk, with an arm twisted between its shoulder blades, the early outlook for a harmonious relationship between the two was less than auspicious. Yet, nearly 30 years on, they're still together. No matter what anyone thought then or thinks now, they can't be completely bad for each other. If not a perfect match, they have at the least developed the art of compromise to a workable degree.

Lately, issues have been in the air to put that to the test over the years immediately ahead. Cricket Australia has had to face the dual facts that the international game in this country has scarcely produced a good contest in a decade and that public response to cricket seems to have flattened. With a new rights agreement to be negotiated, television was entitled to feel it wanted more bang for its buck.

Against that backdrop, Cricket Australia has sold the right to have future international matches in Sydney and Melbourne televised live against the gate. It's a considerable risk, flying in the face of the wisdom of half a century of televised sports coverage in this country.

While the Australian Formula One Grand Prix and the Melbourne Cup draw six-figure crowds despite live television coverage in their city of origin, they are once-a-year, one-day events. The Australian Open Tennis is also televised live and the crowds continue to pour into Melbourne Park, but they do this for the sense of mid-summer festival the tennis offers and for the matches that television doesn't show. The circumstances of each of these events are quite different from those of cricket, which has ongoing exposure across the summer and therefore doesn't have novelty appeal.

No one at Cricket Australia or Melbourne Cricket Club, which hosts international matches at the MCG, dares predict what the impact on crowds of "against the gate" television might be. Perhaps the AFL, Melbourne's other bread-and-butter sporting competition, provides the most useful comparison.

During the 2005 season, Channel Nine was allowed live coverage in Melbourne of a Friday night match between Collingwood and Port Adelaide that would normally have been subject to a one-hour delay. The match was played at Telstra Dome, where Collingwood's average crowd for three Friday night matches against non-Victorian clubs over the two preceding seasons had been of the order of 42,000. This match drew an attendance of slightly below 36,000, a drop of around 14%.

Cricket Australia says it is acting to increase the game's exposure, particularly to the young, in the country's two largest cities. It believes the extra television coverage in each city, of up to 20 hours per Test match and about ten hours across two one-day internationals, will justify the risk. The decision has been taken in line with the view of James Sutherland, Cricket Australia's CEO, that the game must, between now and the year 2020, consolidate its position as the first-choice summer sport of Australia's youth.

There's no doubt that 20 to 30 hours of additional coverage per summer in Sydney and Melbourne, even on top of more than 200 hours already provided, represents a significant growth in the game's exposure. Whether, though, it outweighs the risk to crowd support – ultimately the lifeblood not only of the game but also of the telecasts – only time will tell.

It's all fine, however, for the Nine Network as it will undoubtedly draw much bigger audiences in its two major markets for two of the summer's five Tests. Consequently, it will have paid more for the television rights and confirmed a commitment to cricket extending beyond the mere purchase of exclusive access to international games.

That's important, for no matter how long-standing any relationship may be, there are times and issues through which one partner requires particular support. Cricket might find itself in that position as it seeks to generate status for its annual Allan Border Medal event.

Instituted at the urging of Australia's players through the Australian Cricketers' Association, the Border has now been a date on the calendar for six seasons. Hands up all those who can immediately reel off winners and years!

In these individualistic times, it stands to reason that modern cricket would have a champion player award, ostentatiously presented at a spectacular televised dinner. Cricket is, after all, a sport in which individual achievements are acknowledged, recorded and often striven for as consciously and enthusiastically as team results. Many other team sports, with an even greater emphasis on group cohesion, honour outstanding individual achievement.

So why does the concept of the Allan Border Medal seem contrived and unsatisfactory? Why, in this event-mad world, does its place on the calendar fail to arouse as great excitement as other comparable events? Why, after six presentations, does it feel as though the concept needs a good gulp of oxygen?

The least questioning response would be that it is still in its infancy – that it wouldn't be unusual for the best idea to have teething problems on the way to becoming an institution. When Banker won the 1863 Melbourne Cup there were only seven starters and the stake money was lower than for the inaugural race two years earlier. That event kicked on a bit. The modern Olympic Games almost fell over in the first decade of their reincarnation, but at the last report they were still managing to survive. When Albert Collier became the sixth winner of Australian football's coveted Brownlow Medal, it probably created less fuss than Michael Clarke's capturing of the sixth Border Medal last summer.

Allan Border Medal Winners

2000	Glenn McGrath
2001	Steve Waugh
2002	Matthew Hayden
2003	Adam Gilchrist
2004	Ricky Ponting
2005	Michael Clarke

One obvious hurdle for the Border is that there's a lot with which to compare it. It has entered a crowded market late in the day. In this country, the Melbourne Cup, Test cricket, football competitions and awards like the Brownlow Medal are examples of long-established and seemingly secure sporting traditions. Invariably, they have their origins in earlier times, when the concept of sport as entertainment for the masses was taking root. Cricket's attempt to start something new with its outstanding player awards is to an extent disadvantaged by time and history.

Not that modernity is all bad. As Tim Rice wrote, of the selling of another message in *Jesus Christ Superstar:* "If you'd come today you could have reached a whole nation: Israel in 4 BC had no mass communication." The Border has mass communication coming out its ears. That's not the problem.

The problem is the nature of the award. It is available only to the players of one team, and in any one year is likely to be vied for by a very small number of contenders. The fact that they all play for the same outfit limits any sense of rivalry that observers might experience during the count. Speaking of which, the voting process lacks clarity and transparency. The public are told that votes are cast by different groups, including umpires, players and media, but exactly who casts what remains a blur.

This is an award for cricket's elite, designed, one suspects, more for their fulfilment than for the satisfaction of supporters of the game. As such, it fails to arouse anticipation before the event, excitement on the night or – so far – any sense of history in retrospect.

Whatever ultimately becomes of it, the attempt by CA and the ACA to create their own slice of tradition will provide a useful test case in years to come. When students not just of sport, but of life's other rituals, try to understand how and why traditions form, this will be an example of a well-resourced, modern-day attempt that either succeeded or failed.

This is the kind of issue that can make a relationship feel like hard work. It will take uncharacteristic patience from the Nine Network, as well as all its renowned skill as a creator of variety television, and perhaps something more, if the Allan Border Medal is to become a major event in Australian cricket in the years ahead.

Tim Lane is a long-time cricket and football commentator, now with Channel 10.

Grounds for change

by JOHN HARMS

When you're a kid in the country, city life seems a world away. And city sport seems a world away, because important sport – Test cricket and football – is played in the city on stages that young minds just aren't equipped to grasp. These places hold such significance because the events in them are discussed with reverence. And even though you see them on TV, you just can't quite imagine what it's like to be there.

I first went to a grand sports venue in January 1971. I was nine, and it was one of the grandest: the MCG for an Australia-England Test. We drove down from Shepparton, two hours north of Melbourne, stayed at our uncle's place, and got the train in from Croydon. We got off at Richmond. I was amazed by the size and shape of the entire structure of the stadium as we walked through the park surrounding it. As we stood on the footpath outside, a taxi pulled up and out jumped a late Colin Cowdrey. We helped him with his many bags and he signed my autograph book.

Inside the grass was so green; even greener than I had imagined. And perfect. We sat in the Southern Stand, which was then like a massive primary school shelter shed. I remember the rise and fall of the noise of the crowd. Noise which is local and immediate and where individual voices can be heard, and also a global roar so enormous that your nine-year-old heart is lifted to new heights. Especially when Rod Marsh struck boundary after boundary, until Bill Lawry declared when the young keeper was 92.

As a kid, it's assumed that cricket grounds had always been the same; that the MCG had always been as it was in January 1971. You come to realise they're not. They are forever being renovated; changed, according to the whim of the age, the desire of those who control them. Great sports grounds continue to attract me. All sports grounds attract me. Recently, I went to the MCG and the Gabba within a couple of days. Both prompted memories, and reflections.

In Brisbane, I saw the Lions beat Hawthorn in front of more than 30,000 people. It is very much the new Gabba. Now that the Lions Social Club gap has been filled in with a standardised grandstand, it has become a classic little stadium: uniform and text-book. The buildings go up rather than back, so that the view is outstanding. The whole complex is a triumph of function, and could quite easily be anywhere in the world – a far cry from the old Gabba which was a triumph of local eccentricity and character.

Our family moved to Queensland in 1972, and I first saw cricket at the Gabba in 1975-76 when the Chappell brothers gathered the runs to defeat West Indies. I was so focused on the game I don't remember much about the ground, except for the Hill and how beautiful the breeze was in the Clem Jones Stand.

I fell in love with the Gabba when I went to university. It had so many different places to watch from and I would vary my choice according to who I was going with, and what the day held. Some mornings I would start on the eastern side, under the huge Moreton Bay figs, and as the sun moved around, and the throat parched, I'd go across to the Hill with its celebrated ratbaggery. Often I'd just start on the Hill and stay there – throwing empties at the Leo Muller Toyota bins, looking out over the concourse, the hedge, the dog track (who would believe a Test ground would have a dog track?), the equipment area, and out to the wicket. When you think about it, the Hill was actually a very long way away.

The garden seats behind the 704-metre starting boxes weren't. They were at gully and there were days when Thommo was bowling that you felt you could reach out and touch Bruce Yardley's bum. Nor was the balcony of the Queensland Cricketers' Club, one of the greatest places to watch in the universe. It was an old wooden verandah that seemed to overhang the slips, and when Patrick Patterson was bowling from the Stanley Street End you felt a chance of snaring one yourself. The Cricketers' Club was full of blokes in shorts and long socks drinking rum and Coke while reading the *Tele*.

Downstairs was the restaurant where it became a short tradition for the University C-Grade to reunite and tell the story – yet again – of how we never fulfilled our potential. The ginger bugs were always the go. In 1984-85 lunch extended into the evening session. Richie Richardson and Clive Lloyd were batting so imperiously that I abandoned the Varsity table and took the nearest steps up into the

The Adelaide Oval, always pretty as a picture.

Mark Dadswell/Getty Images

daylight. I kept climbing but halfway up decided just to sit and watch. There were no security zombies in those days. If you check the tapes you will find that a six lands very near to a happy young man brandishing a glass of fair red. That is me.

Then there were the stands – all gloriously unplanned, and all over the place, as if every time the family had another child a new bedroom was tacked on. The venue had character. All very Queensland. The so-called dictates of sport as enterprise have necessitated the change, and the new stadium has its own character and is developing its own mythology. Nine-year-olds will think it's been like that forever, and they will garner their own memories.

Around the same time as I was at the Gabba, the Melbourne Cricket Club took me on a tour of their new facilities. The structures were all complete and in the process of being fitted out. I had visited the old members' areas, watching cricket and football, working in the old MCC library, and having a quiet beer in the bar under the pavilion. I knew the brilliant old press room with its oblong shallow window giving a spectacular and unusual vista. I knew the old Long Room from various book launches and attended the final function there, which was a lunch at which the historian Geoffrey Blainey brilliantly delivered the Bob Rose Lecture.

I have never been a member of the MCC, although sportswriters are granted access to all parts of the ground. But, based on those earlier visits, I can see why many members felt a sense of loss when the decision was made to pull it down and start again. The red bricks of the gates and the areas beneath the stands had an historical ambience, such that you could almost hear the applause for Ponsford. The dining rooms and bars breathed history. And nothing connects you with the past like a porcelain urinal.

But it has all changed. And it was a daunting burden that fell on the shoulders of the committee – and their architects and designers – responsible for capturing a sense of the past in something new. I imagine there will be years of conversation over gin and tonics.

The new members' area is certainly big. The entrance is huge. The atrium is huge. There are bars everywhere, wood-panelled and clubby. Any sense of Melbourne as a city of wowsers won't be found at the MCC.

There are four levels. The top one is largely seating and the view, although from well above ground level, is fantastic. The roof is high – so you can see the sky – and you feel very much in an outdoor stadium, unlike many modern grandstands closed in by concrete. The media areas are on Level 3: TV studios, radio boxes, and the press room. The MCC Library is on the outside of the floor and faces the city and Yarra Park, as do the MCC offices. The new Long Room on Level 2 will no doubt generate debate. The view from the long window is terrific and you can almost hear the clinking chat already. But the room is only Long-ish. In fact, the members' dining room, which is enormous, pillar-less and overlooking the playing arena on one side and the cityscape on the other, is more impressive. It will be the scene of many a function. This second level also accommodates the committee room and the coaches' boxes. Level 1 is for the players: dressing-rooms, gym, and a palatial area of indoor nets. In the finest tradition of Australian sport, the Besser brick is featured in the dressing-rooms.

It will take time for members to feel at home in their new facilities and there will be much argument. But good cricket and footy may provide a suitable distraction.

After all, it is the reason we go. However, there is a certain sameness creeping into sports stadia. It's why we should treasure the WACA with its grandstands that point in every direction except directly at the wicket. And the Adelaide Oval. If nothing else they will transport us back to another time, and evoke those memories that have made this sporting life so rich.

John Harms is a Melbourne-based writer and the author of Confessions of a Thirteenth Man.

Keith Miller
"The best-loved Australian"

by TONY CHARLTON

Richie Benaud said that everything you read about Keith Miller was true. When he was asked who might be Keith's parallel today, he replied: "No one. He was a one-off."

When the original inductions into the Australian Cricket Hall of Fame were made in November 1996, this was part of the commentary: "The record books do not remotely reflect the marvellous talent of a strokemaking, fast-bowling all-rounder who might have earned his place in any team of any period for batting or bowling alone." You can add: "For comradeship and good company" too.

He was the cricketer everyone wanted to be. He caught the imagination of crowds everywhere. He could bowl ferocious bouncers, hit towering sixes and take marvellous catches.

In 2003 he invited me to his place and said: "I've put aside a few treasured things that I would like to show you." Among them was an article from *The Times* headed "The heroic figure of Keith Miller". Another was from *The Hindu* in India: its bold heading was "The best-loved Australian".

Part of that article read: "It was how he conducted himself as much as how he looked." It went on: "Like the great Victor Trumper, he didn't always carry his own kit and was prone to picking up the first bat he saw lying around. In the Calcutta Test, he picked up a new bat belonging to Dick Whitington. Three of the first four balls he faced were deposited into a lily pond that lay beyond the stand at long-on."

Miller was unanimously chosen as one of the ten most outstanding heroes in the long, long history of sporting achievers at the MCG. Paradoxically, there was no statue, bust or bronze of Miller

> Keith Miller bowled more than 10,000 balls and took 170 wickets in Text cricket, yet he was never hit for six by any batsmen.

Keith Miller, and why he is an immortal.

THE GREAT ALL-ROUNDERS OF ALL TIME

	M	Runs	Avrge	Wkts	Avrge
I. T. Botham (England)	102	5200	33.55	383	28.40
C. L. Cairns (New Zealand)	62	3320	33.54	218	29.40
R. J. Hadlee (New Zealand)	86	3124	27.17	431	22.30
Imran Khan (Pakistan)	88	3807	37.69	362	22.81
J. H. Kallis (South Africa)	93	7337	56.88	183	31.60
Kapil Dev (India)	131	5248	31.05	434	29.65
K. R. Miller (Australia)	**55**	**2958**	**36.98**	**170**	**22.98**
G. S. Sobers (West Indies)	93	8032	57.78	235	34.04
Wasim Akram (Pakistan)	104	2898	22.64	414	23.63

until the unveiling of a statue at the MCG in 2003. He is honoured by the room named after him at our great ground, and also has a room named after him at The Oval in London. But how many know that the wind vane that for years stood on top of the old Olympic stand at the MCG featured Keith, with the image captured from one of the most famous cricket photographs ever taken? Former Prime Minister Sir Robert Menzies, in a foreword to a book, declared that the same photo hung in his office, and that it "refreshed" him.

"It is not only the greatest action photograph of a cricketer I have ever seen, it is in two dimensions a beautiful piece of sculpture, and it would have provided immense joy in ancient Athens," Sir Robert wrote.

At the unveiling of his statue at the MCG, Keith suddenly caught a glimpse of Les Fehr, who has been around the traps at South Melbourne forever and used to carry Keith's bat and pads. When Keith sighted him after all those years, everything stopped while he called Les to the rostrum and embraced him. That was Keith Miller: the captains, the kings – and the ordinary man.

Who knew that two or three times a week at the Covent Garden Hotel in Sydney the garbage collectors would gather for a drink and Keith was always there? He noted that if you were ever down on your luck, their money would be on the table first.

On the sideboard in Keith's lounge room are two trophies only. One is a cup presented to Keith in 1936 for his "sterling performance" as a 16-year-old whippet when he played for South Melbourne against Carlton, led by Bill Woodfull. Carlton had to win the game to get into the finals. Young Keith came in when

South Melbourne were five wickets down for nothing, heroically held up an end and made 56. The trophy is only the size of an egg-cup, yet he said it meant more to him than any other trophy he had received. It contrasts with the other trophy, a magnificent Waterford crystal bowl which marked his induction into the International Hall of Fame.

Who knew that when war broke out the great man intended to enlist in the Navy, and went along to the Navy recruiting office with his mate? One requirement was that you had achieved your merit certificate at school. Keith had, but his mate had not. The recruiting officer said: "Miller, you're in. Stoker, you're not." Keith responded: "If he's not in, neither am I." Out they strode, and Keith joined the Air Force.

He flew many operations and thankfully came back unscathed. Of course, there were narrow squeaks. Once, he was returning to base in a Mosquito when one of the Rolls-Royce engines caught fire over the coast of England. He crash-landed, but somehow survived.

> "We do well to acclaim Keith. He was a free spirit who played for the joy of the game."

It is well known that he loved England and its manner of things. He had many English friends. He said that the late Paul Getty, heir to a great oil fortune, was his best friend. Getty's death in April 2003 greatly upset Keith, who with his wife Marie attended the memorial service in Westminster Abbey.

Keith was walking through London's Piccadilly Circus one day when a Cockney newspaper boy he knew introduced him to a certain David Leney. "'e drives the Concorde," the boy said. In fact, Leney was second only to Brian Trubshaw in the hierarchy of Concorde fliers. This elite pilot then invited Keith to fly with him on the supersonic plane, sat him in the dickey seat behind the command seat and flew him to New York and back. Keith said he was amazed that you could see the curvature of the earth from 60,000 feet. For the seven-hour turnaround in New York, he stayed at the airport and bought a couple of bottles of grog, before boarding the return flight. Then the fun really started. "You, sir," said the Customs man in London. "You're Australian – yes? You've been in America – yes? For seven hours? What do you mean, seven hours? Where's your luggage?" Keith replied that he had none, and then waved the two plonk bottles. "This is all I've got," he said.

Why did Keith leave Victoria and play so much of his cricket for New South Wales? The answer is simple. When he went to war, he had been working for an oil company. When he came back, his superior (who did not go to war) said: "Miller, you've been away long enough – it's about time you did some work." Keith resisted turning the desk upside down on this ignorant chap and left the room. It was certainly a big gain for NSW. They won nine straight Sheffield Shields. No wonder: that side featured Arthur Morris, Alan Davidson and Richie Benaud.

Cricket owed much to Keith, but Keith owed much to cricket. Cricket saved his life once. In the Air Force in England, he knocked around with a group of ten mates. One day, he was asked to play cricket at Dulwich. He did, not knowing that while he was away playing cricket the Focke-Wulfs came over, shot up the base and killed all but one of his ten mates.

Keith always loved music. Whether it was Brahms or Mozart or Chopin, he derived deep satisfaction from it. When asked his favourite, his response was unequivocal: "Beethoven." His favourite Beethoven work was the Choral Symphony. When he was in this mood, he declared his love for poetry, and showed me a book of poems he was reading. He did not like to talk about cricket, but this discussion led him to speak of the high regard in which he held the Bradman family. He told me how attached he was to Lady Jessie and young John and Shirley. He said he babysat them several times.

Finally, what of stoic and devoted Marie? Such a selfless person, she said it was a pleasure to nurse Keith 24 hours a day for the last five and a half years of his life. She was upset by media reports that he died in a nursing home. He was never in a nursing home: he was always in her loving care. Keith was her life.

We do well to acclaim Keith. He was a free spirit who played for the joy of the game. As he leaves us to fly again among the clouds, those of us who knew him and watched him will forever be uplifted by indelible memories, and by the warmth of his company. Neville Cardus, who he knew well, once described him as "an Australian *in excelsis*".

I know Keith liked what Ray Robinson wrote about him: "The erect set of his capless head on his square shoulders, the loose swing of his long legs, the half smile on his handsome face and his general ease of manner all signify that no ordinary cricketer approaches. Long before Keith Miller gets near the wicket, you can tell something extraordinary is going to happen."

May he of blithe spirit, who fought the good fight – in everything – in his unique way of dash and splendour and decency and good fellowship, dwell among those who follow. Let us all thank him for the marvellous memories captured by the name of Keith Ross Miller. It remains a constant that the best teachers of humanity are the lives of great men.

This is an edited version of Tony Charlton's eulogy-in-chief to Keith Miller at his funeral service, St Paul's Anglican Cathedral, Melbourne, October 2004. Charlton is an immensely respected broadcaster and was a close friend to Miller.

Pickers of the crop

by JOHN BENAUD

Cricket selectors are generally such mild mannered, intelligent and selfless blokes that it surprises when those who rush to judge them offer such passionate and even divisive views. Like Greg Shipperd, the 2005 Victorian coach. It would be good news for Australian cricket if he pulled no weight in the choosing of future national selection panels.

When he was a player, Greg was a slowcoach, master of the dead bat. This old Australian selector was rostered for duty at Launceston in the 1989-90 season and remains numbed by the memory of every one of the 494 minutes Greg the Grit took to score 100 for Tasmania against Victoria. More unhappily, this was not the match where a snorting Merv Hughes, his searing short stuff absorbed by the well-padded body of Greg, referred to the opener as "the human mattress", a light moment that could have stirred us watchers from our moribund slumber, however briefly.

But as a coach, Shipperd has been transformed into an administrative slogger. No sooner had seven-term national selector Allan Border slipped his resignation under the door of Cricket Australia than Shipperd was publicly advocating his replacement should be a Victorian, implying a kinder deal was due for his charges. Greg said: "They [home selectors] just tend to see more of the team and the people who live in their state. They know more about the players and there can be a personal link."

This rather cynical burst of one-eyed marketing had its genesis in Victoria's 2003-04 Pura Cup win and the outspokenness of the then coach, the late David Hookes, who was never one to let a chance go by when lauding his own favourite players, and whose claims ignited a fierce debate over whether Victorian cricketers had got the rough end of the pineapple from a panel said to be heavily influenced by two Queenslanders – chairman Trevor Hohns and Border – plus a coach from Queensland, John Buchanan.

Ah, a conspiracy, or at the very least bias. Conspiracy theories and cricket selectors share headlines. Take the case of Clarrie Grimmett, a hero worth a brass plaque in any hall of Australian leg-spinning fame. When the Test selectors sacked him late in his career the colourful scuttlebutt was that it was all the work of Don Bradman – a plot.

It unfolded this way: in 1935-36, on the tour to South Africa, Grimmett took 44 wickets, highlighted by 7 for 100 and 6 for 73 in the final Test. Meanwhile, back in Australia, another leg-spinner had invaded Grimmett's home turf, Adelaide, to make his Sheffield Shield debut. His name was Frank Ward, from Don Bradman's old Sydney club St George. That summer, Ward and his captain Bradman – who was unavailable for the South African tour through illness – were the dominant players in South Australia's first Shield win for ten years. Ward took 50 wickets and Bradman made a thousand-plus runs. The whisper on cricket's grapevine was that Bradman thought Ward a "more penetrating spinner than Grimmett".

The next season, 1936-37, South Australia offered Ward a contract worth £5 to stay in Adelaide (conspiracy alert: Bradman must have organised that!). Also, Ward was named in Bradman's XI to oppose Richardson's XI, which included Grimmett and other South African tourists, in the season opener, the Bardsley-Gregory benefit match at the Sydney Cricket Ground.

RECENT AUSTRALIAN CRICKET SELECTORS

Lawrie Sawle (W Aust)	1983-84 to 1994-95
Dick Guy (NSW)	1984-85 to 1986-87
Greg Chappell (Qld)	1982-83 to 1988-89
Jim Higgs (Vic)	1984-85 to 1995-96
Bob Simpson (NSW)	1987-88 to 1993-94
John Benaud (NSW)	1989-90 to 1992-93
Trevor Hohns (Qld)	1993-94 to date
Steve Bernard (NSW)	1993-94 to 1995-96
Peter Taylor (Qld)	1994-95 to 1995-96
Geoff Marsh (W Aust)	1995-96 to 1997-98
Andrew Hilditch (S Aust)	1996-97 to date
Allan Border (Qld)	1998-99 to 2004-05
David Boon (Tas)	2000-01 to date
Merv Hughes (Vic)	2005-06 to date

Ward's match figures were 12 for 227, Grimmett's 7 for 228. Two weeks before the first Test, South Australia played Victoria at the Melbourne Cricket Ground. Jack Fingleton didn't play in the game but later wrote: "The Old Fox [Grimmett] wanted a man on the straight-hit fence, but Bradman disagreed with him and wouldn't give him what he wanted. Twice [Len] Darling lofted him to the straight-hit outfield, a stroke he would not have attempted had a fieldsman been there. In between overs Bradman said to Darling: 'I think the old man's finished, isn't he?'" Grimmett didn't play in the 1936-37 Ashes Tests against Gubby Allen's team, then wasn't selected to tour England in 1938.

Intrigue is a constant in the selection process, which is a cobweb of theories about every analytical assessment of a player's performance under pressure, all complicated by the selectors' (quite reasonable) decision not to go into too much detail publicly when they name a team.

The fact is, the Great Clarrie Conspiracy never was. Grimmett was 45 years old by then and being mightily challenged by Ward, comparatively just a lad at 30. First-class performances in 1936-37 favoured Ward, with 53 wickets to Grimmett's 48 (in 1937-38 it was Ward 51, Grimmett 41). The panel (on which Bradman was making his debut as a national selector) simply got the balance right, in terms of planning for the future – the age/form factor – and attack variation. The spinners who went to England under Bradman's captaincy were O'Reilly and Ward and "Chuck" Fleetwood-Smith, the left-arm wristy.

Of all the criticisms levelled at selectors, bias is the silliest, and rather juvenile. It merely echoes a fan's tribal instinct – "Go the Bushrangers" – and where in that nanosecond of emotion is there room for a considered judgment like team balance or the national good? But snaky fans frustrate administrators and the outcome is predictable: "Let's get our own selector on the panel!"

There's muddled thinking for you. Taken to its logical conclusion we could have a panel of six – one selector from each state: ludicrously unworkable, as anyone who has ever been to a local council meeting knows. Or noted the chaos that often besets Indian cricket where multi-representation will surely test Greg Chappell's enthusiasm for coaching.

Grumpy observers demanding "one of their own" at the selection table might try to explain how the squad of 15 that toured India and

South Africa in 1969-70 included Bill Lawry, the captain, Alan Connolly, Ray Jordon, Ian Redpath, Paul Sheahan and Keith Stackpole – six Victorians – yet was chosen by Bradman of South Australia, Neil Harvey of New South Wales and Phil Ridings of South Australia!

From 1988-93, on a panel of four, I was one of "too many selectors from New South Wales" (with Bob Simpson). Yet Mike Whitney, the season's leading wicket-taker from NSW, was omitted from the 1989 Ashes team, and in that period – arguably one trigger-point for this winning era – of the 36 Test players selected, only eight came from NSW.

Shipperd and his supporters are on a bumpy pitch. Objectivity is an essential quality in any selector, yet Shipperd creates the perception that he wants none of it. First-class experience, a good eye for the stand-out player, and an acute awareness of the challenges likely to be tossed up by an aging Australian squad are other traits the next lot of selectors might possess. Selecting, it should be conceded, is a tougher business in these modern times. The game has changed and, more to the point, so have the circumstances and conditions under which it is played. And players are more outspoken, emboldened by a union, influential managers and a halo of invincibility.

There is a much more substantive debate to be had about the impacts that mix can have on selection than whether or not there should be fewer Queenslanders in the mix. Certainly a national panel should be more diverse, more talent-balanced, like a cricket team. The old panel was capital-C conservative: similar ages and personalities, three disciplined top-order batsmen and a steady all-rounder – and a conservative coach to advise. When offered the most obvious futuristic moment, it dilly-dallied over Michael Clarke. And in 2005 it could find no room for rampaging Brett Lee against the shell-shocked Kiwis, although in 1959 a Bradman panel gob-smacked Richie Benaud by giving him four fast bowlers to drive a stake further into a demoralised England.

Maybe conservatism was good for these very good times and, confronted by a worldwide weakness in the Test game, there was no real pressure to make "potential judgments" (a contraposition to the 1980s, strong world cricket and a wobbly Australia in need of an engine rebuild).

But the next panel is being confronted by an era change, which West Indies botched in the mid-1990s. If it is conceded there should be room in the mix for an extrovert – a broad thinker, a bowler, maybe a fast bowler because they are less conservative – then Merv Hughes is the right man for the job.

It is likely the high-wage, contract system has dampened selectorial flair. There is a predisposition to remain inside the contract list – today a public document, but which in the old days was simply that little black book in the selectors' back pocket. Selection today has a public service feel to it, a pecking order. But so what if a choice from outside the contracts exposed the panel to an accusation of sloppy forward planning? The pity is that the cricketing public may never again see exciting, imaginative Test selections such as Ian Craig (aged 17) and Doug Walters (19).

There is pressure from ageing, rich players to stay in the game longer, and high-profile players even go public to express resentment at speculation that a team-mate in poor form might be dropped. The adage "never change a winning team" satisfies player egos but is dangerous territory for selectors. And what is this heady team preoccupation with win-loss records – "if we win this Test series 3–0 it will be the first time" – and so on? Arguably this "trophy mindset" has compromised what might be called dead-Test adventurism and may nobble era change.

Bradman's 1948 Invincibles' triumph (team average age 30 years, four months) ushered in era change. In 1951-52 Australia took a 3–1 series lead against West Indies, but in the dead fifth Test Bradman's selectors chose three debutants: two, Richie Benaud (aged 21) and Colin McDonald (23), became major forces in Australia's re-emergence. Dead-Test selection is just another form of player rotation, earnestly practised by this panel in the limited-overs form of the game, so why not in Test series?

And what are the ramifications for Test selection now that the World Cup is the Holy Grail? Summers ago, when the limited-overs game was the bastard child, the domestic World Series was occasionally used to slide a prospective Test player into the international pressure cooker. Now, visionary selectors looking for ways to toughen potential Test players are handcuffed by a World Cup whose status demands a more rigid preparatory selection process, by a decline in A-team international tours, and by a Pura Cup where international players rarely figure.

Lost also is the opportunity to educate players on what were once long tours like the Ashes, now grossly abbreviated to accommodate yet another limited-overs dash for cash. When Frank Ward went to England in 1938, Australia played 25 long matches, other than Tests. In 2005, Ponting's team played just four such matches where a rookie tourist could develop his skills.

When the squad for the 2005 Ashes tour was announced, the headline could have been "Ashes team shock": shock, because there was no shock. The modern orthodox balance in an Ashes line-up was strictly adhered to – seven batsmen, two keepers, two spinners and five fast bowlers – and every player deserved selection. There wasn't a name from left-field, not a whiff of risk just in case England did turn out to be its most competitive since 1987.

So, imagine if this conservative panel had decided that the batsmen-wicket-keepers Haddin and Gilchrist could quite adequately cover the reserve batting spot and, in an outbreak of enthusiastic futurism, had given the last spot not to Brad Hodge from Victoria, but to the rookie off-spinner Dan Cullen (aged 21) from South Australia.

Now, would that have been bias against Victoria, a conspiracy, an unwarranted gamble? Or just a good, old-fashioned example of how to forward plan in case the inevitable retirements of today's match-winning spinners, Warne and MacGill, come sooner rather than later?

John Benaud is a former Australian player, selector, journalist, editor and brother of Richie.

Lunatics' coup in the asylum

by JOHN TOWNSEND

The few remaining Colonel Blimps on the Western Australian Cricket Association membership list might have feared that the lunatics had finally taken over the asylum with the appointment of Dennis Lillee as president. But since Lillee, he of the aluminium bat-flinging, the nasty run-in with Javed Miandad and the bane of administrators across the land, was elected in September 2004 nothing could be further from the truth.

The WACA might still sometimes resemble a mad house, particularly in the world's worst press box where journalists crane across each other to get a glimpse of the pitch and scoreboard, but it has rarely been in better hands. Lillee, the great and flamboyant fast bowler, has turned gamekeeper, and the sport in Western Australia is showing the same signs of stirring as when he turned at the top of his mark.

Lillee was the most prominent member of a small group of influential former players that had been concerned for several years about the state's direction. Last winter, he decided to do something about it. He organised an election ticket and even ran a campaign, which admittedly amounted to little more than a couple of well-placed newspaper stories on the well-worn theme that it was time for a change. But he was acting like the leader of a powerful lobby.

Sam Gannon, who took his chance during World Series Cricket to play three Tests, is a millionaire several times over on the back of his financial services business, and he became the balance-sheet number-cruncher. The former Test opener Graeme Wood, who led Western Australia to a hat-trick of Sheffield Shield titles but was later dumped during a clumsy player coup, was also heavily involved. A senior employee at Carlton and United Beverages, one of Australian cricket's main sponsors, Wood remains one of the game's clearest thinkers. Daryl Foster, a highly successful coach, began his career with the state soon after Lillee, has been a constant ever since, and is a precise back-room planner and organiser. Although Foster and Lillee hold fundamentally opposite positions on the legality of Muttiah Muralidaran's action, Foster's ability to massage support proved crucial to the campaign.

Behind Lillee, the most significant yet least-known member of the ticket was David Williams, the former lawyer and hotel executive. A decent club spinner, Williams was vice-president at the University club and a WACA delegate in the 1970s, but he made his name in sports administration as the president of Subiaco football club at the time the West Coast Eagles joined the then VFL. The club was based at Subiaco Oval and Williams was one of the first to see the benefits of tying long-term ticketing and sponsorship deals to the ground. His foresight has paid massive dividends for Subiaco, who are now based at another inner city ground but earn $1 million a year from their links to Subiaco Oval.

Although Williams had little of the profile of his running mates, his acumen helped drive the campaign. His advice that Lillee should run as president was crucial. With a Perth grandstand named in his honour, Lillee is the biggest name in Western Australian cricket. However, he was originally content to push for a place on the new board with Williams leading the charge. Cannily reversing the positions, Williams had his eye on the chairmanship, where the real WACA power resided.

> "Lillee was the most prominent member of a small group of influential former players concerned about the state's direction. Last winter, he decided to do something about it"

No gesture from the new faces was more symbolic than the one on the day they were elected to office. Williams and Lillee, who shared an abhorrence of the previous ties, swiftly brushed aside the old guard. Brian Rakich, the president and a WACA blue-blood, was out. A member of the executive for a quarter of a century, Rakich was a superb public spruiker for the values of cricket in general and, in particular, the WACA. Nonetheless, he was a key target for replacement – along with the vice-president Bob Paulsen and the chairman Charles Fear – if Western Australia were to regenerate.

The association had made a loss for four consecutive years, it was seen to drive out the young and talented batsman Simon Katich, the best player produced in the state for a decade, and was clearly on the nose in government, media, sponsorship, membership and public circles. Anchored by a $13 million debt used to redevelop the ground, the former administration had also put significant store in attracting the new Super 14 rugby union franchise. Even when it was blatantly apparent that rugby's preference was the neighbouring Perth Oval, a former football ground since redeveloped with $25 million of state government support for the Perth Glory soccer team, the WACA continued to promote itself as a superior venue.

Inextricably linked to the past, the old guard had a bloated sense of importance not supported by reality or reflected in their standing in the cricket community. However, for all the perception that it was time for a change, Lillee and his cohorts received a free kick of enormous magnitude shortly

> "Lillee has startled old friends and colleagues who never thought they would see a fire-breathing dragon morph into a silk-tongued persuader"

before the election ballot. In July 2004, the WACA uncovered a fraud by one of its employees that had resulted in at least $170,000 being siphoned out over several years. The worker was later jailed and the money recovered under insurance, but the shock of the crime, which was immediately seen as an analogy for the WACA's woes, resonated throughout the state. There was no surprise when the regular ballot three months later ended in Lillee and his team being elected in a landslide.

Lillee knew his task would be difficult, but he surprised the members, many of whom had taken a punt on a big name, with a concise and warm acceptance speech. He has become increasingly comfortable in the position and startled old friends and colleagues who never thought they would see a fire-breathing dragon morph into a silk-tongued persuader. "My role will be one of a person who has lots of contacts and who will be able to convince people to join the WACA – the new WACA that we are heading for," Lillee said at the time. "I am under no illusions that I can walk in and swan around. I have to get the gloves on and get dirty. But I'm not averse to that.

I know I have to work hard. Instead of being one of the critics, I thought I should get in there and have a go."

The success of a membership drive, a project given immediate impetus when 300 people re-joined the day his election was announced, was immediate, but it was the activity the scenes that spoke of an organisation fixed on its goals and capable of achieving them. Lillee, Williams and Tony Dodemaide, the chief executive appointed four months before the ballot, were to push the specifics of immediate discussions with the state government, negotiations that were to prove fruitful just before Christmas 2004 when it was announced that a $5 million package would be provided to help retire some of the crippling debt. Although not directly related to the funding package, the WACA had previously announced it would embrace the burgeoning East Perth residential district, a booming inner-city precinct, by making the ground available as a public green space during winter and perhaps selling off some of the unused corners for commercial or residential use.

The most recent project for Williams and Gannon was an 82-part revamp of the WACA's operations, moves that included the dumping of the cricket manager Rob Langer, the uncle of the captain Justin Langer and a former team-mate of Lillee's, and his off-sider Darrin Ramshaw. Up to 15 jobs would go and operations would become more centralised under the new scheme as the board attempted to slash its annual costs by $200,000 and increase efficiency. "We have to cut our coat to suit our cloth," Williams said. "The WACA has no winter tenant and is heavy with bureaucracy. We have inherited this situation and we have to do something about it."

Lillee has achieved much and relishes a new leadership role, although as Western Australia's most successful Sheffield Shield captain – two wins from three matches – it should not come as a surprise. But few would have believed he would laud Cricket Australia for running the game well, as he did recently during an unguarded moment. That should be music to the ears of CA's chairman Bob Merriman, a Lillee fan who once pronounced sentence against the fast bowler over that incident with Miandad. Times really have changed.

John Townsend writes on cricket for The West Australian.

The one that didn't get away

by BELINDA CLARK

Entering the 2005 Women's World Cup there was much talk about Australia making amends for our four-run loss to New Zealand in the final almost five years earlier. It was a lurking memory, especially because an agonisingly small defeat is worse than a thrashing. We had been dominant throughout that tournament in New Zealand and this time in South Africa there was a real sense that we were not going to let things slip or fail to face up to match-day challenges.

The determination to make up for lost opportunity was a thought we carried through the campaign and it was clearly evident in the squad. Karen Rolton highlighted the mindset in the final against India with her unbeaten 107 as we went through the event undefeated. After our tour of the subcontinent in December 2004 I realised that India would be a bigger threat than other teams expected. We knew they would be difficult to beat, especially in a final.

Gathering for the national anthems and preparing to represent your country is the most nerve-wracking moment. There was such a great sense of anticipation on April 10 at Centurion's SuperSport Park of what was about to unfold. But they didn't play the Australian anthem. Instead of *Advance Australia Fair* we got one of our warm-up training songs, *The Time Is Now* by Moloko. Fortunately it was a mistake that helped break the tension – we all laughed – and it allowed us to escape from the tight pre-match experience.

As an opening batter I was starting to hit the ball well in the second half of the tournament, when things began to click and I moved into some good form. So I was pretty disappointed when I was caught behind off Amita Sharma because I was starting to break the shackles. However, we all felt a little more at ease after Rolton's innings, which was supported superbly by Lisa Sthalekar's 55. At the change of innings we knew that if we stuck to our plans and bowled and fielded well the game was locked up, which was the way it panned out with India 98 runs short of our 4 for 215.

Paul Kane/Getty Images

Australian women's captain Belinda Clark with the World Cup trophy safe in her grasp.

Following a big victory, particularly a final, all we want to do is sit in the dressing-room with the people who have put in the hard work. The reality is different and there is always an official function. There was a quick chance to relax before we were rushed off to our other commitments and a long night of celebrating. Winning a World Cup is the ultimate team achievement because the tournament places every side under the same conditions and requires players to peak at the same time. That doesn't happen on a tour-by-tour basis, making it the absolute test.

One of the most important breakthroughs from this event was that the final was shown on Australian television. The decision made an unbelievable difference as young girls – even players in the state sides – got to watch instead of only hearing about it. That was inspirational. For the junior women in the side, the ones who want to take the reins in the future, it was a time to get a picture of where they were as international cricketers and realise what was necessary to take the game to the next level. After winning back the trophy it is now their challenge to defend the World Cup in four years and avoid the need to make up for lost opportunity.

Belinda Clark has captained Australia to two Women's World Cups and scored 1,151 runs in the tournament at an average of 60.57.

WOMEN'S WORLD CUP WINNERS

Series	Venue	Result
1973	Birmingham (England)	England defeated Australia by 92 runs
1977-78	Hyderabad (India)	Australia defeated England by eight wickets
1981-82	Christchurch (New Zealand)	Australia defeated England by three wickets
1988-89	Melbourne (Australia)	Australia defeated England by eight wickets
1993	Lord's (England)	England defeated New Zealand by 67 runs
1997-98	Calcutta (India)	Australia defeated New Zealand by five wickets
2000-01	Lincoln (New Zealand)	New Zealand defeated Australia by four runs
2004-05	Centurion (South Africa)	Australia defeated India by 98 runs

DAMIEN MARTYN on his way to a seemingly effortless century against Pakistan in Melbourne, rounding off a replete calendar year.
Photo by William West, Getty Images.

2

The Players

Glenn McGrath

by GEOFF LAWSON

Throughout Australia's dominance of world cricket, there has been much talk of the batting genius of Ponting, the broadening skills of Martyn, the determination and luck of Langer, the relative decline of Hayden and the striking purity of Gilchrist. The batsmen have broken records in huge volume, increased their scoring pace to un-matched levels and returned more newspaper and magazine column inches than their bowling counterparts. It is true that dynamic and aggressive batting have been significant ingredients of Australia's table-topping position. Other countries manage it only in spits and spurts – and, until this year, not consistently against the world champions. However, what is regularly overlooked is the perform-ance of quality bowlers and Glenn McGrath, the attack's durable and outstanding leader.

Old timers would say "batsmen save games, bowlers win them". The one-day contest has bent that maxim out of shape, but when it comes to the longer format very little has changed. Yes, Australia score quickly. Yes, they give themselves more time to bowl out the opposition. But – it is an important but – they must still knock over their rivals twice. Having a quality leg-spinner is handy; owning the bowler of the century is much better. But before Shane Warne gets the ball, the swing, seam and snarl of McGrath and his first-class sidekicks come into play. It is something that has happened with astounding success for more than a decade.

At 35, McGrath looked at the start of the Ashes series, like a well-preserved middle-aged fast bowler rather than a greybeard having his last tilt at the English windmills. Not many international pacemen bowl into their mid-30s. A small number such as Courtney Walsh and Sir Richard Hadlee have become legends at a similar age, but they are the exceptions justifying Rule 1a of the quick brigade: "The more overs you bowl, the faster you will fall apart." For most of his career McGrath has kept himself together. While his colleagues have fallen to deteriorating backs, knees and shoulders – repetitive strain injuries

Glenn McGrath: the cap still fits.

are common in teenagers, not just 35-year-olds – McGrath's recent weakness has been the ankles.

From mid-2003 McGrath was forced into a 12-month hiatus due to problems with three bone spurs causing unbearable pain when he put his left foot down. Two operations were required and while his comeback was reportedly aborted on many occasions, McGrath was happy that it went to plan. However, by the time of his selection for the Sri Lanka Top End series in July 2004 there were doubts over his powers of recovery – except from the man himself.

The decision was controversial as his main gallops were limited to an end-of-season Pura Cup match, the one-day tour to Zimbabwe and a warm-up against the Sri Lankans for the Northern Territory Chief Minister's XI. McGrath's performances were not impressive, but as a veteran of more than 400 Test wickets he had up his sleeve a benefit-of-the-doubt card. Already a couple had been played, but he was entitled to another and the national selectors agreed. Fast bowlers rely on their legs and they gain strength from matches, not just the nets. McGrath needed more work and, most importantly, had to test his vital feet, which would carry him to the crease and support the pressure of up to 20 times his body weight at release. Bleeding toes and aching ankles are part of the job description, but he had to know if his cleaned-up bones could sustain the Test load.

While struggling to find quickly the death-and-taxes rhythm, McGrath openly doubted his ability to make a full comeback aged 34. In his initial outings his pace was down on the modest 130 kph he usually bowls; it was not the only thing that had seemingly diminished. The hitherto infallible radar was finding the middle of the bat instead of the edge. As he hit the crease he looked to be decelerating, he was lacking energy, his body was creaking and the results were poor. Pundits saw all the signs of rust and retirement. Who would begrudge the most successful Australian seam bowler of all time a cup of tea and a good lie down? He had surely earned it. But that was not his way.

McGrath soldiered on with the kind of self-belief that is at the core of any real champion. The recovery improved, the pain in the ankle faded and he was rapidly back to his best. In his first Test innings he took five wickets against Sri Lanka and then passed 450 on the unfriendly pitches of India, where a serious drought that started the year before he was born ended. Back in the southern hemisphere he destroyed New Zealand with 27 home-and-away wickets at

17.29 and sandwiched career-best figures of 8 for 24 against Pakistan in Perth. Each series was won and there were no longer arguments about his health. The feeling was so good that he even hit 61 not out against New Zealand at the Gabba.

The body that had been brittle as a NSW rookie had become resilient through hard work with Kevin Chevell, his fitness training mentor who had once again whipped him into shape. Through the programme the thigh, hamstring and calf strains that beset the pigeon legs have been eradicated. McGrath's work ethic has always been strong; his training load, just like his bowling, might embarrass a Benedictine monk. Kostya Tszyu and Mike Tyson recently realised that comebacks on the edge of the age envelope were not easy, but McGrath showed they were possible with a steel-trap mental approach.

There was also another incentive: his Cricket Australia contract ranking dropped while he was injured and his earnings and ego were affected. Money certainly acts as a carrot to the contemporary cricketer and McGrath makes millions from the game. Players of not-so-long-ago would retire so they could earn a living that didn't require the body to be a temple rather than spend months or years recuperating and rehabilitating. McGrath had the support of Cricket Australia's medical team, the board and a full-time contract that allowed him to train, recover and still pay the mortgage.

Glenn McGrath reaches 500 Test wickets, Lord's, 2005.

Hamish Blair/Getty Images

He used the resources well. The dedication and discipline came as no surprise – the completeness of the comeback surely has. Leaving for England with 499 wickets, he became the second fast bowler to step to 500 at Lord's in July. Only then did his body begin to betray him.

What had helped propel McGrath so far is an advantage that few other bowlers have carried. Simply, it is simplicity. The simplicity of his action, his bowling mechanics, is a large part of this successful comeback. He puts a minimal amount of stress on his body because he has an action that doesn't have a lot of stress points. He doesn't bowl fast because he doesn't try to bowl fast, therefore the pressure on his frame is low. McGrath's front leg – the left one – rises only centimetres above the ground in delivery. The true fast bowlers such as Lillee, Thomson and Hogg had theirs almost parallel to the turf, spikes pointing menacingly at the trembling batsmen. This position created huge strain on the hamstrings, groin and the back.

McGrath has a principally front-on action with almost no trunk rotation so his back has been preserved. When he delivers he uses all of his 183 cm height with a braced and extended front leg: there is little impact on the crease because of that lack of leg-lift, the long, tensile arms rotate smoothly and the whip-cord wrist keeps the seam perfect and adds the maximum pace. It is a beautiful and simple movement, the Swiss watch of the timekeepers and the Ernie Els of golf. Perhaps it is the deceptive yet stealthy action that has batsmen not quite cocked to repel another line and length delivery. The term "false sense of security" comes to mind, but how could any rational batsmen feel secure with 'Pigeon' creeping to the crease?

Tactic-wise McGrath's methods are similarly simple. He hits the wicket hard, unlike the kissing-the-pitch and sliding-along styles of Brett Lee or the late Malcolm Marshall. This way he makes the margins for error larger and the "good length" a wider concept. Aiming just outside off-stump, he lands the ball on the seam almost every time, increasing the chances of late movement, and in between delivering a loose ball every leap year waits for batsmen to err. He has been helped by wonderful support bowling and some of the best fieldsmen and catchers of all time, who contribute to the never-slackening pressure. The quality of his opponents could be legitimately questioned with strong arguments pointing to the decline in world batting standards, but his victories over the superstars of any era – Lara, Tendulkar, Kirsten, Fleming et al. – are significant.

McGrath, who grew up in Narromine in central NSW, comes from an uncomplicated rural background where hard work and perseverance were essential for survival in a harsh and unforgiving climate. They are conditions similar to elite sport. While the dash and flair of Australia's batsmen are up in neon lights, McGrath has helped haul the side to the top with his simplicity, hard work, adherence to a fundamental yet almost unique bowling discipline and wonderful tactical sense. He is the true colossus of the early 21st century bowlers.

Geoff Lawson took 180 wickets in 46 Tests for Australia between 1980 and 1989.

WISDEN AUSTRALIA CRICKETER OF THE YEAR

1998	Belinda Clark
1999	Glenn McGrath
2000-01	Steve Waugh
2001-02	Glenn McGrath
2002-03	Adam Gilchrist
2003-04	Ricky Ponting
2004-05	Darren Lehmann
2005-06	Glenn McGrath

WISDEN AUSTRALIA PURA CUP CRICKETER OF THE YEAR

Michael Bevan

by MARTIN BLAKE

Cricket is a mind game above all others with the possible exception of golf, the ultimate masochists' pursuit. It is something Michael Bevan, the most driven of Australian players, knows only too well. Bevan spent more than a decade trying to prove himself on the world stage while fighting a losing battle against certain perceptions of his batting, notably that he had a weakness against the short ball and was thus the dreaded "one-day specialist".

So when he lost his lucrative Cricket Australia contract at the end of 2003-04 and went back to negotiate the relative pittance of a salary with his beloved New South Wales, his cricketing life reached a genuine flashpoint. He knew his international career was probably finished at 34, unfair as that might have been given his one-day average of 53.58 and a reputation for owning three or four shots to every ball.

Always a different card, Bevan chose to pack up and play in Tasmania, who also offered an assistant coaching job. He arrived in Hobart with a mindset that reflected the fact he was no longer required to prove anything to anyone beyond himself. Brian McFadyen, the coach, soon noticed the change. While it was different from before, there was also a familiarity about it. McFadyen, now ensconced as a senior coach at the Centre of Excellence in Brisbane, sensed Bevan wanted to play like he had all those years ago, when it was just another game. In essence, he had gone back to the swashbuckling kid from Canberra who lit up NSW upon his arrival at the end of the 1980s. The result was astonishing. Jamie Cox, the state's veteran top-order batsman, called it "phenomenal". McFadyen preferred "out of this world".

Bevan played nine Pura Cup matches for Tasmania in 2004-05 after missing the opening game with an Achilles injury. He made eight centuries, an Australian record for a single season. He accumulated 1,464 runs, breaking the all-time domestic mark of 1,381, which was set only the season before by Matthew Elliott, another

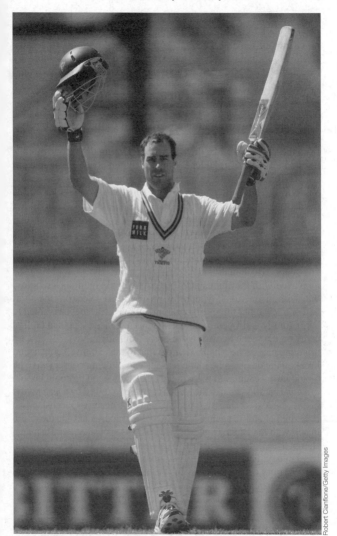

Michael Bevan: more runs, more milestones, more records, more plaudits

left-hander. He averaged 97.60 and Phil Jaques, the next best player, was 273 runs behind. Tasmania's poor season meant he had no chance of making the final, and combined with his first-game absence, four potential hits were sacrificed. It is said that there are lies, damned lies and statistics, but there is no disguising this one. It is a big number, a significant number, and one for the ages.

Beginning with a muffled 19 and a magnificent, unbeaten 167 against Victoria at Bellerive Oval, Bevan scarcely stopped. Tasmania's season at four-day level was dreadful as they finished last in a competition won by NSW. At least they could watch Bevan from the sanctuary of the dressing-room. During the second innings he and the feisty all-rounder Damien Wright met at 6 for 46 and put on 215 for the seventh wicket, a record for Tasmania, who defied Victoria for hour after hour. Bevan survived 439 minutes in the maelstrom and was still there when the Bushrangers secured their first win in Hobart for 25 years. Despite the loss, he was on a roll.

A match later he conjured 106 and 100, from only 137 balls, against South Australia as the Tigers won by 195 runs. Around this point McFadyen spotted the change in Bevan's batting from previous years. "He actually backed himself more," he says. "I suppose he played with the chains off. I've got no doubt he'd played before that with distractions, whether it was national selection, the short ball or a few other things around him." It was clear that he wanted to bat naturally and fluently, like he had as a teenager. "When he first came on the scene he was aggressive," McFadyen says. "Like a lot of young players he's had to temper that to make himself consistent. I reckon the decision he made was instead of being conservative he would throw caution to the wind and see how good he could be."

Twin centuries against the Redbacks were followed by a lean period in the context of his summer: 11 and 93 against Queensland in Brisbane; 21 and 12 against NSW in Sydney; and 42 and 4 in the return match with the Bulls. However, the rest was special. After Tasmania slumped to 3 for 23 against West Australia at Bellerive Oval in late January, he peeled off a first-innings 190. As they aimed to set the Warriors a target, Bevan hit the ball even better in the second innings, gleaning an unbeaten 114 out of 5 for 226. Symptomatic of their season, they lost despite setting a monumental 396.

The runaway train was still motoring when, confronted by a Victoria attack headed by Shane Warne, he toiled for 434 minutes over 144, then gathered 86 of Tasmania's limp 198 as they were again defeated. When the Tigers met NSW in Hobart, Bevan smashed an unbeaten 170 against Stuart MacGill and his impressive company. As the Blues rolled to victory on the final day MacGill had his revenge, dismissing Bevan for 26, which was a rare failure on his new home deck.

Bellerive Oval has a reputation as a batsman's paradise, but Bevan was not getting it easy. McFadyen said the curator at the beautiful ground beside the Derwent estuary was urged to prepare "result wickets" and duly delivered. "There was juice left in and the first hour of each first innings was always difficult," he says. "It was not a traditional batsman-friendly wicket. The scores don't reflect that because it dried out on the third and fourth days. I can tell you it was bloody difficult." In the tough conditions, against quality opposition, and on surfaces helping the pace bowlers, Bevan was unflappable. Even McFadyen was slightly surprised. "There's been a question mark about him when it's difficult and he's been labelled a one-day player," he says. "He did not look like missing a ball, didn't look like playing and missing for the whole season."

Cox recognised an old look in Bevan's eye. "I played under-age cricket with Michael and even then he had the aloofness, if you like, that a lot of special players have," he says. "There's this zone where they go and you wonder what they're thinking. You look at them and you know they're ready to go." By the final game Bevan's mind was still churning, and as they arrived in Adelaide he needed another 76 runs to overtake Elliott's landmark. With 115 and 44 he succeeded in another loss, which won the wooden spoon, and completed a four-game streak of centuries in the world's toughest domestic competition.

The Pura Cup had ended for Tasmania but their season wasn't entirely over. In the ING Cup final Bevan hit a typically inventive 47 not out from 52 balls that helped them to a famous victory over Queensland, the state's first one-day trophy since the Gillette Cup in 1978-79. Enjoying a fine season on that stage, too, he captured 519 runs at 86.50. "In the end, it got ridiculous," Cox says. "We were almost taking it for granted. He'd score a hundred late in the year, and you could see the blokes almost forgetting to pat him on the back."

Bevan told the media he was still improving, and that he remained hopeful of a berth at the 2007 World Cup. He refused to make a retirement announcement, a fact that surprised no one who knew him well. "I'm a better player than when I was in the Australian side, no doubt about it," he says. "The World Cup is a long way off but I don't think it's out of the question. I hope it isn't. It's nice to know that at this stage of my life I'm hitting the ball the best I've ever hit it."

All of which must make people wonder why Bevan, the artist and sometimes cantankerous player, completed his international career with only 18 Tests, an average of 29.07, and precisely zero centuries. The answer is in the timing. Bevan played in an era when Australian batting opportunities were limited, a fact the likes of Cox, Jamie Siddons, Stuart Law and even Dean Jones could attest, too. Then there was the short-ball perception and the associated mind games and battles. Devon Malcolm, the very-quick English bowler, made him flinch a couple of times in the 1994-95 Ashes series. Bevan paid a massive price for those moments of discomfort, and the irony was that nearing the end of his career he was flaying the short ball.

"It's a myth, there's no doubt about it," Cox says of the weakness-against-the-short-ball theory. "It was exposed on one trip by one bowler. If you watched him last year he pulled and hooked beautifully. People tested him out because they thought he was weak, but he smacked them."

Everyone already knew that Bevan was a fine player and a highly-charged individual. In a sense he was ahead of his time because he did not fit the archetypal Australian cricket legend of the beer-swilling man's man, the image cultivated by the Chappells, Lillee, Marsh and Walters. He was a gym rat and a fitness fanatic long before it became the norm of the modern

> "I'm a better player than when I was in the Australian side, no doubt about it" says Bevan

professionals. What was not so widely known was that his hunger was undiminished by the vagaries of selection and the bodyblow of losing his contract.

"His strength is his ability to remain focused on the job at hand," McFadyen says, "but he probably expects that of everyone." While he has been labelled as difficult, last season he was a role model who would spend a couple of hours on the bowling machine the day before a game.

Sitting back watching the show, McFadyen reasoned that if Bevan was picked for Australia again he would thrive. It probably won't happen, but it's a nice thought. "Most of us who witnessed it felt his batting was as good as anything we'd ever seen," he says. "It wasn't just one or two performances, it was every time he went out. It was out of this world."

Martin Blake writes on sport for The Age.

WISDEN AUSTRALIA PURA CUP CRICKETER OF THE YEAR

1998	Colin Miller (Tas)
1999	Simon Katich (WAust)
2000-01	Paul Reiffel (Vic)
2001-02	Jamie Cox (Tas)
2002-03	Jimmy Maher (Qld)
2003-04	Wade Seccombe (Qld)
2004-05	Matthew Elliott (Vic)
2005-06	Michael Bevan (Tas)

Player Profiles

The players in this section appeared in first-class or limited-overs matches during 2004-05, or are scheduled to feature in the 2005-06 Australian season. Statistics are accurate to July 20, 2005.

Profiles written by
Phil Wilkins (New South Wales)
Stephen Gray (Queensland)
Nabila Ahmed (Victoria)
Daniel Brettig (South Australia)
Ric Finlay (Tasmania)
Ken Casellas (West Australia)

NATHAN ADCOCK *Right-hand batsman, right-arm fast-medium bowler*   **SA**
Occasionally Adcock has looked as if he might make the leap from extra to reliable middle-order cast member. Given an extended run in 2004-05 ahead of flashier players like Mark Higgs, Adcock contributed an admirably gritty innings to cancel out Doug Bollinger's ING hat-trick for NSW at Manuka, while a similarly stubborn display against the same side stretched a home Pura Cup defeat well into the fourth day. The balance of his performances, however, did not provide consistent evidence that he could achieve a regular position at state level. With only two scores above 50 in a first-class career now eight years old, Adcock will have to produce something special to interest the selectors in 2005-06.

	M	I	NO	Runs	HS	100s	50s	Avge	Ct	St	W	Avge	BB
First-class	18	32	1	700	114	1	1	22.58	19	0	2	108.00	1/19
Dom. first-class	16	30	1	585	67	0	1	20.17	13	0	2	108.00	1/19
Dom. limited-overs	26	25	1	456	62*	0	4	19.00	9	0	0	–	

*Denotes not out.

JASON ARNBERGER *Right-hand batsman*   **Victoria**
No one was more realistic than Arnberger when he was ruled out early in the season with a back injury just before his 32nd birthday. With Graeme Rummans bearing down upon him, Arnberger hoped only for another chance, and he did not have to wait long. Continuing from his sparkling Pura Cup final performance in 2003-04, Arnberger enjoyed a resurgence, finishing the season as Victoria's second-highest run-scorer despite playing only six matches. His role in the victory in Brisbane was critical, and when Victoria were trying to transform their mathematical possibility to an actual finals berth late in the season, it was the seasoned right-hander who stood up in a struggling batting line-up. With Matthew Elliott departing to South Australia, Arnberger will become even more vital to Victoria's chances in 2005-06.

	M	I	NO	Runs	HS	100s	50s	Avge	Ct	St	W	Avge	BB
First-class	78	146	10	5,328	214	11	30	39.18	55	0	0	–	–
Dom. first-class	74	140	10	5,178	214	11	29	39.83	51	0	0	–	–
Dom. limited-overs	27	26	1	541	79	0	4	21.64	0	0	–	–	–

CULLEN BAILEY *Right-arm leg-spinner* **SA**

An intelligent, skilful deliverer of flighted leg-breaks, Bailey was handed a state cap for the final match of the season against Tasmania. With loop, bounce and turn he bagged the wickets of Jamie Cox and Damien Wright. He shares Daniel Cullen's name and enthusiasm: spectators enjoyed the spectacle of two 20-year-olds trying to twirl the ball past Michael Bevan. Bailey's outstanding return for Sturt last summer (44 wickets at 20.36) was comparable to the season Daniel Cullen enjoyed before playing at first-class level, and there is every chance "Cullen and Cullen" will operate in tandem for SA in future seasons. A media student at the University of Adelaide, Bailey has penned many thoughtful articles for the SACA's website.

	M	I	NO	Runs	HS	100s	50s	Avge	Ct	St	W	Avge	BB
First-class	1	1	0	0	0	0	0	0.00	0	0	2	41.00	2/82
Dom. first-class	1	1	0	0	0	0	0	0.00	0	0	2	41.00	2/82

GEORGE BAILEY *Right-hand batsman* **Tasmania**

Bailey marked his first-class debut with a typically breezy 70 at the SCG, but only made 115 runs in his other eight innings. He is part of Tasmania's future in the Pura Cup, but he will be expected to shoulder more of the burden next season, especially given his experience in ING Cup ranks. He played in all ten matches in the latter competition, contributing some useful runs in the middle order, and saving many more in the field with his athletic agility. His appearance in the Twenty20 match at Bellerive wearing what looked to be a hairpiece stolen from Tiny Tim's wardrobe received some bemused comment from onlookers.

	M	I	NO	Runs	HS	100s	50s	Avge	Ct	St	W	Avge	BB
First-class	5	9	1	185	70	0	1	23.13	3	0	0	–	–
Dom. first-class	5	9	1	185	70	0	1	23.13	3	0	0	–	–
Dom. limited-overs	23	21	6	423	57*	0	2	28.20	9	0	1	38.00	1/19

MICHAEL BEVAN *Left-hand batsman* **Tasmania**

The marriage of Bevan and Bellerive was consummated in style in 2004-05 as he smashed the old record for most runs in a season at Tasmania's home venue by more than 200 runs, pushing the new mark out to 938. Bevan also holds the corresponding record for the SCG (741 in 1993-94) and only Bill Ponsford's record of 1,013 at the MCG in 1927-28 heads him at any Australian venue. What makes his feat more extraordinary was that none of his colleagues seemed inclined to join him in this run spree, and he scored more than a quarter of his team's output. Record after record fell to him as he took at least one century from every domestic attack except Queensland (nipped in the bud at 93), and in the case of South Australia, three. He won the Pura Cup Player of the Year award, and might have done the same in the ING Cup, since he was the heaviest run-scorer in the competition, and played for the winning team. However, calls for his re-instatement in the Australian team fail to recognise Bevan's fielding, which used to be brilliant but now befits a man in his mid-thirties.

	M	I	NO	Runs	HS	100s	50s	Avge	Ct	St	W	Avge	BB
First-class	227	382	66	18,502	216	67	77	58.55	120	0	117	45.32	6/82
Dom. first-class	108	193	36	9,976	216	41	37	63.54	47	0	23	63.48	3/40
Test	18	30	3	785	91	0	6	29.07	8	0	29	24.24	6/82
Int'l limited-overs	232	196	67	6,912	108*	6	46	53.58	69	0	36	45.97	3/36
Dom. limited-overs	70	70	24	2,997	135*	2	24	65.15	18	0	5	38.80	2/24

ANDY BICHEL *Right-arm fast-medium bowler*   **Queensland**

Although Bichel is playing cricket of international standard he seems unlikely to play for Australia again. Once more he rolled up his sleeves and got the job done for Queensland. He broke a record held by Craig McDermott, one of his early mentors, by taking 60 wickets for the season at 22.10. Starting with ten wickets against NSW in the opening game, he was often the difference between winning and losing for Queensland, with two of his five-wicket hauls coming in the second innings. He also topped the Queensland bowling in the one-day competition with 14 at 26.21. He did receive some recognition, called up for the FICA World XI against New Zealand in January 2005. In a short stint with Hampshire over winter he scored a remarkable 138 on debut after his team had been 7 for 81. The innings was all the more noteworthy considering he had needed laser surgery on his eye after a gardening mishap.

	M	I	NO	Runs	HS	100s	50s	Avge	Ct	St	W	Avge	BB
First-class	143	188	18	4,010	142	5	14	23.59	76	0	584	25.81	9/93
Dom. first-class	67	93	9	1,840	112	2	6	21.90	35	0	334	22.27	7/77
Test	19	22	1	355	71	0	1	16.90	16	0	58	32.24	5/60
Int'l limited-overs	67	36	13	471	64	0	1	20.48	19	0	78	31.59	7/20
Dom. limited-overs	57	37	10	608	62	0	2	22.52	17	0	61	34.05	4/45

TRAVIS BIRT *Left-hand batsman* **Tasmania**

Birt emerged from 2004-05 as Tasmania's best long-term prospect, a reputation built upon some rollicking innings opening in the one-day side. He hit 13 sixes in both competitions over the summer. He extended by some distance the Tasmanian record for an individual innings in the one-day competition, making 145 against South Australia, while his 55 off 26 balls in the Twenty20 match against Western Australia left spectators gasping. His record in the Pura Cup was more modest, averaging only a sedately-compiled 20.69 in eight matches and frequently falling to catches behind the stumps before he got started. He will, however, have fond memories of his first full season at senior level, playing an integral role in Tasmania's ING Cup victory.

	M	I	NO	Runs	HS	100s	50s	Avge	Ct	St	W	Avge	BB
First-class	8	16	0	331	57	0	2	20.69	3	0	–	–	–
Dom. first-class	8	16	0	331	57	0	2	20.69	3	0	–	–	–
Dom. limited-overs	11	11	0	358	145	1	0	32.55	2	0	–	–	–

GREG BLEWETT *Right-hand batsman, right-arm medium bowler*   **SA**

Though he had an outstanding all-round season in the ING Cup, Blewett struggled with the four-day game in 2004-05. Without reliable batting partners, he found it difficult to make flowing starts, seldom batted with anything like his former authority, and failed to make a century. Always a languid, relaxed cricketer, Blewett appeared bereft of inspiration at times, though his mood improved towards the end of the summer. A dominant ING Cup match against NSW (125 and 4 for 16) helped, as did the run-scoring of Shane Deitz, who relieved a little of Blewett's top-order burden. With Darren Lehmann and Matthew Elliott ready to keep him company, there is reason to hope Blewett will return to the business of making hundreds in 2005-06.

	M	I	NO	Runs	HS	100s	50s	Avge	Ct	St	W	Avge	BB
First-class	225	406	27	17,082	268	43	85	45.07	176	0	139	42.69	5/29
Dom. first-class	110	210	11	9,412	268	23	47	47.30	67	0	89	40.88	4/39
Test	46	79	4	2,552	214	4	15	34.03	45	0	14	51.43	2/9
Int'l limited-overs	32	30	3	551	57*	0	2	20.41	7	0	14	46.14	2/6
Dom. limited-overs	88	86	8	3,212	125	5	18	41.18	29	0	60	32.23	4/16

ANDY BLIGNAUT *Left-hand batsman, right-arm fast-medium bowler* **Tasmania**
Blignaut's brief experience in Australia last summer highlighted the yawning gap between Australian and Zimbabwean cricket. Recruited from the internal schism that all but destroyed the game in Zimbabwe, it was assumed that a man who could bowl quickly and bat even faster in the middle order for his country would be ideally suited to a domestic team in Australia. Mutual disillusionment soon set in, however, for Blignaut was discarded from the senior Tasmanian team after just one Pura Cup match in which he scored nine runs and had his bowling collared mercilessly. His subsequent failure to find any sort of form in lower levels of the game resulted in his early return to his native country. It was fortunate that Tasmania's other major recruit, Michael Bevan, was able to cover for the disappointing outcome of this experiment.

	M	I	NO	Runs	HS	100s	50s	Avge	Ct	St	W	Avge	BB
First-class	46	72	4	1,866	194	2	9	27.44	31	0	114	36.52	5/73
Dom. first-class	1	2	0	9	9	0	0	4.50	1	0	0	–	–
Test	17	32	2	759	92	0	5	25.30	13	0	51	34.94	5/73
Int'l limited-overs	47	36	8	533	63*	0	4	19.04	10	0	41	43.39	4/43

DOUG BOLLINGER *Left-arm fast-medium bowler* **NSW**
An important part of NSW's successes in his initial season in 2003-04, Bollinger was unfortunate to find himself behind three experienced pace bowlers, and played only two first-class games for two expensive wickets, and three ING Cup games. When he replaced the injured Stuart Clark in the ING Cup against South Australia, Bollinger shared the new ball and captured only the fourth hat-trick in the competition's history. Three weeks later, he failed to take a wicket against Western Australia, and made only one more ING Cup appearance. He was one of the game-breakers in the Sydney competition, with 35 wickets at 13.54 by Christmas. With no immediate opening into the state team available, Bollinger, a supple, lively bowler and capable outfielder with a strong arm, must be tempted to look further afield, as so many NSW cricketers have done.

	M	I	NO	Runs	HS	100s	50s	Avge	Ct	St	W	Avge	BB
First-class	11	13	7	28	7	0	0	4.67	5	0	16	66.19	4/50
Dom. first-class	10	12	7	21	4*	0	0	4.20	4	0	15	63.13	4/50
Dom. limited-overs	10	3	1	6	5	0	0	3.00	4	0	10	36.70	4/24

CAMERON BORGAS *Right-hand batsman* **SA**
Recalled after a four-year absence for the final Pura Cup match against Tasmania, Borgas batted without undue hurry. His lack of haste was influenced by the accuracy of Damien Wright's bowling, but it was refreshing to see someone prepared to take his time. His rewards were a maiden first-class fifty, victory for South Australia, and glowing words from his skipper Graham Manou that suggested he would figure in future batting orders. With a compact defence and useful array of strokes, Borgas may be about to follow through on the promise that had him debuting for his state at the age of 17.

	M	I	NO	Runs	HS	100s	50s	Avge	Ct	St	W	Avge	BB
First-class	3	5	0	81	53	0	1	16.20	0	0	–	–	–
Dom. first-class	3	5	0	81	53	0	1	16.20	0	0	–	–	–

NATHAN BRACKEN *Left-arm fast-medium bowler* **NSW**
Stung by his exclusion from the national list of contracted players after 2003-04, the tall paceman responded with an outstanding season for NSW, and was recalled to the national squad at the end of the summer. Bracken's ability to swing the ball at pace, especially on a seaming pitch in humid conditions, led to an astonishing performance in Sydney when he took 7 for 4 from seven overs as South Australia collapsed for 29. No

less impressive in the Pura Cup final in Brisbane, Bracken routed Queensland, claiming 6 for 27 from 13.2 overs. With 43 wickets at 18.79 he headed the Pura Cup averages, and was also easily the most economical bowler in the competition, conceding only 2.21 runs per over. Selection for three of the four home Tests against India in 2003-04 whetted his appetite for international recognition and now, more experienced and in his prime, Bracken's career is set to blossom anew.

	M	I	NO	Runs	HS	100s	50s	Avge	Ct	St	W	Avge	BB
First-class	49	66	25	716	38*	0	0	17.46	13	0	155	26.83	7/4
Dom. first-class	43	59	21	676	38*	0	0	17.79	11	0	139	26.19	7/4
Test	3	3	1	9	6*	0	0	4.50	1	0	6	58.50	2/12
Int'l limited-overs	17	1	1	7	7*	0	0	–	5	0	28	19.71	4/29
Dom. limited-overs	46	20	7	96	16*	0	0	7.38	7	0	59	29.24	5/38

SHAWN BRADSTREET *Right-hand batsman, right-arm medium bowler*   **NSW**

At 33, the Manly–Warringah all-rounder's first-class career appears to be on the wane, but forever strong and combative, Bradstreet appeared in eight of NSW's ING Cup matches, only to see the team he helped to three successive limited-overs titles plunge from first to last. His typically gritty unbeaten 53 from 74 balls gave NSW some respectability in the opening game against Queensland. Thereafter, he found runs more difficult to come by, although his late-innings bowling and sure fielding remained of value. The state selectors recognised his leadership qualities by appointing him to take charge of a NSW Under-23 team on an end-of-season limited-overs tour of India.

	M	I	NO	Runs	HS	100s	50s	Avge	Ct	St	W	Avge	BB
First-class	9	17	4	296	60	0	1	22.77	6	0	12	62.00	2/32
Dom. first-class	8	16	4	281	60	0	1	23.42	6	0	11	52.18	2/32
Dom. limited-overs	49	39	16	663	75*	0	2	28.83	17	0	45	32.84	4/23

LUKE BUTTERWORTH *Left-hand batsman, right-arm medium bowler*
Tasmania

Having played a handful of ING Cup matches in 2003-04, all-rounder Butterworth was afforded an extended run in the team in 2004-05, and became an important cog in the bowling attack that eventually triumphed. His batting was not as impressive as the first brief glimpses a year before had suggested, but in scoring 44 off 58 balls and taking 3 for 38 in ten tight overs at Adelaide, he showed what he is capable of, and what yet might be tapped as this young player's career unfolds. He was frequently asked to keep the middle overs tight, and he usually obliged, conceding runs at around five an over for the season. He hasn't played a first-class match, but the coming season might see him break into the four-day side as a player who can turn his hand to any facet of the game.

	M	I	NO	Runs	HS	100s	50s	Avge	Ct	St	W	Avge	BB
Dom. limited-overs	13	11	2	159	44	0	0	17.67	2	0	16	30.00	3/33

BEN CAMERON *Right-hand batsman*   **SA**

Cameron endured a wretched summer. After a puzzling demotion from opener to No. 3, his inability to follow up a strong first season in the early games was one of the warning signs that South Australia were still a long way from having a bankable batting side. He managed a determined if scratchy 77 against Queensland in the ING Cup, but otherwise Cameron could not make adequate scores. He developed trouble covering his off stump effectively, and lost his place in the state side by Christmas. His subsequent grade form for Tea Tree Gully was only moderate, pushing him further back in a batting queue that has been lengthened by the acquisition of Matthew Elliott and the return of Darren Lehmann.

	M	I	NO	Runs	HS	100s	50s	Avge	Ct	St	W	Avge	BB
First-class	6	12	1	252	81	0	3	22.91	4	0	–	–	–
Dom. first-class	6	12	1	252	81	0	3	22.91	4	0	–	–	–
Dom. limited-overs	7	7	0	178	77	0	2	25.43	2	0	–	–	–

RYAN CAMPBELL *Right-hand batsman, wicket-keeper* WA

Now in the twilight of a successful career, Campbell has set his own agenda. Disenchanted after being pushed aside for Western Australia's limited-overs matches in 2004-05, with the selectors opting for Luke Ronchi, ten years his junior, he considered retiring at the end of the season. But buoyed by encouragement from coach Wayne Clark, he plans to continue and make 2005-06 his farewell. His batting and keeping in four-day cricket was of a high standard. He batted with admirable responsibility for a player whose natural instincts have earned him a reputation as a cavalier. Injuries sustained in a traffic accident did not keep him out of action, but they did have a slightly detrimental effect on his wicket-keeping for a couple of games. His 533 Pura Cup runs at 35.53 were a valuable contribution.

	M	I	NO	Runs	HS	100s	50s	Avge	Ct	St	W	Avge	BB
First-class	92	159	6	5,617	203	10	35	36.71	43	13	0	–	–
Dom. first-class	81	141	5	5,029	203	9	33	36.98	42	9	0	–	–
Int'l limited-overs	2	2	0	54	38	0	0	27.00	0	1	–	–	–
Dom. limited-overs	70	68	1	1,475	108	1	6	22.01	9	6	–	–	–

ROB CASSELL *Right-arm fast-medium bowler* Victoria

After a two-year absence, Cassell found his way back to the Victorian team for its final one-day match of the season against New South Wales. His selection followed a string of strong performances for the state 2nd XI and an impressive season with his club, Melbourne, where he had taken 27 wickets at 20.48. He acted as 12th man in that match, but the swing bowler who Darren Berry labelled the "most exciting talent I've kept for Victoria since Damien Fleming" should become a regular fixture in the side.

	M	I	NO	Runs	HS	100s	50s	Avge	Ct	St	W	Avge	BB
First-class	2	3	1	20	18	0	0	10.00	0	0	7	22.71	4/33
Dom. first-class	2	3	1	20	18	0	0	10.00	0	0	7	22.71	4/33
Dom. limited-overs	3	–	–	–	–	–	–	–	0	0	4	22.50	2/32

BEAU CASSON *Left-arm wrist-spinner* WA

This outstanding youngster endured a frustrating season in which the state selectors faced a dilemma every time Brad Hogg was available. Further, on a couple of occasions Casson was overlooked when the selectors opted for a four-man new-ball attack on the fast Perth pitches. He played only three Pura Cup matches, taking his nine wickets at an average of 40.33. In only four ING Cup matches he performed grandly, with eight wickets at 17.75 at a little over four an over. His position as Hogg's understudy early in the season denied him opportunities to experience much-needed long stints at the bowling crease in first-class cricket. However, he is held in high regard by the Western Australian cricket establishment as a vital ingredient in the state's future.

	M	I	NO	Runs	HS	100s	50s	Avge	Ct	St	W	Avge	BB
First-class	15	25	5	290	35	0	0	14.50	6	0	46	38.80	6/64
Dom. first-class	13	23	4	283	35	0	0	14.89	5	0	43	37.49	6/64
Dom. limited-overs	13	6	1	38	18	0	0	7.60	3	0	12	27.42	4/31

MICHAEL CLARK *Left-arm fast-medium bowler*   **WA**

Continuing back problems wrecked another season for the lithe fast bowler. A screw had been inserted in a lower spinal fracture in February 2004. After getting through opening-round fixtures in one-day and four-day cricket against Tasmania in Perth, Clark broke down in an ING Cup match in Sydney in October. Clark was cleared of further structural damage to his spine, the latest problem being diagnosed as ankylosing spondylitis, which causes back muscles to spasm. During these spasms Clark's back locks. With this knowledge, and with the constant use of anti-inflammatory drugs, he can manage the problem by having a spell from bowling for 30 minutes, and he is confident of returning to interstate action in the summer of 2005-06. Using a shortened run-up for a start, Clark eased back into club cricket and helped Subiaco–Floreat to beat Joondalup in the final of the Sunday League competition with 4 for 49 off ten overs.

	M	I	NO	Runs	HS	100s	50s	Avge	Ct	St	W	Avge	BB
First-class	17	23	10	139	26	0	0	10.69	11	0	49	28.71	5/47
Dom. first-class	16	21	9	135	26	0	0	11.25	11	0	46	28.20	5/47
Dom. limited-overs	9	4	2	58	27	0	0	29.00	5	0	14	24.86	3/34

STUART CLARK *Right-arm fast-medium bowler*   **NSW**

The former Australia A pace bowler was an indispensable member of the four-pronged NSW attack that dominated the Pura Cup in 2004-05. Clark's bounce, accuracy and ability to seam the ball disconcertingly make him a thorny opponent, especially with moisture and humidity about. An ideal bowler for English conditions, he was called into the Ashes squad as a cover for Glenn McGrath while playing for Middlesex. In 11 first-class games, Clark claimed 40 wickets at 25.97, including a remarkable return of 5 for 10 from 13.5 overs in Victoria's second innings at the Junction Oval, his sixth five-wicket haul. Strangely for such an accurate, guileful bowler, his seven ING Cup appearances yielded only one wicket a game at 38 each, although he made a difference in Perth when his early breakthroughs gave NSW the advantage in a close game, and he finished with 4 for 24 from ten overs.

	M	I	NO	Runs	HS	100s	50s	Avge	Ct	St	W	Avge	BB
First-class	52	72	20	663	35	0	0	12.75	13	0	168	31.70	6/84
Dom. first-class	46	66	19	590	35	0	0	12.55	12	0	152	31.46	6/84
Dom. limited-overs	60	16	3	66	14	0	0	5.08	12	0	72	29.76	4/24

MICHAEL CLARKE *Right-hand batsman, slow left-arm orthodox bowler*   **NSW and Australia**

Clarke began his Test career with a bang in Bangalore, striking four sixes and 18 fours in his century. He also scored 91 and 73 in the third Test in Nagpur to help Australia to victory in the series. His remarkable 6 for 9 in the fourth Test at Mumbai capped an outstanding debut series. Although he claimed a regular position in the national team, success did not automatically follow. Clarke's sense of responsibility and growing maturity has led the dashing young right-hander to curb his ways and lose some of his youthful gloss. He hit a five-hour 141 in the first Test against New Zealand at the Gabba, completing the rare double of hundreds in his first Tests abroad and at home, and sharing a double-century stand with Adam Gilchrist. His six subsequent Test appearances against Pakistan and New Zealand passed without the distinction of a half-century. Despite his success in Mumbai he was given few opportunities with the ball, but his catching and fielding remained on the highest plane. He continued his international limited-overs success by heading the run-scorers in the VB Series and won the Allan Border Medal.

	M	I	NO	Runs	HS	100s	50s	Avge	Ct	St	W	Avge	BB
First-class	62	106	6	3,805	151	13	14	38.05	64	0	15	40.47	6/9
Dom. first-class	31	57	2	2,020	134	7	8	36.73	28	0	5	48.20	2/25
Test	12	17	1	669	151	2	2	41.81	14	0	8	7.63	6/9
Int'l limited-overs	57	51	13	1,686	105*	2	10	44.37	21	0	18	36.33	5/35
Dom. limited-overs	29	27	5	841	101*	1	5	38.23	8	0	7	25.57	3/57

MARK CLEARY *Left-hand batsman, right-arm fast-medium bowler* **SA**
A back injury robbed Cleary of half the 2004-05 season, and his all-round abilities were missed by the South Australia side, which was striving for balance. He found wickets harder to come by than previously, however, and did not achieve the batting results of which he is capable. Cleary was last out in the side razed for 29 by NSW in Sydney, and his dismissal (yorked by a sharply swerving Nathan Bracken inswinger to which he did not offer a stroke) summed up the combination of difficult conditions and poor technique that brought about the procession of wickets. Ryan Harris made a few notable impressions in Cleary's absence, and it will be interesting to see if both all-rounders can fit into the side.

	M	I	NO	Runs	HS	100s	50s	Avge	Ct	St	W	Avge	BB
First-class	28	42	10	592	58	0	1	18.50	14	0	81	31.42	7/80
Dom. first-class	17	28	2	413	58	0	1	15.88	11	0	54	29.61	5/102
Dom. limited-overs	22	22	7	234	70	0	1	15.60	8	0	30	31.63	4/55

SEAN CLINGELEFFER *Left-hand batsman, wicket-keeper* **Tasmania**
No one can accuse Clingeleffer of inconsistency. In 2004-05, he took exactly the same number of Pura Cup catches, scored much the same number of runs, at roughly the same average, with the same number of fifties, as in 2003-04. As a consequence, he did better with the bat than five of his better-credentialed batting team-mates, and played an important part, along with Damien Wright, in stemming the frequent collapses that afflicted the upper order. He batted with pleasing authority with some elegant driving, especially in a mid-season purple patch that brought him, consecutively, 68, 73, 25, 92 and 46. Behind the stumps, he continued to be unobtrusively effective, seeing off any challenge that might have come from having young wicket-keeper-batsman David Dawson in the same side. He is still some four seasons away from reaching Mark Atkinson's Tasmanian career wicket-keeping dismissals record, but Clingeleffer, still only 25, has plenty of time – and form – on his side.

	M	I	NO	Runs	HS	100s	50s	Avge	Ct	St	W	Avge	BB
First-class	51	80	8	1,875	141*	2	9	26.04	1	10	–	–	–
Dom. first-class	51	80	8	1,875	141*	2	9	26.04	1	10	–	–	–
Dom. limited-overs	40	32	16	362	48	0	0	22.63	0	3	–	–	–

MARK COSGROVE *Left-hand batsman, right-arm medium bowler* **SA**
It was a decidedly sheepish Cosgrove who shuffled up to accept the Bradman Young Cricketer of the Year award. At the time he had just been dropped from the South Australian side. He began 2004-05 as he ended the previous summer, in sublime form, and it was hard to tell exactly when things went wrong. His square drives were blocked by opposition sides, and his ability to pick up the ball early – so crucial for a batsman with a minimalist approach to footwork – was momentarily lost. The result was a run of six Pura Cup innings for 10 runs including a trio of ducks. Critical eyes wandered down to Cosgrove's waistline, and most agreed that a concerted fitness regime would not hurt his chances of returning to the middle of South Australia's batting order.

	M	I	NO	Runs	HS	100s	50s	Avge	Ct	St	W	Avge	BB
First-class	17	31	1	950	144	2	6	31.67	19	0	6	28.17	1/0
Dom. first-class	17	31	1	950	144	2	6	31.67	19	0	6	28.17	1/0
Dom. limited-overs	22	22	0	480	73	0	3	21.82	5	0	0	–	–

ED COWAN *Right-hand batsman* **NSW**
Having fielding in a Test for several minutes as Australia's emergency in front of a near-capacity crowd at the SCG before his maiden first-class appearance, Cowan eventually made his Pura Cup debut for NSW before a few hundred at Adelaide Oval. Days before, chosen to strengthen NSW's vulnerable ING Cup middle order, he nursed his team to victory over Western Australia in Perth. Cowan impressed again with his

maturity and temperament by coming in with the score at 3 for 8 against Queensland to make a defiant top score of 57 from 88 balls. His measured three-hour Pura Cup second innings of 66 saw NSW fall just one wicket short of victory over Queensland. Regarded as a batsman of the future by state coach Trevor Bayliss, his summer's experience will serve him and NSW well in the years ahead. Cowan is an investment bank analyst, holds a commerce degree and is studying for a law degree at Sydney University. He played for Oxford UCCE in 2003.

	M	I	NO	Runs	HS	100s	50s	Avge	Ct	St	W	Avge	BB
First-class	7	13	2	502	137*	1	2	45.64	1	0	0	–	–
Dom. first-class	3	6	0	132	66	0	1	22.00	0	0	–	–	–
Dom. limited-overs	4	3	1	79	57	0	1	39.50	3	0	0	–	–

JAMIE COX *Right-hand batsman* **Tasmania**
Cox's profile here last year hinted that the end of his career was in sight, but that failed to take into account his determination to remain at the highest possible level of the game for as long as possible. Twice during 2004-05 he picked himself off the floor, following two finger injuries, to put himself back into first-team contention, and he finished the season with two elegant Pura Cup half-centuries, and a strong claim to be in the side when the 2005-06 season kicks off. He only once failed to make double figures, and was one of the few Tasmanians to average over 30. After sustaining a severe finger injury during a club match in late November, he scored 106 in a 2nd XI game. When this failed to sway the selectors, he made 162 in the next 2nd XI match. The selectors understandably reinstated him, with happy results. It would be foolish to try to predict when this vastly experienced batsman will call it a day, but when he does, he has a blossoming commentator's career before him.

	M	I	NO	Runs	HS	100s	50s	Avge	Ct	St	W	Avge	BB
First-class	261	461	31	18,554	250	51	81	43.15	123	0	5	94.00	3/46
Dom. first-class	158	289	17	10,761	245	30	47	39.56	77	0	1	202.00	1/44
Dom. limited-overs	75	73	4	1,879	99	0	14	27.23	19	0	0	–	–

ADAM CROSTHWAITE *Right-hand batsman, wicket-keeper* **Victoria**
The player who moved to a different school for lack of wicket-keeping opportunities at Ivanhoe Grammar broke into the state team aged 20. His stunning 54 not out off 38 balls in Victoria's tense one-day win over Queensland at the Gabba was fittingly rewarded with the Man of the Match award. In his three first-class matches Crosthwaite performed solidly. Anointed by former captain Darren Berry as a star of the future, the effervescent youngster said he sought to emulate Adam Gilchrist in his batting, Berry in his determination and Ian Healy's all-round keeping style.

	M	I	NO	Runs	HS	100s	50s	Avge	Ct	St	W	Avge	BB
First-class	3	4	0	60	24	0	0	15.00	0	2	–	–	–
Dom. first-class	3	4	0	60	24	0	0	15.00	0	2	–	–	–
Dom. limited-overs	11	6	3	66	54*	0	1	22.00	0	3	–	–	–

DAN CULLEN *Right-arm off-spin bowler* **SA**

David Hussey bowled through the gate. Justin Langer caught in close. Michael Bevan caught at slip. Though just three of the 43 wickets off-spinner Cullen snatched in his first season, they speak volumes of the impact the 20-year-old had. No off-spinner has enjoyed such a prolific year of wicket-taking in the Pura Cup since Greg Matthews retired, and none has performed so well at a young age since Ashley Mallett pocketed 32 wickets in 1967-68 at the age of 22. As important as the number of wickets Cullen captured was how he took them. Employing generous flight, vicious turn and even a doosra, he managed one of the hardest tasks in Australian cricket – bowling finger spin with an element of mystery. Cullen's combative attitude, no doubt a result of being schooled by Terry Jenner, also had an impact, as he surprised several older players with his lip. Given the dearth of good young spinners in Australia, it is likely Cullen will be called up sooner rather than later. His first challenge, though, is to maintain his debut season form now that batsmen know what a threat he poses.

	M	I	NO	Runs	HS	100s	50s	Avge	Ct	St	W	Avge	BB
First-class	10	18	5	219	42	0	0	16.85	5	0	43	30.37	5/38
Dom. first-class	10	18	5	219	42	0	0	16.85	5	0	43	30.37	5/38
Dom. limited-overs	6	5	2	33	13*	0	0	11.00	2	0	9	24.56	3/55

JOHN DAVISON *Right-arm off-spin bowler* **SA**

The best way to sum up Davison's season is to say that he ended it playing club cricket in another state, and pondering a greater role in the Canadian game. Though he began the summer as South Australia's one-day vice-captain, there were few positives in his performances in the early games of the ING Cup. Pressure brought to bear by Daniel Cullen, as well as Davison's inability to replicate his whirlwind batting displays for Canada in the 2003 World Cup, led the state selectors to discard the 34-year-old. Davison elected to move back to NSW, the state where his cricket career began, and quickly ran up a number of tall scores for Mosman.

	M	I	NO	Runs	HS	100s	50s	Avge	Ct	St	W	Avge	BB
First-class	47	71	7	861	84	0	3	13.45	20	0	100	47.49	9/76
Dom. first-class	45	67	7	732	84	0	2	12.20	19	0	81	55.01	5/81
Int'l limited-overs	6	6	0	226	111	1	1	37.67	1	0	10	18.70	3/15
Dom. limited-overs	21	19	3	355	59	0	2	22.19	7	0	15	41.53	5/26

JOE DAWES *Right-arm fast-medium bowler* **Queensland**

The burly Dawes operates off half the run-up these days but with the same effectiveness as he used to derive from his old Fred Flintstone-like charge from near the boundary. He took 46 wickets at 21.93, his best season since 2000-01 when he took 49. On the way, he passed 200 first-class career wickets for Queensland, just the eighth bowler to do so. In keeping with a season where Glenn McGrath and Jason Gillespie raised the bat to acclaim, Dawes did his bit for the run-challenged. He and Nathan Hauritz defied NSW for 11 overs in a last-wicket stand at Bankstown Oval to snatch a draw. He also produced his highest first-class score, with a gleeful 34 not out against Western Australia at the Gabba. He hopes to team up again with fellow 35-year-old Andy Bichel for another season.

	M	I	NO	Runs	HS	100s	50s	Avge	Ct	St	W	Avge	BB
First-class	75	94	36	612	34*	0	0	10.55	12	0	285	25.08	7/67
Dom. first-class	63	79	30	503	34*	0	0	10.27	9	0	238	24.58	7/67
Dom. limited-overs	13	1	1	1	1*	0	0	–	2	0	16	29.13	3/26

DAVID DAWSON *Right-hand batsman, wicket-keeper*   **Tasmania**

Dawson, a young batsman who learned his cricket in the ACT, enjoyed an unforgettable Pura Cup debut by scoring a century and carrying his bat through the innings, a unique achievement in Australian first-class cricket. He never reached the same heights again, and ended the season with 476 runs at 28, but his composure at the top of the order should stand Tasmania in good stead in the years to come. His ability to rotate the strike needs to be addressed; his strike rate of 30 runs per hundred balls was the lowest in the country of anyone who scored 200 runs, and the two innings of 6 he played during the summer occupied between them exactly 100 balls. His initial selection to bat at No. 3 in the one-day team was a mistake, and even the wicket-keeping string to his bow was not enough to prevent him from being left out after six matches. Until he expands his shot-making selection, he looks a prospect in only the longer form of the game.

	M	I	NO	Runs	HS	100s	50s	Avge	Ct	St	W	Avge	BB
First-class	9	18	1	476	123*	1	2	28.00	8	0	–	–	–
Dom. first-class	9	18	1	476	123*	1	2	28.00	8	0	–	–	–
Dom. limited-overs	6	5	0	55	20	0	0	11.00	0	0	–	–	–

SHANE DEITZ *Left-hand batsman*   **SA**

Having survived the contractual cut by a hair's breadth at the end of 2003-04, Deitz was forced to wait most of the season while younger openers were tried. Fast running out of options following the failures of Ben Cameron, Tom Plant and Luke Williams, the selectors reinstated Deitz in March, and he responded with the best batting form of his career. Unimpeachable opening hands of 90 in Perth and 141 in Adelaide were exactly what the team had been crying out for all summer. His time out of the team appeared to have stiffened his resolve to bat for long periods, and he combined defence and attack with more success than in previous seasons. Deitz's place is still not quite assured, but he has shown he has a future.

	M	I	NO	Runs	HS	100s	50s	Avge	Ct	St	W	Avge	BB
First-class	38	75	2	2,238	141	3	14	30.66	27	1	2	46.50	2/17
Dom. first-class	37	73	2	2,226	141	3	14	31.35	25	1	2	46.50	2/17
Dom. limited-overs	14	14	0	412	60	0	2	29.43	3	0	–	–	–

GERARD DENTON *Right-arm fast-medium bowler*   **Victoria**

There were a few grumbles in state pace bowling circles about the Tasmanian's move to Victoria. But Denton managed only a solitary one-day game for his new state before being struck down by recurring stress fractures in his left foot. He played just a handful of matches for Footscray during a season that he will be keen to put behind him.

	M	I	NO	Runs	HS	100s	50s	Avge	Ct	St	W	Avge	BB
First-class	32	44	19	179	34	0	0	7.16	6	0	85	37.79	5/40
Dom. first-class	30	43	18	177	34	0	0	7.08	6	0	80	38.66	5/40
Dom. limited-overs	12	1	1	2	2*	0	0	–	2	0	13	40.62	3/53

MICHAEL DI VENUTO *Left-hand batsman*   **Tasmania**

Di Venuto, now a vastly experienced cricketer, was clearly the best batsman in the Tasmanian set-up after Michael Bevan, and it was unfortunate that injury again ate into his season, causing the talented left-hander to miss six of the 20 matches. He batted with pleasing consistency in the ING Cup, averaging 32 in his seven matches, and fell just short of 500 runs in the Pura Cup, at 37.62 an innings. He was seen at his best during a magnificent partnership of 277 with Bevan against NSW at Bellerive, Di Venuto's share being an undefeated 157. His catching at slip is as safe as ever and his appetite for cricket remained unbounded as he returned to Derbyshire in 2005 for his sixth season with the county.

	M	I	NO	Runs	HS	100s	50s	Avge	Ct	St	W	Avge	BB
First-class	204	361	19	14,521	230	31	90	42.46	226	0	5	96.00	1/0
Dom. first-class	111	196	8	7,532	189	12	54	40.06	110	0	2	122.00	1/0
Int'l limited-overs	9	9	0	241	89	0	2	26.78	1	0	–	–	–
Dom. limited-overs	82	80	7	2,233	129*	3	10	30.59	41	0	3	37.00	1/10

MICHAEL DIGHTON *Right-hand batsman*   **Tasmania**

Dighton experienced a frustrating year, only getting to 30 once in 12 Pura Cup innings after scoring nearly 1,000 runs in 2003-04. The selectors lost patience and he was discarded for the last four matches, despite some heavy scoring in 2nd XI cricket. He will better remember his contribution to the ING Cup triumph, where he scored most runs after Michael Bevan, and, in partnership with Travis Birt, often gave the team a rousing start with his big hitting in the first 15 overs. Batting at nearly 80 runs per 100 balls, he seemed happier trying to dispatch the white ball out of sight than defending against the red one. He also stepped in to fill the wicket-keeping role for the last four ING Cup matches, in the interest of team balance.

	M	I	NO	Runs	HS	100s	50s	Avge	Ct	St	W	Avge	BB
First-class	47	82	4	2,776	182*	6	12	35.59	36	0	0	–	–
Dom. first-class	46	80	3	2,726	182*	6	12	35.40	34	0	0	–	–
Dom. limited-overs	41	40	1	1,176	113	1	9	30.15	15	1	–	–	–

XAVIER DOHERTY *Slow left-arm orthodox bowler*   **Tasmania**

Xavier Doherty is another Tasmanian who will remember his ING Cup season with considerably more affection than his first-class one. He was one of a stable selection of five bowlers that Tasmania used in bringing home the trophy, and he delivered more overs than any other spinner in the land, plying his left-arm slows with accuracy and occasional penetration. His batting was crucial in winning a tight tussle against Western Australia at Devonport, and at that point of the summer, he looked to be on top of his game. Thereafter, however, his performances with bat and ball dropped off – in the Pura Cup he rounded off the season with seven consecutive single-figure scores and three wickets for 558. His overall Pura Cup average of 63.69 was more reminiscent of the demoralising figures sustained by Tasmanian spinners of the 1980s than of Doherty's true ability.

	M	I	NO	Runs	HS	100s	50s	Avge	Ct	St	W	Avge	BB
First-class	21	31	5	293	52	0	1	11.27	6	0	51	52.59	6/149
Dom. first-class	21	31	5	293	52	0	1	11.27	6	0	51	52.59	6/149
Dom. limited-overs	24	16	3	142	37	0	0	10.92	10	0	20	38.20	4/41

BRETT DOREY *Right-arm fast-medium bowler*   **WA**

At the start of the 2004-05 season, this tall right-armer was virtually unknown. Stress fractures to his back in 1999 kept him out of club cricket for four years, but a stellar 2003-04 season for Fremantle when he took 48 first-grade wickets at an average of 11.46 earned him selection in the Western Australian 2nd XI against South Australia where he took 4 for 28 off 16 overs. He made his first-class debut against Queensland at the WACA with 1 for 110 off 31 overs. However, his steepling bounce, a genuine outswinger and great accuracy soon made him a player to note. Apart from his 15 Pura Cup wickets at 28.40 and four at 37.75 in ING Cup matches, Dorey made an impression with his dynamic bowling in the four-day match against Pakistan at the WACA when he took 3 for

38 and 5 for 41. A side injury and groin problems forced him to miss three Pura Cup matches late in the season. He is an athletic outfielder and a capable big hitter at the tail.

	M	I	NO	Runs	HS	100s	50s	Avge	Ct	St	W	Avge	BB
First-class	6	9	1	112	22	0	0	14.00	1	0	23	21.96	5/41
Dom. first-class	5	8	1	91	22	0	0	13.00	1	0	15	28.40	4/53
Dom. limited-overs	5	3	0	19	17	0	0	6.33	4	0	4	37.75	2/27

ANDREW DOWNTON *Left-arm fast-medium bowler* **Tasmania**
The Sydney-born Andrew Downton has had a chequered career since he joined Tasmania six years ago, and just when it seemed he was set for an extended period at the senior level, following an outstanding season in 2003-04, a knee injury terminated his season abruptly after four Pura Cup games. The effects from this problem might keep him out of cricket in 2005-06, after which his present contract expires. The tenacious left-armer, who can bowl all day when fit, now sits on 94 Pura Cup wickets, and at 28, still stands a chance of becoming the tenth bowler to take 100 wickets for Tasmania.

	M	I	NO	Runs	HS	100s	50s	Avge	Ct	St	W	Avge	BB
First-class	33	43	8	296	45	0	0	8.46	8	0	102	34.13	6/56
Dom. first-class	31	42	7	295	45	0	0	8.43	8	0	94	35.51	6/56
Dom. limited-overs	4	2	1	15	9	0	0	15.00	0	0	3	40.67	1/26

CHRIS DUVAL *Right-arm fast-medium bowler* **SA**
When Andrew Symonds was thrashing him to every part of Adelaide Oval in the ING Cup, Duval may have wondered whether he should have pursued the baseball-pitching career a talent scout said he was capable of the previous summer. Duval, however, knuckled down at grade level for Northern Districts to collect 33 wickets at 22.06, as well as heading the wicket-takers in the Cricket Australia Cup with 16 at 24.31. That was enough to earn the strapping paceman a second stint at the Cricket Australia Centre of Excellence in Brisbane during the winter. He has since moved to Tasmania, where he has been awarded a contract for 2005-06.

	M	I	NO	Runs	HS	100s	50s	Avge	Ct	St	W	Avge	BB
Dom. limited-overs	2	1	1	1	1*	0	0	–	1	0	1	125.00	1/61

BEN EDMONDSON *Right-arm fast-medium bowler* **WA**
An enigmatic character, Edmondson is still coming to terms with the demands of first-class cricket after his dramatic recruitment from Brisbane in December 2003, which followed a stint playing and coaching in Denmark. An untimely side strain forced him to miss Western Australia's first three Pura Cup matches in 2004-05. This affected his general fitness for the rest of the season, and towards the end of the summer he was weary and bowling well below top pace. A confidence bowler, he is one of the fastest in Australia at his best. He was Western Australia's most successful bowler in Pura Cup matches with 29 wickets at 36.41 from seven matches. However, against Tasmania at Bellerive in January he lost everything – rhythm, pace, direction – and finished the first innings with 0 for 138 off 22 overs. Otherwise he had the happy knack of taking a wicket when the side needed a breakthrough. The national selectors showed their interest by picking him for the Prime Minister's XI against Pakistan.

	M	I	NO	Runs	HS	100s	50s	Avge	Ct	St	W	Avge	BB
First-class	15	15	8	35	13	0	0	5.00	5	0	62	33.06	5/90
Dom. first-class	14	14	7	32	13	0	0	4.57	5	0	57	34.05	5/90
Dom. limited-overs	6	4	3	8	3*	0	0	8.00	1	0	9	32.22	2/34

MATTHEW ELLIOTT *Left-hand batsman* **Victoria and Australia**
Included for the first time in many summers in the list of Australian contracted players, Elliott could not match the dizzy heights of his previous, record-breaking summer. He held the Victorian batting together on several occasions, but seemed to lack the freedom of the previous season, when he had played just for enjoyment. However, he continued to provide support to Cameron White and publicly expressed disappointment in past players who criticised the team. At the end of the season, the 33-year-old stunned Victoria and South Australia alike when he approached the Redbacks for a combined batsman/mentor role similar to Michael Bevan's at Tasmania. His explanation – that he was looking for a new challenge – was quickly dismissed by Victorians convinced he just wanted the extra financial rewards. But Elliott effectively became a free agent when he came out of his Cricket Australia contract and Victoria was left powerless when Cricket Australia turned down its appeal against his decision to move.

	M	I	NO	Runs	HS	100s	50s	Avge	Ct	St	W	Avge	BB
First-class	190	349	26	16,141	203	50	76	49.97	206	0	13	58.00	3/68
Dom. first-class	103	197	16	9,470	203	32	43	52.32	125	0	10	42.40	3/68
Test	21	36	1	1,172	199	3	4	33.49	14	0	0	–	–
Int'l limited-overs	1	1	0	1	1	0	0	1.00	0	0	–	–	–
Dom. limited-overs	78	76	6	2,640	118*	6	17	37.71	31	0	0	–	–

CALLUM FERGUSON *Right-hand batsman* **SA**
Circumstances heaped a great deal of responsibility on Ferguson during 2004-05. Making his first-class debut at the start of the summer, Ferguson soon became South Australia's only in-form batsman. It was a heavy burden on young shoulders, but Ferguson responded with character. In the second innings of the match in which South Australia were infamously dismissed for 29, he ground out a stand of 218 with Tom Plant and made his maiden first-class hundred. By doing so, he proved there was considerable grit to complement a plush strokeplay range. Ferguson maintained his form throughout the rest of the summer and finished among the top ten Pura Cup run-scorers, an outstanding performance by a young man in a battling team. He radiates ease at the crease, and among his stylish shots the cover drive is among the most elegant around.

	M	I	NO	Runs	HS	100s	50s	Avge	Ct	St	W	Avge	BB
First-class	10	19	0	733	114	2	4	38.58	2	0	–	–	–
Dom. first-class	10	19	0	733	114	2	4	38.58	2	0	–	–	–
Dom. limited-overs	13	13	1	296	72*	0	3	24.67	2	0	–	–	–

BRETT GEEVES *Right-arm fast bowler* **Tasmania**
After several seasons of one-day cricket, Geeves was given his opportunity at first-class level in 2004-05, and did enough to engender enthusiastic anticipation of a profitable career. A wholehearted trier, he sometimes bowled a wayward width which led to heavy punishment, but just when you were casting your eye around the field to see who might relieve him, he would produce an unplayable ball and claim a vital wicket. His in-swinging yorker upset five sets of stumps over the summer, and a combined total of 43 wickets in both competitions was a creditable haul from an inexperienced first-change bowler. In the ING Cup he took more

wickets than anyone in the country save Shaun Tait, and played a crucial role in Tasmania's trophy victory. He also showed some impressive hitting ability at No. 11, which could well be nurtured to produce something more substantial in the future.

	M	I	NO	Runs	HS	100s	50s	Avge	Ct	St	W	Avge	BB
First-class	7	12	8	64	28	0	0	16.00	0	0	23	40.35	4/94
Dom. first-class	7	12	8	64	28	0	0	16.00	0	0	23	40.35	4/94
Dom. limited-overs	28	12	5	28	6	0	0	4.00	5	0	37	28.54	5/45

ADAM GILCHRIST *Left-hand batsman, wicket-keeper*   **WA and Australia**

Gilchrist's breathtaking feats with the bat strengthen the claims that he is the greatest match-winner in world cricket. The pugnacious left-hander has added a new dimension to the game and his exhilarating strokeplay continues to rescue Australia and turn the possibility of defeat into victory. He ended the tour of New Zealand in March 2005 as Australia's most prolific wicket-keeper-batsman, and his 79 Test sixes had him in third place behind New Zealand's Chris Cairns (87) and West Indian Viv Richards (84). He was 60 not out when Australia were dismissed for 383 in the first innings against New Zealand at Eden Park, foiling his bid to become only the fifth batsman to score four successive Test centuries. In the absence of Ricky Ponting in India in late 2004 Gilchrist handled the burdensome task of leading the side, keeping wickets and batting with considerable aplomb. So famous are his spectacular feats that he has been targeted by American Major League champions the Boston Red Sox, whose coaches believe that Gilchrist has the key ingredients to succeed in baseball – remarkable hand-eye co-ordination and hitting power.

	M	I	NO	Runs	HS	100s	50s	Avge	Ct	St	W	Avge	BB
First-class	159	235	43	9,087	204*	28	36	47.33	18	45	–	–	–
Dom. first-class	60	95	13	3,196	203*	8	12	38.98	14	8	–	–	–
Test	68	97	17	4,452	204*	15	20	55.65	1	27	–	–	–
Int'l limited-overs	219	213	9	7,362	172	11	42	36.09	0	42	–	–	–
Dom. limited-overs	38	35	3	996	115	1	7	31.13	0	6	–	–	–

JASON GILLESPIE *Right-arm fast-medium bowler*   **SA and Australia**

For a man whose early career was beset by injuries, Gillespie has shown remarkable durability. As last summer drew to a close, it actually seemed he was in need of a break from cricket – something that was regularly forced on him when his body was not so hardy. Gillespie, however, had exerted himself fully on Australia's spell-breaking tour of India, where he played some of the best cricket of his life. In the first two Tests he delivered tight spells and broke partnerships on unresponsive pitches, and in Chennai he helped scratch out the runs that salvaged a draw. When the Nagpur groundsman prepared a sporting wicket for the deciding match, Gillespie became irresistible. Match figures of 9 for 80 were the best of his career, and he was unlucky to miss the match and series awards. While team-mates enjoyed themselves in subsequent series against New Zealand and Pakistan, Gillespie took a back seat. His star waned, and after struggling in the first Test of the Ashes series he was dropped.

	M	I	NO	Runs	HS	100s	50s	Avge	Ct	St	W	Avge	BB
First-class	114	147	38	1,716	58	0	5	15.74	45	0	419	24.92	8/50
Dom. first-class	26	43	6	504	58	0	2	13.62	13	0	107	22.96	8/50
Test	66	84	26	940	54*	0	2	16.21	24	0	248	25.73	7/37
Int'l limited-overs	97	39	16	289	44*	0	0	12.57	10	0	142	25.43	5/22
Dom. limited-overs	24	16	7	70	19	0	0	7.78	2	0	39	23.44	4/46

MURRAY GOODWIN *Right-hand batsman*   **WA**

For the second successive season Goodwin was Western Australia's leading run-getter in Pura Cup matches, but his 2004-05 season fell well short of his record-breaking 1,183 runs at 65.72 the previous summer. Two centuries and five half-centuries in his 840 Pura

Cup runs at 49.41 certainly made him a valuable member of the side. However, he was disappointed at his results in the ING Cup, where he managed only one half-century from ten innings that produced an unsatisfactory 214 runs at 21.40. In 2004-05 he was under more pressure, with early wickets falling cheaply in both forms of the game. This forced adjustments to his natural game, and he suffered the consequences. His fielding, at times, was brilliant, but uncharacteristically he spilt several catches during the season. He made a splendid contribution in a leadership role in support of deputy captain Mike Hussey. Goodwin has signed to play county cricket with Sussex through to the end of the 2007 English season, and at 32, the former Zimbabwe international still has much to offer Western Australian cricket.

	M	I	NO	Runs	HS	100s	50s	Avge	Ct	St	W	Avge	BB
First-class	168	294	23	12,925	335*	39	55	47.69	109	0	7	51.00	2/23
Dom. first-class	56	103	8	4,013	201*	10	18	42.24	35	0	0	–	–
Test	19	37	4	1,414	166*	3	8	42.85	10	0	0	–	–
Int'l limited-overs	71	70	3	1,818	112*	2	8	27.13	20	0	4	52.50	1/12
Dom. limited-overs	50	46	7	1,465	167	1	10	37.56	17	0	–	–	–

ADAM GRIFFITH *Right-arm fast-medium bowler*   **Tasmania**

Tempted by an offer to follow the sun to Perth over the winter after a less-than-glamorous second season with Tasmania, Griffith was persuaded to stay put, with pleasing results. He snared 45 Pura Cup wickets, regaining the respect that batsmen around the country had for him after his successful first season in 2002-03. Rediscovering his McGrath-like metronomic consistency of line and length, he was one of a handful of bowlers in the country with a strike-rate of under 50 balls per wicket. Taking more than half of his wickets on the placid Bellerive pitch, he was an admirable foil for the hard-working Damien Wright, and whatever the failures of the Tasmanian cricket system in 2004-05, their work together wasn't one of them. Having had a taste of Australia A cricket, he might be motivated to try for further opportunities.

	M	I	NO	Runs	HS	100s	50s	Avge	Ct	St	W	Avge	BB
First-class	20	33	10	254	37	0	0	11.04	4	0	74	33.26	7/54
Dom. first-class	20	33	10	254	37	0	0	11.04	4	0	74	33.26	7/54
Dom. limited-overs	29	11	5	14	5*	0	0	2.33	5	0	34	35.29	3/14

BRAD HADDIN *Right-hand batsman, wicket-keeper*   **NSW and Australia**

Brad Haddin's struggle to assert himself as heir apparent to Adam Gilchrist was fulfilled at last when he gained a full Cricket Australia contract and a spot on the Ashes tour after captaining NSW to success in the Pura Cup. Always the most effortless strokemaker, Haddin's development was due to his wicket-keeping improvement from long hours of practice, initially with Steve Rixon and then with new state coach Trevor Bayliss. Appearing in all 12 first-class games for NSW, he hit two centuries and five half-centuries in an outstanding season for 916 runs at 57.25 as well as taking 36 catches and making three stumpings, leading the side with imagination and verve in Simon Katich's absence. Few batsmen in the season were as enjoyable to watch. Haddin was chosen to captain the Australia A team in limited-overs games against West Indies and Pakistan, opening the innings against the Pakistanis for a blazing 129 from 123 balls in Adelaide. When Gilchrist was unavailable, Haddin performed enterprisingly in the limited-overs internationals.

	M	I	NO	Runs	HS	100s	50s	Avge	Ct	St	W	Avge	BB
First-class	60	103	12	3,351	154	4	21	36.82	0	16	–	–	–
Dom. first-class	54	96	11	3,165	154	4	20	37.24	0	14	–	–	–
Int'l limited-overs	11	9	0	158	32	0	0	17.56	0	3	–	–	–
Dom. limited-overs	60	59	2	1,765	133	3	12	30.96	0	23	–	–	–

DANIEL HARRIS *Right-hand batsman*   **SA**
Neat with the bat, useful in the field and productive off it as a doctor, Harris deserves to
do well. But as Clint Eastwood said in *Unforgiven*: "Deserve's got nothin' to do with
it." Six years after his debut, Harris's first half-century for South Australia (a stout 82
at the WACA in March) was long overdue. Always considered a tidy player of good
character, Harris's results had to that point been poor, and even now he nurses a first-
class average of 14.29. None of his other innings were long or memorable, but his
opening stand of 165 with Shane Deitz in the Perth match was significant, and gives
Harris the impetus for a more productive future.

	M	I	NO	Runs	HS	100s	50s	Avge	Ct	St	W	Avge	BB
First-class	9	18	1	243	82	0	1	14.29	10	0	–	–	–
Dom. first-class	8	16	1	207	82	0	1	13.80	8	0	–	–	–
Dom. limited-overs	1	1	0	5	5	0	0	5.00	1	0	–	–	–

RYAN HARRIS *Right-hand batsman, right-arm fast-medium bowler*   **SA**
Outstanding at grade level for Northern Districts, all-rounder Harris made some subtle
advances in the first-class arena last summer. A return of 4 for 92 helped South Australia
log an outright win in Perth, while a rearguard 47 at the MCG showed Harris could also
prosper with the bat. After a poor new-ball spell at the Gabba, he provided improved
value in the ING Cup too, and a frugal analysis of 2 for 31 in the final match against
Tasmania neatly illustrated his ability. Turning 26 as the new season gets under way,
Harris must work towards the consistent performances required of a more senior
performer. Narrowing the gap between his grade (10.81) and first-class (43.88) bowling
averages last summer would be a good start.

	M	I	NO	Runs	HS	100s	50s	Avge	Ct	St	W	Avge	BB
First-class	12	21	1	259	47	0	0	12.95	10	0	22	44.32	4/92
Dom. first-class	12	21	1	259	47	0	0	12.95	10	0	22	44.32	4/92
Dom. limited-overs	25	17	7	152	31*	0	0	15.20	14	0	29	32.48	4/43

CHRIS HARTLEY *Left-hand batsman, wicket-keeper*   **Queensland**
Wade Seccombe's cycling accident gave Hartley his chance, and he gloved it. A neat and
proficient wicket-keeper, Hartley took nine catches in the match against Tasmania to
reinforce his reputation as one of the brightest of Australia's next generation of
glovemen. He claimed 19 dismissals from his three Pura Cup appearances, and while his
batting did not reach the heights of the previous season when he scored a hundred on
debut, he was efficient, with a highest score of 50. He was named as the stand-by keeper
for the Australia A tour of Pakistan.

	M	I	NO	Runs	HS	100s	50s	Avge	Ct	St	W	Avge	BB
First-class	6	8	1	205	103	1	1	29.29	0	2	–	–	–
Dom. first-class	6	8	1	205	103	1	1	29.29	0	2	–	–	–
Dom. limited-overs	4	2	0	19	14	0	0	9.50	0	3	–	–	–

IAN HARVEY *Right-hand batsman, right-arm fast-medium bowler*   **Victoria**
Harvey was at his enigmatic best throughout the season. One day, he was manfully
taking blows on the body and batting Victoria out of trouble; the next he played like
someone who would rather be elsewhere. His innings at the Gabba, dubbed "unnatural"
by state coach Greg Shipperd, was further proof of the super-relaxed Harvey's ability.
But after being discarded by the national limited-overs selectors he appeared to find the
return to being just a state cricketer an anticlimax. At season's end, Harvey became
embroiled in a pay dispute with Cricket Victoria before accepting a contract. Then,

during the winter, the 33-year-old signed a two-year contract to play in South Africa for Western Province-Boland, and will now probably play the remainder of his career there and for Yorkshire.

	M	I	NO	Runs	HS	100s	50s	Avge	Ct	St	W	Avge	BB
First-class	143	237	22	7,067	209*	10	40	32.87	100	0	391	27.62	8/101
Dom. first-class	78	133	14	4,065	136	4	29	34.16	52	0	182	32.82	7/44
Int'l limited-overs	73	51	11	715	48*	0	0	17.88	17	0	85	30.32	4/16
Dom. limited-overs	69	64	5	1,137	72	0	6	19.27	20	0	81	27.41	5/34

KADE HARVEY *Right-hand batsman, right-arm fast-medium bowler* **WA**
A hat-trick against Tasmania in an ING Cup match in Devonport in January 2005 was the icing on the cake of a wonderful interstate career for this wholehearted competitor who, a month later, surprisingly retired from all forms of interstate cricket at the age of 29. Hampered by dodgy knees in recent years, he was once again Western Australia's leading wicket-taker in ING Cup matches in 2004-05, with 16 at 25.37. He retires with a one-day domestic record of 103 wickets at 27.12, one of only two players in the competition's history to reach 100 wickets. Harvey made four Pura Cup appearances, taking 11 wickets at 30.18 in his farewell season. The full-time pharmacist will continue to play first-grade cricket with Scarborough and is sure to have an important role as a specialist coach. A splendid team man, he has always been willing to share his knowledge.

	M	I	NO	Runs	HS	100s	50s	Avge	Ct	St	W	Avge	BB
First-class	27	40	10	740	100*	1	2	24.67	18	0	60	35.35	4/43
Dom. first-class	23	36	9	645	100*	1	1	23.89	16	0	55	33.93	4/43
Dom. limited-overs	80	56	18	806	53*	0	1	21.21	13	0	103	27.13	4/8

SHANE HARWOOD *Right-arm fast-medium bowler* **Victoria**
Injury found new parts of Harwood's body to attack. While he was riding his bike with his dog on a leash, the dog ran off, pulling the paceman off the bike and breaking his hand. No sooner had he recovered to take his place in the team than he strained his hamstring in a dashing one-day innings in Hobart, then suffered multiple fractures to his jaw in a match at the Junction Oval. Later in the season, the right-armer succumbed to an eye problem, though he did find some of his old venom at various stages, claiming 13 wickets at 34. With several younger pace bowlers vying for positions in the Victorian side his future seemed bleak, but he may have earned a reprieve with Mathew Inness's departure for Western Australia.

	M	I	NO	Runs	HS	100s	50s	Avge	Ct	St	W	Avge	BB
First-class	16	19	5	219	35	0	0	15.64	5	0	49	31.92	5/54
Dom. first-class	15	17	3	208	35	0	0	14.86	5	0	48	31.44	5/54
Dom. limited-overs	16	8	2	67	50*	0	1	11.17	4	0	12	41.00	3/22

NATHAN HAURITZ *Right-arm off-spin bowler* **Queensland and Australia**
Hauritz quickly fell from grace with the cricketing gods. A surprise choice for the tour of India, he had a dream start by taking a wicket with the third ball of his first over in Tests, emulating his effort of a first-over wicket on his one-day international debut. He finished with five victims in the match, including the scalps of Sachin Tendulkar and V.V.S. Laxman, in a losing side. On his return to Queensland he battled to make an impact. His six Pura Cup wickets came at an average of 96, and he was eventually omitted from the side. His first-class high point came when he and Joe Dawes defied

NSW at Bankstown Oval in January to salvage a vital draw. Fortunately his one-day form was better, and he remains a key figure for the Queenslanders in that format.

	M	I	NO	Runs	HS	100s	50s	Avge	Ct	St	W	Avge	BB
First-class	32	43	9	543	94	0	1	15.97	17	0	59	47.31	4/95
Dom. first-class	26	37	9	454	94	0	1	16.21	11	0	46	51.39	4/95
Test	1	2	0	15	15	0	0	7.50	1	0	5	20.60	3/16
Int'l limited-overs	8	4	3	35	20*	0	0	35.00	2	0	9	34.22	4/39
Dom. limited-overs	42	22	7	199	39*	0	0	13.27	11	0	61	24.05	4/39

MATTHEW HAYDEN *Left-hand batsman*   Queensland and Australia

Enjoys yoga, bakes bread for his friends, author of a best-selling cookbook and a doting dad of two young children – little wonder that when Hayden's batting lost some of its bite in 2004-05 some people questioned where his focus lay. Until the last Test of the Ashes series in England he had gone 23 Test innings without a century, and had got past 50 on just five occasions for a highest score of 70. On the limited-overs front, he was dropped from the national team last summer but rebounded to score a century during the tour of New Zealand. Illness ruled him out of his only game for Queensland, and the chance for the young players to rub shoulders with the great batsman vanished for another year.

	M	I	NO	Runs	HS	100s	50s	Avge	Ct	St	W	Avge	BB
First-class	250	432	43	20,983	380	68	87	53.94	233	0	17	39.47	3/10
Dom. first-class	83	150	17	7,332	234	24	30	55.13	75	0	3	31.00	2/17
Test	67	117	10	5,721	380	20	20	53.47	77	0	0	–	–
Int'l limited-overs	119	115	12	4,131	146	5	26	40.11	46	0	0	–	–
Dom. limited-overs	51	51	9	2,231	152*	8	11	53.12	16	0	3	10.67	2/16

IAN HEWETT *Left-hand batsman, left-arm fast-medium bowler*   Victoria

Hewett fought his way back into the ING Cup team after smashing 82 from 52 balls and impressing with the ball against New Zealand in a one-day tour match. He played three one-day games for Victoria with little success, although he enjoyed a solid year as captain of Richmond.

	M	I	NO	Runs	HS	100s	50s	Avge	Ct	St	W	Avge	BB
First-class	3	3	2	41	34*	0	0	41.00	1	0	6	51.83	3/63
Dom. first-class	3	3	2	41	34*	0	0	41.00	1	0	6	51.83	3/63
Dom. limited-overs	25	19	5	116	29*	0	0	8.29	7	0	29	30.79	4/22

MARK HIGGS *Left-hand batsman, left-arm slow bowler* SA

At 29, Higgs remains a prodigious yet unrealised talent. He retained his SACA contract last summer, but was still made to pay for his poor season in 2003-04. Banished entirely from first-class cricket, Higgs tantalised in limited-overs matches. His highest score of 48 roused Greg Blewett from a scratchy start to post 125 against NSW. But a season return of 182 runs at 26.00 was inadequate, regardless of how clean and poised those runs were. It would be a shame if Higgs's career petered out after showing such immense promise.

	M	I	NO	Runs	HS	100s	50s	Avge	Ct	St	W	Avge	BB
First-class	38	66	7	1,915	181*	3	9	32.46	21	0	31	56.16	4/25
Dom. first-class	37	65	7	1,892	181*	3	9	32.62	20	0	29	56.38	4/25
Dom. limited-overs	57	53	5	1,166	77	0	3	24.29	20	0	31	32.48	4/15

BRAD HODGE *Right-hand batsman, right-arm off-spin bowler*   Victoria

Not one to die wondering, Hodge rang the Australian selectors from his beach holiday to confirm his availability when he heard of Ricky Ponting's injured thumb just before the tour of India. In the end, Hodge's trip to India proved fruitless and he returned to Australia feeling that he needed to prove himself again. At first he struggled, and it was not until Christmas, when a friend pointed out that perhaps he was trying too hard, that Hodge rediscovered his best form. In three Pura Cup games he hit a masterly 204 not out against South Australia in January, 140 and 88 against Tasmania, and 5 and 151 against Queensland. Played with grace, fluency and power, these innings gained him a place on the tours to New Zealand and England. He was courted in the off-season by New South Wales, but after thorough consideration decided to stay.

	M	I	NO	Runs	HS	100s	50s	Avge	Ct	St	W	Avge	BB
First-class	161	287	26	12,258	302*	37	45	46.97	90	0	61	41.82	4/17
Dom. first-class	106	195	19	7,435	204*	21	33	42.24	58	0	32	51.28	4/92
Dom. limited-overs	84	82	9	2,987	118*	7	19	40.92	34	0	8	48.13	2/25

BRAD HOGG *Left-hand batsman, left-arm slow bowler*   **WA and Australia**
Abounding with enthusiasm, Hogg is a sportsman in perpetual motion who is showing no signs of slowing down despite celebrating his 34th birthday in 2005. Soon after scoring an unbeaten 41 and taking 3 for 45 to win Man of the Match honours for Australia against New Zealand in Sydney in December, Hogg declared that he wanted to keep playing at the top level until he was 40. But despite two match-winning performances in Pura Cup matches, Hogg was controversially relegated to 12th man for Western Australia's final qualifying match against Queensland at the Gabba. This decision, following the move by the selectors to leave him out of the side in a dead rubber ING Cup match against Queensland, angered Hogg, who could move interstate if he continues to receive similar shabby treatment. Hogg remains a regular and successful member of the Australian one-day side. He was outstanding in two of the four Pura Cup matches in which he appeared, taking 6 for 44 in the second innings against Tasmania in Perth, and then dominating a low-scoring contest against South Australia in Adelaide, hitting 109 and 61 and taking 3 for 46.

	M	I	NO	Runs	HS	100s	50s	Avge	Ct	St	W	Avge	BB
First-class	89	130	27	3,571	158	4	24	34.67	50	0	145	42.38	6/44
Dom. first-class	63	98	19	2,493	111*	2	16	31.56	40	0	94	41.44	6/44
Test	4	5	1	38	17*	0	0	9.50	0	0	9	50.22	2/40
Int'l limited-overs	68	42	20	503	71*	0	2	22.86	18	0	82	29.10	5/32
Dom. limited-overs	65	51	20	930	59	0	2	30.00	27	0	48	30.44	4/50

JAMES HOPES *Right-hand batsman, right-arm fast-medium bowler*   **Queensland and Australia**
Even though he had been assured that he and Shane Watson were not competing for a spot in the Queensland side, Hopes took no chances and raised his game to another level. He produced career-best performances on the way to making his Australian limited-overs debut on the 2004-05 New Zealand tour after representing Australia A and the Prime Minister's XI. Ironically, it was an injury to Watson that saw a "like-for-like" selection which presented Hopes with his first national cap. Moving to the opening position in the ING Cup, he caught the eye almost immediately with a 33-ball half-century against Tasmania in Launceston. He went on to win the ING Cup Player of the Year award, and for good measure, the Ian Healy Trophy as Queensland Player of the Year. His one-day returns were 293 runs at 32.56 and 11 wickets at 32.36, while he finished with 609 first-class runs at 40.60 and 18 wickets at 26.44. His selection for the Australia A tour of Pakistan in September 2005 suggests the national selectors have an eye on him as a 2006-07 World Cup contender.

	M	I	NO	Runs	HS	100s	50s	Avge	Ct	St	W	Avge	BB
First-class	27	46	1	1,277	111	2	5	28.38	12	0	41	46.76	4/39
Dom. first-class	27	46	1	1,277	111	2	5	28.38	12	0	41	46.76	4/39
Int'l limited-overs	1	–	–	–	–	–	–	–	0	0	1	38.00	1/38
Dom. limited-overs	47	37	4	782	73	0	3	23.70	13	0	66	25.83	5/29

DAVID HUSSEY *Right-hand batsman* **Victoria**
Hussey returned from a successful stint with Nottinghamshire a shadow of his confident self, getting out to unnecessarily aggressive shots. By the time he reached his last chance in the Pura Cup, against Western Australia in Melbourne, his average had slumped to less than 15. He conjured a sparkling century, but failed again in Perth and found himself out of favour with the selectors despite excellent form for Australia A. Bitterly disappointed, Hussey refused to play in a 2nd XI match, and by season's end was considering a return home to Western Australia. But he was selected for the final Pura Cup match of the season and told he would not be released from his contract. He played in all Victoria's games in the ING Cup, where he contributed three fifties. In England, Hussey sparkled once again after his Nottinghamshire batting coach adjusted an alignment problem in his first net session.

	M	I	NO	Runs	HS	100s	50s	Avge	Ct	St	W	Avge	BB
First-class	48	70	8	3,346	212*	13	14	53.97	58	0	12	55.50	4/105
Dom. first-class	21	34	3	1,263	212*	5	5	40.74	14	0	2	34.00	1/6
Dom. limited-overs	23	21	5	653	113	1	3	40.81	13	0	1	104.00	1/37

MIKE HUSSEY *Left-hand batsman* **WA and Australia**
In the absence of Justin Langer, Hussey proved to be an outstanding captain. Tactically he was sound and his positive approach rubbed off on his charges. He excelled in limited-overs matches, scoring 383 runs at 38.30 in the ING Cup, to earn a recall to the national one-day side. So well did he perform for Australia that he enhanced his prospects of appearing in the 2007 World Cup. Hussey played two magnificent Pura Cup innings at the WACA – 210 against Tasmania, and carrying his bat for an unbeaten 223 against Victoria – but he was dismissed for fewer than 25 in nine of his other innings to finish with 721 Pura Cup runs at 55.46. He also scored a fine century in Western Australia's first-class match against Pakistan. A bonus was his improved and lively medium-paced bowling. He delivered only 20 overs in his side's first seven Pura Cup matches, but when Brett Dorey broke down early in the final match at the Gabba, Hussey filled the breach and took three wickets in each innings to finish the season with seven at 19.57.

	M	I	NO	Runs	HS	100s	50s	Avge	Ct	St	W	Avge	BB
First-class	168	302	24	14,645	331*	37	63	52.68	174	0	17	37.29	3/34
Dom. first-class	99	181	10	7,192	223*	15	35	42.06	85	0	12	35.00	3/34
Int'l limited-overs	15	10	7	387	84	0	3	129.00	7	0	1	92.00	1/31
Dom. limited-overs	75	71	10	2,603	106	3	21	42.67	40	0	10	32.10	3/52

MATHEW INNESS *Left-arm fast-medium bowler* **Victoria**
Despite the recruitment of Gerard Denton, the Victorian selectors kept their word by starting Inness in the 1st XI. But the big-hearted, burly paceman, who was shattered to have been overlooked for the Pura Cup final in 2003-04, appeared not to have recovered his spark and lacked penetration. He was dropped from Victoria's match against Western Australia in Perth to make room for Shane Warne and told to review his bowling plan. Devastated, Inness poured his heart and soul into his club, Essendon, finishing the season with a phenomenal 50 wickets at 10.68 apiece, including match figures of 14 for 84. Despite announcing his engagement to Joanna Kurek, a marketing officer at Cricket Victoria, he decided to move to Western Australia.

	M	I	NO	Runs	HS	100s	50s	Avge	Ct	St	W	Avge	BB
First-class	67	74	27	293	27	0	0	6.23	23	0	229	25.78	7/19
Dom. first-class	59	69	26	224	27	0	0	5.21	17	0	199	25.62	7/19
Dom. limited-overs	21	2	1	1	1*	0	0	1.00	3	0	13	54.00	3/33

PHIL JAQUES *Left-hand batsman* **NSW**
All of the run-making prowess and flair which accompanied Jaques' English County Championship ventures emerged in the most opportune season for the dashing left-hander. He became the first NSW batsman since Bob Simpson in 1963-64 to hit two double-centuries, amassing an inspirational 1,269 runs at 66.78 from 12 first-class games. After a moderate start to the season, he announced his arrival with a commanding 217 against South Australia in Sydney, and never looked back. Jaques rose to the challenge of NSW's loss of four batting luminaries, cutting and pulling in devastating manner. In 2003, Jaques alerted the cricket world to his emerging talent with 1,409 runs for Northamptonshire, and in 2004 he made 1,118 runs for Yorkshire. Given his opportunity at the head of the batting order, Jaques doubled his run output of the previous season for NSW and by season's end was attracting attention as a probable international of the near future.

	M	I	NO	Runs	HS	100s	50s	Avge	Ct	St	W	Avge	BB
First-class	59	104	5	5,261	243	13	26	53.14	46	0	0	–	–
Dom. first-class	23	43	1	1,913	240*	4	9	45.55	17	0	0	–	–
Dom. limited-overs	19	19	0	592	75	0	3	31.16	2	0	–	–	–

NICK JEWELL *Right-hand batsman* **Victoria**
Strong performances in the state 2nd XI led to Jewell's inclusion in Victoria's squad for the final match of the Pura Cup season. The gifted batsman had been on the fringe of selection for some years, and made the most of his solitary appearance. In the first innings he came in at 2 for 9 and scored 80 out of a team total of 169. His all-round form for St Kilda helped the club to the premiership for the third consecutive season.

	M	I	NO	Runs	HS	100s	50s	Avge	Ct	St	W	Avge	BB
First-class	5	9	0	179	80	0	1	19.89	1	0	0	–	–
Dom. first-class	5	9	0	179	80	0	1	19.89	1	0	0	–	–
Dom. limited-overs	14	14	0	384	60	0	2	27.43	1	0	0	–	–

MITCHELL JOHNSON *Left-hand batsman, left-arm fast bowler* **Queensland**
Johnson completed his first full season in four years, putting a string of back stress fractures behind him. He played only a handful of matches, with nothing startling in terms of wickets (although his 4 for 45 in a one-day match against Western Australia featured some seriously rapid deliveries), but the sheer fact of seeing him bowl quickly again would have pleased many observers. Among the pleased were the national selectors, who included him in the 2005 Commonwealth Bank Cricket Centre of Excellence tour of India and Sri Lanka. While his ability to bowl fast is his biggest attraction, he is developing into a capable lower-order batsman, scoring his maiden first-class half-century with a valuable 51 not out against South Australia at the Gabba.

	M	I	NO	Runs	HS	100s	50s	Avge	Ct	St	W	Avge	BB
First-class	6	8	3	152	51*	0	1	30.40	0	0	17	35.29	3/23
Dom. first-class	5	7	2	146	51*	0	1	29.20	0	0	14	35.29	3/23
Dom. limited-overs	6	2	0	35	27	0	0	17.50	1	0	10	28.70	4/37

BRENDAN JOSELAND *Right-hand batsman* **Victoria**
A composed half-century against South Australia in his only Pura Cup match of the season left Joseland with two fifties in his two first-class appearances for his state. He excelled for his club, leading Melbourne University to the final against St Kilda and finishing third in the Ryder Medal count. The 29-year-old, who balances a full-time

career as an engineer and extensive charity work for his church with cricket, was also chosen in the Premier Cricket team of the year.

	M	I	NO	Runs	HS	100s	50s	Avge	Ct	St	W	Avge	BB
First-class	2	4	0	110	51	0	2	27.50	2	0	1	19.00	1/19
Dom. first-class	2	4	0	110	51	0	2	27.50	2	0	1	19.00	1/19
Dom. limited-overs	8	6	0	72	23	0	0	12.00	2	0	1	95.00	1/24

SHANE JURGENSEN *Right-arm fast*   Queensland

The strapping former Tasmanian and Western Australian paceman played four ING Cup games in 2004-05 with only moderate success, and made regular Cricket Australia Cup appearances without playing a first-class match. He was in outstanding form for his club Sandgate–Redcliffe. He runs his own coaching business, High Performance Cricket, with a special interest in nurturing young fast bowlers.

	M	I	NO	Runs	HS	100s	50s	Avge	Ct	St	W	Avge	BB
First-class	22	30	9	250	56	0	1	11.90	3	0	69	30.07	6/65
Dom. first-class	21	29	8	237	56	0	1	11.29	2	0	68	29.22	6/65
Dom. limited-overs	13	3	2	4	3*	0	0	4.00	1	0	8	62.38	2/31

MICHAEL KASPROWICZ *Right-arm fast*   Queensland and Australia

After a shellacking at the hands of New Zealand in a one-day loss in Melbourne, Kasprowicz was pursued the next day by the media, prompting him to wonder aloud whether his bad day at the office had resulted in physical harm to others. Apart from that one spell, Kasprowicz's summer was typically workmanlike. He played more home Tests than ever before, and took his 100th Test wicket on the tour of New Zealand. Despite being dubbed "fashionable for unfashionable tours" a few years ago, he was selected for the Ashes tour of England but had a nightmare time. Popular with team-mates, whether at national, state or club level, he made certain he was available for selection for his only game for Queensland, and took 4 for 37 in the ING Cup against Western Australia at the Gabba.

	M	I	NO	Runs	HS	100s	50s	Avge	Ct	St	W	Avge	BB
First-class	222	298	63	4,121	92	0	11	17.54	87	0	883	26.43	9/36
Dom. first-class	89	114	20	1,393	52*	0	2	14.82	34	0	387	24.31	6/47
Test	33	46	10	379	25	0	0	10.53	12	0	102	31.12	7/36
Int'l limited-overs	43	13	9	74	28*	0	0	18.50	13	0	67	24.99	5/45
Dom. limited-overs	67	33	16	235	34	0	0	13.82	14	0	84	28.37	4/19

SIMON KATICH *Left-hand batsman, slow left-arm bowler*   NSW and Australia

After he had played a leading part in Australia's victory in India, Katich's omission from the Australian team in favour of Darren Lehmann was a frustration that he bore with patience and application. He batted at No. 3 in India, making an important four-hour 81 in the first Test and 99 in the third Test. His recall was inevitable upon Lehmann's omission, returning for the three-Test series in New Zealand. In Christchurch, his 118 in 229 minutes and 212-run stand with Adam Gilchrist led on to victory. Always a superb fieldsman in close or in the deep, his versatility with his left-arm spinners and capacity to bat in all conditions sealed Katich's selection for the Ashes tour. Appointed captain of New South Wales upon Steve Waugh's retirement, he was ever a thoughtful, imaginative leader. He appeared in two Pura Cup games, as well as three ING Cup matches in which he again showed his consistency with half-centuries in each appearance. Has the rare combination of talent and leadership qualities to captain his country.

	M	I	NO	Runs	HS	100s	50s	Avge	Ct	St	W	Avge	BB
First-class	135	233	33	10,100	228*	28	51	50.50	129	0	77	37.68	7/130
Dom. first-class	65	116	14	5,133	228*	14	27	50.32	57	0	36	32.00	7/130
Test	16	26	3	1,010	125	2	6	43.91	10	0	11	32.36	6/65
Int'l limited-overs	18	15	3	344	76	0	2	28.67	8	0	–	–	–
Dom. limited-overs	58	56	7	2,105	136*	4	13	42.96	21	0	5	47.00	3/43

TRENT KELLY *Right-arm fast-medium bowler* **SA**
Now resigned to reserve status behind regular new-ball bowlers
Shaun Tait and Paul Rofe, Trent Kelly performed creditably when
called up to plug the gap left by Mark Cleary at Bellerive in
November. Kelly bowled tidily without luck in the first innings,
then collected three wickets in the second. He was not a regular
wicket-taker at grade level after that game, however, and when
Cleary was injured a second time Ryan Harris was preferred. There
is much to like about Kelly's zippy pace and occasional swing, and
there is every chance he will get more opportunities in the likely
event of Tait winning an Australian berth.

	M	I	NO	Runs	HS	100s	50s	Avge	Ct	St	W	Avge	BB
First-class	1	2	0	9	6	0	0	4.50	1	0	3	40.67	3/59
Dom. first-class	1	2	0	9	6	0	0	4.50	1	0	3	40.67	3/59
Dom. limited-overs	3	1	0	1	1	0	0	1.00	2	0	1	104.00	1/30

BRAD KNOWLES *Right-hand batsman, right-arm fast* **Victoria**
Knowles emerged from the state's rookie list to play all but one of
Victoria's ING Cup matches, building on the promise he had
displayed the season before. Recovering from the osteitis pubis that
had restricted him previously, Knowles bowled with pace and
accuracy to pick up nine wickets at 32, and also managed one first-
class match. But his season ended badly when he broke down
during the Premier Cricket semi-finals, requiring a knee
reconstruction and throwing his preparation for 2005-06 into
disarray.

	M	I	NO	Runs	HS	100s	50s	Avge	Ct	St	W	Avge	BB
First-class	1	2	1	22	18	0	0	22.00	2	0	1	69.00	1/69
Dom. first-class	1	2	1	22	18	0	0	22.00	2	0	1	69.00	1/69
Dom. limited-overs	10	5	2	35	17	0	0	11.67	1	0	11	30.09	2/14

JASON KREJZA *Right-arm off-spin bowler* **NSW**
The son of a Czechoslovakian who played soccer in Australia and New Zealand, and a
mother from Poland, Jason Krejza attended St Francis Xavier School in Liverpool in
outer Sydney. Visions of a career as a fast bowler were cut short by a double stress
fracture of the back, leading him to take up spin. Krejza won selection in both the Pura
Cup and ING Cup teams with his all-round skills, especially his variation of flight and
willingness to loop the ball above eye level in challenging the batsman. Twelve wickets
at 40.75 from nine first-class games hardly indicates it, but his season was an outstanding
investment for the future, and he showed his potential by claiming the wicket of the
prolific Michael Bevan three times. A genuine all-rounder, the 185cm Krejza batted at
No. 7 for a determined half-century for New South Wales against the New Zealanders
and made a three-hour 63 in the win over Victoria in Melbourne.

	M	I	NO	Runs	HS	100s	50s	Avge	Ct	St	W	Avge	BB
First-class	10	15	2	271	63	0	2	20.85	9	0	12	52.08	2/11
Dom. first-class	8	12	2	160	63	0	1	16.00	7	0	9	46.22	2/11
Dom. limited-overs	4	3	1	26	19	0	0	13.00	0	0	5	34.60	3/45

SCOTT KREMERSKOTHEN *Left-hand batsman, right-arm medium bowler* **Tasmania**
Kremerskothen has found himself on the periphery of the Tasmanian team in recent years,
and last season saw him slip back even further. He played only three ING Cup games, and,
for the first time since his debut in 1999, no Pura Cup matches at all. He was not in the first-
choice side in the one-day competition, generally playing when injury forced someone else

out, but he still kept in touch by being perennial 12th man. His fielding continues to shine, but he probably suffers from the idea that neither his batting nor his bowling is, on its own, strong enough for him to command a regular place. Still, at only 26, his best days are potentially ahead of him if he is prepared to work at his game.

	M	I	NO	Runs	HS	100s	50s	Avge	Ct	St	W	Avge	BB
First-class	34	50	9	1,146	82*	0	4	27.95	22	0	33	40.70	3/53
Dom. first-class	33	49	8	1,145	82*	0	4	27.93	21	0	31	40.94	3/53
Dom. limited-overs	41	33	6	508	64	0	1	18.81	14	0	29	32.59	3/33

GRANT LAMBERT *Right-hand batsman, right-arm fast-medium bowler*   **NSW**
Widely regarded as the best all-round club cricketer of the last decade in Sydney, the dual Bill O'Reilly Medallist at last had the satisfaction of winning recognition at the critical moment for the Pura Cup final against Queensland. In conditions ideally suited to seam bowling, Lambert acted as NSW's fourth pace bowler, capturing the wickets of Martin Love in the first innings and Shane Watson in the second. Batting at No. 7, he struck five boundaries in an hour-long innings of 23 in his team's grim progress for a crucial first-innings lead. It was his only game for the season, although he captained the NSW 2nd XI. At 28, he is still young enough and sufficiently skilled to become a first-class regular, perhaps for another state.

	M	I	NO	Runs	HS	100s	50s	Avge	Ct	St	W	Avge	BB
First-class	6	10	1	183	45*	0	0	20.33	1	0	9	60.67	3/86
Dom. first-class	6	10	1	183	45*	0	0	20.33	1	0	9	60.67	3/86
Dom. limited-overs	4	4	2	13	7	0	0	6.50	1	0	6	30.00	2/33

JUSTIN LANGER *Left-hand batsman*   **WA and Australia**
For sheer determination, unwavering concentration and the skill to master the fastest bowlers, Langer has few peers. The compact left-handed opener reached the pinnacle of his career in 2004 when he was Test cricket's leading run-getter, scoring five centuries in his 1,481 runs at an average of 54.85. He and Matthew Hayden also became only the third Test opening pair to pass 4,000 runs in aggregate stands. A bulging spinal disc seemed certain to keep him out of the Boxing Day Test against Pakistan at the MCG, but he worked for 18 hours a day to overcome the affliction and take his place in the team. The man who declared that he trained for the 2004 tour of India as if for a world title fight continues to set the standard for dedication, self-discipline and a passionate approach to training and playing. Running, boxing, karate, yoga, weight sessions and bike riding help to prepare Langer for any challenge. In three Pura Cup matches in 2004-05 he hit two superb centuries, including 134 off 114 deliveries against NSW in Perth, when he hammered 65 runs from the 24 balls he faced from Stuart MacGill.

	M	I	NO	Runs	HS	100s	50s	Avge	Ct	St	W	Avge	BB
First-class	271	474	45	21,951	274*	70	83	51.17	222	0	5	40.80	2/17
Dom. first-class	86	155	12	7,685	274*	24	27	53.74	71	0	0	–	–
Test	88	150	8	6,607	250	21	26	46.53	58	0	0	–	–
Int'l limited-overs	8	7	2	160	36	0	0	32.00	1	1	–	–	–
Dom. limited-overs	80	76	6	2,828	146	6	19	40.40	35	0	–	–	–

RYAN LE LOUX *Right-arm leg-spinner*   **Queensland**
When he made his Pura Cup debut against Tasmania at the Gabba, Ryan Le Loux became the first wrist-spinner selected for Queensland since Bruce Oxenford in 1992-93. It was an inauspicious debut, scoring 5 in his only innings and getting just one over as pace dominated the match, yet it marked a significant shift in thinking from the state selectors. Disquiet over the form of Nathan Hauritz and lack of playing time for Chris Simpson prompted them to try something more venturesome. Le Loux (the family name is Dutch) had made his mark in taking ten wickets in

two Cricket Australia Cup matches. Brisk through the air off a short, bustling approach, he has good control with his stock leg-break. He represented the Northern Territory at Under-17 and Under-19 levels, and was a Commonwealth Bank Cricket Academy scholar in 2004.

	M	I	NO	Runs	HS	100s	50s	Avge	Ct	St	W	Avge	BB
First-class	1	1	0	5	5	0	0	5.00	0	0	0	–	–
Dom. first-class	1	1	0	5	5	0	0	5.00	0	0	0	–	–

BRETT LEE *Right-hand batsman, right-arm fast* **NSW and Australia**

Lee experienced the most frustrating time of his career as he waited for a Test recall behind Australia's preferred trio of pacemen, Glenn McGrath, Jason Gillespie and Michael Kasprowicz. He got his chance again in England, but made more impact with bat than ball. He remained an automatic choice in the limited-overs international side, and that combined with his seemingly permanent 12th man status in the Test team to allow him only one first-class match – for NSW against the touring New Zealanders – for the season, as well as three ING Cup games. Despite his lack of match practice, he shone in Australia's limited-overs team, being named player of the VB Series. He continued to take the new ball as Australia routed the Black Caps in New Zealand. During the tour, one Lee delivery was timed at 160.8 kph, second only for speed to Shoaib Akhtar's 161 kph. Lee attracted adverse publicity for his occasional delivery of beamers, which he said were attempted yorkers that slipped.

	M	I	NO	Runs	HS	100s	50s	Avge	Ct	St	W	Avge	BB
First-class	71	78	13	1,139	79	0	4	17.52	19	0	295	26.59	7/114
Dom. first-class	18	25	4	306	74*	0	1	14.57	8	0	87	24.28	7/114
Test	37	36	6	593	62*	0	2	19.77	9	0	139	31.68	5/47
Int'l limited-overs	112	47	18	511	51*	0	1	17.62	27	0	200	22.17	5/27
Dom. limited-overs	17	9	5	92	44*	0	0	23.00	3	0	21	32.43	3/41

DARREN LEHMANN *Left-hand batsman, slow left-arm orthodox bowler* **SA and Australia**

There were shades of Mark Taylor about Lehmann last summer. His high regard as an Australian team tactician was compromised by low returns as a batsman, and he lost his place in both forms of the game. He had declared in India, with typical frankness, that he would voluntarily make way for Michael Clarke if required. Back in Australia, he again made the news when Shoaib Akhtar bowled him behind his pads in Perth. After he flicked the same bowler into short leg's hands at the MCG, Lehmann was "rested" – according to his loyal skipper Ricky Ponting – from the SCG Test, but most people sensed his international career was over. That was confirmed during the VB Series, as early good scores gave way to later poor ones. When he returned to play for South Australia, Lehmann promptly spanked 104 from 85 balls on a Gabba green-top before withdrawing for shoulder surgery that he had postponed all season.

	M	I	NO	Runs	HS	100s	50s	Avge	Ct	St	W	Avge	BB
First-class	248	420	28	21,991	255	70	100	56.10	129	0	96	34.99	4/35
Dom. first-class	127	231	14	11,636	255	39	44	53.62	80	0	24	49.08	3/42
Test	27	42	2	1,798	177	5	10	44.95	11	0	15	27.47	3/42
Int'l limited-overs	117	101	22	3,077	119	4	17	38.95	26	0	52	27.81	4/7
Dom. limited-overs	77	76	10	3,240	142*	6	24	49.09	24	0	19	30.63	3/16

MICHAEL LEWIS *Right-arm fast-medium bowler* **Victoria**

A menacing spell of seriously fast bowling against South Australia in Victoria's first match at the MCG suggested that Lewis would not merely edge out his pace bowling rivals for a state spot but could press for higher honours. In the end, after almost single-handedly carrying Victoria's attack through both Pura Cup and ING Cup in a season of discontent, this old-fashioned competitor was rewarded with his first Cricket Australia contract. At 31, it may have appeared that Lewis had left his run too late, but the national selectors have obviously been impressed by the combination of fire, accuracy, stamina and determination that make him such a formidable opponent.

	M	I	NO	Runs	HS	100s	50s	Avge	Ct	St	W	Avge	BB
First-class	51	67	17	438	54*	0	1	8.76	26	0	182	28.34	6/59
Dom. first-class	45	63	16	429	54*	0	1	9.13	23	0	158	28.59	6/59
Dom. limited-overs	47	13	6	72	19	0	0	10.29	13	0	64	25.98	4/41

RHETT LOCKYEAR *Right-hand batsman*   **Tasmania**

Arriving in Hobart from New South Wales in 2003-04, this young right-hander has done well to make his first-class debut in only his second season in the state. He showed composure in making 24 on his debut at the Gabba, and made another 20 when the team moved south to Sydney. When Michael Di Venuto regained fitness, Lockyear was consigned to the 2nd XI, where he continued to bat well. With the senior team disappointing in its batting in 2004-05, Lockyear can expect to be considered once again next season.

	M	I	NO	Runs	HS	100s	50s	Avge	Ct	St	W	Avge	BB
First-class	2	4	0	46	24	0	0	11.50	0	0	–	–	–
Dom. first-class	2	4	0	46	24	0	0	11.50	0	0	–	–	–

MARTIN LOVE *Right-hand batsman*   **Queensland**

Normally one of Queensland's most bankable batsmen, Love suffered a downturn that quickly became a depression as a spate of hand injuries led to a form collapse. For much of the season, he was averaging single figures. But he was the outstanding batsman in the low-scoring Pura Cup final, scoring a defiant second-innings century in six hours of dedication, the third time he had scored a century in a final. Part of Love's post-season review with coach Terry Oliver revealed that his hand injuries had caused him to make subtle changes to his grip that might have contributed to his horror run. His prolific subsequent form for Northamptonshire suggested that he had overcome his problems and could look forward to a more typical season in 2005-06.

	M	I	NO	Runs	HS	100s	50s	Avge	Ct	St	W	Avge	BB
First-class	177	309	30	14,042	300*	35	64	50.33	213	0	1	11.00	1/5
Dom. first-class	110	192	16	7,963	300*	19	34	45.24	124	0	1	11.00	1/5
Test	5	8	3	233	100*	1	1	46.60	7	0	–	–	–
Dom. limited-overs	82	79	11	2,412	127*	4	9	35.47	31	0	–	–	–

STUART MacGILL *Right-arm leg-spinner*   **NSW and Australia**

MacGill experienced the bitter disappointment of omission from the tour of India and was essentially not required for home international duty until his call-up for the Sydney Test. He had the satisfaction there of match figures of 8 for 170 in Australia's nine-wicket victory over Pakistan, compared with Shane Warne's 5 for 195. MacGill remained one of the best spinners in world cricket, as his 62 wickets at 23.24 in 12 domestic first-class games showed and his Steve Waugh Medal as the outstanding cricketer for NSW verified. Three times he took five wickets or better in a Pura Cup innings. If his batting was often gung-ho, he showed his nerveless temperament at No. 11 by defying Queensland for 24 minutes for 11 not out to secure victory for his team in the Pura Cup final. Likewise, he contributed a sterling 27 of the famous 219-run partnership for the tenth wicket with Dominic Thornely against Western Australia.

Strong-minded, articulate and never short of a viewpoint, he is a popular guest on television.

	M	I	NO	Runs	HS	100s	50s	Avge	Ct	St	W	Avge	BB
First-class	149	178	46	1,288	53	0	1	9.76	66	0	646	29.45	8/111
Dom. first-class	67	89	26	627	53	0	1	9.95	30	0	260	32.72	6/64
Test	33	38	7	272	43	0	0	8.77	16	0	160	28.82	7/50
Int'l limited-overs	3	2	1	1	1	0	0	1.00	2	0	6	17.50	4/19
Dom. limited-overs	54	22	11	93	18	0	0	8.45	12	0	109	21.91	5/40

STEVE MAGOFFIN *Right-arm fast-medium bowler* **WA**

A towering beanpole whose new team-mates fondly called him Mal (as in malnutrition), Magoffin proved to be a wonderful acquisition after he was poached from Queensland, where he was unable to break into first-class ranks. He belied his flimsy, slender frame by playing in all Western Australia's Pura Cup matches and bowling 335.3 overs for his 28 wickets at 35.10. As well, he took four wickets in the first-class match against Pakistan and another six at a somewhat costly economy rate of 5.23 runs an over in the ING Cup. He gives every indication of becoming a better bowler with that experience. Recruited as a support bowler, Magoffin frequently had to be used as a strike weapon, which did not suit him. His stock  delivery angles into a right-hander, but he has been working on his outswinger, which he bowled to great effect to help Melville beat Scarborough in the first-grade final.

	M	I	NO	Runs	HS	100s	50s	Avge	Ct	St	W	Avge	BB
First-class	11	14	6	125	29*	0	0	15.63	4	0	32	34.47	5/76
Dom. first-class	10	13	5	111	29*	0	0	13.88	4	0	28	35.11	5/76
Dom. limited-overs	6	3	1	3	2*	0	0	1.50	0	0	6	45.33	3/40

JIMMY MAHER *Left-hand batsman* **Queensland**

It was a frustrating season for the Queensland captain, as Queensland lost both interstate finals. Since taking over from Stuart Law, Maher has held the reins in five losing finals. His personal performances underscore his will to succeed – his season included a remarkable innings of 170 out of a team total of 271 against Tasmania in Hobart which was probably the difference between victory and defeat. His dashing century in the ING Cup final took him to 490 runs at 44.54 for the summer – making him the all-time leading run-scorer in domestic one-day cricket. Vastly experienced and still only 31, Maher appears caught in a selection eddy when it comes to the national scene, as others have consistently been preferred in recent seasons despite poorer statistical returns.

	M	I	NO	Runs	HS	100s	50s	Avge	Ct	St	W	Avge	BB
First-class	149	264	27	10,006	217	21	49	42.22	154	2	10	50.40	3/11
Dom. first-class	112	200	20	7,271	209	13	37	40.39	126	0	10	30.20	3/11
Int'l limited-overs	26	26	3	438	95	0	1	25.76	11	0	–	–	–
Dom. limited-overs	84	84	9	3,627	187	8	20	48.36	43	0	2	43.50	2/43

GREG MAIL *Right-hand batsman, right-arm medium bowler* **NSW**

The angular opener played all 12 games for NSW without doing himself justice, save for his pugnacious second-innings century in Perth when his team was fighting to stave off defeat. Mail's five-and-a-half-hour defiance could not prevent the loss, but enabled him to retain his position throughout the campaign, culminating in his appearance in the Pura Cup final when he made a resolute 30 in 97 minutes as NSW struggled to avoid a second-innings collapse. He finished with a disappointing aggregate of 448 runs at 22.40. A fieldsman with sure hands, he held 15 catches. His slow-medium deliveries, so valuable in the Pura Cup final of 2002-03, were rarely required. Mail opened in four of NSW's ING Cup games without satisfying the selectors with his output and scoring speed. Industrious and intelligent, Mail applies himself so well to the game that he can look forward to more prosperous times.

	M	I	NO	Runs	HS	100s	50s	Avge	Ct	St	W	Avge	BB
First-class	51	93	5	2,984	176	6	15	33.91	47	0	12	32.17	4/18
Dom. first-class	48	87	5	2,774	176	6	13	33.83	45	0	11	33.64	4/18
Dom. limited-overs	7	6	1	115	58	0	1	23.00	2	1	0	–	–

GRAHAM MANOU *Right-hand batsman, wicket-keeper* SA

When defending champions Victoria were comfortably beaten in South Australia's Pura Cup opener, newly appointed acting captain Manou probably harboured thoughts of a calm and quietly successful summer. It wasn't for him to know that horrors – including the now infamous team total of 29 and the concession of an ING Cup double bonus point – lay ahead, and when they eventuated he looked as surprised as anyone. Manou, however, earned respect as a gracious and frank team spokesman and a thoughtful captain. His batting gained a hitherto unseen level of grit not reflected in his runs tally. Admirably, his keeping was better than ever, 34 catches and two stumpings setting a new personal benchmark in the Pura Cup, and his 16 catches topped the dismissals in the ING Cup. Opening the innings in the final ING Cup match he scored 43 off 36 balls, setting up victory and winning the match award. Darren Lehmann afforded him some rest from captaincy late in proceedings, and Manou can reasonably expect the new season to offer him a better hand than the old one did.

	M	I	NO	Runs	HS	100s	50s	Avge	Ct	St	W	Avge	BB
First-class	55	95	9	1,643	130	1	7	19.10	0	14	–	–	–
Dom. first-class	51	88	7	1,547	130	1	7	19.10	0	14	–	–	–
Dom. limited-overs	55	49	14	767	63	0	2	21.91	0	3	–	–	–

DAN MARSH *Right-hand batsman, slow left-arm orthodox bowler* **Tasmania**

Whatever else Dan Marsh achieves in cricket, his emulation of Jack Simmons' giant-killing feat of 1978-79 will put him on a pedestal in Tasmania above all those before him who have tried and failed. His brutal half-century as Tasmania rushed to victory in the ING Cup final had more than a touch of Simmons' brawn to it, and for this affable and loyal cricketer it will be favourite memory of 2004-05, when little else went right for him personally. Despite one trademark century in the Pura Cup, his output in that competition was more than halved compared with 2003-04, his first season effectively in charge of the Tasmanian side. He began the ING campaign with an 85-ball century at Perth, but until the vital climax at the Gabba four months later, did little else with the bat. As he is now in his 33rd year, the question has to be asked: have we seen the best of him?

	M	I	NO	Runs	HS	100s	50s	Avge	Ct	St	W	Avge	BB
First-class	106	178	29	5,582	157	11	28	37.46	120	0	146	44.55	7/57
Dom. first-class	94	158	25	4,668	134	8	23	35.10	107	0	135	44.45	7/57
Dom. limited-overs	82	75	16	1,831	106*	3	7	31.03	40	0	44	45.77	3/33

SHAUN MARSH *Left-hand batsman* WA

The stylish Shaun Marsh made significant strides forward in the summer of 2004-05. After a winter playing for Walsden in the Central Lancashire League, Marsh showed he was prepared to fight and make it difficult for bowlers. The signs were clear that he was starting to understand his game and was prepared to build an innings. He was rewarded with two centuries and 503 runs at 35.33 in the Pura Cup. However, the selectors did not give him a chance in the ING Cup even though he had shown in previous seasons that he is a talented, free-scoring batsman in that form of the game. Marsh also excelled for Fremantle in club cricket and headed the first-grade averages with 722 runs at 80.22. In a semi-final against Scarborough he played a lone hand in blazing his way to 131 not out in a total of 241, posting his century off only 58 balls.

	M	I	NO	Runs	HS	100s	50s	Avge	Ct	St	W	Avge	BB
First-class	22	38	5	1,016	119	3	1	30.79	20	0	2	39.00	2/20
Dom. first-class	20	35	4	966	119	3	1	31.16	18	0	2	39.00	2/20
Dom. limited-overs	11	9	0	182	42	0	0	20.22	2	0	1	14.00	1/14

DAMIEN MARTYN *Right-hand batsman, right-arm medium bowler* **WA and Australia**
Martyn's six centuries and 1,353 runs at 56.38 made him the second most prolific run-getter in Test cricket in 2004. That also earned him the WACA's Gold Cup (beating Justin Langer and Adam Gilchrist) as Western Australia's outstanding cricketer for the year. Before the tour of Sri Lanka in early 2004 he had gone 16 Tests without scoring a century, and many critics were questioning his place in the side. The Ashes tour proved to be a trial, as it was for many. A wonderfully fluent and unhurried batsman, Martyn delights spectators with his exquisite square drives and soft deflections. Four of his six hundreds in 2004 were scored on the sub-continent, and another, his 142 against Pakistan, was his first century at the MCG. While he has flourished in the Test arena, Martyn also continues to shine in limited-overs cricket and is looking forward to the 2007 World Cup in the Caribbean. Quiet and almost reclusive, he prepares diligently, both physically and mentally, and sets a high standard of fielding either close to the bat or in the outfield.

	M	I	NO	Runs	HS	100s	50s	Avge	Ct	St	W	Avge	BB
First-class	189	315	44	13,966	238	43	70	51.54	144	2	36	42.64	4/30
Dom. first-class	93	163	16	6,705	203*	20	33	45.61	87	1	32	38.69	4/30
Test	56	89	12	3,947	165	12	21	51.26	26	0	2	84.00	1/0
Int'l limited-overs	181	157	48	4,604	144*	5	30	42.24	57	0	12	58.67	2/21
Dom. limited-overs	53	50	7	1,880	140	3	13	43.72	16	0	18	16.33	3/3

ANDREW MCDONALD *Right-hand batsman, right-arm fast-medium bowler* **Victoria**
Hampered by injury and kept out of the team by Ian Harvey, McDonald was an occasional contributor to Victoria's effort. He enjoyed a fruitful year in his debut as captain of Melbourne, although the team was lost in the semi-finals. He has struggled to live up to his initial promise, and was entertaining thoughts of a move interstate before accepting a Cricket Victoria contract.

	M	I	NO	Runs	HS	100s	50s	Avge	Ct	St	W	Avge	BB
First-class	17	28	6	401	51*	0	1	18.23	12	0	37	29.78	6/67
Dom. first-class	16	27	6	400	51*	0	1	19.05	11	0	36	29.42	6/67
Dom. limited-overs	25	20	6	361	55*	0	2	25.79	5	0	17	44.29	2/23

GLENN McGRATH *Right-hand batsman, right-arm fast bowler* **NSW and Australia**
The champion bowler of one of the game's great sides, McGrath showed no sign of flagging or his career deteriorating until he suffered ankle and elbow injuries on the Ashes tour. The modern demands of the Test and limited-over fields restricted his appearances for New South Wales to a single ING Cup match. On this occasion, McGrath took the new ball with Brett Lee, delivered ten lethal overs and claimed 4-36 in a resounding defeat of Victoria at the Sydney Cricket Ground in mid-February to deprive Victoria of a cup final position. So influential was McGrath that he dismissed Victoria's first four batsmen without saving New South Wales from the competition wooden spoon. It was a mark of McGrath's prodigious ability and durability that he took the new ball in all four Tests as Australia won a series on the "last frontier tour" of India for the first time since 1969 as well as for all five successful Tests at home against New Zealand and Pakistan, and then again in the two-nil series success in New Zealand at an

age when most fast bowlers are finished. Swing bowling was never his fancy, rather precision in line and length and subtlety of movement off the seam at pace which he has combined to devastating effect. Selection was automatic for the World XI in a tsunami appeal match against an Asian XI in Melbourne though his promotion to No. 6 in the batting order was an extravagance. His dismissal for a first-ball duck merely added to his batting reputation.

	M	I	NO	Runs	HS	100s	50s	Avge	Ct	St	W	Avge	BB
First-class	173	175	58	892	61	0	2	7.62	49	0	767	20.52	8/24
Dom. first-class	22	22	8	113	26	0	0	8.07	3	0	83	26.82	5/36
Test	109	120	42	556	61	0	1	7.13	34	0	499	21.23	8/24
Int'l limited-overs	214	58	31	102	11	0	0	3.78	30	0	324	22.30	7/15
Dom. limited-overs	20	–	–	–	–	–	–	–	5	0	26	24.04	4/17

DARREN McNEES *Right-arm fast-medium bowler*   **Tasmania**

After an extended stint as 12th man for Tasmania, this fast bowler from country Victoria received his chance against his native state at Bellerive in a late-season match, and found the going tough. He did take Brad Hodge's wicket, but not before Hodge had plundered 228 runs in the match. The selectors had taken the opportunity to rest Brett Geeves, but were quick to restore him to the team in the next match. However, McNees has something to work with: he was the ACT's leading wicket-taker in 2002-03, and has played with a premiership club side in Melbourne. His 193 cm frame gives him a natural advantage, and he has plenty of time to learn about bowling at the top level.

	M	I	NO	Runs	HS	100s	50s	Avge	Ct	St	W	Avge	BB
First-class	1	2	0	0	0	0	0	0.00	0	0	1	142.00	1/19
Dom. first-class	1	2	0	0	0	0	0	0.00	0	0	1	142.00	1/19

SCOTT MEULEMAN *Right-hand batsman*   **WA**

The cricketing gods were not smiling on Meuleman in 2004-05. He was injured in the first over of Western Australia's first match of the season, an ING Cup contest against Tasmania in Perth. Diving in the field, he landed awkwardly on his left elbow, dislocating his shoulder. He was back in action within a fortnight and scored 59 against NSW in a limited-overs match at North Sydney Oval. But he was out cheaply in his next four innings and was replaced in both forms of the game by Chris Rogers. Some rival states are putting out feelers for the competent right-hand batsman, but Western Australian officials hope he will resist these overtures and stay in his home state.

	M	I	NO	Runs	HS	100s	50s	Avge	Ct	St	W	Avge	BB
First-class	19	34	0	742	109	2	3	21.82	10	0	2	49.00	1/38
Dom. first-class	16	30	0	564	106	1	3	18.80	10	0	2	49.00	1/38
Dom. limited-overs	13	11	0	372	71	0	2	33.82	2	0	–	–	–

MICK MILLER *Left-hand batsman, right-arm fast-medium bowler*   **SA**

Miller's decision to retire from first-class cricket in order to go fishing for a living was understandable. The mystery lay in his timing. An uncomplicated outdoors boy at heart, Miller said he was thinking about family and future income when he made his choice, but he announced it in November, just two games into the season. Miller's exit cast something of a cloud over the young and impressionable South Australia playing group as they drifted into a period of on-field misadventures. Miller had lost his Pura Cup place but would surely have regained it had he stuck around. A genuine swing merchant with the ball and a stolid customer with the bat, he enjoyed moments of brilliance, but never the consistency that his talent warranted.

	M	I	NO	Runs	HS	100s	50s	Avge	Ct	St	W	Avge	BB
First-class	18	32	2	745	112	1	4	24.83	15	0	28	39.50	7/55
Dom. first-class	18	32	2	745	112	1	4	24.83	15	0	28	39.50	7/55
Dom. limited-overs	22	22	6	354	82*	0	2	22.13	7	0	13	59.77	3/27

JON MOSS *Right-hand batsman, right-arm fast-medium bowler*   **Victoria**

Moss made a point of denying that he was tired from having played for almost two years straight, thanks to commitments with Derbyshire. That something was missing, though, was clear from the first match in Adelaide, when, captaining Victoria, he was dropped four times on his way to 50 on a final day that called for cool heads and steady hands. In a struggling team, Moss, who went close to 1,000 runs the previous season, managed a single century for the summer and asked to be released to his native New South Wales in April. His move was delayed by at least another year, when he decided to stay after Matthew Elliott's departure. He had more success in the ING Cup, where he hit three fifties at a brisk rate.

	M	I	NO	Runs	HS	100s	50s	Avge	Ct	St	W	Avge	BB
First-class	57	96	8	3,336	172*	6	21	37.91	27	0	85	32.20	4/40
Dom. first-class	36	60	5	2,234	172*	4	15	40.62	16	0	57	27.70	4/50
Dom. limited-overs	40	35	3	840	77	0	7	26.25	11	0	31	32.52	5/47

BRENDAN NASH *Left-hand batsman, left-arm medium* **Queensland**

Nash re-established himself in Queensland's one-day team, where he played nine games and shone in the field, though he was seldom required to bat. His new-found confidence stood him in good stead in his two Pura Cup games, where he had a top score of 92. Nash will be hoping he can continue to ascend to the sort of form he displayed a few years ago and expunge the taint of his barnacle-like innings of 2002-03 when he took 88 minutes to get off the mark, just shy of the world record. He was awarded a full contract for the 2005-06 season. A jackrabbit in the field, it is apt that Nash works in the state government's "Get Active Queensland Schools" program.

	M	I	NO	Runs	HS	100s	50s	Avge	Ct	St	W	Avge	BB
First-class	23	43	4	1106	176	2	4	28.36	13	0	1	32.00	1/22
Dom. first-class	22	42	4	1088	176	2	4	28.63	13	0	1	32.00	1/22
Dom. limited-overs	29	18	4	326	63	0	1	23.29	12	0	2	23.50	2/31

MATTHEW NICHOLSON *Right-arm fast-medium bowler*   **NSW**

An integral member of an attack which paved the way for New South Wales' Pura Cup final triumph and brought about a nine-wicket defeat of the touring New Zealanders, Nicholson enjoyed a superlative season without attracting sufficient attention to suggest he will receive a second Test cap. In 11 first-class games he took 47 wickets at a splendid average of 20.06, taking the new ball in each game, often with genuine pace and hostility. An ankle injury early in Queensland's second innings at Bankstown Oval prevented him appearing in all first-class games, troubling him throughout February and forcing him out of the Perth match against his former team, Western Australia, and at least two ING Cup games in Hobart and Sydney. Nicholson capped his season with seven wickets in the Pura Cup final at the Gabba including 5 for 60 in the second innings. If his bowling retained its sharp edge, the batting skills appeared to have deserted him as he failed to register a half-century for the state. Captaincy at Gordon club in Sydney proved beneficial, leading to his important counselling of James Packman, which led to a more responsible attitude from the young batsman and his eventual selection in the New South Wales team.

	M	I	NO	Runs	HS	100s	50s	Avge	Ct	St	W	Avge	BB
First-class	63	94	17	1,518	101*	1	3	19.71	34	0	236	27.46	7/77
Dom. first-class	54	84	15	1,235	59*	0	1	17.90	32	0	197	28.96	6/76
Test	1	2	0	14	9	0	0	7.00	0	0	4	28.75	3/56
Dom. limited-overs	22	15	3	142	25	0	0	11.83	9	0	23	36.70	3/34

ASHLEY NOFFKE *Right-hand batsman, right-arm fast*   **Queensland**
Noffke continued to struggle to regain the form that took him to the fringe of Australian
selection a few years ago. He took 23 Pura Cup wickets at 37.91 and ten ING Cup
wickets at 43.50, an improvement on his previous season. At times he bowled
impressively without luck, and his decisive second-innings spell of 4 for 78 against
Victoria at the MCG, to inspire an unlikely outright win, showed what he is capable of.
Carl Rackemann is mentoring Noffke, and one suspects that his form could easily
blossom if a few breaks go his way early. A back injury during the Pura Cup final was
an added concern, although it did not prevent him accepting a contract with Durham. He
performed solidly there before another back scare brought him home early.

	M	I	NO	Runs	HS	100s	50s	Avge	Ct	St	W	Avge	BB
First-class	69	85	17	1,694	114*	1	6	24.91	24	0	228	31.01	8/24
Dom. first-class	40	54	13	1,090	114*	1	4	26.59	15	0	134	30.37	6/24
Dom. limited-overs	44	18	7	163	24	0	0	14.82	15	0	46	39.67	4/32

MARCUS NORTH *Left-hand batsman, right-arm off-spin bowler*   **WA**
On the surface, a summer without a first-class century for one of the state's top batsmen
would appear to be a disappointing season. On the contrary, North enjoyed a bountiful
summer, with nine first-class fifties in a tally of 826 runs at 55.06. He was involved in
many important partnerships and excelled in tough situations. His consistency was
admired by his peers, and whether he graduates to the next level probably will be
determined by opportunity. North was also his state's leading scorer in the ING Cup,
with 412 runs at 45.77. Overcoming an injury to his right shoulder, North was able to
resume bowling his off-spinners, and he gave a most encouraging performance with his
3 for 93 off 34 overs against NSW in Perth.

	M	I	NO	Runs	HS	100s	50s	Avge	Ct	St	W	Avge	BB
First-class	68	119	10	4,366	219	9	26	40.06	43	0	34	43.26	4/16
Dom. first-class	44	78	6	2,990	200*	7	17	41.53	32	0	26	49.00	3/23
Dom. limited-overs	30	27	7	872	134*	1	7	43.60	9	0	8	43.75	2/15

AARON NYE *Right-hand batsman*   **Queensland**
Nye added three more Pura Cup games to his career, with unremarkable results, and also
made his ING Cup debut, playing six games. Usually batting late in the innings, he
thumped 113 runs at 28.25 and revealed himself to be an asset in the field. He helped
claim an exceptional catch in the opening match against NSW. A hefty blow by Brad
Haddin to mid-wicket was caught by the running Nye just inside the rope, but with
momentum carrying him forward, he just had time to throw the ball over his shoulder
to Martin Love before he crossed the boundary. Nye captained the QAS 2nd XI as well
as leading his club team, Wests, to a first-grade premiership.

	M	I	NO	Runs	HS	100s	50s	Avge	Ct	St	W	Avge	BB
First-class	4	6	0	176	102	1	0	29.33	5	0	2	30.00	1/15
Dom. first-class	4	6	0	176	102	1	0	29.33	5	0	2	30.00	1/15
Dom. limited-overs	6	6	2	113	35	0	0	28.25	3	0	–	–	–

AARON O'BRIEN *Left-hand batsman, slow left-arm orthodox bowler*   **NSW**
O'Brien broke into the New South Wales team in 2001-02, and was considered the
long-term left arm spin-bowling partner for leg-spinner Stuart MacGill. But so
dependably destructive proved New South Wales' attack that he did not bowl a single
over in four first-class games, even against the touring New Zealanders. Entrusted with
the No. 5 Pura Cup batting position, he failed to live up to expectations for the capable
run-scorer he is at club level, contributing 40 runs at an average of 8.00. O'Brien had
more misfortune in the ING Cup, capturing a single wicket and again failing to make a
half-century in four matches. Lucklessly run out for eight followed by four overs for 29
runs, with three consecutive wides in the 48th over which enabled Tasmania to scramble

home in the ING Cup game at Newcastle, was not the evidence the selectors wished to see and they dropped him from both teams before the New Year. A better all-rounder than cold statistics indicate, O'Brien is still young enough to play an important role in New South Wales cricket in years ahead.

	M	I	NO	Runs	HS	100s	50s	Avge	Ct	St	W	Avge	BB
First-class	6	8	0	53	21	0	0	6.63	1	0	2	114.50	1/54
Dom. first-class	5	7	0	32	7	0	0	4.57	1	0	2	114.50	1/54
Dom. limited-overs	12	10	3	193	62*	0	1	27.57	2	0	4	70.00	2/14

JAMES PACKMAN *Right-hand batsman* NSW

A year after being demoted by Gordon club selectors from first to reserve grade for lackadaisical inconsistency, Packman was promoted to the New South Wales representative team from outside the contracted 26-man state squad against the ING Cup leaders, Queensland. A Shore School product from Sydney who represented New South Wales Schools after helping his team to a joint G.P.S. premiership in 1996-97, Packman was reminded of the need for application and discipline in the off-season by Matthew Nicholson, his Gordon captain. Two centuries and 600 runs in the Sydney competition by the New Year and a stunning innings of 165 for the New South Wales 2nd XI at Melbourne's Albert Ground, against
a Victorian 2nd XI attack led by the Pura Cup pair of Shane Harwood and Gerard Denton when no other batsman of his side reached 50, brought attention to Packman. Promoted for Simon Katich for the Telstra Stadium ING Cup game, he batted at No. 6 and with New South Wales under pressure at 3 for 8 in reply to Queensland's 267, Packman made 33 from 47 balls in trying circumstances. A failure against South Australia in Adelaide soon after and the internationals' return led to Packman's ING Cup exclusion, but he played in the last five Pura Cup games including the final in Brisbane. In Perth he justified the selectors' confidence with a stirring second innings century as New South Wales fought to avoid an innings defeat. Packman hit 15 fours and two sixes for 107 in just under three hours of daring counter-attack, sharing a last wicket stand of 49 with Doug Bollinger. A commerce graduate, Packman planned to resign as a funds manager to become a full-time professional cricketer.

	M	I	NO	Runs	HS	100s	50s	Avge	Ct	St	W	Avge	BB
First-class	5	10	0	267	107	1	0	26.70	1	0	–	–	–
Dom. first-class	5	10	0	267	107	1	0	26.70	1	0	–	–	–
Dom. limited-overs	2	2	0	35	33	0	0	17.50	1	0	–	–	–

CLINTON PERREN *Right-hand batsman* Queensland

Increasingly at home as an opener, Perren scored 708 runs in first-class cricket last season – the third season in a row in which he has made more than 700 runs – although his average of 33.71 was disappointing. He scored two vastly differing but valuable centuries. One was a dogged 103 to avert a collapse against NSW at Bankstown, and the other was a free-wheeling 105 against Western Australia at the Gabba, again scored while wickets fell around him. A clean striker and stylish timer of the ball when set, he produced his maiden ING Cup century against Tasmania at the Gabba batting at No. 3. However, that innings accounted for nearly half his ING Cup tally.

	M	I	NO	Runs	HS	100s	50s	Avge	Ct	St	W	Avge	BB
First-class	52	90	6	2,903	224	7	11	34.56	46	0	1	129.00	1/15
Dom. first-class	49	85	5	2,774	224	7	11	34.68	43	0	0	–	–
Dom. limited-overs	58	51	11	1,659	117	1	13	41.48	17	0	4	49.00	1/10

MATTHEW PHELPS *Right-hand batsman*   **NSW**

One of only three players with Phil Jaques and Dominic Thornely to represent New South Wales in all 12 first-class games and the nine limited-over matches played, Phelps had a valuable season while not providing the bountiful return he has promised since beginning his first-class career in 1998-99. Resolute, technically well-equipped and strong in his strokeplay, he made a century and four half-centuries, his second innings six-hour 127 not out contributing to the Blues' win over South Australia in Adelaide. Rarely a batsman to plunder an attack, it was only Phelps' third first-class century, a remarkable statistic for the quality top-order batsman the evidence suggests he is. Likewise, his innings of 84 in gruelling Gabba conditions against an Andy Bichel-led attack almost brought victory. Phelps complemented his first-class aggregate of 677 runs at 35.63 with some of the smartest close-in catching of the entire competition, specialising at slip, with 20 first-class catches. Three times in an innings he held three catches. His innings in the ING Cup where he made only 195 runs at 21.66 reflected the team's performances and suggested there was still much to be achieved for a man of his talent.

	M	I	NO	Runs	HS	100s	50s	Avge	Ct	St	W	Avge	BB
First-class	29	52	3	1,745	192	3	10	35.61	28	0	0	–	–
Dom. first-class	28	50	2	1,689	192	3	10	35.19	27	0	0	–	–
Dom. limited-overs	18	18	0	430	136	1	2	23.89	6	0	–	–	–

CRAIG PHILIPSON *Right-hand batsman*   **Queensland**

Sage observers like what they see in this stocky young right-hander, who has drawn comparisons with the youthful Greg Ritchie with his aggressive stroke-play. Darren Lehmann was impressed by Philipson's hard-hitting 73 in the second innings of the outright win over South Australia, seeking him out after the match to compliment him on his knock. Philipson scored his second first-class century last season, adding 119 against Tasmania to the ton he produced on debut in 2003-04, on the way to 447 runs at 37.25 in seven games. His ING Cup campaign netted 208 briskly-scored runs at 41.60.

	M	I	NO	Runs	HS	100s	50s	Avge	Ct	St	W	Avge	BB
First-class	10	19	3	645	119	2	3	40.31	7	0	0	–	–
Dom. first-class	10	19	3	645	119	2	3	40.31	7	0	0	–	–
Dom. limited-overs	12	11	2	288	70	0	2	32.00	4	0	1	12.00	1/2

TOM PLANT *Right-hand batsman*   **SA**

It takes rare form to earn state team selection from outside the contracted squad, but 20-year-old Plant managed it last summer. It takes nerve to pull a new-ball delivery from Andy Bichel into the stands during the last over of the day, but Plant managed that too. It takes guts to grind out a six-hour century against the bowlers who chopped up your team for 29 in the first innings, but Plant did that as well. It was an impressive trio of achievements, yet the man who achieved them also had extended periods when he looked unready for first-class cricket. After eight games, Plant was eventually withdrawn from the firing line with only 286 runs to his credit. While clearly a considerable talent, he needs time to iron out the faults keenly exploited by experienced bowlers. If that can happen, the promise he showed last summer will bloom into plentiful runs.

	M	I	NO	Runs	HS	100s	50s	Avge	Ct	St	W	Avge	BB
First-class	8	16	0	286	125	1	0	17.88	3	0	–	–	–
Dom. first-class	8	16	0	286	125	1	0	17.88	3	0	–	–	–
Dom. limited-overs	1	1	0	9	9	0	0	9.00	0	0	–	–	–

RICKY PONTING *Right-hand batsman* **Tasmania and Australia**

Ricky Ponting in 2004-05 was unable to match his output of the two previous southern hemisphere summers, each producing more than 1,000 Test runs, but he still scored 931 runs at an average of 71, better than any other batsman except Shivnarine Chanderpaul. His remarkable consistency is reflected in the fact that he failed to reach double figures only three times in 18 innings. He has now built up an enviable recent record; in the 41 Tests between the England tours of and 2005, he amassed 4,120 runs at 72.28. Add this to more than 800 ODI runs at 41 in 2004-05, and it can be seen that the Australian captain is shouldering his share of the team's batting responsibilities. Following manfully in Steve Waugh's big footsteps, Ponting presided over 15 ODI wins in 20 starts, and seven Test wins out of ten in year leading into the Ashes series. His maturation as a player and person is self-evident; his measured and articulate public utterances as Australia's leader are in sharp contrast to those of the feisty young player who first appeared a dozen years ago. But his captaincy was tested in the winter as England provided steely resistance for the first time for many years. His Old Trafford innings of 156 was a masterpiece of determined batting, but his leadership skills will come under increasing scrutiny if his ageing team disintegrates over the next year.

	M	I	NO	Runs	HS	100s	50s	Avge	Ct	St	W	Avge	BB
First-class	181	302	44	15,202	257	55	60	58.92	185	0	13	57.00	2/10
Dom. first-class	48	89	13	4,756	233	20	14	62.58	32	0	5	74.00	1/7
Test	88	143	20	6,950	257	22	27	56.50	103	0	4	53.75	1/0
Int'l limited-overs	232	226	28	8,290	145	18	45	41.87	93	0	3	34.67	1/12
Dom. limited-overs	32	32	4	942	102	1	6	33.64	13	0	5	28.60	3/34

PETER ROACH *Right-hand batsman, wicket-keeper* **Victoria**

Beginning a season for the first time as Victoria's official wicket-keeper, Roach was solid in his keeping but failed to score the sort of runs that had come so easily when he was filling in for Darren Berry throughout the previous decade. After seven matches he made way for Adam Crosthwaite. Roach was gracious in his departure, full of praise for Crosthwaite and realistic about his own chances of a return to the side.

	M	I	NO	Runs	HS	100s	50s	Avge	Ct	St	W	Avge	BB
First-class	25	42	12	829	108*	1	4	27.63	0	2	0	–	–
Dom. first-class	22	37	10	685	108*	1	3	25.37	0	1		–	–
Dom. limited-overs	9	6	1	64	26	0	0	12.80	0	0	–	–	–

PAUL ROFE *Right-arm fast* **SA**

Paul Rofe has developed into the most predictable component of an erratic South Australian team. He can now be relied upon to collect 30 to 40 well-priced Pura Cup wickets each season, and operate for long spells in all conditions. Of course, anyone as subtly efficient as Rofe will only be noticed when he has gone, but so far he has managed to remain free of injuries. If there was any indication in 2004-05 that Rofe is under-appreciated, it came through his puzzlingly rare selection for limited-overs matches. His batting and fielding have been cited as areas of concern, but it is hard to imagine how an extra all-rounder (particularly those available) would be more valuable than a pace bowler with the ability to tie down as well as penetrate. At 24, Rofe still has ample time to make an international claim, but it is unlikely to happen before Glenn McGrath retires.

	M	I	NO	Runs	HS	100s	50s	Avge	Ct	St	W	Avge	BB
First-class	48	73	26	312	19*	0	0	6.64	13	0	155	30.41	7/52
Dom. first-class	41	65	21	287	19*	0	0	6.52	11	0	142	29.00	7/52
Dom. limited-overs	30	12	7	14	6*	0	0	2.80	2	0	27	39.11	3/33

CHRIS ROGERS *Left-hand batsman* **WA**

Rogers' experience of county cricket with Derbyshire in 2004 was cut short by nagging injuries. He had corrective surgery on his right shoulder in July, and in September he underwent an operation on his right hamstring. This disjointed preparation affected his performances in a season in which he scored one century, a 95, 83 and 74 in a tally of 645 Pura Cup runs at 43.00. His four ING Cup appearances netted a disappointing 68 runs at 17.00. He celebrated his selection in the Prime Minister's XI against Pakistan by top-scoring with 46. A gutsy, hard-working cricketer, with high levels of concentration, a positive approach and an ability to make big scores, Rogers has plenty to offer in the seasons to come, and showed it during a double-century for Leicestershire against the touring Australians.

	M	I	NO	Runs	HS	100s	50s	Avge	Ct	St	W	Avge	BB
First-class	51	92	6	3,912	209	11	18	45.49	51	0	0	–	–
Dom. first-class	36	65	4	2,784	194	9	12	45.64	38	0	0	–	–
Dom. limited-overs	29	28	4	786	117*	1	4	32.75	11	0	–	–	–

LUKE RONCHI *Right-hand batsman, wicket-keeper* **WA**

Western Australia's deputy wicket-keeper is rapidly earning a reputation as one of Australia's most exciting limited-overs cricketers. A polished, natural gloveman, both standing back or up to the stumps, Ronchi has the potential to become a very good batsman in any form of cricket. The state selectors preferred him ahead of Ryan Campbell as wicket-keeper in ING Cup matches in a season in which he did not appear in first-class ranks. Perhaps the feeling that he was fighting for his spot influenced him against playing his natural free-flowing game, and he managed only 140 runs at 17.50 from nine ING Cup innings. However, he shone in the new Twenty20 game, scoring 67 off 24 deliveries against Victoria and 52 off 25 balls against Tasmania. He also hammered 51 off 43 balls against the Pakistanis in the Lilac Hill festival match and 40 from 13 balls for the Prime Minister's XI against the Pakistanis.

	M	I	NO	Runs	HS	100s	50s	Avge	Ct	St	W	Avge	BB
First-class	4	7	0	275	90	0	3	39.29	0	1	–	–	–
Dom. first-class	4	7	0	275	90	0	3	39.29	0	1	–	–	–
Dom. limited-overs	11	10	1	140	75	0	1	15.56	0	3	–	–	–

GRAEME RUMMANS *Left-hand batsman* **Victoria**

The quietly-spoken former New South Welshman made his name with a classy 188 against Tasmania in Hobart that ultimately handed victory to Victoria. It was second first-class century, something Rummans felt he was running out of time to achieve, as it was his 31st match. Aside from that one big innings, though, he was inconsistent and had trouble settling, scoring only one other fifty. He was not helped by having to occupy three different batting positions in his eight matches.

	M	I	NO	Runs	HS	100s	50s	Avge	Ct	St	W	Avge	BB
First-class	37	62	8	1,583	188	2	8	29.31	17	0	7	35.14	3/24
Dom. first-class	35	60	8	1,386	188	1	7	26.65	15	0	4	55.00	2/71
Dom. limited-overs	46	42	8	1,075	75	0	8	31.62	10	0	0	–	–

WADE SECCOMBE *Right-hand batsman, wicket-keeper* **Queensland**

A broken foot from a freak cycling accident during the 2004-05 season produced a chink in the otherwise impregnable armour of Seccombe. But on recovery he returned to the team and, as usual, did not let Queensland down, finishing with the most Pura Cup dismissals (40) in 2004-05. His first-class haul of 255 runs at 18.21 was below par, but his double of 69 and 84 against Western Australia at the Gabba in the last Pura Cup game of the season, with the Queenslanders needing to win on the first innings, then not lose outright, to host the final, underscored his fighting quality.

	M	I	NO	Runs	HS	100s	50s	Avge	Ct	St	W	Avge	BB
First-class	115	175	30	3,559	151	4	12	24.54	0	21	0	–	–
Dom. first-class	101	155	27	3,207	151	4	11	25.05	0	14	0	–	–
Dom. limited-overs	77	56	16	794	67*	0	3	19.85	0	22	–	–	–

CHRIS SIMPSON *Right-hand batsman, right-arm off-spin bowler*   **Queensland**
After starting the season in Queensland's Pura Cup and ING Cup line-ups, a blow on the wrist during his third one-day appearance effectively ruined Simpson's season. He missed more than three months, and by the time he was back in contention, the Queensland side was settled. The 23-year-old off-spinning all-rounder remains a project player for the Bulls, and with Nathan Hauritz's immediate future unclear and rookie leg-spinner Ryan Le Loux taking his first tentative steps, the opportunity is there for Simpson to make a mark. He twice took three cheap wickets in an innings in the ING Cup last season, and the limited-overs arena looks his most likely launching pad.

	M	I	NO	Runs	HS	100s	50s	Avge	Ct	St	W	Avge	BB
First-class	8	15	0	231	83	0	2	15.40	9	0	7	62.00	3/8
Dom. first-class	8	15	0	231	83	0	2	15.40	9	0	7	62.00	3/8
Dom. limited-overs	8	6	1	43	15	0	0	8.60	3	0	11	19.55	3/30

DANIEL SMITH *Left-hand batsman, wicket-keeper*   **NSW**
Brad Haddin's elevation to become Adam Gilchrist's national understudy and the departure of Nathan Pilon for Victoria enabled Daniel Smith to appear for New South Wales in two ING Cup games. A thick-set, hard-hitting, right-hand opening batsman-wicketkeeper, he had the misfortune to be dismissed for a first-ball duck when opening in his initial game against Queensland. With Haddin promoted for Australia's VB Series, Smith had better fortune a week later when he held his first catch for New South Wales from Ryan Harris at the Adelaide Oval. Batting at No 7 with New South Wales 5 for 93 and chasing 286, Smith made a robust unbeaten 49 from 60 balls with three fours and a six in another losing cause. Smith accompanied a New South Wales Under-23 team captained by Shawn Bradstreet on a six-game tour to India in mid-2005, impressing with his swift, neat glovework and powerful drives and pulls, and was awarded a full contract with Cricket New South Wales upon his return. A graduate from the Australian Cricket Academy in Adelaide in 2001, he represented New South Wales Colts from 2000-2005. Initially with Petersham-Marrickville club before their Randwick merger, he then moved to Western Suburbs club and is seen as long-term successor to Brad Haddin.

	M	I	NO	Runs	HS	100s	50s	Avge	Ct	St	W	Avge	BB
Dom. limited-overs	2	2	1	49	49*	0	0	49.00	0	1	–	–	–

JACK SMITH *Right-hand batsman*   **SA**
Trumped as a potential team leader after captaining Adelaide to the A-Grade premiership in 2003-04, Smith failed to achieve what had been expected. What he brought to the team in terms of tactics was hard to deduce, but his batting fell short of requirements. He stroked one decent innings, a smart 57 to set up a winning target against Victoria in the first match of the Pura Cup, but otherwise he struggled. He fared worse still in the ING Cup, averaging single figures and suffering the ignominy of being the middle man in a hat-trick for Doug Bollinger. He was not seen in South Australian colours after Christmas, and he will have a fight on his hands to regain his place.

	M	I	NO	Runs	HS	100s	50s	Avge	Ct	St	W	Avge	BB
First-class	4	8	1	173	57	0	1	24.71	3	0	–	–	–
Dom. first-class	4	8	1	173	57	0	1	24.71	3	0	–	–	–
Dom. limited-overs	4	4	0	36	23	0	0	9.00	1	0	–	–	–

LACHLAN STEVENS *Left-hand batsman* **Queensland**

For the Queensland selectors, Lachlan Stevens' appearance in state colours' in 2004-05 was akin to poking about in your wine cellar and rediscovering a bottle put aside several years earlier that had suddenly come into vogue. A talented youth player who played for Queensland and Australian Under-19s in 1997-98, Stevens moved to South Australia for employment reasons and played in the ING Cup for the South Australians in 2002-03. Job opportunities lured him back to Brisbane and he was appointed in 2004 as the High Performance Co-ordinator at the Cricket Australia Centre of Excellence. He scored a valuable 46 against South Australia on his first-class debut, and 37 and 67 in his second match, against

Victoria in Melbourne. A free-swinging left-handed batsman capable of batting up the order or in the middle, and a useful left-arm spinner (his mentor was Paul Jackson), the 26-year-old should find a niche within the Queensland set-up.

	M	I	NO	Runs	HS	100s	50s	Avge	Ct	St	W	Avge	BB
First-class	2	4	0	158	67	0	1	39.50	2	0	0	–	–
Dom. first-class	2	4	0	158	67	0	1	39.50	2	0	0	–	–
Dom. limited-overs	4	4	0	31	18	0	0	7.75	0	0	0	–	–

ANDREW SYMONDS *Right-hand batsman, right-arm off-spin bowler* **Queensland and Australia**

On the cricket field, Symonds is increasingly delivering the goods. Among a string of consistent one-day international performances, he scored a disciplined 91 in the first final of the VB Series. For Queensland he hit four half-centuries in six innings in the ING Cup on the way to making 339 runs at a strike-rate of 110 and an average of 84.75. After being named the Australian One-Day Player of the Year in 2004-05, Symonds' career hit a low point in June when his over-enthusiastic celebration of Shane Watson's birthday led to a suspension. He responded with Man of the Match efforts in his next two appearances, including a career-best 5 for 18 against Bangladesh, on the way to winning the Player of the Series award. Significantly, Australia lost none of the matches in which he played. His form surge continued when he joined his new county Lancashire.

	M	I	NO	Runs	HS	100s	50s	Avge	Ct	St	W	Avge	BB
First-class	180	303	28	11,646	254*	34	48	42.35	129	0	181	37.15	6/105
Dom. first-class	77	126	9	4,287	163	11	16	36.64	48	0	93	31.37	4/39
Test	2	4	0	53	24	0	0	13.25	4	0	1	85.00	1/68
Int'l limited-overs	124	96	19	2,833	143*	2	15	36.79	48	0	93	36.70	5/18
Dom. limited-overs	61	57	8	1,491	91	0	9	30.43	27	0	34	33.91	3/32

SHAUN TAIT *Right-arm fast* **SA and Australia**

His 2004 winter may have been spoiled by a brief nightmare with Durham in the County Championship, but Tait was more devastating than ever by the time the Australian summer commenced. Averaging nearly seven wickets a match, Tait blasted his way through 65 batsmen to have the most prolific season ever enjoyed by any South Australian bowler. While most of his wickets were taken with deadly speed and damaging swing, Tait showed signs he was developing other attributes. His best innings figures of 7 for 99 were achieved despite suffering from a virus, while late in the season as he tired, Tait reduced his pace and relied upon rhythm and accuracy. His reward was a place on the Ashes tour, and a debut Test cap at Trent Bridge.

	M	I	NO	Runs	HS	100s	50s	Avge	Ct	St	W	Avge	BB
First-class	26	41	17	252	58	0	1	10.50	6	0	118	24.53	7/99
Dom. first-class	23	39	17	248	58	0	1	11.27	6	0	115	22.71	7/99
Dom. limited-overs	20	10	5	10	4*	0	0	2.00	5	0	39	21.08	8/43

DOMINIC THORNELY *Right-hand batsman, right-arm medium bowler* **NSW**
One of the revelations of the Australian summer, Thornely made it his resolve to occupy a top-order position left vacant by the retirement of the Waugh brothers, and he did so with distinction. Rod Marsh sang Thornely's praises as one of the best of all Cricket Academy graduates in Adelaide. Yet it took several long seasons with Northern District club in Sydney for him to fulfill the predictions made of him. A raw-boned, tough, all-rounder whose batting provided much of the backbone in the State's middle-order, his powerful batting was seen at its best when he eclipsed David Hookes' Australian record of ten first-class sixes with 11 in an unbeaten 261 against Western Australia at the Sydney Cricket Ground in November, cutting, driving and pulling sixes from point to square leg. With Stuart MacGill (27), Thornely added 219 runs for the highest 10th-wicket partnership for 75 years, taking New South Wales' 9 for 200 to a dominant 419, from which the visitors never recovered. The performance came at a most critical stage for New South Wales after early-season setbacks, the inspiration to transform the Blues' first-class season and lead on to Cup final success. Thornely added another three first-class centuries and five half-centuries in passing 1,000 runs for the first time, although a solitary half century in eight ING Cup innings was much less satisfying. His slow-medium bowling was used infrequently due to the team's splendid attack, but his fielding remained at a high level and he was suitably rewarded with selection for the Australia A team.

	M	I	NO	Runs	HS	100s	50s	Avge	Ct	St	W	Avge	BB
First-class	20	34	3	1,562	261*	5	9	50.39	12	0	9	53.11	3/52
Dom. first-class	17	31	3	1,349	261*	5	6	48.18	10	0	7	52.86	3/52
Dom. limited-overs	33	29	3	656	78	0	4	25.23	15	0	19	36.53	3/32

SHANNON TUBB *Left-arm slow bowler* **SA**
As a Tasmanian teenager in the late 1990s, Tubb was thought a contender for future national selection as a promising chinaman bowler. It says much about the tenuous nature of wrist spin that Tubb has since moved states, and in three ING Cup matches for South Australia last season did not deliver a single ball. Instead he batted, with the same mixture of aggression and ill luck that characterised his performances for Tasmania. A feisty 29 from 30 balls against Western Australia demonstrated what Tubb could do, but it was offset by ducks in his other two innings, including the briefest of innings against his former state when he smacked his first ball straight to short cover. Selection at least gave Tubb the knowledge that he was being watched, and some solid displays at grade level will ensure that continues.

	M	I	NO	Runs	HS	100s	50s	Avge	Ct	St	W	Avge	BB
First-class	8	13	0	151	42	0	0	11.62	2	0	8	50.88	3/57
Dom. first-class	8	13	0	151	42	0	0	11.62	2	0	8	50.88	3/57
Dom. limited-overs	10	10	0	207	79	0	1	20.70	0	0	0	–	–

ADAM VOGES *Right-hand batsman, left-arm slow bowler* **WA**
The summer of 2004-05 was a landmark season for this tall, slim and graceful batsman. Voges hit the headlines early in the season when he pulverised the NSW attack in scoring a spectacular unbeaten 62-ball century at North Sydney Oval, the fastest in the history of the domestic limited-overs competition. One of his seven sixes earned the Western Australian team a $50,000 bonus by hitting a sponsor's sign. Even though he scored an unbeaten 52 in his side's opening Pura Cup match against Tasmania, he was omitted for the next four games. The highlight in his five matches after his return at the end of the season was his maiden first-class century (against NSW in Perth). His 362 runs at 72.40 (Pura Cup) and 287 at 31.88 (ING Cup) were accurate reflections of his worth to the side.

He captained an AIS side on a successful tour of India in July-August 2004 and finished the summer by leading Melville to a premiership victory in the Western Australian first-grade competition.

	M	I	NO	Runs	HS	100s	50s	Avge	Ct	St	W	Avge	BB
First-class	10	16	4	481	128	1	2	40.08	11	0	8	33.88	2/16
Dom. first-class	10	16	4	481	128	1	2	40.08	11	0	8	33.88	2/16
Dom. limited-overs	10	10	1	287	100*	1	2	31.89	1	0	0	–	–

SHANE WARNE *Right-hand batsman, right-arm leg-spin bowler*   **Victoria and Australia**

It took just one series for Warne to dismiss the doubters who had questioned his ability to return from his year-long drug ban, as he swept aside 26 Sri Lankan batsmen in three Tests, along the way collecting his 500th Test wicket. A much simpler bowler now who relies more on accuracy and control than any new mystery ball, Warne also conquered India, New Zealand and Pakistan on his relentless way to becoming the first Test bowler to take 600 wickets. At the end of the Australian summer he announced a permanent move to England. Warne made headlines constantly during the English season with his statesmanlike leadership of Hampshire, his maiden first-class century, a budding friendship with England's new batsman Kevin Pietersen, endorsement of an anti-balding program once spruiked by Greg Matthews and Graham Gooch, high-class bowling in the Ashes tests and the by-now customary adverse personal publicity.

	M	I	NO	Runs	HS	100s	50s	Avge	Ct	St	W	Avge	BB
First-class	243	330	41	5,388	107*	2	20	18.64	204	0	1,054	25.92	8/71
Dom. first-class	40	52	7	751	75	0	3	16.69	32	0	135	35.39	6/42
Test	123	169	15	2,518	99	0	10	16.35	107	0	583	25.52	8/71
Int'l limited-overs	194	107	29	1,018	55	0	1	13.05	80	0	293	25.74	5/33
Dom. limited-overs	28	22	1	210	32	0	0	10.00	12	0	42	26.40	5/35

DARREN WATES *Right-hand batsman, right-arm fast-medium bowler*   **WA**

A qualified lawyer, Wates made a major commitment to his chosen sport by quitting full-time employment to concentrate on a make-or-break effort to become a regular interstate cricketer. This enabled him to work much harder on his fitness and his skills. He would have made more than four Pura Cup and seven ING Cup appearances during 2004-05 if he had not been affected by hamstring problems. A genuine swing bowler, Wates showed the ability to take early wickets when given the opportunity at first-class level, and he was one of Western Australia's leading bowlers in both competitions. His batting is steady, but shows the potential for improvement.

	M	I	NO	Runs	HS	100s	50s	Avge	Ct	St	W	Avge	BB
First-class	12	15	3	392	99	0	3	32.67	6	0	31	36.48	4/77
Dom. first-class	11	15	3	392	99	0	3	32.67	6	0	27	36.33	4/77
Dom. limited-overs	29	17	8	141	29*	0	0	15.67	5	0	33	34.61	3/32

SHANE WATSON *Right-hand batsman, right-arm fast*   **Queensland and Australia**

By and large, Watson enjoyed his return to his home state after beginning his interstate career in Tasmania. A player whose potential is still being converted to results, he nonetheless made his Test debut against Pakistan on the SCG. But injury, which has been the bane of his career so far, intervened in the second final of the VB Series with a side strain that ruled him out of the New Zealand tour. He returned to the Australian team for the one-day leg of the Ashes tour. His efforts in 2004-05 for Queensland included 136 against Western Australia at the WACA, 94 against Victoria at the MCG, and 60 and 4 for 25 against South Australia in Adelaide on debut. For Queensland, he seems most comfortable batting at No. 4 and bowling second or even third change. For

Australia, he bats lower in the order and is regarded as a third seamer to enable a second spinner. He is intent on adding more variation to his bowling, and admits he is still coming to grips with an action that has been remodelled more times than an inner-city terrace house.

	M	I	NO	Runs	HS	100s	50s	Avge	Ct	St	W	Avge	BB
First-class	38	66	7	2,657	157	8	13	45.03	18	0	72	28.74	6/32
Dom. first-class	34	61	5	2,390	157	6	13	42.68	18	0	66	28.76	6/32
Test	1	1	0	31	31	0	0	31.00	0	0	1	60.00	1/32
Int'l limited-overs	37	23	10	380	77*	0	1	29.23	10	0	25	45.00	3/27
Dom. limited-overs	33	32	2	876	96	0	8	29.20	7	0	22	39.41	3/42

MATTHEW WEEKS *Right-hand batsman, right-arm medium bowler* **SA**

The sort of spare-parts cricketer often seen in one-day cricket, Matthew Weeks was unsuccessful when tried in South Australia's first two ING Cup matches. Opposition batsmen took to him easily, while not enough was seen of his batting to assess its quality. Weeks had more success for Port Adelaide at grade level, averaging 42 with the bat and 22 with the ball, but he was not called upon at state level after November. Still a young man, he is clearly behind fellow all-rounders Ryan Harris and Mark Cleary in the race for a place in the state side.

	M	I	NO	Runs	HS	100s	50s	Avge	Ct	St	W	Avge	BB
Dom. limited-overs	2	2	1	17	11	0	0	17.00	0	0	1	69.00	1/25

TIM WELSFORD *Right-hand batsman, right-arm fast-medium bowler* **Victoria**

Eight times 12th man for Victoria's ING Cup team, Welsford played just one match, but did not bat or bowl because of rain. He was appointed captain of a Victorian XI assembled to give the touring New Zealanders some much-needed practice, but the highlight of his season came in January when, with a delivery he described as "not great", he dismissed Brian Lara in another tour match. His all-round form for Northcote twice won him the Premier Cricket Player of the Round Award in 2004-05.

	M	I	NO	Runs	HS	100s	50s	Avge	Ct	St	W	Avge	BB
Dom. limited-overs	1	–	–	–	–	–	–	–	0	0	–	–	–

CAMERON WHITE *Right-hand batsman, right-arm leg-spinner* **Victoria**

Effectively reduced to drinks waiter for most of Australia's tour of India, White, who was overlooked in favour of Nathan Hauritz to replace the injured Shane Warne in the fourth Test, returned to Victoria in November tired and frustrated. While he led his team to victory in Tasmania after a humiliating first-up loss to South Australia in his absence, Victoria all but fell out of finals contention by Christmas and the young captain was regularly at a loss to explain the decline of the Pura Cup title-holders. Although he steadied personally to enjoy a reasonably fruitful season, the highlight of which was his classy maiden first-class century in the grand fightback at the Gabba, and retained his Cricket Australia contract, he was more hesitant with the ball upon Warne's return to the side. Without his strongest supporter, David Hookes, and team disciplinarian Darren Berry, the leadership at times proved burdensome for White, particularly without a vice-captain.

	M	I	NO	Runs	HS	100s	50s	Avge	Ct	St	W	Avge	BB
First-class	37	58	6	1,443	119	1	8	27.75	44	0	88	35.25	6/66
Dom. first-class	35	55	6	1,384	119	1	8	28.24	43	0	84	35.48	6/66
Dom. limited-overs	30	23	3	349	61	0	1	17.45	7	0	28	35.43	4/15

BRAD WILLIAMS *Right-arm fast* WA

Once again Williams was cursed by injuries, which stalled his international career. After back problems kept him out of contention for Australia's Tests against Sri Lanka in the winter of 2004, he was hurt in Western Australia's opening Pura Cup match against Tasmania. Running in to bowl in Tasmania's second innings, Williams jumped a bit wider on the crease and collapsed in agony. He had dislocated his right knee as well as tearing the calf muscle. He missed the next five first-class matches. He resumed in good form, but back and hamstring problems began to affect him and he managed only two wickets at a cost of 269 runs in the last five innings in which he bowled. He needs a full pre-season preparation to be at peak fitness for 2005-06.

	M	I	NO	Runs	HS	100s	50s	Avge	Ct	St	W	Avge	BB
First-class	63	79	21	742	41*	0	0	12.79	24	0	215	31.55	6/74
Dom. first-class	47	61	16	571	41*	0	0	12.69	15	0	173	30.94	6/74
Test	4	6	3	23	10*	0	0	7.67	4	0	9	45.11	4/53
Int'l limited-overs	25	6	4	27	13*	0	0	13.50	4	0	35	23.26	5/22
Dom. limited-overs	38	12	5	85	23	0	0	12.14	7	0	53	25.58	4/29

LUKE WILLIAMS *Right-hand batsman* SA

Like Daniel Harris and Cameron Borgas, Williams was recalled in 2004-05 some years after his debut, as South Australia grappled with deep batting problems. Unlike the other two, Williams was unable to make even a single fifty, and generally looked short of the grade. His recall came after a handsome 172 against ACT for the South Australia 2nd XI, for whom he scored 591 runs in three matches. Though a consistently heavy scorer at lower levels, Williams does not appear comfortable against first-class bowling.

	M	I	NO	Runs	HS	100s	50s	Avge	Ct	St	W	Avge	BB
First-class	5	10	0	114	37	0	0	11.40	1	0	0	–	–
Dom. first-class	5	10	0	114	37	0	0	11.40	1	0	0	–	–

ALLAN WISE *Left-arm fast-medium bowler* Victoria

Allan Wise was brought back down to earth after his breathtaking debut season. Although he bowled accurately and retained his ability to break partnerships, Wise lacked the penetration of the previous summer. He was consistently good for Richmond in Premier Cricket, but a successful career in financial management off the field means Wise has always taken his cricket as a bonus.

	M	I	NO	Runs	HS	100s	50s	Avge	Ct	St	W	Avge	BB
First-class	16	19	13	44	8	0	0	7.33	5	0	48	27.38	5/47
Dom. first-class	16	19	13	44	8	0	0	7.33	5	0	48	27.38	5/47
Dom. limited-overs	8	2	1	0	0*	0	0	0.00	0	0	10	28.70	2/31

PETER WORTHINGTON *Right-hand batsman, right-arm fast-medium bowler* WA

A wholehearted competitor, this remarkable all-rounder remains on the periphery of the Western Australian side. But he is an honest battler who is a handy player to have on the fringe. Though he works hard on his game, he struggles to be good enough as a batsman or bowler to demand a spot in the side. He did not show up in his only ING Cup match in 2004-05, but gave a strong all-round performance in his only Pura Cup appearance, against New South Wales in Perth late in the season. He enjoyed a good season in club cricket with Midland-Guildford, scoring two centuries in his 603 first-grade runs at 60.30 and taking 30 wickets at 19.00.

	M	I	NO	Runs	HS	100s	50s	Avge	Ct	St	W	Avge	BB
First-class	7	13	1	250	73	0	2	20.83	8	0	15	38.53	6/59
Dom. first-class	6	11	0	175	73	0	2	15.91	7	0	15	34.80	6/59
Dom. limited-overs	11	7	5	113	49*	0	0	56.50	2	0	12	34.33	3/45

DAMIEN WRIGHT *Right-hand batsman, right-arm fast-medium bowler*
Tasmania

For the third consecutive season, this wholehearted performer claimed more than 30 wickets for his adopted state, and he has now moved into third place on the Tasmanian wicket-taking list behind Colin Miller and Shaun Young. Another season like last, when he took 36 wickets, will put him close to top of that tree, fair reward for his work over the last six seasons. The Tasmanian press lobby has been strong for his inclusion in national teams, and it was rewarded with two more Australia A matches to go with the half-dozen he had previously accumulated. He also struck his maiden first-class century, adding a record 215 with Michael Bevan for the seventh wicket against Victoria at Bellerive, and in scoring 534 Pura Cup runs, actually exceeded the output of everyone above him in the batting line-up bar Bevan. But Wright has just turned 30, and although it is not unknown for a bowler of that age to reach the pinnacle of cricketing achievement, it is unusual. The national selectors may be looking elsewhere to replace McGrath, Gillespie and Kasprowicz when they step down.

	M	I	NO	Runs	HS	100s	50s	Avge	Ct	St	W	Avge	BB
First-class	70	106	19	2,082	111	1	10	23.93	34	0	217	32.18	8/60
Dom. first-class	57	90	16	1,722	111	1	8	23.27	27	0	175	33.22	6/25
Dom. limited-overs	52	37	11	392	52	0	1	15.08	11	0	62	28.61	4/23

Births and Deaths of Cricketers

The following list details information on the 3,209 players to have represented an Australian first-class cricket team.

STATE REPRESENTATION
New South Wales   697
Queensland   453
South Australia   576
Tasmania   508
Victoria   798
Western Australia   386
Other Teams   32

The compiler of this section welcomes any information from readers regarding the details contained therein.

Key to abbreviations

Australian states and territories: ACT – Australian Capital Territory, NSW – New South Wales, NT – Northern Territory, Qld – Queensland, S Aust – South Australia, Tas – Tasmania, Vic – Victoria, WAust – Western Australia.

*Denotes Test player.

**Denotes Test player for two countries.

There is a full list of Australian Test players from page 212.

a'Beckett, Edward Clive (Vic) b Jan. 18, 1940 East Melbourne (Vic)

a'Beckett, Edward Fitzhayley (Vic) b April 16, 1836 Holborn, London, (England) d March 25, 1922 Upper Beaconsfield (Vic)

* a'Beckett, Edward Lambert (Vic) b Aug. 11, 1907 East St Kilda (Vic) d June 2, 1989 Terang (Vic)

a'Beckett, Malwyn (Vic) b Sept. 26, 1834 London, Middlesex (England) d June 25, 1906 Sale (Vic)

Abell, William (Qld) b April 16, 1874 Leeds, Yorkshire (England) d June 10, 1960 Herston (Qld)

Achurch, Claude Septimus (NSW) b Aug. 16, 1896 Dubbo (NSW) d Aug. 15, 1979 Nambour (Qld)

Adams, Edward William (NSW) b July 10, 1896 Bathurst (NSW) d May 25, 1977 Bexley (NSW)

Adams, Francis (NSW) b Feb. 12, 1835 Doohat, County Fermanagh (Ireland) d Feb. 10, 1911 North Sydney (NSW)

Adams, James William (Qld) b Feb. 22, 1904 Toowong (Qld) d Jan. 8, 1988 Willoughby (NSW)

Adamson, Charles Young (Qld) b April 18, 1875 Neville's Cross, Durham (England) d Sept. 17, 1918 Salonica (Greece)

Adcock, Nathan Tennyson (S Aust) b April 22, 1978 Campbelltown (S Aust)

Addison, Alexander Gollan (Tas) b Sept. 29, 1877 Adelaide (S Aust) d Oct. 12, 1935 Double Bay (NSW)

Ainslie, James (Vic) b June 9, 1880 Elsternwick (Vic) d Dec. 31, 1953 St Kilda (Vic)

Albury, William Douglas (Qld) b Feb. 9, 1947 Herston (Qld)

* Alderman, Terence Michael (WAust) b June 12, 1956 Subiaco (WAust)

Aldridge, Keith John (Tas) b March 13, 1935 Evesham, Worcestershire (England)

Alexander, Francis James (WAust) b April 15, 1911 Perth (WAust)

* Alexander, George (Vic) b April 22, 1851 Oxfordshire (England) d Nov. 6, 1930 East Melbourne (Vic)

* Alexander, Henrry Houston (Vic) b June 9, 1905 Ascot Vale (Vic) d April 15, 1993 East Melbourne (Vic)

Alexander, Leonard James (Tas) b Sept. 1, 1922 Hobart (Tas)

Alexander, William Colin (S Aust) b Sept. 14, 1907 Gawler (S Aust) d Feb. 8, 1993 Melbourne (Vic)

* Allan, Francis Erskine (Vic) b Dec. 2, 1849 Allansford (Vic) d Feb. 9, 1917 East Melbourne (Vic)

Allan, George Harold (Tas) b Feb. 18, 1887 Albury (NSW) d Nov. 2, 1932 Adelaide (S Aust)

Allan, Henry Alexander (NSW) b Jan. 6, 1846 Westminster, London, Middlesex (England) d Apr. 26, 1926 East Melbourne (Vic)

* Allan, Peter John (Qld) b Dec. 31, 1935 Coorparoo (Qld)

Allanby, Nicholas John (Tas) b Aug. 24, 1957 Hobart (Tas)

Allanby, Richard Andrew (Tas) b July 26, 1971 Hobart (Tas)

Allanson, Noel Laurence (Vic) b Dec. 25, 1925 North Carlton (Vic)

Allardice, Geoffrey John (Vic) b May 7, 1967 Melbourne (Vic)

Allee, Charles George (Vic) b Feb. 10, 1848 Melbourne (Vic) d June 7, 1896 East Melbourne (Vic)

Allen, Donald John (Qld) b Feb. 26, 1947 Lismore (NSW)

Allen, Donald Radford (Vic) b Dec. 13, 1926 East St Kilda (Vic)

Allen, Harold Eric (Tas) b Oct. 13, 1886 Invercargill (New Zealand) d July 9, 1939 West Hobart (Tas)

Allen, Harold Hedley (Tas) b Nov. 15, 1940 Latrobe (Tas)

Allen, Jeremy Michael (WAust) b June 11, 1971 Subiaco (WAust)

Allen, Leslie Graham (Tas) b Sept. 13, 1954 Wynyard (Tas)

* Allen, Reginald Charles (NSW) b July 2, 1858 Glebe (NSW) d May 2, 1952 Sydney (NSW)

Allen, Ross Thomas (Qld) b Aug. 12, 1939 Toowoomba (Qld)

Allen, Thomas (Qld) b Sept. 5, 1912 Toowoomba (Qld) d March 18, 1954 Cambooya (Qld)

Allen, Thorpe (Qld) b March 7, 1870 Oxley (Qld) d Jan. 25, 1950 East Brisbane (Qld)

Allen, William Miller (Vic) b July 7, 1889 Ballarat (Vic) d Nov. 13, 1948 Ringwood (Vic)

Alley, Phillip John Sydney (S Aust & NSW) b July 26, 1970 Orange (NSW)

Alley, William Edward (NSW) b Feb. 3, 1919 Hornsby (NSW) d Nov. 26, 2004 Taunton, Somerset (England)

Alleyne, John Placid (NSW) b Aug. 1, 1908 Glebe (NSW) d June 24, 1980 Glebe (NSW)

Allison, Henry (Tas) b July 14, 1828 Campbell Town (Tas) d May 12, 1881 Coupeville Island, Washington (USA)

Allsopp, Arthur Henry (NSW & Vic) b March 1, 1908 Lithgow (NSW) d Feb. 6, 1993 Chadstone (Vic)

Alsop, Charles James (Vic) b Nov. 24, 1868 Moonee Ponds (Vic) d Sept. 17, 1948 Melbourne (Vic)

Amalfi, Anthony John (Vic) b Jan. 19, 1967 East Melbourne (Vic)

Ambler, Albert Mark (S Aust) b Sept. 27, 1892 Murray Bridge (S Aust) d Nov. 27, 1970 Prospect (S Aust)

Amos, Gordon Stanley (NSW & Qld) b April 4, 1905 Newtown (NSW) d April 7, 1995 Labrador (Qld)

Amos, William (S Aust) b April 20, 1860 Glen Osmond (S Aust) d May 14, 1935 North Adelaide (S Aust)

Anderson, Allan David (NSW) b April 22, 1949 Greenwich (NSW)

Anderson, Dale Thomas (Tas) b June 10, 1931 Latrobe (Tas)

Anderson, David John (Vic) b Jan. 26, 1940 Warrnambool (Vic) d June 17, 2005 Sydney (NSW)

Anderson, James William Falconer (Qld) b Feb. 25, 1889 birth place unknown (Qld) d Dec. 8, 1951 Bellevue Hill (NSW)

Anderson, John Gregory (Vic) b Feb. 15, 1955 East Melbourne (Vic)

Anderson, John Theodore (WAust) b Aug. 10, 1878 Warrnambool (Vic) d Aug. 29, 1926 South Yarra (Vic)

Anderson, Matthew Allan (Qld) b Nov. 30, 1976 Darwin (NT)

Anderson, Peter Gordon (NSW) b Oct. 4, 1933 Hawthorn (Vic)

Anderson, Peter McKenzie (Vic) b Sept. 17, 1968 Geelong (Vic)

Anderson, Peter William (Qld & S Aust) b May 22, 1961 South Brisbane (Qld)

Andrew-Street, Alfred Gordon (Vic) b April 8, 1914 Bondi (NSW) d Dec. 13, 1984 Concord (NSW)

* Andrews, Thomas James Edwin (NSW) b Aug. 26, 1890 Newtown (NSW) d Jan. 28, 1970 Croydon (NSW)

Andrews, Wayne Stewart (WAust) b Nov. 19, 1958 Melbourne (Vic)

Andrews, William Charles (NSW & Qld) b July 14, 1908 West Maitland (NSW) d June 9, 1962 Bombay (India)

* Angel, Jo (WAust) b April 22, 1968 Mt Lawley (WAust)

Antill, Thomas Wills (Vic) b Nov. 20, 1830 Jarvisfield (NSW) d May 11, 1865 Nelson (New Zealand)

Appleton, Leslie Joseph Francis (Tas) b Sept. 28, 1947 Hobart (Tas)

Archer, Daniel John Lancelot (Tas) b June 17, 1939 Launceston (Tas)

* Archer, Kenneth Alan (Qld) b Jan. 17, 1928 Yeerongpilly (Qld)

* Archer, Ronald Graham (Qld) b Oct. 25, 1933 Highgate Hill (Qld)

Armstrong, Edward Killeen (Qld) b Feb. 15, 1881 Milton (Qld) d April 28, 1963 Brisbane (Qld)

Armstrong, George Gort (Qld) b Dec. 29, 1882 Milton (Qld) d Jan. 12, 1956 Brisbane (Qld)

Armstrong, Glenarvon Huntley (S Aust) b Nov. 17, 1969 Hobart (Tas)

Armstrong, Thomas Goldsmith (Vic) b Oct. 31, 1889 Caulfield (Vic) d April 15, 1963 Bairnsdale (Vic)

* Armstrong, Warwick Windridge (Vic) b May 22, 1879 Kyneton (Vic) d July 13, 1947 Darling Point (NSW)

Armstrong, William Anthony (Qld) b May 2, 1886 Milton (Qld) d May 29, 1955 Brisbane (Qld)

Arnberger, Jason Lee (NSW & Vic) b Nov. 18, 1972 Penrith (NSW)

Arnold, Colin Robert (Tas) b Aug. 19, 1957 Devonport (Tas)

Arnold, Evan Matthew Campbell (S Aust) b Aug. 20, 1974 North Adelaide (S Aust)

Arnold, Weller John b Sept. 23, 1882 North Hobart (Tas) d Oct. 28, 1957 Hobart (Tas)

Arnott, Percival Sinclair (NSW) b July 9, 1889 Newcastle (NSW) d Dec. 23, 1950 Camperdown (NSW)

Arthur, Charles (Tas) b Feb. 5, 1808 Plymouth, Devon (England) d July 29, 1884 Longford (Tas)

Arthur, George Henry (Tas) b March 10, 1849 Longford (Tas) d Oct. 13, 1932 Longford (Tas)

Arthur, Gerald Charles (WAust) b July 25, 1913 Yarloop (WAust)

Arthur, John Lake Allen (Tas) b April 7, 1847 Longford (Tas) d April 26, 1877 Longford (Tas)

Asher, Oswald Philip (NSW) b May 21, 1891 Paddington (NSW) d July 16, 1970 Waverton (NSW)

Ashley, Nathan William (Cricket Academy) b Oct. 3, 1973 St Leonard's (NSW)

Astley, Graeme Patrick (Tas) b March 31, 1957 Sydney (NSW)

Atkins, Arthur Alfred (Qld & NSW) b April 22, 1874 (NSW) death details unknown

Atkinson, James Archibald (Vic & Tas) b April 4, 1896 North Fitzroy (Vic) d June 11, 1956 Beaconsfield (Tas)

Atkinson, Mark Neville (Tas) b Feb. 11, 1969 Sydney (NSW)

Atkinson, Mark Peter (WAust) b Nov. 27, 1970 Bentley (WAust)

Attenborough, Geoffrey Robert (S Aust) b Jan. 17, 1951 Mile End (S Aust)

Austen, Ernest Thomas (Vic) b Sept. 23, 1906 Hawthorn (Vic) d June 21, 1983 Donvale (Vic)

Austen, Victor Cecil (S Aust) b Nov. 30, 1918 Kew (Vic)

Austin, Harold MacPherson (Vic) b March 8, 1903 Skipton (Vic) d July 31, 1981 Timboon (Vic)

Austin, Sydney Walter (NSW & Qld) b Nov. 16, 1866 Sydney (NSW) d Sept. 11, 1932 Randwick (NSW)

Auty, Clinton (WAust) b Oct. 29, 1969 Auckland (New Zealand)

Aylett, Allen James (Vic) b April 24, 1934 Melbourne (Vic)

Ayres, Ryall Sydney (Qld) b Sept. 1, 1931 Clayfield (Qld) d Nov. 24, 1991 Sydney (NSW)

Ayres, Sydney William (Qld) b Aug. 7, 1889 Enmore (NSW) d Aug. 7, 1974 Castle Hill (NSW)

Ayres, Warren Geoffrey (Vic) b Oct. 25, 1965 Moorabbin (Vic)

Back, William (WAust) b c. 1856 Rottnest Island (WAust) d Feb. 15, 1911 Perth (WAust)

Backman, Charles James (S Aust) b April 11, 1884 Adelaide (S Aust) d April 25, 1915 Gallipoli (Turkey)

* Badcock, Clayvel Lindsay (Tas & S Aust) b April 10, 1914 Exton (Tas) d Dec. 13, 1982 Exton (Tas)

Badcock, Kevin Bruce (Tas) b March 24, 1951 Launceston (Tas)

Bagshaw, Kenneth James (S Aust) b Oct. 22, 1920 Kadina (S Aust) d Oct. 8, 1985 Watson (ACT)

Bailey, Alfred John Thomas Slater (S Aust) b March 3, 1932 North Adelaide (S Aust)

Bailey, Bertram Theodore (S Aust) b Dec. 5, 1874 Adelaide (S Aust) d Oct. 3, 1964 Payneham (S Aust)

Bailey, Cullen Benjamin (S Aust) b Feb. 26, 1985 Bedford Park (S Aust)

Bailey, Ernest Albert (S Aust) b Nov. 15, 1881 Adelaide (S Aust) d Aug. 16, 1966 Northfield (S Aust)

Bailey, George Herbert (Tas) b Oct. 29, 1853 Colombo (Ceylon) d Oct. 10, 1926 Hobart (Tas)

Bailey, George John (Tas) b Sept. 7, 1982 Launceston (Tas)

Bailey, George Keith Brooke (Tas) b Jan. 3, 1882 Hobart (Tas) d June 17, 1964 Hobart (Tas)

Bailey, Peter George (Vic) b Aug. 16, 1939 Glenhuntly (Vic)

Bailey, Rowland Herbert (Vic) b Oct. 5, 1876 Melbourne (Vic) d March 24, 1950 Ivanhoe (Vic)

Bailey, William Henry (Vic) b July 20, 1898 Condoblin (NSW) d Feb. 27, 1983 Geelong (Vic)

Baird, James George (Vic) b Nov. 9, 1920 Parkville (Vic) d Nov. 4, 2003 Sandringham (Vic)

Baird, Keith Hugh (WAust) b Dec. 27, 1911 Perth (WAust) d July 18, 1965 Peppermint Grove (WAust)

Baker, Charles Michael (Vic) b June 18, 1880 Ballarat East (Vic) d May 4, 1962 Ballarat (Vic)

Baker, Charles Ronald (NSW) b March 24, 1939 Islington (NSW)

Baker, Dennis James (WAust & Tas) b Dec. 29, 1947 Norseman (WAust)

Baker, Everard Audley (Vic) b July 28, 1913 Cohuna (Vic) d March 30, 1987 Melbourne (Vic)

Baker, Frederick (Vic) b Aug. 5, 1851 (England) d Sept. 14, 1939 Perth (WAust)

Baker, Glen George (Qld) b Aug. 9, 1915 Townsville (Qld) d Dec. 15, 1943 Buna (Papua New Guinea) on active service

Baker, Leigh James (Vic) b Sept. 20, 1951 Oakleigh (Vic)

Baker, Robert Michael (WAust) b July 24, 1975 Osborne Park (WAust)

Bakker, Jason Richard (Vic) b Nov. 12, 1967 Geelong (Vic)

Balcam, Leonard Frank (Qld & Vic) b Aug. 20, 1957 Footscray (Vic)

Baldock, Darrel John (Tas) b Sept. 29, 1938 Devonport (Tas)

Baldry, Robert John (Vic) b Nov. 30, 1950 Warragul (Vic)

Ball, Thomas Edward (Qld) b Dec. 3, 1921 Atherton (Qld) d Jan. 13, 2002 Cairns (Qld)

Ballans, David Murray (S Aust) b June 30, 1868 at sea d June 26, 1957 Goodwood Park (S Aust)

Bandy, Lawrence Henry (WAust) b Sept. 3, 1911 Perth (WAust) d July 18, 1984 Scarborough (WAust)

Banks, Albert James (WAust) b Dec. 10, 1883 Maryborough (Vic) d July 5, 1930 Toodyay (WAust)

* Bannerman, Alexander Chalmers (NSW) b March 21, 1854 Paddington (NSW) d Sept. 19, 1924 Paddington (NSW)

* Bannerman, Charles (NSW) b July 23, 1851 Woolwich, Kent (England) d Aug. 20, 1930 Surry Hills (NSW)

Barbour, Eric Pitty (NSW) b Jan. 27, 1891 Ashfield (NSW) d Dec. 7, 1934 Darlinghurst (NSW)

Barbour, Robert Roy (Qld) b March 29, 1899 Ashfield (NSW) d Dec. 29, 1994 Berwick (Vic)

Bardsley, Raymond (NSW) b Jan. 19, 1894 Glebe Point (NSW) d June 25, 1983 Rose Bay (NSW)

* Bardsley, Warren (NSW) b Dec. 6, 1882 Nevertire (NSW) d Jan. 20, 1954 Collaroy (NSW)

Baring, Frederick Albert (Vic) b Dec. 15, 1890 Hotham East (Vic) d Dec. 10, 1961 Doncaster (Vic)

Baring, Hugh Thomas (Vic) b Aug. 17, 1906 East Melbourne (Vic) d July 9, 1968 Fitzroy (Vic)

Barnard, Francis George Allman (Vic) b Dec. 26, 1857 Kew (Vic) d June 1, 1932 Melbourne (Vic)

Barnes, James Charles (NSW) b Oct. 16, 1882 Alexandria (NSW) death details unknown

Barnes, Jeffrey Robert (S Aust) b Jan. 9, 1948 Glenelg (S Aust)

Barnes, John Francis (Qld) b Sept. 27, 1916 Rockhampton (Qld)

Barnes, John Robert (Vic) b May 20, 1905 Williamstown (Vic) d Oct. 6, 1999 Williamstown (Vic)

Barnes, Richard (Tas) b 1849 (Ireland) d April 30, 1902 Heidelberg (Vic)

* Barnes, Sydney George (NSW) b June 5, 1916 Annandale (NSW) d Dec. 16, 1973 Collaroy (NSW)

* Barnett, Benjamin Arthur (Vic) b March 23, 1908 Auburn (Vic) d June 27, 1979 Newcastle (NSW)

Barras, Alexander Edward Owen (WAust) b Jan. 26, 1914 Auburn (Vic) d Aug. 15, 1986 Mt Lawley (WAust)

Barrett, Edgar Alfred (Vic) b June 26, 1869 Emerald Hill (Vic) d April 29, 1959 Kew (Vic)

Barrett, Henry (Tas) b Aug. 19, 1837 Launceston (Tas) d Sept. 10, 1910 Westbury (Tas)

* Barrett, John Edward (Vic) b Oct. 15, 1866 Emerald Hill (Vic) d Feb. 6, 1916 Peak Hill (WAust)

Barsby, Trevor John (Qld) b Jan. 16, 1964 Herston (Qld)

Barstow, Charles Banks (Qld) b March 13, 1883 Brisbane (Qld) d July 12, 1935 Eagle Junction (Qld)

Bartlett, Albert James (S Aust) b April 23, 1900 Parkside (S Aust) d Oct. 6, 1968 Woodville South (S Aust)

Bartlett, Robert Andrew (Vic) b Jan. 2, 1972 Melbourne (Vic)

Bassano, Christopher Warwick Godfrey (Tas) b Sept. 11, 1975 East London (South Africa)

Bateman, William Augustus (WAust) b Sept. 11, 1866 Fremantle (WAust) d July 27, 1935 South Perth (WAust)

Bates, Barry (NSW) b July 1, 1939 Mayfield (NSW)

Bayles, Robert Charles Alfred Vivian (Tas) b July 7, 1892 Ross (Tas) d May 16, 1959 Launceston (Tas)

Bayles, William Headlam (Tas) b Jan. 8, 1896 Ross (Tas) d Dec. 17, 1960 Launceston (Tas)

Bayliss, Trevor Harley (NSW) b Dec. 21, 1962 Goulburn (NSW)

Bayly, Henry Vincent (Tas) b Nov. 19, 1850 Dulcot (Tas) d Jan. 7, 1903 New Town (Tas)

Beacham, George (Vic) b Oct. 27, 1867 (Qld) d Jan. 11, 1925 South Fitzroy (Vic)

Beagley, John William (S Aust) b March 23, 1933 Adelaide (S Aust)

Beal, Charles William (Australians) b June 24, 1855 Sydney (NSW) d Feb. 5, 1921 Randwick (NSW)

Beal, James Charles (NSW) b May 26, 1830 Sydney (NSW) d Aug. 24, 1904 Milton (Qld)

Beames, Percy James (Vic) b July 27, 1911 Ballarat (Vic) d April 28, 2004 Kew (Vic)

Bean, Ernest Edward (Vic) b April 17, 1866 Miner's Rest, near Ballarat (Vic) d March 22, 1939 Hampton (Vic)

Beard, Barry Allan (Tas) b Dec. 21, 1941 Bothwell (Tas) d June 9, 2001 Ulverstone (Tas)

* Beard, Graeme Robert (NSW) b Aug. 19, 1950 Auburn (NSW)

Beath, Neville Ray James (NSW) b Nov. 12, 1921 Goolagong (NSW) d Nov. 22, 1987 Richmond (NSW)

Beattie, Simon Guy (Qld) b Dec. 10, 1958 Junee (NSW)

Beatty, Christopher (NSW) b Oct. 21, 1952 Newcastle (NSW)

Beatty, Reginald George (NSW) b Dec. 24, 1913 Wickham (NSW) d May 27, 1957 Waratah (NSW)

Becker, Gordon Charles (WAust) b March 14, 1935 Katanning (WAust)

Bedford, Albert Austen (S Aust) b Sept. 12, 1932 Rose Park (S Aust) d March 25, 2001 Noarlunga (S Aust)

Bedford, Peter Lawrence Anthony (Vic) b April 11, 1947 Melbourne (Vic)

Bednall, Philip Malcolm (S Aust) b Jan. 27, 1931 Burra (S Aust)

Beeston, John Lievesley (NSW) b Jan. 17, 1831 Bingley Locks, Yorkshire (England) d June 1, 1873 Newcastle (NSW)

Beeston, Norman Charles (Qld) b Sept. 29, 1900 Brisbane (Qld) d Feb. 4, 1985 Brisbane (Qld)

Belcher, Samuel Harborne (NSW) b Nov. 1, 1834 (England) d Aug. 22, 1920 Garroorigang (NSW)

Bell, John Clifford (Qld) b Jan. 18, 1949 Ipswich (Qld)

* Benaud, John (NSW) b May 11, 1944 Auburn (NSW)

* Benaud, Richard (NSW) b Oct. 6, 1930 Penrith (NSW)

Benbow, Ernest Aldred (Qld) b March 14, 1888 Mt Walker (Qld) d Dec. 28, 1940 Springsure (Qld)

Bendixen, Hilton Fewtrell (Qld) b Feb. 21, 1910 Nambour (Qld) d April 15, 1962 Nambour (Qld)

Benjamin, Emmanuel (Tas) b Feb. 2, 1955 Jullundur City (India)

Bennett, Albert (NSW) b May 21, 1910 St Helens, Lancashire (England) d c. 1985 full death details unknown

Bennett, Floyd Chester (S Aust & WAust) b April 12, 1919 North Perth (WAust) d Nov. 26, 1997 Stirling (S Aust)

Bennett, George Henry (NSW) b Aug. 16, 1906 Brookvale (NSW) d c. 1984 full death details unknown

Bennett, Harry Francis (WAust) b June 22, 1859 Prahran (Vic) d Oct. 4, 1898 Guildford (WAust)

Bennett, Joseph (Vic) birth and death details unknown

* Bennett, Murray John (NSW) b Oct. 6, 1956 Brisbane (Qld)

Bennett, Rex Leland (S Aust & Tas) b June 25, 1896 Snowtown (S Aust) d Dec. 14, 1963 Collaroy (NSW)

Bennett, Richard John (Tas) b June 5, 1965 Launceston (Tas)

Bennett, Thomas (S Aust) b Oct. 11, 1866 Littlehampton (S Aust) d Dec. 26, 1942 Northfield (S Aust)

Bennetts, Gordon Kissack (Vic) b March 26, 1909 Wellington (NSW) d April 4, 1987 Geelong (Vic)

Benneworth, Anthony John (Tas) b Dec. 12, 1949 Launceston (Tas)

Bennison, James Ernest (Tas) b Feb. 16, 1854 Hobart (Tas) d Nov. 14, 1916 Hobart (Tas)

Bensley, Gary Robert (NSW) b Oct. 17, 1958 Inverell (NSW)

Bensted, Eric Charles (Qld) b Feb. 11, 1901 Killarney (Qld) d March 24, 1980 Brisbane (Qld)

Benton, Jeffrey John (S Aust) b Oct. 9, 1953 Mildura (Vic)

Bernard, Stephen Russell (NSW) b Dec. 28, 1949 Orange (NSW)

Berrie, Edward Bruce (NSW) b April 8, 1884 Tomenbil, near Forbes (NSW) d Dec. 8, 1963 Tamworth (NSW)

Berry, Darren Shane (Vic & S Aust) b Dec. 10, 1969 Melbourne (Vic)

Berry, Walter Lyall (NSW) b April 9, 1893 Woolwich (NSW) d April 20, 1970 Ettalong Beach (NSW)

Bessen, Mervyn Oscar (WAust) b Aug. 29, 1913 Tambellup (WAust) d July 13, 2002 Mandurah (WAust)

Best, Leslie (NSW) b Nov. 20, 1893 Seven Hills (NSW) d Aug. 27, 1925 Sydney (NSW)

Bettington, Brindley Cecil John (NSW) b Sept. 2, 1898 Parramatta (NSW) d Aug. 26, 1931 Merriwa (NSW)

Bettington, Reginald Henshall Brindley (NSW) b Feb. 24, 1900 Parramatta (NSW) d June 24, 1969 Gisborne (New Zealand)

Betts, Arthur John (Tas) b Feb. 26, 1880 Launceston (Tas) d Aug. 4, 1948 Belgrave (Vic)

Bevan, Hubert George (WAust) b Dec. 21, 1932 Perth (WAust) d June 15, 2005 East Fremantle (WAust)

Bevan, John Lawrence (S Aust) b May 10, 1846 Swansea, Glamorgan (Wales) d March 31, 1918 Portland Estate (S Aust)

* Bevan, Michael Gwyl (S Aust, NSW & Tas) b May 8, 1970 Belconnen (ACT)

Beven, Ian Robert (Tas) b Nov. 27, 1958 Hobart (Tas)

* Bichel, Andrew John (Qld) b Aug. 27, 1970 Laidley (Qld)

Bichel, Donald Alan (Qld) b May 4, 1935 Lowood (Qld) d Oct. 11, 2004 Auchenflower (Qld))

Bidstrup, Trevor Allan (WAust) b Dec. 29, 1937 Midland (WAust)

Biffin, Raymond Leo (Tas) b May 6, 1949 Launceston (Tas)

Biggs, Malcolm (Qld) b July 7, 1904 Caboolture (Qld) d Aug. 1, 1972 Ipswich (Qld)

Bill, Oscar Wendell (NSW) b April 8, 1909 Waverley (NSW) d May 10, 1988 Sydney (NSW)

Bingham, John Edmund (Tas) b July 15, 1864 Forcett (Tas) d July 23, 1946 Hobart (Tas)

Binney, Edgar James (Vic) b May 31, 1885 Port Tremayne (S Aust) d Sept. 9, 1978 Brighton (Vic)

Birch, William Thomas (Tas) b Oct. 26, 1849 Hobart (Tas) d Aug. 18, 1897 Hobart (Tas)

Birchall, James Thomas Wardlaw (S Aust) b Nov. 23, 1962 North Adelaide (S Aust)

Bird, Thomas Robert (Vic) b Aug. 31, 1904 Collingwood (Vic) d April 12, 1979 Thornbury (Vic)

Birt, Travis Rodney (Tas) b Dec. 9, 1981 Sale (Vic)

Bishop, Edward George (WAust) b Aug. 4, 1872 birthplace unknown d Feb. 16, 1943 Nedlands (WAust)

Bishop, Glenn Andrew (S Aust) b Feb. 25, 1960 North Adelaide (S Aust)

Bishop, Henry Symons (Vic) b Dec. 15, 1849 Torrington, Devon (England) d July 18, 1891 Prahran (Vic)

Bitmead, Robert Clyde (Vic) b July 17, 1942 Fitzroy (Vic)

Bizzell, Graham Maurice (Qld) b Nov. 19, 1941 Beenleigh (Qld)

Black, Alfred A. (Vic) birth details unknown d c. 1859

Black, George Gordon (NSW) b Jan. 19, 1885 Darling Point (NSW) d Dec. 6, 1954 Orange (NSW)

Black, Graham Ash (S Aust) b May 14, 1924 Unley (S Aust)

* Blackham, John McCarthy (Vic) b May 11, 1854 North Fitzroy (Vic) d Dec. 28, 1932 Melbourne (Vic)

* Blackie, Donald Dearness (Vic) b April 5, 1882 Bendigo (Vic) d April 18, 1955 South Melbourne (Vic)

Blackman, Oswald Colin (NSW) b March 9, 1942 Griffith (NSW)

Blackstock, John MacDonald (Qld) b Jan. 16, 1871 Drum, Thornhill, Edinburgh (Scotland) d post-1945 Sydney (NSW)

Blair, Dennis John (Tas) b Sept. 27, 1934 Bulawayo (Southern Rhodesia)

Blair, Gregory David (Tas & Vic) b Dec. 15, 1947 Launceston (Tas)

Blanchard, Charles Joseph (Surrey) b circa 1842 (Australia) d circa 1919 Newtown (NSW)

Blaxland, Marcus Herbert (NSW & Qld) b April 29, 1884 Callan Park (NSW) d July 31, 1958 Clayfield (Qld)

* Blewett, Gregory Scott (S Aust) b Oct. 29, 1971 North Adelaide (S Aust)

Blewett, Robert Kevin (S Aust) b March 30, 1943 Prospect (S Aust)

* Blignaut, Arnoldus Mauritius (Tas) b Aug. 1, 1979 Salisbury (Rhodesia)

Blinman, Harry (S Aust) b Dec. 30, 1861 Adelaide (S Aust) d July 23, 1950 Adelaide (S Aust)

Blizzard, Phillip Ashley (Tas & NSW) b Feb. 6, 1958 Burnie (Tas)

Bloomfield, George Thomas (S Aust) b Feb. 5, 1882 Bowden (S Aust) d Nov. 1, 1958 Adelaide (S Aust)

Blundell, George Robert (WAust) b April 19, 1896 Perth (WAust) d Feb. 11, 1940 West Perth (WAust)

Blundell, Norman Charles (Vic) b Sept. 2, 1917 North Carlton (Vic)

Blundell, Rex Pole (S Aust) b May 8, 1942 Adelaide (S Aust)

Blundell, William Walter (Vic) b Dec. 30, 1866 Majorca (Vic) d Feb. 28, 1946 Kensington (Vic)

Boag, Kenneth John (Qld) b Sept. 6, 1914 Toowoomba (Qld) d July 10, 1984 Port Kembla (NSW)

Boddam, Edmund Tudor (Tas) b Nov. 23, 1879 Hobart (Tas) d Sept. 9, 1959 New Town (Tas)

Bogle, James (NSW) b Jan. 4, 1893 Mossgiel (NSW) d Oct. 19, 1963 Southport (Qld)

Bollinger, Douglas (NSW) b July 24, 1981 Baulkham Hills (NSW)

Bolton, John Turner (Qld) b Oct. 3, 1888 Riverstone (NSW)

* Bonnor, George John (Vic & NSW) b Feb. 25, 1855 Bathurst (NSW) d June 27, 1912 East Orange (NSW)

* Boon, David Clarence (Tas) b Dec. 29, 1960 Launceston (Tas)

* Booth, Brian Charles (NSW) b Oct. 19, 1933 Perthville (NSW)

Booth, Ernest Brian Nelson (Tas) b Sept. 30, 1924 Scottsdale (Tas)

* Border, Allan Robert (NSW & Qld) b July 27, 1955 Cremorne (NSW)

Borgas, Cameron James (S Aust) b Sept. 1, 1983 Flinders (S Aust)

Bosley, Marcus Williams (NSW) b Aug. 10, 1897 Liverpool (NSW) d June 12, 1982 Ashfield (NSW)

* Botham, Ian Terence (Qld) b Nov. 24, 1955 Heswall, Cheshire (England)

Botham, Leslie John (Vic) b May 5, 1930 Hawthorn (Vic) d April 17, 1999 Melbourne (Vic)

Bott, Leonidas Cecil (WAust) b July 14, 1889 Adelaide (S Aust) d Aug. 21, 1968 Perth (WAust)

Botten, Robert Dyas (S Aust) b Oct. 11, 1853 Lewisham, Kent (England) d April 26, 1935 Medindie (S Aust)

Boulter, Edward Samuel (Vic) b March 23, 1886 North Fitzroy (Vic) d June 10, 1968 North Balwyn (Vic)

Bourne, Gordon Alister (Qld) b April 21, 1913 Tintenbar (NSW) d Sept. 13, 1993 Goomeri (Qld)

Bovell, Henry Edward Joseph (WAust) b March 15, 1936 East Fremantle (WAust)

Bowden, Albert John (NSW) b Sept. 28, 1874 Sydney (NSW) d Aug. 8, 1943 Northwood (NSW)

Bowden, Samuel Hedskis (Qld) b Sept. 29, 1867 Sydney (NSW) d Aug. 25, 1945 Manly (NSW)

Bowe, Ronald Doig (WAust) b Dec. 10, 1939 Beaconsfield (WAust)

Bower, Rodney John (NSW) b Nov. 30, 1959 Bankstown (NSW)

Bower, Timothy Donald (Tas) b Sept. 10, 1968 Devonport (Tas)

Bowler, Peter Duncan (Tas) b July 30, 1963 Plymouth, Devon (England)

Bowley, Bruce Leonard (S Aust) b Jan. 1, 1922 Clare (S Aust)

Bowley, Edwin Leonard (S Aust) b Feb. 27, 1888 Clare (S Aust) d April 22, 1963 Woodville (S Aust)

Bowman, Alcon Ninus Ascot (Vic) b May 10, 1862 Ascot Vale (Vic) d June 30, 1938 Surrey Hills (Vic)

Box, Henry (Vic) b c. Sept. 1837 Walshall, London, Middlesex (England) death details unknown

Boyce, Raymond Charles Manning (NSW) b June 28, 1891 Taree (NSW) d Jan. 20, 1941 Northwood (NSW)

Boyd, David Laurence (WAust) b Nov. 21, 1955 Kalgoorlie (WAust)

Boyd, Trevor Joseph (NSW) b Oct. 22, 1944 Nyngan (NSW)

* Boyle, Henry Frederick (Vic) b Dec. 10, 1847 Sydney (NSW) d Nov. 21, 1907 Bendigo (Vic)

Brabon, George William (Qld) b Aug. 2, 1957 Ayr (Qld)

Bracher, Herbert Henry Gladstone (Vic) b Aug. 28, 1886 Footscray (Vic) d Feb. 25, 1974 Donvale (Vic)

* Bracken, Nathan Wade (NSW) b Sept. 12, 1977 Penrith (NSW)

Bradbridge, John Sidney (NSW) b Dec. 1, 1831 Sydney (NSW) d July 14, 1905 Dulwich Hill (NSW)

Bradley, Craig Edwin (S Aust & Vic) b Oct. 23, 1964 Ashford (S Aust)

Bradley, William Francis (Qld) b Oct. 8, 1867 Brisbane (Qld) d Sept. 7, 1948 Ipswich (Qld)

* Bradman, Donald George (NSW & S Aust) b Aug. 27, 1908 Cootamundra (NSW) d Feb. 25, 2001 Kensington Park (S Aust)

Bradridge, John Sidney (NSW) b Dec. 1, 1831 Sydney (NSW) d July 14, 1905 Dulwich Hill (NSW)

Bradshaw, Keith (Tas) b Oct. 2, 1963 Hobart (Tas)

Bradstreet, Shawn David (NSW) b Feb. 28, 1972 Wollongong (NSW)

Braid, Rupert Lee (Vic) b March 3, 1888 Talbot (Vic) d Nov. 11, 1963 Upper Ferntree Gully (Vic)

Brain, Desmond Morrah (Tas) b Dec. 16, 1909 Hobart (Tas) d March 1, 1990 Tumut (NSW)

Brain, John Heather (Tas) b Feb. 9, 1905 Hobart (Tas) d June 21, 1961 Hobart (Tas)

Brain, Roy Albert (Tas) b Sept. 2, 1926 Hobart (Tas)

Braithwaite, Arthur (Tas) b Sept. 2, 1880 Rushworth (Vic) d Dec. 19, 1953 Cheltenham (Vic)

Brakey, Gary Leslie (Combined XI) b Oct. 8, 1942 Wynyard (Tas) d Feb. 3, 1987 Killarney Heights (NSW)

Brant, Scott Andrew (Qld) b Jan. 26, 1983 Harare (Zimbabwe)

Braslin, Leon Anthony (Tas) b May 12, 1938 New Norfolk (Tas)

Bratchford, James Douglas (Qld) b Feb. 2, 1929 Cleveland (Qld) d Oct. 5, 1997 on flight from USA to Australia

Braybrook, Clive (S Aust) b Sept. 27, 1901 Goodwood (S Aust) d July 16, 1985 Swan Hill (Vic)

Brayshaw, Ian James (WAust) b Jan. 14, 1942 South Perth (WAust)

Brayshaw, James Antony (WAust & S Aust) b May 11, 1967 Subiaco (WAust)

Breman, Todd George (WAust) b Oct. 28, 1965 Subiaco (WAust)

Bremner, Colin David (Services) b Jan. 29, 1920 Hawthorn (Vic) d June 13, 2002 Canberra (ACT)

Brew, Francis Malcolm (Qld) b Jan. 5, 1903 Petrie Terrace (Qld) d Jan. 13, 1974 Sandgate (Qld)

Brewster, Robert Colin (NSW) b Aug. 17, 1867 Sydney (NSW) d Nov. 8, 1962 Killara (NSW)

Briant, George William (Tas) b c. 1828 Hackney, London, Middlesex (England) d May 10, 1914 Hobart (Tas)

Brideson, John Holmes (S Aust) b July 9, 1856 Rushworth (Vic) d Feb. 1, 1898 Belair (S Aust)

Bridgman, Hugh Hossick Mackay (S Aust) b Feb. 1, 1890 Findon (S Aust) d Dec. 3, 1953 Torrensville (S Aust)

Bridson, John (S Aust) b Feb. 2, 1863 Fitzroy (Vic) d Feb. 1, 1898 Belair (S Aust)

Briggs, Ronald Edward (NSW) b Sept. 22, 1927 Belmore (NSW) d Oct. 10, 2003 Katoomba (NSW)

* Bright, Raymond James (Vic) b July 13, 1954 Footscray (Vic)

Britt, Harold James (Vic) b May 6, 1911 Doncaster (Vic) d Sept. 20, 1988 Healesville (Vic)

Broad, David John (Vic) b Sept. 25, 1953 Kew (Vic)

Broad, Wayne Ronald (Qld) b June 20, 1956 Herston (Qld)

Broadby, Christopher Laurence (Tas) b March 17, 1959 Hobart (Tas)

Brodie, James Chalmers (Vic) b Sept. 28, 1820 Perth, Perthshire (Scotland) d Feb. 19, 1912 Balwyn (Vic)

Brodie, Richard Sinclair (Vic) b Sept. 9, 1813 County Caithness (Scotland) d Jan. 18, 1872 Bulla Bulla (Vic)

* Bromley, Ernest Harvey (WAust & Vic) b Sept. 3, 1912 Fremantle (WAust) d Feb. 1, 1967 Clayton (Vic)

Brooks, Gordon Victor (S Aust) b May 30, 1938 Ceduna (S Aust) d Jan. 31, 2004 Chermside (Qld)

Brooks, Thomas Francis (NSW) b March 28, 1919 Paddington (NSW)

Broomby, Reginald Arthur (Tas) b Jan. 6, 1905 Launceston (Tas) d May 10, 1984 Southport (Qld)

Broster, Paul Alexander (Vic) b Jan. 31, 1973 Wangaratta (Vic)

Broughton, Donald Ean (Tas) b Feb. 4, 1931 Hobart (Tas) d Dec. 11, 1987 Hobart (Tas)

Brown, Albert Ernest (Vic) b Dec. 22, 1890 Clifton Hill (Vic) d Nov. 17, 1954 Northcote (Vic)

Brown, Anthony Norman (Qld) b March 30, 1961 Herston (Qld)

Brown, Craig Franklin Archer (Tas) b Jan. 25, 1954 Hobart (Tas)

Brown, Edward (NSW) b c. Jan. 1837 Uppingham, Rutland (England) d full death details unknown

Brown, Edward Keith Faulkner (NSW) b March 7, 1891 Newcastle (NSW) d March 12, 1949 Bowenfels (NSW)

Brown, Graham Campbell (Vic) b May 9, 1944 Burwood (Vic)

Brown, Guy Archibald Loeman (Qld) b July 31, 1884 Dalby (Qld) d March 21, 1958 New Farm (Qld)

Brown, John (Qld) b May 13, 1943 Mt Morgan (Qld)

Brown, Kevin Ronald (Tas) b July 1, 1941 Devonport (Tas)

Brown, Norman Eric (Vic) b April 1, 1889 North Fitzroy (Vic) d July 7, 1962 Carrum (Vic)

Brown, Raymond Kinnear (Tas) b Nov. 3, 1950 New Norfolk (Tas)

Brown, Roger Leedham (Tas) b Aug. 9, 1959 Launceston (Tas)

Brown, Vallancey Kennedy (Vic) b Dec. 7, 1912 Ashfield (NSW) d Oct. 24, 1987 Melbourne (Vic)

Brown, Walter Graham Fairfax (NSW) b April 12, 1899 Summer Hill (NSW) d May 21, 1931 Mosman (NSW)

Brown, Wilfred Martin (Qld) b March 21, 1930 Warwick (Qld)

Brown, William (Tas) b c. 1807 (England) d Aug. 28, 1859 Hobart (Tas)

* Brown, William Alfred (NSW & Qld) b July 31, 1912 Toowoomba (Qld)

Browne, William Creighton (Qld) b Nov. 6, 1898 Toowoomba (Qld) d Oct. 25, 1980 Southport (Qld)

Browning, George Richard (Vic) b Dec. 12, 1858 Hepburn (Vic) d Oct. 9, 1900 North Carlton (Vic)

Brownlow, Bertie (Tas) b May 20, 1920 Portland (NSW) d Oct. 22, 2004 Hobart (Tas)

* Bruce, William (Vic) b May 22, 1864 South Yarra (Vic) d Aug. 3, 1925 Elwood (Vic)

Bryant, Francis Joseph (WAust) b Nov. 7, 1907 Perth (WAust) d March 11, 1984 Glendalough (WAust)

Bryant, James Mark (Vic) b 1826 birth day and month unknown Caterham, Surrey (England) d Dec. 10, 1881 Sale (Vic)

Bryant, Richard (NSW) b c. 1847 Maitland (NSW) d Oct. 27, 1931 Stockton (NSW)

Bryant, Richard John (WAust) b May 8, 1904 Perth (WAust) d Aug. 17, 1989 Mt Lawley (WAust)

Bryant, William James (WAust) b Jan. 15, 1906 Perth (WAust) d Jan. 1, 1995 Perth (WAust)

Bryce, William Cecil James (Qld) b Aug. 18, 1911 Maryborough (Qld) d Feb. 8, 1986 Spring Hill (Qld)

Bubb, Ernest Reinhard (NSW) b Dec. 6, 1884 Summer Hill (NSW) d Nov. 26, 1946 Neutral Bay (NSW)

Bubb, Roy Alfred Reinhard (NSW) b June 23, 1900 Darlinghurst (NSW) d April 4, 1965 Hamilton (NSW)

Buchanan, John Marshall (Qld) b April 5, 1953 Ipswich (Qld)

Buckingham, Danny James (Tas) b Dec. 2, 1964 Burnie (Tas)

Buckle, Frank (NSW) b Nov. 11, 1891 Pyrmont (NSW) d June 4, 1982 Sydney (NSW)

Buckle, William Harvey (Qld) b June 3, 1943 Wooloowin (Qld)

Buggins, Bruce Leonard (WAust) b Jan. 29, 1935 Perth (WAust)

Bull, Desmond Frederick Earl (Qld) b Aug, 13, 1935 South Brisbane (Qld)

Bull, Eric Alister (NSW) b Sept. 28, 1886 Bourke (NSW) d May 14, 1954 Mt Kuring-Gai (NSW)

Bullough, Walter (S Aust) b Oct. 21, 1855 Hunslet, Yorkshire (England) d Sept. 17, 1888 Hindmarsh (S Aust)

Burchett, Alfred (Vic) b May 22, 1831 London, Middlesex (England) d Nov. 12, 1888 St Kilda (Vic)

Burchett, Frederick (Vic) b April 27, 1824 London, Middlesex (England) d July 16, 1861 Melbourne (Vic)

* Burge, Peter John Parnell (Qld) b May 17, 1932 Kangaroo Point (Qld) d Oct. 5, 2001 Main Beach (Qld)

* Burke, James Wallace (NSW) b June 12, 1930 Mosman (NSW) d Feb. 2, 1979 Manly (NSW)

* Burn, Edwin James Kenneth (Tas) b Sept. 17, 1862 Richmond (Tas) d July 20, 1956 Hobart (Tas)

Burn, James Henry (Tas) b July 31, 1849 Hobart (Tas), death details unknown

Burns, Harold Vincent (Qld) b May 20, 1908 Ebagoolah (Qld) d June 6, 1944 Cairns (Qld)

Burrows, Arthur Owen (Tas) b Oct. 17, 1903 Hobart (Tas) d Jan. 4, 1984 Sandy Bay (Tas)

Burrows, Ian Donald (Combined XI) b Nov. 20, 1944 Hobart (Tas)

Burrows, J. (NSW) birth and death details unknown

Burt, Selby John Wright (NSW) b Dec. 12, 1903 Hillgrove (NSW) d Feb. 14, 1959 Camperdown (NSW)

* Burton, Frederick John (NSW & Vic) b Nov. 2, 1865 Collingwood (Vic) d Aug. 25, 1929 Wanganui (New Zealand)

Burton, Garth (S Aust) b Jan. 21, 1913 Black Forest (S Aust) d Sept. 6, 1993 South Brighton (S Aust)

Burton, Jack Richard (S Aust) b Nov. 3, 1923 Cleve (S Aust) d Oct. 30, 2001 Elizabeth Vale (S Aust)

Bush, Giles Edmund Wreford (WAust) b Sept. 9, 1956 Subiaco (WAust)

* Butcher, Roland Orlando (Tas) b Oct. 14, 1953 East Point, St Philip (Barbados)

Butler, Charles William (Tas) b Sept. 18, 1854 Battery Point (Tas) d June 10, 1937 Sandy Bay (Tas)

Butler, Edward Henry (Tas & Vic) b March 15, 1851 Battery Point (Tas) d Jan. 5, 1928 Lower Sandy Bay (Tas)

Butler, Edward Lionel Austin (Tas) b April 10, 1883 Hobart (Tas) d Aug. 23, 1916 Puchevillers (France)

Butler, Frank (Tas) b Nov. 13, 1889 Brighton (Vic) d May 8, 1965 Kew (Vic)

Butler, Walter John (WAust) b May 30, 1882 Port Adelaide (S Aust) d March 12, 1966 Bruce Rock (WAust)

Butterworth, Benjamin (Vic) b 1832 birth day and month unknown Rochdale, Lancashire (England) d Jan. 6, 1879 Chiswick, Middlesex (England)

Butterworth, Thomas (Vic) b Dec. 17, 1828 Rochdale, Lancashire (England) d July 15, 1877 Kensington, London (England)

Buttsworth, Frederick James (WAust) b May 29, 1927 North Perth (WAust)

Buttsworth, Frederick Richard (WAust) b April 28, 1880 Wilberforce (NSW) d Feb. 26, 1974 Perth (WAust)

Buttsworth, Wallace Francis (WAust) b Jan. 21, 1917 North Perth (WAust) d May 22, 2002 Milton (NSW)

Byfield, Arnold Stanley (WAust) b Nov. 1, 1923 Northam (WAust)

Byrne, Thomas (Qld) b July 11, 1866 Paterson (NSW) d Dec. 19, 1951 Herston (Qld)

Caban, Timothy Kenneth (Qld) b Feb. 15, 1952 Cessnock (NSW)

Caffyn, William (NSW) b Feb. 2, 1828 Reigate, Surrey (England) d Aug. 28, 1919 Reigate, Surrey (England)

Cahill, Keyran William Jack (Tas) b Dec. 3, 1911 Hobart (Tas) d March 7, 1966 Launceston (Tas)

Cain, William (Qld) b Dec. 17, 1899 Paddington (Qld) d Dec. 24, 1981 Sherwood (Qld)

Calder, Henry (WAust) b July 3, 1906 Guildford (WAust) d Aug. 27, 1970 South Perth (WAust)

Caldwell, Tim Charles John (NSW) b Oct. 29, 1913 Clayfield (Qld) d June 17, 1994 Orange (NSW)

Callachor, John Joseph Casimir (NSW) b Nov. 10, 1857 Woolloomooloo (NSW) d Feb. 20, 1924 Lane Cove (NSW)

Callaway, Norman Frank (NSW) b April 5, 1896 Hay (NSW) d May 3, 1917 Bullecourt (France)

* Callaway, Sydney Thomas (NSW) b Feb. 6, 1868 Redfern (NSW) d Nov. 25, 1923 Christchurch (New Zealand)

* Callen, Ian Wayne (Vic) b May 2, 1955 Alexandra (Vic)

Calvert, Derreck (Tas) b Dec. 22, 1919 South Arm (Tas) d Dec. 25, 2003 Hobart (Tas)

Cameron, Benjamin Peter (S Aust) b Feb. 21, 1981 Hobart (Tas)

Cameron, Mark Alan (NSW) b Jan. 31, 1981 Waratah (NSW)

Cameron, Robert Alastair (S Aust) b Sept. 6, 1938 North Adelaide (S Aust)

Cameron, Verney Lovett (Vic) b c. 1842 Sorrento (Vic) d May 27, 1881 Richmond (Vic)

Campbell, Blair Maismore (Vic & Tas) b Aug. 20, 1946 Kew (Vic)

Campbell, Colin Mansfield (Tas) b Aug. 13, 1872 Cressy (Tas) d April 3, 1907 Winlaton, Northumberland (Eng)

Campbell, Donald (Vic) b Sept. 18, 1851 Loddon Plains (Vic) d Sept. 14, 1887 South Yarra (Vic)

Campbell, Francis Beresford (Tas) b April 20, 1867 Hobart (Tas) d May 14, 1929 Gladesville (NSW)

Campbell, Gordon Cathcart (S Aust) b June 4, 1885 Myrtle Bank (S Aust) d Aug. 13, 1961 Woodville South (S Aust)

* Campbell, Gregory Dale (Tas) b March 10, 1964 Launceston (Tas)

Campbell, Ivan James (WAust) b Oct. 29, 1908 Perth (WAust) d Jan. 22, 1962 Hollywood (WAust)

Campbell, James Norval (NSW) b Sept. 21, 1908 Chatswood (NSW) d Sept. 11, 1973 St Ives (NSW)

Campbell, Leslie Percy (NSW) b Oct. 14, 1902 Marrickville (NSW) d Aug. 19, 1970 Southport (Qld)

Campbell, Malcolm MacDonald (Qld) b Jan. 7, 1881 Ipswich (Qld) d Dec. 14, 1967 Ipswich (Qld)

Campbell, Ryan John (WAust) b Feb. 7, 1972 Osborne Park (WAust)

Campbell, Stoddart William Grylls (Vic) b Sept. 19, 1846 Melbourne (Vic) d Sept. 2, 1903 East Melbourne (Vic)

Camphin, William Joseph (NSW) b Nov. 13, 1867 Sydney (NSW) d Sept. 11, 1942 Quirindi (NSW)

Campling, Campbell Roy (NSW) b April 3, 1892 Burwood (NSW) d April 21, 1977 Greenwich (NSW)

Canning, Tamahau Karangatukituki (Cricket Academy) b April 7, 1977 Adelaide (S Aust)

Cannon, William Henry (Vic) b Sept. 11, 1871 Eaglehawk (Vic) d April 29, 1933 North Fitzroy (Vic)

Cantrell, Peter Edward (Qld) b Oct. 28, 1962 Gunnedah (NSW)

Cantwell, Hubert Richard (WAust) b Oct. 24, 1905 Warbleton, Sussex (England) d April 22, 1956 Esperance (WAust)

Capes, Peter Andrew (WAust) b Feb. 26, 1962 East Fremantle (WAust)

Carew, James (Qld) b Jan. 23, 1872 Pine Mountain (Qld) d Sept. 4, 1950 Kelvin Grove (Qld)

Carew, Patrick (Qld) b Sept. 8, 1875 Pine Mountain (Qld) d March 31, 1942 Queanbeyan (NSW)

Carew, Paul John (Qld & S Aust) b July 9, 1967 South Brisbane (Qld)

* Carkeek, William (Vic) b Oct. 17, 1878 Walhalla (Vic) d Feb. 20, 1937 Prahran (Vic)

* Carlson, Phillip Henry (Qld) b Aug. 8, 1951 Nundah (Qld)

Carlson, Victor Charles (WAust) b July 16, 1893 Adelaide (S Aust) d Feb. 23, 1974 Perth (WAust)

Carlton, Alfred Robert (Vic) b Nov. 13, 1867 Bacchus Marsh (Vic) d Sept. 10, 1941 Camberwell (Vic)

Carlton, John (Vic & Qld) b July 6, 1866 Bacchus Marsh (Vic) d Aug. 13, 1945 Parkville (Vic)

Carlton, Thomas Andrew (Vic & S Aust) b Dec. 8, 1890 Footscray (Vic) d Dec. 17, 1973 Brunswick (Vic)

Carlton, William (Vic) b May 22, 1876 Fitzroy (Vic) d Dec. 23, 1959 Parkville (Vic)

Carlyon, Norman Murdoch (Vic) b May 5, 1938 East Melbourne (Vic)

Carmichael, Ian Robert (S Aust) b Dec. 17, 1960 Hull, Yorkshire (England)

Carmody, Douglas Keith (NSW & WAust) b Feb. 16, 1919 Mosman (NSW) d Oct. 21, 1977 Concord (NSW)

Carney, Brian William (Tas) b June 2, 1931 Launceston (Tas)

Carr, Charles Seymour (Vic) b Nov. 22, 1849 (Jamaica) d March 30, 1921 East Melbourne (Vic)

Carr, William Niall (Vic) b June 1, 1976 Box Hill (Vic)

Carracher, Arthur James (S Aust) b July 7, 1867 Heywood (Vic) d Oct. 15, 1935 North Adelaide (S Aust)

Carragher, Edward John (S Aust) b June 1, 1891 Broken Hill (NSW) d Nov. 28, 1977 Broken Hill (NSW)

Carrigan, Aubrey Herbert (Qld) b Aug. 26, 1917 Zillmere (Qld)

Carroll, Edmund Louis (Vic) b Oct. 22, 1886 Albert Park (Vic) d June 6, 1959 Ormond (Vic)

Carroll, Eugene Vincent (Vic) b Jan. 17, 1885 South Melbourne (Vic) d Sept. 18, 1965 Elsternwick (Vic)

Carroll, Sidney Joseph (NSW) b Nov. 28, 1922 Willoughby (NSW) d Oct. 12, 1984 Willoughby (NSW)

Carroll, Thomas Davis (Tas) b Feb. 26, 1884 Hobart (Tas) d June 3, 1957 Hobart (Tas)

Carseldine, Lee Andrew (Qld) b Nov. 17, 1975 Nambour (Qld)

Carter, Alfred Snowden (Vic) b March 1, 1869 Kew (Vic) d June 7, 1920 Camberwell (Vic)

Carter, Edmund Sardinson (Vic) b Feb. 3, 1845 Malton, Yorkshire (England) d May 23, 1923 Scarborough, Yorkshire (England)

Carter, Edwin Lewis (Vic) b May 2, 1925 Caulfield (Vic)

* Carter, Hanson (NSW) b March 15, 1878 Halifax, Yorkshire (England) d June 8, 1948 Bellevue Hill (NSW)

Carter, Reginald Clarence (WAust) b March 1, 1888 Brunswick East (Vic) d July 16, 1970 Subiaco (WAust)

Carter, William Jack Sydney (NSW) b Dec. 7, 1907 Randwick (NSW) d Aug. 19, 1995 Penshurst (NSW)

Cartledge, Brian Lewis (Tas) b March 3, 1941 Smithton (Tas)

Cary, Sean Ross (WAust) b March 10, 1971 Subiaco (WAust)

Cass, George Rodney (Tas) b April 23, 1940 Overton, Yorkshire (Eng)

Cassell, Jerry Lee (Qld) b Jan. 12, 1975 Mona Vale (NSW)

Cassell, Robert James (Vic) b April 28, 1983 Melbourne (Vic)

Casson, Beau (WAust) b Dec. 7, 1982 Subiaco (WAust)

Castle, David James (Tas) b May 25, 1972 Launceston (Tas)

Catchlove, Walter Evered (S Aust) b Feb. 24, 1907 North Adelaide (S Aust) d April 12, 1997 Glen Osmond (S Aust)

Caterer, Thomas Ainslie (S Aust) b May 16, 1858 Woodville (S Aust) d Aug. 25, 1924 Walkerville (S Aust)

Causby, Barry Leon (S Aust) b Sept. 11, 1948 Adelaide (S Aust)

Causby, John Phillip (S Aust) b Oct. 27, 1942 Hindmarsh (S Aust)

Cavenagh, George (Vic) b June 16, 1836 Sydney (NSW) d Nov. 23, 1922 Albert Park (Vic)

Chadwick, Derek (WAust) b March 21, 1941 Busselton (WAust)

Chamberlain, Cornelius Thomas (S Aust) b c. 1882 (Ireland) d Nov. 14, 1943 Rose Park (S Aust)

Chamberlain, John Aloysius (WAust) b Aug. 29, 1884 Glanville (S Aust) d April 1941 Leabrook (S Aust)

Chamberlain, William Leonard (S Aust) b Jan. 15, 1889 Port Adelaide (S Aust) d March 21, 1956 Darlinghurst (NSW)

Chambers, John Lindsay (Vic) b Oct. 14, 1930 Geelong (Vic)

Chancellor, Frederick Edgar (Tas) b Aug. 28 1878 Hobart (Tas) d June 16, 1939 Hobart (Tas)

Chapman, Frederick Douglas (Vic) b March 21, 1901 Clifton Hill (Vic) d June 27, 1964 Northcote (Vic)

Chapman, George Arthur Northcote (NSW) b April 21, 1904 Chatswood (NSW) d May 22, 1986 Sydney (NSW)

Chapman, Henry William (Qld) b Jan. 7, 1866 Tredegar, Monmouthshire (Wales) d May 5, 1942 Herston (Qld)

Chapman, Lawrence Gordon (Qld) b June 25, 1928 Tingalpa (Qld)

Chapman, Ross Albert (NSW) b Oct. 22, 1952 New Lambton (NSW)

* Chappell, Gregory Stephen (S Aust & Qld) b Aug. 7, 1948 Unley (S Aust)

* Chappell, Ian Michael (S Aust) b Sept. 26, 1943 Unley (S Aust)

* Chappell, Trevor Martin (S Aust, WAust & NSW) b Oct. 12, 1952 Glenelg (S Aust)

Chardon, David Michael (NSW) b Dec. 8, 1951 Newtown (NSW)

Charlesworth, Lester (WAust) b Oct. 11, 1916 Kanowna (WAust) d Jan. 15, 1980 Perth (WAust)

Charlesworth, Richard Ian (WAust) b Dec. 6, 1952 Subiaco (WAust)

* Charlton, Percie Chater (NSW) b April 9, 1867 Surry Hills (NSW) d Sept. 30, 1954 Pymble (NSW)

Chee Quee, Richard (NSW) b Jan. 4, 1971 Camperdown (NSW)

Cheetham, Albert George (NSW) b Dec. 7, 1915 Ryde (NSW) d May 23, 1997 Sandringham (Vic)

Chegwyn, John William (NSW) b March 18, 1909 Botany (NSW) d May 26, 1992 Sydney (NSW)

Chillingworth, Garry Andrew (S Aust) b Jan. 23, 1970 Sutherland (NSW)

Chilvers, Hugh Cecil (NSW) b Oct. 26, 1902 Sawbridgeworth, Hertfordshire (England) d Dec. 1, 1994 Sydney (NSW)

Chinner, Hubert George Williams (S Aust) b Aug. 30, 1870 Brighton (S Aust) d June 12, 1953 Unley Park (S Aust)

* Chipperfield, Arthur Gordon (NSW) b Nov. 17, 1905 Ashfield (NSW) d July 29, 1987 Ryde (NSW)

Chittleborough, Henry Carew (S Aust) b April 14, 1861 Wallaroo (S Aust) d June 25, 1925 Malvern (S Aust)

Chivers, Alfred Percy (Vic) b Aug. 15, 1908 Templestowe (Vic) d July 11, 1997 Templestowe (Vic)

Christ, Charles Percival (Qld) b June 10, 1911 Paddington (Qld) d Jan. 22, 1998 Redcliffe (Qld)

Christensen, Robert Thomas (S Aust) b Oct. 31, 1959 Hindmarsh (S Aust)

Christian, Arthur Hugh (Vic & WAust) b Jan. 22, 1877 Richmond (Vic) d Sept. 8, 1950 Claremont (WAust)

Christy, Frederick Collier (Surrey) b Sept. 9, 1822 Asperfield, Kent (England) d Jan. 17, 1909 South Yarra (Vic)

* Christy, James Alexander Joseph (Qld) b Dec. 12, 1904 Pretoria (South Africa) d Feb. 1, 1971 Durban (South Africa)

Chyer, Darren Scott (S Aust) b July 28, 1966 Glenelg (S Aust)

Clark, Anthony Michael (NSW) b March 23, 1977 St Leonard's (NSW)

Clark, Donald Jack (Tas) b Jan. 19, 1914 Hobart (Tas) d Aug. 16, 1994 Hobart (Tas)

Clark, Henry Judge (WAust) b April 23, 1892 Sydney (NSW) d Feb. 8, 1973 Perth (WAust)

Clark, James Patrick (Qld) b March 14, 1871 (Qld) d June 6, 1941 Coolangatta (Qld)

Clark, John Lawrence (Qld & NSW) b Oct. 14, 1928 Paddington (NSW)

Clark, Michael Wayne (WAust) b March 31, 1978 Perth (WAust)

Clark, Stuart Rupert (NSW) b Sept. 28, 1975 Caringbah (NSW)

* Clark, Wayne Maxwell (WAust) b Sept. 19, 1953 Perth (WAust)

Clarke, Alfred Edward (NSW) b April 6, 1868 Surry Hills (NSW) d Sept. 16, 1940 Wellington (New Zealand)

Clarke, David Alexander (S Aust) b Jan. 25, 1970 Adelaide (S Aust)

Clarke, Gerard John (Vic) b Dec. 31, 1966 Malvern (Vic)

Clarke, Gother Robert Carlisle (NSW) b April 27, 1875 North Sydney (NSW) d Oct. 12, 1917 Zonnebeke (Belgium)

Clarke, Graham Cornelius (S Aust) b July 10, 1939 Laura (S Aust)

Clarke, John (NSW) birth and death details unknown

* Clarke, Michael John (NSW) b April 2, 1981 Liverpool (NSW)

Claxton, Norman (S Aust) b Nov. 2, 1877 North Adelaide (S Aust) d Dec. 5, 1951 North Adelaide (S Aust)

Claxton, William David Hambridge (S Aust) b June 2, 1857 Kensington (S Aust) d March 12, 1937 Glenelg (S Aust)

Clay, Ivor Thomas (Tas) b May 7, 1915 Bendigo (Vic) d Aug. 12, 1958 Essendon (Vic)

Clayton, Nicholas George (Tas) b March 11, 1826 Norfolk Plains (Tas) d April 23, 1867 Auckland (New Zealand)

Cleary, Edward Joseph (Vic) b April 18, 1913 Benalla (Vic) d April 6, 1985 Benalla (Vic)

Cleary, Mark Francis (S Aust) b July 19, 1980 Moorabbin (Vic)

Cleeve, James Oatley (NSW) b Feb. 14, 1864 Sydney (NSW) d Feb. 8, 1909 Moree (NSW)

Clem, Gordon Rex (Qld) b July 5, 1909 Milora (Qld) d March 3, 1970 Melbourne (Vic)

Clements, Peter John (S Aust) b Jan. 23, 1953 Glenelg (S Aust)

Clements, Shane Clifton (WAust) b June 28, 1958 Middle Swan (WAust) d April 22, 2001 Inglewood (WAust)

Clews, Mark Lindsay (NSW) b Jan. 13, 1952 Grange (S Aust)

Clifford, Peter Stanley (NSW & Qld) b Nov. 4, 1959 Bellingen (NSW)

Clingeleffer, Sean Geoffrey (Tas) b May 9, 1980 Hobart (Tas)

Clingly, Michael Thomas (S Aust) b April 18, 1932 Prospect (S Aust) d Aug. 16, 2004 Adelaide (S Aust)

Clough, Peter Michael (Tas & WAust) b Aug. 17, 1956 Sydney (NSW)

Clutterbuck, Stanley Herwin (S Aust) b May 27, 1888 Kapunda (S Aust) d Jan. 24, 1972 Adelaide (S Aust)

Coates, Joseph (NSW) b Nov. 13, 1844 Huddersfield, Yorkshire (England) d Sept. 9, 1896 Sydney (NSW)

Coats, James (Qld) b Feb. 26, 1914 Annerley (Qld) d June 8, 2002 Wynnum West (Qld)

Cobcroft, Leslie Thomas (NSW) b Feb. 12, 1867 Muswellbrook (NSW) d March 9, 1938 Wellington (New Zealand)

Cockburn, James Sydney David (Qld) b May 20, 1916 Maryborough (Qld) d Nov. 13, 1990 Herston (Qld)

Cockburn, William Frederick (Vic) b Nov. 28, 1916 Richmond (Vic) d July 16, 2004 Corowa (NSW)

Cody, Leslie Alwyn (NSW & Vic) b Oct. 11, 1889 Paddington (NSW) d Aug. 10, 1969 Toorak (Vic)

Cohen, Bertram Louis (Vic) b Sept. 25, 1892 London (England) d June 30, 1955 North Caulfield (Vic)

Cohen, Morton Barnett (NSW) b Sept. 19, 1913 Paddington (NSW) d Jan. 14, 1968 Vaucluse (NSW)

Colegrave, Mark David (Tas) b July 1, 1970 Hobart (Tas)

Colgan, Gregory (WAust) b Nov. 5, 1953 Subiaco (WAust)

* Colley, David John (NSW) b March 15, 1947 Mosman (NSW)

Colley, Timothy Peter Michael (S Aust) b July 10, 1935 Sydney (NSW)

Collins, Frank Henry Kenneth (S Aust) b Dec. 16, 1910 Queenstown (S Aust) d Jan 24, 2001 Penola (S Aust)

Collins, Frederick Bisset (Vic) b Feb. 25, 1881 Richmond (Vic) d Oct. 4, 1917 Ypres (Belgium)

* Collins, Herbert Leslie (NSW) b Jan. 21, 1888 Randwick (NSW) d May 28, 1959 Little Bay (NSW)

Collins, Ross Phillip (NSW) b Dec. 9, 1945 Paddington (NSW)

Collins, Vincent Aloysius (NSW) b Sept. 23, 1917 Newtown (NSW) d Oct. 30, 1989 Sunnybank (Qld)

Collins, William Anthony (Tas) b Dec. 9, 1837 Launceston (Tas) d Jan. 12, 1876 Launceston (Tas)

Colreavy, Bernard Xavier (NSW) b June 30, 1871 Dripstone (NSW) d Nov. 30, 1946 Dubbo (NSW)

Combes, Geoffrey Arthur (Tas) b May 19, 1913 Greymouth (New Zealand) d Feb. 4, 1997 Woodstock near Huonville (Tas)

Combes, Maxwell James (Tas) b July 29, 1911 Greymouth (New Zealand) d March 10, 1983 Longley (Tas)

* Coningham, Arthur (NSW & Qld) b July 14, 1863 South Melbourne (Vic) d June 13, 1939 Gladesville (NSW)

Connell, Thomas William (NSW) b March 4, 1869 Invercargill (New Zealand) death details unknown

* Connolly, Alan Norman (Vic) b June 29, 1939 Skipton (Vic)

Connor, Gerald O'Grady (WAust & Tas) b Sept. 15, 1932 Perth (WAust) d Sept. 5, 1993 Perth (WAust)

Considine, Bernard Thomas (Vic & Tas) b April 8, 1925 Ararat (Vic) d June 4, 1989 (Qld)

Conway, John (Vic) b Feb. 3, 1842 Fyansford (Vic) d Aug. 22, 1909 Frankston (Vic)

Cook, Bernard William (Qld) b March 15, 1879 Torquay, Devon (England) d March 15, 1944 Sherwood (Qld)

Cook, Bruce (NSW) b Oct. 24, 1914 Orange (NSW) d Jan. 2, 1981 Balgowlah (NSW)

Cook, Geoffrey Glover (Qld) b June 29, 1910 Chelmer (Qld) d Sept. 12, 1982 Chelmer (Qld)

Cook, Russell Frederick (Vic) b Sept. 23, 1947 South Melbourne (Vic)

* Cook, Simon Hewitt (Vic & NSW) b Jan. 29, 1972 Hastings (Vic)

Cooke, Colin John (Qld) b Nov. 21, 1947 Harrisville (Qld)

Cooley, Troy James (Tas) b Dec. 9, 1965 Launceston (Tas)

Coombe, Ephraim Henry (S Aust) b Aug. 26, 1858 Gawler (S Aust) d April 5, 1917 Semaphore (S Aust)

Coombe, Percy Howard (S Aust) b Jan. 7, 1880 Brompton (S Aust) d July 28, 1947 Prospect (S Aust)

Coombe, Thomas Melrose (WAust) b Dec. 3, 1873 Gladstone (S Aust) d July 22, 1959 London (England)

Cooper, Allan Ferguson (NSW) b March 18, 1916 Sydney (NSW) d Sept. 7, 1970 Concord (NSW)

* Cooper, Bransby Beauchamp (Vic) b March 15, 1844 Dacca (India) d Aug. 7, 1914 Geelong (Vic)

Cooper, Bryce Arnot (NSW) b Dec. 19, 1905 Lewisham (NSW) d May 19, 1995 Gordon (NSW)

Cooper, Duncan Elphinstone (Vic) b c. 1813 (India) d Nov. 22, 1904 Paddington, London (England)

Cooper, George Henry (Qld) b Feb. 15, 1907 Gympie (Qld) d Jan. 3, 2000 Mudgeeraba (Qld)

Cooper, John Richard (Qld) b July 11, 1922 Lilydale (Vic)

Cooper, Lewis Dale (Qld) b May 14, 1937 Mackay (Qld)

* Cooper, William Henry (Vic) b Sept. 11, 1849 Maidstone, Kent (England) d April 5, 1939 Malvern (Vic)

Cooper, William Osborne (S Aust) b Feb. 13, 1891 North Adelaide (S Aust) d June 28, 1930 Glenelg (S Aust)

Corbett, Troy Frederick (Vic) b Oct. 11, 1972 Ouyen (Vic)

Cordner, John Pruen (Vic) b March 20, 1929 Diamond Creek (Vic)

Cordner, Laurence Osmaston (Vic) b Feb. 7, 1911 Warrnambool (Vic) d July 11, 1992 Penshurst (Vic)

* Corling, Grahame Edward (NSW) b July 13, 1941 Newcastle (NSW)

Cormack, Geoffrey Fairhurst (Vic) b Feb. 26, 1929 Camberwell (Vic)

Cornelius, William John (Vic) b Feb. 17, 1915 Port Melbourne (Vic)

Corstorphin, Colin James (Vic) b July 20, 1954 Bairnsdale (Vic) d Sept. 4, 1998 Melbourne (Victoria)

Cosgrave, Bryan (Vic) b March 23, 1903 Clifton Hill (Vic) d Nov. 22, 1992 Melbourne (Vic)

Cosgrave, James (Vic) b March 16, 1932 Parkville (Vic)

Cosgrove, Mark James (S Aust) b June 14, 1984 Elizabeth (S Aust)

* Cosier, Gary John (Vic, S Aust & Qld) b April 25, 1953 Richmond (Vic)

Cossart, Charles Edward (Qld) b Sept. 2, 1885 Rosewood (Qld) d June 6, 1963 Boonah (Qld)

Costick, Samuel (Vic & NSW) b Jan. 1, 1836 Croydon, Surrey (England) d April 8, 1896 West Maitland (NSW)

* Cottam, John Thomas (NSW) b Sept. 5, 1867 Strawberry Hills (NSW) d Jan. 30, 1897 Coolgardie (WAust)

* Cotter, Albert (NSW) b Dec. 3, 1884 Sydney (NSW) d Oct. 31, 1917 Beersheba (Palestine)

Cotter, Denis Francis (Vic) b c. 1862 Fitzroy (Vic) d Nov. 18, 1905 North Fitzroy (Vic)

Cotton, Edward Kenneth (NSW) b Aug. 8, 1927 Paddington (NSW) d March 26, 2002 Kogarah (NSW)

Cotton, Harold Norman Jack (S Aust) b Dec. 3, 1914 Prospect (S Aust) d April 6, 1966 Malvern (S Aust)

Coulson, Craig Edward (WAust) b June 13, 1967 South Perth (WAust)

Coulstock, Richard (Vic) b c. 1823 Surrey (England) d Dec. 15, 1870 South Melbourne (Vic)

* Coulthard, George (Vic) b Aug. 1, 1856 Boroondara (Vic) d Oct. 22, 1883 Carlton (Vic)

Courtice, Brian Andrew (Qld) b March 30, 1961 South Brisbane (Qld)

Courtney, Nicholas Charles Palliser (Tas) b July 18, 1967 Launceston (Tas)

Coverdale, Miles Colquhoun (Tas) b Aug. 4, 1846 Richmond (Tas) d April 3, 1898 Hobart (Tas)

Cowan, Edward James McKenzie (NSW) b June 16, 1982 Paddington (NSW)

Cowan, Robert Francis (S Aust) b May 3, 1880 Angaston (S Aust) d Nov. 11, 1962 Neutral Bay (NSW)

Cowley, Ian Arthur (Tas) b March 20, 1937 Launceston (Tas)

Cowley, Owen William (NSW & Qld) b Dec. 14, 1868 Port Louis (Mauritius) d Feb. 27, 1922 Brisbane (Qld)

Cowley, Terence John (Tas) b July 17, 1928 Evandale (Tas)

Cowmeadow, Garry John (Tas) b Aug. 21, 1954 Huonville (Tas)

Cowper, David Raymond (Vic) b Jan. 25, 1939 Kew (Vic)

Cowper, George (NSW) b c. 1858 full birth and death details unknown

* Cowper, Robert Maskew (Vic & WAust) b Oct. 5, 1940 Kew (Vic)

Cox, Douglas Edward (Qld) b July 9, 1919 West End (Qld) d Jan. 9, 1982 Dakabin (Qld)

Cox, Jamie (Tas) b Oct. 15, 1969 Burnie (Tas)

Cox, John (Tas & Vic) b 1823 birth day and month unknown Norfolk Plains (Tas) full birth and death details unknown

Cox, Michael John (WAust) b April 26, 1957 Newcastle (NSW)

Cox, Peter John (Vic) b Jan. 13, 1954 Mildura (Vic)

Cox, Richard (Tas) b April 21, 1830 Hobart (Tas) d March 27, 1865 Fingal (Tas)

Coyle, Timothy Charles (Tas) b July 27, 1960 Launceston (Tas)

Coyne, Thomas Harold (WAust) b Oct. 12, 1873 Tornagullah (Vic) d April 8, 1955 Christchurch (New Zealand)

* Craig, Ian David (NSW) b June 12, 1935 Yass (NSW)

Craig, Reginald Jack (S Aust) b Aug. 3, 1916 North Adelaide (S Aust) d April 17, 1985 Walker Flat (S Aust)

Craig, Shawn Andrew Jacob (Vic) b June 23, 1973 Carlton (Vic)

Craigie, John Edwin (S Aust) b Aug. 25, 1866 Adelaide (S Aust) d Sept. 11, 1948 Gilberton (S Aust)

Crane, Frederick Robert (Qld) b July 10, 1942 Mullumbimby (NSW)

Cranney, Harold (NSW) b Oct. 23, 1886 Parramatta (NSW) d Jan. 29, 1971 North Rocks (NSW)

* Crawford, John Neville (S Aust) b Dec. 1, 1886 Cane Hill, Surrey (England) d May 2, 1963 Epsom, Surrey (England)

* Crawford, William Patrick Anthony (NSW) b Aug. 3, 1933 Dubbo (NSW)

Creevey, Brendan Neville (Qld) b Feb. 18, 1970 Charleville (Qld)

Cresswick, Ernest Albert (Qld) b Oct. 16, 1867 Newcastle (NSW) d Sept. 23, 1939 Waverley (NSW)

Creswick, Henry (Vic) b April 13, 1824 Sheffield, Yorkshire (England) d Oct. 24, 1892 Hawthorn (Vic)

Crippin, Ronald James (NSW) b April 23, 1947 Darlinghurst (NSW)

Cripps, Alan Edward (WAust) b Aug. 11, 1930 Lakemba (NSW)

Cristofani, Desmond Robert (NSW) b Nov. 14, 1920 Waverley (NSW) d Aug. 22, 2002 Fleet, Hampshire (England)

Crompton, Colin Neil (Vic) b Aug. 16, 1937 Dandenong (Vic) d Dec. 11, 2003 Malvern (Vic)

Crook, Andrew Richard (S Aust) b Oct. 14, 1980 Modbury (S Aust)

Crossan, Ernest Eric (NSW) b Nov. 3, 1914 Footscray (Vic)

Crosthwaite, Adam John (Vic) b Sept. 22, 1984 Melbourne (Vic)

Crouch, Edward Robert (Qld) b Jan. 11, 1873 Holborn, London, (England) d Aug. 8, 1962 South Brisbane (Qld)

Crouch, George Stanton (Qld) b Aug. 20, 1878 Strand, London, Middlesex (England) d Aug. 21, 1952 Indooroopilly (Qld)

Crow, Thomas Leslie (Vic) b Aug. 23, 1931 Hawthorn (Vic)

Crowden, Ian Bruce (Tas) b Feb. 22, 1933 Deloraine (Tas)

Crowder, Arthur Beaumont (Tas) b July 4, 1892 Sorell (Tas) d Feb. 16, 1964 Hobart (Tas)

* Crowe, Jeffrey John (S Aust) b Sept. 14, 1958 Cornwall Park, Auckland (New Zealand)

Cruse, Bruce Andrew (Tas) b April 26, 1967 Launceston (Tas)

Cuff, Alan Gordon (Tas) b June 7, 1908 Launceston (Tas) d April 23, 1995 Launceston (Tas)

Cuff, Leonard Albert (Tas) b March 28, 1866 Christchurch (New Zealand) d Oct. 9, 1954 Launceston (Tas)

Cuffe, John Alexander (NSW) b June 26, 1880 Dubbo (NSW) d May 16, 1931 Burton-on-Trent, Staffordshire (England)

Cullen, Daniel James (S Aust) b April 10, 1984 Woodville (S Aust)

Cullen, Daniel Robert (NSW) b April 27, 1889 Balmain (NSW) d July 21, 1971 Concord (NSW)

Cullen, Geoff Ian (WAust) b March 16, 1977 Claremont (WAust)

Cullen, William (NSW) b c. 1887 Wellington (New Zealand) d May 7, 1945 Double Bay (NSW)

Cullinan, Thomas (WAust) b (S Aust) full birth details unknown d July 31, 1907 Fremantle (WAust)

Cumberland, Charles Brownlow (Vic) b c. 1801 d Nov. 27, 1882 Leamington, Warwickshire (England)

Cumming, Kenneth Roy (WAust) b April 12, 1916 East Coolgardie (WAust) d Oct. 11, 1988 Perth (WAust)

Cummins, Frank Septimus (NSW) b Aug. 8, 1906 West Maitland (NSW) d April 27, 1966 North Sydney (NSW)

Cunningham, Graeme Timothy (Tas) b Jan. 25, 1975 Goulburn (NSW)

Cunningham, Kenneth George (S Aust) b July 26, 1939 Adelaide (S Aust)

Currie, Ernest William (Qld) b April 9, 1873 Dunedin (New Zealand) d Oct. 23, 1932 Little Bay (NSW)

Curtin, Barry George (S Aust) b June 30, 1951 Rose Park (S Aust)

Curtin, Paul (S Aust) b May 10, 1954 Rose Park (S Aust)

Curtin, Pearce William Edward (WAust) b Sept. 27, 1907 Boulder (WAust) d May 17, 1997 Canberra (ACT)

Curtin, Peter Donald (S Aust) b Sept. 22, 1949 Rose Park (S Aust)

Curtis, George Thomas (NSW) b Aug. 17, 1837 Sydney (NSW) d April 2, 1885 Darlinghurst (NSW)

Curtis, Louis David (S Aust) b Aug. 5, 1928 Loxton (S Aust)

Cush, Norman Lloyd (NSW) b Oct. 4, 1911 Glebe Point (NSW) d Jan. 22, 1983 Maroubra (NSW)

Cuthbert, Daniel Charles (Tas) b Feb. 2, 1846 Franklin (Tas) d July 6, 1912 Hobart (Tas)

* Dale, Adam Craig (Qld) b Dec. 30, 1968 Greensborough (Vic)

Daly, Anthony John (Tas) b July 25, 1969 Newcastle (NSW)

Daly, Thomas (Tas) b c. 1847 d Sept. 23, 1887 Inveresk (Tas)

Daniel, Jack (Vic) b Dec. 9, 1923 Leeds, Yorkshire (England) d Oct. 12, 2002 Tugan (Qld)

* Daniel, Wayne Wendell (WAust) b Jan. 16, 1956 Brereton Village, St Philip (Barbados)

Dansie, Hampton Neil (S Aust) b July 2, 1928 Nuriootpa (S Aust)

D'Arcy, D (NSW) birth and death details unknown

Darke, William Floyd (Vic) b July 24, 1846 Sydney (NSW) d Jan. 24, 1925 Elsternwick (Vic)

* Darling, Joseph (S Aust) b Nov. 21, 1870 Glen Osmond (S Aust) d Jan. 2, 1946 Hobart (Tas)

* Darling, Leonard Stuart (Vic) b Aug. 14, 1909 South Yarra (Vic) d June 24, 1992 Daw Park (S Aust)

* Darling, Warrick Maxwell (S Aust) b May 1, 1957 Waikerie (S Aust)

Davey, John Richard (S Aust) b Aug. 26, 1957 Bournemouth, Hampshire (England)

Davey, John Ryan (S Aust) b Sept. 20, 1913 Broken Hill (NSW) d Sept. 6, 1992 Unley (S Aust)

Davidson, Alan Andrew (Vic) b July 14, 1897 Brunswick (Vic) d Aug. 1, 1962 Ringwood (Vic)

* Davidson, Alan Keith (NSW) b June 14, 1929 Lisarow (NSW)

Davidson, Hugh Lavery (NSW) b May 17, 1907 South Yarra (Vic) d April 22, 1960 Wamberal (NSW)

Davidson, Thomas Rex (Tas) b July 30, 1927 Campbell Town (Tas)

Davie, Bert Joseph James (Tas & Vic) b May 2, 1899 Hobart (Tas) d June 3, 1979 Melbourne (Vic)

Davies, Christopher James (S Aust) b Nov. 15, 1978 Bedford Park (S Aust)

Davies, George Arthur (Vic) b March 19, 1892 Maindample (Vic) d Nov. 27, 1957 Essendon (Vic)

Davies, Geoffrey Robert (NSW) b July 22, 1946 Randwick (NSW)

Davies, Gerald Stanley (Tas) b Jan. 29, 1949 Cinderford, Gloucestershire (England)

Davies, John George (Tas) b Feb. 17, 1846 Melbourne (Vic) d Nov. 12, 1913 New Town (Tas)

Davies, Peter John (Vic) b Aug. 18, 1957 Melbourne (Vic)

Davis, Arthur Hugh (Tas) b Nov. 6, 1898 Launceston (Tas) d March 5, 1943 Camberwell (Vic)

Davis, Frank Alexander (Tas) b May 29, 1904 Launceston (Tas) d Sept. 12, 1973 Launceston (Tas)

Davis, Horace Hyman (NSW) b Feb. 1, 1889 Darlinghurst (NSW) d Feb. 4, 1960 Sydney (NSW)

* Davis, Ian Charles (NSW & Qld) b June 25, 1953 North Sydney (NSW)

Davis, Jonas J. (NSW) b May 12, 1859 Goulburn (NSW) d May 18, 1911 Waverley (NSW)

Davis, Neil Wilton (Tas) b Aug. 1, 1900 Launceston (Tas) d April 25, 1974 Evans Head (NSW)

Davis, Reginald Augur (Tas) b Oct. 22, 1892 Invermay (Tas) d July 11, 1957 Launceston (Tas)

* Davis, Simon Peter (Vic) b Nov. 8, 1959 Brighton (Vic)

* Davis, Winston Walter (Tas) b Sept. 18, 1958 Sion Hill, Kingstown (St Vincent)

Davison, Brian Fettes (Tas) b Dec. 21, 1946 Bulawayo (Southern Rhodesia)

Davison, John Michael (Vic & S Aust) b May 9, 1970 Campbell River, Vancouver Island, British Columbia (Canada)

Davison, Lindsay John (Vic) b Oct. 11, 1941 Malvern (Vic)

Davison, Rodney John (NSW) b June 26, 1969 Kogarah (NSW)

Dawes, Joseph Henry (Qld) b Aug. 29, 1970 Herston (Qld)

Dawson, David Graham (Tas) b March 7, 1982 Canberra (ACT)

Day, Arthur Charles (Vic) b Aug. 8, 1933 Sunshine (Vic)

Day, Herbert John (S Aust) b April 1, 1868 Bowden (S Aust) d Oct. 14, 1947 Hindmarsh (S Aust)

* De Courcy, James Harry (NSW) b April 18, 1927 Newcastle (NSW) d June 20, 2000 Newcastle (NSW)

De Gruchy, Henry William (Vic) b May 15, 1898 Sydney (NSW) d May 2, 1952 Parkville (Vic)

De Jong, Howard Keith (Qld) b Feb. 12, 1956 Mt Lavinia, Colombo (Ceylon)

De Winter, Allister John (Tas) b March 12, 1968 Launceston (Tas)

Dean, Archibald Herbert (Vic) b Oct. 3, 1885 Hawthorn (Vic) d Sept. 3, 1939 Norfolk Island (NSW)

Dean, Arthur Edgar (Vic) b July 23, 1931 Williamstown (Vic)

Dean, Oscar Hessel (NSW) b April 30, 1886 Windsor (NSW) d May 11, 1962 Windsor (NSW)

Deane, Norman Younger (NSW) b Aug. 29, 1875 Neutral Bay (NSW) d Sept. 30, 1950 Lindfield (NSW)

Deane, Sydney Leslie (NSW) b March 1, 1863 Sydney (NSW) d March 20, 1934 Brooklyn, New York (United States of America)

Deely, Patrick Joseph (Vic) b Feb. 18, 1864 North Melbourne (Vic) d Feb. 28, 1925 Brighton (Vic)

Deitz, Shane Alan (S Aust) b May 4, 1975 Bankstown (NSW)

Delaney, William (S Aust) b Jan. 17, 1866 Kapunda (S Aust) d Dec. 16, 1921 Port Augusta (S Aust)

* Dell, Anthony Ross (Qld) b Aug. 6, 1945 Lymington, Hampshire (England)

Dell, Christopher Ronald (Tas) b Oct. 27, 1960 Devonport (Tas)

Delves, Thomas Frederick (Vic) b Aug. 23, 1876 Carlton (Vic) d July 28, 1944 Heidelberg (Vic)

Delves, Walter Frederick (Vic) b Feb. 17, 1891 Brunswick (Vic) d May 27, 1955 Canterbury (Vic)

Dempsey, Darren Michael (S Aust) b Oct. 17, 1975 Mount Gambier (S Aust)

Dempster, Robert Alexander (Vic) b March 11, 1915 Hotham West (Vic) d April 2, 1974 Fitzroy (Vic)

Denton, Gerard John (Tas) b Aug. 7, 1975 Mt Isa (Qld)

Desmazeures, Pitre Cesar (Vic & S Aust) b Aug. 17, 1880 Collingwood (Vic) d Oct. 7, 1942 New Norfolk (Tas)

Deveney, Frank Barclay (Vic) b Aug. 16, 1910 Berwick (Vic) d Oct. 30, 1998 Melbourne (Vic)

Devenish-Meares, Frank (WAust & NSW) b April 25, 1873 Surry Hills (NSW) d July 4, 1952 Petersham (NSW)

Deverson, Charles Sydney (S Aust) b Nov. 2, 1905 Alberton (S Aust) d Feb. 2, 1945 Port Adelaide (S Aust)

Di Venuto, Michael James (Tas) b Dec. 12, 1973 Hobart (Tas)

Diamond, Austin (NSW) b July 10, 1874 Huddersfield, Yorkshire (England) d Aug. 5, 1966 Concord (NSW)

Dick, Alexander Williamson (WAust) b Nov. 30, 1922 Boulder (WAust)

Dick, Andrew M. (Vic) birth and death details unknown

Dick, Ian Robinson (WAust) b Aug. 30, 1926 Boulder (WAust)

Dick, William Allan (Vic) b Nov. 10, 1922 Newcastle (NSW) d March 27, 2004 Melbourne (Vic)

Dickson, George D. (NSW) birth and death details unknown

Dighton, Michael Gray (WAust & Tas) b July 24, 1976 Toowoomba (Qld)

Dillon, Marshall (Vic) b July 22, 1925 Ballarat (Vic) d Oct. 11, 1979 Beaumaris (Vic)

Dimattina, Michael Gerard David (Vic) b May 11, 1965 Malvern (Vic)

Diprose, Noel Vertigan (Tas) b March 5, 1922 Glenorchy (Tas)

Ditchburn, Albert James (WAust) b Aug. 24, 1908 Boulder (WAust) d March 7, 1964 Perth (WAust)

Dive, Percy William (NSW) b July 10, 1881 Paddington (NSW) d Sept. 17, 1965 Roseville (NSW)

Dixon, Joseph Black (Tas) b Sept. 26, 1836 Hobart (Tas) d March 6, 1882 Battery Point (Tas)

Dixon, Patrick Leslie (Qld) b Jan. 13, 1916 Eagle Junction (Qld) d Nov. 5, 1996 Goulburn (NSW)

Dixon, Troy James (Qld) b Dec. 22, 1969 Geelong (Vic)

Doble, Alan William (Vic) b Dec. 27, 1942 Glenhuntly (Vic)

Docker, Arthur Robert (NSW) b June 3, 1848 Thornthwaite (NSW) d April 8, 1929 Enfield, Middlesex (England)

Docker, Cyril Talbot (NSW) b March 3, 1884 Ryde (NSW) d March 26, 1975 Double Bay (NSW)

Docker, Ernest Brougham (NSW) b April 1, 1842 Thornthwaite (NSW) d Aug. 12, 1923 Elizabeth Bay (NSW)

Docker, Keith Brougham (NSW) b Sept. 1, 1888 Ryde (NSW) d May 16, 1977 Ashfield (NSW)

Docker, Phillip Wybergh (NSW) b April 8, 1886 Ryde (NSW) d Oct. 29, 1978 Concord (NSW)

Docking, Trevor William (Tas) b Dec. 22, 1952 Burnie (Tas)

Dodds, Norman (Tas) b Aug. 30, 1876 Hobart (Tas) d Dec. 15, 1916 Hobart (Tas)

* Dodemaide, Anthony Ian Christopher (Vic) b Oct. 5, 1963 Williamstown (Vic)

Doherty, Xavier John (Tas) b Nov. 22, 1982 Scottsdale (Tas)

Doig, Ronald Oldham (WAust) b July 10, 1909 Fremantle (WAust) d Sept. 17, 1932 Beaconsfield (WAust)

Dollery, Keith Robert (Qld & Tas) b Dec. 9, 1924 Cooroy (Qld)

Dolling, Charles Edward (S Aust) b Sept. 4, 1886 Wokurna (S Aust) d June 11, 1936 Adelaide (S Aust)

Dolman, Michael Charles (S Aust) b June 14, 1960 North Adelaide (S Aust)

Donahoo, Sydney John (Vic & Qld) b April 14, 1871 St Kilda (Vic) d Jan. 14, 1946 St Kilda (Vic)

Donaldson, John Stuart (S Aust) b April 14, 1950 Adelaide (S Aust)

Donaldson, William Peter James (NSW) b Oct. 26, 1923 Lilyfield (NSW) d Aug. 8, 1999 Sydney (NSW)

Done, Richard Phillip (NSW) b Aug. 5, 1955 Ryde (NSW)

* Donnan, Henry (NSW) b Nov. 12, 1864 Liverpool (NSW) d Aug. 13, 1956 Bexley (NSW)

Donnelly, James Louis (NSW) b June 24, 1906 Merimbula (NSW) d March 2, 1978 Koorawatha (NSW)

Doolan, Bruce Richard (Tas) b Sept. 9, 1947 Launceston (Tas)

* Dooland, Bruce (S Aust) b Nov. 1, 1923 Cowandilla (S Aust) d Sept. 8, 1980 Bedford Park (S Aust)

Dorey, Brett Raymond (WAust) b Oct. 3, 1977 East Fremantle (WAust)

Douglas, Adye (Tas) b May 31, 1815 Thorpe-next-Norwich (England) d April 10, 1906 Hobart (Tas)

Douglas, Alfred Jamieson (Tas) b Feb. 4, 1872 Newstead (Tas) d June 9, 1938 Malvern (Vic)

Douglas, John Raymond (Vic) b Oct. 24, 1951 East Brunswick (Vic)

Douglas, Osborne Henry (Tas) b March 14, 1880 Launceston (Tas) d April 24, 1918 Dernancourt, near Albert (France)

Dowling, Gerard Patrick (Vic) b Nov. 10, 1964 Preston (Vic)

Down, Granville James Stuart (S Aust) b May 24, 1883 Dubbo (NSW) d May 14, 1970 St Kilda (Vic)

Downes, Francis (NSW) b June 11, 1864 Redfern (NSW) d May 20, 1916 Little Bay (NSW)

Downey, Donnell Raymond (S Aust) b April 12, 1907 Parkside (S Aust) d Jan. 23, 1966 Adelaide (S Aust)

Downey, Joseph Aloysius (Qld) b Feb. 4, 1895 (Qld) d April 18, 1934 Kangaroo Point (Qld)

Downton, Andrew Graham (Tas) b July 17, 1977 Auburn (NSW)

Dowsley, Harcourt (Vic) b July 15, 1919 Essendon (Vic)

Doyle, Bryan Bernard John (Vic) b Oct. 20, 1968 Carlton (Vic)

Draney, John Davis Rodney (Qld) b May 10, 1927 Indooroopilly (Qld)

Drape, Isaac Selby (Vic & Qld) b May 13, 1864 Hotham (Vic) d Feb. 7, 1916 St Kilda (Vic)

Drennan, John (S Aust) b Nov. 13, 1932 West Croydon (S Aust)

Drew, Albert David (WAust) b Oct. 30, 1906 West Leederville (WAust) d Feb. 20, 1984 Shenton Park (WAust)

Drew, Charles Francis (S Aust) b April 24, 1888 Kooringa, now Burra (S Aust) d Feb. 19, 1960 Adelaide (S Aust)

Drew, James Leggat (Vic) b Jan. 20, 1872 Williamstown (Vic) d Jan. 22, 1944 Maryborough (Vic)

Drew, Richard (Vic) b Jan. 20, 1871 Creswick (Vic) death details unknown

Drew, Thomas Mitchell (S Aust) b June 9, 1875 Kooringa, now Burra (S Aust) d Jan. 9, 1928 Toowoomba (Qld)

Drewer, Richard Harris (S Aust) b June 12, 1946 Parkside (S Aust)

Drinnen, Peter John (Qld) b Oct. 5, 1967 Bundaberg (Qld)

Driscoll, Clarence Rheuben (Tas) b Sept. 4, 1895 Glebe (Tas) d May 1, 1948 Hobart (Tas)

Driscoll, Vernon Reginald (Tas) b April 11, 1891 Glebe (Tas) d March 19, 1967 Bellerive (Tas)

Driver, Richard (NSW) b Sept. 16, 1829 Cabramatta (NSW) d July 8, 1880 Moore Park (NSW)

Driver, Walter George (Vic & WAust) b Sept. 25, 1922 Glenhuntly (Vic) d Jan. 11, 1994 Mooloolooba (Qld)

Druery, William Lance (Qld) b May 14, 1927 Townsville (Qld) d Aug. 10, 1993 Carina (Qld)

Drysdale, John (Vic) b Aug. 1, 1862 Castlemaine (Vic) d Feb. 15, 1922 Kew (Vic)

Du Croz, Gervase Bedford (Tas & Vic) b c. 1830 (England) d Feb. 19, 1855 Launceston (Tas)

Ducker, John Robert (S Aust) b June 12, 1934 Prospect (S Aust)

Dudgeon, Keith Edward (Qld) b Sept. 5, 1946 Cairns (Qld)

Dudley, Walter John (Vic) b May 29, 1918 Carlton North (Vic) d April 5, 1978 Northcote (Vic)

* Duff, Reginald Alexander (NSW) b Aug. 17, 1878 Sydney (NSW) d Dec. 13, 1911 North Sydney (NSW)

Duff, Walter Scott (NSW) b April 22, 1876 Sydney (NSW) d Nov. 11, 1921 Sydney (NSW)

Duffy, Joseph Thomas (Vic) b c. 1860 Ballarat (Vic) d May 30, 1936 Ballarat (Vic)

Duffy, William Vincent (WAust) b July 8, 1866 Doutta Galla (Vic) d June 13, 1959 Subiaco (WAust)

Dufty, Ross (Tas) b Aug. 13, 1927 Bingara (NSW)

Dugan, Roger Wayne (S Aust) b Aug. 10, 1959 Broken Hill (NSW)

Duldig, Lance Desmond (S Aust) b Feb. 21, 1922 Eudunda (S Aust) d Sept. 14, 1998 Beaumont (SA)

Dulling, Philip (Tas) b May 5, 1909 Launceston (Tas) d Sept. 1, 1974 Launceston (Tas)

Dumaresq, Henry Rowland Gascoigne (Tas) b Feb. 28, 1839 Longford (Tas) d Oct. 31, 1924 Ulverstone (Tas)

Dummett, Arthur William (Vic) b Nov. 18, 1900 Clifton Hill (Vic) d June 4, 1968 Ivanhoe (Vic)

Dummett, William (NSW) b July 18, 1840 Sydney (NSW) d May 3, 1900 (NSW)

* Duncan, John Ross Frederick (Qld & Vic) b March 25, 1944 Herston (Qld)

Duncan, William (Qld) b Oct. 19, 1912 Brisbane (Qld) d July 27, 1943 South Brisbane (Qld)

Dunn, Martin Matthew Francis (Qld) b May 10, 1884 Maryborough (Qld) d Dec. 31, 1942 Woollahra (NSW)

Dunn, Wallace Peter (WAust) b Aug. 8, 1921 Westonia (WAust) d Feb. 1, 2004 Nedlands (WAust)

Dunstan, William John (WAust) b Dec. 4, 1878 Glen Osmond (S Aust) d April 11, 1955 Perth (WAust)

Dupain, Francois Henri (NSW) b Aug. 19, 1889 Ashfield (NSW) d Sept. 29, 1959 Burradoo (NSW)

Duperouzel, Bruce (WAust) b April 21, 1950 Northam (WAust)

Dwyer, Christopher (Vic) b c. 1879 Albury (NSW) d July 21, 1961 Kew (Vic)

Dwyer, Edmund Alfred (NSW) b Oct. 19, 1894 Mosman (NSW) d Sept. 10, 1975 Mosman (NSW)

Dwyer, Eric William (Tas) b June 15, 1917 St Helen's (Tas) d May 15, 1997 Canberra (ACT)

* Dyer, Gregory Charles (NSW) b March 16, 1959 Parramatta (NSW)

Dyer, Robert Henry (S Aust) b c. 1860 (England) d Aug. 31, 1950 Nailsworth (S Aust)

Dykes, James Andrew (Tas) b Nov. 15, 1971 Hobart (Tas)

* Dymock, Geoffrey (Qld) b July 21, 1945 Maryborough (Qld)

* Dyson, John (NSW) b June 11, 1954 Kogarah (NSW)

* Eady, Charles John (Tas) b Oct. 29, 1870 Hobart (Tas) d Dec. 20, 1945 Hobart (Tas)

Easton, Frank Alexander (NSW) b Feb. 19, 1910 Waterloo (NSW) d May 5, 1989 Sydney (NSW)

Easton, Robert Peter (Qld) b Oct. 21, 1936 Windsor (Qld)

* Eastwood, Kenneth Humphrey (Vic) b Nov. 23, 1935 Chatswood (NSW)

Eaton, Anthony Mark (S Aust) b June 11, 1953 Prospect (S Aust)

Eaton, George Melville (Vic) b Oct. 23, 1904 Durban (South Africa) d May 28, 1938 East Melbourne (Vic)

Eaton, Harry Ronald (NSW) b c. 1909 St Leonard's (NSW) d May 13, 1960 Castlecrag (NSW)

* Ebeling, Hans Irvine (Vic) b Jan. 1, 1905 Avoca (Vic) d Jan. 12, 1980 East Bentleigh (Vic)

Ebsworth, Norman (NSW) b Jan. 2, 1878 Sydney (NSW) d Nov. 19, 1949 Kirribilli (NSW)

Edmondson, Ben Matthew (WAust) b Sept. 28, 1978 Southport (Qld)

Edmondson, Henry Pudsey Dawson (WAust) b Nov. 25, 1872 Hobart (Tas) d Aug. 18, 1946 Perth (WAust)

Edwards, Alan Robert (WAust) b Dec. 24, 1921 Perth (WAust)

Edwards, Allen Crisp (S Aust) b Nov. 18, 1868 Brighton (S Aust) d Jan. 1, 1961 Adelaide (S Aust)

Edwards, Edmund Keane (WAust) b Jan. 6, 1910 Cottesloe (WAust) d Aug. 18, 1990 Cottesloe (WAust)

Edwards, Frederick Raymond (S Aust) b Feb. 28, 1908 Sydney (NSW) d April 27, 1982 St Leonards (NSW)

* Edwards, John Dunlop (Vic) b June 12, 1860 Prahran (Vic) d July 31, 1911 Hawksburn (Vic)

Edwards, John Neild (Vic) b Aug. 16, 1928 Ormond (Vic) d Dec. 29, 2002 Malvern (Vic)

* Edwards, Ross (WAust & NSW) b Dec. 1, 1942 Cottesloe (WAust)

* Edwards, Walter John (WAust) b Dec. 23, 1949 Subiaco (WAust)

Egan, Grahame Maxwell (Qld) b June 8, 1941 Armidale (NSW)

Egan, Thomas Charles Wills (NSW) b Oct. 5, 1906 Warren (NSW) d Nov. 29, 1979 Double Bay (NSW)

Egglestone, John Waterhouse (Vic) b July 7, 1847 Hobart (Tas) d Oct. 17, 1912 Malvern (Vic)

Eime, Andrew Barry (S Aust) b July 3, 1971 North Adelaide (S Aust)

Elliott, Edward Hudspith (Vic) b April 19, 1851 Sunderland, Durham (England) d March 19, 1885 North Carlton (Vic)

Elliott, Gideon (Vic) b April 17, 1828 Merstham, Surrey (England) d Feb. 15, 1869 Richmond (Vic)

* Elliott, Matthew Thomas Gray (Vic) b Sept. 28, 1971 Chelsea (Vic)

Elliott, Raymond Allister (Tas) b Jan. 1, 1918 New Norfolk (Tas) d Sept. 8, 1997 New Town (Tas)

Elliott, Thomas Henry (Tas) b March 22, 1879 Hobart (Tas) d Oct. 21, 1939 Launceston (Tas)

Ellis, David Leigh (Qld) b Jan. 2, 1951 Herston (Qld)

Ellis, Donald George (Tas) b Oct. 5, 1917 Launceston (Tas) d Sept. 4, 2001 Launceston (Tas)

Ellis, John Albert (Qld) b June 10, 1914 Spring Hill (Qld) d Oct. 17, 1994 Greenslopes (Qld)

Ellis, John Leslie (Vic) b May 9, 1890 Malvern (Vic) d July 26, 1974 Glen Iris (Vic)

Ellis, Leslie George (NSW) b March 2, 193 New Lambton (NSW)

Ellis, Matthew (Vic) b Feb. 3, 1870 Melbourn (Vic) d Nov. 19, 1940 Fitzroy (Vic)

Ellis, Percy Arthur (Vic) b May 10, 190 Abbotsford (Vic) d April 25, 1992 Lilydal (Vic)

Ellis, Reginald Newnham (Vic) b Feb. 22 1891 Randwick (NSW) d May 26, 195 Cheltenham (Vic)

Ellis, Reginald Sidney (S Aust) b Nov. 26 1917 Angaston (S Aust)

* Ellison, Richard Mark (Tas) b Sept. 21, 195 Willesborough, Kent (England)

Eltham, William Keith (Tas) b Oct. 10, 1886 Hobart (Tas) d Dec. 31, 1916 Lesboeufs (France)

Emerson, David Alan (Vic) b March 10, 1961 Malvern (Vic)

Emerson, Norman Leonard (Vic) b Oct. 26, 1939 Ararat (Vic)

* Emery, Philip Allen (NSW) b June 25, 1964 St Ives (NSW)

* Emery, Sidney Hand (NSW) b Oct. 16, 1885 Macdonaldtown (NSW) d Jan. 7, 1967 Petersham (NSW)

Emery, Victor Rupert (NSW) b Dec. 24, 1920 St Leonard's (NSW) d Feb. 14, 2005 Narrabeen (NSW)

Eneberg, Alfred (S Aust) b Nov. 30, 1928 Birkenhead (S Aust)

England, Ernest James (WAust & S Aust) b May 26, 1927 Bunbury (WAust)

Englefield, William (S Aust) b Oct. 6, 1917 Leichhardt (NSW) d June 3, 1988 Ryde (NSW)

Epstein, Jan (WAust) b Oct. 1, 1918 West Perth (WAust) d March 24, 1988 Melbourne (Vic)

Evan, Laurence William (S Aust) b Oct. 27, 1864 Adelaide (S Aust) d Aug. 12, 1894 North Adelaide (S Aust)

Evans, Arthur Ernest (S Aust) b July 12, 1871 East Adelaide (S Aust) d March 26, 1950 Bordertown (S Aust)

Evans, Charles F (Tas) birth and death details unknown

* Evans, Edwin (NSW) b March 26, 1849 Emu Plains (NSW) d July 2, 1921 Walgett (NSW)

Evans, George Nicholas (WAust) b Dec. 24, 1915 Boulder (WAust) d April 11, 1965 Hollywood (WAust)

Evans, Henry (Tas) b Aug. 6, 1846 Launceston (Tas) death details unknown

Evans, Richard (S Aust) b Sept. 9, 1867 Hindmarsh (S Aust) d Nov. 1, 1939 Hindmarsh (S Aust)

Evans, Royston Macauley (WAust) b Jan. 13, 1884 Semaphore (S Aust) d March 12, 1977 Perth (WAust)

Evans, Walter Allan (WAust) b Sept. 29, 1897 Gympie (Qld) d Jan. 15, 1955 Hollywood (WAust)

Evans, William Thomas (Qld) b April 9, 1876 Indooroopilly (Qld) d July 19, 1964 Woolloongabba (Qld)

Everett, Charles Samuel (NSW) b June 17, 1901 Marrickville (NSW) d Oct. 10, 1970 Concord (NSW)

Everett, Dudley Tabor (WAust) b March 9, 1912 Perth (WAust) d May 3, 1943 Ontario (Canada) on active service

Everett, James Seabrook (WAust) b July 20, 1884 Toodyay (WAust) d June 19, 1968 Nedlands (WAust)

Evers, Harold Albert (NSW & WAust) b Feb. 28, 1876 Newcastle (NSW) d Feb. 6, 1937 Perth (WAust)

Eyres, Gordon (WAust) b Dec. 20, 1912 Kalgoorlie (WAust) d Aug. 21, 2004 Peppermint Grove (WAust)

Facy, Ashley Cooper (Tas & Vic) b Jan. 26, 1886 Bellerive (Tas) d Dec. 2, 1954 Hobart (Tas)

Fagan, Arthur Mervyn (NSW) b April 24, 1931 birthplace unknown

Fairbairn, Clive Lindsay (Vic) b Aug. 25, 1919 Geelong (Vic)

* Fairfax, Alan George (NSW) b June 16, 1906 Summer Hill (NSW) d May 17, 1955 Kensington, London (England)

Fairweather, Robert John (NSW) b July 24, 1845 Pyrmont (NSW) d May 31, 1925 Waverley (NSW)

Faithfull, Henry Montague (NSW) b June 16, 1847 Springfield (NSW) d Oct. 22, 1908 Elizabeth Bay (NSW)

Fallowfield, Leslie John (NSW) b March 12, 1914 North Sydney (NSW) d May 29, 1999 North Ryde (NSW)

Fanning, Edward (Vic) b March 16, 1848 Sydney (NSW) d Nov. 30, 1917 St Kilda (Vic)

Farnsworth, Andrew William (NSW) b Jan. 14, 1887 Sydney (NSW) d Oct. 30, 1966 Waterfall (NSW)

Farquhar, Barclay Wallace (NSW) b Feb. 22, 1875 West Maitland (NSW) d Jan. 23, 1961 Queanbeyan (NSW)

Farquhar, John Kennedy (Qld) b Jan. 30, 1887 Home Hill (Qld) d July 31, 1977 Chermside (Qld)

Farrar, Frank Martindale (NSW) b March 29, 1893 Rylstone (NSW) d May 30, 1973 Waverley (NSW)

Farrell, Graeme Ian (Tas) b Nov. 2, 1947 Launceston (Tas)

Farrell, Graeme Stanley (S Aust) b Feb. 4, 1943 Norwood (S Aust)

Farrell, Michael Graeme (Tas) b Sept. 24, 1968 Melbourne (Vic)

Farrell, Steven James (Qld) b Feb. 6, 1980 Townsville (Qld)

Faulkner, Peter Ian (Tas) b April 18, 1960 Launceston (Tas)

Faull, Martin Peter (S Aust) b May 10, 1968 Darwin (NT)

Faunce, Thomas Bowman (Qld) b March 19, 1883 (Qld) d May 27, 1968 Greenslopes (Qld)

Favell, Alan Leslie (S Aust) b June 6, 1960 North Adelaide (S Aust)

* Favell, Leslie Ernest (S Aust) b Oct. 6, 1929 Rockdale (NSW) d June 14, 1987 Magill (S Aust)

Fennelly, Sidney James (Qld) b March 22, 1887 Sydney (NSW) d Aug. 25, 1964 Brighton (Qld)

Fenton, Arthur (Vic) b Feb. 27, 1870 Tarnagulla (Vic) d May 20, 1950 Melbourne (Vic)

Ferguson, Callum James (S Aust) b Nov. 21, 1984 North Adelaide (S Aust)

Ferguson, James Alexander (Tas) b Feb. 19, 1848 Launceston (Tas) d May 10, 1913 Brisbane (Qld)

Ferguson, Leslie Drummond (Vic) b Dec. 8, 1892 North Brighton (Vic) d Jan. 30, 1957 East Melbourne (Vic)

Ferrall, Raymond Alfred (Tas) b May 27, 1906 Launceston (Tas) d June 1, 2000 Launceston (Tas)

Ferries, Kenneth Ian (WAust) b May 7, 1936 Wyalkatchem (WAust)

* Ferris, John James (NSW & S Aust) b May 21, 1867 Sydney (NSW) d Nov. 17, 1900 Durban (South Africa)

Fett, Frederick (Qld) b May 2, 1886 Toowoomba (Qld) d Aug. 27, 1979 Woolloongabba (Qld)

Fewin, Henry (Qld) b Jan. 25, 1896 Townsville (Qld) d Aug. 25, 1980 Bongaree (Qld)

Fidock, Harold Edward (WAust) b Aug. 24, 1902 Adelaide (S Aust) d Feb. 9, 1986 Nedlands (WAust)

Field, William (Tas) b March 17, 1816 Port Dalrymple (Tas) d June 22, 1890 Bishopsbourne (Tas)

Fielke, Noel Robert (S Aust) b Dec. 23, 1966 Blackwood (S Aust)

Findlay, Algernon Percy (Tas) b March 17, 1892 Launceston (Tas) d Jan. 9, 1956 Launceston (Tas)

* Fingleton, John Henry Webb (NSW) b April 28, 1908 Waverley (NSW) d Nov. 22, 1981 St Leonards (NSW)

Fisher, Alexander (Qld) b March 14, 1908 Gatton (Qld) d Oct. 6, 1968 Maryborough (Qld)

Fisher, Arthur Donnelly Wentworth (NSW) b Dec. 14, 1882 Lavender Bay (NSW) d July 9, 1968 Neutral Bay (NSW)

Fisher, Barry (Qld) b Jan. 20, 1934 Brisbane (Qld) d April 6, 1980 Inverell (NSW)

Fisher, Harry Medcalf (S Aust) b May 28, 1899 North Adelaide (S Aust) d Oct. 14, 1982 South Launceston (Tas)

Fisher, William Thornton (Qld) b Aug. 31, 1865 Brisbane (Qld) d June 1, 1945 Herston (Qld)

Fitchett, Michael King (Vic) b Nov. 30, 1927 Hawthorn (Vic)

Fitness, Gavin Arthur James (Qld) b June 4, 1968 Maryborough (Qld)

Fitzgerald, David Andrew (WAust & S Aust) b Nov. 30, 1972 Osborne Park (WAust)

Fitzgerald, James (Qld) b Feb. 19, 1874 Surry Hills (NSW) d Aug. 20, 1950 Graceville (Qld)

Fitzmaurice, Desmond Michael John (Vic) b Oct. 16, 1917 Carlton (Vic) d Jan. 19, 1981 Prahran (Vic)

Fitzmaurice, Dudley James Anthony (Vic) b May 21, 1913 Carlton (Vic) d June 28, 2001 Frankston (Vic)

Fitzpatrick, Jack Herbert (NSW) b Sept. 18, 1911 Bankstown (NSW) d Jan. 23, 1999 Bankstown (NSW)

Fitzpatrick, John Milling (Vic) b June 26, 1889 Waverley (NSW) d Aug. 16, 1952 Coogee (NSW)

Fleay, Clarence William Edward James (WAust) b Dec. 27, 1886 Gilgering (WAust) d Aug. 6, 1955 Katanning (WAust)

* Fleetwood-Smith, Leslie O'Brien (Vic) b March 30, 1908 Stawell (Vic) d March 16, 1971 Fitzroy (Vic)

Flegler, Shawn Leonard (Qld) b March 23, 1972 Darwin (NT)

* Fleming, Damien William (Vic & S Aust) b April 24, 1970 Bentley (WAust)

Fletcher, John Henry (Qld) b Oct. 27, 1893 Brisbane (Qld)

Fletcher, John William (Qld) b Jan. 25, 1884 Woollahra (NSW) d March 13, 1965 South Brisbane (Qld)

Flint, Kerry Royce (Tas) b Sept. 17, 1946 Smithton (Tas)

Flockton, Raymond George (NSW) b March 14, 1930 Paddington (NSW)

* Flower, Andrew (S Aust) b April 28, 1968 Cape Town (South Africa)

Flynn, Brian James (Qld) b June 7, 1929 Darlinghurst (NSW) d Aug. 3, 1986 Vesty's Beach, Darwin (NT)

Flynn, John Paul (NSW) b June 29, 1890 Paddington (NSW) d May 28, 1952 Chatswood (NSW)

Foley, Geoffrey Ian (Qld) b Oct. 11, 1967 Jandowae (Qld)

Foley, Maurice Hinton (WAust) b Feb. 4, 1930 Perth (WAust)

Folkard, Bernard James (NSW) b May 17, 1878 Ryde (NSW) d Jan. 31, 1937 Leichhardt (NSW)

Fontaine, Frederick Ernest (Vic) b Dec. 14, 1912 Northcote (Vic) d Oct. 24, 1982 Greensborough (Vic)

Foot, Charles Francis (Vic) b Aug. 14, 1855 Brighton (Vic) d July 2, 1926 East Melbourne (Vic)

Foot, Henry Boorn (Vic) b Nov. 21, 1805 Romsey, Hampshire (England) d May 14, 1857 Brighton (Vic)

Ford, Douglas Allan (NSW) b Dec. 16, 1928 Maryville (NSW)

Forsaith, Geoffrey Milner (WAust) b Jan. 5, 1931 Perth (WAust)

Forssberg, Edward Ernest Brackley (NSW) b Dec. 10, 1894 Sydney (NSW) d May 23, 1953 Bondi (NSW)

Forster, William Robert (Tas) b March 1, 1884 Gateshead-on-Tyne, Durham (England) d Feb. 7, 1930 Richmond (Tas)

Foster, Michael Robert (Vic) b March 5, 1973 East Melbourne (Vic)

Foster, Norman Kelk (Qld) b Jan. 19, 1878 Brisbane (Qld) d March 15, 1960 Clayfield (Qld)

Foster, Thomas Henry (NSW) b Sept. 30, 1883 Glebe (NSW) d June 27, 1947 Leichhardt (NSW)

Fothergill, Desmond Hugh (Vic) b July 15, 1920 Northcote (Vic) d March 16, 1996 Melbourne (Vic)

Fowler, Edwin (Vic) b c. 1841 London (England) d May 31, 1909 St Kilda (Vic)

Fox, Albert Henry Newnham (Vic) b April 20, 1867 Battery Point (Tas) d Dec. 24, 1946 Brighton (Vic)

Fox, Norman Henry (NSW) b July 29, 1904 Longueville (NSW) d May 7, 1972 Castle Cove (NSW)

* Francis, Bruce Colin (NSW) b Feb. 18, 1948 Sydney (NSW)

Francis, Craig Lawrence (S Aust) b Nov. 25, 1966 North Adelaide (S Aust)

Francis, John Charles (Vic) b June 22, 1908 Hawthorn (Vic) d July 6, 2001 Camberwell (Vic)

Francis, Keith Raymond (NSW) b Nov. 14, 1933 Arncliffe (NSW)

Francis, Stanley George (WAust) b April 14, 1906 Geelong (Vic) d Jan. 25, 1994 Nedlands (WAust)

Francke, Fredrick Malcolm (Qld) b March 21, 1939 Mt Lavinia, Colombo (Ceylon)

Frankish, Ronald Richard (WAust) b Oct. 6, 1925 Perth (WAust)

Fraser, Neville Graham (Qld) b Sept. 28, 1930 Cleveland (Qld)

Fraser, Robert Alexander (S Aust) b Feb. 13, 1954 Parkside (S Aust)

Frazer, Ian Douglas (Vic) b Sept. 7, 1966 Lilydale (Vic)

Frederick, John (Vic) b Dec. 18, 1910 Armadale (Vic)

Free, Ernest Peardon (Tas) b Sept. 7, 1867 Rokeby (Tas) d July 5, 1946 Hobart (Tas)

Freedman, David Andrew (NSW) b June 19, 1964 Darlinghurst (NSW)

Freeman, Edward John (Tas) b Nov. 7, 1848 Hobart (Tas) d Aug. 11, 1905 Hobart (Tas)

* Freeman, Eric Walter (S Aust) b July 13, 1944 Largs Bay (S Aust)

Freeman, Harry Septimus (Vic & Qld) b June 11, 1860 Carlton (Vic) d Nov. 7, 1933 Brunswick (Vic)

Freeman, John Edward (Qld) b June 28, 1935 Nundah (Qld)

Freeman, Thomas Daniel (Tas) b June 13, 1894 Hobart (Tas) d June 19, 1965 Heidelberg (Vic)

Freemantle, Leslie Francis (Vic & WAust) b May 11, 1898 Canterbury (Vic) d June 6, 1963 Kew (Vic)

* Freer, Frederick Alfred William (Vic) b Dec. 4, 1915 North Carlton (Vic) d Nov. 2, 1998 Frankston (Vic)

Frei, Harald (Qld) b May 1, 1951 Nuremberg (Germany)

Frick, John (S Aust) b March 24, 1957 Medindie (S Aust)

Friend, Raymond Grattan (Tas) b April 11, 1898 Prahran (Vic) death details unknown

Frost, Albert Edgar (Tas) b March 19, 1878 Launceston (Tas) d Oct. 25, 1951 Launceston (Tas)

Frost, Allan Russell (S Aust) b Dec. 2, 1942 Adelaide (S Aust)

Frost, Sydney Robert (Tas) b Jan. 21, 1881 Launceston (Tas) d Dec. 19, 1952 Middle Park (Vic)

Fry, Herbert James (Vic) b Oct. 28, 1870 Morphett Vale (S Aust) d Jan. 19, 1953 Hawthorn (Vic)

Furlong, Ronald William (Vic) b May 16, 1936 Ballarat (Vic)

Furness, Arthur John (NSW) b Jan. 11, 1873 Sydney (NSW) d Oct. 31, 1948 Strathfield (NSW)

Gaggin, William Wakeham (Vic) b Nov. 23, 1847 County Cork (Ireland) d July 5, 1925 Elsternwick (Vic)

Gallagher, Ian Noel (Qld) b Nov. 20, 1950 Greenslopes (Qld)

Gallash, Ian (WAust) b June 17, 1936 Perth (WAust)

Galloway, Paul Warren (S Aust) b Sept. 14, 1943 North Sydney (NSW) d Aug. 20, 1996 Loxton (S Aust)

Gamble, Herbert Spencer (Vic & Qld) b March 2, 1903 Sunbury (Vic) d June 15, 1962 Shorncliffe (Qld)

Gandy, Michael George (Tas) b Aug. 28, 1944 Hobart (Tas)

* Gannon, John Bryant (WAust) b Feb. 8, 1947 Subiaco (WAust)

Gardiner, George Alan (WAust) b Nov. 27, 1914 Perth (WAust) d Oct. 17, 1989 Melbourne (Vic)

Gardiner, Grant Bruce (Vic) b Feb. 26, 1965 Melbourne (Vic)

Gardiner, Jack (Tas) b May 20, 1913 Hobart (Tas) d Sept. 11, 1976 Hobart (Tas)

Gardner, Charles Allan (Vic) b Oct. 28, 1908 Brighton East (Vic) d Dec. 9, 2001 Frankston (Vic)

Gardner, Roy (Vic) b Jan. 18, 1914 Hotham West (Vic) d April 2, 2004 Mount Eliza (Vic)

Garland, John George Morton (Vic) b Aug. 22, 1875 Hotham (Vic) d Feb. 23, 1938 Hawthorn (Vic)

Garlick, Paul Anthony (Vic) b Sept. 21, 1968 Sandringham (Vic)

Garnaut, Matthew Stuart (WAust) b Nov. 7, 1973 Subiaco (WAust)

* Garner, Joel (S Aust) b Dec. 16, 1952 Enterprise, Christ Church (Barbados)

Garnsey, George Leonard (NSW) b Feb. 10, 1881 Sydney (NSW) d April 18, 1951 Canberra (ACT)

* Garrett, Thomas William (NSW) b July 26, 1858 Wollongong (NSW) d Aug. 6, 1943 Warrawee (NSW)

Gartrell, Kevin Boyd (WAust) b March 4, 1936 Midland (WAust)

Gartrell, Robert Boyd (WAust & Tas) b March 9, 1962 Middle Swan (WAust)

Garwood, Rex Elvyn (Tas) b May 15, 1930 Hobart (Tas)

Gaskell, Mark Andrew (Qld) b Oct. 17, 1956 Herston (Qld)

Gatehouse, George Henry (Tas) b June 20, 1864 Sorell (Tas) d Jan. 25, 1947 Toorak (Vic)

Gatenby, David John (Tas) b Feb. 12, 1952 Launceston (Tas)

Gatenby, Lawrence Frank (Tas) b April 10, 1889 Epping Forest (Tas) d Jan. 14, 1917 Armentieres (France)

Gatenby, Peter Robert (Tas) b May 26, 1949 Launceston (Tas)

* Gaunt, Ronald Arthur (WAust & Vic) b Feb. 26, 1934 Yarloop (WAust)

Geary, Alfred (NSW) b Aug. 8, 1849 birthplace unknown d Oct. 14, 1911 Brisbane (Qld)

Gee, Daniel Albert (NSW) b Sept. 30, 1875 Sydney (NSW) d Jan. 16, 1947 Adelaide (S Aust)

Geeves, Brett (Tas) b June 13, 1982 Hobart (Tas)

Gehan, Rodney Arthur Howard (S Aust) b Nov. 12, 1942 Werribee (Vic) d Feb. 8, 2001 Hope Island (Qld)

* Gehrs, Donald Raeburn Algernon (S Aust) b Nov. 29, 1880 Port Victor (S Aust) d June 25, 1953 Kings Park (S Aust)

Geise, Gregory Gordon (NSW) b April 3, 1960 Wallsend (NSW)

Gentle, Steven Robert (S Aust) b May 30, 1955 Rose Park (S Aust)

George, Shane Peter (S Aust) b Oct. 20, 1970 Adelaide (S Aust)

Germaine, Lewis (Vic & WAust) b March 1, 1935 Glenhuntly (Vic) d April 8, 1992 Melbourne (Vic)

Geyer, Kevin James (NSW) b Oct. 11, 1973 Bathurst (NSW)

Gibaud, Henry Peter (Vic) b May 1, 1892 Carlton (Vic) d July 29, 1964 Fitzroy (Vic)

Gibbs, Charles H. (S Aust) b c. 1841 full birth and death details unknown

* Gibbs, Lancelot Richard (S Aust) b Sept. 29, 1934 Georgetown (British Guiana)

Giblin, Vincent Wanostrocht (Tas) b Nov. 13, 1817 Kingston upon Thames, Surrey (England) d May 15, 1884 Milsons Point (NSW)

Gibson, George (Tas) b 1827 birth day and month unknown Norfolk Plains (Tas) d Oct. 8, 1873 Sandy Bay (Tas)

Gibson, George Watson Hogg (Vic) b Jan. 16, 1828 Thakambau (Jamaica) d Sept. 5, 1910 Carlton (Vic)

Gibson, Gordon Galloway (Tas) b Nov. 1, 1908 Hobart (Tas) d July 7, 1967 Melbourne (Vic)

Gibson, Vincent Roy (S Aust) b May 14, 1916 Rose Park (S Aust) d Nov. 28, 1983 Neutral Bay (NSW)

* Giffen, George (S Aust) b March 27, 1859 Adelaide (S Aust) d Nov. 29, 1927 Parkside (S Aust)

* Giffen, Walter Frank (S Aust) b Sept. 21, 1861 Adelaide (S Aust) d June 28, 1949 North Unley (S Aust)

Gilbert, Ashley Stephen (Vic) b Nov. 26, 1971 Melbourne (Vic)

* Gilbert, David Robert (NSW & Tas) b Dec. 19, 1960 Darlinghurst (NSW)

Gilbert, Eddie (Qld) b 1904 birth day and month unknown Woodford (Qld) d Jan. 9, 1978 Wacol (Qld)

Gilbert, George Henry Bailey (NSW) b Sept. 7, 1829 Cheltenham, Gloucestershire (England) d June 16, 1906 Summer Hill (NSW)

Gilbourne, Robert James (S Aust) b July 16, 1943 Adelaide (S Aust)

* Gilchrist, Adam Craig (NSW & WAust) b Nov. 14, 1971 Bellingen (NSW)

Giles, Leonard George (S Aust) b June 17, 1921 Yorketown (S Aust) d Aug. 23, 1994 Glandore (S Aust)

Gill, Lynwood Laurence (Tas & Qld) b Nov. 19, 1891 Macquarie Plains (Tas) d Dec. 4, 1986 Pullenvale (Qld)

Giller, James Frederick (Vic) b May 1, 1870 Melbourne (Vic) d June 13, 1947 Albert Park (Vic)

* Gillespie, Jason Neil (S Aust) b April 19, 1975 Darlinghurst (NSW)

Gilmore, Francis Patrick John (NSW) b Sept. 12, 1909 Yass (NSW) d April 26, 1955 Camperdown (NSW)

* Gilmour, Gary John (NSW) b June 26, 1951 Waratah (NSW)

Gladigau, Peter Wayne (S Aust) b May 23, 1965 Whyalla (S Aust)

Glassock, Craig Anthony (NSW) b Nov. 29, 1973 Mona Vale (NSW)

* Gleeson, John William (NSW) b March 14, 1938 Kyogle (NSW)

Glew, Steven Adam (Cricket Academy) b March 11, 1977 Perth (WAust)

Glynn, William Thomas (Tas) b c. 1846 d June 18, 1895 Fitzroy (Vic)

Goddard, Henry (NSW) b Nov. 16, 1885 Sydney (NSW) d May 13, 1925 Maroubra (NSW)

Godfrey, Charles George (S Aust) b Nov. 17, 1860 Adelaide (S Aust) d March 27, 1940 Rose Park (S Aust)

Goffet, Gordon (NSW) b March 4, 1941 Speers Point (NSW) d July 29, 2004 Waratah (NSW)

Goggin, Peter John Thomas (Qld) b Oct. 30, 1965 Roma (Qld)

Gogler, Keith Geoffrey (S Aust) b May 1, 1923 Port Augusta (S Aust) d Aug. 24, 1983 Glenelg (S Aust)

Goldman, Albert Edward Arms (Qld) b Oct. 4, 1868 Wee Waa (NSW) d Jan. 30, 1937 Sydney (NSW)

Goldsmith, Louis (Vic) b Sept. 14, 1846 Melbourne (Vic) d Sept. 15, 1911 East Melbourne (Vic)

Gonnella, Peter (WAust) b Jan. 14, 1963 Canberra (ACT)

Good, Robert Norman Scott (WAust) b March 29, 1885 East Melbourne (Vic) d June 16, 1962 Camberwell (Vic)

Goode, Benjamin Ryall (S Aust) b Jan. 23, 1924 Port Lincoln (S Aust)

Gooden, Henry Alfred (S Aust) b Jan. 12, 1858 Adelaide (S Aust) d March 30, 1904 North Fitzroy (Vic)

Gooden, James Edward (S Aust) b Dec. 23, 1845 Brentford, Middlesex (England) d July 17, 1913 Norwood (S Aust)

Gooden, Norman Leslie (S Aust) b Dec. 27, 1889 Norwood (S Aust) d July 5, 1966 Unley Park (S Aust)

Goodfellow, James Edward (S Aust) b Aug. 21, 1850 Surrey (England) d July 22, 1924 Malvern (S Aust)

Goodman, Gary Weech (Tas & S Aust) b Dec. 6, 1953 Sydney (NSW)

Goodrick, Garnet Gordon (Tas) b Feb. 19, 1895 Franklin (Tas) d Jan. 26, 1929 South Melbourne (Vic)

Goodwin, Charles Geoffrey (Tas) b Feb. 12, 1923 Hobart (Tas) d Sept. 20, 1981 Fitzroy (Vic)

* Goodwin, Murray William (WAust) b Dec. 11, 1972 Salisbury (Southern Rhodesia)

Goodwin, Victor Henry Vallance (Qld) b Oct. 26, 1906 Newtown (NSW) d Sept. 22, 1957 Leichhardt (NSW)

Gooma, George Arlington (Qld) b June 25, 1918 Fortitude Valley (Qld) d Oct. 1, 1985 Greenslopes (Qld)

Gooneseena, Gamini (NSW) b Feb. 16, 1931 Mt Lavinia, Colombo (Ceylon)

Gordon, Charles Steward (Vic) b Sept. 8, 1849 Oakleaze, Gloucestershire (England) d March 24, 1930 Nottington, Dorset (England)

Gordon, Evan Shawn (NSW) b Sept. 26, 1960 Pinelands, Cape Town (South Africa)

Gordon, George Birnie (Vic) b Aug. 12, 1860 South Melbourne (Vic) d March 5, 1946 Rose Bay (NSW)

Gordon, George Hollinworth (NSW) b Sept. 20, 1846 New England District (NSW) d May 18, 1923 Darling Point (NSW)

Gordon, Trevor Fairburn (Tas) b Feb. 18, 1915 Hobart (Tas)

Gorman, Frederick Owen (NSW) b Feb. 15, 1843 Sydney (NSW) death details unknown

Gorringe, Harrison Reginald (WAust) b March 7, 1928 Carlisle (WAust)

Gorry, Charles Richard (NSW) b Sept. 18, 1878 Auckland (New Zealand) d Sept. 13, 1950 Petersham (NSW)

Goss, Edward Alfred (Vic) b Nov. 28, 1875 Richmond (Vic) d Sept. 1, 1955 Camberwell (Vic)

Gostelow, Reginald Edwin Potter (NSW) b July 26, 1900 Darlinghurst (NSW) d Aug. 2, 1984 Darling Point (NSW)

Gott, Douglas Lawrence (Vic) b June 30, 1950 Melbourne (Vic)

Gough, Francis Joseph (Qld) b July 26, 1898 Sandgate (Qld) d Jan. 30, 1980 Sandgate (Qld)

Gould, Fred Keen (S Aust) b Sept. 18, 1891 Hindmarsh (S Aust) d Feb. 15, 1954 Kingswood (S Aust)

Gould, John William (NSW) b Oct. 1, 1868 Sydney (NSW) d Dec. 4, 1908 Lewisham (NSW)

Gouly, Lionel (WAust) b Feb. 12, 1873 Woolloomooloo (NSW) d April 15, 1911 Perth (WAust)

Gourlay, Kenneth Garrett (Tas) b June 27, 1914 Hobart (Tas) d Jan. 28, 1999 Lenah Valley (Tas)

Govan, John Macmillan (Qld) b Dec. 30, 1914 Coorparoo (Qld) d July 20, 1996 South Brisbane (Qld)

Gow, Frederick Kingswood (NSW) b Dec. 18, 1882 Richmond (NSW) d Oct. 11, 1961 Randwick (NSW)

Grace, Brian James David (Qld) b Dec. 30, 1945 Herston (Qld)

Graf, Shaun Francis (Vic & WAust) b May 19, 1957 Somerville (Vic)

* Graham, Henry (Vic) b Nov. 22, 1870 Carlton (Vic) d Feb. 7, 1911 Dunedin (New Zealand)

Grangel, Horace Henry Eric (Vic) b Nov. 23, 1908 Burwood (NSW)

Grant, Bartholomew (Vic) b Aug. 13, 1876 St Kilda (Vic) death details unknown

Grant, Colin Spicer (S Aust) b June 22, 1927 Alberton (S Aust) d Sept. 3, 1998 Clare (S Aust)

Grant, John William (Vic) b Feb. 9, 1941 Essendon (Vic)

Grant, Norman Frederic (Qld) b Jan. 15, 1891 Sydney (NSW) d Sept. 17, 1966 Coorparoo (Qld)

Grant, Thomas Christopher (Vic) b Dec. 20, 1878 St Kilda (Vic) d c. 1934 Kurri Kurri (NSW)

* Graveney, Thomas William (Qld) b June 16, 1927 Riding Mill, Northumberland (England)

Gray, Arthur Thomas (NSW) b June 12, 1892 Glebe (NSW) d July 19, 1977 Glebe (NSW)

Gray, Cecil Douglas (S Aust) b April 28, 1902 Henley Beach (S Aust) d c. 1976

Gray, Geoffrey Thomas (Qld) b Aug. 27, 1943 Ipswich (Qld)

Greaves, William Henry (Vic) b c. 1830 (England) d Aug. 6, 1869 Warrnambool (Vic)

Green, Albert (S Aust) b Jan. 28, 1874 Medindie (S Aust) d c. 1913

Green, Braddon Clive (Vic) b Jan. 18, 1958 Benalla (Vic)

Green, Donald William (Vic) b Nov. 22, 1933 Canterbury (Vic) d Nov. 7, 1994 Sydney (NSW)

Green, Douglas Carling (Tas) b May 19, 1902 Hobart (Tas) d Nov. 28, 1990 Hobart (Tas)

Green, Jack Godfrey (Vic) b Oct. 4, 1921 Brighton (Vic)

Green, Randal James (NSW) b July 15, 1961 Hawthorn (Vic)

Gregg, Donald Malcolm (S Aust) b Sept. 17, 1924 Tumby Bay (S Aust)

Gregg, Norman McAlister (NSW) b March 7, 1892 Burwood (NSW) d July 27, 1966 Woollahra (NSW)

Gregory, Arthur Herbert (NSW) b July 7, 1861 Sydney (NSW) d Aug. 17, 1929 Chatswood (NSW)

Gregory, Charles Smith (NSW) b June 5, 1847 Wollongong (NSW) d April 5, 1935 Chatswood (NSW)

Gregory, Charles William (NSW) b Sept. 30, 1878 Randwick (NSW) d Nov. 14, 1910 Darlinghurst (NSW)

* Gregory, David William (NSW) b April 15, 1845 Fairy Meadow (NSW) d Aug. 4, 1919 Turramurra (NSW)

* Gregory, Edward James (NSW) b May 29, 1839 Waverley (NSW) d April 22, 1899 Randwick (NSW)

* Gregory, Edward Sydney (NSW) b April 14, 1870 Randwick (NSW) d Aug. 1, 1929 Randwick (NSW)

* Gregory, Jack Morrison (NSW) b Aug. 14, 1895 North Sydney (NSW) d Aug. 7, 1973 Bega (NSW)

* Gregory, Ross Gerald (Vic) b Feb. 28, 1916 Malvern (Vic) d June 10, 1942 in action over Ghafargon, Assam (India)

Grew, Ernest Sadler (Qld) b Aug. 11, 1867 Birmingham, Warwickshire (England) d Sept. 3, 1954 Brisbane (Qld)

Grieves, Kenneth John (NSW) b Aug. 27, 1925 Burwood (NSW) d Jan. 3, 1992 Rawtenstall, Lancashire (England)

Griffith, Adam Richard (Tas) b Feb. 11, 1978 Launceston (Tas)

Griffith, Harold Bickerton (Qld) b Oct. 10, 1879 Manly (NSW) d May 30, 1947 Herston (Qld)

Griffiths, Charles Samuel (Qld) b May 28, 1889 Townsville (Qld) d May 12, 1928 Rockhampton (Qld)

Griffiths, George Edward (NSW & S Aust) b April 9, 1938 Glebe (NSW)

Grigg, Henry Tattersall (WAust) b May 24, 1906 Fremantle (WAust) d July 9, 1991 Inglewood (WAust)

* Grimmett, Clarence Victor (Vic & S Aust) b Dec. 25, 1891 Caversham, Dunedin (New Zealand) d May 2, 1980 Kensington (S Aust)

Grinrod, Barton (Vic) b April 25, 1834 Liverpool , Lancashire (England) d May 23, 1895 Great Crosby, Lancashire (England)

Grosser, John William (NSW) b Aug. 29, 1942 Gunnedah (NSW)

* Groube, Thomas Underwood (Vic) b Sept. 2, 1857 New Plymounth, Taranaki (New Zealand) d Aug. 5, 1927 Hawthorn (Vic)

Grounds, William Thomas (NSW) b Jan. 14, 1878 Surry Hills (NSW) d July 21, 1950 Mortdale (NSW)

* Grout, Arthur Theodore Wallace (Qld) b March 30, 1927 Mackay (Qld) d Nov. 9, 1968 Spring Hill (Qld)

Grove, Percival Brian (S Aust) b Feb. 23, 1921 Adelaide (S Aust)

* Guest, Colin Ernest John (Vic & WAust) b Oct. 7, 1937 Melbourne (Vic)

Gulliver, Kenneth Charles (NSW) b Aug. 14, 1913 East Maitland (NSW) d June 11, 2001 Collaroy (NSW)

Gumley, William Dudgeon (Qld) b June 28, 1923 Bangalow (NSW) d Aug. 14, 1988 Redcliffe (Qld)

Gun, Lancelot Townsend (S Aust) b April 13, 1903 Port Adelaide (S Aust) d May 25, 1958 North Adelaide (S Aust)

Gunston, Edward Claude (Vic) b May 7, 1913 Brunswick (Vic) d Feb. 28, 1991 Melbourne (Vic)

Gunthorpe, Gilbert Dudley (Qld) b Aug. 9, 1910 Mt Morgan (Qld) d June 3, 1998 Casino (NSW)

Gurr, Gordon Caleb (S Aust) b Dec. 22, 1881 Hyde Park (S Aust) d Aug. 11, 1960 Loxton (S Aust)

Guthrie, Herbert France (Vic) b Sept. 29, 1902 Brisbane (Qld) d Jan. 26, 1951 Bellevue Hill (NSW)

Guttormsen, Maurice Stewart (Qld) b July 29, 1916 Coorpooroo (Qld) d Aug. 8, 1998 Redcliffe (Qld)

Guy, Richard Henry (NSW) b April 4, 1937 St Leonard's (NSW)

Gwynne, Leslie William (NSW) b Jan. 26, 1893 Sydney (NSW) d Oct. 25, 1962 Keith (S Aust)

Hack, Alfred Thomas (S Aust) b June 12, 1905 Glenelg (S Aust) d Feb. 4, 1933 Adelaide (S Aust)

Hack, Frederick Theodore (S Aust) b Aug. 24, 1877 Aldinga (S Aust) d April 10, 1939 Brisbane (Qld)

Hack, Norman Reginald (S Aust) b Feb. 25, 1907 Glenelg (S Aust) d Oct. 13, 1971 Keith (S Aust)

Hackett, James Victor (Qld) b Oct. 8, 1917 Perth (WAust) d Nov. 13, 2004 Wavell Heights (Qld)

Haddin, Bradley James (NSW) b Oct. 23, 1977 Cowra (NSW)

Haddrick, Alfred Page (Vic) b July 14, 1868 Adelaide (S Aust) d Feb. 15, 1939 Brisbane (Qld)

Haddrick, Ronald Norman (S Aust) b April 9, 1929 Glenelg (S Aust)

* Hadlee, Richard John (Tas) b July 3, 1951 St Albans, Christchurch (New Zealand)

Hagdorn, Kim John (WAust) b April 8, 1955 Subiaco (WAust)

Halbert, John Arno (S Aust) b Sept. 5, 1937 Hyde Park (S Aust)

Halcombe, Ronald Andrewes (S Aust & WAust) b March 19, 1906 Petersburg (S Aust) d Aug. 1, 1993 Geelong (Vic)

Haldane, Harry (S Aust) b July 13, 1865 Kent Town (S Aust) d Aug. 12, 1951 Ararat (Vic)

Hale, David John (Qld) b Nov. 11, 1941 Ashgrove (Qld)

Hale, Harold (Tas) b March 27, 1867 Perth (WAust) d Aug. 2, 1947 Melbourne (Vic)

Hall, Melmoth (Vic) b April 26, 1811 Horringer, Suffolk (England) d Oct. 4, 1885 Ashfield (NSW)

Hall, Richard (NSW) birth and death details unknown

* Hall, Wesley Winfield (Qld) b Sept. 12, 1937 Glebe Land, Station Hill, St Michael (Barbados)

Hallebone, Jeffrey (Vic) b Aug. 3, 1929 East Coburg (Vic)

* Hamence, Ronald Arthur (S Aust) b Nov. 25, 1915 Hindmarsh (S Aust)

Hamilton, James (Tas) b May 16, 1843 birthplace unknown d July 28, 1881 Launceston (Tas)

Hamilton, Thomas Ferrier (Vic) b March 31, 1821 Cairnhill, Aberdeenshire (Scotland) d Aug. 7, 1905 St Kilda (Vic)

Hammelmann, Andrew John (Qld) b May 9, 1966 Corinda (Qld)

Hammersley, William Josiah Sumner (Vic) b Sept. 26, 1828 Ash, Surrey (England) d Nov. 15, 1886 Fitzroy (Vic)

Hammond, Ashley James (S Aust) b Sept. 27, 1969 Burnside (S Aust)

Hammond, Charles Pitt (Tas) b Aug. 31, 1868 Hobart (Tas) d Sept. 25, 1955 Hollywood, California (United States of America)

* Hammond, Jeffrey Roy (S Aust) b April 19, 1950 North Adelaide (S Aust)

* Hampshire, John Harry (Tas) b Feb. 10, 1941 Thurnscoe, Yorkshire (England)

Hand, Walter Charles (NSW) b July 22, 1847 Richmond, Surrey (England) death details unknown

Handrickan, Anthony John (S Aust) b Jan. 6, 1959 Largs Bay (S Aust)

Hanify, Cecil Page (Qld) b Aug. 1, 1887 Brisbane (Qld) d Oct. 28, 1964 Manly (Qld)

Hanlin, David Walter (NSW) b Dec. 8, 1928 Chester (England) d June 6, 2001 Chester (England)

Hanna, Brian Leslie (WAust) b Oct. 7, 1946 Katanning (WAust)

Hansen, Christopher Desmond Petrie (Qld) b May 20, 1912 Childers (Qld)

Hanson, Frederick James (Tas) b April 7, 1872 Hobart (Tas) d Sept. 24, 1917 Moonah (Tas)

Hanson, Leopole Harry (S Aust) b Sept. 27, 1883 Woodville (S Aust) d April 27, 1952 Kingscote (S Aust)

Hantke, Theodore Charles Muncaster (WAust) b Aug. 1, 1875 Blinman (S Aust) d May 22, 1931 South Perth (WAust)

Harburn, Colin Malcolm (WAust) b Sept. 3, 1938 Subiaco (WAust)

Hardcastle, Gilbert William (Qld) b Feb. 26, 1910 Bowen Hills (Qld) d Feb. 14, 2000 Currimundi (Qld)

Hardie, Archibald Edward (WAust) b April 14, 1892 Warrnambool (Vic) d March 31, 1976 Nedlands (WAust)

Hardie, J. (Australians) birth and death details unknown

Hargrave, Christopher George (Tas) b Aug. 31, 1951 Kiverton, Yorkshire (England)

Harms, Christopher Louis (S Aust) b April 21, 1956 Albury (NSW)

Harper, Barry James (Tas) b Oct. 30, 1938 Launceston (Tas) d April 28, 2003 Launceston (Tas)

Harper, Charles Walter (WAust) b Jan. 27, 1880 Guildford (WAust) d July 1, 1956 South Perth (WAust)

Harper, Laurence Damien (Vic) b Dec. 10, 1970 Deniliquin (NSW)

Harper, Peter Quinton (Vic) b Dec. 11, 1977 Burwood (Vic)

Harris, Daniel Joseph (S Aust) b Dec. 31, 1979 Adelaide (S Aust)

Harris, David (S Aust) b Dec. 19, 1930 Alberton (S Aust)

Harris, David Andrew (Vic) b March 17, 1966 Newtown (Vic)

Harris, Douglas James (WAust) b Dec. 20, 1962 Subiaco (WAust)

Harris, Errol John (Tas) b May 2, 1963 Cairns (Qld)

Harris, Gordon William (S Aust) b Dec. 11, 1897 Alberton (S Aust) d June 30, 1974 Kensington Park (S Aust)

Harris, Henry Vere Poulett (Tas & WAust) b April 22, 1865 Hobart (Tas) d March 7, 1933 Perth (WAust)

Harris, Kim Phillip (S Aust) b Jan. 24, 1952 North Adelaide (S Aust)

Harris, Ryan James (S Aust) b Oct. 11, 1979 Nowra (NSW)

Harrison, Colin William (S Aust) b May 10, 1928 West Croydon (S Aust)

Harrison, Ernest Weedon (Tas) b July 22, 1874 Campbell Town (Tas) d Nov. 14, 1968 New Norfolk (Tas)

Harrity, Mark Andrew (S Aust) b March 9, 1974 Semaphore (S Aust)

Harrold, Hubert Walton (WAust) b March 9, 1898 East Perth (WAust) d April 14, 1968 Hollywood (WAust)

Harrop, Brett David (Vic) b Dec. 11, 1979 Frankston (Vic)

* Harry, John (Vic) b Aug. 1, 1857 Ballarat (Vic) d Oct. 27, 1919 Surrey Hills (Vic)

Harry, Rex Alexander (Vic) b Oct. 19, 1936 Melbourne (Vic)

Hart, Harold William (Vic) b Jan. 4, 1889 Fitzroy South (Vic) d Jan. 2, 1953 Yarraville (Vic)

Hart, Trevor Herbert (Vic) b Nov. 18, 1935 Morwell (Vic)

Harten, James Thomas (Qld) b Nov. 11, 1924 Brisbane (Qld) d Sept. 11, 2001 Everton Hills (Qld)

* Hartigan, Michael Joseph (NSW & Qld) b Dec. 12, 1879 Chatswood (NSW) d June 7, 1958 Brisbane (Qld)

Hartigan, Thomas Joseph (NSW) b Dec. 8, 1877 Chatswood (NSW) d May 2, 1963 Mosman (NSW)

* Hartkopf, Albert Ernest Victor (Vic) b Dec. 28, 1889 South Fitzroy (Vic) d May 20, 1968 Kew (Vic)

Hartley, Christopher Desmond (Qld) b May 24, 1982 Nambour (Qld)

Harvey, Clarence Edgar (Vic & Qld) b March 17, 1921 Newcastle (NSW)

Harvey, Ernest (WAust) b Dec. 14, 1880 Redfern (NSW) d Oct. 19, 1923 Perth (WAust)

Harvey, George Graham (NSW) b May 7, 1885 Mudgee (NSW) death details unknown

Harvey, Ian Joseph (Vic) b April 10, 1972 Wonthaggi (Vic)

Harvey, Kade Murray (WAust) b Oct. 7, 1975 Subiaco (WAust)

* Harvey, Mervyn Roye (Vic) b April 29, 1918 Broken Hill (NSW) d March 18, 1995 Footscray (Vic)

Harvey, Raymond (Vic) b Jan. 3, 1926 Sydney (NSW)

* Harvey, Robert Neil (Vic & NSW) b Oct. 8, 1928 Fitzroy (Vic)

Harvey, Ronald Mason (NSW) b Oct. 26, 1933 Newcastle (NSW)

Harwood, Shane Michael (Vic) b March 1, 1974 Ballarat (Vic)

* Hassett, Arthur Lindsay (Vic) b Aug. 28, 1913 Geelong (Vic) d June 16, 1993 Batehaven (NSW)

Hassett, Richard Joseph (Vic) b Sept. 7, 1909 Geelong (Vic)

Hastings, Edward Percival (Vic) b June 16, 1849 (England) d May 31, 1905 Brighton East (Vic)

Hastings, Thomas James (Vic) b Jan. 16, 1865 Melbourne (Vic) d June 14, 1938 North Brighton (Vic)

Hatton, Mark Aaron (Tas) b Jan. 24, 1974 Waverley (NSW)

* Hauritz, Nathan Michael (Qld) b Oct. 18, 1981 Wondai (Qld)

* Hawke, Neil James Napier (WAust, S Aust & Tas) b June 27, 1939 Cheltenham (S Aust) d Dec. 25, 2000 Adelaide (S Aust)

Hawkins, George William (Vic) b Dec. 7, 1908 Brunswick (Vic) d July 20, 1979 Chiltern (Vic)

Hawson, Edgar Stanley (Tas) b July 25, 1878 Hobart (Tas) d Sept. 29, 1946 Hobart (Tas)

Hawson, Reginald James (Tas) b Sept. 2, 1880 Hobart (Tas) d Feb. 20, 1928 Hobart (Tas)

Hay, Henry (S Aust) b March 30, 1874 Adelaide (S Aust) d May 16, 1960 Adelaide (S Aust)

* Hayden, Matthew Lawrence (Qld) b Oct. 29, 1971 Kingaroy (Qld)

Hayes, William Bede (Qld) b Oct. 16, 1883 Surry Hills (NSW) d Nov. 5, 1926 Corinda (Qld)

Haymes, Frederick George (Tas) b April 5, 1849 Launceston (Tas) d March 12, 1928 Lakes Entrance (Vic)

Hayne, Greg John (NSW) b Oct. 2, 1971 Moree (NSW)

Haysman, Michael Donald (S Aust) b April 22, 1961 North Adelaide (S Aust)

Hayward, Charles Waterfield (S Aust) b June 6, 1867 Norwood (S Aust) d Feb. 2, 1934 North Adelaide (S Aust)

Haywood, Martin Thomas (NSW) b Oct. 7, 1969 Tamworth (NSW)

* Hazlitt, Gervys Rignold (Vic & NSW) b Sept. 4, 1888 Enfield (NSW) d Oct. 30, 1915 Parramatta (NSW)

Head, Lindsay Hudson (S Aust) b Sept. 16, 1935 North Adelaide (S Aust)

Headlam, Eustace Slade (Tas) b May 20, 1892 Bothwell (Tas) d May 25, 1958 Launceston (Tas)

Headlam, Felix Emerson (Tas) b June 20, 1897 Bothwell (Tas) d Oct. 5, 1965 Bowral (NSW)

Heairfield, Herbert Venters (S Aust) b Feb. 28, 1907 Adelaide (S Aust)

Heal, Aaron Keith (WAust) b March 13, 1983 Armadale (WAust)

Healy, Edwin Francis (Vic) b Sept. 26, 1909 Hawthorn (Vic) d June 14, 1995 Camberwell (Vic)

Healy, Eric Nicholas (WAust) b Nov. 5, 1888 Elizabeth Bay (NSW) d Oct. 9, 1954 Cottesloe (WAust)

Healy, Gerald Edward James (Vic) b March 26, 1885 Prahran (Vic) d July 12, 1946 Armadale (Vic)

* Healy, Ian Andrew (Qld) b April 30, 1964 Spring Hill (Qld)

Healy, John Joseph (Vic) b June 23, 1851 Burra (S Aust) d May 17, 1916 East Melbourne (Vic)

Healy, Kenneth James (Qld) b Oct. 15, 1967 South Brisbane (Qld)

Heath, Henry Francis Trafford (S Aust) b Dec. 19, 1885 Kadina (S Aust) d July 9, 1967 Edinburgh (Scotland)

Heath, Jamie Matthew (NSW) b April 25, 1977 Belmont (NSW)

Heather, Edward Drinkall (Vic) b Oct. 6, 1848 Marylebone, London (England) d July 10, 1935 South Melbourne (Vic)

Heather, Percival Jackson (Vic) b Oct. 6, 1882 Emerald Hill (Vic) d June 29, 1956 Melbourne (Vic)

Hefferan, Francis Urban (Qld) b May 25, 1901 Bowen (Qld) d Sept. 21, 1974 Tweed Heads (NSW)

Heffernan, Ray Leslie (Tas) b Oct. 13, 1935 Hobart (Tas)

Heindrichs, Adolphos Heinrich Julius Carl (WAust) b April 28, 1883 (Germany) d June 24, 1967 Adelaide (S Aust)

Henderson, Frank (NSW) b June 1, 1908 Wickham (NSW) d Dec. 6, 1954 Heidelberg (Vic)

Hendricks, Michael (NSW & S Aust) b Dec. 12, 1942 Corrimal (NSW)

Hendrie, Charles Richard (Vic) b July 5, 1886 Richmond (Vic) death details unknown

* Hendry, Hunter Scott Thomas Laurie (NSW & Vic) b May 24, 1895 Woollahra (NSW) d Dec. 16, 1988 Rose Bay (NSW)

Hennah, Walter Henry (WAust) b March 16, 1880 Ballarat (Vic) d Aug. 13, 1946 Perth (WAust)

Henri, Harry James Tepapa (Tas) b July 27, 1865 Tauranga (New Zealand) d Feb. 5, 1947 Lindisfarne (Tas)

Henry, Albert (Qld) b c. 1880 Boonah (Qld) d March 13, 1909 Yarrabah (Qld)

Henry, Donald McKenzie (S Aust) b June 24, 1885 Parkside (S Aust) d July 31, 1973 Felixstow (S Aust)

Henschell, Allan Brett (Qld) b June 6, 1961 Dalby (Qld)

Henty, Philip Guy (Tas) b Feb. 4, 1883 Pakenham (Vic) d Oct. 21, 1949 Hobart (Tas)

Henty, William (Tas) b Sept. 23, 1808 West Tarring, Sussex (England) d July 11, 1881 Hove, Sussex (England)

Hepburn, Thomas Robert (Vic) b Dec. 20, 1839 Collingwood (Vic) d April 22, 1921 St Kilda (Vic)

Herbert, Henry James (WAust) b April 24, 1895 Fremantle (WAust) d Nov. 21, 1957 Claremont (WAust)

Herbert, Morgan Uriah (WAust) b Aug. 4, 1918 Albany (WAust) d June 15, 2000 Duncraig (WAust)

Herbert, Peter Jeffrey (S Aust) b Jan. 8, 1947 Adelaide (S Aust)

Herman, Richard John (Vic) b July 31, 1967 Melbourne (Vic)

Herring, Llewellyn Lloyd (WAust) b April 3, 1871 Clunes (Vic) d Aug. 5, 1922 Fremantle (WAust)

Herring, Robert Wolseley (Vic) b June 8, 1898 Maryborough (Vic) d Oct. 8, 1964 Melbourne (Vic)

Hervey, Matthew (Vic) b Jan. 27, 1820 Glasgow, Lanarkshire (Scotland) d Dec. 1, 1874 Turnbull Plains (Vic)

Herzberg, Steven (WAust & Tas) b May 25, 1967 Carshalton, Surrey (England)

Hetherington, Henry Francisco (Vic) b Sept. 3, 1874 West Melbourne (Vic) d July 11, 1950 Malvern (Vic)

Hewer, William Albert (S Aust) b May 7, 1877 Goodwood (S Aust) d June 2, 1948 Wayville (S Aust)

Hewett, Ian Stephen Louis (Vic) b Jan. 24, 1976 East Melbourne (Vic)

Hewitt, Albert Hedley Vickers (Qld) b Jan. 21, 1866 Nowra (NSW) d July 11, 1947 Brisbane (Qld)

Hewitt, Richard Child (NSW) b Feb. 13, 1844 Beverley, Yorkshire (England) d March 21, 1920 Granville (NSW)

Hewson, Robert Henry (WAust) b Aug. 4, 1893 Carlton (Vic) d Oct. 21, 1972 Melbourne (Vic)

* Hibbert, Paul Anthony (Vic) b July 23, 1952 Brunswick (Vic)

* Hick, Graeme Ashley (Qld) b May 23, 1966 Salisbury (Rhodesia)

Hickey, Denis Jon (Vic & S Aust) b Dec. 31, 1964 Mooroopna (Vic)

Hickson, Robert Newburgh (NSW) b May 2, 1884 Newcastle (NSW) d June 21, 1963 Armidale (NSW)

Hiddleston, Hugh Charles Stewart (NSW) b c. 1855 full birth details unknown d May 14, 1934 Coolgardie (WAust)

Hide, Jesse Bollard (S Aust) b March 12, 1857 Eastbourne, Sussex (England) d March 19, 1924 Edinburgh (Scotland)

Hiern, Barry Neil (S Aust) b Aug. 8, 1951 North Adelaide (S Aust)

Hiern, Ross Noel (S Aust) b Aug. 2, 1922 Parkside (S Aust) d Aug. 21, 1999 Morphettville (S Aust)

Higgins, Benjamin Hugh (S Aust) b March 8, 1972 Rose Park (S Aust)

Higgins, Henry James Roy (Qld) b Jan. 27, 1900 Rosalie (Qld) d Feb. 24, 1990 Chermside (Qld)

Higgins, James (Qld) b Nov. 14, 1874 Ormiston (Qld) d Nov. 24, 1957 Sandgate (Qld)

* Higgs, James Donald (Vic) b July 11, 1950 Kyabram (Vic)

Higgs, Mark Anthony (NSW & S Aust) b June 30, 1976 Queanbeyan (NSW)

* Hilditch, Andrew Mark Jefferson (NSW & S Aust) b May 20, 1956 North Adelaide (S Aust)

Hill, Arthur (S Aust) b May 28, 1871 Adelaide (S Aust) d June 22, 1936 Glenelg (S Aust)

* Hill, Clement (S Aust) b March 18, 1877 Hindmarsh (S Aust) d Sept. 5, 1945 Parkville (Vic)

Hill, Clement John (NSW) b July 2, 1904 Beryl (NSW) d May 21, 1988 Belmont (NSW)

Hill, Henry John (S Aust) b July 7, 1878 Adelaide (S Aust) d Oct. 30, 1906 Kensington Park (S Aust)

* Hill, John Charles (Vic) b June 25, 1923 Murrumbeena (Vic) d Aug. 11, 1974 Caulfield (Vic)

Hill, John Gerard (Qld) b Nov. 11, 1956 Waratah (NSW)

Hill, Kenneth Michael (NSW) b Jan. 26, 1945 Merewether (NSW)

Hill, Leon Trevor (S Aust & Qld) b Feb. 28, 1936 West Croydon (S Aust)

Hill, Leslie Roy (S Aust) b April 27, 1884 Adelaide (S Aust) d Dec. 15, 1952 North Adelaide (S Aust)

Hill, Mark Anthony (Tas) b July 27, 1964 Perth (WAust)

Hill, Percy (S Aust) b July 4, 1868 Kent Town (S Aust) d July 24, 1950 Adelaide (S Aust)

Hill, Peter Distin (S Aust) b Jan. 28, 1923 North Adelaide (S Aust) d Oct. 3, 2002 Adelaide (S Aust)

Hill, Roland James (S Aust) b Oct. 18, 1868 Parkside (S Aust) d Jan. 10, 1929 Glenelg (S Aust)

Hill, Stanley (S Aust & NSW) b Aug. 22, 1885 Adelaide (S Aust) d May 10, 1970 Englefield Green, Surrey (England)

Hill, Wayne Douglas (WAust) b Dec. 5, 1953 Subiaco (WAust)

Hill-Smith, Wyndham (WAust) b Feb. 16, 1909 Angaston (S Aust) d Oct. 25, 1990 Angaston (S Aust)

Hilliard, Henry (NSW) b Nov. 7, 1826 Sydney (NSW) d March 19, 1914 Willoughby (NSW)

Hills, Dene Fleetwood (Tas) b Aug. 27, 1970 Wynyard (Tas)

Hird, Sydney Francis (NSW) b Jan. 7, 1910 Balmain (NSW) d Dec. 20, 1980 Bloemfontein (South Africa)

Hird, William (Tas) b Sept. 23, 1921 Stanley, Durham (England)

Hiscock, Ernest John (S Aust) b April 9, 1868 Penrice (S Aust) d Dec. 16, 1894 Alberton (S Aust)

Hitchcock, Oswould Charles (Qld) b Sept. 9, 1859 Greenhill, Shoalhaven (NSW) d July 13, 1948 Brisbane (Qld)

Hitchcock, Robert Alan (S Aust) b May 14, 1938 North Adelaide (S Aust)

* Hoare, Desmond Edward (WAust) b Oct. 19, 1934 Perth (WAust)

Hoare, William (Qld) b Oct. 23, 1868 Brisbane (Qld) d Dec. 16, 1954 Salt Lake City, Utah (USA)

Hodge, Bradley John (Vic) b Dec. 29, 1974 Sandringham (Vic)

Hodge, Malcolm Gordon Fergurson (S Aust) b Aug. 28, 1934 Adelaide (S Aust)

* Hodges, John Robart (Vic) b Aug. 11, 1855 Knightsbridge (London) death details unknown

Hodgetts, Bruce Frederick (Tas) b Jan. 25, 1947 Burnie (Tas)

Hodgkinson, John Ernest (NSW) b Feb. 7, 1873 Surry Hills (NSW) d Nov. 19, 1939 Burwood (NSW)

Hodgson, Robert William (Tas) b Feb. 22, 1973 Launceston (Tas)

* Hogan, Tom George (WAust) b Sept. 23, 1956 Merredin (WAust)

Hogg, Geoffrey Charles Huxtable (NSW) b Sept. 28, 1909 Goulburn (NSW) d Aug. 14, 1959 Coorparoo (Qld)

* Hogg, George Bradley (WAust) b Feb. 6, 1971 Narrogin (WAust)

Hogg, James Edgar Phipps (NSW & Qld) b Oct. 16, 1906 Goulburn (NSW) d Dec. 2, 1975 West Ryde (NSW)

* Hogg, Rodney Malcolm (S Aust & Vic) b March 5, 1951 Richmond (Vic)

Hogg, Thomas (Combined XIII) b March 12, 1845 Hobart (Tas) d July 13, 1890 Trevallyn (Tas)

Hogue, Thomas Herbert (NSW & WAust) b Oct. 5, 1877 Wickham (NSW) d May 6, 1956 Nedlands (WAust)

Hogue, Wallace White (WAust) b Dec. 9, 1879 Wickham (NSW) d June 1, 1946 Cook's Hill (NSW)

* Hohns, Trevor Victor (Qld) b Jan. 23, 1954 Nundah (Qld)

* Holding, Michael Anthony (Tas) b Feb. 16, 1954 Half Way Tree, Kingston (Jamaica)

Holdsworth, Wayne John (NSW) b Oct. 5, 1968 Paddington (NSW)

* Hole, Graeme Blake (NSW & S Aust) b Jan. 6, 1931 Concord West (NSW) d Feb. 14, 1990 Kensington Gardens (S Aust)

* Holland, Robert George (NSW) b Oct. 19, 1946 Camperdown (NSW)

Holman, Raymond Sidney (S Aust) b Sept. 17, 1919 Largs Bay (S Aust) d Sept. 19, 1989 Woodville South (S Aust)

Holten, Charles Valentine (Vic) b Sept. 15, 1927 Brighton (Vic)

Holton, Leslie George (S Aust) b March 13, 1903 Carlton (Vic) d Feb. 1, 1956 Hawthorn (Vic)

Holyman, Josef Michael (Tas) b June 10, 1970 Launceston (Tas)

Homburg, Robert Otto (S Aust) b Jan. 31, 1876 Norwood (S Aust) d Oct. 21, 1948 Medindie (S Aust)

Hone, Brian William (S Aust) b July 1, 1907 Semaphore (S Aust) d May 28, 1978 Paris (France)

Hone, Garton Maxwell (S Aust) b Feb. 21, 1901 Morphett Vale (S Aust) d May 28, 1991 Myrtle Bank (S Aust)

Honeybone, George Alfred (Vic) b April 2, 1875 London (England) d Nov. 1, 1956 Ashburton (Vic)

Honour, Victor Gerald (Qld) b Oct. 25, 1910 Bierton, Buckinghamshire (England) d Jan. 3, 2001 Brookfield (Qld)

Hook, Benjamin James (S Aust) b March 5, 1973 Kingswood (S Aust)

Hooker, John Edward Halford (NSW) b March 6, 1898 Summer Hill (NSW) d Feb. 12, 1982 Winmalee (NSW)

* Hookes, David William (S Aust) b May 3, 1955 Mile End (S Aust) d Jan. 19, 2004 Prahran (Vic)

Hookey, Scott Gregory (NSW & Tas) b Feb. 10, 1967 Sydney (NSW)

Hooper, Kerry (Tas) b June 9, 1942 Launceston (Tas)

Hooper, Victor Leonard (Tas) b April 23, 1905 Mt Stuart (Tas) d Sept. 3, 1990 New Town (Tas)

Hope, Adam (Vic) b c. 1834 (England) d Oct. 9, 1916 East Melbourne (Vic)

Hopes, James Redfern (Qld) b Oct. 24, 1978 Townsville (Qld)

* Hopkins, Albert John Young (NSW) b May 3, 1874 Young (NSW) d April 25, 1931 North Sydney (NSW)

Hopkins, Isaac (Vic) b Nov. 9, 1870 Collingwood (Vic) d Oct. 25, 1913 Richmond (Vic)

Hopkinson, Samuel Good (Vic) b Oct. 1, 1825 Thorne, Yorkshire (England) d June 26, 1887 South Melbourne (Vic)

Horan, James Francis (Vic) b June 8, 1880 Fitzroy (Vic) d Nov. 1, 1945 Malvern (Vic)

Horan, Thomas Ignatius Bernard (Vic) b April 7, 1886 Fitzroy (Vic) d May 26, 1952 East Camberwell (Vic)

* Horan, Thomas Patrick (Vic) b March 8, 1854 Midleton, County Cork (Ireland) d April 16, 1916 Malvern (Vic)

* Hordern, Herbert Vivian (NSW) b Feb. 10, 1883 North Sydney (NSW) d June 17, 1938 Darlinghurst (NSW)

Horley, John Rasalle (S Aust) b Jan. 23, 1936 Medindie (S Aust)

* Hornibrook, Percival Mitchell (Qld) b July 27, 1899 Obi Obi (Qld) d Aug. 25, 1976 Spring Hill (Qld)

Horrocks, William John (WAust) b June 18, 1905 Warrington, Lancashire (England) d Nov. 15, 1985 Parkdale (Vic)

Horsell, Jack Aymat James (S Aust) b July 12, 1914 Stepney (S Aust) d April 20, 1985 Sydney (NSW)

Horsfield, Gordon Cameron (NSW) b March 24, 1913 Balmain (NSW) d Aug. 25, 1982 Mosman (NSW)

Horsley, Daniel, Anthony (NSW) b July 20, 1972 Sydney (NSW)

Horsnell, Kenneth George (S Aust) b Sept. 3, 1933 Joslin (S Aust)

Horton, Arnell Stanley (Tas) b Sept. 21, 1892 Burnie (Tas) d Sept. 15, 1987 Newstead (Tas)

Hosie, Robert (Vic) b Sept. 8, 1858 Collingwood (Vic) d Sept. 29, 1932 Richmond (Vic)

Hosking, Peter Mowat (Vic) b Sept. 30, 1932 Fairfield (Vic)

Hoskings, Arthur G. W. (WAust) b c. 1872 d Sept. 2, 1919 Dunella, New Jersey (United States of America)

Hotchin, Mortimer Douglas (Vic) b May 20, 1889 Prahran (Vic) d June 21, 1958 East Melbourne (Vic)

Hotham, Augustus Thomas (Vic) b c. 1817 (christened Jan. 25) Denningston, Suffolk (England) d Dec. 24, 1896 Tunbridge Wells, Kent (England)

Hourn, David William (NSW) b Sept. 9, 1949 Bondi (NSW)

House, Graham Warwick Charles (WAust & S Aust) b Sept. 4, 1950 Busselton (WAust)

Houston, Richard Shinnock (Vic) b June 30, 1863 Brighton (Vic) d Nov. 27, 1921 Williamstown (Vic)

Howard, Craig (Vic) b April 8, 1974 Lilydale (Vic)

Howard, Harry Cecil (WAust) b June 30, 1885 Adelaide (S Aust) d Sept. 18, 1960 Perth (WAust)

Howard, Leonard Easther (S Aust) b April 18, 1886 Adelaide (S Aust) d Aug. 14, 1945 Prospect (S Aust)

Howard, Roy (Vic) b Nov. 15, 1922 Terang (Vic)

Howard, Stephen John (Tas) b Feb. 7, 1949 Launceston (Tas)

Howard, Thomas Harris (NSW) b May 2, 1877 Sydney (NSW) d Oct. 6, 1965 Randwick (NSW)

Howe, John Sidney (Tas) b Dec. 27, 1868 Kotree (India) d July 29, 1939 Neutral Bay (NSW)

Howell, George (NSW) b June 9, 1822 Sydney (NSW) d Nov. 18, 1890 Sydney (NSW)

Howell, William Hunter (NSW) b Jan. 12, 1902 Penrith (NSW) d Jan. 23, 1987 Penrith (NSW)

* Howell, William Peter (NSW) b Dec. 29, 1869 Penrith (NSW) d July 14, 1940 Castlereagh (NSW)

Howlett, John Thomas (Vic) b April 8, 1868 North Melbourne (Vic) d June 15, 1931 East Melbourne (Vic)

Howson, Herbert (Vic) b Aug. 11, 1872 Newstead (Vic) d May 8, 1948 Murrumbeena (Vic)

Hubbard, Edward Francis (Qld) b June 27, 1906 Brisbane (Qld) d Oct. 1, 1969 Herston (Qld)

Hubble, James Merrick (WAust) b Aug. 12, 1942 Beaconsfield (WAust)

Huddleston, John (Vic) b Nov. 25, 1837 Nottingham, Nottinghamshire (England) d July 29, 1904 Brunswick (Vic)

Hudson, Graeme Charles (Tas) b June 16, 1930 Wynyard (Tas) d Sept. 23, 1974 Launceston (Tas)

Hudson, John Lambert (Tas) b July 23, 1882 Launceston (Tas) d March 16, 1961 Hobart (Tas)

Hughes, David Paul (Tas) b April 13, 1947 Newton-le-Willows, Lancashire (England)

Hughes, Glenn Arthur (Tas) b Nov. 23, 1959 Goomalling (WAust)

Hughes, Graeme Christopher (NSW) b Dec. 6, 1955 Stanmore (NSW)

* Hughes, Kimberley John (WAust) b Jan. 26, 1954 Margaret River (WAust)

* Hughes, Mervyn Gregory (Vic) b Nov. 23, 1961 Euroa (Vic)

Hughes, Walter Cecil (WAust) b Aug. 13, 1882 Adelaide (S Aust) d Aug. 16, 1917 Perth (WAust)

Hughson, Desmond George (Qld) b May 27, 1941 Herston (Qld)

Hugo, Victor (S Aust) b Nov. 25, 1877 Adelaide (S Aust) d April 8, 1930 Malvern (S Aust)

Hume, Andrew Ernest (NSW) b Feb. 5, 1869 Redfern (NSW) d June 22, 1912 London (England)

Humphreys, Anthony John Rolph (Tas) b June 9, 1971 Launceston (Tas)

Humphreys, John (NSW) birth and death details unknown

Hunt, Horace Charles (Vic) b July 15, 1907 Stawell (Vic) d Oct. 15, 1984 Melbourne (Vic)

* Hunt, William Alfred (NSW) b Aug. 26, 1908 Balmain (NSW) d Dec. 30, 1983 Balmain (NSW)

Huntington, Ian Ross (Vic) b Oct. 18, 1931 Coburg (Vic)

Hurburgh, Clifton Maurice (Tas) b Jan. 15, 1917 Hobart (Tas)

Hurn, Brian Morgan (S Aust) b March 4, 1939 Angaston (S Aust)

* Hurst, Alan George (Vic) b July 15, 1950 Altona (Vic)

* Hurwood, Alexander (Qld) b June 17, 1902 Kangaroo Point (Qld) d Sept. 26, 1982 Coffs Harbour (NSW)

Hussey, David John (Vic) b July 15, 1977 Morley (WAust)

Hussey, Michael Edward Killeen (WAust) b May 27, 1975 Morley (WAust)

Hussey, Percival Leitch (WAust) b June 23, 1869 Perth (WAust) d May 13, 1944 Adelaide (S Aust)

Hutcheon, Ernest Henry (Qld) b June 17, 1889 Toowoomba (Qld) d June 9, 1937 Brisbane (Qld)

Hutcheon, John Silvester (Qld) b April 5, 1882 Warwick (Qld) d June 18, 1957 Albion Heights (Qld)

Hutchison, Paul James (S Aust & Tas) b Feb. 17, 1968 Glen Innes (NSW)

Hutton, Ernest Hamilton (Vic & Qld) b March 29, 1867 Mt Rouse (Vic) d July 12, 1929 Ascot (Qld)

Hutton, Henry George (S Aust) b Aug. 26, 1878 Masterton (New Zealand) d Aug. 13, 1968 Norwood (S Aust)

Hutton, Maurice Percy (S Aust) b March 21, 1903 Parkside (S Aust) d Feb. 20, 1940 Ararat (Vic)

Hutton, Mervyn Douglas (S Aust) b Aug. 24, 1911 Port Augusta (S Aust) d Sept. 28, 1988 Melbourne (Vic)

Hutton, Norman Harvey (S Aust) b Aug. 10, 1911 Unley (S Aust) d Aug. 27, 1965 Fullarton (S Aust)

Hutton, William Frederick Percy (S Aust) b Oct. 2, 1876 Mintaro (S Aust) d Oct. 1, 1951 Millswood (S Aust)

Hyatt, Roland Shane (Tas) b Dec. 30, 1961 Hobart (Tas)

Hyde, Phillip Andrew (Vic) b Oct. 22, 1958 Melbourne (Vic)

Hyett, Francis William (Vic) b Feb. 9, 1882 Bolwarra (Vic) d April 25, 1919 Fitzroy (Vic)

Hyland, Byron John (Tas) b Jan. 14, 1930 New Norfolk (Tas)

Hynes, Lincoln Carruthers (NSW) b April 12, 1912 Balmain (NSW) d Aug. 7, 1977 Killara (NSW)

Hyslop, Hector Henry (Australians) b Dec. 13, 1840 Southampton, Hampshire (England) d Sept. 11, 1920 Cosham, Hampshire (England)

* Ibadulla, Khalid (Tas) b Dec. 20, 1935 Lahore (Pakistan)

Iceton, Thomas Henry (NSW) b Oct. 12, 1849 Sydney (NSW) d May 19, 1908 Ashfield (NSW)

Illingworth, Edward Philip (Vic) b Nov. 27, 1938 Fairfield (Vic)

Illman, Brian Kevin (S Aust) b Oct. 23, 1937 Unley Park (S Aust)

* Imran Khan (NSW) b Nov. 25, 1952 Lahore (Pakistan)

Ingleton, Walter George (Vic) b Feb. 16, 1867 Collingwood (Vic) d Feb. 4, 1923 East Melbourne (Vic)

Inkster, Gordon Bradford (S Aust) b June 30, 1893 Portland Estate (S Aust) d March 22, 1957 Darlinghurst (NSW)

Inness, Mathew William Hunter (Vic) b Jan. 13, 1978 East Melbourne (Vic)

Inverarity, Mervyn (WAust) b Oct. 25, 1907 Claremont (WAust) d March 17, 1979 Cottesloe (WAust)

* Inverarity, Robert John (WAust & S Aust) b Jan. 31, 1944 Subiaco (WAust)

Inwood, Bradley Phillip (Qld) b July 23, 1963 Gladstone (Qld)

* Iredale, Francis Adams (NSW) b June 19, 1867 Surry Hills (NSW) d April 15, 1926 Crows Nest (NSW)

Ireland, Gary John (WAust) b Oct. 3, 1961 Collie (WAust)

* Ironmonger, Herbert (Qld & Vic) b April 7, 1882 Pine Mountain (Qld) d June 1, 1971 St Kilda (Vic)

Irvine, John Taylor (WAust) b April 13, 1944 Subiaco (WAust)

* Iverson, John Bryan (Vic) b July 27, 1915 Melbourne (Vic) d Oct. 23, 1973 Brighton (Vic)

Ives, William Francis (NSW) b Nov. 14, 1896 Glebe (NSW) d March 23, 1975 Newport Beach (NSW)

Ivory, Wilfred Charles (Rest of Australia) b Sept. 12, 1888 South Yarra (Vic) d Oct. 13, 1975 North Brighton (Vic)

Jack, Keith Mayall (Qld) b April 25, 1927 Tambo (Qld) d Nov. 22, 1982 Buderim (Qld)

Jackman, Darrell (Tas) b May 31, 1921 Hobart (Tas) d April 5, 1991 Cheltenham (Vic)

* Jackson, Archibald (NSW) b Sept. 5, 1909 Rutherglen, Lanarkshire (Scotland) d Feb. 16, 1933 Clayfield (Qld)

Jackson, Arthur Enderby (WAust) b Jan. 6, 1872 Kapunda (S Aust) d June 29, 1935 Cottesloe (WAust)

Jackson, Paul William (Vic & Qld) b Nov. 1, 1961 East Melbourne (Vic)

Jackson, Victor Edward (NSW) b Oct. 25, 1916 Woollahra (NSW) d Jan. 30, 1965 Manildra (NSW)

Jacobson, Alan Melville (Tas) b Nov. 12, 1942 Sydney (NSW)

Jacomb, John Newton (Vic) b 1841 Hobart (Tas) d Nov. 5, 1891 Walhalla (Vic)

Jakins, James Albert (Tas) b Oct. 1, 1886 Hawthorn (Vic) d Dec. 12, 1948 Wivenhoe (Tas)

James, Alec Pearce (S Aust) b May 22, 1889 Neath, Glamorgan (Wales) d Aug. 14, 1961 Torquay, Devon (England)

James, Eric Lisle (Tas) b Oct. 21, 1881 Low Head (Tas) d Aug. 28, 1948 Malvern (Vic)

James, Eric Pearse (WAust) b Feb. 27, 1923 Albany (WAust) d March 28, 1999 Albany (WAust)

James, Gerald Thomas Henry (Tas) b March 22, 1908 New Norfolk (Tas) d Dec. 24, 1967 Hobart (Tas)

James, Ronald Victor (NSW & S Aust) b May 23, 1920 Paddington (NSW) d April 28, 1983 Auburn (NSW)

James, Sidney Victor Austin (Tas) b Oct. 26, 1895 Adelaide (S Aust) d Aug. 3, 1966 Canterbury (Vic)

Jamieson, Dudley Garfield (S Aust) b July 4, 1912 Redruth (S Aust) d Jan. 14, 1979 Burnside (S Aust)

Jamieson, Walter Angus Bethune (Tas) b 1828 birth day and month unknown Plenty (Tas) d Dec. 28, 1881 Plenty (Tas)

Jansan, Ernest William (NSW) b Aug. 26, 1874 Gulgong (NSW) d May 31, 1945 Leichhardt (NSW)

Jaques, Philip Anthony (NSW) b May 3, 1979 Wollongong (NSW)

* Jarman, Barrington Noel (S Aust) b Feb. 17, 1936 Hindmarsh (S Aust)

Jarvis, Alfred (S Aust) b Feb. 15, 1868 Hindmarsh (S Aust) d Aug. 12, 1938 Semaphore (S Aust)

* Jarvis, Arthur Harwood (S Aust) b Oct. 19, 1860 Hindmarsh (S Aust) d Nov. 15, 1933 Hindmarsh (S Aust)

Jarvis, Carlisle Melrose Byron (WAust) b Dec. 10, 1906 East Fremantle (WAust) d Nov. 6, 1979 Mt Lawley (WAust)

Jarvis, Harwood Samuel Coombe (S Aust) b Aug. 30, 1884 Brompton (S Aust) d Oct. 10, 1936 Port Pirie (S Aust)

Jeffrey, Clifton Linley (Tas) b Jan. 10, 1913 Hobart (Tas) d Feb. 11, 1987 Launceston (Tas)

Jeffrey, Robert Frederick (NSW & Tas) b Sept. 19, 1953 Goulburn (NSW)

Jeffreys, Arthur Frederick (NSW) b April 7, 1848 London (England) d Feb. 4, 1906 Lasham, Hampshire (England)

Jeffreys, John Alan (WAust) b April 17, 1913 Fremantle (WAust) d Nov. 3, 1943 Shipham, Somerset (England)

Jeffreys, Keith Stanley (WAust) b Jan. 18, 1921 Bridgetown (WAust) d May 16, 2000 Mandurah (WAust)

Jelich, Neville (Qld & Tas) b March 11, 1962 Orasje, near Belgrade (Yugoslavia)

* Jenner, Terrence James (WAust & S Aust) b Sept. 8, 1944 Mt Lawley (WAust)

* Jennings, Claude Burrows (S Aust & Qld) b June 5, 1884 East St Kilda (Vic) d June 20, 1950 Adelaide (S Aust)

Jennings, Henry John (Vic) b April 9, 1849 Launceston (Tas) d June 6, 1925 St Kilda (Vic)

Jewell, Nicholas (Vic) b Aug. 27, 1977 East Melbourne (Vic)

Jinks, Allan (Vic) b Dec. 29, 1913 Carlton North (Vic) d Nov. 7, 1997 Melbourne (Vic)

Jinks, Frederick (Vic) b May 6, 1909 Eaglehawk (Vic) d Aug. 16, 1996 Pakenham (Vic)

John, Bruce Duncanson (Tas) b July 20, 1937 Launceston (Tas)

Johns, Alfred Edward (Vic) b Jan. 22, 1868 Hawthorn (Vic) d Feb. 13, 1934 Melbourne (Vic)

Johnson, Benjamin Andrew (S Aust) b Aug. 1, 1973 Naracoorte (S Aust)

Johnson, Eric Alfred (S Aust) b July 11, 1902 North Norwood (S Aust) d Jan. 10, 1976 Adelaide (S Aust)

Johnson, Francis Barry (NSW) b May 21, 1882 Redfern (NSW) d May 28, 1951 Longueville (NSW)

* Johnson, Ian William Geddes (Vic) b Dec. 8, 1917 Hotham West (Vic) d Oct. 9, 1998 Malvern (Vic)

Johnson, James William (Vic) b Sept. 22, 1884 Footscray (Vic) d Aug. 14, 1941 Middle Park (Vic)

* Johnson, Leonard Joseph (Qld) b March 18, 1919 Ipswich (Qld) d April 20, 1977 Silkstone (Qld)

Johnson, Mitchell Guy (Qld) b Nov. 2, 1981 Townsville (Qld)

Johnston, Aubrey Edmund (NSW) b Sept. 7, 1882 Canterbury (NSW) d June 16, 1960 Manly (NSW)

Johnston, Clive William (NSW) b Aug. 4, 1925 Petersham (NSW) d May 11, 1991 Petersham (NSW)

Johnston, David Alexander Hughes (NSW) b July 10, 1955 Maitland (NSW)

Johnston, David Allan (S Aust) b Dec. 4, 1954 Melbourne (Vic)

Johnston, David Trent (NSW) b April 29, 1974 Wollongong (NSW)

Johnston, Frederick Bourke (NSW) b Sept. 10, 1915 Sydney (NSW) d Sept. 6, 1977 Hillsdale (NSW)

* Johnston, William Arras (Vic) b Feb. 26, 1922 Beeac (Vic)

Johnstone, Richard Gordon (Vic) b Feb. 9, 1885 Malvern (Vic) d Nov. 9, 1961 Geelong (Vic)

Jolly, Harvey Bruce (S Aust) b Aug. 1, 1960 Naracoorte (S Aust)

Jones, Alan (WAust) b Nov. 4, 1938 Velindre, Glamorgan (Wales)

Jones, Alan Robert (Qld) b June 11, 1948 Greenslopes (Qld)

Jones, Arthur Harold (Qld) b Dec. 17, 1874 Brisbane (Qld) d Dec. 2, 1917 Salisbury Plain, Wiltshire (England)

Jones, Charles Frederick (Vic) b Feb. 9, 1870 Williamstown (Vic) d March 25, 1957 Williamstown (Vic)

* Jones, Dean Mervyn (Vic) b March 24, 1961 Coburg (Vic)

* Jones, Ernest (S Aust & WAust) b Sept. 30, 1869 East Auburn (S Aust) d Nov. 23, 1943 Norwood (S Aust)

Jones, John Raymond (WAust) b May 10, 1899 Clunes (Vic) d March 14, 1991 Hamilton Hill (WAust)

Jones, Neil Richard (NSW) b July 12, 1966 Stourport-on-Severn, Worcestershire (England)

Jones, Ronald Andrew (NSW) b March 28, 1964 Dubbo (NSW)

* Jones, Samuel Percy (NSW & Qld) b Aug. 1, 1861 Sydney (NSW) d July 14, 1951 Auckland (New Zealand)

Jones, Sidney (NSW) birth and death details unknown

Jones, Stephen Alexander (WAust) b July 1, 1949 Sydney (NSW)

Jones, Victor Clarence (WAust) b May 11, 1881 Ballarat (Vic) d July 20, 1923 Mt Lawley (WAust)

Jones, William George (S Aust) b May 13, 1864 Hindmarsh (S Aust) d July 16, 1924 Adelaide (S Aust)

Jordan, Frank Slater (NSW) b Sept. 19, 1905 Darlington (NSW) d Oct. 22, 1995 Vaucluse (NSW)

Jordan, Grant Leigh (Vic) b March 18, 1965 Ivanhoe (Vic)

Jordon, Raymond Clarence (Vic) b Feb. 17, 1936 Melbourne (Vic)

Jose, Anthony Douglas (S Aust) b Feb. 17, 1929 Knoxville (S Aust) d Feb. 3, 1972 Los Angeles, California (United States of America)

Jose, Gilbert Edgar (S Aust) b Nov. 1, 1898 Taichow (China) d March 27, 1942 Changi POW Camp (Singapore)

Joseland, Brendan Richard (Vic) b April 2, 1976 Upper Ferntree Gully (Vic)

Joseph, Joel P. (NSW) b c. 1867 d c. 1942 Canterbury (NSW)

* Joslin, Leslie Ronald (Vic) b Dec. 13, 1947 Yarraville (Vic)

Joyce, Robert Eric (Qld) b Dec. 11, 1947 Auchenflower (Qld)

Joynt, Hartley Kelly (WAust) b June 14, 1938 Subiaco (WAust)

* Julian, Brendon Paul (WAust) b Aug. 10, 1970 Hamilton (New Zealand)

Junor, John Leonard (Vic) b April 27, 1914 Northcote (Vic) d April 6, 2005 Frankston (Vic)

Junor, Robert Johnston (Vic) b Jan. 10, 1888 Marcus Hill (Vic) d July 26, 1957 Heidelberg (Vic)

Jurgensen, Shane John (WAust, Tas & Qld) b April 28, 1976 Redcliffe (Qld)

Kahler, Lance Warren (Qld) b June 27, 1977 Crows Nest (Qld)

* Kallicharran, Alvin Isaac (Qld) b March 21, 1949 Paidama (British Guiana)

* Kanhai, Rohan Bholal (WAust & Tas) b Dec. 26, 1935 Port Mourant, Berbice (British Guiana)

Karppinen, Stuart James (WAust) b June 13, 1973 Townsville (Qld)

* Kasprowicz, Michael Scott (Qld) b Feb. 10, 1972 South Brisbane (Qld)

* Katich, Simon Mathew (WAust & NSW) b Aug. 21, 1975 Middle Swan (WAust)

Kay, William Malcolm (Qld) b May 4, 1893 Gympie (Qld) d July 7, 1973 Taringa (Qld)

Keating, James Leslie (Vic) b Oct. 1, 1891 Brunswick East (Vic) d March 13, 1962 Fitzroy (Vic)

Kekwick, Edwin Huntley (S Aust) b March 5, 1875 Port MacDonell (S Aust) d Aug. 29, 1950 Adelaide (S Aust)

* Kelleway, Charles (NSW) b April 25, 1886 Lismore (NSW) d Nov. 16, 1944 Lindfield (NSW)

Kellick, Charles Moore (NSW) b Nov. 21, 1842 Sydney (NSW) d March 27, 1918 Strathfield (NSW)

Kellick, James (NSW) b Aug. 24, 1840 Sydney (NSW) d Aug. 8, 1926 Sydney (NSW)

Kelly, David John (S Aust) b Jan. 28, 1959 North Adelaide (S Aust)

Kelly, Ian Donald Cameron (Qld) b May 5, 1959 Herston (Qld)

* Kelly, James Joseph (NSW) b May 10, 1867 Sandridge (Vic) d Aug. 14, 1938 Bellevue Hill (NSW)

Kelly, Otto Harvey (WAust) b May 15, 1880 Sandridge (Vic) d July 30, 1946 Mt Lawley (WAust)

Kelly, Peter Charles (NSW & WAust) b April 28, 1942 Mosman (NSW)

Kelly, Richard Terence Bonynge (Vic) b March 21, 1870 Ballan (Vic) d Dec. 27, 1941 St Kilda (Vic)

Kelly, Robert Charles (WAust) b May 18, 1969 Subiaco (WAust)

* Kelly, Thomas Joseph Dart (Vic) b May 3, 1844 County Waterford (Ireland) d July 20, 1893 Hawthorn (Vic)

Kelly, Trent Peter (S Aust) b March 24, 1984 Henley Beach (S Aust)

Kelly, William Harvey (WAust) b March 24, 1883 St Kilda (Vic) d July 30, 1944 Croydon (Vic)

Kelly, William Lucius Usna (Vic) b Jan. 20, 1875 Rosedale (Vic) d Dec. 27, 1968 Bulla (Vic)

Kelton, Matthew David (S Aust) b April 9, 1974 Woodville South (S Aust)

Kemp, Benjamin Charles Ernest (S Aust & Vic) b Jan. 30, 1864 Plymouth, Devon (England) d Dec. 3, 1940 Albert Park (Vic)

Kemp, Leonard Denton (Vic) b June 6, 1909 Malvern (Vic)

Kendall, Keith Harold Dudley (Vic) b March 16, 1929 South Melbourne (Vic)

* Kendall, Thomas Kingston (Vic & Tas) b Aug. 24, 1851 Bedford, Bedfordshire (England) d Aug. 17, 1924 Hobart (Tas)

Kenneally, Cornelius James (S Aust) b July 28, 1926 Edwardstown (Vic) d Jan. 18, 1995 Ashford (S Aust)

Kenny, Arthur (Vic) b Aug. 9, 1878 Emerald Hill (Vic) d Aug. 2, 1934 South Melbourne (Vic)

Kenny, Justin Dean (NSW) b Sept. 24, 1966 Camperdown (NSW)

* Kent, Martin Francis (Qld) b Nov. 23, 1953 Mossman (Qld)

Keogh, Ernest John (WAust) b 1869 South Melbourne (Vic) d c. 1951 South Yarra (Vic)

Kermode, Alexander (NSW) b May 15, 1876 Sydney (NSW) d July 17, 1934 Balmain (NSW)

Kerr, Eric Alan David (Vic) b June 28, 1923 Auburn (Vic) d Feb. 16, 1989 Melbourne (Vic)

* Kerr, Robert Byers (Qld) b June 16, 1961 Herston (Qld)

Kershler, Anthony John (NSW) b July 6, 1968 St Leonard's (NSW)

Kessey, Gwilym Taf (WAust) b Jan. 13, 1919 Meekatharra (WAust) d June 25, 1986 Perth (WAust)

Kettle, John Louis (NSW) b Dec. 3, 1830 Sydney (NSW) d Oct. 30, 1891 Newtown (NSW)

Kiernan, Christopher (Vic) b March 23, 1878 Fitzroy (Vic) d Dec. 2, 1925 North Fitzroy (Vic)

Kierse, John Michael (S Aust) b Jan. 11, 1918 Nhill (Vic)

Kildey, Edward Keith (Tas) b April 30, 1919 Leeton (NSW) d Feb. 12, 2005 Melbourne (Vic)

Killen, Christopher Michael (S Aust) b Sept. 23, 1967 Dubbo (NSW)

Kimber, Adam Patrick (S Aust) b Sept. 30, 1969 North Adelaide (S Aust)

Kimpton, Robert Webb (WAust) b Jan. 5, 1914 Essendon (Vic)

King, Darryl James (Qld) b June 6, 1942 East Brisbane (Qld) d March 3, 2002 Buderim (Qld)

King, Ian Harold (Qld) b June 1, 1943 Herston (Qld)

King, James Francis (S Aust) b May 23, 1851 Hindmarsh (S Aust) d June 28, 1921 Hindmarsh (S Aust)

King, Norman Reginald (S Aust) b April 9, 1915 Mile End (S Aust) d April 25, 1973 Linden Park (S Aust)

King, Percy Macgregor (NSW) b Sept. 2, 1889 Richmond (Vic) d Dec. 9, 1967 Rose Bay (NSW)

King, Peter Denis (Vic) b May 24, 1959 Melbourne (Vic)

King, Stuart Patrick (Vic) b April 22, 1906 Ararat (Vic) d Feb. 28, 1943 in action on the Coral Sea

Kingdon, Darren Robert (Qld) b Sept. 24, 1969 Dubbo (NSW)

Kington, Philip Oliphant (Vic) b Dec. 17, 1832 Clifton, Gloucestershire (England) d July 2, 1892 Dachet, Buckinghamshire (England)

Kinloch, John (NSW) b c. 1833 Dublin (Ireland) d April 9, 1897 Camperdown (NSW)

Kinnear, Joseph David (Vic) b Feb. 12, 1912 West Brunswick (Vic) d Dec. 14, 1981 Moreland (Vic)

Kinnear, William George (Vic) b Aug. 19, 1914 West Brunswick (Vic) d Dec. 7, 1982 West Brunswick (Vic)

* Kippax, Alan Falconer (NSW) b May 25, 1897 Sydney (NSW) d Sept. 5, 1972 Bellevue Hill (NSW)

Kirby, Keith William (Vic) b Oct. 1, 1939 Essendon (Vic)

Kirby, Richard George (Tas) b Jan. 28, 1861 Hobart (Tas) d Aug. 26, 1947 Hobart (Tas)

Kirkman, William Stanley (Tas) b Feb. 14, 1961 Launceston (Tas)

Kirkwood, Harold Peter (S Aust) b Sept. 15, 1882 Orroroo (S Aust) d May 19, 1943 Unley (S Aust)

Kissell, Ronald Keith (NSW) b Aug. 9, 1928 Camperdown (NSW)

Kitson, Eugene Henry (S Aust) b Nov. 28, 1889 Adelaide (S Aust) d Aug. 4, 1962 Heidelberg (Vic)

* Kline, Lindsay Francis (Vic) b Sept. 29, 1934 Camberwell (Vic)

Klinger, Michael (Vic) b July 4, 1980 Kew (Vic)

Klose, Tom Elliott (S Aust) b Jan. 21, 1918 North Adelaide (S Aust) d June 13, 1986 Nailsworth (S Aust)

* Knight, David Jeffrey (Vic) b Aug. 21, 1956 Coburg (Vic)

Knight, Gary William (Combined XI) b July 20, 1950 Launceston (Tas)

Knight, Robert Leonard (Tas) b Nov. 20, 1957 Launceston (Tas)

Knill, William (S Aust) b Jan. 28, 1859 Prospect Village (S Aust) d July 8, 1940 North Adelaide (S Aust)

* Knott, Alan Philip Eric (Tas) b April 9, 1946 Belvedere, Kent (England)

Knowles, Brad Aaron (Vic) b Oct. 29, 1981 Moe (Vic)

Knowles, Eric Charles (Qld) b March 9, 1896 Toowoomba (Qld) d Sept. 15, 1978 Southport (Qld)

Kortlang, Henry Frederick Lorenz (Vic) b March 12, 1880 Carlton (Vic) d Feb. 15, 1961 Cottesloe (WAust)

Kowalick, Jeffrey Peter (S Aust) b July 22, 1946 Maylands (S Aust)

Krejza, Jason John (NSW) b Jan. 14, 1983 Newtown (NSW)

Kremerskothen, Scott Paul (Tas) b Jan. 5, 1979 Launceston (Tas)

Kroger, Henry Jack (Vic) b June 27, 1906 Caulfield (Vic) d July 16, 1987 Malvern (Vic)

Kruger, Nicholas James (Qld) b Aug. 14, 1983 Paddington (NSW)

Kyle, James Henderson (Vic) b May 29, 1880 Bacchus Marsh (Vic) d Jan. 11, 1919 Albert Park (Vic)

La Frantz, Errold Campbell (Qld) b May 25, 1919 Wooloowin (Qld)

* Laird, Bruce Malcolm (WAust) b Nov. 21, 1950 Mt Lawley (WAust)

Lambert, Daryl John (S Aust) b Oct. 8, 1946 Prospect (S Aust)

Lambert, Grant Michael (NSW) b Aug. 5, 1977 Parramatta (NSW)

Lambert, Henry Francis (Vic) b July 8, 1918 Bairnsdale (Vic) d June 19, 1995 Grange (S Aust)

Lambert, Oswald (NSW) b Aug. 23, 1926 New Lambton (NSW)

Lampard, Albert Wallis (Vic) b July 3, 1885 Richmond (Vic) d Jan. 11, 1984 Armadale (Vic)

Lampe, William Henry Warwick (NSW) b Aug. 29, 1902 Albert Park (Vic) d Dec. 22, 1987 Wagga Wagga (NSW)

Lane, John Bayley (NSW) b Jan. 7, 1886 Petersham (NSW) d Aug. 30, 1937 Manly (NSW)

Lang, Harold King (WAust) b Aug. 23, 1905 Banyena (Vic) d April 23, 1991 Nedlands (WAust)

Langdon, Christopher Walter (WAust) b July 4, 1922 Boulder (WAust) d May 2, 2004 Nedlands (WAust)

* Langer, Justin Lee (WAust) b Nov. 21, 1970 Subiaco (WAust)

Langer, Robert Samuel (WAust) b Oct. 3, 1948 Subiaco (WAust)

Langford, Ian Frederick (Vic) b June 2, 1936 Kew (Vic)

* Langley, Gilbert Roche Andrews (S Aust) b Sept. 14, 1919 North Adelaide (S Aust) d May 14, 2001 Fullarton (S Aust)

Langley, Jeffrey Noel (S Aust & Qld) b Oct. 28, 1948 Adelaide (S Aust)

Lanigan, Emmet Robert (Vic) b Sept. 6, 1909 Maffra (Vic)

Lanigan, Joseph Patrick (WAust) b July 8, 1891 Mogumber (WAust) d Sept. 30, 1972 Glendalough (WAust)

Lansdown, Albert Joseph Walter (Vic) b March 10, 1897 Fitzroy South (Vic) d Jan. 7, 1979 Frankston (Vic)

Lansdown, Harold Charles (Vic) b Feb. 18, 1900 North Fitzroy (Vic) d April 18, 1957 Ivanhoe (Vic)

Larkin, Rohan Patrick (Vic) b Oct. 19, 1969 Seymour (Vic)

* Laughlin, Trevor John (Vic) b Jan. 30, 1951 Nyah West (Vic)

Lavender, Mark Philip (WAust) b Aug. 28, 1967 Madras (India)

* Laver, Frank (Vic) b Dec. 7, 1869 Castlemaine (Vic) d Sept. 24, 1919 East Melbourne (Vic)

Laver, John Francis Lee (Tas) b March 9, 1917 Malvern (Vic)

Law, Ian Kennon (Vic) b Sept. 27, 1938 Richmond (Vic)

Law, Rupert William (Qld) b Feb. 24, 1890 Sydney (NSW) d May 5, 1942 Randwick (NSW)

* Law, Stuart Grant (Qld) b Oct. 18, 1968 Herston (Qld)

Lawes, Charles Henry Wickham (NSW) b Dec. 9, 1899 Cobar (NSW) d Oct. 23, 1980 (NSW)

Lawlor, John (Vic) b Jan. 25, 1864 Castleisland, County Kerry (Ireland) d Jan. 29, 1908 Melbourne (Vic)

Lawrence, Charles (NSW) b Dec. 16, 1828 Hoxton, London (England) d Dec. 20, 1916 Canterbury (Vic)

Lawrence, Rodney John (Qld) b Aug. 8, 1954 Herston (Qld)

* Lawry, William Morris (Vic) b Feb. 11, 1937 Thornbury (Vic)

* Lawson, Geoffrey Francis (NSW) b Dec. 7, 1957 Wagga Wagga (NSW)

Lawson, Robert James (Vic) b March 23, 1901 South Melbourne (Vic) d Nov. 28, 1974 West Brunswick (Vic)

Laycock, Henry (S Aust) b Oct. 31, 1901 Edwardstown (S Aust) d Aug. 6, 1983 Port Noarlunga (S Aust)

Le Couteur, Philip Ridgeway (Vic) b June 26, 1885 Kyneton (Vic) d June 30, 1958 Gunnedah (NSW)

Leabeater, Leonard Raymond (NSW) b July 10, 1906 Parramatta (NSW) d June 1, 1996 Port Macquarie (NSW)

Leak, Brian Headley (S Aust) b May 5, 1917 Hawthorn (S Aust)

Leak, Ernest Howard (S Aust) b Oct. 28, 1872 Finniss Vale (S Aust) d Aug. 22, 1945 Adelaide (S Aust)

Leak, Stanley Garfield (S Aust) b March 12, 1886 Goodwood (S Aust) d Jan. 10, 1963 Millswood (S Aust)

Leary, John Denis (Qld) b c. 1862 Picton (NSW) d Jan. 16, 1940 Herston (Qld)

Leather, Thomas William (Vic) b June 2, 1910 Rutherglen, Lanarkshire (Scotland) d May 10, 1991 Prahran (Vic)

Ledger, Scott Norman (Qld) b Sept. 1, 1952 Nambour (Qld)

Ledward, John Allan (Vic) b April 22, 1909 East Melbourne (Vic) d July 22, 1997 Box Hill (Vic)

* Lee, Brett (NSW) b Nov. 8, 1976 Wollongong (NSW)

Lee, Clarence Leslie (Tas) b Dec. 28, 1890 Cressy (Tas) d Feb. 5, 1959 Invermay (Tas)

Lee, Ian Somerville (Vic) b March 24, 1914 Brunswick North (Vic) d April 14, 1976 Port Melbourne (Vic)

* Lee, Philip Keith (S Aust) b Sept. 15, 1904 Gladstone (S Aust) d Aug. 8, 1980 Woodville South (S Aust)

Lee, Robert William (S Aust) b Jan. 31, 1927 Hindmarsh (S Aust) d June 9, 2001 Adelaide (S Aust)

Lee, Shane (NSW) b Aug. 8, 1973 Wollongong (NSW)

Lee, Terence Henderson (NSW) b Aug. 31, 1940 Manly (NSW)

Leedham, Michael John (Tas) b Feb. 22, 1950 Campbell Town (Tas)

Leehane, John Francis (Vic) b Dec. 11, 1950 Coburg (Vic)

Leehane, John Thomas (Vic) b Oct. 20, 1921 Brunswick (Vic) d July 22, 1991 Caulfield (Vic)

Leeson, Henry Follie (Qld) b July 20, 1908 Mount Morgan (Qld) d May 24, 1950 Logan River (Qld)

Lehmann, Charles Albert (WAust) b Sept. 16, 1878 Caltowie (S Aust) d April 27, 1940 Melbourne (Vic)

* Lehmann, Darren Scott (S Aust & Vic) b Feb. 5, 1970 Gawler (S Aust)

Le Loux, Ryan Nicholas (Qld) b April 30, 1984 Darlinghurst (NSW)

Leslie, Peter Glen (NSW) b Feb. 24, 1947 Bexley (NSW)

Letcher, Charles (Vic) b Dec. 22, 1868 Collingwood (Vic) d Nov. 30, 1916 Perth (WAust)

Lethborg, Gordon John (Tas) b Nov. 23, 1907 Scottsdale (Tas) d Aug. 31, 1989 Launceston (Tas)

Lette, Henry Elms (Tas) b 1829 birth day and month unknown Curramore (Tas) d Aug. 15, 1892 Launceston (Tas)

* Lever, Peter (Tas) b Sept. 17, 1940 Todmorden, Yorkshire (England)

Levingston, Raydon Charles (Qld) b Jan. 17, 1946 Toowoomba (Qld)

Levy, Graham Bruce (S Aust) b Feb. 10, 1938 North Adelaide (S Aust)

Levy, Roy Mark (Qld) b April 20, 1906 Waverley (NSW) d Dec. 12, 1965 Clayfield (Qld)

Lewis, Arthur (Vic) b c. 1830 full birth details unknown d June 1, 1907 Alexandra (Vic)

Lewis, John William (Qld) b Nov. 21, 1867 St George (Qld) d Sept. 19, 1939 Brisbane (Qld)

Lewis, Keith (S Aust) b Feb. 4, 1923 Prospect (S Aust)

Lewis, Kevin John (S Aust) b Nov. 27, 1947 Hindmarsh (S Aust)

Lewis, Laurence Robert (S Aust) b May 24, 1889 Cherry Gardens (S Aust) d Sept. 2, 1947 Prospect (S Aust)

Lewis, Michael Llewellyn (Vic) b June 29, 1974 Greensborough (Vic)

Lewis, Oswald Hoddle (NSW) b Feb. 28, 1833 Sydney (NSW) d April 28, 1895 Darlinghurst (NSW)

Lewis, Percy Markham (Vic) b March 13, 1864 Hamilton (Vic) d Nov. 24, 1922 St Kilda (Vic)

Lewis, Thomas Harvie (NSW) b c. 1828 London (England) d June 19, 1901 Darlinghurst (NSW)

Liddicut, Arthur Edward (Vic) b Oct. 17, 1891 Fitzroy (Vic) d April 8, 1983 Parkdale (Vic)

Lihou, Jack (Qld) b Sept. 9, 1930 Sandgate (Qld)

Lill, John Charles (S Aust) b Dec. 7, 1933 Maylands (S Aust)

* Lillee, Dennis Keith (WAust & Tas) b July 18, 1949 Subiaco (WAust)

Lillie, Dennis John (Qld) b Oct. 28, 1945 Auchenflower (Qld)

Lilly, Kenneth Edward (WAust) b Dec. 25, 1959 Perth (WAust)

Limb, Allen (Tas) b Sept. 29, 1886 Gawler (S Aust) d July 1, 1975 Battery Point (Tas)

* Lindwall, Raymond Russell (NSW & Qld) b Oct. 3, 1921 Mascot (NSW) d June 22, 1996 Greenslopes (Qld)

Linney, George Frederick (Tas) b Nov. 18, 1869 Guildford, Surrey (England) d Nov. 5, 1927 Weston-super-Mare, Somerset (England)

Lister, Charles (Vic) b Nov. 7, 1811 Armitage Park, Staffordshire (England) d Aug. 18, 1873 Laverstock Asylum, Alderbury, Wiltshire (England)

Liston, George Grieve (S Aust) b April 29, 1860 Tanunda (S Aust) d June 6, 1929 Kent Town (S Aust)

Litster, John Lewis (Qld) b Feb. 2, 1904 Townsville (Qld) d March 11, 1982 Railway Estate, Townsville (Qld)

Little, Raymond Cecil James (NSW) b Oct. 7, 1914 Armidale (NSW) d April 28, 1995 Burwood (NSW)

Living, Gary Francis (Vic) b Oct. 1, 1952 Dandenong (Vic)

Livingston, Bruce Arthur Lionel (NSW) b May 11, 1927 Marrickville (NSW)

Livingston, Leonard (NSW) b May 3, 1920 Hurlstone Park (NSW) d Jan. 16, 1998 Hurlstone Park (NSW)

Lloyd, Robert Grantley (S Aust) b Oct. 24, 1940 Gladstone (S Aust)

* Loader, Peter James (WAust) b Oct. 25, 1929 Wallington, Surrey (England)

Lochner, Augustus Meyer (Tas) b Oct. 1, 1827 Enfield, Middlesex (England) d Feb. 20, 1865 Plumstead Common, Kent (England)

* Lock, Graham Anthony Richard (WAust) b July 5, 1929 Limpsfield, Surrey (England) d March 29, 1995 Beechboro (WAust)

Lockie, George William (Qld) b Feb. 18, 1910 Mt Morgan (Qld) d Nov. 2, 1971 Northgate (Qld)

Lockwood, William Thomas (WAust) b June 26, 1868 Geelong (Vic) d Aug. 29, 1953 Tuart Hill (WAust)

Lockyear, Rhett John Gaven (Tas) b Feb. 28, 1983 Mudgee (NSW)

Lodding, Brent Andrew (Vic) b March 20, 1973 Upper Ferntree Gully (Vic)

Loder, Robert Roy (NSW) b Dec. 17, 1896 East Maitland (NSW) d Feb. 13, 1964 French's Forest (NSW)

Lodge, Arthur Oliver (WAust) b April 7, 1933 Guildford (WAust)

Logan, William (Vic) birth and death details unknown

Lonergan, Albert Roy (S Aust & NSW) b Dec. 6, 1909 Maylands (WAust) d Oct. 22, 1956 Adelaide (S Aust)

Loney, Geoffrey Souter (Tas) b March 31, 1894 Campbelltown (NSW) d April 7, 1985 Hobart (Tas)

Long, Edmund James (NSW) b March 28, 1883 Darlinghurst (NSW) d Dec. 8, 1947 Leichhardt (NSW)

Long, Gordon Hillhouse (Combined XI) b May 6, 1934 Hobart (Tas)

Long, Thomas Tasman Thompson (Qld) b Sept. 11, 1875 at sea d Oct. 20, 1926 Spring Hill (Qld)

Longney, Geoffrey Wallace (Vic) b May 25, 1935 Oakleigh (Vic)

Lord, John Carr (Tas) b Aug. 17, 1844 Hobart (Tas) d May 25, 1911 Antill Ponds (Tas)

Lord, Sidney (Tas) b Oct. 20, 1886 birthplace and death details unknown

Loton, Cecil Vernon (WAust) b Jan. 5, 1906 Upper Swan (WAust) d June 8, 1986 Pinjarra (WAust)

Loton, Morris William (WAust) b March 18, 1905 Springhill (WAust) d March 2, 1976 Northam (WAust)

Lough, William David (NSW) b Oct. 31, 1886 Bourke (NSW) d c. 1939 Newtown (NSW)

Loughnan, Austin Robert (Vic) b June 15, 1851 Hobart (Tas) d Oct. 9, 1926 Cheltenham (Vic)

* Love, Hampden Stanley Bray (NSW & Vic) b Aug. 10, 1895 Lilyfield (NSW) d July 22, 1969 Sydney (NSW)

* Love, Martin Lloyd (Qld) b March 30, 1974 Mundubbera (Qld)

Lovell, David Cameron (S Aust) b Feb. 17, 1955 North Adelaide (S Aust)

Lovelock, Oswald Ifould (WAust) b Aug. 28, 1911 Highgate (WAust) d Aug. 1, 1981 Subiaco (WAust)

Loveridge, Eustace Alfred (S Aust) b April 14, 1891 Yongala (S Aust) d July 29, 1959 Adelaide (S Aust)

Loveridge, Walter David (NSW) b Sept. 13, 1867 Redfern (NSW) d Jan. 6, 1940 East Brisbane (Qld)

Lovett, Arthur Frederick (Tas & WAust) b June 1, 1920 St Kilda (Vic) d July 1, 1990 Coffs Harbour (NSW)

Lovett, Henry Charles (Tas) b March 3, 1856 Battery Point (Tas) d May 20, 1937 Hobart (Tas)

Lowe, Frederick (Vic) b Sept. 7, 1827 Holme Pierrepont, Nottinghamshire (England) d Oct. 15, 1887 Ararat (Vic)

Lowry, Jack Brown (Vic) b Nov. 25, 1916 Lambton (NSW)

Loxton, Colin Cameron (Qld) b Jan. 1, 1914 Beecroft (NSW) d Sept. 2, 2000 Greenslopes (Qld)

Loxton, John Frederick Cameron (Qld) b Nov. 26, 1945 Ashgrove (Qld)

* Loxton, Samuel John Everett (Vic) b March 29, 1921 Albert Park (Vic)

Lucas, Clyde Edward (Tas) b Aug. 11, 1898 Kingston (Tas) d Jan. 12, 1988 Palm Beach (Qld)

Lucas, Edward (Tas) b June 16, 1848 Kingston (Tas) d April 19, 1916 Kingston (Tas)

Lucas, Frank Russell (S Aust) b Nov. 9, 1888 Port Pirie (S Aust) d Aug. 31, 1941 Adelaide (S Aust)

Lucas, Michael John (Qld) b April 14, 1944 Ashgrove (Qld)

Lucas, Thomas Turland (S Aust) b Feb. 18, 1852 Eyres Flat (S Aust) d March 13, 1945 Norwood (S Aust)

Lugton, Frank Leslie (Vic) b Nov. 4, 1893 Northcote (Vic) d July 29, 1916 near Villers-Bretonneux (France)

Lukeman, Eric William (NSW) b March 11, 1923 Drummoyne (NSW) d April 18, 1993 Palm Beach (Qld)

Lush, John Grantley (NSW) b Oct. 14, 1913 Prahran (Vic) d Aug. 23, 1985 Sydney (NSW)

* Lyons, John James (S Aust) b May 21, 1863 Gawler (S Aust) d July 21, 1927 Magill (S Aust)

Lyons, Rodney Bernard (Qld) b April 24, 1924 Cairns (Qld)

* McAlister, Peter Alexander (Vic) b July 11, 1869 Williamstown (Vic) d May 10, 1938 Richmond (Vic)

McAllen, Charles (Tas) b July 2, 1860 Hobart (Tas) d Jan. 15, 1924 Hobart (Tas)

McAllister, Donald Ernest (S Aust) b Nov. 19, 1935 Hindmarsh (S Aust)

McAndrew, John William (Qld) b Nov. 4, 1889 Berrima (NSW) d April 10, 1961 Ipswich (Qld)

McArdle, Brendan Joseph (Vic) b March 2, 1952 Preston (Vic)

* Macartney, Charles George (NSW) b June 27, 1886 West Maitland (NSW) d Sept. 9, 1958 Little Bay (NSW)

McAullay, Kenneth James (WAust) b Sept. 29, 1949 Subiaco (WAust)

McBeath, Arthur (NSW & S Aust) b June 17, 1876 Mudgee (NSW) d March 17, 1945 Surry Hills (NSW)

* McCabe, Stanley Joseph (NSW) b July 16, 1910 Grenfell (NSW) d Aug. 25, 1968 Beauty Point (NSW)

McCaffrey, Michael Francis (Qld) b Feb. 18, 1878 Rockhampton (Qld) d March 17, 1949 Brisbane (Qld)

McCaffrey, Victor William (NSW) b Aug. 11, 1918 Goulburn (NSW)

* McCague, Martin John (WAust) b May 24, 1969 Larne (Northern Ireland)

McCarthy, John Edward (Qld) b Feb. 22, 1917 Maryborough (Qld) d Feb. 18, 1998 Southport (Qld)

McCarthy, Kevin Joseph (S Aust) b Oct. 11, 1945 Rose Park (S Aust)

McCarthy, Patrick Covell Derrick (WAust) b Oct. 24, 1919 (Ceylon)

McCarthy, Richard Charles Arthur Marum (Vic) b Dec. 21, 1961 Geelong (Vic)

McCauley, Bede Vincent (NSW) b June 11, 1909 Coogee (NSW) d Oct. 14, 1994 Sydney (NSW)

McCloy, William Stanley Swain (Qld & NSW) b Nov. 10, 1886 Paddington (NSW) d Nov. 10, 1975 Young (NSW)

McCooke, Steven Milne (Vic) b Jan. 31, 1960 South Caulfield (Vic)

* McCool, Colin Leslie (NSW & Qld) b Dec. 9, 1916 Paddington (NSW) d April 5, 1986 Concord (NSW)

McCoombe, Clarence Arthur (Qld) b Feb. 23, 1904 Cooktown (Qld) d Sept. 6, 1955 Sydney (NSW)

McCormack, William Henry (Vic) b May 5, 1877 St Kilda (Vic) d April 26, 1946 Stawell (Vic)

* McCormick, Ernest Leslie (Vic) b May 16, 1906 North Carlton (Vic) d June 28, 1991 Tweed Heads (NSW)

McCormick, Raymond Vincent (S Aust) b Jan. 30, 1931 Mile End (S Aust)

* McCosker, Richard Bede (NSW) b Dec. 11, 1946 Inverell (NSW)

McCoy, Bernard Leslie (NSW) b March 26, 1896 Kangaroo Valley (NSW) d June 11, 1970 Sydney (NSW)

McCurdy, Rodney John (Tas, Vic & S Aust) b Dec. 30, 1959 Melbourne (Vic)

* McDermott, Craig John (Qld) b April 14, 1965 Ipswich (Qld)

McDonald, Andrew Barry (Vic) b June 5, 1981 Wodonga (Vic)

* McDonald, Colin Campbell (Vic) b Nov. 17, 1928 Glen Iris (Vic)

* McDonald, Edgar Arthur (Tas & Vic) b Jan. 6, 1891 Launceston (Tas) d July 22, 1937 Blackrod, near Bolton, Lancashire (England)

McDonald, Ian Hamilton (Vic) b July 28, 1923 Windsor (Vic)

Macdonald, Kenneth Locke (Tas) b Jan. 3, 1934 Premaydena (Tas) d July 1, 1999 Hobart (Tas)

Macdonald, Robert (Qld) b Feb. 14, 1870 Clunes (Vic) d March 7, 1946 Victoria, British Columbia (Canada)

McDonald, Walter Hugh (Vic, Qld & Tas) b March 24, 1884 Shepparton (Vic) d March 22, 1955 Kew (Vic)

* McDonnell, Percy Stanislaus (Vic, NSW & Qld) b Nov. 13, 1858 Kennington, Kent (England) d Sept. 24, 1896 South Brisbane (Qld)

McDowall, Robert Murray (Tas) b Nov. 21, 1821 Edinburgh (Scotland) d Nov. 5, 1894 (New Zealand)

Mace, Christopher (Vic) b Dec. 24, 1830 Bedale, Yorkshire (England) d Nov. 23, 1907 Sydenham (New Zealand)

Mace, John (Vic) b Dec. 28, 1828 Bedale, Yorkshire (England) d April 30, 1905 Te Aroha (New Zealand)

Mace, John Cruttenden (Tas) b May 7, 1839 Sydney (NSW) d April 18, 1906 Hawley-with-Minley, Hampshire (England)

McElhone, Frank Eric (NSW) b June 27, 1887 Waverley (NSW) d July 21, 1981 Darlinghurst (NSW)

McEvoy, Daniel Michael (WAust) b Aug. 19, 1946 Mount Lawley (WAust)

McEvoy, Frederick Aloysius (Vic) b July 4, 1856 Gundagai (NSW) d Nov. 5, 1913 Brighton (Vic)

McEvoy, William Joseph (Vic) b c. 1845 Sydney (NSW) d July 14, 1930 (England)

McEwan, Kenneth Scott (WAust) b July 16, 1952 Bedford, Cape Province (South Africa)

McEwan, W. (Tas) b 1815 birth day and month unknown Perth, Perthshire (Scotland) d c. 1862 (Vic)

McFarland, Robert (Vic) b July 9, 1847 Coleraine (Vic) d July 4, 1876 Carlton (Vic)

McFarlane, Clement Basil Patrick (Qld) b Aug. 20, 1900 New Farm (Qld) d March 2, 1946 Grange (Qld)

McFarlane, Robert Donald (WAust) b Feb. 7, 1955 Corrigin (WAust)

McGain, Bryce Edward (Vic) b March 25, 1972 Mornington (Vic)

McGan, Bryan (Vic) b March 19, 1847 Melbourne (Vic) d July 9, 1894 South Melbourne (Vic)

McGhee, Robert William (Qld) b March 24, 1963 Richmond (Qld)

MacGill, Charles William Terry (WAust) b June 16, 1916 Perth (WAust) d Oct. 31, 1999 Perth (WAust)

* MacGill, Stuart Charles Glyndwr (WAust & NSW) b Feb. 25, 1971 Mt Lawley (WAust)

MacGill, Terry Mornington David (WAust) b Dec. 22, 1945 Moreland (Vic)

McGilvray, Alan David (NSW) b Dec. 6, 1909 Paddington (NSW) d July 17, 1996 Darlinghurst (NSW)

McGinn, Albert Howard (Qld) b Nov. 11, 1913 Upper Kedron (Qld)

McGinty, Adam David (Vic) b March 24, 1971 Melbourne (Vic)

McGlinchy, William Walter (NSW & Qld) b Jan. 31, 1864 Newcastle (NSW) d July 1, 1946 Sydney (NSW)

* McGrath, Glenn Donald (NSW) b Feb. 9, 1970 Dubbo (NSW)

McGregor, William (Australians) b Feb. 23, 1888 St Kilda (Vic) d Oct. 5, 1980 Benalla (Vic)

McGuire, David Victor (Tas) b Nov. 13, 1931 Hobart (Tas)

McGuirk, Harold Vincent (NSW) b Oct. 17, 1906 Crookwell (NSW) death details unknown

McGuirk, Leo Daniel (NSW) b May 3, 1908 Crookwell (NSW) d June 15, 1974 Sydney (NSW)

* McIlwraith, John (Vic) b Sept. 7, 1857 Collingwood (Vic) d July 5, 1938 Camberwell (Vic)

McInnes, Alan Roderick (Vic) b May 29, 1907 Kensington (Vic) d Sept. 16, 1991 Dandenong (Vic)

McInnes, Mark William (Cricket Academy) b April 16, 1977 Wagga Wagga (NSW)

McIntyre, Ernest John (Vic) b April 19, 1921 Albert Park (Vic) d April 10, 2003 Melbourne (Vic)

* McIntyre, Peter Edward (Vic & S Aust) b April 27, 1966 Gisborne (Vic)

McIntyre, William Robert (NSW) b April 10, 1877 Forbes (NSW) d c. 1943 Drummoyne (NSW)

Mack, Christopher David (WAust) b June 30, 1970 Subiaco (WAust)

McKay, Douglas Gordon (S Aust) b July 2, 1904 North Adelaide (S Aust) d April 9, 1994 North Adelaide (S Aust)

Mackay, George (Vic) b July 6, 1860 Castlemaine (Vic) d May 22, 1948 Bendigo (Vic)

McKay, Henry James (S Aust) b Jan. 1, 1883 Goodwood (S Aust) d Feb. 12, 1926 Hawthorn (S Aust)

Mackay, James Rainey Munro (NSW) b Sept. 9, 1880 Armidale (NSW) d June 13, 1953 Walcha (NSW)

Mackay, John Robert Edward (Qld) b Nov. 24, 1937 Rockhampton (Qld)

* Mackay, Kenneth Donald (Qld) b Oct. 24, 1925 Windsor (Qld) d June 13, 1982 Point Lookout, Stradbroke Island (Qld)

Mackay, Kerry (NSW) b May 7, 1949 Brighton-Le-Sands (NSW)

MacKenzie, Alexander Cecil Knox (NSW) b Aug. 7, 1870 Sydney (NSW) d April 11, 1947 Epping (NSW)

McKenzie, Colin (Vic) b Dec. 12, 1880 Trawool (Vic) d Aug. 31, 1930 Avenel (Vic)

MacKenzie, Damien Robert (Qld) b July 21, 1980 Herston (Qld)

McKenzie, Douglas Charles (WAust) b March 15, 1906 Kew (Vic) d July 1, 1979 Perth (WAust)

McKenzie, Eric Norman (WAust) b Dec. 9, 1910 Kalgoorlie (WAust) d April 28, 1994 Cottesloe (WAust)

* McKenzie, Graham Douglas (WAust) b June 24, 1941 Cottesloe (WAust)

McKenzie, John (S Aust) b Oct. 11, 1862 Aldinga (S Aust) d June 3, 1944 Hazelwood Park (S Aust)

McKenzie, Matthew Stanley (Tas) b May 17, 1890 Launceston (Tas) d Dec. 8, 1915 Alexandria (Egypt)

McKew, Cecil George (NSW) b Aug. 12, 1887 Leichhardt (NSW) d Oct. 12, 1974 Lilli Pilli (NSW)

* McKibbin, Thomas Robert (NSW) b Dec. 10, 1870 Raglan (NSW) d Dec. 15, 1939 Bathurst (NSW)

McKone, John James (NSW) b Oct. 3, 1835 Sydney (NSW) d Aug. 7, 1882 Sydney (NSW)

McLachlan, Ian Murray (S Aust) b Oct. 2, 1936 North Adelaide (S Aust)

* McLaren, John William (Qld) b Dec. 22, 1886 Toowong (Qld) d Nov. 17, 1921 Highgate Hill (Qld)

McLaughlin, John Joseph (Qld) b Feb. 18, 1930 Corinda (Qld)

McLay, Gregory Francis (NSW) b May 7, 1969 Wagga Wagga (NSW)

McLean, Allan Robert Charles (S Aust) b Feb. 1, 1914 Mile End (S Aust) d Nov. 9, 1989 Christies Beach (S Aust)

McLean, Hugh (Vic) b Nov. 26, 1864 Woodford (Vic) d Feb. 19, 1915 East Melbourne (Vic)

McLean, Ian Robert (S Aust) b Jan. 30, 1954 Semaphore (S Aust)

* Maclean, John Alexander (Qld) b April 27, 1946 Herston (Qld)

MacLeay, Kenneth Hervey (WAust) b April 2, 1959 Bedford-on-Avon, Wiltshire (England)

McLellan, Ross Malcolm (S Aust) b Feb. 20, 1955 Glenhuntly (Vic)

* McLeod, Charles Edward (Vic) b Oct. 24, 1869 Sandridge (Vic) d Nov. 26, 1918 Armadale (Vic)

McLeod, Daniel Hutton (Vic) b March 29, 1872 Sandridge (Vic) d Nov. 25, 1901 Port Melbourne (Vic)

* McLeod, Robert William (Vic) b Jan. 19, 1868 Sandridge (Vic) d June 14, 1907 Middle Park (Vic)

McMahon, John Terrence (Qld) b May 18, 1932 Five Dock (NSW)

McMahon, Vincent Gerald (Qld) b Jan. 18, 1918 Chinchilla (Qld) d Jan. 23, 1988 Greenslopes (Qld)

McMichael, Samuel Albert (Vic) b July 18, 1869 Collingwood (Vic) d July 21, 1923 Elsternwick (Vic)

McNamara, Bradley Edward (NSW) b Dec. 30, 1965 Sydney (NSW)

McNamee, Raymond Leonard Alphonsus (NSW) b Aug. 26, 1895 Orange (NSW) d Sept. 18, 1949 Little Bay (NSW)

McNaughton, John Leonard (Vic) b Jan. 15, 1884 Richmond (Vic) d Dec. 26, 1970 Lower Kingswood, Surrey (England)

McNees, Darren Alexander (Tas) b June 14, 1979 Nhy West (Vic)

MacNish, William George (NSW) b Oct. 29, 1842 Paddington (NSW) d Nov. 29, 1873 Bundaberg (Qld)

McPetrie, William Martin (Vic) b Feb. 15, 1880 Emerald Hill (Vic) d June 30, 1951 Hawthorn (Vic)

McPhee, Mark William (WAust) b Jan. 25, 1964 Katanning (WAust) d Aug. 15, 1999 Gingin (WAust)

McPhee, Peter Thomas (Tas) b July 29, 1963 South Brisbane (Qld)

MacPherson, Herbert James Keele (NSW) b Feb. 20, 1869 Mudgee (NSW) d Nov. 12, 1953 Mudgee (NSW)

McPherson, James Philip (Vic) b Nov. 20, 1842 Moonee Ponds (Vic) d Aug. 23, 1891 Melbourne (Vic)

McPhillamy, Keith (NSW) b June 20, 1882 Bathurst (NSW) d May 3, 1937 Bowral (NSW)

McRae, Donald (S Aust) b June 13, 1873 Aldinga (S Aust) d Oct. 22, 1940 Prospect (S Aust)

McRae, William Alexander (WAust) b June 18, 1904 Geelong (Vic) d July 25, 1973 Subiaco (WAust)

MacRow, William Reginald Fairbairn (Vic) b July 7, 1889 Kew (Vic) d May 19, 1970 Heidelberg (Vic)

* McShane, Patrick George (Vic) b April 18, 1858 Keilor (Vic) d Dec. 11, 1903 Kew (Vic)

Mace, Christopher (Vic) b Dec. 24, 1830 Bedale, Yorkshire (England) d Nov. 23, 1907 Sydenham (New Zealand)

Madden, Robert Harold (NSW) b Dec. 12, 1928 Camperdown (NSW)

Maddern, James Gregory (Qld) b March 22, 1914 Crows Nest (Qld) d March 27, 1987 Nambour (Qld)

Madders, Garry James (Qld) b Jan. 21, 1953 Maryborough (Qld)

Maddock, Charles Edward Rokeby (Qld) b Aug. 14, 1887 (Qld) d Feb. 14, 1957 Herston (Qld)

Maddocks, Ian Leonard (Vic) b April 12, 1951 Ashburton (Vic)

* Maddocks, Leonard Victor (Vic & Tas) b May 24, 1926 Beaconsfield (Vic)

Maddocks, Richard Ivor (Vic) b July 30, 1928 Carnegie (Vic) d Sept. 10, 1968 Blackburn (Vic)

Maddox, George (Tas) b c. 1811 (Ireland) d July 7, 1867 Melbourne (Vic)

Maddox, John Montgomery (Tas) b Dec. 30, 1930 St Mary's (Tas)

Magarey, William Ashley (S Aust) b Jan. 30, 1868 North Adelaide (S Aust) d Oct. 18, 1929 North Adelaide (S Aust)

Magoffin, Steven James (WAust) b Dec. 17, 1979 Corinda (Qld)

* Maguire, John Norman (Qld) b Sept. 15, 1956 Murwillumbah (NSW)

Maher, James Patrick (Qld) b Feb. 27, 1974 Innisfail (Qld)

Mahoney, Hector James Henry (Qld) b Sept. 8, 1913 Maryborough (Qld) d Sept. 25, 1991 Maryborough (Qld)

Mail, Gregory John (NSW) b April 29, 1978 Penrith (NSW)

Mailer, David (Vic) b Aug. 18, 1874 Coburg (Vic) d Dec. 21, 1937 Shepparton (Vic)

* Mailey, Arthur Alfred (NSW) b Jan. 3, 1886 Zetland (NSW) d Dec. 31, 1967 Kirrawee (NSW)

Mainhardt, Michael Shane (Qld) b Jan. 6, 1960 Clermont (Qld)

Mair, Frederick (NSW) b April 15, 1901 Balmain (NSW) d Dec. 25, 1959 Sydney (NSW)

Majewski, Neil John (Tas) b May 27, 1954 Footscray (Vic)

* Majid Jahangir Khan (Qld) b Sept. 28, 1946 Ludhiana (India)

Major, Albert George (Vic) b March 20, 1851 Langport, Somerset (England) d Oct. 16, 1921 Caulfield (Vic)

Makin, James Charles (Vic) b Feb. 11, 1904 Collingwood (Vic) d Jan. 15, 1973 Heidelberg (Vic)

Makin, William (NSW) birth details unknown d Jan. 11, 1962 West Kogarah (NSW)

Makinson, Charles (Vic) b c. 1831 Salford, Lancashire (England) d June 12, 1895 Rugeley, Staffordshire (England)

* Mallett, Ashley Alexander (S Aust) b July 13, 1945 Chatswood (NSW)

* Malone, Michael Francis (WAust) b Oct. 9, 1950 Perth (WAust)

Maloney, Peter Ivan (NSW) b Nov. 5, 1950 Ballina (NSW)

Mancell, Peter John (Tas) b March 15, 1958 Goulburn (NSW)

* Mann, Anthony Longford (WAust) b Nov. 8, 1945 Middle Swan (WAust)

Mann, John Lewis (S Aust) b April 26, 1919 Strathalbyn (S Aust) d Sept. 24, 1969 Lockleys (S Aust)

Manning, John Stephen (S Aust) b June 11, 1923 Ethelton (S Aust) d May 31, 1988 Belair (S Aust)

Manou, Graham Allan (S Aust) b April 23, 1979 Modbury (S Aust)

Mansfield, Graeme Edward (Tas) b Dec. 27, 1942 Hobart (Tas)

Mansfield, J. (Tas) birth and death details unknown

Maplestone, Henry Carman (Vic) b Jan. 11, 1870 Parkville (Vic) d Dec. 10, 1949 Moonee Ponds (Vic)

Maranta, Michael Gerard (Qld) b March 20, 1961 South Brisbane (Qld)

Marjoribanks, Hugh Lynch (NSW) b Aug. 12, 1933 Mackay (Qld)

Marks, Alexander Edward (NSW) b Dec. 9, 1910 Toowong (Qld) d July 28, 1983 Wahroonga (NSW)

Marks, Lynn Alexander (NSW & S Aust) b Aug. 15, 1942 Randwick (NSW) d Dec. 7, 1997 Mona Vale (NSW)

Marks, Neil Graham (NSW) b Sept. 13, 1938 Randwick (NSW)

Marks, Phillip Henry (NSW) b April 30, 1961 Salisbury (Southern Rhodesia)

* Marks, Victor James (WAust) b June 25, 1955 Middle Chinnock, Somerset (England)

Marquet, Joshua Phillip (Tas) b Dec. 3, 1968 Melbourne (Vic)

* Marr, Alfred Percy (NSW) b March 28, 1862 Pyrmont (NSW) d March 15, 1940 Arncliffe (NSW)

Marriott, Arthur John (Tas) b c. 1821 (England) d March 31, 1866 Nice (France)

Marsden, Albert John (Qld) b June 13, 1887 Maryborough (Qld) d Dec. 17, 1971 Kallista (Vic)

Marsden, Frederick William (Vic) b c. 1819 Lewisham, London (England) d March 20, 1870 Fitzroy (Vic)

Marsh, Daniel James (S Aust & Tas) b June 14, 1973 Subiaco (WAust)

* Marsh, Geoffrey Robert (WAust) b Dec. 31, 1958 Northam (WAust)

Marsh, Jack (NSW) b c. 1874 Yugilbar (NSW) d May 25, 1916 Orange (NSW)

* Marsh, Rodney William (WAust) b Nov. 4, 1947 Armadale (WAust)

Marsh, Shaun Edwards (WAust) b July 9, 1983 Narrogin (WAust)

Marshal, Alan (Qld) b June 12, 1883 Warwick (Qld) d July 23, 1915 Imtarfa Military Hospital (Malta)

Marshall, Angus Neil (Qld) b Jan. 7, 1906 Essequibo (British Guiana) d Aug. 29, 1969 Nundah (Qld)

Marshall, George (Tas) b 1832 birth day and month unknown Sorell (Tas) d July 13, 1905 Sorell (Tas)

Marshall, George (Vic) b Dec. 20, 1829 Nottingham, Nottinghamshire (England) d March 6, 1868 Melbourne (Vic)

Marshall, John (Tas) b c. 1796 (England) d Sept. 7, 1876 New Town (Tas)

Martin, Charles (Qld) b May 15, 1867 Ipswich (Qld) d c. 1942 Sydney (NSW)

Martin, Charles Albert (S Aust) b March 29, 1863 Adelaide (S Aust) d May 14, 1955 St Georges (S Aust)

Martin, Charles William Beresford (Tas) b Oct. 6, 1888 Launceston (Tas) d Oct. 30, 1951 Camberwell (Vic)

Martin, Edmund John (W Aust) b Sept. 26, 1902 Eaglehawk (Vic) d June 9, 2004 Perth (W Aust)

Martin, Geoffrey Bernard (Tas) b July 16, 1927 Launceston (Tas)

Martin, Geoffrey William (Tas) b March 7, 1896 Launceston (Tas) d March 7, 1968 Launceston (Tas)

Martin, Gordon Francis (Qld) b Jan. 14, 1885 Clunes (Vic) d Aug. 19, 1974 Canberra (ACT)

Martin, Hugh (NSW) b Aug. 3, 1947 Enkeldoorn (Southern Rhodesia)

Martin, James Macfie (Tas) b Feb. 25, 1851 Launceston (Tas) d Oct. 22, 1930 Launceston (Tas)

Martin, John Frank (NSW) b May 8, 1942 Alton, Hampshire (England)

* Martin, John Wesley (NSW & S Aust) b July 28, 1931 Wingham (NSW) d July 15, 1992 Burrell Creek (NSW)

Martin, William (Tas) b June 21, 1856 Westbury (Tas) d July 10, 1938 Launceston (Tas)

* Martyn, Damien Richard (W Aust) b Oct. 21, 1971 Darwin (NT)

Mason, Matthew Sean (W Aust) b March 20, 1974 Claremont (W Aust)

Mason, Scott Robert (Tas) b July 27, 1976 Launceston (Tas) d April 9, 2005 Hobart (Tas)

Massey, Richard Eric Charles (S Aust) b June 5, 1961 Tamworth (NSW)

* Massie, Hugh Hamon (NSW) b April 11, 1854 near Belfast (Vic) d Oct. 12, 1938 Point Piper (NSW)

* Massie, Robert Arnold Lockyer (W Aust) b April 14, 1947 Subiaco (W Aust)

Massie, Robert John Allwright (NSW) b July 8, 1890 North Sydney (NSW) d Feb. 14, 1966 Mosman (NSW)

Mateljan, Tony (W Aust) b Feb. 18, 1934 Middle Swan (W Aust)

Mather, Adam (NSW) b Nov. 26, 1860 Paterson (NSW) d Aug. 31, 1917 Singleton (NSW)

Mather, John Henry (Vic) b Nov. 19, 1822 Everton, Lancashire (England) d Aug. 4, 1870 Iquique (Chile)

Mathers, James (Vic) b June 30, 1894 Minmi (NSW) d March 28, 1977 Eastwood (NSW)

Mathieson, Donald Kenneth (Vic) b April 24, 1931 Nhill (Vic)

Matson, George (Tas) b Dec. 5, 1817 Rochester, Kent (England) d July 22, 1898 Brighton, Sussex (England)

* Matthews, Christopher Darrell (W Aust & Tas) b Sept. 22, 1962 Cunderdin (W Aust)

* Matthews, Gregory Richard John (NSW) b Dec. 15, 1959 Newcastle (NSW)

Matthews, James George Facey (S Aust) b Sept. 27, 1876 Roseworthy (S Aust) d Oct. 8, 1963 Prospect (S Aust)

Matthews, Robert Graham (Vic) b April 17, 1953 Camberwell (Vic)

Matthews, Thomas Harold (Tas) b Feb. 9, 1905 Longley (Tas) d May 11, 1990 Longley (Tas)

* Matthews, Thomas James (Vic) b April 3, 1884 Mt Gambier (S Aust) d Oct. 14, 1943 Caulfield (Vic)

Maxwell, Eustace (Tas) b Jan. 20, 1864 Hobart (Tas) d May 18, 1939 Hobart (Tas)

Maxwell, Neil Donald (Vic & NSW) b June 12, 1967 Lautoka (Fiji)

* May, Timothy Brian Alexander (S Aust) b Jan. 26, 1962 North Adelaide (S Aust)

Mayes, Alexander Dunbar Aitken (NSW & Qld) b July 24, 1901 Toowoomba (Qld) d Feb. 8, 1983 Spring Hill (Qld)

* Mayne, Lawrence Charles (W Aust) b Jan. 23, 1942 Westonia (W Aust)

* Mayne, Richard Edgar (S Aust & Vic) b July 2, 1882 Jamestown (S Aust) d Oct. 26, 1961 Richmond (Vic)

* Meckiff, Ian (Vic) b Jan. 6, 1935 Mentone (Vic)

Meech, James Robert (Tas) b Dec. 16, 1884 Hobart (Tas) d Oct. 31, 1955 Hobart (Tas)

Meek, Andrew Bonar (W Aust) b Dec. 7, 1889 Gulgong (NSW) d Feb. 13, 1957 Perth (W Aust)

Meikle, George Stanley (Vic) b Oct. 22, 1916 Footscray (Vic) d July 25, 1991 Brighton (Vic)

Melville, Paul (Vic) b Dec. 27, 1956 South Shields, Durham (England) d Nov. 21, 1978 Vermont South (Vic)

Menegon, Lyndon John (Tas) b Feb. 11, 1948 Burnie (Tas)

Mengel, Douglas Charles (Qld) b March 2, 1933 Brisbane (Qld)

Metcalfe, Evelyn James (Qld) b Sept. 29, 1865 Kennington, Kent (England) d June 14, 1951 Cambridge, Cambridgeshire (England)

* Meuleman, Kenneth Douglas (Vic & WAust) b Sept. 5, 1923 Melbourne (Vic) d Sept. 9, 2004 Nedlands (Waust)

Meuleman, Robert Douglas (WAust) b Sept. 6, 1949 Melbourne (Vic)

Meuleman, Scott William (WAust) b July 17, 1980 Subiaco (WAust)

Michael, Constantine Anthony (WAust) b Jan. 12, 1953 Victoria Park (WAust)

Michael, Leonard (S Aust) b June 3, 1921 Medindie (S Aust) d March 16, 1996 Adelaide (S Aust)

Middleton, Frederick Stewart (NSW) b May 28, 1883 Burrowa (now Booroowa) (NSW) d July 21, 1956 Auckland (New Zealand)

Middleton, Roy Foster (S Aust) b Sept. 18, 1889 Kent Town (S Aust) d March 19, 1975 Adelaide (S Aust)

**Midwinter, William Evans (Vic) b June 19, 1851 St Briavel's, Gloucestershire (England) d Dec. 3, 1890 Kew Asylum (Vic)

Mihell, Robert William (Qld) b Jan. 8, 1937 Lismore (NSW)

* Milburn, Colin (WAust) b Oct. 23, 1941 Burnopfield, Durham (England) d Feb. 28, 1990 Newton Aycliffe, Durham (England)

Miles, Geoffrey John (Vic) b Aug. 7, 1957 Kew (Vic)

Millar, Geoffrey Alan (WAust) b Nov. 22, 1955 Subiaco (WAust)

Millar, Keith James (Vic) b Aug. 15, 1906 Richmond (Vic) d July 13, 1971 Camberwell (Vic)

* Miller, Colin Reid (Vic, S Aust & Tas) b Feb. 6, 1964 Footscray (Vic)

Miller, David Lawson (NSW & Qld) b Jan. 30, 1870 Holytown, Lanarkshire (Scotland) d April 12, 1943 Clayfield (Qld)

Miller, Graeme Geoffrey (Combined XI) b Sept. 24, 1940 Launceston (Tas)

Miller, Ivan Derness (Vic) b Dec. 30, 1913 Ivanhoe (Vic) d May 6, 1966 Heidelberg (Vic)

* Miller, Keith Ross (Vic & NSW) b Nov. 28, 1919 Sunshine (Vic) d Oct. 11, 2004 Mornington (Vic)

Miller, Kevin Roy (Tas) b Oct. 12, 1936 Launceston (Tas)

Miller, Leslie Percy Robert (Vic) b June 16, 1880 St Kilda (Vic) d July 2, 1963 death place unknown

Miller, Michael Christian (Qld & S Aust) b May 30, 1979 Toowoomba (Qld)

Miller, Noel Keith (NSW) b July 1, 1913 Wyong (NSW)

Miller, William Edward (WAust) b March 9, 1905 East Perth (WAust) d July 24, 1974 Perth (WAust)

Milliken, Geoffrey Scott (NSW) b May 6, 1964 Hay (NSW)

Millns, David James (Tas) b Feb. 27, 1965 Clipstone, Nottinghamshire (England)

Mills, John (NSW) b June 3, 1836 Botley Hampshire (England) d Feb. 24, 1899 Bisterne, Hampshire (England)

Mills, Rowland Leslie (WAust) b July 14, 1914 Leederville (WAust) d Feb. 27, 2000 Perth (WAust)

Milosz, Stephen Joseph (WAust & Tas) b Dec. 26, 1955 Northam (WAust)

Minagall, Matthew John Peter (S Aust) b Nov. 13, 1971 Woodville (S Aust)

Minchin, James Melbourne (Vic) b Aug. 15, 1859 Emerald Hill (Vic) d Feb. 13, 1919 Cheltenham (Vic)

Minnett, Leslie Alma (NSW) b May 19, 1883 St Leonard's (NSW) d Aug. 8, 1934 Collaroy (NSW)

* Minnett, Roy Baldwin (NSW) b June 13, 1886 St Leonard's (NSW) d Oct. 21, 1955 Manly (NSW)

Minnett, Rupert Villiers (NSW) b Sept. 2, 1884 St Leonard's (NSW) d June 24, 1974 Cremorne (NSW)

Minter, Eric James (NSW) b Sept. 13, 1917 Kempsey (NSW) d July 1, 1985 Vincentia (NSW)

* Misson, Francis Michael (NSW) b Nov. 19, 1938 Darlinghurst (NSW)

Mitchell, Brian Gordon (S Aust) b March 15, 1959 Glenelg (S Aust)

Mitchell, Norman Frederick (Vic) b Feb. 19, 1900 Collingwood (Vic) d March 8, 1973 Melbourne (Vic)

Mitchell, Robert (Vic) b April 11, 1863 Campbellfield (Vic) d Sept. 17, 1926 West Preston (Vic)

Moffat, William (S Aust) b July 22, 1858 Byethorne (S Aust) d July 30, 1922 Jamestown (S Aust)

Moffatt, Alfred Augustine (WAust) b March 15, 1870 Perth (WAust) d Dec. 8, 1956 Perth (WAust)

Moir, Bruce Graeme (Vic) b Nov. 10, 1960 Melbourne (Vic)

Monfries, John Elliott (Vic) b Dec. 25, 1873 Gumeracha (S Aust) d Sept. 2, 1954 Hobart (Tas)

Monohan, Vincent Clifford (Vic) b April 22, 1896 Collingwood (Vic) d July 9, 1974 Linden Park (S Aust)

Monty, Stephen (Qld) b March 3, 1963 Glenelg (S Aust)

* Moody, Thomas Masson (WAust) b Oct. 2, 1965 Adelaide (S Aust)

Moore, David John Arthur (NSW) b Oct. 16, 1964 Sydney (NSW)

Moore, George (NSW) b April 18, 1820 Ampthill, Bedfordshire (England) d Sept. 29, 1916 West Maitland (NSW)

Moore, George Stanley (NSW & Qld) b April 18, 1886 North Sydney (NSW) d March 22, 1948 Bundaberg (Qld)

Moore, Henry Thomas (S Aust) b c. 1860 Plomesgate (England) death details unknown

Moore, James (NSW) b c. 1839 Ampthill, Bedfordshire (England) d April 19, 1890 West Maitland (NSW)

Moore, Leonard David (NSW) b Feb. 8, 1871 West Maitland (NSW) d Sept. 11, 1934 Maitland (NSW)

Moore, William Henry (NSW & WAust) b Oct. 16, 1863 West Maitland (NSW) d Feb. 25, 1956 Lane Cove (NSW)

Morcom, Samuel (Combined XIII) b c. 1847 full birth details unknown d Jan. 15, 1888 Adelaide (S Aust)

Morgan, Charles Edward (Vic) b Aug. 10, 1900 Collingwood (Vic) d Dec. 8, 1965 Preston (Vic)

Morgan, Charles William (Qld) b Jan. 10, 1877 Hotham (Vic) d April 15, 1937 death place unknown

Morgan, George (NSW) b July 7, 1844 Bathurst (NSW) d July 17, 1896 Sydney (NSW)

Morgan, John Gordon (NSW) b March 6, 1893 Camperdown (NSW) d May 7, 1967 Concord (NSW)

Morgan, Oliver John (Qld) b June 7, 1945 Herston (Qld)

Morgan, Walter Millard (Vic) b Nov. 1, 1871 Ballarat (Vic) d July 10, 1941 Ballarat (Vic)

Morgan, Wayne Geoffrey (Qld) b July 10, 1955 Greenslopes (Qld)

* Moroney, John (NSW) b July 24, 1917 Macksville (NSW) d July 1, 1999 Orange (NSW)

Moroney, Robert (S Aust) b Jan. 23, 1885 Upper Sturt (S Aust) d Aug. 4, 1958 Parkside (S Aust)

Morres, Thomas Furley (Vic) b Sept. 12, 1829 Wokingham, Berkshire (England) d Sept. 28, 1884 East Melbourne (Vic)

* Morris, Arthur Robert (NSW) b Jan. 19, 1922 Bondi (NSW)

Morris, John Humphrey (NSW) b June 5, 1831 Sydney (NSW) d Dec. 9, 1921 Glebe Point (NSW)

Morris, Maesmore Alfred (Vic) b April 30, 1868 Northcote (Vic) d Aug. 31, 1917 Heidelberg (Vic)

Morris, Norman O'Neil (NSW) b May 9, 1907 Camperdown (NSW) d July 15, 1982 Leichhardt (NSW)

* Morris, Samuel (Vic) b June 22, 1855 Hobart (Tas) d Sept. 20, 1931 South Melbourne (Vic)

Morris, William Wallace (Qld) b March 6, 1918 Thornleigh (NSW)

Morrisby, Ronald Orlando George (Tas) b Jan. 12, 1915 Hobart (Tas) d June 12, 1995 Hobart (Tas)

Morrissey, Charles Vincent (NSW) b April 26, 1903 Corowa (NSW) d Feb. 20, 1938 Quirindi (NSW)

Morse, Eric George Arnold (Tas) b Aug. 26, 1918 Sheffield (Tas)

Morton, Francis Lonsdale (S Aust & Vic) b Dec. 21, 1901 Fullarton (S Aust) d Oct. 14, 1971 Caulfield (Vic)

Morton, Hugh Gilbert Stuart (Qld) b Oct. 14, 1881 Maryborough (Qld) d Jan. 28, 1936 Herston (Qld)

* Moses, Henry (NSW) b Feb. 13, 1858 Windsor (NSW) d Dec. 7, 1938 Strathfield (NSW)

* Moss, Jeffrey Kenneth (Vic) b June 29, 1947 Melbourne (Vic)

Moss, Jonathan (Vic) b May 4, 1975 Manly (NSW)

Moss, Ronald Barbar (NSW) b June 13, 1922 Alexandria (NSW)

Mossop, Kenneth Leonard Mario (Qld) b Aug. 15, 1909 New Farm (Qld) d Sept. 18, 1975 Surfers Paradise (Qld)

Mott, Matthew Peter (Qld & Vic) b Oct. 3, 1973 Charleville (Qld)

* Moule, William Henry (Vic) b Jan. 31, 1858 Brighton (Vic) d Aug. 24, 1939 St Kilda (Vic)

Moyes, Alban George (S Aust & Vic) b Jan. 2, 1893 Gladstone (S Aust) d Jan. 18, 1963 Chatswood (NSW)

Moyle, Charles Rule (S Aust) b April 16, 1884 Adelaide (S Aust) d Aug. 2, 1952 Adelaide (S Aust)

Moyle, Edward James Ross (S Aust) b Oct. 15, 1913 Moonta Mines (S Aust) d Oct. 24, 1942 Cairo (Egypt) on active service

Moysey, George Bickford (WAust) b May 14, 1874 Battery Point (Tas) d May 18, 1932 Canterbury (Vic)

Muddle, Donald Gordon (Qld) b July 26, 1937 The Grange (Qld)

Mudge, Harold (NSW) b Feb. 14, 1914 Stanmore (NSW)

Mueller, Mervyn Edward Christopher Edgar (S Aust) b Oct. 3, 1914 Yatala (S Aust) d July 22, 1984 South Plympton (S Aust)

Muggleton, Mervyn Brian (WAust) b Sept. 4, 1941 Unley (S Aust)

Muhl, Arthur Henry (Qld) b Feb. 12, 1913 South Brisbane (Qld) d April 17, 1994 South Brisbane (Qld)

Muir, William Frederick (Vic) b Feb. 8, 1907 Prahran (Vic) d Nov. 27, 1964 Box Hill (Vic)

Mulder, Brett (WAust) b Feb. 6, 1964 Subiaco (WAust)

Mulherin, Wayne Michael (NSW) b June 17, 1957 Canterbury (NSW)

Mullagh, Johnny (Unaarrimin) (Vic) b Aug. 13, 1841 Harrow (Vic) d Aug. 14, 1891 Pine Hills Station (Vic)

* Mullally, Alan David (WAust) b July 12, 1969 Southend-on-Sea, Essex (England)

Mullarkey, Desmond Antony (NSW) b Sept. 19, 1899 Rockdale (NSW) d July 30, 1975 Randwick (NSW)

* Muller, Scott Andrew (Qld) b July 11, 1971 Herston (Qld)

Mullett, David Anthony (Tas) b Aug. 18, 1958 Burnie (Tas)

Mullett, Leonard Thomas (Vic) b Nov. 27, 1894 Moonee Ponds (Vic) d April 22, 1944 Toorak (Vic)

Mullooly, Thomas Cade (WAust) b Jan. 30, 1954 Mt Lawley (WAust)

Mundy, David Lloyd (S Aust) b June 30, 1947 Enfield (S Aust)

Munn, Arthur Reginald (NSW) b Feb. 22, 1888 Paddington (NSW) d Sept. 15, 1975 Sydney (NSW)

Munro, Charles (WAust) b March 21, 1871 Wallan (Vic) d Feb. 7, 1969 North Fremantle (WAust)

Munro, John Knox Ewing (WAust) b Dec. 27, 1928 Perth (WAust)

Munro, William (Qld) b Aug. 7, 1862 Ardwick, Lancashire (England) d Feb. 18, 1896 Stanthorpe (Qld)

Murch, Stewart Nigel Clifford (Vic) b June 27, 1944 Warrnambool (Vic)

**Murdoch, William Lloyd (NSW) b Oct. 18, 1854 Sandhurst (Vic) d Feb. 18, 1911 Melbourne (Vic)

Murfett, Julian Ivor (Tas) b July 2, 1915 Dunorlan (Tas) d April 27, 1982 Hobart (Tas)

Murphy, James Joseph (NSW) b Sept. 29, 1911 Bega (NSW) d May 7, 1984 Glenfield (NSW)

Murphy, Michael Augustus (Vic) b June 12, 1854 Sydney (NSW) d Sept. 2, 1890 Richmond (Vic)

Murray, Alfred Wynyatt (Vic) b Feb. 4, 1868 Long Gully (Vic) d July 29, 1936 Regent (Vic)

Murray, George Ian (WAust) b Nov. 6, 1940 South Perth (WAust)

Murray, John Tinline (S Aust) b Dec. 1, 1892 Norwood (S Aust) d Sept. 19, 1974 Stirling (S Aust)

Murray, Norman Eric (Tas) b Nov. 2, 1908 Perth (WAust) d Aug. 21, 1967 Manly (NSW)

Murray, Richard (NSW) b c. 1831 Sydney (NSW) d Nov. 21, 1861 Manly (NSW)

Murray, William Walter Bruce (Vic) b Sept. 4, 1929 Red Cliffs (Vic)

* Musgrove, Henry Alfred (Vic) b Nov. 27, 1860 Surbiton, Surrey (England) d Nov. 2, 1931 Darlinghurst (NSW)

Musgrove, John (S Aust) b July 28, 1861 Adelaide (S Aust) d June 9, 1940 death place unknown

Mutton, Howard James Charles (S Aust) b Oct. 21, 1924 Angaston (S Aust) d Nov. 20 1992 Adelaide (S Aust)

Myers, Hubert (Tas) b Jan. 2, 1875 Yeadon Yorkshire (England) d June 12, 1944 Hobart (Tas)

* Nagel, Lisle Ernest (Vic) b March 26, 1905 Bendigo (Vic) d Nov. 23, 1971 Mornington (Vic)

Nagel, Vernon George (Vic) b March 26, 1905 Bendigo (Vic) d April 27, 1974 Sandringham (Vic)

Nash, Brendan Paul (Qld) b Dec. 14, 1977 Bentley (WAust)

Nash, Don Anthony (NSW) b March 29, 1978 Dubbo (NSW)

Nash, John Eric (S Aust) b April 16, 1950 North Adelaide (S Aust)

* Nash, Laurence John (Tas & Vic) b May 2, 1910 Fitzroy (Vic) d July 24, 1986 Heidelberg (Vic)

Neill, Bruce William (Tas) b Feb. 23, 1949 Cabramatta (NSW)

Nettelton, Robert Glanville (Vic) b Sept. 16, 1909 Newport (Vic) d April 6, 1972 Newport (Vic)

Neville, Kevin John (Vic) b March 24, 1968 Numurkah (Vic)

Neville, Warwick John (Qld) b Dec. 31, 1948 Melbourne (Vic)

Newcombe, Henry Charles Edwin (NSW) b c. 1835 Sydney (NSW) d Oct. 26, 1908 Randwick (NSW)

Newell, Andrew Livingstone (NSW) b Nov. 13, 1865 Dungog (NSW) death details unknown

Newland, Philip Mesmer (S Aust) b Feb. 2, 1875 Kensington (S Aust) d Aug. 11, 1916 Knightsbridge (S Aust)

Newman, Charles Frederick (WAust) b Nov. 7, 1909 Fremantle (WAust) d March 28, 1977 Fremantle (WAust)

Newman, Henry Albert (WAust) b March 13, 1907 Fremantle (WAust) d April 23, 1988 Riverton (WAust)

Newman, Richard Nelson (Tas) b Aug. 9, 1924 Brunswick (Vic)

Newstead, George Holt (Vic) b Aug. 11, 1910 Brighton (Vic) d July 21, 2000 Deepdene (Vic)

Newton, Alan Colin (Tas) b April 6, 1894 Longford (Tas) d March 27, 1979 Narrabeen (NSW)

Newton, Percy Allen (NSW) b Dec. 21, 1880 Newtown (NSW) d April 25, 1946 Rose Bay (NSW)

Nichols, Arthur Joseph (NSW) b Sept. 3, 1881 Sydney (NSW) d Nov. 19, 1937 North Sydney (NSW)

Nicholls, Charles Omer (NSW) b Dec. 5, 1901 Freeman's Reach (NSW) d Jan. 14, 1983 Freeman's Reach (NSW)

Nicholls, Paul Allen (WAust) b Nov. 10, 1946 East Fremantle (WAust)

Nicholls, Ronald Charles (Vic) b Sept. 1, 1951 Footscray (Vic)

* Nicholson, Matthew James (WAust & NSW) b Oct. 2, 1974 St Leonard's (NSW)

Nicolson, John Norman Walter (Tas) b April 14, 1917 Campbell Town (Tas) d Oct. 7, 1992 Launceston (Tas)

Niehuus, Richard Dudley (S Aust) b July 6, 1917 St Peters (S Aust)

Nielsen, Timothy John (S Aust) b May 5, 1968 Forest Gate, London (England)

Nikitaras, Steven (NSW & WAust) b Aug. 31, 1970 Port Kembla (NSW)

* Nitschke, Holmesdale Carl (S Aust) b April 14, 1905 Adelaide (S Aust) d Sept. 29, 1982 North Adelaide (S Aust)

Nobes, Paul Christopher (Vic & S Aust) b April 20, 1964 West Heidelberg (Vic)

Noble, Edward George (NSW) b Jan. 16, 1865 Brickfield Hill (NSW) d May 4, 1941 Balmain (NSW)

* Noble, Montague Alfred (NSW) b Jan. 28, 1873 Sydney (NSW) d June 22, 1940 Randwick (NSW)

* Noblet, Geffery (S Aust) b Sept. 14, 1916 Evandale (S Aust)

Noel, John (S Aust) b March 28, 1856 Hindmarsh (S Aust) d Jan. 9, 1938 Largs Bay (S Aust)

Noffke, Ashley Allan (Cricket Academy) b April 30, 1977 Nambour (Qld)

Nolan, Francis Edward (Qld) b June 27, 1920 Manly (Qld)

Noonan, Daniel Francis (Vic) b May 11, 1873 North Melbourne (Vic) d May 30, 1910 North Melbourne (Vic)

Noonan, David James (NSW) b Jan. 8, 1876 Newtown (NSW) d March 10, 1929 Sydney (NSW)

Norman, Michael John (Tas) b Aug. 17, 1952 Launceston (Tas)

Norman, Hercules Rex Clive (NSW) b Aug. 8, 1891 North Annandale (NSW) d Dec. 30, 1961 Parramatta (NSW)

North, Frederic Dudley (WAust) b Nov. 9, 1866 Kensington, London, Middlesex (England) d Aug. 22, 1921 Cottesloe (WAust)

North, Marcus James (WAust) b July 28, 1979 Melbourne (Vic)

* Nothling, Otto Ernest (NSW & Qld) b Aug. 1, 1900 Teutoburg (Qld) d Sept. 26, 1965 Chelmer (Qld)

Noyes, Alfred William Finch (Vic) b c. 1835 Torquay, Devon (England) d Sept. 30, 1902 Deniliquin (NSW)

Noyes, Harold David (Qld) b Aug. 12, 1892 Warwick (Qld) d July 14, 1968 Brisbane (Qld)

Numa, Herbert Leslie (Vic) b June 22, 1925 Carlton (Vic) d April 17, 1984 Heidelberg (Vic)

Nunn, Thomas (NSW) b Jan. 21, 1846 Penshurst, Kent (England) d May 31, 1889 Bexley (NSW)

Nutt, Richard Nathaniel (NSW) b June 25, 1911 Balmain (NSW) d Feb. 5, 1985 Gladesville (NSW)

Nye, Aaron James (Qld) b Nov. 9, 1978 Herston (Qld)

Oakes, Cecil James Grellis (Tas) b March 1, 1915 Hobart (Tas) d Oct. 10, 1994 Canberra (ACT)

Oakley, Hector Herbert (Vic) b Jan. 10, 1909 North Fitzroy (Vic) d Dec. 19, 1998 Sandringham (Vic)

Oatley, James Napoleon (NSW) b Aug. 12, 1845 Newtown (NSW) d Dec. 17, 1925 Cremorne (NSW)

O'Brien, Aaron Warren (NSW) b Oct. 2, 1981 St Leonard's (NSW)

O'Brien, Charles Joseph (NSW) b May 19, 1921 d Dec. 15, 1980 Coal Point (NSW)

O'Brien, Ernest Francis (NSW) b Aug. 26, 1900 Paddington (NSW) d Nov. 2, 1935 Newcastle (NSW)

* O'Brien, Leo Patrick Joseph (Vic) b July 2, 1907 West Melbourne (Vic) d March 13, 1997 Mentone (Vic)

O'Brien, Leslie John (NSW) d c. 1968 full birth and death details unknown

O'Brien, Matthew Evanson (Anderson's XI) details unknown

O'Brien, Robert (Qld) b July 16, 1869 Redfern (NSW) d Oct. 2, 1922 Brisbane (Qld)

O'Connell, Thomas Reginald (S Aust) b March 10, 1916 Parkside (S Aust)

O'Connor, Brian Redmond Devereaux (Qld) b July 5, 1913 South Brisbane (Qld) d Dec. 17, 1963 Red Hill (Qld)

O'Connor, Donald Frederick Gregory (S Aust & Tas) b July 20, 1958 Gilgandra (NSW)

* O'Connor, John Denis Alphonsus (NSW & S Aust) b Sept. 9, 1875 Booroowa (NSW) d Aug. 23, 1941 Lewisham (NSW)

O'Connor, John William (Vic) b Aug. 19, 1868 Geelong (Vic) d Feb. 2, 1952 Windsor (Vic)

O'Connor, Leo Patrick Devereaux (Qld) b April 11, 1890 Murtoa (Vic) d Jan. 16, 1985 Melbourne (Vic)

* O'Donnell, Simon Patrick (Vic) b Jan. 26, 1963 Deniliquin (NSW)

O'Dwyer, Thomas Edmund (WAust) b Nov. 5, 1919 Bridgetown (WAust)

* Ogilvie, Alan David (Qld) b June 3, 1951 Southport (Qld)

Ogilvy, David Skene (NSW) b June 7, 1859 Wollongong (NSW) d Aug. 6, 1917 Liverpool (NSW)

O'Halloran, Dale Francis (Tas) b Feb. 15, 1955 Smithton (Tas)

O'Halloran, James Patrick (Vic) b Jan. 12, 1872 Richmond (Vic) d April 28, 1943 East Melbourne (Vic)

O'Halloran, William Matthew (Vic) b June 18, 1934 Corowa (NSW) d Dec. 13, 1994 East Melbourne (Vic)

O'Hanlon, William James (NSW) b March 10, 1863 Carlton (Vic) d June 23, 1940 Randwick (NSW)

Ohlstrom, Patrick Andreas Paul (S Aust) b Dec. 16, 1890 Warooka (S Aust) d June 10, 1940 Adelaide (S Aust)

O'Keeffe, Francis Aloysius (NSW & Vic) b May 11, 1896 Waverley (NSW) d March 26, 1924 Hampstead, London (England)

* O'Keeffe, Kerry James (NSW) b Nov. 25, 1949 Hurstville (NSW)

O'Leary, Scott James (Qld) b Dec. 17, 1977 South Brisbane (Qld)

* Oldfield, William Albert Stanley (NSW) b Sept. 9, 1894 Alexandria (NSW) d Aug. 10, 1976 Killara (NSW)

Oldroyd, Bradley John (WAust) b Nov. 5, 1973 Bentley (WAust)

Oliver, Benjamin Carl (Vic & Tas) b Oct. 24, 1979 Castlemaine (Vic)

Oliver, Charles Nicholson Jewel (NSW) b April 24, 1848 Hobart (Tas) d June 14, 1920 Manly (NSW)

Oliver, Stuart Bradley (Tas) b March 20, 1972 Launceston (Tas)

O'Meara, Phillip Anthony (WAust) b June 13, 1951 Kellerberrin (WAust)

O'Mullane, George Jeremiah Patrick (Vic) b Dec. 3, 1842 Melbourne (Vic) d Dec. 20, 1866 East Melbourne (Vic)

O'Neill, Kevin Ignatius (S Aust) b Aug. 16, 1919 Hectorville (S Aust)

O'Neill, Mark Dorian (WAust & NSW) b March 5, 1959 Sutherland (NSW)

* O'Neill, Norman Clifford (NSW) b Feb. 19, 1937 Carlton (NSW)

Onyons, Basil Austin (Vic) b March 14, 1887 Prahran (Vic) d May 31, 1967 Glen Iris (Vic)

O'Regan, James Bernard (NSW) b April 23, 1938 Ashfield (NSW) d May 15, 1998 Randwick (NSW)

O'Reilly, John William (NSW) b Nov. 16, 1930 Mosman (NSW)

* O'Reilly, William Joseph (NSW) b Dec. 20, 1905 White Cliffs (NSW) d Oct. 6, 1992 Sutherland (NSW)

Orr, Herbert Richard (WAust) b Feb. 3, 1865 Kensington, London (England) d May 22, 1940 Sevenoaks, Kent (England)

Osborn, Francis James (S Aust) b Feb. 13, 1935 Alberton (S Aust)

Osborne, Mark (Vic) b Oct. 8, 1961 Kogarah (NSW)

Osborne, Noton Michael (Vic) b c. 1844 (England) d Dec. 10, 1878 Hobart (Tas)

Osborne, Robert Henry (NSW) b Feb. 4, 1897 Redfern (NSW) d Feb. 21, 1975 Long Jetty (NSW)

Osborne, Robert Moorhead (Vic) b Sept. 29, 1881 St Kilda (Vic) d Nov. 19, 1927 Wesburn (Vic)

O'Shannassy, Robert Martin (S Aust) b March 7, 1949 Hindmarsh (S Aust)

O'Shaughnessy, Barney (WAust) b Feb. 28, 1912 Wiluna (WAust)

Oswald, Norman Hamilton (S Aust) b Oct. 31, 1916 Prospect (S Aust) d June 22, 1970 Adelaide (S Aust)

Outridge, Thomas Michael (WAust) b Sept. 8, 1927 Perth (WAust) d July 21, 2003 Bunbury (WAust)

Over, Willie (Vic) b Jan. 20, 1862 Richmond (Vic) d Nov. 10, 1910 Krugersdorp, Transvaal (South Africa)

Owen, Christopher John (S Aust) b Dec. 21, 1963 Henley Beach (S Aust)

Owen, Kerry Alfred (NSW) b June 23, 1943 Bondi Beach (NSW)

Oxenford, Bruce Nicholas James (Qld) b March 5, 1960 Southport (Qld)

Oxenford, Ian Bruce (Qld) b Sept. 3, 1932 South Brisbane (Qld)

Oxenham, Lionel Emmanuel (Qld) b Jan. 27, 1888 Nundah (Qld) d Jan. 10, 1970 Clayfield (Qld)

* Oxenham, Ronald Keven (Qld) b July 28, 1891 Nundah (Qld) d Aug. 16, 1939 Nundah (Qld)

Packman, James Russell (NSW) b Aug. 21, 1979 Paddington (NSW)

Packham, Leonard (WAust) b Sept. 15, 1891 Norwood (S Aust) d Oct. 4, 1958 Swanbourne (WAust)

Page, Clive Basil (Qld) b May 25, 1894 Rockhampton (Qld) d July 1, 1967 Greenslopes (Qld)

Palfreyman, Brent Avis Hardcastle (Tas) b Jan. 20, 1945 Hobart (Tas)

* Palmer, George Eugene (Vic & Tas) b Feb. 22, 1859 Mulwala (NSW) d Aug. 22, 1910 Benalla (Vic)

Palmer, George Hamilton (S Aust) b Aug. 2, 1903 Eastwood (S Aust) d Aug. 24, 1986 Woodville South (S Aust)

Palmer, Jack Stirling (S Aust) b Oct. 20, 1903 East Adelaide (S Aust) d Dec. 11, 1979 Glenelg (S Aust)

Panitzki, Robert James (Tas) b April 29, 1948 Hobart (Tas)

Park, Alfred Leath (NSW) b April 15, 1840 Oatlands (Tas) d Jan. 16, 1924 Liverpool (NSW)

* Park, Roy Lindsay (Vic) b July 30, 1892 Charlton (Vic) d Jan. 23, 1947 Middle Park (Vic)

Parker, Alec David (Qld) b June 12, 1955 Dalby (Qld)

Parker, Ernest Frederick (WAust) b Nov. 5, 1883 Perth (WAust) d May 2, 1918 Caestre (France)

Parker, Geoffrey Ross (Vic & S Aust) b March 31, 1968 Malvern (Vic)

Parker, John Francis (WAust) b March 13, 1936 South Perth (WAust)

Parker, Robert Ernest (Qld) b Sept. 18, 1942 Toowoomba (Qld)

Parker, Ronald Arthur (S Aust) b Feb. 23, 1916 Goodwood (S Aust) d Aug. 27, 1993 San Francisco, California (United States of America)

Parker, Russell John (S Aust) b Aug. 3, 1952 Sudbury, Middlesex (England)

Parkin, George Thomas (S Aust) b Oct. 11, 1864 Adelaide (S Aust) d Aug. 6, 1933 Adelaide (S Aust)

Parkinson, Henry (Tas) b June 10, 1882 Port Arthur (Tas) d c. 1962 death place unknown

Parkinson, Samuel David Haslam (S Aust) b July 8, 1960 Adelaide (S Aust)

Parry, Cyril Norman (S Aust & Tas) b Oct. 14, 1900 Queenstown (S Aust) d July 6, 1984 Kew (Vic)

Parsonage, Thomas Griffiths (NSW) b Nov. 13, 1910 Chatswood (NSW) d Feb. 3, 1951 Manly (NSW)

Parsons, Herbert Fulton (Vic) b May 21, 1875 Hawthorn (Vic) d Dec. 20, 1937 Canterbury (Vic)

* Pascoe, Len Stephen (NSW) b Feb. 13, 1950 Bridgetown (WAust)

Pascoe, Matthew David (Qld) b Jan. 10, 1977 Camperdown (NSW)

Pateman, Robert (Vic) b Aug. 28, 1856 Magpie (Vic) death details unknown

Patfield, Alfred Samuel (WAust) b Sept. 6, 1884 Paterson (WAust) d Nov. 9, 1961 Perth (WAust)

Paton, George Douglas (Tas) b March 1, 1879 Hobart (Tas) d Oct. 5, 1950 Hobart (Tas)

Patrick, Charles Wright (NSW & Qld) b Jan. 13, 1866 Sydney (NSW) d Nov. 29, 1919 Coogee (NSW)

* Patterson, Balfour Patrick (Tas) b Sept. 15, 1961 Portland (Jamaica)

Patterson, Brian Clifford (Tas) b June 28, 1937 Hobart (Tas)

Patterson, Mark Winston (NSW) b Nov. 15, 1966 Dubbo (NSW)

Patterson, Thomas Francis (Tas) b Sept. 16, 1839 Hobart (Tas)

Paulsen, Robert George (Qld & WAust) b Oct. 18, 1947 Herston (Qld)

Pavy, Leonard (WAust) b Aug. 21, 1936 Boulder (WAust)

Pawley, Michael Bernard (NSW) b March 10, 1944 Glen Innes (NSW)

Payne, Charles Percy (Tas) b July 31, 1876 Hobart (Tas) d Jan. 28, 1938 Lower Sandy Bay (Tas)

Payne, Daniel Martin (Qld) b Oct. 27, 1978 Herston (Qld)

Peachey, Mark (Qld) b Oct. 31, 1900 Tannymorel (Qld) d Nov. 23, 1987 Ipswich (Qld)

Peake, Clinton John (Vic) b March 25, 1977 Geelong (Vic)

Pearce, Donald Rex (Tas) b Feb. 21, 1941 Ulverstone (Tas) d Feb. 13, 1999 Burnie (Tas)

Pearce, Kevin Dudley (Tas) b Feb. 29, 1960 Devonport (Tas)

Pearce, Reginald Manus (NSW) b April 20, 1918 Tumbarumba (NSW) d June 19, 1995 Sydney (NSW)

Pearsall, Alan Louden (Tas) b May 24, 1915 Hobart (Tas) d March 8, 1941 in action in English Channel

Pearson, Trevor John (S Aust) b Oct. 13, 1943 Goodwood (S Aust)

Pearson, William Ernest (Vic) b Nov. 10, 1912 Kerang (Vic) d Sept. 11, 1987 Melbourne (Vic)

Pegg, Harry Robert Edgar (Qld) b March 19, 1916 Moorooka (Qld)

Pellew, Arthur Howard (S Aust) b Jan. 20, 1878 Riverton (S Aust) d Aug. 21, 1948 Rose Park (S Aust)

* Pellew, Clarence Everard (S Aust) b Sept. 21, 1893 Port Pirie (S Aust) d May 9, 1981 Adelaide (S Aust)

Pellew, John Harold (S Aust) b July 17, 1882 Truro (S Aust) d Oct. 17, 1946 Unley (S Aust)

Pellew, Lancelot Vivian (S Aust) b Dec. 15, 1899 Port Elliott (S Aust) d Dec. 8, 1970 Adelaide (S Aust)

Penman, Arthur Percival (NSW) b Jan. 23, 1885 Ultimo (NSW) d Sept. 11, 1944 Rockley (NSW)

Pennefather, George Shirley (Tas) b Sept. 28, 1864 Launceston (Tas) d Oct. 16, 1945 Launceston (Tas)

Pennycuick, Rupert James (Tas) b April 11, 1893 Jericho (Tas) d Jan. 17, 1963 Concord (NSW)

Penter, Colin Edward (WAust) b July 20, 1955 Albany (WAust)

Pepper, Cecil George (NSW) b Sept. 15, 1916 Forbes (NSW) d March 24, 1993 Littleborough, Lancashire (England)

Perraton, Jack Oldfield (Vic) b Feb. 26, 1909 Prahran (Vic) d Oct. 1, 1950 Kings Cross (NSW)

Perraton, William Thomas Crooke (Vic) b Aug. 27, 1867 Collingwood (Vic) d Sept. 23, 1952 Elsternwick (Vic)

Perren, Clinton Terrence (Qld) b Feb. 22, 1975 Herston (Qld)

Perrin, Thomas Henry (Vic) b Oct. 27, 1928 Prahran (Vic)

Perrins, Keith Robinson (Qld) b Jan. 17, 1931 Rockhampton (Qld)

Perry, Cecil Thomas Henry (Tas) b March 3, 1846 Battery Point (Tas) d Aug. 4, 1917 Timaru (New Zealand)

Perryman, Charles Henry (Vic) b Jan. 20, 1872 Richmond (Vic) d Aug. 30, 1950 St Kilda (Vic)

Peters, Arthur Ernest (S Aust) b March 8, 1872 Adelaide (S Aust) d Sept. 24, 1903 Henley Beach (S Aust)

Pettiford, Jack (NSW) b Nov. 29, 1919 Freshwater (NSW) d Oct. 11, 1964 North Sydney (NSW)

Pettinger, Aldam Murr (S Aust) b July 30, 1859 Kent Town (S Aust) d Aug. 18, 1950 Lower Mitcham (S Aust)

Phelps, Leslie Roy (Tas) details unknown

Phelps, Matthew James (Tas) b Sept. 1, 1972 Lismore (NSW)

Philipson, Craig Andrew (Qld) b Nov. 18, 1982 Herston (Qld)

Phillips, Edward George (S Aust) b March 1, 1851 Port Adelaide (S Aust) d Feb. 8, 1933 North Adelaide (S Aust)

Phillips, Edward Lauriston (S Aust) b Sept. 2, 1892 North Adelaide (S Aust) d Jan. 8, 1971 Adelaide (S Aust)

Phillips, James (Vic) b Sept. 1, 1860 Pleasant Creek (Vic) d April 21, 1930 Burnaby, Vancouver, British Columbia (Canada)

Phillips, Joseph (Vic) b April 22, 1840 Parramatta (NSW) d May 7, 1901 Heidelberg (Vic)

Phillips, Norbert Eugene (NSW) b July 9, 1896 Cowra (NSW) d Oct. 3, 1961 Sydney (NSW)

Phillips, Raymond Berry (NSW & Qld) b May 23, 1954 Paddington (NSW)

* Phillips, Wayne Bentley (S Aust) b March 1, 1958 Adelaide (S Aust)

* Phillips, Wayne Norman (Vic) b Nov. 7, 1962 Geelong (Vic)

Philpott, Albert John William (Vic) b March 14, 1873 Gaffneys Creek (Vic) d Nov. 25, 1950 Kew (Vic)

* Philpott, Peter Ian (NSW) b Nov. 21, 1934 Manly (NSW)

Philpott, Richard (Vic) b Feb. 7, 1813 West Farleigh, Kent (England) d June 8, 1888 Brenchley, Kent (England)

Philpott, William (Vic) b Jan. 24, 1819 West Farleigh, Kent (England) d Nov. 4, 1891 Linton, Kent (England)

Pickering, George Thomas (Vic) b c. 1832 Sydney (NSW) d Dec. 1, 1858 Sandridge (Vic)

Pickering, Kelby Sinclair (S Aust) b Jan. 3, 1973 Lameroo (S Aust)

Pickett, Alfred William (Tas) b c. 1871 Ulverstone (Tas) d March 19, 1953 Ulverstone (Tas)

Pickett, Edward Arthur (Tas) b April 2, 1909 Ulverstone (Tas)

Pictet, Francis Stewart (Tas) b June 4, 1866 Bath, Somerset (England) death details unknown

Pierce, Michael (NSW & Qld) b Sept. 3, 1869 Paddington (NSW) d Feb. 4, 1913 Sydney (NSW)

Pilon, Nathan Steven (NSW) b Oct. 27, 1976 Dubbo (NSW)

Pinch, Colin John (NSW & S Aust) b June 23, 1921 Brownsville (NSW)

Pinkus, Harold William (Tas) b Sept. 27, 1934 Smithton (Tas)

Pinnington, Todd Andrew (Tas) b March 21, 1971 Hobart (Tas)

Pitcher, Franklyn Joseph (Vic) b June 24, 1879 Collingwood (Vic) d Jan. 23, 1921 Northcote (Vic)

Pite, Walter Edward (NSW) b Sept. 24, 1876 Sydney (NSW) d May 7, 1955 Waverley (NSW)

Pittman, Brian Harold (S Aust) b June 17, 1930 Rose Park (S Aust)

Plant, Hugh Joseph (Vic) b Oct. 12, 1907 Narrandera (NSW) d Aug. 30, 1993 Geelong (Vic)

Plant, Thomas Christopher (S Aust) b March 31, 1984 Ashford (S Aust)

* Playle, William Rodger (WAust) b Dec. 1, 1938 Palmerston North (New Zealand)

Plummer, Neil Robert (S Aust) b July 6, 1955 Lobethal (S Aust)

Pocock, William Johnstone (NSW) b c. 1848 Clifton, Gloucestershire (England) d Sept. 27, 1928 East Brighton (Vic)

Poeppel, George Augustus (Qld) b Nov. 6, 1893 Bundaberg (Qld) d Feb. 2, 1917 Hermies (France)

Poidevin, Leslie Oswald Sheridan (NSW) b Nov. 5, 1876 Merrilla (NSW) d Nov. 19, 1931 Waverley (NSW)

Polkinghorne, Adam William (Tas) b Aug. 23, 1975 Karoonda (S Aust)

Polzin, Michael Allan (Qld) b June 23, 1964 Wondai (Qld)

* Ponsford, William Harold (Vic) b Oct. 19, 1900 North Fitzroy (Vic) d April 6, 1991 Kyneton (Vic)

* Ponting, Ricky Thomas (Tas) b Dec. 19, 1974 Launceston (Tas)

Poon, Hunter Robert George (Qld) b May 14, 1894 Pimlico (NSW) d Jan. 25, 1980 Greenslopes (Qld)

* Pope, Roland James (NSW) b Feb. 18, 1864 Ashfield (NSW) d July 27, 1952 Manly (NSW)

Porter, Brian Clifford (Vic) b Dec. 20, 1942 Carlton (Vic)

Porter, Graham David (WAust) b March 18, 1955 Middle Swan (WAust)

Potter, Jack (Vic) b April 13, 1938 Melbourne (Vic)

Powell, George (NSW) b April 12, 1918 Newtown (NSW) d April 11, 1994 Clovelly (NSW)

Powell, Ronald Hartley (Tas) b Sept. 27, 1883 New Norfolk (Tas) d Aug. 22, 1922 (Qld)

Powell, Theodore (NSW) b July 10, 1852 Berrima (NSW) d Sept. 3, 1913 Sydney (NSW)

Power, John Francis (Vic) b March 23, 1932 Port Melbourne (Vic) d May 6, 2005 Kogarah (NSW)

Power, Laurence James (S Aust) b July 31, 1898 Ovingham (S Aust) d March 20, 1963 Glenelg (S Aust)

Power, Louis Bertrand (S Aust) b Oct. 10, 1905 Ovingham (S Aust) d Sept. 30, 1988 Bedford Park (S Aust)

Power, Robert (Vic) b c. 1833 Galway (Ireland) d Nov. 4, 1914 Toorak (Vic)

Powlett, Frederick Armand (Vic) b Jan. 6, 1811 Shrewsbury, Shropshire (England) d June 9, 1865 Kyneton (Vic)

Pratten, Herbert Graham (NSW) b April 22, 1892 Ashfield (NSW) d Sept. 11, 1979 Neutral Bay (NSW)

Preen, Alan Thomas (WAust) b July 4, 1935 Fremantle (WAust)

Prentice, Warden Selby (NSW) b July 30, 1886 Homebush (NSW) d Feb. 26, 1969 Rosebery (NSW)

Prescott, Shaun St Aubyn (Vic) b Sept. 7, 1966 Melbourne (Vic)

Prestwidge, Scott Arthur (Qld) b May 15, 1968 Bankstown (NSW)

Pretty, Alfred Henry (S Aust) b Jan. 29, 1874 Willunga (S Aust) d June 21, 1929 Mile End (S Aust)

Price, Charles Frederick Thomas (Services) b Feb. 17, 1917 Sydney (NSW) d Jan. 19, 1997 Avalon (NSW)

Price, Henry Alexander (Qld) b March 31, 1913 Spring Hill (Qld) d May 3, 1999 Wavell Heights (Qld)

Price, Reuben Henry (WAust) b April 27, 1923 London (England) d Feb. 26, 1991 Perth (WAust)

Price, Walter Davies (S Aust) b March 24, 1886 Hawthorn (Vic) d July 29, 1944 Adelaide (S Aust)

Prindiville, Kevin Joseph (WAust) b Sept. 18, 1949 Subiaco (WAust)

Prindiville, Terence John (WAust) b Nov. 20, 1942 Subiaco (WAust)

Prior, Wayne (S Aust) b Sept. 30, 1952 Salisbury (S Aust)

Pritchard, David Edward (S Aust) b Jan. 5, 1893 Queenstown (S Aust) d July 4, 1983 Myrtle Bank (S Aust)

Prout, James Alexander (Qld) b Aug. 12, 1889 Flemington (Vic) d Feb. 18, 1952 Double Bay (NSW)

Pryor, David Godfrey (NSW) b Feb. 3, 1870 Maitland (NSW) d Jan. 3, 1937 Gosford (NSW)

Puckett, Charles William (WAust) b Feb. 21, 1911 Beddington Corner, Surrey (England) d Jan. 22, 2002 Morphett Vale (S Aust)

Puckett, Maxwell Charles (S Aust) b June 3, 1935 Unley Park (S Aust) d Aug. 25, 1991 North Adelaide (S Aust)

Punch, Austin Thomas Eugene (NSW & Tas) b Aug. 16, 1894 North Sydney (NSW) d Aug. 25, 1985 Cremorne (NSW)

Punch, Keith Francis (WAust) b Oct. 19, 1940 Subiaco (WAust)

Putman, Sydney William Leslie (Tas) b March 25, 1912 Hobart (Tas) d Sept. 20, 1947 Hobart (Tas)

Pye, Leslie Walter (NSW) b July 6, 1871 Windsor (NSW) d March 9, 1949 Parramatta (NSW)

Pyke, James Kendrick (S Aust) b June 7, 1966 Cottesloe (WAust)

Pyke, Richard Dimond (Qld) b Aug. 15, 1877 Collingwood (Vic) d Dec. 4, 1914 Gympie (Qld)

Pynor, Ernest Ivan (S Aust) b April 23, 1920 Essendon (Vic) d Oct. 23, 1999 East Doncaster (Vic)

Quelch, Leslie Norman (Qld) b Feb. 26, 1918 Maryborough (Qld) d April 13, 1987 Paddington (Qld)

Quick, Ian William (Vic) b Nov. 5, 1933 Geelong (Vic)

Quigley, Brian Maxwell (S Aust) b Dec. 27, 1935 Henley Beach (S Aust)

Quilty, John (S Aust) b c. 1860 Adelaide (S Aust) d May 9, 1942 Kent Town (S Aust)

Quin, Stanley Oldfield (Vic) b April 17, 1908 Caulfield (Vic) d Nov. 27, 1967 Brighton (Vic)

Quinlan, Francis Patrick (WAust) b March 17, 1891 Perth (WAust) d Aug. 15, 1935 Perth (WAust)

Quinn, Michael Brian (Vic) b July 2, 1962 Adelaide (S Aust)

Quist, Karl Hugo (NSW, WAust & S Aust) b Aug. 18, 1875 Milson's Point (NSW) d March 31, 1957 Plympton (S Aust)

* Rackemann, Carl Gray (Qld) b June 3, 1960 Wondai (Qld)

Rahmann, Herbert William (Qld) b Aug. 23, 1886 Maryborough (Qld) d Oct. 12, 1957 Nundah (Qld)

Rainey, Leslie Newburn (Vic) b Jan. 10, 1881 South Yarra (Vic) d Aug. 27, 1962 Melbourne (Vic)

Ramsay, John (Tas) b Dec. 26, 1872 Glasgow, Lanarkshire (Scotland) d Feb. 6, 1944 Launceston (Tas)

Ramsay, Marmaduke Francis (Qld) b Dec. 8, 1860 Cheltenham, Gloucestershire (England) d Dec. 31, 1947 Lee, Canterbury, Kent (England)

Ramshaw, Darrin Joseph (WAust & Vic) b Nov. 29, 1965 Subiaco (WAust)

Randell, Alfred Charles (WAust) b May 10, 1884 Perth (WAust) d Sept. 13, 1958 Sydney (NSW)

Randell, Ernest Arthur (WAust) b Jan. 25, 1873 Perth (WAust) d May 12, 1938 Perth (WAust)

Randell, James Arthur (NSW) b Aug. 4, 1880 Gulgong (NSW) d Dec. 7, 1952 Balgowlah (NSW)

* Ransford, Vernon Seymour (Vic) b March 20, 1885 South Yarra (Vic) d March 19, 1958 Brighton (Vic)

Ratcliffe, Andrew Thomas (NSW) b April 3, 1891 Leichhardt (NSW) d Aug. 31, 1974 Banksia (NSW)

Rathie, David Stewart (Qld) b May 29, 1951 Roma (Qld)

Rawle, Keith Trevillian (Vic) b Oct. 29, 1924 Essendon (Vic) d March 6, 2005 Maryborough (Qld)

Ray, Mark (NSW & Tas) b Oct. 2, 1952 Surry Hills (NSW)

Raymer, Vincent Norman (Qld) b May 4, 1918 Toowoomba (Qld)

Raymond, Ralph Cossart (Qld) b Nov. 28, 1912 Boonah (Qld) d Oct. 11, 1982 Murgon (Qld)

Rayson, Maxwell William (Vic) b Aug. 26, 1912 Kew (Vic) d May 11, 1993 Heidelberg (Vic)

Rayson, Roger William (Vic) b Feb. 17, 1942 Windsor (Vic)

Rayson, William Jones (Vic) b Dec. 18, 1889 Malmsbury (Vic) d Sept. 8, 1957 Parkdale (Vic)

Read, Arthur Edwin (WAust) b May 26, 1908 Unley (S Aust) d March 1, 2001 Bentley (WAust)

Rebbeck, Phillip Douglas (S Aust) b July 31, 1948 North Adelaide (S Aust)

Reddrop, Walter William (Vic) b Sept. 9, 1901 Kyneton (Vic) d March 31, 1983 Parkville (Vic)

Redfearn, James (Vic) b c. 1836 Yorkshire (England) d March 10, 1916 Glenhuntly (Vic)

Redgrave, John Sidney (NSW & Qld) b Aug. 5, 1878 North Sydney (NSW) d Aug. 3, 1958 West End (Qld)

* Redpath, Ian Ritchie (Vic) b May 11, 1941 Geelong (Vic)

* Reedman, John Cole (S Aust) b Oct. 9, 1865 Taminda (S Aust) d March 25, 1924 Gilberton (S Aust)

Rees, John Newman Stace (S Aust) b Sept. 2 1880 Hindmarsh (S Aust) d Jan. 17, 1959 S Peters (S Aust)

Rees, Robert Blackie Colston (S Aust) April 15, 1882 Hindmarsh (S Aust) Sept. 20, 1966 Bowmans Green Hertfordshire (England)

Rees, William Gilbert (NSW) b April 6, 1827 St Issell's, Pembrokeshire (Wales) d Oct. 31 1898 Marlborough (New Zealand)

Rees, William Lee (Vic) b Dec. 16, 1836 Bristol, Gloucestershire (England) d May 13 1912 Gisborne (New Zealand)

Reeves, Damion Albert (S Aust) b July 12, 1971 Darwin (NT)

Reeves, William Henry (Vic) b Aug. 11, 1881 Fitzroy (Vic) d Sept. 13, 1962 Kew (Vic)

Regeling, Donald Carl (Qld) b Aug. 13, 1955 Boonah (Qld)

Reid, Alan Walter (Qld) b June 30, 1931 Maryborough (Qld)

Reid, Basil Stanley (Tas) b May 17, 1924 Launceston (Tas) d July 16, 2000 Launceston (Tas)

* Reid, Bruce Anthony (WAust) b March 14, 1963 Osborne Park (WAust)

Reid, Curtis Alexander (Vic) b July 16, 1836 Inverary Park (NSW) d July 1, 1886 Hawthorn (Vic)

Reid, Douglas Clement (NSW) b Sept. 23, 1886 St Peters (NSW) d Aug. 21, 1959 Wahroonga (NSW)

Reid, Stanley John (Tas) b May 5, 1955 St Helen's (Tas)

Reid, William (Tas) details unknown

Reid, William (S Aust) b c. 1871 North Adelaide (S Aust) full birth and death details unknown

* Reiffel, Paul Ronald (Vic) b April 19, 1966 Box Hill (Vic)

Renfrey, Leslie Cotswold (WAust) b Feb. 15, 1893 Wallaroo Mines (S Aust) d Sept. 23, 1958 Mt Lawley (WAust)

* Renneberg, David Alexander (NSW) b Sept. 23, 1942 Rozelle (NSW)

Reynolds, George Raymond (Qld) b Aug. 24, 1936 Bundaberg (Qld)

Rhodes, Brian Leslie (NSW) b March 7, 1951 Paddington (NSW)

Ricci, Brendan Paul (Vic) b April 24, 1965 East Melbourne (Vic)

* Richards, Barry Anderson (S Aust) b July 21, 1945 Morningside, Durban, Natal (South Africa)

Richards, Corey John (NSW) b Aug. 25, 1975 Camden (NSW)

Richards, Frank Hitchen (Vic) d Fremantle (WAust) full birth and death details unknown

* Richards, Isaac Vivian Alexander (Qld) b March 7, 1952 St John's (Antigua)

Richards, Thomas Oliver (S Aust) b July 5, 1855 Norwood (S Aust) d Dec. 14, 1923 Cottonville (Qld)

Richardson, Arthur John (S Aust & WAust) b July 24, 1888 Sevenhills (S Aust) d Dec. 23, 1973 Semaphore (S Aust)

Richardson, Brian Douglas (Tas) b May 15, 1932 Hobart (Tas)

Richardson, Charles Augustus (NSW) b Feb. 22, 1864 Sydney (NSW) d Aug. 17, 1949 Waipara, Canterbury (New Zealand)

Richardson, Colin George (Tas) b June 6, 1920 Hobart (Tas) d Dec. 22, 1993 Hobart (Tas)

Richardson, Edward Noel (Tas) b Dec. 8, 1929 Hobart (Tas)

Richardson, Frederick William (Tas) b March 29, 1878 Campbell Town (Tas) d March 7, 1955 Campbell Town (Tas)

Richardson, Geoffrey William (Vic) b Dec. 7, 1956 Koo Wee Rup (Vic)

Richardson, George Biggs (NSW) b May 28, 1834 Bathurst (NSW) d May 1, 1911 Dandaloo (NSW)

Richardson, Howard James (Vic) b Oct. 29, 1894 Berwick (Vic) d Dec. 21, 1959 Richmond (Vic)

Richardson, Joseph (S Aust) b Feb. 28, 1878 Kooringa (S Aust) d June 13, 1951 Glenelg (S Aust)

Richardson, Leonard Martin (NSW & Qld) b May 5, 1950 Paddington (NSW)

Richardson, Leslie Lambert (Tas) b Jan. 9, 1887 Ralph's Bay (Tas) d Nov. 15, 1962 Hobart (Tas)

Richardson, Leslie Walter (Tas) b Sept. 5, 1911 New Town (Tas) d Nov. 1, 1981 Hobart (Tas)

Richardson, Reginald Maxwell (Tas) b Oct. 6, 1922 Hobart (Tas) d June 2, 2003 Lenah Valley (Tas)

* Richardson, Victor York (S Aust) b Sept. 7, 1894 Parkside (S Aust) d Oct. 29, 1969 Fullarton (S Aust)

Richardson, Walter Barrett (Tas) b Oct. 24, 1876 Ralph's Bay (Tas) d May 30, 1962 Hobart (Tas)

Richardson, William Alfred (NSW) b Aug. 22, 1866 Sydney (NSW) d Jan. 3, 1930 Mosman (NSW)

Richter, Arthur Frederick (S Aust) b Sept. 1, 1908 Telowie (S Aust) d Aug. 16, 1936 Adelaide (S Aust)

Rickman, Wilfred (Vic) b c. 1856 South Yarra (Vic) d June 6, 1911 Frankston (Vic)

Ridge, Frank Macquarie (NSW) b Jan. 10, 1873 Dubbo (NSW) d May 25, 1959 Manly (NSW)

Ridgway, Mark William (Tas) b May 21, 1960 Warragul (Vic)

Ridings, Kenneth Lovett (S Aust) b Feb. 7, 1920 Malvern (S Aust) d May 17, 1943 in action over Bay of Biscay, France

Ridings, Phillip Lovett (S Aust) b Oct. 2, 1917 Malvern (S Aust) d Sept. 13, 1998 Adelaide (S Aust)

Rigaud, Stephen (S Aust) b Nov. 25, 1856 Kenton Valley, Talunga (S Aust) d Nov. 13, 1922 Claremont (WAust)

Rigby, Albert (WAust) b c. 1901 Lancashire (England) d Oct. 10, 1963 Hollywood (WAust)

Rigg, Basil Augustus (WAust) b Aug. 12, 1926 Highgate (WAust)

Rigg, Herbert William Hardy (WAust) b Aug. 18, 1923 Highgate (WAust)

* Rigg, Keith Edward (Vic) b May 21, 1906 Malvern (Vic) d Feb. 28, 1995 Malvern (Vic)

Riley, William Norman (S Aust) b April 9, 1894 Hyde Park (S Aust) d Oct. 2, 1960 North Adelaide (S Aust)

Rimington, Stanley Garnet (Vic) b Jan. 22, 1892 Kew (Vic) d Nov. 23, 1991 Kew (Vic)

* Ring, Douglas Thomas (Vic) b Oct. 14, 1918 Hobart (Tas) d June 23, 2003 Melbourne (Vic)

* Ritchie, Gregory Michael (Qld) b Jan. 23, 1960 Stanthorpe (Qld)

Ritossa, David John (S Aust) b Jan. 22, 1971 Rose Park (S Aust)

* Rixon, Stephen John (NSW) b Feb. 25, 1954 Albury (NSW)

Roach, Peter John (Vic) b May 19, 1975 Kew (Vic)

Roach, William Alexander (WAust) b Dec. 12, 1914 South Fremantle (WAust) d June 8, 1944 in action over Friesian Islands (Netherlands)

* Roberts, Anderson Montgomery Everton (NSW) b Jan. 29, 1951 Urlings Village (Antigua)

Roberts, Kevin Joseph (NSW) b July 2, 1972 North Sydney (NSW)

Roberts, Peter Gerald (Tas) b Feb. 16, 1952 Hobart (Tas)

Roberts, William (NSW) birth and death details unknown

Roberts, William Maurice (S Aust) b Aug. 26, 1916 Wallaroo Mines (S Aust) d Jan. 21, 1989 Adelaide (S Aust)

Robertson, Ashley Peter Scott (Vic) b March 9, 1972 Footscray (Vic)

Robertson, David Alexander (S Aust) b March 4, 1959 North Adelaide (S Aust)

* Robertson, Gavin Ron (NSW & Tas) b May 28, 1966 St Leonard's (NSW)

Robertson, George Pringle (Vic) b Aug. 22, 1842 Hobart (Tas) d June 23, 1895 East Melbourne (Vic)

Robertson, Trevor John (S Aust) b Nov. 20, 1947 Rose Park (S Aust)

* Robertson, William Roderick (Vic) b Oct. 6, 1861 Deniliquin (NSW) d June 24, 1938 Brighton (Vic)

Robins, Donnell (S Aust) b March 7, 1934 Blackwood (S Aust)

Robinson, Alexander (WAust) b Aug. 19, 1886 Brighton (Vic) d Oct. 4, 1967 Perth (WAust)

Robinson, Alexander William (WAust) b Aug. 14, 1924 Boulder (WAust)

Robinson, Brian Anthony (Tas) b Nov. 22, 1967 Devonport (Tas)

Robinson, Charles Henry (Tas & WAust) b Feb. 18, 1879 Dubbo (NSW) d Sept. 23, 1951 Ashfield (NSW)

Robinson, David Brian (Tas & Vic) b March 20, 1958 Devonport (Tas)

Robinson, George David (WAust) b Jan. 21, 1921 Boulder (WAust) d March 12, 1999 Kew (Vic)

Robinson, Henry Joseph Wickham (NSW) b March 11, 1864 Watsons Bay (NSW) d March 24, 1931 Mascot (NSW)

* Robinson, Rayford Harold (NSW & S Aust) b March 26, 1914 Stockton (NSW) d Aug. 10, 1965 Stockton (NSW)

* Robinson, Richard Daryl (Vic) b June 8, 1946 East Melbourne (Vic)

Robison, William Carr (NSW) b Dec. 14, 1874 Camden (NSW) d July 5, 1916 Darlinghurst (NSW)

Robran, Barrie Charles (S Aust) b Sept. 25, 1947 Whyalla (S Aust)

Roche, William (Vic) b July 20, 1871 Brunswick (Vic) d Jan. 2, 1950 East Brunswick (Vic)

Rocher, Thomas Walter (Tas) b June 17, 1930 Scottsdale (Tas)

Rock, Claude William (Tas) b June 9, 1863 Deloraine (Tas) d July 27, 1950 Longford (Tas)

Rock, Harry Owen (NSW) b Oct. 18, 1896 Scone (NSW) d March 9, 1978 Manly (NSW)

Rock, Norman Vosper (Tas) b Aug. 30, 1864 Deloraine (Tas) d Feb. 7, 1945 Brighton (Vic)

Rockliffe, Thornton Francis Edward (Tas) b July 5, 1887 Sassafras (Tas) d March 18, 1961 East Devonport (Tas)

Rodwell, Edwin Emerson (Tas) b April 12, 1921 Hobart (Tas)

Roe, Richard (WAust) b Jan. 22, 1913 Geraldton (WAust)

Rofe, Paul Cameron (S Aust) b Jan. 16, 1981 Adelaide (S Aust)

Rogers, Christopher John Llewellyn (WAust) b Aug. 31, 1977 Kogarah (NSW)

Rogers, John Edward (Vic) b Feb. 8, 1858 Botany (NSW) d July 8, 1935 South Melbourne (Vic)

Rogers, Noel Thomas (Qld) b Dec. 28, 1923 Spring Hill (Qld) d May 27, 1982 Annerley (Qld)

Rogers, Rex Ernest (Qld) b Aug. 24, 19[?] Cairns (Qld) d May 22, 1996 Coorparo[?] (Qld)

Rogers, William John (NSW) b May 7, 194[?] Gosford (NSW)

Rolfe, Douglas John (Vic & S Aust) b Feb. 2[?] 1953 Wheelers Hill (Vic)

Ronchi, Luke (WAust) b April 23, 198[?] Dannevirke (New Zealand)

Roper, Arthur William (NSW) b Feb. 20, 191[?] Petersham (NSW) d Sept. 4, 1972 Woy Woy (NSW)

* Rorke, Gordon Frederick (NSW) b June 27[?] 1938 Neutral Bay (NSW)

Rose, Robert Peter (Vic) b Feb. 6, 1952 Eastern Hill (Vic) d May 12, 1999 Heidelberg (Vic)

Rosen, Marshall Frederick (NSW) b Sept. 17, 1948 Paddington (NSW)

Rosman, Arthur Victor (S Aust) b Nov. 26, 1870 Barossa Goldfields (S Aust) d Feb. 10, 1948 Kent Town (S Aust)

Ross, Charles Howard (Vic) b May 10, 1863 St Kilda (Vic) d Feb. 5, 1935 Sydney (NSW)

Ross, Graeme Thomson (Vic) b Feb. 5, 1955 Geelong (Vic)

Ross, William A. (Vic) birth and death details unknown

Rosser, John (Vic) b April 22, 1862 Fremantle (WAust) d Dec. 25, 1925 Toowoomba (Qld)

Rothwell, Barry Alan (NSW) b Aug. 18, 1939 Ryde (NSW)

Rothwell, John Wilson (Tas) b Oct. 1, 1913 Hobart (Tas)

Rowan, Robert Keith (Vic) b Sept. 14, 1947 Coburg (Vic)

Rowe, Raymond Curtis (NSW) b Dec. 9, 1913 Harris Park (NSW) d May 14, 1995 Parramatta (NSW)

Rowe, Samuel Harold Drew (WAust) b Nov. 5, 1883 Perth (WAust) d Oct. 29, 1968 Perth (WAust)

Rowe, William Denis (Qld) b Jan. 10, 1892 East Brisbane (Qld) d Sept. 3, 1972 South Brisbane (Qld)

Rowell, Gregory John (NSW, Qld & Tas) b Sept. 1, 1966 Lindfield (NSW)

Rowland, Frank Walter (NSW) b March 1, 1893 Inverell (NSW) d Feb. 25, 1957 Mosman (NSW)

Rowlands, Edward Richard (Vic) b c. 1826 Claines, Worcestershire (England) d c. 1860

Rowlands, William Trevor (WAust) b May 7, 1904 Echuca (Vic) d May 18, 1984 Subiaco (WAust)

Rowley, Francis (NSW) b Sept. 27, 1835 Burwood (NSW) d June 23, 1862 Woolloomooloo (NSW)

Roxby, Robert Charles (NSW & S Aust) b March 16, 1926 Newcastle (NSW)

Rummans, Graeme Clifford (NSW & Vic) b Dec. 13, 1976 Camperdown (NSW)

Rundell, Joshua Upcott (S Aust) b May 6, 1858 Sandhurst (Vic) d Jan. 7, 1922 Alberton (S Aust)

Rundell, Percy Davies (S Aust) b. Nov. 20, 1890 Alberton (S Aust) d March 24, 1979 North Adelaide (S Aust)

Rush, Edward Reynolds (Vic) b March 29, 1868 Flemington (Vic) d May 6, 1936 Malvern (Vic)

Rush, John (Vic) b April 5, 1910 Malvern (Vic) d Jan. 13, 1982 Adelaide (S Aust)

Rush, Thomas Reynolds (Vic) b Dec. 7, 1874 Collingwood (Vic) d Oct. 29, 1926 Malvern (Vic)

Rushbrook, Roy Francis Kerr (Qld) b Sept. 29, 1911 Spring Hill (Qld) d March 31, 1987 Mackay (Qld)

Rushforth, Alfred William (Tas) b April 23, 1898 Hobart (Tas) d Dec. 30, 1985 Taroona (Tas)

Russell, Bernard (NSW) b Aug. 1, 1891 Leichhardt (NSW) d July 13, 1961 Belmore (NSW)

Russell, Richard Stevan (WAust) b Jan. 22, 1968 Helensville (New Zealand)

Russen, Charles Gordon (Tas) b May 9, 1886 Launceston (Tas) d Dec. 16, 1969 Newstead (Tas)

* Rutherford, John Walter (WAust) b Sept. 25, 1929 Bungulluping (WAust)

Ryan, Alfred James (S Aust) b April 27, 1904 Adelaide (S Aust) d July 10, 1990 Semaphore (S Aust)

Ryan, Gregory William (NSW) b March 13, 1913 Wallsend (NSW) d May 10, 1986 Randwick (NSW)

Ryan, Peter Andrew (Qld) b Feb. 18, 1951 East Melbourne (Vic)

Ryan, Roderick Thomas (WAust) b Nov. 15, 1909 Cannington (WAust) d Oct. 23, 1979 Toronto, Ontario (Canada)

Ryan, Thomas Patrick (Tas) b May 4, 1865 Hobart (Tas) d April 20, 1921 Hobart (Tas)

* Ryder, John (Vic) b Aug. 8, 1889 Collingwood (Vic) d April 3, 1977 Fitzroy (Vic)

Rymill, Jack Westall (S Aust) b March 20, 1901 North Adelaide (S Aust) d Feb. 11, 1976 Adelaide (S Aust)

Saballus, Andrew William (Tas) b June 1, 1969 Hobart (Tas)

Sacristani, Peter Geoffrey (Vic) b Sept. 5, 1957 Melbourne (Vic)

Saddler, Edward (NSW) d Oct. 28, 1874 full birth and death details unknown

* Sadiq Mohammad (Tas) b May 5, 1945 Junagadh (India)

* Saggers, Ronald Arthur (NSW) b May 15, 1917 Sydenham (NSW) d March 17, 1987 Harbord (NSW)

Sainsbury, Andrew John (NSW) b May 11, 1974 Gosford (NSW)

Saint, John Michael (Tas) b Jan. 31, 1969 Auburn (NSW)

Saker, David James (Vic & Tas) b May 29, 1966 Oakleigh (Vic)

Salmon, Benjamin Melville (NSW) b Jan. 9, 1906 Footscray (Vic) d Jan. 24, 1979 Mosman (NSW)

Salmon, John Lionel (Vic) b March 31, 1934 Canterbury (Vic)

Salvado, John Frederick (Vic) b Nov. 11, 1939 Carlton (Vic)

Salvana, Louis Charles (Vic) b Jan. 20, 1897 Hawthorn (Vic) d Dec. 8, 1974 Mitcham (Vic)

Sams, Louis Robert (Tas) b Sept. 26, 1863 Westbury (Tas) d July 6, 1941 Redcliffe (Qld)

Sams, Richard Horace (Tas) b c. 1864 Westbury (Tas) d March 5, 1933 Roseville (NSW)

Samuels, Edward (NSW) b May 25, 1833 Sydney (NSW)

Sanders, Leyland Arthur (Qld) b Oct. 17, 1927 Sandgate (Qld) d Jan. 3, 2005 Forestville (NSW)

Sandford, Horace Charles Augustus (Vic) b Oct. 14, 1891 St Leonard's (NSW) d Aug. 16, 1967 Heidelberg (Vic)

Sands, Ronald Francis (WAust) b Sept. 16, 1921 Perth (WAust) d Sept. 5, 1995 Nedlands (WAust)

Sangster, Christopher Bagot (S Aust) b May 1, 1908 Kooringa (S Aust) d Feb. 27, 1995 North Adelaide (S Aust)

Sangster, John Fraser (S Aust) b Jan. 21, 1942 Adelaide (S Aust)

Sankey, Clarence Joseph (Tas) b Oct. 27, 1913 Northtown (Tas) d March 12, 1996 Launceston (Tas)

Sargent, Murray Alfred James (S Aust) b Aug. 23, 1928 Adelaide (S Aust)

Sarovich, Theodor Keith (Vic) b May 20, 1915 Port Melbourne (Vic) d Nov. 23, 1987 Atherton (Qld)

Sarre, Ronald Basil (WAust) b Jan. 20, 1932 Midland (WAust)

Sartori, Ronald Joseph (WAust) b March 23, 1915 Fremantle (WAust) d July 1, 1991 Perth (WAust)

* Saunders, John Victor (Vic) b March 21, 1876 Melbourne (Vic) d Dec. 21, 1927 Toorak (Vic)

Saunders, Stuart Lucas (Tas) b June 27, 1960 Hobart (Tas)

Saunders, Warren Joseph (NSW) b July 18, 1934 Arncliffe (NSW)

Savage, Harry Milton (NSW) b July 1, 1887 Ermington (NSW) d Nov. 14, 1964 (NSW)

Savage, Keith Douglas (Qld) b Sept. 19, 1926 Brisbane (Qld) d Jan. 18, 1979 Mt Morgan (Qld)

Savigny, John Horatio (Tas) b Aug. 25, 1867 Bathurst (NSW) d Feb. 11, 1923 Carrick (Tas)

Savigny, William Henry (Tas) b Feb. 17, 1864 Sydney (NSW) d Aug. 6, 1922 Burwood (NSW)

Sawle, Lawrence Michael (WAust) b Aug. 19, 1925 East Fremantle (WAust)

Sayers, Dean Keith (S Aust) b June 11, 1954 Hindmarsh (S Aust)

Sayers, Mervyn Gerald (WAust) b March 5, 1958 Subiaco (WAust)

Scaife, John Willie (Vic) b Nov. 14, 1908 Haslingden, Lancashire (England) d Oct. 27, 1995 Melbourne (Vic)

Scanes, Albert Edward (NSW) b Aug. 6, 1900 Erskineville (NSW) d Nov. 1, 1969 death place unknown

Scanlan, Edmund (NSW) b c. 1848 Newcastle on Tyne, Northumberland (England) d Jan. 9, 1916 Erskineville (NSW)

Scannell, Timothy Francis (Vic) b Nov. 12, 1882 Hotham (Vic) d July 9, 1939 Royal Park (Vic)

Scarff, Clark Steven (WAust) b Nov. 19, 1948 Subiaco (WAust)

Schade, Matias Anderson (Vic) b March 25, 1887 Huntly (Vic) d June 9, 1959 Williamstown (Vic)

Schenscher, Peter Malcolm (S Aust) b May 4, 1962 Murray Bridge (S Aust)

Schmidt, Keith Ernest (Tas) b Dec. 19, 1921 Hobart (Tas)

Schneider, Karl Joseph (Vic & S Aust) b Aug. 15, 1905 Hawthorn (Vic) d Sept. 5, 1928 Kensington Park (S Aust)

Scholes, Mark Bradley (Tas) b July 1, 1957 Carlton (Vic)

Scholes, Walter John (Vic) b Jan. 5, 1950 East Brunswick (Vic) d July 14, 2003 North Eltham (Vic)

Schrader, Heinrich Christian (Vic) b Dec. 5, 1893 East Prahran (Vic) d June 10, 1980 Kew (Vic)

Schreiber, Sidney Arthur (Qld) b April 7, 1873 birth and death details unknown

Schuller, Denis Clemenceau (Qld) b May 5, 1948 Herston (Qld)

Schultz, Bruce (S Aust) b March 13, 1913 Royston Park (S Aust) d Jan. 11, 1980 Modbury (S Aust)

Schultz, Julius William Eugene (S Aust) b Sept. 25, 1888 Summer Town (S Aust) d Aug. 8, 1966 Berri (S Aust)

Scott, Darryl Bryan (S Aust) b March 9, 1961 Glenelg (S Aust)

* Scott, Henry James Herbert (Vic) b Dec. 26, 1858 Prahran (Vic) d Sept. 23, 1910 Scone (NSW)

Scott, Jack A. (S Aust) b Jan. 14, 1910 Sydney (NSW) d May 22, 1980 Collaroy Beach (NSW)

Scott, John Drake (NSW & S Aust) b Jan. 31, 1888 Petersham (NSW) d April 7, 196. Springbank (S Aust)

Scott, Robert Barrington (Vic & NSW) b Oct. 9, 1916 South Melbourne (Vic) d April 6, 1984 Melbourne (Vic)

Scott, Walter Aubrey (Vic) b Feb. 19, 1907 Camberwell (Vic) d Oct. 23, 1989 death place unknown

Scott, William John (Vic) b June 14, 1882 Hotham (Vic) d Sept. 30, 1965 Ferntree Gully (Vic)

Scrymgour, Bernard Vincent (S Aust) b July 31, 1864 Adelaide (S Aust) d April 16, 1943 Medindie (S Aust)

Scuderi, Joseph Charles (S Aust) b Dec. 24, 1968 Ingham (Qld)

Seabrook, Wayne John Stephen (NSW) b Sept. 6, 1961 Ryde (NSW)

Seale, Joseph (NSW) b April 18, 1855 Grafton (NSW) d Aug. 19, 1941 Waratah (NSW)

Searle, James (NSW) b Aug. 8, 1861 Surry Hills (NSW) d Dec. 28, 1936 Manly (NSW)

Searle, Richard Henry (Qld) b Jan. 16, 1934 Red Hill (Qld)

Seccombe, Donald Harry (Qld) b April 3, 1942 Goomeri (Qld)

Seccombe, Wade Anthony (Qld) b Oct. 30, 1971 Murgon (Qld)

Seddon, Cecil Dudley (NSW) b July 3, 1902 Campbelltown (NSW) d April 18, 1978 Dulwich Hill (NSW)

Seib, Ian Martin (Qld) b Sept. 15, 1946 Herston (Qld)

Seitz, John Arnold (Vic) b Sept. 19, 1883 Carlton (Vic) d May 1, 1963 St Kilda (Vic)

Selk, Rudolph Albert (WAust) b Oct. 6, 1871 Omeo (Vic) d Jan. 31, 1940 Pickering Brook (WAust)

Sellers, Michael John (Tas) b July 5, 1952 Launceston (Tas)

* Sellers, Reginald Hugh Durning (S Aust) b Aug. 20, 1940 Bulsar (India)

Selth, Victor Poole (S Aust) b June 1, 1895 Parkside (S Aust) d Sept. 2, 1967 Daw Park (S Aust)

* Serjeant, Craig Stanton (WAust) b Nov. 1, 1951 Nedlands (WAust)

Serjeant, David Maurice (Vic) b Jan. 18, 1830 Ramsey, Huntingdonshire (England) d Jan. 12, 1929 Camberwell, London (England)

Sewart, William Isaac (Qld & Vic) b Nov. 12, 1881 Allendale East (S Aust) d Dec. 13, 1928 Caulfield (Vic)

Shade, Eric (Vic) b Aug. 27, 1943 Brighton (Vic)

Sharman, Baden Eric (Tas) b Aug. 11, 1939 Beulah (Tas)

* Sharpe, Duncan Albert (S Aust) b Aug. 3, 1937 Rawalpindi (India)

Shaw, John Hilary (Vic) b Oct. 18, 1932 Geelong (Vic)

Shaw, Noel Clyde (Vic) b May 10, 1937 Euroa (Vic)

Shawe, Patrick Henry Villiers Washington (Tas) b Bangalore (India) d Sept. 24, 1945 East Melbourne (Vic)

Shea, John Adrian (WAust) b May 8, 1913 Boulder (WAust) d Feb. 7, 1986 Claremont (WAust)

Shea, Morris (NSW) b c. 1869 Campbelltown (NSW) death details unknown

Shea, Patrick Augustus (Vic) b March 17, 1886 Clunes (Vic) d May 29, 1954 Northbridge (NSW)

* Sheahan, Andrew Paul (Vic) b Sept. 30, 1948 Werribee (Vic)

Sheen, Brian Lawrence (Tas) b Dec. 30, 1938 Hobart (Tas)

Shelton, Herbert John (Tas) b Jan. 21, 1924 Launceston (Tas)

Shepard, David John (Vic) b Dec. 30, 1970 Berwick (Vic)

Shephard, Athol Lennard (Tas) b Aug. 16, 1920 Burnie (Tas)

Shepherd, Alan Gordon (S Aust) b Sept. 29, 1912 Kilkenny (S Aust) d Oct. 9, 1998 Marion (S Aust)

* Shepherd, Barry Kenneth (WAust) b April 23, 1937 Donnybrook (WAust) d Sept. 17, 2001 Fremantle (WAust)

Shepherd, David Stanmore (Vic) b Aug. 3, 1956 Melbourne (Vic)

Shepherd, James (NSW) b May 24, 1856 Steiglitz (Vic) death details unknown

Shepherdson, Hartley Robert (S Aust) b Sept. 4, 1913 Mt Gambier (S Aust) d Aug. 19, 1992 Fitzroy (Vic)

Shepley, Herbert Neil (S Aust) b Oct. 7, 1899 Knightsbridge (S Aust) d Nov. 14, 1953 Tranmere (S Aust)

Sheppard, Benjamin Joseph (Vic) b June 23, 1892 Fitzroy (Vic) d Sept. 9, 1931 Fitzroy (Vic)

Sheppard, James Francis (Qld) b Jan. 16, 1888 Brisbane (Qld) d Dec. 10, 1944 Hendra (Qld)

Sheridan, Edward Orwell (NSW) b Jan. 3, 1842 Sydney (NSW) d Nov. 30, 1923 West End (Qld)

Sherriff, Rowan James (Tas) b July 7, 1951 Sheffield (Tas)

Shewan, Leslie James (Qld) b June 12, 1892 Rushworth (Vic) d Sept. 25, 1977 Windsor (Vic)

Shiell, Alan Bruce (S Aust) b April 25, 1945 St Peters (S Aust)

Shillinglaw, Harold Arthur Edward (Vic) b Dec. 2, 1927 Fitzroy (Vic)

Shipperd, Gregory (WAust & Tas) b Nov. 13, 1956 Subiaco (WAust)

Short, Henry William (S Aust) b March 31, 1874 Morphett Vale (S Aust) d May 11, 1916 Lower Mitcham (S Aust)

Shortland, Herbert (NSW) b April 7, 1881 Sydney (NSW) d July 17, 1946 death place unknown

Shugg, Albert William (Tas) b July 5, 1894 Hawthorn (Vic) d July 20, 1941 Hobart (Tas)

Siddons, James Darren (Vic & S Aust) b April 25, 1964 Robinvale (Vic)

Sidebottom, William Lemuel (Tas) b Sept. 24, 1862 Evandale (Tas) d April 11, 1948 Launceston (Tas)

Sides, Francis William (Qld & Vic) b Dec. 15, 1913 Mackay (Qld) d Aug. 25, 1943 Kunai Spur, Salamaua (Papua New Guinea) in action

Sieler, Alan John (Vic) b July 17, 1948 Arncliffe (NSW)

* Sievers, Morris William (Vic) b April 13, 1912 Powlett River (Vic) d May 10, 1968 Parkville (Vic)

Siggs, Douglas (Qld) b Aug. 11, 1920 Fortitude Valley (Qld)

Sim, Charles Wallace (Qld) b March 30, 1895 Brisbane (Qld) d July 3, 1971 Woodville South (S Aust)

Simmonds, William (Anderson's XI) details unknown

Simmons, Arthur Harry (NSW) b Nov. 13, 1909 Croydon (NSW) d Feb. 28, 1990 Mirrabooka (NSW)

Simmons, Craig Joseph (WAust) b Dec. 1, 1982 Paddington (NSW)

Simmons, Jack (Tas) b March 28, 1941 Clayton-le-Moors, Lancashire (England)

Simpson, Charles Edward (Qld & NSW) b March 27, 1882 Parramatta (NSW) d June 26, 1956 Sydney (NSW)

Simpson, Christopher Patrick (Qld) b Jan. 9, 1982 South Brisbane (Qld)

* Simpson, Robert Baddeley (NSW & WAust) b Feb. 3, 1936 Marrickville (NSW)

Sims, Alfred Edward (Qld) b Nov. 8, 1875 birthplace and death details unknown

Sims, Arthur (Australians) b July 27, 1877 Spridlington, Lincolnshire (England) d April 27, 1969 East Hoathly, Sussex (England)

Simunsen, Robert Francis (S Aust) b June 7, 1941 Adelaide (S Aust)

Sinclair, Arthur (NSW) birth details unknown d Nov. 29, 1869 Sydney (NSW)

Sincock, Andrew Thomas (S Aust) b June 7, 1951 Adelaide (S Aust)

* Sincock, David John (S Aust) b Feb. 1, 1942 North Adelaide (S Aust)

Sincock, Harrold Keith (S Aust) b Dec. 10, 1907 Eastwood (S Aust) d Feb. 2, 1982 Plympton (S Aust)

Sincock, Peter Damien (S Aust) b July 8, 1948 North Adelaide (S Aust)

Sincock, Russell John (Vic) b Dec. 28, 1947 Kew (Vic)

Sindrey, Clive Alexander Hazell (Vic) b Aug. 10, 1903 Richmond (Vic) d June 26, 1981 Vermont (Vic)

Single, Clive Vallack (NSW) b Sept. 17, 1888 Penrith (NSW) d July 10, 1931 Woollahra (NSW)

Sismey, Stanley George (NSW) b July 15, 1916 Junee (NSW)

Skilbeck, Andrew John (NSW) b July 21, 1958 St Leonard's (NSW)

Skuse, Alan Raymond (Qld) b March 28, 1942 Herston (Qld)

Sladen, Charles (Vic) b Aug. 28, 1816 Walmer, Kent (England) d Feb. 22, 1884 Geelong (Vic)

* Slater, Keith Nichol (WAust) b March 12, 1935 Midland (WAust)

* Slater, Michael Jonathon (NSW) b Feb. 21, 1970 Wagga Wagga (NSW)

* Sleep, Peter Raymond (S Aust) b May 4, 1957 Penola (S Aust)

Slight, Alexander Frank (S Aust) b March 13, 1861 Emerald Hill (Vic) d July 5, 1930 Maylands (S Aust)

* Slight, James (Vic) b Oct. 20, 1855 Ashby, Geelong (Vic) d Dec. 9, 1930 Elsternwick (Vic)

Slight, William (Vic & S Aust) b Sept. 19, 1858 Emerald Hill (Vic) d Dec. 22, 1941 Toorak Gardens (S Aust)

Small, Gladstone Cleophas (S Aust) b Oct. 18, 1961 Brighton, St George (Barbados)

Small, Stephen Mark (NSW & Tas) b March 2, 1955 Canterbury (NSW)

Smart, Christopher Boddington (Qld) b Oct. 17, 1958 Port Moresby (Papua New Guinea)

Smart, Hadyn Warren Gavin (S Aust) b Nov. 26, 1958 Hobart (Tas)

Smart, Lawrence Maxwell (S Aust) b Feb. 16, 1928 Narridy (S Aust)

Smith, Adam Matthew (Vic) b April 6, 1976 Greensborough (Vic)

Smith, Alfred Edward Charles (WAust) b Oct. 4, 1908 Prahran (WAust) d Jan. 17, 1989 Fremantle (WAust)

Smith, Andrew (S Aust) b Sept. 1, 1889 Port Adelaide (S Aust) d May 18, 1983 Adelaide (S Aust)

Smith, Carey Kenneth (Vic) b Oct. 16, 1960 Moreland (Vic)

Smith, Cyril Robert (Qld) b Nov. 1, 1926 South Brisbane (Qld)

Smith, Darryl Donald (WAust) b June 8, 1960 Adelaide (S Aust)

Smith, David Anthony (Tas) b Sept. 1, 1957 Launceston (Tas)

* Smith, David Betram Miller (Vic) b Sept. 14, 1884 Richmond (Vic) d July 29, 1963 Hawthorn (Vic)

Smith, Douglas Roy (Tas) b Oct. 9, 1888 Fingal (Tas) d Feb. 27, 1933 Port Fairy (Vic)

Smith, Edward Henry (Tas) b July 30, 1911 Nook (Tas) d Dec. 26, 1999 Launceston (Tas)

Smith, George Elms (Vic) b July 22, 1855 Emerald Hill (Vic) d April 7, 1897 St Kilda (Vic)

Smith, Harry Oxley (Tas & Vic) b Oct. 27, 1887 Launceston (Tas) d Aug. 24, 1916 Pinewood, London (England)

Smith, Herbert George (Vic) b March 21, 1914 Richmond (Vic) d Feb. 23, 1997 Caulfield (Vic)

Smith, Horace Clitheroe (Tas) b Oct. 31, 1892 Sandy Bay (Tas) d April 6, 1977 Hobart (Tas)

Smith, Hubert George Selwyn (Qld) b Oct. 9, 1891 Beaudesert (Qld) d June 7, 1917 Messines (France)

Smith, James Halliburton (NSW) b March 20, 1880 Parramatta (NSW) d June 18, 1958 Killara (NSW)

Smith, James Kevin (S Aust) b May 22, 1977 Port Noarlunga (S Aust)

Smith, John Phillips (Vic) b March 6, 1936 Ballarat (Vic)

Smith, Lavington Albert (S Aust) b Oct. 9, 1904 Medindie (S Aust) d May 9, 1953 Adelaide (S Aust)

Smith, Leonard Angus (Vic) b Oct. 25, 1882 Hotham (Vic) d July 29, 1943 Heidelberg (Vic)

Smith, Lloyd Harold James (Tas) b Aug. 5, 1928 Hobart (Tas) d Aug. 26, 2004 Hobart (Tas)

Smith, Michael John (S Aust) b July 17, 1973 Rose Park (S Aust)

Smith, Peter Julian (Vic) b Feb. 8, 1968 Greensborough (Vic)

Smith, Robert Thomas (Vic) b May 27, 1868 Harrow (Vic) d Aug. 21, 1927 East Melbourne (Vic)

Smith, Stanley Arthur John (Vic) b Jan. 8, 1910 Footscray (Vic) d c. 1984 Ryde (NSW)

* Smith, Stephen Barry (NSW) b Oct. 18, 1961 Sydney (NSW)

Smith, Struan McKinley (Rest of Australia) b June 4, 1907 St Leonard's (NSW)

Smith, Thomas Henry (Qld) b Sept. 19, 1898 Talgai (Qld) d March 6, 1926 Warwick (Qld)

Smith, Warren Robert (WAust) b Dec. 29, 1941 Guildford (WAust)

Smyth, Neil Weston (Vic) b June 6, 1928 South Yarra (Vic)

* Sobers, Garfield St Aubrun (S Aust) b July 28, 1936 Chelsea Road, Bay Land, Bridgetown (Barbados)

Solomon, Cyril Moss (NSW) b March 11, 1911 Cootamundra (NSW) d July 15, 1995 Manly (NSW)

Soule, Richard Eric (Tas) b Sept. 5, 1966 Launceston (Tas)

Souter, Vernon John (Vic) b Feb. 26, 1894 Uranquinty (NSW) d July 17, 1915 Elsternwick (Vic)

Spalding, Earl George (WAust) b March 13, 1965 South Perth (WAust)

Speirs, Norman Lennox (Vic) b May 31, 1886 Caulfield (Vic) d Aug. 1, 1960 Noosa Heads (Qld)

Spencer, Duncan John (WAust) b April 5, 1972 Burnley, Lancashire (England)

Spencer, Ernest Lott (Vic) b May 1, 1888 Hotham West (Vic) d Nov. 4, 1953 Essendon (Vic)

* Spofforth, Frederick Robert (NSW & Vic) b Sept. 9, 1853 Balmain (NSW) d June 4, 1926 Ditton Hill, Surrey (England)

Spring, Graham Allan (NSW) b April 20, 1961 Sydney (NSW)

Spry, Richard (Qld) b July 18, 1862 Melbourne (Vic) d Nov. 10, 1920 Linville (Qld)

Squires, Philip Horley (S Aust) b June 18, 1939 Marden (S Aust)

Stacey, Bradley John (Vic) b June 11, 1972 Geelong (Vic)

Stack, George Bagot (NSW) b March 12, 1846 West Maitland (NSW) d Oct. 7, 1930 Orange (NSW)

Stack, Walter Jaques (NSW) b Oct. 31, 1884 Croydon (NSW) d March 26, 1972 Bathurst (NSW)

* Stackpole, Keith Raymond (Vic) b July 10, 1940 Collingwood (Vic)

Stackpole, Keith William (Vic) b July 31, 1916 Melbourne (Vic) d Sept. 19, 1992 Heidelberg (Vic)

Stackpoole, John (Qld) b Nov. 23, 1916 Jundah (Qld)

Stalker, Walter (Vic) b Oct. 29, 1909 Elaine (Vic) d Jan. 13, 1977 Ballarat (Vic)

Stanes, John Gladstone (Vic) b Dec. 15, 1910 South Melbourne (Vic) d Sept. 2, 1997 Narrabeen (NSW)

Stanford, Graham Edwin (S Aust) b April 25, 1948 Adelaide (S Aust)

Stanford, Ross Milton (S Aust) b Sept. 25, 1917 Fulham (S Aust)

Stapleton, Harold Vincent (NSW) b Jan. 7, 1915 Kyogle (NSW)

Starr, Cecil Leonard Berry (S Aust) b July 20, 1907 Quorn (S Aust) d Jan. 25, 2005 North Plympton (S Aust)

Staunton, Andrew Michael (S Aust) b May 18, 1979 Canterbury (NSW)

Steele, Donald Macdonald (S Aust) b Aug. 17, 1892 East Adelaide (S Aust) d July 13, 1962 Adelaide (S Aust)

Steele, Harry Cornwall (NSW) b April 22, 1901 East Sydney (NSW) d Nov. 9, 1985 Sydney (NSW)

Steele, John Anthony (NSW) b Nov. 13, 1942 Waverley (NSW)

Steele, Kenneth Nagent (S Aust) b Dec. 17, 1889 East Adelaide (S Aust) d Dec. 19, 1956 North Adelaide (S Aust)

Stephens, Jack Lawson (Vic) b Aug. 31, 1913 Majorca (Vic) d Sept. 2, 1967 Daylesford (Vic)

Stephens, John Raymond (Vic) b Sept. 15, 1950 East Melbourne (Vic)

Stephens, Reginald Stanley (Vic) b April 16, 1883 Creswick (Vic) d Sept. 7, 1965 Malvern (Vic)

Stephenson, Franklyn Dacosta (Tas) b April 8, 1959 Halls, St James (Barbados)

Stepto, Paul Douglas (NSW) b Dec. 23, 1966 Sydney (NSW)

* Stevens, Gavin Byron (S Aust) b Feb. 29, 1932 Glenelg (S Aust)

Stevens, John Grenfell (NSW) b Feb. 22, 1948 Muswellbrook (NSW)

Stevens, John Whitehall (Vic) birth and death details unknown

Stevens, Lachlan McRae (Qld) b Dec. 31, 1978 Toowoomba (Qld)

Stevens, Robert Barry (Vic) b Nov. 5, 1929 Melbourne (Vic)

Stewart, Barry James (Tas) b May 6, 1940 Wynyard (Tas) d July 23, 1975 Wynyard (Tas)

Stewart, Gordon Lionel (NSW) b June 16, 1906 Petersham (NSW) d Oct. 21, 1984 Katoomba (NSW)

Stewart, James (WAust & NSW) b Aug. 22, 1970 East Fremantle (WAust)

Stewart, James C. (Vic) birth and death details unknown

Stewart, Trevor George (Qld) b March 15, 1940 Mt Isa (Qld)

Stewart, William (Vic) b c. 1844 full birth and death details unknown

Stibe, Colin George Reinzi (Qld) b April 22, 1916 Bundaberg (Qld) d Jan. 6, 1970 Sydney (NSW)

Still, Robert Stuart (Tas) b March 15, 1822 Bathurst (NSW) d July 5, 1907 Launceston (Tas)

Still, William Cathcart (NSW) b c. 1820 (England) d July 5, 1910 Sydney (NSW)

Stillman, William Leslie (Vic & S Aust) b Oct. 5, 1949 Alexandra (Vic)

Stirling, William Stuart (S Aust) b March 19, 1891 Jamestown (S Aust) d July 18, 1971 Adelaide (S Aust)

Stobo, Richard Montagu (NSW) b June 20, 1965 Toowoomba (Qld)

Stokes, George William (Vic) b Dec. 11, 1857 South Yarra (Vic) d Aug. 16, 1929 Brighton (Vic)

Stokes, Raymond Gordon (Tas) b May 21, 1924 Longford (Tas)

Stokes, William (WAust) b July 28, 1886 Geraldton (WAust) d Oct. 4, 1954 Perth (WAust)

Storey, Stephen Craig (Qld) b Nov. 23, 1964 Mona Vale (NSW)

Stratford, H. E. (Vic) birth and death details unknown

Strauss, Raymond Bernard (WAust) b Nov. 4, 1927 Perth (WAust)

Strudwick, David Charles (S Aust) b Jan. 11, 1934 Adelaide (S Aust)

Stuart, Anthony Mark (NSW) b Jan. 2, 1970 Waratah (NSW)

Stuart, William Percy (S Aust) b March 7, 1871 Goolwa (S Aust) d Aug. 20, 1956 Unley Park (S Aust)

Stubbs, John Robert Marshall (WAust) b Oct. 15, 1931 Collie (WAust)

Stuckey, George (Vic) b July 6, 1871 Walhalla (Vic) d March 15, 1932 North Melbourne (Vic)

Stuckey, John Henry (Vic) b July 3, 1869 Walhalla (Vic) d Aug. 10, 1952 Cheltenham (Vic)

Such, Bruce Vincent (Qld) b c. 1907 Sydney (NSW) d April 14, 1933 Townsville (Qld)

Sullivan, Alfred Ernest (NSW) b Dec. 10, 1872 Balmain (NSW) d Sept. 25, 1942 Balmain (NSW)

Sullivan, William (Qld) b Aug. 19, 1877 Hotham (Vic) d Aug. 29, 1924 Albury (NSW)

Suppel, James Thomas (NSW) b Oct. 19, 1914 Warren (NSW) d March 9, 1994 Lidcombe (NSW)

* Surti, Rusi Framroz (Qld) b May 25, 1936 Surat (India)

Sutherland, David (Vic) b June 4, 1873 Boroondara (Vic) d Oct. 6, 1971 Hawthorn (Vic)

Sutherland, Donald John (S Aust) b Nov. 28, 1949 Adelaide (S Aust)

Sutherland, James Alexander (Vic) b July 14, 1965 East Melbourne (Vic)

Swain, Brett Andrew (S Aust) b Feb. 14, 1974 Stirling (S Aust)

Swan, Gavin Graham (WAust) b Oct. 30, 1970 Subiaco (WAust)

Swanson, John David (Vic) b April 5, 1940 Brunswick (Vic)

Swendsen, Robert Charles (Qld) b Oct. 18, 1929 Charters Towers (Qld)

Swift, John Sheddon (Vic) b Feb. 3, 1852 birthplace unknown d Feb. 28, 1926 Kew (Vic)

* Symonds, Andrew (Qld) b June 9, 1975 Birmingham, West Midlands (England)

Symonds, Crawford (S Aust) b Feb. 15, 1915 North Adelaide (S Aust) d July 20, 2000 Bedford Park (S Aust)

Taaffe, Frederick Herbert (WAust) b Jan. 7, 1899 Deolali (India) d April 2, 196 Ulladulla (NSW)

Tabart, John Lewis Benjamin (Tas) b Nov. 30 1827 St Pancras, London (England) d Sept. 9, 1894 Launceston (Tas)

Tabart, Thomas Alfred (Tas) b Aug. 10, 1877 Campbell Town (Tas) d Aug. 29, 1950 East Melbourne (Vic)

* Taber, Hedley Brian (NSW) b April 29, 1940 Wagga Wagga (NSW)

Tait, Alan Houston (Qld) b Feb. 17, 1908 Toowoomba (Qld) d July 27, 1988 Indooroopilly (Qld)

Tait, George (Parr's XI) b April 12, 1844 Parramatta (NSW) d Dec. 21, 1934 East Malvern (Vic)

Tait, Shaun William (S Aust) b Feb. 22, 1983 Bedford Park (S Aust)

* Tallon, Donald (Qld) b Feb. 17, 1916 Bundaberg (Qld) d Sept. 7, 1984 Bundaberg (Qld)

Tallon, Leslie William Thomas (Qld) b July 9, 1914 Bundaberg (Qld) d Sept. 18, 1972 Coopers Plains (Qld)

Tamblyn, Geoffrey Leonard (Vic) b April 8, 1949 Melbourne (Vic)

Tamblyn, Gordon Erle (Vic) b April 23, 1918 Wallaroo Mines (S Aust) d Dec. 31, 2001 Melbourne (Vic)

Tame, Michael Philip (Tas) b Jan. 6, 1956 Hobart (Tas)

Tardif, Joseph Henry (S Aust) b May 17, 1860 Gawler (S Aust) d June 14, 1920 Prospect (S Aust)

Targett, Benjamin Stuart (Tas) b Dec. 27, 1972 Paddington (NSW)

Tarrant, Francis Alfred (Vic) b Dec. 11, 1880 Fitzroy (Vic) d Jan. 29, 1951 Upper Hawthorn (Vic)

Tarrant, William Ambrose (Vic) b Sept. 22, 1866 Fitzroy (Vic) d Nov. 1, 1938 North Fitzroy (Vic)

Tatchell, Thomas (Vic) b June 13, 1867 Inglewood (Vic) d Oct. 18, 1936 East Melbourne (Vic)

Taylor, Bruce William (Qld) b June 14, 1924 Brisbane (Qld) d Oct. 16, 1984 New Farm (Qld)

Taylor, David (NSW) b May 2, 1881 Sydney (NSW) death details unknown

Taylor, John James (WAust) b April 3, 1979 Essendon (Vic)

* Taylor, John Morris (NSW) b Oct. 10, 1895 Stanmore (NSW) d May 12, 1971 Turramurra (NSW)

Taylor, Joseph Stanley (NSW) b Nov. 1, 1887 Leichhardt (NSW) d Sept. 3, 1954 Waratah (NSW)

* Taylor, Mark Anthony (NSW) b Oct. 27, 1964 Leeton (NSW)

Taylor, Michael David (Vic & Tas) b June 9, 1955 Chelsea (Vic)

Taylor, Peter Laurence (NSW & Qld) b Aug. 22, 1956 North Sydney (NSW)

Taylor, Ross Simeon (NSW) b May 8, 1938 Mudgee (NSW) d Dec. 7, 1996 Tamworth (NSW)

Taylor, Stuart Gifford (Tas) b April 13, 1900 Prahran (Vic) d Feb. 2, 1978 Mosman Park (WAust)

Tazelaar, Dirk (Qld) b Jan. 13, 1963 Ipswich (Qld)

Teagle, Reginald Crump (S Aust) b Feb. 27, 1909 Parkside (S Aust) d June 8, 1987 Adelaide (S Aust)

Teece, Richard (Combined XIII) b April 29, 1847 Paihia (New Zealand) d Dec. 13, 1928 Point Piper (NSW)

Teisseire, Francis Lawrence (S Aust) b July 8, 1917 Rose Park (S Aust) d Nov. 23, 1998 Glenelg (S Aust)

Templeton, Robert Ian (Vic) b March 15, 1957 Hamilton (Vic)

Tennent, Hector Norman (Australians) b April 6, 1843 Hobart (Tas) d April 16, 1904 Westminster, London (England)

Tennent, John Pattison (Vic) b July 31, 1846 Hobart (Tas) d Oct. 31, 1893 Clifton Hill (Vic)

Terry, Richard Benjamin (Vic) birth and death details unknown

Thamm, Carl Friedrich Wilhelm (S Aust) b Nov. 1, 1874 Nuriootpa (S Aust) d July 4, 1944 Subiaco (WAust)

Thatcher, Allen Norman (NSW) b April 17, 1899 Sydney (NSW) d Feb. 12, 1932 Dulwich Hill (NSW)

Theak, Henry John Thomas (NSW) b March 19, 1909 Pyrmont (NSW) d Sept. 14, 1979 Narwee (NSW)

Thistle, Michael James (WAust) b Aug. 5, 1980 Perth (WAust)

Thollar, Douglas Hugh (Tas) b Feb. 13, 1919 George Town (Tas) d June 14, 2005 Kyeemagh (NSW)

Thomas, Arthur Churchill (S Aust) b May 4, 1869 Unley (S Aust) d April 28, 1934 Unley (S Aust)

Thomas, Brad John (Tas) b Jan. 18, 1972 Hobart (Tas)

Thomas, George Alexander (NSW) b April 22, 1881 Sydney (NSW)

* Thomas, Grahame (NSW) b March 21, 1938 Croydon Park (NSW)

Thomas, Jeffrey Mark (Qld) b Oct. 19, 1971 Toowoomba (Qld)

Thomas, John Oliver (Tas) b April 12, 1852 Merthyr Tydfil (Wales) d May 29, 1915 Carlton (Vic)

Thomas, Josiah (Vic) b Aug. 27, 1910 Golden Square, Bendigo (Vic) d May 28, 1960 Essendon (Vic)

Thomas, Kenneth Bruce (Vic) b Oct. 5, 1942 East Melbourne (Vic)

Thomas, Llewellyn (Tas) b April 1, 1883 Fitzroy (Vic) d Nov. 2, 1962 Evandale (Tas)

Thomas, Maxwell Raymond (Tas) b June 28, 1921 Launceston (Tas) d May 20, 2001 Lenah Valley (Tas)

Thomas, Ramon Cedric (S Aust) b Nov. 18, 1932 Mile End (S Aust)

Thomas, Ronald Vivian (Tas) b Sept. 21, 1915 Longford (Tas) d May 28, 1987 Launceston (Tas)

Thomlinson, Arthur (Tas) b c. 1887 full birth and death details unknown

Thompson, C.D. (NSW) birth and death details unknown

Thompson, Francis Cecil (Qld) b Aug. 17, 1890 Stanwell (Qld) d Sept. 24, 1963 Southport (Qld)

Thompson, Horace Malcolm (S Aust) b Nov. 29, 1913 Malvern (S Aust) d March 19, 1936 Kalgoorlie (WAust)

Thompson, James Bogne (Vic) b c. 1829 Yorkshire (England) d July 18, 1877 Melbourne (Vic)

Thompson, Kerry William (NSW) b Dec. 12, 1949 Wallsend (NSW)

Thompson, Scott Michael (NSW) b May 4, 1972 Bankstown (NSW)

Thompson, William James (Qld) b Jan. 2, 1891 (Qld)

* Thoms, George Ronald (Vic) b March 22, 1927 Footscray (Vic) d Aug. 29, 2003 Melbourne (Vic)

Thomsett, Harold King (Qld) b Oct. 23, 1913 Yarraman (Qld) d April 12, 1991 Spring Hill (Qld)

* Thomson, Alan Lloyd (Vic) b Dec. 2, 1945 Reservoir (Vic)

Thomson, Alan Ogilvie (Vic) b Sept. 1, 1899 Tibooburra (NSW) d c. 1938 Tibooburra (NSW)

Thomson, Alfred Taddy (Vic) b 1818 birth day and month unknown Paddington, London, Middlesex (England) d Oct. 12, 1895 London (England)

Thomson, Geoffrey David (WAust) b April 21, 1959 Subiaco (WAust)

* Thomson, Jeffrey Robert (NSW & Qld) b Aug. 16, 1950 Greenacre (NSW)

Thomson, Joseph (Qld) b May 27, 1877 South Brisbane (Qld) d July 5, 1953 (Qld)

Thomson, Kenneth Stephen (Tas) b Jan. 5, 1947 Hobart (Tas)

* Thomson, Nathaniel Frampton Davis (NSW) b May 29, 1839 Surry Hills (NSW) d Sept. 2, 1896 Burwood (NSW)

Thorn, Frank Leslie Oliver (Vic) b Aug. 16, 1912 St Arnaud (Vic) d Feb. 11, 1942 Gasmata (New Britain) in action

Thornely, Dominic John (NSW) b Oct. 1, 1978 Albury (NSW)

Thornton, Barry Thomas (WAust) b June 3, 1941 South Perth (WAust)

Thornton, John (Vic) b Jan. 16, 1835 Huddersfield, Yorkshire (England) d Dec. 15, 1919 Camperdown (Vic)

Thorp, Callum David (WAust) b Feb. 11, 1975 Mount Lawley (WAust)

Thorpe, Henry (Combined XI) b June 15, 1862 Parramatta (NSW) d April 18, 1937 Artarmon (NSW)

Thorpe, Linsley James (Qld) b Feb. 15, 1923 Alpha (Qld)

Thurgarland, Wilfred John (S Aust) b March 11, 1892 Queenstown (S Aust) d July 12, 1974 Campbelltown (S Aust)

* Thurlow, Hugh Morley (Qld) b Jan. 10, 1903 Townsville (Qld) d Dec. 3, 1975 Rosalie (Qld)

Thwaites, Colin Geoffrey (Vic) b Jan. 23, 1955 Lang Lang (Vic)

Thwaites, Thomas Edwin (Qld) b July 1, 1910 Nindooinbah (Qld) d May 24, 2000 Beaudesert (Qld)

Tilyard, Gregory Almeria Sydney (Tas) b March 19, 1932 Sandford (Tas)

Timbury, Fredrick Richard Vaughan (Qld) b July 12, 1885 Gladstone (Qld) d April 14, 1945 Sydney (NSW)

Tindall, Edwin (NSW) b March 31, 1851 Liverpool (NSW) d Jan. 16, 1926 Marrickville (NSW)

Tobin, Bertrandt Joseph (S Aust) b Nov. 11, 1910 North Adelaide (S Aust) d Oct. 19, 1969 Adelaide (S Aust)

Tobin, William Andrew (Vic) b June 7, 1859 Kensington, London, Middlesex (England) d Feb. 17, 1904 South Melbourne (Vic)

Toby, Frederick James (Tas) b Dec. 9, 1888 Redfern (NSW) d c. 1963 death details unknown

Tolhurst, Edward Keith (Vic) b Oct. 29, 1895 St Kilda (Vic) d May 24, 1982 East Prahran (Vic)

Tooher, John Andrew (NSW) b Nov. 18, 1846 Sydney (NSW) d May 23, 1941 Neutral Bay (NSW)

* Toohey, Peter Michael (NSW) b April 20, 1954 Blayney (NSW)

Tooley, Mark Victor (Qld) b April 29, 1965 Toowoomba (Qld)

Toovey, Ernest Albert (Qld) b May 16, 1922 Warwick (Qld)

* Toshack, Ernest Raymond Herbert (NSW) b Dec. 8, 1914 Cobar (NSW) d May 11, 2003 Bobbin Head (NSW)

Tovey, Edward Richard (Qld) b Dec. 25, 1930 Kings Cross (NSW) d May 31, 2002 St Leonard's (NSW)

Townley, Reginald Colin (Tas) b April 15, 1904 Hobart (Tas) d May 3, 1982 Hobart (Tas)

Townsend, Richard James Bruce (S Aust) Aug. 12, 1886 Mt Torrens (S Aust) d Jan. 1? 1960 Waikerie (S Aust)

Tozer, Claude John (NSW) b Sept. 27, 189€ Sydney (NSW) d Dec. 21, 1920 Lindfiel€ (NSW)

Tozer, George Bruce (Vic) b June 27, 192€ Hopetoun (Vic)

Trapp, Vincent Burney (Vic) b Jan. 26, 186? Prahran (Vic) d Oct. 21, 1929 Armadale (Vic)

* Travers, Joseph Patrick Francis (S Aust) b Jan. 10, 1871 Adelaide (S Aust) d Sept. 15, 1942 Adelaide (S Aust)

Traves, Roger Norman (Qld) b Oct. 15, 1961 Cairns (Qld)

Treanor, John Cassimar (NSW) b Aug. 17, 1922 Darlinghurst (NSW) d Nov. 7, 1993 East Ballina (NSW)

Trebilcock, Arthur Joseph (Tas) b Dec. 13, 1907 Zeehan (Tas) d May 2, 1972 Hobart (Tas)

Tregoning, Jack (S Aust) b June 13, 1919 West Adelaide (S Aust) d June 26, 1989 North Adelaide (S Aust)

Trembath, Thomas James (Vic) b Jan. 16, 1912 Moonta (S Aust) d April 2, 1978 West Brunswick (Vic)

Trenerry, Edwin (NSW) b Feb. 24, 1897 Queanbeyan (NSW) d July 8, 1983 Woollahra (NSW)

Trenerry, William Leo (NSW) b Nov. 29, 1892 Queanbeyan (NSW) d Sept. 4, 1975 Mosman (NSW)

Trethewey, Peter Grant (S Aust & Qld) b May 12, 1935 Croydon (S Aust)

* Tribe, George Edward (Vic) b Oct. 4, 1920 Footscray (Vic)

Triffitt, Arthur James (Tas) b March 17, 1914 Branxholm (Tas) d March 12, 1973 Cuckoo (Tas)

Trimble, Glenn Samuel (Qld) b Jan. 1, 1963 Herston (Qld)

Trimble, Samuel Christy (Qld) b Aug. 16, 1934 Lismore (NSW)

Tringrove, James (Tas) b Nov. 25, 1907 Blackmans Bay (Tas) d Sept. 11, 1979 Blackmans Bay (Tas)

Trinnick, James (Vic) b Dec. 13, 1853 Kingsbridge, Devon (England) d July 12, 1928 Northcote (Vic)

**Trott, Albert Edwin (Vic) b Feb. 6, 1873 Collingwood (Vic) d July 30, 1914 Willesden Green, London (England)

* Trott, George Henry Stephens (Vic) b Aug. 5, 1866 Collingwood (Vic) d Nov. 10, 1917 South Melbourne (Vic)

Trowse, Dean Frederick (S Aust) b Oct. 18, 1931 Rose Park (S Aust)

Trueman, Geoffrey Stanley (NSW) b Jan. 7, 1926 Double Bay (NSW) d June 28, 1981 Sydney (NSW)

Truman, Frederick George (Vic) b Dec. 6, 1886 Carlton (Vic) d June 17, 1955 Brighton (Vic)

* Trumble, Hugh (Vic) b May 12, 1867 Abbotsford (Vic) d Aug. 14, 1938 Hawthorn (Vic)

* Trumble, John William (Vic) b Sept. 16, 1863 Collingwood (Vic) d Aug. 17, 1944 Brighton (Vic)

Trumper, Victor (NSW) b Oct. 7, 1913 Chatswood (NSW) d Aug. 31, 1981 Sydney (NSW)

* Trumper, Victor Thomas (NSW) b Nov. 2, 1877 Sydney (NSW) d June 28, 1915 Darlinghurst (NSW)

Truscott, William John (WAust) b Oct. 9, 1886 Lithgow (NSW) d June 20, 1966 Bayswater (WAust)

Tubb, Shannon Benjamin (Tas) b May 11, 1980 Bracknell (Tas)

Tucker, Adrian Edward (NSW) b Sept. 19, 1969 Ryde (NSW)

Tucker, Rodney James (NSW & Tas) b Aug. 28, 1964 Auburn (NSW)

Tuckwell, Bertie Joseph (Vic) b Oct. 6, 1882 Carlton (Vic) d Jan. 2, 1943 Wellington (New Zealand)

Tumilty, Leonard Ross (Tas) b June 12, 1884 Launceston (Tas) d March 27, 1962 Launceston (Tas)

Tunks, William (NSW) b April 8, 1816 Castlereagh (NSW) d April 12, 1883 St Leonards (NSW)

* Turner, Alan (NSW) b July 23, 1950 Camperdown (NSW)

* Turner, Charles Thomas Byass (NSW) b Nov. 16, 1862 Bathurst (NSW) d Jan. 1, 1944 Manly (NSW)

Turner, Dale Andrew (NSW) b Jan. 30, 1974 Bankstown (NSW)

Turner, Edward (Vic) b Aug. 8, 1858 Northcote (Vic) d Jan. 26, 1893 Prahran (Vic)

Turner, J. B. (Vic) birth and death details unknown

Turner, Thomas (S Aust & Vic) b March 7, 1865 Nuriootpa (S Aust) d Oct. 27, 1936 Prospect (S Aust)

Turner, Wilfred Herbert (Vic) b July 6, 1921 Woodvale near Bendigo (Vic) d Feb. 24, 2002 Bendigo (Vic)

Tuttle, Roy Thomas (Vic) b Sept. 11, 1920 Carlton (Vic) d c. 1997 Canberra (ACT)

Tweeddale, Ernest Richard (NSW) b Aug. 23, 1895 Newtown (NSW) d April 28, 1956 Dover Heights (NSW)

Twible, Paul William (Qld) b Dec. 14, 1957 Herston (Qld)

Twopenny (Murrumgunarriman) (NSW) b c. 1845 Bathurst (NSW) d March 12, 1883 West Maitland (NSW)

Van Deinsen, Brett Paul (NSW) b Dec. 28, 1977 Bankstown (NSW)

Varis, Leslie (WAust) b May 13, 1947 Kalgoorlie (WAust)

Vaughan, Frederick (Vic) b Nov. 8, 1876 Croydon, Surrey (England) d Sept. 30, 1926 Elsternwick (Vic)

Vaughan, Jeffrey Mark (S Aust) b March 26, 1974 Blacktown (NSW)

Vaughan, Leonard J. (NSW) b March 16, 1908 Waverley (NSW) d c. 1960 full death details unknown

Vaughan, Robert (NSW) b c. 1834 d July 12, 1865 at sea between Australia and New Zealand

Vaughton, Roland William (S Aust) b May 5, 1914 Ardrossan (S Aust) d Jan. 5, 1979 Adelaide (S Aust)

Vautin, Charles Edwin (Tas) b June 24, 1867 Sorell (Tas) d Dec. 11, 1942 Moonah (Tas)

Vautin, Douglas Maynard (Tas) b July 26, 1896 Hobart (Tas) d Jan. 11, 1976 Mt Martha (Vic)

Vautin, George James Phillips (Tas & Vic) b April 23, 1869 Orielton (Tas) d Jan. 9, 1949 West Preston (Vic)

Vawser, Bruce Forbes (Vic) b June 17, 1929 Mitcham (Vic) d May 1, 2004 Melbourne (Vic)

* Veivers, Thomas Robert (Qld) b April 6, 1937 Beenleigh (Qld)

* Veletta, Michael Robert John (WAust) b Oct. 30, 1963 Subiaco (WAust)

Vernon, Edward Henry George (Vic) b Oct. 11, 1911 Northcote (Vic) d May 8, 1968 Kew (Vic)

Vernon, Leslie Phillip (Vic) b May 29, 1880 Melbourne (Vic) d May 11, 1957 Ashwood (Vic)

Vernon, Murray Trevor (WAust) b Feb. 9, 1937 Kondinin (WAust)

Vidler, Robert Trevor (NSW) b Feb. 5, 1957 Cronulla (NSW)

Vimpani, Graeme Ronald (Vic) b Jan. 27, 1972 Herston (Qld)

Vincent, Brian Alfred (S Aust) b Feb. 16, 1960 Unley (S Aust)

Vincent, Norman Hill (Tas) b Nov. 10, 1883 Sunderland, Durham (England) d Feb. 12, 1958 Prahran (Vic)

Vincent, Russell George (S Aust) b March 25, 1954 Jamestown (S Aust)

Vint, William (Vic) b June 30, 1851 Belfast (Ireland) d March 28, 1897 Helens Bay (Ireland)

Voges, Adam Charles (WAust) b Oct. 4, 1979 Perth (WAust)

Waddy, Edgar Lloyd (NSW) b Dec. 3, 1879 Morpeth (NSW) d Aug. 2, 1963 Collaroy (NSW)

Waddy, Ernest Frederick (NSW) b Oct. 5, 1880 Morpeth (NSW) d Sept. 23, 1958 Evesham , Worcestershire (England)

Wade, Frank Hainsworth (NSW) b Sept. 1, 1871 Farsley, Yorkshire (England) d Oct. 4, 1940 Lindfield (NSW)

Wainwright, Edmund George Chalwin (S Aust) b May 18, 1903 North Adelaide (S Aust) d Aug. 8, 1995 North Geelong (Vic)

* Waite, Mervyn George (S Aust) b Jan. 7, 1911 Kent Town (S Aust) d Dec. 16, 1985 Georgetown (S Aust)

Waldron, Alfred Edward (S Aust) b Feb. 26, 1857 Moorooduc (Vic) d June 7, 1929 Adelaide (S Aust)

Wales, Isaac (NSW) b Jan. 31, 1865 Auckland Park, near Bishop Auckland, Durham (England) d Jan. 11, 1949 death place unknown

Walford, Sydney Rundle (NSW) b Nov. 19, 1857 Darlinghurst (NSW) d July 2, 1949 Woollahra (NSW)

Walker, Alan Keith (NSW) b Oct. 4, 1925 Manly (NSW) d June 19, 2005 Balgowah Heights (NSW)

Walker, Charles William (S Aust) b Feb. 19, 1909 Brompton Park (S Aust) d Dec. 18, 1942 in action over Soltau (Germany)

Walker, Darren Kenneth (Vic) b June 8, 1966 Bendigo (Vic)

Walker, Jeffrey Milton (Qld) b Sept. 11, 1960 Beaudesert (Qld)

Walker, Kenneth Victor John (Vic) b June 25, 1941 Melbourne (Vic)

* Walker, Maxwell Henry Norman (Vic) b Sept. 12, 1948 West Hobart (Tas)

Walker, Ronald Radford (Vic) b Jan. 1, 1926 Collingwood (Vic)

Walker, William Holden (Tas) b Dec. 16, 1835 Islington, London (England) d June 14, 1886 Hobart (Tas)

Walkerden, Henry Ernest (WAust) b Nov. 20, 1885 Brunswick (Vic) d May 16, 1966 Richmond (Vic)

Walkley, Edwin (S Aust) b May 10, 1876 Wallaroo (S Aust) d April 18, 1950 Randwick (NSW)

Wall, John Craik Lyall Sydney (NSW) b Oct. 25, 1891 Balmain (NSW) d June 9, 1969 West Pymble (NSW)

* Wall, Thomas Welbourn (S Aust) b May 13, 1904 Semaphore (S Aust) d March 26, 1981 Adelaide (S Aust)

Wallace, Percival Henry (Vic) b Oct. 6, 1891 Bendigo (Vic) d Oct. 3, 1959 Glen Iris (Vic)

Wallace, Richard Miscamble (Tas) b March 22, 1934 Melbourne (Vic)

Walmsley, Walter Thomas (NSW, Tas & Qld) b March 16, 1916 Homebush (NSW) d Feb. 25, 1978 Hamilton (New Zealand)

Walsh, James Michael (Tas) b May 28, 1913 Launceston (Tas) d July 5, 1986 Launceston (Tas)

Walsh, John Edward (NSW) b Dec. 4, 1912 Walcha (NSW) d May 20, 1980 Wallsend (NSW)

Walsh, Lawrence Stanley (S Aust) b Feb. 8, 1902 North Adelaide (S Aust) d Jan. 12, 1976 St Georges (S Aust)

Walsh, Mark Jason (WAust) b April 28, 1972 Townsville (Qld)

Walsh, Norman Arthur (S Aust) b Feb. 8, 1902 North Adelaide (S Aust) d Dec. 7, 1969 Adelaide (S Aust)

Walshe, John Hamilton (Tas) b c. 1841 (England) d April 17, 1893 Sandy Bay (Tas)

* Walters, Francis Henry (Vic & NSW) b Feb. 9, 1860 Richmond (Vic) d June 1, 1922 at sea near Bombay

* Walters, Kevin Douglas (NSW) b Dec. 21, 1945 Dungog (NSW)

Walters, Maxwell John (Qld) b July 28, 1953 Bundaberg (Qld)

Walton, Douglas John (Tas) b April 9, 1927 New Norfolk (Tas) d Feb. 18, 2001 Glenorchy (Tas)

Ward, Edward Wolstenholme (NSW) b Aug. 17, 1823 Calcutta (India) d Feb. 5, 1890 Cannes (France)

* Ward, Francis Anthony (S Aust) b Feb. 23, 1906 Leichhardt (NSW) d May 25, 1974 Brooklyn (NSW)

Ward, Harry Alexander (Tas) b Dec. 8, 1924 Hobart (Tas) d Dec. 8, 1993 Sandy Bay (Tas)

Ward, John Charles (Vic) b Nov. 15, 1946 Melbourne (Vic)

Ward, Leonard Keith (Tas) b Feb. 17, 1879 South Kingston (S Aust) d Sept. 30, 1964 Heathpool (S Aust)

Ward, Maxwell John (NSW) b Feb. 3, 1907 Randwick (NSW) d Oct. 24, 1983 New Lambton Heights (NSW)

Ward, Ronald Egbert (Tas) b May 7, 1905 Adelaide (S Aust) d Nov. 8, 2000 Launceston (Tas)

Ward, William George (Tas) b May 15, 1863 West Hobart (Tas) d June 22, 1948 East Malvern (Vic)

Warden, Lester Griffith (Qld) b April 14, 1940 Wooloowin (Qld) d April 3, 1989 Greenslopes (Qld)

Wardill, Benjamin Johnson (Vic) b Oct. 15, 1842 Everton, Lancashire (England) d Oct. 15, 1917 Sandringham (Vic)

Wardill, Richard Wilson (Vic) b Nov. 3, 1840 Everton, Lancashire (England) d Aug. 17, 1873 Melbourne (Vic)

Wardlaw, Douglas McLaren Searl (Tas) b July 19, 1904 Hobart (Tas) d May 20, 1968 St Marys (Tas)

Wardlaw, Robert Bruce Searl (Tas) b Jan. 9, 1914 Hobart (Tas) d Sept. 12, 1986 Launceston (Tas)

Ware, Joseph Maitland (Tas) b Sept. 8, 1822 London (England) d Sept. 21, 1868 Lausanne (Switzerland)

Warne, Frank Belmont (Vic) b Oct. 3, 1906 North Carlton (Vic) d May 29, 1994 Edenvale (South Africa)

* Warne, Shane Keith (Vic) b Sept. 13, 1969 Ferntree Gully (Vic)

Warne, Tom Summerhayes (Vic) b Jan. 13, 1870 North Melbourne (Vic) d July 7, 1944 Carlton (Vic)

Warr, Gerald Gerrard (Qld) b May 17, 1939 Casino (NSW)

Warren, Peter Charles (Tas) b May 13, 1953 Launceston (Tas)

Wasley, Mark Andrew (WAust & Tas) b Oct. 6, 1965 Subiaco (WAust)

Waterman, Leonard William (Qld) b Feb. 18, 1892 Brisbane (Qld) d Jan. 1, 1952 Kangaroo Point (Qld)

Waters, Glen Wayne (Tas) b May 3, 1943 Launceston (Tas)

Waters, Robert William (S Aust) b April 29, 1874 Gravesend, Kent (England) d Feb. 20, 1912 Woodville (S Aust)

Wates, Darren Jude (WAust) b July 2, 1977 Subiaco (WAust)

* Watkins, John Russell (NSW) b April 16, 1943 Hamilton (NSW)

Watling, Walter Herbert (S Aust) b March 13, 1864 Unley (S Aust) d Dec. 19, 1928 Randfontein (South Africa)

Watmuff, Frederick John (Vic) b Sept. 16, 1915 St Kilda (Vic) d Aug. 10, 1972 Castlemaine (Vic)

Watsford, Goulburn (S Aust) b July 1, 1859 Goulburn (NSW) d May 16, 1951 Melbourne (Vic)

Watson, Alfred Edward (Tas) b Aug. 31, 1888 Carlton (Vic) d May 6, 1957 South Melbourne (Vic)

Watson, Andrew Simon (S Aust) b Oct. 14, 1955 Woomera (S Aust)

Watson, Bertie Francis (NSW) b March 13, 1898 Maclean (NSW) d Nov. 18, 1987 Canberra (ACT)

* Watson, Graeme Donald (Vic, WAust & NSW) b March 8, 1945 Kew (Vic)

Watson, Gregory George (NSW & WAust) b Jan. 29, 1955 Gulgong (NSW)

Watson, John Wentworth (Tas) b 1828 birth day and month unknown Sorell (Tas) d June 26, 1920 Scottsdale (Tas)

Watson, Roy Clarence William (WAust) b June 21, 1933 Fremantle (WAust)

* Watson, Shane Robert (Tas & Qld) b June 17, 1981 Ipswich (Qld)

Watson, William (NSW) b Nov. 10, 1881 Lambton (NSW) d Feb. 12, 1926 North Sydney (NSW)

* Watson, William James (NSW) b Jan. 31, 1931 Randwick (NSW)

Watt, Arthur David (WAust) b Nov. 24, 1913 Edinburgh (Scotland)

Watt, Arthur Kenneth Elwyn (Tas) b Dec. 12, 1891 Hobart (Tas) d Oct. 8, 1973 Hobart (Tas)

Watt, Donald (Qld) b March 15, 1920 Southport (Qld)

Watt, John (Tas) b Feb. 16, 1858 Hobart (Tas) d Nov. 14, 1918 Glebe (Tas)

Watt, John Charles (Tas) b July 6, 1884 Hobart (Tas) d Aug. 4, 1961 Hobart (Tas)

Watters, John Charles (Vic) b Oct. 6, 1924 Footscray (Vic)

Watts, Colin Arthur (S Aust) b Jan. 9, 1921 St Peters (S Aust)

Watts, Gary Maxwell (Vic) b Oct. 22, 1958 Dunolly (Vic)

Waugh, Dean Parma (NSW) b Feb. 3, 1969 Campsie (NSW)

* Waugh, Mark Edward (NSW) b June 2, 1965 Canterbury (NSW)

Waugh, Russell Frederick (NSW & WAust) b Sept. 29, 1941 Sydney (NSW)

* Waugh, Stephen Rodger (NSW) b June 2, 1965 Canterbury (NSW)

Waye, Libby Sibly (S Aust) b Jan. 14, 1885 Willunga (S Aust) d June 10, 1951 Frewville (S Aust)

Wearne, William Stewart (NSW) b Jan. 18, 1857 Campbelltown (NSW) d Jan. 28, 1929 Kalk Bay (South Africa)

Webb, Berrowes Littleton (Qld) b April 15, 1915 Brisbane (Qld) d Feb. 7, 1983 Greenslopes (Qld)

Webb, Colin Ralph (S Aust) b Jan. 20, 1926 North Adelaide (S Aust)

Webb, Kenneth Norman (S Aust) b Feb. 27, 1921 Unley (S Aust) d March 7, 1994 Daw Park (S Aust)

Webber, Darren Scott (S Aust) b Aug. 18, 1971 Burnside (S Aust)

Webster, Alexander Miles Clifton (WAust) b Nov. 25, 1908 East Fremantle (WAust) d March 28, 1964 Shenton Park (WAust)

Webster, Harold Wynne (S Aust) b Feb. 17, 1887 Randwick (NSW) d Oct. 7, 1949 Randwick (NSW)

Webster, Stuart Edward (NSW) b June 11, 1946 Orange (NSW)

Wedgwood, Walter Bernard (Vic) b Oct. 23, 1912 Clifton Hill (Vic) d Dec. 2, 1977 Mornington (Vic)

Weekley, Leonard Rex (S Aust) b July 21, 1922 Port Wakefield (S Aust)

Weeks, Albert Edmund (S Aust) b July 23, 1864 Bowden (S Aust) d April 21, 1948 Hollywood (WAust)

Weeks, Matthew Craig (S Aust) b Oct. 4, 1982 Adelaide (S Aust)

Weir, Alexander John (S Aust) b March 5, 1921 Largs Bay (S Aust)

Weir, Harold Stanley (Qld) b April 23, 1904 Croydon Junction (Qld) d June 11, 2002 Maryborough (Qld)

Welch, Charles William (Vic) b June 9, 1907 birthplace unknown d April 11, 1983 Melbourne (Vic)

* Wellham, Dirk Macdonald (NSW, Tas & Qld) b March 13, 1959 Marrickville (NSW)

Wellham, Walter Arthur (NSW) b Sept. 17, 1932 Belmont (NSW)

Wellington, Clement Wellesley (WAust) b Aug. 17, 1880 Yongala (S Aust) d July 26, 1956 Underdale (S Aust)

Wellington, Stephen Leslie (Tas) b July 4, 1899 Beaconsfield (Tas) d June 11, 1974 Scotts Head (NSW)

Wells, Arthur Phillip (NSW) b Sept. 4, 1900 Paddington (NSW) d Dec. 27, 1964 South Coogee (NSW)

**Wessels, Kepler Christoffel (Qld) b Sept. 14, 1957 Bloemfontein, Orange Free State (South Africa)

West, Neville Leonard (Vic) b Nov. 9, 1933 Marysville (Vic) d Aug. 8, 1987 Belrose (NSW)

Westaway, Colin Edward (Qld) b Aug. 27, 1936 Indooroopilly (Qld)

Westbrook, Keith Raymond (Tas) b May 28, 1887 Scottsdale (Tas) d Jan. 20, 1982 Burnie (Tas)

Westbrook, Norman Russell (Tas) b June 25, 1868 Launceston (Tas) d May 29, 1931 Launceston (Tas)

Westbrook, Roy Austin (Tas) b Jan. 3, 1889 Ringarooma (Tas) d Aug. 7, 1961 Wellington (New Zealand)

Westbrook, Thomas (Tas) b 1827 birth day and month unknown Hobart (Tas) d Sept. 13, 1911 Sandy Bay (Tas)

Westbrook, Walter Horatio (Tas) b Nov. 21, 1827 Hobart (Tas) d Jan. 3, 1897 Launceston (Tas)

Whalley, John (Qld) b Nov. 27, 1872 Spring Hill (Qld) d Oct. 29, 1925 Brisbane (Qld)

* Whatmore, Davenell Frederick (Vic) b March 16, 1954 Colombo (Ceylon)

Whiddon, Henry (NSW) b Nov. 20, 1878 Sydney (NSW) d Dec. 19, 1935 Manly (NSW)

White, Alfred Becher Stewart (NSW) b Oct. 4, 1879 Mudgee (NSW) d Dec. 15, 1962 Karuah (NSW)

White, Alfred Henry Ebsworth (NSW) b Oct. 18, 1901 Scone (NSW) d March 6, 1964 Darling Point (NSW)

White, Cameron Leon (Vic) b Aug. 18, 1983 Bairnsdale (Vic)

* White, Craig (Vic) b Dec. 16, 1969 Morley Yorkshire (England)

White, Edward Clive Stewart (NSW) b April 17, 1913 Mosman (NSW) d Oct. 10, 1999 Hornsby (NSW)

Whiteside, Warren Gregory (Vic) b Nov. 1, 1961 Box Hill (Vic)

Whitesides, Thomas (Tas) b 1836 birth day and month unknown Hobart (Tas) d Sept. 24, 1919 Hobart (Tas)

Whitfield, Henry Edward (S Aust) b Feb. 25, 1903 Kent Town (S Aust) d Jan. 14, 1937 Royston Park (S Aust)

Whitfield, Stephen Bourke John (NSW) b Nov. 21, 1950 Ryde (NSW)

Whitford, Graham Sydney (Vic) b July 25, 1938 Ascot Vale (Vic)

Whiting, Albert William Harley (NSW) b May 31, 1866 Darlinghurst (NSW) death details unknown

Whitington, Richard Smallpeice (S Aust) b June 30, 1912 Unley Park (S Aust) d March 13, 1984 Sydney (NSW)

Whitlow, Edward Hardmond (Vic) b c. 1832 Manchester, Lancashire (England) d Nov. 29, 1870 South Melbourne (Vic)

Whitney, Gary Reginald (Tas) b March 19, 1951 Campbell Town (Tas)

* Whitney, Michael Roy (NSW) b Feb. 24, 1959 Surry Hills (NSW)

Whitting, William Charles (NSW) b July 9, 1884 Drummoyne (NSW) d Oct. 26, 1936 Bellevue Hill (NSW)

* Whitty, William James (NSW & S Aust) b Aug. 15, 1886 Sydney (NSW) d Jan. 30, 1974 Tantanoola (S Aust)

Whyte, Graham Keith (Qld) b March 29, 1952 Herston (Qld)

* Wiener, Julien Mark (Vic) b May 1, 1955 Melbourne (Vic)

Wigley, Robert Strangways (S Aust) b March 15, 1864 Windsor (Vic) d April 20, 1926 Glenelg (S Aust)

Wigney, Bradley Neil (S Aust) b June 30, 1965 Leongatha (Vic)

Wilberforce, Robert James (WAust) b July 31, 1910 Subiaco (WAust) d Oct. 10, 1987 Woodlands (WAust)

Wildsmith, Andrew (Vic) b Jan. 9, 1958 East Melbourne (Vic)

Wildsmith, John (Vic) b July 1, 1939 Fitzroy (Vic)

Wilkes, Alfred Ernest (Tas) b Nov. 15, 1922 Launceston (Tas) d Aug. 27, 1998 Evandale (Tas)

Wilkie, Daniel (Vic) b Dec. 1, 1843 Melbourne (Vic) d May 11, 1917 St Kilda (Vic)

Wilkin, John Winstanley Symons (S Aust) b April 28, 1924 North Adelaide (S Aust)

Wilkins, Roy (Tas) b April 18, 1892 North Hobart (Tas) d July 17, 1965 Hobart (Tas)

Wilkinson, Alfred (S Aust) b Jan. 2, 1863 Kooringa (S Aust) d Jan. 22, 1922 Lower Mitcham (S Aust)

Wilkinson, James Scott (Tas) b Dec. 4, 1951 Hobart (Tas)

Wilkinson, Robert B. (Vic) birth and death details unknown

Wilkinson, William Archer (Vic) b Sept. 1, 1899 Clifton Hill (Vic) d May 5, 1974 Mildura (Vic)

Willcocks, Robert James (Qld) b Dec. 23, 1891 Brisbane (Qld) d March 21, 1965 Toowoomba (Qld)

* Williams, Bradley Andrew (Vic & WAust) b Nov. 20, 1974 Frankston (Vic)

Williams, Brett Douglas (S Aust) b Dec. 15, 1967 Camden (NSW)

Williams, Douglas Samuel Thomas (WAust) b July 3, 1919 Elwood (Vic)

Williams, Edward Alexander (Vic) b Sept. 18, 1915 North Fitzroy (Vic)

Williams, Luke (S Aust) b Dec. 24, 1979 Henley Beach (S Aust)

* Williams, Neil Fitzgerald (Tas) b July 2, 1962 Hope Well (St Vincent)

Williams, Norman Leonard (S Aust) b Sept. 23, 1899 Exeter (S Aust) d May 31, 1947 Semaphore (S Aust)

Williams, Owen Charles (Vic) b June 20, 1847 Impression Bay (Tas) d Nov. 18, 1917 Kandy (Ceylon)

Williams, Peter David (Vic) b Feb. 9, 1942 Brighton (Vic)

Williams, Robert Graham (S Aust) b April 4, 1911 St Peters (S Aust) d Aug. 31, 1978 Medindie (S Aust)

Williams, Scott Bradley (Qld) b Feb. 1, 1971 Herston (Qld)

Williams, Vaughan Morgan (NSW) b Dec. 19, 1977 Blaxland (NSW)

Williamson, Cameron John (S Aust) b March 26, 1970 Ryde (NSW)

Willis, Carl Bleackley (Vic) b March 23, 1893 Daylesford (Vic) d May 12, 1930 Berrigan (NSW)

Wills, Thomas Wentworth (Vic) b Dec. 19, 1835 Molonglo Plains (NSW) d May 2, 1880 Heidelberg (Vic)

Willsmore, Hurtle Binks (S Aust) b Dec. 26, 1889 Beverley (S Aust) d Sept. 17, 1985 Kings Park (S Aust)

Wilson, Charles Geldart (Vic) b Jan. 9, 1869 Carngham (Vic) d June 28, 1952 Rosenerth (New Zealand)

Wilson, George Lindsay (Vic) b April 27, 1868 Collingwood (Vic) d March 9, 1920 St Kilda (Vic)

Wilson, Gregory James (Tas) b Jan. 4, 1958 Launceston (Tas)

Wilson, Henry (Tas) b March 31, 1865 Westbury (Tas) d Aug. 18, 1914 Sydney (NSW)

Wilson, Horace (WAust) b June 28, 1864 Kadina (S Aust) d May 15, 1923 West Perth (WAust)

Wilson, John Thomas (Tas) b Nov. 27, 1868 Westbury (Tas) d July 24, 1906 Launceston (Tas)

Wilson, John Warwick (NSW) b Sept. 1, 1947 Paddington (NSW)

* Wilson, John William (Vic & S Aust) b Aug. 20, 1921 Albert Park (Vic) d Oct. 13, 1985 Bayswater (Vic)

Wilson, Joseph Cameron (NSW) b Feb. 11, 1869 Braidwood (NSW) d Aug. 26, 1938 Wollongong (NSW)

* Wilson, Paul (S Aust & WAust) b Jan. 12, 1972 Newcastle (NSW)

Wilson, Richard (Qld) b Jan. 14, 1869 Paddington (NSW) d Oct. 8, 1937 Parramatta (NSW)

Wilson, Stanley Vincent (WAust & S Aust) b Sept. 23, 1948 Midland (WAust)

Wilson, William John (Vic) b c. 1912 Mildura (Vic)

Wilson, William Young (Vic) b Dec. 13, 1909 Essendon (Vic) d Sept. 30, 1976 Ascot Vale (Vic)

Windsor, Edward Arthur Cartwright (Tas) b March 9, 1869 Launceston (Tas) d Dec. 23, 1953 Launceston (Tas)

Wingrove, Francis William (Combined XI) b April 20, 1863 Eltham (Vic) d May 27, 1892 Rupanyup (Vic)

Winning, Charles Samuel (AIF) b July 17, 1889 Paddington (NSW) d April 20, 1967 Newport (NSW)

Winser, Cyril Legh (S Aust) b Nov. 27, 1884 High Legh, Staffordshire (England) d Dec. 20, 1983 Barwon Heads (Vic)

Winter, Graham John (S Aust) b Nov. 6, 1955 Medindie (S Aust)

Wise, Allan Brett (Vic) b Feb. 24, 1979 Melbourne (Vic)

Wishart, Peter William (WAust) b June 18, 1937 Perth (WAust)

Wishart, Warren Keith (WAust) b Feb. 17, 1971 Subiaco (WAust)

Wolfe, Malcolm Frederick (WAust) b July 28, 1952 Gnowangerup (WAust)

Wood, Cecil Clunas (Tas) b April 8, 1896 Erin Bay (Tas) death details unknown

* Wood, Graeme Malcolm (WAust) b Nov. 6, 1956 East Fremantle (WAust)

Wood, Hartley Lionel (S Aust) b April 5, 1930 Flinders Park (S Aust) d Dec. 16, 1988 Elizabeth Vale (S Aust)

Wood, John Robert (NSW) b April 11, 1865 Newcastle (NSW) d Feb. 14, 1928 Putney, London (England)

Wood, Percy Barnes (WAust) b Dec. 22, 1901 Wellington (New Zealand) d June 9, 1941 Litani River (Syria) in action

Young, Shaun (Tas) b June 13, 1970 Burnie (Tas)

Younis Mohammad Ahmed (S Aust) b Oct. 20, 1947 Jullundur (India)

Zachariah, Harry (Vic) b June 4, 1911 Stirling (S Aust)

Zadow, Robert John (S Aust) b Jan. 17, 1954 Mannun (S Aust)

Zammit, Liam Aaron (NSW) b Jan. 27, 1981 Camden (NSW)

Zesers, Andris Karlis (S Aust) b March 11, 1967 Medindie (S Aust)

Ziebell, Keith Percy (Qld) b July 26, 1942 Rosewood (Qld)

Zimbulis, Anthony George (WAust) b Feb. 11, 1918 Perth (WAust) d May 17, 1963 Palm Beach (WAust)

* Zoehrer, Timothy Joseph (WAust) b Sept. 25, 1961 Armadale (WAust)

Zschorn, Paul William (S Aust) b July 16, 1886 North Unley (S Aust) d June 13, 1953 Glen Iris (Vic)

Births and Deaths of Other Cricketing Notables

The following list shows the births and deaths of people who have made a significant contribution to cricket in Australia but did not play first-class cricket for an Australian team. It includes umpires, administrators, curators, writers, coaches, managers and many more besides.

Abbott, Roy William *WACA curator 1951-81* b Nov. 14, 1915 d Sept. 25, 1993

Alcott, Errol Laurence *Physiotherapist* b Dec. 2, 1955

Allen, Joseph *ACB chairman 1913-18* b c. 1861 d Nov. 5, 1932

Argall, Philip *Test umpire* b Feb. 27, 1855 d April 3, 1912

Armstrong, Henry James *Test umpire* b not known

Bailhache, Robin Carl *Test umpire* b May 4, 1937

Barbour, George Pitty *ACB chairman 1907-08* b Jan. 27, 1867 d Sept. 7, 1951

Barlow, Andrew Nicholas *Test umpire* b July 3, 1899 d July 13, 1961

Barnes, Alan Robert *ACB secretary 1960-81; NSWCA secretary 1950-76* b Sept. 16, 1916 d Mar. 14, 1989

Barton, Edmund *Cricket-loving prime minister, first-class umpire* b Jan. 18, 1849 d Jan. 7, 1920

Battersby, Dr Arthur Cameron "Cam" *QCA chairman 1993-2000* b Jan. 21, 1935.

Bennett, Frederick William Cecil *ACB chairman 1983-86* b Sept. 5, 1915 d Jan. 26, 1995

Borwick, George Eric *Test umpire* b Apr. 2, 1896 d Aug. 1, 1981

Bowden, Percy Kelly *NSWCA secretary 1894-1914* b Dec. 11, 1861 d Feb. 23, 1922

Brereton, Henry Evan *VCA secretary 1925-50* b June 13, 1887 d Dec. 31, 1950

Buggy, Edward Hugh *Journalist; coined the word "Bodyline"* b June 9, 1896 d June 17, 1974

Bunning, Charles Robert *WACA president 1963-80* b Mar. 1, 1905 d June 3, 1994

Burdett, Les Underwood *Adelaide Oval curator 1980-* b Jan. 11, 1951

Burge, Thomas John *Test team manager* b Sept. 23, 1903 d Jan. 7, 1957

Bushby, Charles Harold *ACB chairman 1919, 1925-26; NTCA chairman 1924-74; Test team manager* b Dec. 3, 1887 d Oct. 3, 1975

Butler, Keith *Journalist* b c. 1912 d May 29, 1990

Callaway, Richard *Test umpire* b Aug. 2, 1860 d Mar. 19, 1935

Cameron, John Daniel "Jack" *Scorer* b Aug. 24, 1923

Cameron, John Laurence *Scorer* b Aug. 2, 1893 d Jan. 4, 1980

Casellas, Kenneth Francis John *Journalist* b Nov. 8, 1936.

Charlton, John Michael *Radio commentator* b May 1, 1927

Creswell, John *SACA secretary 1883-1909* b Dec. 8, 1858 d Mar. 24, 1909

Coady, P. *Test umpire* b not known d not known

Cocks, Arthur F. *Test umpire* b not known d not known

Cohen, Victor *Test team manager* b Aug. 5, 1851 d not known

Cole, Nicholas "Tom" *Test umpire* b July 12, 1844 d Jan. 27, 1924

Collins, John Richard *Test umpire* b Aug. 1, 1932

Cooper, George Stephen *Test umpire* b Mar. 1, 1907 d Dec. 29, 1980

Copeland, William John *Test umpire* b Aug. 16, 1929

Coward, Michael John *Journalist* b Aug. 2, 1946

Crafter, Anthony Ronald *Test umpire* b Dec. 5, 1940

Crockett, Robert Maxwell *Test umpire* b 1863 d Dec. 11, 1935

Crompton, Alan Barons *ACB chairman 1992-95; Test team manager* b Feb. 28, 1941

Cronin, Peter Michael *Test umpire* b Feb. 21, 1947

Curran, William Gregory *Test umpire* b not known d Dec. 21, 1921

Cush, Frank Maitland *ACB chairman 1955-57* b Aug. 10, 1893 d Nov. 1985

Davis, John Corbett *Journalist* b Apr. 11, 1868 d Feb. 16, 1941

Davis, Stephen James *Test umpire* b Apr. 9, 1952

Deare, Michael John *SACA chief executive 1996-* b Feb. 14, 1947

Dixon, Graham *Queensland Cricket chief executive 1997-* b Nov. 15, 1952

Dowling, William Joseph *ACB chairman 1957-60; VCA president 1963-73; Test team manager* b Sept. 23, 1904 d Aug. 24, 1973

Downs, George Edward *Test umpire* b July 25, 1856 d Apr. 2, 1936

Drysdale, George Russell *Painter of "The Cricketers"* b Feb. 7, 1912 d June 29, 1981

Dundas, Ross Lloyd *Statistician* b Sept. 7, 1953

Edwards, John Ernest "Jack" *VCA president 1992-97; Test team manager* b Aug. 29, 1930 d May 23, 2005

Egan, Jack *Film researcher* b Jan. 28, 1941

Egar, Colin John *Test umpire; ACB chairman 1989-92; Test team manager* b Mar. 30, 1928

Elder, David Alexander *Test umpire* b Apr. 29, 1865 d Apr. 20, 1954

Elphinston, Herbert Alfred Rhys *Test umpire* b Feb. 25, 1905 d July 8, 1966

Enright, Peter Robert *Test umpire* b Jan. 18, 1925

Evan, Griffith Mostyn *ACB chairman 1910-11; SACA president 1920-24* b 1861 d Dec. 25, 1924

Evans, Richard James "Ric" *Test umpire* b Nov. 20, 1942

Evatt, Dr Herbert Vere "Doc" *ALP leader, cricket enthusiast* b Apr. 30, 1894 d Nov. 2, 1965

Ferguson, William Henry *Scorer, baggageman* b June 6, 1880 d Sept. 22, 1957

Fisher, Isaac Alfred *Test umpire* b Apr. 12, 1851 d June 19, 1944

Flynn, Thomas *Test umpire* b 1869 d Apr. 21, 1931

Foster, Daryl Hugh *Coach* b Dec. 9, 1938

Foxton, Justin Fox Greenlaw *ACB chairman 1908-10; QCA president 1902-16* b Sept. 24, 1849 d June 23, 1916

French, Richard Allan "Dick" *Test umpire* b Aug. 7, 1938

French, Walter G. *Test umpire* b not known d 1961

Frith, David Edward John *Author, editor* b Mar. 16, 1937

Garing, Clement *Test umpire* b Dec. 17, 1873 d 1951

Gibbs, Barry Montgomery *SACA secretary 1960-66* b Mar. 11, 1933

Goodman, Thomas Lyall *Journalist, author* b c. 1902 d Sept. 28, 1989

Gray, Malcolm Alexander *ACB chairman 1986-89* b May 30, 1940

Gregory, Henry *ACB chairman 1919-20, 1922-23, 1926-27* b Mar 15, 1860 d Nov. 15, 1940

Greig, Anthony William *TV commentator* b Oct. 6, 1946

Grose, James Robert *SACA president 1987-99* b Aug. 21, 1930

Haigh, Gideon Clifford Jeffrey Davidson *Journalist, author* b Dec. 29, 1965

Hair, Darrell Bruce *Test umpire* b Sept. 30, 1952

Halbish, Graham Wilfred *ACB chief executive 1993-97* b Dec. 31, 1948

Hannah, William *Test umpire* b 1867 d Oct. 18, 1942

Harburg, Clive Henry *Radio commentator* b July 13, 1912 d July 21, 2002

Harmer, John *Coach* b June 2, 1942

Harper, Daryl John *Test umpire* b Oct. 23, 1951

Hedley, Harry Wharton *Journalist* b Jan. 7, 1848 d Nov. 20, 1911

Hele, George Alfred *Test umpire* b July 16, 1892 d Aug. 28, 1982

Heydon, Harold *NSWCA secretary 1926-50* b Oct. 9, 1893 d Dec. 14, 1967

Hiley, Thomas Alfred *QCA president 1965-69* b Nov. 25, 1905 d Nov. 6, 1990

Hodges, George James *Test umpire* b not known d not known

Holroyd, Henry North (Lord Sheffield) *Founded the Sheffield Shield* b Jan. 18, 1832 d Apr. 21, 1909

Hoy, Colin *Test umpire* b May 9, 1922 d Mar. 24, 1999

Hughes, Canon Ernest Selwyn *VCA president 1932-42* b May 12, 1860 d June 16, 1942

Ingamells, Christopher Robert *TCC chairman* b Aug. 9, 1914 d Oct. 27, 1986

Ironside, Frederick James *Invented matting wickets* b Mar. 3, 1836 d Dec. 24, 1912

Isherwood, Raymond Charles *Test umpire* b Jan. 20, 1938

Jacobs, Kenneth William *VCA secretary/chief exec 1980-* b July 6, 1952

Jacobs, William Lawson *Test team manager* b Jan. 5, 1918

James, Arthur Edward *Masseur* b not known d Sept. 1974

James, John Charles Horsey *WACA president 1885-97* b Jan. 30, 1841 d Feb. 3, 1899

Jeanes, William Henry *ACB secretary 1927-54; SACA secretary 1926-55; Test team manager* b May 19, 1883 d Sept. 1, 1958

Jenkins, Arthur George *Test umpire* b c. 1886 d May 19, 1963

Jillett, Maxwell John *TCA chairman 1967-79* b Sept. 15, 1915 d Feb. 27, 1999

Johnson, Melville William *Test umpire* b May 17, 1942

Jones, Alfred Charles *Test umpire* b June 6, 1859 d Feb. 10, 1949

King, Bennett Alfred *Academy coach* b Dec. 19, 1964

King, Leonard John *Test umpire* b July 31, 1941

Laing, James *Test umpire* b Apr. 21, 1833 d Sept. 11, 1913

Lance, Arthur Alfred *Adelaide Oval curator* 1953-80 b Dec. 9, 1913 d Sept. 11, 1999

Lane, Timothy Paul *Radio commentator* b Sept. 18, 1951

Ledwidge, Reginald Ross *Test umpire* b *c.* 1922 d Dec. 10, 1977

Leroy, Peter *SCG curator 1983-* b Nov. 16, 1949

Lillywhite, Jas jnr *Test umpire* b Feb. 23, 1842 d Oct. 25, 1929

Luttrell, Albert John Wesley "Bert"*MCG curator 1920-46* b 1875 d July 29, 1951

McAlpine, Walter *MCG curator 1880-88* b 1826 d Apr. 7, 1888

McConnell, Peter John *Test umpire* b Nov. 11, 1944

McElhone, William Percy *ACB chairman/ secretary 1911-12* b Dec. 22, 1870 d Apr. 21, 1932

McFarline, Peter Muir *Journalist* b Mar. 27, 1945 d Apr. 7, 2002

McInnes, Melville James *Test umpire* b June 30, 1915 d July 23, 1996

McKenzie, John Reginald *Helped found Country Championships* b Dec. 23, 1918 d Mar. 20, 1985

Mackinnon, Hon. Donald *VCA president 1906-32* b Sept. 29, 1859 d Apr. 25, 1932

Mackley, Allan E. *Test umpire* b 1913 d 1982

Maley, John Kennedy *Curator who pioneered drop-in pitches* b May 2, 1947

McMahon, Norman Thomas *QCA chairman 1967-87* b Feb. 21, 1922 d Dec. 21, 1991

Macmillan, Ewart Gladstone *ACB chairman 1963-66* b July 31, 1898 d Nov. 26, 1970

McQuillan, Anthony John *Test umpire* b Mar. 19, 1951

Martin, Bruce Edward *Test umpire* b June 11, 1942

Maxwell, James Edward *Radio commentator* b July 28, 1950

Menzies, Sir Robert Gordon *Cricket-loving prime minister, patron* b Dec. 20, 1894 d May 15, 1978

Merriman, Robert Frederick *CA chairman 2001-; VCA president 1997-; Test team manager* b Aug. 22, 1935

Mitchell, Kevin Michael *Gabba curator 1991-* b Sept.2, 1959

Mitchell, Kevin Vincent *Gabba curator 1982-91* b June 11, 1935

Moody, Clarence Percival *Journalist* b Aug. 11, 1867 d Nov. 28, 1937

Morton, Dr Reginald Lonsdale *VCA president 1942-47* b 1878 d May 26, 1947

Mullins, Patrick Joseph *Collector* b Jan 12, 1923 d Sept. 7, 2002

Mulvaney, Richad *Bradman Museum curator* b Mar 8, 1957

Norton, John Edward "Jack" *Test team manager* b 1910 d Jan. 28, 1992

O'Connell, Maxwell George *Test umpire* b Apr. 4, 1936

O'Reilly, Charles Bernard *Journalist* b Nov. 2, 1871 d Oct. 30, 1960

Orr, James Patrick *Test umpire* b July 18, 1868 d Dec. 26, 1940

Oxlade, Robert Aubrey *ACB chairman 1927-30, 1933-36, 1945-48, 1951-52* b 1886 d Sept. 13, 1955

Packer, Kerry Francis Bullmore *Creator of World Series Cricket* b Dec. 17, 1937

Page, Roger *Bookseller* b June 25, 1936

Parish, Robert James *ACB chairman 1966-69, 1975-80; VCA vice-pres 1970-1992; Test team manager* b May 7, 1916 d May 11, 2005

Parker, Peter Douglas *Test umpire* b July 20, 1959

Payne, John William *Test umpire* b 1844 d May 12, 1908

Pettigrew, Alan Charles *QCA chairman 1988-93* b Dec. 12, 1935 d Dec. 16, 1993

Piesse, Kendrick Bruce *Author* b Aug. 7, 1955

Pollard, Jack Ernest *Journalist, author* b Jul. 31, 1926 d May 25, 2002

Prue, Terry Arthur *Test umpire* b Dec. 11, 1948

Pyke, Dr Frank Sherman *Sports scientist* b Dec. 1, 1941

Radford, Robert Michael *NSWCA secretary/ chief exec 1976-95* b Nov. 18, 1943 d Feb. 28, 2004

Randell, Stephen Grant *Test umpire* b Feb. 19, 1956

Rawlinson, Elisha Barker *Test umpire* b Apr. 10, 1837 d Feb. 17, 1892

Richards, David Lyle *ACB chief exec 1981-93; VCA secretary 1973-80* b July 28, 1946

Richards, Joseph *Test umpire* b not known d not known

Robertson, Dr Allen William David *ACB chairman 1930-33, 1936-45, 1948-51* b 1867 d 1954

Robinson, Raymond John *Journalist, author* b July 8, 1905 d July 6, 1982

Roebuck, Peter Michael *Journalist* b Mar. 6, 1956

Rogers, Denis Walsh *ACB chairman 1995-2001; TCA chairman 1986-2004* b June 20, 1940

Rowan, Louis Patrick *Test umpire* b May 2, 1925

Rush, Henry Reynolds *ACB chairman 1920-22* b 1865 d Sept. 28, 1928

Searcy, George Henry Graff *Test umpire* b Jan. 15, 1855 d Jan. 6, 1927

Sheahan, William Peter *Test umpire* b Jan. 12, 1953

Sheridan, Philip *SCG Trust secretary 1877-1910* b Feb. 17, 1834 d Jan. 15, 1910

Sherwood, David Knox Patrick *Scorer* b *c.* 1911 d Mar. 12, 1985

Smeaton, John Henry *Test umpire* b Aug. 31 1948

Smith, Edwin Thomas *SACA president 1897-1919* b Apr. 6, 1830 d 237Dec. 25, 1919

Smith, Sydney *ACB jnr sec 1911-27; NSWCA president 1936-66; Test team manager* b Mar. 1, 1880 d Apr. 11, 1972

Smyth, William Joseph *Test umpire* b July 8, 1916

Speed, Malcolm Walter *ACB chief exec 1997-2001* b Sept. 14, 1948

Steele, Raymond Charles *VCA president 1973-1992; Test team manager* b May 19, 1917 d Nov. 22, 1993

Swift, James *Test umpire* b Jan. 5, 1848 d June 27, 1910

Taufel, Simon James Arthur *Test umpire* b Jan. 21, 1971

Timmins, Colin Douglas *Test umpire* b Apr. 2, 1947

Torrens, Warwick William *Historian, statistician* b Jan 14, 1935

Townsend, Leslie Hyde *Test umpire* b Oct. 4, 1914 d Jan. 30, 1986

Townsend, Norman E. *Test umpire* b Oct. 24, 1924

Tresidder, Phillip Lyle *Journalist* b Sept. 20, 1928 d Oct. 19, 2003

Truman, Leslie Ernest *WACA secretary 1947-73* b Oct. 11, 1919 d Jan. 13, 1973

Tyson, Frank Holmes *Author, coach* b June 6, 1930

Ware, Anthony *MCG curator 1990-* b Dec. 25, 1957

Watkins, Athol George *SCG curator 1958-84* b Apr. 11, 1919 d Apr. 9, 2001

Watson, George Albert *Test umpire* b not known d 237not known

Watt, William Brockbank *SCG curator 1951-57; MCG curator 1958-78* b Aug. 3, 1918

Webb, Sydney George *Test team manager* b Jan. 31, 1900 d Aug. 5, 1976

Webster, Raymond Mervyn *Historian, statistician* b Apr. 22, 1941

Weser, Donald Gordon *Test umpire* b Feb. 8, 1937

Whitehead, Rex Vernon *Test umpire* b Oct. 26, 1948

Whitridge, William Oswald *Test umpire; SACA adminstrator* b Aug. 14, 1853 d Feb. 12, 1919

Wilkins, Philip Laurence *Journalist* b June 26, 1939.

Williams, Alfred Percy *Test umpire* b not known d 237May 22, 1933

Winning, Clifford McGregor *Librarian* b Dec. 8, 1909 d 237Aug. 1, 2002

Wright, Ronald James John *Test umpire* b 1913 d June 14, 1968

Wyeth, Arthur Edwin *Test umpire* b July 3, 1887 d Oct. 18, 1971

Wykes, Edgar Frederick "Ted" *Test umpire* b Apr. 28, 1921

"Yabba" (Gascoigne, Stephen Harold) *Barracker* b Mar. 19, 1878 d Jan. 8, 1942

Yeomans, Ernest Charles *Test team manager* b May 3, 1883 d Oct. 28, 1955

Young, W. A. *Test umpire* b not known d not known

Births and Deaths of Women Cricketers

The following list shows the births and deaths of the women cricketers who have represented Australia in a first-class cricket team.

Key to abbreviations

Australian states and territories: ACT – Australian Capital Territory, NSW – New South Wales, NT – Northern Territory, Qld – Queensland, S Aust – South Australia, Tas – Tasmania, Vic –Victoria, W Aust – Western Australia

* Denotes Test player.

Albon, Leanne Margaret (Vic) b Nov. 7, 1959 Melbourne (Vic)

* Allitt (nee Loy), Mary (NSW) b Nov. 1, 1925 Deniliquin (NSW)

* Amos, Elizabeth (Vic) b May 26, 1938 Melbourne (Vic)

* Annetts (nee Anderson), Denise Audrey (NSW) b Jan. 30, 1964 Sydney (NSW)

* Antonio (nee Howard), Peggy (Vic) b June 2, 1917 Melbourne (Vic) d Jan. 11, 2002 Bundoora (Vic)

Bambury, Cherie (W Aust) b July 24, 1976 unknown

* Banfield, Shirley Adele (Vic) b Oct. 16, 1937 Richmond (Vic)

* Bath, Joyce (Vic) b Feb. 27, 1925 Kangaroo Flats (Vic)

* Batty, Valma (Vic) b Sept. 23, 1928 Port Melbourne (Vic) d 1995 death day and month unknown Sth Melbourne (Vic)

* Baylis (nee Craddock), Myrtle (Vic) b May 1, 1920 Footscray (Vic)

* Blackwell, Alexandra Joy (NSW) b Aug. 31, 1983 Wagga Wagga (NSW)

* Blackwell, Katherine Anne (NSW) b Aug. 31, 1983 Wagga Wagga (NSW)

* Blade (nee Shevill), Fernie Leone (NSW) b Aug. 20, 1910 Sydney (NSW) d Sept. 28, 1988 Forster (NSW)

* Blunsden, Wendy (S Aust) b Sept. 2, 1942 Adelaide (S Aust)

Bow, Sharyn Lena (Qld) b Oct. 16, 1971 birth place unknown

Bradley, Kim (Vic) b Sept. 7, 1967 Melbourne (Vic)

* Bray, Elaine Joy (Vic) b March 22, 1940 Kew (Vic) d Jan. 10, 1988 Ballarat (Vic)

* Brewer (nee Bonwick), Joyce Phyllis (Qld) b March 22, 1915 Cordalba (Qld)

* Britt, Kris Lynsey (S Aust) b April 13, 1983 Canberra (ACT)

* Broadbent, Joanne (S Aust &Qld) b Nov. 29, 1965 Adelaide (S Aust)

* Broadfoot, Louise Catherine (Vic) b Feb. 26, 1978 Melbourne (Vic)

* Brown, Karen Maree (Vic) b Sept. 9, 1963 Upfield (Vic)

* Buck (nee Ronay), Hazel (NSW) b March 8, 1932 Wyong (NSW)

* Buckstein, Ruth (Vic) b July 28, 1955 Melbourne (Vic)

Bulow, Melissa Jane (Qld) b June 13, 1950 Ipswich (Qld)

Callaghan, Leonie (NSW) b 1959 full birth details unknown

* Calver, Bronwyn Lianne (ACT & NSW) b Sept. 22, 1969 Footscray (Vic)

Calvert, Julie (Vic) b Sept. 23, 1964 Melbourne (Vic)

* Christ (nee McCulloch), Joyce (NSW) b March 7, 1921 Waverley (NSW) d Oct. 17, 1997 Arncliffe (NSW)

* Clark, Belinda Jane (NSW & Vic) b Sept. 10, 1970 Newcastle (NSW)

Coleman, Leonie Anne (NSW) b Feb. 5, 1979 Tamworth (NSW)

Cook, Lynette Gai (ACT) b May 4, 1959 Penrith (NSW)

Cooper, Sally Ann (Qld) b Oct. 12, 1978 b Melbourne (Vic)

* Cornish (nee Lutschini), Marie Janice (NSW) b Nov. 1, 1956 Wellington (NSW)

* Coulthard (nee Thomas), Faith (S Aust) b 1933 birth day and month unknown Neppabunna (S Aust)

Cunneen, Shannon Brooke (NSW) March 2, 1977 Orange (NSW)

* Dalton, Joyce (NSW) b May 20, 1933 Gayndah (Qld)

Dannatt, Jodi Maree (Qld) b April 26, 1971 Sunshine (Vic)

Davis, Jodie Elizabeth (ACT) b Dec. 25, 1966 Canberra (ACT)

* Dawson (nee Kelly), Patricia Carmel (NSW) b July 9, 1959 Lilyfield (NSW)

* Deane (nee Hassett), Elsie May (Vic) b June 22, 1910 Brighton (Vic) d July 22, 1978 Healsville (Vic)

* Denholm, Lynn (Vic) b Oct. 22, 1939 Melbourne (Vic)

* Dive, Mary (Molly) Clouston (NSW) b June 26, 1913 Five Dock (NSW) d Sept. 10, 1997 Roseville (NSW)

* Dow, (Lorna) Ruth (S Aust) b June 28, 1926 Ouyen (Vic) d 1989 full death details unknown

* Edwards, Myrtle (Vic) b June 7, 1921 Clifton Hill (Vic)

Edwards, Sarah Jane (Vic) b Jan. 4, 1982 birth place unknown

* Emerson (nee Alderman), Denise (NSW & W Aust) b May 13, 1960 Subiaco (W Aust)

Esmond, Judy (W Aust) b Jan. 27, 1960 Perth (W Aust)

* Fahey, Avril Joy (W Aust) b June 22, 1974 Subiaco (W Aust)

Farrell, Valerie (Vic) b Dec. 15, 1946 Carlton (Vic)

* Fazackerley, Kim (Tas, ACT & Qld) b Feb. 16, 1967 Hobart (Tas)

* Fellows, Annette (S Aust) b April 8, 1955 Adelaide (S Aust)

* Fitzpatrick, Cathryn Lorraine (Vic) b March 4, 1968 Melbourne (Vic)

* Flaherty, Molly (NSW) b May 10, 1914 birthplace unknown d Jan. 13, 1989 death place unknown

* Franklin, Jane Allanah (Vic) b Jan. 11, 1974 Mansfield (Vic)

* Fullston, Lynette Ann (S Aust) b March 3, 1956 Karoonda (S Aust)

* Garey, Joanne Kathleen (NSW) b May 1, 1974 Sydney (NSW)

* George (nee O'Meara), Winifred Una Margaretta (S Aust) b Jan. 19, 1914 Mordialloc (Vic) d March 19, 1988 Dandenong (Vic)

* Goldsmith, Joyce (Vic & W Aust) b Jan. 8, 1942 Melbourne (Vic)

* Gordon (nee Lonsdale), (Dorothy) Anne (Vic) b Dec. 24, 1941 birthplace unknown

* Goss, Zoe Jean (W Aust & Vic) b Dec. 6, 1968 Perth (W Aust)

* Goszko, Michelle Ann Jane (NSW) b Oct. 7, 1977 Blacktown (NSW)

* Griffiths, Sally Jane (NSW) b April 9, 1963 Newcastle (NSW)

* Haggett (nee Robertson), Belinda Jane (NSW) b Oct. 12, 1964 Sydney (NSW)

* Hall, Glenda Joy (ACT & Qld) b May 5, 1964 Brisbane (Qld)

* Hayes, Julie (NSW) b May 2, 1973 Ryde (NSW)

Heywood, Sharlene Inez (Vic) b Feb. 22, 1963 Carlton (Vic)

* Hill, Lorraine (Vic) b Oct. 24, 1946 Perth (W Aust)

* Hill (nee Fitzsimmons), Sharyn (Vic) b May 19, 1954 Melbourne (Vic)

* Hills (nee Spicer), Hilda Mary (Vic) b July 18, 1913 Northcote (Vic) d March 2003 death day and place unknown

* Hills (nee Chalner), Wendy Joan (W Aust) b Aug. 1, 1954 Merredin (W Aust)

* Holmes (nee Stuart), Patricia (NSW) b 1917 full birth details unknown d 1992 full death details unknown

* Hudson, Amy (NSW) b Feb. 5, 1916 Sydney (NSW) d Aug. 2003 death day and place unknown

* Hunter, Lee-Anne (S Aust) b July 14, 1964 Adelaide (S Aust)

* Jacobs, Jennifer Mary (S Aust & Vic) b March 8, 1956 Adelaide (S Aust)

* James (nee Morey), June (W Aust) b April 22, 1925 South Perth (W Aust)

* Jennings, Margaret Jean (Vic) b June 1, 1949 Essendon (Vic)

* Johnston (nee Dennis), Lesley (Vic) b June 9, 1937 Wedderburn (Vic)

* Jones, Mavis (Vic) b Dec. 10, 1922 Melbourne (Vic) d 1990 death day & month unknown Lakes Entrance (Vic)

* Jones, Melanie (Vic) b Aug. 11, 1972 Barnstaple (England)

* Jude, Margaret Bowman (S Aust) b Aug. 1, 1940 Adelaide (S Aust)

* Juhasz, Tunde (S Aust) b June 25, 1969 Adelaide (S Aust)

* Keightley, Lisa Maree (NSW) b Aug. 26, 1971 Mudgee (NSW)

Kendall, Rhonda Joy (W Aust & S Aust) b March 17, 1962 Perth (W Aust)

* Kennare, Jill (S Aust) b Aug. 16, 1956 Karoonda (S Aust)

* Kettels (nee Smith), Lorna Winifred (Vic) b April 5, 1912 Nagambie (Vic)

* Knee, Miriam (Vic) b Jan. 19, 1938 Ringwood (Vic)

* Kutcher (nee Morris), Lorraine (Vic) b Jan. 9, 1938 Sunshine (Vic)

* Laing, Judith (NSW) b May 27, 1957 Darlinghurst (NSW)

* Larsen, Lynette Ann (NSW & ACT) b Feb. 3, 1963 Lismore (NSW)

* Larter (nee Beal), Lorna (Vic) b Nov. 28, 1923 Hawthorn (Vic)

* Laughton (nee Watts), (Irene) Doris (S Aust) b Sept. 29, 1913 Adelaide (S Aust) d March 8, 1982 Adelaide (S Aust)
* Lee (nee Taylor), Helen (NSW) b Jan. 3, 1943 Sydney (NSW)
  Leonard (nee Mitchell), Frances Jane (ACT & W Aust) b Aug. 23, 1964 Mildura (Vic)
* Liddell (nee Twining), Emma (NSW) b March 30, 1980 Sydney (NSW)
* Lumsden, Janette Kennedy (S Aust & NSW) b Oct. 2, 1945 Musselborough (Scotland)
* Macpherson (nee Lawson), Tina (NSW) b Aug. 20, 1949 Strathfield (NSW)
* Magno, Olivia Jane (NSW & S Aust) Nov. 4, 1972 Darlinghurst (NSW)
* Martin, Deborah Leila (NSW) b Feb. 23, 1955 Sydney (NSW)
* Martin (nee Plain), Denise (W Aust) b March 4, 1959 Mt Lawley (W Aust)
* Marvell (nee Berry), Marjorie Evelyn (NSW) b July 7, 1938 Sydney (NSW)
* Mason, Charmaine Lea (Vic) b Sept. 20, 1970 Sydney (NSW)
* Massey (nee Ubergang), Eileen (Vic) b Dec. 28, 1933 Albany (W Aust)
* Massey (nee Crouch), Nell (Vic) b Feb. 21, 1938 Mount Barker (W Aust)
* Matthews (nee White), Christina (Vic, ACT & NSW) b Dec. 26, 1959 Kew (Vic)
* May (nee Fayne), Patricia (NSW) b Aug. 22, 1947 Camberwell (Vic)
* McCauley, Andrea (S Aust) b Sept. 23, 1965 Maitland (S Aust)
* McClintock, Florence (NSW) b 1918 full birth details unknown
* McDonald, Betty (W Aust) b 1950 birth day and month unknown (W Aust)
* McDonough, Marie (W Aust) b Nov 15, 1977 Perth (W Aust)
* McGregor, Therese Ann (NSW) b July 5, 1977 Sydney (NSW)
* McKenzie (nee Murdoch), Thelma (NSW) b April 6, 1915 Wallerawang (NSW)
* McLarty, Ellen Mary (W Aust) b Jan. 5, 1912 North Fremantle (W Aust) d Dec. 26, 1998 South Melbourne (Vic)
* Moffat, Sally Ann (NSW) Dec. 29, 1964 Sydney (NSW)
* Monaghan (nee Lee), Ruby (NSW) b May 24, 1917 Coniston (NSW)
  Mortimer, Kerry Lynne (S Aust) b July 30, 1955 Adelaide (S Aust)
* Napier, Wendy (Vic) b Oct. 1, 1957 Caulfield (Vic)
* Need, Jillian (S Aust) b March 11, 1944 Adelaide (S Aust) d March 8, 1997 Hawthorn (S Aust)
* Newman, Dawn (W Aust) b April 8, 1942 Mount Hawthorn (W Aust)
* Nitschke, Shelley (S Aust) b Dec. 3, 1976 Adelaide (S Aust)

* Orchard, Barbara (S Aust) b Aug. 14, 1930 Adelaide (S Aust)
* Owens, Jennifer (W Aust) b June 1, 1963 Subiaco (W Aust)
* Paisley, Una Lillian (Vic) b Nov. 18, 1922 Kew (Vic) d 1977 death day and month unknown Kew (Vic)
* Palmer, Anne (Vic) b 1915 full birth details unknown
  Papworth, Melissa Mary (Vic) b June 18, 1966 Melbourne (Vic)
* Parker (nee Wady), Janice (Vic) b Nov. 13, 1937 birth place unknown
* Peden (nee Munro), Barbara Constance Coyburn (NSW) b Oct. 18, 1905 Chatswood (NSW) d March 18, 1981 Sydney (NSW)
* Peden, Margaret Elizabeth Maynard (NSW) b Aug. 2, 1907 Chatswood (NSW) d Aug. 31, 1984 Sydney (NSW)
* Picton, Muriel (NSW) b Oct. 31, 1930 Singelton (NSW)
  Pike, Kirsten Elizabeth (Qld) b Nov. 12, 1984 Brisbane (Qld)
* Piltz, Wendy (S Aust) b Aug. 24, 1956 Adelaide (S Aust)
* Potter, Jackie (NSW) b April 9, 1948 Sydney (NSW)
* Price, Julia Clare (Qld) b Jan. 11, 1972 Sydney (NSW)
* Price (nee Hill), Karen (NSW) b May 7, 1955 Sydney (NSW)
* Pritchard (nee Scanlon), Hazel Doreen (NSW) b Dec. 23, 1913 Sydney (NSW) d Nov. 3, 1967 Sydney (NSW)
* Rae (nee Adams), Dawn (Vic) b Jan, 4, 1941 North Fitzroy (Vic)
* Raymond, Kit Arthurine (NSW) b May 21, 1930 Winton (Qld)
* Raymont, Katherine Gayle (Qld) b Oct. 31, 1959 Laidley (Qld)
* Read, Karen (W Aust) b Aug. 31, 1959 Nth Fremantle (W Aust)
* Reeler, Lindsay Anne (NSW) b March 18, 1961 (Zambia)
* Rolton, Karen Louise (S Aust) b Nov. 21, 1974 Adelaide (S Aust)
  Russell, Terri Lynn (W Aust) b June 3, 1974 Kalgoorlie (W Aust)
  Saunders, Kerry (Vic) b Dec. 6, 1960 Melbourne (Vic)
* Schmidt (nee Tyson), Joan (Vic) b Jan. 24, 1920 Mardown (Vic) d March 2003 death day and place unknown
* Shevill (nee Nann), Essie Mabel (NSW) b April 6, 1908 Sydney (NSW) d Oct. 19, 1989 Sydney (NSW)
* Shevill (nee Harris), Irene Henrietta (NSW) b Aug. 20, 10 Sydney (NSW) d Sept. 28, 1988 Sydney (NSW)
* Slater, Valmai (Qld) b Jan. 16, 1933 Norman Park (Qld)

Smith, Catherine Margaret (ACT & NSW) b Jan. 12, 1961 Yagoona (NSW)

* Smith, Clea Rosemary (Vic) b Jan. 6, 1979 Melbourne (Vic)

* Smith, Kathleen Mary (Qld) b Oct. 16, 1915 Brisbane (Qld) d July 20, 1993 Greenslopes (Qld)

* Smith, Olive (NSW) b May 17, 1923 Belmore (NSW)

* Sthalekar, Lisa Caprini (NSW) b Aug. 13, 1979 Pune (India)

* Stockton (nee Robinson), Julie (NSW) b April 19, 1959 Sydney (NSW)

* Theodore, Stephanie Rena (Vic) b Sept. 30, 1970 (France)

* Thompson, Raelee (Vic) b Aug. 3, 1945 Shepparton (Vic)

* Thomson, Patricia Ann (Vic) b Nov. 26, 1937 Leeton (NSW)

* Tredrea (nee Roberts), Janetta (Vic) b July 24, 1956 Carlton (Vic)

* Tredrea, Sharon Ann (Vic) b June 30, 1954 Melbourne (Vic)

* Tsakiris, Isabelle (S Aust) b Nov. 19, 1960 Adelaide (S Aust)

* Verco (nee Cook), Peta (W Aust) b March 2, 1956 Moora (W Aust)

* Vogt, Alma (Vic) b Feb. 25, 1925 Melbourne (Vic)

* Walsh (nee Alcorn), Alicia (NSW) b Feb. 14, 1911 Hunters Hill (NSW) d May 4, 1984 Mosman (NSW)

* Ward, Caroline (S Aust) b Sept. 30, 1969 Adelaide (S Aust)

* Wegemund (nee Smallman), Alice (NSW) b June 7, 1907 birthplace unknown

* Weir, Wendy (NSW) b Nov. 12, 1948 Cronulla (NSW)

* White, Christine Helen (Vic) b Nov. 16, 1952 Melbourne (Vic)

White, Megan Lisa (Qld & Vic) b July 30, 1980 birthplace unknown

* Whiteman (nee Johnston), (Betty) Norma (NSW) b Dec. 28, 1927 Bathurst (NSW)

* Wilson, Beverley (NSW) b Jan. 1, 1949 Sydney (NSW)

* Wilson, Deborah Lea (NSW & W Aust) b March 23, 1961

* Wilson, Elizabeth (Betty) Rebecca (Vic) b Nov. 21, 1921 Melbourne (Vic)

* Wilson (nee Edwards), Margaret (NSW) b June 25, 1946 Auburn (NSW)

* Wilson (nee Gardner), Norma (Vic) b Sept. 14, 1929 Colac (Vic)

Winch, Martha (NSW) b Oct. 31, 1978 Sydney (NSW)

THESE ARE THE DAYS OF OUR LIVES

When Rod Marsh helmed the Australian Cricket Academy in Adelaide, he made a point of ensuring his charges had something to do when they weren't developing their games. All were asked to find jobs, with several gravitating, quite understandably, towards odd jobs at Adelaide Oval. So it was that Ricky Ponting spent a good deal of time working with Les Burdett on the ground staff, while Shane Warne served in the unlikely role of office assistant for then SACA chief executive Barry Gibbs. Burdett said most stuck dutifully to their tasks, but there was one amusing exception – Ian Harvey. "We have about 60 television sets around the oval, and each afternoon without fail, Harv would go missing for an hour," Burdett said. "I wondered what it was all about until one day I found him watching *Days Of Our Lives*. He loved that show."

– DANIEL BRETTIG

"When you win the toss, usually you bat. At other times, you think about sending the opponents in to bat, and then you choose to bat first."

Generations of captains have followed, by word or deed, this piece of conventional cricketing wisdom. Traditionally, they have been supported by the fact that teams batting first have won more often than they lose. Yet, slowly but surely, this pattern has changed, and changed so gradually that few commentators have noticed. The fact is that, these days, Test cricket favours the team batting second. The traditional advantage of batting first, which before WWII gave rise to a 59:41 win:loss ratio, has virtually been reversed in the last ten years (400 Test matches). Since 2000, teams batting first have won 83 and lost 117 Tests.

There are various factors at play which may be deserving of a detailed analysis, for another time perhaps. However, one observation: there is a little-recognised problem in winning cricket matches for teams batting first. This is because teams batting first must usually score an excess of runs to secure victory, and this uses up precious time. (Tests won by teams batting first are, on average, 10% longer than those won by teams batting second.) When time constraints come into play, most captains will delay second-innings declarations until the probability of defeat is minimal. Quite often, this presents the team batting last with the chance to escape with a draw.

– CHARLES DAVIS

JASON GILLESPIE sees Glenn McGrath's half-century and raises him one, first Test against New Zealand in Brisbane. *Picture by Jonathan Wood, Getty Images.*

3

Records

Records

Compiled by ROSS DUNDAS

Records are accurate to 15 July, 2005, and excludes the Ashes series.

* Denotes not out or an unbroken partnership.

Key to abbreviations
Australian States: NSW – New South Wales, Qld – Queensland, SAust – South Australia,
Tas – Tasmania, Vic – Victoria, WAust – Western Australia.
Countries: Aust – Australia, Ban – Bangladesh, Can – Canada, Eng – England, HK – Hong Kong, Ind – India,
Ire – Ireland, Kya – Kenya, NAmer – North America, Nam – Namibia, Net – Netherlands, NZ – New Zealand,
Pak – Pakistan, SAf – South Africa, Sco – Scotland, SL – Sri Lanka, UAE – United Arab Emirates, WI – West Indies,
Zim – Zimbabwe.
Australian Grounds: Bel – Bellerive Oval, DS Docklands Stadium, Ex – Exhibition Ground, LRG – Lower Railway
Ground, TCA – Tasmanian Cricket Association Ground.
Other Grounds: BS Bradbourne Stadium (Mumbai), Chepauk – M. A. Chidambaram Stadium (Chennai),
Corp – Corporation Stadium (Chennai), EP – Ellis Park (Johannesburg), OW – Old Wanderers (Johannesburg),
PIS – R. Premadasa (Khettarama) International Stadium (Colombo), PSS – P.Saravanamuttu Stadium (Colombo),
SSC – Sinhalese Sports Club Ground (Colombo), WS – Wanderers Stadium (Johannesburg), Wankhede Stadium
(Bombay/Mumbai).

CONTENTS

AUSTRALIAN TEST MATCH RECORDS

BOWLING

ALL-ROUNDERS

WICKET-KEEPING

FIELDING

TEAM

ALL-ROUNDERS

WICKET-KEEPING

FIELDING

TEAM

APPEARANCES

CAPTAINCY

AUSTRALIAN LIMITED-OVERS INTERNATIONALS

AUSTRALIAN FIRST-CLASS RECORDS

BATTING

BOWLING

ALL-ROUNDERS

WICKET-KEEPING

FIELDING

TEAM

MISCELLANEOUS

Australian Test Match Records

AUSTRALIAN TEST PLAYERS IN ORDER OF APPEARANCE

	M	I	NO	R	HS	Avge	100s	50s	Ct	St	Balls	Mdns	R	W	Avge	S-R	RPO	BB	5	10
1 C. Bannerman ...1876-77 to 1878-79	3	6	2	239	165+	59.75	1	4	—	—	—	—	—	—	—	—	—	—	—	—
2 J.M. Blackham ...1876-77 to 1894-95	35	62	11	800	74	15.69	—	—	37	24	—	—	—	—	—	—	—	—	—	—
3 B.B. Cooper ...1876-77	1	2	—	18	15	9.00	—	—	1	—	—	—	—	—	—	—	—	—	—	—
4 T.W. Garrett ...1876-77 to 1887-88	19	33	6	339	51*	12.56	—	1	7	—	2,728	297	970	36	26.94	75.78	2.13	6-78	2	—
5 D.W. Gregory ...1876-77 to 1878-79	3	5	2	60	43	20.00	—	—	1	—	20	—	9	0	—	—	2.70	—	—	—
6 E.J. Gregory ...1876-77	1	2	—	11	11	5.50	—	—	—	—	—	—	—	—	—	—	—	—	—	—
7 J.R. Hodges †‡ ...1876-77	2	4	1	10	8	3.33	—	—	1	—	136	9	84	6	14.00	22.67	3.71	2-7	—	—
8 T.P. Horan ...1876-77 to 1884-85	15	27	2	471	124	18.84	1	1	6	—	373	45	143	11	13.00	33.91	2.30	6-40	—	—
9 T.K. Kendall †‡ ...1876-77	2	4	1	39	17*	13.00	—	—	2	—	563	56	215	14	15.36	40.21	2.29	7-55	1	—
10 W.E. Midwinter ...1876-77 to 1886-87	8	14	1	174	37	13.38	—	—	5	—	949	104	333	14	23.79	67.79	2.11	5-78	1	—
11 N.F.D. Thomson ...1876-77	2	4	—	67	41	16.75	—	—	3	—	112	16	31	1	31.00	112.00	1.66	1-14	—	—
12 T.J.D. Kelly ...1876-77 to 1878-79	2	3	—	64	35	21.33	—	—	1	—	—	—	—	—	—	—	—	—	—	—
13 W.L. Murdoch ...1876-77 to 1890	18	33	5	896	211	32.00	2	1	14	1	—	—	—	—	—	—	—	—	—	—
14 F.R. Spofforth ...1876-77 to 1886-87	18	29	6	217	50	9.43	—	1	11	—	4,185	416	1,731	94	18.41	44.52	2.48	7-44	7	4
15 F.E. Allan †‡ ...1878-79	1	2	—	5	5	5.00	—	—	—	—	180	15	80	4	20.00	45.00	2.67	2-30	—	—
16 A.C. Bannerman ...1878-79 to 1893	28	50	2	1,108	94	23.08	—	8	21	—	292	17	163	4	40.75	73.00	3.35	3-111	—	—
17 H.F. Boyle ...1878-79 to 1884-85	12	16	4	153	36*	12.75	—	—	10	—	1,744	175	641	32	20.03	54.50	2.21	6-42	1	—
18 G. Alexander ...1880 to 1884-85	2	4	—	52	33	13.00	—	—	2	—	168	13	93	2	46.50	84.00	3.32	2-69	—	—
19 G.J. Bonnor ...1880 to 1888	17	30	—	512	128	17.07	1	2	16	—	164	16	84	2	42.00	82.00	3.07	1-5	—	—
20 T.U. Groube ...1880	1	2	—	11	11	5.50	—	—	—	—	—	—	—	—	—	—	—	—	—	—
21 P.S. McDonnell ...1880 to 1888	19	34	1	955	147	28.94	3	2	6	—	52	1	53	0	—	—	6.12	—	—	—
22 W.H. Moule ...1880	1	1	—	40	34	20.00	—	—	—	—	51	4	23	3	7.67	17.00	2.71	3-23	—	—
23 G.E. Palmer ...1880 to 1886	17	25	4	296	48	14.10	—	—	13	—	4,517	452	1,678	78	21.51	57.91	2.23	7-65	6	2
24 J. Slight ...1880	1	2	—	11	7	5.50	—	—	—	—	—	—	—	—	—	—	—	—	—	—
25 W.H. Cooper ...1881-82 to 1884-85	2	3	1	13	7	6.50	—	—	1	—	466	31	226	9	25.11	51.78	2.91	6-120	1	—
26 E. Evans ...1881-82 to 1886	6	10	2	82	33	10.25	—	—	5	—	1,247	166	332	7	47.43	178.14	1.60	3-64	—	—

No.	Player	Career	M	I	NO	Runs	HS	Avge	100	50	Ct	St	Balls	Mdns	Runs	Wkts	Avge	SR	Econ	BB	5	10
27	G. Giffen	1881-82 to 1896	31	53	–	1,238	161	23.36	1	6	24	–	6,391	434	2,791	103	27.10	62.05	2.62	6-103	7	1
28	H.H. Massie	1881-82 to 1884-85	9	16	–	249	55	15.56	–	1	5	–	–	–	–	–	–	–	–	–	–	–
29	G. Coulthard	1881-82	1	1	1	6	6*	–	–	–	–	–	–	–	–	–	–	–	–	–	–	–
30	S.P. Jones	1881-82 to 1887-88	12	24	4	428	102	21.40	1	1	12	–	262	26	112	6	18.67	43.67	2.56	4-47	–	–
31	H.J.H. Scott	1884 to 1886	8	14	1	359	102	27.62	1	1	8	–	28	1	26	0	–	–	5.57	–	–	–
32	W. Bruce	1884-85 to 1894-95	14	26	2	702	80	29.25	–	5	12	–	988	72	440	12	36.67	82.33	2.67	3-88	–	–
33	A.H. Jarvis	1884-85 to 1894-95	11	21	3	303	82	16.83	–	1	9	–	–	–	–	–	–	–	–	–	–	–
34	A.P. Marr	1884-85	1	2	–	5	5	2.50	–	–	1	–	48	6	14	0	–	–	1.75	–	–	–
35	S. Morris	1884-85	1	2	1	14	10*	14.00	–	–	–	–	136	14	73	2	36.50	68.00	3.22	2-73	–	–
36	H.A. Musgrove	1884-85	1	2	–	13	9	6.50	–	–	1	–	–	–	–	–	–	–	–	–	–	–
37	R.J. Pope	1884-85	1	2	–	3	2	1.50	–	–	–	–	–	–	–	–	–	–	–	–	–	–
38	W.R. Robertson	1884-85	1	2	–	2	2	1.00	–	–	1	–	44	3	24	0	–	–	3.27	–	–	–
39	J.W. Trumble	1884-85 to 1886	7	13	1	243	59	20.25	–	1	5	–	600	29	222	10	22.20	60.00	2.22	3-29	–	–
40	J. Worrall	1884-85 to 1899	11	22	3	478	76	25.16	–	2	13	–	255	9	127	1	127.00	255.00	2.99	1-97	–	–
41	P.G. McShane	1884-85 to 1887-88	3	6	1	26	12*	5.20	–	–	2	–	108	9	48	1	48.00	108.00	2.67	1-39	–	–
42	F.H. Walters	1884-85	1	2	–	12	7	6.00	–	–	1	–	–	–	–	–	–	–	–	–	–	–
43	J. McIlwraith	1886	1	2	–	9	7	4.50	–	–	1	–	–	–	–	–	–	–	–	–	–	–
44	J.J. Ferris	1886-87 to 1890	8	16	4	98	20*	8.17	–	–	4	–	2,030	224	684	48	14.25	42.29	2.02	5-26	4	1
45	H. Moses	1886-87 to 1894-95	6	16	6	198	33	19.80	–	–	1	–	–	–	–	–	–	–	–	–	–	–
46	C.T.B. Turner	1886-87 to 1894-95	17	32	4	323	29	11.54	–	–	8	–	5,179	457	1,670	101	16.53	51.28	1.93	7-43	11	2
47	R.C. Allen	1886-87	1	2	–	44	30	22.00	–	–	2	–	–	–	–	–	–	–	–	–	–	–
48	F.J. Burton	1886-87 to 1887-88	2	4	2	4	2*	2.00	–	–	2	1	–	–	–	–	–	–	–	–	–	–
49	J.T. Cottam	1886-87	1	2	–	4	3	2.00	–	–	1	–	–	–	–	–	–	–	–	–	–	–
50	W.F. Giffen	1886-87 to 1891-92	3	6	–	11	3	1.83	–	–	3	–	–	–	–	–	–	–	–	–	–	–
51	J.J. Lyons	1886-87 to 1897-98	14	27	–	731	134	27.07	1	4	3	–	316	17	149	6	24.83	52.67	2.83	5-30	1	–
52	J.D. Edwards	1888	3	6	1	48	26	9.60	–	–	–	–	–	–	–	–	–	–	–	–	–	–
53	G.H.S. Trott	1888 to 1897-98	24	42	–	921	143	21.93	1	4	21	–	1,891	48	1,019	29	35.14	65.21	3.23	4-71	1	–
54	S.M.J. Woods	1888	3	6	–	32	18	5.33	–	–	1	–	217	18	121	5	24.20	43.40	3.35	2-35	–	–
55	J.E. Barrett	1890	2	4	1	80	67*	26.67	–	1	–	–	–	–	–	–	–	–	–	–	–	–
56	E.J.K. Burn	1890	2	4	–	41	19	10.25	–	–	1	–	–	–	–	–	–	–	–	–	–	–
57	P.C. Charlton	1890	2	4	–	29	11	7.25	–	–	3	–	45	1	24	3	8.00	15.00	3.20	3-18	–	–
58	S.E. Gregory	1890 to 1912	58	100	7	2,282	201	24.54	4	8	25	–	30	–	33	0	–	–	6.60	–	–	–
59	H. Trumble	1890 to 1903-04	32	57	14	851	70	19.79	–	4	45	–	8,099	452	3,072	141	21.79	57.44	2.28	8-65	9	3
60	S.T. Callaway	1891-92 to 1894-95	5	6	1	87	41	17.40	–	–	1	–	471	33	142	6	23.67	78.50	1.81	5-37	1	–
61	H. Donnan	1891-92 to 1896	5	10	1	75	19	8.33	–	–	–	–	54	2	22	0	–	–	2.44	–	–	–
62	R.W. McLeod	1891-92 to 1893	6	11	1	146	31	13.27	–	–	3	–	1,089	67	382	12	31.83	90.75	2.10	5-53	1	–
63	H. Graham	1893 to 1896	6	10	–	301	107	30.10	1	1	3	–	–	–	–	–	–	–	–	–	–	–

Player	Career	M	I	NO	R	HS	Avge	100s	50s	Ct	St	Balls	Mdns	R	W	Avge	S-R	RPO	BB	5	10
64 J. Darling †	1894-95 to 1905	34	60	2	1,657	178	28.57	3	8	27	—	12	1	—	0	—	—	1.50	—	—	—
65 F. A. Iredale	1894-95 to 1899	14	23	1	807	140	36.68	2	4	16	—		—	—	—	—	—	—	—	—	—
66 E. Jones	1894-95 to 1902-03	19	26	5	126	29	5.04	—	—	21	—	3,754	161	1,857	64	29.02	58.66	2.97	7-88	3	1
67 C. E. McLeod	1894-95 to 1905	17	29	5	573	112	23.88	—	1	21	—	3,374	171	1,325	33	40.15	102.24	2.36	5-65	3	—
68 J. C. Reedman	1894-95		2	—	21	17	10.50	—	—	4	—	57	2	24	1	24.00	57.00	2.53	1-12	—	—
69 A. Coningham ††	1894-95		2	—	13	10	6.50	—	—	1	—	186	9	76	2	38.00	93.00	2.45	2-17	—	—
70 J. Harry	1894-95		2	—	6	6	4.00	—	—	1	—		—	—	—	—	—	—	—	—	—
71 A. E. Trott	1894-95	5	8	3	205	85*	102.50	—	2	4	—	474	17	192	9	21.33	52.67	2.43	8-43	1	—
72 T. R. McKibbin	1894-95 to 1897-98	5	8	2	88	28*	14.67	—	—	4	—	1,032	41	496	17	29.18	60.71	2.88	3-35	—	—
73 C. J. Eady	1896 to 1901-02	3	5	2	20	10*	6.67	—	—	2	—	223	14	112	7	16.00	31.86	3.01	3-30	—	—
74 C. Hill †	1896 to 1911-12	49	89	2	3,412	191	39.22	7	19	33	—		—	—	—	—	—	—	—	—	—
75 J. J. Kelly	1896 to 1905	36	56	17	664	46*	17.03	—	—	43	20		—	—	—	—	—	—	—	—	—
76 M. A. Noble	1897-98 to 1909	42	73	7	1,997	133	30.26	1	16	26	—	7,159	361	3,025	121	25.00	59.17	2.54	7-17	9	2
77 W. P. Howell †	1897-98 to 1903-04	27	29	6	158	35	7.52	—	—	14	—	3,892	245	1,407	49	28.71	79.43	2.17	5-81	1	—
78 F. Laver	1899 to 1909	15	23	6	196	45	11.53	—	1	8	—	2,361	121	964	37	26.05	63.81	2.45	8-31	2	—
79 V. T. Trumper	1899 to 1911-12	48	89	8	3,163	214*	39.05	8	13	31	—	546	20	317	8	39.63	68.25	3.48	3-60	—	—
80 W. W. Armstrong	1901-02 to 1921	50	84	10	2,863	159*	38.69	6	8	44	—	8,022	407	2,923	87	33.60	92.21	2.19	6-35	6	—
81 R. A. Duff	1901-02 to 1905	22	40	3	1,317	146	35.59	4	6	14	—	180	9	85	4	21.25	45.00	2.83	2-43	—	—
82 A. J. Y. Hopkins	1901-02 to 1909	20	33	2	509	51	16.42	—	2	11	—	1,327	49	696	26	26.77	51.04	3.15	6-35	2	—
83 J. V. Saunders ††	1901-02 to 1907-08	14	23	6	39	11*	2.29	—	—	5	—	3,565	116	1,796	79	22.73	45.13	3.02	7-34	6	3
84 J. P. F. Travers ††	1901-02		2	—	10	5	5.00	—	—	—	—	48	2	14	1	14.00	48.00	1.75	1-14	—	—
85 A. Cotter	1903-04 to 1911-12	21	37	2	457	45	13.06	—	1	8	—	4,639	86	2,549	89	28.64	52.12	3.30	7-148	7	—
86 P. A. McAlister	1903-04 to 1909	8	16	1	252	41	16.80	—	2	10	—		—	—	—	—	—	—	—	—	—
87 D. R. A. Gehrs	1903-04 to 1910-11	6	11	1	221	67	20.09	—	1	6	—		—	—	—	—	—	—	—	—	—
88 H. Carter	1907-08 to 1921-22	28	47	9	873	72	22.97	—	4	44	21	6	—	4	0	—	—	4.00	—	—	—
89 G. R. Hazlitt	1907-08 to 1912	9	12	4	89	34*	11.13	—	—	9	—	1,563	74	623	23	27.09	67.96	2.39	7-25	1	—
90 C. G. Macartney ‡	1907-08 to 1926	35	55	4	2,131	170	41.78	7	9	17	—	3,561	177	1,240	45	27.56	79.13	2.09	7-58	2	1
91 V. S. Ransford ††	1907-08 to 1911-12	20	38	6	1,211	143*	37.84	1	7	10	—	43	3	28	1	28.00	43.00	3.91	1-9	—	—
92 M. J. Hartigan	1907-08	4	8	4	170	42	42.50	—	1	5	—	12	—	7	0	—	—	3.50	—	—	—
93 J. D. A. O'Connor †	1907-08 to 1909	4	8	1	86	20	12.29	—	—	3	—	692	24	340	13	26.15	53.23	2.95	5-40	1	—
94 W. Bardsley †	1909 to 1926	41	66	5	2,469	193*	40.48	6	14	12	—		—	—	—	—	—	—	—	—	—
95 W. J. Whitty †	1909 to 1912	14	19	7	161	39*	13.42	—	—	14	—	3,357	163	1,373	65	21.12	51.65	2.45	6-17	3	—
96 C. Kelleway	1910-11 to 1928-29	26	42	4	1,422	147	37.42	3	6	24	—	4,363	146	1,683	52	32.37	83.90	2.31	5-33	1	—
97 H. V. Hordern †	1910-11 to 1911-12	7	13	2	254	50	23.09	—	1	6	—	2,148	49	1,075	46	23.37	46.70	3.00	7-90	5	2
98 R. B. Minnett	1911-12 to 1912	9	15	1	391	90	26.07	—	3	7	—	589	26	290	11	26.36	53.55	2.95	4-34	1	—
99 T. J. Matthews	1911-12	8	10	1	153	53	17.00	—	1	7	—	1,081	46	419	16	26.19	67.56	2.33	4-29	1	—

No.	Player	Career	M	I	NO	HS	Runs	Avge	100	50	0	Ct	St	Balls	Mdns	Runs	Wkts	Avge	S/R	Econ	Best	5w	10w
100	J.W. McLaren	1911-12	1	2	1	0*	0	0.00	—	—	—	—	—	144	3	70	1	70.00	144.00	2.92	—	—	—
101	W. Carkeek †	1912	6	5	2	6*	16	5.33	—	—	—	6	2	—	—	—	—	—	—	—	—	—	—
102	S.H. Emery	1912	4	5	3	5	6	3.00	—	—	—	2	—	462	13	249	5	49.80	92.40	3.23	2-46	—	—
103	C.B. Jennings	1912	6	8	2	32	107	17.83	—	—	—	5	—	—	—	—	—	—	—	—	—	—	—
104	D.B.M. Smith	1912	2	2	0	24	30	15.00	—	—	—	—	—	—	—	—	—	—	—	—	—	—	—
105	R.E. Mayne	1912	4	4	0	25	64	16.00	—	—	—	—	—	—	—	—	—	—	—	—	—	—	—
106	H.L. Collins ‡	1920-21 to 1926	19	31	1	203	1,352	45.07	4	6	—	13	—	654	31	252	4	63.00	163.50	2.31	—	—	—
107	J.M. Gregory †	1920-21 to 1928-29	24	34	3	119	1,146	36.97	2	7	—	37	—	5,582	138	2,648	85	31.15	65.67	2.85	7-69	4	—
108	A.A. Mailey	1920-21 to 1926	21	29	9	46*	222	11.10	—	—	—	14	—	6,119	115	3,358	99	33.92	61.81	3.29	9-121	6	2
109	W.A.S. Oldfield	1920-21 to 1936-37	54	80	17	65*	1,427	22.65	—	4	—	78	52	—	—	—	—	—	—	—	—	—	—
110	C.E. Pellew	1920-21 to 1921-22	10	14	1	116	484	37.23	2	1	—	4	—	—	—	—	—	—	—	—	—	—	—
111	J. Ryder	1920-21 to 1928-29	20	32	5	201*	1,394	51.63	3	9	—	17	—	1,897	71	743	17	43.71	111.59	2.35	2-20	—	—
112	J.M. Taylor	1920-21 to 1926	20	28	0	108	997	35.61	1	8	—	11	—	114	5	45	1	45.00	114.00	2.37	1-25	—	—
113	R.L. Park	1920-21	1	1	0	0	0	0.00	—	—	—	—	—	—	—	—	—	—	—	—	—	—	—
114	E.A. McDonald	1920-21	11	12	5	36	116	16.57	—	—	—	3	—	2,885	90	1,431	43	33.28	67.09	2.98	5-32	2	—
115	T.J.E. Andrews	1921	16	23	1	94	592	26.91	—	3	—	12	—	156	4	116	1	116.00	156.00	4.46	1-23	—	—
116	H.S.T.L. Hendry	1921 to 1928-29	11	18	2	92	335	20.94	—	3	—	10	—	1,706	73	640	16	40.00	106.63	2.25	3-36	—	—
117	W.H. Ponsford	1924-25 to 1934	29	48	4	266	2,122	48.23	7	6	—	21	—	—	—	—	—	—	—	—	—	—	—
118	A.J. Richardson	1924-25 to 1926	9	13	0	100	403	31.00	1	2	—	6	—	1,812	91	521	12	43.42	151.00	1.73	2-20	—	—
119	V.Y. Richardson	1924-25 to 1935-36	19	30	0	138	706	23.53	1	4	—	24	—	—	—	—	—	—	—	—	—	—	—
120	A.E.V. Hartkopf	1924-25	1	2	0	80	80	40.00	—	1	—	—	—	240	5	134	1	134.00	240.00	3.35	1-120	—	—
121	C.V. Grimmett	1924-25 to 1935-36	37	50	10	50	557	13.93	—	1	—	17	—	14,513	736	5,231	216	24.22	67.19	2.16	7-40	21	7
122	A.F. Kippax	1924-25 to 1934	22	34	1	146	1,192	36.12	2	8	—	13	—	—	—	—	—	—	—	—	—	—	—
123	W.M. Woodfull	1926 to 1934	35	54	4	161	2,300	46.00	7	13	—	7	—	—	—	—	—	—	—	—	—	—	—
124	D.G. Bradman	1928-29 to 1948	52	80	10	334	6,996	99.94	29	13	7	32	—	160	3	72	2	36.00	80.00	2.70	1-8	—	—
125	H. Ironmonger ††	1928-29 to 1932-33	14	21	5	12	42	2.63	—	—	—	3	—	4,695	328	1,330	74	17.97	63.45	1.70	7-23	4	2
126	D.D. Blackie †	1928-29 to 1928-29	3	6	3	11*	24	8.00	—	—	—	2	—	1,260	51	444	14	31.71	90.00	2.11	6-94	1	—
127	O.E. Nothling	1928-29	1	2	0	44	52	26.00	—	—	—	—	—	276	15	72	0	—	—	1.57	—	—	—
128	E.L. a'Beckett	1928-29 to 1931-32	4	7	0	41	143	20.43	—	—	—	4	—	1,062	47	317	3	105.67	354.00	1.79	1-41	—	—
129	R.K. Oxenham	1928-29 to 1931-32	7	10	0	48	151	15.10	—	—	—	4	—	1,802	112	522	14	37.29	128.71	1.74	4-39	—	—
130	A. Jackson	1928-29 to 1930-31	8	11	1	164	474	47.40	1	2	—	7	—	—	—	—	—	—	—	—	—	—	—
131	A.G. Fairfax	1928-29 to 1930-31	10	12	4	65	410	51.25	—	4	—	15	—	1,520	54	645	21	30.71	72.38	2.55	4-31	1	—
132	P.M. Hornibrook ††	1928-29 to 1930	6	7	1	26	60	10.00	—	—	—	4	—	1,579	63	664	17	39.06	92.88	2.52	7-92	1	—
133	T.W. Wall	1928-29 to 1934	18	24	5	20	121	6.37	—	—	—	11	—	4,812	154	2,010	56	35.89	85.93	2.51	5-14	2	—
134	S.J. McCabe	1930 to 1938	39	62	5	232	2,748	48.21	6	13	—	41	—	3,746	127	1,543	36	42.86	104.06	2.47	4-13	—	—
135	A. Hurwood	1930 to 1930-31	2	2	0	5	5	2.50	—	—	—	1	—	517	28	170	11	15.45	47.00	1.97	4-22	1	—
136	K.E. Rigg	1930-31 to 1936-37	8	12	0	127	401	33.42	1	1	—	5	—	—	—	—	—	—	—	—	—	—	—

		M	I	NO	R	HS	Avge	100s	50s	Ct	St	Balls	Mdns	R	W	Avge	S-R	RPO	BB	5	10
137 H.C. Nitschke †	1931-32	2	2	–	53	47	26.50	–	–	3	–	–	–	–	–	–	–	–	–	–	–
138 P.K. Lee	1931-32 to 1932-33	2	3	–	57	42	19.00	–	–	–	–	436	19	212	5	42.40	87.20	2.92	4-111	–	–
139 W.A. Hunt ‡	1931-32	1	2	–	0	0	0.00	–	–	–	–	96	–	39	0	–	–	2.44	–	–	–
140 W.J. O'Reilly	1931-32 to 1945-46	27	39	7	410	56*	12.81	–	1	7	–	10,024	585	3,254	144	22.60	69.61	1.95	7-54	11	3
141 H.M. Thurlow	1931-32	1	1	1	0	0*	0.00	–	–	–	–	234	7	86	0	–	–	2.21	–	–	–
142 J.H.W. Fingleton	1931-32 to 1938	18	29	1	1,189	136	42.46	5	3	13	–	–	–	–	–	–	–	–	–	–	–
143 L.J. Nash	1931-32 to 1936-37	2	2	–	30	17	15.00	–	–	6	–	311	12	126	10	12.60	31.10	2.43	4-18	–	–
144 L.E. Nagel	1932-33	1	2	1	21	21*	21.00	–	–	–	–	262	9	110	2	55.00	131.00	2.52	2-110	–	–
145 L.P.J. O'Brien †	1932-33 to 1936-37	5	8	–	211	61	26.38	–	2	3	–	–	–	–	–	–	–	–	–	–	–
146 E.H. Bromley †‡	1932-33 to 1934	2	4	–	38	26	9.50	–	–	2	–	60	4	19	0	–	–	1.90	–	–	–
147 L.S. Darling †	1932-33 to 1936-37	12	18	1	474	85	27.88	–	3	8	–	162	7	65	0	–	–	2.41	–	–	–
148 H.S.B. Love	1932-33	1	2	–	8	5	4.00	–	–	3	3	–	–	–	–	–	–	–	–	–	–
149 H.H. Alexander	1932-33	1	2	1	17	17*	17.00	–	–	–	–	276	3	154	1	154.00	276.00	3.35	1-129	–	–
150 W.A. Brown	1934 to 1948	22	35	1	1,592	206*	46.82	4	9	14	–	–	–	–	–	–	–	–	–	–	–
151 A.G. Chipperfield	1934 to 1938	14	20	3	552	109	32.47	1	2	15	–	924	28	437	5	87.40	184.80	2.84	3-91	–	–
152 H.I. Ebeling	1934	1	2	–	43	41	21.50	–	–	–	–	186	9	89	3	29.67	62.00	2.87	3-74	–	–
153 L.O. Fleetwood-Smith†	1935-36 to 1938	10	11	5	54	16*	9.00	–	–	–	–	3,093	78	1,570	42	37.38	73.64	3.05	6-110	2	1
154 E.L. McCormick	1935-36 to 1938	12	14	5	54	17*	6.00	–	–	8	–	2,107	50	1,079	36	29.97	58.53	3.07	4-101	–	–
155 C.L. Badcock	1936-37 to 1938	7	12	1	160	118	14.55	1	–	3	–	–	–	–	–	–	–	–	–	–	–
156 R.H. Robinson	1936-37	1	2	–	5	3	2.50	–	–	–	–	–	–	–	–	–	–	–	–	–	–
157 M.W. Sievers	1936-37 to 1936-37	3	6	1	67	25*	13.40	–	–	4	–	602	25	161	9	17.89	66.89	1.60	5-21	1	–
158 F.A. Ward	1936-37 to 1938	4	8	2	36	18	6.00	–	–	1	–	1,268	30	574	11	52.18	115.27	2.72	6-102	1	–
159 R.G. Gregory	1936-37	2	3	–	153	80	51.00	–	2	1	–	24	–	14	0	–	–	3.50	–	–	–
160 B.A. Barnett †	1938	4	8	1	195	57	27.86	–	1	3	2	–	–	–	–	–	–	–	–	–	–
161 A.L. Hassett	1938 to 1953	43	69	3	3,073	198*	46.56	10	11	30	–	111	2	78	0	–	–	4.22	–	–	–
162 M.G. Waite	1938	2	3	–	11	8	3.67	–	–	1	–	552	23	190	1	190.00	552.00	2.07	1-150	–	–
163 S.G. Barnes	1938 to 1948	13	19	2	1,072	234	63.06	3	5	14	–	594	11	218	4	54.50	148.50	2.20	2-25	–	–
164 I.W.G. Johnson	1945-46 to 1956-57	45	66	12	1,000	77	18.52	–	6	30	–	8,780	330	3,182	109	29.19	80.55	2.17	7-44	3	–
165 R.R. Lindwall	1945-46 to 1959-60	61	84	13	1,502	118	21.15	2	5	26	–	13,650	419	5,251	228	23.03	59.87	2.31	7-38	12	–
166 C.L. McCool	1945-46 to 1949-50	14	17	4	459	104*	35.31	1	1	14	–	2,504	44	958	36	26.61	69.56	2.30	5-41	3	–
167 K.D. Meuleman	1945-46	1	2	–	0	0	0.00	–	–	–	–	–	–	–	–	–	–	–	–	–	–
168 K.R. Miller	1945-46 to 1956-57	55	87	7	2,958	147	36.98	7	13	38	–	10,389	337	3,906	170	22.98	61.11	2.26	7-60	7	1
169 D. Tallon	1945-46 to 1953	21	26	3	394	92	17.13	–	2	50	8	–	–	–	–	–	–	–	–	–	–
170 E.R.H. Toshack ‡	1945-46 to 1948	12	11	6	73	20*	14.60	–	–	4	–	3,140	155	989	47	21.04	66.81	1.89	6-29	4	1
171 A.R. Morris †‡	1946-47 to 1954-55	46	79	3	3,533	206	46.49	12	12	15	–	111	1	50	2	25.00	55.50	2.70	1-5	–	–
172 G.E. Tribe ††	1946-47 to 1946-47	3	3	1	35	25*	17.50	–	–	–	–	760	9	330	2	165.00	380.00	2.61	2-48	–	–

No.	Player	Career	Tests	I	NO	Runs	HS	Avg	100	50	Ct	St	Balls	Runs	Wkts	Avg	SR	Econ	BB	5wi	10wm
173	F. W. Freer	1946-47	1	1	1	28	28*	–	–	–	–	–	160	74	3	24.67	53.35	2.78	2-49	–	–
174	B. Dooland	1946-47 to 1947-48	3	5	1	76	31	19.00	–	–	3	–	880	419	9	46.56	97.78	2.86	4-69	–	–
175	M. R. Harvey	1946-47	1	2	–	43	31	21.50	–	–	1	–	–	–	–	–	–	–	–	–	–
176	R. A. Hamence	1946-47 to 1947-48	3	4	1	81	30*	27.00	–	–	1	–	–	–	–	–	–	–	–	–	–
177	W. A. Johnston †‡	1947-48 to 1954-55	40	49	25	273	29	11.38	–	1	16	–	11,048	3,826	160	23.91	69.05	2.08	6-44	7	–
178	R. N. Harvey †	1947-48 to 1962-63	79	137	10	6,149	205	48.42	21	24	64	–	414	120	3	40.00	138.00	1.74	1-8	–	–
179	L. J. Johnson	1947-48	1	1	1	25	25*	–	–	–	2	–	282	74	6	12.33	47.00	1.57	3-8	–	–
180	S. J. E. Loxton	1947-48 to 1950-51	12	15	–	554	101	36.93	1	3	7	–	906	349	8	43.63	113.25	2.31	3-55	–	–
181	D. T. Ring	1947-48 to 1953	13	21	2	426	67	22.42	–	3	5	–	3,024	1,305	35	37.29	86.40	2.59	6-72	2	–
182	R. A. Saggers	1948 to 1949-50	6	5	2	30	14	10.00	–	–	16	8	–	–	–	–	–	–	–	–	–
183	J. Moroney	1949-50 to 1951-52	7	12	1	383	118	34.82	2	1	1	–	–	–	–	–	–	–	–	–	–
184	G. Noblet	1949-50 to 1952-53	3	3	1	22	13*	7.33	–	–	–	–	774	183	7	26.14	110.57	1.42	3-21	–	–
185	J. B. Iverson	1950-51	5	7	3	3	1*	0.75	–	–	2	–	1,108	320	21	15.24	52.76	1.73	6-27	1	–
186	K. A. Archer	1950-51 to 1951-52	5	9	–	234	48	26.00	–	–	–	–	–	–	–	–	–	–	–	–	–
187	J. W. Burke	1950-51 to 1958-59	24	44	7	1,280	189	34.59	3	5	18	–	814	230	8	28.75	101.75	1.70	4-37	–	–
188	G. B. Hole	1950-51 to 1954-55	18	33	2	789	66	25.45	1	6	21	–	398	126	3	42.00	132.67	1.90	1-9	–	–
189	G. R. A. Langley	1951-52 to 1956-57	26	37	12	374	53	14.96	–	1	83	15	–	–	–	–	–	–	–	–	–
190	R. Benaud	1951-52 to 1963-64	63	97	7	2,201	122	24.46	3	9	65	–	19,108	6,704	248	27.03	77.05	2.11	7-72	16	1
191	C. C. McDonald	1951-52 to 1961	47	83	4	3,107	170	39.33	5	17	14	–	8	3	0	–	–	2.25	–	–	–
192	G. R. Thoms	1951-52	1	2	–	44	28	22.00	–	–	–	–	–	–	–	–	–	–	–	–	–
193	R. G. Archer	1952-53 to 1956-57	19	30	1	713	128	24.59	1	2	20	–	3,576	1,318	48	27.46	74.50	2.21	5-53	1	–
194	I. D. Craig	1952-53 to 1957-58	11	18	–	358	53	19.89	–	2	2	–	–	–	–	–	–	–	–	–	–
195	A. K. Davidson †‡	1953 to 1962-63	44	61	7	1,328	80	24.59	–	5	42	–	11,587	3,819	186	20.53	62.30	1.98	7-93	14	2
196	J. C. Hill	1953 to 1954-55	3	6	3	21	8*	7.00	–	–	3	–	606	273	8	34.13	75.75	2.70	3-35	–	–
197	J. H. de Courcy	1953	3	6	1	81	41	16.20	–	1	3	–	–	–	–	–	–	–	–	–	–
198	L. E. Favell	1954-55 to 1960-61	19	31	3	757	101	27.04	1	5	9	–	–	–	–	–	–	–	–	–	–
199	L. V. Maddocks	1954-55 to 1956-57	7	12	1	177	69	17.70	–	1	18	1	–	–	–	–	–	–	–	–	–
200	P. J. P. Burge	1954-55 to 1965-66	42	68	8	2,290	181	38.17	4	12	23	–	6	5	0	–	–	–	–	–	–
201	W. J. Watson	1954-55	4	7	1	106	30	17.67	–	–	2	–	–	–	–	–	–	–	–	–	–
202	W. P. A. Crawford	1956	4	5	2	53	34	17.67	–	–	1	–	437	107	7	15.29	62.43	1.47	3-28	–	–
203	K. D. Mackay †	1956 to 1962-63	37	52	7	1,507	89	33.49	–	13	16	–	5,792	1,721	50	34.42	115.84	1.78	6-42	2	–
204	J. W. Rutherford	1956-57	1	1	–	30	30	30.00	–	–	–	–	36	15	1	15.00	36.00	2.50	1-11	–	–
205	J. W. Wilson ‡	1956-57	1	1	1	–	–	–	–	–	2	–	216	64	1	64.00	216.00	1.78	1-25	–	–
206	A. T. W. Grout	1957-58 to 1965-66	51	67	8	890	74	15.08	–	3	163	24	–	–	–	–	–	–	–	–	–
207	L. F. Kline †‡	1957-58 to 1960-61	13	16	9	58	15*	8.29	–	–	9	–	2,373	776	34	22.82	69.79	1.96	7-75	1	–
208	I. Meckiff ‡	1957-58 to 1963-64	18	20	7	154	45*	11.85	–	–	9	–	3,734	1,423	45	31.62	82.98	2.38	6-38	2	–
209	R. B. Simpson	1957-58 to 1977-78	62	111	7	4,869	311	46.82	10	27	110	–	6,881	3,001	71	42.27	96.92	2.62	5-57	2	–

No.	Player	Career	M	I	NO	R	HS	Avge	100s	50s	Ct	St	Balls	Mdns	R	W	Avge	S-R	RPO	BB	5	10
210	R. A. Gaunt †	1957-58 to 1963-64	3	4	2	6	3	3.00	–	–	1	–	716	14	310	7	44.29	102.29	2.60	3-53	–	–
211	N. C. O'Neill	1958-59 to 1964-65	42	69	8	2,779	181	45.56	6	15	21	–	1,392	48	667	17	39.24	81.88	2.88	4-41	–	–
212	K. N. Slater	1958-59	1	1	1	1	1*	–	–	–	–	–	256	9	101	2	50.50	128.00	2.37	2-40	–	–
213	G. F. Rorke †	1958-59	4	4	2	9	7	4.50	–	–	–	–	703	26	203	10	20.30	70.30	1.73	3-23	–	–
214	G. B. Stevens	1959-60	4	7	1	112	28	16.00	–	–	2	–	–	–	–	–	–	–	–	–	–	–
215	B. N. Jarman	1959-60 to 1968-69	19	30	3	400	78	14.81	–	–	50	4	–	–	–	–	–	–	–	–	–	–
216	J. W. Martin †‡	1960-61 to 1966-67	8	13	1	214	55	17.83	–	1	3	–	1,846	57	832	17	48.94	108.59	2.70	3-56	–	–
217	F. M. Misson	1960-61 to 1961	5	5	3	38	25*	19.00	–	–	6	–	1,197	30	616	16	38.50	74.81	3.09	4-58	–	–
218	D. E. Hoare	1960-61	1	2	–	35	35	17.50	–	–	–	–	232	–	156	2	78.00	116.00	4.03	2-68	–	–
219	W. M. Lawry †	1961 to 1970-71	68	123	12	5,234	210	47.15	13	27	30	–	14	–	6	0	–	–	2.57	–	–	–
220	G. D. McKenzie	1961 to 1970-71	61	89	12	945	76	12.27	–	2	34	–	17,684	547	7,328	246	29.79	71.89	2.49	8-71	16	3
221	B. C. Booth	1961 to 1965-66	29	48	6	1,773	169	42.21	5	10	17	–	436	15	146	3	48.67	145.33	2.01	2-33	–	–
222	C. E. J. Guest	1962-63	1	1	–	11	11	11.00	–	–	–	–	144	1	59	0	–	–	2.46	–	–	–
223	B. K. Shepherd †	1962-63 to 1964-65	9	14	2	502	96	41.83	–	5	2	–	26	1	9	0	–	–	2.08	–	–	–
224	N. J. N. Hawke	1962-63 to 1968	27	37	15	365	45*	16.59	–	–	9	–	6,974	238	2,677	91	29.42	76.64	2.30	7-105	6	–
225	A. N. Connolly	1963-64 to 1970-71	30	45	20	260	37	10.40	–	–	17	–	7,818	289	2,981	102	29.23	76.65	2.29	6-47	4	–
226	T. R. Veivers †	1963-64 to 1966-67	21	30	4	813	88	31.27	–	4	7	–	4,191	195	1,375	33	41.67	127.00	1.97	4-68	–	–
227	I. R. Redpath	1963-64 to 1975-76	67	120	11	4,737	171	43.46	8	31	83	–	64	2	41	0	–	–	3.84	–	–	–
228	G. E. Corling	1964	5	5	2	5	3	1.67	–	–	1	–	1,159	50	447	12	37.25	96.58	2.31	4-60	–	–
229	R. M. Cowper †	1964 to 1968	27	46	2	2,061	307	46.84	5	10	21	–	3,005	138	1,139	36	31.64	83.47	2.27	4-48	–	–
230	R. H. D. Sellers	1964-65	1	1	–	0	0	0.00	–	–	–	–	30	1	17	0	–	–	3.40	–	–	–
231	I. M. Chappell	1964-65 to 1979-80	76	136	10	5,345	196	42.42	14	26	105	–	2,873	87	1,316	20	65.80	143.65	2.75	2-21	–	–
232	D. J. Sincock ‡	1964-65 to 1965-66	3	4	1	80	29	26.67	–	–	2	–	724	37	410	8	51.25	90.50	3.40	3-67	–	–
233	L. C. Mayne †	1964-65 to 1969-70	6	11	3	76	13	9.50	–	–	3	–	1,251	37	628	19	33.05	65.84	3.01	4-43	–	–
234	P. I. Philpott	1964-65 to 1965-66	8	10	1	93	22	10.33	–	–	5	–	2,262	67	1,000	26	38.46	87.00	2.65	5-90	1	–
235	G. Thomas	1964-65 to 1965-66	8	12	1	325	61	29.55	–	3	3	–	–	–	–	–	–	–	–	–	–	–
236	P. J. Allan	1965-66	1	–	–	–	–	–	–	–	–	–	192	6	83	2	41.50	96.00	2.59	2-58	–	–
237	K. D. Walters	1965-66 to 1980-81	75	125	14	5,357	250	48.26	15	33	43	–	3,295	79	1,425	49	29.08	67.24	2.59	5-66	1	–
238	K. R. Stackpole †	1965-66 to 1973-74	44	80	5	2,807	207	37.43	7	14	47	–	2,321	86	1,001	15	66.73	154.73	2.59	2-33	–	–
239	D. A. Renneberg	1966-67 to 1967-68	8	13	7	22	9	3.67	–	–	2	–	1,598	42	830	23	36.09	69.48	3.12	5-39	1	–
240	H. B. Taber	1966-67 to 1969-70	16	27	5	353	48	16.05	–	–	56	4	–	–	–	–	–	–	–	–	–	–
241	J. W. Gleeson	1967-68 to 1972	29	46	8	395	45	10.39	–	–	17	–	8,857	378	3,367	93	36.20	95.24	2.28	5-61	3	–
242	G. D. Watson †	1967-68 to 1972	5	9	–	97	50	10.78	–	1	2	–	552	23	254	6	42.33	92.00	2.76	2-67	–	–
243	A. P. Sheahan †	1967-68 to 1973-74	31	53	6	1,594	127	33.91	2	7	17	–	–	–	–	–	–	–	–	–	–	–
244	E. W. Freeman	1967-68 to 1969-70	11	18	–	345	76	19.17	–	2	5	–	2,183	58	1,128	34	33.18	64.21	3.10	4-52	–	–
245	L. R. Joslin ††	1967-68	1	2	–	9	7	4.50	–	–	–	–	–	–	–	–	–	–	–	–	–	–

No.	Player	Career	M	I	NO	Runs	HS	Avge	100	50	Ct	St	Balls	Mdns	Runs	Wkts	Avge	SR	Econ	BB	5wi	10wm
246	R.J. Inverarity ‡	1968 to 1972	6	11	1	174	56	17.40	–	1	4	–	372	26	93	4	23.25	93.00	1.50	–	–	–
247	A.A. Mallett	1968 to 1980	39	50	13	430	43*	11.62	–	–	30	–	9,990	419	3,940	132	29.85	75.68	2.37	8-59	6	1
248	T.J. Jenner	1970-71 to 1975-76	9	14	5	208	74	23.11	–	1	5	–	1,881	62	749	24	31.21	78.38	2.39	5-90	1	–
249	R.W. Marsh †	1970-71 to 1983-84	97	150	13	3,633	132	26.52	3	16	343	12	72	–	54	0	–	–	4.50	–	–	–
250	A.L. Thomson	1970-71 to 1970-71	4	4	3	22	12*	22.00	–	–	–	–	1,519	33	654	12	54.50	126.58	2.58	3-79	–	–
251	G.S. Chappell	1970-71 to 1983-84	87	151	19	7,110	247*	53.86	24	31	122	–	5,327	208	1,913	47	40.70	113.34	2.15	5-61	1	–
252	J.R.F. Duncan	1970-71 to 1970-71	1	1	–	3	3	3.00	–	–	–	–	112	4	30	0	–	–	1.61	–	–	–
253	K.J. O'Keeffe	1970-71 to 1977	24	34	9	644	85	25.76	–	1	15	–	5,384	189	2,018	53	38.08	101.58	2.25	3-65	–	–
254	D.K. Lillee	1970-71 to 1983-84	70	90	24	905	73*	13.71	–	1	23	–	18,467	652	8,493	355	23.92	52.02	2.76	7-83	23	7
255	A.R. Dell ‡	1970-71 to 1973-74	2	2	2	6	3*	–	–	–	–	–	559	18	160	6	26.67	93.17	1.72	3-65	–	–
256	K.H. Eastwood †‡	1970-71 to 1970-71	1	2	–	5	5	2.50	–	–	1	–	40	–	21	1	21.00	40.00	3.15	1-21	–	–
257	D.J. Colley	1972	3	4	1	84	54	21.00	–	1	1	–	729	20	312	6	52.00	121.50	2.57	3-83	–	–
258	B.C. Francis	1972 to 1972	3	5	–	52	27	10.40	–	–	3	–	–	–	–	–	–	–	–	–	–	–
259	R. Edwards	1972 to 1975	20	32	1	1,171	170*	40.38	2	9	7	–	12	–	20	0	–	–	10.00	–	–	–
260	R.A.L. Massie †	1972 to 1972-73	6	8	1	78	42	11.14	–	–	1	–	1,739	74	647	31	20.87	56.10	2.23	8-53	2	1
261	J. Benaud	1972 to 1972-73	3	5	–	223	142	44.60	1	–	2	–	24	–	12	2	6.00	12.00	3.00	2-12	–	–
262	J.R. Thomson	1972-73 to 1985	51	73	20	679	49	12.81	–	–	20	–	10,535	300	5,602	200	28.01	52.68	3.19	6-46	8	–
263	M.H.N. Walker	1972-73 to 1977	34	43	13	586	78*	19.53	–	1	12	–	10,094	380	3,792	138	27.48	73.14	2.25	8-143	6	–
264	J.R. Watkins	1972-73 to 1972-73	1	2	1	39	36	39.00	–	–	–	–	48	–	21	0	–	–	2.63	–	–	–
265	J.R. Hammond	1972-73 to 1972-73	5	5	2	28	19	9.33	–	–	4	–	1,031	47	488	15	32.53	68.73	2.84	4-38	–	–
266	I.C. Davis	1973-74 to 1977	15	27	1	692	105	26.62	1	4	9	–	–	–	–	–	–	–	–	–	–	–
267	G.J. Gilmour †‡	1973-74 to 1976-77	15	22	1	483	101	23.00	1	3	8	–	2,661	51	1,406	54	26.04	49.28	3.17	6-85	3	1
268	G. Dymock ‡	1973-74 to 1979-80	21	32	11	236	31*	9.44	–	–	3	–	5,545	179	2,116	78	27.13	71.09	2.29	7-67	5	1
269	A.G. Hurst	1973-74 to 1979-80	12	20	3	102	26	6.00	–	–	1	–	3,054	74	1,200	43	27.91	71.02	2.36	5-28	2	–
270	A.J. Woodcock	1973-74 to 1973-74	1	1	–	27	27	27.00	–	–	–	–	–	–	–	–	–	–	–	–	–	–
271	W.J. Edwards †	1974-75 to 1974-75	3	6	–	68	30	11.33	–	–	–	–	–	–	–	–	–	–	–	–	–	–
272	R.B. McCosker	1974-75 to 1979-80	25	46	5	1,622	127	39.56	4	9	21	–	–	–	–	–	–	–	–	–	–	–
273	A. Turner †	1975 to 1976-77	14	27	–	768	136	28.44	1	3	15	–	–	–	–	–	–	–	–	–	–	–
274	G.J. Cosier	1975-76 to 1978-79	18	32	1	897	168	28.94	2	3	14	–	899	30	341	5	68.20	179.80	2.28	2-26	–	–
275	G.N. Yallop †‡	1975-76 to 1984-85	39	70	3	2,756	268	41.13	8	9	23	–	192	4	116	1	116.00	192.00	3.63	1-21	–	–
276	D.W. Hookes †‡	1976-77 to 1985-86	23	41	3	1,306	143*	34.37	1	8	12	–	96	4	41	1	41.00	96.00	2.56	1-4	–	–
277	L.S. Pascoe	1976-77 to 1981-82	14	19	9	106	30*	10.60	–	–	2	–	3,403	112	1,668	64	26.06	53.17	2.94	5-59	1	–
278	R.D. Robinson	1977 to 1977	3	6	–	100	34	16.67	–	–	4	–	–	–	–	–	–	–	–	–	–	–
279	C.S. Serjeant ‡	1977 to 1977-78	12	23	1	522	124	23.73	1	2	13	–	–	–	–	–	–	–	–	–	–	–
280	R.J. Bright ‡	1977 to 1986-87	25	39	8	445	33	14.35	–	–	13	–	5,541	298	2,180	53	41.13	104.55	2.36	7-87	4	1
281	K.J. Hughes ‡	1977 to 1984-85	70	124	6	4,415	213	37.42	9	22	50	–	85	1	28	0	–	–	1.98	–	–	–
282	M.F. Malone	1977	1	1	1	46	46*	–	–	–	–	–	342	24	77	6	12.83	57.00	1.35	5-63	1	–

No.	Player	Span	M	I	NO	R	HS	Avge	100s	50s	Ct	St	Balls	Mdns	R	W	Avge	S-R	RPO	BB	5	10
283	W. M. Clark	1977-78 to 1978-79	10	19	2	98	33	5.76	—	—	6	—	2,793	63	1,264	44	28.73	63.48	2.72	4-46	—	—
284	P. A. Hibbert ††	1977-78	1	2	—	15	13	7.50	—	—	1	—										
285	A. L. Mann †	1977-78	4	8	—	189	105	23.63	1	—	2	—	552	4	316	4	79.00	138.00	3.43	3-12	—	—
286	A. D. Ogilvie	1977-78	5	10	—	178	47	17.80	—	—	5	—										
287	S. J. Rixon	1977-78 to 1984-85	13	24	3	394	54	18.76	—	1	42	5										
288	P. M. Toohey	1977-78 to 1979-80	15	29	1	893	122	31.89	1	5	9	—	2	—	4	0	—	—	12.00	—	—	—
289	J. Dyson	1977-78 to 1984-85	30	58	7	1,359	127*	26.65	2	5	10	—										
290	J. B. Gannon ‡	1977-78	3	5	4	3	3*	3.00	—	—	—	—	726	13	361	11	32.82	66.00	2.98	4-77	—	—
291	I. W. Callen †	1977-78	1	2	2	26	22*	—	—	—	1	—	440	5	191	6	31.83	73.33	2.60	3-83	—	—
292	W. M. Darling	1977-78 to 1979-80	14	27	1	697	91	26.81	—	6	5	—										
293	G. M. Wood †	1977-78 to 1988-89	59	112	6	3,374	172	31.83	9	13	41	—										
294	B. Yardley	1977-78 to 1982-83	33	54	4	978	74	19.56	—	1	31	—	8,909	379	3,986	126	31.63	70.71	2.68	7-98	6	1
295	J. D. Higgs	1977-78 to 1980-81	22	36	16	111	16	5.55	—	—	3	—	4,752	176	2,057	66	31.17	72.00	2.60	7-143	2	1
296	T. J. Laughlin †	1977-78 to 1978-79	3	6	1	87	35	17.40	—	—	3	—	516	16	262	6	43.67	86.00	3.05	5-101	1	—
297	R. M. Hogg	1978-79 to 1984-85	38	58	13	439	52	9.76	—	1	6	—	7,633	230	3,503	123	28.48	62.06	2.75	6-74	6	—
298	J. A. Maclean	1978-79	4	7	—	79	33*	11.29	—	—	18	—										
299	A. R. Border ††	1978-79 to 1993-94	156	265	44	11,174	205	50.56	27	63	156	—	4,009	199	1,525	39	39.10	102.79	2.28	7-46	2	1
300	P. H. Carlson	1978-79	2	4	—	23	21	5.75	—	—	3	—	368	10	99	2	49.50	184.00	1.61	2-41	—	—
301	K. J. Wright	1978-79 to 1979-80	10	21	8	219	55*	16.85	—	1	31	4										
302	A. M. J. Hilditch	1978-79 to 1985-86	18	34	—	1,073	119	31.56	2	6	13	—										
303	P. R. Sleep	1978-79 to 1989-90	14	21	1	483	90	24.15	—	2	13	—	2,982	132	1,397	31	45.06	96.19	2.81	5-72	1	—
304	D. F. Whatmore	1978-79 to 1979-80	7	13	—	293	77	22.54	—	2	13	—	30	2	11	0	—	—	2.20	—	—	—
305	J. K. Moss †	1978-79	1	2	1	60	38*	60.00	—	—	2	—										
306	B. M. Laird	1979-80 to 1982-83	21	40	2	1,341	92	35.29	—	11	16	—										
307	J. M. Wiener	1979-80	6	11	—	281	93	25.55	—	2	6	—	18	1	12	0	—	—	4.00	—	—	—
308	G. R. Beard	1979-80	3	6	1	114	26*	22.80	—	—	2	—	259	17	109	1	109.00	259.00	2.53	1-26	—	—
309	G. F. Lawson	1980-81 to 1989-90	46	68	12	894	74	15.96	—	1	10	—	11,118	386	5,501	180	30.56	61.77	2.97	8-112	11	2
310	T. M. Alderman	1981 to 1990-91	41	53	22	203	26*	6.55	—	—	27	—	10,181	432	4,616	170	27.15	59.89	2.72	6-47	14	1
311	T. M. Chappell	1981	3	6	1	79	27	15.80	—	—	2	—										
312	M. F. Kent	1981	3	6	—	171	54	28.50	—	2	6	—										
313	M. R. Whitney ‡	1981 to 1992-93	12	19	8	68	13	6.18	—	—	6	—	2,672	90	1,325	39	33.97	68.51	2.98	7-27	2	—
314	D. M. Wellham	1981 to 1986-87	6	11	—	257	103	23.36	1	—	2	—										
315	G. M. Ritchie	1982-83 to 1986-87	30	53	5	1,690	146	35.21	3	7	14	—	6	—	10	0	—	—	10.00	—	—	—
316	C. G. Rackemann	1982-83 to 1990-91	12	14	4	53	15*	5.30	—	—	2	—	2,719	132	1,137	39	29.15	69.72	2.51	6-86	3	1
317	K. C. Wessels †	1982-83 to 1985-86	24	42	1	1,761	179	42.95	4	9	18	—	90	—	42	0	—	—	2.80	—	—	—
318	T. G. Hogan ‡	1982-83 to 1983-84	7	12	1	205	42*	18.64	—	—	9	—	1,436	54	706	15	47.07	95.73	2.95	5-66	1	—

No.	Player	Span	M	I	NO	Runs	HS	Avge	100	50	Ct	St	Balls	Mdns	Runs	Wkts	Avge	SR	Econ	BB	5wi	10wm
319	R. D. Woolley	1982-83 to 1983-84	2	2	—	21	13	10.50	—	—	7	—										
320	W. B. Phillips †	1983-84 to 1985-86	27	48	1	1,485	159	32.28	2	7	52	—										
321	J. N. Maguire	1983-84	2	2	1	28	15*	7.00	—	—	1	—	616	21	323	10	32.30	61.60	3.15	4-57	—	—
322	G. R. J. Matthews †	1983-84 to 1992-93	33	53	8	1,849	130	41.09	4	12	17	—	6,271	256	2,942	61	48.23	102.80	2.81	5-103	2	1
323	S. B. Smith	1983-84	3	3	—	41	12	13.66	—	—	—	—										
324	D. M. Jones	1983-84 to 1992-93	52	89	11	3,631	216	46.55	11	14	34	—	198	15	64	1	64.00	198.00	1.94	1-5	—	—
325	D. C. Boon	1984-85 to 1995-96	107	190	20	7,422	200	43.66	21	32	99	—										
326	R. G. Holland	1984-85 to 1985-86	11	19	10	35	10	3.18	—	—	5	—	2,889	124	1,352	34	39.76	84.97	2.81	6-54	3	—
327	M. J. Bennett	1984-85 to 1985	3	5	2	71	23	23.67	—	—	3	—	665	24	325	6	54.17	110.83	2.93	3-79	—	—
328	C. J. McDermott	1984-85 to 1995-96	71	90	13	940	42*	12.21	—	—	19	—	16,586	581	8,332	291	28.63	57.00	3.01	8-97	14	2
329	S. P. O'Donnell	1985 to 1985-86	6	10	3	206	48	29.43	—	—	4	—	940	37	504	6	84.00	156.67	3.22	3-37	—	—
330	D. R. Gilbert	1985 to 1986-87	9	12	4	57	15	7.13	—	—	1	—	1,647	37	843	16	52.69	102.94	3.07	3-48	—	—
331	R. B. Kerr	1985-86	2	4	—	31	17	7.75	—	—	1	—										
332	M. G. Hughes	1985-86 to 1993-94	53	70	8	1,032	72*	16.65	—	2	23	—	12,285	499	6,017	212	28.38	57.95	2.94	8-87	7	1
333	G. R. Marsh	1985-86 to 1991-92	50	93	7	2,854	138	33.19	4	15	38	—										
334	B. A. Reid †‡	1985-86 to 1992-93	27	34	14	93	13	4.65	—	—	5	—	6,244	245	2,784	113	24.64	55.26	2.68	7-51	5	2
335	S. R. Waugh	1985-86 to 2003-04	168	260	46	10,927	200	51.06	32	50	112	—	7,805	332	3,445	92	37.45	84.84	2.65	5-28	3	—
336	S. P. Davis	1985-86	1	—	—	—	—	—	—	—	—	—	150	18	70	0	—	—	2.80	—	—	—
337	T. J. Zoehrer	1985-86 to 1986-87	10	14	2	246	52*	20.50	—	1	18	1										
338	C. D. Matthews †‡	1986-87 to 1988-89	3	6	1	54	32	10.80	—	—	—	—	570	18	313	6	52.17	95.00	3.29	3-95	—	—
339	G. C. Dyer	1986-87 to 1987-88	6	9	1	131	60	18.82	—	1	22	2										
340	P. L. Taylor	1986-87 to 1991-92	13	19	3	431	42*	26.94	—	2	10	—	2,227	101	1,068	27	39.56	82.48	2.88	6-78	1	—
341	M. R. J. Veletta	1987-88 to 1989-90	8	11	—	207	39	18.82	—	—	12	—										
342	T. B. A. May	1987-88 to 1994-95	24	28	12	225	42*	14.06	—	—	6	—	6,577	322	2,606	75	34.75	87.69	2.38	5-9	5	1
343	A. I. C. Dodemaide	1987-88 to 1992-93	10	15	6	202	50	22.44	—	1	6	—	2,184	92	953	34	28.03	64.24	2.62	6-58	1	—
344	I. A. Healy	1988-89 to 1999-00	119	182	23	4,356	161*	27.40	4	22	366	29										
345	T. V. Hohns †	1988-89 to 1989	7	7	1	136	40	22.67	—	—	1	—	1,528	42	580	17	34.12	89.88	2.28	3-59	—	—
346	M. A. Taylor †	1988-89 to 1998-99	104	186	13	7,525	334*	43.50	19	40	157	—	42	—	26	1	26.00	42.00	3.71	1-11	—	—
347	G. D. Campbell	1989 to 1989-90	4	4	—	10	6	2.50	—	—	2	—	951	29	503	13	38.69	73.15	3.17	3-79	—	—
348	T. M. Moody	1989-90 to 1992-93	8	14	—	456	106	32.57	2	3	9	—	432	19	147	2	73.50	216.00	2.04	1-17	—	—
349	M. E. Waugh	1990-91 to 2002-03	128	209	17	8,029	153*	41.82	20	47	181	—	4,853	170	2,429	59	41.17	82.25	3.00	5-40	1	—
350	S. K. Warne	1991-92 to 2004-05	112	199	17	2,326	99	16.27	—	8	93	—	31,489	1,479	14,793	527	28.07	59.75	2.82	8-71	27	8
351	W. N. Phillips	1991-92	1	2	—	22	14	11.00	—	—	—	—										
352	P. R. Reiffel	1991-92 to 1997-98	35	50	14	955	79*	26.53	—	6	15	—	6,403	279	2,804	104	26.96	61.57	2.63	6-71	5	—
353	D. R. Martyn	1992-93 to 2004-05	44	72	11	2,875	161	47.13	7	17	21	—	348	16	168	2	84.00	174.00	2.90	1-0	—	—
354	J. L. Langer †	1992-93 to 2004-05	76	128	6	5,488	250	44.98	17	21	50	—	6	—	3	0	—	—	3.00	—	—	—
355	J. Angel †	1992-93 to 1994-95	4	7	1	35	11	5.83	—	—	—	—	748	22	463	10	46.30	74.80	3.71	3-54	—	—

No. Name	Career	M	I	NO	R	HS	Avge	100s	50s	Ct	St	Balls	Mdns	R	W	Avge	S-R	RPO	BB	5	10
356 B. P. Julian ‡	1993 to 1995-96	7	9	1	128	56*	16.00	—	1	4	—	1,098	43	599	15	39.93	73.20	3.27	4-36	—	—
357 M. J. Slater	1993 to 2001	74	131	7	5,312	219	42.84	14	21	33	—	25	—	10	—	—	—	2.40	1-4	—	—
358 G. D. McGrath	1993-94 to 2004-05	97	107	38	450	39	6.52	—	—	29	—	22,860	1146	9,509	440	21.61	51.95	2.50	8-38	24	3
359 M. L. Hayden †	1993-94 to 2004-05	55	95	8	5,059	380	58.15	20	15	67	—	54	—	40	—	—	—	4.44	—	—	—
360 M. G. Bevan †	1994-95 to 1997-98	18	30	3	785	91	29.07	—	6	8	—	1,285	30	703	29	24.24	44.31	3.28	6-82	1	—
361 D. W. Fleming	1994-95 to 2000-01	20	19	3	305	71*	19.06	—	—	8	—	4,129	153	1,942	75	25.89	55.05	2.82	5-30	3	—
362 P. A. Emery †	1994-95	1	—	—	8	8*	—	—	—	5	1										
363 G. S. Blewett	1994-95 to 1999-00	46	79	4	2,552	214	34.03	4	15	45	—	1,436	60	720	14	51.43	102.57	3.01	2-9	—	—
364 P. E. McIntyre	1994-95 to 1996-97	2	4	1	22	16	7.33	—	—	—	—	393	10	194	5	38.80	78.60	2.96	3-103	—	—
365 S. G. Law	1995-96	1	1	—	54	54*	54.00	—	1	—	—	18	—	9	—	—	—	3.00	—	—	—
366 R. T. Ponting	1995-96 to 2004-05	79	127	15	6,086	257	54.34	20	22	91	—	437	18	190	4	47.50	109.25	2.61	1-0	—	—
367 G. B. Hogg †‡	1996-97 to 2003-04	4	5	1	38	17*	9.50	—	—	—	—	774	26	452	9	50.22	86.00	3.50	2-40	—	—
368 M. T. G. Elliott †‡	1996-97 to 2004-05	21	36	1	1,172	199	33.49	3	4	14	—	12	—	4	—	—	—	2.00	—	—	—
369 M. S. Kasprowicz	1996-97 to 2004-05	22	33	8	282	25	11.28	—	—	10	—	4,391	153	2,242	67	33.46	65.54	3.06	7-36	3	—
370 J. N. Gillespie	1996-97 to 2004-05	54	69	22	685	48*	14.57	—	1	16	—	11,143	509	5,298	206	25.72	54.09	2.85	7-37	7	—
371 A. J. Bichel	1996-97 to 2003-04	19	22	5	355	71*	16.90	—	1	16	—	3,337	112	1,870	58	32.24	57.53	3.36	5-60	3	—
372 S. Young †	1997	1	2	2	4	4*	4.00	—	—	—	—	48	3	13	—	—	—	1.63	—	—	—
373 S. H. Cook †	1997-98	2	2	1	3	3*	3.00	—	—	—	—	224	10	142	7	20.29	32.00	3.80	5-39	1	—
374 S. C. G. MacGill	1997-98 to 2003-04	32	37	6	263	43	8.48	—	—	16	—	8,447	291	4,441	152	29.22	55.57	3.15	7-50	9	2
375 G. R. Robertson	1997-98	4	7	1	140	57	20.00	—	—	—	—	898	20	515	13	39.62	69.08	3.44	4-72	—	—
376 P. Wilson	1997-98	1	2	2	0	0*	—	—	—	—	—	72	2	50	—	—	—	4.17	—	—	—
377 A. C. Dale †	1997-98 to 1998-99	2	2	—	5	5	2.00	—	—	1	—	348	19	187	6	31.17	58.00	3.22	3-71	—	—
378 D. S. Lehmann †‡	1997-98 to 2004-05	20	32	3	1,549	177	53.63	5	8	9	—	740	29	287	13	22.08	56.92	2.33	3-42	—	—
379 C. R. Miller	1998-99 to 2000-01	18	24	4	174	43	8.29	—	—	6	—	4,091	163	1,805	69	26.16	59.29	2.65	5-32	3	1
380 M. J. Nicholson	1998-99	1	2	—	14	9	7.00	—	—	—	—	150	4	115	4	28.75	37.50	4.60	3-56	—	—
381 A. C. Gilchrist †	1999-00 to 2004-05	56	80	14	3,485	204*	52.80	10	17	217	24										
382 S. A. Muller	1999-00	2	2	—	6	6*	—	—	—	2	—	348	8	258	7	36.86	49.71	4.45	3-68	—	—
383 B. Lee	1999-00 to 2003-04	37	36	6	593	62*	19.77	—	2	9	—	7,380	256	4,403	139	31.68	53.09	3.58	5-47	4	—
384 S. M. Katich †‡	2001	9	15	2	546	125	42.00	1	4	6	—	575	9	349	11	31.73	52.27	3.64	6-65	—	—
385 M. L. Love	2002-03 to 2003-04	5	8	—	233	100*	46.60	1	1	7	—										
386 B. A. Williams	2003-04	4	3	3	23	10*	7.67	—	—	1	—	852	43	406	9	45.11	94.67	2.86	4-53	—	—
387 N. W. Bracken ‡	2003-04	3	4	1	9	6*	4.50	—	—	4	—	768	38	351	6	58.50	128.00	2.74	2-12	—	—
388 A. Symonds	2003-04	2	4	—	53	24	13.25	—	—	—	—	144	4	85	1	85.00	144.00	3.54	1-68	—	—
389 M. J. Clarke ‡	2004-05	12	17	1	669	151	41.81	2	2	14	—	110	4	61	8	7.63	13.75	3.33	6-9	1	—
390 N. M. Hauritz	2004-05	1	2	—	15	15	7.50	—	—	1	—	162	4	103	3	20.60	32.40	3.81	3-16	—	—
391 S. R. Watson	2004-05	1	1	—	31	31	31.00	—	—	—	—	114	5	60	1	60.00	114.00	3.16	1-32	—	—

† denotes left-hand batsman; ‡ denotes left-arm bowler; + denotes retired hurt.

BATTING RECORDS

HIGHEST INDIVIDUAL INNINGS

380	M. L. Hayden	v Zimbabwe at Perth	2003-04
334	D. G. Bradman	v England at Leeds	1930
334*	M. A. Taylor	v Pakistan at Peshawar	1998-99
311	R. B. Simpson	v England at Manchester	1964
307	R. M. Cowper	v England at Melbourne	1965-66
304	D. G. Bradman	v England at Leeds	1934
299*	D. G. Bradman	v South Africa at Adelaide	1931-32
270	D. G. Bradman	v England at Melbourne	1936-37
268	G. N. Yallop	v Pakistan at Melbourne	1983-84
266	W. H. Ponsford	v England at The Oval	1934
257	R. T. Ponting	v India at Melbourne	2003-04
254	D. G. Bradman	v England at Lord's	1930
250	K. D. Walters	v New Zealand at Christchurch	1976-77
250	J. L. Langer	v England at Melbourne	2002-03
247*	G. S. Chappell	v New Zealand at Wellington	1973-74
244	D. G. Bradman	v England at The Oval	1934
242	K. D. Walters	v West Indies at Sydney	1968-69
242	R. T. Ponting	v India at Adelaide	2003-04
235	G. S. Chappell	v Pakistan at Faisalabad	1979-80
234	D. G. Bradman	v England at Sydney	1946-47
234	S. G. Barnes	v England at Sydney	1946-47
232	D. G. Bradman	v England at The Oval	1930
232	S. J. McCabe	v England at Nottingham	1938
226	D. G. Bradman	v South Africa at Brisbane	1931-32
225	R. B. Simpson	v England at Adelaide	1965-66
223	D. G. Bradman	v West Indies at Brisbane (Ex)	1930-31
223	J. L. Langer	v India at Sydney	1999-00
219	M. A. Taylor	v England at Nottingham	1989
219	M. J. Slater	v Sri Lanka at Perth	1995-96
216	D. M. Jones	v West Indies at Adelaide	1988-89
215	J. L. Langer	v New Zealand at Adelaide	2004-05
214*	V. T. Trumper	v South Africa at Adelaide	1910-11
214	G. S. Blewett	v South Africa at Johannesburg (WS)	1996-97
213	K. J. Hughes	v India at Adelaide	1980-81
212	D. G. Bradman	v England at Adelaide	1936-37
211	W. L. Murdoch	v England at The Oval	1884
210	W. M. Lawry	v West Indies at Bridgetown	1964-65
210	D. M. Jones	v India at Chennai (Chepauk)	1986-87
207	K. R. Stackpole	v England at Brisbane	1970-71
207	R. T. Ponting	v Pakistan at Sydney	2004-05
206*	W. A. Brown	v England at Lord's	1938
206	A. R. Morris	v England at Adelaide	1950-51
206	R. T. Ponting	v West Indies at Port-of-Spain	2002-03
205	R. N. Harvey	v West Indies at Melbourne	1952-53
205	W. M. Lawry	v West Indies at Melbourne	1968-69
205	A. R. Border	v New Zealand at Adelaide	1987-88
204	R. N. Harvey	v West Indies at Kingston	1954-55
204	G. S. Chappell	v India at Sydney	1980-81
204*	A. C. Gilchrist	v South Africa at Johannesburg (WS)	2001-02
203	H. L. Collins	v South Africa at Johannesburg (OW)	1921-22
203	M. L. Hayden	v India at Chennai	2000-01
201	S. E. Gregory	v England at Sydney	1894-95
201*	J. Ryder	v England at Adelaide	1924-25
201	D. G. Bradman	v India at Adelaide	1947-48
201	R. B. Simpson	v West Indies at Bridgetown	1964-65
201	G. S. Chappell	v Pakistan at Brisbane	1981-82
200	D. C. Boon	v New Zealand at Perth	1989-90

| 200* | A.R. Border | v England at Leeds | 199. |
| 200 | S.R. Waugh | v West Indies at Kingston | 1994-95 |

HIGHEST INDIVIDUAL INNINGS AGAINST AUSTRALIA

281	L. Hutton	for England at The Oval	1938
287	R.E. Foster	for England at Sydney	1903-04
281	V.V.S. Laxman	for India at Kolkata	2000-01
277	B.C. Lara	for West Indies at Sydney	1992-93
274	R.G. Pollock	for South Africa at Durban (Kingsmead)	1969-70

HUNDRED ON DEBUT

†C. Bannerman (165*)	v England at Melbourne	1876-77
H. Graham (107)	v England at Lord's	1893
R.A. Duff (104)	v England at Melbourne	1901-02
M.J. Hartigan (116)	v England at Adelaide	1907-08
H.L. Collins (104)	v England at Sydney	1920-21
W.H. Ponsford (110)	v England at Sydney	1924-25
A. Jackson (164)	v England at Adelaide	1928-29
J.W. Burke (101*)	v England at Adelaide	1950-51
K.D. Walters (155)	v England at Brisbane	1965-66
G.S. Chappell (108)	v England at Perth	1970-71
G.J. Cosier (109)	v West Indies at Melbourne	1975-76
D.M. Wellham (103)	v England at The Oval	1981
K.C. Wessels (162)	v England at Brisbane	1982-83
W.B. Phillips (159)	v Pakistan at Perth	1983-84
M.E. Waugh (138)	v England at Adelaide	1990-91
G.S. Blewett (102*)	v England at Adelaide	1994-95
M.J. Clarke (151)	v India at Bangalore	2004-05

† Retired hurt

HUNDRED IN EACH INNINGS OF A MATCH

	1st	2nd		
W. Bardsley	136	130	v England at The Oval	1909
A.R. Morris	122	124*	v England at Adelaide	1946-47
D.G. Bradman	132	127*	v India at Melbourne	1947-48
J. Moroney	118	101*	v South Africa at Johannesburg (EP)	1949-50
R.B. Simpson	153	115	v Pakistan at Karachi	1964-65
K.D. Walters	242	103	v West Indies at Sydney	1968-69
I.M. Chappell	145	121	v New Zealand at Wellington	1973-74
G.S. Chappell	247*	133	v New Zealand at Wellington	1973-74
G.S. Chappell	123	109*	v West Indies at Brisbane	1975-76
A.R. Border	150*	153	v Pakistan at Lahore	1979-80
A.R. Border	140	114*	v New Zealand at Christchurch	1985-86
D.M. Jones	116	121*	v Pakistan at Adelaide	1989-90
S.R. Waugh	108	116	v England at Manchester	1997
M.L. Hayden	197	103	v England at Brisbane	2002-03
M.L. Hayden	117	132	v Sri Lanka at Cairns	2004-05

MOST HUNDREDS

	100s	Eng	SAf	WI	NZ	Ind	Pak	SL	Zim	Ban
S.R. Waugh	32	10	2	7	2	2	3	3	1	2
D.G. Bradman	29	19	4	2	0	4	0	0	0	0
A.R. Border	27	8	0	3	5	4	6	1	0	0
G.S. Chappell	24	9	0	5	3	1	6	0	0	0
R.T. Ponting	22	4	2	4	2	4	4	1	1	0
R.N. Harvey	21	6	8	3	0	4	0	0	0	0
D.C. Boon	21	7	0	3	3	6	1	1	0	0

	100s	Eng	SAf	WI	NZ	Ind	Pak	SL	Zim	Ban
, L. Langer	21	3	2	3	4	3	4	2	0	0
A. E. Waugh	20	6	4	4	1	1	3	1	0	0
R. T. Ponting	20	4	2	4	1	4	3	1	1	0
M. L. Hayden	20	3	4	3	1	3	1	3	2	0
M. A. Taylor	19	6	2	1	2	2	4	2	0	0
J. L. Langer	19	3	2	3	3	3	3	2	0	0
K. D. Walters	15	4	0	6	3	1	1	0	0	0
A. C. Gilchrist	15	2	2	1	4	2	2	1	1	0
I. M. Chappell	14	4	0	5	2	2	1	0	0	0
M. J. Slater	14	7	0	1	2	0	3	1	0	0
W. M. Lawry	13	7	1	4	0	1	0	0	0	0
A. R. Morris	12	8	2	1	0	1	0	0	0	0
D. R. Martyn	12	2	3	0	1	2	2	2	0	0
D. M. Jones	11	3	0	1	0	2	2	3	0	0
A. L. Hassett	10	4	3	2	0	1	0	0	0	0
R. B. Simpson	10	2	1	1	0	4	2	0	0	0

MOST HUNDREDS AGAINST AUSTRALIA

	100s	In Australia	Elsewhere
J. B. Hobbs (England)	12	9	3
W. R. Hammond (England)	9	7	2
D. I. Gower (England)	9	5	4
R. B. Richardson (West Indies)	9	4	5
H. Sutcliffe (England)	8	6	2
S. M. Gavaskar (India)	8	5	3
B. C. Lara (West Indies)	8	3	5

MOST DOUBLE-HUNDREDS

	200s	Eng	SAf	WI	NZ	Ind	Pak	SL	Zim	Ban
D. G. Bradman	12	8	2	1	0	1	0	0	0	0
G. S. Chappell	4	0	0	0	1	1	2	0	0	0
R. T. Ponting	4	0	0	1	0	2	1	0	0	0
R. B. Simpson	3	2	0	1	0	0	0	0	0	0

CARRYING BAT THROUGH AN INNINGS

(Figures in brackets show side's total)

J. E. Barrett	67*	(176)	v England at Lord's	1890
W. W. Armstrong	159*	(309)	v South Africa at Johannesburg (OW)	1902-03
W. Bardsley	193*	(383)	v England at Lord's	1926
W. M. Woodfull	30*	(66)†	v England at Brisbane (Ex)	1928-29
W. M. Woodfull	73*	(193)†	v England at Adelaide	1932-33
W. A. Brown	206*	(422)	v England at Lord's	1938
W. M. Lawry	49*	(107)	v India at Delhi	1969-70
W. M. Lawry	60*	(116)†	v England at Sydney	1970-71
I. R. Redpath	159*	(346)	v New Zealand at Auckland	1973-74
D. C. Boon	58*	(103)	v New Zealand at Auckland	1985-86
M. A. Taylor	169*	(350)	v South Africa at Adelaide	1997-98

† *Denotes one or more batsmen absent or retired.*

MOST RUNS IN A SERIES

	M	I	NO	R	HS	100s	Avge	Series
D. G. Bradman	5	7	0	974	334	4	139.14	1930 v England in England
M. A. Taylor	6	11	1	839	219	2	83.90	1989 v England in England
R. N. Harvey	5	9	0	834	205	4	92.66	1952-53 v South Africa in Australia

	M	I	NO	R	HS	100s	Avge	Series
D. G. Bradman ...	5	9	0	810	270	3	90.00	1936-37 v England in Australia
D. G. Bradman ...	5	5	1	806	299*	4	201.50	1931-32 v South Africa in Australia
D. G. Bradman ...	5	8	0	758	304	2	94.75	1934 v England in England
D. G. Bradman ...	5	6	2	715	201	4	178.75	1947-48 v India in Australia
R. T. Ponting	4	8	1	706	257	2	100.86	2002-03 v West Indies in West Indies
G. S. Chappell ...	6	11	5	702	182*	3	117.00	1975-76 v West Indies in Australia
K. D. Walters	4	6	0	699	242	4	116.50	1968-69 v West Indies in Australia
A. R. Morris	5	9	1	696	196	3	87.00	1948 v England in England
D. G. Bradman ...	5	8	1	680	234	2	97.14	1946-47 v England in Australia
W. M. Lawry	5	8	0	667	205	3	83.38	1968-69 v West Indies in Australia
V. T. Trumper ...	5	9	2	661	214*	2	94.43	1910-11 v South Africa in Australia
R. N. Harvey	5	8	3	660	178	4	132.00	1949-50 v South Africa in S. Africa
R. N. Harvey	5	7	1	650	204	3	108.33	1954-55 v West Indies in West Indies
K. R. Stackpole ..	7	12	0	627	207	2	52.25	1970-71 v England in Australia
M. J. Slater	5	10	0	623	176	3	62.30	1994-95 v England in Australia
G. S. Chappell ...	6	11	0	608	144	2	55.27	1974-75 v England in Australia

Most runs in a series against opponents not mentioned above:

v Bangladesh

	M	I	NO	R	HS	100s	Avge	Series
D. S. Lehmann ...	2	2	0	287	177	2	143.50	2003-04 in Australia
S. R. Waugh	2	2	2	256	156*	2	–	2003-04 in Australia
M. L. Love	2	2	1	100	100*	1	100.00	2003-04 in Australia

v New Zealand

	M	I	NO	R	HS	100s	Avge	Series
G. S. Chappell ...	3	6	1	449	247*	2	89.30	1973-74 in New Zealand
I. R. Redpath	3	6	1	413	159*	1	82.60	1973-74 in New Zealand
I. M. Chappell ...	3	6	0	359	145	2	59.83	1973-74 in New Zealand

v Pakistan

	M	I	NO	R	HS	100s	Avge	Series
G. N. Yallop	5	6	0	554	268	2	92.33	1983-84 in Australia
M. A. Taylor	3	5	1	513	334*	1	128.25	1998-99 in Pakistan
A. R. Border	5	6	1	429	118	2	85.80	1983-84 in Australia

v Sri Lanka

	M	I	NO	R	HS	100s	Avge	Series
D. S. Lehmann ...	3	6	0	375	153	2	62.50	2003-04 in Sri Lanka
S. R. Waugh	2	3	2	362	170	2	362.00	1995-96 in Australia
D. R. Martyn	3	6	0	333	161	2	55.50	2003-04 in Sri Lanka

v Zimbabwe

	M	I	NO	R	HS	100s	Avge	Series
M. L. Hayden	2	3	1	501	380	2	250.50	2003-04 in Australia
R. T. Ponting	2	3	1	259	169	1	129.50	2003-04 in Australia
S. R. Waugh	1	1	1	151	151*	0	–	1999-00 in Zimbabwe

MOST RUNS IN A SERIES AGAINST AUSTRALIA

	M	I	NO	R	HS	100s	Avge	Series
W. R. Hammond .	5	9	1	905	251	4	113.13	1928-29 for England in Australia
C. L. Walcott ...	5	10	0	827	155	5	82.70	1954-55 for West Indies in West Indies
H. Sutcliffe	5	9	0	734	176	4	81.56	1924-25 for England in Australia
G. A. Faulkner ..	5	10	0	732	204	2	73.20	1910-11 for South Africa in Australia
D. I. Gower	6	9	0	732	215	3	81.33	1985 for England in England

MOST RUNS IN A THREE-TEST SERIES

	M	I	NO	R	HS	100s	Avge	Series
M. L. Hayden	3	6	1	549	203	2	109.80	2000-01 v India in India
M. A. Taylor	3	5	1	513	334*	1	128.25	1998-99 v Pakistan in Pakistan
A. C. Gilchrist ..	3	5	2	473	204*	2	157.67	2001-02 v SAf in South Africa
G. S. Chappell ...	3	6	1	449	247*	2	89.80	1973-74 v NZ in New Zealand
M. L. Hayden	3	6	0	429	138	3	107.25	2001-02 v South Africa in Australia

Note: M. L. Hayden scored 501 runs in a two-Test series against Zimbabwe in Australia in 2003-04.

MOST RUNS IN A FOUR-TEST SERIES

	M	I	NO	R	HS	100s	Avge	Series
R.T. Ponting	4	8	1	706	257	2	100.86	2002-03 v West Indies in West Indies
R.M. Cowper ...	4	7	–	485	165	2	69.29	1967-68 v India in Australia
I.M. Chappell ...	4	6	–	429	192	1	71.50	1975 v England in England
S.R. Waugh	4	6	2	429	200	1	107.25	1994-95 v West Indies in West Indies
R.B. McCosker ..	4	7	2	414	127	1	82.80	1975 v England in England
S.R. Waugh	4	8	1	409	199	2	58.43	1998-99 v West Indies in West Indies

MOST RUNS IN A CALENDAR YEAR

	M	I	NO	R	HS	100s	Avge	Year
R.T. Ponting	11	18	3	1,503	257	4	100.20	2003
J.L. Langer	14	27	0	1,481	215	5	54.85	2004
M.L. Hayden	14	25	3	1,391	203	5	63.23	2001
R.B. Simpson	14	26	3	1,381	311	3	60.04	1964
D.R. Martyn	14	26	2	1,353	161	6	56.37	2004
M.L. Hayden	12	21	4	1,312	380	5	77.17	2003
D.C. Boon	16	25	2	1,241	164*	4	62.05	1993
M.A. Taylor	11	20	1	1,219	219	4	64.16	1989
K.J. Hughes	15	28	4	1,163	130*	2	48.45	1979
M.L. Hayden	11	17	1	1,160	197	6	72.50	2002
M.A. Taylor	12	22	3	1,112	334*	3	58.53	1998
M.L. Hayden	14	27	1	1,123	132	3	43.19	2004
M.A. Taylor	15	23	2	1,106	170	4	52.67	1993
A.R. Border	11	20	3	1,099	196	4	64.65	1985
D.M. Jones	11	18	3	1,099	216	4	73.27	1989
A.R. Border	14	27	3	1,073	162	3	44.70	1979
G.S. Blewett	15	25	0	1,067	214	2	42.68	1997
R.T. Ponting	11	16	1	1,064	154	5	70.93	2002
C. Hill	12	21	2	1,060	142	2	55.79	1902
W.M. Lawry	14	27	2	1,056	157	2	42.24	1964
M.J. Slater	14	25	2	1,051	169	3	45.70	1999
M.E. Waugh	12	22	6	1,034	153	4	64.63	1998
D.G. Bradman	8	13	4	1,025	201	5	113.89	1948
A.R. Border	11	19	3	1,000	140	5	62.50	1986

MOST RUNS IN A CAREER

		M	I	NO	R	HS	100s	Avge
1	A.R. Border	156	265	44	11,174	205	27	50.56
2	**S.R. Waugh**	**168**	**260**	**46**	**10,927**	**200**	**32**	**51.06**
3	M.E. Waugh	128	209	17	8,029	153*	20	41.82
4	M.A. Taylor	104	186	13	7,525	334*	19	43.50
5	D.C. Boon	107	190	20	7,422	200	21	43.66
6	G.S. Chappell	88	151	19	7,110	247*	24	53.86
7	D.G. Bradman	52	80	10	6,996	334	29	99.94
8	R.T. Ponting	88	143	20	6,950	257	22	56.50
9	J.L. Langer	88	150	8	6,607	250	21	46.53
10	R.N. Harvey	79	137	10	6,149	205	21	48.42
11	M.L. Hayden	67	117	10	5,721	380	20	53.47
12	K.D. Walters	75	125	14	5,357	250	15	48.26
13	I.M. Chappell	76	136	10	5,345	196	14	42.42
14	M.J. Slater	74	131	7	5,312	219	14	42.84
15	W.M. Lawry	68	123	12	5,234	210	13	47.15
16	R.B. Simpson	62	111	7	4,869	311	10	46.82
17	I.R. Redpath	67	120	11	4,737	171	8	43.46
18	A.C. Gilchrist	68	97	17	4,452	204*	15	55.65
19	K.J. Hughes	70	124	6	4,415	213	9	37.42
20	I.A. Healy	119	182	23	4,356	161*	4	27.40

MOST RUNS AGAINST OPPONENT

	M	I	NO	R	HS	100s	Avge
v England							
D. G. Bradman	37	63	7	5,028	334	19	89.79
A. R. Border	47	82	19	3,548	200*	8	56.32
S. R. Waugh	46	73	18	3,200	177*	10	58.18
v South Africa							
R. N. Harvey	14	23	3	1,625	205	8	81.25
S. R. Waugh	16	25	2	1,147	164	2	49.87
M. E. Waugh	18	29	2	1,135	116	4	42.04
v West Indies							
S. R. Waugh	32	51	7	2,192	200	7	49.82
A. R. Border	31	59	7	2,052	126	3	39.46
M. E. Waugh	28	48	3	1,858	139*	4	41.29
v New Zealand							
A. R. Border	23	32	3	1,500	205	5	51.72
J. L. Langer	14	23	4	1,196	215	4	62.95
D. C. Boon	17	27	2	1,187	200	3	47.48
v India							
A. R. Border	20	35	5	1,567	163	4	52.23
R. T. Ponting	15	27	3	1,253	257	4	52.21
M. L. Hayden	11	22	2	1,244	203	3	62.20
v Pakistan							
A. R. Border	22	36	8	1,666	153	6	59.50
G. S. Chappell	17	27	2	1,581	235	6	63.24
M. A. Taylor	12	20	3	1,347	334*	4	79.24
v Sri Lanka							
R. T. Ponting	10	16	1	711	105*	1	47.40
S. R. Waugh	8	11	3	701	170	3	87.63
M. A. Taylor	8	15	1	611	164	2	43.64
v Zimbabwe							
M. L. Hayden	2	3	1	501	380	2	250.50
R. T. Ponting	3	4	1	290	169	1	96.67
S. R. Waugh	3	3	1	290	151*	1	145.00
v Bangladesh							
D. S. Lehmann	2	2	0	287	177	2	143.50
S. R. Waugh	2	2	2	256	156*	2	–
M. L. Love	2	2	1	100	100*	1	100.00

MOST RUNS AGAINST AUSTRALIA

	M	I	NO	R	HS	100s	Avge
for England							
J. B. Hobbs	41	71	4	3,636	187	12	54.27
D. I. Gower	42	77	4	3,269	215	9	44.78
G. Boycott	39	71	9	2,945	191	7	47.50
for South Africa							
R. G. Pollock	14	23	2	1,453	274	5	69.19
E. J. Barlow	14	26	2	1,149	201	5	47.88
G. Kirsten	18	34	1	1,134	153	2	34.36

	M	I	NO	R	HS	100s	Avge
for West Indies							
B. C. Lara	27	50	2	2,470	277	8	51.46
I. V. A. Richards	34	54	3	2,266	208	5	44.43
D. L. Haynes	33	59	6	2,233	145	5	42.13
for New Zealand							
J. G. Wright	19	36	3	1,277	141	2	38.70
M. D. Crowe	17	29	3	1,255	188	3	48.27
N. J. Astle	14	27	3	930	156*	1	38.75
for India							
S. R. Tendulkar	21	39	4	1,859	241*	7	53.11
S. M. Gavaskar	20	31	1	1,550	172	8	51.67
G. R. Viswanath	18	31	2	1,538	161*	4	53.03
for Pakistan							
Javed Miandad	25	40	2	1,797	211	6	47.29
Zaheer Abbas	20	34	2	1,411	126	2	44.09
Salim Malik	15	26	2	1,106	237	2	46.08
for Sri Lanka							
P. A. de Silva	12	19	2	803	167	1	47.24
A. Ranatunga	12	19	3	673	127	1	42.06
S. T. Jayasuriya	11	20	2	592	131	2	32.89
	M	I	NO	R	HS	100s	Avge
for Zimbabwe							
T. R. Gripper	3	6	0	179	60	0	29.83
M. A. Vermeulen	2	4	0	166	63	0	41.50
S. V. Carlisle	2	4	0	160	118	1	40.00
for Bangladesh							
Hannan Sarkar	2	4	0	166	76	0	41.50
Habibul Bashar	2	4	0	141	54	0	35.25
Khaled Mashud	2	4	0	75	44	0	18.75

MOST RUNS AT EACH AUSTRALIAN VENUE

	M	I	NO	R	HS	100s	Avge
Melbourne Cricket Ground (Melbourne)							
D. G. Bradman	11	17	4	1,671	270	9	128.54
S. R. Waugh	17	30	6	1,284	131*	3	53.30
A. R. Border	20	36	3	1,272	163	4	38.55
Most by non-Australian							
J. B. Hobbs (Eng)	10	18	4	1,178	178	5	69.29
Sydney Cricket Ground (Sydney)							
A. R. Border	17	29	8	1,177	89	0	56.05
G. S. Chappell	12	22	4	1,150	204	4	63.89
D. C. Boon	11	21	3	1,127	184*	4	62.61
Most by non-Australian							
W. R. Hammond (Eng)	5	7	2	808	251	4	161.60
Adelaide Oval (Adelaide)							
A. R. Border	16	29	5	1,415	205	4	58.96
S. R. Waugh	15	26	2	1,056	170	3	44.00
D. G. Bradman	7	11	2	970	299*	3	107.78
Most by non-Australian							
J. B. Hobbs (Eng)	5	10	1	601	187	3	66.78
Brisbane Exhibition Ground (Brisbane)							
D. G. Bradman	2	3	0	242	223	1	80.67
E. H. Hendren (Eng) . .	1	2	0	214	169	1	107.00
G. A. Headley (WI) . . .	1	2	1	130	102*	1	130.00

	M	I	NO	R	HS	100s	Avge
Brisbane Cricket Ground (Brisbane)							
G. S. Chappell	7	11	2	1,006	201	5	111.78
S. R. Waugh	17	26	4	915	147*	3	41.59
M. A. Taylor	10	18	2	912	164	2	57.00
Most by non-Australian							
R. B. Richardson (WI)	3	6	1	314	138	1	62.80
WACA Ground (Perth)							
A. R. Border	16	26	3	931	125	2	40.48
D. C. Boon	11	19	2	846	200	2	49.76
S. R. Waugh	15	21	2	843	99*	0	44.37
Most by non-Australian							
D. I. Gower (Eng)	5	10	1	471	136	2	52.33
Bellerive Oval (Hobart)							
M. A. Taylor	4	7	1	405	123	2	67.50
M. J. Slater	3	5	0	365	168	1	73.00
J. L. Langer	2	3	0	309	127	2	103.00
M. E. Waugh	5	8	0	309	111	1	38.63
Most by non-Australian							
Inzamam-ul-Haq (Pak)	2	4	0	197	149*	1	49.25
Marrara Cricket Ground (Darwin)							
D. S. Lehmann	2	3	0	218	110	1	72.67
A. C. Gilchrist	2	3	0	123	80	0	41.00
J. L. Langer	2	3	0	111	71	0	37.00
Most by non-Australian							
Habibul Bashar (Ban)	1	2	0	70	54	0	35.00
	M	I	NO	R	HS	100s	Avge
Cazaly's Stadium (Cairns)							
M. L. Hayden	2	3	0	299	132	2	99.67
D. S. Lehmann	2	3	0	248	177	1	82.67
J. L. Langer	2	3	0	171	162	1	57.00
Most by non-Australian							
M. S. Atapattu (SL)	1	2	0	142	133	1	71.00

HIGHEST CAREER AVERAGE

(Qualification: 1,000 runs)

	M	I	NO	R	HS	100s	Avge
D. G. Bradman	52	80	10	6,996	334	29	99.94
S. G. Barnes	13	19	2	1,072	234	3	63.06
R. T. Ponting	88	143	20	6,950	257	22	56.50
A. C. Gilchrist	68	97	17	4,452	204*	15	55.65
G. S. Chappell	88	151	19	7,110	247*	24	53.86
M. L. Hayden	67	117	10	5,721	380	20	53.47
J. Ryder	20	32	5	1,394	201*	3	51.63
D. R. Martyn	56	89	12	3,947	165	12	51.26
S. R. Waugh	168	260	46	10,927	200	32	51.06
A. R. Border	156	265	44	11,174	205	27	50.56

FASTEST FIFTIES

Minutes

22	V. T. Trumper	v South Africa at Johannesburg (OW)	1902-03
31	W. J. O'Reilly	v South Africa at Johannesburg (OW)	1935-36
35	C. G. Macartney	v South Africa at Sydney	1910-11
38	R. Benaud	v West Indies at Kingston	1954-55
40	J. Darling	v England at Sydney	1897-98
40	S. J. McCabe	v South Africa at Johannesburg (OW)	1935-36

Balls

37	S. K. Warne	v New Zealand at Wellington	2004-05
42	J. L. Langer	v New Zealand at Hamilton	1999-00
43	J. M. Gregory	v South Africa at Johannesburg (OW)	1921-22
43	D. R. Martyn	v England at The Oval	2001
45	W. J. O'Reilly	v South Africa at Johannesburg (OW)	1935-36
46	A. C. Gilchrist	v Pakistan at Brisbane	1999-00

FASTEST HUNDREDS

Minutes

70	J. M. Gregory	v South Africa at Johannesburg (OW)	1921-22
78	R. Benaud	v West Indies at Kingston	1954-55
91	J. Darling	v England at Sydney	1897-98
91	S. J. McCabe	v South Africa at Johannesburg (OW)	1935-36
94	V. T. Trumper	v England at Sydney	1903-04

Balls

67	J. M. Gregory	v South Africa at Johannesburg (OW)	1921-22
84	A. C. Gilchrist	v India at Mumbai	2000-01
84	A. C. Gilchrist	v Zimbabwe at Perth	2003-04
84	M. L. Hayden	v Zimbabwe at Sydney	2003-04
86	A. C. Gilchrist	v New Zealand at Wellington	2004-05

FASTEST DOUBLE-HUNDREDS

Minutes

214	D. G. Bradman	v England at Leeds	1930
223	S. J. McCabe	v England at Nottingham	1938
226	V. T. Trumper	v South Africa at Adelaide	1910-11
234	D. G. Bradman	v England at Lord's	1930
241	S. E. Gregory	v England at Sydney	1894-95

Balls

212	A. C. Gilchrist	v South Africa at Johannesburg (WS)	2001-02
242	D. G. Bradman	v England at The Oval	1934
258	S. J. McCabe	v England at Nottingham	1938
259	D. G. Bradman	v England at Leeds	1930
266	D. G. Bradman	v England at Lord's	1934

FASTEST TRIPLE-HUNDREDS

Minutes

336	D. G. Bradman	v England at Leeds	1930
425	D. G. Bradman	v England at Leeds	1934
529	M. L. Hayden	v Zimbabwe at Perth	2003-04
681	M. A. Taylor	v Pakistan at Peshawar	1998-99
693	R. W. Cowper	v England at Melbourne	1965-66
752	R. B. Simpson	v England at Manchester	1964

Balls

362	M. L. Hayden	v Zimbabwe at Perth	2003-04
410	D. G. Bradman	v England at Leeds	1930
458	D. G. Bradman	v England at Leeds	1934
520	M. A. Taylor	v Pakistan at Peshawar	1998-99
580	R. W. Cowper	v England at Melbourne	1965-66
737	R. B. Simpson	v England at Manchester	1964

Note: Cowper's 580 balls are approximate based on his innings details.

MOST RUNS OFF AN OVER

Eight Balls

21	V. Y. Richardson	off J. W. H. T Douglas v England at Melbourne ...	1924-25
21	R. N. Harvey and C. L. McCool	off J. C. Watkins v South Africa at Cape Town ...	1949-50
21	K. R. Miller and R. R. Lindwall	off S. Ramadhin v West Indies at Brisbane	1951-52
21	I. M. Chappell	off Intikhab Alam v Pakistan at Adelaide	1972-73
21	G. J. Cosier and G. S. Chappell	off Saleem Altaf v Pakistan at Melbourne	1976-77
21	J. R. Thomson and A. G. Hurst	off Madan Lal v India at Brisbane	1977-78

Six Balls

22	A. C. Gilchrist	off M. A. Butcher v England at Birmingham	2001
21	D. G. Bradman and S. G. Barnes	off J. C. Laker v England at Lord's	1948
21	R. T. Ponting and M. L. Hayden	off A. M. Blignaut v Zimbabwe at Sydney	2003-04
21	D. R. Martyn and M. J. Clarke	off A. B. Agarkar v India at Nagpur	2004-05

MOST RUNS IN A DAY'S PLAY

309	D. G. Bradman	v England at Leeds	1930
271	D. G. Bradman	v England at Leeds	1934
244	D. G. Bradman	v England at The Oval	1934
223	D. G. Bradman	v West Indies at Brisbane (Ex)	1930-31
222	M. A. Taylor	v Pakistan at Peshawar	1998-99
213	S. J. McCabe	v England at Nottingham	1938
208	V. T. Trumper	v South Africa at Adelaide	1910-11
205	W. H. Ponsford	v England at The Oval	1934
203	H. L. Collins	v South Africa at Johannesburg (OW)	1921-22
201	D. G. Bradman	v India at Adelaide	1947-48
200	D. G. Bradman	v South Africa at Brisbane	1931-32

LONGEST TO GET OFF THE MARK

Minutes

72	C. G. Rackemann	v England at Sydney	1990-91
70	W. L. Murdoch	v England at Sydney	1882-83
69	R. M. Hogg	v West Indies at Adelaide	1984-85
62	M. A. Taylor	v England at Sydney	1994-95

SLOWEST FIFTIES

Minutes

310	A. R. Border	v West Indies at Sydney	1988-89
304	P. L. Taylor	v Pakistan at Karachi	1988-89
275	W. M. Lawry	v England at Melbourne	1962-63

SLOWEST HUNDREDS

Minutes

388	J. L. Langer	v Pakistan at Hobart	1999-00
385	D. M. Jones	v India at Chennai (Chepauk)	1986-87
384	M. A. Taylor	v India at Adelaide	1991-92
378	D. R. Martyn	v Sri Lanka at Kandy	2003-04

MOST CAREER DUCKS

	Total	Eng	SAf	WI	NZ	Ind	Pak	SL	Zim	Ban
G. D. McGrath ...31		8	4	6	3	3	5	2	0	0
S. K. Warne 30		8	3	4	0	6	4	5	0	0
S. R. Waugh 22		6	2	3	3	3	5	0	0	0
M. E. Waugh 19		0	1	4	1	4	4	5	0	0
I. A. Healy 18		3	1	10	2	0	1	1	0	0
D. C. Boon 16		5	0	3	3	0	2	3	0	0
G. D. McKenzie ..15		7	3	1	0	4	0	0	0	0

HIGHEST PARTNERSHIPS FOR EACH WICKET

First Wicket
382 W. M. Lawry (210) and R. B. Simpson (201) v West Indies at Bridgetown .. 1964-65
329 G. R. Marsh (138) and M. A. Taylor (219) v England at Nottingham 1989
269 M. J. Slater (169) and G. S. Blewett (89) v Pakistan at Brisbane 1999-00

Second Wicket
451 W. H. Ponsford (266) and D. G. Bradman (244) v England at The Oval 1934
301 A. R. Morris (182) and D. G. Bradman (173*) v England at Leeds 1948
298 W. M. Lawry (205) and I. M. Chappell (165) v West Indies at Melbourne .. 1968-69

Third Wicket
315 R. T. Ponting (206) and D. S. Lehmann (160) v West Indies at Port-of-Spain . 2002-03
295 C. C. McDonald (172) and R. N. Harvey (204) v West Indies at Kingston 1954-55
276 D. G. Bradman (187) and A. L. Hassett (128) v England at Brisbane 1946-67

Fourth Wicket
388 W. H. Ponsford (181) and D. G. Bradman (304) v England at Leeds 1934
336 W. M. Lawry (151) and K. D. Walters (242) v West Indies at Sydney 1968-69
251 G. M. Wood (126) and C. S. Serjeant (124) v West Indies at Georgetown .. 1977-78

Fifth Wicket
405 S. G. Barnes (234) and D. G. Bradman (234) v England at Sydney 1946-47
385 S. R. Waugh (160) and G. S. Blewett (214*) v SAf at Johannesburg (WS) .. 1996-97
332*A. R. Border (200*) and S. R. Waugh (157*) v England at Leeds 1993

Sixth Wicket
346 J. H. W. Fingleton (136) and D. G. Bradman (270) v England at Melbourne 1936-37
317 D. R. Martyn (133) and A. C. Gilchrist (204*) v SAf at Johannesburg (WS) .. 2001-02
260*D. M. Jones (118*) and S. R. Waugh (134*) v Sri Lanka at Hobart 1989-90

Seventh Wicket
217 K. D. Walters (250) and G. J. Gilmour (101) v New Zealand at Christchurch 1976-77
212 S. M. Katich (118) and A. C. Gilchrist (118) v New Zealand at Christchurch 2004-05
185 G. N. Yallop (268) and G. R. J. Matthews (75) v Pakistan at Melbourne 1983-84

Eighth Wicket
243 M. J. Hartigan (116) and C. Hill (160) v England at Adelaide 1907-08
173 C. E. Pellew (116 and J. M. Gregory (100) v England at Melbourne 1920-21
154 G. J. Bonnor (128) and S. P. Jones (40) v England at Sydney 1884-85
154 D. Tallon (92) and R. R. Lindwall (100) v England at Melbourne 1946-47

Ninth Wicket
154 S. E. Gregory (201) and J. M. Blackham (74) v England at Sydney 1894-95
133 S. R. Waugh (110) and J. N. Gillespie (46) v India at Kolkata 2000-01
130 S. R. Waugh (152*) and G. F. Lawson (74) v England at Lord's 1989

Tenth Wicket
127 J. M. Taylor (108) and A. A. Mailey (46*) v England at Sydney 1924-25
120 R. A. Duff (104) and W. W. Armstrong (45*) v England at Melbourne 1901-02
114 J. N. Gillespie (54*) and G. D. McGrath (61) v New Zealand at Brisbane 2004-05

BOWLING RECORDS

MOST WICKETS IN AN INNINGS

9-121	A. A. Mailey	v England at Melbourne	1920-21
8-24	G. D. McGrath	v Pakistan at Perth	2004-05
8-31	F. Laver	v England at Manchester	1909
8-38	G. D. McGrath	v England at Lord's	1997
8-43	A. E. Trott	v England at Adelaide	1894-95
8-53	R. A. L. Massie	v England at Lord's	1972
8-59	A. A. Mallett	v Pakistan at Adelaide	1972-73
8-65	H. Trumble	v England at The Oval	1902
8-71	G. D. McKenzie	v West Indies at Melbourne	1968-69
8-71	S. K. Warne	v England at Brisbane	1994-95
8-84	R. A. L. Massie	v England at Lord's	1972
8-87	M. G. Hughes	v West Indies at Perth	1988-89
8-97	C. J. McDermott	v England at Perth	1990-91
8-112	G. F. Lawson	v West Indies at Adelaide	1984-85
8-141	C. J. McDermott	v England at Manchester	1985
8-143	M. H. N. Walker	v England at Melbourne	1974-75

MOST WICKETS IN AN INNINGS AGAINST AUSTRALIA

9-37	J. C. Laker	for England at Manchester	1956
9-52	R. J. Hadlee	for New Zealand at Brisbane	1985-86
9-69	J. M. Patel	for India at Kanpur	1959-60
9-86	Sarfraz Nawaz	for Pakistan at Melbourne	1978-79
8-35	G. A. Lohmann	for England at Sydney	1886-87

MOST WICKETS IN A MATCH

16-137	R. A. L. Massie	v England at Lord's	1972
14-90	F. R. Spofforth	v England at The Oval	1882
14-199	C. V. Grimmett	v South Africa at Adelaide	1931-32
13-77	M. A. Noble	v England at Melbourne	1901-02
13-110	F. R. Spofforth	v England at Melbourne	1878-79
13-148	B. A. Reid	v England at Melbourne	1990-91
13-173	C. V. Grimmett	v South Africa at Durban (Kingsmead)	1935-36
13-217	M. G. Hughes	v West Indies at Perth	1988-89
13-236	A. A. Mailey	v England at Melbourne	1920-21
12-87	C. T. B. Turner	v England at Sydney	1887-88
12-89	H. Trumble	v England at The Oval	1896
12-107	S. C. G. MacGill	v England at Sydney	1998-99
12-124	A. K. Davidson	v India at Kanpur	1959-60
12-126	B. A. Reid	v India at Melbourne	1991-92
12-128	S. K. Warne	v South Africa at Sydney	1993-94
12-166	G. Dymock	v India at Kanpur	1979-80
12-173	H. Trumble	v England at The Oval	1902
12-175	H. V. Hordern	v England at Sydney	1911-12

MOST WICKETS IN A MATCH AGAINST AUSTRALIA

19-90	J. C. Laker	for England at Manchester	1956
15-104	H. Verity	for England at Lord's	1934
15-123	R. J. Hadlee	for New Zealand at Brisbane	1985-86
15-124	W. Rhodes	for England at Melbourne	1903-04
15-217	Harbhajan Singh	for India at Chennai (Chepauk)	2000-01

MOST WICKETS IN AN INNINGS ON DEBUT

8-43	A. E. Trott	v England at Adelaide	1894-95
8-53	R. A. L. Massie	v England at Lord's (2nd innings)	1972
8-84	R. A. L. Massie	v England at Lord's (1st innings)	1972
7-55	T. K. Kendall	v England at Melbourne	1876-77

Note: I. W. G. Johnson (6-42 v Eng at Sydney, 1946-47) and S. M. Katich (6-65 v Zim at Sydney, 2003-04) took six wickets in their first match at the crease but not on debut.

MOST WICKETS IN A MATCH ON DEBUT

16-137	R. A. L. Massie	v England at Lord's	1972
11-82	C. V. Grimmett	v England at Sydney	1924-25
9-103	J. J. Ferris	v England at Sydney	1886-87
9-130	T. M. Alderman	v England at Nottingham	1981
9-162	J. V. Saunders	v England at Sydney	1901-02
9-200	W. H. Cooper	v England at Melbourne	1881-82

HAT-TRICKS

F. R. Spofforth	v England at Melbourne	1878-79
H. Trumble	v England at Melbourne	1901-02
H. Trumble	v England at Melbourne	1903-04
T. J. Matthews (1st Inns)	v South Africa at Manchester	1912
T. J. Matthews (2nd Inns)	v South Africa at Manchester	1912
L. F. Kline	v South Africa at Cape Town	1957-58
M. G. Hughes	v West Indies at Perth	1988-89
D. W. Fleming	v Pakistan at Rawalpindi	1994-95
S. K. Warne	v England at Melbourne	1994-95
G. D. McGrath	v West Indies at Perth	2000-01

MOST WICKETS IN A SERIES

	M	O	Mdns	R	W	BB	5 W/i	10 W/m	Avge	
C. V. Grimmett	5	346.1	140	642	44	7-40	5	3	14.59	1935-36 v SAf in South Africa
T. M. Alderman	6	325	76	893	42	6-135	4	0	21.26	1981 v England in England
R. M. Hogg	6	217.4	60	527	41	6-74	5	2	12.85	1978-79 v England in Australia
T. M. Alderman	6	269.2	68	712	41	6-128	6	1	17.37	1989 v England in England
D. K. Lillee	6	311.4	81	870	39	7-89	2	1	22.31	1981 v England in England
W. J. Whitty	5	232.3	55	632	37	6-17	2	0	17.08	1910-11 v SAf in Australia
A. A. Mailey	5	244.1	27	946	36	9-121	4	2	26.28	1920-21 v England in Australia
G. D. McGrath	6	249.5	67	701	36	8-38	2	0	19.47	1997 v England in England

Most wickets in a series against opponents not mentioned above:

v Bangladesh

	M	O	Mdns	R	W	BB	5 W/i	10 W/m	Avge	
S. C. G. MacGill	2	70.1	17	219	17	5-56	3	1	24.76	2003-04 in Australia
J. N. Gillespie	2	61.4	14	170	11	4-38	0	0	15.45	2003-04 in Australia
B. Lee	2	49.2	10	190	6	3-23	0	0	31.67	2003-04 in Australia

v India

	M	O	Mdns	R	W	BB	5 W/i	10 W/m	Avge	
C. J. McDermott	5	264.2	75	670	31	5-54	3	1	21.61	1991-92 in Australia
A. K. Davidson	5	244.5	85	431	29	7-93	2	1	14.86	1959-60 in India
R. Benaud	5	322.2	146	568	29	5-43	2	0	19.58	1959-60 in India

v New Zealand

	M	O	Mdns	R	W	BB	5 W/i	10 W/m	Avge	
S. K. Warne	3	170.4	36	476	19	5-88	1	0	25.05	1997-98 in Australia
S. K. Warne	3	151.3	49	305	18	6-31	1	0	16.94	1993-94 in Australia
B. Lee	3	100.4	26	315	18	5-77	1	0	17.50	1999-00 in New Zealand
G. D. McGrath	3	126.2	47	283	18	6-115	1	0	15.72	2004-05 in New Zealand

	M	O	Mdns	R	W	BB	5 W/i	10 W/m	Avge	
v Pakistan										
S. K. Warne	3	124	29	342	27	7-94	2	1	12.67	2002-03 in SRL/U.A.E.
G. F. Lawson	5	188.3	40	580	24	5-49	2	0	24.17	1983-84 in Australia
D. K. Lillee	3	173.4	16	540	21	6-82	2	1	25.71	1976-77 in Australia
v Sri Lanka										
S. K. Warne	3	169	37	521	26	5-43	4	2	20.03	2003-04 in Sri Lanka
G. D. McGrath	3	154.5	35	438	21	5-40	1	0	20.86	1995-96 in Australia
C. J. McDermott	3	124	30	342	14	4-53	0	0	24.43	1992-93 in Sri Lanka
v West Indies										
C. V. Grimmett	5	239.2	60	593	33	7-87	2	1	17.96	1930-31 in Australia
A. K. Davidson	4	231.5	25	612	33	6-53	5	1	18.55	1960-61 in Australia
G. D. McGrath	4	199.4	59	508	30	5-28	4	1	16.93	1998-99 in West Indies
v Zimbabwe										
A. J. Bichel	2	92.4	29	255	10	4-63	0	0	55.60	2003-04 in Australia
G. D. McGrath	1	54	19	90	6	3-44	0	0	15.00	1999-00 in Zimbabwe
S. K. Warne	2	53.1	13	137	6	3-68	0	0	22.83	1999-00 in Zimbabwe
B. Lee	2	73	17	222	6	3-48	0	0	37.00	2003-04 in Australia
S. M. Katich	2	32.5	3	90	6	6-65	1	0	15.00	2003-04 in Australia

MOST WICKETS IN A SERIES AGAINST AUSTRALIA

	M	O	Mdns	R	W	BB	5 W/i	10 W/m	Avge	
J. C. Laker	5	283.5	127	442	46	10-53	4	2	9.61	1956 for England in England
A. V. Bedser	5	265.1	58	682	39	7-44	5	1	17.49	1953 for England in England
M. W. Tate	5	421.2	62	881	38	6-99	5	1	23.18	1924-25 for Eng in Australia
S. F. Barnes	5	297	64	778	34	5-44	3	0	22.88	1911-12 for Eng in Australia
I. T. Botham	6	272.3	81	700	34	6-95	3	1	20.59	1981 for England in England

MOST WICKETS IN A THREE-TEST SERIES

	M	O	Mdns	R	W	BB	5 W/i	10 W/m	Avge	
S. K. Warne	3	124	29	342	27	7-94	2	1	12.67	2002-03 v Pakistan in SL/UAE
S. K. Warne	3	168	37	521	26	5-43	4	2	20.04	2003-04 v SL in Sri Lanka
R. Benaud	3	169.5	52	388	23	7-72	3	1	16.87	1956-57 v India in India
D. K. Lillee	3	155.1	41	388	23	6-60	2	1	16.87	1979-80 v England in Australia

MOST WICKETS IN A FOUR-TEST SERIES

	M	O	Mdns	R	W	BB	5 W/i	10 W/m	Avge	
G. D. McGrath	4	199.4	59	508	30	5-28	4	1	16.93	1998-99 v WI in West Indies
G. E. Palmer	4	243.4	145	522	24	7-68	2	1	21.75	1881-82 v England in Australia
W. J. O'Reilly	4	263	78	610	22	5-56	2	1	27.73	1938 v England in England
G. E. Palmer	4	180.1	113	397	21	7-65	2	1	18.90	1882-83 v England in Australia
D. K. Lillee	4	207	72	460	21	5-15	1	0	21.90	1975 v England in England
A. N. Connolly	4	214.2	57	522	20	6-47	2	0	26.10	1969-70 v SA in South Africa
S. C. G. MacGill	4	204.1	46	678	20	5-75	1	0	33.90	2002-03 v WI in West Indies

MOST WICKETS IN A CALENDAR YEAR

	M	Balls	Mdns	R	W	BB	5W/i	10W/m	Avge	Year
D. K. Lillee	13	3,710	162	1,781	85	7-83	5	2	20.95	1981
S. K. Warne	16	5,054	316	1,697	72	6-31	2	0	23.56	1993
G. D. McKenzie	14	4,106	119	1,737	71	7-153	4	1	24.46	1964
S. K. Warne	10	3,773	217	1,274	70	8-71	6	2	18.20	1994
S. K. Warne	12	3,472	123	1,685	70	6-125	5	2	24.07	2004

	M	Balls	Mdns	R	W	BB	5Wi	10W/m	Avge	Year
G. D. McGrath	14	3,508	196	1,473	68	7-78	4	0	21.68	2001
S. K. Warne	15	4,091	194	1,661	68	6-48	2	0	24.42	1997
S. K. Warne	10	2,874	109	1,310	67	7-94	3	1	19.55	2002
G. D. McGrath	14	3,364	169	1,425	67	5-28	4	1	21.26	1999
G. D. McGrath	13	3,113	151	1,347	63	8-38	4	0	21.38	1997
S. K. Warne	13	3,501	113	1,809	58	7-165	4	1	31.19	2001
M. G. Hughes	12	3,033	127	1,448	57	5-64	2	0	25.40	1993
S. C. G. MacGill	11	3,148	107	1,688	57	5-56	4	1	29.61	2003
C. J. McDermott	9	2,416	84	1,188	56	8-97	4	1	21.21	1991
R. Benaud	9	3,248	177	1,031	55	5-76	4	0	18.74	1959
A. A. Mailey	10	2,849	63	1,567	55	9-121	4	2	28.49	1921
J. N. Gillespie	14	3,087	130	1,369	55	5-56	1	0	24.89	2004

MOST WICKETS IN A CAREER

		M	Balls	Mdns	R	W	BB	5Wi	10W/m	Avge
1	S. K. Warne	123	34,437	1,571	14,878	583	8-71	29	8	25.52
2	G. D. McGrath	109	25,509	1,289	10,592	499	8-24	26	3	21.23
3	D. K. Lillee	70	18,467	652	8,493	355	7-83	23	7	23.92
4	C. J. McDermott	71	16,586	581	8,332	291	8-97	14	2	28.63
5	R. Benaud	63	19,108	805	6,704	248	7-72	16	1	27.03
6	J. N. Gillespie	66	13,574	611	6,380	248	7-37	8	0	25.73
7	G. D. McKenzie	61	17,684	547	7,328	246	8-71	16	3	29.79
8	R. R. Lindwall	61	13,650	419	5,251	228	7-38	12	0	23.03
9	C. V. Grimmett	37	14,513	736	5,231	216	7-40	21	7	24.22
10	M. G. Hughes	53	12,285	499	6,017	212	8-87	7	1	28.38
11	J. R. Thomson	51	10,535	300	5,602	200	6-46	8	0	28.01

MOST WICKETS AGAINST OPPONENTS

	M	Balls	Mdns	R	W	BB	5Wi	10W/m	Avge
v England									
D. K. Lillee	29	8,516	361	3,507	167	7-89	11	4	21.00
H. Trumble	31	7,895	448	2,945	141	8-65	9	3	20.89
S. K. Warne	26	7,792	408	3,040	132	8-71	7	2	23.03
v South Africa									
S. K. Warne	18	6,130	303	2,257	101	7-56	6	2	22.35
C. V. Grimmett	10	3,913	248	1,199	77	7-40	8	4	15.57
R. Benaud	13	4,136	116	1,413	52	5-49	5	0	27.17
v West Indies									
G. D. McGrath	20	4,701	248	1,847	97	6-17	8	2	19.04
J. R. Thomson	14	2,774	56	1,818	62	6-50	3	0	29.32
C. J. McDermott	14	3,036	84	1,703	59	5-80	1	0	28.86
v New Zealand									
S. K. Warne	20	5,770	252	2,511	103	6-31	3	0	24.38
G. D. McGrath	14	3,427	172	1,444	57	6-115	2	0	25.33
C. J. McDermott	13	3,214	130	1,460	48	5-97	1	0	30.42
v India									
R. Benaud	8	2,953	198	956	52	7-72	5	1	18.38
G. D. McGrath	11	2,558	157	951	51	5-48	2	1	18.65
G. D. McKenzie	10	2,563	106	967	47	7-66	4	2	20.57
v Pakistan									
S. K. Warne	15	4,050	192	1,816	90	7-23	6	2	20.18
G. D. McGrath	17	3,835	173	1,736	80	8-24	3	0	21.70
D. K. Lillee	17	4,433	127	2,161	71	6-82	5	1	30.44
v Sri Lanka									
S. K. Warne	13	3,167	133	1,507	59	5-43	5	2	25.54
G. D. McGrath	8	1,828	84	823	37	5-37	2	0	22.24
C. J. McDermott	7	1,534	60	735	27	4-53	0	0	27.22

	M	Balls	Mdns	R	W	BB	5W/i	10W/m	Avge
v Zimbabwe									
A. J. Bichel	2	556	29	255	10	4-63	0	0	25.50
S. M. Katich	1	197	3	90	6	6-65	1	0	15.00
G. D. McGrath	1	324	19	90	6	3-44	0	0	15.00
B. Lee	2	438	17	222	6	3-48	0	0	37.00
v Bangladesh									
S. C. G. MacGill	2	421	17	219	17	5-56	3	1	12.88
J. N. Gillespie	2	370	14	170	11	4-38	0	0	15.45
B. Lee	2	296	10	190	6	3-23	0	0	31.67

MOST WICKETS AGAINST AUSTRALIA

	M	Balls	Mdns	R	W	BB	5W/i	10W/m	Avge
for England									
I. T. Botham	36	8,479	297	4,093	148	6-78	9	2	27.66
R. G. D. Willis	36	7,294	200	3,346	128	8-43	7	0	26.14
W. Rhodes	41	5,790	234	2,616	109	8-68	6	1	24.00
for South Africa									
H. J. Tayfield	15	6,027	179	2,208	64	7-23	4	1	34.50
T. L. Goddard	18	5,089	259	1,462	53	6-53	2	0	27.58
A. A. Donald	14	3,266	115	1,647	53	6-59	2	0	31.08
for West Indies									
C. A. Walsh	38	8,560	286	3,872	135	6-54	4	0	28.68
C. E. L. Ambrose	27	6,696	279	2,718	128	7-25	8	1	21.23
L. R. Gibbs	24	9,358	361	3,222	103	6-29	6	0	31.28
for New Zealand									
R. J. Hadlee	23	6,099	213	2,674	130	9-52	14	3	20.57
D. L. Vettori	13	3,441	114	1,706	51	7-87	6	1	33.45
C. L. Cairns	14	2,623	88	1,636	39	5-146	1	0	41.95
for India									
A. R. Kumble	14	4,836	149	2,390	88	8-141	9	2	27.16
Kapil Dev	20	4,746	198	2,003	79	8-106	7	0	25.35
E. A. S. Prasanna	13	4,331	173	1,637	57	6-74	5	1	28.72
for Pakistan									
Imran Khan	18	3,994	140	1,598	64	6-63	3	1	24.97
Iqbal Qasim	13	3,957	206	1,490	57	7-49	2	1	26.14
Sarfraz Nawaz	15	4,520	151	1,828	52	9-86	1	1	35.15
for Sri Lanka									
M. Muralidaran	10	3,093	83	1,571	50	6-59	5	1	31.42
W. P. U. J. C. Vaas	11	2,425	87	1,127	37	5-31	1	0	30.46
C. P. H. Ramanayake	6	1,384	35	744	21	5-82	1	0	35.43
for Zimbabwe									
H. H. Streak	3	540	18	353	7	5-93	1	0	50.43
R. W. Price	2	538	11	371	6	6-121	1	0	61.83
S. M. Ervine	1	186	4	146	4	4-146	0	0	36.50
for Bangladesh									
Mashrafe Bin Mortaza	2	288	14	134	4	3-74	0	0	33.50
Sanwar Hossain	1	180	2	128	2	2-128	0	0	64.00
Tapash Baisya	2	287	9	165	2	1-69	0	0	82.50

MOST WICKETS AT EACH AUSTRALIAN VENUE

	M	Balls	Mdns	R	W	BB	5W/i	10W/m	Avge
Melbourne Cricket Ground (Melbourne)									
D. K. Lillee	14	3,833	105	1,798	82	7-83	7	4	21.93
H. Trumble	7	1,708	71	646	46	7-28	3	0	14.04
G. D. McKenzie	8	2,370	35	1,019	45	8-71	3	2	22.64
Most by non-Australian									
S. F. Barnes (Eng)	5	1,723	83	632	35	7-121	5	1	18.06

Sydney Cricket Ground (Sydney)

S. K. Warne	11	3,420	149	1,486	54	7-56	4	2	27.52
C. T. B. Turner	6	2,106	209	602	45	7-43	4	1	13.38
D. K. Lillee	8	2,191	61	1,036	43	4-40	0	0	24.09
Most by non-Australian									
G. A. Lohmann (Eng)	4	1,219	114	331	35	8-35	3	2	9.46

Adelaide Oval (Adelaide)

D. K. Lillee	9	2,479	63	1,206	45	6-171	4	0	26.80
S. K. Warne	11	3,241	145	1,332	44	5-113	1	0	30.27
C. J. McDermott	8	2,325	98	1,162	42	5-76	3	1	27.67
Most by non-Australian									
Kapil Dev (Ind)	3	984	38	439	19	8-106	2	0	23.11

Brisbane Exhibition Ground (Brisbane)

C. V. Grimmett	2	841	24	442	18	6-131	2	0	24.56
H. Larwood (Eng)	1	130	4	62	8	6-32	1	0	7.75
H. Ironmonger	2	813	61	236	7	2-43	0	0	33.71

Brisbane Cricket Ground (Brisbane)

S. K. Warne	9	2,882	145	1,183	59	8-71	2	2	20.05
G. D. McGrath	11	2,787	133	1,217	54	6-17	3	1	22.54
C. J. McDermott	8	1,887	69	905	40	6-53	2	0	22.63
Most by non-Australian									
R. J. Hadlee (NZ)	3	807	29	343	21	9-52	2	1	16.33

WACA Ground (Perth)

G. D. McGrath	10	2,466	119	1,045	47	8-24	1	0	22.23
M. G. Hughes	6	1,618	63	752	39	8-87	3	1	19.28
C. J. McDermott	8	1,781	67	847	38	8-97	2	1	22.29
Most by non-Australian									
C. E. L. Ambrose (WI)	3	639	28	310	24	7-25	3	0	12.91

Bellerive Oval (Hobart)

S. K. Warne	5	1,073	44	461	24	6-31	1	0	19.21
G. D. McGrath	3	693	39	274	13	5-61	1	0	21.08
P. R. Reiffel	3	449	21	195	11	4-38	0	0	17.73
Most by non-Australian									
Mushtaq Ahmed (Pak)	1	408	13	198	9	5-115	1	0	22.00

Marrara Cricket Ground (Darwin)

G. D. McGrath	2	324	19	106	11	5-37	1	0	9.64
S. C. G. MacGill	1	157	5	86	7	5-65	1	0	12.29
M. S. Kasprowicz	1	148	4	54	7	7-39	1	0	7.71
Most by non-Australian									
W. P. U. J. C. Vaas (SL)	1	195	10	82	7	5-31	1	0	11.71

Cazaly's Stadium (Cairns)

J. N. Gillespie	2	560	22	250	12	4-38	0	0	20.82
S. C. G. MacGill	1	264	12	133	10	5-56	2	1	13.30
U. D. U. Chandana (SL)	1	268	3	210	10	5-101	2	1	21.00

LOWEST CAREER AVERAGE

(Qualification: 20 wickets)

	M	Balls	Mdns	R	W	BB	5W/i	10W/m	Avge
J. J. Ferris	8	2,030	224	684	48	5-26	4	0	14.25
J. B. Iverson	5	1,108	29	320	21	6-27	1	0	15.24
C. T. B. Turner	17	5,179	457	1,670	101	7-43	11	2	16.53
H. Ironmonger	14	4,695	328	1330	74	7-23	4	2	17.97
F. R. Spofforth	18	4,185	416	1,731	94	7-44	7	4	18.41
H. F. Boyle	12	1,743	175	641	32	6-42	1	0	20.03
A. K. Davidson	44	11,587	431	3,819	186	7-93	14	2	20.53
R. A. L. Massie	6	1,739	74	647	31	8-53	2	1	20.87
E. R. H. Toshack	12	3,140	155	989	47	6-29	4	1	21.04
W. J. Whitty	14	3,357	163	1,373	65	6-17	3	0	21.12

MOST ECONOMICAL

(Qualification: 20 wickets, and calculated on six-ball overs)

	Wkts	RPO	Eng	SAf	WI	NZ	Ind	Pak	SL	Zim	Ban
H. Ironmonger ..	74	1.70	1.74	1.33	2.11	–	–	–	–	–	–
J.B. Iverson	21	1.73	1.73	–	–	–	–	–	–	–	–
K.D. Mackay ...	50	1.78	1.86	1.54	2.28	–	1.55	1.47	–	–	–
E.R.H. Toshack .	47	1.89	1.95	–	–	0.62	2.04	–	–	–	–
C.T.B. Turner ..	101	1.93	1.93	–	–	–	–	–	–	–	–
W.J. O'Reilly ..	144	1.95	1.97	1.86	–	1.74	–	–	–	–	–
L.F. Kline	34	1.96	–	1.62	3.05	–	1.72	1.61	–	–	–
T.R. Veivers ...	33	1.97	2.19	1.95	–	–	1.64	1.77	–	–	–
A.K. Davidson .	186	1.98	2.00	1.58	2.64	–	1.77	1.91	–	–	–
J.J. Ferris	48	2.02	2.02	–	–	–	–	–	–	–	–

MOST WICKETS PER MATCH

(Qualification: 20 wickets)

	Wkts	WPM	Eng	SAf	WI	NZ	Ind	Pak	SL	Zim	Ban
H.V. Hordern ..	46	6.57	6.40	7.00	–	–	–	–	–	–	–
J.J. Ferris	48	6.00	6.00	–	–	–	–	–	–	–	–
C.T.B. Turner ..	101	5.94	5.94	–	–	–	–	–	–	–	–
C.V. Grimmett .	216	5.84	4.82	7.70	6.60	–	–	–	–	–	–
J.V. Saunders ..	79	5.64	5.33	7.50	–	–	–	–	–	–	–
W.J. O'Reilly ..	144	5.33	5.37	4.86	–	8.00	–	–	–	–	–
H. Ironmonger ..	74	5.29	3.50	7.75	5.50	–	–	–	–	–	–
F.R. Spofforth .	94	5.22	5.22	–	–	–	–	–	–	–	–
R.A.L. Massie .	31	5.17	5.75	–	–	–	–	4.00	–	–	–
D.K. Lillee	355	5.07	5.76	–	4.58	4.75	7.00	4.18	3.00	–	–

MOST MAIDENS

	Mdns	Eng	SAf	WI	NZ	Ind	Pak	SL	Zim	Ban
S.K. Warne	1,571	408	303	132	252	139	192	132	13	–
G.D. McGrath	1,289	245	174	248	172	157	173	84	19	17
R. Benaud	805	289	116	103	–	198	99	–	–	–
C.V. Grimmett	736	427	248	61	–	–	–	–	–	–
D.K. Lillee	652	361	–	62	63	33	127	6	–	–

MOST BALLS IN A CAREER

	Balls	Eng	SAf	WI	NZ	Ind	Pak	SL	Zim	Ban
S.K. Warne	34,437	7,792	6,130	3,284	5,770	3,925	4,050	3,167	319	–
G.D. McGrath	25,509	5,221	3,284	4,701	3,427	2,558	3,835	1,828	324	331
R. Benaud	19,108	7,284	4,136	3,289	–	2,953	1,446	–	–	–
D.K. Lillee	18,467	8,516	–	2,677	1,770	891	4,433	180	–	–
G.D. McKenzie ...	17,684	7,489	3,745	3,185	–	2,563	702	–	–	–

MOST BALLS IN A MATCH

708	G. Giffen	v England at Sydney	1894-95
672	W.A. Johnston	v South Africa at Melbourne	1952-53
656	C.V. Grimmett	v England at The Oval	1930
656	F.A. Ward	v England at Brisbane	1936-37
654	H. Trumble	v England at Adelaide	1901-02
654	C.V. Grimmett	v South Africa at Melbourne	1931-32

ALL-ROUNDERS

HUNDRED AND FIVE WICKETS IN AN INNINGS

C. Kelleway	114	5-33	v South Africa at Manchester	1912
J. M. Gregory	100	7-69	v England at Melbourne	1920-21
K. R. Miller	109	6-107	v West Indies at Kingston	1954-55
R. Benaud	100	5-84	v South Africa at Johannesburg (WS)	1957-58

HUNDRED RUNS AND TEN WICKETS IN A MATCH

A.K. Davidson	44	5-135	v West Indies at Brisbane	1960-61
	and 80	and 6-87		

1,000 RUNS AND 100 WICKETS IN A CAREER

	M	R	W	Tests for Double
R. Benaud	63	2,201	248	32
A. K. Davidson	44	1,328	186	34
G. Giffen	31	1,238	103	30
M.G. Hughes	53	1,032	212	52
I. W. G. Johnson	45	1,000	109	45
R. R. Lindwall............	61	1,502	228	38
K. R. Miller	55	2,958	170	33
M. A. Noble..............	42	1,997	121	27
S. K. Warne	123	2,518	583	58

WICKET-KEEPING RECORDS

MOST DISMISSALS IN AN INNINGS

6	(all ct)	A. T. W. Grout	v South Africa at Johannesburg (WS)	1957-58
6	(all ct)	R. W. Marsh	v England at Brisbane	1982-83
6	(all ct)	I. A. Healy	v England at Birmingham	1997

Note: There are 43 instances of five dismissals in an innings.

MOST DISMISSALS IN A MATCH

10	(all ct)	A. C. Gilchrist	v New Zealand at Hamilton	1999-00
9	(8ct, 1st)	G. R. A. Langley	v England at Lord's........................	1956
9	(all ct)	R. W. Marsh	v England at Brisbane	1982-83
9	(all ct)	I. A. Healy	v England at Brisbane	1994-95

Note: There are 14 instances of eight dismissals in a match.

MOST DISMISSALS IN A SERIES

28	(all ct)	5 Tests	R. W. Marsh .	v England in Australia	1982-83
27	(25ct, 2st)	6 Tests	I. A. Healy ...	v England in England	1997
26	(all ct)	6 Tests	R. W. Marsh .	v West Indies in Australia	1975-76
26	(21ct, 5st)	6 Tests	I. A. Healy ..	v England in England	1993
26	(24ct, 2st)	5 Tests	A. C. Gilchrist	v England in England	2001
25	(23ct, 2st)	5 Tests	I. A. Healy ...	v England in Australia	1994-95
25	(23ct, 2st)	5 Tests	A. C. Gilchrist	v England in Australia	2002-03

Note: There are 22 instances of 20 or more dismissals in a series

MOST DISMISSALS IN A THREE-TEST SERIES

19	(17ct, 2st)	I. A. Healy	v Sri Lanka in Australia	1995-96
18	(17ct, 1st)	A. C. Gilchrist	v New Zealand in New Zealand	1999-00
17	(16ct, 1st)	R. W. Marsh	v New Zealand in Australia	1973-74
16	(all ct)	R. W. Marsh	v Pakistan in Australia	1972-73
16	(15ct, 1st)	R. W. Marsh	v India in Australia	1980-81

MOST DISMISSALS IN A CAREER

		M	Ct	St	Total
1	I. A. Healy	119	366	29	395
2	R. W. Marsh	97	343	12	355
3	A. C. Gilchrist	68	260	27	287
4	A. T. W. Grout	51	163	24	187
5	W. A. S. Oldfield	54	78	52	130
6	G. R. A. Langley	26	83	15	98
7	H. Carter	28	44	21	65
8	J. J. Kelly	36	43	20	63
9	{ J. M. Blackham	35	36	24	60
	H. B. Taber	16	56	4	60
11	D. Tallon	21	50	8	58
12	B. N. Jarman	19	50	4	54

MOST DISMISSALS AGAINST OPPONENTS

		M	Ct	St	Dismissals
v England	R. W. Marsh	43	141	7	148
v South Africa	H. B. Taber	9	35	3	38
v West Indies	I. A. Healy	28	72	6	78
v New Zealand	R. W. Marsh	14	57	1	58
v India	A. C. Gilchrist	14	48	2	50
v Pakistan	R. W. Marsh	20	66	2	68
v Sri Lanka	I. A. Healy	11	32	2	34
v Zimbabwe	A. C. Gilchrist	2	9	2	11
v Bangladesh	A. C. Gilchrist	2	9	0	9

MOST DISMISSALS AGAINST AUSTRALIA

		M	Ct	St	Dismissals
for England	A. P. E. Knott	35	97	8	105
for South Africa	D. J. Richardson	12	39	1	40
for West Indies	P. J. L. Dujon	21	83	1	84
for New Zealand	I. D. S. Smith	15	34	5	39
for India	S. M. H. Kirmani	17	29	12	41
for Pakistan	Wasim Bari	19	56	10	66
for Sri Lanka	R. S. Kaluwitharana	9	15	6	21
for Zimbabwe	A. Flower	1	3	0	3

MOST DISMISSALS IN A CALENDAR YEAR

	M	Ct	St	Dismissals	Year
I. A. Healy	16	58	9	67	1993
A. C. Gilchrist	14	52	5	57	2001
I. A. Healy	15	55	4	59	1997
R. W. Marsh	13	52	1	53	1981
A. C. Gilchrist	14	58	8	66	2004

MOST DISMISSALS PER MATCH

	D/M	Eng	SAf	WI	NZ	Ind	Pak	SL	Zim	Ban
▸.A. Emery	6.00	–	–	–	–	–	6.00	–	–	–
▸.A. Maclean	4.50	4.50	–	–	–	–	–	–	–	–
▸.C. Gilchrist	4.22	5.10	4.00	4.00	3.72	3.57	4.22	5.40	5.50	4.50
R.A. Saggers	4.00	3.00	4.20	–	–	–	–	–	–	–
▸.C. Dyer	4.00	2.50	–	–	4.33	–	–	6.00	–	–

MOST STUMPINGS IN A MATCH

4	J. M. Blackham	v England at Lord's	1888
4	A. H. Jarvis	v England at Sydney	1894-95
4	W. A. S. Oldfield	v England at Melbourne	1924-25
4	W. A. S. Oldfield	v England at Sydney	1924-25
4	W. A. S. Oldfield	v West Indies at Adelaide	1930-31
4	R. A. Saggers	v South Africa at Port Elizabeth	1949-50
4	G. R. A. Langley	v West Indies at Brisbane	1951-52

BEST KEEPER–BOWLER COMBINATIONS

Dismissals
- 95 . . . . R. W. Marsh – D. K. Lillee
- 75 . . . . A. C. Gilchrist - G. D. McGrath
- 58 . . . . I. A. Healy – G. D. McGrath
- 56 . . . . A. C. Gilchrist - J. N. Gillespie
- 55 . . . . I. A. Healy – C. J. McDermott

Dismissals
- 49 . . . . . I. A. Healy – S. K. Warne
- 47 . . . . . A. C. Gilchrist – J. N. Gillespie
- 46 . . . . . I. A. Healy – M. G. Hughes
- 45 . . . . . A. T. W. Grout – A. K. Davidson

FIELDING RECORDS

MOST CATCHES IN AN INNINGS

5	V. Y. Richardson	v South Africa at Durban (Kingsmead)	1935-36

Note: There are 19 instances of four catches in an innings.

MOST CATCHES IN A MATCH

7	G. S. Chappell	v England at Perth	1974-75
7	M. L. Hayden	v Sri Lanka at Galle	2003-04
6	J. M. Gregory	v England at Sydney	1920-21
6	V. Y. Richardson	v South Africa at Durban (Kingsmead)	1935-36
6	R. N. Harvey	v England at Sydney	1962-63
6	I. M. Chappell	v New Zealand at Adelaide	1973-74
6	D. F. Whatmore	v India at Kanpur	1979-80
6	M. E. Waugh	v India at Chennai (Chepauk)	2000-01

Note: There are 12 instances of five catches in a match.

MOST CATCHES IN A SERIES

15	J. M. Gregory	v England in Australia	1920-21
14	G. S. Chappell	v England in Australia	1974-75
13	R. B. Simpson	v South Africa in South Africa	1957-58
13	R. B. Simpson	v West Indies in Australia	1960-61
12	D. F. Whatmore	v India in India	1979-80
12	A. R. Border	v England in England	1981

Note: There are 7 instances of eleven catches in a series.

MOST CATCHES IN A CAREER

1	M. E. Waugh	....	181 in 128 matches
2	M. A. Taylor	....	157 in 104 matches
3	A. R. Border	....	156 in 156 matches
4	G. S. Chappell	....	122 in 88 matches
5	R. B. Simpson	....	110 in 62 matches
5	S. R. Waugh	....	112 in 168 matches
6	R. B. Simpson	....	110 in 62 matches
7	S. K. Warne	....	107 in 123 matches
8	I. M. Chappell	....	105 in 76 matches
9	R. T. Ponting	....	103 in 88 matches
10	D. C. Boon	....	99 in 107 matches

MOST CATCHES AGAINST OPPONENTS

v England	G. S. Chappell	61 in 36 matches
v South Africa	R. B. Simpson	27 in 15 matches
v West Indies	M. E. Waugh	45 in 28 matches
v New Zealand	A. R. Border	31 in 23 matches
v India	M. E. Waugh	29 in 14 matches
v Pakistan	M. E. Waugh	23 in 15 matches
v Sri Lanka	S. K. Warne	15 in 13 matches
v Zimbabwe	M. E. Waugh	5 in 1 match
v Bangladesh	J. L. Langer	3 in 2 matches

MOST CATCHES AGAINST AUSTRALIA

for England	I. T. Botham	57 in 36 matches
for South Africa	T. L. Goddard	21 in 18 matches
for West Indies	C. L. Hooper	38 in 25 matches
for New Zealand	J. V. Coney	24 in 15 matches
for India	R. S. Dravid	32 in 18 matches
for Pakistan	Mudassar Nazar	16 in 19 matches
for Sri Lanka	S. T. Jayasuriya	11 in 11 matches
for Zimbabwe	S. V. Carlisle	3 in 2 matches
	N. C. Johnson	3 in 1 match
for Bangladesh	Javed Omar	3 in 2 matches

MOST CATCHES IN A CALENDAR YEAR

J. M. Gregory	27 in 12 matches	1921
M. A. Taylor	27 in 15 matches	1997
R. B. Simpson	26 in 14 matches	1964
M. E. Waugh	26 in 14 matches	1999
R. T. Ponting	25 in 14 matches	2001
M. A. Taylor	25 in 15 matches	1993

BEST FIELDER–BOWLER COMBINATION

Catches		*Catches*	
51	M. A. Taylor – S. K. Warne	25	S. K. Warne - G. D. McGrath
39	M. E. Waugh – S. K. Warne	22	G. S. Chappell – D. K. Lillee
34	M. E. Waugh – G. D. McGrath	22	R. T. Ponting – G. D. McGrath
28	R. T. Ponting - S. K. Warne		

TEAM

HIGHEST INNINGS TOTALS

8-758 dec.	v West Indies at Kingston	1954-55
6-735 dec.	v Zimbabwe at Perth	2003-04
5-729 dec.	v England at Lord's	1930
701	v England at The Oval	1934
695	v England at The Oval	1930
674	v India at Adelaide	1947-48
668	v West Indies at Bridgetown	1954-55
8-659 dec.	v England at Sydney	1946-47
8-656 dec.	v England at Manchester	1964
4-653 dec.	v England at Leeds	1993
7-652 dec.	v South Africa at Johannesburg (WS)	2001-02
6-650 dec.	v West Indies at Bridgetown	1964-65
645	v England at Brisbane	1946-47
7-641 dec.	v England at The Oval	2001
4-632 dec.	v England at Lord's	1993
8-628 dec.	v South Africa at Johannesburg (WS)	1996-97
619	v West Indies at Sydney	1968-69
617	v Pakistan at Faisalabad	1979-80
5-617 dec.	v Sri Lanka at Perth	1995-96
6-607 dec.	v New Zealand at Brisbane	1993-94
9-605 dec.	v West Indies at Bridgetown	2002-03
604	v England at Melbourne	1936-37
6-602 dec.	v England at Nottingham	1989
8-601 dec.	v England at Brisbane	1954-55
7-601 dec.	v England at Leeds	1989
600	v England at Melbourne	1924-25
9-600 dec.	v West Indies at Port-of-Spain	1954-55

HIGHEST INNINGS TOTALS AGAINST AUSTRALIA

7-903 dec.	for England at The Oval	1938
7-705 dec.	for India at Sydney	2003-04
8-658 dec.	for England at Nottingham	1938
7-657 dec.	for India at Kolkata	2000-01
636	for England at Sydney	1928-29

HIGHEST FOURTH-INNINGS TOTALS

3-404	v England (won) at Leeds	1948
402	v England (set 505) at Manchester	1981
7-381	v New Zealand (set 439) at Perth	2001-02
6-369	v Pakistan (won) at Hobart (Bel)	1999-00
7-362	v West Indies (won) at Georgetown	1977-78
6-357	v India (set 443) at Sydney	2003-04
7-344	v England (set 448) at Sydney	1994-95
8-342	v India (won) at Perth	1977-78

LOWEST COMPLETED INNINGS TOTALS

36	v England at Birmingham	1902
42	v England at Sydney	1887-88
44	v England at The Oval	1896
53	v England at Lord's	1896

58	v England at Brisbane	....	1936-?
60	v England at Lord's	....	18??
63	v England at The Oval	....	18??
65	v England at The Oval	....	19??
66	v England at Brisbane	....	1928-2?
68	v England at The Oval	....	188?
70	v England at Manchester	....	188?
74	v England at Birmingham	....	190?
75	v South Africa at Durban (Kingsmead)	....	1949-5?
76	v West Indies at Perth	....	1984-8?

Lowest completed innings totals for opponents not mentioned above:

v New Zealand

103	at Auckland	....	1985-86
110	at Wellington	....	1989-90
139	at Auckland	....	1992-93

v Sri Lanka

120	at Kandy	....	2003-04
188	at Kandy	....	1998-99
201	at Darwin	....	2004-05

v Zimbabwe

403	at Sydney	....	2003-04
422	at Harare	....	1999-00
6d-735	at Perth	....	2003-04

v Bangladesh

7d-407	at Darwin	....	2003-04
4d-556	at Cairns	....	2003-04

LOWEST COMPLETED INNINGS TOTALS AGAINST AUSTRALIA

36	for South Africa at Melbourne	1931-32
42	for New Zealand at Wellington	1945-46
45	for England at Sydney	1886-87
45	for South Africa at Melbourne	1931-32
51	for West Indies at Port-of-Spain	1998-99

MOST RUNS IN A DAY'S PLAY

6-494	1st day	v South Africa at Sydney	1910-11
2-475	1st day	v England at The Oval	1934
3-458	1st day	v England at Leeds	1930
1-455	2nd day	v England at Leeds	1934
450	1st day	v South Africa at Johannesburg (OW)	1921-22

HIGHEST MATCH AGGREGATE

1,028-20	v England at The Oval	1934
1,013-18	v West Indies at Sydney	1968-69
971-14	v New Zealand at Wellington	1973-74
936-20	v England at Adelaide	1920-21
917-20	v West Indies at Bridgetown	1954-55

LOWEST COMPLETED MATCH AGGREGATE

124-20	v England at Sydney	1887-88
151-20	v England at Manchester	1888
163-20	v England at The Oval	1896
176-20	v England at Lord's	1888
176-20	v England at The Oval	1912

LARGEST VICTORIES

By Innings and Runs Margin

Innings and 360	v South Africa at Johannesburg (WS)	2001-02
Innings and 332	v England at Brisbane	1946-47
Innings and 259	v South Africa at Port Elizabeth	1949-50
Innings and 226	v India at Brisbane	1947-48
Innings and 222	v New Zealand at Hobart	1993-94
Innings and 217	v West Indies at Brisbane (Ex)	1930-31
Innings and 200	v England at Melbourne	1936-37

By Runs Margin

562 runs	v England at The Oval	1934
530 runs	v South Africa at Melbourne	1910-11
491 runs	v Pakistan at Perth	2004-05
409 runs	v England at Lord's	1948
384 runs	v England at Brisbane	2002-03
382 runs	v England at Adelaide	1894-95
382 runs	v West Indies at Sydney	1968-69
377 runs	v England at Sydney	1920-21
365 runs	v England at Melbourne	1936-37

NARROWEST VICTORIES

By One Wicket

v West Indies at Melbourne (*Last Wkt:* 38 – D. T. Ring 32* and W. A. Johnston 7*)	1951-52

By 20 Runs or Less

3	v England at Manchester	1902
6	v England at Sydney	1884-85
7	v England at The Oval	1882
11	v England at Adelaide	1924-25
16	v India at Brisbane	1977-78
16	v Sri Lanka at Colombo (SSC)	1992-93

HEAVIEST DEFEATS

By Innings and Runs Margin

Innings and 579	by England at The Oval	1938
Innings and 230	by England at Adelaide	1891-92
Innings and 225	by England at Melbourne	1911-12
Innings and 219	by India at Calcutta	1997-98
Innings and 217	by England at The Oval	1886

By Runs Margin

675 runs	by England at Brisbane (Ex)	1928-29
408 runs	by West Indies at Adelaide	1979-80
343 runs	by West Indies at Bridgetown	1990-91
338 runs	by England at Adelaide	1932-33
323 runs	by South Africa at Port Elizabeth	1969-70
322 runs	by England at Brisbane	1936-37
307 runs	by South Africa at Johannesburg (WS)	1969-70

NARROWEST DEFEATS

By One Wicket

v England at The Oval (*Last Wkt:* 15 – G. H. Hirst 58* and W. Rhodes 6*) 1900
v England at Melbourne (*Last Wkt:* 39 – S. F. Barnes 38* and A. Fielder 18*) 1907-0
v Pakistan at Karachi (*Last Wkt:* 57 – Inzamam-ul-Haq 58* and Mushtaq Ahmed 20*) . . . 1994-9
v West Indies at Bridgetown (*Last Wkt:* 9 – B. C. Lara 153* and C. A. Walsh 0*) 1998-9

By 20 Runs or Less

1	by West Indies at Adelaide	1992-9.
3	by England at Melbourne	1982-8:
5	by South Africa at Sydney	1993-9·
10	by England at Sydney	1894-9!
12	by England at Adelaide	1928-29
12	by England at Melbourne	1998-99
13	by England at Sydney	1886-87
13	by India at Mumbai	2003-04
18	by England at Leeds	1981
19	by England at The Oval	1997

TIED TESTS

Australia (505 and 232) tied with West Indies (453 and 284) at Brisbane 1960-61
India (397 and 347) tied with Australia (7d-574 and 5d-170) at Chennai (Chepauk) 1986-87

APPEARANCE RECORDS

MOST TEST APPEARANCES

	M	Eng	SAf	WI	NZ	Ind	Pak	SL	Zim	Ban
S. R. Waugh	168	46	16	32	23	18	20	8	3	2
A. R. Border	156	47	6	31	23	20	22	7	0	0
M. E. Waugh	128	29	18	28	14	14	15	9	1	0
S. K. Warne	123	26	18	16	20	14	15	13	1	0
I. A. Healy	119	33	12	28	11	9	14	11	1	0
G. D. McGrath	109	22	14	20	14	11	17	8	1	2
D. C. Boon	107	31	6	22	17	11	11	9	0	0
M. A. Taylor	104	33	11	20	11	9	12	8	0	0

MOST TEST APPEARANCES AGAINST AUSTRALIA

M. C. Cowdrey (England) 44
G. A. Gooch (England) 42
D. I. Gower (England) 42
J. B. Hobbs (England) 41
W. Rhodes (England) 41
G. Boycott (England) 39
C. A. Walsh (West Indies) 38
I. T. Botham (England) 36
R. G. D. Willis (England) 36
A. C. MacLaren (England) 35

YOUNGEST PLAYERS ON DEBUT

Years	Days			
17	239	I. D. Craig	v South Africa at Sydney	1952-53
18	232	T. W. Garrett	v England at Melbourne	1876-77
19	54	A. Cotter	v England at Sydney	1903-04

19	96	C. Hill .... v England at Lord's	1896
19	100	G. R. Hazlitt .... v England at Sydney	1907-08
19	104	R. G. Archer .... v South Africa at Melbourne	1952-53
19	107	R. N. Harvey .... v India at Adelaide	1947-48
19	149	A. Jackson .... v England at Adelaide	1928-29
19	173	J. T. Cottam .... v England at Sydney	1886-87
19	252	J. J. Ferris .... v England at Sydney	1886-87
19	252	C. J. McDermott ..... v West Indies at Melbourne	1984-85
19	331	S. J. McCabe .... v England at Nottingham	1930
19	354	K. D. Walters .... v England at Brisbane	1965-66
19	363	G. D. McKenzie ..... v England at Lord's	1961

OLDEST PLAYERS ON DEBUT

Years	Days		
46	253	D. D. Blackie .... v England at Sydney	1928-29
46	237	H. Ironmonger .... v England at Brisbane (Ex)	1928-29
38	328	N. F. D. Thomson .... v England at Melbourne	1876-77
38	35	R. G. Holland .... v West Indies at Brisbane	1984-85
37	290	E. J. Gregory .... v England at Melbourne	1876-77
37	184	H. S. B. Love .... v England at Brisbane	1932-33
37	163	J. Harry .... v England at Adelaide	1894-95
37	154	R. K. Oxenham .... v England at Melbourne	1928-29
36	148	A. J. Richardson ..... v England at Sydney	1924-25

OLDEST PLAYERS

Years	Days		
50	327	H. Ironmonger .... v England at Sydney	1932-33
46	309	D. D. Blackie .... v England at Adelaide	1928-29
44	69	C. V. Grimmett ...... v South Africa at Durban (Kingsmead)	1935-36
43	259	H. Carter .... v South Africa at Cape Town	1921-22
43	255	W. Bardsley .... v England at The Oval	1926
42	224	C. Kelleway .... v England at Brisbane (Ex)	1928-29
42	130	S. E. Gregory .... v England at The Oval	1912
42	86	W. W. Armstrong ..... v England at The Oval	1921
42	74	W. A. S. Oldfield ..... v England at Melbourne	1936-37
41	178	V. Y. Richardson ..... v South Africa at Durban (Kingsmead)	1935-36
40	227	A. A. Mailey .... v England at The Oval	1926
40	223	J. M. Blackham ...... v England at Sydney	1894-95
40	127	R. K. Oxenham ...... v South Africa at Brisbane	1931-32
40	100	W. J. O'Reilly .... v New Zealand at Wellington	1945-46
40	52	C. G. Macartney ..... v England at The Oval	1926

UMPIRES

MOST APPEARANCES BY AUSTRALIAN UMPIRES

D. B. Hair	64	1995-96	to	
D. J. Harper	51	1998-99	to	
S. G. Randell	36	1990-91	to	1997-98
A. R. Crafter	33	1978-79	to	1981-82
R. M. Crockett	32	1903-04	to	1907-08
J. Phillips	29	1895-96	to	1905-06
C. J. Egar	29	1962-63	to	1968-69
R. C. Bailhache	27	1974-75	to	1988-89
L. P. Rowan	26	1962-63	to	1968-69
T. F. Brooks	24	1970-71	to	1975-76
S. J. A. Taufel	24	2000-01	to	

CAPTAINCY

THE CAPTAINS

		M	W	L	D	T	% Won
1	D. W. Gregory	3	2	1	0	0	66.66
2	W. L. Murdoch	16	5	7	4	0	31.25
3	T. P. Horan	2	0	2	0	0	0.00
4	H. H. Massie	1	1	0	0	0	100.00
5	J. M. Blackham	8	3	3	2	0	37.50
6	H. J. H. Scott	3	0	3	0	0	0.00
7	P. S. McDonnell	6	1	5	0	0	16.66
8	G. Giffen	4	2	2	0	0	50.00
9	G. H. S. Trott	8	5	3	0	0	62.50
10	J. Darling	21	7	4	10	0	33.33
11	H. Trumble	2	2	0	0	0	100.00
12	M. A. Noble	15	8	5	2	0	53.33
13	C. Hill	10	5	5	0	0	50.00
14	E. S. Gregory	6	2	1	3	0	33.33
15	W. W. Armstrong	10	8	0	2	0	80.00
16	H. L. Collins	11	5	2	4	0	45.45
17	W. Bardsley	2	0	0	2	0	0.00
18	J. Ryder	5	1	4	0	0	20.00
19	W. M. Woodfull	25	14	7	4	0	56.00
20	V. Y. Richardson	5	4	0	1	0	80.00
21	D. G. Bradman	24	15	3	6	0	62.50
22	W. A. Brown	1	1	0	0	0	100.00
23	A. L. Hassett	24	14	4	6	0	58.33
24	A. R. Morris	2	0	2	0	0	0.00
25	I. W. G. Johnson	17	7	5	5	0	41.17
26	R. R. Lindwall	1	0	0	1	0	0.00
27	I. D. Craig	5	3	0	2	0	60.00
28	R. Benaud	28	12	4	11	1	42.85
29	R. N. Harvey	1	1	0	0	0	100.00
30	R. B. Simpson	39	12	12	15	0	30.76
31	B. C. Booth	2	0	1	1	0	0.00
32	W. M. Lawry	26	9	8	9	0	34.61
33	B. N. Jarman	1	0	0	1	0	0.00
34	I. M. Chappell	30	15	5	10	0	50.00
35	G. S. Chappell	48	21	13	14	0	43.75
36	G. N. Yallop	7	1	6	0	0	14.28
37	K. J. Hughes	28	4	13	11	0	14.28
38	A. R. Border	93	32	22	38	1	34.40
39	M. A. Taylor	50	26	13	11	0	52.00
40	S. R. Waugh	57	41	9	7	0	71.92
41	A. C. Gilchrist	6	4	1	1	0	66.66
42	R. T. Ponting	13	10	1	2	0	76.92

SUMMARY OF AUSTRALIAN TEST CRICKET

Note: The Third Test at the Melbourne Cricket Ground from December 31, 1970, to January 5, 1971, has been sanctioned by Cricket Australia as an official Test match. In consultation with the MCC tour management, the Test was declared a 'DRAW'. This decision was determined as the two teams had been officially announced, including the 12th men, and the toss had been made. The umpires were walking out to the ground when rain began to fall, thus preventing any further play in the match.

Opponent	First Test	Tests	Won	Lost	Drawn	Tied	%Won
England	Mar 15, 1877	307	125	95	87	0	40.71
South Africa	Oct 11, 1902	71	39	15	17	0	54.49
West Indies	Dec 12, 1930	99	45	32	21	1	45.45
New Zealand	Mar 29, 1946	46	22	7	17	0	47.82
India	Nov 28, 1947	68	32	15	20	1	47.05
Pakistan	Oct 11, 1956	52	24	11	17	0	46.15
Sri Lanka	Apr 22, 1983	18	11	1	6	0	61.11
Zimbabwe	Oct 14, 1999	3	3	0	0	0	100.00
Bangladesh	Jly 18, 2003	2	2	0	0	0	100.00
Total		666	303	176	185	2	45.49

TEST MATCHES

Venue	Opponent	Result for Australia	Captain	Test/Opp
1876-77 in Australia				
Melbourne	England	Won by 45 runs	D. W. Gregory	1/1
Melbourne	England	Lost by four wickets	D. W. Gregory	2/2
1878-79 in Australia				
Melbourne	England	Won by 10 wickets	D. W. Gregory	3/3
Venue	Opponent	Result for Australia	Captain	Test/Opp
1880 in England				
The Oval	England	Lost by five wickets	W. L. Murdoch	4/4
1881-82 in Australia				
Melbourne	England	Drawn	W. L. Murdoch	5/5
Sydney	England	Won by five wickets	W. L. Murdoch	6/6
Sydney	England	Won by six wickets	W. L. Murdoch	7/7
Melbourne	England	Drawn	W. L. Murdoch	8/8
1882 in England				
The Oval	England	Won by seven runs	W. L. Murdoch	9/9
1882-83 in Australia				
Melbourne	England	Won by nine wickets	W. L. Murdoch	10/10
Melbourne	England	Lost by an innings and 27 runs	W. L. Murdoch	11/11
Sydney	England	Lost by 69 runs	W. L. Murdoch	12/12
Sydney	England	Won by four wickets	W. L. Murdoch	13/13
1884 in England				
Manchester	England	Drawn	W. L. Murdoch	14/14
Lord's	England	Lost by an innings and five runs	W. L. Murdoch	15/15
The Oval	England	Drawn	W. L. Murdoch	16/16
1884-85 in Australia				
Adelaide	England	Lost by eight wickets	W. L. Murdoch	17/17
Melbourne	England	Lost by 10 wickets	T. P. Horan	18/18
Sydney	England	Won by six runs	H. H. Massie	19/19
Sydney	England	Won by eight wickets	J. M. Blackham	20/20
Melbourne	England	Lost by an innings and 98 runs	T. P. Horan	21/21

Venue	Opponent	Result for Australia	Captain	Test/Opp
1886 in England				
Manchester	England	Lost by four wickets	H. J. H. Scott	22/22
Lord's	England	Lost by an innings and 106 runs	H. J. H. Scott	23/23
The Oval	England	Lost by an innings and 217 runs	H. J. H. Scott	24/24
1886-87 in Australia				
Sydney	England	Lost by 13 runs	P. S. McDonnell	25/25
Sydney	England	Lost by 71 runs	P. S. McDonnell	26/26
1887-88 in Australia				
Sydney	England	Lost by 126 runs	P. S. McDonnell	27/27
1888 in England				
Lord's	England	Won by 61 runs	P. S. McDonnell	28/28
The Oval	England	Lost by an innings and 137 runs	P. S. McDonnell	29/29
Manchester	England	Lost by an innings and 21 runs	P. S. McDonnell	30/30
1890 in England				
Lord's	England	Lost by seven wickets	W. L. Murdoch	31/31
The Oval	England	Lost by two wickets	W. L. Murdoch	32/32
1891-92 in Australia				
Melbourne	England	Won by 54 runs	J. M. Blackham	33/33
Sydney	England	Won by 72 runs	J. M. Blackham	34/34
Adelaide	England	Lost by an innings and 230 runs	J. M. Blackham	35/35
1893 in England				
Lord's	England	Drawn	J. M. Blackham	36/36
The Oval	England	Lost by an innings and 43 runs	J. M. Blackham	37/37
Manchester	England	Drawn	J. M. Blackham	38/38
1894-95 in Australia				
Sydney	England	Lost by 10 runs	J. M. Blackham	39/39
Melbourne	England	Lost by 94 runs	G. Giffen	40/40
Adelaide	England	Won by 382 runs	G. Giffen	41/41
Sydney	England	Won by an innings and 147 runs	G. Giffen	42/42
Melbourne	England	Lost by six wickets	G. Giffen	43/43
1896 in England				
Lord's	England	Lost by six wickets	G. H. S. Trott	44/44
Manchester	England	Won by three wickets	G. H. S. Trott	45/45
The Oval	England	Lost by 66 runs	G. H. S. Trott	46/46
1897-98 in Australia				
Sydney	England	Lost by nine wickets	G. H. S. Trott	47/47
Melbourne	England	Won by an innings and 55 runs	G. H. S. Trott	48/48
Adelaide	England	Won by an innings and 13 runs	G. H. S. Trott	49/49
Melbourne	England	Won by eight wickets	G. H. S. Trott	50/50
Sydney	England	Won by six wickets	G. H. S. Trott	51/51
1899 in England				
Nottingham	England	Drawn	J. Darling	52/52
Lord's	England	Won by 10 wickets	J. Darling	53/53
Leeds	England	Drawn	J. Darling	54/54
Manchester	England	Drawn	J. Darling	55/55
The Oval	England	Drawn	J. Darling	56/56
1901-02 in Australia				
Sydney	England	Lost by an innings and 124 runs	J. Darling	57/57
Melbourne	England	Won by 229 runs	J. Darling	58/58
Adelaide	England	Won by four wickets	J. Darling	59/59
Sydney	England	Won by seven wickets	H. Trumble	60/60
Melbourne	England	Won by 32 runs	H. Trumble	61/61
1902 in England				
Birmingham	England	Drawn	J. Darling	62/62
Lord's	England	Drawn	J. Darling	63/63
Sheffield	England	Won by 143 runs	J. Darling	64/64

Venue	Opponent	Result for Australia	Captain	Test/Opp
Manchester	England	Won by three runs	J. Darling	65/65
The Oval	England	Lost by one wicket	J. Darling	66/66

1902-03 in South Africa

Johannesburg (OW)	South Africa	Drawn	J. Darling	67/1
Johannesburg (OW)	South Africa	Won by 159 runs	J. Darling	68/2
Cape Town	South Africa	Won by 10 wickets	J. Darling	69/3

1903-04 in Australia

Sydney	England	Lost by five wickets	M. A. Noble	70/67
Melbourne	England	Lost by 185 runs	M. A. Noble	71/68
Adelaide	England	Won by 216 runs	M. A. Noble	72/69
Sydney	England	Lost by 157 runs	M. A. Noble	73/70
Melbourne	England	Won by 218 runs	M. A. Noble	74/71

1905 in England

Nottingham	England	Lost by 213 runs	J. Darling	75/72
Lord's	England	Drawn	J. Darling	76/73
Leeds	England	Drawn	J. Darling	77/74
Manchester	England	Lost by an innings and 80 runs	J. Darling	78/75
The Oval	England	Drawn	J. Darling	79/76

1907-08 in Australia

Sydney	England	Won by two wickets	M. A. Noble	80/77
Melbourne	England	Lost by one wicket	M. A. Noble	81/78
Adelaide	England	Won by 245 runs	M. A. Noble	82/79
Melbourne	England	Won by 308 runs	M. A. Noble	83/80
Sydney	England	Won by 49 runs	M. A. Noble	84/81

1909 in England

Birmingham	England	Lost by 10 wickets	M. A. Noble	85/82
Lord's	England	Won by nine wickets	M. A. Noble	86/83
Leeds	England	Won by 126 runs	M. A. Noble	87/84
Manchester	England	Drawn	M. A. Noble	88/85
The Oval	England	Drawn	M. A. Noble	89/86

1910-11 in Australia

Sydney	South Africa	Won by an innings and 114 runs	C. Hill	90/4
Melbourne	South Africa	Won by 89 runs	C. Hill	91/5
Adelaide	South Africa	Lost by 38 runs	C. Hill	92/6
Melbourne	South Africa	Won by 530 runs	C. Hill	93/7
Sydney	South Africa	Won by seven wickets	C. Hill	94/8

1911-12 in Australia

Sydney	England	Won by 146 runs	C. Hill	95/87
Melbourne	England	Lost by eight wickets	C. Hill	96/88
Adelaide	England	Lost by seven wickets	C. Hill	97/89
Melbourne	England	Lost by an innings and 225 runs	C. Hill	98/90
Sydney	England	Lost by 70 runs	C. Hill	99/91

1912 in England

Manchester	South Africa	Won by an innings and 88 runs	S. E. Gregory	100/9
Lord's	England	Drawn	S. E. Gregory	101/92
Lord's	South Africa	Won by 10 wickets	S. E. Gregory	102/10
Manchester	England	Drawn	S. E. Gregory	103/93
Nottingham	South Africa	Drawn	S. E. Gregory	104/11
The Oval	England	Lost by 244 runs	S. E. Gregory	105/94

1920-21 in Australia

Sydney	England	Won by 377 runs	W. W. Armstrong	106/95
Melbourne	England	Won by an innings and 91 runs	W. W. Armstrong	107/96
Adelaide	England	Won by 119 runs	W. W. Armstrong	108/97
Melbourne	England	Won by eight wickets	W. W. Armstrong	109/98
Sydney	England	Won by nine wickets	W. W. Armstrong	110/99

Venue	Opponent	Result for Australia	Captain	Test/Opp
1921 in England				
Nottingham	England	Won by 10 wickets	W. W. Armstrong	111/100
Lord's	England	Won by eight wickets	W. W. Armstrong	112/101
Leeds	England	Won by 219 runs	W. W. Armstrong	113/102
Manchester	England	Drawn	W. W. Armstrong	114/103
The Oval	England	Drawn	W. W. Armstrong	115/104
1921-22 in South Africa				
Durban (Lord's)	South Africa	Drawn	H. L. Collins	116/12
Johannesburg (OW)	South Africa	Drawn	H. L. Collins	117/13
Cape Town	South Africa	Won by 10 wickets	H. L. Collins	118/14
1924-25 in Australia				
Sydney	England	Won by 193 runs	H. L. Collins	119/105
Melbourne	England	Won by 81 runs	H. L. Collins	120/106
Adelaide	England	Won by 11 runs	H. L. Collins	121/107
Melbourne	England	Lost by an innings and 29 runs	H. L. Collins	122/108
Sydney	England	Won by 307 runs	H. L. Collins	123/109
1926 in England				
Nottingham	England	Drawn	H. L. Collins	124/110
Lord's	England	Drawn	H. L. Collins	125/111
Leeds	England	Drawn	W. Bardsley	126/112
Manchester	England	Drawn	W. Bardsley	127/113
The Oval	England	Lost by 289 runs	H. L. Collins	128/114
1928-29 in Australia				
Brisbane (Ex)	England	Lost by 675 runs	J. Ryder	129/115
Sydney	England	Lost by eight wickets	J. Ryder	130/116
Melbourne	England	Lost by three wickets	J. Ryder	131/117
Adelaide	England	Lost by 12 runs	J. Ryder	132/118
Melbourne	England	Won by five wickets	J. Ryder	133/119 *Venue*
1930 in England				
Nottingham	England	Lost by 93 runs	W. M. Woodfull	134/120
Lord's	England	Won by seven wickets	W. M. Woodfull	135/121
Leeds	England	Drawn	W. M. Woodfull	136/122
Manchester	England	Drawn	W. M. Woodfull	137/123
The Oval	England	Won by an innings and 39 runs	W. M. Woodfull	138/124
1930-31 in Australia				
Adelaide	West Indies	Won by 10 wickets	W. M. Woodfull	139/1
Sydney	West Indies	Won by an innings and 172 runs	W. M. Woodfull	140/2
Brisbane (Ex)	West Indies	Won by an innings and 217 runs	W. M. Woodfull	141/3
Melbourne	West Indies	Won by an innings and 122 runs	W. M. Woodfull	142/4
Sydney	West Indies	Lost by 30 runs	W. M. Woodfull	143/5
1931-32 in Australia				
Brisbane	South Africa	Won by an innings and 163 runs	W. M. Woodfull	144/15
Sydney	South Africa	Won by an innings and 155 runs	W. M. Woodfull	145/16
Melbourne	South Africa	Won by 169 runs	W. M. Woodfull	146/17
Adelaide	South Africa	Won by 10 wickets	W. M. Woodfull	147/18
Melbourne	South Africa	Won by an innings and 72 runs	W. M. Woodfull	148/19
1932-33 in Australia				
Sydney	England	Lost by 10 wickets	W. M. Woodfull	149/125
Melbourne	England	Won by 111 runs	W. M. Woodfull	150/126
Adelaide	England	Lost by 338 runs	W. M. Woodfull	151/127
Brisbane	England	Lost by six wickets	W. M. Woodfull	152/128
Sydney	England	Lost by eight wickets	W. M. Woodfull	153/129
1934 in England				
Nottingham	England	Won by 238 runs	W. M. Woodfull	154/130
Lord's	England	Lost by an innings and 38 runs	W. M. Woodfull	155/131
Manchester	England	Drawn	W. M. Woodfull	156/132
Leeds	England	Drawn	W. M. Woodfull	157/133
The Oval	England	Won by 562 runs	W. M. Woodfull	158/134

Venue	Opponent	Result for Australia	Captain	Test/Opp
1935-36 in South Africa				
Durban (Kingsmead)	South Africa	Won by nine wickets	V. Y. Richardson	159/20
Johannesburg (OW)	South Africa	Drawn	V. Y. Richardson	160/21
Cape Town	South Africa	Won by an innings and 78 runs	V. Y. Richardson	161/22
Johannesburg (OW)	South Africa	Won by an innings and 184 runs	V. Y. Richardson	162/23
Durban (Kingsmead)	South Africa	Won by an innings and six runs	V. Y. Richardson	163/24
1936-37 in Australia				
Brisbane	England	Lost by 322 runs	D. G. Bradman	164/135
Sydney	England	Lost by an innings and 22 runs	D. G. Bradman	165/136
Melbourne	England	Won by 365 runs	D. G. Bradman	166/137
Adelaide	England	Won by 148 runs	D. G. Bradman	167/138
Melbourne	England	Won by an innings and 200 runs	D. G. Bradman	168/139
1938 in England				
Nottingham	England	Drawn	D. G. Bradman	169/140
Lord's	England	Drawn	D. G. Bradman	170/141
Leeds	England	Won by five wickets	D. G. Bradman	171/142
The Oval	England	Lost by an innings and 579 runs	D. G. Bradman	172/143
1945-46 in New Zealand				
Wellington	New Zealand	Won by an innings and 103 runs	W. A. Brown	173/1
1946-47 in Australia				
Brisbane	England	Won by an innings and 332 runs	D. G. Bradman	174/144
Sydney	England	Won by an innings and 33 runs	D. G. Bradman	175/145
Melbourne	England	Drawn	D. G. Bradman	176/146
Adelaide	England	Drawn	D. G. Bradman	177/147
Sydney	England	Won by five wickets	D. G. Bradman	178/148
1947-48 in Australia				
Brisbane	India	Won by an innings and 226 runs	D. G. Bradman	179/1
Sydney	India	Drawn	D. G. Bradman	180/2
Melbourne	India	Won by 233 runs	D. G. Bradman	181/3
Adelaide	India	Won by an innings and 16 runs	D. G. Bradman	182/4
Melbourne	India	Won by an innings and 177 runs	D. G. Bradman	183/5
1948 in England				
Nottingham	England	Won by eight wickets	D. G. Bradman	184/149
Lord's	England	Won by 409 runs	D. G. Bradman	185/150
Manchester	England	Drawn	D. G. Bradman	186/151
Leeds	England	Won by seven wickets	D. G. Bradman	187/152
The Oval	England	Won by an innings and 149 runs	D. G. Bradman	188/153
1949-50 in South Africa				
Johannesburg (EP)	South Africa	Won by an innings and 85 runs	A. L. Hassett	189/25
Cape Town	South Africa	Won by eight wickets	A. L. Hassett	190/26
Durban (Kingsmead)	South Africa	Won by five wickets	A. L. Hassett	191/27
Johannesburg (EP)	South Africa	Drawn	A. L. Hassett	192/28
Port Elizabeth	South Africa	Won by an innings and 259 runs	A. L. Hassett	193/29
1950-51 in Australia				
Brisbane	England	Won by 70 runs	A. L. Hassett	194/154
Melbourne	England	Won by 28 runs	A. L. Hassett	195/155
Sydney	England	Won by an innings and 13 runs	A. L. Hassett	196/156
Adelaide	England	Won by 274 runs	A. L. Hassett	197/157
Melbourne	England	Lost by eight wickets	A. L. Hassett	198/158
1951-52 in Australia				
Brisbane	West Indies	Won by three wickets	A. L. Hassett	199/6
Sydney	West Indies	Won by seven wickets	A. L. Hassett	200/7
Adelaide	West Indies	Lost by six wickets	A. R. Morris	201/8
Melbourne	West Indies	Won by one wicket	A. L. Hassett	202/9
Sydney	West Indies	Won by 202 runs	A. L. Hassett	203/10

Venue	Opponent	Result for Australia	Captain	Test/Opp
1952-53 in Australia				
Brisbane	South Africa	Won by 96 runs	A. L. Hassett	204/30
Melbourne	South Africa	Lost by 82 runs	A. L. Hassett	205/31
Sydney	South Africa	Won by an innings and 38 runs	A. L. Hassett	206/32
Adelaide	South Africa	Drawn	A. L. Hassett	207/33
Melbourne	South Africa	Lost by six wickets	A. L. Hassett	208/34
1953 in England				
Nottingham	England	Drawn	A. L. Hassett	209/159
Lord's	England	Drawn	A. L. Hassett	210/160
Manchester	England	Drawn	A. L. Hassett	211/161
Leeds	England	Drawn	A. L. Hassett	212/162
The Oval	England	Lost by eight wickets	A. L. Hassett	213/163
1954-55 in Australia				
Brisbane	England	Won by an innings and 154 runs	I. W. G. Johnson	214/164
Sydney	England	Lost by 38 runs	A. R. Morris	215/165
Melbourne	England	Lost by 128 runs	I. W. G. Johnson	216/166
Adelaide	England	Lost by five wickets	I. W. G. Johnson	217/167
Sydney	England	Drawn	I. W. G. Johnson	218/168
1954-55 in West Indies				
Kingston	West Indies	Won by nine wickets	I. W. G. Johnson	219/11
Port-of-Spain	West Indies	Drawn	I. W. G. Johnson	220/12
Georgetown	West Indies	Won by eight wickets	I. W. G. Johnson	221/13
Bridgetown	West Indies	Drawn	I. W. G. Johnson	222/14
Kingston	West Indies	Won by an innings and 82 runs	I. W. G. Johnson	**1956 in**
England				
Nottingham	England	Drawn	I. W. G. Johnson	224/169
Lord's	England	Won by 185 runs	I. W. G. Johnson	225/170
Leeds	England	Lost by an innings and 42 runs	I. W. G. Johnson	226/171
Manchester	England	Lost by an innings and 170 runs	I. W. G. Johnson	227/172
The Oval	England	Drawn	I. W. G. Johnson	228/173
1956-57 in Pakistan				
Karachi	Pakistan	Lost by nine wickets	I. W. G. Johnson	229/1
1956-57 in India				
Madras (Corp)	India	Won by an innings and five runs	I. W. G. Johnson	230/6
Bombay (BS)	India	Drawn	R. R. Lindwall	231/7
Calcutta	India	Won by 94 runs	I. W. G. Johnson	232/8
1957-58 in South Africa				
Johannesburg (WS)	South Africa	Drawn	I. D. Craig	233/35
Cape Town	South Africa	Won by an innings and 141 runs	I. D. Craig	234/36
Durban (Kingsmead)	South Africa	Drawn	I. D. Craig	235/37
Johannesburg (WS)	South Africa	Won by 10 wickets	I. D. Craig	236/38
Port Elizabeth	South Africa	Won by eight wickets	I. D. Craig	237/39
1958-59 in Australia				
Brisbane	England	Won by eight wickets	R. Benaud	238/174
Melbourne	England	Won by eight wickets	R. Benaud	239/175
Sydney	England	Drawn	R. Benaud	240/176
Adelaide	England	Won by 10 wickets	R. Benaud	241/177
Melbourne	England	Won by nine wickets	R. Benaud	242/178
1959-60 in Pakistan				
Dacca	Pakistan	Won by eight wickets	R. Benaud	243/2
Lahore	Pakistan	Won by seven wickets	R. Benaud	244/3
Karachi	Pakistan	Drawn	R. Benaud	245/4

Venue	Opponent	Result for Australia	Captain	Test/Opp
1959-60 in India				
Delhi	India	Won by an innings and 127 runs	R. Benaud	246/9
Kanpur	India	Lost by 119 runs	R. Benaud	247/10
Bombay (BS)	India	Drawn	R. Benaud	248/11
Madras (Corp)	India	Won by an innings and 55 runs	R. Benaud	249/12
Calcutta	India	Drawn	R. Benaud	250/13
1960-61 in Australia				
Brisbane	West Indies	Tied	R. Benaud	251/16
Melbourne	West Indies	Won by seven wickets	R. Benaud	252/17
Sydney	West Indies	Lost by 222 runs	R. Benaud	253/18
Adelaide	West Indies	Drawn	R. Benaud	254/19
Melbourne	West Indies	Won by two wickets	R. Benaud	255/20
1961 in England				
Birmingham	England	Drawn	R. Benaud	256/179
Lord's	England	Won by five wickets	R. N. Harvey	257/180
Leeds	England	Lost by eight wickets	R. Benaud	258/181
Manchester	England	Won by 54 runs	R. Benaud	259/182
The Oval	England	Drawn	R. Benaud	260/183
1962-63 in Australia				
Brisbane	England	Drawn	R. Benaud	261/184
Melbourne	England	Lost by seven wickets	R. Benaud	262/185
Sydney	England	Won by eight wickets	R. Benaud	263/186
Adelaide	England	Drawn	R. Benaud	264/187
Sydney	England	Drawn	R. Benaud	265/188
1963-64 in Australia				
Brisbane	South Africa	Drawn	R. Benaud	266/40
Melbourne	South Africa	Won by eight wickets	R. B. Simpson	267/41
Sydney	South Africa	Drawn	R. B. Simpson	268/42
Adelaide	South Africa	Lost by 10 wickets	R. B. Simpson	269/43
Sydney	South Africa	Drawn	R. B. Simpson	270/44
1964 in England				
Nottingham	England	Drawn	R. B. Simpson	271/189
Lord's	England	Drawn	R. B. Simpson	272/190
Leeds	England	Won by seven wickets	R. B. Simpson	273/191
Manchester	England	Drawn	R. B. Simpson	274/192
The Oval	England	Drawn	R. B. Simpson	275/193
1964-65 in India				
Madras (Corp)	India	Won by 139 runs	R. B. Simpson	276/14
Bombay (BS)	India	Lost by two wickets	R. B. Simpson	277/15
Calcutta	India	Drawn	R. B. Simpson	278/16
1964-65 in Pakistan				
Karachi	Pakistan	Drawn	R. B. Simpson	279/5
1964-65 in Australia				
Melbourne	Pakistan	Drawn	R. B. Simpson	280/6
1964-65 in West Indies				
Kingston	West Indies	Lost by 179 runs	R. B. Simpson	281/21
Port-of-Spain	West Indies	Drawn	R. B. Simpson	282/22
Georgetown	West Indies	Lost by 212 runs	R. B. Simpson	283/23
Bridgetown	West Indies	Drawn	R. B. Simpson	284/24
Port-of-Spain	West Indies	Won by 10 wickets	R. B. Simpson	285/25
1965-66 in Australia				
Brisbane	England	Drawn	B. C. Booth	286/194
Melbourne	England	Drawn	B. C. Booth	287/195
Sydney	England	Lost by an innings and 93 runs	B. C. Booth	288/196
Adelaide	England	Won by an innings and nine runs	R. B. Simpson	289/197
Melbourne	England	Drawn	R. B. Simpson	290/198

Venue	Opponent	Result for Australia	Captain	Test/Opp
1966-67 in South Africa				
Johannesburg (WS)	South Africa	Lost by 233 runs	R. B. Simpson	291/45
Cape Town	South Africa	Won by six wickets	R. B. Simpson	292/46
Durban (Kingsmead)	South Africa	Lost by eight wickets	R. B. Simpson	293/47
Johannesburg (WS)	South Africa	Drawn	R. B. Simpson	294/48
Port Elizabeth	South Africa	Lost by seven wickets	R. B. Simpson	295/49
1967-68 in Australia				
Adelaide	India	Won by 146 runs	R. B. Simpson	296/17
Melbourne	India	Won by an innings and four runs	R. B. Simpson	297/18
Brisbane	India	Won by 39 runs	W. M. Lawry	298/19
Sydney	India	Won by 144 runs	W. M. Lawry	299/20
1968 in England				
Manchester	England	Won by 159 runs	W. M. Lawry	300/199
Lord's	England	Drawn	W. M. Lawry	301/200
Birmingham	England	Drawn	W. M. Lawry	302/201
Leeds	England	Drawn	B. N. Jarman	303/202
The Oval	England	Lost by 226 runs	W. M. Lawry	304/203
1968-69 in Australia				
Brisbane	West Indies	Lost by 125 runs	W. M. Lawry	305/26
Melbourne	West Indies	Won by an innings and 30 runs	W. M. Lawry	306/27
Sydney	West Indies	Won by 10 wickets	W. M. Lawry	307/28
Adelaide	West Indies	Drawn	W. M. Lawry	308/29
Sydney	West Indies	Won by 382 runs	W. M. Lawry	309/30
1969-70 in India				
Bombay (BS)	India	Won by eight wickets	W. M. Lawry	310/21
Kanpur	India	Drawn	W. M. Lawry	311/22
Delhi	India	Lost by seven wickets	W. M. Lawry	312/23
Calcutta	India	Won by 10 wickets	W. M. Lawry	313/24
Madras (Chepauk)	India	Won by 77 runs	W. M. Lawry	314/25
1969-70 in South Africa				
Cape Town	South Africa	Lost by 170 runs	W. M. Lawry	315/50
Durban (Kingsmead)	South Africa	Lost by an innings and 129 runs	W. M. Lawry	316/51
Johannesburg (WS)	South Africa	Lost by 307 runs	W. M. Lawry	317/52
Port Elizabeth	South Africa	Lost by 323 runs	W. M. Lawry	318/53
1970-71 in Australia				
Brisbane	England	Drawn	W. M. Lawry	319/204
Perth	England	Drawn	W. M. Lawry	320/205
Melbourne	England	Drawn	W. M. Lawry	321/206
Sydney	England	Lost by 299 runs	W. M. Lawry	322/207
Melbourne	England	Drawn	W. M. Lawry	323/208
Adelaide	England	Drawn	W. M. Lawry	324/209
Sydney	England	Lost by 62 runs	I. M. Chappell	325/210
1972 in England				
Manchester	England	Lost by 89 runs	I. M. Chappell	326/211
Lord's	England	Won by eight wickets	I. M. Chappell	327/212
Nottingham	England	Drawn	I. M. Chappell	328/213
Leeds	England	Lost by nine wickets	I. M. Chappell	329/214
The Oval	England	Won by five wickets	I. M. Chappell	330/215
1972-73 in Australia				
Adelaide	Pakistan	Won by an innings and 114 runs	I. M. Chappell	331/7
Melbourne	Pakistan	Won by 92 runs	I. M. Chappell	332/8
Sydney	Pakistan	Won by 52 runs	I. M. Chappell	333/9
1972-73 in West Indies				
Kingston	West Indies	Drawn	I. M. Chappell	334/31
Bridgetown	West Indies	Drawn	I. M. Chappell	335/32
Port-of-Spain	West Indies	Won by 44 runs	I. M. Chappell	336/33
Georgetown	West Indies	Won by 10 wickets	I. M. Chappell	337/34
Port-of-Spain	West Indies	Drawn	I. M. Chappell	338/35

Venue	Opponent	Result for Australia	Captain	Test/Opp
1973-74 in Australia				
Melbourne	New Zealand	Won by an innings and 25 runs	I. M. Chappell	339/2
Sydney	New Zealand	Drawn	I. M. Chappell	340/3
Adelaide	New Zealand	Won by an innings and 57 runs	I. M. Chappell	341/4
1973-74 in New Zealand				
Wellington	New Zealand	Drawn	I. M. Chappell	342/5
Christchurch	New Zealand	Lost by five wickets	I. M. Chappell	343/6
Auckland	New Zealand	Won by 297 runs	I. M. Chappell	344/7
1974-75 in Australia				
Brisbane	England	Won by 166 runs	I. M. Chappell	345/216
Perth	England	Won by nine wickets	I. M. Chappell	346/217
Melbourne	England	Drawn	I. M. Chappell	347/218
Sydney	England	Won by 171 runs	I. M. Chappell	348/219
Adelaide	England	Won by 163 runs	I. M. Chappell	349/220
Melbourne	England	Lost by an innings and four runs	I. M. Chappell	350/221
1975 in England				
Birmingham	England	Won by an innings and 85 runs	I. M. Chappell	351/222
Lord's	England	Drawn	I. M. Chappell	352/223
Leeds	England	Drawn	I. M. Chappell	353/224
The Oval	England	Drawn	I. M. Chappell	354/225
1975-76 in Australia				
Brisbane	West Indies	Won by eight wickets	G. S. Chappell	355/36
Perth	West Indies	Lost by an innings and 87 runs	G. S. Chappell	356/37
Melbourne	West Indies	Won by eight wickets	G. S. Chappell	357/38
Sydney	West Indies	Won by seven wickets	G. S. Chappell	358/39
Adelaide	West Indies	Won by 190 runs	G. S. Chappell	359/40
Melbourne	West Indies	Won by 165 runs	G. S. Chappell	360/41
1976-77 in Australia				
Adelaide	Pakistan	Drawn	G. S. Chappell	361/10
Melbourne	Pakistan	Won by 348 runs	G. S. Chappell	362/11
Sydney	Pakistan	Lost by eight wickets	G. S. Chappell	363/12
1976-77 in New Zealand				
Christchurch	New Zealand	Drawn	G. S. Chappell	364/8
Auckland	New Zealand	Won by 10 wickets	G. S. Chappell	365/9
1976-77 in Australia				
Melbourne	England	Won by 45 runs	G. S. Chappell	366/226
1977 in England				
Lord's	England	Drawn	G. S. Chappell	367/227
Manchester	England	Lost by nine wickets	G. S. Chappell	368/228
Nottingham	England	Lost by seven wickets	G. S. Chappell	369/229
Leeds	England	Lost by an innings and 85 runs	G. S. Chappell	370/230
The Oval	England	Drawn	G. S. Chappell	371/231
1977-78 in Australia				
Brisbane	India	Won by 16 runs	R. B. Simpson	372/26
Perth	India	Won by two wickets	R. B. Simpson	373/27
Melbourne	India	Lost by 222 runs	R. B. Simpson	374/28
Sydney	India	Lost by an innings and two runs	R. B. Simpson	375/29
Adelaide	India	Won by 47 runs	R. B. Simpson	376/30
1977-78 in West Indies				
Port-of-Spain	West Indies	Lost by an innings and 106 runs	R. B. Simpson	377/42
Bridgetown	West Indies	Lost by nine wickets	R. B. Simpson	378/43
Georgetown	West Indies	Won by three wickets	R. B. Simpson	379/44
Port-of-Spain	West Indies	Lost by 198 runs	R. B. Simpson	380/45
Kingston	West Indies	Drawn	R. B. Simpson	381/46

Venue	Opponent	Result for Australia	Captain	Test/Opp
1978-79 in Australia				
Brisbane	England	Lost by seven wickets	G. N. Yallop	382/232
Perth	England	Lost by 166 runs	G. N. Yallop	383/233
Melbourne	England	Won by 103 runs	G. N. Yallop	384/234
Sydney	England	Lost by 93 runs	G. N. Yallop	385/235
Adelaide	England	Lost by 205 runs	G. N. Yallop	386/236
Sydney	England	Lost by nine wickets	G. N. Yallop	387/237
Melbourne	Pakistan	Lost by 71 runs	G. N. Yallop	388/13
Perth	Pakistan	Won by seven wickets	K. J. Hughes	389/14
1979-80 in India				
Madras (Chepauk)	India	Drawn	K. J. Hughes	390/31
Bangalore	India	Drawn	K. J. Hughes	391/32
Kanpur	India	Lost by 153 runs	K. J. Hughes	392/33
Delhi	India	Drawn	K. J. Hughes	393/34
Calcutta	India	Drawn	K. J. Hughes	394/35
Bombay (WS)	India	Lost by an innings and 100 runs	K. J. Hughes	395/36
1979-80 in Australia				
Brisbane	West Indies	Drawn	G. S. Chappell	396/47
Perth	England	Won by 138 runs	G. S. Chappell	397/238
Melbourne	West Indies	Lost by 10 wickets	G. S. Chappell	398/48
Sydney	England	Won by six wickets	G. S. Chappell	399/239
Adelaide	West Indies	Lost by 408 runs	G. S. Chappell	400/49
Melbourne	England	Won by eight wickets	G. S. Chappell	401/240
1979-80 in Pakistan				
Karachi	Pakistan	Lost by seven wickets	G. S. Chappell	402/15
Faisalabad	Pakistan	Drawn	G. S. Chappell	403/16
Lahore	Pakistan	Drawn	G. S. Chappell	404/17
1980 in England				
Lord's	England	Drawn	G. S. Chappell	405/241
1980-81 in Australia				
Brisbane	New Zealand	Won by 10 wickets	G. S. Chappell	406/10
Perth	New Zealand	Won by eight wickets	G. S. Chappell	407/11
Melbourne	New Zealand	Drawn	G. S. Chappell	408/12
Sydney	India	Won by an innings and four runs	G. S. Chappell	409/37
Adelaide	India	Drawn	G. S. Chappell	410/38
Melbourne	India	Lost by 59 runs	G. S. Chappell	411/39
1981 in England				
Nottingham	England	Won by four wickets	K. J. Hughes	412/242
Lord's	England	Drawn	K. J. Hughes	413/243
Leeds	England	Lost by 18 runs	K. J. Hughes	414/244
Birmingham	England	Lost by 29 runs	K. J. Hughes	415/245
Manchester	England	Lost by 103 runs	K. J. Hughes	416/246
The Oval	England	Drawn	K. J. Hughes	417/247
1981-82 in Australia				
Perth	Pakistan	Won by 286 runs	G. S. Chappell	418/18
Brisbane	Pakistan	Won by 10 wickets	G. S. Chappell	419/19
Melbourne	Pakistan	Lost by an innings and 82 runs	G. S. Chappell	420/20
Melbourne	West Indies	Won by 58 runs	G. S. Chappell	421/50
Sydney	West Indies	Drawn	G. S. Chappell	422/51
Adelaide	West Indies	Lost by five wickets	G. S. Chappell	423/52
1981-82 in New Zealand				
Wellington	New Zealand	Drawn	G. S. Chappell	424/13
Auckland	New Zealand	Lost by five wickets	G. S. Chappell	425/14
Christchurch	New Zealand	Won by eight wickets	G. S. Chappell	426/15

Venue	*Opponent*	*Result for Australia*	*Captain*	*Test/Opp*
1982-83 in Pakistan				
Karachi	Pakistan	Lost by nine wickets	K. J. Hughes	427/21
Faisalabad	Pakistan	Lost by an innings and three runs	K. J. Hughes	428/22
Lahore	Pakistan	Lost by nine wickets	K. J. Hughes	429/23
1982-83 in Australia				
Perth	England	Drawn	G. S. Chappell	430/248
Brisbane	England	Won by seven wickets	G. S. Chappell	431/249
Adelaide	England	Won by eight wickets	G. S. Chappell	432/250
Melbourne	England	Lost by three runs	G. S. Chappell	433/251
Sydney	England	Drawn	G. S. Chappell	434/252
1982-83 in Sri Lanka				
Kandy	Sri Lanka	Won by an innings and 38 runs	G. S. Chappell	435/1
1983-84 in Australia				
Perth	Pakistan	Won by an innings and nine runs	K. J. Hughes	436/24
Brisbane	Pakistan	Drawn	K. J. Hughes	437/25
Adelaide	Pakistan	Drawn	K. J. Hughes	438/26
Melbourne	Pakistan	Drawn	K. J. Hughes	439/27
Sydney	Pakistan	Won by 10 wickets	K. J. Hughes	440/28
Venue	*Opponent*	*Result for Australia*	*Captain*	*Test/Opp*
1983-84 in West Indies				
Georgetown	West Indies	Drawn	K. J. Hughes	441/53
Port-of-Spain	West Indies	Drawn	K. J. Hughes	442/54
Bridgetown	West Indies	Lost by 10 wickets	K. J. Hughes	443/55
St John's	West Indies	Lost by an innings and 36 runs	K. J. Hughes	444/56
Kingston	West Indies	Lost by 10 wickets	K. J. Hughes	445/57
1984-85 in Australia				
Perth	West Indies	Lost by an innings and 112 runs	K. J. Hughes	446/58
Brisbane	West Indies	Lost by eight wickets	K. J. Hughes	447/59
Adelaide	West Indies	Lost by 191 runs	A. R. Border	448/60
Melbourne	West Indies	Drawn	A. R. Border	449/61
Sydney	West Indies	Won by an innings and 55 runs	A. R. Border	450/62
1985 in England				
Leeds	England	Lost by five wickets	A. R. Border	451/253
Lord's	England	Won by four wickets	A. R. Border	452/254
Nottingham	England	Drawn	A. R. Border	453/255
Manchester	England	Drawn	A. R. Border	454/256
Birmingham	England	Lost by an innings and 118 runs	A. R. Border	455/257
The Oval	England	Lost by an innings and 94 runs	A. R. Border	456/258
1985-86 in Australia				
Brisbane	New Zealand	Lost by an innings and 41 runs	A. R. Border	457/16
Sydney	New Zealand	Won by four wickets	A. R. Border	458/17
Perth	New Zealand	Lost by six wickets	A. R. Border	459/18
Adelaide	India	Drawn	A. R. Border	460/40
Melbourne	India	Drawn	A. R. Border	461/41
Sydney	India	Drawn	A. R. Border	462/42
1985-86 in New Zealand				
Wellington	New Zealand	Drawn	A. R. Border	463/19
Christchurch	New Zealand	Drawn	A. R. Border	464/20
Auckland	New Zealand	Lost by eight wickets	A. R. Border	465/21
1986-87 in India				
Madras (Chepauk)	India	Tied	A. R. Border	466/43
Delhi	India	Drawn	A. R. Border	467/44
Bombay (WS)	India	Drawn	A. R. Border	468/45

Venue	Opponent	Result for Australia	Captain	Test/Opp
1986-87 in Australia				
Brisbane	England	Lost by seven wickets	A. R. Border	469/259
Perth	England	Drawn	A. R. Border	470/260
Adelaide	England	Drawn	A. R. Border	471/261
Melbourne	England	Lost by an innings and 14 runs	A. R. Border	472/262
Sydney	England	Won by 55 runs	A. R. Border	473/263
1987-88 in Australia				
Brisbane	New Zealand	Won by nine wickets	A. R. Border	474/22
Adelaide	New Zealand	Drawn	A. R. Border	475/23
Melbourne	New Zealand	Drawn	A. R. Border	476/24
Sydney	England	Drawn	A. R. Border	477/264
Perth	Sri Lanka	Won by an innings and 108 runs	A. R. Border	478/2
1988-89 in Pakistan				
Karachi	Pakistan	Lost by an innings and 188 runs	A. R. Border	479/29
Faisalabad	Pakistan	Drawn	A. R. Border	480/30
Lahore	Pakistan	Drawn	A. R. Border	481/31
1988-89 in Australia				
Brisbane	West Indies	Lost by eight wickets	A. R. Border	482/63
Perth	West Indies	Lost by 169 runs	A. R. Border	483/64
Melbourne	West Indies	Lost by 285 runs	A. R. Border	484/65
Sydney	West Indies	Won by seven wickets	A. R. Border	485/66
Adelaide	West Indies	Drawn	A. R. Border	486/67
Venue	*Opponent*	*Result for Australia*	*Captain*	*Test/Opp*
1989 in England				
Leeds	England	Won by 210 runs	A. R. Border	487/265
Lord's	England	Won by six wickets	A. R. Border	488/266
Birmingham	England	Drawn	A. R. Border	489/267
Manchester	England	Won by nine wickets	A. R. Border	490/268
Nottingham	England	Won by an innings and 180 runs	A. R. Border	491/269
The Oval	England	Drawn	A. R. Border	492/270
1989-90 in Australia				
Perth	New Zealand	Drawn	A. R. Border	493/25
Brisbane	Sri Lanka	Drawn	A. R. Border	494/3
Hobart	Sri Lanka	Won by 173 runs	A. R. Border	495/4
Melbourne	Pakistan	Won by 92 runs	A. R. Border	496/32
Adelaide	Pakistan	Drawn	A. R. Border	497/33
Sydney	Pakistan	Drawn	A. R. Border	498/34
1989-90 in New Zealand				
Wellington	New Zealand	Lost by nine wickets	A. R. Border	499/26
1990-91 in Australia				
Brisbane	England	Won by 10 wickets	A. R. Border	500/271
Melbourne	England	Won by eight wickets	A. R. Border	501/272
Sydney	England	Drawn	A. R. Border	502/273
Adelaide	England	Drawn	A. R. Border	503/274
Perth	England	Won by nine wickets	A. R. Border	504/275
1990-91 in West Indies				
Kingston	West Indies	Drawn	A. R. Border	505/68
Georgetown	West Indies	Lost by 10 wickets	A. R. Border	506/69
Port-of-Spain	West Indies	Drawn	A. R. Border	507/70
Bridgetown	West Indies	Lost by 343 runs	A. R. Border	508/71
St John's	West Indies	Won by 157 runs	A. R. Border	509/72
1991-92 in Australia				
Brisbane	India	Won by 10 wickets	A. R. Border	510/46
Melbourne	India	Won by eight wickets	A. R. Border	511/47
Sydney	India	Drawn	A. R. Border	512/48
Adelaide	India	Won by 38 runs	A. R. Border	513/49
Perth	India	Won by 300 runs	A. R. Border	514/50

Venue	Opponent	Result for Australia	Captain	Test/Opp
1992-93 in Sri Lanka				
Colombo (SSC)	Sri Lanka	Won by 16 runs	A. R. Border	515/5
Colombo (PIS)	Sri Lanka	Drawn	A. R. Border	516/6
Moratuwa	Sri Lanka	Drawn	A. R. Border	517/7
1992-93 in Australia				
Brisbane	West Indies	Drawn	A. R. Border	518/73
Melbourne	West Indies	Won by 139 runs	A. R. Border	519/74
Sydney	West Indies	Drawn	A. R. Border	520/75
Adelaide	West Indies	Lost by one run	A. R. Border	521/76
Perth	West Indies	Lost by an innings and 25 runs	A. R. Border	522/77
1992-93 in New Zealand				
Christchurch	New Zealand	Won by an innings and 60 runs	A. R. Border	523/27
Wellington	New Zealand	Drawn	A. R. Border	524/28
Auckland	New Zealand	Lost by five wickets	A. R. Border	525/29
1993 in England				
Manchester	England	Won by 179 runs	A. R. Border	526/276
Lord's	England	Won by an innings and 62 runs	A. R. Border	527/277
Nottingham	England	Drawn	A. R. Border	528/278
Leeds	England	Won by an innings and 148 runs	A. R. Border	529/279
Birmingham	England	Won by eight wickets	A. R. Border	530/280
The Oval	England	Lost by 161 runs	A. R. Border	531/281
1993-94 in Australia				
Perth	New Zealand	Drawn	A. R. Border	532/30
Hobart	New Zealand	Won by an innings and 222 runs	A. R. Border	533/31
Brisbane	New Zealand	Won by an innings and 96 runs	A. R. Border	534/32
Melbourne	South Africa	Drawn	A. R. Border	535/54
Sydney	South Africa	Lost by five runs	A. R. Border	536/55
Adelaide	South Africa	Won by 191 runs	A. R. Border	537/56
1993-94 in South Africa				
Johannesburg (WS)	South Africa	Lost by 197 runs	A. R. Border	538/57
Cape Town	South Africa	Won by nine wickets	A. R. Border	539/58
Durban (Kingsmead)	South Africa	Drawn	A. R. Border	540/59
1994-95 in Pakistan				
Karachi	Pakistan	Lost by one wicket	M. A. Taylor	541/35
Rawalpindi	Pakistan	Drawn	M. A. Taylor	542/36
Lahore	Pakistan	Drawn	M. A. Taylor	543/37
1994-95 in Australia				
Brisbane	England	Won by 184 runs	M. A. Taylor	544/282
Melbourne	England	Won by 295 runs	M. A. Taylor	545/283
Sydney	England	Drawn	M. A. Taylor	546/284
Adelaide	England	Lost by 106 runs	M. A. Taylor	547/285
Perth	England	Won by 329 runs	M. A. Taylor	548/286
1994-95 in West Indies				
Bridgetown	West Indies	Won by 10 wickets	M. A. Taylor	549/78
St John's	West Indies	Drawn	M. A. Taylor	550/79
Port-of-Spain	West Indies	Lost by nine wickets	M. A. Taylor	551/80
Kingston	West Indies	Won by an innings and 53 runs	M. A. Taylor	552/81
1995-96 in Australia				
Brisbane	Pakistan	Won by an innings and 126 runs	M. A. Taylor	553/38
Hobart	Pakistan	Won by 155 runs	M. A. Taylor	554/39
Sydney	Pakistan	Lost by 74 runs	M. A. Taylor	555/40
Perth	Sri Lanka	Won by an innings and 36 runs	M. A. Taylor	556/8
Melbourne	Sri Lanka	Won by 10 wickets	M. A. Taylor	557/9
Adelaide	Sri Lanka	Won by 148 runs	M. A. Taylor	558/10

Venue	Opponent	Result for Australia	Captain	Test/Opp
1996-97 in India				
Delhi	India	Lost by seven wickets	M. A. Taylor	559/51
1996-97 in Australia				
Brisbane	West Indies	Won by 123 runs	M. A. Taylor	560/82
Sydney	West Indies	Won by 124 runs	M. A. Taylor	561/83
Melbourne	West Indies	Lost by six wickets	M. A. Taylor	562/84
Adelaide	West Indies	Won by an innings and 183 runs	M. A. Taylor	563/85
Perth	West Indies	Lost by 10 wickets	M. A. Taylor	564/86
1996-97 in South Africa				
Johannesburg (WS)	South Africa	Won by an innings and 196 runs	M. A. Taylor	565/60
Port Elizabeth	South Africa	Won by two wickets	M. A. Taylor	566/61
Centurion	South Africa	Lost by eight wickets	M. A. Taylor	567/62
1997 in England				
Birmingham	England	Lost by nine wickets	M. A. Taylor	568/287
Lord's	England	Drawn	M. A. Taylor	569/288
Manchester	England	Won by 268 runs	M. A. Taylor	570/289
Leeds	England	Won by an innings and 61 runs	M. A. Taylor	571/290
Nottingham	England	Won by 264 runs	M. A. Taylor	572/291
The Oval	England	Lost by 19 runs	M. A. Taylor	573/292
1997-98 in Australia				
Brisbane	New Zealand	Won by 186 runs	M. A. Taylor	574/33
Perth	New Zealand	Won by an innings and 70 runs	M. A. Taylor	575/34
Hobart	New Zealand	Drawn	M. A. Taylor	576/35
Melbourne	South Africa	Drawn	M. A. Taylor	577/63
Sydney	South Africa	Won by an innings and 21 runs	M. A. Taylor	578/64
Adelaide	South Africa	Drawn	M. A. Taylor	579/65
1997-98 in India				
Chennai (Chepauk)	India	Lost by 179 runs	M. A. Taylor	580/52
Calcutta	India	Lost by an innings and 219 runs	M. A. Taylor	581/53
Bangalore	India	Won by eight wickets	M. A. Taylor	582/54
1998-99 in Pakistan				
Rawalpindi	Pakistan	Won by an innings and 99 runs	M. A. Taylor	583/40
Peshawar	Pakistan	Drawn	M. A. Taylor	584/41
Karachi	Pakistan	Drawn	M. A. Taylor	585/42
1998-99 in Australia				
Brisbane	England	Drawn	M. A. Taylor	586/293
Perth	England	Won by seven wickets	M. A. Taylor	587/294
Adelaide	England	Won by 205 runs	M. A. Taylor	588/295
Melbourne	England	Lost by 12 runs	M. A. Taylor	589/296
Sydney	England	Won by 98 runs	M. A. Taylor	590/297
1998-99 in West Indies				
Port-of-Spain	West Indies	Won by 312 runs	S. R. Waugh	591/87
Kingston	West Indies	Lost by 10 wickets	S. R. Waugh	592/88
Bridgetown	West Indies	Lost by one wicket	S. R. Waugh	593/89
St John's	West Indies	Won by 176 runs	S. R. Waugh	594/90
1999-2000 in Sri Lanka				
Kandy	Sri Lanka	Lost by six wickets	S. R. Waugh	595/11
Galle	Sri Lanka	Drawn	S. R. Waugh	596/12
Colombo (SSC)	Sri Lanka	Drawn	S. R. Waugh	597/13
1999-2000 in Zimbabwe				
Harare	Zimbabwe	Won by 10 wickets	S. R. Waugh	598/1

Venue	*Opponent*	*Result for Australia*	*Captain*	*Test/Opp*
1999-2000 in Australia				
Brisbane	Pakistan	Won by 10 wickets	S.R. Waugh	599/44
Hobart (Bel)	Pakistan	Won by four wickets	S.R. Waugh	600/45
Perth	Pakistan	Won by an innings and 20 runs	S.R. Waugh	601/46
Adelaide	India	Won by 285 runs	S.R. Waugh	602/55
Melbourne	India	Won by 180 runs	S.R. Waugh	603/56
Sydney	India	Won by an innings and 141 runs	S.R. Waugh	604/57
1999-2000 in New Zealand				
Auckland	New Zealand	Won by 62 runs	S.R. Waugh	605/36
Wellington	New Zealand	Won by six wickets	S.R. Waugh	606/37
Hamilton	New Zealand	Won by six wickets	S.R. Waugh	607/38
2000-01 in Australia				
Brisbane	West Indies	Won by an innings and 126 runs	S.R. Waugh	608/91
Perth	West Indies	Won by an innings and 27 runs	S.R. Waugh	609/92
Adelaide	West Indies	Won by five wickets	A.C. Gilchrist	610/93
Melbourne	West Indies	Won by 352 runs	S.R. Waugh	611/94
Sydney	West Indies	Won by six wickets	S.R. Waugh	612/95
2000-01 in India				
Mumbai (WS)	India	Won by 10 wickets	S.R. Waugh	613/58
Kolkata	India	Lost by 171 runs	S.R. Waugh	614/59
Chennai (Chepauk)	India	Lost by two wickets	S.R. Waugh	615/60
2001 in England				
Birmingham	England	Won by an innings and 126 runs	S.R. Waugh	616/298
Lord's	England	Won by eight wickets	S.R. Waugh	617/299
Nottingham	England	Won by seven wickets	S.R. Waugh	618/300
Leeds	England	Lost by six wickets	A.C. Gilchrist	619/301
The Oval	England	Won by an innings and 25 runs	S.R. Waugh	620/302
2001-02 in Australia				
Brisbane	New Zealand	Drawn	S.R. Waugh	621/39
Hobart (Bel)	New Zealand	Drawn	S.R. Waugh	622/40
Perth	New Zealand	Drawn	S.R. Waugh	623/41
Adelaide	South Africa	Won by 246 runs	S.R. Waugh	624/66
Melbourne	South Africa	Won by nine wickets	S.R. Waugh	625/67
Sydney	South Africa	Won by 10 wickets	S.R. Waugh	626/68
2001-02 in South Africa				
Johannesburg (WS)	South Africa	Won by an innings and 360 runs	S.R. Waugh	627/69
Cape Town	South Africa	Won by four wickets	S.R. Waugh	628/70
Durban (Kingsmead)	South Africa	Lost by five wickets	S.R. Waugh	629/71
2002-03 in Sri Lanka and United Arab Emirates				
Colombo	Pakistan	Won by 41 runs	S.R. Waugh	630/47
Sharjah	Pakistan	Won by an innings and 198 runs	S.R. Waugh	631/48
Sharjah	Pakistan	Won by an innings and 20 runs	S.R. Waugh	632/49
2002-03 in Australia				
Brisbane	England	Won by 384 runs	S.R. Waugh	633/303
Adelaide	England	Won by an innings and 51 runs	S.R. Waugh	634/304
Perth	England	Won by an innings and 48 runs	S.R. Waugh	635/305
Melbourne	England	Won by five wickets	S.R. Waugh	636/306
Sydney	England	Lost by 225 runs	S.R. Waugh	637/307
2002-03 in West Indies				
Georgetown	West Indies	Won by nine wickets	S.R. Waugh	638/96
Port-of-Spain	West Indies	Won by 118 runs	S.R. Waugh	639/97
Bridgetown	West Indies	Won by nine wickets	S.R. Waugh	640/98
St John's	West Indies	Lost by seven wickets	S.R. Waugh	641/99

Venue	Opponent	Result for Australia	Captain	Test/Opp
2003-04 in Australia				
Darwin	Bangladesh	Won by an innings and 132 runs	S. R. Waugh	642/1
Cairns	Bangladesh	Won by an innings and 98 runs	S. R. Waugh	643/2
Perth	Zimbabwe	Won by an innings and 175 runs	S. R. Waugh	644/2
Sydney	Zimbabwe	Won by nine wickets	S. R. Waugh	645/3
Brisbane	India	Drawn	S. R. Waugh	646/61
Adelaide	India	Lost by four wickets	S. R. Waugh	647/62
Melbourne	India	Won by nine wickets	S. R. Waugh	648/63
Sydney	India	Drawn	S. R. Waugh	649/64
2003-04 in Sri Lanka				
Galle	Sri Lanka	Won by 197 runs	R. T. Ponting	650/14
Kandy	Sri Lanka	Won by 27 runs	R. T. Ponting	651/15
Colombo (SSC)	Sri Lanka	Won by 121 runs	R. T. Ponting	652/16
2004-05 in Australia				
Darwin	Sri Lanka	Won by 149 runs	A. C. Gilchrist	653/17
Cairns	Sri Lanka	Drawn	R. T. Ponting	654/18
2004-05 in India				
Bangalore	India	Won by 217 runs	A. C. Gilchrist	655/65
Chennai (Chepauk)	India	Drawn	A. C. Gilchrist	656/66
Nagpur	India	Won by 342	A. C. Gilchrist	657/67
Mumbai	India	Lost by 13 runs	R. T. Ponting	658/68
2004-05 in Australia				
Brisbane	New Zealand	Won by an innings and 156 runs	R. T. Ponting	659/42
Adelaide	New Zealand	Won by 213 runs	R. T. Ponting	660/43
Perth	Pakistan	Won by 491 runs	R. T. Ponting	661/50
Melbourne	Pakistan	Won by nine wickets	R. T. Ponting	662/51
Sydney	Pakistan	Won by nine wickets	R. T. Ponting	663/52
2004-05 in New Zealand				
Christchurch	New Zealand	Won by nine wickets	R. T. Ponting	664/44
Wellington	New Zealand	Match drawn	R. T. Ponting	665/45
Auckland	New Zealand	Won by nine wickets	R. T. Ponting	666/46

Australian Limited-Overs International Records

AUSTRALIAN ONE-DAY PLAYERS IN ORDER OF APPEARANCE

	Player	Career	M	I	NO	R	HS	Avge	S-R	100s	50s	Ct/St	Balls	Mdns	R	W	Avge	S-R	RPO	BB	5i
1	G. S. Chappell	1970-71 to 1982-83	74	72	14	2,331	138*	40.19	75.44	3	14	23	3,108	41	2,096	72	29.11	43.17	4.05	5-15	2
2	I. M. Chappell	1970-71 to 1979-80	16	16	2	673	86	48.07	77.00	–	8	5	42	1	23	2	11.50	21.00	3.29	2-14	–
3	A. N. Connolly	1970-71	1	–	–	–	–	–	–	–	–	–	64	–	62	0	–	–	5.81	–	–
4	W. M. Lawry †	1970-71	1	1	–	27	27	27.00	55.10	–	–	–	–	–	–	–	–	–	–	–	–
5	A. A. Mallett †	1970-71 to 1975-76	9	3	1	14	8	7.00	38.89	–	–	4	502	7	341	11	31.00	45.64	4.08	3-34	–
6	R. W. Marsh †	1970-71 to 1983-84	92	76	15	1,225	66	20.08	80.28	–	4	120/4	–	–	–	–	–	–	–	–	–
7	G. D. McKenzie	1970-71	1	–	–	–	–	–	–	–	–	–	60	–	22	2	11.00	30.00	2.20	2-22	–
8	I. R. Redpath	1970-71 to 1975-76	5	5	–	46	24	9.20	68.66	–	–	2	–	–	–	–	–	–	–	–	–
9	K. R. Stackpole	1970-71 to 1973-74	6	6	–	224	61	37.33	57.88	–	3	1	77	–	54	3	18.00	25.67	4.21	3-40	–
10	A. L. Thomson	1970-71	1	–	–	–	–	–	–	–	–	–	64	–	22	1	22.00	64.00	2.06	1-22	–
11	K. D. Walters	1970-71 to 1980-81	28	24	6	513	59	28.50	70.18	–	2	10	314	3	273	4	68.25	78.50	5.22	2-24	–
12	R. Edwards	1972 to 1975	9	8	1	255	80*	36.43	73.07	–	3	3	–	–	–	–	–	–	–	–	–
13	D. K. Lillee	1972 to 1983	63	34	8	240	42*	9.23	75.47	–	–	10	3,593	80	2,145	103	20.83	34.88	3.58	5-34	1
14	R. A. L. Massie †	1972	3	1	1	16	16*	–	66.67	–	–	1	183	5	129	3	43.00	61.00	4.23	2-35	–
15	A. P. Sheahan	1972	3	3	–	75	50	25.00	60.48	–	1	1	–	–	–	–	–	–	–	–	–
16	G. D. Watson	1972	2	2	1	11	11*	11.00	68.75	–	–	–	48	1	28	2	14.00	24.00	3.50	2-28	–
17	D. J. Colley	1972	1	1	1	15	15*	–	53.57	–	–	–	66	–	72	1	72.00	66.00	6.55	1-72	–
18	J. R. Hammond	1972	1	–	–	–	–	–	–	–	–	–	54	–	41	1	41.00	54.00	4.56	1-41	–
19	R. J. Bright ‡	1973-74 to 1985-86	11	8	4	66	19*	16.50	54.10	–	–	2	462	3	350	3	116.67	154.00	4.55	1-28	–
20	I. C. Davis	1973-74 to 1977	3	3	1	12	11*	6.00	33.33	–	–	1	–	–	–	–	–	–	–	–	–
21	G. Dymock ‡	1973-74 to 1980	15	5	2	35	14*	11.67	42.68	–	–	2	806	16	412	15	27.47	53.73	3.07	2-21	–
22	G. J. Gilmour ‡	1973-74 to 1975-76	5	3	2	42	28*	42.00	107.69	–	–	1	320	9	165	16	10.31	20.00	3.09	6-14	2
23	M. H. N. Walker	1973-74 to 1980-81	17	12	4	79	20	9.88	46.75	–	–	6	1,006	24	546	20	27.30	50.30	3.26	4-19	–
24	A. J. Woodcock	1973-74	1	1	–	53	53	53.00	79.10	–	1	–	–	–	–	–	–	–	–	–	–
25	W. J. Edwards †	1974-75	1	1	–	2	2	2.00	14.29	–	–	1	1	–	0	0	–	–	0.00	–	–
26	A. G. Hurst	1974-75 to 1979	8	5	2	7	3*	2.33	36.84	–	–	1	402	11	203	12	16.92	33.50	3.03	5-21	1

No. Player	Career	M	I	NO	R	HS	Avge	100	50	Ct/St	Balls	Md	R	W	Avge	S-R	RPO	BB	5i
27 T. J. Jenner	1974-75	1	1	-	12	12	12.00	-	-	-	64	1	28	0	-	-	2.63	-	-
28 J. R. Thomson	1974-75 to 1985	50	30	6	181	21	7.54	-	-	9	2,696	37	1,942	55	35.31	49.02	4.32	4-67	-
29 R. B. McCosker	1975 to 1981-82	14	14	-	320	95	22.86	-	1	3	-	-	-	-	-	-	-	-	-
30 A. Turner†	1975	6	6	-	247	101	41.17	1	2	3	-	-	-	-	-	-	-	-	-
31 G. J. Cosier	1975-76 to 1979	9	9	2	154	84	30.80	-	1	4	409	9	248	14	17.71	29.21	3.64	5-18	1
32 D. W. Hookes †‡	1977 to 1985-86	39	36	2	826	76	24.29	-	5	11	29	-	28	1	28.00	29.00	5.79	1-2	-
33 M. F. Malone	1977 to 1981-82	10	7	3	36	15*	9.00	-	-	-	612	16	315	11	28.64	55.64	3.09	2-9	-
34 K. J. O'Keeffe	1977	2	2	1	16	16*	16.00	-	-	1	132	3	79	2	39.50	66.00	3.59	1-36	-
35 L. S. Pascoe	1977 to 1981-82	29	11	7	39	15*	9.75	-	-	6	1,568	21	1,066	53	20.11	29.58	4.08	5-30	1
36 C. S. Serjeant	1977	3	3	-	73	46	24.33	-	-	1	-	-	-	-	-	-	-	-	-
37 K. J. Hughes	1977 to 1977-78	97	88	6	1,968	98	24.00	-	17	27	1	-	4	0	-	-	24.00	-	-
38 R. D. Robinson	1977	2	2	-	82	70	41.00	-	1	3/1	-	-	-	-	-	-	-	-	-
39 I. W. Callen †	1977-78 to 1982-83	5	3	2	6	3*	6.00	-	-	2	180	2	148	5	29.60	36.00	4.93	3-24	-
40 W. M. Clark	1977-78	2	2	1	6	6	6.00	-	-	-	100	3	61	3	20.33	33.33	3.66	2-39	-
41 W. M. Darling	1977-78 to 1981-82	18	18	1	363	74	21.35	-	1	3	-	-	-	-	-	-	-	-	-
42 T. J. Laughlin †	1977-78 to 1979-80	6	6	1	105	74	26.25	-	1	2	308	3	224	8	28.00	38.50	4.36	3-54	-
43 S. J. Rixon	1977-78 to 1984-85	6	6	3	40	20*	13.33	-	-	9/2	-	-	-	-	-	-	-	-	-
44 R. B. Simpson	1977-78	2	2	-	36	23	18.00	-	-	-	102	-	95	2	47.50	51.00	5.59	2-30	-
45 P. M. Toohey	1977-78 to 1978-79	5	4	2	105	54*	52.50	-	1	2	-	-	-	-	-	-	-	-	-
46 G. M. Wood †	1977-78 to 1988-89	83	77	11	2,219	114*	33.62	3	11	17	-	-	-	-	-	-	-	-	-
47 G. N. Yallop †‡	1977-78 to 1984-85	30	27	6	823	66*	39.19	-	7	5	138	3	119	3	39.67	46.00	5.17	2-28	-
48 B. Yardley	1977-78 to 1982-83	7	4	-	58	28	14.50	-	-	4	2,661	11	2,071	73	28.37	36.45	4.67	3-28	-
49 A. R. Border †‡	1978-79 to 1993-94	273	252	39	6,524	127*	30.63	3	39	127	168	3	70	2	35.00	84.00	2.50	1-21	-
50 P. H. Carlson	1978-79	4	2	-	11	11	5.50	-	-	1	-	-	-	-	-	-	-	-	-
51 J. A. Maclean	1978-79	2	2	1	11	11	11.00	-	-	2	-	-	-	-	-	-	-	-	-
52 A. M. J. Hilditch	1978-79 to 1985	8	8	-	226	72	28.25	-	1	3	-	-	-	-	-	-	-	-	-
53 R. M. Hogg	1978-79 to 1984-85	71	35	20	137	22	9.13	-	-	8	3,677	57	2,418	85	28.45	43.26	3.95	4-29	-
54 K. J. Wright	1978-79	5	2	-	29	23	14.50	-	-	5	-	-	-	-	-	-	-	-	-
55 J. K. Moss †	1979	1	2	-	7	7	7.00	-	-	1	-	-	-	-	-	-	-	-	-
56 G. D. Porter	1979	2	1	-	3	3	3.00	-	-	1	108	5	33	3	11.00	36.00	1.83	2-13	-
57 B. M. Laird	1979-80 to 1982-83	23	23	3	594	117*	29.70	1	2	5	-	-	-	-	-	-	-	-	-
58 J. M. Wiener	1979-80	7	7	-	140	50	20.00	-	1	5	24	-	34	0	-	-	8.50	-	-
59 D. F. Whatmore	1979-80	1	1	-	2	2	2.00	-	-	-	-	-	-	-	-	-	-	-	-
60 J. Dyson	1980 to 1982-83	29	27	4	755	79	32.83	-	4	12	-	-	-	-	-	-	-	-	-
61 T. M. Chappell	1980-81 to 1983	20	13	-	229	110	17.62	1	-	8	736	4	538	19	28.32	38.74	4.39	3-31	-
62 S. F. Graf †	1980-81 to 1981-82	11	6	-	24	18	4.00	-	-	1	522	4	345	8	43.13	65.25	3.97	2-23	-

No.	Player	Career	M	I	NO	Runs	HS	Avge	S-R	100	50	Ct/St	Balls	Runs	Wkts	Avge	Best	4w/5w
63	G. F. Lawson	1980-81 to 1989-90	79	52	18	378	33*	11.12	77.21	–	–	18	4,259	2,592	88	29.45	4-26	1
64	M. F. Kent	1980-81 to 1981	5	5	1	78	33*	19.50	58.65	–	–	4			–			
65	G. R. Beard	1980-81	2	–	–	–	–	–	–	–	–	–	112	70	4	17.50	2-20	–
66	T. M. Alderman	1981 to 1990-91	65	18	6	32	9*	2.67	32.99	–	–	28	3,371	2,056	88	23.36	5-17	2
67	D. M. Wellham	1981-82 to 1986-87	17	17	2	379	97	25.27	54.22	–	2	8			–			
68	G. M. Ritchie	1982-83 to 1986-87	44	42	6	959	84	27.40	61.95	–	9	9			–			
69	W. B. Phillips †	1982-83 to 1985-86	48	41	6	852	75*	24.34	85.80	–	6	42/7			–			
70	C. G. Rackemann	1982-83 to 1990-91	52	18	6	34	9*	2.83	44.16	–	–	7	2,791	1,833	82	22.35	5-16	1
71	K. C. Wessels †	1982-83 to 1985	54	51	3	1,740	107	36.25	58.97	1	14	14	737	655	18	36.39	2-16	–
72	J. N. Maguire	1982-83 to 1984-85	23	5	2	42	14*	7.00	59.15	–	–	2	1,009	769	19	40.47	2-20	–
73	T. G. Hogan ‡	1982-83 to 1984-85	16	11	1	72	27	9.00	78.82	–	–	10	917	574	23	24.96	4-33	1
74	K. H. MacLeay	1982-83 to 1986-87	16	12	1	139		12.64	84.31	–	–	2	857	626	15	41.73	6-39	1
75	S. B. Smith	1982-83 to 1984-85	28	24	2	861	117	39.14	65.28	1	8	8	7	5	0			
76	M. R. Whitney ‡	1982-83 to 1992-93	38	13	7	40	9*	6.67	44.44	–	–	11	2,106	1,249	46	27.15	4-34	1
77	R. D. Woolley	1982-83	2	2	1	31	16	31.00	81.58	–	–	1/1			–			
78	G. R. J. Matthews †	1983-84 to 1992-93	59	50	13	619	54*	16.73	63.42	–	–	23	2,808	1,999	57	35.07	3-27	–
79	D. M. Jones	1983-84 to 1993-94	164	161	16	6,068	145	44.62	72.49	7	46	54	106	106	3	35.33	2-34	–
80	D. C. Boon	1983-84 to 1994-95	181	177	16	5,964	122	37.04	65.12	5	37	45	86	82	0		6.29	
81	M. J. Bennett	1984-85	8	2	1		6*	3.00	42.86	–	–	1	275		6	68.75	2-27	–
82	C. J. McDermott	1984-85 to 1995-96	138	78	17	432	37	7.08	87.80	–	–	27	7,460	5,020	203	24.73	5-44	1
83	S. P. O'Donnell	1984-85 to 1991-92	87	64	15	1,242	74*	25.35	80.54	–	9	22	4,350	3,102	108	28.72	5-13	1
84	R. G. Holland	1984-85	4	2	1				46.48	–	–	1	126	99	2	49.50	2-49	–
85	R. J. McCurdy	1984-85	11	6	1	33	13*	8.25	61.01	–	1	5	515	375	12	31.25	3-19	–
86	R. B. Kerr	1984-85	4	4	–		87*	32.33	58.82	–	1	1			–			
87	S. P. Davis	1985-86 to 1987-88	39	11	7	97	6	5.00	38.24	–	–	5	2,019	1,133	44	25.75	3-10	–
88	D. R. Gilbert	1985-86	14	7	1	20	8	5.00	38.89	–	–	5	684	552	18	30.67	5-46	1
89	B. A. Reid †‡	1985-86 to 1991-92	61	21	7	49	10	3.77	55.81	–	–	18	3,250	2,201	63	34.94	5-53	1
90	S. R. Waugh	1985-86 to 2001-02	325	288	58	7,569	120*	32.91	75.81	1	45	111	8,883	6,764	195	34.69	4-33	–
91	G. R. Marsh	1985-86 to 1991-92	117	115	6	4,357	126*	39.97	55.77	9	22	37	6	4	0			
92	G. S. Trimble	1985-86	2	2	–	4	4	4.00	80.00	–	–	–	24	32	0			
93	T. J. Zoehrer	1985-86 to 1993-94	22	15	3	130	50	10.83	71.04	–	–	21/2			–			
94	G. C. Dyer	1986-87 to 1987-88	23	13	2	174	45*	15.82	76.99	–	–	24/4			–			
95	G. A. Bishop	1986-87	2	2	–	13		6.50	29.55	–	–	1			–			
96	P. L. Taylor	1986-87 to 1991-92	83	47	25	437	54*	19.86	75.87	–	1	34	3,937	2,740	97	28.25	4-38	–
97	M. R. J. Veletta	1986-87 to 1989	20	19	4	484	68*	32.27	75.39	–	2	8			–			
98	T. M. Moody	1987-88 to 1999-00	76	64	12	1,211	89	23.29	69.00	–	8	21	2,797	2,014	52	38.73	3-25	–
99	T. B. A. May	1987-88 to 1994-95	47	12	8	39	15	9.75		–	–	3	2,504	1,772	39	45.44	3-19	–

No. & Name	Span	M	I	NO	R	HS	Avge	S-R	100	50	Ct/St	Balls	Md	R	W	Avge	S-R	RPO	BB	5i
100 A.K. Zesers	1987-88	2	2	2	10	8*	–	71.43	–	–	1	90	1	74	1	74.00	90.00	4.93	1-37	–
101 A.I.C. Dodemaide	1987-88 to 1992-93	24	16	7	124	30	13.78	77.99	–	–	7	1,327	30	753	36	20.92	36.86	3.40	5-21	1
102 I.A. Healy	1988-89 to 1997	168	120	36	1,764	56	21.00	83.64	–	–	194/39	–	–	–	–	–	–	–	–	–
103 J.D. Siddons	1988-89	1	1	–	32	32	32.00	86.49	–	–	1	–	–	–	–	–	–	–	–	–
104 M.G. Hughes	1988-89 to 1993	33	17	8	100	20	11.11	72.99	–	–	6	1,639	22	1,115	38	29.34	43.13	4.08	4-44	–
105 M.E. Waugh	1988-89 to 2001-02	244	236	20	8,500	173	39.35	76.54	18	50	108	3,687	10	2,938	85	34.56	43.38	4.78	5-24	1
106 G.D. Campbell	1989-90	12	8	6	6	4*	3.00	30.00	–	–	4	613	9	404	18	22.44	34.06	3.95	3-17	–
107 M.A. Taylor †	1989-90 to 1997	113	110	1	3,514	105	32.24	59.42	1	28	56	–	–	–	–	–	–	–	–	–
108 P.R. Reiffel	1991-92 to 1999	92	57	21	503	57	13.97	71.25	–	1	25	4,732	84	3,095	106	29.20	44.64	3.92	4-13	–
109 D.R. Martyn	1992-93 to 2003-04	151	130	40	3,713	144*	41.26	79.22	5	22	50	794	1	704	12	58.67	66.17	5.32	2-21	–
110 S.K. Warne	1992-93 to 2002-03	193	106	28	1,016	55	13.03	71.75	–	1	80	10,600	109	7,514	291	25.82	36.43	4.25	5-33	1
111 M.L. Hayden †	1993 to 2003-04	95	91	11	3,366	146	42.08	77.93	4	22	34	6	–	18	0	–	–	18.00	–	–
112 B.P. Julian ‡	1993 to 1999	25	17	–	224	35	13.18	89.96	–	–	8	1,146	11	997	22	45.32	52.09	5.22	3-40	–
113 G.D. McGrath	1993-94 to 2003-04	188	50	27	94	11	4.09	49.21	–	–	26	9,940	221	6,443	285	22.61	34.88	3.89	7-15	6
114 M.J. Slater	1993-94 to 1997	42	42	1	987	73	24.07	60.22	–	9	9	12	–	11	0	–	–	5.50	–	–
115 D.W. Fleming	1993-94 to 2001	88	31	18	152	21*	11.69	67.86	–	–	14	4,619	62	3,402	134	25.39	34.47	4.42	5-36	1
116 M.G. Bevan ‡†	1993-94 to 2003-04	232	196	67	6,912	108*	53.58	73.96	6	46	69	1,966	9	1,655	36	45.97	54.61	5.05	3-36	–
117 J.L. Langer †	1993-94 to 1997	8	7	2	160	36	32.00	88.89	–	1	2	–	–	–	–	–	–	–	–	–
118 J. Angel †	1994-95 to 1994-95	7	3	1	0	0*	0.00	0.00	–	–	3	162	3	113	4	28.25	40.50	4.19	2-47	–
119 G.R. Robertson	1994-95 to 1997-98	13	7	4	45	15*	15.00	–	–	–	3	597	3	430	8	53.75	74.63	4.32	3-29	–
120 P.A. Emery †	1994-95	1	1	1	11	11*	–	–	–	–	2/1	–	–	–	–	–	–	–	–	–
121 S.G. Law	1994-95 to 1998-99	54	51	5	1,237	110	26.89	74.74	1	7	12	807	3	635	12	52.92	67.25	4.72	2-22	–
122 G.S. Blewett	1994-95 to 1998-99	32	30	3	551	57*	20.41	61.63	–	2	7	749	3	646	14	46.14	53.50	5.17	2-6	–
123 R.T. Ponting	1994-95 to 2003-04	201	196	25	7,255	145	42.43	77.64	15	41	82	150	1	104	3	34.67	50.00	4.16	1-12	–
124 S. Lee	1995-96 to 2000-01	45	35	8	477	47	17.67	90.52	–	–	23	1,706	14	1,245	48	25.94	35.54	4.38	5-33	1
125 M.S. Kasprowicz	1995-96 to 2003-04	24	10	7	62	28*	20.67	80.52	–	–	4	1,267	14	952	37	25.73	34.24	4.51	5-45	1
126 G.B. Hogg ‡†	1996-97 to 2003-04	48	29	13	334	71*	20.88	78.77	–	2	17	2,287	7	1,650	53	31.13	43.15	4.33	4-27	–
127 J.N. Gillespie	1996-97 to 2003-04	72	30	13	223	33*	13.12	75.08	–	–	22	3,903	68	2,688	111	24.22	35.16	4.13	5-22	3
128 D.S. Lehmann ‡†	1996-97 to 2003-04	102	89	19	2,780	119	39.71	82.32	4	15	22	1,364	5	1,080	42	25.71	32.48	4.75	4-7	–
129 A.C. Gilchrist †	1996-97 to 2003-04	193	187	6	6,468	172	35.73	94.11	10	37	283/39	–	–	–	–	–	–	–	–	–
130 A.J. Bichel	1996-97 to 2003-04	67	36	13	471	64	20.48	78.50	–	2	28	3,257	19	2,464	78	31.59	41.76	4.54	7-20	2
131 A.M. Stuart	1996-97	3	2	1	1	1*	1.00	14.29	–	–	1	180	2	109	8	13.63	22.50	3.63	5-26	1
132 A.C. Dale †	1996-97 to 1999-00	30	12	8	78	15*	19.50	56.12	–	–	11	1,596	34	979	32	30.59	49.88	3.68	3-18	–
133 M.J. Di Venuto †	1996-97	9	9	–	241	89	26.78	84.86	–	2	2	–	–	–	–	–	–	–	–	–
134 M.T.G. Elliott †	1997	1	1	–	1	1	1.00	20.00	–	–	–	–	–	–	–	–	–	–	–	–
135 I.J. Harvey	1997-98 to 2003-04	73	51	11	715	48*	17.88	88.05	–	–	17	3,279	29	2,577	85	30.32	38.58	4.72	4-16	–

No.	Player	Career	M	I	NO	Runs	HS	Avge	S/R	100	50	Ct/St	Balls	Runs	Wkts	Avge	BB	5w	S/R	R/O
136	P. Wilson	1997-98	11	5	2	4	2	1.33	33.33	—	—	—	562	450	13	34.62	4-25	—	43.23	4.80
137	J.P. Maher †	1997-98 to 2003-04	26	20	3	438	95	25.76	64.89	—	—	—	—	—	—	—	—	—	—	—
138	B.E. Young ‡	1997-98 to 1998-99	6	3	1	31	18	15.50	65.96	—	—	—	234	251	1	251.00	1-26	—	234.00	6.44
139	A. Symonds	1998-99 to 2003-04	96	72	15	2,064	143*	36.21	89.23	1	10	—	3,157	2,591	72	35.99	4-11	—	43.85	4.92
140	B. Lee	1999-00 to 2003-04	84	35	11	347	51*	14.46	80.70	—	1	—	4,291	3,344	151	22.15	5-27	3	28.42	4.68
141	S.C.G. MacGill	1999-00	3	2	1	1	1	1.00	33.33	—	—	—	180	105	6	17.50	4-19	—	30.00	3.50
142	N.W. Bracken ‡	2000-01 to 2003-04	6	2	2	7	7*	—	70.00	—	—	—	852	552	28	19.71	4-29	—	30.43	3.89
143	S.M. Katich †	2000-01 to 2003-04	4	4	2	44	18*	22.00	73.33	—	—	—	—	—	—	—	—	—	—	—
144	B.J. Haddin †	2000-01 to 2003-04	4	4	—	68	32	17.00	71.58	—	—	1/2	—	—	—	—	—	—	—	—
145	B.A. Williams	2001-02 to 2003-04	25	6	4	27	13*	13.50	58.70	—	—	—	1,203	814	35	23.26	5-22	2	34.37	4.06
146	R.J. Campbell	2001-02	2	2	—	54	38	27.00	77.14	—	—	4/1	—	—	—	—	—	—	—	—
147	N.M. Hauritz	2001-02 to 2002-03	8	3	2	35	20*	35.00	89.74	—	—	—	360	308	9	34.22	4-39	—	40.00	5.13
148	S.R. Watson	2001-02 to 2003-04	24	16	8	306	77*	38.25	66.96	—	1	—	869	670	18	37.22	3-27	—	48.28	4.63
149	M.J. Clarke ‡	2002-03 to 2003-04	28	26	8	784	105*	43.56	87.40	1	4	—	581	496	17	29.18	5-35	1	34.18	5.12
150	M.E.K. Hussey †	2003-04	1	1	1	17	17*	—	73.91	—	—	—	18	15	0	—	—	—	—	5.00
151	J.R. Hopes	2004-05	1	—	—	—	—	—	—	—	—	—	60	38	1	38.00	1-38	—	60.00	3.80

† denotes left-hand batsman; ‡ denotes left-arm bowler.

BATTING RECORDS

MOST RUNS IN A CAREER

	M	I	NO	R	HS	100s	Avge	S-R
M. E. Waugh	244	236	20	8,500	173	18	39.35	76.54
R. T. Ponting	231	225	28	8,175	145	17	41.50	77.50
S. R. Waugh	325	288	58	7,569	120*	3	32.91	75.81
A. C. Gilchrist	218	212	9	7,338	172	11	36.15	95.14
M. G. Bevan	232	196	67	6,912	108*	6	53.58	73.93
A. R. Border	273	252	39	6,524	127*	3	30.63	71.26
D. M. Jones	164	161	25	6,068	145	7	44.62	72.49
D. C. Boon	181	177	16	5,964	122	5	37.04	65.12
D. R. Martyn	181	157	48	4,604	144*	5	42.24	78.23
G. R. Marsh	117	115	6	4,357	126*	9	39.97	55.77
M. L. Hayden	118	114	12	4,129	146	5	40.48	75.93
M. A. Taylor	113	110	1	3,514	105	1	32.24	59.42
D. S. Lehmann	117	101	22	3,077	119	4	38.95	81.38
A. Symonds	124	96	19	2,833	143*	2	36.79	89.74
G. S. Chappell	74	72	14	2,331	138*	3	40.19	75.44
G. M. Wood	83	77	11	2,219	114*	3	33.62	59.43

HIGHEST CAREER STRIKE-RATE

(Qualification: 500 runs)

	M	I	NO	R	HS	100s	Avge	S-R
A. C. Gilchrist	218	212	9	7,338	172	11	36.15	95.14
A. Symonds	124	96	19	2,833	143*	2	36.79	89.74
I. J. Harvey	73	51	11	715	48*	0	17.88	88.05
W. B. Phillips	48	41	6	852	75*	0	24.34	85.80
M. J. Clarke	57	51	13	1,686	105*	2	44.37	85.24
I. A. Healy	168	120	36	1,764	56	0	21.00	83.64
B. Lee	112	47	18	511	51*	0	17.62	83.22
R. W. Marsh	92	76	15	1,225	66	0	20.08	81.94
D. S. Lehmann	117	101	22	3,077	119	4	38.95	81.38
S. P. O'Donnell	87	64	15	1,242	74*	0	25.35	80.54

HIGHEST CAREER AVERAGE

(Qualification: 500 runs)

	M	I	NO	R	HS	100s	Avge	S-R
M. G. Bevan	232	196	67	6,912	108*	6	53.58	73.93
I. M. Chappell	16	16	2	673	86	0	48.07	77.00
D. M. Jones	164	161	25	6,068	145	7	44.62	72.49
M. J. Clarke	57	51	13	1,686	105*	2	44.37	85.24
D. R. Martyn	181	157	48	4,604	144*	5	42.24	78.23
R. T. Ponting	231	225	28	8,175	145	17	41.50	77.50
M. L. Hayden	118	114	12	4,129	146	5	40.48	75.93
G. S. Chappell	74	72	14	2,331	138*	3	40.19	75.44

CENTURY-MAKERS

M. G. Bevan (6)	103	v South Africa at Centurion	1996-97
	108*	v England at The Oval	1997
	101*	v India at Sharjah	1997-98
	107	v New Zealand at Napier	1999-00
	106	v South Africa at Melbourne (DS)	2000-01
	102*	v New Zealand at Melbourne	2001-02
D. C. Boon (5)	111	v India at Jaipur	1986-87
	122	v Sri Lanka at Adelaide	1987-88
	102*	v India at Hobart	1991-92
	100	v New Zealand at Auckland	1991-92
	100	v West Indies at Melbourne	1991-92
A. R. Border (3)	105*	v India at Sydney	1980-81
	118*	v Sri Lanka at Adelaide	1984-85
	127*	v West Indies at Sydney	1984-85
T. M. Chappell	110	v India at Nottingham	1983
G. S. Chappell (3)	125*	v England at The Oval	1977
	138*	v New Zealand at Sydney	1980-81
	108	v New Zealand at Auckland	1981-82
A. C. Gilchrist (11)	100	v South Africa at Sydney	1997-98
	118	v New Zealand at Christchurch	1997-98
	103	v Pakistan at Lahore	1998-99
	131	v Sri Lanka at Sydney	1998-99
	154	v Sri Lanka at Melbourne	1998-99
	128	v New Zealand at Christchurch	1999-00
	105	v South Africa at Durban (Kingsmead)	2001-02
	124	v England at Melbourne	2002-03
	111	v India at Bangalore	2003-04
	172	v Zimbabwe at Hobart	2003-04
	121*	v England at The Oval	2005
M. J. Clarke (2)	105*	v Zimbabwe at Harare	2003-04
	103*	v Pakistan at Sydney	2004-05
M. L. Hayden (5)	111	v India at Visakhapatnam	2003-04
	146	v Pakistan at Nairobi	2003-04
	109	v India at Brisbane	2003-04
	126	v India at Sydney	2003-04
	114	v New Zealand at Christchurch	2004-05
D. M. Jones (7)	104	v England at Perth	1986-87
	121	v Pakistan at Perth	1986-87
	101	v England at Brisbane	1986-87
	107	v New Zealand at Christchurch	1989-90
	102*	v New Zealand at Auckland	1989-90
	117*	v Sri Lanka at Sharjah	1989-90
	145	v England at Brisbane	1990-91
B. M. Laird	117*	v West Indies at Sydney	1981-82
S. G. Law	110	v Zimbabwe at Hobart	1994-95
D. S. Lehmann (4)	103	v Pakistan at Karachi	1998-99
	110*	v West Indies at St George's	1998-99
	119	v Sri Lanka at Perth	2002-03
	107	v West Indies at St George's	2002-03
G. R. Marsh (9)	125	v India at Sydney	1985-86
	104	v India at Jaipur	1986-87
	110	v India at Chennai	1987-88
	126*	v New Zealand at Chandigarh	1987-88
	101	v New Zealand at Sydney	1987-88
	125*	v Pakistan at Melbourne	1988-89
	111*	v England at Lord's	1989
	113	v West Indies at Bridgetown	1990-91
	106*	v West Indies at Georgetown	1990-91

D. R. Martyn (5)	116*	v New Zealand at Auckland	1999-00
	144*	v Zimbabwe at Perth	2000-01
	104*	v South Africa at Brisbane	2001-02
	101*	v England at Hobart	2002-03
	100	v India at Mumbai	2003-04
R. T. Ponting (17)	123	v Sri Lanka at Melbourne	1995-96
	102	v West Indies at Jaipur	1995-96
	100	v New Zealand at Melbourne	1997-98
	145	v Zimbabwe at Delhi	1997-98
	124*	v Pakistan at Lahore	1998-99
	115	v India at Melbourne	1999-00
	101	v India at Visakhapatnam	2000-01
	102	v England at Bristol	2001
	129	v South Africa at Bloemfontein	2001-02
	119	v England at Melbourne	2002-03
	106*	v Sri Lanka at Melbourne	2002-03
	114	v Sri Lanka at Centurion	2002-03
	140*	v India at Johannesburg	2002-03
	101	v Bangladesh at Darwin	2003-04
	108*	v India at Bangalore	2003-04
	141*	v New Zealand at Napier	2004-05
	111	v England at Lord's	2005
S. B. Smith (2)	117	v New Zealand at Melbourne	1982-83
	106	v Pakistan at Sydney	1983-84
A. Symonds (2)	143*	v Pakistan at Johannesburg (WS)	2002-03
	104*	v Pakistan at Lord's	2004
M. A. Taylor	105	v India at Bangalore	1996-97
A. Turner	101	v Sri Lanka at The Oval	1975
M. E. Waugh (18)	108	v New Zealand at Hamilton	1992-93
	113	v England at Birmingham	1993
	107	v South Africa at Sydney	1993-94
	121*	v South Africa at Rawalpindi	1994-95
	130	v Sri Lanka at Perth	1995-96
	130	v Kenya at Visakhapatnam	1995-96
	126	v India at Mumbai	1995-96
	110	v New Zealand at Chennai (Chepauk)	1995-96
	102	v West Indies at Brisbane	1996-97
	115*	v South Africa at Port Elizabeth	1996-97
	104	v New Zealand at Adelaide	1996-97
	104	v Zimbabwe at Lord's	1999
	106	v Zimbabwe at Bulawayo	1999-00
	116	v India at Adelaide	1999-00
	112*	v West Indies at Brisbane	2000-01
	102	v Zimbabwe at Hobart (Bel)	2000-01
	173	v West Indies at Melbourne	2000-01
	133*	v India at Pune	2000-01
S. R. Waugh (3)	102*	v Sri Lanka at Melbourne	1995-96
	120*	v South Africa at Birmingham	1999
	114*	v South Africa at Melbourne (DS)	2000-01
K. C. Wessels	107	v India at New Delhi	1984-85
G. M. Wood (3)	108	v England at Leeds	1981
	104*	v West Indies at Adelaide	1984-85
	114*	v England at Lord's	1985

FASTEST FIFTIES

Balls

18	S. P. O'Donnell	v Sri Lanka at Sharjah	1989-90
22	D. R. Martyn	v Bangladesh at Cairns	2003-04
26	W. B. Phillips	v New Zealand at Wellington	1985-86
27	A. C. Gilchrist	v South Africa at Port Elizabeth	2001-02
28	T. M. Moody	v Bangladesh at Chester-le-Street	1999
28	A. C. Gilchrist	v India at Margoa	2000-01
28	A. C. Gilchrist	v Pakistan at Nottingham	2001

FASTEST HUNDREDS

Balls

78	A. R. Border	v Sri Lanka at Adelaide	1984-85
78	A. C. Gilchrist	v New Zealand at Christchurch	1999-00
81	A. C. Gilchrist	v England at The Oval	2005
82	G. S. Chappell	v New Zealand at Auckland	1981-82
85	A. C. Gilchrist	v Sri Lanka at Melbourne	1998-99
88	D. S. Lehmann	v West Indies at St George's	1998-99

MOST RUNS OFF AN OVER

28	(444646)	D. S. Lehmann	off R. J. Van Vuuren v Namibia at Potchestroom	2002-03
27	(164646)	D. S. Lehmann and B. Lee	off A. A. Donald v South Africa at Perth	2001-02
26	(64646.)	R. W. Marsh	off B. L. Cairns v New Zealand at Adelaide	1980-81
24	(66624x)	I. J. Harvey	off D. P. Viljoen v Zimbabwe at Perth	2000-01

SLOWEST FIFTIES

Balls

116	K. C. Wessels	v West Indies at Sydney	1984-85
111	G. R. Marsh	v West Indies at Sydney	1991-92
108	D. M. Jones	v India at Adelaide	1991-92
107	G. R. Marsh	v India at Hamilton	1989-90
106	B. M. Laird	v New Zealand at Dunedin	1981-82
106	G. R. Marsh	v India at Sydney	1991-92

SLOWEST HUNDREDS

Balls

166	D. C. Boon	v India at Hobart (Bel)	1991-92
156	G. R. Marsh	v England at Lord's	1989
150	G. R. Marsh	v West Indies at Georgetown	1990-91
146	G. R. Marsh	v New Zealand at Sydney	1987-88
146	D. C. Boon	v West Indies at Melbourne	1991-92

MOST CAREER DUCKS

16	M. E. Waugh
15	C. J. McDermott
15	S. R. Waugh
14	R. T. Ponting
13	A. C. Gilchrist

HIGHEST PARTNERSHIPS

234* for 3rd	R. T. Ponting and D. R. Martyn	v India at Johannesburg (WS)	2002-03
225 for 2nd	A. C. Gilchrist and R. T. Ponting	v England at Melbourne	2002-03
224* for 3rd	D. M. Jones and A. R. Border	v Sri Lanka at Adelaide	1984-85
222 for 4th	M. G. Bevan and S. R. Waugh	v South Africa at Melbourne (DS)	2000-01
219 for 2nd	M. E. Waugh and R. T. Ponting	v Zimbabwe at Delhi	1997-98
219 for 2nd	M. L. Hayden and R. T. Ponting	v India at Viskhapatnam	2000-01
212 for 1st	G. R. Marsh and D. C. Boon	v India at Jaipur	1986-87
207 for 3rd	M. E. Waugh and S. R. Waugh	v Kenya at Viskhapatnam	1995-96
206 for 1st	A. C. Gilchrist and M. E. Waugh	v West Indies at Brisbane	2000-01
193 for 2nd	A. C. Gilchrist and R. T. Ponting	v Pakistan at Lahore	1998-99

HIGHEST PARTNERSHIPS FOR EACH WICKET

212 for 1st	G. R. Marsh and D. C. Boon	v India at Jaipur	1986-87
225 for 2nd	A. C. Gilchrist and R. T. Ponting	v England at Melbourne	2002-03
234* for 3rd	R. T. Ponting and D. R. Martyn	v India at Johannesburg (WS)	2002-03
222 for 4th	M. G. Bevan and S. R. Waugh	v South Africa at Melbourne (DS)	2000-01
172* for 5th	D. S. Lehmann and M. G. Bevan	v West Indies at Kingstown	1998-99
136* for 6th	M. J. Clarke and M. E. K. Hussey	v New Zealand at Auckland	2004-05
102* for 7th	S. R. Waugh and G. C. Dyer	v India at Delhi	1986-87
119 for 8th	P. R. Reiffel and S. K. Warne	v South Africa at Port Elizabeth	1993-94
77 for 9th	M. G. Bevan and S. K. Warne	v West Indies at Port-of-Spain	1998-99
63 for 10th	A. J. Bichel and S. R. Watson	v Sri Lanka at Sydney	2002-03

BOWLING RECORDS

MOST WICKETS IN A CAREER

	M	Balls	Mdns	R	W	BB	5W/i	Avge
G. D. McGrath	213	11,173	253	7,188	323	7-15	7	22.25
G. D. McGrath	188	9,940	221	6,443	285	7-15	6	22.61
B. Lee	112	5,688	74	4,433	200	5-27	4	22.17
C. J. McDermott	138	7,460	99	5,020	203	5-44	1	24.73
S. R. Waugh	325	8,883	54	6,764	195	4-33	0	34.69
J. N. Gillespie	97	5,144	80	3,611	142	5-22	3	25.43
D. W. Fleming	88	4,619	62	3,402	134	5-36	1	25.39
J. N. Gillespie	72	3,903	68	2,688	111	5-22	3	24.22
S. P. O'Donnell	87	4,350	49	3,102	108	5-13	1	28.72
P. R. Reiffel	92	4,732	84	3,095	106	4-13	0	29.20
D. K. Lillee	63	3,593	80	2,145	103	5-34	1	20.83

BEST CAREER STRIKE-RATE

(Qualification: 25 wickets)

	M	Balls	Mdns	R	W	BB	5W/i	Avge	S-R
B. Lee	112	5,688	74	4,433	200	5-27	4	22.17	28.44
L. S. Pascoe	29	1,568	21	1,066	53	5-30	1	20.11	29.58
N. W. Bracken	17	852	18	552	28	4-29	0	19.71	30.43
M. S. Kasprowicz	43	2,225	28	1,674	67	5-45	2	24.99	33.21
C. G. Rackemann	52	2,791	51	1,833	82	5-16	1	22.35	34.04
B. A. Williams	25	1,203	19	814	35	5-22	2	23.26	34.37
G. D. McGrath	213	11,173	253	7,188	323	7-15	7	22.25	34.59
D. W. Fleming	88	4,619	62	3,402	134	5-36	1	25.39	34.47
D. S. Lehmann	117	1,793	2	1,446	52	4-7	0	27.81	34.48
D. K. Lillee	63	3,593	80	2,145	103	5-34	1	20.83	34.88

Every year
we make our mark
on the record books.

www.albionsports.com.au

CRICKE
AUSTRALI
Official Suppli
Cricket Headwe
Cricket Austra

BEST CAREER ECONOMY-RATE

(Qualification: 25 wickets)

	M	Balls	Mdns	R	W	BB	5W/i	Avge	RPO
.P. Davis	39	2,019	46	1,133	44	3-10	0	25.75	3.37
..I.C. Dodemaide	24	1,327	30	753	36	5-21	1	20.92	3.40
.I.R. Whitney	38	2,106	42	1,249	46	4-34	0	27.15	3.56
).K. Lillee	63	3,593	80	2,145	103	5-34	1	20.83	3.58
ì.F. Lawson	79	4,259	94	2,592	88	4-26	0	29.45	3.65
".M. Alderman	65	3,371	75	2,056	88	5-17	2	23.36	3.66
.A.C. Dale	30	1,596	34	979	32	3-18	0	30.59	3.68
ì.D. McGrath	213	11,173	253	7,188	323	7-15	7	22.25	3.86
.N.W. Bracken	17	852	18	552	28	4-29	0	19.71	3.89
?.R. Reiffel	92	4,732	84	3,095	106	4-13	0	29.20	3.92

BEST CAREER AVERAGE

(Qualification: 25 wickets)

	M	Balls	Mdns	R	W	BB	5W/i	Avge
N.W. Bracken	17	852	18	552	28	4-29	0	19.71
L.S. Pascoe	29	1,568	21	1,066	53	5-30	1	20.11
D.K. Lillee	63	3,593	80	2,145	103	5-34	1	20.83
A.I.C. Dodemaide	24	1,327	30	753	36	5-21	1	20.92
B. Lee	112	5,688	74	4,433	200	5-27	4	22.17
G.D. McGrath	213	11,173	253	7,188	323	7-15	7	22.25
C.G. Rackemann	52	2,791	51	1,833	82	5-16	1	22.35
B.A. Williams	25	1,203	19	814	35	5-22	2	23.26
T.M. Alderman	65	3,371	75	2,056	88	5-17	2	23.36
C.J. McDermott	138	7,460	99	5,020	203	5-44	1	24.73

FIVE WICKETS IN AN INNINGS

T.M. Alderman (2)	5-17	v New Zealand at Wellington	1981-82
	5-32	v India at Christchurch	1989-90
A.J. Bichel (2)	5-19	v South Africa at Sydney	2001-02
	7-20	v England at Port Elizabeth	2002-03
G.S. Chappell (2)	5-20	v England at Birmingham	1977
	5-15	v India at Sydney	1980-81
M.J. Clarke	5-35	v Sri Lanka at Dambulla	2003-04
G.J. Cosier	5-18	v England at Birmingham	1977
A.I.C. Dodemaide	5-21	v Sri Lanka at Perth	1979-80
D.W. Fleming	5-36	v India at Mumbai	1995-96
D.R. Gilbert	5-46	v New Zealand at Sydney	1985-86
J.N. Gillespie (3)	5-22	v Pakistan at Nairobi	2002-03
	5-70	v Pakistan at Nairobi	2002-03
	5-32	v Zimbabwe at Harare	2003-04
G.J. Gilmour (2)	6-14	v England at Leeds	1975
	5-48	v West Indies at Lord's	1975
A.G. Hurst	5-21	v Canada at Birmingham	1979
G.B. Hogg (2)	5-41	v Sri Lanka at Dambulla	2003-04
	5-32	v West Indies at Melbourne	2004-05
B. Lee (4)	5-27	v India at Adelaide	1999-00
	5-30	v England at Melbourne	2002-03
	5-42	v New Zealand at Port Elizabeth	2002-03
	5-41	v England at Lord's	2005
S. Lee	5-33	v Sri Lanka at Melbourne	1998-99
D.K. Lillee	5-34	v Pakistan at Leeds	1975
K.H. MacLeay	6-39	v India at Nottingham	1983
C.J. McDermott	5-44	v Pakistan at Lahore	1987-88

G. D. McGrath (7)	5-52	v Pakistan at Lahore	1994-95
	5-40	v Sri Lanka at Adelaide	1998-99
	5-14	v West Indies at Manchester	1999
	5-49	v Pakistan at Sydney	1999-00
	5-37	v New Zealand at Colombo	2002-03
	7-15	v Namibia at Potchefstroom	2002-03
	5-27	v Pakistan at Sydney	2004-05
S. P. O'Donnell	5-13	v New Zealand at Christchurch	1989-90
L. S. Pascoe	5-30	v New Zealand at Sydney	1980-81
C. G. Rackemann	5-16	v Pakistan at Adelaide	1983-84
B. A. Reid	5-53	v India at Adelaide	1985-86
A. M. Stuart	5-26	v Pakistan at Melbourne	1996-97
A. Symonds	5-18	v Bangladesh at Manchester	2005
S. K. Warne	5-23	v West Indies at Sydney	1996-97
M. E. Waugh	5-24	v West Indies at Melbourne	1992-93
B. A. Williams (2)	5-53	v New Zealand at Pune	2003-04
	5-22	v Zimbabwe at Sydney	2003-04

HAT-TRICKS

B. A. Reid	v New Zealand at Sydney	1985-86
A. M. Stuart	v Pakistan at Melbourne	1996-97
B. Lee	v Kenya at Durban	2002-03

ALL-ROUND RECORDS

FIFTY RUNS AND THREE WICKETS IN A MATCH

G. S. Chappell	90 and 3-43	v New Zealand at Melbourne	1980-81
G. R. J. Matthews	54 and 3-33	v New Zealand at Auckland	1985-86
S. R. Waugh	82 and 4-48	v Pakistan at Perth	1986-87
S. R. Waugh	54 and 3-57	v West Indies at Melbourne	1988-89
S. P. O'Donnell	57* and 4-36	v Sri Lanka at Melbourne	1989-90
M. E. Waugh	57 and 5-24	v West Indies at Melbourne	1992-93
M. G. Bevan	79* and 3-36	v Pakistan at Melbourne	1996-97
T. M. Moody	56* and 3-25	v Bangladesh at Chester-le-Street	1999
D. S. Lehmann	67 and 4-7	v Zimbabwe at Harare	2003-04

1,000 RUNS AND 50 WICKETS IN A CAREER

	Runs	Batting Average	Wickets	Bowling Average	Games for the Double
G. S. Chappell	2,331	40.19	72	29.11	44
S. P. O'Donnell	1,242	25.35	108	28.72	40
S. R. Waugh	7,569	32.91	195	34.69	46
A. R. Border	6,524	30.63	73	28.37	199
M. E. Waugh	8,500	39.35	85	34.56	93
S. K. Warne	1,016	13.03	291	25.82	104
T. M. Moody	1,211	23.29	52	38.73	75
A. Symonds	2,833	36.79	93	36.70	70
D. S. Lehmann	3,077	38.95	52	27.81	114

WICKET-KEEPING RECORDS

MOST DISMISSALS IN A CAREER

	M	Ct	St	Total
A. C. Gilchrist	219	320	41	361
I. A. Healy	168	194	39	233
R. W. Marsh	92	120	4	124
W. B. Phillips	42	42	7	49
G. C. Dyer	23	24	4	28
T. J. Zoehrer	22	21	2	23

MOST DISMISSALS IN AN INNINGS

6	(all ct)	A. C. Gilchrist	v South Africa at Cape Town	1999-00
6	(5ct, 1st)	A. C. Gilchrist	v England at Sydney	2002-03
6	(all ct)	A. C. Gilchrist	v Namibia at Potchefstroom	2002-03
6	(all ct)	A. C. Gilchrist	v Sri Lanka at Colombo (PIS)	2003-04

Note: There are 4 instances of five dismissals in an innings.

MOST DISMISSALS PER MATCH

	M	Ct	St	Dismissals	Dismissals per Match
A. C. Gilchrist	219	320	41	361	1.64
I. A. Healy	168	194	39	233	1.39
R. W. Marsh	92	120	4	124	1.35
G. C. Dyer	23	24	4	28	1.22
W. B. Phillips	42	42	7	49	1.17
T. J. Zoehrer	22	21	2	23	1.05

FIELDING RECORDS

MOST CATCHES IN A CAREER

A. R. Border	127 in 273 matches	M. G. Bevan	69 in 232 matches
S. R. Waugh	111 in 325 matches	D. R. Martyn	57 in 181 matches
M. E. Waugh	108 in 244 matches	M. A. Taylor	56 in 113 matches
R. T. Ponting	92 in 231 matches	D. M. Jones	54 in 164 matches
S. K. Warne	80 in 193 matches	A. Symonds	48 in 124 matches

MOST CATCHES IN AN INNINGS

| 4 | M. A. Taylor | v West Indies at Sydney | 1992-93 |
| 4 | M. J. Clarke | v India at Melbourne | 2003-04 |

Note: There are 24 instances of three catches in an innings.

TEAM RECORDS

HIGHEST INNINGS TOTALS

Batting first (result for Australia)
2-359 v India at Johannesburg (WS) (Won) 2002-03
5-359 v India at Sydney (Won) 2003-04
6-349 v New Zealand at Christchurch (Won) 1999-00
2-347 v India at Bangalore (Won) 2003-04

5-347 v New Zealand at Napier (Won) 2004-0
7-344 v Zimbabwe at Hobart (Bel) (Won) 2003-0
6-338 v West Indies at Melbourne (Won) 2000-0
4-338 v India at Visakhapatnam (Won) 2000-0
7-337 v Pakistan at Sydney (Won) 1999-0

    Note: Australia's highest losing total batting first: 9-286, v West Indies, Georgetown, 1994-95.

Batting Second (result for Australia)

7-330 v South Africa at Port Elizabeth (Won) .... 2001-0.
4-316 v Pakistan at Lahore (Won) .... 1998-9'
4-289 v New Zealand at Chennai (Chepauk) (Won) 1995-9
5-287 v South Africa at Centurion (Won) .... 1996-9'
284   v India at Chandigarh (Lost) .... 1996-9'
284   v India at Brisbane (Lost) 2003-0-
4-282 v Zimbabwe at Hobart (Bel) (Won) 2000-0
4-280 v England at Birmingham (Won) .... 199.
4-279 v England at Lord's (Won) 1989
6-275 v England at Sydney (Lost) 1998-99

LOWEST COMPLETED INNINGS TOTALS

101   v England at Melbourne 1978-79
139   v India at Sharjah 1984-85
146   v West Indies at Melbourne 1981-82
147   v West Indies at Melbourne 1992-93
154   v South Africa at Durban 1993-94

    Note: Australia's lowest total defended: 9-101, v West Indies, Sydney, 1992-93.

LARGEST VICTORIES

By Runs

256   v Namibia at Potchefstroom 2002-03
232   v Sri Lanka at Adelaide 1984-85
224   v Pakistan at Nairobi 2002-03
208   v India at Sydney 2003-04
164   v New Zealand at Colombo 2002-03

By Wickets

10   v West Indies at Adelaide 2000-01
10   v England at Sydney 2002-03
10   v Bangladesh at Manchester 2005

    Note: 19 instances of a victory by nine wickets.

NARROWEST VICTORIES

By Runs

1   v India at Chennai (Chepauk) 1987-88
1   v India at Brisbane 1991-92
1   v South Africa at Bloemfontein 1993-94
1   v Zimbabwe at Perth 2000-01
1   v New Zealand at Christchurch 1992-93
1   v West Indies at Sydney 1995-96

by Wickets

1   v New Zealand at Christchurch 1992-93
1   v West Indies at Sydney 1995-96

HEAVIEST DEFEATS

By Runs

206	by New Zealand at Adelaide	1985-86
164	by West Indies at Perth	1986-87
133	by West Indies at Port-of-Spain	1994-95
128	by West Indies at Melbourne	1981-82
118	by India at Chelmsford	1983
118	by India at Indore	2000-01
109	by South Africa at Bloemfontein	1996-97
107	by India at Perth	1991-92
101	by England at Birmingham	1977
101	by West Indies at Leeds	1983

By Wickets

9	by West Indies at Sydney	1983-84
9	by West Indies at Kingston	1983-84
9	by South Africa at Sydney	1991-92
9	by West Indies at Perth	1992-93
9	by Pakistan at Rawalpindi	1994-95
9	by West Indies at St George's	2002-03
9	by England at Birmingham	2005

NARROWEST DEFEATS

By Runs

1	by New Zealand at Sydney	1980-81
1	by New Zealand at Perth	1987-88
1	by West Indies at Sydney	1988-89
1	by New Zealand at Hobart (Bel)	1990-91
1	by Sri Lanka at Dambulla	2003-04

By Wickets

1	by Pakistan at Perth	1986-87

TIED MATCHES

Australia (9-222) tied West Indies (5-222) at Melbourne	1983-84
England (5-226) tied Australia (8-226) at Nottingham	1989
Australia (7-228) tied Pakistan (9-228) at Hobart (Bel)	1992-93
West Indies (5-173) tied Australia (7-173) at Georgetown	1998-99
Australia (213) tied South Africa (213) at Birmingham	1999
South Africa (8-226) tied Australia (9-226) at Melbourne (DS)	2000-01
South Africa (7-259) tied Australia (9-259) at Potchefstroom	2001-02
Australia (196) tied England (196) at Lord's	2005

APPEARANCE RECORDS

MOST LIMITED-OVERS APPEARANCES

	M	Eng	NZ	Pak	SL	WI	Can	Ind	Zim	SAf	Ban	Kya	Sco	Net	Nam	USA
S. R. Waugh	325	30	60	43	24	50	–	53	14	47	2	1	1	–	–	–
A. R. Border	273	43	52	34	23	61	1	38	5	15	1	–	–	–	–	–
M. E. Waugh	244	21	39	29	23	47	–	27	13	42	1	1	1	–	–	–
M. G. Bevan	232	18	28	28	30	29	–	35	18	35	5	3	1	1	1	–
R. T. Ponting	231	23	28	28	26	31	–	34	20	26	8	3	1	1	1	1
A. C. Gilchrist	218	27	32	24	18	22	–	32	15	34	8	3	1	–	1	1
G. D. McGrath	213	26	26	32	20	25	–	22	14	37	4	3	1	1	1	1
S. K. Warne	193	18	27	22	18	27	–	18	12	45	2	3	1	–	–	–
D. C. Boon	181	21	39	19	16	32	–	29	5	19	1	–	–	–	-1	–
D. R. Martyn	181	24	28	28	15	12	–	27	15	20	6	3	–	1	1	1

YOUNGEST PLAYERS ON DEBUT

Years	Days			
19	260	R. J. Bright	v New Zealand at Dunedin	1973-74
19	267	C. J. McDermott	v West Indies at Melbourne	1984-85
20	58	R. T. Ponting	v South Africa at Wellington	1994-95
20	155	N. M. Hauritz	v South Africa at Johannesburg (WS)	2002-03
20	221	S. R. Waugh	v New Zealand at Melbourne	1985-86
20	225	A. K. Zesers	v India at Delhi	1987-88
20	278	I. C. Davis	v New Zealand at Dunedin	1973-74
20	280	S. R. Watson	v South Africa at Centurion	2002-03
20	297	W. M. Darling	v West Indies at St John's	1977-78

OLDEST PLAYERS ON DEBUT

Years	Days			
42	20	R. B. Simpson	v West Indies at St John's	1977-78
38	88	R. G. Holland	v West Indies at Sydney	1984-85
33	328	W. M. Lawry	v England at Melbourne	1970-71
32	261	J. A. Maclean	v England at Sydney	1978-79
31	349	J. K. Moss	v Pakistan at Nottingham	1979
31	190	A. N. Connolly	v England at Melbourne	1970-71

OLDEST PLAYERS

Years	Days			
42	69	R. B. Simpson	v West Indies at Castries	1977-78
38	255	A. R. Border	v South Africa at Bloemfontein	1993-94
38	223	R. G. Holland	v England at Manchester	1985
36	246	S. R. Waugh	v South Africa at Perth	2001-02
36	246	M. E. Waugh	v South Africa at Perth	2001-02
36	110	I. M. Chappell	v England at Sydney	1979-80
36	100	R. W. Marsh	v West Indies at Melbourne	1983-84

CAPTAINCY

THE CAPTAINS

	M	W	L	NR	T	% Won
W. M. Lawry	1	1	0	0	0	100.00
I. M. Chappell	11	6	5	0	0	54.44
G. S. Chappell	49	21	25	3	0	42.86
R. B. Simpson	2	1	1	0	0	50.00
G. N. Yallop	4	2	1	1	0	50.00
K. J. Hughes	49	21	23	4	1	42.86
D. W. Hookes	1	0	1	0	0	0.00
A. R. Border	178	107	67	3	1	60.11
R. J. Bright	1	0	1	0	0	0.00
G. R. Marsh	4	3	1	0	0	75.00
M. A. Taylor	67	37	29	0	1	53.73
I. A. Healy	8	5	3	0	0	62.50
S. R. Waugh	106	67	35	1	3	63.21
S. K. Warne	11	10	1	0	0	90.91
A. C. Gilchrist	8	7	1	0	0	87.50
R. T. Ponting	100	76	17	5	2	76.00

SUMMARY OF AUSTRALIAN LIMITED-OVERS INTERNATIONALS

	First Game	M	W	L	NR	T	% Won
England	1970-71	85	48	33	1	2	56.47
New Zealand	1973-74	97	68	26	3	-	70.10
Pakistan	1975	74	43	27	3	1	58.10
Sri Lanka	1975	55	36	17	2	-	65.45
West Indies	1975	108	49	55	2	2	45.53
Canada	1979	1	1	-	-	-	100.00
India	1980-81	80	49	27	4	-	61.25
Zimbabwe	1983	27	25	1	1	-	92.59
Bangladesh	1989-90	9	8	-	-	-	88.88
South Africa	1991-92	56	29	24	-	3	51.78
Kenya	1995-96	4	4	-	-	-	100.00
Scotland	1999	1	1	-	-	-	100.00
Netherlands	2002-03	1	1	-	-	-	100.00
Namibia	2002-03	1	1	-	-	-	100.00
USA	2004	1	1	-	-	-	100.00
Total		600	364	211	17	8	60.66

AUSTRALIAN LIMITED-OVERS INTERNATIONAL MATCHES

Date	Venue	Opponent	Result for Australia	Captain	Team/Opp
1970-71 in Australia					
Jan 5	Melbourne	England	Won by five wickets	W. M. Lawry	1/1
1972 in England					
Aug 24	Manchester	England	Lost by six wickets	I. M. Chappell	2/2
Aug 26	Lord's	England	Won by five wickets	I. M. Chappell	3/3
Aug 28	Birmingham	England	Lost by two wickets	I. M. Chappell	4/4
1973-74 in New Zealand					
Mar 30	Dunedin	New Zealand	Won by seven wickets	I. M. Chappell	5/1
Mar 31	Christchurch	New Zealand	Won by 31 runs	I. M. Chappell	6/2
1974-75 in Australia					
Jan 1	Melbourne	England	Lost by three wickets	I. M. Chappell	7/5
1975 World Cup in England					
Jun 7	Leeds	Pakistan	Won by 73 runs	I. M. Chappell	8/1
Jun 11	The Oval	Sri Lanka	Won by 52 runs	I. M. Chappell	9/1
Jun 14	The Oval	West Indies	Lost by seven wickets	I. M. Chappell	10/1
Jun 18	Leeds	England	Won by four wickets	I. M. Chappell	11/6
Jun 21	Lord's	West Indies	Lost by 17 runs	I. M. Chappell	12/2
1975-76 in Australia					
Dec 20	Adelaide	West Indies	Won by five wickets	G. S. Chappell	13/3
1977 in England					
Jun 2	Manchester	England	Lost by two wickets	G. S. Chappell	14/7
Jun 4	Birmingham	England	Lost by 99 runs	G. S. Chappell	15/8
Jun 6	The Oval	England	Won by two wickets	G. S. Chappell	16/9
1977-78 in West Indies					
Feb 22	St John's	West Indies	Lost on run-rate	R. B. Simpson	17/4
Apr 12	Castries	West Indies	Won by two wickets	R. B. Simpson	18/5
1978-79 in Australia					
Jan 13	Sydney	England	No result	G. N. Yallop	19/10
Jan 24	Melbourne	England	Lost by seven wickets	G. N. Yallop	20/11
Feb 4	Melbourne	England	Won by four wickets	G. N. Yallop	21/12
Feb 7	Melbourne	England	Won by six wickets	G. N. Yallop	22/13

Date	Venue	Opponent	Result for Australia	Captain	Team/Opp
1979 World Cup in England					
Jun 9	Lord's	England	Lost by six wickets	K. J. Hughes	23/14
Jun 13–14	Nottingham	Pakistan	Lost by 89 runs	K. J. Hughes	24/2
Jun 16	Birmingham	Canada	Won by seven wickets	K. J. Hughes	25/1
1979-80 World Series Cup in Australia					
Nov 27	Sydney	West Indies	Won by five wickets	G. S. Chappell	26/6
Dec 8	Melbourne	England	Lost by three wickets	G. S. Chappell	27/15
Dec 9	Melbourne	West Indies	Lost by 80 runs	G. S. Chappell	28/7
Dec 11	Sydney	England	Lost by 72 runs	G. S. Chappell	29/16
Dec 21	Sydney	West Indies	Won by seven runs	G. S. Chappell	30/8
Dec 26	Sydney	England	Lost by four wickets	G. S. Chappell	31/17
Jan 14	Sydney	England	Lost by two wickets	G. S. Chappell	32/18
Jan 18	Sydney	West Indies	Won by nine runs	G. S. Chappell	33/9
1980 in England					
Aug 20	The Oval	England	Lost by 23 runs	G. S. Chappell	34/19
Aug 22	Birmingham	England	Lost by 47 runs	G. S. Chappell	35/20
1980-81 World Series Cup in Australia					
Nov 23	Adelaide	New Zealand	Lost by three wickets	G. S. Chappell	36/3
Nov 25	Sydney	New Zealand	Won by 94 runs	G. S. Chappell	37/4
Dec 6	Melbourne	India	Lost by 66 runs	G. S. Chappell	38/1
Dec 7	Melbourne	New Zealand	Won by four wickets	G. S. Chappell	39/5
Dec 18	Sydney	India	Won by nine wickets	G. S. Chappell	40/2
Jan 8	Sydney	India	Won by nine wickets	G. S. Chappell	41/3
Jan 11	Melbourne	India	Won by seven wickets	G. S. Chappell	42/4
Jan 13	Sydney	New Zealand	Lost by one run	G. S. Chappell	43/6
Jan 15	Sydney	India	Won by 27 runs	G. S. Chappell	44/5
Jan 21	Sydney	New Zealand	No result	G. S. Chappell	45/7
Jan 29	Sydney	New Zealand	Lost by 78 runs	G. S. Chappell	46/8
Jan 31	Melbourne	New Zealand	Won by seven wickets	G. S. Chappell	47/9
Feb 1	Melbourne	New Zealand	Won by six runs	G. S. Chappell	48/10
Feb 3	Sydney	New Zealand	Won by six wickets	G. S. Chappell	49/11
1981 in England					
Jun 4	Lord's	England	Lost by six wickets	K. J. Hughes	50/21
Jun 6	Birmingham	England	Won by two runs	K. J. Hughes	51/22
Jun 8	Leeds	England	Won by 71 runs	K. J. Hughes	52/23
1981-82 World Series Cup in Australia					
Nov 21	Melbourne	Pakistan	Lost by four wickets	G. S. Chappell	53/3
Nov 24	Sydney	West Indies	Won by seven wickets	G. S. Chappell	54/10
Dec 6	Adelaide	Pakistan	Won by 38 runs	G. S. Chappell	55/4
Dec 17	Sydney	Pakistan	Lost by six wickets	G. S. Chappell	56/5
Dec 20	Perth	West Indies	Lost by eight wickets	G. S. Chappell	57/11
Jan 20	Melbourne	Pakistan	Lost by 25 runs	G. S. Chappell	58/6
Jan 10	Melbourne	West Indies	Lost by five wickets	G. S. Chappell	59/12
Jan 14	Sydney	Pakistan	Won by 76 runs	G. S. Chappell	60/7
Jan 17	Brisbane	West Indies	Lost by five wickets	G. S. Chappell	61/13
Jan 19	Sydney	West Indies	Won on run-rate	G. S. Chappell	62/14
Jan 23	Melbourne	West Indies	Lost by 86 runs	G. S. Chappell	63/15
Jan 24	Melbourne	West Indies	Lost by 128 runs	G. S. Chappell	64/16
Jan 26	Sydney	West Indies	Won by 46 runs	G. S. Chappell	65/17
Jan 27	Sydney	West Indies	Lost by 18 runs	G. S. Chappell	66/18
1981-82 in New Zealand					
Feb 13	Auckland	New Zealand	Lost by 46 runs	G. S. Chappell	67/12
Feb 17	Dunedin	New Zealand	Won by six wickets	G. S. Chappell	68/13
Feb 9	Wellington	New Zealand	Won by eight wickets	G. S. Chappell	69/14

Date	Venue	Opponent	Result for Australia	Captain	Team/Opp

1982-83 in Pakistan

Sep 20	Hyderabad	Pakistan	Lost by 59 runs	K. J. Hughes	70/8
Oct 8	Lahore	Pakistan	Lost by 28 runs	K. J. Hughes	71/9
Oct 22	Karachi	Pakistan	No result	K. J. Hughes	72/10

1982-83 World Series Cup in Australia

Jan 9	Melbourne	New Zealand	Won by eight wickets	K. J. Hughes	73/15
Jan 11	Sydney	England	Won by 31 runs	K. J. Hughes	74/24
Jan 16	Brisbane	England	Won by seven wickets	K. J. Hughes	75/25
Jan 18	Sydney	New Zealand	Lost by 47 runs	K. J. Hughes	76/16
Jan 22	Melbourne	New Zealand	Lost by 58 runs	K. J. Hughes	77/17
Jan 23	Melbourne	England	Won by five wickets	K. J. Hughes	78/26
Jan 26	Sydney	England	Lost by 98 runs	K. J. Hughes	79/27
Jan 30	Adelaide	England	Lost by 14 runs	K. J. Hughes	80/28
Jan 31	Adelaide	New Zealand	Lost by 46 runs	K. J. Hughes	81/18
Feb 6	Perth	New Zealand	Won by 27 runs	K. J. Hughes	82/19
Feb 9	Sydney	New Zealand	Won by six wickets	K. J. Hughes	83/20
Feb 13	Melbourne	New Zealand	Won by 149 runs	K. J. Hughes	84/21

1982-83 in Australia

Mar 17	Sydney	New Zealand	Lost by 14 runs	K. J. Hughes	85/22

1982-83 in Sri Lanka

Apr 13	Colombo (PSS)	Sri Lanka	Lost by two wickets	G. S. Chappell	86/2
Apr 16	Colombo (PSS)	Sri Lanka	Lost by four wickets	G. S. Chappell	87/3
Apr 20	Colombo (SSC)	Sri Lanka	No result	G. S. Chappell	88/4
Apr 30	Colombo (SSC)	Sri Lanka	No result	G. S. Chappell	89/5

1983 World Cup in England

Jun 9	Nottingham	Zimbabwe	Lost by 13 runs	K. J. Hughes	90/1
Jun 11–12	Leeds	West Indies	Lost by 101 runs	K. J. Hughes	91/19
Jun 13	Nottingham	India	Won by 162 runs	K. J. Hughes	92/6
Jun 16	Southampton	Zimbabwe	Won by 32 runs	K. J. Hughes	93/2
Jun 18	Lord's	West Indies	Lost by seven wickets	K. J. Hughes	94/20
Jun 20	Chelmsford	India	Lost by 118 runs	D. W. Hookes	95/7

1983-84 World Series Cup in Australia

Jan 8	Melbourne	West Indies	Lost by 27 runs	K. J. Hughes	96/21
Jan 10	Sydney	Pakistan	Won by 34 runs	K. J. Hughes	97/11
Jan 15	Brisbane	Pakistan	No result	K. J. Hughes	98/12
Jan 17	Sydney	West Indies	Lost by 28 runs	K. J. Hughes	99/22
Jan 21	Melbourne	Pakistan	Won by 45 runs	K. J. Hughes	100/13
Jan 22	Melbourne	West Indies	Lost by 26 runs	K. J. Hughes	101/23
Jan 25	Sydney	Pakistan	Won by 87 runs	K. J. Hughes	102/14
Jan 29	Adelaide	West Indies	Lost by six wickets	K. J. Hughes	103/24
Jan 30	Adelaide	Pakistan	Won by 70 runs	K. J. Hughes	104/15
Feb 5	Perth	West Indies	Won by 14 runs	K. J. Hughes	105/25
Feb 8	Sydney	West Indies	Lost by nine wickets	K. J. Hughes	106/26
Feb 11	Melbourne	West Indies	Tied	K. J. Hughes	107/27
Feb 12	Melbourne	West Indies	Lost by six wickets	K. J. Hughes	108/28

1983-84 in West Indies

Feb 29	Berbice	West Indies	Lost by eight wickets	K. J. Hughes	109/29
Mar 14	Port-of-Spain	West Indies	Won by four wickets	K. J. Hughes	110/30
Apr 19	Castries	West Indies	Lost by seven wickets	K. J. Hughes	111/31
Apr 26	Kingston	West Indies	Lost by nine wickets	K. J. Hughes	112/32

Date	Venue	Opponent	Result for Australia	Captain	Team/Opp
1984-85 in India					
Sep 28	New Delhi	India	Won by 48 runs	K. J. Hughes	113/8
Oct 1	Trivandrum	India	No result	K. J. Hughes	114/9
Oct 3	Jamshedpur	India	No result	K. J. Hughes	115/10
Oct 5	Ahmedabad	India	Won by seven wickets	K. J. Hughes	116/11
Oct 6	Indore	India	Won by six wickets	K. J. Hughes	117/12
1984-85 World Series Cup in Australia					
Jan 6	Melbourne	West Indies	Lost by seven wickets	A. R. Border	118/33
Jan 8	Sydney	Sri Lanka	Won by six wickets	A. R. Border	119/6
Jan 13	Brisbane	West Indies	Lost by five wickets	A. R. Border	120/34
Jan 15	Sydney	West Indies	Lost by five wickets	A. R. Border	121/35
Jan 19	Melbourne	Sri Lanka	Lost by four wickets	A. R. Border	122/7
Jan 20	Melbourne	West Indies	Lost by 65 runs	A. R. Border	123/36
Jan 23	Sydney	Sri Lanka	Won by three wickets	A. R. Border	124/8
Jan 27	Adelaide	West Indies	Lost by six wickets	A. R. Border	125/37
Jan 28	Adelaide	Sri Lanka	Won by 232 runs	A. R. Border	126/9
Feb 3	Perth	Sri Lanka	Won by nine wickets	A. R. Border	127/10
Feb 6	Sydney	West Indies	Won by 26 runs	A. R. Border	128/38
Feb 10	Melbourne	West Indies	Lost by four wickets	A. R. Border	129/39
Feb 12	Sydney	West Indies	Lost by seven wickets	A. R. Border	130/40
1984-85 World Championship of Cricket in Australia					
Feb 17	Melbourne	England	Won by seven wickets	A. R. Border	131/29
Feb 24	Melbourne	Pakistan	Lost by 62 runs	A. R. Border	132/16
Mar 3	Melbourne	India	Lost by eight wickets	A. R. Border	133/13
1984-85 in United Arab Emirates					
Mar 24	Sharjah	England	Won by two wickets	A. R. Border	134/30
Mar 29	Sharjah	India	Lost by three wickets	A. R. Border	135/14
1985 in England					
May 30	Manchester	England	Won by three wickets	A. R. Border	136/31
Jun 1	Birmingham	England	Won by four wickets	A. R. Border	137/32
Jun 3	Lord's	England	Lost by eight wickets	A. R. Border	138/33
1985-86 World Series Cup in Australia					
Jan 9	Melbourne	New Zealand	No result	A. R. Border	139/23
Jan 12	Brisbane	India	Won by four wickets	A. R. Border	140/15
Jan 14	Sydney	New Zealand	Won by four wickets	A. R. Border	141/24
Jan 16	Melbourne	India	Lost by eight wickets	A. R. Border	142/16
Jan 19	Perth	New Zealand	Won by four wickets	A. R. Border	143/25
Jan 21	Sydney	India	Won by 100 runs	A. R. Border	144/17
Jan 26	Adelaide	India	Won by 36 runs	A. R. Border	145/18
Jan 27	Adelaide	New Zealand	Lost by 206 runs	A. R. Border	146/26
Jan 29	Sydney	New Zealand	Won by 99 runs	A. R. Border	147/27
Jan 31	Melbourne	India	Lost by six wickets	A. R. Border	148/19
Feb 5	Sydney	India	Won by 11 runs	A. R. Border	149/20
Feb 9	Melbourne	India	Won by seven wickets	A. R. Border	150/21
1985-86 in New Zealand					
Mar 19	Dunedin	New Zealand	Lost by 30 runs	A. R. Border	151/28
Mar 22	Christchurch	New Zealand	Lost by 53 runs	A. R. Border	152/29
Mar 26	Wellington	New Zealand	Won by three wickets	A. R. Border	153/30
Mar 29	Auckland	New Zealand	Won by 44 runs	A. R. Border	154/31
1985-86 in United Arab Emirates					
Apr 11	Sharjah	Pakistan	Lost by eight wickets	R. J. Bright	155/17
1986-87 in India					
Sep 7	Jaipur	India	Lost by seven wickets	A. R. Border	156/22
Sep 9	Srinagar	India	Won by three wickets	A. R. Border	157/23
Sep 24	Hyderabad	India	No result	A. R. Border	158/24

Date		Venue	Opponent	Result for Australia	Captain	Team/Opp
Oct	2	Delhi	India	Lost by three wickets	A. R. Border	159/25
Oct	5	Ahmedabad	India	Lost by 52 runs	A. R. Border	160/26
Oct	7	Rajkot	India	Won by seven wickets	A. R. Border	161/27

1986-87 World Challenge in Australia

Jan	1	Perth	England	Lost by 37 runs	A. R. Border	162/34
Jan	2	Perth	Pakistan	Lost by one wicket	A. R. Border	163/18
Jan	4	Perth	West Indies	Lost by 164 runs	A. R. Border	164/41

1986-87 World Series Cup in Australia

Jan	18	Brisbane	England	Won by 11 runs	A. R. Border	165/35
Jan	20	Melbourne	West Indies	Lost by seven wickets	A. R. Border	166/42
Jan	22	Sydney	England	Lost by three wickets	A. R. Border	167/36
Jan	25	Adelaide	West Indies	Lost by 16 runs	A. R. Border	168/43
Jan	26	Adelaide	England	Won by 33 runs	A. R. Border	169/37
Jan	28	Sydney	West Indies	Won by 36 runs	A. R. Border	170/44
Feb	1	Melbourne	England	Won by 109 runs	A. R. Border	171/38
Feb	6	Sydney	West Indies	Won by two wickets	A. R. Border	172/45
Feb	8	Melbourne	England	Lost by six wickets	A. R. Border	173/39
Feb	11	Sydney	England	Lost by eight runs	A. R. Border	174/40

1986-87 in United Arab Emirates

Apr	3	Sharjah	Pakistan	Lost by six wickets	A. R. Border	175/19
Apr	6	Sharjah	India	Lost by seven wickets	G. R. Marsh	176/28
Apr	9	Sharjah	England	Lost by 11 runs	A. R. Border	177/41

1987-88 World Cup in India and Pakistan

Oct	9	Chennai	India	Won by one run	A. R. Border	178/29
Oct	13	Chennai	Zimbabwe	Won by 96 runs	A. R. Border	179/3
Oct	19	Indore	New Zealand	Won by three runs	A. R. Border	180/32
Oct	22	New Delhi	India	Lost by 56 runs	A. R. Border	181/30
Oct	27	Chandigarh	New Zealand	Won by 17 runs	A. R. Border	182/33
Oct	30	Cuttack	Zimbabwe	Won by 70 runs	A. R. Border	183/4
Nov	4	Lahore	Pakistan	Won by 18 runs	A. R. Border	184/20
Nov	8	Calcutta	England	Won by seven runs	A. R. Border	185/42

1987-88 World Series Cup in Australia

Jan	2	Perth	Sri Lanka	Won by 81 runs	A. R. Border	186/11
Jan	3	Perth	New Zealand	Lost by one run	A. R. Border	187/34
Jan	7	Melbourne	New Zealand	Won by six runs	A. R. Border	188/35
Jan	10	Adelaide	Sri Lanka	Won by 81 runs	A. R. Border	189/12
Jan	14	Melbourne	Sri Lanka	Won by 38 runs	A. R. Border	190/13
Jan	17	Brisbane	New Zealand	Won by five wickets	A. R. Border	191/36
Jan	19	Sydney	Sri Lanka	Won by three wickets	A. R. Border	192/14
Jan	20	Sydney	New Zealand	Won by 78 runs	A. R. Border	193/37
Jan	22	Melbourne	New Zealand	Won by eight wickets	A. R. Border	194/38
Jan	24	Sydney	New Zealand	Won by six wickets	A. R. Border	195/39

1987-88 in Australia

Feb	4	Melbourne	England	Won by 22 runs	A. R. Border	196/43

1988-89 in Pakistan

Oct	14	Lahore	Pakistan	Lost on fewer wickets	A. R. Border	197/21

1988-89 World Series Cup in Australia

Dec	11	Adelaide	Pakistan	Won by nine wickets	A. R. Border	198/22
Dec	13	Sydney	West Indies	Lost by one run	A. R. Border	199/46
Dec	15	Melbourne	West Indies	Lost by 34 runs	A. R. Border	200/47
Jan	2	Perth	Pakistan	Lost by 38 runs	A. R. Border	201/23
Jan	5	Melbourne	West Indies	Won by eight runs	A. R. Border	202/48
Jan	8	Brisbane	Pakistan	Won by five wickets	A. R. Border	203/24

Date	Venue	Opponent	Result for Australia	Captain	Team/Opp
Jan 10	Melbourne	Pakistan	Won on run-rate	A. R. Border	204/25
Jan 12	Sydney	West Indies	Won by 61 runs	A. R. Border	205/49
Jan 14	Melbourne	West Indies	Won by two runs	A. R. Border	206/50
Jan 16	Sydney	West Indies	Lost by 92 runs	A. R. Border	207/51
Jan 18	Sydney	West Indies	Lost on run-rate	A. R. Border	208/52

1989 in England

May 25	Manchester	England	Lost by 95 runs	A. R. Border	209/44
May 27	Nottingham	England	Tied	A. R. Border	210/45
May 29	Lord's	England	Won by six wickets	A. R. Border	211/46

1989-90 in India

Oct 19	Hyderabad	England	Lost by seven wickets	A. R. Border	212/47
Oct 21	Chennai	West Indies	Won by 99 runs	A. R. Border	213/53
Oct 23	Bombay	Pakistan	Lost by 66 runs	A. R. Border	214/26
Oct 25	Goa	Sri Lanka	Won by 28 runs	A. R. Border	215/15
Oct 27	Bangalore	India	Lost by three wickets	A. R. Border	216/31

1989-90 World Series in Australia

Dec 26	Melbourne	Sri Lanka	Won by 30 runs	A. R. Border	217/16
Dec 30	Perth	Sri Lanka	Won by nine wickets	A. R. Border	218/17
Jan 3	Melbourne	Pakistan	Won by seven wickets	A. R. Border	219/27
Jan 4	Melbourne	Sri Lanka	Won by 73 runs	A. R. Border	220/18
Feb 11	Brisbane	Pakistan	Won by 67 runs	A. R. Border	221/28
Feb 13	Sydney	Pakistan	Lost by five wickets	A. R. Border	222/29
Feb 18	Adelaide	Sri Lanka	Won by seven wickets	A. R. Border	223/19

Date	Venue	Opponent	Result for Australia	Captain	Team/Opp
Feb 20	Sydney	Pakistan	Lost by two runs	A. R. Border	224/30
Feb 23	Melbourne	Pakistan	Won by seven wickets	A. R. Border	225/31
Feb 25	Sydney	Pakistan	Won by 69 runs	A. R. Border	226/32

1989-90 in New Zealand

Mar 3	Christchurch	India	Won by 18 runs	A. R. Border	227/32
Mar 4	Christchurch	New Zealand	Won by 150 runs	A. R. Border	228/40
Mar 8	Hamilton	India	Won by seven wickets	A. R. Border	229/33
Mar 10	Auckland	New Zealand	Won on run-rate	G. R. Marsh	230/41
Mar 11	Auckland	New Zealand	Won by eight wickets	A. R. Border	231/42

1989-90 in United Arab Emirates

Apr 26	Sharjah	New Zealand	Won by 63 runs	A. R. Border	232/43
Apr 30	Sharjah	Bangladesh	Won by seven wickets	A. R. Border	233/1
May 2	Sharjah	Sri Lanka	Won by 114 runs	A. R. Border	234/20
May 4	Sharjah	Pakistan	Lost by 36 runs	A. R. Border	235/33

1990-91 World Series in Australia

Nov 29	Sydney	New Zealand	Won by 61 runs	A. R. Border	236/44
Dec 2	Adelaide	New Zealand	Won by six wickets	A. R. Border	237/45
Dec 9	Perth	England	Won by six wickets	A. R. Border	238/48
Dec 11	Melbourne	New Zealand	Won by 39 runs	A. R. Border	239/46
Dec 16	Brisbane	England	Won by 37 runs	A. R. Border	240/49
Dec 18	Hobart (Bel)	New Zealand	Lost by one run	A. R. Border	241/47
Jan 1	Sydney	England	Won by 68 runs	A. R. Border	242/50
Jan 10	Melbourne	England	Won by three runs	A. R. Border	243/51
Jan 13	Sydney	New Zealand	Won by six wickets	G. R. Marsh	244/48
Jan 15	Melbourne	New Zealand	Won by seven wickets	G. R. Marsh	245/49

1990-91 in West Indies

Feb 26	Kingston	West Indies	Won by 35 runs	A. R. Border	246/54
Mar 9	Port-of-Spain	West Indies	Won by 45 runs	A. R. Border	247/55
Mar 10	Port-of-Spain	West Indies	Lost on run-rate	A. R. Border	248/56
Mar 13	Bridgetown	West Indies	Won by 46 runs	A. R. Border	249/57
Mar 20	Georgetown	West Indies	Won by six wickets	A. R. Border	250/58

Date	Venue	Opponent	Result for Australia	Captain	Team/Opp
1991-92 World Series in Australia					
Dec 8	Perth	India	Lost by 107 runs	A. R. Border	251/34
Dec 10	Hobart (Bel)	India	Won by eight wickets	A. R. Border	252/35
Dec 12	Melbourne	West Indies	Won by nine runs	A. R. Border	253/59
Dec 15	Adelaide	India	Won by six wickets	A. R. Border	254/36
Dec 18	Sydney	West Indies	Won by 51 runs	A. R. Border	255/60
Jan 9	Melbourne	West Indies	No result	A. R. Border	256/61
Jan 12	Brisbane	West Indies	Lost by 12 runs	A. R. Border	257/62
Jan 14	Sydney	India	Won by nine wickets	A. R. Border	258/37
Jan 18	Melbourne	India	Won by 88 runs	A. R. Border	259/38
Jan 20	Sydney	India	Won by six runs	A. R. Border	260/39
1991-92 World Cup in Australia and New Zealand					
Feb 22	Auckland	New Zealand	Lost by 37 runs	A. R. Border	261/50
Feb 26	Sydney	South Africa	Lost by nine wickets	A. R. Border	262/1
Mar 1	Brisbane	India	Won by one run	A. R. Border	263/40
Mar 5	Sydney	England	Lost by eight wickets	A. R. Border	264/52
Mar 7	Adelaide	Sri Lanka	Won by seven wickets	A. R. Border	265/21
Mar 11	Perth	Pakistan	Lost by 48 runs	A. R. Border	266/34
Mar 14	Hobart (Bel)	Zimbabwe	Won by 128 runs	A. R. Border	267/5
Mar 18	Melbourne	West Indies	Won by 57 runs	A. R. Border	268/63
1992-93 in Sri Lanka					
Aug 15	Colombo (PSS)	Sri Lanka	Lost by four wickets	A. R. Border	269/22
Sep 4	Colombo (PIS)	Sri Lanka	Lost on run-rate	A. R. Border	270/23
Sep 5	Colombo (PIS)	Sri Lanka	Won by five wickets	A. R. Border	271/24
1992-93 World Series in Australia					
Dec 6	Perth	West Indies	Lost by nine wickets	A. R. Border	272/64
Dec 8	Sydney	West Indies	Won by 14 runs	M. A. Taylor	273/65
Dec 10	Hobart (Bel)	Pakistan	Tied	M. A. Taylor	274/35
Dec 13	Adelaide	Pakistan	Won by eight wickets	M. A. Taylor	275/36
Dec 15	Melbourne	West Indies	Won by four runs	M. A. Taylor	276/66
Jan 10	Brisbane	West Indies	Lost by seven runs	A. R. Border	277/67
Jan 12	Melbourne	Pakistan	Won by 32 runs	A. R. Border	278/37
Jan 14	Sydney	Pakistan	Won by 23 runs	A. R. Border	279/38
Jan 16	Sydney	West Indies	Lost by 25 runs	A. R. Border	280/69
Jan 18	Melbourne	West Indies	Lost by four wickets	A. R. Border	281/69
1992-93 in New Zealand					
Mar 19	Dunedin	New Zealand	Won by 129 runs	A. R. Border	282/51
Mar 21-22	Christchurch	New Zealand	Won by one wicket	M. A. Taylor	283/52
Mar 24	Wellington	New Zealand	Lost by 88 runs	A. R. Border	284/53
Mar 27	Hamilton	New Zealand	Lost by three wickets	M. A. Taylor	285/54
Mar 28	Auckland	New Zealand	Won by three runs	A. R. Border	286/55
1993 in England					
May 19	Manchester	England	Won by four runs	A. R. Border	287/53
May 21	Birmingham	England	Won by six wickets	A. R. Border	288/54
May 23	Lord's	England	Won by 19 runs	M. A. Taylor	289/55
1993-94 World Series in Australia					
Dec 9	Melbourne	South Africa	Lost by seven wickets	A. R. Border	290/2
Dec 12	Adelaide	New Zealand	Won by eight wickets	A. R. Border	291/56
Dec 14	Sydney	South Africa	Won by 103 runs	A. R. Border	292/3
Dec 16	Melbourne	New Zealand	Won by three runs	A. R. Border	293/57
Jan 9	Brisbane	South Africa	Won by 48 runs	A. R. Border	294/4
Jan 11	Sydney	New Zealand	Lost by 13 runs	A. R. Border	295/58
Jan 16	Perth	South Africa	Lost by 82 runs	M. A. Taylor	296/5
Jan 19	Melbourne	New Zealand	Won by 51 runs	A. R. Border	297/59

Date		Venue	Opponent	Result for Australia	Captain	Team/Op
Jan	21	Melbourne	South Africa	Lost by 28 runs	A. R. Border	298/6
Jan	23	Sydney	South Africa	Won by 69 runs	A. R. Border	299/7
Jan	25	Sydney	South Africa	Won by 35 runs	A. R. Border	300/8

1993-94 in South Africa

Feb	19	Johannesburg	South Africa	Lost by five runs	A. R. Border	301/9
Feb	20	Pretoria	South Africa	Lost by 56 runs	A. R. Border	302/10
Feb	22	Port Elizabeth	South Africa	Won by 88 runs	A. R. Border	303/11
Feb	24	Durban	South Africa	Lost by seven wickets	A. R. Border	304/12
Apr	2	East London	South Africa	Won by seven wickets	A. R. Border	305/13
Apr	4	Port Elizabeth	South Africa	Lost by 26 runs	A. R. Border	306/14
Apr	6	Cape Town	South Africa	Won by 36 runs	A. R. Border	307/15
Apr	8	Bloemfontein	South Africa	Won by one run	A. R. Border	308/16

1993-94 in United Arab Emirates

Apr	14	Sharjah	Sri Lanka	Won by nine wickets	M. A. Taylor	309/25
Apr	16	Sharjah	New Zealand	Won by seven wickets	M. A. Taylor	310/60
Apr	19	Sharjah	India	Lost by seven wickets	M. A. Taylor	311/41

1994-95 in Sri Lanka

Sep	7	Colombo (SSC)	Pakistan	Won by 28 runs	M. A. Taylor	312/39
Sep	9	Colombo (PIS)	India	Lost by 31 runs	M. A. Taylor	313/42
Sep	13	Colombo (SSC)	Sri Lanka	Lost on run-rate	M. A. Taylor	314/26

1994-95 in Pakistan

Oct	12	Lahore	South Africa	Won by six wickets	M. A. Taylor	315/17
Oct	14	Multan	Pakistan	Won by seven wickets	M. A. Taylor	316/40
Oct	18	Faisalabad	South Africa	Won by 22 runs	M. A. Taylor	317/18
Oct	22	Rawalpindi	Pakistan	Lost by nine wickets	M. A. Taylor	318/41
Oct	24	Peshawar	South Africa	Won by three wickets	M. A. Taylor	319/19
Oct	30	Lahore	Pakistan	Won by 64 runs	M. A. Taylor	320/42

1994-95 World Series in Australia

Dec	2	Perth	Zimbabwe	Won by two wickets	M. A. Taylor	321/6
Dec	6	Sydney	England	Won by 28 runs	M. A. Taylor	322/56
Dec	8	Hobart (Bel)	Zimbabwe	Won by 85 runs	M. A. Taylor	323/7
Jan	10	Melbourne	England	Lost by 37 runs	M. A. Taylor	324/57

1994-95 in New Zealand

Feb	15	Wellington	South Africa	Won by three wickets	M. A. Taylor	325/20
Feb	19	Auckland	New Zealand	Won by 27 runs	M. A. Taylor	326/61
Feb	22	Dunedin	India	Lost by five wickets	M. A. Taylor	327/43
Feb	26	Auckland	New Zealand	Won by six wickets	M. A. Taylor	326/62

1994-95 in West Indies

Mar	8	Bridgetown	West Indies	Lost by six runs	M. A. Taylor	329/70
Mar	11	Port-of-Spain	West Indies	Won by 26 runs	M. A. Taylor	330/71
Mar	12	Port-of-Spain	West Indies	Lost by 133 runs	M. A. Taylor	331/72
Mar	15	Kingstown	West Indies	Lost on run-rate	M. A. Taylor	332/73
Mar	18	Georgetown	West Indies	Lost by five wickets	M. A. Taylor	333/74

1995-96 World Series in Australia

Dec	17	Adelaide	West Indies	Won by 121 runs	M. A. Taylor	334/75
Dec	19	Melbourne	West Indies	Won by 24 runs	M. A. Taylor	335/76
Dec	21	Sydney	Sri Lanka	Won by five wickets	M. A. Taylor	336/27
Jan	1	Sydney	West Indies	Won by one wicket	M. A. Taylor	337/77
Jan	7	Brisbane	West Indies	Lost by 14 runs	M. A. Taylor	338/78
Jan	9	Melbourne	Sri Lanka	Lost by three wickets	M. A. Taylor	339/28
Jan	12	Perth	Sri Lanka	Won by 83 runs	M. A. Taylor	340/29
Jan	16	Melbourne	Sri Lanka	Lost by three wickets	M. A. Taylor	341/30
Jan	18	Melbourne	Sri Lanka	Won by 18 runs	M. A. Taylor	342/31
Jan	20	Sydney	Sri Lanka	Won on run-rate	M. A. Taylor	343/32

ate	Venue	Opponent	Result for Australia	Captain	Team/Opp
1995-96 World Cup in India, Pakistan and Sri Lanka					
Feb 23	Vishakhapatnam	Kenya	Won by 97 runs	M. A. Taylor	344/1
Feb 27	Bombay	India	Won by 16 runs	M. A. Taylor	345/44
Mar 1	Nagpur	Zimbabwe	Won by eight wickets	M. A. Taylor	346/8
Mar 4	Jaipur	West Indies	Lost by four wickets	M. A. Taylor	347/79
Mar 11	Chennai	New Zealand	Won by six wickets	M. A. Taylor	348/63
Mar 14	Chandigarh	West Indies	Won by five runs	M. A. Taylor	349/80
Mar 17	Lahore	Sri Lanka	Lost by seven wickets	M. A. Taylor	350/33
1996-97 in Sri Lanka					
Aug 26	Colombo (PIS)	Zimbabwe	Won by 125 runs	I. A. Healy	351/9
Aug 30	Colombo (PIS)	Sri Lanka	Lost by four wickets	I. A. Healy	352/34
Sep 6	Colombo (SSC)	India	Won by three wickets	I. A. Healy	353/45
Sep 7	Colombo (SSC)	Sri Lanka	Lost by 50 runs	I. A. Healy	354/35
1996-97 in India					
Oct 19	Indore	South Africa	Lost by seven wickets	M. A. Taylor	355/21
Oct 21	Bangalore	India	Lost by two wickets	M. A. Taylor	356/46
Oct 25	Faridabad	South Africa	Lost by two wickets	M. A. Taylor	357/22
Nov 1	Guwahati	South Africa	Lost by eight wickets	M. A. Taylor	358/23
Nov 3	Chandigarh	India	Lost by five runs	M. A. Taylor	359/47
1996-97 Carlton & United Series in Australia					
Dec 6	Melbourne	West Indies	Won by five wickets	M. A. Taylor	360/81
Dec 8	Sydney	West Indies	Won by eight wickets	M. A. Taylor	361/82
Dec 15	Adelaide	Pakistan	Lost by 12 runs	M. A. Taylor	362/43
Jan 1	Sydney	Pakistan	Lost by four wickets	M. A. Taylor	363/44
Jan 5	Brisbane	West Indies	Lost by seven wickets	M. A. Taylor	364/83
Jan 7	Hobart (Bel)	Pakistan	Lost by 29 runs	M. A. Taylor	365/45
Jan 12	Perth	West Indies	Lost by four wickets	M. A. Taylor	366/84
Jan 16	Melbourne	Pakistan	Won by three wickets	M. A. Taylor	367/46
1996-97 in South Africa					
Mar 29	East London	South Africa	Lost by six wickets	M. A. Taylor	368/24
Mar 31	Port Elizabeth	South Africa	Won by seven wickets	M. A. Taylor	369/25
Apr 3	Cape Town	South Africa	Lost by 46 runs	I. A. Healy	370/26
Apr 5	Durban	South Africa	Won by 15 runs	I. A. Healy	371/27
Apr 8	Johannesburg	South Africa	Won by eight runs	I. A. Healy	372/28
Apr 10	Centurion	South Africa	Won by five wickets	I. A. Healy	373/29
Apr 13	Bloemfontein	South Africa	Lost by 109 runs	S. R. Waugh	374/30
1997 in England					
May 22	Leeds	England	Lost by six wickets	M. A. Taylor	375/58
May 24	The Oval	England	Lost by six wickets	M. A. Taylor	376/59
May 25	Lord's	England	Lost by six wickets	S. R. Waugh	377/60
1997-98 Carlton & United Series in Australia					
Dec 4	Sydney	South Africa	Lost by 67 runs	S. R. Waugh	378/31
Dec 7	Adelaide	New Zealand	Won by three wickets	S. R. Waugh	379/64
Dec 9	Melbourne	South Africa	Lost by 45 runs	S. R. Waugh	380/32
Dec 17	Melbourne	New Zealand	Won by six wickets	S. R. Waugh	381/65
Jan 11	Brisbane	South Africa	Lost by five wickets	S. R. Waugh	382/33
Jan 14	Sydney	New Zealand	Won by 131 runs	S. K. Warne	383/66
Jan 18	Perth	South Africa	Lost by seven wickets	S. R. Waugh	384/34
Jan 21	Melbourne	New Zealand	Lost by four wickets	S. R. Waugh	385/67
Jan 23	Melbourne	South Africa	Lost by six runs	S. R. Waugh	386/35
Jan 26	Sydney	South Africa	Won by seven wickets	S. R. Waugh	387/36
Jan 27	Sydney	South Africa	Won by 14 runs	S. R. Waugh	388/37
1997-98 in New Zealand					
Feb 8	Christchurch	New Zealand	Won by seven wickets	S. R. Waugh	389/68
Feb 10	Wellington	New Zealand	Won by 66 runs	S. R. Waugh	390/69
Feb 12	Napier	New Zealand	Lost by seven wickets	S. R. Waugh	391/70
Feb 14	Auckland	New Zealand	Lost by 30 runs	S. R. Waugh	392/71

Date	Venue	Opponent	Result for Australia	Captain	Team/Opp
1997-98 in India					
Apr 1	Kochi	India	Lost by 41 runs	S.R. Waugh	393/48
Apr 3	Ahmedabad	Zimbabwe	Won by 13 runs	S.R. Waugh	394/10
Apr 7	Kanpur	India	Lost by six wickets	S.R. Waugh	395/49
Apr 11	Delhi	Zimbabwe	Won by 16 runs	S.R. Waugh	396/11
Apr 14	Delhi	India	Won by four wickets	S.R. Waugh	397/50
1997-98 in United Arab Emirates					
Apr 18	Sharjah	New Zealand	Won by six wickets	S.R. Waugh	398/72
Apr 19	Sharjah	India	Won by 58 runs	S.R. Waugh	399/51
Apr 21	Sharjah	New Zealand	Won by five wickets	S.R. Waugh	400/73
Apr 22	Sharjah	India	Won on run-rate	S.R. Waugh	401/52
Apr 24	Sharjah	India	Lost by six wickets	S.R. Waugh	402/53
1998-99 in Bangladesh					
Oct 28	Dhaka	India	Lost by 44 runs	S.R. Waugh	403/54
1998-99 in Pakistan					
Nov 6	Karachi	Pakistan	Won by 86 runs	S.R. Waugh	404/47
Nov 8	Peshawar	Pakistan	Won by five wickets	S.R. Waugh	405/48
Nov 10	Lahore	Pakistan	Won by six wickets	S.R. Waugh	406/49
1998-99 Carlton & United Series in Australia					
Jan 10	Brisbane	England	Won on run-rate	S.K. Warne	407/61
Jan 13	Sydney	Sri Lanka	Won by eight wickets	S.K. Warne	408/36
Jan 15	Melbourne	England	Won by nine wickets	S.K. Warne	409/62
Jan 17	Sydney	England	Lost by seven runs	S.K. Warne	410/63
Jan 21	Hobart (Bel)	Sri Lanka	Lost by three wickets	S.K. Warne	411/37
Jan 24	Adelaide	Sri Lanka	Won by 80 runs	S.K. Warne	412/38
Jan 26	Adelaide	England	Won by 16 runs	S.K. Warne	413/64
Jan 31	Perth	Sri Lanka	Won by 45 runs	S.K. Warne	414/39
Feb 5	Sydney	England	Won by four wickets	S.K. Warne	415/65
Feb 7	Melbourne	Sri Lanka	Won by 43 runs	S.K. Warne	416/40
Feb 10	Sydney	England	Won by 10 runs	S.K. Warne	417/66
Feb 13	Melbourne	England	Won by 162 runs	S.K. Warne	418/67
1998-99 in West Indies					
Apr 11	Kingstown	West Indies	Lost by 44 runs	S.R. Waugh	419/85
Apr 14	St George's	West Indies	Won by 46 runs	S.R. Waugh	420/86
Apr 17	Port-of-Spain	West Indies	Lost by five wickets	S.R. Waugh	421/87
Apr 18	Port-of-Spain	West Indies	Won by 20 runs	S.R. Waugh	422/88
Apr 21	Georgetown	West Indies	Tied	S.R. Waugh	423/89
Apr 24	Bridgetown	West Indies	Won by four wickets	S.R. Waugh	424/90
Apr 25	Bridgetown	West Indies	Lost on run-rate	S.R. Waugh	425/91
1999 World Cup in England					
May 16	Worcester	Scotland	Won by six wickets	S.R. Waugh	426/1
May 20	Cardiff	New Zealand	Lost by five wickets	S.R. Waugh	427/74
May 23	Leeds	Pakistan	Lost by ten runs	S.R. Waugh	428/50
May 27	Chester-le-Street	Bangladesh	Won by seven wickets	S.R. Waugh	429/2
May 30	Manchester	West Indies	Won by six wickets	S.R. Waugh	430/92
Jun 4	The Oval	India	Won by 77 runs	S.R. Waugh	431/55
Jun 9	Lord's	Zimbabwe	Won by 44 runs	S.R. Waugh	432/12
Jun 13	Leeds	South Africa	Won by five wickets	S.R. Waugh	433/38
Jun 17	Birmingham	South Africa	Tied	S.R. Waugh	434/39
Jun 20	Lord's	Pakistan	Won by eight wickets	S.R. Waugh	435/51
1999-2000 in Sri Lanka					
Aug 22	Galle	Sri Lanka	Won on run-rate	S.R. Waugh	436/41
Aug 23	Galle	India	Won on run-rate	S.R. Waugh	437/56
Aug 26	Colombo (PIS)	Sri Lanka	Won by 27 runs	S.R. Waugh	438/42
Aug 28	Colombo (SSC)	India	Won by 41 runs	S.R. Waugh	439/57
Aug 31	Colombo (PIS)	Sri Lanka	Lost by eight wickets	S.R. Waugh	440/43

Date	Venue	Opponent	Result for Australia	Captain	Team/Opp
1999-2000 in Zimbabwe					
Oct 21	Bulawayo	Zimbabwe	Won by 83 runs	S. R. Waugh	441/13
Oct 23	Harare	Zimbabwe	Won by nine wickets	S. R. Waugh	442/14
Oct 24	Harare	Zimbabwe	Won by nine wickets	S. R. Waugh	443/15
1999-2000 Carlton & United Series in Australia					
Jan 9	Brisbane	Pakistan	Lost by 45 runs	S. R. Waugh	444/52
Jan 12	Melbourne	India	Won by 28 runs	S. R. Waugh	445/58
Jan 14	Sydney	India	Won by five wickets	S. R. Waugh	446/59
Jan 16	Melbourne	Pakistan	Won by six wickets	S. R. Waugh	447/53
Jan 19	Sydney	Pakistan	Won by 81 runs	S. R. Waugh	448/54
Jan 23	Melbourne	Pakistan	Won by 15 runs	S. R. Waugh	449/55
Jan 26	Adelaide	India	Won by 152 runs	S. R. Waugh	450/60
Jan 30	Perth	India	Won by four wickets	S. R. Waugh	451/61
Feb 2	Melbourne	Pakistan	Won by six wickets	S. R. Waugh	452/56
Feb 4	Sydney	Pakistan	Won by 152 runs	S. R. Waugh	453/57
1999-2000 in New Zealand					
Feb 17	Wellington	New Zealand	No result	S. R. Waugh	454/75
Feb 19	Auckland	New Zealand	Won by five wickets	S. R. Waugh	455/76
Feb 23	Dunedin	New Zealand	Won by 50 runs	S. R. Waugh	456/77
Feb 26	Christchurch	New Zealand	Won by 48 runs	S. R. Waugh	457/78
Mar 1	Napier	New Zealand	Won by five wickets	S. R. Waugh	458/79
Mar 3	Auckland	New Zealand	Lost by seven wickets	S. R. Waugh	459/80
1999-2000 in South Africa					
Apr 12	Durban	South Africa	Lost by six wickets	S. R. Waugh	460/40
Apr 14	Cape Town	South Africa	Won by five wickets	S. R. Waugh	461/41
Apr 16	Johannesburg	South Africa	Lost by four wickets	S. R. Waugh	462/42
2000-2001 in Australia					
Aug 12	Melbourne (DS)	South Africa	Won by 94 runs	S. R. Waugh	463/43
Aug 14	Melbourne (DS)	South Africa	Tied	S. R. Waugh	464/44
Aug 16	Melbourne (DS)	South Africa	Lost by eight runs	S. R. Waugh	465/45
2000-01 in Kenya					
Oct 7	Nairobi	India	Lost by 20 runs	S. R. Waugh	466/62
2000-01 Carlton Series in Australia					
Jan 11	Melbourne	West Indies	Won by 74 runs	S. R. Waugh	467/93
Jan 14	Brisbane	West Indies	Won by nine wickets	A. C. Gilchrist	468/94
Jan 17	Sydney	West Indies	Won on run-rate	A. C. Gilchrist	469/95
Jan 21	Melbourne	Zimbabwe	Won by eight wickets	A. C. Gilchrist	470/16
Jan 26	Adelaide	West Indies	Won by 10 wickets	S. R. Waugh	471/96
Jan 28	Sydney	Zimbabwe	Won by 86 runs	S. R. Waugh	472/17
Jan 30	Hobart (Bel)	Zimbabwe	Won by six wickets	S. R. Waugh	473/18
Feb 4	Perth	Zimbabwe	Won by one run	S. R. Waugh	474/19
Feb 7	Sydney	West Indies	Won by 134 runs	S. R. Waugh	475/97
Feb 9	Melbourne	West Indies	Won by 39 runs	S. R. Waugh	476/98
2000-01 in India					
Mar 23	Bangalore	India	Lost by 60 runs	S. R. Waugh	477/63
Mar 28	Pune	India	Won by eight wickets	S. R. Waugh	478/64
Mar 31	Indore	India	Lost by 118 runs	S. R. Waugh	479/65
Apr 3	Visakhapatnam	India	Won by 93 runs	S. R. Waugh	480/66
Apr 6	Goa	India	Won by four wickets	S. R. Waugh	481/67
2001 in England					
Jun 9	Cardiff	Pakistan	Won by seven wickets	S. R. Waugh	482/58
Jun 10	Bristol	England	Won by five wickets	S. R. Waugh	483/68
Jun 14	Manchester	England	Won on run-rate	S. R. Waugh	484/69
Jun 19	Nottingham	Pakistan	Lost by 36 runs	S. R. Waugh	485/59
Jun 21	The Oval	England	Won by eight wickets	S. R. Waugh	486/70
Jun 23	Lord's	Pakistan	Won by nine wickets	S. R. Waugh	487/60

2001-02 VB Series in Australia

Jan	11	Melbourne	New Zealand	Lost by 23 runs	S. R. Waugh	488/81
Jan	13	Melbourne	South Africa	Lost by four wickets	S. R. Waugh	489/46
Jan	17	Sydney	New Zealand	Lost by 23 runs	S. R. Waugh	490/82
Jan	20	Brisbane	South Africa	Won by 27 runs	S. R. Waugh	491/47
Jan	22	Sydney	South Africa	Won by eight wickets	S. R. Waugh	492/48
Jan	26	Adelaide	New Zealand	Lost by 77 runs	S. R. Waugh	493/83
Jan	29	Melbourne	New Zealand	Won by two wickets	S. R. Waugh	494/84
Feb	3	Perth	South Africa	Lost by 33 runs	S. R. Waugh	495/49

2001-02 in South Africa

Mar	23	Johannesburg	South Africa	Won by 19 runs	R. T. Ponting	496/50
Mar	24	Centurion	South Africa	Won by 45 runs	R. T. Ponting	497/51
Mar	27	Potchefstroom	South Africa	Tied	R. T. Ponting	498/52
Mar	30	Bloemfontein	South Africa	Won by 37 runs	R. T. Ponting	499/53
Apr	4	Durban	South Africa	Won by eight wickets	R. T. Ponting	500/54
Apr	6	Port Elizabeth	South Africa	Won by three wickets	R. T. Ponting	501/55
Apr	9	Cape Town	South Africa	Lost on run-rate	R. T. Ponting	502/56

2001-02 in Australia

Jun	12	Melbourne (DS)	Pakistan	Won by seven wickets	R. T. Ponting	503/61
Jun	15	Melbourne (DS)	Pakistan	Lost by two wickets	R. T. Ponting	504/62
Jun	19	Brisbane	Pakistan	Lost by 91 runs	R. T. Ponting	505/63

2002-03 in Kenya

Aug	30	Nairobi	Pakistan	Won by 224 runs	R. T. Ponting	506/64
Sep	2	Nairobi	Kenya	Won by eight wickets	R. T. Ponting	507/2
Sep	4	Nairobi	Pakistan	Won by nine wickets	R. T. Ponting	508/65
Sep	5	Nairobi	Kenya	Won by five wickets	A. C. Gilchrist	509/3
Sep	7	Nairobi	Pakistan	No result	R. T. Ponting	510/66

2002-03 in Sri Lanka

Sep	15	Colombo (SSC)	New Zealand	Won by 164 runs	R. T. Ponting	511/85
Sep	19	Colombo (SSC)	Bangladesh	Won by nine wickets	R. T. Ponting	512/3
Sep	27	Colombo (PIS)	Sri Lanka	Lost by seven wickets	R. T. Ponting	513/44

2002-03 VB Series in Australia

Dec	13	Sydney	England	Won by seven wickets	R. T. Ponting	514/71
Dec	15	Melbourne	England	Won by 89 runs	R. T. Ponting	515/72
Dec	22	Perth	Sri Lanka	Won by 142 runs	R. T. Ponting	516/45
Jan	9	Sydney	Sri Lanka	Lost by 79 runs	R. T. Ponting	517/46
Jan	11	Hobart (Bel)	England	Won by seven runs	R. T. Ponting	518/73
Jan	15	Brisbane	Sri Lanka	Won by four wickets	R. T. Ponting	519/47
Jan	19	Adelaide	England	Won by four wickets	A. C. Gilchrist	520/74
Jan	21	Melbourne	Sri Lanka	Won by nine wickets	R. T. Ponting	521/48
Jan	23	Sydney	England	Won by 10 wickets	R. T. Ponting	522/75
Jan	25	Melbourne	England	Won by five wickets	R. T. Ponting	523/76

2002-03 World Cup in South Africa and Zimbabwe

Feb	11	Johannesburg	Pakistan	Won by 82 runs	R. T. Ponting	524/67
Feb	15	Centurion	India	Won by nine wickets	R. T. Ponting	525/68
Feb	20	Potchefstroom	Netherlands	Won by 75 runs	R. T. Ponting	526/1
Feb	24	Bulawayo	Zimbabwe	Won by seven wickets	R. T. Ponting	527/20
Feb	27	Potchefstroom	Namibia	Won by 256 runs	R. T. Ponting	528/1
Mar	2	Port Elizabeth	England	Won by two wickets	R. T. Ponting	529/77
Mar	7	Centurion	Sri Lanka	Won by 96 runs	R. T. Ponting	530/49
Mar	11	Port Elizabeth	New Zealand	Won by 96 runs	R. T. Ponting	531/86
Mar	15	Durban	Kenya	Won by five wickets	R. T. Ponting	532/4
Mar	18	Port Elizabeth	Sri Lanka	Won by 48 runs	R. T. Ponting	533/50
Mar	23	Johannesburg	India	Won by 125 runs	R. T. Ponting	534/69

Date	Venue	Opponent	Result for Australia	Captain	Team/Opp
2002-03 in West Indies					
May 17	Kingston	West Indies	Won by two runs	R. T. Ponting	535/99
May 18	Kingston	West Indies	Won by eight wickets	R. T. Ponting	536/100
May 21	St Lucia	West Indies	Won by 25 runs	R. T. Ponting	537/101
May 24	Port-of-Spain	West Indies	Won by 67 runs	R. T. Ponting	538/102
May 25	Port-of-Spain	West Indies	Won by 39 runs	R. T. Ponting	539/103
May 30	St George's	West Indies	Lost by three wickets	R. T. Ponting	540/104
Jun 1	St George's	West Indies	Lost by nine wickets	R. T. Ponting	541/105
2003-04 in Australia					
Aug 2	Cairns	Bangladesh	Won by eight wickets	R. T. Ponting	542/4
Aug 3	Cairns	Bangladesh	Won by nine wickets	R. T. Ponting	543/5
Aug 6	Darwin	Bangladesh	Won by 112 runs	R. T. Ponting	544/6
2003-04 in India					
Oct 26	Gwalior	India	Lost by 37 runs	R. T. Ponting	545/70
Oct 29	Faridabad	New Zealand	Won by eight wickets	R. T. Ponting	546/87
Nov 1	Mumbai	India	Won by 77 runs	R. T. Ponting	547/71
Nov 3	Pune	New Zealand	Won by two wickets	R. T. Ponting	548/88
Nov 9	Guwahati	New Zealand	Won by 44 runs	R. T. Ponting	549/89
Nov 12	Bangalore	India	Won by 61 runs	R. T. Ponting	550/72
Nov 18	Kolkata	India	Won by 18 runs	R. T. Ponting	551/73
2003-04 VB Series					
Jan 9	Melbourne	India	Won by 18 runs	R. T. Ponting	552/74
Jan 11	Sydney	Zimbabwe	Won by 99 runs	R. T. Ponting	553/21
Jan 16	Hobart (Bel)	Zimbabwe	Won by 148 runs	R. T. Ponting	554/22
Jan 18	Brisbane	India	Lost by 19 runs	R. T. Ponting	555/75
Jan 22	Sydney	India	Won by two wickets	R. T. Ponting	556/76
Jan 26	Adelaide	Zimbabwe	Won by 13 runs	R. T. Ponting	557/23
Jan 29	Melbourne	Zimbabwe	No result	R. T. Ponting	558/24
Feb 1	Perth	India	Won by five wickets	A. C. Gilchrist	559/77
Feb 6	Melbourne	India	Won by seven wickets	R. T. Ponting	560/78
Feb 8	Sydney	India	Won by 208 runs	R. T. Ponting	561/79
2003-04 in Sri Lanka					
Feb 20	Dambulla	Sri Lanka	Won by 84 runs	R. T. Ponting	562/51
Feb 22	Dambulla	Sri Lanka	Lost by one run	R. T. Ponting	563/52
Feb 25	Colombo (PIS)	Sri Lanka	Won by five wickets	R. T. Ponting	564/53
Feb 27	Colombo (PIS)	Sri Lanka	Won by 40 runs	R. T. Ponting	565/54
Feb 29	Colombo (SSC)	Sri Lanka	Lost by three wickets	A. C. Gilchrist	566/55
2003-04 in Zimbabwe					
May 25	Harare	Zimbabwe	Won by seven wickets	R. T. Ponting	567/25
May 27	Harare	Zimbabwe	Won by 139 runs	R. T. Ponting	568/26
May 29	Harare	Zimbabwe	Won by eight wickets	R. T. Ponting	569/27
2004-05 in Netherlands					
Aug 23	Amstelveen	India	No result	R. T. Ponting	570/80
Aug 28	Amstelveen	Pakistan	Won by 17 runs	R. T. Ponting	571/68
2004 in England					
Sep 4	Lord's	Pakistan	Won by ten runs	R. T. Ponting	572/69
Sep 13	Southampton	U.S.A.	Won by nine wickets	R. T. Ponting	573/1
Sep 16	The Oval	New Zealand	Won by seven wickets	R. T. Ponting	574/90
Sep 21	Birmingham	England	Lost by six wickets	R. T. Ponting	575/78
2004-05 in Australia					
Dec 5	Melbourne DS	New Zealand	Lost by four wickets	R. T. Ponting	576/91
Dec 8	Sydney	New Zealand	Won by 17 runs	R. T. Ponting	577/92

Date	Venue	Opponent	Result for Australia	Captain	Team/Opp
2004-05 VB Series					
Jan 14	Melbourne	West Indies	Won by 116 runs	R. T. Ponting	578/106
Jan 16	Hobart	Pakistan	Won by four wickets	R. T. Ponting	579/70
Jan 21	Brisbane	West Indies	No result	R. T. Ponting	580/107
Jan 23	Sydney	Pakistan	Won by nine wickets	R. T. Ponting	581/71
Jan 26	Adelaide	West Indies	Won by 73 runs	R. T. Ponting	582/108
Jan 30	Perth	Pakistan	Lost by three wickets	R. T. Ponting	583/72
Feb 4	Melbourne	Pakistan	Won by 18 runs	R. T. Ponting	584/73
Feb 6	Sydney	Pakistan	Won by 31 runs	R. T. Ponting	585/74
2004-05 in New Zealand					
Feb 19	Wellington WS	New Zealand	Won by 10 runs	R. T. Ponting	586/93
Feb 22	Christchurch	New Zealand	Won by 106 runs	R. T. Ponting	587/94
Feb 26	Auckland	New Zealand	Won by 86 runs	R. T. Ponting	588/95
Mar 1	Wellington	New Zealand	Won by seven wickets	A. C. Gilchrist	589/96
Mar 5	Napier	New Zealand	Won by 122 runs	R. T. Ponting	590/97
2005 in England					
Jun 18	Cardiff	Bangladesh	Lost by five wickets	R. T. Ponting	591/7
Jun 19	Bristol	England	Lost by three wickets	R. T. Ponting	592/79
Jun 23	Chester-le-Street	England	Lost by 57 runs	R. T. Ponting	593/80
Jun 25	Manchester	Bangladesh	Lost by 10 wickets	R. T. Ponting	594/8
Jun 28	Birmingham	England	No result	R. T. Ponting	595/81
Jun 30	Canterbury	Bangladesh	Won by six wickets	R. T. Ponting	596/9
Jly 2	Lord's	England	Match tied	R. T. Ponting	597/82
Jly 7	Leeds	England	Lost by nine wickets	R. T. Ponting	598/83
Jly 10	Lord's	England	Won by seven wickets	R. T. Ponting	599/84
Jly 12	The Oval	England	Won by eight wickets	R. T. Ponting	600/85

Australian First-Class Records

BATTING RECORDS

HIGHEST INDIVIDUAL SCORES

452*	D. G. Bradman	New South Wales v Queensland at Sydney	1929-30
437	W. H. Ponsford	Victoria v Queensland at Melbourne	1927-28
429	W. H. Ponsford	Victoria v Tasmania at Melbourne	1922-23
383	C. W. Gregory	New South Wales v Queensland at Brisbane	1906-07
380	M. L. Hayden	Australia v Zimbabwe at Perth	2003-04
369	D. G. Bradman	South Australia v Tasmania at Adelaide	1935-36
365*	C. Hill	South Australia v New South Wales at Adelaide	1900-01
364	L. Hutton	England v Australia at The Oval	1938
359	R. B. Simpson	New South Wales v Queensland at Brisbane	1963-64
357	D. G. Bradman	South Australia v Victoria at Melbourne	1935-36
356	B. A. Richards	South Australia v Western Australia at Perth	1970-71
355*	G. R. Marsh	Western Australia v South Australia at Perth	1989-90
352	W. H. Ponsford	Victoria v New South Wales at Melbourne	1926-27
345	C. G. Macartney	Australians v Nottinghamshire at Nottingham	1921
340*	D. G. Bradman	New South Wales v Victoria at Sydney	1928-29
336	W. H. Ponsford	Victoria v South Australia at Melbourne	1927-28
335*	M. W. Goodwin	Sussex v Leicestershire at Hove	2003
334	D. G. Bradman	Australia v England at Leeds	1930
334*	M. A. Taylor	Australia v Pakistan at Peshawar	1998-99
331*	M. E. K. Hussey	Northamptonshire v Somerset at Taunton	2003
329*	M. E. K. Hussey	Northamptonshire v Essex at Northampton	2001
325*	H. S. T. L. Hendry	Victoria v New Zealanders at Melbourne	1925-26
325	C. L. Badcock	South Australia v Victoria at Adelaide	1935-36
324*	D. M. Jones	Victoria v South Australia at Melbourne	1994-95
321	W. L. Murdoch	New South Wales v Victoria at Sydney	1881-82
315*	A. F. Kippax	New South Wales v Queensland at Sydney	1927-28
311	R. B. Simpson	Australia v England at Manchester	1964
310*	M. E. K. Hussey	Northamptonshire v Gloucestershire at Bristol	2002
307	M. C. Cowdrey	MCC v South Australia at Adelaide	1962-63
307	R. M. Cowper	Australia v England at Melbourne	1965-66
306*	D. W. Hookes	South Australia v Tasmania at Adelaide	1986-87
305*	F. E. Woolley	MCC v Tasmania at Hobart (TCA)	1911-12
304	D. G. Bradman	Australia v England at Leeds	1934
303*	W. W. Armstrong	Australians v Somerset at Bath	1905
302*	B. J. Hodge	Leicestershire v Nottinghamshire at Nottingham	2003
300*	V. T. Trumper	Australians v Sussex at Hove	1899
300*	M. L. Love	Queensland v Victoria at St Kilda	2003-04

HUNDRED ON FIRST-CLASS DEBUT
FOR AUSTRALIAN TEAMS

C. S. Gordon	121	Victoria v New South Wales at Melbourne	1869-70
J. P. O'Halloran	128*	Victoria v South Australia at Melbourne	1896-97
L. W. Pye	166	New South Wales v Queensland at Brisbane (Ex)	1896-97
H. G. S. Morton	135*	Queensland v Victoria at Melbourne	1904-05
W. M. McPetrie	123	Victoria v Tasmania at Melbourne	1904-05
A. G. Moyes	104	South Australia v Western Australia at Adelaide	1912-13
N. L. Gooden	102	South Australia v Western Australia at Adelaide	1912-13
F. W. Hyett	108*	Victoria v Tasmania at Melbourne	1914-15
N. F. Callaway	207	New South Wales v Queensland at Sydney	1914-15
J. Bogle	145	New South Wales v Victoria at Sydney	1918-19
E. E. B. Forssberg	143	New South Wales v Queensland at Sydney	1920-21
D. A. Mullarkey	130	New South Wales v Queensland at Brisbane (Ex)	1923-24
S. E. Wootton	105	Victoria v Tasmania at Hobart (TCA)	1923-24
H. O. Rock	127	New South Wales v South Australia at Sydney	1924-25
L. T. Gun	136*	South Australia v New South Wales at Adelaide	1924-25
H. C. Steele	130	New South Wales v Queensland at Brisbane	1926-27
D. G. Bradman	118	New South Wales v South Australia at Adelaide	1927-28
R. N. Ellis	100	Victoria v Tasmania at Hobart (TCA)	1927-28
B. W. Hone	137	South Australia v Victoria at Adelaide	1928-29
R. M. Levy	129	Queensland v Victoria at Brisbane (Ex)	1928-29
A. H. Allsopp	117	New South Wales v MCC at Sydney	1929-30
O. W. Bill	115	New South Wales v Tasmania at Sydney	1929-30
L. R. Leabeater	128	New South Wales v Tasmania at Sydney	1929-30
F. E. Fontaine	118	Victoria v Tasmania at Hobart (TCA)	1930-31
R. J. Lawson	119	Victoria v Tasmania at Hobart (TCA)	1930-31
R. N. Nutt	102	New South Wales v South Australia at Adelaide	1931-32
J. C. Francis	135	Victoria v Tasmania at Launceston	1932-33
H. H. E. Grangel	108	Victoria v Tasmania at Melbourne	1935-36
R. A. Hamence	121	South Australia v Tasmania at Adelaide	1935-36
K. R. Miller	181	Victoria v Tasmania at Melbourne	1937-38
A. E. O. Barras	113	Western Australia v Victoria at Perth	1938-39
A. R. Morris	148	New South Wales v Queensland at Sydney	1940-41
M. R. Thomas	164	Tasmania v Australian Services at Hobart (TCA)	1945-46
S. J. E. Loxton	232*	Victoria v Queensland at Melbourne	1946-47
E. W. Lukeman	118	New South Wales v South Australia at Adelaide	1946-47
E. A. D. Kerr	112	Victoria v Tasmania at Launceston	1946-47
J. L. Chambers	122	Victoria v Tasmania at Melbourne	1949-50
L. E. Favell	164	South Australia v New South Wales at Adelaide	1951-52
J. Hallebone	202	Victoria v Tasmania at Melbourne	1951-52
R. E. Briggs	121	New South Wales v Western Australia at Perth	1952-53
B. K. Shepherd	103*	Western Australia v Queensland at Perth	1955-56
R. B. Lyons	102	Queensland v Victoria at Brisbane	1955-56
H. W. Pinkus	102*	Tasmania v South Australia at Hobart (TCA)	1956-57
N. G. Marks	180*	New South Wales v South Australia at Sydney	1958-59
D. Chadwick	129	Western Australia v Queensland at Brisbane	1963-64
J. F. C. Loxton	100	Queensland v Western Australia at Perth	1966-67
M. J. Lucas	107	Queensland v New South Wales at Brisbane	1968-69
R. W. Marsh	104	Western Australia v West Indians at Perth	1968-69
G. J. Gilmour	122	New South Wales v South Australia at Sydney	1971-72
M. F. Kent	140	Queensland v New South Wales at Brisbane	1974-75
K. J. Hughes	119	Western Australia v New South Wales at Perth	1975-76
J. M. Wiener	106	Victoria v Queensland at Brisbane	1977-78
M. D. Taylor	107	Victoria v Queensland at Melbourne	1977-78
C. E. Penter	112	Western Australia v New South Wales at Sydney	1979-80
D. M. Wellham	100	New South Wales v Victoria at Melbourne	1980-81
M. D. Haysman	126	South Australia v Queensland at Adelaide	1982-83
S. P. O'Donnell	130	Victoria v South Australia at Melbourne	1983-84
W. J. S. Seabrook	165	New South Wales v Victoria at Melbourne	1984-85

?. J. Harris	118	Tasmania v South Australia at Adelaide	1985-86
W. N. Phillips	111	Victoria v West Indians at Melbourne	1988-89
M. G. Bevan	114	South Australia v Western Australia at Perth	1989-90
G. I. Foley	155	Queensland v Pakistanis at Brisbane	1989-90
M. P. Lavender	118	Western Australia v Victoria at St Kilda	1990-91
M. L. Hayden	149	Queensland v South Australia at Brisbane	1991-92
R. J. Davison	133*	New South Wales v Tasmania at Sydney	1993-94
C. D. Hartley	103	Queensland v South Australia at Brisbane	2003-04
C. A. Philipson	101*	Queensland v Tasmania at Hobart	2003-04
A. J. Nye	102	Queensland v New South Wales at Sydney	2003-04
D. J. Dawson	123*	Tasmania v Western Australia at Perth	2004-05

Note: A. R. Morris scored a century (111) in the second innings of his debut match, thus becoming the first player in world cricket to achieve such a feat.

HUNDRED IN EACH INNINGS OF A MATCH FOR AUSTRALIAN TEAMS

C. J. Eady	116	112*	Tasmania v Victoria at Hobart (TCA)	1894-95
V. T. Trumper	109	119	Australians v Essex at Leyton	1902
J. R. M. Mackay	105	102*	New South Wales v South Australia at Sydney	1905-06
D. R. A. Gehrs	148*	100*	South Australia v Western Australia at Fremantle	1905-06
M. A. Noble	176	123	New South Wales v Victoria at Sydney	1907-08
V. S. Ransford	182	110	Victoria v New South Wales at Sydney	1908-09
W. Bardsley	136	130	Australia v England at The Oval	1909
A. Kenny	164	100*	Victoria v Queensland at Brisbane	1909-10
C. G. Macartney	119	126	New South Wales v South Africans at Sydney	1910-11
C. G. Macartney	142	121	Australians v Sussex at Hove	1912
R. S. Stephens	108	181	Victoria v Tasmania at Launceston	1913-14
J. M. Gregory	122	102	AIF Team v New South Wales at Sydney	1919-20
W. W. Armstrong	157*	245	Victoria v South Australia at Melbourne	1920-21
F. A. O'Keefe	177	141	The Rest v Australian XI at Sydney	1921-22
W. H. Ponsford	110	110*	Victoria v New South Wales at Sydney	1923-24
V. Y. Richardson	100	125	South Australia v New South Wales at Sydney	1924-25
A. F. Kippax	127	131	New South Wales v Queensland at Brisbane (Ex)	1926-27
L. P. D. O'Connor	103	143*	Queensland v New South Wales at Sydney	1926-27
A. Jackson	131	122	New South Wales v South Australia at Sydney	1927-28
D. G. Bradman	131	133*	New South Wales v Queensland at Brisbane (Ex)	1928-29
B. A. Onyons	105	122	Victoria v Queensland at Brisbane (Ex)	1928-29
D. G. Bradman	124	225	W. M. Woodfull's XI v J. Ryder's XI at Sydney	1929-30
A. F. Kippax	158	102*	Australians v Sussex at Hove	1930
S. J. McCabe	106	103*	New South Wales v Victoria at Sydney	1931-32
A. R. Lonergan	115	100	South Australia v Victoria at Melbourne	1933-34
K. E. Rigg	100	167*	Victoria v New South Wales at Melbourne	1936-37
D. G. Bradman	107	113	South Australia v Queensland at Brisbane	1937-38
A. L. Hassett	122	122	Victoria v New South Wales at Sydney	1939-40
C. L. Badcock	120	102	South Australia v Victoria at Melbourne	1940-41
R. A. Hamence	130	103*	South Australia v Victoria at Melbourne	1940-41
A. R. Morris	148	111	New South Wales v Queensland at Sydney	1940-41
A. L. Hassett	187	124*	Australian Services v Prince's XI at Delhi	1945-46
A. R. Morris	122	124*	Australia v England at Adelaide	1946-47
R. A. Hamence	132	101*	South Australia v New South Wales at Adelaide	1946-47
D. G. Bradman	132	127*	Australia v India at Melbourne	1947-48
J. Moroney	118	101*	Australia v South Africa at Johannesburg (EP)	1949-50
A. R. Edwards	103	105	Western Australia v Queensland at Perth	1950-51
K. R. Miller	100	101	A. L. Hassett's XI v A. R. Morris's XI at Melbourne	1953-54
J. W. Burke	138	125*	Australians v Somerset at Taunton	1956
L. E. Favell	112	114	South Australia v New South Wales at Sydney	1956-57
C. J. Pinch	110	100	South Australia v Western Australia at Perth	1956-57
C. J. Pinch	102	102	South Australia v Victoria at Melbourne	1957-58
G. B. Stevens	164	111	South Australia v New South Wales at Sydney	1957-58

L. E. Favell 104	145	South Australia v Western Australia at Adelaide	1958-59
S. C. Trimble 113	136*	Queensland v Victoria at Brisbane	1963-64
R. B. Simpson 153	115	Australia v Pakistan at Karachi	1964-65
R. B. Simpson 121	142*	New South Wales v South Australia at Sydney	1964-65
P. C. Kelly 119	108*	Western Australia v MCC at Perth	1965-66
K. G. Cunningham. 107	101*	South Australia v Western Australia at Adelaide	1966-67
K. D. Walters..... 242	103	Australia v West Indies at Sydney	1968-69
G. S. Chappell ... 129	156*	South Australia v Queensland at Brisbane	1969-70
I. M. Chappell ... 145	106	Australians v World XI at Brisbane	1971-72
A. J. Sieler....... 157	105	Victoria v Queensland at Brisbane	1973-74
G. S. Chappell ... 180	101	Queensland v Victoria at Brisbane	1973-74
I. M. Chappell ... 141*	130	South Australia v Victoria at Adelaide	1973-74
I. M. Chappell ... 145	121	Australia v New Zealand at Wellington	1973-74
G. S. Chappell ... 247*	133	Australia v New Zealand at Wellington	1973-74
R. B. McCosker... 138	136*	New South Wales v Western Australia at Sydney	1974-75
R. B. McCosker... 115	115	Australians v Sussex at Hove	1975
G. S. Chappell ... 123	109*	Australia v West Indies at Brisbane	1975-76
D. W. Hookes 185	105	South Australia v Queensland at Adelaide	1976-77
D. W. Hookes 135	156	South Australia v New South Wales at Adelaide	1976-77
G. N. Yallop 105	114*	Victoria v New South Wales at Sydney	1977-78
A. R. Border 150*	153	Australia v Pakistan at Lahore	1979-80
R. B. McCosker... 123*	118*	New South Wales v Victoria at Sydney	1981-82
R. B. Kerr 158	101	Queensland v Western Australia at Perth	1981-82
D. W. Hookes 137	107	South Australia v Victoria at Adelaide	1982-83
G. N. Yallop 113	145*	Victoria v Western Australia at Melbourne	1983-84
S. B. Smith...... 105	116	Australians v Guyana at Georgetown	1983-84
A. R. Border 140	114*	Australia v New Zealand at Christchurch	1985-86
K. C. Wessels ... 135	105*	Australians v South Africans at Port Elizabeth	1986-87
D. C. Boon 108	143	Tasmania v Queensland at Launceston	1987-88
M. A. Taylor 107	152*	New South Wales v Western Australia at Perth	1988-89
T. M. Moody 162	159	Western Australia v South Australia at Perth	1988-89
D. M. Jones 116	121*	Australia v Pakistan at Adelaide	1989-90
J. Cox 175	102	Tasmania v New South Wales at Hobart (Bel)	1989-90
M. A. Taylor 127	100	New South Wales v Queensland at Brisbane	1989-90
S. M. Small 115	126	New South Wales v Wellington at North Sydney	1990-91
S. G. Law....... 142*	105	Queensland v Western Australia at Perth	1990-91
D. R. Martyn 132*	112	Western Australia v Queensland at Brisbane	1992-93
R. T. Ponting 107	100*	Tasmania v Western Australia at Hobart (Bel)	1992-93
D. C. Boon....... 108	106	Australians v Worcestershire at Worcester	1993
M. L. Hayden..... 165	116	Queensland v South Australia at Adelaide	1993-94
P. C. Nobes 140	106	South Australia v Queensland at Adelaide	1993-94
M. L. Hayden..... 126	155	Queensland v Victoria at Brisbane	1993-94
D. M. Jones 145	152*	Victoria v South Australia at Melbourne	1993-94
D. F. Hills 114	126	Tasmania v South Australia at Adelaide	1993-94
M. L. Love...... 187	116	Queensland v Tasmania at Brisbane	1994-95
S. G. Law....... 102	138	Queensland v Tasmania at Hobart (Bel)	1994-95
R. T. Ponting 118*	100*	Tasmania v Queensland at Brisbane	1995-96
M. T. G. Elliott.... 104*	135	Victoria v Western Australia at Perth	1995-96
R. T. Ponting 126	145*	Tasmania v Queensland at Hobart (Bel)	1996-97
J. Cox 143	125	Tasmania v New South Wales at Sydney	1996-97
S. R. Waugh..... 108	116	Australia v England at Manchester	1997
A. Symonds...... 163	100*	Queensland v South Australia at Adelaide	1997-98
D. S. Lehmann.... 103	100†	Australians v Rawalpindi Cricket Assn at Rawalpindi .	1998-99
M. T. G. Elliott.... 108	103*	Victoria v New South Wales at Melbourne	1998-99
G. S. Blewett 169*	213*	Australian XI v England XI at Hobart (Bel)	1998-99
D. S. Lehmann.... 101*	113	South Australia v Tasmania at Adelaide	1999-00
J. Cox 106	128*	Tasmania v New South Wales at Hobart (Bel)	2000-01
R. T. Ponting 102	102*	Australians v BCCI President's XI at Delhi	2000-01
B. J. Hodge 140	110*	Victoria v South Australia at Adelaide	2001-02
R. T. Ponting 126	154	Tasmania v New South Wales at Sydney	2001-02
C. J. L. Rogers 101*	102*	Western Australia v South Australia at Perth	2001-02

L. Arnberger.... 172*	102*	Victoria v Tasmania at Melbourne	2002-03
.L. Hayden.... 197	103	Australia v England at Brisbane	2002-03
.J. Mail..... 128	152*	New South Wales v South Australia at Sydney	2003-04
.T. G. Elliott.. 166	102*	Victoria v Tasmania at Melbourne	2003-04
.L. Hayden.... 117	132	Australia v Sri Lanka at Cairns	2004-05
.G. Bevan 106	100	Tasmania v South Australia at Hobart (Bel)	2004-05
.G. Bevan 190	114*	Tasmania v Western Australia at Hobart (Bel)	2004-05
.L. Arnberger.... 103	126	Victoria v Queensland at Melbourne	2004-05

† *Retired hurt.*

MOST HUNDREDS IN CONSECUTIVE INNINGS

	1st	*2nd*		
Six				
D. G. Bradman	118	dnb	D. G. Bradman's XI v K. E. Rigg's XI at Melbourne ...	1938-39
	143	dnb	South Australia v New South Wales at Adelaide	1938-39
	225	dnb	South Australia v Queensland at Adelaide	1938-39
	107	dnb	South Australia v Victoria at Melbourne	1938-39
	186	dnb	South Australia v Queensland at Brisbane	1938-39
	135*	dnb	South Australia v New South Wales at Sydney	1938-39
Five				
M. E. K. Hussey	100	dnb	Northamptonshire v Hampshire at Southampton	2003
	331*	dnb	Northamptonshire v Somerset at Taunton	2003
	115	dnb	Northamptonshire v Derbyshire at Derby	2003
	187	dnb	Northamptonshire v Durham at Northampton	2003
	147	dnb	Northamptonshire v Glamorgan at Cardiff	2003

Note: The following batsmen achieved four hundreds in consecutive innings: C. G. Macartney, D. G. Bradman (twice), D. W. Hookes, A. R. Border, M. G. Bevan and G. S. Blewett.

HUNDREDS IN A CAREER

	100s	*I*	*400+*	*300+*	*200+*
D. G. Bradman	117	338	1	6	37
M. E. Waugh	81	591	0	0	5
S. R. Waugh	79	551	0	0	5
G. S. Chappell	74	542	0	0	4
A. R. Border	70	625	0	0	3
D. S. Lehmann	70	420	0	0	9
J. L. Langer	69	473	0	0	10
S. G. Law	69	520	0	0	5
D. C. Boon	68	585	0	0	3
M. L. Hayden	68	431	0	1	5
R. N. Harvey	67	461	0	0	7
M. G. Bevan	67	382	0	0	5
K. C. Wessels	66	539	0	0	4
T. M. Moody	64	501	0	0	4
R. B. Simpson	60	436	0	2	10
A. L. Hassett	59	322	0	0	8
I. M. Chappell	59	448	0	0	3
M. G. Bevan	59	359	0	0	4
D. M. Jones	55	415	0	1	8
R. T. Ponting	54	301	0	0	6
W. Bardsley	53	376	0	0	7
W. H. Ponsford	51	282	2	2	9
J. Cox	51	461	0	0	4
W. M. Lawry	50	417	0	0	4
M. T. G. Elliott	50	349	0	0	2
C. G. Macartney	49	360	0	1	3
W. M. Woodfull	49	245	0	0	7
A. R. Morris	46	250	0	0	4
C. Hill	45	416	0	1	3

	100s	I	400+	300+	200+
W. W. Armstrong	45	406	0	6	1
N. C. O'Neill	45	306	0	0	2
K. D. Walters	45	426	0	0	4
A. F. Kippax	43	256	0	1	6
G. S. Blewett	43	406	0	0	5
V. T. Trumper	42	401	0	1	7
D. R. Martyn	42	314	0	0	2
K. R. Miller	41	326	0	0	7
M. A. Taylor	41	435	0	1	1

MOST RUNS IN AN AUSTRALIAN SEASON

	Season	M	I	NO	R	HS	100s	50s	Avge
D. G. Bradman (New South Wales) . .	1928-29	13	24	6	1,690	340*	7	5	93.88
R. N. Harvey (Victoria)	1952-53	16	27	1	1,659	205	5	8	63.80
D. G. Bradman (New South Wales) . .	1929-30	11	16	2	1,586	452*	5	4	113.28
W. R. Hammond (MCC)	1928-29	13	18	1	1,553	251	7	1	91.35
D. G. Bradman (South Australia)	1936-37	12	19	1	1,552	270	6	2	86.22
G. S. Chappell (Queensland)	1975-76	15	26	8	1,547	182*	6	7	85.94
R. B. Simpson (Western Australia) . .	1960-61	15	26	2	1,541	221*	4	9	64.21
B. A. Richards (South Australia)	1970-71	10	16	2	1,538	356	6	3	109.85
G. Boycott (MCC)	1970-71	13	22	6	1,535	173	6	7	95.93
G. A. Faulkner (South Africans)	1910-11	14	27	1	1,534	204	3	13	59.00
R. B. Simpson (New South Wales) . .	1963-64	14	25	2	1,524	359	4	4	66.26
E. J. Barlow (South Africans)	1963-64	14	25	2	1,523	209	6	4	66.21
G. S. Chappell (Queensland)	1980-81	14	22	2	1,502	204	5	6	75.10

1,000 RUNS IN A SEASON

12 Times: D. G. Bradman 1928-29 (1,690), 1929-30 (1,586), 1930-31 (1,422), 1931-32 (1,403), 1932-33 (1,171), 1933-34 (1,192), 1935-36 (1,173), 1936-37 (1,552), 1937-38 (1,437), 1939-40 (1,475), 1946-47 (1,032), 1947-48 (1,296).

6 Times: I. M. Chappell 1965-66 (1,019), 1968-69 (1,476), 1970-71 (1,210), 1971-72 (1,140), 1973-74 (1,074), 1975-76 (1,310).

5 Times: G. S. Chappell 1973-74 (1,288), 1974-75 (1,484), 1975-76 (1,547), 1979-80 (1,066), 1980-81 (1,502); A. R. Border 1978-79 (1,220), 1982-83 (1,081), 1985-86 (1,247), 1986-87 (1,002), 1987-88 (1,164); D. S. Lehmann 1989-90 (1,142), 1993-94 (1,087), 1994-95 (1,104), 1995-96 (1,237), 1999-00 (1,142); G. S. Blewett 1993-94 (1,036), 1995-96 (1,173), 1998-99 (1,187), 2000-01 (1,162), 2001-02 (1,025); M. L. Hayden 1991-92 (1,028), 1992-93 (1,249), 1993-94 (1,136), 2001-02 (1,243), 2003-04 (1,022); M. T. G. Elliott 1994-95 (1,029), 1995-96 (1,233), 1998-99 (1,014), 1999-00 (1,028), 2003-04 (1,429); J. L. Langer 1993-94 (1,198), 1997-98 (1,075), 1999-00 (1,108), 2001-02 (1,030), 2004-05 (1,245); M. L. Love 1994-95 (1,097), 2001-02 (1,189), 2002-03 (1,120), 2003-04 (1,098).

MOST RUNS ON AN AUSTRALIAN OVERSEAS TOUR

		Season	M	I	NO	R	HS	100s	50s	Avge
D. G. Bradman	England	1930	27	36	6	2,960	334	10	5	98.66
V. T. Trumper	England	1902	36	53	0	2,570	128	11	11	48.49
D. G. Bradman	England	1938	20	26	5	2,429	278	13	5	115.66
D. G. Bradman	England	1948	23	31	4	2,428	187	11	8	89.92
W. Bardsley	England	1912	36	52	6	2,365	184*	8	9	51.41
C. G. Macartney . . .	England	1921	31	41	2	2,317	345	8	6	59.41
C. G. Macartney . . .	England	1912	33	49	1	2,187	208	6	8	45.56
S. J. McCabe	England	1934	26	37	7	2,078	240	8	7	69.26
W. Bardsley	England	1909	33	49	4	2,072	219	6	7	46.04
M. A. Noble	England	1905	31	46	2	2,053	267	6	13	46.66
R. N. Harvey	England	1953	25	35	4	2,040	202*	10	5	65.80

		Season	M	I	NO	R	HS	100s	50s	Avge
D. G. Bradman.....	England	1934	22	27	3	2,020	304	7	6	84.16
W. M. Lawry......	England	1961	23	39	6	2,019	165	9	7	61.18
W. Bardsley.......	England	1921	30	41	4	2,005	209	8	10	54.18

Most in countries other than England:

R. N. Harvey	South Africa	1949-50	19	25	5	1,526	178	8	4	76.30
A. R. Border	India	1979-80	15	28	3	1,423	178	5	4	56.92
G. S. Chappell ...	West Indies	1972-73	10	17	1	1,109	154	4	6	69.31
W. M. Woodfull .	New Zealand	1927-28	6	9	3	781	284	3	2	130.16
A. R. Border	Pakistan	1979-80	5	9	3	674	178	3	1	112.33
W. Bardsley	North America	1913-14	5	6	2	437	142*	3	0	109.25
D. S. Lehmann ..	Sri Lanka	2003-04	4	7	0	509	153	3	1	72.71
S. R. Waugh	Zimbabwe	1999-00	2	3	1	339	161	2	0	169.50

LEADING BATSMEN IN EACH AUSTRALIAN SEASON
(Qualification for top of averages: 8 completed innings)

Season	Leading Scorer	Runs	Avge	Top of Averages	Runs	Avge
1850-51	T. F. Hamilton (Vic)	45	22.50	n/a		
1851-52	T. F. Hamilton (Vic)	84	42.00	n/a		
1853-54	G. Cavenagh (Vic)	45	22.50	n/a		
1854-55	no games played					
1855-56	{ J. J. McKone (NSW)	18	18.00	n/a		
	{ R. Driver (NSW)	18	9.00	n/a		
1856-57	G. H. B. Gilbert (NSW)	33	16.50	n/a		
1857-58	T. W. Wills (Vic)	94	23.50	n/a		
1858-59	O. W. Lewis (NSW)	53	26.50	n/a		
1859-60	T. W. Wills (Vic)	24	12.00	n/a		
1860-61	J. M. Bryant (Vic)	32	16.00	n/a		
1861-62	W. Caffyn (England)	88	88.00	n/a		
1862-63	D. D'Arcy (NSW)	51	51.00	n/a		
1863-64	T. Lockyer (England)	84	84.00	n/a		
1864-65	no games played					
1865-66	E. J. Gregory (NSW)	61	30.50	n/a		
1866-67	S. Cosstick (Vic)	29	14.50	n/a		
1867-68	R. W. Wardill (Vic)	155	155.00	n/a		
1868-69	J. Phillips (Vic)	133	44.33	n/a		
1869-70	C. S. Gordon (Vic)	143	71.50	n/a		
1870-71	A. R. Loughnan (Vic)	71	23.67	n/a		
1871-72	N. F. D. Thomson (NSW) ...	46	23.00	n/a		
1872-73	J. L. A. Arthur (Tas)	86	28.67	n/a		
1873-74	no games played					
1874-75	C. Bannerman (NSW)	113	113.00	n/a		
1875-76	D. W. Gregory (NSW)	116	38.67	n/a		
1876-77	C. Bannerman (NSW)	243	48.60	n/a		
1877-78	N. F. D. Thomson (NSW) ...	101	33.67	n/a		
1878-79	G. Ulyett (England)	306	34.00	G. Ulyett (England)	306	34.00
1879-80	A. C. Bannerman (NSW) ...	103	25.75	n/a		
1880-81	T. P. Horan (Vic)	318	35.33	H. H. Massie (NSW)	299	37.38
1881-82	W. L. Murdoch (NSW)	679	61.73	W. L. Murdoch (NSW) ...	679	61.73
1882-83	A. C. Bannerman (NSW) ...	434	54.25	A. C. Bannerman (NSW) ..	434	54.25
1883-84	W. L. Murdoch (NSW)	567	113.40	n/a		
1884-85	W. Barnes (England)	520	43.33	W. Barnes (England)	520	43.33
1885-86	J. McIlwraith (Vic)	315	78.75	n/a		
1886-87	A. Shrewsbury (England) ...	721	48.07	A. Shrewsbury (England) .	721	48.07
1887-88	H. Moses (NSW)	815	62.69	H. Moses (NSW)	815	62.69
1888-89	G. H. S. Trott (Vic)	507	39.00	G. H. S. Trott (Vic)	507	39.00
1889-90	J. J. Lyons (SAust)	254	63.50	n/a		
1890-91	G. Giffen (SAust)	275	91.67	n/a		
1891-92	J. J. Lyons (SAust)	557	55.70	J. J. Lyons (SAust)	557	55.70

Season	Leading Scorer	Runs	Avge	Top of Averages	Runs	Avge
1892-93	G. Giffen (SAust)	468	58.50	G. Giffen (SAust)	468	58.5
1893-94	G. Giffen (SAust)	526	75.14	G. Giffen (SAust)	526	75.1
1894-95	A. Ward (England)	916	41.64	A. E. Stoddart (England)	870	51.1
1895-96	H. Donnan (NSW)	626	69.56	H. Donnan (NSW)	626	69.5
1896-97	J. J. Lyons (SAust)	404	57.71	G. H. S. Trott (Vic)	323	40.3
1897-98	C. Hill (SAust)	1,196	66.44	C. Hill (SAust)	1,196	66.4
1898-99	V. T. Trumper (NSW)	873	62.36	C. Hill (SAust)	841	64.6
1899-00	V. T. Trumper (NSW)	721	72.10	V. T. Trumper (NSW)	721	72.1
1900-01	C. Hill (SAust)	620	103.33	n/a		
1901-02	C. Hill (SAust)	1,035	51.75	A. C. MacLaren (England)	929	58.06
1902-03	R. A. Duff (NSW)	786	87.33	R. A. Duff (NSW)	786	87.33
1903-04	V. T. Trumper (NSW)	990	55.00	M. A. Noble (NSW)	961	56.33
1904-05	W. W. Armstrong (Vic)	460	57.50	W. W. Armstrong (Vic)	460	57.50
1905-06	J. R. M. Mackay (NSW)	902	112.75	J. R. M. Mackay (NSW)	902	112.75
1906-07	A. J. Y. Hopkins (NSW)	617	56.09	A. J. Y. Hopkins (NSW)	617	56.09
1907-08	J. Hardstaff sr (MCC)	1,360	52.30	F. A. Tarrant (Vic)	762	76.20
1908-09	V. S. Ransford (Vic)	825	103.13	V. S. Ransford (Vic)	825	103.13
1909-10	H. H. L. Kortlang (Vic)	656	131.20	C. McKenzie (Vic)	377	47.13
1910-11	G. A. Faulkner (SAf)	1,534	59.00	V. T. Trumper (NSW)	1,246	69.22
1911-12	W. Rhodes (MCC)	1,098	54.90	R. B. Minnett (NSW)	882	63.00
1912-13	V. T. Trumper (NSW)	843	84.30	V. T. Trumper (NSW)	843	84.30
1913-14	C. G. Macartney (NSW)	892	111.50	C. G. Macartney (NSW)	892	111.50
1914-15	J. Ryder (Vic)	445	74.17	C. E. Pellew (SAust)	287	35.88
1915-16	no games played					
1916-17	no games played					
1917-18	no games played					
1918-19	W. W. Armstrong (Vic)	249	83.00	n/a		
1919-20	R. L. Park (Vic)	648	72.00	R. L. Park (Vic)	648	72.00
1920-21	E. H. Hendren (MCC)	1,178	62.00	W. W. Armstrong (Vic)	1,069	89.08
1921-22	F. A. O'Keefe (Vic)	708	118.00	H. S. B. Love (NSW)	424	43.00
1922-23	A. P. F. Chapman (MCC)	782	65.17	A. J. Richardson (SAust)	758	75.80
1923-24	W. H. Ponsford (Vic)	777	111.00	F. C. Thompson (Qld)	397	49.63
1924-25	H. Sutcliffe (MCC)	1,250	69.44	A. F. Kippax (NSW)	853	77.55
1925-26	A. J. Richardson (SAust)	904	50.22	C. G. Macartney (NSW)	795	88.33
1926-27	W. H. Ponsford (Vic)	1,229	122.90	W. H. Ponsford (Vic)	1,229	122.90
1927-28	W. H. Ponsford (Vic)	1,217	152.12	W. H. Ponsford (Vic)	1,217	152.12
1928-29	D. G. Bradman (NSW)	1,690	93.88	D. G. Bradman (NSW)	1,690	93.88
1929-30	D. G. Bradman (NSW)	1,586	113.28	D. G. Bradman (NSW)	1,586	113.28
1930-31	D. G. Bradman (NSW)	1,422	79.00	D. G. Bradman (NSW)	1,422	79.00
1931-32	D. G. Bradman (NSW)	1,403	116.91	D. G. Bradman (NSW)	1,403	116.91
1932-33	H. Sutcliffe (MCC)	1,318	73.22	H. Sutcliffe (MCC)	1,318	73.22
1933-34	D. G. Bradman (NSW)	1,192	132.44	D. G. Bradman (NSW)	1,192	132.44
1934-35	J. H. W. Fingleton (NSW)	880	58.67	L. S. Darling (Vic)	634	70.44
1935-36	D. G. Bradman (SAust)	1,173	130.33	D. G. Bradman (SAust)	1,173	130.33
1936-37	D. G. Bradman (SAust)	1,552	86.22	D. G. Bradman (SAust)	1,552	86.22
1937-38	D. G. Bradman (SAust)	1,437	89.81	D. G. Bradman (SAust)	1,437	89.81
1938-39	W. A. Brown (Qld)	1,057	105.70	W. A. Brown (Qld)	1,057	105.70
1939-40	D. G. Bradman (SAust)	1,475	122.91	D. G. Bradman (SAust)	1,475	122.91
1940-41	S. G. Barnes (NSW)	1,050	75.00	S. G. Barnes (NSW)	1,050	75.00
1941-42	V. N. Raymer (Qld)	130	130.00	n/a		
1942-43	no games played					
1943-44	no games played					
1944-45	no games played					
1945-46	S. G. Barnes (NSW)	794	88.22	S. G. Barnes (NSW)	794	88.22
1946-47	D. C. S. Compton (MCC)	1,432	65.09	D. G. Bradman (SAust)	1,032	79.38
1947-48	D. G. Bradman (SAust)	1,296	129.60	D. G. Bradman (SAust)	1,296	129.60
1948-49	A. R. Morris (NSW)	1,069	66.81	J. Moroney (NSW)	897	81.55
1949-50	A. R. C. McLean (SAust)	660	50.77	A. R. C. McLean (SAust)	660	50.77
1950-51	A. L. Hassett (Vic)	1,423	64.68	K. R. Miller (NSW)	1,332	78.35
1951-52	A. L. Hassett (Vic)	855	61.07	A. L. Hassett (Vic)	855	61.07

Season	Leading Scorer	Runs	Avge	Top of Averages	Runs	Avge
1952-53	R. N. Harvey (Vic)	1,659	63.80	R. N. Harvey (Vic)	1,659	63.80
1953-54	C. C. McDonald (Vic)	857	57.13	K. D. Mackay (Qld)	723	72.30
1954-55	R. N. Harvey (Vic)	1,009	45.86	D. C. S. Compton (MCC)	799	57.07
1955-56	J. W. Burke (NSW)	979	61.19	K. R. Miller (NSW)	638	70.89
1956-57	C. J. Pinch (SAust)	840	52.50	R. N. Harvey (Vic)	836	104.50
1957-58	N. C. O'Neill (NSW)	1,005	83.75	N. C. O'Neill (NSW)	1,005	83.75
1958-59	P. B. H. May (MCC)	1,197	57.00	C. C. McDonald (Vic)	990	61.87
1959-60	R. B. Simpson (WAust)	902	300.66	R. G. Flockton (NSW)	617	77.12
1960-61	R. B. Simpson (WAust)	1,541	64.21	B. C. Booth (NSW)	981	65.40
1961-62	R. B. Simpson (NSW)	704	46.93	B. K. Shepherd (WAust)	808	62.15
1962-63	K. F. Barrington (MCC)	1,451	85.35	K. F. Barrington (MCC)	1,451	85.35
1963-64	R. B. Simpson (NSW)	1,524	66.26	B. C. Booth (NSW)	1,180	90.76
1964-65	S. C. Trimble (Qld)	984	57.87	W. M. Lawry (Vic)	848	84.80
1965-66	W. M. Lawry (Vic)	1,445	72.25	R. M. Cowper (Vic)	1,418	74.63
1966-67	L. E. Favell (SAust)	847	49.82	N. C. O'Neill (NSW)	815	67.91
1967-68	R. B. Simpson (NSW)	1,082	56.94	A. P. Sheahan (Vic)	973	64.86
1968-69	I. M. Chappell (SAust)	1,476	82.00	I. M. Chappell (SAust)	1,476	82.00
1969-70	G. S. Chappell (SAust)	856	65.84	J. A. Steele (NSW)	677	67.70
1970-71	B. A. Richards (SAust)	1,538	109.85	B. A. Richards (SAust)	1,538	109.85
1971-72	I. M. Chappell (SAust)	1,140	60.00	K. D. Walters (NSW)	895	68.84
1972-73	A. P. Sheahan (Vic)	1,002	83.50	A. P. Sheahan (Vic)	1,002	83.50
1973-74	G. S. Chappell (Qld)	1,288	85.86	G. S. Chappell (Qld)	1,288	85.86
1974-75	G. S. Chappell (Qld)	1,484	61.83	G. S. Chappell (Qld)	1,484	61.83
1975-76	G. S. Chappell (Qld)	1,547	85.94	G. S. Chappell (Qld)	1,547	85.94
1976-77	D. W. Hookes (SAust)	861	71.75	R. D. Robinson (Vic)	828	82.80
1977-78	A. D. Ogilvie (Qld)	1,215	50.62	G. M. Wood (WAust)	678	56.50
1978-79	A. R. Border (NSW)	1,220	55.45	J. K. Moss (Vic)	881	67.77
1979-80	G. S. Chappell (Qld)	1,066	71.06	G. S. Chappell (Qld)	1,066	71.06
1980-81	G. S. Chappell (Qld)	1,502	75.10	G. S. Chappell (Qld)	1,502	75.10
1981-82	K. C. Wessels (Qld)	1,094	60.77	H. A. Gomes (West Indians)	712	89.00
1982-83	D. W. Hookes (SAust)	1,424	64.72	G. N. Yallop (Vic)	1,418	67.52
1983-84	G. N. Yallop (Vic)	1,132	113.20	G. N. Yallop (Vic)	1,132	113.20
1984-85	K. C. Wessels (Qld)	1,020	53.68	G. Shipperd (WAust)	823	68.58
1985-86	A. R. Border (Qld)	1,247	73.35	A. R. Border (Qld)	1,247	73.35
1986-87	G. R. Marsh (WAust)	1,200	48.00	M. R. J. Veletta (WAust)	971	74.69
1987-88	D. C. Boon (Tas)	1,287	67.74	M. D. Crowe (NZ)	715	89.38
1988-89	M. A. Taylor (NSW)	1,241	49.64	I. V. A. Richards (WI)	683	68.30
1989-90	M. A. Taylor (NSW)	1,403	70.15	M. E. Waugh (NSW)	1,009	77.62
1990-91	S. G. Law (Qld)	1,204	75.25	S. G. Law (Qld)	1,204	75.25
1991-92	D. M. Jones (Vic)	1,248	96.00	D. M. Jones (Vic)	1,248	96.00
1992-93	M. L. Hayden (Qld)	1,249	52.04	J. D. Siddons (SAust)	1,190	66.51
1993-94	M. G. Bevan (NSW)	1,312	77.18	M. L. Hayden (Qld)	1,136	126.22
1994-95	D. M. Jones (Vic)	1,251	69.50	D. M. Jones (Vic)	1,251	69.50
1995-96	D. S. Lehmann (SAust)	1,237	56.22	M. T. G. Elliott (Vic)	1,233	68.50
1996-97	J. Cox (Tas)	1,349	67.45	J. L. Langer (WAust)	771	77.10
1997-98	D. F. Hills (Tas)	1,220	55.45	T. M. Moody (WAust)	702	78.00
1998-99	G. S. Blewett (SAust)	1,187	118.70	G. S. Blewett (SAust)	1,187	118.70
1999-00	D. S. Lehmann (SAust)	1,142	63.44	R. T. Ponting (Tas)	582	72.75
2000-01	S. M. Katich (WAust)	1,282	71.22	R. T. Ponting (Tas)	726	80.67
2001-02	M. L. Hayden (Qld)	1,243	82.87	N. J. Astle (New Zealanders)	554	110.80
2002-03	M. L. Love (Qld)	1,120	65.88	M. L. Love (Qld)	1,120	65.88
2003-04	M. T. G. Elliott (Vic)	1,429	79.39	R. S. Dravid (Indians)	620	103.33
2004-05	M. G. Bevan (Tas)	1,464	97.60	M. G. Bevan (Tas)	1,464	97.60

HIGHEST AVERAGE IN AN AUSTRALIAN SEASON
(Qualification: 500 runs)

	Season	M	I	NO	R	HS	100s	50s	Avge
R. B. Simpson (Western Australia)....	1959-60	5	6	3	902	236*	3	3	300.66
W. H. Ponsford (Victoria)...........	1922-23	3	4	0	616	429	2	1	154.00
D. G. Bradman (South Australia).....	1938-39	7	7	1	919	225	6	0	153.17
C. Hill (South Australia).............	1909-10	3	4	0	609	205	3	0	152.25
W. H. Ponsford (Victoria)...........	1927-28	6	8	0	1,217	437	4	1	152.13
D. G. Bradman (New South Wales)..	1933-34	7	11	2	1,192	253*	5	3	132.44
H. H. L. Kortlang (Victoria).........	1909-10	5	9	4	656	197	2	3	131.20
D. G. Bradman (South Australia).....	1935-36	8	9	0	1,173	369	4	1	130.33
D. G. Bradman (South Australia).....	1947-48	9	12	2	1,296	201	8	1	129.60
W. M. Woodfull (Victoria)...........	1927-28	5	7	2	645	191*	2	3	129.00
M. L. Hayden (Queensland).........	1993-94	6	12	3	1,136	173*	7	1	126.22
D. G. Bradman (South Australia)....	1939-80	9	15	3	1,475	267	5	4	122.92
W. H. Ponsford (Victoria)...........	1926-27	6	10	0	1,229	352	6	0	122.90

AUSTRALIANS WITH 10,000 FIRST-CLASS RUNS

	Career	M	I	NO	R	HS	100s	50s	Avge
D. G. Bradman	1927-28 - 1948-49	234	338	43	28,067	452*	117	69	95.14
A. R. Border	1976-77 - 1995-96	385	625	97	27,131	205	70	142	51.38
M. E. Waugh	1985-86 - 2003-04	368	591	75	26,855	229*	81	133	52.04
K. C. Wessels	1973-74 - 1999-00	316	539	50	25,738	254	66	132	52.50
G. S. Chappell	1966-67 - 1983-84	322	542	72	24,535	247*	74	111	52.20
S. R. Waugh	1984-85 - 2003-04	356	551	88	24,052	216*	79	97	51.95
S. G. Law	1988-89 -	315	520	57	23,557	263	69	109	50.88
D. C. Boon	1978-79 - 1999	350	585	53	23,413	227	68	114	44.01
K. J. Greives	1945-46 - 1964	490	746	79	22,454	224	29	136	33.66
D. S. Lehmann	1987-88 -	248	420	28	21,991	255	70	100	56.10
J. L. Langer	1991-92 -	270	473	46	21,836	274*	69	83	51.14
R. N. Harvey	1946-47 - 1962-63	306	461	35	21,699	231*	67	94	50.93
R. B. Simpson	1952-53 - 1977-78	257	436	62	21,029	359	60	100	56.22
T. M. Moody	1985-86 - 2000-01	300	501	47	21,001	272	64	94	46.26
M. L. Hayden	1991-92 -	249	431	43	20,908	380	68	86	53.89
I. M. Chappell	1961-62 - 1979-80	263	448	41	19,680	209	59	96	48.35
W. E. Alley	1945-46 - 1968	400	682	67	19,612	221*	31	92	31.88
D. M. Jones	1981-82 - 1997-98	245	415	45	19,188	324*	55	88	51.86
W. M. Lawry	1955-56 - 1971-72	250	417	49	18,734	266	50	100	50.90
J. Cox	1987-98 -	261	461	31	18,554	250	51	81	43.15
M. G. Bevan	1989-90 -	227	382	66	18,502	216	67	77	58.55
F. A. Tarrant	1898-99 - 1936-37	329	541	48	17,952	250*	33	93	36.41
M. A. Taylor	1985-86 - 1998-99	253	435	20	17,415	334*	41	97	41.96
C. Hill	1892-93 - 1924-25	252	416	21	17,213	365*	45	82	43.57
G. S. Blewett	1991-92 -	225	406	27	17,082	268	43	85	45.07
W. Bardsley	1903-04 - 1926-27	250	376	35	17,025	264	53	74	49.92
W. L. Murdoch	1875-76 - 1904	391	679	48	16,953	321	19	85	26.86
V. T. Trumper	1894-95 - 1913-14	255	401	21	16,939	300*	42	87	44.57
A. L. Hassett	1932-33 - 1953-54	216	322	32	16,890	232	59	76	58.24
K. D. Walters	1962-63 - 1980-81	259	426	57	16,180	253	45	81	43.84
W. W. Armstrong ..	1898-99 - 1921-22	269	406	61	16,158	303*	45	57	46.83
M. T. G. Elliott	1992-93 -	190	349	26	16,141	203	50	76	49.97
V. E. Jackson	1936-37 - 1958	354	605	53	15,698	170	21	72	28.43
S. M. J. Woods	1886 - 1910	401	690	35	15,345	215	19	62	23.42
L. Livingston	1941-42 - 1964	236	384	45	15,269	210	34	78	45.04
E. S. Gregory	1889-90 - 1912	368	587	55	15,192	201	25	65	28.55
R. T. Ponting	1992-93 -	180	301	44	15,083	257	54	60	58.69
C. G. Macartney ...	1905-06 - 1935-36	249	360	32	15,019	345	49	53	45.78
I. R. Redpath	1961-62 - 1975-76	226	391	34	14,993	261	32	84	41.99
M. J. Slater	1991-92 - 2003-04	216	384	19	14,912	221	36	69	40.85

	Career	M	I	NO	R	HS	100s	50s	Avge
1. E. K. Hussey	1994-95 -	168	302	25	14,645	331*	37	63	52.87
2. J. P. Burge	1952-53 - 1966-67	233	354	46	14,640	283	38	66	47.53
M. J. Di Venuto	1991-92 -	204	361	19	14,521	230	31	90	42.46
K. R. Miller	1937-38 - 1959	226	326	36	14,183	281*	41	63	48.90
M. L. Love	1992-93 -	177	309	30	14,042	300*	35	64	50.33
M. A. Noble	1893-94 - 1919-20	248	377	34	13,975	284	37	65	40.74
N. C. O'Neill	1955-56 - 1967-68	188	306	34	13,859	284	45	64	50.95
W. A. Brown	1932-33 - 1949-50	189	284	15	13,838	265*	39	65	51.44
W. H. Ponsford	1920-21 - 1934-35	162	235	23	13,819	437	47	42	65.18
D. R. Martyn	1990-91 -	188	314	43	13,812	238	42	70	50.97
W. M. Woodfull	1921-22 - 1934-35	174	245	39	13,388	284	49	58	64.99
G. M. Wood	1976-77 - 1991-92	227	375	42	13,353	186*	35	61	40.09
M. W. Goodwin	1994-95 -	167	292	23	12,836	335*	39	54	47.72
A. F. Kippax	1918-19 - 1935-36	175	256	33	12,762	315*	43	45	57.22
K. J. Hughes	1975-76 - 1990-91	216	368	20	12,711	213	26	69	36.52
D. W. Hookes	1975-76 - 1991-92	178	304	16	12,671	306*	32	65	43.39
A. R. Morris	1940-41 - 1963-64	162	250	15	12,614	290	46	46	53.67
C. L. McCool	1939-40 - 1960	251	412	34	12,420	172	18	66	32.85
L. E. Favell	1951-52 - 1969-70	202	347	9	12,379	190	27	68	36.62
B. J. Hodge	1993-94 -	160	286	26	12,219	302*	37	45	47.00
S. J. McCabe	1928-29 - 1941-42	182	262	20	11,951	240	29	68	49.38
R. J. Inverarity	1962-63 - 1984-85	223	377	49	11,777	187	26	60	35.90
G. R. Marsh	1977-78 - 1993-94	184	323	25	11,760	355*	34	46	39.46
G. Giffen	1877-78 - 1903-04	251	421	23	11,758	271	18	51	29.54
R. Benaud	1948-49 - 1967-68	259	365	44	11,719	187	23	61	36.50
A. Symonds		180	303	28	11,646	254*	34	48	42.35
G. N. Yallop	1972-73 - 1986-87	164	283	30	11,615	268	30	57	45.90
J. D. Siddons	1984-85 - 1999-00	160	280	22	11,587	245	35	53	44.91
C. C. McDonald	1947-48 - 1962-63	192	307	26	11,376	229	24	57	40.48
B. C. Booth	1954-55 - 1968-69	183	283	35	11,265	214*	26	60	45.42
R. W. Marsh	1968-69 - 1983-84	258	396	41	11,067	236	12	54	31.17
K. D. Mackay	1946-47 - 1962-63	201	294	46	10,823	223	23	58	43.64
V. Y. Richardson	1918-19 - 1937-38	184	297	12	10,727	231	27	46	37.63
A. E. Trott	1892-93 - 1911	375	602	53	10,696	164	8	43	19.48
J. Darling	1893-94 - 1907-08	202	333	25	10,635	210	19	55	34.52
R. M. Cowper	1959-60 - 1969-70	147	228	31	10,595	307	26	58	53.78
J. Ryder	1912-13 - 1935-36	177	274	37	10,499	295	24	55	44.29
S. C. Trimble	1959-60 - 1975-76	144	262	16	10,282	252*	26	48	41.79
G. E. Tribe	1945-46 - 1959	308	454	82	10,177	136*	7	48	27.34
G. M. Ritchie	1980-81 - 1991-92	159	255	24	10,171	213*	24	54	44.03
K. R. Stackpole	1959-60 - 1973-74	167	279	22	10,100	207	22	50	39.29
S. M. Katich	1996-97 -	134	232	33	10,096	228*	28	51	50.73
J. P. Maher	1993-94 -	149	264	27	10,006	217	21	49	42.22

HIGHEST CAREER AVERAGE

(Qualification: 500 runs)

	Career	M	I	NO	R	HS	100s	50s	Avge
D. G. Bradman	1927-28 - 1948-49	234	338	43	28,067	452*	117	69	95.14
H. O. Rock	1924-25 - 1925-26	6	9	1	758	235	3	2	94.75
F. A. O'Keeffe	1919-20 - 1921-22	9	13	0	926	180	3	4	71.23
W. H. Ponsford	1920-21 - 1934-35	162	235	23	13,819	437	47	42	65.18
W. M. Woodfull	1921-22 - 1934-35	174	245	39	13,388	284	49	58	64.99
B. A. Onyons	1918-19 - 1928-29	11	17	1	997	136	6	3	62.31
R. T. Ponting	1992-93 -	180	301	44	15,083	257	54	60	58.69
M. G. Bevan	1989-90 -	227	382	66	18,502	216	67	77	58.55
A. L. Hassett	1932-33 - 1953-54	216	322	32	16,890	232	59	76	58.24
A. F. Kippax	1918-19 - 1935-36	175	256	33	12,762	315*	43	45	57.22
R. B. Simpson	1952-53 - 1977-78	257	436	62	21,029	359	60	100	56.22

	Career	M	I	NO	R	HS	100s	50s	Avge
D.S. Lehmann	1987-88 -	248	420	28	21,991	255	70	100	56.01
S.G. Barnes	1936-37 - 1952-53	110	164	10	8,333	234	26	37	54.11
D.J. Hussey	2002-03 -	48	70	8	3,346	212*	13	14	53.97
M.L. Hayden	1991-92 -	249	431	43	20,908	380	68	86	53.89
R.M. Cowper	1959-60 - 1969-70	147	228	31	10,595	307	26	58	53.78
A.R. Morris	1940-41 - 1963-64	162	250	15	12,614	290	46	46	53.67
P.A. Jaques	2000-01 -	59	104	5	5,261	243	13	26	53.14
M.E.K. Hussey	1994-95 -	168	302	25	14,645	331*	37	63	52.87
J.R. Moroney	1945-46 - 1951-52	57	93	16	4,023	217	12	19	52.24
G.S. Chappell	1966-67 - 1983-84	322	542	72	24,535	247*	74	111	52.20
M.E. Waugh	1985-86 - 2003-04	368	591	75	26,855	229*	81	133	52.04
S.R. Waugh	1984-85 - 2003-04	356	551	88	24,052	216*	79	97	51.95
D.M. Jones	1981-82 - 1997-98	245	415	45	19,188	324*	55	88	51.86
C.L. Badcock	1929-30 - 1940-41	97	159	16	7,371	325	26	21	51.54
W.A. Brown	1932-33 - 1949-50	189	284	15	13,838	265*	39	65	51.44
A.R. Border	1976-77 - 1995-96	385	625	97	27,131	205	70	142	51.38
J.R.M. Mackay	1902-03 - 1906-07	20	33	2	1,556	203	6	7	50.19
J.L. Langer	1991-92 -	270	473	46	21,836	274*	69	83	51.14
D.R. Martyn	1990-91 -	188	314	43	13,812	238	42	70	50.97
N.C. O'Neill	1955-56 - 1967-68	188	306	34	13,859	284	45	64	50.95
R.N. Harvey	1946-47 - 1962-63	306	461	35	21,699	231*	67	94	50.93
W.M. Lawry	1955-56 - 1971-72	250	417	49	18,734	266	50	100	50.90
S.G. Law	1988-89 -	315	520	57	23,557	263	69	109	50.88
S.M. Katich	1996-97 -	134	232	33	10,096	228*	28	51	50.73
M.L. Love	1992-93 -	177	309	30	14,042	300*	35	64	50.33
K.C. Wessels	1973-74 - 1999-00	316	539	50	25,738	254	66	132	50.50

FASTEST FIFTIES

Minutes

11	T.M. Moody	Warwickshire v Glamorgan at Swansea	1990
14	S.J. Pegler	South Africans v Tasmania at Launceston	1910-11
15	D.J. Shepherd	Glamorgan v Australians at Swansea	1961
17	D.W. Hookes	South Australia v Victoria at Adelaide	1982-83
18	J.H. Sinclair	South Australians v Tasmania at Launceston	1910-11
18	A. Cotter	New South Wales v Victoria at Sydney	1911-12
18	A. Symonds	Gloucestershire v Durham at Bristol	1995

FASTEST HUNDREDS

Minutes

26	T.M. Moody	Warwickshire v Glamorgan at Swansea	1990
43	R.N.S. Hobbs	Essex v Australians at Chelmsford	1975
43	D.W. Hookes	South Australia v Victoria at Adelaide	1982-83
50	D.R.A. Gehrs	South Australia v Western Australia at Adelaide	1912-13

Balls

34	D.W. Hookes	South Australia v Victoria at Adelaide	1982-83
36	T.M. Moody	Warwickshire v Glamorgan at Swansea	1990

FASTEST DOUBLE-HUNDREDS

Minutes

131	V.T. Trumper	Australians v Canterbury at Christchurch	1913-14
135	S.M.J. Woods	Somerset v Susses at Hove	1895
143	C.G. Macartney	Australians v Nottinghamshire at Nottingham	1921
154	F.E. Woolley	MCC. v Tasmania at Hobart (TCA)	1911-12
154	D.G. Bradman	South Australia v Western Australia at Perth	1939-40

How hard can it be?

FASTEST TRIPLE-HUNDREDS

Minutes

198	C. G. Macartney	Australians v Nottingham at Nottingham	1921
209	F. E. Woolley	MCC v Tasmania at Hobart (TCA)	1911-12
213	D. G. Bradman	South Australia v Tasmania at Adelaide	1935-36
285	W. H. Ponsford	Victoria v New South Wales at Melbourne	1926-27
288	D. G. Bradman	New South Wales v Queensland at Sydney	1929-30

MOST RUNS IN A DAY'S PLAY

Runs

345	C. G. Macartney	Australians v Nottinghamshire at Nottingham	1921
334	W. H. Ponsford	Victoria v New South Wales at Melbourne	1926-27
325	B. A. Richards	South Australia v Western Australia at Perth	1970-71
318	C. W. Gregory	New South Wales v Queensland	1906-07
309	D. G. Bradman	Australia v England at Leeds	1930

LONGEST INNINGS

Minutes

797	L. Hutton	England v Australia at The Oval	1938
766	M. R. J. Veletta	Western Australia v Victoria at Perth	1986-87
762	R. B. Simpson	Australia v England at Manchester	1964
727	R. M. Cowper	Australia v England at Melbourne	1965-66
720	M. A. Taylor	Australia v Pakistan at Peshawar	1998-9

MOST RUNS SCORED OFF AN OVER

Eight Balls

32	(34166066)	D. K. Carmody and I. D. Craig	(off I. W. G. Johnson) A. R. Morris's XI v A. L. Hassett's XI at Melbourne	1953-54

Six Balls

32	(666644)	I. R. Redpath	(off N. Rosendorff) Australians v Orange Free State at Bloemfontein	1969-70
31	(166666)	M. H. Bowditch and M. J. Procter	(off A. A. Mallett) Western Province v Australians at Cape Town	1969-70
30	(466464)	D. G. Bradman	(off A. P. Freeman) Australians v England XI at Folkestone	1934
30	(644646)	T. M. Moody	(off A. E. Tucker) Western Australia v New South Wales at Sydney	1990-91

MOST SIXES IN AN INNINGS

16	A. Symonds	Gloucestershire v Glamorgan at Abergavenny	1995
12	D. M. Jones	Australians v Warwickshire at Birmingham	1989
11	R. Benaud	Australians v T. N. Pearce's XI at Scarborough	1953
11	M. L. Hayden	Australia v Zimbabwe at Perth	2003-04
11	D. J. Thornely	New South Wales v Western Australia at Sydney	2004-05
10	D. W. Hookes	South Australia v New South Wales at Adelaide	1985-86

MOST SIXES IN A MATCH

20	A. Symonds	Gloucestershire v Glamorgan at Abergavenny	1995

SLOWEST FIFTIES

Minutes

357	T. E. Bailey	England v Australia at Brisbane	1958-59
316	D. J. Ramshaw	Victoria v New South Wales at Sydney	1991-92
313	D. J. McGlew	South Africa v Australia at Johannesburg (WS)	1957-58
310	B. A. Edgar	New Zealand v Australia at Wellington	1981-82

SLOWEST HUNDREDS

Minutes

545	D. J. McGlew	South Africa v Australia at Durban	1957-58
481	G. Shipperd	Tasmania v Victoria at Launceston	1989-90
462	M. J. Greatbatch	New Zealand v Australia at Perth	1989-90
460	S. M. Katich	Western Australia v Queensland at Perth	2000-01
449	G. Shipperd	Tasmania v Western Australia at Perth	1989-90

LONGEST TO GET OFF THE MARK

Minutes

97	T. G. Evans	England v Australia at Adelaide	1946-47
93	G. J. Denton	Tasmania v Queensland at Hobart (Bel)	1999-00
88	B. P. Nash	Queensland v Tasmania at Hobart (Bel)	2002-03
74	J. T. Murray	England v Australia at Sydney	1962-63
72	C. G. Rackemann	Australia v England at Sydney	1990-91

HIGHEST PARTNERSHIPS FOR EACH WICKET

First wicket

456	W. H. Ponsford and R. E. Mayne, Victoria v Queensland at Melbourne	1923-24
431	M. R. J. Veletta and G. R. Marsh, Western Australia v South Australia at Perth	1989-90
388	K. C. Wessels and R. B. Kerr, Queensland v Victoria at St Kilda	1982-83
382	W. M. Lawry and R. B. Simpson, Australia v West Indies at Bridgetown	1964-65
375	W. M. Woodfull and W. H. Ponsford, Victoria v New South Wales at Melbourne	1926-27
374	G. R. Marsh and M. R. J. Veletta, Western Australia v Tamil Nadu at Perth	1988-89
353	M. T. G. Elliott and J. L. Arnberger, Victoria v Tasmania at Richmond	1999-00
337	C. C. McDonald and K. D. Meuleman, Victoria v South Australia at Adelaide	1949-50
331	B. A. Courtice and R. B. Kerr, Queensland v Tasmania at Brisbane	1984-85
329	G. R. Marsh and M. A. Taylor, Australia v England at Nottingham	1989

Second wicket

451	W. H. Ponsford and D. G. Bradman, Australia v England at The Oval	1934
386	G. S. Blewett and D. S. Lehmann, South Australia v Tasmania at Hobart (Bel)	2001-02
382	L. Hutton and M. Leyland, England v Australia at The Oval	1938
378	L. A. Marks and K. D. Walters, New South Wales v South Australia at Adelaide	1964-65
374	R. B. Simpson and R. M. Cowper, Australians v N. E. Transvaal at Pretoria	1966-67
369	C. T. Perren and S. G. Law, Queensland v Western Australia at Brisbane	2003-04
368	W. Rhodes and C. A. G. Russell, MCC v South Australia at Adelaide	1920-21
368*	M. L. Hayden and M. L. Love, Queensland v Tasmania at Hobart (Bel)	1995-96
365	M. L. Hayden and M. L. Love, Queensland v Tasmania at Brisbane	1995-96
358	C. McKenzie and H. H. L. Kortlang, Victoria v Western Australia at Perth	1909-10

Third wicket

390*	J. M. Wiener and J. K. Moss, Victoria v Western Australia at St Kilda	1981-82
389	W. H. Ponsford and S. J. McCabe, Australians v MCC at Lord's	1934
363	D. G. Bradman and A. F. Kippax, New South Wales v Queensland at Sydney	1933-34
362	W. Bardsley and C. G. Macartney, Australians v Essex at Leyton	1912
356	D. G. Bradman and R. A. Hamence, South Australia v Tasmania at Adelaide	1935-36
355	W. Bardsley and V. S. Ransford, Australians v Essex at Leyton	1909
349	D. M. Jones and T. M. Moody, Australians v Warwickshire at Birmingham	1989

545 W. Bardsley and J. M. Taylor, New South Wales v South Australia at Adelaide 1920-21
541 E. J. Barlow and R. G. Pollock, South Africa v Australia at Adelaide 1963-64
530 G. M. Wood and G. R. Marsh, Western Australia v New South Wales at Sydney 1983-84

Fourth wicket

462* D. W. Hookes and W. B. Phillips, South Australia v Tasmania at Adelaide 1986-87
424 I. S. Lee and S. O. Quin, Victoria v Tasmania at Melbourne 1933-34
388 W. H. Ponsford and D. G. Bradman, Australia v England at Leeds 1934
377 K. R. Miller and J. H. de Courcy, Australians v Comb. Services at Kingston-on-Thames .. 1953
369 C. J. L. Rogers and M. J. North, Western Australia v New South Wales at Perth ... 2002-03
353 S. R. Tendulkar and V. V. S. Laxman, India v Australia at Sydney 2003-04
336 W. M. Lawry and K. D. Walters, Australia v West Indies at Sydney 1968-69
333 E. H. Hendren and W. R. Hammond, MCC v New South Wales at Sydney 1928-29
325 N. C. O'Neill and B. C. Booth, New South Wales v Victoria at Sydney 1957-58
321 D. R. Martyn and M. W. Goodwin, Western Australia v Tasmania at Perth 2001-02

Fifth wicket

464* M. E. Waugh and S. R. Waugh, New South Wales v Western Australia at Perth 1990-91
405 S. G. Barnes and D. G. Bradman, Australia v England at Sydney 1946-47
397 W. Bardsley and C. Kelleway, New South Wales v South Australia at Sydney 1920-21
385 S. R. Waugh and G. S. Blewett, Australia v South Africa at Johannesburg (WS) 1996-97
377* G. P. Thorpe and M. R. Ramprakash, England XI v South Australia at Adelaide ... 1998-99
376 V. V. S. Laxman and R. S. Dravid, India v Australia at Kolkata 2000-01
344 M. C. Cowdrey and T. W. Graveney, MCC v South Australia at Adelaide 1962-63
344 B. C. Lara, †P. T. Collins and J. C. Adams, West Indies v Australia at Kingston ... 1998-99
343 R. I. Maddocks and J. Hallebone, Victoria v Tasmania at Melbourne 1951-52
336 W. H. Ponsford and H. S. B. Love, Victoria v Tasmania at Melbourne 1922-23

Sixth wicket

428 M. A. Noble and W. W. Armstrong, Australians v Sussex at Hove 1902
365 R. D. Jacobs and B. C. Lara, West Indians v Australia A at Hobart (Bel) 2000-01
346 J. H. W. Fingleton and D. G. Bradman, Australia v England at Melbourne 1936-37
332 N. G. Marks and G. Thomas, New South Wales v South Australia at Sydney 1958-59
323 E. H. Hendren and J. W. H. T. Douglas, MCC v Victoria at Melbourne 1920-21
317 D. R. Martyn and A. C. Gilchrist, Australia v South Africa at Johannesburg (WS) ... 2001-02
298* D. B. Vengsarkar and R. J. Shastri, India v Australia at Bombay 1986-87
290 M. T. G. Elliott and D. S. Berry, Victoria v New South Wales at Sydney 1996-97
289 S. J. E. Loxton and D. T. Ring, Victoria v Queensland at Melbourne 1946-47
279 A. L. Hassett and E. A. Williams, Australian Services v Prince's XI at Delhi 1945-46

Seventh wicket

347 D. S. Atkinson and C. C. Depeiza, West Indies v Australia at Bridgetown 1954-55
335 C. W. Andrews and E. C. Bensted, Queensland v New South Wales at Sydney 1934-35
273* W. W. Armstrong and J. Darling, Australians v Gentlemen of England at Lord's 1905
268 A. H. Kardar and Imtiaz Ahmed, North Zone v Australian Services at Lahore 1945-46
255 G. Thomas and R. Benaud, New South Wales v Victoria at Melbourne 1961-62
244 W. R. Patrick and C. F. W. Allcott, New Zealanders v New South Wales at Sydney .. 1925-26
232 W. Bruce and H. Trumble, Australians v Oxford and Cambridge Univ. at Portsmouth .. 1893
229 K. J. Schneider and W. A. S. Oldfield, Australians v Canterbury at Christchurch 1927-28
222* N. Deonarine and C. S. Baugh, Carib Beer XI v Australians at Georgetown 2002-03
221 D. T. Lindsay and P. L. van der Merwe, South Africa v Australia at Johannesburg (WS) 1966-67

Eighth wicket

433 V. T. Trumper and A. Sims, Australians v Canterbury at Christchurch 1913-14
270 V. T. Trumper and E. P. Barbour, New South Wales v Victoria at Sydney 1912-13
253 N. J. Astle and A. C. Parore, New Zealand v Australia at Perth 2001-02
243 M. J. Hartigan and C. Hill, Australia v England at Adelaide 1907-08
242* T. J. Zoehrer and K. H. MacLeay, Western Australia v New South Wales at Perth ... 1990-91
236 R. A. Duff and A. J. Y. Hopkins, New South Wales v Lord Hawke's XI at Sydney ... 1902-03
222 M. C. Miller and B. E. Young, South Australia v Queensland at Adelaide 2002-03

218 C. G. Macartney and J. D. Scott, New South Wales v Queensland at Sydney .... 1913-1⸱
215 W. W. Armstrong and R. L. Park, Victoria v South Australia at Melbourne .... 1919-2⸱
204 W. A. S. Oldfield and C. O. Nicholls, New South Wales v Victoria at Sydney .... 1927-2⸱

Ninth wicket

232 C. Hill and E. Walkley, South Australia v New South Wales at Adelaide 1900-01
226 C. Kelleway and W. A. S. Oldfield, New South Wales v Victoria at Melbourne 1925-26
225 W. W. Armstrong and E. A. C. Windsor, Australian XI v The Rest at Sydney 1907-08
221 E. F. Waddy and W. P. Howell, New South Wales v South Australia at Adelaide 1904-05
201 E. E. B. Forssberg and H. S. B. Love, New South Wales v Queensland at Sydney 1920-21
172 R. G. Barlow and W. Flowers, Players v Australians at Nottingham 1886
171 D. P. B. Morkel and N. A. Quinn, South Africans v Western Australia at Perth 1931-32
170 T. W. Garrett and T. R. McKibbin, New South Wales v South Australia at Sydney ... 1896-97
169 C. B. Willis and W. A. S. Oldfield, A. I. F. v Nottinghamshire at Nottingham 1919
168* K. H. MacLeay and V. J. Marks, Western Australia v New South Wales at Perth 1986-87

Tenth wicket

307 A. F. Kippax and J. E. H. Hooker, New South Wales v Victoria at Melbourne 1928-29
219 D. J. Thornely and S. C. G. MacGill, New South Wales v Western Australia at Sydney .. 2004-05
211 M. Ellis and T. J. Hastings, Victoria v South Australia at Melbourne 1902-03
169 R. B. Minnett and C. G. McKew, New South Wales v Victoria at Sydney 1911-12
154 F. R. Buttsworth and J. P. Lanigan, Western Australia v Victoria at Perth 1921-22
147 C. G. Macartney and S. C. Everett, Australian XI v Tasmania at Hobart (TCA) 1925-26
145 G. A. Rotherham and J. H. Naumann, Cambridge Univ. v AIF Team at Cambridge .. 1919
138* B. E. McNamara and P. J. S. Alley, New South Wales v Tasmania at Hobart (Bel) ... 1996-97
136 J. P. O'Halloran and A. E. Johns, Victoria v South Australia at Melbourne 1896-97
135 W. A. S. Oldfield and A. A. Mailey, New South Wales v South Australia at Adelaide . 1923-24

BOWLING RECORDS

TEN WICKETS IN AN INNINGS

10-43	E. Barratt	The Players v Australians at The Oval	1878
10-66	G. Giffen	Australian XI v The Rest at Sydney	1883-84
10-69	S. M. J. Woods	Cambridge University v C. I. Thornton's XI at Cambridge ..	1890
10-28	W. P. Howell	Australians v Surrey at The Oval	1899
10-42	A. E. Trott	Middlesex v Somerset at Taunton	1900
10-66	A. A. Mailey	Australians v Gloucestershire at Cheltenham	1921
10-37	C. V. Grimmett	Australians v Yorkshire at Sheffield	1930
10-36	T. W. Wall	South Australia v New South Wales at Sydney	1932-33
10-53	J. C. Laker	England v Australia at Manchester	1956
10-88	J. C. Laker	Surrey v Australians at The Oval	1956
10-61	P. J. Allan	Queensland v Victoria at Melbourne	1965-66
10-44	I. J. Brayshaw	Western Australia v Victoria at Perth	1967-68

BEST BOWLING IN AN INNINGS ON DEBUT

9-55	J. Quilty	South Australia v Victoria at Adelaide	1881-82
9-67	H. P. Hay	South Australia v Lord Hawke's XI at Unley	1902-03
8-31	W. Brown	Tasmania v Victoria at Hobart (LRG)	1857-58
8-35	R. Wilson	Queensland v Auckland at Auckland	1896-97
8-36	J. L. Bevan	South Australia v Tasmania at Adelaide	1877-78
8-81	H. V. Hordern	New South Wales v Queensland at Sydney	1905-06
8-111	M. Pierce	New South Wales v South Australia at Adelaide	1892-93

BEST BOWLING IN A MATCH ON DEBUT

15-73	W. Brown	Tasmania v Victoria at Hobart (LRG)	1857-58

14-59	J. L. Bevan	South Australia v Tasmania at Adelaide	1877-78
13-61	T. W. Antill	Victoria v Tasmania at Launceston	1850-51
13-265	M. Pierce	New South Wales v South Australia at Adelaide	1892-93
11-48	S. Cosstick	Victoria v New South Wales at Sydney	1860-61
11-80	J. E. Barrett	Victoria v South Australia at Melbourne	1884-85
11-97	R. Wilson	Queensland v Auckland at Auckland	1896-97
11-103	M. A. Polzin	Queensland v South Australia at Brisbane	1986-87
11-126	D. J. Noonan	New South Wales v Canterbury at Christchurch	1895-96
10-34	G. Elliott	Victoria v New South Wales at Melbourne	1855-56
10-36	J. J. McKone	New South Wales v Victoria at Melbourne	1855-56
10-46	F. D. Stephenson	Tasmania v Victoria at Melbourne	1981-82
10-97	J. Quilty	South Australia v Victoria at Adelaide	1881-82
10-141	R. B. C. Rees	South Australia v Victoria at Melbourne	1903-04
10-145	L. O. Fleetwood-Smith	Victoria v Tasmania at Hobart (TCA)	1931-32
10-226	A. C. Facy	Tasmania v Victoria at Hobart (TCA)	1908-09

MOST WICKETS IN A MATCH BY AUSTRALIANS

17-50	C. T. B. Turner, Australians v England XI at Hastings	1888
17-54	W. P. Howell, Australians v Western Province at Cape Town	1902-03
17-137	J. M. Davison, Canada v United States of America at Fort Lauderdale	2003-04
17-201	G. Giffen, South Australia v Victoria at Adelaide	1885-86
16-65	G. Giffen, Australians v Lancashire at Manchester	1886
16-69	F. A. Tarrant, England XII v Indian XII at Mumbai	1915-16
16-79	C. T. B. Turner, New South Wales v A. Shrewsbury's XI at Sydney	1887-88
16-83	B. Dooland, Nottinghamshire v Essex at Nottingham	1954
16-86	H. V. Hordern, Philadelphia v Jamaica at Kingston	1908-09
16-101	G. Giffen, Australians v Derbyshire at Derby	1886
16-137	R. A. L. Massie, Australia v England at Lord's	1972
16-166	G. Giffen, South Australia v Victoria at Adelaide	1891-92
16-176	F. A. Tarrant, Middlesex v Lancashire at Manchester	1914
16-186	G. Giffen, South Australia v New South Wales at Adelaide	1894-95
16-201	G. Giffen, Australians v Derbyshire at Derby	1886
16-225	J. E. Walsh, Leicestershire v Oxford University at Oxford	1953
16-289	C. V. Grimmett, South Australia v Queensland at Adelaide	1934-35

HAT-TRICKS FOR OR AGAINST AUSTRALIAN TEAMS

G. H. B. Gilbert	New South Wales v Victoria at Melbourne	1857-58
F. R. Spofforth	Australians v MCC at Lord's	1878
J. Robertson	Middlesex v Australians at Lord's	1878
F. R. Spofforth	Australians v Players of England at The Oval	1878
F. R. Spofforth	Australia v England at Melbourne	1878-79
G. Ulyett (4 in 4)	Lord Hawke's XI v New South Wales at Sydney	1878-79
W. A. Humphreys	Sussex v Australians at Hove	1880
G. E. Palmer	Australians v Sussex at Hove	1882
W. Bates	England v Australia at Melbourne	1882-83
W. A. Humphreys	Sussex v Australians at Hove	1884
G. Giffen	Australians v Lancashire at Manchester	1884
F. R. Spofforth	Australians v South of England at The Oval	1884
C. T. B. Turner	New South Wales v Victoria at Melbourne	1886-87
G. Giffen	South Australia v G. F. Vernon's XI at Adelaide	1887-88
J. Briggs	England v Australia at Sydney	1891-92
H. Trumble	Australians v Gloucestershire at Cheltenham	1896
G. Giffen	Australians v Wembley Park XI at Wembley Park	1896
A. D. Pougher	MCC v Australians at Lord's	1896
T. R. McKibbin	Australians v Lancashire at Liverpool	1896
M. A. Noble	New South Wales v Tasmania at Sydney	1898-99

J. T. Hearne	England v Australia at Leeds	1899
H. Trumble	Australia v England at Melbourne	1901-02
A. J. Y. Hopkins	Australians v Cambridge University at Cambridge	1902
W. P. Howell (4 in 5)	Australians v Western Province at Cape Town	1902-03
W. W. Armstrong	Victoria v New South Wales at Melbourne	1902-03
T. H. Howard (4 in 5)	New South Wales v Queensland at Sydney	1902-03
H. Hay	South Australia v Lord Hawke's XI at Unley	1902-03
A. J. Y. Hopkins	New South Wales v South Australia at Sydney	1903-04
H. Trumble	Australia v England at Melbourne	1903-04
W. P. Howell	Australians v New Zealand XI at Wellington	1904-05
G. A. Wilson	Worcestershire v Australians at Worcester	1905
T. J. Matthews	Victoria v Tasmania at Launceston	1908-09
J. A. Newman	Hampshire v Australians at Southampton	1909
T. J. Matthews (1st inns)	Australia v South Africa at Manchester	1912
T. J. Matthews (2nd inns)	Australia v South Africa at Manchester	1912
T. J. Matthews	Australians v Philadelphia at Philadelphia	1912-13
J. N. Crawford	South Australia v Western Australia at Adelaide	1912-13
C. Kelleway	New South Wales v Queensland at Brisbane	1913-14
J. Horsley	Derbyshire v AIF Team at Derby	1919
J. W. H. T. Douglas	MCC v New South Wales at Sydney	1920-21
A. P. Freeman	MCC v South Australia at Adelaide	1922-23
H. Ironmonger	Victoria v MCC at Melbourne	1924-25
H. I. Ebeling	Victoria v Queensland at Melbourne	1928-29
J. E. H. Hooker (4 in 4)	New South Wales v Victoria at Sydney	1928-29
C. V. Grimmett	South Australia v Queensland at Brisbane (Ex)	1928-29
F. L. Morton	Victoria v Tasmania at Melbourne	1931-32
H. J. Enthoven	Middlesex v Australians at Lord's	1934
R. K. Oxenham	Australians v All Ceylon at Colombo (PSS)	1935-36
M. G. Waite	South Australia v MCC at Adelaide	1935-36
B. Dooland	South Australia v Victoria at Melbourne	1945-46
C. R. Rangachari	Indians v Tasmania at Hobart (TCA)	1947-48
A. K. Walker	New South Wales v Queensland at Sydney	1948-49
H. J. Tayfield	South Africans v Victoria at Melbourne	1952-53
J. C. Treanor	New South Wales v Queensland at Brisbane	1954-55
L. F. Kline	Australia v South Africa at Cape Town	1957-58
G. F. Rorke	New South Wales v Queensland at Sydney	1958-59
L. R. Gibbs	West Indies v Australia at Adelaide	1960-61
A. K. Davidson	New South Wales v Western Australia at Perth	1962-63
A. D. Robins (4 in 4)	South Australia v New South Wales at Adelaide	1965-66
R. F. Surti	Queensland v Western Australia at Perth	1968-69
R. A. Woolmer	MCC v Australians at Lord's	1975
W. Prior	South Australia v New South Wales at Adelaide	1975-76
A. T. Sincock	South Australia v Indians at Adelaide	1977-78
L. S. Pascoe	New South Wales v South Australia at Adelaide	1980-81
P. M. Clough	Tasmania v New South Wales at Hobart (TCA)	1982-83
J. R. Thomson	Queensland v Western Australia at Brisbane	1984-85
D. R. Gilbert	New South Wales v Victoria at Sydney	1984-85
G. S. Le Roux	South Africans v Australian XI at Johannesburg (WS)	1985-86
C. E. B. Rice	South Africans v Australian XI at Johannesburg (WS)	1985-86
J. N. Maguire	Australians v Eastern Province at Port Elizabeth	1986-87
C. A. Walsh	West Indies v Australia at Brisbane	1988-89
M. G. Hughes	Australia v West Indies at Perth	1988-89
W. K. M. Benjamin	Leicestershire v Australians at Leicester	1989
W. J. Holdsworth	Australians v Derbyshire at Derby	1993
D. W. Fleming	Australia v Pakistan at Rawalpindi	1994-95
S. K. Warne	Australia v England at Melbourne	1994-95
N. E. Trescothick	Somerset v Young Australians at Taunton	1995
S. C. G. MacGill	New South Wales v New Zealanders at Newcastle	1997-98
D. Gough	England v Australia at Sydney	1998-99
M. S. Kasprowicz	Queensland v Victoria at Brisbane	1998-99
M. W. H. Inness	Victoria v New South Wales at Melbourne	1999-00
G. D. McGrath	Australia v West Indies at Perth	2000-01

Harbhajan Singh	India v Australia at Kolkata	2000-01
I. J. Harvey	Victoria v South Australia at Adelaide	2001-02
S. J. Jurgensen	Tasmania v New South Wales at Hobart (Bel)	2001-02
S. M. Harwood	Victoria v Tasmania at Melbourne	2002-03
J. J. C. Lawson	West Indies v Australia at Bridgetown	2002-03

FOUR WICKETS IN FOUR BALLS

G. Ulyett	Lord Hawke's XI v New South Wales at Sydney	1878-79
J. E. H. Hooker	New South Wales v Victoria at Sydney	1928-29
D. Robins	South Australia v New South Wales at Adelaide	1965-66

FOUR WICKETS IN FIVE BALLS

F. S. Jackson	Yorkshire v Australians at Leeds	1902
W. P. Howell	Australians v Western Province at Cape Town	1902-03
T. H. Howard	New South Wales v Queensland at Sydney	1902-03
D. J. Hickey	South Australia v England XI at Adelaide	1990-9

MOST HAT-TRICKS

5 times: F. A. Tarrant
4 times: F. R. Spofforth, T. J. Matthews
3 times: G. Giffen, E. A. McDonald, H. Trumble

MOST WICKETS IN AN AUSTRALIAN SEASON

	Season	M	B	Mdns	R	W	BB	5W/i	10W/m	Avge
C. T. B Turner (NSW)	1887-88	12	4,267	473	1,441	106	8-39	13	5	13.59
G. Giffen (S Aust)	1894-95	11	4,787	196	2,097	93	8-77	12	4	22.54
C. V. Grimmett (S Aust) . .	1929-30	11	3,795	51	1,943	82	7-136	9	3	23.69
R. Benaud (NSW)	1958-59	13	4,467	142	1,579	82	7-32	6	1	19.25
A. A. Mailey (NSW)	1920-21	10	2,993	45	1,825	81	9-121	8	3	22.53
M. W. Tate (MCC)	1924-25	14	4,018	93	1,464	77	7-74	7	2	19.01
C. V. Grimmett (S Aust) . .	1931-32	12	4,096	166	1,535	77	7-83	7	1	19.93
E. Jones (S Aust)	1897-98	11	3,529	121	1,653	76	7-80	9	3	21.75
R. M. Hogg (S Aust)	1978-79	14	3,483	97	1,249	76	6-74	6	2	16.43
C. V. Grimmett (S Aust) . .	1930-31	11	3,524	99	1,417	74	7-87	7	1	19.14
C. V. Grimmett (S Aust) . .	1939-40	9	3,543	57	1,654	73	6-118	10	3	22.65
C. V. Grimmett (S Aust) . .	1928-29	10	5,152	135	2,432	71	6-109	5	0	34.25
C. T. B. Turner (NSW) . . .	1886-87	7	2,145	273	538	70	8-32	8	3	7.68
W. J. Whitty (S Aust)	1910-11	11	2,957	109	1,419	70	6-17	4	0	20.27
H. J. Tayfield (SAf)	1952-53	14	4,836	123	1,954	70	7-71	5	1	27.91
D. K. Lillee (W Aust)	1976-77	11	2,832	59	1,368	70	6-26	8	4	19.54
C. R. Miller (Tas)	1997-98	12	3,896	172	1,749	70	7-49	5	2	24.99
S. C. G. MacGill (NSW) . . .	2004-05	13	3,053	99	1611	70	6-85	4	0	23.01

50 WICKETS IN AN AUSTRALIAN SEASON

10 Times: C. V. Grimmett 59 (1924-25), 59 (1925-26), 71 (1928-29), 82 (1929-30), 74 (1930-31), 77 (1931-32), 55 (1932-33), 66 (1933-34), 58 (1934-35), 73 (1939-40).
6 Times: D. K. Lillee 56 (1972-73), 62 (1974-75), 62 (1975-76), 70 (1976-77), 69 (1980-81), 59 (1983-84).
5 Times: L. O. Fleetwood-Smith 50 (1932-33), 53 (1933-34), 63 (1934-35), 53 (1936-37), 64 (1937-38); A. A. Mallett 54 (1971-72), 62 (1972-73), 57 (1974-75), 56 (1975-76), 53 (1979-80); W. J. O'Reilly 62 (1932-33), 51 (1936-37), 64 (1937-38), 55 (1939-40), 55 (1940-41).

4 Times: C. J. McDermott 58 (1986-87), 54 (1989-90), 67 (1990-91), 60 (1991-92).

3 Times: A. A. Mailey 81 (1920-21), 55 (1922-23), 59 (1924-25); F. A. Ward 50 (1935-36), 53 (1936-37), 51 (1937-38); G. D. McKenzie 51 (1962-63), 53 (1967-68), 60 (1968-69); J. R. Thomson 62 (1974-75), 62 (1975-76), 57 (1977-78); C. D. Matthews 57 (1986-87), 57 (1987-88), 53 (1991-92); M. S. Kasprowicz 51 (1992-93), 64 (1995-96), 51 (2001-02); S. C. G. MacGill 50 (1997-98), 60 (2002-03), 58 (2003-04); S. C. G. MacGill 50 (1997-98), 60 (2002-03), 70 (2004-05).

MOST WICKETS ON AN AUSTRALIAN OVERSEAS TOUR

			M	O	Mdns	R	W	BB	5W/i	10W/m	Avge
C. T. B. Turner	England	1888	36	2,427.2	1,127	3,307	283	9-15	31	12	11.69
F. R. Spofforth	England	1884	31	1,538.2	646	2,564	201	8-62	24	11	12.75
J. J. Ferris	England	1888	37	2,080.1	937	2,934	199	8-41	17	3	14.74
J. J. Ferris	England	1890	30	1,545.2	628	2,657	186	7-16	15	5	14.28
C. T. B. Turner	England	1890	31	1,500.1	652	2,526	178	7-23	16	4	14.19
F. R. Spofforth	England	1882	30	1,470	646	2,079	157	9-51	16	6	13.24
G. Giffen	England	1886	35	1,673.2	710	2,674	154	9-60	13	5	17.36
C. T. B. Turner	England	1893	26	1,079	413	2,018	148	8-95	16	5	13.64
H. Trumble	England	1896	30	1,140.1	380	2,340	148	7-67	11	5	15.81
C. V. Grimmett	England	1930	26	1,015.1	262	2,427	144	10-37	15	5	16.85
H. Trumble	England	1899	32	1,246.3	432	2,618	142	8-35	10	3	18.44
E. A. McDonald	England	1921	26	809.2	158	2,284	138	8-41	9	3	16.55
H. Trumble	England	1902	20	912	292	1,921	137	9-39	13	7	14.02
E. Jones	England	1899	28	1,163.2	331	2,849	135	7-31	10	4	21.10
A. A. Mailey	England	1921	20	800	103	2,595	133	10-66	7	1	19.51
G. E. Palmer	England	1884	30	1,214.3	446	2,099	130	7-74	13	5	16.14
A. A. Mailey	England	1926	27	816	162	2,437	126	9-86	12	4	19.34
H. F. Boyle	England	1882	27	1,101.2	488	1,523	125	7-32	13	3	12.18
T. W. Garrett	England	1886	34	1,654.1	778	2,221	123	6-22	5	1	18.06
J. V. Saunders	England	1902	25	710	160	2,085	123	6-9	10	3	16.95
W. W. Armstrong	England	1905	30	990.4	298	2,221	122	8-50	9	2	18.20
E. Jones	England	1896	29	868.3	282	1,940	121	8-39	7	1	16.03

Most in countries other than England:

			M	O	Mdns	R	W	BB	5W/i	10W/m	Avge
R. Benaud	SAf	1957-58	18	743.6	187	2,057	106	7-46	11	2	19.40
R. K. Oxenham	Ind	1935-36	11	303.3	89	555	75	7-13	8	4	7.40
W. W. Armstrong	NZ	1913-14	8	312.0	81	789	52	7-17	7	1	15.17
S. W. Austin	NZ	1893-94	7	1,747.0	85	612	52	8-14	6	1	11.77
P. I. Philpott	WI	1964-65	9	449.0	99	1,207	49	6-86	2	0	24.63
R. J. Bright	Pak	1979-80	5	230.2	72	558	29	7-87	4	2	19.24
J. N. Crawford	NAmer	1913-14	5	116.2	21	359	33	6-40	3	0	10.88
S. K. Warne	SL	2003-04	4	197.2	43	621	29	5-43	4	2	21.41
D. R. Gilbert	Zim	1985-86	2	68.0	14	215	15	7-43	2	1	14.33

LEADING BOWLERS IN EACH AUSTRALIAN SEASON

(Qualification for top of averages: 20 wickets)

Season	Leading Wicket-Taker	W	Avge	Top of Averages	W	Avge
1850-51	T. W. Antill (Vic)	13	4.00	n/a		
1851-52	W. Henty (Tas)	10	10.00	n/a		
1852-53	no games played					
1853-54	R. M. McDowall (Tas)	8	6.25	n/a		
1854-55	no games played					
1855-56	J. J. McKone (NSW)	10	3.60	n/a		
	G. Elliott (Vic)	10	3.20	n/a		
1856-57	T. W. Wills (Vic)	10	6.50	n/a		
1857-58	T. W. Wills (Vic)	26	5.03	T. W. Wills (Vic)	26	5.03
1858-59	T. W. Wills (Vic)	11	4.45	n/a		
1859-60	T. W. Wills (Vic)	9	4.33	n/a		
	G. B. Richardson (NSW)	9	6.00	n/a		
1860-61	S. Cosstick (Vic)	11	4.36	n/a		
1861-62	G. Bennett (The World)	14	8.21	n/a		
1862-63	C. Lawrence (NSW)	14	5.21	n/a		
1863-64	E. M. Grace (Anderson's XI)	9	7.67	n/a		
1864-65	no games played					
1865-66	S. Cosstick (NSW)	8	13.63	n/a		
	J. Conway (Vic)	8	15.25	n/a		
1866-67	D. W. Gregory (NSW)	7	9.57	n/a		
1867-68	T. W. Wills (Vic)	9	16.56	n/a		
1868-69	S. Cosstick (Vic)	23	5.42	S. Cosstick (Vic)	23	5.42
1869-70	S. Cosstick (Vic)	10	7.70	n/a		
1870-71	C. A. Reid (Vic)	16	9.50	n/a		
1871-72	F. E. Allan (Vic)	13	4.62	n/a		
1872-73	S. Cosstick (Vic)	23	6.52	S. Cosstick (Vic)	23	6.52
1873-74	no games played					
1874-75	J. Coates (NSW)	15	10.67	n/a		
1875-76	E. Evans (NSW)	21	5.62	E. Evans (NSW)	21	5.62
1876-77	A. Shaw (Lillywhite's XI)	17	11.76	n/a		
1877-78	E. Evans (NSW)	18	10.72	n/a		
1878-79	T. Emmett (Eng)	44	11.84	T. Emmett (Eng)	44	11.84
1879-80	W. H. Cooper (Vic)	12	10.75	n/a		
1880-81	E. Evans (NSW)	32	11.25	E. Evans (NSW)	32	11.25
1881-82	G. E. Palmer (Vic)	47	21.55	W. Bates (Eng)	30	17.33
1882-83	G. E. Palmer (Vic)	51	11.53	H. F. Boyle (Vic)	24	11.00
1883-84	G. E. Palmer (Vic)	29	17.51	G. E. Palmer (Vic)	29	17.51
1884-85	R. Peel (England)	35	19.22	W. Barnes (England)	26	13.23
1885-86	F. R. Spofforth (NSW)	18	15.22	n/a		
1886-87	C. T. B. Turner (NSW)	70	7.68	C. T. B. Turner (NSW)	70	7.68
1887-88	C. T. B. Turner (NSW)	106	13.59	W. Attewell (Eng)	55	10.72
1888-89	J. J. Ferris (NSW)	36	15.83	G. Giffen (SAust)	22	12.95
1889-90	H. Trumble (Vic)	29	14.21	H. Trumble (Vic)	29	14.21
1890-91	J. Phillips (Vic)	25	10.00	J. Phillips (Vic)	25	10.00
1891-92	G. Giffen (SAust)	50	17.30	W. Attewell (Eng)	44	13.02
1892-93	G. Giffen (SAust)	33	23.00	H. Trumble (Vic)	22	13.55
1893-94	C. T. B. Turner (NSW)	30	12.30	C. T. B. Turner (NSW)	30	12.30
1894-95	G. Giffen (SAust)	93	22.54	T. R. McKibbin (NSW)	44	16.66
1895-96	T. R. McKibbin (NSW)	46	23.87	E. Jones (SAust)	31	17.67
1896-97	T. R. McKibbin (NSW)	44	14.89	T. R. McKibbin (NSW)	44	14.89
1897-98	E. Jones (SAust)	76	21.75	W. Roche (Vic)	33	20.73
1898-99	E. Jones (SAust)	45	27.53	C. E. McLeod (Vic)	36	17.86
1899-00	M. A. Noble (NSW)	37	20.65	M. A. Noble (NSW)	37	20.65
1900-01	J. V. Saunders (Vic)	29	17.14	J. V. Saunders (Vic)	29	17.14
	J. P. F. Travers (SAust)	29	20.76			
1901-02	L. C. Braund (Eng)	62	28.69	S. F. Barnes (Eng)	41	16.49
1902-03	J. V. Saunders (Vic)	32	20.81	L. W. Pye (NSW)	23	19.30

Season	Leading Wicket-Taker	W	Avge	Top of Averages	W	Avge
1903-04	W. Rhodes (MCC)	65	16.23	A. Cotter (NSW)	30	13.47
1904-05	F. B. Collins (Vic)	27	23.37	F. B. Collins (Vic)	27	23.37
1905-06	G. L. Garnsey (NSW)	36	21.03	J. D. A. O'Connor (NSW) .	32	21.70
1906-07	G. L. Garnsey (NSW)	32	21.94	M. A. Noble (NSW)	24	13.92
1907-08	{ J. V. Saunders (Vic)	66	24.04	S. F. Barnes (Eng)	54	21.94
	{ J. N. Crawford (MCC)	66	25.19			
1908-09	J. D. A. O'Connor (SAust) .	40	23.00	A. H. Christian (WAust) ..	25	17.28
1909-10	J. V. Saunders (Vic)	49	17.33	J. D. Scott (NSW)	25	12.56
1910-11	W. J. Whitty (SAust)	70	20.27	H. V. Hordern (NSW)	58	14.83
1911-12	F. R. Foster (MCC)	62	20.19	F. R. Foster (MCC)	62	20.19
1912-13	R. J. A. Massie (Vic)	59	18.66	A. A. Mailey (NSW)	21	16.05
1913-14	C. Kelleway (NSW)	45	12.69	C. Kelleway (NSW)	45	12.69
1914-15	H. Ironmonger (Vic)	36	17.53	H. Ironmonger (Vic)	36	17.53
1915-16	no games played					
1916-17	no games played					
1917-18	no games played					
1918-19	E. A. McDonald (Vic)	25	15.72	E. A. McDonald (Vic)	25	15.72
1919-20	H. S. T. L. Hendry (NSW) ...	29	18.14	H. S. T. L. Hendry (NSW) .	29	18.14
1920-21	A. A. Mailey (NSW)	81	22.53	J. M. Gregory (NSW)	22	22.37
1921-22	E. A. McDonald (Vic)	28	21.50	P. H. Wallace (Vic)	20	17.85
1922-23	A. A. Mailey (NSW)	55	21.64	A. E. Liddicut (Vic)	20	21.05
1923-24	{ A. E. V. Hartkopf (Vic)	26	24.58	A. E. V. Hartkopf (Vic)	26	24.58
	{ N. L. Williams (SAust)	26	26.88			
1924-25	M. W. Tate (MCC)	77	19.01	R. K. Oxenham (Qld)	22	14.50
1925-26	C. V. Grimmett (SAust)	59	30.41	C. G. Macartney (NSW) ...	24	18.88
1926-27	N. L. Williams (SAust)	35	32.03	D. D. Blackie (Vic)	33	24.64
1927-28	C. V. Grimmett (SAust)	42	27.40	D. D. Blackie (Vic)	31	22.23
1928-29	C. V. Grimmett (SAust)	71	34.25	J. C. White (MCC)	65	22.63
1929-30	C. V. Grimmett (SAust)	82	23.69	E. L. A'Beckett (Vic)	27	15.22
1930-31	C. V. Grimmett (SAust)	74	19.14	H. Ironmonger (Vic)	68	14.29
1931-32	C. V. Grimmett (SAust)	77	19.93	L. O. Fleetwood-Smith (Vic)	37	16.27
1932-33	W. J. O'Reilly (NSW)	62	19.95	C. J. Hill (NSW)	25	15.27
1933-34	C. V. Grimmett (SAust)	66	21.83	S. A. J. Smith (Vic)......	20	17.90
1934-35	L. O. Fleetwood-Smith (Vic)	63	20.34	H. C. Chilvers (NSW)	46	18.63
1935-36	F. A. Ward (SAust)	50	20.94	T. W. Wall (SAust)	22	17.09
1936-37	{ L. O. Fleetwood-Smith (Vic)	53	20.25	J. G. Lush (NSW)	27	17.89
	{ F. A. Ward (SAust)	53	28.41			
1937-38	{ W. J. O'Reilly (NSW)	64	12.25	W. J. O'Reilly (NSW)	64	12.25
	{ L. O. Fleetwood-Smith (Vic)	64	22.43			
1938-39	L. O. Fleetwood-Smith (Vic)	30	39.73	C. V. Grimmett (SAust) ...	27	20.85
1939-40	C. V. Grimmett (SAust)	73	22.65	W. J. O'Reilly (NSW)	55	15.13
1940-41	W. J. O'Reilly (NSW)	55	12.43	W. J. O'Reilly (NSW)	55	12.43
1941-42	W. J. O'Reilly (NSW)	9	13.78	n/a		
1942-43	no games played					
1943-44	no games played					
1944-45	no games played					
1945-46	G. E. Tribe (Vic)	40	19.03	W. J. O'Reilly (NSW)	33	14.36
1946-47	D. V. P. Wright (MCC)	51	33.31	R. R. Lindwall (NSW)	39	22.08
1947-48	M. H. Mankad (Ind)	61	26.14	G. Noblet (SAust)	40	19.43
1948-49	I. W. G. Johnson (Vic)	43	24.12	A. K. Walker (NSW)	39	15.31
1949-50	J. B. Iverson (Vic)	46	16.52	J. B. Iverson (Vic)	46	16.52
1950-51	A. V. Bedser (MCC)	51	19.80	R. H. Price (WAust)	24	18.42
1951-52	W. A. Johnston (Vic)	54	20.63	R. R. Lindwall (NSW)	42	17.33
1952-53	H. J. Tayfield (SAf)	70	27.91	G. Noblet (SAust)	55	17.84
1953-54	I. W. G. Johnson (Vic)	45	22.76	R. R. Lindwall (Qld)	22	20.14
1954-55	F. H. Tyson (MCC)	51	19.64	W. P. A. Crawford (NSW) .	34	16.03
1955-56	R. Benaud (NSW)	44	21.61	W. P. A. Crawford (NSW) .	35	19.80
1956-57	L. F. Kline (Vic)	39	28.21	I. Meckiff (Vic)	23	23.67
1957-58	I. W. Quick (Vic)	32	27.25	N. C. O'Neill (NSW)	26	20.42
1958-59	R. Benaud (NSW)	82	19.25	J. C. Laker (MCC)	38	17.23

Season	Leading Wicket-Taker	W	Avge	Top of Averages	W	Avge
1959-60	J. W. Martin (NSW)	45	23.64	R. A. Gaunt (WAust)	24	16.75
1960-61	A. K. Davidson (NSW)	47	20.87	A. K. Davidson (NSW)	47	20.87
1961-62	R. Benaud (NSW)	47	17.97	A. K. Davidson (NSW)	42	13.61
1962-63	I. Meckiff (Vic)	58	19.86	I. Meckiff (Vic)	58	19.86
1963-64	R. H. D. Sellers (SAust)	54	26.57	P. I. Philpott (NSW)	30	25.73
1964-65	N. J. N. Hawke (SAust)	41	26.29	D. E. Hoare (WAust)	29	22.86
1965-66	N. J. N. Hawke (SAust)	49	25.73	O. J. Morgan (Qld)	25	19.20
1966-67	G. A. R. Lock (WAust)	51	21.29	R. C. Bitmead (Vic)	33	19.66
1967-68	A. N. Connolly (Vic)	60	20.18	L. C. Mayne (WAust)	20	15.10
1968-69	G. D. McKenzie (WAust) . .	40	27.66	P. J. Allan (Qld)	46	16.37
1969-70	A. L. Thomson (Vic)	55	18.74	A. L. Thomson (Vic)	55	18.74
1970-71	A. L. Thomson (Vic)	51	30.09	J. R. Hammond (SAust)	34	20.26
1971-72	A. A. Mallett (SAust)	54	19.64	A. A. Mallett (SAust)	54	19.64
1972-73	A. A. Mallett (SAust)	62	19.09	G. D. Watson (WAust)	20	18.40
1973-74	G. Dymock (Qld)	51	19.88	R. J. Bright (Vic)	32	19.66
1974-75 {	J. R. Thomson (Qld)	62	19.37	J. R. Thomson (Qld)	62	19.37
	D. K. Lillee (WAust)	62	25.14			
1975-76 {	J. R. Thomson (Qld)	62	23.75	W. Prior (SAust)	43	19.67
	D. K. Lillee (WAust)	62	24.03			
1976-77	D. K. Lillee (WAust)	70	19.54	J. R. Thomson (Qld)	27	14.00
1977-78	J. R. Thomson (Qld)	62	21.86	I. J. Brayshaw (WAust)	35	18.03
1978-79	R. M. Hogg (SAust)	76	16.43	P. H. Carlson (Qld)	31	15.90
1979-80	A. A. Mallett (SAust)	53	28.30	J. Garner (WI)	32	20.03
1980-81	D. K. Lillee (WAust)	69	21.18	L. S. Pascoe (NSW)	63	19.52
1981-82	B. Yardley (WAust)	49	22.55	J. Garner (WI)	23	16.17
1982-83	G. F. Lawson (NSW)	65	21.04	C. G. Rackemann (Qld)	35	15.80
1983-84	D. K. Lillee (WAust)	59	25.64	C. G. Rackemann (Qld)	28	18.68
1984-85	R. G. Holland (NSW)	58	25.80	Imran Khan (Pak)	28	19.14
1985-86	R. G. Holland (NSW)	48	32.40	R. J. Hadlee (NZ)	37	14.51
1986-87	C. J. McDermott (Qld)	58	22.34	G. C. Small (England)	33	18.97
1987-88	C. D. Matthews (WAust) . .	57	22.40	G. F. Lawson (NSW)	42	18.86
1988-89	M. R. Whitney (NSW)	58	23.62	T. M. Alderman (WAust) . .	48	20.94
1989-90	C. G. Rackemann (Qld) . . .	50	21.48	C. D. Matthews (WAust) . .	42	19.19
1990-91	C. J. McDermott (Qld)	67	19.46	A. I. C. Dodemaide (Vic) . .	20	12.25
1991-92	C. J. McDermott (Qld)	60	20.80	D. A. Freedman (NSW) . . .	22	18.59
1992-93	W. J. Holdsworth (NSW) . .	53	25.96	C. E. L. Ambrose (WI)	38	18.13
1993-94	S. K. Warne (Vic)	63	19.92	S. K. Warne (Vic)	63	19.92
1994-95	C. G. Rackemann (Qld) . . .	52	23.60	S. K. Warne (Vic)	40	20.35
1995-96	M. S. Kasprowicz (Qld) . . .	64	20.47	A. M. Stuart (NSW)	23	13.40
1996-97	M. S. Kasprowicz (Qld) . . .	48	25.54	J. C. Scuderi (SAust)	23	17.34
1997-98	C. R. Miller (Tas)	70	24.99	D. W. Fleming (Vic)	39	18.08
1998-99	D. J. Saker (Vic)	48	23.31	A. C. Dale (Qld)	31	17.10
1999-00	A. J. Bichel (Qld)	60	20.12	M. S. Kasprowicz (Qld) . . .	49	14.41
2000-01 {	A. J. Bichel (Qld)	49	23.35	J. H. Dawes (Qld)	49	20.47
	J. H. Dawes (Qld)	49	20.47			
2001-02	M. S. Kasprowicz (Qld) . . .	51	24.29	M. W. H. Inness (Vic)	31	19.26
2002-03	S. C. G. MacGill (NSW) . . .	60	29.57	D. A. Nash (NSW)	26	16.46
2003-04	S. C. G. MacGill (NSW) . . .	58	35.95	J. N. Gillespie (S Aust)	37	21.54
2004-05	S. C. G. MacGill (NSW) . . .	70	23.01	G. D. McGrath (Australia) .	37	16.62

BEST AVERAGE IN AN AUSTRALIAN SEASON

(Qualification: 30 wickets)

		M	B	Mdns	R	W	BB	5Wi	10Wm	Avge
C. T. B. Turner (NSW)	1886-87	7	2,145	273	538	70	8-32	8	3	7.68
E. Attewell (England)	1887-88	9	3,086	425	590	54	7-15	4	2	10.92
E. Evans (NSW)	1880-81	4	1,749	251	360	32	5-34	5	1	11.25
G. E. Palmer (Vic)	1882-83	7	1,772	201	588	51	7-65	2	2	11.53

		M	B	Mdns	R	W	BB	5Wh	10W/m	Avge
T. Emmett (England)	1878-79	5	1,933	255	521	44	8-47	6	2	11.84
G.A. Lohmann (England)	1887-88	8	2,667	364	755	63	7-43	7	2	11.98
W.J. O'Reilly (NSW)	1937-38	11	2,487	91	784	64	9-41	6	2	12.25
C.T.B. Turner (NSW)	1893-94	3	940	35	369	30	6-51	5	2	12.30
W.J. O'Reilly (NSW)	1940-41	8	1,838	48	684	55	6-60	5	0	12.43
C. Kelleway (NSW)	1913-14	7	1,498	76	571	45	7-35	3	1	12.69
W. Attewell (England)	1891-92	8	2,858	241	573	44	6-34	4	1	13.02
J. Briggs (England))	1891-92	8	1,212	71	420	32	6-49	4	1	13.13
A. Cotter (NSW)	1903-04	5	740	18	404	30	6-40	2	0	13.47
C.T.B. Turner (NSW)	1887-88	12	4,267	473	1,441	106	8-39	12	5	13.59
A.K. Davidson (NSW)	1961-62	9	1,696	52	572	42	7-31	2	0	13.61
H. Ironmonger (Vic)	1930-31	10	3,037	112	972	68	8-31	7	4	14.29
W.J. O'Reilly (NSW)	1945-46	6	1,257	20	474	33	6-43	1	0	14.36
M.S. Kasprowicz (Qld)	1999-00	8	1485	69	706	49	5-32	4	1	14.41
R.J. Hadlee (New Zealanders)	1985-86	5	1,449	65	537	37	9-52	5	2	14.51
J. Briggs (England)	1887-88	8	2,263	215	436	30	6-40	2	1	14.53
J.J. Ferris (NSW)	1886-87	7	1,967	224	689	47	5-28	3	0	14.66
H.V. Hordern (NSW)	1910-11	8	1,448	29	860	58	7-31	6	2	14.83
T.R. McKibbin (NSW)	1896-97	4	1,381	46	655	44	8-74	5	2	14.89

AUSTRALIANS WITH 500 FIRST-CLASS WICKETS

		M	R	W	BB	5Wh	10W/m	Avge
A.E. Trott	1892-93 – 1911	375	35,317	1,674	10-42	131	41	21.09
F.A. Tarrant	1898-99 – 1936-37	329	26,391	1,506	10-90	133	38	17.52
C.V. Grimmett	1911-12 – 1940-41	248	31,740	1,424	10-37	127	33	22.28
E.A. McDonald	1909-10 – 1935	281	28,966	1,395	8-41	119	31	20.76
G.E. Tribe	1945-46 – 1959	308	28,321	1,378	9-43	93	23	20.55
G.D. McKenzie	1959-60 – 1975	383	32,868	1,219	8-71	49	5	26.96
J.E. Walsh	1936-37 – 1956	296	29,226	1,190	9-101	98	26	24.56
S.K. Warne	1990-91 -	243	27,315	1,054	8-71	50	8	25.92
S.M.J. Woods	1886 – 1910	401	21,653	1,040	10-69	77	21	20.82
G. Giffen	1877-78 – 1903-04	251	21,782	1,023	10-66	95	30	21.29
B. Dooland	1945-46 – 1957-58	214	22,332	1,016	8-20	84	23	21.98
C.T.B. Turner	1882-83 – 1909-10	155	14,147	993	9-15	102	35	14.24
V.E. Jackson	1936-37 – 1958	354	23,874	965	8-43	43	6	24.73
T.M. Alderman	1974-75 – 1992-93	245	22,701	956	8-46	53	8	23.74
R. Benaud	1948-49 – 1967-68	259	23,370	945	7-18	56	9	24.73
H. Trumble	1887-88 – 1903-04	344	17,134	929	9-39	69	25	18.44
S.K. Warne	1990-91 – 2004	214	23,872	923	8-71	46	8	25.86
D.K. Lillee	1969-70 – 1988	198	20,696	882	8-29	50	13	23.46
M.S. Kasprowicz	1989-90 -	221	23,234	882	9-36	48	6	26.34
F.R. Spofforth	1874-75 – 1897	155	12,759	853	9-18	84	32	14.95
M.S. Kasprowicz	1989-90 – 2004	208	22,072	845	9-36	47	6	26.12
W.W. Armstrong	1898-99 – 1921-22	269	16,406	832	8-47	50	5	19.71
J.J. Ferris	1886-87 – 1897-98	198	14,260	813	8-41	63	11	17.53
R.R. Lindwall	1941-42 – 1961-62	228	16,956	794	7-20	34	2	21.35
A.A. Mailey	1912-13 – 1930-31	158	18,778	779	10-66	61	16	24.10
W.J. O'Reilly	1927-28 – 1945-46	135	12,850	774	9-38	63	17	16.60
W.E. Alley	1945-46 – 1968	400	17,421	768	8-65	30	1	22.68
G.D. McGrath	1992-93 -	173	15,739	767	8-38	39	7	20.52
J.A. Cuffe	1902-03 – 1914	221	18,798	738	9-38	33	7	25.47
G.D. McGrath	1992-93 – 20045	159	14,546	700	8-38	37	7	20.78
A.A. Mallett	1967-68 – 1980-81	183	18,208	693	8-59	33	5	26.27
C.J. McDermott	1983-84 – 1995-96	174	19,025	677	8-44	37	4	28.10
A.N. Connolly	1959-60 – 1970-71	201	17,974	676	9-67	25	6	26.58
J.R. Thomson	1972-73 – 1985-86	187	17,864	675	7-27	28	3	26.46
A.K. Davidson	1949-50 – 1962-63	193	14,048	672	7-31	33	2	20.90
G.F. Lawson	1977-78 – 1991-92	191	16,564	666	8-112	28	2	24.87

		M	B	Mdns	R	W	BB	5Wi	10Wm	Avge
E. Jones............	1892-93 – 1907-08	144	14,638		641		8-39	47	9	22.83
S. C. G. MacGill	1993-94 -	148	18,839		640		8-111	38	6	29.44
M. A. Noble.........	1893-94 – 1919-20	248	14,445		625		8-48	33	7	23.11
. W. G. Johnson	1935-36 – 1956-57	189	14,423		619		7-42	27	4	23.30
C. G. Rackemann	1979-80 – 1995-96	167	16,629		616		8-84	22	3	26.99
C. L. McCool........	1939-40 – 1960	251	16,542		602		8-74	34	2	27.47
L. O. Fleetwood-Smith	1931-32 – 1939-40	112	13,519		597		9-36	57	18	22.64
G. E. Palmer	1878-79 – 1896-97	133	10,520		594		8-48	54	16	17.71
M. G. Hughes	1981-82 – 1994-95	165	17,249		593		8-87	21	3	29.09
A. J. Bichel	1992-93 -	143	15,073		584		9-93	29	6	25.81
S. C. G. MacGill	1993-94 – 2004	131	16,910		567		8-111	34	6	29.82
W. A. Johnston	1945-46 – 1954-55	142	12,936		554		8-52	29	6	23.35
J. V. Saunders	1899-00 – 1913-14	107	12,064		553		8-106	48	9	21.81
P. R. Reiffel........	1987-88 – 2001-02	167	14,392		545		6-57	16	2	26.41
A. I. C. Dodemaide ...	1983-84 – 1997-98	184	17,096		534		6-58	17	0	32.01
W. P. Howell........	1894-95 – 1905-06	141	11,157		520		10-28	30	5	21.45
G. R. J. Matthews ...	1982-83 – 1997-98	190	16,413		516		8-52	22	5	31.81
J. S. Manning	1951-52 – 1960	146	11,662		513		8-43	25	4	22.73
A. J. Bichel	1992-93 – 2004	128	13,288		509		9-93	24	5	26.11
J. M. Gregory	1919 – 1928-29	129	10,580		504		9-32	33	8	20.99

BEST CAREER AVERAGE

(Qualification: 50 wickets)

		M	R	W	BB	5Wi	10Wm	Avge
S. Cosstick	1860-61 – 1875-76	18	998	106	9-61	11	5	9.41
T. W. Wills	1854 – 1875-76	32	1,217	121	7-44	15	3	10.06
J. Coates	1867-68 – 1879-80	15	885	76	7-39	5	1	11.64
S. W. Austin	1892-93 – 1894-95	10	709	60	8-14	6	1	11.81
F. E. Allan.........	1867-68 – 1882-83	31	1,638	123	8-20	11	2	13.32
C. T. B. Turner	1882-83 – 1909-10	155	14,147	993	9-15	102	35	14.24
F. R. Spofforth.....	1874-75 – 1897	155	12,760	853	9-18	84	32	14.95
H. F. Boyle........	1871-72 – 1890	140	5,692	370	7-32	26	6	15.38
F. S. Middleton	1905-06 – 1921-22	14	911	56	7-36	5	2	16.26
W. J. O'Reilly	1927-28 – 1945-46	135	12,850	774	9-38	63	17	16.60
		M	R	W	BB	5Wi	10Wm	Avge
E. Evans	1874-75 – 1887-88	65	3,356	201	7-16	18	4	16.69
H. V. Hordern......	1905-06 – 1912-13	33	3,644	217	8-31	23	9	16.79
S. T. Callaway......	1888-89 – 1906-07	62	5,460	320	8-33	33	12	17.06
W. E. Midwinter	1874-75 – 1886-87	160	7,298	419	7-27	27	3	17.41
F. A. Tarrant	1898-99 – 1935-36	329	26,450	1,512	10-90	133	38	17.49
J. J. Ferris	1886-87 – 1897-98	198	14,260	813	8-41	63	11	17.53
G. E. Palmer	1878-79 – 1896-97	133	10,520	594	8-48	54	16	17.71
R. J. A. Massie......	1910-11 – 1913-14	16	1,280	99	7-110	7	4	18.38
H. Trumble	1887-88 – 1903-04	344	17,134	929	9-39	69	25	18.44
T. W. Garrett	1876-77 – 1897-98	160	8,353	445	7-38	29	5	18.77
W. W. McGlinchy....	1885-86 – 1899-00	20	1,345	71	6-62	4	2	18.94
D. L. Miller	1892-93 – 1905-06	15	1,045	55	5-38	2	0	19.00
J. B. Iverson.......	1949-50 – 1953-54	34	3,019	157	7-77	9	1	19.23
G. Noblet..........	1945-46 – 1956	71	5,432	282	7-29	13	2	19.26
W. W. Armstrong....	1898-99 – 1921-22	269	16,405	832	8-47	50	5	19.71
T. R. McKibbin......	1894-95 – 1898-99	57	6,297	319	9-68	28	11	19.73
P. C. Charlton	1888-89 – 1897-98	40	1,937	97	7-44	6	1	19.96

MOST WICKETS PER MATCH

(Qualification: 50 wickets)

		M	R	W	BB	5W	10W	Avge	Wkts/Match
H. V. Hordern	1905-06 – 1912-13	33	3,644	217	8-31	23	9	16.79	6.57
C. T. B. Turner	1882-83 – 1909-10	155	14,147	993	9-15	102	35	14.24	6.40
S. W. Austin	1892-93 – 1894-95	10	709	60	8-14	6	1	11.81	6.00
R. J. A. Massie	1910-11 – 1913-14	16	1,280	99	7-110	7	4	18.38	6.18
S. Cosstick	1860-61 – 1875-76	18	998	106	9-61	11	5	9.41	5.88
C. V. Grimmett	1911-12 – 1940-41	248	31,740	1,424	10-37	127	33	22.28	5.74
W. J. O'Reilly	1927-28 – 1945-46	135	12,850	774	9-38	63	17	16.60	5.73
T. R. McKibbin	1894-95 – 1898-99	57	6,297	319	9-68	28	11	19.73	5.59
F. R. Spofforth	1874-75 – 1897	155	12,760	853	9-18	84	32	14.95	5.50
L. O. Fleetwood-Smith	1931-32 – 1939-40	112	13,519	597	9-36	57	18	22.64	5.33
S. T. Callaway	1888-89 – 1906-07	62	5,460	320	8-33	33	12	17.06	5.16
J. V. Saunders	1899-00 – 1913-14	107	12,064	553	8-106	48	9	21.81	5.16
J. Coates	1867-68 – 1879-80	15	885	76	7-39	5	1	11.64	5.06

MOST BALLS BOWLED IN AN INNINGS

Balls	M	R	W		
571	36	155	3	T. R. Veivers, Australia v England at Manchester	1964
522	12	309	5	G. Giffen, South Australia v A. E. Stoddart's XI at Adelaide	1894-95
522	11	298	1	L. O. Fleetwood-Smith, Australia v England at The Oval	1938
512	0	362	4	A. A. Mailey, New South Wales v Victoria at Melbourne	1926-27
510	26	178	3	W. J. O'Reilly, Australia v England at The Oval	1938
501	35	150	6	G. Giffen, South Australia v New South Wales at Adelaide	1890-91

MOST BALLS BOWLED IN A MATCH

Balls	M	R	W		
848	14	394	10	C. V. Grimmett, South Australia v New South Wales at Sydney	1925-26
749	37	256	13	J. C. White, England v Australia at Adelaide	1928-29
743	22	255	10	D. D. Blackie, Victoria v South Australia at Adelaide	1926-27
736	16	267	9	C. V. Grimmett, South Australia v Victoria at Adelaide	1924-25
725	58	152	11	R. W. McLeod, Victoria v New South Wales at Melbourne	1892-93
712	19	228	11	M. W. Tate, England v Australia at Sydney	1924-25
708	42	239	8	G. Giffen, Australia v England at Sydney	1894-95

MOST RUNS CONCEDED IN A MATCH

Runs		
394 (4/192, 6/202)	C. V. Grimmett, South Australia v New South Wales at Sydney	1925-26
362 (4-362)	A. A. Mailey, New South Wales v Victoria at Melbourne	1926-27
345 (3-190, 0-155)	J. D. Scott, South Australia v New South Wales at Sydney	1925-26
326 (6-134, 5-192)	N. L. Williams, South Australia v Victoria at Adelaide	1928-29
322 (5-309, 0-13)	G. Giffen, South Australia v A. E. Stoddart's XI at Adelaide	1894-95
308 (4-129, 3-179)	A. A. Mailey, Australia v England at Sydney	1924-25
302 (5-160, 5-142)	A. A. Mailey, Australia v England at Adelaide	1920-21

ALL-ROUND RECORDS

100 RUNS IN AN INNINGS AND TEN WICKETS IN A MATCH

R. G. Barlow	101	10/48	North of England v Australians at Nottingham	1884
G. Giffen	166	14-125	South Australia v Victoria at Adelaide	1887-88
G. Giffen	135	13-159	South Australia v Victoria at Melbourne	1888-89

G. Giffen	237	12-192	South Australia v Victoria at Melbourne	1890-91
G. Giffen	271	16-165	South Australia v Victoria at Adelaide	1891-92
G. Giffen	120	12-150	South Australia v New South Wales at Sydney	1891-92
G. Giffen	181	11-235	South Australia v Victoria at Adelaide	1892-93
A. E. Trott	101*	11-140	Lord Hawke's XI v Transvaal at Johannesburg (OW)	1898-99
A. E. Trott	123	12-190	Middlesex v Sussex at Lord's	1899
A. E. Trott	112	11-138	Middlesex v Essex at Lord's	1901
W. W. Armstrong	126*	10-52	Australians v New Zealanders at Christchurch	1904-05
F. A. Tarrant	152	12-149	Middlesex v Gloucestershire at Bristol	1908
F. A. Tarrant	101*	16-176	Middlesex v Lancashire at Manchester	1914
F. A. Tarrant	182*	11-112	Behar's XI v Willingdon's XI at Pune	1918-19
V. E. Jackson	108	10-99	Leicestershire v Kent at Gillingham	1954
B. Dooland	115*	10-102	Nottinghamshire v Sussex at Worthing	1957
P. H. Carlson	102*	10-73	Queensland v New South Wales at Brisbane	1978-79
J. C. Scuderi	110	10-165	South Australia v New South Wales at Adelaide	1991-92

500 RUNS AND 50 WICKETS IN AN AUSTRALIAN SEASON

		M	R	Avge	W	Avge
G. Giffen (S Aust)	1891-92	6	509	50.90	50	17.30
G. Giffen (S Aust)	1894-95	11	902	50.11	93	22.55
L. C. Braund (MCC)	1907-08	16	783	35.59	50	32.88
J. N. Crawford (MCC)	1907-08	16	610	26.52	66	25.20
F. R. Foster (MCC)	1911-12	13	641	35.61	62	20.19
M. H. Mankad (Indians)	1947-48	13	889	38.65	61	26.15
G. S. Sobers (S Aust)	1962-63	10	1,001	52.68	51	26.56
G. S. Sobers (S Aust)	1963-64	9	1,128	80.57	51	28.25
G. R. J. Matthews (NSW)	1991-92	12	603	40.20	52	21.46
G. R. J. Matthews (NSW)	1992-93	13	625	36.76	51	28.92

10,000 RUNS AND 500 WICKETS IN A CAREER

	M	R	Avge	W	Avge
W. E. Alley	400	19,612	31.88	768	22.68
W. W. Armstrong	269	16,158	46.83	832	19.71
R. Benaud	259	11,719	36.50	945	23.74
G. Giffen	251	11,758	29.54	1,023	21.29
V. E. Jackson	354	15,698	28.43	965	24.73
C. L. McCool	251	12,420	32.85	602	27.47
M. A. Noble	248	13,975	40.74	625	23.11
F. A. Tarrant	326	17,857	36.37	1,489	17.66
G. E. Tribe	308	10,177	27.34	1,378	20.55
A. E. Trott	375	10,696	19.48	1,674	21.09

WICKET-KEEPING RECORDS

MOST DISMISSALS IN AN INNINGS

8	(all ct)	A. T. W. Grout, Queensland v Western Australia at Brisbane	1959-60
8	(6ct, 2st)	T. J. Zoehrer, Australians v Surrey at The Oval	1993
8	(7ct, 1st)	D. S. Berry, Victoria v South Australia at Melbourne	1996-97

MOST DISMISSALS IN A MATCH

12	(9ct, 3st)	D. Tallon, Queensland v New South Wales at Sydney	1938-39
12	(9ct, 3st)	H. B. Taber, New South Wales v South Australia at Adelaide	1968-69
11	(all ct)	R. W. Marsh, Western Australia v Victoria at Perth	1975-76
11	(all ct)	T. J. Nielsen, South Australia v Western Australia at Perth	1990-91
11	(10ct, 1st)	I. A. Healy, Australians v N. Transvaal at Verwoerdburg	1993-94
11	(all ct)	D. S. Berry, Victoria v Pakistanis at Melbourne	1995-96
11	(10ct, 1st)	W. A. Seccombe, Queensland v Western Australia at Brisbane	1995-96
11	(10ct, 1st)	D. S. Berry, Victoria v South Australia at Melbourne	1996-97

MOST DISMISSALS IN AN AUSTRALIAN SEASON

Total	Ct	St	M		
67	63	4	15	R. W. Marsh (Western Australia)	1975-76
67	64	3	13	W. A. Seccombe (Queensland)	1999-00
64	58	6	14	R. W. Marsh (Western Australia)	1974-75
62	58	4	12	A. C. Gilchrist (Western Australia)	1995-96
62	60	2	12	A. C. Gilchrist (Western Australia)	1996-97
61	59	2	14	R. W. Marsh (Western Australia)	1980-81
61	61	0	13	R. W. Marsh (Western Australia)	1982-83
59	54	5	13	R. W. Marsh (Western Australia)	1983-84
59	57	2	9	W. A. Seccombe (Queensland)	1995-96
58	57	1	11	W. A. Seccombe (Queensland)	2000-01
57	53	4	13	K. J. Wright (Western Australia)	1978-79
56	55	1	12	R. B. Phillips (Queensland)	1984-85
55	55	0	11	A. C. Gilchrist (Western Australia)	1994-95
54	52	2	13	P. A. Emery (New South Wales)	1992-93
54	52	2	11	D. S. Berry (Victoria)	1999-00
53	53	0	11	R. W. Marsh (Western Australia)	1976-77
52	52	0	11	W. A. Seccombe (Queensland)	2001-02

AUSTRALIANS WITH 300 FIRST-CLASS DISMISSALS

	Career	M	Ct	St	Total
R. W. Marsh	1968-69 - 1983-84	257	803	66	869
I. A. Healy	1986-87 - 1999-00	231	698	69	767
A. C. Gilchrist	1992-93 -	158	625	45	670
W. A. S. Oldfield	1919 - 1937-38	245	399	262	661
D. S. Berry	1989-90 - 2003-04	153	552	51	603
A. T. W. Grout	1946-47 - 1965-55	183	473	114	587
B. N. Jarman	1955-56 - 1968-69	191	431	129	560
W. A. Seccombe	1992-93 -	115	516	21	537
S. J. Rixon	1974-75 - 1987-88	151	394	66	460
T. J. Zoehrer	1980-81 - 1993-94	144	411	38	449
J. M. Blackham	1874-75 - 1894-95	250	259	181	440
D. Tallon	1933-34 - 1953-54	150	303	129	432

MOST DISMISSALS PER MATCH

(Qualification: 200 dismissals)

		M	Ct	St	Total	Per match
W. A. Seccombe	1992-93 –	115	576	21	537	4.66
A. C. Gilchrist	1992-93 –	158	625	45	602	4.24
D. S. Berry	1989-90 – 2003-04	153	552	51	603	3.94
J. A. Maclean	1968-69 – 1978-79	108	353	31	384	3.55
K. J. Wright	1974-75 – 1983-84	85	268	26	294	3.45
R. D. Robinson	1971-72 – 1981-82	97	289	40	329	3.39
R. W. Marsh	1968-69 – 1983-84	257	803	66	869	3.38
I. A. Healy	1986-87 – 1999-00	231	698	69	767	3.32
R. B. Phillips	1978-79 – 1985-86	89	271	15	286	3.21
A. T. W. Grout	1946-47 – 1965-55	183	473	114	587	3.20

FIELDING RECORDS

MOST CATCHES IN AN INNINGS

6	F. A. Tarrant	Middlesex v Essex at Leyton	1906
6	J. F. Sheppard	Queensland v New South Wales at Brisbane	1914-15
6	K. J. Grieves	Lancashire v Sussex at Manchester	1951

Note: There are 16 instances of five catches in an innings.

MOST CATCHES IN A MATCH

8	K. J. Grieves	Lancashire v Sussex at Manchester	1951
7	L. O. S. Poidevin	Lancashire v Yorkshire at Manchester	1906
7	F. A. Tarrant	Middlesex v Essex at Leyton	1906
7	J. A. Atkinson	Tasmania v Victoria at Melbourne	1928-29
7	E. W. Freeman	South Australia v Western Australia at Adelaide	1971-72
7	G. S. Chappell	Australia v England at Perth	1974-75
7	M. A. Taylor	New South Wales v Victoria at Melbourne	1995-96
7	M. E. K. Hussey	Northamptonshire v Oxford University at Oxford	2002
7	M. L. Hayden	Australia v Sri Lanka at Galle	2003-04

MOST CATCHES IN AN AUSTRALIAN SEASON

Ct	M		
27	14	I. M. Chappell (South Australia)	1968-69
26	13	G. B. Hole (South Australia)	1952-53
26	13	M. A. Taylor (New South Wales)	1997-98
25	16	L. C. Braund (MCC)	1907-08
25	14	M. A. Taylor (New South Wales)	1991-92

Note: There have been ten instances of 24 catches in a season.

AUSTRALIANS WITH 200 FIRST-CLASS CATCHES

	Career	M	Ct
K. J. Grieves	1945-46 - 1964	490	610
A. E. Trott	1892-93 - 1911	375	452
M. E. Waugh	1985-86 - 2003-04	368	452
R. B. Simpson	1952-53 - 1977-78	257	383
A. R. Border	1976-77 - 1995-96	385	379
G. S. Chappell	1966-67 - 1983-84	322	376
S. G. Law	1988-89 -	315	354
M. A. Taylor	1985-86 - 1998-99	253	350
H. Trumble	1887-88 - 1903-04	213	328
I. M. Chappell	1961-62 - 1979-80	263	312
F. A. Tarrant	1898-99 - 1936-37	329	304
T. M. Moody	1985-86 - 2000-01	300	294
W. E. Alley	1945-46 - 1968	400	293
D. C. Boon	1978-79 - 1999	350	283
S. M. J. Woods	1886 - 1910	401	279
W. W. Armstrong	1898-99 - 1921-22	269	274
S. R. Waugh	1984-85 - 2003-04	356	273
K. C. Wessels	1973-74 - 1999-00	316	268
C. L. McCool	1939-40 - 1960	251	262
R. Benaud	1948-49 - 1967-68	259	255
V. E. Jackson	1936-37 - 1958	354	250
R. J. Inverarity	1962-63 - 1984-85	223	250
G. E. Tribe	1945-46 - 1959	308	242
M. L. Hayden	1991-92 -	249	230

	Career	M	Ct
R. N. Harvey	1946-47 - 1962-63	306	228
M. J. Di Venuto	1991-92 -	204	226
J. L. Langer	1991-92 -	270	222
V. Y. Richardson	1918-19 - 1937-38	184	213
M. L. Love	1992-93 -	177	213
I. R. Redpath	1961-62 - 1975-76	226	211
J. E. Walsh	1936-37 - 1956	296	209
J. D. Siddons	1984-85 - 1999-00	160	206
M. T. G. Elliott	1992-93 -	190	206
S. K. Warne	1990-91 -	243	204
G. D. McKenzie	1959-60 - 1975	383	201

TEAM RECORDS

HIGHEST INNINGS TOTALS

1,107	Victoria v New South Wales at Melbourne	1926-27
1,059	Victoria v Tasmania at Melbourne	1922-23
918	New South Wales v South Australia at Sydney	1900-01
7-903 dec.	England v Australia at The Oval	1938
843	Australians v Oxford and Cambridge Universities at Portsmouth	1893
839	New South Wales v Tasmania at Sydney	1898-99
7-821 dec.	South Australia v Queensland at Adelaide	1939-40
815	New South Wales v Victoria at Sydney	1908-09
807	New South Wales v South Australia at Adelaide	1899-00
805	New South Wales v Victoria at Melbourne	1905-06
803	Non Smokers v Smokers at East Melbourne	1886-87
802	New South Wales v South Australia at Sydney	1920-21
793	Victoria v Queensland at Melbourne	1927-28
786	New South Wales v South Australia at Adelaide	1922-23
775	New South Wales v Victoria at Sydney	1881-82
7-774 dec.	Australians v Gloucestershire at Bristol	1948
770	New South Wales v South Australia at Adelaide	1920-21
769	A. C. MacLaren's XI v New South Wales at Sydney	1901-02
763	New South Wales v Queensland at Brisbane	1906-07
8-761 dec.	New South Wales v Queensland at Sydney	1929-30
8-758 dec.	Australia v West Indies at Kingston	1954-55
8-752 dec.	New South Wales v Otago at Dunedin	1923-24
6-735 dec.	Australia v Zimbabwe at Perth	2003-04
7-734 dec.	MCC v New South Wales at Sydney	1928-29
6-729 dec.	Australia v England at Lord's	1930
724	Victoria v South Australia at Melbourne	1920-21
721	Australians v Essex at Southend	1948
713	New South Wales v South Australia at Adelaide	1908-09
6-713 dec.	New South Wales v Victoria at Sydney	1928-29
710	Victoria v Queensland at Melbourne	2003-04
5-708 dec.	Australians v Cambridge University at Cambridge	1921
7-708 dec.	Australians v Hampshire at Southampton	1938
708	New South Wales v Victoria at Sydney	1925-26
705	New South Wales v Victoria at Melbourne	1925-26
7-705 dec.	India v Australia at Sydney	2003-04
701	Australia v England at The Oval	1934

HIGHEST FOURTH-INNINGS TOTALS

6-506	South Australia (won) v Queensland at Adelaide	1991-92
495	South Australia (set 521 to win) v New South Wales at Sydney	2003-04
7-455	Victoria (won) v New South Wales at Newcastle	2003-04
454	Western Australia (set 497 to win) v South Australia at Perth	2004-05
6-446	New South Wales (won) v South Australia at Adelaide	1926-27
9-529	Combined XI (set 579 to win) v South Africans at Perth	1963-64
572	New South Wales (set 593 to win) v South Australia at Sydney	1907-08
518	Victoria (set 753 to win) v Queensland at Brisbane (Ex)	1926-27
472	New South Wales (set 552 to win) v Australian XI at Sydney	1905-06
466	New South Wales (set 466 to win) v West Indians at Sydney	1930-31

HIGHEST MATCH AGGREGATES

R	W	Avge		
1,929	39	49.46	New South Wales v South Australia at Sydney	1925-26
1,911	34	56.20	New South Wales v Victoria at Sydney	1908-09
1,801	40	45.02	A. L. Hassett's XI v A. R. Morris's XI at Melbourne	1953-54
1,764	39	45.23	Australia v West Indies at Adelaide	1968-69
1,753	40	43.82	Australia v England at Adelaide	1920-21
1,752	34	51.52	New South Wales v Queensland at Sydney	1926-27
1,747	25	69.88	Australia v India at Sydney	2003-04
1,744	30	58.13	New South Wales v South Africans at Sydney	1910-11
1,739	40	43.47	New South Wales v A. E. Stoddart's XI at Sydney	1897-98
1,723	31	55.58	England v Australia at Leeds	1948
1,716	40	42.90	New South Wales v South Australia at Sydney	1907-08
1,704	39	43.69	J. Ryder's XI v W. M. Woodfull's XI at Sydney	1929-30

LOWEST COMPLETED INNINGS TOTALS

15	Victoria v MCC at Melbourne	1903-04
17	Gloucestershire v Australians at Cheltenham	1896
18	Tasmania v Victoria at Melbourne	1868-69
18	Australians v MCC at Lord's	1896
19	MCC v Australians at Lord's	1878
23	South Australia v Victoria at East Melbourne	1882-83
23	Australians v Yorkshire at Leeds	1902
25	Tasmania v Victoria at Hobart (LRG)	1857-58
26	England XI v Australians at Birmingham	1884
27	Lord Sheffield's XI v Australians at Sheffield Park	1890
27	South Australia v New South Wales at Sydney	1955-56

LOWEST COMPLETED MATCH AGGREGATE

R	W	Avge		
105	31	3.38	MCC v Australians at Lord's	1878

LARGEST VICTORIES

By Innings

Inns and 666	Victoria (1,059) v Tasmania at Melbourne	1922-23
Inns and 656	Victoria (1,107) v New South Wales at Melbourne	1926-27
Inns and 605	New South Wales (918) v South Australia at Sydney	1900-01
Inns and 579	England (7 dec 903) v Australia at The Oval	1938
Inns and 572	New South Wales (713) v South Australia at Adelaide	1908-09
Inns and 517	Australians (675) v Nottinghamshire at Nottingham	1921

By Runs

685 runs	New South Wales (235 and 8 dec 761) v Queensland at Sydney	1929-30
675 runs	England (521 and 8 dec 342) v Australia at Brisbane (Ex)	1928-29
638 runs	New South Wales (304 and 770) v South Australia at Adelaide	1920-21
571 runs	Victoria (309 and 649) v South Australia at Melbourne	1926-27
562 runs	Australia (701 and 327) v England at The Oval	1934
550 runs	Victoria (295 and 521) v Tasmania at Launceston	1913-14
541 runs	New South Wales (642 and 593) v South Australia at Sydney	1925-26
530 runs	Australia (328 and 578) v South Africa at Melbourne	1910-11

NARROWEST VICTORIES

Victory by One Wicket

New South Wales defeated Victoria at Sydney (Last Wkt: 16)	1877-78
Nottinghamshire defeated Australians at Nottingham (Last Wkt: 2)	1880
Canterbury defeated Tasmania at Christchurch (Last Wkt: 8)	1883-84
Australians defeated Liverpool and Districts at Liverpool (Last Wkt: 4)	1884
Australians defeated Middlesex at Lord's (Last Wkt: 8)	1886
Victoria defeated New South Wales at Sydney (Last Wkt: 10)	1900-01
England defeated Australia at The Oval (Last Wkt: 15)	1902
Australians defeated England XI at Bournemouth (Last Wkt: 1)	1905
England defeated Australia at Melbourne (Last Wkt: 39)	1907-08
Australians defeated Sussex at Hove (Last Wkt: 22)	1909
AIF Team defeated Yorkshire at Sheffield (Last Wkt: 54)	1919
South Australia defeated New South Wales at Adelaide (Last Wkt: 5)	1927-28
Queensland defeated South Australia at Brisbane (Ex) (Last Wkt: 3)	1928-29
J. Ryder's XI defeated W. M. Woodfull's XI at Sydney (Last Wkt: 8)	1929-30
South Australia defeated West Indians at Adelaide (Last Wkt: 22)	1930-31
Tasmania defeated Victoria at Hobart (TCA) (Last Wkt: 11)	1935-36
Australians defeated Madras Presidency at Chennai (Last Wkt: 77)	1935-36
New South Wales defeated Queensland at Brisbane (Last Wkt: 6)	1936-37
New South Wales defeated Queensland and Victorian XI at Brisbane (Last Wkt: 10)	1940-41
New South Wales defeated Queensland at Sydney (Last Wkt: 17)	1949-50
Western Australia defeated West Indians at Perth (Last Wkt: 48)	1951-52
Australia defeated West Indies at Melbourne (Last Wkt: 38)	1951-52
Western Australia defeated South Australia at Adelaide (Last Wkt: 36)	1961-62
Queensland defeated Victoria at Melbourne (Last Wkt: 11)	1968-69
Queensland defeated Western Australia at Perth (Last Wkt: 2)	1968-69
Victoria defeated New South Wales at Melbourne (Last Wkt: 4)	1969-70
South Australia defeated New South Wales at Sydney (Last Wkt: 51)	1971-72
South Australia defeated Victoria at Adelaide (Last Wkt: 12)	1977-78
Victoria defeated New South Wales at Melbourne (Last Wkt: 6)	1979-80
England XI defeated Western Australia at Perth (Last Wkt: 5)	1982-83
New South Wales defeated Queensland at Sydney (Last Wkt: 14)	1984-85
New South Wales defeated Victoria at Sydney (Last Wkt: 2)	1986-87
Victoria defeated New South Wales at Melbourne (Last Wkt: 2)	1993-94
Pakistan defeated Australia at Karachi (Last Wkt: 57)	1994-95
Victoria defeated Tasmania at Melbourne (Last Wkt: 17)	1996-97
Derbyshire defeated Australians at Derby (Last Wkt: 11)	1997
England XI defeated Queensland at Cairns (Last Wkt: 36)	1998-99
West Indies defeated Australia at Bridgetown (Last Wkt: 9)	1998-99

Victory by Five Runs or Less

1	West Indies defeated Australia at Adelaide	1992-93
2	New South Wales defeated Queensland at Sydney	1903-04
2	Tasmania defeated Victoria at Launceston	1911-12
2	Philadelphia defeated Australians at Mannheim	1912-13
2	Western Australia defeated Victoria at Perth	1998-99
2	South Australia defeated Western Australia at Adelaide	1999-00

3	Australia defeated England at Manchester	1902
3	England defeated Australia at Melbourne	1982-83
3	Victoria defeated Queensland at Melbourne	1993-94
5	Western Australia defeated New South Wales at Fremantle	1906-07
5	Surrey defeated Australians at The Oval	1909
5	South Africa defeated Australia at Sydney	1993-94

VICTORY AFTER FOLLOWING ON

A. Shaw's XI (146 and 198) defeated Victoria (251 and 75) at Melbourne 1881-82
A. Shaw's XI (201 and 264) defeated Australian XI (294 and 114) at Melbourne 1886-87
Victoria (137 and 178) defeated New South Wales (240 and 63) at Sydney 1888-89
South Australia (212 and 330) defeated New South Wales (337 and 148) at Adelaide .. 1892-93
Kent (127 and 198) defeated Australians (229 and 60) at Canterbury 1893
Australians (196 and 319) defeated Cambridge University (290 and 108) at Cambridge ... 1893
England (325 and 437) defeated Australia (586 and 166) at Sydney 1894-95
South Australia (304 and 454) defeated Lord Hawke's XI (553 and 108) at Unley 1902-03
New South Wales (108 and 450) defeated Queensland (307 and 224) at Brisbane 1965-66
England (174 and 356) defeated Australia (9d-401 and 111) at Leeds 1981
India (171 and 7d-657) defeated Australia (445 and 212) at Kolkata 2000-01

TIED MATCHES

Gloucestershire tied with Australians at Bristol 1930
MCC tied with Victoria at Melbourne 1932-33
A. L. Hassett's XI tied with D. G. Bradman's XI at Melbourne 1948-49
Victoria tied with New South Wales at St Kilda 1956-57
West Indies tied with Australia at Brisbane 1960-61
South Australia tied with Queensland at Adelaide 1976-77
New Zealanders tied with Victoria at Melbourne 1982-83
Australia tied with India at Chennai 1986-87

MATCHES COMPLETED IN ONE DAY

Australians (41 and 1-12) defeated MCC (33 and 19) at Lord's .... May 27 1878
Australia (76 and 6-33) defeated England (82 and 26) at Birmingham .... May 26 1884
New South Wales (185 and 1-14) defeated Auckland (93 and 102) at Auckland .... Jan 20 1894

MOST RUNS BY ONE SIDE IN A MATCH

R	W	Avge		
1,235	20	61.75	New South Wales v South Australia at Sydney	1925-26
1,107	10	110.70	Victoria v New South Wales at Melbourne	1926-27
1,074	20	53.70	New South Wales v South Australia at Adelaide	1920-21
1,059	10	105.90	Victoria v Tasmania at Melbourne	1922-23
1,034	20	51.70	Victoria v South Australia at Melbourne	1920-21
1,028	20	51.50	Australia v England at The Oval	1934
1,013	18	56.27	Australia v West Indies at Sydney	1968-69

LONGEST MATCHES

Eight days
Australia v England at Melbourne 1928-29
Seven days
Australia v England at Sydney 1911-12
Australia v England at Sydney 1924-25
Australia v England at Melbourne 1924-25
Australia v England at Adelaide 1924-25
Australia v England at Melbourne 1928-29
Australia v England at Adelaide 1928-29

MISCELLANEOUS

FIRST-CLASS TEAMS IN AUSTRALIA

	First Game	M	W	L	D	T
Tasmania	Feb 11 1851	435	67	195	173	0
Victoria	Feb 11 1851	1,004	389	301	311	3
New South Wales	Mar 26 1856	976	432	279	264	1
English Teams	Mar 1 1862	472	190	124	157	1
Combined Teams/Australian XIs	Dec 26 1872	147	41	44	62	0
Australia	Mar 15 1877	344	187	87	69	1
South Australia	Nov 10 1877	865	250	371	243	1
Western Australia	Mar 17 1893	611	189	188	234	0
Queensland	Apr 3 1893	745	201	277	266	1
New Zealanders	Feb 17 1899	84	11	36	36	1
South Africans	Nov 5 1910	81	20	27	34	0
West Indians	Nov 21 1930	133	43	51	38	1
Indians	Oct 17 1947	67	14	31	22	0
Pakistanis	Nov 27 1964	66	12	28	26	0
World XI	Nov 5 1971	12	5	2	5	0
Sri Lankans	Feb 10 1983	19	1	8	10	0
Zimbweans	Dec 18 1994	5	0	3	2	0
Bangladeshi	Jly 18 2003	2	0	2	0	0
Others		46	14	14	16	2
Total		**3057**	**2067**	**2067**	**984**	**6**

TOURING TEAMS IN AUSTRALIA

			First-Class				All Matches			
		Captain	M	W	L	D	T	M	W	L	D	T
1861-62	H. H. Stephenson's Team	H. H. Stephenson	1	0	1	0	0	14	6	3	5	0
1863-64	G. Parr's Team	G. Parr	1	0	1	0	0	14	7	2	5	0
1873-74	W. G. Grace's Team	W. G. Grace	0	0	0	0	0	15	10	3	2	0
1876-77	J. Lillywhite's Team	J. Lillywhite	3	1	1	1	0	15	5	4	6	0
1878-79	Lord Harris's Team	Lord Harris	5	2	3	0	0	13	5	3	5	0
1881-82	A. Shaw's Team	A. Shaw	7	3	2	2	0	18	8	3	7	0
1882-83	Hon I.F.W. Bligh's Team	Hon I. F. W. Bligh	7	4	3	0	0	17	9	3	5	0
1884-85	A. Shaw's Team	A. Shrewsbury	8	6	2	0	0	33	16	2	15	0
1886-87	A. Shaw's Team	A. Shrewsbury	10	6	2	2	0	30	12	2	16	0
1887-88	G. F. Vernon's Team	G. F. Vernon	8	6	1	1	0	26	11	1	14	0
	A. Shrewsbury's Team	A. Shrewsbury	7	5	2	0	0	22	14	2	6	0
	Combined England	W. W. Read	1	1	0	0	0	1	1	0	0	0
1891-92	Lord Sheffield's Team	W. G. Grace	8	6	2	0	0	27	12	2	13	0
1894-95	A. E. Stoddart's Team	A. E. Stoddart	12	8	4	0	0	23	9	4	10	0
1897-98	A. E. Stoddart's Team	A. E. Stoddart	12	4	5	3	0	22	6	5	11	0
1898-99	New Zealanders	L. T. Cobcroft	2	0	2	0	0	4	1	2	1	0
1901-02	A. C. MacLaren's Team	A. C. MacLaren	11	5	6	0	0	22	8	6	8	0
1902-03	Lord Hawke's Team	P. F. Warner	3	0	2	1	0	3	0	2	1	0
1903-04	MCC	P. F. Warner	14	9	2	3	0	20	10	2	8	0
1907-08	MCC	A. O. Jones	18	7	4	7	0	19	7	4	8	0
1910-11	South Africans	P. W. Sherwell	15	6	7	2	0	22	12	7	3	0
1911-12	MCC	J. W. H. T. Douglas	14	11	1	2	0	18	12	1	5	0
1913-14	New Zealanders	D. Reese	4	1	2	1	0	9	5	2	2	0
1920-21	MCC	J. W. H. T. Douglas	13	5	6	2	0	22	9	6	7	0
1922-23	MCC	A. C. MacLaren	7	0	3	4	0	8	0	3	5	0
1924-25	MCC	A. E. R. Gilligan	17	7	6	4	0	23	8	6	9	0
1925-26	New Zealanders	W. R. Patrick	4	0	1	3	0	9	3	1	5	0
1927-28	New Zealanders	T. C. Lowry	1	0	1	0	0	10	1	0	0	0
1928-29	MCC	A. P. F. Chapman	17	8	1	8	0	24	10	1	13	0
1929-30	MCC	A. H. H. Gilligan	5	2	2	1	0	5	2	2	1	0
1930-31	West Indians	G. C. Grant	14	4	8	2	0	16	5	8	3	0

			First-Class					All Matches				
		Captain	M	W	L	D	T	M	W	L	D	T
1931-32	South Africans	H. B. Cameron	16	4	6	6	0	18	6	6	6	0
1932-33	MCC	D. R. Jardine	17	10	1	5	1	22	10	1	10	1
1935-36	MCC	E. R. T. Holmes	6	3	1	2	0	6	3	1	2	0
1936-37	MCC	G. O. B. Allen	17	5	5	7	0	25	7	5	13	0
1937-38	New Zealanders	M. L. Page	3	0	3	0	0	3	0	3	0	0
1946-47	MCC	W. R. Hammond	17	1	3	13	0	25	4	3	18	0
1947-48	Indians	L. Amarnath	14	2	7	5	0	20	5	7	8	0
1950-51	MCC	F. R. Brown	16	5	4	7	0	25	7	4	14	0
1951-52	West Indians	J. D. C. Goddard	13	4	8	1	0	15	5	8	2	0
1952-53	South Africans	J. E. Cheetham	16	4	3	9	0	23	7	3	13	0
1953-54	New Zealanders	B. Sutcliffe	3	2	0	1	0	3	2	0	1	0
1954-55	MCC	L. Hutton	17	8	2	7	0	23	13	2	8	0
1958-59	MCC	P. B. H. May	17	4	4	9	0	20	7	4	9	0
1960-61	West Indians	F. M. M. Worrell	14	4	5	4	1	22	10	5	5	2
1961-62	New Zealanders	J. R. Reid	3	0	2	1	0	3	0	2	1	0
1962-63	MCC	E. R. Dexter	15	4	3	8	0	26	12	3	11	0
1963-64	South Africans	T. L. Goddard	14	5	3	6	0	28	16	4	8	0
1964-65	Pakistanis	Hanif Mohammad	4	0	0	4	0	4	0	0	4	0
1965-66	MCC	M. J. K. Smith	15	5	2	8	0	23	13	2	8	0
1967-68	New Zealanders	B. W. Sinclair	4	0	2	2	0	7	2	2	3	0
	Indians	Nawab of Pataudi jr	9	0	6	3	0	15	4	6	5	0
1968-69	West Indians	G. S. Sobers	15	4	5	6	0	23	9	5	9	0
1969-70	New Zealanders	G. T. Dowling	3	0	0	3	0	8	3	0	5	0
1970-71	MCC	R. Illingworth	15	3	1	11	0	25	10	2	13	0
	New Zealanders	G. T. Dowling	1	0	0	1	0	2	0	1	1	0
1971-72	World XI	G. S. Sobers	12	5	2	5	0	16	5	3	8	0
	New Zealanders	G. T. Dowling	0	0	0	0	2	1	1	0	0	0
1972-73	Pakistanis	Intikhab Alam	8	2	5	1	0	13	5	6	2	0
	New Zealanders	B. E. Congdon	1	0	0	1	0	3	2	0	1	0
1973-74	New Zealanders	B. E. Congdon	9	2	5	2	0	13	5	6	2	0
1974-75	MCC	M. H. Denness	15	5	5	5	0	23	8	9	6	0
	New Zealanders	B. E. Congdon	0	0	0	0	0	3	3	0	0	0
1975-76	West Indians	C. H. Lloyd	13	3	6	4	0	21	8	7	6	0
1976-77	Pakistanis	Mushtaq Mohammad	5	1	2	2	0	5	1	2	2	0
	MCC	A. W. Greig	2	0	1	1	0	2	0	1	1	0
1977-78	Indians	B. S. Bedi	11	6	5	0	0	20	12	6	2	0
1978-79	England XI	J. M. Brearley	13	8	2	3	0	26	17	4	5	0
	Pakistanis	Mushtaq Mohammad	4	1	1	2	0	5	2	1	2	0
1979-80	England XI	J. M. Brearley	8	3	3	2	0	21	13	5	3	0
	West Indians	C. H. Lloyd	7	5	1	1	0	20	10	7	3	0
1980-81	New Zealanders	G. P. Howarth	7	1	2	4	0	29	14	9	6	0
	Indians	S. M. Gavaskar	8	2	2	4	0	25	8	11	6	0
1981-82	Pakistanis	Javed Miandad	8	2	2	4	0	21	8	8	5	0
	West Indians	C. H. Lloyd	7	4	1	2	0	24	16	5	3	0
1982-83	England XI	R. G. D. Willis	11	4	3	4	0	23	10	9	4	0
	New Zealanders	G. P. Howarth	2	0	0	1	1	22	13	7	1	1
	Sri Lankans	L. R. D. Mendis	2	0	0	2	0	5	1	1	3	0
1983-84	Pakistanis	Imran Khan	11	3	3	5	0	24	7	11	6	0
	West Indians	C. H. Lloyd	0	0	0	0	0	13	10	2	0	1
1984-85	West Indians	C. H. Lloyd	11	4	2	5	0	33	24	4	5	0
	Sri Lankans	L. R. D. Mendis	1	1	0	0	0	22	11	11	0	0
	England XI	D. I. Gower	0	0	0	0	0	3	0	3	0	0
	Indians	S. M. Gavaskar	0	0	0	0	0	5	5	0	0	0
	Pakistanis	Javed Miandad	0	0	0	0	0	5	3	2	0	0
	New Zealanders	G. P. Howarth	0	0	0	0	0	4	1	2	1	0
1985-86	New Zealanders	J. V. Coney	6	2	1	3	0	19	5	7	7	0
	Indians	Kapil Dev	5	1	0	4	0	19	8	7	4	0
1986-87	England XI	M. W. Gatting	11	5	3	3	0	30	19	7	4	0
	Pakistanis	Imran Khan	0	0	0	0	0	4	2	2	0	0
	West Indians	I. V. A. Richards	1	0	0	1	0	13	4	8	1	0

			First-Class					All Matches				
		Captain	M	W	L	D	T	M	W	L	D	T
1987-88	New Zealanders	J.J. Crowe	6	1	2	3	0	19	8	8	3	0
	Sri Lankans	R. S. Madugalle	3	0	1	2	0	18	6	9	3	0
	England XI	M. W. Gatting	1	0	0	1	0	2	0	1	1	0
1988-89	West Indians	I. V. A. Richards	11	4	2	5	0	23	11	7	5	0
	Tamil Nadu	S. Vasudevan	1	0	1	0	0	3	0	3	0	0
	Pakistanis	Imran Khan	1	0	0	1	0	14	6	7	1	0
	New Zealanders	J. G. Wright	0	0	0	0	0	1	0	1	0	0
	Worcestershire	P. A. Neale	0	0	0	0	0	2	0	2	0	0
1989-90	New Zealanders	J. G. Wright	3	0	0	3	0	4	0	1	3	0
	Sri Lankans	A. Ranatunga	6	0	2	4	0	17	5	9	3	0
	Pakistanis	Imran Khan	6	0	3	3	0	27	6	14	7	0
	Lancashire	D. P. Hughes	0	0	0	0	0	8	3	5	0	0
1990-91	England XI	G. A. Gooch	11	1	5	5	0	28	8	14	6	0
	Wellington	E. B. McSweeney	1	0	1	0	0	4	1	1	2	0
	New Zealanders	M. D. Crowe	0	0	0	0	0	11	4	7	0	0
	Lancashire	G. Fowler	0	0	0	0	0	6	4	2	0	0
1991-92	New Zealanders	M. D. Crowe	0	0	0	0	0	6	4	2	0	0
	Indians	M. Azharuddin	7	1	5	1	0	29	7	19	2	1
	West Indians	R. B. Richardson	1	0	0	1	0	22	12	8	1	1
	Pakistanis	Imran Khan	2	0	0	2	0	14	5	6	3	0
	South Africans	K. C. Wessels	0	0	0	0	0	12	7	3	2	0
	Zimbabweans	D. L. Houghton	0	0	0	0	0	6	1	5	0	0
	Sri Lankans	P. A. de Silva	0	0	0	0	0	7	2	4	1	0
	England XI	G. A. Gooch	0	0	0	0	0	9	6	2	1	0
1992-93	West Indians	R. B. Richardson	8	3	1	4	0	22	13	5	4	0
	Pakistanis	Javed Miandad	1	1	0	0	0	12	5	6	0	1
	England A	M. D. Moxon	4	0	2	2	0	11	4	4	3	0
1993-94	New Zealanders	M. D. Crowe	7	2	3	2	0	16	5	9	2	0
	South Africans	K. C. Wessels	5	1	2	2	0	17	6	9	2	0
	Indians	S. R. Tendulkar	0	0	0	0	0	3	0	3	0	0
1994-95	England XI	M. A. Atherton	11	3	4	4	0	24	9	11	4	0
	Zimbabweans	A. Flower	2	0	1	1	0	19	8	10	1	0
1995-96	Western Province	E. O. Simons	2	0	2	0	0	5	1	3	1	0
	Pakistanis	Rameez Raja	6	1	3	2	0	7	2	3	2	0
	Sri Lankans	A. Ranatunga	5	0	4	1	0	17	5	11	1	0
	West Indians	R. B. Richardson	2	0	0	2	0	14	4	8	2	0
1996-97	England A	A. J. Hollioake	3	2	0	1	0	6	3	1	2	0
	West Indians	C. A. Walsh	8	4	4	0	0	25	12	13	0	0
	Pakistanis	Wasim Akram	1	0	1	0	0	10	6	4	0	0
1997-98	Transvaal	K. R. Rutherford	0	0	0	0	0	7	1	6	0	0
	New Zealanders	S. P. Fleming	6	0	5	1	0	21	5	13	2	1
	South Africans	W. J. Cronje	6	0	1	5	0	20	11	4	5	0
1998-99	England XI	A. J. Stewart	10	2	4	4	0	27	10	13	4	0
	Sri Lankans	A. Ranatunga	0	0	0	0	0	15	5	10	0	0
1999-00	Pakistanis	Wasim Akram	5	1	4	0	0	21	6	15	0	0
	Indians	S. R. Tendulkar	6	1	4	1	0	15	2	12	1	0
2000	South Africans	S. M. Pollock	0	0	0	0	0	3	1	1	0	1
2000-01	South Africans	S. M. Pollock	0	0	0	0	0	3	1	1	0	1
	West Indians	J. C. Adams	8	0	7	1	0	18	2	14	2	0
	Zimbabweans	H. H. Streak	0	0	0	0	0	9	1	8	0	0
2001-02	New Zealanders	S. P. Fleming	5	0	1	4	0	18	6	8	4	0
	South Africans	S. M. Pollock	5	0	3	2	0	14	9	3	2	0
	Pakistanis	Waqar Younis	0	0	0	0	0	4	3	1	0	0
2002-03	England XI	N. Hussain	8	1	4	3	0	24	3	16	5	0
	Sri Lankans	S. T. Jayasuriya	0	0	0	0	0	13	4	9	0	0
	South Africa A	G. Dros	2	0	0	2	0	6	1	3	2	0
2003-04	Bangladeshi	Khaled Mahmud	2	0	2	0	0	8	3	5	0	0
	Zimbabweans	H. H. Streak	3	0	2	1	0	16	2	11	3	0
	Indians	S. C. Ganguly	5	1	1	3	0	18	7	6	5	0

			First-Class					All Matches				
			M	W	L	D	T	M	W	L	D	T
2004-05 Sri Lankans		M.S. Atapattu	2	0	1	1	0	3	1	1	1	0
New Zealanders		S.P. Fleming	3	0	3	0	0	6	2	4	0	0
Pakistanis		Inzamam-ul-Haq	4	0	4	0	0	15	5	10	0	0
West Indians		B.C. Lara	0	0	0	0	0	9	2	6	1	0

AUSTRALIANS ON TOUR

		Country	Captain	First-Class					All Matches				
				M	W	L	D	T	M	W	L	D	T
1868	Aboriginals	England	C. Lawrence	0	0	0	0	0	47	14	14	19	0
1877-78	Australians	New Zealand	D.W. Gregory	0	0	0	0	0	7	5	1	1	0
1878	Australians	England	D.W. Gregory	15	7	4	4	0	37	18	7	12	0
1878-79	Australians	North America	D.W. Gregory	1	0	0	1	0	6	4	0	2	0
1880	Australians	England	W.L. Murdoch	9	4	2	3	0	37	21	4	12	0
1880-81	Australians	New Zealand	W.L. Murdoch	0	0	0	0	0	10	6	1	3	0
1882	Australians	England	W.L. Murdoch	33	18	4	11	0	38	23	4	11	0
1882-83	Australians	North America	W.L. Murdoch	0	0	0	0	0	2	2	0	0	0
1883-84	Tasmania	New Zealand	J.G. Davies	4	0	3	1	0	7	2	3	2	0
1884	Australians	England	W.L. Murdoch	31	17	7	7	0	32	18	7	7	0
1886	Australians	England	H.J.H. Scott	37	9	7	21	0	39	9	8	22	0
1886-87	Australians	New Zealand	H.J.H. Scott	0	0	0	0	0	5	2	0	3	0
1888	Australians	England	P.S. McDonnell	37	17	13	7	0	40	19	14	7	0
1889-90	NSW	New Zealand	J. Davis	5	4	0	1	0	7	6	0	1	0
1890	Australians	England	W.L. Murdoch	34	10	16	8	0	38	13	16	9	0
1893	Australians	England	J.M. Blackham	31	14	10	7	0	36	18	10	8	0
1893-94	Australians	North America	J.M. Blackham	2	1	1	0	0	6	4	1	1	0
	NSW	New Zealand	J. Davis	7	4	1	2	0	8	4	1	3	0
1895-96	NSW	New Zealand	L.T. Cobcroft	5	3	1	1	0	5	3	1	1	0
1896	Australians	England	G.H.S. Trott	34	20	6	8	0	34	20	6	8	0
1896-97	Australians	North America	G.H.S. Trott	3	2	1	0	0	6	4	1	1	0
	Australians	New Zealand	G.H.S. Trott	0	0	0	0	0	5	3	0	2	0
	Queensland	New Zealand	O.C. Hitchcock	5	3	1	1	0	8	4	1	3	0
1899	Australians	England	J. Darling	35	16	3	16	0	35	16	3	16	0
1902	Australians	England	J. Darling	37	21	2	14	0	39	23	2	14	0
1902-03	Australians	South Africa	J. Darling	4	3	0	1	0	6	3	0	3	0
1904-05	Australians	New Zealand	M.A. Noble	4	3	0	1	0	6	4	0	2	0
1905	Australians	England	J. Darling	35	15	3	17	0	38	16	3	19	0
1909	Australians	England	M.A. Noble	37	11	4	22	0	39	13	4	22	0
1909-10	Australians	New Zealand	W.W. Armstrong	6	5	0	1	0	9	7	0	2	0
1912	Australians	England	E.S. Gregory	36	9	8	19	0	37	9	8	20	0
1912-13	Australians	North America	E.S. Gregory	2	1	1	0	0	7	5	1	1	0
1913-14	NSW	Ceylon	E.F. Waddy	0	0	0	0	0	9	8	1	0	0
	Australians	North America	A. Diamond	5	4	0	1	0	53	49	1	3	0
	Australians	New Zealand	A. Sims	8	6	0	2	0	16	8	0	8	0
1919	AIF Team	England	H.L. Collins	28	12	4	12	0	32	13	4	15	0
1919-20	AIF Team	South Africa	H.L. Collins	8	6	0	2	0	10	8	0	2	0
1920-21	Australians	New Zealand	V.S. Ransford	9	6	0	3	0	15	12	0	3	0
1921	Australians	England	W.W. Armstrong	34	21	2	11	0	39	23	2	14	0
1921-22	Australians	South Africa	H.L. Collins	6	4	0	2	0	6	4	0	2	0
1923-24	NSW	New Zealand	C.G. Macartney	6	5	0	1	0	12	8	0	4	0
1924-25	Victoria	New Zealand	R.E. Mayne	6	1	1	4	0	12	4	1	7	0
1926	Australians	England	H.L. Collins	33	9	1	23	0	40	12	1	27	0
1927-28	Australians	New Zealand	V.Y. Richardson	6	4	0	2	0	13	6	0	7	0
1930	Australians	England	W.M. Woodfull	31	11	1	18	1	33	12	1	19	1
1932-33	Australians	North America	V.Y. Richardson	0	0	0	0	0	51	46	1	4	0
1934	Australians	England	W.M. Woodfull	30	13	1	16	0	34	15	1	18	0
1935-36	Australians	Ceylon	J. Ryder	1	1	0	0	0	1	1	0	0	0
	Australians	India	J. Ryder	16	9	3	4	0	22	10	3	9	0
	Australians	South Africa	V.Y. Richardson	16	13	0	3	0	16	13	0	3	0
1938	Australians	England	D.G. Bradman	29	15	2	12	0	35	20	2	13	0

	Country	*Captain*	First-Class					All Matches				
			M	W	L	D	T	M	W	L	D	T
1945	Aus. Services	England	A.L. Hassett	6	3	2	1	0	48	24	9	15	0
1945-46	Australians	India	A.L. Hassett	8	1	2	5	0	9	1	2	6	0
	Australians	Ceylon	A.L. Hassett	1	1	0	0	0	1	1	0	0	0
	Australians	New Zealand	W.A. Brown	5	5	0	0	0	5	5	0	0	0
1948	Australians	England	D.G. Bradman	31	23	0	8	0	34	25	0	9	0
1949-50	Australians	South Africa	A.L. Hassett	21	14	0	7	0	25	18	0	7	0
	Australians	New Zealand	W.A. Brown	5	3	0	2	0	14	9	0	5	0
1953	Australians	England	A.L. Hassett	33	16	1	16	0	35	16	1	18	0
1954-55	Australians	West Indies	I.W.G. Johnson	9	5	0	4	0	11	5	0	6	0
1956	Australians	England	I.W.G. Johnson	31	9	3	19	0	35	12	3	20	0
1956-57	Australians	Pakistan	I.W.G. Johnson	1	0	1	0	0	1	0	1	0	0
	Australians	India	I.W.G. Johnson	3	2	0	1	0	3	2	0	1	0
	Australians	New Zealand	I.D. Craig	7	5	0	2	0	12	7	0	5	0
1957-58	Australians	South Africa	I.D. Craig	20	11	0	9	0	22	11	0	11	0
1959-60	Australians	Pakistan	R. Benaud	4	3	0	1	0	4	3	0	1	0
	Australians	India	R. Benaud	7	2	1	4	0	7	2	1	4	0
	Australians	New Zealand	I.D. Craig	6	2	0	4	0	9	4	0	5	0
1961	Australians	England	R. Benaud	32	13	1	18	0	37	14	2	21	0
1964	Australians	England	R.B. Simpson	30	11	3	16	0	36	14	4	18	0
1964-65	Australians	India	R.B. Simpson	3	1	1	1	0	3	1	1	1	0
	Australians	Pakistan	R.B. Simpson	1	0	0	1	0	1	0	0	1	0
	Australians	West Indies	R.B. Simpson	11	3	2	6	0	16	4	3	9	0
1966-67	Australians	South Africa	R.B. Simpson	17	7	5	5	0	24	11	6	7	0
	Australians	New Zealand	L.E. Favell	9	1	2	6	0	10	2	2	6	0
1968	Australians	England	W.M. Lawry	25	8	3	14	0	29	10	3	16	0
1969-70	Australians	Ceylon	W.M. Lawry	1	0	0	1	0	4	1	0	3	0
	Australians	India	W.M. Lawry	10	5	1	4	0	10	5	1	4	0
	Australians	South Africa	W.M. Lawry	12	4	4	4	0	12	4	4	4	0
	Australians	New Zealand	S.C. Trimble	8	2	0	6	0	8	2	0	6	0
1972	Australians	England	I.M. Chappell	26	11	5	10	0	37	14	10	13	0
1972-73	Australians	West Indies	I.M. Chappell	12	7	0	5	0	15	10	0	5	0
1973-74	Australians	New Zealand	I.M. Chappell	7	2	1	4	0	11	6	1	4	0
1974-75	Australians	North America	I.M. Chappell	0	0	0	0	0	5	2	1	2	0
1975	Australians	England	I.M. Chappell	15	8	2	5	0	21	12	4	5	0
1976-77	Australians	New Zealand	G.S. Chappell	6	5	0	1	0	8	5	2	1	0
1977	Australians	England	G.S. Chappell	22	5	4	13	0	31	8	8	15	0
1977-78	Australians	West Indies	R.B. Simpson	11	5	3	3	0	13	6	4	3	0
1979	Australians	England	K.J. Hughes	0	0	0	0	0	6	2	3	1	0
1979-80	Australians	India	K.J. Hughes	11	0	3	8	0	11	0	3	8	0
	Australians	Pakistan	G.S. Chappell	5	0	1	4	0	5	0	1	4	0
1980	Australians	England	G.S. Chappell	5	1	2	2	0	8	1	4	3	0
1980-81	Australians	Sri Lanka	K.J. Hughes	1	0	0	1	0	4	2	1	1	0
1981	Australians	England	K.J. Hughes	17	3	3	11	0	26	7	7	12	0
1981-82	Australians	New Zealand	G.S. Chappell	5	1	1	3	0	11	4	4	3	0
1982-83	Australians	Pakistan	K.J. Hughes	6	0	3	3	0	9	0	5	4	0
	Australians	Zimbabwe	D.M. Wellham	2	1	1	0	0	8	7	1	0	0
	Australians	Sri Lanka	G.S. Chappell	2	1	0	1	0	6	1	2	3	0
1983	Australians	England	K.J. Hughes	0	0	0	0	0	9	3	5	1	0
1983-84	Australians	West Indies	K.J. Hughes	10	1	3	6	0	15	2	6	7	0
1984-85	Australians	India	K.J. Hughes	0	0	0	0	0	6	4	0	2	0
	NSW	New Zealand	D.M. Wellham	0	0	0	0	0	1	1	0	0	0
	Australians	Sharjah, UAE	A.R. Border	0	0	0	0	0	2	1	1	0	0
1985	Australians	England	A.R. Border	20	4	3	13	0	29	9	5	15	0
1985-86	Australians	Zimbabwe	R.B. Kerr	2	1	0	1	0	9	3	5	1	0
	Australians	South Africa	K.J. Hughes	10	2	2	6	0	25	10	9	6	0
	Australians	New Zealand	A.R. Border	5	1	1	3	0	11	5	3	3	0
	Australians	Sharjah, UAE	R.J. Bright	0	0	0	0	0	1	0	1	0	0
1985-86	NSW	Zimbabwe	G.C. Dyer	2	1	0	1	0	8	5	2	1	0
1986-87	Australians	India	A.R. Border	7	0	0	6	1	13	2	3	7	1
	NSW	New Zealand	D.M. Wellham	0	0	0	0	0	2	1	1	0	0
	Australians	South Africa	K.J. Hughes	12	2	3	7	0	25	8	9	8	0

	Country	Captain	First-Class					All Matches				
			M	W	L	D	T	M	W	L	D	T
	SAust	New Zealand	D. W. Hookes									
			0	0	0	0	0	4	4	0	0	0
	Australians	Sharjah, UAE	A. R. Border									
			3	0	3	0	0	3	0	3	0	0
1987-88	NSW	Zimbabwe	D. M. Wellham									
			2	0	0	2	0	8	5	1	2	0
	Australians	India	A. R. Border									
			0	0	0	0	0	7	6	1	0	0
	Australians	Pakistan	A. R. Border									
			0	0	0	0	0	1	1	0	0	0
	Victoria	New Zealand	D. F. Whatmore									
			0	0	0	0	0	2	0	2	0	0
	Queensland	New Zealand	R. B. Kerr									
			0	0	0	0	0	3	3	0	0	0
1988	Aboriginals	England	J. McGuire									
			0	0	0	0	0	27	15	11	1	0
1988-89	Australians	Pakistan	A. R. Border									
			6	0	1	5	0	7	0	2	5	0
1989	Australians	England	A. R. Border									
			20	12	1	7	0	31	20	3	7	1
1989-90	WAust	India	G. M. Wood									
			1	0	0	1	0	4	1	2	1	0
	Australians	India										
			0	0	0	0	0	5	2	3	0	0
	Australians	New Zealand	A. R. Border									
			1	0	1	0	0	6	5	0	1	0
	Australians	Sharjah, UAE	A. R. Border									
			0	0	0	0	0	4	3	1	0	0
1990-91	Australians	West Indies	A. R. Border									
			10	2	2	6	0	19	10	3	6	0
1991	Victoria	England	S. P. O'Donnell									
			1	0	0	1	0	4	1	1	2	0
1991-92	Australians	Zimbabwe	M. A. Taylor									
			2	2	0	0	0	6	5	1	0	0
	Australians	New Zealand	A. R. Border									
			0	0	0	0	0	2	1	1	0	0
1992-93	Australians	Sri Lanka	A. R. Border									
			5	1	0	4	0	8	2	2	4	0
	Australians	New Zealand	A. R. Border									
			4	2	1	1	0	10	5	4	1	0
1993	Australians	England	A. R. Border									
			21	10	2	9	0	30	18	3	9	0
1993-94	Australians	South Africa	A. R. Border									
			6	3	1	2	0	16	7	5	4	0
	NSW	New Zealand	P. A. Emery									
			0	0	0	0	0	1	1	0	0	0
	Australians	Sharjah, UAE	M. A. Taylor									
			0	0	0	0	0	3	2	1	0	0
1994-95	Australians	Sri Lanka	M. A. Taylor									
			0	0	0	0	0	3	1	2	0	0
	Australians	Pakistan	M. A. Taylor									
			4	0	1	3	0	10	5	2	3	0
	Australians	New Zealand	M. A. Taylor									
			0	0	0	0	0	4	3	1	0	0
	Cricket Academy	New Zealand	N. W. Ashley									
			1	1	0	0	0	6	6	0	0	0
	Australians	West Indies	M. A. Taylor									
			7	3	1	3	0	16	8	5	3	0
1995	Young Australia	England	S. G. Law									
			8	5	1	2	0	16	11	3	2	0
	NSW	England	M. A. Taylor									
			1	0	0	1	0	2	1	0	1	0
1995-96	Tasmania	Zimbabwe	D. C. Boon									
			2	0	0	2	0	5	3	0	2	0
	Australians	India	M. A. Taylor									
			0	0	0	0	0	6	5	1	0	0
	Australians	Pakistan	M. A. Taylor									
			0	0	0	0	0	1	0	1	0	0
1996-97	Australians	Sri Lanka	I. A. Healy									
			0	0	0	0	0	6	4	2	0	0
	Australians	India	M. A. Taylor									
			2	0	1	1	0	7	0	6	1	0
	Australians	South Africa	M. A. Taylor									
			6	5	1	0	0	17	13	4	0	0
1997	Australians	England	M. A. Taylor									
			16	6	3	6	1	27	11	7	7	2
1997-98	Australians	New Zealand	S. R. Waugh									
			0	0	0	0	0	4	2	2	0	0
	Australians	India	S. R. Waugh									
			6	1	2	3	0	6	1	2	3	0
	Australians	Sharjah, UAE	S. R. Waugh									
			0	0	0	0	0	5	4	1	0	0
1998	Australians	Scotland	M. J. Di Venuto									
			2	0	0	2	0	5	2	0	3	0
	Australians	Ireland	M. J. Di Venuto									
			1	1	0	0	0	6	5	0	1	0
1998-99	Australians	Pakistan	M. A. Taylor									
			5	2	0	3	0	9	6	0	3	0
	Australians	Bangladesh	M. A. Taylor									
			0	0	0	0	0	1	0	1	0	0
	Australians	West Indies	S. R. Waugh									
			7	4	2	1	0	14	7	5	1	1
	Cricket Academy	Zimbabwe	B. J. Hodge									
			2	2	0	0	0	7	5	2	0	0
1999	Australians	England	S. R. Waugh									
			0	0	0	0	0	10	7	2	0	1
1999-00	Australians	North America	A. C. Gilchrist									
			0	0	0	0	0	5	4	1	0	0
	Australians	Sri Lanka	S. R. Waugh									
			5	2	1	2	0	10	6	2	2	0
	Australians	Zimbabwe	S. R. Waugh									
			2	2	0	0	0	5	5	0	0	0
	Australians	New Zealand	S. R. Waugh									
			5	4	1	0	0	11	8	1	2	0
	Australians	South Africa	S. R. Waugh									
			0	0	0	0	0	3	2	1	0	0
2000-01	Australians	Kenya	S. R. Waugh									
			0	0	0	0	0	2	1	1	0	0
	Australians	India	S. R. Waugh									
			6	1	2	3	0	12	4	5	3	0
2001	Australians	England	S. R. Waugh									
			11	8	2	1	0	20	13	4	2	1
2001-02	Australians	South Africa	S. R. Waugh									
			6	3	2	1	0	13	8	2	2	1

		Country	Captain	First-Class					All Matches				
				M	W	L	D	T	M	W	L	D	T
2001-02	Australians	South Africa	S. R. Waugh	6	3	2	1	0	13	8	2	2	
2002-03	Australians	Kenya	R. T. Ponting	0	0	0	0	0	5	4	0	1	
	Australia A	South Africa	J. L. Langer	0	0	0	0	0	6	5	1	0	
	Australians	Sri Lanka	R. T. Ponting	0	0	0	0	0	4	3	1	0	
	Australians	Sri Lanka/Sh	S. R. Waugh	3	3	0	0	0	3	3	0	0	
	Australians	South Africa	R. T. Ponting	0	0	0	0	0	11	11	0	0	
	Australians	West Indies	S. R. Waugh	6	4	1	1	0	13	8	4	1	
2003-04	Australians	India	R. T. Ponting	0	0	0	0	0	7	6	1	0	
	Australians	Sri Lanka	R. T. Ponting	4	4	0	0	0	9	7	2	0	
	Australians	Zimbabwe	R. T. Ponting	0	0	0	0	0	4	3	0	1	
2004-05	Australians	Netherlands	R. T. Ponting	0	0	0	0	0	2	1	0	1	
	Australians	England	R. T. Ponting	0	0	0	0	0	4	3	1	0	0
	Australians	India	R. T. Ponting	5	2	1	2	0	5	2	1	2	0
	Australians	New Zealand	R. T. Ponting	3	2	0	1	0	9	8	0	1	0

FIRST-CLASS GROUNDS

	First Game	Last Game	Games
N. T. C. A. Ground, Launceston, Tasmania	1850-51	1995-96	82
Emerald Hill Cricket Ground, Emerald Hill, Victoria	*1851-52		1
Melbourne Cricket Ground (MCG), Victoria	1855-56	2004-05	614
The Domain, Sydney, New South Wales	*1856-57	1868-69	6
Lower Domain Ground, Hobart, Tasmania	*1857-58		1
Albert Ground, Redfern, New South Wales	*1870-71	1876-77	5
Adelaide Oval, South Australia	1877-78	2004-05	547
Sydney Cricket Ground (SCG), New South Wales	1877-78	2004-05	621
East Melbourne Cricket Ground, Victoria	*1880-81		4
Tasmanian Cricket Association Ground, Hobart, Tasmania	1889-90	1986-87	86
Exhibition Ground, Brisbane, Queensland	**1892-93	1930-31	28
Brisbane Cricket Ground (The Gabba), Queensland	1897-98	2004-05	427
Western Australian Cricket Association Ground, Perth, WA	1898-99	2004-05	388
Unley Oval, South Australia	*1902-03		1
Fremantle Oval, Western Australia	**1905-06	1909-10	5
South Melbourne Cricket Ground (Lakeside Oval), Victoria	*1907-08	1931-32	2
Fitzroy Cricket Ground (Brunswick Street Oval), Victoria	*1925-26		1
Richmond Cricket Ground (Punt Road Oval), Victoria	1932-33	2001-02	6
Carlton Recreation Ground (Princes Park), Victoria	1945-46	1997-98	7
St Kilda Cricket Ground (Junction Oval), Victoria	1945-46	2004-05	33
Kardinia Park, Geelong, Victoria	*1961-62	1981-92	6
Sydney Cricket Ground No 2, New South Wales	*1966-67		1
Devonport Oval, Tasmania	1977-78	1997-98	27
Manuka Oval, Canberra, Australian Capital Territory	1978-79	1998-99	5
Oakes Oval, Lismore, New South Wales	1979-80	1991-92	2
No 1 Sports Ground, Newcastle, New South Wales	1981-82	2003-04	18
Salter Oval, Bundaberg, Queensland	1982-83		1
Showgrounds Oval, Wangaratta, Victoria	1986-87	1996-97	2
Endeavour Park, Townsville, Queensland	1986-87		1
Bellerive Oval, Tasmania	1987-88	2004-05	99
Sale Oval, Victoria	1989-90		1
Lavington Sports Ground, Albury, New South Wales	1989-90	1990-91	2
North Sydney Oval, New South Wales	1990-91	2000-01	3
Eastern Oval, Ballarat, Victoria	1990-91		1
Carrara Sports Ground, Queensland	**1990-91		1
Queen Elizabeth Oval, Bendigo, Victoria	1991-92	1994-95	2
Henzell Park, Caloundra, Queensland	1992-93		1
Southern Cross Reserve, Toowoomba, Queensland	1994-95		1
Newtown Oval, Maryborough, Queensland	1994-95		1
Hurstville Oval, New South Wales	1995-96		1

	First Game	Last Game	Games
*Harrup Park, Mackay, Queensland	1995-96		1
Bankstown Memorial Oval, New South Wales	1996-97	2004-05	2
Cazaly's Australian Football Park, Cairns, Queensland	1997-98	2004-05	4
Alan Border Field, Albion, Queensland	1999-00	2002-03	7
Marrara Cricket Ground, Darwin	2002-03	2004-05	2

* Denotes the ground no longer exists; ** Denotes the ground is no longer used for cricket.

RUN-OUTS

For some years now, run out credits to fieldsmen have been recorded in Test match scores. It is worth asking, who have been the most prolific fieldsmen when it comes to run outs? Thanks to sources such as Ray Webster's *First-Class Cricket in Australia*, and to research for overseas Tests, it is possible to answer this, up to a point, for Tests involving Australia. The limitation is that about 7% of run-outs have no known credited fieldsmen, mostly involving Tests played long ago, so figures for early players may be a little low.

The most run-out credits for non-wicket-keepers are:

	Run-Outs	Tests	per 10 Tests
J. B. Hobbs	12	41	2.9
S. R. Waugh	12	168	0.7
R. N. Harvey	11	79	1.4
D. G. Bradman	9	52	1.7
D. R. Martyn	9	56	1.6
C. L. Hooper	8	25	3.2
I. M. Chappell	8	75	1.1
R. T. Ponting	8	88	0.9

It is remarkable that an Englishman heads the list, given that we are limited here to Tests involving Australia. Surprising, too, that modern players do not feature more, given the profusion of matches today, and the fact that there are no gaps in modern data.

The most successful keepers have been Rod Marsh and J.J. Kelly (a 19th-century player) on 14, with Gilchrist, Healy, Oldfield, and Grout credited with 13 run outs each.
– CHARLES DAVIS

4

International Summer

New Zealand in Australia, 2004-05

by MAX BONNELL

Stephen Fleming's New Zealanders arrived in Australia in November with optimism and fighting words about the power of team spirit. They left in December with the dignity of a split result in the Chappell-Hadlee Trophy. So the tour was no disaster, except for everything in between.

"We're light," admitted Fleming at the start of the tour. "If you stick us up player to player we're well short of matching up." If anything, the New Zealand captain underplayed his team's underdog role. Perhaps the most telling statistic of the series was that every Australian batsman averaged more than 40 – a mark achieved by only one New Zealander. And the most expensive Australian bowler, Darren Lehmann, had a superior average to the best New Zealander. The gulf between the sides really was that great.

There was never any substance to the idea that the tourists could repeat their efforts of 2001-02, when they held Australia to 0-0. Injuries to Shane Bond and Darryl Tuffey, and the retirement of Chris Cairns from the Test arena, exposed the limited depth of New Zealand cricket and left Fleming with an impotent pace attack. Chris Martin, Jacob Oram and James Franklin all depend on green pitches and heavy skies. Instead they were confronted with hot conditions and flat, bone-hard surfaces. Nothing illustrated the weakness of the tourists' attack more emphatically than the fact that even Jason Gillespie and Glenn McGrath cashed in, scoring their first Test fifties in Brisbane.

For a day and a half, New Zealand were competitive. On the back of Oram's rugged century, they posted a respectable total in Brisbane before reducing Australia to 4 for 128. But that was as good as it got. Michael Clarke and Adam Gilchrist wrested the game away, Gillespie and McGrath heaped indignity upon insult,

nd by the time the visitors batted again, their appetite for the fight
ad evaporated. In Adelaide, Australia's batsmen took control of
he game in the first session, and the highly professional execution
hat followed had a grim inevitability about it.

Few of the New Zealanders emerged with their reputations
nscathed. Fleming may well be one of the most astute captains in the
modern game, but this tour proved that no captain can rise above the
material at his disposal. It was a forgettable series for Fleming the
batsman, too. He led by example with a wonderfully tenacious
effort in Adelaide, but his other three innings yielded only 13 runs.

The pick of the tourists was Daniel Vettori, who has been playing
for so long that it was a surprise to be reminded that he is still only
26. He seemed to have regained confidence, and control of his
action, and relished the responsibility of carrying the attack. He
was the only New Zealander to concede fewer than three runs an
over, and he also had the best strike rate – although one wicket
every 12 overs was nothing much to celebrate. His defiant half-
century in Adelaide emphasised his credentials as an all-rounder
although, in a series in which McGrath and Gillespie made
fifties and Lehmann took wickets, the value of that label became
increasingly dubious.

New Zealand's strategy depended upon the top order wearing
down the Australian pace attack. It never happened, partly because
Mark Richardson had become too fallible around the off-stump.
After scraping 48 runs from four innings, he decided that Test cricket was no longer enjoyable, and announced his retirement. Matthew
Sinclair played adhesively in Brisbane, then failed completely.
Without a sound platform to build upon, the middle order struggled:
the dangerous Nathan Astle was kept in check, while Scott Styris
never seemed likely to play a long innings. Oram's defiant hundred
in Brisbane was full of beefy drives, and helped to make up for his
bowling, which was too plain to trouble anyone.

The Australians went about their work with impeccable professionalism. Ricky Ponting's refusal to enforce the follow-on in
Adelaide was motivated less by a fear of batting last than by a
relentless determination to grind his opponents out of the game.
Australia had the luxury of wondering whether Matthew Hayden's
70 and 54, or the captain's failure to post a century, amounted to a
form slump.

The series proved little about the Australian side that was no already known – Langer's reliability, Gilchrist's strikepower although the team would have been encouraged by Clarke's sparkling century in Brisbane, which came at the only point in the series at which Australia were subjected to real pressure. That innings made Clarke only the third Australian to post a century in his first game both abroad and at home, and confirmed his standing as the most marketable Australian player of his generation. The presence of another blond, gelled-up hairstyle in the Australian team seemed to have a direct influence on Shane Warne, who played the series with an alarmingly vertical hairdo, a cross-breed of mullet and mohawk.

That was the problem with this series. The cricket itself had degenerated into a highly professional demolition job, so the media began to focus on whatever quirks or controversy the games could throw up. So let the record show that when Gillespie reached 50 in Brisbane, he rode his bat down the pitch, that Richardson defeated Lehmann in the slow sprint, and that the umpires made some mistakes.

Gilchrist raised a fuss, not only by walking himself, but by giving the impression that he expected Craig McMillan to follow his example. Fleming grumbled that Gilchrist appeared to be "on a crusade", although a simpler view of that incident was that Gilchrist was merely perpetuating the Australian wicket-keepers' tradition of having a word to a batsman who survived an edge behind the wicket.

The ease of Australia's victory also prompted concern for the future of Test cricket, for it seemed as though the strong countries – Australia, England, India – continued to grow stronger while the others declined. The debate is valid, but it would be unfair to focus entirely on the relative weakness of the New Zealanders. This series was one-sided not only because the New Zealanders were limited, but also because they ran into truly formidable opponents.

NEW ZEALAND TOURING PARTY

S. P. Fleming (*captain*), N. J. Astle, I. G. Butler, J. E. C. Franklin, H. J. H. Marshall, C. S. Martin, B. B. McCullum, K. D. Mills, J. D. P. Oram, M. H. Richardson, M. S. Sinclair, S. B. Styris, D. L. Vettori and P. J. Wiseman.

G. J. Hopkins included to the squad for the New South Wales game only and C. D. McMillan included to the touring squad on November 10.

Manager: R. Dykes; *Coach*: J. G. Bracewell; *Assistant Coach/video analyst*: R. Carter; *Physiotherapist*: D. F. Shackel; *Fitness Conditioner*: G. Owen; *Media manager*: A. Clearwater.

NEW ZEALAND TOUR RESULTS

Test matches – Played 2: Lost 2.
First-class matches – Played 3, Lost 3.
Losses – Australia (2), New South Wales (1).
  Wins: Australia (1); *Losses* – Australia (1).
Limited-over Internationals – Played 2: Won 1, Lost 1.
  Wins: Australia (1); *Losses* – Australia (1).
Other non first-class matches: Played 1: Won 1. *Wins* – Victorian Invitational XI.

TEST BATTING AVERAGES

	M	I	NO	R	HS	100s	50s	Avge	Ct/St	S-R
J. L. Langer (Aust)...	2	3	0	295	215	1	0	98.33	4	53.54
A. C. Gilchrist (Aust)	2	2	0	176	126	1	1	88.00	8/1	76.52
M. J. Clarke (Aust)...	2	2	0	148	141	1	0	74.00	2	68.52
R. T. Ponting (Aust)..	2	3	1	145	68	0	2	72.50	4	65.91
J. N. Gillespie (Aust)..	2	2	1	66	54*	0	1	66.00	1	39.29
S. K. Warne (Aust)...	2	2	1	63	53*	0	1	63.00	4	77.78
J. D. P. Oram (NZ)...	2	4	1	186	126*	1	0	62.00	1	57.06
G. D. McGrath (Aust)	2	1	0	61	61	0	1	61.00	0	66.30
D. S. Lehmann (Aust)	2	2	0	89	81	0	1	44.50	0	48.63
M. L. Hayden (Aust)..	2	3	0	132	70	0	2	44.00	3	48.35
D. R. Martyn (Aust)..	2	3	1	83	70	0	1	41.50	0	49.11
K. D. Mills (NZ).....	1	2	1	33	29	0	0	33.00	1	45.21
N. J. Astle (NZ)......	2	4	0	126	52	0	1	31.50	2	48.84
P. J. Wiseman (NZ)...	1	2	1	26	15*	0	0	26.00	1	37.14
D. L. Vettori (NZ)....	2	4	0	102	59	0	1	25.50	1	52.58
S. P. Fleming (NZ)...	2	4	0	97	83	0	1	24.25	1	49.74
M. S. Sinclair (NZ)...	2	4	0	71	69	0	1	17.75	0	36.41
S. B. Styris (NZ).....	2	4	0	70	28	0	0	17.50	1	39.77
C. D. McMillan (NZ).	1	2	0	32	23	0	0	16.00	1	30.77
B. B. McCullum (NZ).	2	4	0	64	36	0	0	16.00	2/1	61.54
M. H. Richardson (NZ)	2	4	0	48	19	0	0	12.00	1	26.97
J. E. C. Franklin (NZ).	1	2	0	20	13	0	0	10.00	0	28.57
M. S. Kasprowicz (Aust)	2	1	0	5	5	0	0	5.00	0	23.81
C. S. Martin (NZ)....	2	4	1	4	2*	0	0	1.33	1	15.38

  * Denotes not out.

TEST BOWLING AVERAGES

	O	Mdns	R	W	BB	5W/i	10W/m	Avge	Balls/W
G. D. McGrath (Aust)..	67.1	10	184	9	4-66	0	0	20.44	44.78
J. N. Gillespie (Aust)..	74	21	181	8	3-37	0	0	22.63	55.50
S. K. Warne (Aust)....	95.2	17	256	11	4-15	0	0	23.27	52.00
M. S. Kasprowicz (Aust)	66	14	216	9	4-90	0	0	24.00	44.00
D. S. Lehmann (Aust)..	22	2	67	2	2-46	0	0	33.50	66.00
D. L. Vettori (NZ).....	123.2	21	341	10	5-152	1	0	34.10	74.00
P. J. Wiseman (NZ)....	54	10	192	4	3-140	0	0	48.00	81.00
C. S. Martin (NZ).....	72.5	12	281	5	5-152	1	0	56.20	87.40
K. D. Mills (NZ)......	26	8	99	1	1-99	0	0	99.00	156.00
S. B. Styris (NZ).....	8	1	33	0	–	0	0	–	–
J. D. P. Oram (NZ).....	54	12	188	0	–	0	0	–	–
C. D. McMillan (NZ)..	5	1	23	0	–	0	0	–	–
J. E. C. Franklin (NZ)..	22	2	120	0	–	0	0	–	–

Note: Matches in this section that were not first-class are signified by a dagger.

NEW SOUTH WALES v NEW ZEALANDERS

At Sydney Cricket Ground, Sydney, November 11, 12, 13, 14, 2004. New South Wales won by nine wickets. *Toss*: New Zealanders.

New Zealanders

M. H. Richardson c Krejza b Nicholson	14	– b MacGill	5..
M. S. Sinclair c Krejza b Nicholson	88	– b Nicholson	7..
H. J. H. Marshall b Lee	18	– c Thornely b MacGill	..
*S. B. Styris b Lee	10	– lbw b Krejza	18
C. D. McMillan c Haddin b MacGill	14	– b Nicholson	17..
J. D. P. Oram c Mail b Krejza	26	– lbw b Krejza	..
J. E. C. Franklin lbw b MacGill	0	– b Lee	6..
†G. J. Hopkins c Mail b MacGill	4	– c Jaques b MacGill	1..
P. J. Wiseman not out	21	– lbw b MacGill	6..
I. G. Butler lbw b MacGill	0	– lbw b Lee	0..
C. S. Martin c Phelps b Lee	3	– not out	1
B 1, l-b 8, w 1, n-b 5	15	B 4, l-b 10, w 1, n-b 7	22

(72.4 overs, 310 mins) 213
Fall: 39 68 83 98 176 184 184 193 193 213

(73.3 overs, 318 mins) 201
Fall: 110 110 145 183 184 184 192
192 192 201

Bowling: First Innings – Lee 16.4–4–52–3; Nicholson 17–6–41–2; Clark 12–4–29–0; MacGill 21–5–57–4; Krejza 6–2–25–1. *Second Innings* – Lee 16–3–37–2; Nicholson 14–3–31–2; Clark 9–3–19–0; Krejza 13–4–48–2; MacGill 19.3–5–52–4; Thornely 2–2–0–0.

New South Wales

G. J. Mail c Styris b Wiseman	43	– c McMillan b Oram	13
P. A. Jaques b Hopkins b Franklin	8	– not out	70
M. J. Phelps b Butler	17	– not out	39
D. J. Thornely c Sinclair b Franklin	59		
A. W. O'Brien c Hopkins b Butler	21		
*†B. J. Haddin b Wiseman	14		
J. J. Krejza c Styris b Franklin	54		
M. J. Nicholson b Butler	23		
B. Lee b Oram	33		
S. R. Clark not out	3		
S. C. G. MacGill b Oram	0		
B 2, l-b 3, w 1, n-b 5	11	B 4, l-b 2, n-b 1	7

(108 overs, 457 mins) 286
Fall: 8 42 112 142 156 175 229 272 286 286

(43.3 overs, 188 mins) ... (1 wkt) 129
Fall: 29

Bowling: First Innings—Martin 20–7–40–0; Franklin 22–7–70–3; Oram 21–9–37–2; Butler 15–1–51–3; Wiseman 22–4–76–2; Styris 4–1–5–0; McMillan 4–3–2–0. *Second Innings*—Martin 10–3–33–0; Franklin 10.3–2–31–0; Oram 6–2–13–1; Wiseman 5–1–21–0; Butler 5–2–10–0; Styris 7–2–15–0.

Umpires: N. S. D. Fowler and S. A. Reed.

AUSTRALIA v NEW ZEALAND

First Test Match

by ADRIAN McGREGOR

At Brisbane Cricket Ground, Brisbane, November 18, 19, 20, 21, 2004. Australia won by an innings and 156 runs. *Toss*: New Zealand.

The Gabba in Brisbane has witnessed many historic moments, notably when Aboriginal fast bowler Eddie Gilbert bowled Bradman for a duck in 1931; the dramatic tied Test with the West Indies in 1960-61; and Queensland winning the Sheffield Shield in 1994-95 after 69 years of trying.

Of course, the Gabba is no longer the charming ground of yore, its Moreton Bay figs, graceful timber stands and grassy hill replaced by a breeze-less concrete coliseum designed for Australian football. But the Gabba still retains the capacity to surprise and 18,000 turned up on the first day to see Australia's Great Returning Heroes, fresh from victory abroad in India. There's nothing quite like it: the Gabba, first ball of the first Test of the Australian summer.

The pitch had a distinctly greenish tinge and locals smiled knowingly when Kiwi captain Stephen Fleming called correctly and decided to bat. But somebody forgot to tell curator Kevin Mitchell. This was no parochial pitch made to order for the home side in the fashion of some Indian curators. It had bounce, true, but no devil off the seam. It was strange to see Glenn McGrath and Jason Gillespie so easily blunted.

After 33 minutes the scene was set for a local hero. Enter Michael Kasprowicz, all bustle and menace. Suddenly the batsmen were uncomfortable and "Kasper" at lunch had 2 for 18. He took the third wicket too, and you had to feel for twelfth man, fast bowling contender Brett Lee, looking on forlornly. Captain Fleming, who had admitted to sleeping for 20 hours a day recovering from a virus he contracted in Bangladesh, lasted just three balls. He probably shouldn't have played and nor should Darren Lehmann, so obviously distracted by the David Hookes court case.

A foretaste of later tensions arose when opener Mathew Sinclair was caught low by Ricky Ponting but declined to walk until the video umpire confirmed the catch. Ponting established a gentleman's agreement with Sri Lanka to accept the fielder's word, but not with India and nor with New Zealand. It appeared the usual Aussie-Kiwi niggle, nothing more. By day's end Jacob Oram and Daniel Vettori had comfortably taken the score to 7 for 250 on a pitch fearfully full of runs.

Next day Oram nursed his score to 98, and the team to 9 for 325, whereupon we were treated to the ludicrous scene of Shane Warne bowling wide of the leg stump to a field ringing the boundary, all to deny Oram his 100. Umpire Aleem Dar called two balls wide, disputed by Warne, who was then firmly chipped by Dar.

Having made his century, the 198cm Oram, wielding his bat as lightly as Andre Agassi a racquet, lifted Gillespie for six, and then Kasprowicz for two successive sixes. The crowd was enthralled, rows of raised arms signalling the blows. Oram was still not out, on 126, when the innings ended for 353. Ponting showed signs of form for a 51 but Australia stumbled to 4 for 197 at stumps and the Black Caps led two days to nil.

Day three was simply tumultuous. Spinner Vettori, a class act, had trapped opener Justin Langer the day before with a ball that hit a crack, turned and kept low. This day he had Adam Gilchrist, on seven, plumb with an identical ball. The Kiwis were jubilant, still more than 100 ahead and about to trash the Australian parlour.

Until umpire Steve Bucknor ruled otherwise. That was the turning point because Gilchrist never needs two lives, and tyro Michael Clarke took his cue. Gilchrist has the eye of an osprey, the best clean hitter in world cricket, but even he played second fiddle to Clarke who possesses the fastest footwork since Muhammad Ali.

His is not Mark Waugh's relaxed, almost nerveless, timing. Clarke's speed is a lightning nervousness, in position so quickly he gives himself optimum options. And being just 23, he can't wait. Such as during the over before lunch, when he still needed 11 for his century. He got them in three balls, the last, a four, smashed off the final ball. A century in his first Test innings in India, now same again in Australia. Those without cable had heard about Clarke's brilliance on the sub-continent, now they saw it.

Gilchrist's admirable century after lunch was almost an afterthought, and when he departed Australia were 100 ahead. The Black Caps were demoralised, as defeated as their compatriots, the world champion Silver Ferns, who that same afternoon were losing a heart-breaker to Australia's women netballers.

Now came the tipping point, as they say in the parlance. Gillespie, no bunny, and McGrath, of whom the same could not be said to that point, combined to contribute maiden half-centuries. Wonderful as was their achievement, especially "ooo-aah Glenn McGrath", after Clarke and Gilchrist, the Kiwis were ripe for just such humiliation. Proof of this came the next day when the two tailenders added another 21 runs before their marathon 114 partnership ended, with Australia on 585. On this self-same pitch, New Zealand were then bundled out for just 76 runs in three hours. Admittedly by then cracks were widening in the pitch, contributing to several dismissals, but the collapse was psychological.

Australia won by an innings and 156 runs but on-field events on that fourth day raised issues which cricket must urgently address. In the Kiwis' second innings Brendon McCullum played at a ball from Gillespie, missed by a country mile but hit the bottom of his pad. Gilchrist caught it, the Aussies went up, and Bucknor gave it. Subsequent replays, at the ground and on television, showed the error. McCullum didn't quibble at this injustice. He turned and left.

Soon after, Craig McMillan clearly edged Gillespie to Gilchrist but stood his ground and Bucknor rejected the appeals. Gilchrist gave McMillan some old-fashioned sledging to which the Kiwi heatedly objected, provoking the umpires to intervene. McMillan told Gilchrist that not everyone felt obliged to walk just because he did. Gilchrist pleaded innocence, but here's the dilemma. Batsmen may feel that, as a demonstrated "honest" walker, Gilchrist's word – and therefore even his traditional wicket-keeping appeals – may be judged to carry undue weight with umpires.

Volunteering dismissal leads to this provocative suggestion – why not walk on doubtful lbw appeals too? Should Gilly have walked in the first innings if he thought Vettori had him? And what about McCullum? Should captains call such batsmen back when replays show they are clearly wronged? Why limit acts of sportsmanship? England captain Michael Atherton predicted that the walking fad would end in tears and it's heading that way.

Of course cricket's administrators could ameliorate all this by employing technological advances in television to determine a wider range of umpiring decisions. Nothing undermines a game faster than loss of audience trust.

Man of Match: M. J. Clarke. *Attendance*: 52,082.

Close of play: First day, New Zealand (1) 7-250 (Oram 63, Vettori 13); Second day, Australia (1) 4-197 (Martyn 59, Clarke 31); Third day, Australia (1) 9-564 (Gillespie 43, McGrath 54).

New Zealand

	R	B	4/6		R	B	4/6
M. H. Richardson c Ponting b Kasprowicz	19	49	1	– c Gilchrist b McGrath	4	7	1
M. S. Sinclair c Ponting b Gillespie	69	163	9	– lbw b McGrath	0	10	0
*S. P. Fleming c Warne b Kasprowicz	0	3		– c Langer b McGrath	11	18	2
S. B. Styris c Gilchrist b Kasprowicz	27	61	4	– lbw b Warne	7	41	1
N. J. Astle run out (Clarke)	19	62	1	– c Warne b Kasprowicz	17	39	2
C. D. McMillan c Gilchrist b Warne	23	56	2 1	– lbw b Gillespie	9	48	1
J. D. P. Oram not out	126	178	12 3	– c Hayden b Warne	8	23	1
†B. B. McCullum st Gilchrist b Warne	10	16	0	– c Gilchrist b Gillespie	8	12	1
D. L. Vettori c Warne b Kasprowicz	21	46	3	– c Hayden b Warne	2	10	0
K. D. Mills c Hayden b Warne	29	66	2 1	– not out	4	7	1
C. S. Martin c Ponting b Warne	0	9	0	– lbw b Warne	0	7	0
B 1, l-b 2, w 3, n-b 4	10			L-b 2, n-b 4	6		

(117.3 overs, 488 mins) 353
Fall: 26 26 77 138 138 180 206 264 317 353

(36.2 overs, 165 mins) 76
Fall: 6 7 19 42 44 55 69 72 72 76

Bowling: *First Innings*—McGrath 27–4–67–0; Gillespie 29–7–84–1; Kasprowicz 28–5–90–4; Warne 29.3–3–97–4; Lehmann 4–0–12–0. *Second Innings*—McGrath 8–1–19–3; Gillespie 10–5–19–2; Kasprowicz 8–2–21–1; Warne 10.2–3–15–4.

Australia

	R	B	4/6		R	B	4/6
J. L. Langer lbw b Vettori	34	72	6	J. N. Gillespie not out	54	155	7
M. L. Hayden lbw b Mills	8	17	2	M. S. Kasprowicz c Mills b Martin	5	21	0
*R. T. Ponting c Astle b Martin	51	84	7	G. D. McGrath c Astle b Martin	61	92	5 1
D. R. Martyn c McMillan b Martin	70	117	8 1				
D. S. Lehmann c McCullum b Vettori	8	11	0	B 1, l-b 7, w 1, n-b 8	17		
M. J. Clarke b Vettori	141	200	21 1				
†A. C. Gilchrist c Styris b Martin	126	151	14 4	(153.5 overs, 641 mins)	585		
S. K. Warne lbw b Vettori	10	11	2	Fall: 16 85 109 128 222 438			
				450 464 471 585			

Bowling: Martin 39.5–7–152–5; Mills 26–8–99–1; Styris 8–1–33–0; Oram 25–4–116–0; Vettori 50–9–154–4; McMillan 5–1–23–0.

Umpires: Aleem Dar (Pakistan) and S. A. Bucknor (West Indies).
TV Umpire: P. D. Parker.
Referee: M. J. Procter (South Africa).

AUSTRALIA v NEW ZEALAND

Second Test Match

by PETER ENGLISH

At Adelaide Oval, Adelaide, November 26, 27, 28, 29, 30, 2004. Australia won by 213 runs. *Toss*: Australia.

Ricky Ponting revealed a ruthless streak that was almost cruel as Australia humiliated opponents they would face again before the end of the summer. With a three-Test away series due in March, the players lined up with Ponting's blessing to knock down the wilting Black Caps, who were still wondering how two days of competition in Brisbane had ended in what Stephen Fleming sensibly called a "hiding".

Once Australia had piled five half-centuries on top of Justin Langer's sweat-filled double-hundred, survival was New Zealand's only hope, but what the 35-degree heat hadn't already drained was soaked up by a brilliant display of team bowling.

Fleming had tried to revive by catching forty winks in the dressing-room before batting. Unfortunately he woke too soon to the nightmare of facing "three Richard Hadlees and the greatest leg-spinner of all". It was surely the highest praise a Black Cap captain could deliver; dismissal was the only relief, and Australia easily lifted the Trans-Tasman Trophy.

The bowling was aggressive and suffocating. Had Ponting chosen to enforce the follow-on when leading by 324, a day-four finish would have replicated the duration of the first Test. However, while Ponting prodded for signs of life and delicately protected his pacemen from overload – Brett Lee could vouch for the plan's season-long success – interest turned instead to the end-of-series foot race between the side's tortoises Darren Lehmann, the local favourite, and Mark Richardson.

Unlike the novelty event, Australia began as the hare after selecting the same XI from Brisbane, while New Zealand installed Paul Wiseman – the off-spinner picked on the tour specifically for this match – for Craig McMillan and replaced Kyle Mills with James Franklin, who had recovered from a groin strain. Langer opened with a boundary off Chris Martin and followed it with four more in the second over from Franklin, a feat he repeated with the next new ball.

Langer, who still looked exhausted three days later, described his third Test double-century as "gritty" – a term he usually despises when pitched anywhere near his batting. The style was reminiscent of his 1990s incarnation: old-fashioned and patient with patches of punch. On a pitch John Bracewell, the New Zealand coach, said was as good as he'd seen, Langer and Matthew Hayden swatted boundaries alongside Adelaide flies while moving past 4,000 runs as an opening combination in their 13th century stand. From there the local scoring became almost a procession.

Damien Martyn and Michael Clarke were the only two of the top eight not to reach fifty. Hayden firmly and incorrectly stood when caught by the bowler Wiseman, leaving the video umpire an easy decision, and Ponting was again in a rush to post his first hundred as captain. His stumping at 68 was his one act of philanthropy to the opposition. Lehmann, narrowly missing a home-ground century at his last opportunity, found another strange way of getting out when bowled by Wiseman off his pads playing outside leg stump, Gilchrist faced some tricky moments and loud appeals from Daniel Vettori before freeing his arms, and Shane Warne hit out as the declaration approached.

The five-wicket performance of Vettori was the peak for the visitors, but his first did not come until Langer, who passed 200 with one of three sixes, departed at 445 after 499 minutes and 25 fours. Franklin struggled with over-pitching and New Zealand suffered from their fast men's inability to prise a wicket from the match. While Vettori and Wiseman were responsible for all of their bowling success, Warne collected three of 20 breakthroughs, although his 550th wicket – Franklin in the first innings – was one of them.

Facing 575, New Zealand's reply was swift and the resistance only cosmetically stronger than the buckling for 76 at the Gabba. Facing an attack that made the pitch appear in new clothes, Fleming's half-century, ended by a cramping Glenn McGrath delivery that kissed his bat's toe, and a partnership of 73 with Nathan Astle showed that achievement was possible with application. However, passing the follow-on target was unlikely once Fleming and Astle left, but Ponting insisted on inflicting more misery, and then ordered some for the crowd with his conservative outlook.

Langer and Hayden showed no urgency before stumps on day three and the sombre march rolled past Monday lunch with Ponting and Martyn in occupation. Crowd calls targeted the batsmen and captain, which was an unusual experience for a home leader, as they crawled towards a confusing declaration that arrived four runs after the break.

Wanting a surprise, Ponting ran to the dressing-room on closing – it was the fastest anyone moved all innings. "We've entertained a lot better than any other side in the history of the game, but with one two-hour period it's all over the papers," Ponting said. "It was deliberate. We wanted to keep them in the field as long as we could so they had no momentum."

Within 21 overs, New Zealand were 4 for 34 and McGrath, Gillespie and Kasprowicz were being compared with Hadlee. Fleming, the only batsman capable of leading any lengthy resistance, had been bowled by his second precise McGrath delivery. The ball, aimed to exploit Fleming's downswing, deceived even McGrath, who appealed for an lbw when the off bail had been tipped. Jacob Oram and the wicket-keeper Brendon McCullum, who assaulted Warne with a flurry of boundaries out of heavy rough, survived until the final day and Vettori's half-century helped push the contest six balls into the second session.

Those who had not exited the Victor Richardson Gates at lunch waited patiently for the lycra-clad bulges of Lehmann and Richardson. Richardson tore the tape but his batting spirit was also broken. On arriving home he waited a week and then retired. With four failures he had suffered as much as anyone in the short series and was content to miss more Australian hidings and humiliation.

Man of Match: J. L. Langer. *Man of Series:* G. D. McGrath. *Attendance:* 60,689.

Close of play: First day, Australia (1) 3-327 (Langer 144, Lehmann 28); Second day, New Zealand (1) 2-56 (Fleming 38, Wiseman 4); Third day, Australia (2) 0-57 (Langer 31, Hayden 21); Fourth day, New Zealand (2) 5-149 (Oram 40, McCullum 34).

Australia

	R	B	4/6		R	B	4/6
J. L. Langer c Oram b Vettori	215	368	25³	lbw b Wiseman	46	111	3
M. L. Hayden c and b Wiseman	70	124	10	– c McCullum b Vettori	54	132	4
*R. T. Ponting st McCullum b Vettori	68	79	11	– not out	26	57	0
D. R. Martyn c Fleming b Wiseman	7	14	1	– not out	6	38	0
D. S. Lehmann b Wiseman	81	172	10				
M. J. Clarke lbw b Vettori	7	16	1				
†A. C. Gilchrist c and b Vettori	50	79	6				
S. K. Warne not out	53	70	3²				
J. N. Gillespie c Richardson b Vettori	12	13	3				
B 4, l-b 4, n-b 4	12			L-b 6, n-b 1	7		

(155.2 overs, 636 mins) (8 wkts dec) 575   (56 overs, 220 mins) (2 wkts dec) 139

Fall: 137 240 261 445 457 465 543 575   Fall: 93 119

M. S. Kasprowicz and G. D. McGrath (did not bat).

Bowling: *First Innings*—Martin 27–4–118–0; Franklin 17–2–102–0; Oram 24–7–55–0; Vettori 55.2–10–152–5; Wiseman 32–7–140–3. *Second Innings*—Martin 6–1–11–0; Oram 5–1–17–0; Franklin 5–0–18–0; Wiseman 22–3–52–1; Vettori 18–2–35–1.

New Zealand

	R	B	4/6		R	B	4/6
M. H. Richardson b Kasprowicz	9	59	0	– c Langer b Kasprowicz	16	63	1
M. S. Sinclair c Warne b Gillespie	0	10	0	– lbw b Gillespie	2	12	0
*S. P. Fleming c Gilchrist b McGrath	83	161	10	– b McGrath	3	13	0
P. J. Wiseman lbw b Kasprowicz	11	33	2	– (10) not out	15	37	2
N. J. Astle c Langer b McGrath	52	86	7	– c Langer b Lehmann	38	71	6
J. D. P. Oram c Gilchrist b Gillespie	12	28	0	– c Gilchrist b McGrath	40	97	3
†B. B. McCullum lbw b Gillespie	10	23	1	– lbw b McGrath	36	53	5 1
D. L. Vettori lbw b McGrath	20	60	1	– c Gillespie b Lehmann	59	78	7
J. E. C. Franklin lbw b Warne	7	32	0	– c Gilchrist b Kasprowicz	13	38	1
S. B. Styris c Clarke b McGrath	28	40	4 1	– (4) c Clarke b Warne	8	34	2
C. S. Martin not out	2	6	0	– c Ponting b Warne	2	4	0
B 3, l-b 5, n-b 9	17			B 1, l-b 12, n-b 5	18		

(88.1 overs, 377 mins)	251	
Fall: 2 44 80 153 178 183 190 213 242 251		

(82.3 overs, 338 mins)	250	
Fall: 11 18 34 34 97 150 160 206 243 250		

Bowling: *First Innings*—McGrath 20.1–3–66–4; Gillespie 19–4–37–3; Warne 28–5–65–1; Kasprowicz 16–3–66–2; Lehmann 5–2–9–0. *Second Innings*—McGrath 12–2–32–2; Gillespie 16–5–41–2; Kasprowicz 14–4–39–2; Warne 27.3–6–79–2; Lehmann 13–0–46–2.

Umpires: S. A. Bucknor (West Indies) and D. R. Shepherd (England).
TV Umpire: S. J. Davis.
Referee: M. J. Procter (South Africa).

†VICTORIA INVITATIONAL XI v NEW ZEALANDERS

At Albert Ground, South Melbourne, December 2, 2004. New Zealanders won by 34 runs. *Toss*: No Toss – NZ to bat first.

New Zealanders

*S. P. Fleming b Hewett	67	(59)	C. Z. Harris not out	5	(5)
N. J. Astle retired	66	(73)	A. R. Adams not out	14	(10)
H. J. H. Marshall c Lindsay b Sandri	13	(19)			
S. B. Styris retired	39	(26)	B 3, l-b 3, w 7, n-b 6	19	
M. S. Sinclair retired	44	(24)			
C. D. McMillan c Cassell b Welsford	8	(17)	(38.3 overs, 172 mins)	243	
C. L. Cairns run out (Crosthwaite)	3	(8)	Fall: 3 8 10 84 84 166 226 229 242 243		

K. D. Mills, I. G. Butler (did not bat).

Victorian Invitation XI

T. H. Welsford c and b Adams	2	(7)	J. J. Taylor c Marshall b Cairns	2	(2)
A. C. Blizzard c Cairns b Butler	43	(47)	C. S. Sandri b Butler	8	(6)
L. G. L. Buchanan b Mills	5	(5)	R. J. Cassell not out	1	(1)
†A. J. Crosthwaite c Styris b Mills	2	(7)			
S. F. Hill run out (Adams/Butler)	21	(30)	B 3, L-b 3, w 7, n-b 6	19	
S. P. Dart c Astle b Mills	26	(44)			
I. S. L. Hewett c Adams b Cairns	82	(52)	(38.3 overs, 167 mins)	243	
G. P. Lindsay c Astle b Butler	32	(35)	Fall: 112 137 161 228 251 256 260		

Bowling: Bowling: *First Innings*—Cassell 5–0–29–0; Hewett 7–0–41–1; Taylor 6–0–56–0; Lindsay 5–0–40–0; Sandri 6–0–42–1; Welsford 4–0–18–1. *Second Innings*—Mills 8–0–57–3; Adams 8–0–44–1; Butler 7.3–1–48–3; Cairns 6–1–20–2; Harris 5–0–36–0; Styris 4–0–32–0.

Umpires: G. T. D. Morrow and J. D. Ward.

CHAPPELL-HADLEE TROPHY

by ROBERT CRADDOCK

When your one-day series is showing signs of decay and disinterest, there is only one sensible course of action – launch a second one. This was the calculated gamble taken by Cricket Australia and it worked quite well.

The VB series – with three teams fighting for two places in the final over an agonisingly long-winded four weeks in January-February – had produced so many lopsided summers that fans were starting to lose interest. Australia responded by downsizing the VB tournament (each team played six instead of eight qualifying games) and introducing the Chappell-Hadlee Trophy early in the summer as a best-of-three tournament between Australia and New Zealand played over six days – this time in Australia in December.

The new tournament needed a strong start and it got one. The first two games were excellent contests in which the ascendancy flashed in both directions and was just what the summer needed after Australia had overwhelmed the Kiwis in the two-Test series.

The use of indoor facilities at Melbourne's Telstra Dome for the first game was deemed a success, although the modest crowd of 30,753 showed that the concept gained only lukewarm public support.

The series finished deadlocked at one game apiece after a week of rain washed out the decider at the Gabba. But even that week had its colourful moments, with feisty New Zealand coach John Bracewell accusing Gabba curator Kevin Mitchell of pitch-doctoring.

In searching for a name for the trophy organisers did not have to look far – the two families are iconic in their homelands, and fitted nicely. Walter Hadlee played 11 Tests (eight as captain) for New Zealand between 1937 and 1951. His sons, Dayle and Richard, played 112 between them and were part of the first New Zealand side to beat Australia at Lancaster Park in 1973-74. Richard became one of the greatest pace bowlers of all time. Greg and Ian Chappell were two of Australia's most successful captains and the fact that younger brother Trevor delivered the famous under-arm ball to the Kiwis in 1981 gave the trophy naming a spicy twist.

"There is a very close bond between Australia and New Zealand," said New Zealand cricket chief executive Martin Snedden. "I am confident the Chappell-Hadlee Trophy will become as eagerly anticipated as other great sporting events such as the Bledisloe Cup (rugby union series). Time will be the judge of that."

†AUSTRALIA v NEW ZEALAND

First Limited-Overs International

At Docklands Stadium, Melbourne, December 5, 2004. Day/night game. New Zealand won by four wickets. *Toss*: New Zealand.

"Is there a mass murderer behind me?" asked Michael Kasprowicz when blinking into a bank of blinding television lights at Brisbane airport the morning after Australia's dramatic loss at cricket's only international indoor venue, Melbourne's Telstra Dome.

Kasprowicz was painted as the villain of the loss after conceding 22 runs off the 48th over of the innings which included one delivery that went for five wides, two fours to Brendon McCullum and one to Hamish Marshall, who shared a daring 39-run stand off 21 balls.

This was New Zealand's only victory against Australia in 12 contests in both forms of the game throughout the summer, but it was one to remember. New Zealand's run-chase stumbled early when the recalled Brett Lee trapped captain Stephen Fleming lbw second ball, but a studied second-wicket stand of 128 between Mathew Sinclair and Nathan Astle gave them the platform for the late charge.

Australia's innings was typical of many throughout the summer – a flying start, a mid-innings wobble and a late surge with Daniel Vettori (3 for 31) the high-quality handbrake that would test Australia's middle order all summer. With Adam Gilchrist (68 from 54 balls) again providing a super-charged start, Australia were eyeing 300-plus early before Sinclair removed Matthew Hayden to one of the best catches of this or any summer – a diving gem on the square-leg boundary.

Man of Match: H. J. H. Marshall. *Attendance*: 30,753.

Australia

†A. C. Gilchrist b Cairns	68	(54)	G. B. Hogg not out 20 (23)
M. L. Hayden c Sinclair b Oram	13	(21)	B. Lee b Cairns 8 (11)
*R. T. Ponting lbw b Vettori	29	(49)	M. S. Kasprowicz not out 9 (9)
D. S. Lehmann c Butler b Oram	50	(73)	
D. R. Martyn lbw b Vettori	1	(4)	B 2, l-b 2, w 2, n-b 3 9
A. Symonds c Mills b Vettori	0	(3)	
M. J. Clarke b Cairns	36	(49)	(50 overs, 222 mins) (9 wkts) 246
S. R. Watson c McCullum b Butler	3	(7)	Fall: 64 113 121 123 123 194 198 220 236

Bowling: Mills 4–0–28–0; Butler 8–0–58–1; Oram 9–0–51–2; Cairns 10–0–39–3; Vettori 10–1–31–3; Styris 9–0–35–0.

New Zealand

*S. P. Fleming lbw b Lee	0	(2)	C. L. Cairns b Lee 14 (11)
N. J. Astle c Ponting b Lehmann	70	(102)	†B. B. McCullum not out 20 (13)
M. S. Sinclair run out			
(Clarke/Symonds)	48	(86)	L-b 9, w 7 16
S. B. Styris c Lee b Lehmann	5	(10)	
H. J. H. Marshall not out	50	(52)	(49.4 overs, 209 mins) (6 wkts) 247
J. D. P. Oram c Gilchrist b Kasprowicz	24	(22)	Fall: 0 128 131 140 189 208

D. L. Vettori, K. D. Mills, I. G. Butler (did not bat).

Bowling: Lee 8–0–40–2; Kasprowicz 9–1–53–1; Watson 8.4–0–42–0; Hogg 7–0–33–0; Lehmann 9–0–35–2; Symonds 8–0–35–0.

Umpires: S. J. Davis and R. E. Koertzen (South Africa).
TV Umpire: R. L. Parry.
Referee: M. J. Procter (South Africa).

†AUSTRALIA v NEW ZEALAND

Second Limited-Overs International

At Sydney Cricket Ground, Sydney, December 8, 2004. Day/night game. Australia won by 17 runs. *Toss*: Australia.

The story was the same as in so many other clashes between the two nations in recent years ... valiant New Zealand mounting a determined thrust, only to have it snuffed out by a side of superior class.

Australia surged out of the barrier with 86 off 12 overs for the first wicket as a hurricane 60 off 48 balls from Adam Gilchrist rattled New Zealand early. A mid-innings stumble left Australia ripe for a king-hit at 6 for 161 but as so often the champions ducked the knock-out punch to post 7 for 261.

No side had chased more and won at the SCG yet New Zealand gave it a dignified shot. At 6 for 86 they seemed gone, but rousing counter-attacks from Chris Cairns, who aised his 50 off 40 balls, and Kyle Mills (44 from 26) silenced Australian chatter in the field with some pure late hitting.

Veteran Chris Harris, in his 250th one-dayer, was notably brave. He had dislocated nis right shoulder while fielding and was sitting in the dressing-room with his arm in a sling when he decided to answer the call of the moment and bat at No. 11. He made four before being bowled by Glenn McGrath.

Scott Styris, who hit a gate after being given out leg-before in a poor decision, and Brendon McCullum, who also showed displeasure after a similar decision, were charged with dissent but later found not guilty by match referee Mike Procter.

Man of Match: G. B. Hogg. *Attendance*: 28,374.

Australia

†A. C. Gilchrist c Astle b Styris	 60	(48)
M. L. Hayden run out (Sinclair)	 43	(65)
*R. T. Ponting c Fleming b Mills	 32	(36)
D. R. Martyn lbw b Mills	 5	(5)
A. Symonds lbw b Vettori	 0	(2)
D. S. Lehmann run out (Styris/Oram)	. 52	(77)
M. J. Clarke c McCullum b Cairns	... 6	(17)

G. B. Hogg not out 41 (53)
B. Lee not out 10 (5)

L-b 2, w 2, n-b 8 12
                                        —
(50 overs, 229 mins)   (7 wkts) 261
Fall: 86 140 147 148 148 161 235

J. N. Gillespie, G. D. McGrath (did not bat).

Bowling: Mills 10–0–49–2; Oram 10–0–77–0; Cairns 10–0–60–1; Styris 10–0–37–1; Vettori 10–1–36–1.

New Zealand

*S. P. Fleming lbw b Hogg	 34	(44)
N. J. Astle c Gilchrist b Lee	 11	(22)
M. S. Sinclair c Hayden b Gillespie	.. 17	(30)
S. B. Styris lbw b Symonds	 5	(6)
H. J. H. Marshall b Lee	 9	(24)
J. D. P. Oram lbw b Hogg	 2	(8)
C. L. Cairns c McGrath b Gillespie	... 50	(40)
†B. B. McCullum lbw b Hogg	 21	(44)

D. L. Vettori run out (Ponting) 33 (36)
K. D. Mills not out 44 (26)
C. Z. Harris b McGrath 4 (6)

L-b 5, w 6, n-b 3 14
                                       —
(47.1 overs, 219 mins)   244
Fall: 27 63 68 78 84 86 154 166 236 244

Bowling: McGrath 7.1–0–27–1; Lee 9–0–48–2; Gillespie 10–1–41–2; Symonds 10–1–47–1; Hogg 8–0–45–3; Lehmann 3–0–31–0.

Umpires: R. E. Koertzen (South Africa) and P. D. Parker.
TV Umpire: S. J. A. Taufel.
Referee: M. J. Procter (South Africa).

†AUSTRALIA v NEW ZEALAND

Third Limited-Overs International

At Brisbane Cricket Ground, Brisbane, December 10, 2004. Day/night game. Abandoned without a ball bowled due to rain. *Man of the Series*: D. L. Vettori.

Umpires: R. E. Koertzen (South Africa) and S. J. A. Taufel.
TV Umpire: R. L. Parry.
Referee: M. J. Procter (South Africa).

Pakistan in Australia, 2004-05

by MALCOLM CONN

Longing rather than anticipation is the motif of the Australian summer now. The longing for a contest that will force one of the greatest cricket teams ever assembled to gird its collective loins and expend every last drop of sweat in pursuit of hard-fought victory.

When Pakistan arrived in Perth as the feature attraction of the season, Australia had not lost a series at home for a dozen years. Many of those triumphs were completed psychologically in just a day or two as the Australians swarmed all over the opposition, breaking their spirit.

But now there was a tingling feeling that maybe, just maybe, this time would be different, for Pakistan had in their ranks the world's fastest bowler, Shoaib Akhtar. With the first Test in Perth on the game's fastest bowler-friendly surface, Australia's batsmen would face a working-over from an era past.

When Allan Border was king, fast bowlers were rampant and batting averages of 50 were rarer than gold. If a batsmen had survived the sustained West Indian battering from Roberts and Holding through to Ambrose and Walsh, Wasim and Waqar from Pakistan and South Africa's young Allan Donald, then they deserved to stand alongside Richard the Lionheart.

Now most bowlers produce fodder and batsmen gorge themselves, averaging 50 as if it were a birthright against attacks which, in some cases, would struggle for respect in Australian state cricket.

So when the Rawalpindi Express, as Shoaib is known, landed in a blaze of publicity – complete with personal manager – and drove his sponsor's sports car to training while the rest of the team walked, here was a mixture of Errol Flynn and Harold Larwood arriving to save Test cricket.

And so it appeared as a punch-drunk Australia staggered to 5 for 78 soon after lunch on the opening day of the first Test at the WACA. Only a dozen minutes into the match Shoaib won the latest bout in the most animated and agitated rivalry between batsman and bowler in the game, trapping Matthew Hayden leg-before for four. In a display of exaggerated theatre, but with no obvious malice, Shoaib waved both index fingers towards the dressing room as if he was a gunslinger.

Remarkably, chief match referee Ranjan Madugalle, a wonderful man and excellent appointment, fined Shoaib 40 per cent of his match fee for the gesture. In a game that is now too often played without character, this was an unnecessary punishment that threatened to further diminish it.

Inevitably, reality took hold of the match and series. Justin Langer and Adam Gilchrist, the bookends of the Australian front-line batting, added 152 at almost a run a ball to change the complexion of the game. Langer went on to savage 191 in front of an adoring home crowd, batting Pakistan out of the game. In less than three days, the longing had turned to the Ashes series more than seven months away.

Pakistan were bowled out for just 72 in their second innings as Australia won by an unthinkable 491 runs, their biggest margin since World War II. Glenn McGrath claimed career-best figures of 8 for 24 to reinforce a most remarkable comeback. He dismissed Inzamam-ul-Haq for a first-ball duck, to follow a single run in the first innings, compounding a back injury that ruled out Inzamam for the remainder of the series.

Already short of experienced batsmen, the loss of Inzamam appeared the final blow for a team with little experience. However, on the flatter pitches in Melbourne and Sydney, Pakistan batted with renewed spirit despite losing both Tests. Stand-in captain Yousuf Youhana played with freedom and enterprise to make an unfettered century in Melbourne as Pakistan scored more than 300 in three of their last four innings in the series.

Younis Khan averaged 43 for the series despite failing to make a hundred, while Salman Butt scored a century in Sydney and averaged 38. For all his great pace, ability and danger, Shoaib was a disappointment who, at 29, found the dual roles of paceman and playboy less compatible than ever.

McGrath has proved that durability is all about fitness, common-sense and a modest run-up. Shoaib has none of these. He appeared to play for his own greater glory, and when things became too tough, simply limped off, leaving a largely young and inexperienced team to fend for itself. There were significant times in all three Tests when Shoaib appeared half-hearted, or did not appear at all. With Shoaib often *hors de combat*, the bowling workload fell on the feisty shoulders of leg-spinner Danish Kaneria, who led Pakistan's wicket-takers with 15 at 37.

Having failed to score a Test or one-day century in 2004, Ricky Ponting produced the most sublime double-hundred in Sydney and Adam Gilchrist exploded with such ferocity that Bill Lawry claimed the wicket-keeper was more potent than Bradman. There were times as Ponting approached this marvellous milestone that it was easy to forget he was batting at all, such was the carnage created by Gilchrist.

Resuming day three on 17, he smashed a further 96 in just 86 balls to complete an innings that included 14 fours and five sixes, becoming the first Test gloveman to make 13 centuries. Ponting, Damien Martyn, Gilchrist and Langer all had extraordinary averages of between 65 and 103 for the series, with Martyn scoring two more centuries in a golden year.

Yet a somewhat embarrassed Stuart MacGill received the final Man of the Match award for an eight-wicket haul after being recalled for the spinning Sydney surface. MacGill and Shane Warne have rarely been successful together but claimed 15 wickets between them, giving MacGill hope for the future.

MAN OF THE MATCH

When Glenn McGrath took the astonishing figures of 8 for 24 against Pakistan in Perth, he still did not win the Man of the Match. How often does this sort of thing happen?

Batsmen are routinely favoured when it comes to MoM gongs, and wicket-keeping, for most, must remain its own reward. Of the last 282 MoM awards, 60% have gone to batsmen and only 32% to bowlers. 8% went to all-rounders or keepers, but these tended to favour batting feats. If a bowler takes the best bowling figures in a match, he only has a 26% chance of the award, whereas scoring the most runs in the match gives you a 47% chance.

In terms of its rarity, McGrath's 8 for 24 is equivalent to a batsman scoring a triple century, taking into account the extremely low cost of the wickets. Yet the award went to Justin Langer, who scored 191 and 97. I'm sure the judge could justify his choice; its just that these justifications too often seem to work in the favour of batsmen, over bowlers and keepers.

Curiously, as performances even out over a full series, bowlers seem to get more reward. They win about 45% of "Man of the Series" awards, a far better return than the 32% figure for "Man of the Match".

That hope was reinforced by the comfortable but unspectacular debut of all-rounder Shane Watson, 23. Watson shapes as a genuine Test batsman, and his lively seamers give Australia the option of playing two spinners, a prospect which has MacGill licking his lips. But in the end the series was won by the old firm, McGrath and Warne, who claimed 32 wickets between them and left Australian cricket fans longing for the next summer.

Pakistan then became part of the Twenty20 phenomenon in a match against Australia A for which 21,254 confused and delighted spectators crammed into the Adelaide Oval. People poured from the city centre after office hours, seemingly drawn by the siren-like wail of pop music blaring from the historic venue and titillated by the notion of backyard tip-and-run being executed by some of the world's best cricketers.

With free hits for no-balls, Australia A opener Brad Haddin made the bizarre attempt to slog Shoaib from behind the stumps from successive infringements, the second of which shattered his stumps to no avail. After the initial madness Australia A scored 185 from their 20 overs while Pakistan collapsed at the start of their run chase and lost by 56 runs. A quick game was no more a good game for Pakistan than the long game had been.

TOURING PARTY

Inzamam-ul-Haq (*captain*), Yousuf Youhana (*vice-captain*), Abdul Razzaq, Shoaib Akhtar, Shahid Afridi, Younis Khan, Mohammad Sami, Shoaib Malik, Danish Kaneria, Yasir Hameed, Imran Farhat, Kamran Akmal, Asim Kamal, Naved-ul-Hasan, Salman Butt, Mohammad Asif and Mohammad Khalil.

Manager: Haroon Rashid; *Coach*: Bob Woolmer; *Video Analyst*: Coertzen Hendrick; *Physiotherapist*: Darryn Lifson; *Biokineticist*: Murray Stevenson; *Masseur*: Abdur Rauf.

PAKISTAN TOUR RESULTS

Test matches – Played 3: Lost 3.

First-class matches – Played 4, Lost 4.

Losses – Australia (3), Western Australia (1).

Limited-over Internationals – Played 8: Won 3, Lost 5. Wins: Australia (1), West Indies (2); *Losses – Australia (4), West Indies (1).*

Other non first-class matches: Played 6: Won 4, Lost 2. Wins – Cricket Australia's Chairman's XI, Western Australia A, Australia A, Prime Minister's XI; *Losses* – Western Australia Second XI, Australia A.

TEST BATTING AVERAGES

	M	I	NO	R	HS	100s	50s	Avge	Ct/St	S-R
D. R. Martyn (Aust) ..	3	4	1	310	142	2	1	103.33	2	60.90
R. T. Ponting (Aust) ..	3	6	2	403	207	1	2	100.75	4	60.78
A. C. Gilchrist (Aust) .	3	4	1	230	113	1	1	76.67	12/2	92.33
J. L. Langer (Aust)	3	6	0	390	191	1	2	65.00	1	70.14
Asim Kamal (Pak) ...	1	2	0	97	87	0	1	48.50	0	56.40
Younis Khan (Pak)	3	6	0	259	87	0	1	43.17	2	50.49
Salman Butt (Pak)	3	6	0	225	108	1	1	37.50	0	56.96
J. N. Gillespie (Aust) .	3	3	1	74	50*	0	1	37.00	3	41.34
Yasir Hameed (Pak) ..	2	4	0	146	63	0	2	36.50	1	63.20
M. L. Hayden (Aust)..	3	6	2	128	56*	0	1	32.00	3	61.24
Yousuf Youhana (Pak)	3	6	0	189	111	1	0	31.50	2	63.00
S. R. Watson (Aust) ..	1	1	0	31	31	0	0	31.00	0	50.00
Shahid Afridi (Pak)...	1	2	0	58	46	0	0	29.00	0	95.08
Shoaib Malik (Pak)...	1	2	0	47	41	0	0	23.50	2	45.63
M. J. Clarke (Aust) ..	3	4	0	83	35	0	0	20.75	3	53.21
Abdul Razzaq (Pak) ..	2	4	1	45	21	0	0	15.00	0	20.55
Mohammad Sami (Pak)	2	4	0	54	29	0	0	13.50	1	27.27
Kamran Akmal (Pak) .	3	6	0	77	47	0	0	12.83	3/4	55.00
S. K. Warne (Aust)	3	3	0	38	16	0	0	12.67	5	55.07
Imran Farhat (Pak) ...	2	4	0	44	20	0	0	11.00	1	34.11
D. S. Lehmann (Aust).	2	3	0	28	12	0	0	9.33	1	93.33
G. D. McGrath (Aust).	3	3	1	18	9	0	0	9.00	2	64.29
Shoaib Akhtar (Pak) ..	3	6	0	42	27	0	0	7.00	2	28.19
Danish Kaneria (Pak) .	3	6	3	18	9*	0	0	6.00	0	51.43
Naved-ul-Hasan (Pak)	1	2	0	9	9	0	0	4.50	0	128.57
M. S. Kasprowicz (Aust)	2	2	0	8	4	0	0	4.00	2	50.00
Mohammad Khalil (Pak)	1	2	0	5	5	0	0	2.50	0	21.74
Inzamam-ul-Haq (Pak)	1	2	0	1	1	0	0	0.50	2	6.67
S. C. G. MacGill (Aust)	1	1	1	9	9*	0	0	–	0	90.00
Mohammad Asif (Pak)	1	2	2	12	12*	0	0	–	1	19.67

* Denotes not out.

TEST BOWLING AVERAGES

	O	Mdns	R	W	BB	5W/i	10W/m	Avge	Balls/W
G. D. McGrath (Aust)..	107	35	260	18	8-24	1	0	14.44	35.67
M. S. Kasprowicz (Aust)	56	17	142	9	5-30	1	0	15.78	37.33
S. C. G. MacGill (Aust)	47	7	170	8	5-87	1	0	21.25	35.25
S. K. Warne (Aust)	124.3	24	402	14	4-111	0	0	28.71	53.36
Shoaib Akhtar (Pak) ...	77.3	8	334	11	5-99	2	0	30.36	42.27
J. N. Gillespie (Aust) ..	91.2	24	258	7	3-77	0	0	36.86	78.29
Danish Kaneria (Pak) ..	149.2	18	560	15	7-188	2	0	37.33	59.73
Abdul Razzaq (Pak) ...	31.3	1	130	3	2-55	0	0	43.33	63.00
Naved-ul-Hasan (Pak)..	29	3	135	3	3-107	0	0	45.00	58.00
Mohammad Sami (Pak)	67.5	6	283	5	3-104	0	0	56.60	81.40
S. R. Watson (Aust) ...	19	5	60	1	1-32	0	0	60.00	114.00
Mohammad Asif (Pak) .	18	3	88	0	–	0	0	–	–
M. J. Clarke (Aust)	3	0	24	0	–	0	0	–	–
R. T. Ponting (Aust) ..	3	1	15	0	–	0	0	–	–
Mohammad Khalil (Pak)	25.2	0	97	0	–	0	0	–	–
Imran Farhat (Pak)	19	2	82	0	–	0	0	–	–
Shahid Afridi (Pak) ...	29	3	115	0	–	0	0	–	–
D. S. Lehmann (Aust)..	6	2	18	0	–	0	0	–	–

Note: Matches in this section that were not first-class are signified by a dagger.

†WESTERN AUSTRALIA SECOND XI v PAKISTANIS

At James Oval, Perth, December 1, 2, 3, 2004. Western Australia Second XI won by 10 runs. *Toss*: Western Australia Second XI.

Western Australia 2nd XI

C. J. Simmons c Kamran Akmal b Mohammad Sami	1	– c Imran b Danish Kaneria	65
S. W. Meuleman c Younis Khan b Mohammad Khalil	32	– lbw b Shoaib Akhtar	16
L. M. Davis b Mohammad Sami	0	– c Kamran b Abdul Razzaq	9
*A. C. Voges c Kamran Akmal b Shoaib Akhtar	1	– b Danish Kaneria	8
S. M. Ervine b Mohammad Sami	1	– c Kamran b Mohammad Khalil	1
†L. Ronchi lbw b Mohammad Asif	66	– c Yousuf b Danish Kaneria	2
P. C. Worthington st Kamran Akmal b Danish Kaneria	9	– c Imran b Danish Kaneria	25
J. P. Coetzee c Yasir Hameed b Mohammad Asif	8	– c Yasir b Danish Kaneria	30
A. K. Heal c Imran Farhat b Mohammad Khalil	14	– st Kamran b Danish Kaneria	20
S. G. Howman b Mohammad Khalil	2	– not out	1
M. J. Petrie not out	7		
J. R. Sprague (did not bat)	–	lbw b Danish Kaneria	0
B 4, l-b 6, n-b 7	17	L-b 8, w 1, n-b 6	15
	158		**192**

(34 overs, 152 mins) 158
Fall: 1 7 17 18 88 116 116 124 151 158

(58 overs, 244 mins) 192
Fall: 19 50 100 105 107 121 166 187 192 192

Bowling: *First Innings*—Shoaib Akhtar 5–0–22–1; Mohammad Sami 8–3–19–3; Mohammad Khalil 8–0–42–3; Mohammad Asif 9–0–52–2; Danish Kaneria 4–2–13–1. *Second Innings*—Shoaib Akhtar 5–3–15–1; Mohammad Sami 9–1–24–0; Mohammad Asif 7–0–31–0; Abdul Razzaq 8–1–38–1; Mohammad Khalil 7–3–13–1; Danish Kaneria 16–2–45–7; Shahid Afridi 6–1–18–0.

Pakistanis

Yasir Hameed c Voges b Petrie	11	– lbw b Coetzee	0
Imran Farhat c Ervine b Coetzee	10	– b Coetzee	0
Younis Khan c Voges b Coetzee	142	– (8) lbw b Sprague	28
*Yousuf Youhana c Davis b Petrie	0	– (3) b Sprague	41
Asim Kamal c Howman b Coetzee	18	– c Ronchi b Petrie	1
Shoaib Malik b Petrie	9	– (11) not out	6
†Kamran Akmal lbw b Petrie	15	– (6) c Ronchi b Coetzee	6
Mohammad Sami c Meuleman b Voges	29	– (10) lbw b Howman	1
Danish Kaneria c Ronchi b Coetzee	7		
Mohammad b Coetzee	4		
Mohammad Khalil not out	3		
Abdul Razzaq (did not bat)	–	– (4) b Coetzee	0
Salman Butt (did not bat)	–	– (7) c Ronchi b Coetzee	0
Shahid Afridi (did not bat)	–	– (9) c (sub) C. J. Heron b Sprague	0
L-b 7, w 2	9		0
	257		**83**

(60.5 overs, 235 mins) 257
Fall: 19 23 33 78 111 147 224 244 248 257

(28 overs, 119 mins) 83
Fall: 0 9 13 18 25 25 62 62 69 83

Shoaib Akhtar (did not bat).

Bowling: *First Innings*—Coetzee 12.5–0–66–5; Petrie 16–1–29–4; Worthington 7–0–40–0; Howman 6–2–16–0; Sprague 8–0–47–0; Heal 7–2–33–0; Voges 3–1–10–1; Meuleman 1–0–9–0. *Second Innings*—Coetzee 8–3–23–5; Petrie 16–1–29–4; Sprague 6–0–24–3; Howman 4–0–21–1.

Umpires: J. Barton and R. R. Pease.

†WESTERN AUSTRALIA A v PAKISTANIS

At James Oval, Perth, December 3, 2004. Pakistanis won by 126 runs. *Toss*: Pakistanis.

Pakistanis

Salman Butt c Ronchi b Sprague	39	(66)	†Kamran Akmal run out 20 (17)	
Imran Farhat run out	31	(24)	Naved-ul-Hasan not out 12 (4)	
Yasir Hameed run out	4	(12)		
Asim Kamal c Heron b Howman ...	0	(3)	L-b 3, w 15, n-b 6 24	
Shoaib Malik c and b Heal	35	(43)		
Abdul Razzaq c Heron b Worthington	55	(74)	(40 overs, 196 mins) (6 wkts) 273	
*Shahid Afridi c Meuleman				
b Worthington	34	(25)	Fall: 46 63 69 92 171 204	

Mohammad Asif, Mohammad Khalil (did not bat).

Bowling: Petrie 5–0–21–0; Coetzee 5–1–25–0; Howman 7–0–41–1; Sprague 7–0–40–1; Heal 8–0–69–1; Worthington 8–0–74–2.

Western Australia A

S. W. Meuleman b Mohammad Khalil	11	(34)	A. K. Heal c Naved-ul-Hasan	
			b Salman Butt 53 (43)	
L. M. Davis lbw b Naved-ul-Hasan ...	5	(11)	S. G. Howman c Imran Farhat	
			b Salman Butt 10 (13)	
C. J. Heron c Mohammad Khalil			M. J. Petrie not out 0 (3)	
b Shoaib Malik	33	(73)		
*A. C. Voges c Kamran Akmal				
b Mohammad Khalil	0	(2)	L-b 3, w 3 6	
A. C. Bandy c Kamran Akmal				
b Abdul Razzaq	5	(17)		
†L. Ronchi c Salman Butt b Asif Kamal	21	(23)	(38.1 overs, 134 mins) 147	
P. C. Worthington run out	2	(6)		
J. P. Coetzee st Kamran Akmal			Fall: 15 17 17 27 58 64 71 130 144 147	
b Shoaib Malik	1	(5)		

J. R. Sprague (did not bat).

Bowling: Mohammad Khalil 6–1–14–2; Naved–ul–Hasan 6–2–8–1; Abdul Razzaq 3–0–6–1; Shahid Afridi 5–0–14–0; Asim Kamal 3–0–19–1; Mohammad Asif 3–0–19–1; Shoaib Malik 8–0–47–2; Imran Farhat 5–0–28–0; Salman Butt 2.1–0–8–2.

Umpires: J. Barton and J. Pease.

†AUSTRALIAN CHAIRMAN'S XI v PAKISTANIS

At Lilac Hill Park, Caversham, December 7, 2004. Pakistanis won by 43 runs. *Toss*: Pakistanis.

Pakistanis

Salman Butt not out	115	(140)	Naved-ul-Hasan c North b Worthington 10 (7)	
Imran Farhat c Thornely b Lawson ...	25	(29)	Mohammad Khalil b Edmondson ... 4 (3)	
Yasir Hameed c Casson b Dodemaide	4	(15)	Danish Kaneria not out 4 (2)	
*Inzamam-ul-Haq b Worthington	16	(19)		
Yousuf Youhana c Rogers b Casson ..	15	(16)	B 2, l-b 4, w 4 10	
Abdul Razzaq c Rogers b Hussey	24	(44)		
Shahid Afridi c Rogers b Hussey	21	(17)	(50 overs, 198 mins) (9 wkts) 256	
†Kamran Akmal b Hussey	8	(8)	Fall: 54 73 99 130 178 205 217 246 252	

Younis Khan (did not bat).

Bowling: Lawson 6–0–31–1; Edmondson 8–0–47–1; Worthington 9–0–46–2; Dodemaide 5–0–25–1; Casson 8–1–42–1; Thornely 10–1–31–0; Hussey 4–0–28–3.

Australian Cricket Board's Chairman's XI

*J. L. Langer c Inzamam-ul-Haq			B. Casson lbw b Naved-ul-Hasan	0	(1)
b Mohammad Khalil	1	(7)	B. M. Edmondson not out	1	(15)
M. J. North run out	26	(34)			
C. J. L. Rogers c Imran Farhat			A. I. C. Dodemaide c Khalil b Kaneria	1	(8)
b Shahid Afridi	61	(59)			
M. E. K. Hussey c Imran Farhat					
b Shahid Afridi	8	(15)			
D. J. Thornely run out	38	(72)	L-b 10, w 4, n-b 1	15	
M. W. Goodwin c Yousuf Youhana					
b Danish Kaneria	8	(10)			
†L. Ronchi b Naved-ul-Hasan	51	(43)	(45.2 overs, 179 mins)	213	
P. C. Worthington b Naved-ul-Hasan	3	(9)	Fall: 6 45 77 117 133 203 207 207 210 213		

G. F. Lawson (did not bat).

Bowling: Naved–ul-Hasan 10–1–36–3; Mohammad Khalil 7–0–33–1; Abdul Razzaq 10–0–45–0; Shahid Afridi 10–0–49–2; Danish Kaneria 8.2–1–40–2.

Umpires: B. Bennett and I. H. Lock.

WESTERN AUSTRALIA v PAKISTANIS

At WACA Ground, Perth, December 9, 10, 11, 2004. Western Australia won by ten wickets. *Toss*: Pakistanis. Attendance: 3,184.

Close of play: First day, Western Australia (1) 1-20 (Hussey 8, Rogers 6); Second day, Pakistanis (2) 0-4 (Salman Butt 3, Imran Farhat 0).

Pakistanis

Salman Butt c Hussey b Edmondson	42	– c Campbell b Magoffin	47		
Imran Farhat lbw b Dorey	8	– c Goodwin b Dorey	5		
Younis Khan c Goodwin b Dorey	4	– c Goodwin b Edmondson	0		
*Inzamam-ul-Haq b Dorey	4	– c Marsh b Edmondson	14		
Yousuf Youhana c Rogers b Magoffin	77	– c Campbell b Edmondson	32		
Shoaib Malik c Campbell b Edmondson	0	– lbw b Magoffin	20		
Abdul Razzaq not out	83	– not out	35		
†Kamran Akmal c Hussey b Magoffin	0	– c Langer b Dorey	4		
Mohammad Sami c Marsh b Hussey	21	– b Dorey	0		
Shoaib Akhtar c and b Casson	9	– c Langer b Dorey	0		
Danish Kaneria b Casson	0	– b Dorey	10		
B 9, l-b 2, w 1, n-b 2	14	B 1, l-b 5, w 1	7		

(82.1 overs, 352 mins)	262	(54.2 overs, 235 mins)	174
Fall: 19 45 55 78 78 173 173 245 260 262		Fall: 18 31 45 88 117 125 138	
		140 144 174	

Bowling: *First Innings*—Magoffin 16–3–68–2; Dorey 16–4–38–3; Edmondson 17–4–71–2; Hussey 15–8–30–1; Casson 18.1–6–44–2. *Second Innings*—Edmondson 12–2–38–3; Dorey 19.2–5–41–5; Magoffin 16–3–52–2; Casson 7–0–37–0.

Western Australia

*J. L. Langer lbw b Shoaib Akhtar	4	– not out	14
M. E. K. Hussey c Yousuf Youhana			
b Shoaib Akhtar	124	– not out	6
C. J. L. Rogers c Kamran Akmal b Danish Kaneria	46		
M. W. Goodwin c Mohammad Sami b Abdul Razzaq	1		
M. J. North c Kamran Akmal b Mohammad Sami	79		
S. E. Marsh lbw b Imran Farhat	39		
†R. J. Campbell c Younis Khan b Danish Kaneria	49		
B. Casson lbw b Danish Kaneria	0		
B. R. Dorey st Kamran Akmal b Imran Farhat	21		
S. J. Magoffin not out	14		
B. M. Edmondson not out	3		
L-b 5, w 2, n-b 17	24	L-b 2, W 5, n-b 7	14

(92 overs, 385 mins)   (9 wkts dec) 404   (4.5 overs, 24 mins)   (0 wkt) 34

Fall: 4 83 84 250 297 349 350 381 385

Bowling: *First Innings*—Shoaib Akhtar 17–5–41–2; Mohammad Sami 19–3–104–1; Abdul Razzaq 13–2–76–1; Danish Kaneria 34–2–133–3; Shoaib Malik 1–0–15–0; Imran Farhat 8–1–30–2. *Second Innings*—Mohammad Sami 2.5–0–21–0; Abdul Razzaq 2–0–11–0.

Umpires: J. K. Brookes and A. R. Craig.

AUSTRALIA v PAKISTAN

First Test Match

by CHLOE SALTAU

At WACA Ground, Perth, December 16, 17, 18, 19, 2004. Australia won by 491 runs. *Toss*: Pakistan. *Test debut*: Mohammad Khalil.

The Perth Test, more than any other, inspires a preoccupation with pace, so it was not surprising to see the faces of Shoaib Akhtar and Brett Lee, sweaty and straining with effort, all over the glossy promotional material. It was as much as anyone would see of Lee, save for his drink-delivering cameos, for the Australian selectors sagely stuck with the proven combination of Glenn McGrath, Jason Gillespie and Michael Kasprowicz on this WACA strip made in fast bowling heaven.

The premonition that pace and bounce would play their part in the opening Test was not false, for Pakistan failed dismally to acclimatise and were bowled out in the second innings for a shambolic 72, their fourth-lowest Test total. McGrath had his biggest day out in 104 Tests and the second-biggest day out by an Australian bowler ever, tormenting Pakistan to take 8 for 24.

This was despite Pakistan's decision to arrive in Perth almost three weeks early so that coach Bob Woolmer might re-program his batsmen's minds and techniques.

India had been spared the nerve-jangling WACA conditions, so foreign to sub-continental tourists, in the wonderfully competitive series a year earlier; but Pakistan was offered no such respite.

Before the Test, the captains cut contrasting figures. Ricky Ponting spoke frankly and excitedly of how Pakistan batsmen had snicked and been caught behind the wicket 16 times against Western Australia. It was an ominous sign. Inzamam, already labouring with a back and stomach complaint that would sabotage his series, could not have looked less animated as he sighed and expressed faith in the talent and work ethic of his inexperienced batsmen.

By the end, Test cricket seemed horribly out of joint. Even Ponting, whose Australians rejoice in any victory, expressed concern that the world's fourth-ranked Test nation had succumbed so easily, only a few weeks after Australia's two-Test mauling of New Zealand.

Shoaib started with 5 for 99 in 22 overs and a fine for his exuberant, two-handed send-off of Matthew Hayden, but his 33-metre run-up, which left the Rawalpindi Express huffing and puffing from the exertion of only four or five overs, was the subject of intense scrutiny, along with his rock star-like behaviour. The English Woolmer, still relatively new in the job, was the target of some xenophobic mutterings at home, and after the Test effigies of him and Inzamam were torched on the streets of Karachi.

Perhaps the reaction would not have been so violent had Australia not conjured their victory – the fourth biggest by any team in terms of runs – from the uncertain position of 5 for 78 just after lunch on the first day. Shoaib and Mohammad Sami, the world's fastest and most flamboyant bowling partnership, destroyed the Australian top order, and if Shoaib could have mustered another withering wicket-taking spell soon after lunch, the Australian tail might have been bared sooner and the day might have finished on an entirely different note.

Instead, Shoaib faded and Adam Gilchrist, dasher of many an opposition dream, joined Justin Langer to dig Australia out of trouble. By the time Gilchrist was bowled by Abdul Razzaq for a breezy 69, Australia were 6 for 230.

At stumps, Langer was unbeaten on 181, having stood his ground and worn Shoaib's blows for one of the sweetest and most satisfying of his 21 Test centuries, and Australia were 8 for 357. With Pakistan's recent batting fragility in mind, it was a position of considerable strength.

Among the pugilistic Australians, none spoils for a fight more than Langer. Strong of mind and seemingly indestructible in the body after years of martial arts training, his battles with Shoaib provided absorbing theatre that was played out before the Test and in the middle, too. Langer said Shoaib had a way of infiltrating his dreams. Shoaib said Langer was the one he wanted most, more even than Hayden, who only 14 months earlier at the same ground had seemed unconquerable as he crashed through the world record.

Now the powerful Queenslander was heavy-footed and out of sorts, and his cheap dismissals in Perth turned out to be a harbinger of a horrible summer. While Shoaib had Hayden's measure, and began the series full of fire, he couldn't overcome the combative Langer. When the ball was veering in at his pads the Western Australian stood his ground, but his 280-ball innings expanded with brutally struck drives and neatly swivelled pulls.

The total of 381 might have masked a couple of worrying signs in Australia's batting – for example, Darren Lehmann's casual way of wandering across his crease to Shoaib strengthened calls for the veteran left-hander's axing – but it looked all the more imposing compared with Pakistan's 179 in response.

The imbalance would have been much worse if Shoaib and Sami had not shamed their top order colleagues with a resilient partnership of 60. Kasprowicz's 5 for 30, including the crucial wickets of Inzamam and Yousuf Youhana, vindicated his selection ahead of Lee and drove the speedier New South Welshman deeper into the international wilderness.

Ponting curiously bowled himself and Lehmann late in the Pakistan innings as if to preserve his fast bowlers, but did not enforce the follow-on, and Australia proceeded to bat Pakistan out of the match. The captain, although scratchy at first, built a mature innings, the highlight of which was a superb, straight-drive off the kind of ball that had bowled him in the first innings. He was denied his first century since taking over as skipper from Steve Waugh by a crafty piece of leg-spin bowling from the impressive Danish Kaneria and a deft stumping by Kamran Akmal.

Langer, who effortlessly took up where he left off in the first innings, fell three runs short of another ton, too, but Damien Martyn – smooth and stylish as always – cruised to an unbeaten 100, a milestone that triggered Ponting's declaration at 5 for 361.

Without Shoaib, whose fitness is always a point of intrigue and who managed only 6.3 overs in the second innings because of an injured shoulder, Pakistan's lack of bowling depth was obvious.

Pakistan resumed at 1 for 18 on the fourth morning. The target of 564 was impossible, but even the critics gathering to condemn Pakistan could not have imagined the extent of the disaster. It was written all over Inzamam's face as he made perhaps history's slowest and most sullen journey back to the dressing-room after edging McGrath and being caught behind for a golden duck. Only a few months earlier McGrath looked to be in his twilight years as he battled to return from ankle surgery, but as he sensed the cluelessness of the Pakistan batsmen and preyed on it mercilessly. It became clear the champion Australian would enjoy more days in the sun.

He bowled in the feared McGrath zone – about 130 kph, around the top of off-stump with an awkward bounce that proved unfathomable to the batsmen – and only one of his eight victims was caught in front of the wicket. Among Australians, only leg-spinner Arthur Mailey has performed better, with 9 for 121 against England 84 years earlier.

The relentless Kasprowicz chimed in and spoiled McGrath's chances of a perfect 10. "At seven-for, I was looking up, thinking, 'This might be my best chance for a 10-for'. But Kasper came in and ruined it," he said, with a glimmer of a smile.

It was that distinctly Australian certitude, that ability to look 5 for 78 in the eye and win by 491 runs, that later had Woolmer calling for psychological help for his players. The loss of 9 for 54 in 25.4 overs on the fourth morning suggested wounded minds, and the desperate situation from which the Pakistanis would need to resurrect themselves to be competitive in the remaining two Tests.

Man of Match: J. L. Langer. *Attendance*: 42,193.

Close of play: First day, Australia (1) 8-357 (Langer 181, Kasprowicz 4); Second day, Australia (2) 0-15 (Langer 3, Hayden 7); Third day, Pakistan (2) 1-18 (Salmat Butt 8, Younis Khan 7).

Australia

	R	B	4/6		R	B	4/6
J. L. Langer c Younis Khan b Mohammad Sami	191	280	19 3	– b Abdul Razzaq	97	145	14
M. L. Hayden lbw b Shoaib Akhtar	4	5	1	– b Shoaib Akhtar	10	25	1
*R. T. Ponting b Mohammad Sami	25	54	2	– st Kamran b Danish Kaneria	98	176	13
D. R. Martyn c Kamran Akmal b Mohammad Sami	1	9	0	– not out	100	121	11
D. S. Lehmann b Shoaib Akhtar	12	8	2	– b Danish Kaneria	5	10	1
M. J. Clarke c Inzamam-ul-Haq b Shoaib Akhtar	1	11	0	– c Inzamam-ul-Haq b Mohammad Sami	27	42	1 1
†A. C. Gilchrist b Abdul Razzaq	69	78	10	– not out	0	0	0
S. K. Warne c Yousof Youhana b Abdul Razzaq	12	26	1				
J. N. Gillespie c Kamran Akmal b Shoaib Akhtar	24	69	3				
M. S. Kasprowicz lbw b Shoaib Akhtar	4	6	1				
G. D. McGrath not out	8	9	1				
B 1, l-b 14, w 5, n-b 10	30			L-b 15, w 2, n-b 7	24		

(90.5 overs, 413 mins) 381 (85.2 overs, 344 mins) (5 wkts dec) 361
Fall: 6 56 58 71 78 230 253 333 362 381 Fall: 28 191 271 281 360

Bowling: *First Innings*—Shoaib Akhtar 22–1–99–5; Mohammad Sami 25.5–3–104–3; Mohammad Khalil 16–0–59–0; Abdul Razzaq 12–0–55–2; Danish Kaneria 15–2–49–0. *Second Innings*—Shoaib Akhtar 6.3–1–22–1; Mohammad Sami 14–1–55–1; Abdul Razzaq 12.3–1–48–1; Mohammad Khalil 9.2–0–38–0; Danish Kaneria 32–3–130–2; Imran Farhat 11–0–53–0.

Pakistan

	R	B	4/6		R	R	4/6
Salman Butt c Gilchrist b Kasprowicz ..	17	55	2	– c Hayden b McGrath	9	25	1
Imran Farhat c Gilchrist b Gillespie	18	26	4	– lbw b McGrath	1	11	0
Younis Khan c Gillespie b Warne	42	99	5	– c Warne b McGrath	17	33	2
*Inzamam-ul-Haq b Kasprowicz	1	14	0	– (6) c Gilchrist b McGrath ..	0	1	0
Yousuf Youhana c Gilchrist							
b Kasprowicz	1	7	0	– (4) c Gilchrist b McGrath ..	27	31	5
Abdul Razzaq b Warne	21	55	3	– (5) c Gilchrist b McGrath ..	1	14	0
†Kamran Akmal b Kasprowicz	2	15	0	– c Clarke b McGrath	0	13	0
Mohammad Sami c Clarke							
b Kasprowicz	29	94	3 1	– b Kasprowicz	2	19	0
Mohammad Khalil b Warne	0	4	0	– (10) c and b Kasprowicz ...	5	19	1
Shoaib Akhtar c Warne b McGrath ...	27	97	3	– (9) c Lehmann b McGrath .	1	21	0
Danish Kaneria not out	6	3	1	– not out	0	2	0
B 1, l-b 3, w 7, n-b 4	15			L-b 7, W 2	9		

(77.3 overs, 314 mins)   179
Fall: 32 45 55 60 108 110 110 111 171 179

(31.3 overs, 145 mins)   72
Fall: 5 34 43 49 49 61 64 66 72 72

Bowling: *First Innings*—McGrath 19–7–44–1; Gillespie 14–2–43–1; Kasprowicz 16.3–6–30–5; Warne 21–9–38–3; Lehmann 4–2–5–0; Ponting 3–1–15–0. *Second Innings*—McGrath 16–8–24–8; Gillespie 12–3–37–0; Kasprowicz 3.3–2–4–2.

Umpires: B. F. Bowden (New Zealand) and R. E. Koertzen (South Africa).
TV Umpire: S. J. Davis.
Referee: R. S. Madugalle (Sri Lanka).

AUSTRALIA v PAKISTAN

Second Test Match

by RON REED

At Melbourne Cricket Ground, Melbourne, December 26, 27, 28, 29, 2004. Australia won by nine wickets. *Toss*: Pakistan.

Pakistan entered the showpiece Boxing Day Test in undignified, desperate circumstances. At home, angry fans had burned effigies of coach Bob Woolmer, captain Inzamam-ul-Haq and vice-captain Yousuf Youhana in response to the humiliating First Test thrashing, and then big Inzy reported an unfit with a back strain.

To literally add insult to injury, former Australian skipper Steve Waugh, noting that Australia's durable opener Justin Langer had pushed through the pain barrier to take his place despite a similar complaint, suggested that the Pakistanis simply lacked ticker.

By the time the match ended a day early – as usual – with the Australians comfortably triumphant again, current captain Ricky Ponting was dishing out another serve that was just as scathing, but for different reasons.

At least, though, the tourists began as if they meant business, and Inzamam's deputy led the way. Youhana won the toss and took first use of the dry, flat drop-in pitch, which was surrounded by a surprisingly firm greensward relaid only a few days earlier as part of the stadium's redevelopment. Reverting to their more aggressive instincts, the Pakistanis made a fine start with Salman Butt and Imran Farhat putting on 85 for the first wicket and Younis Khan and Youhana adding 192 for the fourth as they finished the first day at a much more resolute 6 for 318.

The 20-year-old Butt survived a chance to the usually reliable Matthew Hayden in the gully in the first over and then hit 10 boundaries before running himself out for a brisk 70. Younis went hard, too, hitting 11 fours in 87 off 157 balls, but Youhana's classy 111 – his 12th century – best exemplified the Pakistanis' determination to take the fight to the Australians. He imparted a rare thrashing to Shane Warne in front of the leg-spinner's home crowd, three times driving him for six. But Warne laughed last, as he so often does. Before the match, he had astutely observed that his remarkable strike-rate against Pakistan was because "they either block you or hit you for six ... there's no in-between".

Sure enough, Youhana was eventually stumped while dancing down in search of another boundary, having already hit four sixes and 11 fours in a 134-ball stay. It gave Warne an unflattering 1 for 100 on the day, but he was far from finished. Youhana said he was unworried about the effigies protest. "It is part of the country," he said. "Our people love cricket and love us as well. We put in a lot of work trying to be more positive and thank God we did it."

Still, the old Pakistan was never far away. The promising start evaporated when late on day one and early the next day they crashed from 3 for 298 to 341 all out, with Glenn McGrath (3 for 77) and Warne (3 for 103) responsible for most of the damage.

However, the visitors had their most explosive shot still to fire. Having been virtually accused by McGrath of being a showpony more interested in bowling fast than well, maverick express bowler Shoaib Akhtar had plenty to prove and duly unleashed a thunderous spell of what Langer described as the fastest bowling he had seen. Operating off his controversially long run-up – which he refused to shorten despite risking his captains being suspended for time-wasting – Shoaib whipped out key rival Hayden (9) for the third time in as many innings and then Darren Lehmann (11) before engaging Langer in a gladiatorial struggle that took the contest to another, rarely seen level.

Langer was struck several painful blows on the fingers but he responded with plenty of verbal by-play. It looked ugly at times but both enjoyed the intensity of the challenge. "It was like two warriors going at each other," said the in-form Langer, who reached an even 50. "He was going at 150 kph and trying to rip the fingers off my hands. It gets your blood going. It is one of the great battles, playing against Shoaib."

Australia were 5 for 203 overnight and the contest was still finely balanced. Damien Martyn (142), Adam Gilchrist (48) and Jason Gillespie (50 not out) – his second Test half-century, both made this summer – stretched the total to 379, a lead of only 38.

But for Pakistan, the cracks were widening. They began the day with a double shock. All-rounder Abdul Razzaq was taken to hospital before play, suffering from a blood pressure problem, leaving the team a bowler short. Then news arrived that all-rounder Shoaib Malik had been adjudged a chucker by Western Australian boffins. Malik was playing as a batsman, but the timing of the announcement was awkward and insensitive.

As rain held up play for 90 minutes, it was shaping as another day in hell for the tourists and Martyn took full advantage to post his sixth ton of the year. Both Shoaib and promising leg-spinner Danish Kaneria took five wickets, the latter from a marathon 39.3 overs.

When Butt fell to McGrath off the fourth ball of the second innings, it was easy to sense that the Pakistani resistance was about to crumble – and at 5 for 85 at stumps, it had. On the fourth morning, the old firm of McGrath (4 for 35) and Warne (3 for 66) dismantled what little was left, leaving Australia a modest victory chase. Ponting smashed Kaneria over his head for six to complete the victory, and then blasted the Pakistani pacemen, especially Shoaib, for not trying hard enough.

The flamboyant paceman delivered his final spell off a run slashed in half and at greatly reduced pace, while Mohammad Sami also bowled tamely, although it was revealed that he was carrying a heel injury.

"I would have been very disappointed if that had been my bowlers running in and bowling like that," Ponting said. Martyn was man of the match, but McGrath, with five wickets, and Warne six, were also hailed as match-winners – again.

Man of Match: D. R. Martyn. *Attendance*: 129,079.
Close of play: First day, Pakistan (1) 6-318 (Abdul Razzaq 1, Kamran Akmal 16); Second day, Australia (1) 5-203 (Martyn 67, Gilchrist 26); Third day, Pakistan (2) 5-85 (Shoaib Malik 11, Mohammad Sami 8).

Pakistan

	R	B	4/6		R	B	4/6
Salman Butt run out (Clarke/Gilchrist) .	70	99	10	– c Kasprowicz b McGrath ..	0	4	0
Imran Farhat c Ponting b Kasprowicz ..	20	76	1	– c Martyn b Gillespie	5	16	0
Yasir Hameed lbw b Gillespie	2	12	0	– c Gilchrist b McGrath ...	23	43	4
Younis Khan c Gilchrist b Gillespie	87	157	11	– c Hayden b Kasprowicz ...	23	55	2
*Yousuf Youhana st Gilchrist b Warne .	111	134	11 4	– c Ponting b Warne	12	28	1
Shoaib Malik c Ponting b Gillespie ...	6	14	0	– c Gillespie b Warne	41	89	4 2
Abdul Razzaq not out	4	76	0	– (8) c Gilchrist b McGrath ...	19	74	1 1
†Kamran Akmal c Gilchrist b McGrath .	24	33	4	– (9) lbw b Warne	0	3	0
Mohammad Sami lbw b Warne	12	37	1	– (7) lbw b Gillespie	11	48	1
Shoaib Akhtar st Gilchrist b Warne ...	0	4	0	– b McGrath	14	18	0 2
Danish Kaneria run out (Clarke/Gilchrist)	0	3	0	– not out	9	10	2
L-b 4, w 1	5			B 4, l-b 1, n-b 1	6		

(107.3 overs, 454 mins)   341   (64.2 overs, 268 mins)   163
Fall: 85 93 94 286 298 301 326 341 341 341   Fall: 0 13 35 60 68 98 101 140 140 163

Bowling: *First Innings*—McGrath 28–12–54–1; Gillespie 26–7–77–3; Kasprowicz 20–6–66–1; Warne 28.3–2–103–3; Clarke 3–0–24–0; Lehmann 2–0–13–0. *Second Innings*—McGrath 11.2–1–35–4; Gillespie 12–7–15–2; Kasprowicz 16–3–42–1; Warne 25–7–66–3.

Australia

	R	B	4/6		R	B	4/6
J. L. Langer c Imran Farhat				– c Kamran Akmal			
b Danish Kaneria	50	82	3 1	b Mohammad Sami ..	5	3	1
M. L. Hayden c Shoaib Malik							
b Shoaib Akhtar	9	20	1	– not out	56	75	6
*R. T. Ponting c Shoaib Malik							
b Shoaib Akhtar	7	9	1	– not out	62	91	5 1
D. R. Martyn lbw b Danish Kaneria	142	245	12				
D. S. Lehmann c Yasir Hameed							
b Shoaib Akhtar	11	12	2				
M. J. Clarke c Shoaib Akhtar							
b Danish Kaneria	20	53	1 1				
†A. C. Gilchrist c M. Sami							
b Danish Kaneria	48	51	4 1				
S. K. Warne c and b Shoaib Akhtar ...	10	17	1				
J. N. Gillespie not out	50	108	4 1				
M. S. Kasprowicz c (sub) Naved							
b Shoaib Akhtar	4	10	0				
G. D. McGrath lbw b Danish Kaneria ..	1	8	0				
B 1, l-b 2, w 5, n-b 19	27			L-b 2, n-b 2	4		

(99.3 overs, 454 mins)   379   (27.5 overs, 110 mins) (1 wkt) 127
Fall: 13 32 122 135 171 230 254 347 368 379   Fall: 11

Bowling: *First Innings*—Shoaib Akhtar 27–4–109–5; Mohammad Sami 23–2–102–0; Abdul Razzaq 7–0–27–0; Danish Kaneria 39.3–5–125–5; Imran Farhat 3–0–13–0. *Second Innings*—Shoaib Akhtar 7–0–35–0; Mohammad Sami 5–0–22–1; Danish Kaneria 10.5–1–52–0; Imran Farhat 5–2–16–0.

Umpires: R. E. Koertzen (South Africa) and J. W. Lloyds (England).
TV Umpire: R. L. Parry.
Referee: R. S. Madugalle (Sri Lanka).

AUSTRALIA v PAKISTAN

Third Test Match

by DAVID FRITH

At Sydney Cricket Ground, Sydney, January 2, 3, 4, 5, 2005. Australia won by nine wickets. *Toss*: Pakistan. *Test debut*: Mohammad Asif, S. R. Watson.

Only for the first three-and-a-half days was Australia's natural superiority obscured. Thereafter the anticipated 3–0 series clean sweep was engineered with professional efficiency and a day to spare.

Conscious of the "dead-rubber syndrome" which had let opponents through Australia's defences several times in recent years after series had been secured, Australia might have felt for a time that it was written in the stars yet again when Yasir Hameed, at the start, gave simple catches to Shane Warne and Adam Gilchrist off consecutive balls from Jason Gillespie, and both were spilt. Shane Watson's Test bowling was launched with a follow-through that catapulted him onto his backside, and Hameed was soon hooking him for six. Poor Pakistan's time had come at last, it seemed.

After a healthy lunchtime score of 0 for 91, it was bewildering to see Glenn McGrath put down a catch off the same batsman at long-off, with Warne the suffering bowler. But, with the century posted, the first breach came as Hameed top-edged a sweep, and just before tea Younis Khan scooped Stuart MacGill's first ball to mid-off. Yousuf Youhana, again standing in as captain for the indisposed Inzamam-ul-Haq, edged the same bowler to slip after the interval, and the slide had begun.

All this time, Salman Butt, the left-hander from Lahore playing in his fourth Test, batted calmly, ever ready to play shots, his well-oiled wristwork the eye-catching feature. His maiden Test century came with a pull-stroke off Warne. McGrath dived for the catch in the deep but grassed it – the 14th drop in the series by Australia.

Butt kissed the pitch in celebration, but was gone soon afterwards, and this precipitated a dismal slide by Pakistan to 304 just when a challenging total seemed imminent. McGrath and MacGill rounded up the rest, only wicket-keeper Kamran Akmal of the recognised batsmen resisting to the second day after an early stoppage for poor light. Wasteful as any was the impulsive Shahid Afridi: a six over cover off McGrath opened his score but he soon clubbed a full-toss for a catch in front of the Ladies Stand. At No. 11, debutant Mohammad Asif's stout 0 not out lasted 41 minutes, shaming some of his betters.

All eyes had been on the comparative performances of MacGill and his senior leg-spinning colleague, world record-holder Warne. It was the ninth time they had played together in a Test, and not for the first time the understudy had taken the honours.

Two big partnerships gave Australia control. Rana Naved-ul-Hasan, one of four changes from the Melbourne Test, pierced Justin Langer's defence with an inswinger, and Matthew Hayden's slog at Danish Kaneria ended an unimpressive hour-and-a-half during which the mountainous Queenslander survived two chances off Mohammad Asif.

Now, though, came the performance the nation had anxiously awaited for a year: not from Damien Martyn, who had been a model of consistency and achievement in that time, but from Ricky Ponting, who was playing his 19th innings since succeeding Steve Waugh as Australia's captain, never in that time having quite made it to three figures. A display of more polished batsmanship at both ends could seldom have been witnessed in Test history. Martyn's precise cutting and Ponting's great range of strokes, especially the on-drive, had the crowd purring with satisfaction.

Shoaib Akhtar, bowling off 22 strides, later left the field with an unspecified strain, and the bulk of the work was undertaken by Kaneria, the tall, aggressive 24-year-old leg-spinner, who later bagged his 100th wicket in this his 23rd Test.

Indeed, the match produced a feast of leg-spin, the 178 overs delivered by Warne, MacGill, Kaneria and Afridi bringing to a modern audience a taste of what it was like when the maestros Bill O'Reilly and Clarrie Grimmett plied their trade for hours on end in the 1930s.

The Ponting-Martyn stand of 174 ended with Martyn's stumping, the first of three in succession, all off the tireless Kaneria. Michael Clarke joyously went for his shots, one going over the fence, before he too advanced and missed. The bowler lost his match fee for delivering a farewell expletive.

By now, Ponting had sealed his first century as captain, for which he had hungered. It was his 21st in Tests, and Adam Gilchrist signed in with a six before stumps were drawn. It was the keeper-batsman's 65th consecutive Test since debut, surpassing Ian Healy's record.

Rain delayed resumption on the third day, but from the start Gilchrist's biffing and clubbing rendered Ponting's role as an almost unseen accomplice. The new ball was soon made old, and the manner in which Gilchrist completed his century – his 13th, surpassing Andy Flower's record for a Test wicket-keeper – was simply staggering. Off Asif he smashed balls for six to midwicket, six wide of long-on, and four just short of the rope at long-on to reach 98. Off Afridi he launched another straightish six to register his hundred, and another one two balls later. Gilchrist's century came off 109 balls in 129 minutes, with 14 fours and four sixes, his second 50 coming off 21 balls. What need was there for Twenty20 cricket?

When Gilchrist became the third consecutive stumping, 86 of his 113 runs had come in boundaries, and this second large stand of the innings, 153, had taken only 139 minutes. In came Watson, on debut, to make a competent 31, and the sturdy young Queenslander was soon witness to his captain's double-hundred, Ponting's fourth, placing him alongside Greg Chappell behind Don Bradman's distant 12.

Soon after a seemingly straightforward caught-and-bowled given by Watson to Kaneria was turned down after referral, Ponting's classic five-hour innings ended with an inside edge into the stumps. The innings subsided, Kaneria coming away with a valiant 7 for 188 off 49.3 overs, Australia with a daunting lead of 264. There was some bold strokeplay that evening from the Pakistan openers, until Butt edged MacGill's first ball into Warne's sure hands. Play went on under lights until 6.35 p.m., and although only 62.1 overs had been bowled on this third day, it was unquestionably one to remember for all present or viewing at home.

Hameed continued to catch the eye, and reached a businesslike half-century off only 55 balls. Several others got started but found ways to get out: Youhana bowled round his legs as he attempted to sweep, Younis Khan leg-before to give an ecstatic Watson his first Test wicket, Afridi wastefully run out by a direct hit after making 46 at close to a run a ball.

The diminutive Asim Kamal, who had made 99 on his Test debut, again fought hard, displaying a range of strokes and reaching 87 in three hours. But yet again it was a countdown. Warne profited among the lower order, until No. 11 Asif again dug in alongside Asim, extending proceedings beyond tea and, after a stand of 55, setting Australia a teasing 62 for victory.

The disappointing Shoaib did not take the field, and in the final act it was left to the defiant Kaneria to bowl Langer behind his pads before Ponting had the pleasure of creaming his first ball through mid-on for the winning runs. There was quite sufficient about this match to save it from being classified as just another Test.

During the four days a creditable $204,789 was donated by SCG spectators to the tsunami disaster relief fund.

Man of Match: S. C. G. MacGill. *Man of the Series*: D. R. Martyn. *Attendance*: 105,417.

Close of play: First day, Pakistan (1) 9-292 (Kamran Akmal 35, Mohammad Asif 0); Second day, Australia (1) 4-340 (Ponting 155, Gilchrist 17); Third day, Pakistan (2) 1-67 (Yasir Hameed 40, Younis Khan 5).

Pakistan

	R	B	4/6		R	B	4/6
Salman Butt c Gilchrist b McGrath	108	185	16	– c Warne b MacGill	21	27	3
Yasir Hameed c Clarke b Warne	58	99	6	1 – lbw b Warne	63	77	9
Younis Khan c McGrath b MacGill	46	67	6	– lbw b Watson	44	102	5
*Yousuf Youhana c Warne b MacGill	8	22	1	– b MacGill	30	78	4
Asim Kamal c Gillespie b MacGill	10	29	1	– c Ponting b Gillespie	87	143	15
Shahid Afridi c McGrath b MacGill	12	9	1	1 – run out (Martyn)	46	52	9
†Kamran Akmal c Warne b McGrath	47	68	8	– c Hayden b Warne	4	8	1
Naved-ul-Hasan lbw b McGrath	0	1	0	– lbw b Warne	9	6	2
Shoaib Akhtar b McGrath	0	5	0	– c Martyn b Warne	0	4	0
Danish Kaneria c Gilchrist b MacGill	3	13	0	– b MacGill	0	4	0
Mohammad Asif not out	0	24	0	– not out	12	37	2
B 6, l-b 2, w 1, n-b 3	12			B 4, l-b 3, n-b 2	9		

(86.4 overs, 366 mins) 304

Fall: 102 193 209 241 241 261 261 261 280 304

(89.2 overs, 374 mins) 325

Fall: 46 104 164 164 238 243 261 269 270 325

Bowling: *First Innings*—McGrath 16.4–5–50–4; Gillespie 14–3–47–0; Watson 10–3–28–0; Warne 24–4–84–1; MacGill 22–4–87–5. *Second Innings*—McGrath 16–2–53–0; Gillespie 13.2–2–39–1; Warne 26–2–111–4; MacGill 25–3–83–3; Watson 9–2–32–1.

Australia

	R	B	4/6		R	B	4/6
J. L. Langer b Naved-ul-Hasan	13	16	3	– b Danish Kaneria	34	30	7
M. L. Hayden b Danish Kaneria	26	57	5	– not out	23	27	3
*R. T. Ponting b Naved-ul-Hasan	207	332	30	– not out	4	1	1
D. R. Martyn st Kamran Akmal b Danish Kaneria	67	134	8				
M. J. Clarke st Kamran Akmal b Danish Kaneria	35	50	5 1				
†A. C. Gilchrist st Kamran Akmal b Danish Kaneria	113	120	14 5				
S. R. Watson c Mohammad Asif b Danish Kaneria	31	62	4				
S. K. Warne c Younis Khan b Danish Kaneria	16	26	1 1				
J. N. Gillespie lbw b Naved-ul-Hasan	0	2	0				
G. D. McGrath c Yousuf Youhana b Danish Kaneria	9	11	1				
S. C. G. MacGill not out	9	10	2				
B 6, l-b 13, w 3, n-b 20	42			N-b 1	1		

(133.3 overs, 554 mins) 568

Fall: 26 83 257 318 471 529 535 537 556 568

(9.3 overs, 38 mins) (1 wkt) 62

Fall: 58

Bowling: *First Innings*—Shoaib Akhtar 15–2–69–0; Naved–ul–Hasan 26–3–107–3; Mohammad Asif 16–3–72–0; Danish Kaneria 49.3–7–188–7; Shahid Afridi 27–3–113–0. *Second Innings*—Naved–ul–Hasan 3–0–28–0; Mohammad Asif 2–0–16–0; Danish Kaneria 2.3–0–16–1; Shahid Afridi 2–0–2–0.

Umpires: B. F. Bowden (New Zealand) and D. R. Shepherd (England).
TV Umpire: S. J. Davis.
Referee: R. S. Madugalle (Sri Lanka).

†AUSTRALIA A v PAKISTANIS

At Adelaide Oval, Adelaide, January 12, 2005. Pakistanis won by 13 runs. *Toss*: Australia A. *Attendance*: 5,604.

Pakistanis

Salman Butt b Wright	15 (24)	Shahid Afridi c Hauritz b Hopes	22 (14)
Yasir Hameed c M. E. K. Hussey b Wright	30 (52)	Azhar Mahmood run out (Hopes)	12 (7)
†Kamran Akmal b Lewis	11 (9)	Naved-ul-Hasan not out	0 (0)
Mohammad Hafeez c D. J. Hussey			
b Hauritz	61 (86)	B 4, l-b 8, w 11, n-b 1	24
*Inzamam-ul-Haq c Hodge b Tait	10 (40)		
Yousuf Youhana c Haddin b Tait	5 (8)	(50 overs, 210 mins) (8 wkts)	279
Abdul Razzaq not out	89 (61)	Fall: 33 48 75 111 117 185 253 271	

Iftikhar Anjum (did not bat).

Bowling: Lewis 10–2–40–1; Tait 10–0–49–2; Wright 10–0–54–2; Hopes 10–1–46–1; Hauritz 8–0–55–1; Thornely 2–0–23–0.

Australia A

J. R. Hopes c Kamran Akmal		N. M. Hauritz b Naved-ul-Hasan	2 (8)
b Iftikhar Anjum	13 (18)	M. L. Lewis not out	1 (1)
*†B. J. Haddin run out (Yasir/Kamran)	129(124)	S. W. Tait c Akmal b Naved-ul-Hasan	0 (1)
B. J. Hodge b Azhar Mahmood	30 (48)		
D. J. Hussey c (sub) Younis Khan			
b Iftikhar Anjum	45 (53)		
M. E. K. Hussey b Abdul Razzaq	5 (5)	L-b 7, w 5, n-b 9	21
D. J. Thornely lbw b Abdul Razzaq	16 (36)		
C. L. White run out (Shahid Afridi)	0 (1)	(48.4 overs, 201 mins)	266
D. G. Wright b Naved-ul-Hasan	4 (4)	Fall: 31 96 205 210 254 254 260 264 266 266	

Bowling: Naved–ul–Hasan 9.4–0–42–3; Iftikhar Anjum 10–0–52–2; Azhar Mahmood 6–0–34–1; Shahid Afridi 9–0–55–0; Abdul Razzaq 10–0–45–2; Mohammad Hafeez 4–0–31–0.

Umpires: I. H. Lock and B. N. J. Oxenford.
TV Umpire: S. J. Davis.

TWENTY20 INTERNATIONAL

†AUSTRALIA A v PAKISTANIS

At Adelaide Oval, Adelaide, January 13, 2005. Australia A won by 56 runs. *Toss*: Australia A. *Attendance*: 21,254.

Australia A

J. R. Hopes b Shoaib Akhtar	8 (8)	M. J. North not out	9 (6)
*†B. J. Haddin b Shoaib Akhtar	2 (5)		
B. J. Hodge c Taufeeq Umar			
b Mohammad Khalil	13 (8)	B 5, l-b 2, w 1, n-b 10	24
M. E. K. Hussey c Azhar Mahmood			
b Iftikhar Anjum	21 (17)		
D. J. Hussey c Shoaib Akhtar			
b Abdul Razzaq	50 (43)	(20 overs, 83 mins) (5 wkts)	185
C. L. White not out	58 (38)	Fall: 9 27 39 69 148	

D. J. Thornely, N. W. Bracken, D. G. Wright, S. W. Tait (did not bat).

Bowling: Shoaib Akhtar 4–0–37–2; Mohammad Khalil 3–0–29–1; Iftikhar Anjum 4–0–23–1; Abdul Razzaq 3–0–22–1; Shahid Afridi 2–0–23–0; Azhar Mahmood 3–0–24–0; Mohammad Hafeez 1–0–14–0.

Pakistanis

Yasir Hameed c White b Wright	5	(6)	†Younis Khan not out 28 (27)
Taufeeq Umar b Tait	31	(20)	Iftikhar Anjum not out 21 (24)
Shahid Afridi c M. E. K. Hussey b Wright	2	(3)	
Mohammad Hafeez run out (Hodge/Haddin)	3	(7)	L-b 3, w 7 16
Abdul Razzaq b Bracken	1	(9)	
Inzamam-ul-Haq run out (Tait/Hopes)	21	(22)	(20 overs, 86 mins) (7 wkts) 129
Azhar Mahmood lbw b White	1	(2)	Fall: 9 11 15 17 67 69 71

Mohammad Khalil, Shoaib Akhtar (did not bat).

Bowling: Bracken 4–0–15–1; Wright 4–0–27–2; Hopes 4–0–29–0; White 4–0–23–1; Tait 4–0–26–1.

Umpires: I. H. Lock and B. N. J. Oxenford.
TV Umpire: S. D. Fry.

Pakistan matches v Australia and West Indies in the VB Series (January 14-February 6) may be found in that section.

†PRIME MINISTER'S XI v PAKISTANIS

At Manuka Oval, Canberra, January 25, 2005. Pakistanis won by five wickets. *Toss*: Pakistanis.

Man of Match: Younis Khan. *Attendance*: 9,684.

Prime Minister's XI

T. R. Birt c Yasir Hameed b Mohammad Khalil	20	(39)	M. L. Lewis st Kamran Akmal b Younis Khan 1 (6)
†L. Ronchi c Shoaib Malik b Azhar Mahmood	40	(13)	D. J. Cullen hit wicket b Salman Butt 1 (3)
J. R. Hopes c Kamran Akmal b Azhar Mahmood	5	(6)	B. M. Edmondson run out (Yousuf Youhana) 0 (3)
D. J. Thornely c Salman Butt b Shoaib Malik	12	(29)	
C. J. L. Rogers c Taufeeq Umar b Shoaib Malik	46	(81)	
S. P. Heaney c Mohammad Hafeez b Shoaib Malik	35	(60)	L-b 3, w 8 11
B. G. Weare not out	13	(28)	(46.4 overs, 172 mins) 191
*M. G. Bevan b Mohammad Hafeez	7	(13)	Fall: 57 64 75 103 164 169 184 188 191 191

Bowling: Azhar Mahmood 7–3–23–2; Mohammad Khalil 6–0–51–1; Iftikhar Anjum 6–0–23–0; Shoaib Malik 10–0–29–3; Mohammad Hafeez 10–1–34–1; Salman Butt 6.4–0–24–1; Younis Khan 1–0–4–1.

Pakistanis

Salman Butt c Ronchi b Edmondson	23	(38)	Shoaib Malik not out 1 (2)
Taufeeq Umar b Edmondson	5	(16)	
*Yousuf Youhana run out (Ronchi/Cullen)	50	(69)	L-b 3, w 5, n-b 2 10
Yasir Hameed c Ronchi b Lewis	5	(14)	
Younis Khan not out	62	(73)	(42.5 overs, 160 mins) (5 wkts) 192
Mohammad Hafeez c Ronchi b Edmondson	36	(49)	Fall: 26 47 70 106 182

Azhar Mahmood, Mohammad Khalil, Iftikhar Anjum, † Kamran Akmal (did not bat).

Bowling: Lewis 8–0–28–1; Edmondson 9–1–38–3; Hopes 10–1–47–0; Cullen 9.5–1–49–0; Thornely 4–0–20–0; Weare 2–0–7–0.

Umpires: A. I. Shelley and J. H. Smeaton.
TV Umpire: G. R. Clifton.

VB Series, 2004-05

By ANDREW WEBSTER

n this space last year, we concluded provocatively that one-day cricket – particularly the triangular series in Australia – needed an enema. After another season, we scarcely dare to think what the 50-over game needs, for the crisis has grown. Dwindling crowds during the 2004-05 VB Series reinforced the notion that it was becoming irrelevant. But in many respects the most damaging signal for the suits at Cricket Australia was all the talk of an even shorter version of the game.

Twenty20 is here, and means to stay. While traditionalists (and many non-traditionalists) questioned the merits of Twenty20, it ensured public and media focus during the VB Series was on what to do about revamping the competition rather than the exploits on the field. After another one-way series, it seemed the right time for this focus. Australian coach John Buchanan nailed the effect the new micro-format would have on its 27-year-old brother: "What Twenty20 cricket will do is question why the 50-over format continues to be the way it is," he told the *Sydney Morning Herald*. "The 20-over game can accelerate that whole format change." Pakistan coach Bob Woolmer, who played for England in the 1970s, told the *Courier-Mail*: "It's not necessarily outlived its popularity, but it needs to be looked at in terms of changing how it's done. I don't know how quickly Cricket Australia and the television people will come up with an answer."

Among the ideas mooted was a shortening of the game to 40 overs, as suggested by former Australian dynamo Doug Walters. His one-time team-mate, Greg Chappell, believes the 50-over game needs to be split into two innings. But after another flat and lopsided series, interspersed with odd memorable moments, it might be thought that the problem is not with imperfections in the game, but with the gulf between the combatants. Australia was always supposed to flog the bejesus out of Pakistan and the West Indies. It was no surprise when it did.

Ricky Ponting's side lost just one match on the way to the finals against Pakistan, who folded when it mattered as they had done in the

Test series. Still, it must be said that while enigmatic and permanently injured paceman Shoaib Akhtar was perched at fashionable bars around the country, his team-mates were trying as hard as they could, no doubt tired as they came to the end of an arduous tour.

Australian selectors decided at the end of this VB Series to abandon the rotation policy they had implemented in 2001, notwithstanding that there had been an upside to the policy throughout the summer. While weary opener Matthew Hayden was rested – and slid into a form slump – his replacement, Michael Clarke, sparkled, scoring 41 runs at an average of 68.50. With the ball, Brett Lee tore through Pakistan and the Windies, the fire in his eyes clearly evident after being overlooked for the Test series against Pakistan.

While the tournament did not reach any great crescendo, it was not without its moments: Pakistan batsman Kamran Akmal's spanking 124 – his maiden ODI ton – against the West Indies in Brisbane; Lee's frightening pace in the opening match of the preliminaries and final; Australia's fightback from 4 for 38 against the Windies on Australia Day; Yousuf Youhana's century to smuggle Pakistan into the finals. But as for the single highlight, this was no contest: Brian Lara's 156 in Adelaide. Lara and some of his team-mates almost decided not to come to Australia because of a pay dispute. For the sake of that knock alone, it was fortunate that the boycott was averted.

Woolmer was livid at the end of the series, citing myriad numbers to prove his team had been dudded by poor decisions, and calling for neutral umpires. The ICC reprimanded him – and then said it would take his comments on board. But perhaps the most telling numbers were the ones Cricket Australia's accountant would have dwelled on in the finals. Not so long ago, these games were the hottest tickets in town. Sell-outs. But only 27,502 turned up for the first final in Melbourne, and 38,279 for the second final in Sydney. This should speak volumes to administrators about the need for another one-day revolution.

VB SERIES RUN SCORERS, 2004-05

	M	I	NO	R	HS	100s	50s	Avge	Ct/St	S-R
M. J. Clarke (Aust) . . .	8	8	2	411	103*	1	3	68.50	5	85.45
Inzamam-ul-Haq (Pak)	8	8	1	364	74	0	5	52.00	4	91.46
Yousuf Youhana (Pak)	8	8	1	318	105	1	2	45.43	0	85.48
S. Chanderpaul (WI) . .	6	6	1	314	85	0	3	62.80	1	81.35
B. C. Lara (WI)	6	6	0	307	156	1	1	51.17	2	99.03
D. R. Martyn (Aust) . .	7	6	2	240	95*	0	2	60.00	3	82.76
R. R. Sarwan (WI) . . .	6	6	1	235	87	0	2	47.00	0	77.30
Shahid Afridi (Pak) . .	8	7	1	231	56*	0	1	38.50	2	167.39
W. W. Hinds (WI). . . .	6	6	1	201	107	1	0	40.20	0	76.43
Shoaib Malik (Pak). . .	8	8	1	195	66	0	2	27.86	4	72.49
Abdul Razzaq (Pak) . .	8	7	1	188	63*	0	1	31.33	1	87.04
R. T. Ponting (Aust) . .	8	8	1	184	78	0	1	26.29	4	64.79
A. Symonds (Aust) . . .	7	6	0	165	91	0	1	27.50	2	75.00
S. M. Katich (Aust). . .	5	5	0	128	76	0	1	25.60	3	79.01
Kamran Akmal (Pak) .	7	7	0	183	124	1	0	26.14	5/2	78.54
C. H. Gayle (WI).	6	6	0	119	82	0	1	19.83	3	79.33
Salman Butt (Pak). . . .	7	7	0	111	61	0	1	15.86	1	56.06
D. S. Lehmann (Aust).	7	6	3	89	49*	0	0	29.67	2	92.71
Naved-ul-Hasan (Pak)	8	6	1	87	29	0	0	17.40	3	70.73
B. Lee (Aust).	8	4	2	87	38*	0	0	43.50	2	82.86
Mohammad Hafeez (Pak)	6	6	0	75	41	0	0	12.50	4	47.17
Azhar Mahmood (Pak)	5	4	2	57	40*	0	0	28.50	0	95.00
D. J. J. Bravo (WI) . . .	5	5	1	52	27	0	0	13.00	4	80.00
J. N. Gillespie (Aust) .	6	4	2	51	44*	0	0	25.50	2	130.77
A. C. Gilchrist (Aust) .	5	5	0	117	47	0	0	23.40	7	87.97
R. L. Powell (WI)	3	3	0	46	23	0	0	15.33	0	73.02
M. L. Hayden (Aust). .	4	4	0	42	27	0	0	10.50	2	41.58
Yasir Hameed (Pak) . .	2	2	0	36	24	0	0	18.00	0	78.26
M. N. Samuels (WI) . .	4	3	0	36	14	0	0	12.00	1	64.29
C. O. Browne (WI) . . .	6	4	1	56	36	0	0	18.67	9/1	75.68
B. J. Haddin (Aust). . .	3	2	0	62	32	0	0	31.00	3/1	77.50
Iftikhar Anjum (Pak). .	6	4	4	32	19*	0	0	–	1	65.31
G. B. Hogg (Aust). . . .	5	4	1	29	13	0	0	9.67	3	78.38
I. D. R. Bradshaw (WI)	6	4	0	28	15	0	0	7.00	0	59.57
S. R. Watson (Aust) . .	5	2	0	25	21	0	0	12.50	1	83.33
M. Dillon (WI)	4	3	1	12	6	0	0	6.00	0	60.00
G. D. McGrath (Aust).	6	3	1	6	5*	0	0	3.00	2	150.00
Younis Khan (Pak) . . .	1	1	0	6	6	0	0	6.00	3	42.86
X. M. Marshall (WI). .	1	1	0	5	5	0	0	5.00	0	50.00
R. D. King (WI)	2	1	1	3	3*	0	0	–	0	30.00
Taufeeq Umar (Pak) . .	1	1	0	3	3	0	0	3.00	0	25.00
P. T. Collins (WI)	5	3	2	2	1*	0	0	2.00	0	33.33
Shoaib Akhtar (Pak) . .	2	0	0	–	–	0	0	–	0	–
M. S. Kasprowicz (Aust)	4	0	0	–	–	0	0	–	1	–
Mohammad Khalil (Pak)	3	1	1	0	0*	0	0	–	2	0.00

* *Denotes not out.*

WICKET-TAKERS

	M	O	Mdns	R	W	BB	5W/i	Avge	RPO
B. Lee (Aus)	8	74.2	4	341	16	4-38	0	21.31	4.59
G. D. McGrath (Aus) . .	6	54.4	11	178	15	5-27	1	11.87	3.26
Naved-ul-Hasan (Pak). .	8	70.1	0	409	14	4-29	0	29.21	5.83
Abdul Razzaq (Pak) . . .	8	70.5	2	366	13	4-53	0	28.15	5.17
Shahid Afridi (Pak). . .	8	77	0	348	10	2-38	0	34.80	4.52
G. B. Hogg (Aus)	5	43	0	227	10	5-32	1	22.70	5.28
I. D. R. Bradshaw (WI).	6	50	4	237	9	3-47	0	26.33	4.74

	M	O	Mdns	R	W	BB	5W/i	Avge	RPO
J. N. Gillespie (Aus) . . .	6	53.5	2	233	8	3-62	0	29.13	4.33
P. T. Collins (WI)	5	38	3	160	8	5-43	1	20.00	4.21
D. S. Lehmann (Aus) . .	7	33.3	0	196	5	3-44	0	39.20	5.85
Iftikhar Anjum (Pak). . .	6	49	2	256	5	2-67	0	51.20	5.22
Mohammad Khalil (Pak)	3	24	0	144	5	2-55	0	28.80	6.00
M. S. Kasprowicz (Aus)	4	30.2	1	124	5	2-38	0	24.80	4.09
D. J. J. Bravo (WI) . . .	5	38	0	209	5	2-39	0	41.80	5.50
W. W. Hinds (WI).	6	25	0	176	4	2-62	0	44.00	7.04
Mohammad Hafeez (Pak)	6	39	1	194	4	1-17	0	48.50	4.97
M. Dillon (WI)	4	27	2	167	3	2-46	0	55.67	6.19
A. Symonds (Aus).	7	47	0	264	3	2-65	0	88.00	5.62
R. D. King (WI)	2	20	0	111	3	2-51	0	37.00	5.55
S. R. Watson (Aus)	5	36.5	3	168	3	2-52	0	56.00	4.56
Azhar Mahmood (Pak) .	5	28.4	4	168	2	1-33	0	84.00	5.86
R. L. Powell (WI)	3	4	0	30	1	1-30	0	30.00	7.50
M. N. Samuels (WI) . . .	4	31	0	175	1	1-45	0	175.00	5.65
Taufeeq Umar (Pak) . . .	1	1	0	8	0	–	0	–	8.00
C. H. Gayle (WI).	6	12	0	107	0	–	0	–	8.92
R. R. Sarwan (WI)	6	13	0	80	0	–	0	–	6.15
Shoaib Akhtar (Pak) . . .	2	10.5	0	61	0	–	0	–	5.63
Salman Butt (Pak).	7	6	0	42	0	–	0	–	7.00

AUSTRALIA v WEST INDIES

At Melbourne Cricket Ground, Melbourne, January 14, 2005. Day/night game. Australia won by 116 runs. *Toss*: Australia. Australia 6 pts. *Limited-overs international debut*: X. M. Marshall.

Those who adore this bold and beautiful brand of cricket made their way to the MCG brimming with renewed belief that they would be witnessing a Windies renaissance, in this form of the game anyway. They had trumped England in the final of the Champions Trophy. They had averted a player revolt weeks before the series began, and boasted a full deck. This was a new era ... then Australia won the toss, batted on a friendly pitch, and posted 4 for 301. Game over, good night Windies. While Damien Martyn (95), captain Ricky Ponting (78) and makeshift opener Michael Clarke (66) – standing in for the weary Matthew Hayden – took the early honours, the white-hot pace of Brett Lee ensured there would be no Brian Lara-inspired comeback. Bowling every bit like an expressman who had been consigned to drinks-waiting in the Test series, Lee nudged the 150 kph speed limit like a young rev-head who had been given the keys to dad's Ferrari. He pounced three times as the Windies sagged to 4 for 33. Just when it seemed that Lara (58) and Shivnarine Chanderpaul (46) were mounting a spirited rearguard action, Brad Hogg swooped, took both their wickets within three overs, and went on to claim career-best figures of 5 for 32.

Man of Match: G. B. Hogg. *Attendance*: 51,543.

Australia

†A. C. Gilchrist c Bravo b Bradshaw	0	(7)	D. S. Lehmann not out 20 (14)
M. J. Clarke b Samuels	66	(77)	B 2, l-b 5, w 11, n-b 4 22
*R. T. Ponting run out			
(Chanderpaul/Browne)	78	(92)	
D. R. Martyn not out	95	(93)	(50 overs, 202 mins) (4 wkts) 301
A. Symonds c Gayle b Bradshaw	20	(21)	Fall: 4 119 207 254

S. R. Watson, G. B. Hogg, B. Lee, J. N. Gillespie, M. S. Kasprowicz (did not bat).

Bowling: Bradshaw 10–1–46–2; Dillon 8–0–69–0; Samuels 10–0–45–1; Hinds 3–0–20–0; Gayle 3–0–21–0; Sarwan 8–0–49–0; Bravo 8–0–44–0.

West Indies

C. H. Gayle lbw b Lee	0	(3)	†C. O. Browne not out 20 (39)
W. W. Hinds run out (Symonds)	5	(10)	I. D. R. Bradshaw c Clarke b Hogg . . 12 (19)
R. R. Sarwan c Gilchrist b Lee	4	(10)	M. Dillon c Ponting b Kasprowicz . . 6 (10)
*B. C. Lara c Symonds b Hogg	58	(68)	
X. M. Marshall c Gilchrist b Lee	5	(10)	B 1, l-b 13, w 3 17
S. Chanderpaul c and b Hogg	46	(73)	
M. N. Samuels c and b Hogg	9	(26)	(46.2 overs, 201 mins) 185
D. J. J. Bravo c Gilchrist b Hogg	3	(10)	Fall: 0 17 21 33 131 136 143 144 167 185

Bowling: Lee 10–1–36–3; Gillespie 8–0–29–0; Kasprowicz 6.2–0–26–1; Watson 7–0–37–0; Hogg 10–0–32–5; Symonds 5–0–11–0.

Umpires: S. J. Davis and R. E. Koertzen (South Africa).
TV Umpire: R. L. Parry.
Referee: B. C. Broad (England).

AUSTRALIA v PAKISTAN

At Bellerive Oval, Hobart, January 16, 2005. Australia won by four wickets. *Toss*: Pakistan. Australia 5 pts and Pakistan 1 pt.

Michael Clarke saw off Antarctic conditions, rain delays and a batting collapse to give Australian selectors the first pangs of a headache that would develop into a migraine later in the series. The Sydney wunderkind was again filling in for Matthew Hayden. Batting alongside Simon Katich, who replaced the injured Adam Gilchrist, they put the home side in the slot. Chasing a target of 253 from 45 overs (reduced from Pakistan's 7 for 272 after a 40-minute rain delay), they cruised to 107 without loss before the rot set in. But as harder heads around him failed, Clarke remained belligerent in the mist. He tore his way to 97 before he also fell. After slipping nervously to 5 for 185, Australia needed the hardest and baldest head of all – Darren Lehmann's – to carry them across the line. Pakistan had lost, yet they displayed some spine not evident during the Test series. Shahid Afridi smacked four sixes and four fours to post 56 from 26 balls late in the innings. And while captain Inzamam-ul-Haq looked like he could have happily slipped into a coma in the icy climate, his 68 was an early indication that Ricky Ponting's side would have to fight for this series.

Man of Match: M. J. Clarke. *Attendance*: 15,503.

Pakistan

Salman Butt c Lehmann b Hogg	61	(87)
†Kamran Akmal c Clarke b McGrath	5	(8)
Mohammad Hafeez c Hogg b Lee	0	(9)
Shoaib Malik lbw b Symonds	31	(43)
*Inzamam-ul-Haq lbw b Kasprowicz	68	(64)
Yousuf Youhana c Martyn b Kasprowicz	30	(47)
Abdul Razzaq c Clarke b McGrath	12	(14)

Shahid Afridi not out	56	(26)
Azhar Mahmood not out	3	(3)
L-b 1, w 4, n-b 1	6	
(50 overs, 209 mins) (7 wkts)	272	
Fall: 15 30 83 117 191 204 251		

Shoaib Akhtar, Naved-ul-Hasan (did not bat).

Bowling: McGrath 10–2–54–2; Lee 10–0–66–1; Kasprowicz 9–0–38–2; Symonds 9–0–55–1; Hogg 7–0–28–1; Lehmann 5–0–30–0.

Australia

M. J. Clarke c Naved-ul-Hasan b Mohammad Hafeez	97	(99)
S. M. Katich b Azhar Mahmood	38	(48)
*R. T. Ponting c Kamran Akmal b Shahid Afridi	6	(8)
D. R. Martyn b Abdul Razzaq	11	(18)
D. S. Lehmann not out	49	(57)
A. Symonds b Abdul Razzaq	0	(5)

†B. J. Haddin c M. Hafeez b Naved-ul-Hasan	30	(30)
G. B. Hogg not out	3	(1)
L-b 5, w 6, n-b 8	19	
(43 overs, 223 mins) (6 wkts)	253	
Fall: 107 118 141 184 185 243		

B. Lee, G. D. McGrath, M. S. Kasprowicz (did not bat).

Bowling: Shoaib Akhtar 8–0–54–0; Naved–ul–Hasan 8–0–60–1; Azhar Mahmood 6–0–33–1; Shahid Afridi 9–0–43–1; Abdul Razzaq 8–0–41–2; Mohammad Hafeez 4–0–17–1.

Umpires: B. F. Bowden (New Zealand) and D. J. Harper.
TV Umpire: P. D. Parker.
Referee: B. C. Broad (England).

PAKISTAN v WEST INDIES

At Brisbane Cricket Ground, Brisbane, January 19, 2005. Pakistan won by six wickets. *Toss:* Pakistan. Pakistan 5 pts and West Indies 1 pt.

Pakistan won this match, but consternation hung thick in the dressing-room afterwards. The off-again-on-again-off-again career of their lethal showman/paceman Shoaib Akhtar was again interrupted when he left the field in the fifth over with a hamstring strain. Body language in the middle says much. In this game, captain Inzamam-ul-Haq did not bat an eyelid in concern when Shoaib trudged off. More drama ensued. Off-spinner Mohammad Hafeez was reported for a suspected illegal bowling action after the game, a victim of the ICC's new hard-nosed stance on dodgy deliveries. But as is often the case with Pakistani cricket, calamity inspired cohesion. Somehow, they overhauled the Windies' imposing 5 for 273 with six wickets to spare. Enigmatic opener Kamran Akmal had tested the selectors' patience for three years – he'd been dropped and reinstated four times – but finally he delivered with 124 from 125 deliveries, his maiden one-day ton. Pakistan needed it as much as he did. After winning the toss, they had sent in the Windies, only to see opener Chris Gayle (82) finally display some form. Brian Lara (39 from 30) and Ramnaresh Sarwan (76 from 91) put on a vicious 60-run stand as the Windies posted a respectable total, but not the 300 that was in prospect. Ultimately, it was Kamran's day. He opened his innings with a crisp cover drive and reached his century with the same shot.

Man of Match: Kamran Akmal. *Attendance*: 10,458.

West Indies

C. H. Gayle c Shoaib Malik b Abdul Razzaq 82 (99)	S. Chanderpaul not out 25 (22)
W. W. Hinds c Salman Butt b Mohammad Hafeez 29 (62)	L-b 8, w 9, n-b 5 22
R. R. Sarwan c Naved-ul-Hasan b Azhar Mahmood 76 (91)	—
*B. C. Lara c Mohammad Hafeez b Naved-ul-Hasan 39 (30)	(50 overs, 212 mins) (5 wkts) 273
R. L. Powell c Kamran Akmal b Naved-ul-Hasan 0 (1)	Fall: 86 149 209 211 273

M. N. Samuels, †C. O. Browne, I. D. R. Bradshaw, M. Dillon, P. T. Collins (did not bat).

Bowling: Shoaib Akhtar 2.5–0–7–0; Naved–ul–Hasan 10–0–55–2; Azhar Mahmood 9.1–1–57–1; Shahid Afridi 10–0–39–0; Mohammad Hafeez 10–0–54–1; Abdul Razzaq 7–0–43–1; Salman Butt 1–0–10–0.

Pakistan

Salman Butt b Dillon 10 (18)	Yousuf Youhana not out 9 (22)
†Kamran Akmal c Lara b Bradshaw ..124 (125)	L-b 1, w 3, n-b 3 7
Mohammad Hafeez c Gayle b Dillon .. 2 (9)	—
Shoaib Malik c Browne b Bradshaw .. 60 (60)	(47 overs, 204 mins) (4 wkts) 274
*Inzamam-ul-Haq not out 62 (51)	Fall: 28 36 159 239

Abdul Razzaq, Shahid Afridi, Azhar Mahmood, Shoaib Akhtar, Naved-ul-Hasan (did not bat).

Bowling: Collins 10–0–50–0; Bradshaw 10–1–49–2; Dillon 10–1–46–2; Samuels 9–0–72–0; Sarwan 5–0–31–0; Hinds 3–0–25–0.

Umpires: R. E. Koertzen (South Africa) and P. D. Parker.
TV Umpire: S. J. A. Taufel.
Referee: B. C. Broad (England).

AUSTRALIA v WEST INDIES

At Brisbane Cricket Ground, Brisbane, January 21, 2005. Day/night game. No result.
Toss: West Indies. Australia 3 pts and West Indies 3 pts.

Cricket can shatter a team like few sports can. It does not need any help from an untimely thunderstorm to crush spirits at the most inappropriate time. The Windies smashed Australia in this game, but still walked away with only a share of the points, without a victory in the series, and drenched. After compiling a defendable 9 for 263, they had Australia's nose hard-pressed on the canvas awaiting the count at 5 for 43. At 2 for 12, Australia were already punch-drunk before the heavens opened. When play resumed after 141 minutes, they lost captain Ricky Ponting and Andrew Symonds (his fifth duck in six innings) in rapid succession as Australia chased a reduced target of 195 from 28 overs. When Michael Clarke's awful attempted pull shot went straight to Marlon Samuels at mid-on (5 for 30), Australia prayed to the rain gods. They were answered minutes later. Windies seamer Pedro Collins (3 for 8) and opening batsman Wavel Hinds (107 from 138 balls) had every right to be filthy. Sadly for the Windies, moral victories did not earn them much-needed points on the ladder.

Man of Match: No award. *Attendance*: 32,618.

West Indies

C. H. Gayle b Gillespie	26	(22)	
W. W. Hinds c Gilchrist b Watson	107	(138)	
R. R. Sarwan lbw b Lehmann	27	(38)	
*B. C. Lara c Gilchrist b Lee	6	(16)	
S. Chanderpaul c Ponting b Kasprowicz	45	(48)	
M. N. Samuels run out (Martyn/Kasprowicz)	13	(10)	
D. J. J. Bravo c Kasprowicz b Gillespie	27	(22)	
†C. O. Browne b Gillespie	0	(1)	

M. Dillon not out	1	(3)	
I. D. R. Bradshaw b Watson	1	(3)	
P. T. Collins not out	0	(1)	
L-b 4, w 4, n-b 2	10		
(50 overs, 228 mins)	(9 wkts)	263	

Fall: 29 84 92 181 210 253 260 260 263

Bowling: Lee 7–1–30–1; Gillespie 9–1–62–3; Kasprowicz 10–1–43–1; Watson 10–0–52–2; Lehmann 7–0–34–1; Symonds 7–0–38–0.

Australia

†A. C. Gilchrist c Browne b Bradshaw	6	(8)	
M. L. Hayden c Gayle b Collins	6	(14)	
*R. T. Ponting lbw b Collins	2	(10)	
D. R. Martyn not out	14	(16)	
A. Symonds c Browne b Collins	0	(3)	
M. J. Clarke c Samuels b Dillon	2	(10)	

D. S. Lehmann not out	10	(6)	
L-b 1, w 1, n-b 1	3		
(11 overs, 54 mins)	(5 wkts)	43	

Fall: 8 12 24 25 30

S. R. Watson, B. Lee, J. N. Gillespie, M. S. Kasprowicz (did not bat).

Bowling: Collins 4–1–8–3; Bradshaw 2–0–6–1; Dillon 3–1–15–1; Samuels 2–0–13–0.

Umpires: B. F. Bowden (New Zealand) and S. J. A. Taufel.
TV Umpire: P. D. Parker.
Referee: B. C. Broad (England).

AUSTRALIA v PAKISTAN

At Sydney Cricket Ground, Sydney, January 23, 2005. Day/night game. Australia won by nine wickets. *Toss:* Australia. Australia 6 pts.

Michael Clarke declared that he expected to be shunted down the order after the selectors' experiment of using him as an opener in the first two matches of the series. When he slugged another century, the selectors were again confounded. After rain sullied the start, Ricky Ponting sent in the visitors. Less than 40 overs and 163 runs later, they were back in the rooms, with Inzamam-ul-Haq (50) and Shahid Afridi (48) providing the only resistance. Glenn McGrath resisted anything fanciful on the moist wicket and was typically miserly (2 for 18 from 10) as Brett Lee (2 for 54) and Darren Lehmann (3 for 44 with his left-arm spin) took greater gambles. Clarke gave Pakistan two chances to halt his ride to his second one-day century, but their fieldsman fumbled as their batsmen had. Ponting blocked out overs at a time to give Clarke a chance to finish his hundred before the runs ran out. He did.

Man of Match: M. J. Clarke. *Attendance:* 30,942.

Pakistan

Salman Butt lbw b McGrath	0	(8)	Azhar Mahmood c Hayden b Lehmann	1	(7)
†Kamran Akmal b Lee	2	(7)	Naved-ul-Hasan b Lee	6	(20)
Shoaib Malik b McGrath	8	(29)	Iftikhar Anjum not out	1	(3)
*Inzamam-ul-Haq c Clarke b Lehmann	50	(61)			
Yousuf Youhana c Ponting b Kasprowicz	4	(6)	L-b 4, w 10	14	
Mohammad Hafeez c Hayden b Watson	13	(36)			
Abdul Razzaq run out (Clarke)	16	(21)	(39.2 overs, 172 mins)	163	
Shahid Afridi st Haddin b Lehmann	48	(37)	Fall: 2 2 38 44 68 98 103 115 161 163		

Bowling: McGrath 10–3–18–2; Lee 10–0–54–2; Kasprowicz 5–0–17–1; Watson 7–2–26–1; Lehmann 7.2–0–44–3.

Australia

M. J. Clarke not out	103	(107)			
M. L. Hayden c Naved-ul-Hasan b Abdul Razzaq	27	(65)			
*R. T. Ponting not out	17	(51)	B 3, l-b 5, w 7, n-b 5	20	
			(36.2 overs, 138 mins) (1 wkt)	167	
			Fall: 79		

D. R. Martyn, A. Symonds, D. S. Lehmann, †B. J. Haddin, S. R. Watson, B. Lee, M. S. Kasprowicz, G. D. McGrath (did not bat).

Bowling: Naved–ul–Hasan 6–0–20–0; Iftikhar Anjum 3–0–22–0; Abdul Razzaq 7–0–43–1; Shahid Afridi 8–0–22–0; Mohammad Hafeez 4–1–17–0; Azhar Mahmood 4.2–2–14–0; Salman Butt 4–0–21–0.

Umpires: D. J. Harper and R. E. Koertzen (South Africa).
TV Umpire: S. J. A. Taufel.
Referee: B. C. Broad (England).

AUSTRALIA v WEST INDIES

At Adelaide Oval, Adelaide, January 26, 2005. Day/night game. Australia won by 73 runs. *Toss*: Australia. Australia 6 pts.

It would have been so West Indian to crush Australia on their national day, in searing heat, on the billiard-green oval of Adelaide. It looked on the cards as Pedro Collins (5 for 43) bowled two wicked spells to set Australia on their heels. At 4 for 38, it could have been all over. Instead, stand-in bat Simon Katich (76), a near Australian-record ninth-wicket partnership between Jason Gillespie (44 not out) and Brett Lee (38 not out), and some docile fielding from the Windies ensured Australia accumulated 269 when they had no right. The West Indians started their chase as they had started in the field. At 6 for 153, with Brian Lara sitting pretty at No. 5, the crowd should have been looking for a nearby bar – even if they had been 2 for 3 at one stage. Instead, Lee came back for another lethal spell and finished with 4 for 38. But the calamitous run out of Shivnarine Chanderpaul (55), thanks to a combination of Michael Clarke and his batting partner Wavell Hinds, meant that just when it seemed these Calypso Kings had risen – again – they fell on their faces – again.

Man of Match: B. Lee. *Attendance*: 26,539.

Australia

M. J. Clarke b Collins	21 (16)	G. B. Hogg c Browne b Bravo	3 (6
M. L. Hayden c Browne b Collins	3 (6)	B. Lee not out	38 (44
*R. T. Ponting c Bravo b Collins	0 (2)	J. N. Gillespie not out	44 (32
A. Symonds c Browne b Hinds	31 (49)	L-b 3, w 8, n-b 6	17
D. S. Lehmann c Browne b Collins	4 (6)		
S. M. Katich lbw b Collins	76 (86)	(50 overs, 224 mins) (8 wkts)	269
†B. J. Haddin b Bravo	32 (50)	Fall: 24 24 34 38 85 167 182 196	

G. D. McGrath (did not bat).

Bowling: Collins 10–1–43–5; Bradshaw 10–1–45–0; Dillon 6–0–37–0; Hinds 4–0–25–1; Bravo 10–0–71–2; Samuels 10–0–45–0.

West Indies

C. H. Gayle c Haddin b Lee	2 (11)	I. D. R. Bradshaw b Gillespie	15 (21)
W. W. Hinds c Haddin b Lee	0 (1)	M. Dillon b Gillespie	5 (7)
R. R. Sarwan c Haddin b Hogg	39 (62)	P. T. Collins not out	1 (2)
S. Chanderpaul run out (Clarke)	55 (87)		
*B. C. Lara c and b Lee	29 (38)	L-b 7, w 6, n-b 5	18
M. N. Samuels c Ponting b Lehmann	14 (20)		
D. J. J. Bravo b McGrath	18 (24)	(44.5 overs, 204 mins)	196
†C. O. Browne lbw b Lee	0 (1)	Fall: 1 3 95 110 147 153 153 185 195 196	

Bowling: Lee 10–1–38–4; McGrath 8–1–18–1; Gillespie 6.5–0–25–2; Symonds 10–0–50–0; Hogg 6–0–33–1; Lehmann 4–0–25–1.

Umpires: B. F. Bowden (New Zealand) and S. J. Davis.
TV Umpire: D. J. Harper.
Referee: B. C. Broad (England).

PAKISTAN v WEST INDIES

At Adelaide Oval, Adelaide, January 28, 2005. West Indies won by 58 runs. *Toss*: Pakistan. Pakistan 1 pt and West Indies 5 pts.

Sadly, the wallpaper quality of one-day cricket will mean that Brian Lara's innings on this day is likely to fade into obscurity. It should not, for his explosive and inspiring 156 was classic Lara. He had nothing to lose and batted that way, taking 81 runs to reach his half-century and then launching a blitzkrieg not seen from him on the international scene for years. He slogged five sixes and 12 fours despite a wrist injury that saw him playing many shots with one hand, some for singles, some for sixes. Lara and Shivnarine Chanderpaul (85) guided the Windies to a monstrous 4 for 339 – the highest ODI score at Adelaide Oval. Pakistan came within 58 runs of the monolithic total, but they were never in it. Opener Salman Butt went in the second over. Reon King (2 for 51) strangled Pakistan early, his dismissal of Mohammad Hafeez his first wicket since August 2002. Inzamam-ul-Haq (30), Yousuf Youhana (45) and Abdul Razzaq (44) came, tried, and were sent on their way. The Windies won their first match of the series, giving themselves a slim hope of reaching the finals. With one knock, Lara ensured he would be leaving Australia with his batting mojo intact.

Man of Match: B. C. Lara. *Attendance*: 5,023.

West Indies

C. H. Gayle b Iftikhar Anjum	9	(12)	D. J. J. Bravo not out	3	(3)
R. L. Powell lbw b Naved-ul-Hasan	23	(36)			
R. R. Sarwan retired hurt	2	(12)			
*B. C. Lara b Mohammad Hafeez	156	(138)	B 1, l-b 9, w 10, n-b 11	31	
S. Chanderpaul c Mohammad Hafeez					
b Shahid Afridi	85	(92)	(50 overs, 219 mins) (4 wkts)	339	
W. W. Hinds not out	30	(18)	Fall: 17 56 243 327		

†C. O. Browne, I. D. R. Bradshaw, P. T. Collins, R. D. King (did not bat).

Bowling: Naved–ul–Hasan 9–0–77–1; Iftikhar Anjum 9–1–50–1; Azhar Mahmood 9–1–63–0; Abdul Razzaq 10–0–41–0; Shahid Afridi 10–0–64–1; Mohammad Hafeez 3–0–34–1.

Pakistan

Salman Butt c Chanderpaul b Bradshaw	1	(4)	Azhar Mahmood not out	40	(36)
†Kamran Akmal b Hinds	19	(34)	Naved-ul-Hasan b Powell	10	(17)
Mohammad Hafeez c (sub)					
M. N. Samuels b King	41	(41)	Iftikhar Anjum not out	7	(8)
Shoaib Malik b King	7	(18)			
*Inzamam-ul-Haq c Bravo b Hinds	30	(31)			
Yousuf Youhana run out			L-b 7, w 12, n-b 1	20	
(King/Browne/Powell)	45	(46)			
Abdul Razzaq c Lara b Bravo	44	(49)	(50 overs, 216 mins) (9 wkts)	281	
Shahid Afridi c Browne b Bravo	17	(16)	Fall: 1 65 65 87 107 179 205 218 254		

Bowling: Collins 4–1–13–0; Bradshaw 8–0–44–1; King 10–0–51–2; Hinds 10–0–62–2; Bravo 10–0–39–2; Powell 4–0–30–1; Gayle 4–0–35–0.

Umpires: D. J. Harper and R. E. Koertzen (South Africa).
TV Umpire: S. J. Davis.
Referee: B. C. Broad (England).

AUSTRALIA v PAKISTAN

At WACA Ground, Perth, January 30, 2005. Day/night game. Pakistan won by three wickets. *Toss:* Australia. Australia 1 pt and Pakistan 5 pts. *Limited-overs international debut*: Mohammad Khalil.

Facing McGrath, Lee and Gillespie on a classical WACA wicket, without their own strike bowler and coming to the end of an arduous tour, Pakistan could have folded like deckchairs in Perth. Instead, they snuck home in the 48th over with three wickets to spare to inflict on Australia their first defeat of the series. Abdul Razzaq – bowling first change and batting at No. 7 – was an unlikely hero. Australia won the toss, backed themselves and batted. Plenty got starts, but Razzaq (4 for 53) bedazzled the Australian top order. Again, it was Michael Clarke, with an unbeaten 75, who ensured Australia posted a winnable total of 265, his 50 coming from a spanking pull shot off Razzaq. Pakistan were faltering at 3 for 49 until Inzamam-ul-Haq (29) and Yousuf Youhana (72) cautiously guided them back into the game. Inzy crunched trademark back-front cover drives, but his departure and then Youhana's – trying to loft a six over mid-off – put the onus on to Razzaq and Shahid Afridi. As Razzaq (63 not out from 61 balls) combined tempestuousness with controlled temperament, Afridi simply went berserk, slashing 30 from 13 balls. When Afridi top-edged Symonds to Lee at square leg, Razzaq took Pakistan to victory with 16 balls to spare. The visitors had finally beaten Australia – someone who had finally beaten Australia – but most importantly they gave themselves one last match to qualify for the finals. They deserved it.

Man of Match: Abdul Razzaq. *Attendance*: 18,751.

Australia

†A. C. Gilchrist b Abdul Razzaq	47	(46)	B. Lee c Mohammad Khalil	
			b Abdul Razzaq	22 (35
M. L. Hayden c Shahid Afridi				
b Naved-ul-Hasan	6	(16)	J. N. Gillespie c Younis Khan	
			b Abdul Razzaq	4 (3
*R. T. Ponting b Abdul Razzaq	29	(45)	G. D. McGrath b Naved-ul-Hasan	0 (1
D. R. Martyn c Shoaib Malik				
b Shahid Afridi	24	(25)		
A. Symonds c Shoaib Malik				
b Shahid Afridi	23	(41)	B 1, l-b 5, w 16, n-b 3	25
M. J. Clarke not out	75	(75)		—
S. M. Katich c Younis Khan				
b Mohammad Khalil	0	(3)	(50 overs, 223 mins)	265
G. B. Hogg c Younis Khan				
b Mohammad Khalil	10	(13)	Fall: 30 63 111 113 164 167 192 246 251 265	

Bowling: Naved–ul-Hasan 10–0–49–2; Iftikhar Anjum 10–0–57–0; Abdul Razzaq 10–0–53–4; Mohammad Khalil 10–0–55–2; Shahid Afridi 10–0–45–2.

Pakistan

Salman Butt c Gillespie b McGrath	20	(36)	Shahid Afridi c Lee b Symonds	30 (13)
Yasir Hameed c Symonds b Lee	12	(15)	Naved-ul-Hasan not out	20 (18)
†Younis Khan c Martyn b McGrath	6	(14)		
Yousuf Youhana c Katich b Symonds	72	(90)	L-b 7, w 6, n-b 2	15
*Inzamam-ul-Haq lbw b Hogg	29	(38)		
Shoaib Malik run out (Symonds)	1	(1)	(47.2 overs, 204 mins) (7 wkts)	268
Abdul Razzaq not out	63	(61)	Fall: 27 41 49 123 125 170 223	

Iftikhar Anjum, Mohammad Khalil (did not bat).

Bowling: Lee 9.2–0–63–1; McGrath 9–2–27–2; Gillespie 10–1–35–0; Hogg 10–0–71–1; Symonds 9–0–65–2.

Umpires: B. F. Bowden (New Zealand) and P. D. Parker.
TV Umpire: S. J. Davis.
Referee: B. C. Broad (England).

PAKISTAN v WEST INDIES

At WACA Ground, Perth, February 1, 2005. Pakistan won by 30 runs. *Toss*: West Indies. Pakistan 5 pts and West Indies 1 pt.

Would the thought of imminent defeat or a finals appearance spark something from these indifferent sides that appeared incapable of defeating the all-conquering Australians? It did as they produced their best performances of the series. It was Pakistan, tired, emotional, and worse still under siege from former captain Imran Khan, that prevailed. Just. A brilliant century from middle-order batsman Yousuf Youhana (105 from 100 balls) set them up; he was the bedrock in an imposing total of 8 for 307. Ultimately, though, the dismissal of Windies batsman Ramnesh Sarwan (87 from 91) in the 33rd over sealed a Pakistan win. Sarwan had survived in the 25th over when Salman Butt grassed a simple chance, but when Pakistan keeper Kamran Akmal cleverly stumped him eight overs later off the bowling of Shahid Afridi (2 for 47), it caused a series-ending slide for the West Indies as they lost 3 for 9 to slip to 6 for 203. Rana Naved-ul-Hasan (4 for 29) had been the chief destroyer, but the accolades rightly went to Youhana, a brilliant but inconsistent talent. Brian Lara appeared justified in sending Pakistan in after winning the toss when they meandered to 3 for 90 and not much more by the 25-over halfway mark. But Youhana played with control, resisting a slaughter and scoring only nine boundaries, preferring to let captain Inzamam-ul-Haq (74 from 67) smash balls on the leg side. Pakistan won, but more importantly they displayed heart when some – including former captains – wondered aloud if they had one.

Man of Match: Yousuf Youhana. *Attendance*: 5,742.

Pakistan

Salman Butt c Browne b Bradshaw	19	(43)
†Kamran Akmal c Bravo b Bradshaw	17	(36)
Yasir Hameed b King	24	(31)
Yousuf Youhana run out (Bravo/Browne)	105	(100)
*Inzamam-ul-Haq b Bravo	74	(67)
Abdul Razzaq st Browne b Hinds	7	(9)
Shahid Afridi b Bradshaw	23	(10)
Shoaib Malik not out	8	(6)
Naved-ul-Hasan run out (Bravo/Browne)	3	(1)
L-b 4, w 19, n-b 4	27	
(50 overs, 230 mins) (8 wkts)	307	

Fall: 37 44 90 224 248 279 300 307

Iftikhar Anjum, Mohammad Khalil (did not bat).

Bowling: Collins 10–0–46–0; Bradshaw 10–1–47–3; King 10–0–60–1; Hinds 5–0–44–1; Bravo 10–0–55–1; Gayle 5–0–51–0.

West Indies

C. H. Gayle c Kamran Akmal b Naved-ul-Hasan	0	(3)
R. L. Powell c Kamran Akmal b Naved-ul-Hasan	23	(26)
R. R. Sarwan st Kamran Akmal b Shahid Afridi	87	(91)
*B. C. Lara c Iftikhar Anjum b Mohammad Khalil	19	(20)
S. Chanderpaul c Inzamam-ul-Haq b Iftikhar Anjum	58	(64)
W. W. Hinds c Inzamam-ul-Haq b Mohammad Khalil	30	(34)
D. J. J. Bravo b Shahid Afridi	1	(6)
†C. O. Browne b Naved-ul-Hasan	36	(33)
I. D. R. Bradshaw b Naved-ul-Hasan	0	(4)
P. T. Collins c Moh. Khalil b Iftikhar Anjum	1	(3)
R. D. King not out	3	(10)
L-b 3, w 11, n-b 5	19	
(48.1 overs, 223 mins)	277	

Fall: 0 67 99 194 198 203 257 259 260 277

Bowling: Naved–ul–Hasan 9.1–0–29–4; Iftikhar Anjum 9–0–67–2; Mohammad Khalil 10–0–59–2; Abdul Razzaq 9–0–61–0; Shahid Afridi 10–0–47–2; Salman Butt 1–0–11–0.

Umpires: S. J. Davis and R. E. Koertzen (South Africa).
TV Umpire: P. D. Parker.
Referee: B. C. Broad (England).

QUALIFYING TABLE

	Played	W on	Lost	No Result	Bonus Points	Points	Net Run-Rate
Australia	6	4	1	1	4	27	1.0817
Pakistan	6	3	3	0	2	17	-0.2950
West Indies	6	1	4	1	2	10	-0.7176

Net run-rate was calculated by subtracting runs conceded per over from runs scored per over.

FIRST FINAL

AUSTRALIA v PAKISTAN

At Melbourne Cricket Ground, Melbourne, February 4, 2005. Day/night game. Australia won by 18 runs. *Toss*: Australia.

There were sub-plots aplenty heading into the first final. After snaring the Allan Border Medal just days before, Michael Clarke was selected and Matthew Hayden dumped; Windies captain Brian Lara tried to plant a seed of doubt by declaring that Australia had batting faults and Pakistan had the firepower to cause a boilover. But the real question was: did Pakistan have any chance whatsoever? After holding Australia to 237, they certainly did. But while Clarke had been the flavour of the series, all-rounder Andrew Symonds' savage 91 from 101 will linger longest in the minds of spectators, along with the frightening pace of Brett Lee (3 for 23) in the opening three overs, which halted any thought of a shock Pakistan win. Earlier, Australia had faltered initially when they struggled to 3 for 53. The question was immediately asked: had the selectors got it all wrong with Clarke, the first to go on nine? It required the fuzzy-haired Symonds to haul Australia out of the mire. Only during his time at the crease did Australia seem capable of setting a defendable total, his self-belief and a 137-run partnership with Damien Martyn (53) lifting Australia. How quickly the summer changes. Symonds had scored five ducks in his six previous innings, and was also named the Australian One-Day Player of the Year. Any notion of a Pakistan victory was quickly dashed as soon as Lee and Glenn McGrath (3 for 34), playing his 200th ODI, were unleashed on Pakistan's batsmen. McGrath became the eighth bowler in history to tally 300 wickets when Mohammad Hafeez skied a simple catch to Shane Watson. That scalp had Pakistan reeling at 4 for 27 and beyond a point of any return – in this match and the finals series.

Man of Match: A. Symonds. *Attendance*: 27,502.

Australia

†A. C. Gilchrist c Abdul Razzaq b Mohammad Khalil	24 (42)	B. Lee b Naved-ul-Hasan	13 (12)
M. J. Clarke lbw b Naved-ul-Hasan	9 (22)	J. N. Gillespie not out	3 (3)
*R. T. Ponting b Iftikhar Anjum	11 (15)	G. D. McGrath run out (Kamran /Iftikhar)	1 (1)
D. R. Martyn st Kamran Akmal b Shahid Afridi	53 (78)		
A. Symonds c Inzamam-ul-Haq b Abdul Razzaq	91 (101)	B 1, l-b 8, w 7, n-b 3	19
D. S. Lehmann c Kamran Akmal b Shahid Afridi	0 (1)		—
S. M. Katich c (sub) Yasir Hameed b Abdul Razzaq	9 (17)	(49 overs, 199 mins)	237
S. R. Watson c Mohammad Hafeez b Abdul Razzaq	4 (5)	Fall: 29 51 53 190 190 213 213 220 235 237	

Bowling: Naved–ul–Hasan 9–0–50–2; Iftikhar Anjum 8–1–27–1; Mohammad Khalil 4–0–30–1; Shahid Afridi 10–0–50–2; Abdul Razzaq 10–0–33–3; Mohammad Hafeez 8–0–38–0.

Pakistan

Salman Butt lbw b Lee	0	(2)	Naved-ul-Hasan c Martyn b McGrath	29	(29)
†Kamran Akmal c Gillespie b McGrath	4	(4)	Iftikhar Anjum not out	19	(32)
Mohammad Hafeez c Watson b McGrath	13	(39)	Mohammad Khalil not out	0	(0)
Yousuf Youhana b Lee	2	(4)			
*Inzamam-ul-Haq c McGrath b Lee	51	(83)	L-b 3, w 2, n-b 1	6	
Shoaib Malik c Lehmann b Gillespie	66	(89)			
Abdul Razzaq run out (Symonds)	3	(4)	(50 overs, 214 mins) (9 wkts)	219	
Shahid Afridi c Katich b Gillespie	26	(15)	Fall: 1 7 9 27 118 123 153 171 216		

Bowling: Lee 10–0–23–3; McGrath 10–3–34–3; Gillespie 10–0–47–2; Watson 9–1–38–0; Lehmann 4–0–29–0; Symonds 7–0–45–0.

Umpires: B. F. Bowden (New Zealand) and S. J. Davis.
TV Umpire: R. L. Parry.
Referee: B. C. Broad (England).

SECOND FINAL

AUSTRALIA v PAKISTAN

At Sydney Cricket Ground, Sydney, February 6, 2005. Day/night game. Australia won by 31 runs. *Toss*: Australia.

Andrew Symonds' match-winning innings in Melbourne came at a price: a strained Achilles tendon that ruled him out of the second final. Again, Australia battled with the bat and relied on the brutality of Glenn McGrath (5 for 27) and Brett Lee (1 for 31) to seal a series win that always looked on the cards but wasn't as perfunctory as many had presumed. Australia did not have the run of the match and had to survive a dangerous ninth-wicket stand of 48 between Abdul Razzaq and Naved-ul-Hasan before Ricky Ponting could lift the trophy. Adam Gilchrist (40) and Michael Clarke (38) were belligerent despite a tricky, turning SCG deck. Spinners Shahid Afridi (2 for 38) and Mohammad Hafeez (1 for 34) eventually applied the brakes until Damien Martyn (43) stepped up as Symonds had in the first final. The Australians limped to 239 and, after a summer in which they had swept everything before them, appeared to have stalled at the precise moment when the one-day series was on the line. For the second game in a row, Pakistan had applied the slow choke and it had worked. Enter McGrath, who claimed three wickets from the opening six overs. That should have been enough to secure victory, but Yousuf Youhana (51) dug in, scoring at a run a ball for most of his innings, while Razzaq (43), Afridi (31) and Naved-ul-Hasan (19) kept nudging away. Lee and Gilchrist combined to run out Afridi with the score on 7 for 133, but McGrath cemented it, dismissing Razzaq and Naved-ul-Hasan in quick succession to give Australia victory. Afterwards Ponting said: "We haven't been at our best in the two finals but we've bowled really well. Pakistan pushed us all the way but we were lucky to keep our noses in front." In front is always enough.

Man of Match: G. D. McGrath. *Man of the Series*: B. Lee. *Attendance*: 38,279.

Australia

†A. C. Gilchrist c Shoaib Malik b Abdul Razzaq	40	(30)	
M. J. Clarke b Mohammad Hafeez	38	(75)	
*R. T. Ponting c Inzamam-ul-Haq b Shahid Afridi	41	(61)	
D. R. Martyn b Abdul Razzaq	43	(60)	
D. S. Lehmann b Shahid Afridi	6	(12)	
S. M. Katich run out (Shoaib Malik/Kamran)	5	(8)	
S. R. Watson c Shahid Afridi b Iftikhar Anjum	21	(25)	
G. B. Hogg b Naved-ul-Hasan	13	(17)	
B. Lee not out	14	(14)	
J. N. Gillespie b Naved-ul-Hasan	0	(1)	
G. D. McGrath not out	5	(2)	

B 1, l-b 4, w 3, n-b 5   13

(50 overs, 196 mins)   (9 wkts) 239

Fall: 55 118 146 156 166 203 207 230 230

Bowling: Naved–ul–Hasan 9–0–69–2; Iftikhar Anjum 10–0–33–1; Abdul Razzaq 9.5–2–51–2; Shahid Afridi 10–0–38–2; Mohammad Hafeez 10–0–34–1; Taufeeq Umar 1–0–8–0; Azhar Mahmood 0.1–0–1–0.

Pakistan

Kamran Akmal c Gilchrist b McGrath	12	(19)	
Taufeeq Umar c McGrath b Lee	3	(12)	
Mohammad Hafeez c Clarke b McGrath	6	(25)	
Yousuf Youhana b Hogg	51	(57)	
*Inzamam-ul-Haq lbw b McGrath	0	(3)	
Shoaib Malik c Katich b Hogg	14	(23)	
Abdul Razzaq c Gilchrist b McGrath	43	(58)	
Shahid Afridi run out (Lee)	31	(21)	
Azhar Mahmood lbw b Gillespie	13	(14)	
Naved-ul-Hasan b McGrath	19	(38)	
Iftikhar Anjum not out	5	(6)	

L-b 3, w 6, n-b 2   11

(45.4 overs, 203 mins)   208

Fall: 13 17 38 38 74 97 133 153 201 208

Bowling: Lee 8–1–31–1; McGrath 7.4–0–27–5; Gillespie 10–0–35–1; Watson 3.5–0–15–0; Hogg 10–0–63–2; Lehmann 6.1–0–34–0.

Umpires: D. J. Harper and R. E. Koertzen (South Africa).
TV Umpire: P. D. Parker.
Referee: B. C. Broad (England).

VB/World Series Records

TOURNAMENT RESULTS

Benson & Hedges World Series Cup

Season	Winners	Runners-Up	Third Team	Fourth Team
1979-80	West Indies	England	Australia	–
1980-81	Australia	New Zealand	India	–
1981-82	West Indies	Australia	Pakistan	–
1982-83	Australia	New Zealand	England	–
1983-84	West Indies	Australia	Pakistan	–
1984-85	West Indies	Australia	Sri Lanka	–
1985-86	Australia	India	New Zealand	–
1986-87	England	Australia	West Indies	–
1987-88	Australia	New Zealand	Sri Lanka	–
1988-89	West Indies	Australia	Pakistan	–

Benson & Hedges World Series

1989-90	Australia	Pakistan	Sri Lanka	–
1990-91	Australia	New Zealand	England	–
1991-92	Australia	India	West Indies	–
1992-93	West Indies	Australia	Pakistan	–
1993-94	Australia	South Africa	New Zealand	–
1994-95	Australia	Australia A	England	Zimbabwe
1995-96	Australia	Sri Lanka	West Indies	–

Carlton & United Series

1996-97	Pakistan	West Indies	Australia	–
1997-98	Australia	South Africa	New Zealand	–
1998-99	Australia	England	Sri Lanka	–
1999-00	Australia	Pakistan	India	–

Carlton Series

2000-01	Australia	West Indies	Zimbabwe	–

VB Series

2001-02	South Africa	New Zealand	Australia	–
2002-03	Australia	England	Sri Lanka	–
2003-04	Australia	India	Zimbabwe	–
2004-05	Australia	Pakistan	West Indies	–

TEAM RESULTS

	Debut	M	W	L	NR	T
Australia	Nov 27, 1979	273	176	89	6	2
West Indies	Nov 27, 1979	120	68	48	2	2
England	Nov 28, 1979	65	27	38	0	0
New Zealand	Nov 23, 1980	81	31	48	2	0
India	Dec 6, 1980	50	17	32	0	1
Pakistan	Nov 21, 1981	74	26	46	1	1
Sri Lanka	Jan 8, 1985	54	12	42	0	0
South Africa	Jan 9, 1993	31	18	13	0	0
Zimbabwe	Dec 2, 1994	22	2	19	1	0
Australia A	Dec 4, 1994	8	3	5	0	0
Total		389				

HIGHEST INDIVIDUAL SCORES

173	M. E. Waugh	Australia v West Indies at Melbourne	2000-01
172	A. C. Gilchrist	Australia v Zimbabwe at Hobart (Bellerive)	2003-04
158	D. I. Gower	England v New Zealand at Brisbane	1982-83
156	B. C. Lara	West Indies v Pakistan at Adelaide	2004-05
154	A. C. Gilchrist	Australia v Sri Lanka at Melbourne	1998-99
153*	I. V. A. Richards	West Indies v Australia at Melbourne	1979-80
145	D. M. Jones	Australia v England at Brisbane	1990-91
144*	D. R. Martyn	Australia v Zimbabwe at Perth	2000-01
141	S. C. Ganguly	India v Pakistan at Adelaide	1999-00
139	Yuvraj Singh	India v Australia at Sydney	2003-04

* Denotes not out.

MOST RUNS

	M	I	NO	R	HS	100s	50s	Avge	S-R
A. R. Border (Aust)	160	148	22	3,899	127*	3	23	30.94	69.67
M. E. Waugh (Aust)	116	110	9	3,730	173	8	22	36.93	73.56
D. M. Jones (Aust)	93	90	16	3,456	145	2	28	46.70	70.26
R. T. Ponting (AuA/Aust)	92	91	8	3,210	123	5	20	38.67	77.31
D. C. Boon (Aust)	94	91	9	3,016	122	2	20	36.78	63.31
S. R. Waugh (Aust)	142	126	31	2,801	102*	1	14	29.48	70.77
M. G. Bevan (Aust/AuA)	89	78	28	2,785	105	2	19	55.70	73.19
D. L. Haynes (WI)	83	83	8	2,782	123*	4	21	37.09	59.42
I. V. A. Richards (WI)	65	60	5	2,563	153*	3	22	46.60	85.25
A. C. Gilchrist (Aust)	70	67	3	2,399	172	5	9	37.48	95.69

* Denotes not out

HIGHEST PARTNERSHIPS FOR EACH WICKET

237	for 1st	S. T. Jayasuriya and M. S. Atapattu	Sri Lanka v Australia at Sydney	2002-03
225	for 2nd	A. C. Gilchrist and R. T. Ponting	Australia v England at Melbourne	2002-03
224*	for 3rd	D. M. Jones and A. R. Border	Australia v Sri Lanka at Adelaide	1984-85
213	for 4th	V. V. S. Laxman and Yuvraj Singh	India v Australia at Sydney	2003-04
159	for 5th	R. T. Ponting and M. G. Bevan	Australia v Sri Lanka at Melbourne	1995-96
124	for 6th	C. D. McMillan and C. Z. Harris	New Zealand v South Africa at Adelaide	1997-98
110	for 7th	P. D. Collingwood and C. White	England v Sri Lanka at Perth	2002-03
88*	for 8th	D. S. Lehmann and B. Lee	Australia v South Africa at Perth	2001-02
73*	for 9th	B. Lee and J. N. Gillespie	Australia v West Indies at Adelaide	2004-05
63	for 10th	S. R. Watson and A. J. Bichel	Australia v Sri Lanka at Sydney	2002-03

* Denotes unbroken partnership.

HIGHEST INNINGS TOTALS

Batting first

5-359 Australia v India at Sydney	2003-04
7-344 Australia v Zimbabwe at Hobart (Bellerive)	2003-04
5-343 Sri Lanka defeated Australia at Adelaide	2002-03
4-339 West Indies defeated Pakistan at Adelaide	2004-05
6-338 Australia defeated West Indies at Melbourne	2000-01
7-337 Australia defeated Pakistan at Sydney	1999-00
329 Australia defeated India at Adelaide	1999-00
2-323 Australia defeated Sri Lanka at Adelaide	1984-85
6-318 Australia defeated England at Melbourne	2002-03
3-315 Pakistan defeated Sri Lanka at Adelaide	1989-90

Batting second

9-303	Sri Lanka defeated England at Adelaide	1998-99
6-301	Zimbabwe lost to Australia at Perth	2000-01
299	West Indies lost to Australia at Melbourne	2000-01
9-298	New Zealand lost to South Africa at Brisbane	1997-98
6-297	New Zealand defeated England at Adelaide	1982-83
8-288	Sri Lanka lost to Pakistan at Adelaide	1989-90
3-284	West Indies defeated Australia at Brisbane	1996-97
284	Australia lost to India at Brisbane	2003-04
4-282	Australia defeated Zimbabwe at Hobart	2000-01
9-281	Pakistan lost to West Indies at Adelaide	2004-05

LOWEST INNINGS TOTALS

Batting first

63	India lost to Australia at Sydney	1980-81
71	Pakistan lost to West Indies at Brisbane	1992-93
100	India lost to Australia in Sydney	1999-00
102	Sri Lanka lost to West Indies at Brisbane	1995-96
106	South Africa lost to Australia at Sydney	2001-02

Batting second

69	South Africa lost to Australia	1993-94
70	Australia lost to New Zealand at Adelaide	1985-86
81	Pakistan lost to West Indies at Sydney	1992-93
87	West Indies lost to Australia at Sydney	1992-93
91	Sri Lanka lost to Australia at Adelaide	1984-85
91	West Indies lost to Zimbabwe at Sydney	2000-01

BEST BOWLING FIGURES

6-42	A. B. Agarkar	India v Australia at Melbourne	2003-04
5-15	G. S. Chappell	Australia v India at Sydney	1980-81
5-15	R. J. Shastri	India v Australia at Perth	1991-92
5-16	C. G. Rackemann	Australia v Pakistan at Adelaide	1983-84
5-17	C. E. L. Ambrose	West Indies v Australia at Melbourne	1988-89
5-19	A. J. Bichel	Australia v South Africa at Sydney	2001-02
5-21	A. I. C. Dodemaide	Australia v Sri Lanka at Perth	1987-88
5-22	A. M. E. Roberts	West Indies v England at Adelaide	1979-80
5-22	B. A. Williams	Australia v Zimbabwe at Sydney	2003-04
5-24	M. E. Waugh	Australia v West Indies at Melbourne	1992-93
5-24	L. Klusener	South Africa v Australia at Melbourne	1997-98

MOST WICKETS

	M	O	Mdns	R	W	BB	5Wi	Avge	RPO
G. D. McGrath (Aust)	78	705.2	91	2,692	143	5-27	3	18.83	3.82
S. K. Warne (Aust)	81	754.5	40	3,183	132	5-33	1	24.11	4.22
C. J. McDermott (Aust)	82	728	67	2,805	122	4-25	0	22.99	3.85
S. R. Waugh (Aust)	142	648.5	27	2,775	86	4-33	0	32.27	4.28
B. Lee (Aust)	43	380.3	24	1,722	76	5-27	2	22.66	4.53
M. A. Holding (WI)	49	459.4	44	1,602	74	5-26	1	21.65	3.49
P. L Taylor (Aust)	54	465.1	23	1,878	71	4-38	0	26.45	4.04
J. Garner (WI)	48	435.5	62	1,381	70	5-31	1	19.73	3.17
M. D. Marshall (WI)	56	497	50	1,748	69	4-18	0	25.33	3.52
S. P. O'Donnell (Aust)	52	432	26	1,826	69	4-19	0	26.46	4.23

MOST CATCHES

A. R. Border (Aust) .. 83 in 160 matches
S. R. Waugh (Aust) .. 55 in 142 matches
M. E. Waugh (Aust) .. 48 in 116 matches
S. K. Warne (Aust) ... 41 in 81 matches
M. G. Bevan (Aust) .. 35 in 89 matches
M. R. Martyn (Aust) .. 34 in 77 matches

M. A. Taylor (Aust) . 32 in 53 matches
D. M. Jones (Aust) .. 29 in 93 matches
R. T. Ponting (Aust) . 29 in 92 matches
P. L. Taylor (Aust) .. 28 in 54 matches
I. V. A. Richards (WI) 28 in 65 matches

MOST DISMISSALS

A. C. Gilchrist (Aust) . 131 (116ct, 15st)
I. A. Healy (Aust) 124 (108ct, 16st)
R. W. Marsh (Aust) .. 79 (78ct, 1st)
P. J. L. Dujon (WI) ... 69 (60ct, 9st)
Moin Khan (Pak) 31 (24ct, 7st)
A. J. Stewart (Eng) .. 31 (30ct, 1st)

D. J. Richardson (SAf) 30 (27ct, 3st)
W. B. Phillips (Aust) 29 (26ct, 3st)
C. O. Browne (WI) 29 (25ct, 4st)
A. C. Parore (NZ) 25 (23ct, 2st)
R. S. Kaluwitharana (SL) .. 25 (19ct, 6st)

MOST APPEARANCES

	M	Aust	AustA	Eng	Ind	NZ	Pak	SL	SAf	WI	Zim
A. R. Border (Aust) ..	160	–	–	19	18	35	22	6	13	47	–
S. R. Waugh (Aust) ..	142	–	3	12	17	27	23	14	16	27	3
M. E. Waugh (Aust) ..	116	–	4	13	7	17	16	13	16	27	5
D. C. Boon (Aust) ...	94	–	4	6	13	21	9	7	10	22	2
D. M. Jones (Aust) ...	93	–	–	10	8	15	14	5	11	30	–
R. T Ponting (Aust) ..	92	4	–	13	9	7	12	13	10	14	10
M. G. Bevan (Aust) ..	89	3	1	13	7	8	10	14	10	14	9
I. A. Healy (Aust) ...	86	–	3	6	6	10	18	6	10	25	2
D. L. Haynes (WI) ...	83	49	–	8	4	–	18	4	–	–	–
C. J. McDermott (Aust)	82	–	4	1	13	13	8	6	11	25	1

Tsunami Appeal Match

by GREG BAUM

This match was hastily arranged to raise funds for victims of the Boxing Day tsunami. Due to the goodwill of the players and the almost entirely voluntary workforce it proved a resounding success, drawing more than 70,000 spectators and bringing $14.6 million for World Vision. Old tensions were left behind as Shane Warne and Muttiah Muralidaran cheerfully shared a stage (and later toured Sri Lanka together), and Muralidaran was made welcome by a previously hostile Australian crowd and, for that matter, a previously disdainful Prime Minister. South Africa and Zimbabwe were the only Test countries not represented. The day was made more meaningful by the fact that many of the Sri Lankans were personally affected by the tragedy – Sanath Jayasuriya's mother had only survived by clinging to a tree.

The cricket was strictly exhibition in nature. Glenn McGrath batted at No. 6 in Ricky Ponting's side and Matthew Hayden at No. 8. Nonetheless, Ponting's scintillating century and cameo half-centuries from Brian Lara and Chris Cairns were fine innings from champion players. Two wickets for Shane Warne, two years after his one-day retirement, and three for Daniel Vettori circumscribed the Asian XI's reply and denied the match a grandstand finish. It did not matter. The ICC had accorded the match full one-day international status, the first time this had happened for a match not between ICC nations. This displeased some statisticians and purists, but the fact that the match was staged and so well supported was its triumph, not its style or outcome.

ACC ASIA WORLD XI v ICC WORLD XI

At Melbourne Cricket Ground, Melbourne, January 10, 2005. Day/night game. ICC World XI won by 112 runs. *Toss*: ICC World XI.

Man of Match: R. T. Ponting. *Attendance*: 70,101.

ICC World XI

C. H. Gayle c Sangakkara		
b Zaheer Khan	1	(9)
†A. C. Gilchrist c Sangakkara		
b Zaheer Khan	24	(20)
*R. T. Ponting st Sangakkara b Kumble	115	(102)
B. C. Lara c Vaas b Kumble	52	(77)
C. L. Cairns st Sangakkara b Muralidaran	69	(47)
G. D. McGrath c Yousuf Youhana		
b Muralidaran	0	(1)
S. P. Fleming b Vaas	30	(28)

D. Gough (did not bat).

M. L. Hayden st Sangakkara		
b Muralidaran	2	(6)
D. L. Vettori not out	27	(17)
S. K. Warne not out	2	(2)
L-b 3, w 7, n-b 12	22	

(50 overs, 219 mins)   (8 wkts) 344

Fall: 1 50 172 263 264 286 292 337

Bowling: Vaas 9-1-59-1; Zaheer Khan 8-0-46-2; Abdul Razzaq 5-0-50-0; Muralidaran 10-0-59-3; Kumble 10-0-73-2; Sehwag 7-0-46-0; Jayasuriya 1-0-8-0.

ACC Asian XI

S. T. Jayasuriya c Fleming b Cairns	28	(29)
V. Sehwag c Gayle b Warne	45	(39)
*S. C. Ganguly c Gough b Vettori	22	(40)
R. S. Dravid not out	75	(71)
Yousuf Youhana c Ponting b Warne	4	(5)
†K. C. Sangakkara c Gilchrist b Gough	24	(24)
Abdul Razzaq st Gilchrist b Vettori	11	(12)
W. P. U. J. C. Vaas c Gayle b Vettori	7	(11)

Zaheer Khan run out (Gayle/Gilchrist)	0	(0)
A. R. Kumble b McGrath	11	(7)
M. Muralidaran run out (Vettori)	0	(2)
L-b 2, w 2, n-b 1	5	

(39.5 overs, 172 mins)   232

Fall: 59 76 107 114 156 173 197 199 226 232

Bowling: McGrath 7-0-37-1; Gough 8-0-55-1; Cairns 6-0-37-1; Warne 7-0-27-2; Vettori 10-0-58-3; Gayle 1.5-0-16-0.

Umpires: B. F. Bowden (New Zealand) and R. E. Koertzen (South Africa).
TV Umpire: R. L. Parry.
Referee: B. C. Broad (England).

IT WAS A LONG TIME BETWEEN DRINKS
for new ING Cup champions Tasmania,
and a thirst was upon them.
Picture by Sean Garnsworthy, Getty Images.

5

The
Domestic
Scene

First-Class Season

FEATURES OF 2004-05

(Seasons run from July 1 to June 30)

Highest Individual Scores

261*	D.J. Thornely	New South Wales v Western Australia at Sydney.
240*	P.A. Jaques	New South Wales v Queensland at Bankstown.
223*	M.E.K. Hussey	Western Australia v Victoria at Perth.
217	P.A. Jaques	New South Wales v South Australia at Sydney.
215	J.L. Langer	Australia v New Zealand at Adelaide.
207	R.T. Ponting	Australia v Pakistan at Sydney.
204*	B.J. Hodge	Victoria v South Australia at Melbourne.
201	M.E.K. Hussey	Western Australia v Tasmania at Perth.
191	J.L. Langer	Australia v Pakistan at Perth.
190	M.G. Bevan	Tasmania v Western Australia at Hobart (Bel).

Denotes not out.

Leading Runs-Makers

		M	I	NO	R	HS	100s	50s	Avge
1.	M.G. Bevan (Tas)	9	18	3	1,464	190	8	2	97.60
2.	P.A. Jaques (NSW)	12	21	2	1,269	240*	3	6	66.79
3.	J.L. Langer (W Aust/Aust)	11	20	1	1,245	215	5	3	65.3
4.	D.J. Thornely (NSW)	12	20	3	1,065	261*	4	5	62.65
5.	B.J. Haddin (NSW)	12	19	3	916	154	2	5	57.25
6.	B.J. Hodge (Vic)	8	15	1	891	204*	3	4	63.64
7.	M.E.K. Hussey (W Aust)	9	17	3	851	223*	3	2	60.79
8.	J.P. Maher (Qld)	11	21	0	841	170	2	4	40.05
9.	M.W. Goodwin (W Aust)	11	20	2	841	138	2	5	46.72
10.	M.J. North (W Aust)	10	18	3	826	94*	0	9	55.07

Leading Batting Averages

(Qualification: 500 Runs)

		M	I	NO	R	HS	100s	50s	Avge
1.	M.G. Bevan (Tas)	9	18	3	1,464	190	8	2	97.60
2.	R.T. Ponting (Aust)	6	11	3	615	207	3	6	66.78
3.	P.A. Jaques (NSW)	12	21	2	1,269	240*	3	6	66.79
4.	D.R. Martyn (Aust)	7	11	2	596	142	2	4	66.22
5.	J.L. Langer (/Aust/W Aust)	11	20	1	1,245	215	5	3	65.53
6.	B.J. Hodge (Vic)	8	15	1	891	204*	3	4	63.64
7.	D.J. Thornely (NSW)	12	20	3	1,065	261*	4	5	62.65
8.	M.E.K. Hussey (W Aust)	9	17	3	851	223*	3	2	60.79
9.	J.L. Arnberger (W Aust)	6	11	0	639	152	3	4	58.09
10.	A.C. Gilchrist (Aust)	7	10	1	521	126	2	3	57.88

Notable Partnerships

First Wicket

55 J. L. Langer/M. L. Hayden, Australia v Sri Lanka at Cairns
57 J. L. Arnberger/M. T. G. Elliott, Victoria v Queensland at Brisbane
65 D. J. Harris/S. A. Deitz, South Australia v Western Australia at Perth
55 J. L. Langer/M. E. K. Hussey, Western Australia v Victoria at Perth
48 M. T. G. Elliott/J. L. Arnberger, Victoria v Tasmania at Melbourne

Second Wicket

56 J. L. Arnberger/B. J. Hodge, Victoria v Queensland at Melbourne
18 P. A. Jaques/M. J. Phelps, New South Wales v Queensland at Bankstown
79 D. G. Dawson/M. G. Bevan, Tasmania v South Australia at Hobart
66 G. C. Rummans/B. J. Hodge, Victoria v Tasmania at Hobart
63 J. L. Langer/R. T. Ponting, Australia v Pakistan at Perth

Third Wicket

277* M. G. Bevan/M. J. Di Venuto, Tasmania v New South Wales at Hobart
231 P. A. Jaques/D. J. Thornely, New South Wales v South Australia at Sydney
96 S. R. Watson/A. Symonds, Queensland v Western Australia at Perth
186 M. J. Phelps/D. J. Thornely, New South Wales v South Australia at Adelaide
174 R. T. Ponting/D. R. Martyn, Australia v Pakistan at Sydney

Fourth Wicket

319 M. G. Bevan/D. J. Marsh, Tasmania v Western Australia at Hobart
274 M. E. K. Hussey/S. E. Marsh, Western Australia v Tasmania at Perth
218 T. C. Plant/C. J. Ferguson, South Australia v New South Wales at Sydney
192 Younis Khan/Yousuf Youhana, Pakistan v Australia at Melbourne
191 B. P. Nash/C. A. Philipson, Queensland v Tasmania at Hobart

Fifth Wicket

153 R. T. Ponting/A. C. Gilchrist, Australia v Pakistan at Sydney
146 B. J. Hodge/I. J. Harvey, Victoria v South Australia at Melbourne
139 C. A. Philipson/L. M. Stevens, Queensland v Victoria at Melbourne
130 B. J. Hodge/C. L. White, Victoria v Tasmania at Melbourne
121 D. J. Hussey/C. L. White, Victoria v Western Australia at St Kilda

Sixth Wicket

216 M. J. Clarke/A. C. Gilchrist, Australia v New Zealand at Brisbane
152 J. L. Langer/A. C. Gilchrist, Australia v Pakistan at Perth
127 C. J. Ferguson/G. A. Manou, South Australia v Queensland at Adelaide
125 A. C. Voges/R. J. Campbell, Western Australia v New South Wales at Perth
111 J. R. Hopes/C. D. Hartley, Queensland v Victoria at Brisbane

Seventh Wicket

215 M. G. Bevan/D. G. Wright, Tasmania v Victoria at Hobart
205 C. L. White/I. J. Harvey, Victoria v Queensland at Brisbane
159 S. G. Clingeleffer/D. G. Wright, Tasmania v New South Wales at Sydney
136 A. C. Voges/P. C. Worthington, Western Australia v New South Wales at Perth
131 B. J. Haddin/J. J. Krejza, New South Wales v Victoria at St Kilda

Eighth Wicket

184 R. J. Campbell/D. J. Wates, Western Australia v Queensland at Perth
150 B. J. Hodge/S. K. Warne, Victoria v South Australia at Melbourne
133 G. A. Manou/D. J. Cullen, South Australia v Tasmania at Hobart
104 C. J. Ferguson/D. J. Cullen, South Australia v Western Australia at Perth

Ninth Wicket

119 M. J. Di Venuto/X. J. Doherty, Tasmania v South Australia at Hobart

Tenth Wicket

219 D. J. Thornely/S. C. G. MacGill, New South Wales v Western Australia at Sydney
114 J. N. Gillespie/G. D. McGrath, Australia v New Zealand at Brisbane

Highest Innings Totals

8-607 dec.	Western Australia v New South Wales at Perth
585	Australia v New Zealand at Brisbane
8-575 dec.	Australia v New Zealand at Adelaide
568	Australia v Pakistan at Sydney
561	Queensland v Western Australia
517	Australia v Sri Lanka at Cairns
512	Western Australia v Queensland at Perth
8-508 dec.	Victoria v Queensland at Brisbane
500	Tasmania v Western Australia at Hobart

Highest Fourth-Innings Totals

454	Western Australia (set 497) v South Australia at Perth
408	Victoria (set 455) v Western Australia at St Kilda
4-397	Western Australia (set 396) v Tasmania at Hobart
392	South Australia (set 446) v Queensland at Adelaide
366	Tasmania (set 494) v Victoria at Hobart

Lowest Complete Innings Totals

29	South Australia v New South Wales at Sydney
72	Pakistan v Australia at Perth
76	New Zealand v Australia at Brisbane
91	Victoria v New South Wales at St Kilda
97	Sri Lanka v Australia at Darwin
101	Tasmania v Victoria at Hobart
102	Queensland v New South Wales at Brisbane
133	South Australia v Western Australia at Adelaide
135	South Australia v New South Wales at Adelaide
143	South Australia v Queensland at Brisbane

Best Innings Analyses

8-24	G. D. McGrath	Australia v Pakistan at Perth
7-4	N. W. Bracken	New South Wales v South Australia at Sydney
7-39	M. S. Kasprowicz	Australia v Sri Lanka at Darwin
7-54	A. R. Griffith	Tasmania v Victoria at Hobart
7-77	A. J. Bichel	Queensland v New South Wales at Brisbane
7-99	S. W. Tait	South Australia v Queensland at Adelaide
7-188	Danish Kaneria	Pakistan v Australia at Sydney
6-25	D. G. Wright	Tasmania v South Australia at Hobart
6-27	N. W. Bracken	New South Wales v Queensland at Brisbane

Leading Wicket-Takers

		M	O	Mds	R	W	BB	5Wi	10W/m	Avge
1.	S. C. G. MacGill (NSW/Aust)	13	508.5	99	1,611	70	6-85	4	0	23.01
2.	S. W. Tait (S Aust)	10	391.1	77	1,311	65	7-99	3	0	20.17
3.	A. J. Bichel (Qld)	11	417.2	99	1,326	60	7-77	4	1	22.10
4.	M. J. Nicholson (NSW)	11	343.4	89	943	47	5-60	1	0	20.06
5.	S. K. Warne (Aust/Vic)	11	476.1	95	1,341	46	4-15	0	0	29.15
6.	J. H. Dawes (Qld)	11	347.5	84	1,009	46	6-49	3	0	21.93
7.	A. R. Griffith (Tas)	9	365.2	81	1,295	45	7-54	4	1	28.78
8.	N. W. Bracken (NSW)	11	365	124	808	43	7-4	3	0	18.79
9.	D. J. Cullen (S Aust)	10	409.4	76	1,306	43	5-38	2	0	30.37
10.	S. R. Clark (NSW)	11	342.4	74	1,039	40	5-10	2	0	25.98

Leading Bowling Averages

(Qualification: 20 wickets)

		M	O	Mds	R	W	BB	5W/i	10W/m	Avge
1.	G. D. McGrath (Aust)	7	255.1	75	615	37	8-24	2	0	16.62
2.	N. W. Bracken (NSW)	11	365	124	808	43	7-4	3	0	18.79
3.	M. J. Nicholson (NSW)	11	343.4	88	943	47	5-60	1	0	20.06
4.	S. W. Tait (S Aust)	10	391.1	77	1,311	65	7-99	3	0	20.16
5.	M. S. Kasprowicz (Aust)	6	189.4	44	559	26	7-39	2	0	21.50
6.	J. H. Dawes (Qld)	11	346.5	83	1,009	46	6-49	3	0	21.93
7.	B. R. Dorey (W Aust)	6	182.1	47	505	23	5-41	1	0	21.95
8.	M. L. Lewis (Vic)	8	297.4	76	838	38	6-84	2	0	22.05
9.	A. J. Bichel (Qld)	11	417.2	99	1,326	60	7-77	4	1	22.10
0.	S. C. G. MacGill (NSW/Aust)	13	508.5	99	1,611	70	6-85	4	0	23.01

Most Catches in an Innings – Fielders

3	S. E. Marsh	Western Australia v New South Wales at Sydney
3	R. T. Ponting	Australia v New Zealand at Brisbane
3	M. J. Phelps	New South Wales v Victoria at St Kilda
3	G. S. Blewett	South Australia v New South Wales at Sydney
3	S. E. Marsh	Western Australia v South Australia at Adelaide
3	G. J. Mail	New South Wales v South Australia at Adelaide
3	J. P. Maher	Queensland v Tasmania at Hobart
3	M. J. Phelps	New South Wales (1st inns) v Victoria at Sydney
3	P. A. Jaques	New South Wales v Victoria at Sydney
3	M. J. Phelps	New South Wales (2nd inns) v Victoria at Sydney
3	D. J. Harris	South Australia v Tasmania at Adelaide

Most Catches in a Match – Fielders

6	M. J. Phelps	New South Wales v Victoria at Sydney
5	M. J. Phelps	New South Wales v Victoria at St Kilda
4	S. E. Marsh	Western Australia v South Australia at Adelaide
4	P. A. Jaques	New South Wales v Victoria at Sydney
4	M. L. Hayden	Australia v India at Brisbane.

Most Dismissals in an Innings

5	(5ct)	A. C. Gilchrist	Australia v Sri Lanka at Darwin
5	(4ct, 1st)	R. J. Campbell	Western Australia v Tasmania at Perth
5	(5ct)	C. D. Hartley	Queensland v Western Australia at Perth
5	(5ct)	C. D. Hartley	Queensland v Tasmania at Brisbane
5	(5ct)	G. A. Manou	South Australia v New South Wales at Adelaide
5	(5ct)	G. A. Manou	South Australia v Victoria at Melbourne
5	(5ct)	R. J. Campbell	Western Australia v South Australia at Perth

Most Dismissals in a Match

9	(9ct)	C. D. Hartley	Queensland v Tasmania at Brisbane
9	(9ct)	R. J. Campbell	Western Australia v South Australia at Perth
8	(8ct)	A. C. Gilchrist	Australia v Sri Lanka at Darwin
8	(8ct)	W. A. Seccombe	Queensland v New South Wales at Bankstown
7	(7ct)	P. A. Roach	Victoria v South Australia at Adelaide
7	(6ct, 1st)	R. J. Campbell	Western Australia v Tasmania at Perth
7	(6ct, 1st)	S. G. Clingeleffer	Tasmania v Queensland at Hobart

FIRST-CLASS AVERAGES, 2004-05

BATTING

*Denotes not out. † Denotes left-handed batsman.

	M	I	NO	R	HS	100s	50s	Avge	Ct	St
Abdul Razzaq (Pakistanis)	3	6	3	163	83*	–	1	54.33	–	–
N. T. Adcock (S Aust)	7	13	–	247	67	–	1	19.00	8	–
J. L. Arnberger (Vic)	6	11	–	639	152	3	4	58.09	2	–
† R. P. Arnold (Sri Lankans)	1	2	–	17	11	–	–	8.50	2	–
† Asim Kamal (Pakistanis)	1	2	–	97	87	–	1	48.50	–	–
N. J. Astle (New Zealanders)	2	4	–	126	52	–	1	31.50	2	–
M. S. Atapattu (Sri Lankans)	2	4	–	156	133	1	–	39.00	1	1
C. B. Bailey (S Aust)	1	1	–	0	0	–	–	0.00	–	–
G. J. Bailey (Tas)	5	9	1	185	70	–	1	23.13	3	–
† M. G. Bevan (Tas)	9	18	3	1,464	190	8	2	97.60	3	–
A. J. Bichel (Qld)	11	18	4	311	69	–	1	22.214	–	–
† T. R. Birt (Tas)	8	16	–	331	57	–	2	20.69	3	–
G. S. Blewett (S Aust)	10	20	1	618	89	–	4	32.53	7	–
† A. M. Blignaut (Tas)	1	2	–	9	9	–	–	4.50	1	–
† D. Bollinger (NSW)	2	3	3	9	4*	–	–	–	–	–
C. J. Borgas (S Aust)	1	1	–	53	53	–	1	53.00	–	–
N. W. Bracken (NSW)	11	15	4	267	35	–	–	24.27	3	–
I. G. Butler (New Zealanders)	1	2	–	0	0	–	–	0.00	–	–
B. P. Cameron (S Aust)	3	6	–	53	31	–	–	8.83	–	–
R. J. Campbell (W Aust)	11	17	1	582	144	1	3	36.38	36	–
B. Casson (W Aust)	4	5	–	36	31	–	–	7.20	2	–
U. D. U. Chandana (Sri Lankans)	2	4	–	64	19	–	–	16.00	1	–
M. W. Clark (W Aust)	1	1	–	1	1	–	–	1.00	1	–
S. R. Clark (NSW)	11	13	4	106	25	–	–	11.78	2	–
M. J. Clarke (Aust)	5	6	–	231	141	1	–	38.50	5	–
† M. F. Cleary (S Aust)	4	8	2	112	40	–	–	18.67	3	–
† S. G. Clingeleffer (Tas)	10	18	–	472	92	–	3	26.22	27	2
† M. J. Cosgrove (S Aust)	6	12	–	223	82	–	3	18.58	6	–
E. J. M. Cowan (NSW)	3	6	–	132	66	–	1	22.00	–	–
J. Cox (Tas)	5	10	–	302	84	–	3	30.20	5	–
A. J. Crosthwaite (Vic)	3	4	–	60	24	–	–	15.00	10	2
D. J. Cullen (S Aust)	10	18	5	219	42	–	–	16.85	5	–
Danish Kaneria (Pakistanis)	4	8	3	28	10	–	–	5.60	–	–
J. H. Dawes (Qld)	11	17	7	117	34*	–	–	11.70	–	–
D. G. Dawson (Tas)	9	18	1	476	123*	1	2	28.00	8	–
† S. A. Deitz (S Aust)	2	4	–	260	141	1	1	65.00	4	–
† M. J. Di Venuto (Tas)	7	14	1	489	157*	1	2	37.62	9	–
M. G. Dighton (Tas)	6	12	–	166	42	–	–	13.83	4	–
T. M. Dilshan (Sri Lankans)	2	4	1	87	35	–	–	29.00	2	–
X. J. Doherty (Tas)	8	14	–	142	35	–	–	10.14	3	–
B. R. Dorey (W Aust)	6	9	1	112	22	–	–	14.00	1	–
A. G. Downton (Tas)	4	8	3	49	14	–	–	9.80	1	–
† B. M. Edmondson (W Aust)	8	8	5	23	13	–	–	7.67	3	–
† M. T. G. Elliott (Aust/Vic)	11	21	–	586	120	1	5	27.90	6	–
C. J. Ferguson (S Aust)	10	19	–	733	114	2	4	38.58	2	–
† S. P. Fleming (New Zealanders)	2	4	–	97	83	–	1	24.25	1	–
† J. E. C. Franklin (New Zealanders)	2	4	–	26	13	–	–	6.50	–	–
B. Geeves (Tas)	7	12	8	64	28	–	–	16.00	–	–
† A. C. Gilchrist (Aust)	7	10	1	521	126	2	3	57.89	31	5
J. N. Gillespie (Aust)	7	9	2	162	54*	–	2	23.14	6	–
M. W. Goodwin (W Aust)	11	20	2	841	138	2	5	46.72	6	–
A. R. Griffith (Tas)	9	16	3	119	37	–	–	9.15	4	–
B. J. Haddin (NSW)	12	19	3	916	154	2	5	57.25	36	3
D. J. Harris (S Aust)	4	8	1	148	82	–	1	21.14	7	–

	M	I	NO	R	HS	100s	50s	Avge	Ct	St
R. J. Harris (S Aust)	4	8	–	161	47	–	–	20.13	3	–
† C. D. Hartley (Qld)	3	4	–	71	50	–	1	17.75	19	–
I. J. Harvey (Vic)	9	15	3	434	90*	–	3	36.17	3	–
K. M. Harvey (W Aust)	4	7	1	47	14*	–	–	7.83	5	–
S. M. Harwood (Vic)	5	5	1	64	35	–	–	16.00	1	–
N. M. Hauritz (Qld)	6	10	4	121	45*	–	–	20.17	2	–
† M. L. Hayden (Aust)	7	13	2	548	132	2	3	49.82	8	–
B. J. Hodge (Vic)	8	15	1	891	204*	3	4	63.64	5	–
† G. B. Hogg (W Aust)	4	6	–	243	109	1	1	40.50	1	–
J. R. Hopes (Qld)	9	16	1	609	107	1	3	40.60	3	–
G. J. Hopkins (New Zealanders)	1	2	–	5	4	–	–	2.50	2	–
D. J. Hussey (Vic)	7	14	1	318	109*	1	2	24.46	3	–
† M. E. K. Hussey (W Aust)	9	17	3	851	223*	3	2	60.79	11	–
† Imran Farhat (Pakistanis)	3	6	–	57	20	–	–	9.50	1	–
† M. W. H. Inness (Vic)	6	11	2	85	24	–	–	9.44	1	–
Inzamam-ul-Haq (Pakistanis)	2	4	–	19	14	–	–	4.75	2	–
† P. A. Jaques (NSW)	12	21	2	1,269	240*	3	6	66.79	10	–
† S. T. Jayasuriya (Sri Lankans)	2	4	–	59	22	–	–	14.75	3	–
D. P. M. Jayawardene (Sri Lankans) . .	2	4	–	107	44	–	–	26.75	2	–
N. Jewell (Vic)	1	2	–	83	80	–	1	41.50	1	–
† M. G. Johnson (Qld)	3	4	1	108	51*	–	1	36.00	–	–
B. R. Joseland (Vic)	1	2	–	53	51	–	1	26.50	–	–
R. S. Kaluwitharana (Sri Lankans) . .	1	2	–	48	34	–	–	24.00	4	2
Kamran Akmal (Pakistanis)	4	8	–	81	47	–	–	10.13	5	5
M. S. Kasprowicz (Aust)	6	7	2	42	15	–	–	8.40	4	–
† S. M. Katich (Aust/NSW)	4	7	–	146	78	–	1	20.86	1	–
T. P. Kelly (S Aust)	1	2	–	9	6	–	–	4.50	1	–
B. A. Knowles (Vic)	1	2	1	22	18	–	–	22.00	2	–
J. J. Krejza (NSW)	9	13	2	214	63	–	2	19.45	9	–
G. M. Lambert (NSW)	1	2	–	23	23	–	–	11.50	–	–
† J. L. Langer (Aust/W Aust)	11	20	1	1,245	215	5	3	65.53	9	–
R. N. Le Loux (Qld)	1	1	–	5	5	–	–	5.00	–	–
B. Lee (NSW)	1	1	–	33	33	–	–	33.00	–	–
† D. S. Lehmann (Aust/S Aust)	8	13	–	465	104	1	4	35.77	4	–
M. L. Lewis (Vic)	8	13	2	72	21	–	–	6.55	2	–
R. J. G. Lockyear (Tas)	2	4	–	46	24	–	–	11.50	–	–
M. L. Love (Qld)	8	16	–	295	116	1	1	18.44	7	–
S. C. G. MacGill (NSW/Aust)	13	14	5	106	27	–	–	11.78	3	–
† S. J. Magoffin (W Aust)	11	14	6	125	29*	–	–	15.63	4	–
† J. P. Maher (Qld)	11	21	–	841	170	2	4	40.05	16	–
G. J. Mail (NSW)	12	21	1	448	101	1	1	22.40	15	–
S. L. Malinga (Sri Lankans)	2	3	–	0	0	–	–	0.00	1	–
G. A. Manou (S Aust)	10	19	–	433	97	–	3	22.79	34	2
D. J. Marsh (Tas)	9	17	1	373	121	1	1	23.31	16	–
† S. E. Marsh (W Aust)	11	18	2	569	103*	2	1	35.56	13	–
H. J. H. Marshall (New Zealanders) .	1	2	–	18	18	–	–	9.00	–	–
C. S. Martin (New Zealanders)	3	6	2	8	3	–	–	2.00	–	–
D. R. Martyn (Aust)	7	11	2	596	142	2	4	66.22	2	–
B. B. McCullum (New Zealanders) . .	2	4	–	64	36	–	–	16.00	2	1
A. B. McDonald (Vic)	2	4	–	51	36	–	–	12.75	1	–
G. D. McGrath (Aust)	7	7	3	79	61	–	1	19.75	2	–
C. D. McMillan (New Zealanders) . .	2	4	–	63	23	–	–	15.75	2	–
D. A. McNees (Tas)	1	2	–	0	0	–	–	0.00	–	–
S. W. Meuleman (W Aust)	1	2	–	23	21	–	–	11.50	2	–
K. D. Mills (New Zealanders)	1	2	1	33	29	–	–	33.00	1	–
† Mohammad Asif (Pakistanis)	1	2	2	12	12*	–	–	–	1	–
† Mohammad Khalil (Pakistanis)	1	2	–	5	5	–	–	2.50	–	–
Mohammad Sami (Pakistanis)	3	6	–	75	29	–	–	12.50	2	–
J. Moss (Vic)	9	17	1	401	114	1	2	25.06	5	–
† B. P. Nash (Qld)	2	4	–	130	92	–	1	32.50	2	–

	M	I	NO	R	HS	100s	50s	Avge	Ct	St
Naved-ul-Hasan (Pakistanis)	1	2	–	9	9	–	–	4.50	–	–
M.J. Nicholson (NSW)	11	16	2	155	28	–	–	11.07	9	–
A. A. Noffke (Qld)	9	15	3	273	53	–	1	22.75	4	–
† M.J. North (W Aust)	10	18	3	826	94*	–	9	55.07	4	–
A.J. Nye (Qld)	3	5	–	74	31	–	–	14.80	5	–
† A. W. O'Brien (NSW)	4	5	–	40	21	–	–	8.00	1	–
† J.D. P. Oram (New Zealanders)	3	6	1	213	126*	1	–	42.60	1	–
J. R. Packman (NSW)	5	10	–	267	107	1	–	26.70	1	–
C. T. Perren (Qld)	11	21	–	708	105	2	4	33.71	10	–
M.J. Phelps (NSW)	12	21	2	677	127*	1	4	35.63	20	–
C. A. Philipson (Qld)	7	14	2	447	119	1	2	37.25	5	–
T. C. Plant (S Aust)	8	16	–	286	125	1	–	17.88	3	–
R. T. Ponting (Aust)	6	11	3	615	207	1	4	76.88	10	–
† M. H. Richardson (New Zealanders) .	3	6	–	112	50	–	1	18.67	1	–
P.J. Roach (Vic)	7	13	2	122	29	–	–	11.09	27	1
P. C. Rofe (S Aust)	10	17	6	87	19*	–	–	7.91	3	–
† C.J. L. Rogers (W Aust)	9	16	–	691	153	1	3	43.19	11	–
† G. C. Rummans (Vic)	8	15	2	398	188	1	1	30.62	3	–
† Salman Butt (Pakistanis)	4	8	–	314	108	1	1	39.25	–	–
T. T. Samaraweera (Sri Lankans) ...	2	4	–	103	70	–	1	25.75	4	–
† K. C. Sangakkara (Sri Lankans) ...	2	4	–	142	74	–	2	35.50	7	–
W. A. Seccombe (Qld)	8	16	2	255	84	–	2	18.21	38	2
Shahid Afridi (Pakistanis)	1	2	–	58	46	–	–	29.00	–	–
Shoaib Akhtar (Pakistanis)	4	8	–	51	27	–	–	6.38	2	–
Shoaib Malik (Pakistanis)	2	4	–	67	41	–	–	16.75	2	–
C. P. Simpson (Qld)	1	2	–	8	8	–	–	4.00	1	–
M. S. Sinclair (New Zealanders) ...	3	6	–	238	88	–	3	39.67	1	–
J. K. Smith (S Aust)	4	8	1	173	57	–	1	24.71	3	–
† L. M. Stevens (Qld)	2	4	–	158	67	–	1	39.50	2	–
S. B. Styris (New Zealanders)	3	6	–	98	28	–	–	16.33	3	–
A. Symonds (Aust)	7	13	–	516	126	1	3	39.69	8	–
S. W. Tait (S Aust)	10	18	7	190	58	–	1	17.27	3	–
D.J. Thornely (NSW)	12	20	3	1,065	261*	4	5	62.65	7	–
† W. P. U. J. C. Vaas (Sri Lankans) ...	2	4	2	28	11*	–	–	14.00	–	–
† D. L. Vettori (New Zealanders)	2	4	–	102	59	–	1	25.50	1	–
A. C. Voges (W Aust)	6	9	4	362	128	1	2	72.40	7	–
S. K. Warne (Aust/Vic)	11	14	1	223	75	–	2	17.15	19	–
D.J. Wates (W Aust)	4	5	1	94	53	–	1	23.50	1	–
S. R. Watson (Qld/Aust)	9	16	1	619	136	1	3	41.27	5	–
C. L. White (Vic)	9	16	1	465	119	1	1	31.00	8	–
B. A. Williams (W Aust)	6	6	–	23	13	–	–	3.83	2	–
L. Williams (S Aust)	3	6	–	79	37	–	–	13.17	1	–
A. B. Wise (Vic)	6	11	7	25	8	–	–	6.25	–	–
P.J. Wiseman (New Zealanders)	2	4	2	53	21*	–	–	26.50	1	–
P. C. Worthington (W Aust)	1	1	–	73	73	–	1	73.00	2	–
D. G. Wright (Tas)	10	19	2	534	111	1	2	31.41	7	–
Yasir Hameed (Pakistanis)	2	4	–	146	63	–	2	36.50	1	–
Younis Khan (Pakistanis)	4	8	–	263	87	–	1	32.88	3	–
Yousuf Youhana (Pakistanis)	4	8	–	298	111	1	1	37.25	3	–
† D. N. T. Zoysa (Sri Lankans)	2	4	2	16	12	–	–	8.00	–	–

BOWLING

† Denotes left-arm bowler.

	M	O	Mdns	R	W	BB	5W/i	10W/m	Avge
Abdul Razzaq (Pakistanis)	3	46.3	3	217	4	2-55	–	–	54.25
N.T. Adcock (S Aust)	7	1	–	7	–	–	–	–	–
J.L. Arnberger (Vic)	6	3	–	12	–	–	–	–	–
R.P. Arnold (Sri Lankans) ...	1	1	–	9	–	–	–	–	–
C.B. Bailey (S Aust)	1	19	2	82	2	2-82	–	–	41.00
G.J. Bailey (Tas)	5	1	1	0	–	–	–	–	–
† M.G. Bevan (Tas)	9	23	–	96	2	2-19	–	–	48.00
A.J. Bichel (Qld)	11	417.2	99	1,326	60	7-77	4	1	22.10
G.S. Blewett (S Aust)	10	76	17	249	4	2-64	–	–	62.25
A.M. Blignaut (Tas)	1	12	–	79	–	–	–	–	–
† D. Bollinger (NSW)	2	58.5	11	204	2	1-34	–	–	102.00
† N.W. Bracken (NSW)	11	365	124	808	43	7-4	3	–	18.79
I.G. Butler (New Zealanders) .	1	20	3	61	3	3-51	–	–	20.33
† B. Casson (W Aust)	4	127.1	22	444	11	3-88	–	–	40.36
U.D.U. Chandana (Sri Lankans)	2	61.4	4	270	12	5-101	2	1	22.50
† M.W. Clark (W Aust)	1	36	10	94	1	1-50	–	–	94.00
S.R. Clark (NSW)	11	342.4	74	1,039	40	5-10	2	–	25.98
† M.J. Clarke (Aust)	5	3	–	24	–	–	–	–	–
M.F. Cleary (S Aust)	4	109.3	23	356	8	2-40	–	–	44.50
M.J. Cosgrove (S Aust)	6	28	9	98	3	1-26	–	–	32.67
J. Cox (Tas)	5	2	–	20	–	–	–	–	–
D.J. Cullen (S Aust)	10	409.4	76	1,306	43	5-38	2	–	30.37
Danish Kaneria (Pakistanis) ...	4	183.2	20	693	18	7-188	2	–	38.50
J.H. Dawes (Qld)	11	347.5	84	1,009	46	6-49	3	–	21.93
M.G. Dighton (Tas)	6	15	3	52	–	–	–	–	–
T.M. Dilshan (Sri Lankans) ...	2	2	–	4	2	2-4	–	–	2.00
† X.J. Doherty (Tas)	8	283.1	48	1,019	16	5-66	1	–	63.69
B.R. Dorey (W Aust)	6	182.1	47	505	23	5-41	1	–	21.96
† A.G. Downton (Tas)	4	117.1	31	396	10	5-94	1	–	39.60
B.M. Edmondson (W Aust) ...	8	270.5	51	1,165	34	3-38	–	–	34.26
† M.T.G. Elliott (Aust/Vic)	11	17	1	68	3	3-68	–	–	22.67
† J.E.C. Franklin (New Zealanders)	2	54.3	11	221	3	3-70	–	–	73.67
B. Geeves (Tas)	7	218.3	28	928	23	4-94	–	–	40.35
J.N. Gillespie (Aust)	7	247	63	649	22	3-37	–	–	29.50
M.W. Goodwin (W Aust)	11	1	–	2	–	–	–	–	–
A.R. Griffith (Tas)	9	365.2	81	1,295	45	7-54	4	1	28.78
R.J. Harris (S Aust)	4	113	23	395	9	4-92	–	–	43.89
I.J. Harvey (Vic)	9	214.5	58	599	21	4-83	–	–	28.52
K.M. Harvey (W Aust)	4	99.2	23	332	11	4-89	–	–	30.18
S.M. Harwood (Vic)	5	144.2	37	442	13	3-47	–	–	34.00
N.M. Hauritz (Qld)	6	147	23	576	6	2-16	–	–	96.00
B.J. Hodge (Vic)	8	31	3	111	3	1-8	–	–	37.00
† G.B. Hogg (W Aust)	9	118.3	18	341	16	6-44	1	–	21.31
J.R. Hopes (Qld)	9	179.2	60	476	18	4-39	–	–	26.44
M.E.K. Hussey (W Aust)	9	64.2	13	167	8	3-34	–	–	20.88
† Imran Farhat (Pakistanis) ...	3	27	3	112	2	2-30	–	–	56.00
† M.W.H. Inness (Vic)	6	161.5	37	549	14	3-41	–	–	39.21
† S.T. Jayasuriya (Sri Lankans) .	2	26	7	58	1	1-21	–	–	58.00
† M.G. Johnson (Qld)	3	81	14	325	9	3-23	–	–	36.11
M.S. Kasprowicz (Aust)	6	189.4	44	559	26	7-39	2	–	21.50
T.P. Kelly (S Aust)	1	39	8	122	3	3-59	–	–	40.67
B.A. Knowles (Vic)	1	19	3	69	1	1-69	–	–	69.00
J.J. Krejza (NSW)	9	128.2	25	489	12	2-11	–	–	40.75
G.M. Lambert (NSW)	1	15	3	52	2	1-17	–	–	26.00
R.N. Le Loux (Qld)	1	1	–	1	–	–	–	–	–
B. Lee (NSW)	1	32.4	7	89	5	3-52	–	–	17.80
† D.S. Lehmann (Aust/S Aust) ..	8	39	4	111	2	2-46	–	–	55.50

	M	O	Mdns	R	W	BB	5W/i	10W/m	Avge
M. L. Lewis (Vic)	8	297.4	76	838	38	6-84	2	–	22.05
S. C. G. MacGill (NSW/Aust)	13	508.5	99	1,611	70	6-85	4	–	23.01
S. J. Magoffin (W Aust)	11	367.3	85	1,103	32	5-76	1	–	34.47
G. J. Mail (NSW)	12	11	1	60	1	1-32	–	–	60.00
S. L. Malinga (Sri Lankans) ...	2	63.3	8	264	10	4-42	–	–	26.40
† D. J. Marsh (Tas)	9	96.3	14	340	6	3-72	–	–	56.67
† S. E. Marsh (W Aust)	11	2	–	26	–	–	–	–	–
C. S. Martin (New Zealanders) .	3	102.5	22	354	5	5-152	1	–	70.80
A. B. McDonald (Vic)	2	44	12	129	1	1-48	–	–	129.00
G. D. McGrath (Aust)	7	255.1	75	615	37	8-24	2	–	16.62
C. D. McMillan (New Zealanders)	2	9	4	25	–	–	–	–	–
D. A. McNees (Tas)	1	28	3	142	1	1-19	–	–	142.00
K. D. Mills (New Zealanders) ..	1	26	8	99	1	1-99	–	–	99.00
Mohammad Asif (Pakistanis) ..	1	18	3	88	–	–	–	–	–
† Mohammad Khalil (Pakistanis)125.2		–	97		–	–	–	–	–
Mohammad Sami (Pakistanis) .	3	89.4	9	408	6	3-104	–	–	68.00
J. Moss (Vic)	9	140.2	45	362	11	3-66	–	–	32.91
Naved-ul-Hasan (Pakistanis) ..	1	29	3	135	3	3-107	–	–	45.00
M. J. Nicholson (NSW)	11	343.4	89	943	47	5-60	1	–	20.06
A. A. Noffke (Qld)	9	282.1	56	872	23	4-58	–	–	37.91
M. J. North (W Aust)	10	86.1	15	300	6	3-93	–	–	50.00
A. J. Nye (Qld)	3	11	–	45	1	1-39	–	–	45.00
J. D. P. Oram (New Zealanders)	3	81	23	238	3	2-37	–	–	79.33
M. J. Phelps (NSW)	12	2	–	3	–	–	–	–	–
R. T. Ponting (Aust)	6	3	1	15	–	–	–	–	–
P. C. Rofe (S Aust)	10	403.3	115	1,079	35	5-93	1	–	30.83
† G. C. Rummans (Vic)	8	22	2	106	2	1-1	–	–	53.00
T. T. Samaraweera (Sri Lankans)	2	37	3	148	2	1-43	–	–	74.00
Shahid Afridi (Pakistanis)	1	29	3	115	–	–	–	–	–
Shoaib Akhtar (Pakistanis)	4	94.3	13	375	13	5-99	2	–	28.85
Shoaib Malik (Pakistanis)	2	1	–	15	–	–	–	–	–
C. P. Simpson (Qld)	1	2	–	6	–	–	–	–	–
† L. M. Stevens (Qld)	2	19	3	69	–	–	–	–	–
S. B. Styris (New Zealanders) .	3	19	4	53	–	–	–	–	–
A. Symonds (Qld)	7	145.4	34	446	11	2-14	–	–	40.55
S. W. Tait (S Aust)	10	391.1	77	1,311	65	7-99	3	–	20.17
D. J. Thornely (NSW)	12	29	8	91	–	–	–	–	–
† W. P. U. J. C. Vaas (Sri Lankans)272.3		15	236	7	5-31		1	–	33.71
† D. L. Vettori (New Zealanders)2123.2		21	341	10	5-152		1	–	34.10
† A. C. Voges (W Aust)	6	69	18	223	6	2-16	–	–	37.17
S. K. Warne (Aust/Vic)	11	476.1	95	1,341	46	4-15	–	–	29.15
D. J. Wates (W Aust)	4	106.5	21	384	13	3-59	–	–	29.54
S. R. Watson (Qld/Aust)	9	156.4	37	559	17	4-25	–	–	32.88
C. L. White (Vic)	9	219.4	38	755	19	4-105	–	–	39.74
B. A. Williams (W Aust)	6	223	53	678	18	4-53	–	–	37.67
† A. B. Wise (Vic)	6	162	41	513	15	4-63	–	–	34.20
P. J. Wiseman (New Zealanders)	2	81	15	289	6	3-140	–	–	48.17
P. C. Worthington (W Aust) ...	1	26.2	3	107	3	2-37	–	–	35.67
D. G. Wright (Tas)	10	442	133	1,223	39	6-25	3	–	31.36
† D. N. T. Zoysa (Sri Lankans) .	2	62	18	187	3	2-34	–	–	62.33

INDIVIDUAL SCORES OF 100 AND OVER

There were 77 three-figure innings in 40 first-class matches in 2004-05, 24 less than in 2003-04 when the four more matches were played. Of these, eight were double-hundreds compared with 13 in 2003-04. This list includes 61 hundreds hit in the Pura Cup, 15 less than in the 2003-04 season.

Denotes not out.

M. G. Bevan (8)
67*	Tasmania v Victoria, Hobart
106	Tasmania v South Australia, Hobart
100	Tasmania v South Australia, Hobart
90	Tasmania v Western Australia, Hobart
114*	Tasmania v Western Australia, Hobart
144	Tasmania v Victoria, Melbourne
170*	Tasmania v New South Wales, Hobart
115	Tasmania v South Australia, Adelaide

J. L. Langer (5)
162	Australia v Sri Lanka, Cairns
215	Australia v New Zealand, Adelaide
191	Australia v Pakistan, Perth
134	Western Australia v New South Wales, Perth
120	Western Australia v South Australia, Perth

D. J. Thornely (4)
261*	New South Wales v Western Australia, Sydney
102	New South Wales v South Australia, Sydney
100	New South Wales v Western Australia, Perth
135*	New South Wales v Tasmania, Hobart

J. L. Arnberger (3)
152	Victoria v Queensland, Brisbane
103	Victoria v Queensland, Melbourne
126	Victoria v Queensland, Melbourne

B. J. Hodge (3)
204*	Victoria v South Australia, Melbourne
140	Victoria v Tasmania, Melbourne
151	Victoria v Queensland, Melbourne

M. E. K. Hussey (3)
210	Western Australia v Tasmania, Perth
124	Western Australia v Pakistanis, Perth
223*	Western Australia v Victoria, Perth

P. A. Jaques (3)
217	New South Wales v South Australia, Sydney
116	New South Wales v Victoria, Sydney

C. J. Ferguson (2)
103	South Australia v New South Wales, Sydney
114	South Australia v Western Australia, Perth

A. C. Gilchrist (2)
126	Australia v New Zealand, Brisbane
113	Australia v Pakistan, Sydney

M. W. Goodwin (2)
130	Western Australia v Victoria, Perth
138	Western Australia v Tasmania, Hobart

B. J. Haddin (2)
154	New South Wales v Victoria, St Kilda
114	New South Wales v Tasmania, Sydney

M. L. Hayden (2)
117	Australia v Sri Lanka, Cairns
132	Australia v Sri Lanka, Cairns

J. P. Maher (2)
148	Queensland v Tasmania, Brisbane
170	Queensland v Tasmania, Brisbane

S. E. Marsh (2)
101	Western Australia v Tasmania, Perth
103*	Western Australia v South Australia, Perth

D. R. Martyn (2)
100*	Australia v Pakistan, Perth
142	Australia v Pakistan, Melbourne

C. T. Perren (2)
103	Queensland v New South Wales, Bankstown
105	Queensland v Western Australia, Brisbane

The following each played one three-figure innings:

M. S. Atapattu 133, Sri Lanka v Australia, Cairns.

R. J. Campbell 144, Western Australia v Queensland, Perth; M. J. Clarke 141, Australia v New Zealand, Brisbane.

D. G. Dawson 123*, Tasmania v Western Australia, Perth; S. A. Deitz 141, South Australia v Tasmania, Adelaide; M. J. Di Venuto 157*, Tasmania v New South Wales, Hobart.

M. T. G. Elliott 120, Victoria v Western Australia, St Kilda.

G. B. Hogg 109, Western Australia v South Australia, Adelaide; J. R. Hopes 107, Queensland v Victoria, Brisbane; D. J. Hussey 109*, Victoria v Western Australia, St Kilda.

D. S. Lehmann 104, South Australia v Queensland, Brisbane; M. L. Love 116, Queensland v New South Wales, Brisbane.

G. J. Mail 101, New South Wales v Western Australia, Perth; D. J. Marsh 121; Tasmania v Western Australia, Hobart; J. Moss 114, Victoria v New South Wales, St Kilda.

J. D. P. Oram 126*, New Zealand v Australia, Brisbane.
J. R. Packman 107, New South Wales v Western Australia, Perth; M. J. Phelps 127*, New South Wales v South Australia, Sydney; C. A. Philipson 119, Queensland v Tasmania, Brisbane; T. C. Plant 125, South Australia v New South Wales, Sydney; R. T. Ponting 207, Australia v Pakistan, Sydney.
C. J. L. Rogers 153, Western Australia v Victoria, St Kilda; G. C. Rummans 188, Victoria v Tasmania, Hobart.
Salman Butt 108, Pakistan v Australia, Sydney; A. Symonds 126, Queensland v Western Australia, Perth.
A. C. Voges 128, Western Australia v New South Wales, Perth.
S. R. Watson 136, Queensland v Western Australia, Perth; C. L. White 119, Victoria v Queensland, Brisbane; D. G. Wright 111, Tasmania v Victoria, Hobart.
Yousuf Youhana 111, Pakistan v Australia, Melbourne.

TEN OR MORE WICKETS IN A MATCH

A. J. Bichel (1)
10-127 Queensland v New South Wales, Brisbane.

U. D. U. Chandana (1)
11-210 Sri Lanka v Australia, Cairns.

A. R. Griffith (1)
10-173 Tasmania v Victoria, Hobart.

FIVE OR MORE WICKETS IN AN INNINGS

A. J. Bichel (4)
7-77   Queensland v New South Wales, Brisbane.
5-73   Queensland v South Australia, Adelaide.
5-70   Queensland v Tasmania, Hobart.
6-108 Queensland v Victoria, Brisbane.

J. H. Dawes (3)
6-49   Queensland v New South Wales, Brisbane.
5-54   Queensland v Victoria, Brisbane.
5-49   Queensland v South Australia, Brisbane.

A. R. Griffith (3)
7-54   Tasmania v Victoria, Hobart.
5-109 Tasmania v Queensland, Brisbane.
5-128 Tasmania v Queensland, Hobart.
6-124 Tasmania v Victoria, Melbourne.

S. C. G. MacGill (3)
5-73   New South Wales v South Australia, Adelaide.
5-87   Australia v Pakistan, Sydney.
5-72   New South Wales v Queensland, Queensland.
6-85   New South Wales v Tasmania, Hobart.

S. W. Tait (3)
5-39   South Australia v Victoria, Adelaide.
7-99   South Australia v Queensland, Adelaide.
5-71   South Australia v Tasmania, Adelaide.

D. G. Wright (3)
5-93   Tasmania v Western Australia, Perth.
6-25   Tasmania v South Australia, Hobart.
5-108 Tasmania v South Australia, Adelaide.

U. D. U. Chandana (2)
5-109 Sri Lanka v Australia, Cairns.
5-101 Sri Lanka v Australia, Cairns.

S. R. Clark (2)
5-10   New South Wales v Victoria, St Kilda.
5-91   New South Wales v South Australia, Adelaide.

D. J. Cullen (2)
5-79   South Australia v Queensland, Brisbane.
5-38   South Australia v Western Australia, Perth.

Danish Kaneria (2)
5-125 Pakistan v Australia, Melbourne.
7-188 Pakistan v Australia, Sydney.

M. S. Kasprowicz (2)
7-39   Australia v Sri Lanka, Darwin.
5-30   Australia v Pakistan, Perth.

M. L. Lewis (2)
6-84   Victoria v Tasmania, Hobart.
5-46   Victoria v South Australia, Melbourne.

G. D. McGrath (2)
5-37   Australia v Sri Lanka, Darwin.
8-24   Australia v Pakistan, Perth.

Shoaib Akhtar (2)
5-99   Pakistan v Australia, Perth.
5-109 Pakistan v Australia, Melbourne.

The following each took five wickets or more in an innings on one occasion:

X. J. Doherty 5-66, Tasmania v South Australia, Hobart; B. R. Dorey 5-41, Western Australia v Pakistanis, Perth; A. G. Downton 5-94 Tasmania v Victoria, Hobart.
G. B. Hogg 6-44, Western Australia v Tasmania, Perth.
S. J. Magoffin 5-76, Western Australia v Tasmania, Hobart; C. S. Martin 5-152, New Zealand v Australia, Brisbane.
M. J. Nicholson 5-60, New South Wales v Queensland, Brisbane.
P. C. Rofe 5-93, South Australia v Queensland, Adelaide.
W. P. U. J. C. Vaas 5-31, Sri Lanka v Australia, Darwin; D. L. Vettori 5-152, New Zealand v Australia, Adelaide.

Pura Cup, 2004-05

by PETER ENGLISH

Despite the recent departures or regular absences of a virtual World XI, New South Wales drew on a deep pool of talent to take their 44th domestic four-day trophy. A season of gentle twists and not-so-subtle turnarounds kept its most dramatic moment for the final afternoon. For three days the Pura Cup decider drew interest away from the Test team in New Zealand to prove that the domestic first-class race could still enthrall Australian cricket followers. During the season the states had jostled for position in echoing venues, despite a final-round scenario in which Queensland, NSW and Western Australia could all make, miss or host the final.

Scheduled for five days, the final ended late on the third evening on a lively surface with the faces of 2,025 supporters reflecting the Gabba lights. It was a fitting climax between sides that had pecked at each other through a summer of gripping contests. They had earlier fought a close tussle in Brisbane, where Queensland won by two wickets, before sharing a tense draw at Bankstown Oval, when the last pair of Nathan Hauritz and Joe Dawes held on for 69 balls for a draw. The two teams then produced a thrilling third act.

Wanting only a draw to claim the title, Queensland were 86 behind on the first innings after collapsing for 102 on losing the toss. Martin Love dragged them ahead with his first hundred of an awful summer before NSW stumbled chasing 183. From the safety of 4 for 158 they lost 5 for 3 in 18 balls. At 5.50 p.m., in artificial light and moist conditions, the No. 11, Stuart MacGill, swiped an ugly lofted pull shot behind square leg and NSW secured victory by a wicket, equalling the narrowest margin in the 23 finals. Before the game MacGill had cheekily suggested he was considering relocating for the Queensland lifestyle, but by stumps he was persona non grata there. It was Queensland's third consecutive final loss. "With 30 runs to go the scales looked like going our way but it just didn't happen," the Queensland captain, Jimmy Maher, said.

In October, NSW had begun their first summer in two decades without a Waugh, and Michael Bevan had also waved goodbye – the state's three top scorers carried away 22,015 runs. The captain, Simon Katich, was available for just two games, and Glenn McGrath, Brett Lee and Michael Clarke did not play at all. What remained were the self-styled "Baby Blues" and they were cradled by Brad Haddin, the deputy captain, and the new coach, Trevor Bayliss. "Not much was expected of us from outside," Haddin said, "but we always knew we would compete. If the young guys got on a roll they would be hard to beat."

The 2004-05 season arrived like springtime after the previous autumn's shedding of veterans and venerables. Apart from Steve and Mark Waugh, there were farewells from Michael Slater, Stuart Law, Darren Berry and Jo Angel. Realising the opportunities of a new generation, the replacements quickly created their own folk tales.

Dominic Thornely beat David Hookes's domestic six-hitting record during an explosive 261 for NSW against Western Australia at the SCG. His 11 sixes raised by one the mark set by Hookes for South Australia against NSW in 1985-86. With four hundreds helping him past 1,000 runs, Thornely and the impressively consistent Phil Jaques, who scored 1,191 runs at 66.17, spectacularly reinforced the batting line-up which had looked shaky after the departures of the Waughs and Bevan.

Over in Adelaide the quality off-spinning berth vacant since Tim May's retirement was filled by Dan Cullen, and by April he had replaced Nathan Hauritz in Cricket Australia's contracted-player squad. Shaun Tait won an Ashes place and the bill as Australia's first pace prospect since Brett Lee. As the Test attack greys, Tait will now be closely watched by hopeful selectors and spectators. Tait's 65 victims toppled Clarrie Grimmett's 1939-40 mark for the most first-class wickets in a South Australia season and put him ahead of his rival for an Ashes tour, Andy Bichel, who passed Craig McDermott's Queensland record with 60 scalps.

After the run-munching of the previous year, the bowlers fought their way back. Twelve months earlier no man had scraped above 40 wickets, but this time nine players did so, including MacGill as he cleared Bill O'Reilly from the New South Wales board after 65 years with 54 victims at 24.67. After eight batsmen scored 900 runs or more in 2003-04, this time there were only four.

Two of the three batsmen to top 1,000 runs and four of the bowlers to pass 40 wickets came from New South Wales. Powered by the competition's most feared attack – Stuart Clark, Nathan Bracken, Matthew Nicholson and MacGill – they soon shattered predictions that they would be also-rans. While Thornely and Jaques, who became the first NSW batsman since Bob Simpson to score two double-centuries in a season, were starring, Haddin, the wicket-keeper, was prepared to chip in from the middle order. During January, Haddin must have felt he was playing almost every day as he bounced from Australia A duty to the national one-day side and back to NSW. None of his innings were more crucial than the 68 and 41 in the final that showed how well he was suited to cap-taincy and responsibility.

In the post-season mop-up Queensland could compare them-selves to Hauritz: both suffered momentous failures when success had seemed likely. Hauritz dipped suddenly from the glorious wick-ets of Sachin Tendulkar and V.V.S. Laxman on Test debut in November to grade cricket by the autumn; Queensland led the field into the final before being cruelly denied. Wade Seccombe's dropped catch from Bracken two runs before NSW celebrated would be replayed by the Queenslanders well beyond the off-season.

Victoria's summer was also one of regrets following their do-it-for-Hookesy win in 2003-04. After they limped into fourth spot, Greg Shipperd, the coach, complained they played at "extremes" all year. A winter of discontent followed as high-profile players chased extra money in their contract talks and dreamed of fresh scenery. Matthew Elliott was bound for South Australia and Mathew Inness flew further west; Ian Harvey went furthest west of all, to South Africa; Jon Moss and Brad Hodge received better offers before eventually deciding to stay.

The dire state of West Australia's attack forced it to be propped up by two former Queensland 2nd XI imports. Fast and fresh, Ben Edmondson and Steve Magoffin performed admirably but ultimately well below the roaring standards set by Dennis Lillee, Terry Alderman, Angel and Brendon Julian. However, Western Australia were flying high for much of the season and led the table at the end of February, only to become the bystanders by mid-March. The absence of Brad Hogg, who collected 16 wickets at 21.23 in four games, added to problems that were often papered over by a well-performing batting order. Several bowling recruits headed west in the off-season, while Brad Williams stayed after considering a leap back to the MCG, but it is unlikely this collection will generate the fears of previous generations.

Two outright victories in South Australia's final matches added sparkle to a horror season made notorious by their dismissal for 29 against New South Wales. However, in Tait and Cullen they have the seeds of revival. A new-look top order of Elliott, Greg Blewett and a full-time Darren Lehmann also gives South Australia reason to be hopeful about the immediate future. In 2004-05 South Australia failed to pass 200 in the first innings in six matches and lost outright each time.

Despite their dreadful batting displays, South Australia still managed to leap over Tasmania, who stayed in the cellar even with the stellar performance of Bevan. He hit a record eight centuries on his way to a competition record aggregate of 1,464 runs at an average of 97.60. In Sydney, Bevan had talented support, but in Hobart he was a one-man batting band. Earning the unofficial title as the best domestic recruit since South Australia lured Don Bradman, Bevan collected the official award as the Pura Cup Player of the Season. Despite missing one match with a heel injury, he comfortably dismantled Elliott's 2003-04 record total of 1,381 when he finished the season with a streak of 190, 114 not out, 144, 86, 170 not out, 26, 115 and 44. The numbers did much for calls to return him to Australia's national teams but little to stave off defeat for Tasmania. As New South Wales's former veteran hungrily plundered, he could have been forgiven envious glances at the team of youngsters in Sydney who were stepping towards group glory rather than individual success.

2004-05 POINTS TABLE

	Played	Won	Lost	Drawn	1st-inns Points	Points	Quotient
Queensland	10	6	1	3	6	42	1.033
New South Wales	10	6	2	2	4	40	1.454
Western Australia	10	6	2	2	0	36	1.177
Victoria	10	4	6	0	2	24	0.932
South Australia	10	3	7	0	0	18	0.807
Tasmania	10	1	6	3	4	10	0.762

Outright win 6 pts; lead on first innings in a drawn or lost game 2 pts.
Quotient runs per wicket scored divided by runs per wicket conceded.

Under Cricket Australia playing conditions, a penalty of one run for a no-ball and a wide shall be scored. This penalty shall stand in addition to any other runs which are scored or awarded.

PURA CUP FINAL, 2004-05

QUEENSLAND v NEW SOUTH WALES

At Brisbane Cricket Ground, Brisbane, March 18, 19, 20, 2005. New South Wales won by one wicket. *Toss:* New South Wales.

Since the home side can bat for days in the knowledge that a draw is enough to secure the title, Pura Cup finals can be drab affairs. This one was anything but. It may even have been the best yet. In three wildly fluctuating days at the Gabba, each team must have thought it was home and hosed several times, only to see its advantage slip away again. As the match reached a heart-stopping climax under floodlights, New South Wales were coasting to victory with 25 runs needed and six wickets in hand. Then they lost 5 for 3, seemingly to surrender the title; finally they were hauled over the line by the unlikely batting heroes Stuart MacGill and Nathan Bracken, who conjured up 22 runs to secure a one-wicket victory.

Queensland went in as bookmakers' favourites to end their maddening run of outs in finals against NSW, having lost all five. The most memorable was probably the first, in 1984-85, which NSW won by one wicket, leaving Queensland still without a Sheffield Shield and Carl Rackemann walking off the SCG in tears. This time, the tears would flow from Jimmy Maher after Queensland let slip their best chance yet to shake the Blue monkey from their back. In truth, however, after the first few hours, when Brad Haddin's bold decision to send Queensland in was handsomely rewarded, this was NSW's match to lose – and they almost managed to do exactly that.

The Queenslanders have often been accused of juicing up their pitches to suit home bowlers, but while this one was tinged with green, and was perhaps slightly too sporting, it was refreshing nonetheless to see a Pura Cup final pitch that helped bowlers. It was the conditions – humid and overcast – more than the deck that helped Bracken destroy Queensland for just 102 in less than three hours (giving Queensland the four lowest innings totals in finals, each suffered against NSW). Following a rain break after six undramatic overs, the left-armer produced some unplayable late swing. He took 4 for 8 in a second spell of 4.2 overs, including three wickets in four balls to close the innings. NSW had already lost Greg Mail cheaply when their batsmen gratefully accepted a dubious offer of the light by Peter Parker and Steve Davis.

As the sun shone on day two NSW should have dominated, but they collapsed in a shambles to 8 for 128 at lunch. Bounce and seam helped Ashley Noffke make things difficult for the batsmen, but they largely contributed to their own demise. Phil Jaques played an ungainly cut shot to a wide short ball and was well caught by Andrew Symonds, James Packman was run out without facing a ball when Dominic Thornely called for a needless single, then Thornely played no shot at Noffke and was caught off the glove. Without Haddin's calm, unbeaten 68 off 92 balls and Stuart Clark's assistance in a 60-run ninth-wicket partnership, NSW's lead would have been far smaller than 86.

The conditions aided Bracken far less on the second day and after two early setbacks for Queensland, Martin Love – choosing the most important match of the season to find form at last – and Shane Watson put Queensland into what appeared a strong position at 2 for 111. But Grant Lambert, in his only match of the summer, and Bracken struck back to have Watson and Symonds caught behind by Haddin, leaving Queensland four down and 64 in front when the light was taken again.

On day three every run was priceless. With Love en route to the only century of the match, Queensland edged to 6 for 236, 150 in front, before Haddin wisely took the new ball despite the temptation to continue with MacGill. The move paid off, only 32 more runs being added as Matthew Nicholson took the last four wickets to complete a deserved five-wicket haul. Love was ninth out after applying himself with determination and skill for six hours.

NSW needed just 183 to win and were well poised at 1 for 50 after the long first session, before two quick wickets to Symonds' medium-pacers, and Noffke's second dismissal for the match of the dangerous Thornely, left the visitors wobbling at 4 for 97. Stability came from Haddin – of course – and the impressive rookie Packman, who put NSW within reach of victory at 4 for 158, before yet another stunning twist. The ball was 48 overs old, but suddenly was moving under evening clouds, and 34-year-old pacemen Andy Bichel and Joe Dawes claimed five wickets in 18 balls. First Bichel and second-slip Maher combined to remove Packman and Lambert three balls apart, then two balls later Dawes grabbed the vital wicket of Haddin, a seaming ball gaining the edge to slip. Next over, Dawes had Nicholson and Clark caught behind the wicket off successive balls. NSW were 9 for 161, and the Cup was almost within Queensland's grasp.

MacGill joined Bracken, vowing to triumph despite the pandemonium, and with a few serviceable swings of the bat took NSW to within two runs of victory as Dawes and Bichel grew more desperate. Then came the moment when Queensland should have won, only for one of their most trusted servants, wicket-keeper Wade Seccombe, to drop Bracken to his right off Bichel, a chance he probably would have held under less pressure and in better light. Moments later, MacGill swung a pull shot at Dawes, the ball sped through the vacant square leg, and the last pair ran two for a memorable triumph. "We should never have lost it, and then we should never have won it," said Haddin. It was an appropriate last word. – TREVOR MARSHALLSEA

Man of Match: N.W. Bracken.   *Attendance:* 4,723.

Close of play: First day, New South Wales (1) 1-26 (Jaques 11, Phelps 0); Second day, Queensland (2) 4-150 (Love 61, Philipson 7).

Queensland

*J. P. Maher c Haddin b Bracken	4	– (2) c Jaques b Bracken	1
C. T. Perren c Nicholson b Bracken	9	– (1) lbw b MacGill	17
M. L. Love c Haddin b Lambert	24	– c Bracken b Nicholson	116
S. R. Watson c Haddin b Nicholson	0	– c Haddin b Lambert	39
A. Symonds b Nicholson	36	– c Haddin b Bracken	14
C. A. Philipson b Clark	0	– b Nicholson	13
J. R. Hopes c Nicholson b Bracken	6	– c Jaques b MacGill	33
†W. A. Seccombe lbw b Bracken	2	– c Haddin b Nicholson	5
A. J. Bichel not out	16	– c Haddin b Nicholson	1
A. A. Noffke b Bracken	0	– c Phelps b Nicholson	5
J. H. Dawes b Bracken	0	– not out	0
L-b 5	5	L-b 17, w 3, n-b 4	24

(35.2 overs, 162 mins)   102   (95 overs, 394 mins)   268

Fall: 14 17 18 60 61 80 84 90 90 102   Fall: 4 31 111 135 156 222 243 257
                                               266 268

Bowling: *First Innings*—Nicholson 9–3–28–2; Bracken 13.2–8–27–6; Clark 9–1–25–1; Lambert 4–0–17–1. *Second Innings*—Nicholson 23–7–60–5; Bracken 27–9–54–2; Clark 17–6–59–0; Lambert 11–3–35–1; MacGill 17–6–43–2.

New South Wales

G. J. Mail c Perren b Watson	12	– lbw b Symonds	30
P. A. Jaques c Symonds b Noffke	18	– c Symonds b Bichel	21
M. J. Phelps b Noffke	3	– c and b Symonds	3
D. J. Thornely c Watson b Noffke	10	– c Seccombe b Noffke	20
J. R. Packman run out (Perren)	0	– c Maher b Bichel	25
*†B. J. Haddin not out	68	– c Love b Dawes	41
G. M. Lambert c Seccombe b Watson	23	– c Maher b Bichel	0
M. J. Nicholson c Love b Hopes	0	– c Seccombe b Dawes	1
N. W. Bracken c and b Bichel	12	– not out	11
S. R. Clark lbw b Hopes	25	– c Perren b Dawes	0
S. C. G. MacGill c Seccombe b Noffke	0	– not out	11
L-b 7, w 8, n-b 2	17	B 1, l-b 12, w 1, n-b 6	20

(53.2 overs, 243 mins)	188	(57.2 overs, 250 mins) (9 wkts) 183

Fall: 21 32 43 43 48 94 102 127 187 188

Fall: 34 60 67 97 158 158 158 161 161

Bowling: *First Innings*—Bichel 19–4–58–1; Dawes 4–0–6–0; Watson 9–1–36–2; Noffke 13.2–3–58–4; Hopes 8–1–23–2. *Second Innings*—Bichel 15–2–48–3; Dawes 10.2–3–30–3; Noffke 10–3–30–1; Symonds 14–3–30–2; Watson 6–1–20–0; Hopes 2–0–12–0.

Umpires: S. J. Davis and P. D. Parker.

DOMESTIC COMPETITION RECORDS

STATISTICS, 2004-05

	M	Runs	For Wickets	Avge	Runs	Against Wickets	Avge
New South Wales	11	5,760	160	35.78	5,042	199	25.34
Queensland	11	5,976	191	31.29	5,864	192	30.54
Western Australia	10	5,685	147	38.67	5,651	172	32.85
Victoria	10	5,099	170	29.99	5,086	158	32.19
South Australia	10	4,522	185	24.44	5,270	174	30.29
Tasmania	10	5,579	186	29.99	5,708	145	39.37

OVERS BOWLED AND RUNS SCORED, 2004-05

	Overs bowled per hour	Runs scored/ 100 balls
New South Wales	14.66	57.26
Queensland	14.81	57.41
Western Australia	14.90	54.24
Victoria	15.10	55.24
South Australia	14.97	50.88
Tasmania	15.08	50.75

LEADING BATTING AVERAGES, 2004-05

(Qualification: 500 runs)

	M	I	NO	R	HS	100s	50s	Avge	S-R
M. G. Bevan (Tas)	9	18	3	1,464	190	8	2	97.60	54.08
P. A. Jaques (NSW)	11	19	1	1,191	240*	3	5	66.17	59.85
B. J. Hodge (Vic)	8	15	1	891	204*	3	4	63.64	67.14
D. J. Thornely (NSW)..	11	19	3	1,006	261*	4	4	62.88	55.76
B. J. Haddin (NSW)	11	18	3	902	154	2	5	60.13	83.29
J. L. Arnberger (Vic) ...	6	11	0	639	152	3	4	58.09	56.40
M. E. K. Hussey (W Aust)	8	15	2	721	223*	2	2	55.46	54.83
M. J. North (W Aust) ...	9	17	3	747	94*	0	8	53.36	51.70
M. W. Goodwin (W Aust)	10	19	2	840	138	2	5	49.41	55.05
C. J. L. Rogers (W Aust).	8	15	0	645	153	1	3	43.00	62.38

* Denotes not out.

LEADING BOWLING AVERAGES, 2004-05

(Qualification: 15 wickets)

	M	O	Mdns	R	W	BB	5W/i	10W/m	Avge	Balls/W
N. W. Bracken (NSW)	11	365	124	808	43	7-4	3	0	18.79	50.93
S. W. Tait (S Aust)	10	391.1	77	1,311	65	7-99	3	0	20.17	36.11
M. J. Nicholson (NSW)	10	312.4	80	871	43	5-60	1	0	20.26	43.63
G. B. Hogg (W Aust)	4	118.3	18	341	16	6-44	1	0	21.31	44.44
J. H. Dawes (Qld)	11	347.5	84	1,009	46	6-49	3	0	21.93	45.37
M. L. Lewis (Vic)	8	297.4	76	838	38	6-84	2	0	22.05	47.00
A. J. Bichel (Qld)	11	417.2	99	1,326	60	7-77	4	1	22.10	41.73
S. C. G. MacGill (NSW)	11	421.2	82	1,332	54	6-85	3	0	24.67	46.81
S. R. Clark (NSW)	10	321.4	67	991	40	5-10	2	0	24.78	48.25
J. R. Hopes (Qld)	9	179.2	60	476	18	4-39	0	0	26.44	59.78

MOST CATCHES, 2004-05

	M	Catches
M. J. Phelps (NSW)	11	19
J. P. Maher (Qld)	11	16
D. J. Marsh (Tas)	9	16
G. J. Mail (NSW)	11	13
S. E. Marsh (W Aust)	10	11
C. T. Perren (Qld)	11	10
C. W. J. Rogers (W Aust)	8	10

MOST DISMISSALS, 2004-05

	M	Catches	Stumpings	Dismissals
W. A. Seccombe (Qld)	8	38	2	40
B. J. Haddin (NSW)	11	35	3	38
G. A. Manou (S Aust)	10	34	2	36
R. J. Campbell (W Aust)	10	33	1	34
S. G. Clingeleffer (Tas)	10	27	2	29
P. J. Roach (Vic)	7	27	1	28
C. D. Hartley (Qld)	3	19	0	19
A. J. Crosthwaite (Vic)	3	10	2	12

AUSTRALIAN DOMESTIC FIRST-CLASS COMPETITION WINNERS

Sheffield Shield

1892-93	Victoria
1893-94	South Australia
1894-95	Victoria
1895-96	New South Wales
1896-97	New South Wales
1897-98	Victoria
1898-99	Victoria
1899-00	New South Wales
1900-01	Victoria
1901-02	New South Wales
1902-03	New South Wales
1903-04	New South Wales
1904-05	New South Wales
1905-06	New South Wales
1906-07	New South Wales
1907-08	Victoria
1908-09	New South Wales
1909-10	South Australia
1910-11	New South Wales
1911-12	New South Wales
1912-13	South Australia
1913-14	New South Wales
1914-15	Victoria
1915-16	–
1916-17	–
1917-18	–
1918-19	–
1919-20	New South Wales
1920-21	New South Wales
1921-22	Victoria
1922-23	New South Wales
1923-24	Victoria
1924-25	Victoria
1925-26	New South Wales
1926-27	South Australia
1927-28	Victoria
1928-29	New South Wales
1929-30	Victoria
1930-31	Victoria
1931-32	New South Wales
1932-33	New South Wales
1933-34	Victoria
1934-35	Victoria
1935-36	South Australia
1936-37	Victoria
1937-38	New South Wales
1938-39	South Australia
1939-40	New South Wales
1940-41	–
1941-42	–
1942-43	–
1943-44	–
1944-45	–
1945-46	–
1946-47	Victoria
1947-48	Western Australia
1948-49	New South Wales
1949-50	New South Wales
1950-51	Victoria
1951-52	New South Wales
1952-53	South Australia
1953-54	New South Wales
1954-55	New South Wales
1955-56	New South Wales
1956-57	New South Wales
1957-58	New South Wales
1958-59	New South Wales
1959-60	New South Wales
1960-61	New South Wales
1961-62	New South Wales
1962-63	Victoria
1963-64	South Australia
1964-65	New South Wales
1965-66	New South Wales
1966-67	Victoria
1967-68	Western Australia
1968-69	South Australia
1969-70	Victoria
1970-71	South Australia
1971-72	Western Australia
1972-73	Western Australia
1973-74	Victoria
1974-75	Western Australia
1975-76	South Australia
1976-77	Western Australia
1977-78	Western Australia
1978-79	Victoria
1979-80	Victoria
1980-81	Western Australia
1981-82	South Australia
1982-83	New South Wales
1983-84	Western Australia
1984-85	New South Wales
1985-86	New South Wales
1986-87	Western Australia
1987-88	Western Australia
1988-89	Western Australia
1989-90	New South Wales
1990-91	Victoria
1991-92	Western Australia
1992-93	New South Wales
1993-94	New South Wales
1994-95	Queensland
1995-96	South Australia
1996-97	Queensland
1997-98	Western Australia
1998-99	Western Australia

Pura Milk Cup

1999-00	Queensland

Pura Cup

2000-01	Queensland
2001-02	Queensland
2002-03	New South Wales
2003-04	Victoria
2004-05	New South Wales

Note: The Sheffield Shield was not played during the First and Second World Wars.

FINALS

1982-83	Western Australia lost to New South Wales at Perth by 54 runs.
1983-84	Western Australia defeated Queensland at Perth by 4 wickets.
1984-85	New South Wales defeated Queensland at Sydney by one wicket.
1985-86	New South Wales drew with Queensland at Sydney.
1986-87	Western Australia drew with Victoria at Perth.
1987-88	Western Australia defeated Queensland at Perth by five wickets.
1988-89	Western Australia drew with South Australia at Perth.
1989-90	New South Wales defeated Queensland at Sydney by 345 runs.
1990-91	Victoria defeated New South Wales at Melbourne by eight wickets.
1991-92	Western Australia defeated New South Wales at Perth by 44 runs.
1992-93	New South Wales defeated Queensland at Sydney by eight wickets.
1993-94	New South Wales defeated Tasmania at Sydney by an innings and 61 runs.
1994-95	Queensland defeated South Australia at Brisbane by an innings and 101 runs.
1995-96	South Australia drew with Western Australia at Adelaide.
1996-97	Western Australia lost to Queensland at Perth by 160 runs.
1997-98	Western Australia defeated Tasmania at Perth by seven wickets.
1998-99	Queensland lost to Western Australia at Brisbane by an innings and 131 runs.
1999-00	Queensland drew with Victoria at Brisbane.
2000-01	Queensland defeated Victoria at Brisbane by four wickets.
2001-02	Queensland defeated Tasmania at Brisbane by 235 runs.
2002-03	Queensland lost to New South Wales at Brisbane by 246 runs.
2003-04	Victoria defeated Queensland at Melbourne by 321 runs.
2004-05	Queensland lost to New South Wales by one wicket.

Note: Since 1982-83 the winner of the season's competition has been decided by the two top teams playing a final at the top of the table's choice of venue.

MATCH RESULTS, 1892-93 to 2004-05

	Debut Season	Played	Won	Lost	Drawn	Tied
South Australia	1892-93	709	202	317	189	1
New South Wales	1892-93	720	310	201	208	1
Victoria	1892-93	712	266	208	237	1
Queensland	1926-27	604	175	207	221	1
Western Australia	1947-48	487	169	139	179	0
Tasmania	1977-78	258	47	97	114	0
Total		1,745	1,169	1,169	574	2

PLACINGS

	1st	2nd	3rd	4th	5th	6th	Seasons
South Australia	13	21	32	12	20	5	103
New South Wales	44	22	18	10	6	3	103
Victoria	26	33	22	8	7	7	103
Queensland	5	17	15	23	12	1	73
Western Australia	15	7	12	15	9	0	58
Tasmania	0	3	4	5	4	12	28
Total	103	103	103	73	58	28	103

LAST TEN YEARS' PLACINGS

	95-96	96-97	97-98	98-99	99-00	00-01	01-02	02-03	03-04	04-05
South Australia ...	1	6	6	4	4	4	4	4	6	5
New South Wales .	5	3	4	6	6	3	6	1	5	1
Victoria	6	5	5	3	2	2	5	3	1	4
Queensland	3	1	3	2	1	1	1	2	2	2
Western Australia .	2	2	1	1	3	5	3	5	4	5
Tasmania	4	4	2	5	5	4	2	6	3	6

MOST RUNS IN A SEASON

	Season	M	I	NO	R	HS	100s	50s	Avge
M. G. Bevan (Tas)	2004-05	9	18	3	1,464	190	8	2	97.60
M. T. G. Elliott (Vic)	2003-04	11	20	3	1,381	182	7	3	81.24
G. N. Yallop (Vic)	1982-83	10	18	0	1,254	246	4	5	69.66
M. G. Bevan (NSW)	1993-94	11	20	5	1,240	203*	5	7	82.67
W. H. Ponsford (Vic)	1927-28	5	8	0	1,217	437	4	1	152.12
D. M. Jones (Vic)	1994-95	10	19	3	1,216	324*	4	3	76.00
P. A. Jaques (NSW)	2004-05	11	19	1	1,191	240*	3	5	66.17
M. W. Goodwin (W Aust)	2003-04	10	20	2	1,183	201*	4	5	65.72
G. S. Blewett (S Aust)	2000-01	9	18	1	1,162	260*	3	6	68.35
J. Cox (Tas)	1996-97	10	20	1	1,149	143	4	7	60.47

* Denotes not out.

MOST RUNS IN A CAREER

	M	I	NO	R	HS	100s	50s	Avge
D. S. Lehmann (S Aust/Vic)	127	231	14	11,636	255	39	44	53.62
J. Cox (Tas)	158	289	17	10,761	245	30	47	39.56
J. D. Siddons (Vic/S Aust)	146	259	21	10,643	245	30	50	44.72
M. G. Bevan (S Aust/NSW/Tas)	108	193	36	9,976	216	41	37	63.54
D. M. Jones (Vic)	110	194	16	9,622	324*	31	40	54.06
M. T. G. Elliott (Vic)	103	197	16	9,470	203	32	43	52.32
G. S. Blewett (S Aust)	110	210	11	9,412	268	23	47	47.30
D. W. Hookes (S Aust)	120	205	9	9,364	306*	26	44	47.78
R. J. Inverarity (W Aust/S Aust)	159	275	32	9,341	187	22	46	38.44
S. G. Law (Qld)	141	232	28	8,944	216	24	46	43.84
D. G. Bradman (NSW/S Aust)	62	96	15	8,926	452*	36	20	110.19
T. M. Moody (W Aust)	132	228	22	8,853	272	20	46	42.98
G. S. Chappell (S Aust/Qld)	101	173	20	8,762	194	27	44	57.27
S. C. Trimble (Qld)	123	230	13	8,647	252*	22	40	39.85
A. R. Border (NSW/Qld)	108	181	19	8,497	200	19	47	52.45
L. E. Favell (S Aust)	121	220	4	8,269	164	20	43	38.28
D. C. Boon (Tas)	119	203	7	8,029	227	20	43	40.96

* Denotes not out.

HIGHEST PARTNERSHIPS FOR EACH WICKET

431	for 1st	M. R. J. Veletta and G. R. Marsh W Aust v S Aust at Perth	1989-90
386	for 2nd	G. S. Blewett and D. S. Lehmann S Aust v Tas at Hobart (Bel)	2001-02
390*	for 3rd	J. M. Weiner and J. K. Moss Vic v W Aust at St. Kilda	1981-82
462*	for 4th	D. W. Hookes and W. B. Phillips S Aust v Tas at Adelaide	1986-87
464*	for 5th	M. E. Waugh and S. R. Waugh NSW v W Aust at Perth	1990-91
332	for 6th	N. G. Marks and G. Thomas NSW v S Aust at Sydney	1958-59
335	for 7th	C. W. Andrews and E. C. Bensted Qld v NSW at Sydney	1934-35
270	for 8th	V. T. Trumper and E. P. Barbour NSW v Vict at Sydney	1912-13
232	for 9th	C. Hill and E. A. Walkley S Aust v NSW at Adelaide	1900-01
307	for 10th	A. F. Kippax and J. E. H. Hooker NSW v Vic at Melbourne	1928-29

* Denotes unbroken partnership.

MOST WICKETS IN A SEASON

	Season	M	Balls	Mdns	R	W	BB	5W/i	10W/m	Avge
C. R. Miller (Tas)	1997-98	11	3,590	159	1,642	67	7-49	5	0	24.51
S. R. Tait (S Aust)	2004-05	10	2,347	77	1,311	65	7-99	3	0	20.17
L. O. Fleetwood-Smith (Vic)	1934-35	6	2,164	25	1,137	60	8-113	8	0	18.95
A. J. Bichel (Qld)	2004-05	11	2,504	99	1,326	60	7-77	4	1	22.10
P. R. Reiffel (Vic)	1999-00	11	2,552	118	982	59	5-65	1	0	16.64
C. D. Matthews (W Aust) ...	1987-88	11	2,553	81	1,215	56	8-101	3	0	21.70
J. Garner (S Aust)	1982-83	8	2,419	131	976	55	7-78	4	0	17.74
C. J. McDermott (Qld)	1989-90	10	1,392	100	1,375	54	8-44	4	0	25.46
S. C. G. MacGill (NSW)	2004-05	11	2,528	82	1,332	54	6-85	3	0	24.67
A. J. Bichel (Qld)	1999-00	11	2,421	124	989	53	6-45	2	1	18.66
W. J. O'Reilly (NSW)	1939-40	6	1,766	48	705	52	8-23	6	0	13.55
G. R. A. Lock (W Aust)	1966-67	8	2,392	104	1,086	51	6-85	3	0	21.29
B. A. Williams (W Aust) ...	1999-00	10	2,194	94	1,151	50	6-74	5	0	23.02

MOST WICKETS IN A CAREER

	M	Balls	Mdns	R	W	BB	5W/i	10W/m	Avge
C. V. Grimmett (Vic/S Aust)	79	28,465	446	12,976	513	9-180	48	13	25.29
J. Angel (W Aust)	105	22,351	1,033	10,418	419	6-35	13	0	24.86
M. S. Kasprowicz (Qld) ...	89	19,599	843	9,409	387	6-47	24	2	24.31
T. M. Alderman (W Aust) ..	97	19,288	778	9,299	384	7-28	17	3	24.21
C. G. Rackemann (Qld) ...	102	22,400	920	10,079	383	7-43	12	1	26.32
G. F. Lawson (NSW)	103	21,391	873	8,742	367	6-31	12	0	23.82
G. R. J. Matthews (NSW) .	116	26,764	1,376	10,518	363	8-52	19	4	28.98
J. R. Thomson (NSW-Qld) .	84	16,939	429	8,591	355	7-27	18	3	24.20
A. A. Mallett (S Aust)	77	20,906	673	8,173	344	7-57	19	2	23.76
D. K. Lillee (W Aust/Tas) ..	75	17,814	475	8,086	338	7-36	18	4	23.92
A. R. Bichel (Qld)	67	14,959	624	7,438	334	7-77	19	4	22.27
P. R. Reiffel (Vic)	86	19,137	843	8,242	318	6-57	7	2	25.92
C. D. Matthews (W Aust/Tas)	79	17,663	614	8,912	307	8-101	18	0	29.03
C. R. Miller (S Aust/Vic/Tas)	84	20,285	624	9,738	304	7-49	11	2	32.03
C. J. McDermott (Qld)	67	14,974	541	7,605	303	8-44	22	2	25.10
G. A. R. Lock (W Aust)	63	20,107	544	7,210	302	7-53	16	2	23.87

MOST CATCHES IN A CAREER – FIELDER

R. J. Inverarity (W Aust/S Aust) .... 189 in 159 matches
J. D. Siddons (Vic/S Aust) .... 189 in 146 matches
M. R. J. Veletta (W Aust) .... 138 in 114 matches
S. G. Law (Qld) .... 126 in 142 matches
J. P. Maher (Qld) .... 126 in 112 matches
M. T. G. Elliott (Vic) .... 125 in 103 matches
M. L. Love (Qld) .... 124 in 110 matches
D. W. Hookes (S Aust) .... 123 in 120 matches
M. A. Taylor (NSW) .... 120 in 85 matches
A. R. Border (NSW/Qld) .... 117 in 108 matches
I. M. Chappell (S Aust) .... 114 in 89 matches
T. M. Moody (W Aust) .... 114 in 132 matches
M. E. Waugh (NSW) .... 112 in 93 matches
M. J. Di Venuto (Tas) .... 110 in 111 matches
D. F. Whatmore (Vic) .... 109 in 85 matches
D. J. Marsh (S Aust/Tas) .... 107 in 94 matches
G. S. Chappell (S Aust/Qld) .... 103 in 101 matches
G. R. J. Matthews (NSW) .... 102 in 116 matches

MOST DISMISSALS IN A CAREER

	M	Catches	Stumpings	Dismissals
D. S. Berry (S Aust/Vic)	139	499	47	546
W. A. Seccombe (Qld)	101	474	14	488
T. J. Zoehrer (W Aust)	107	331	28	359
R. W. Marsh (W Aust)	81	311	33	344
P. A. Emery (NSW)	109	298	41	339
J. A. Maclean (Qld)	86	289	24	313
T. J. Nielsen (S Aust)	92	255	29	284
A. T. W. Grout (Qld)	84	213	63	276
S. J. Rixon (NSW)	94	219	42	261
M. N. Atkinson (Tas)	84	236	25	261
A. C. Gilchrist (NSW/W Aust)	51	250	8	258
B. N. Jarman (S Aust)	77	193	57	250

MOST APPEARANCES

159	R. J. Inverarity (W Aust/S Aust)	1962-63 – 1984-85
158	J. Cox (Tas)	1987-88 – 2004-05
146	J. D. Siddons (Vic/S Aust)	1984-85 – 1999-00
142	S. G. Law (Qld)	1988-89 – 2003-04
139	D. S. Berry (S Aust/Vic)	1989-90 – 2003-04
132	T. M. Moody (W Aust)	1985-86 – 2000-01
127	P. R. Sleep (S Aust)	1976-77 – 1992-93
127	D. S. Lehmann (S Aust/Vic)	1987-88 – 2004-05
123	S. C. Trimble (Qld)	1959-60 – 1975-76
121	L. E. Favell (S Aust)	1951-52 – 1969-70
120	D. W. Hookes (S Aust)	1975-76 – 1991-92
119	D. C. Boon (Tas)	1978-79 – 1998-99
116	G. R. J. Matthews (NSW)	1982-83 – 1997-98
114	M. R. J. Veletta (W Aust)	1983-84 – 1994-95
112	J. P. Maher (Qld)	1993-94 – 2004-05
111	M. J. Di Venuto (Tas)	1991-92 – 2004-05
110	D. M. Wellham (NSW/Tas/Qld)	1980-81 – 1993-94
110	D. M. Jones (Vic)	1981-82 – 1997-98
110	G. S. Blewett (S Aust)	1991-92 – 2004-05
110	M. L. Love (Qld)	1992-93 – 2004-05
109	G. M. Wood (W Aust)	1977-78 – 1991-92
109	A. M. J. Hilditch (NSW/S Aust)	1976-77 – 1991-92
109	P. A. Emery (NSW)	1989-90 – 1998-99
108	A. R. Border (NSW/Qld)	1976-77 – 1995-96
108	M. G. Bevan (S Aust/NSW/Tas)	1989-90 – 2004-05
107	H. N. Dansie (S Aust)	1949-50 – 1966-67
107	T. J. Zoehrer (W Aust)	1980-81 – 1993-94
106	B. J. Hodge (Vic)	1993-94 – 2004-05
105	T. V. Hohns (Qld)	1972-73 – 1990-91
105	J. Angel (W Aust)	1991-92 – 2003-04
104	S. Young (Tas)	1991-92 – 2001-02
103	G. F. Lawson (NSW)	1977-78 – 1991-92
103	M. T. G. Elliott (Vic)	1992-93 – 2004-05
102	C. G. Rackemann (Qld)	1979-80 – 1995-96
101	G. S. Chappell (S Aust/Qld)	1966-67 – 1983-84
101	R. J. Bright (Vic)	1972-73 – 1987-88
101	W. A. Seccombe (Qld)	1993-94 – 2004-05
100	K. D. Mackay (Qld)	1946-47 – 1963-64
100	G. R. Marsh (W Aust)	1977-78 – 1993-94
100	T. J. Barsby (Qld)	1984-85 – 1996-97
100	D. F. Hills (Tas)	1991-92 – 2001-02

PLAYED FOR THREE OR MORE STATES

			M	R	*Batting* Avge	W	*Bowling* Avge	Ct
G. D. Watson	Vic	(1964-65 – 1970-71)	34	1,555	32.40	53	26.57	20
	W Aust	(1971-72 – 1974-75)	22	997	31.16	54	24.37	25
	NSW	(1976–77)	4	122	20.33	8	22.50	1
	Total		60	2,674	31.09	115	25.25	46
G. J. Cosier	Vic	(1971-72 & 1980-81)	4	133	22.17	2	43.00	2
	S Aust	(1974-75 – 1976-77)	20	1,059	29.42	34	22.18	17
	Qld	(1977-78 – 1979-80)	22	1,295	35.97	16	36.75	22
	Total		46	2,487	31.88	52	27.46	41
T. M. Chappell	S Aust	(1972-73 – 1975-76)	14	473	18.92	1	60.00	6
	W Aust	(1976–77)	4	160	40.00	–	–	2
	NSW	(1979-80 – 1984-85)	45	2,320	32.68	51	21.06	29
	Total		63	2,953	29.53	52	21.90	37
R. J. McCurdy	Tas	(1980-81)	5	45	4.50	17	34.82	3
	Vic	(1981-82 – 1983-84)	20	239	12.58	67	34.19	7
	S Aust	(1984-85)	8	128	12.80	36	29.47	5
	Total		33	412	10.56	120	32.87	15
D. M. Wellham ...	NSW	(1980-81 – 1986-87)	59	3,812	44.33	0	–	28
	Tas	(1988-89 – 1989-90)	30	1,600	41.03	0	–	12
	Qld	(1991-92 – 1993-94)	21	1,327	39.03	0	–	13
	Total		110	6,739	42.38	0	–	53
C. R. Miller	Vic	(1985-86 – 2001-02)	10	88	7.33	27	42.46	2
	S Aust	(1988-89 – 1991-92)	20	274	13.05	67	28.96	
	Tas	(1992-93 – 1999-00)	54	783	15.35	210	31.70	17
	Total		84	1,145	13.63	304	32.03	25
G. J. Rowell	NSW	(1989-90 – 1990-91)	3	77	25.67	11	26.09	1
	Qld	(1991-92 – 1997-98)	34	400	10.81	116	29.80	18
	Tas	(1998-99)	6	12	4.00	18	25.50	3
	Total		43	489	11.37	145	28.99	22
S. J. Jurgensen	W Aust	(1998-99)	1	3	–	1	135.00	0
	Tas	(2000-01 – 2002-03)	17	228	12.67	54	28.72	1
	Qld	(2003-04)	3	6	2.00	13	23.15	1
	Total		21	237	11.29	68	29.22	2
M. G. Bevan	S Aust	(1989-99)	6	338	33.80	0	–	1
	NSW	(1990-91 – 2003-04)	93	8,174	61.92	21	64.48	43
	Tas	(2004-05)	9	1,464	97.60	2	48.00	3
	Total		108	9,976	63.54	23	63.48	47

NEW SOUTH WALES

Long live the new kings

by PHIL WILKINS

Pura Cup: Champions
ING Cup: Sixth
Captain: Simon Katich
Coach: Trevor Bayliss

Simon Katich

The sun shone again on the Sydney Cricket
Ground and Cricket New South Wales after
all following the closure of Waugh Bros.
Corporation.

Disappearing into retirement with Steve
and Mark Waugh went former Test opener,
Michael Slater, while Michael Bevan turned south to continue his
ever-prolific batting and develop coaching skills for Tasmania, and
Steve Rixon, mastermind of New South Wales' hat-trick of ING
Cup wins and the treasured "Cups double" in 2002-2003, departed
overseas on another coaching mission.

Despite these apparently insurmountable losses, the rebirth of the
Blues and founding of a new era and path to success by new coach
Trevor Bayliss did not become the long torture trail anticipated.

Built on the foundations of a quartet of bowlers, who modestly
described themselves as 'the fab four', New South Wales claimed
the Sheffield Shield-Pura Cup for the 44th time since the first-class
interstate competition began in 1892-93.

Likewise, the Blues' prosperity in a season expected to be one of
travail and hardship came about through the 1,000-run contributions of formidable opener Phil Jaques and rawboned, robust middle
order allrounder Dominic Thornely, both of whom, until this
season, were largely cast in the shadow of more illustrious international team-mates.

The original Fab Four, the Beatles, enjoyed their many hey-days
back in the 60s and New South Wales' modern equivalent, pacemen
Nathan Bracken, Stuart Clark and Matthew Nicholson and leg-spinner

Stuart MacGill, revelled in theirs in moist conditions on a green-tipped Gabba wicket in March of 2005.

That their one-wicket victory in an enthralling three-day Pura Cup final against Queensland eventuated at all was due to the batting heroics of the inglorious last-wicket pair of batsmen, Bracken and MacGill, who added 22 runs to drive Queensland to despair and deprive them of a home win and their first against New South Wales in six first-class finals.

After Bracken dismantled Queensland for 102 with 6 for 27 on the first day, it was astonishing to hear the optimistic greeting which MacGill, New South Wales' No. 11 batsman, delivered as he and Bracken conferred in the last frantic minutes: "Mate, we're going to win this!"

Never one with pretensions of batting elegance, MacGill said later: "I'm not a nervous person, particularly with my batting because I'm not very good. On the last ball I knew they'd brought the field up and I decided it was back to the old school and that I'd swing like a maniac."

MacGill, who came to the wicket to thwart a hat-trick by paceman Joe Dawes, lashed out appropriately, succeeding in yanking the ball through square leg for the two runs needed for the win, prompting an emotional rival captain Jimmy Maher to remark: "It feels like someone's ripped a great big piece out of your heart."

Any final win is priceless, but this was an extraordinary success, providing yet another chapter of tension, drama and nerve-racking excitement to the history book of interstate finals which began in 1982-83 when New South Wales upset the applecart by defeating Western Australia in Perth by 54 runs.

Quite apart from being without the Waugh twins, Bevan and Slater, New South Wales proved to have a most astute tactician in Trevor Bayliss, a composed, meticulous, painstaking new coach, formerly an invaluable middle order batsman for New South Wales before he became Rixon's understudy.

Bayliss played for eight seasons for New South Wales, appearing in 58 games and assisting the Blues to the Sheffield Shield and limited-over double in 1992-93, retiring to take up the position of coach of the NSW Second XI for four seasons.

With Brad Haddin, who led the side in the spirited fashion of his batting in the international absence of Simon Katich, New South Wales were blessed to have an established, versatile battery of bowlers in left arm swing bowler Bracken (43 first-class wickets a~ 18.79), the right arm pair of Clark (40 at 24.77) and Nicholson (4~ at 20.25) and leg-spinner MacGill, whose 54 wickets at 24.66 broke the state record of Bill O'Reilly, which had stood for 65 years.

When Queensland eliminated New South Wales from the Pura~ Cup a year earlier in March, 2004, Steve Waugh observed gratefully as he bade farewell to the Sydney Cricket Ground and first-class cricket: "In a way, I'm glad it's over." All too apparently, there was no reciprocity of sentiment from the public.

But if genuine, heartfelt sadness accompanied the departure of the twins with a metaphorical wreath of understanding dropped on Cricket New South Wales' doorstep in the expectation of hard times to follow, it failed to take into account the resilience of the state's squad.

The summer did not begin that way as the Blues lost their first Pura Cup and first three ING Cup matches of the summer. Ultimately, the Blues won only three games of their ING Cup program to finish last in an interstate limited-overs competition they had won in the previous three seasons. The first-class situation was happily different.

No instance of a season turning on a single performance was better illustrated than with Dominic Thornely's unbeaten 261 early in November, 2004, the highest innings by a New South Wales batsman against Western Australia and a 405-minute performance which contained a domestic record equalling 11 sixes.

Things just got better from that week with opener Jaques (1,269 runs at 66.78) eventually hitting two double-centuries and a hundred in first-class matches while Thornely (1,065 at 62.64) added another three centuries to his double-hundred and skipper Haddin (916 at 57.25) struck two centuries, all in the most responsible but entertaining fashion.

A season which began as one of experimentation and blind faith in the tradition of the state with three new players introduced to first-class cricket in middle-order batsmen Ed Cowan and James Packman and off-spinning allrounder Jason Krejza, finished as one of resounding success and morale-soaring stature.

Late in 2004, it was announced that Cricket NSW would continue playing the bulk of its representative games at the Sydney Cricket Ground, the game's traditional home being preferred to Telstra Stadium for the period from the end of 2004-2005 until the season ending 2009-2010.

The reported figure that the Sydney Cricket Ground Trust offered Cricket NSW to remain at its old headquarters was between $60 million and $70 million.

NEW SOUTH WALES RESULTS, 2004-05

All first-class matches – Played 12: Won 8, Lost 2, Drawn 2.
Pura Cup – Played 11: Won 9, Lost 2.
ING Cup matches – Played 10: Won 3, Lost 6, No Result 1.

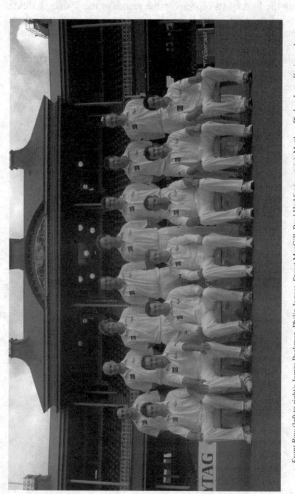

Front Row (left to right): James Packman, Philip Jaques, Stuart MacGill, Brad Haddin (*captain*), Matthew Phelps, Jason Krejza and Aaron O'Brien. *Back Row* (left to right): Ed Cowan, Doug Bollinger, Nathan Bracken, Stuart Clark, Matthew Nicholson, Grant Lambert, Dominic Thornely and Greg Mail.

PURA CUP AVERAGES, 2004-05

BATTING

	M	I	NO	R	HS	100s	50s	Avge	Ct/St	S-R
*.A. Jaques	11	19	1	1,191	240*	3	5	66.17	9	59.85
).J. Thornely	11	19	3	1,006	261*	4	4	62.88	6	55.76
3.J. Haddin	11	18	3	902	154	2	5	60.13	35/3	83.29
S.M. Katich	2	3	0	120	78	0	1	40.00	1	44.94
M.J. Phelps	11	19	1	621	127*	1	4	34.50	19	37.73
♦.R. Packman	5	10	0	267	107	1	0	26.70	1	53.71
N.W. Bracken	11	15	4	267	35	0	0	24.27	3	86.41
E.J.M. Cowan	3	6	0	132	66	0	1	22.00	0	37.50
G.J. Mail	11	19	1	392	101	1	1	21.78	13	35.80
J.J. Krejza	8	12	2	160	63	0	1	16.00	7	42.22
S.C.G. MacGill	11	12	4	97	27	0	0	12.13	3	67.83
G.M. Lambert	1	2	0	23	23	0	0	11.50	0	57.50
S.R. Clark	10	12	3	103	25	0	0	11.44	2	66.88
M.J. Nicholson	10	15	2	132	28	0	0	10.15	9	43.56
A.W. O'Brien	3	4	0	19	7	0	0	4.75	0	38.78
D. Bollinger	2	3	3	9	4*	0	0	–	0	24.32

Denotes not out.

BOWLING

	O	Mdns	R	W	BB	5W/i	10W/m	Avge	Balls/W
N.W. Bracken.......	365	124	808	43	7-4	3	0	18.79	50.93
S.R. Clark..........	321.4	67	991	40	5-10	2	0	24.78	48.25
J.J. Krejza..........	109.2	19	416	9	2-11	0	0	46.22	72.89
G.M. Lambert.......	15	3	52	2	1-17	0	0	26.00	45.00
S.C.G. MacGill	421.2	82	1,332	54	6-85	3	0	24.67	46.81
G.J. Mail...........	11	1	60	1	1-32	0	0	60.00	66.00
M.J. Nicholson......	312.4	80	871	43	5-60	1	0	20.26	43.63
D. Bollinger	58.5	11	204	2	1-34	0	0	102.00	176.50
M.J. Phelps.........	2	0	3	0	–	0	0	–	–
D.J. Thornely	27	6	91	0	–	0	0	–	–

At Brisbane Cricket Ground, Brisbane, October 15, 16, 17, 18, 2004. NEW SOUTH WALES lost to QUEENSLAND by two wickets.

NEW SOUTH WALES v WESTERN AUSTRALIA

At Sydney Cricket Ground, Sydney, November 2, 3, 4, 2004. New South Wales won by an innings and 134 runs. *Toss:* New South Wales. New South Wales 6 pts.

A phenomenal game which illuminated the summer for New South Wales and inspired a young team to extraordinary heights. With his team 9 for 200, Dominic Thornely continued on from 76 not out with such flourish and power that he finished with 261 not out in only his second first-class hundred. Thornely shared a 10th-wicket partnership of 219 with Stuart MacGill, striking 11 sixes in his 405-minute innings, equalling the Australia first-class record held by Matthew Hayden against Zimbabwe in Perth, October 2003. With the meticulously restrained MacGill, Thornely shared the highest first-class 10th wicket partnership since Alan Kippax and Hal Hooker added 307 for New South Wales against Victoria in 1928-29. MacGill contributed a single run to their first century stand and in all 27 runs while no other New South Wales batsman made a half-century. Western Australia were shattered psychologically, collapsing before the pace of Nathan Bracken, Matthew Nicholson and Stuart Clark for 137 in just over four hours, MacGill chiming in as he did throughout the season for the important

wicket of top-scorer Murray Goodwin and completing a rare all-round match with five
wickets. Clark claimed seven wickets for the match and Nicholson six for an
overwhelming New South Wales win in three days.

Match reports by PHILWILKINS.

Man of Match: D. J. Thornely.   *Attendance:* 1,261.

Close of play: First day, New South Wales (1) 9-351 (Thornely 204, MacGill 16)
Second day, Western Australia (2) 0-23 (Meuleman 16, Hussey 5).

New South Wales

G. J. Mail b Wates	3	N. W. Bracken c Marsh b Hogg	4
P. A. Jaques c Harvey b Wates	18	S. R. Clark c Marsh b Casson	6
M. J. Phelps lbw b Harvey	22	S. C. G. MacGill lbw b North	27
D. J. Thornely not out	261		
A. W. O'Brien c Meuleman b Magoffin	6	L-b 3, w 7, n-b 7	17
*†B. J. Haddin c Meuleman b Casson	45		
J. J. Krejza lbw b Casson	0	(110 overs, 442 mins)	419
M. J. Nicholson c Marsh b Hogg	10	Fall: 3 34 66 78 146 146 161 165 200 419	

Bowling: Magoffin 22–1–95–1; Wates 16–3–71–2; Harvey 21–5–67–1; Hogg 22–0–87–2; Hussey
1–0–1–0; Casson 25–5–88–3; North 3–0–7–1.

Western Australia

*M. E. K. Hussey c Haddin b Nicholson	8	– (2) lbw b MacGill	5
S. W. Meuleman c Haddin b Bracken	2	– (1) lbw b Clark	21
M. W. Goodwin st Haddin b MacGill	55	– lbw b Bracken	58
M. J. North c Haddin b Clark	24	– c Thornely b Clark	3
S. E. Marsh b Clark	0	– c Nicholson b Clark	6
†R. J. Campbell b Nicholson	28	– lbw b MacGill	0
K. M. Harvey b Nicholson	0	– b Nicholson	14
G. B. Hogg lbw b MacGill	7	– c Haddin b Nicholson	22
B. Casson b Clark	4	– c Haddin b Nicholson	0
D. J. Wates lbw b Clark	2	– not out	12
S. J. Magoffin not out	0	– c Bracken b MacGill	1
B 2, l-b 4, w 1	7	B 4, l-b 2	6

(62.3 overs, 251 mins)   137   (59.5 overs, 247 mins)   148
Fall: 10 10 58 62 105 105 128 129 134 137   Fall: 23 54 66 76 77 106 122 122
                                                      137 148

Bowling: *First Innings*—Nicholson 14–8–18–3; Bracken 13–7–22–1; Krejza 13–4–47–0; Clark
12.3–2–24–4; MacGill 10–3–20–2. *Second Innings*—Nicholson 19–3–41–3; Bracken 9–3–18–1;
MacGill 19.5–7–52–3; Krejza 2–0–11–0; Thornely 1–1–0–0; Clark 9–3–20–3.

Umpires: N. S. D. Fowler and G. T. D. Morrow.

At Junction Oval, St Kilda, November 23, 24, 25, 2004. NEW SOUTH WALES
defeated VICTORIA by an innings and 88 runs.

NEW SOUTH WALES v SOUTH AUSTRALIA

At Sydney Cricket Ground, Sydney, December 2, 3, 4, 2004. New South Wales won by an innings and 133 runs. *Toss:* South Australia. New South Wales 6 pts.

Having won the toss and batted under cloudy conditions on what appeared a reasonable pitch, South Australia's captain Graham Manou could only look back at the wreckage of his team's first innings of 29 and wonder at the cruelty of the game. Humiliation was the only description fit for 80 minutes of shame. From seven overs of swing and seaming spite, left-arm pace-bowler Nathan Bracken finished with the amazing analysis of seven wickets for four runs, dismissing five of his victims without scoring. Nathan Adcock top-scored with eight runs for the innings, the second lowest score in the 112-year history of interstate first-class cricket in Australia. South Australia were dismissed within the space of 88 balls, second only behind 73 balls as the briefest first-class innings in Australian cricket history when Victoria's total was 15 runs against the M.C.C. team in 1903-04. South Australia also registered the lowest innings score of 27 against New South Wales at the Sydney Cricket Ground in 1955-56. Adding to the visitors' woe, Phil Jaques broke out of his unproductive Australian shell and smashed 30 fours and a six for 217 from 340 balls in 430 minutes for his second Pura Cup century and the 10th of his first-class career, sharing a third-wicket partnership of 231 runs in just over four hours with Dominic Thornely, thriving on his new responsibility at No. 4 for 78 runs from 202 balls with 11 fours and a six. There was to be no capitulation in South Australia's second innings with opener Tom Plant gaining his maiden century in measured circumstances in just over six hours with 15 boundaries from 290 balls and sharing a stand of 218 for the fourth wicket with another 20-year-old maiden century-maker in Callum Ferguson. Matthew Nicholson engineered the breakthrough by trapping Plant leg before wicket and Stuart MacGill struck again soon after for Ferguson's wicket, the pair completing South Australia's misery by dismissing nine batsmen in the innings and the last seven batsmen for 17 runs. It was New South Wales's third successive innings win in the Pura Cup and their fourth first-class win in successive matches.

Man of Match: N.W. Bracken.   *Attendance:* 1,438.

Close of play: First day, New South Wales (1) 2-233 (Jaques 154, Thornely 37); Second day, South Australia (2) 3-122 (Plant 64, Ferguson 41).

South Australia

T. C. Plant c Krejza b Bracken	0	–	(2) lbw b Nicholson	125
G. S. Blewett b Bracken	4	–	(1) lbw b MacGill	11
M. J. Cosgrove c Phelps b Bracken	0	–	c Phelps b MacGill	0
N. T. Adcock b Nicholson	8	–	lbw b Nicholson	4
C. J. Ferguson lbw b Bracken	0	–	c Thornely b MacGill	103
J. K. Smith c Haddin b Clark	5	–	run out (Thornely/Haddin)	0
*†G. A. Manou c Krejza b Bracken	4	–	lbw b MacGill	5
M. F. Cleary b Bracken	0	–	b MacGill	2
D. J. Cullen not out	3	–	not out	4
S. W. Tait b Bracken	0	–	b Nicholson	6
P. C. Rofe b Clark	2	–	c Krejza b Nicholson	0
L-b 2, n-b 1	3		L-b 4, n-b 4	8
(14.4 overs, 80 mins)	29		(103 overs, 409 mins)	268

Fall: 1 3 15 15 16 20 24 24 24 29

Fall: 26 26 33 251 251 256 258 259 268 268

Bowling: *First Innings*—Nicholson 5–2–13–1; Bracken 7–5–4–7; Clark 2.4–0–10–2. *Second Innings*—Nicholson 26–8–81–4; Bracken 17–3–45–0; MacGill 33–8–73–5; Clark 9–2–14–0; Krejza 13–2–40–0; Thornely 5–2–11–0.

New South Wales

G. J. Mail c Blewett b Cleary 31	N. W. Bracken not out 34
P. A. Jaques c Blewett b Cullen 217	S. R. Clark b Tait 11
M. J. Phelps lbw b Cullen 0	S. C. G. MacGill not out 0
D. J. Thornely c and b Blewett 78	
A. W. O'Brien lbw b Tait 6	L-b 11, n-b 3 14
*†B. J. Haddin b Rofe 32	
J. J. Krejza b Tait 0	(121 overs, 479 mins) (9 wkts dec) 430
M. J. Nicholson b Tait 7	Fall: 92 93 324 333 376 376 376 395 419

Bowling: Tait 34–3–137–4; Rofe 28–6–104–1; Cullen 32–8–91–2; Cleary 22–4–74–1; Blewe 5–1–13–1.

Umpires: J. H. Smeaton and R. J. Tucker.

NEW SOUTH WALES v TASMANIA

At Sydney Cricket Ground, Sydney, December 16, 17, 18, 19, 2004. Match drawn
Toss: Tasmania. New South Wales 2 pts. *First-class debut:* G. J. Bailey.

Tasmania provided worthy opposition throughout four days of hard, uncompromising cricket. Despite new-ball bowler Nathan Bracken's early successes, opener David Dawson defied New South Wales' splendidly varied attack for almost two sessions before leg-spinner Stuart MacGill had him caught at the wicket, his 600th first-class victim. Debutant George Bailey then introduced some vigorous counter-punching to Tasmania's middle order with a 137-minute innings of 70 from 105 balls with 11 boundaries, sharing stubborn stands of 77 with Sean Clingeleffer and 41 with Damien Wright. New South Wales experienced their own new-ball difficulties against Wright and Adam Griffith until a 127-run partnership by Matthew Phelps and Dominic Thornely steadied the ship. Brad Haddin swept his team to a valuable first-innings lead with his fourth first-class hundred, cracking two sixes and 11 fours in three boisterous hours for 114 after which Matthew Nicholson unsettled Tasmania with his pace and reverse swing on a deteriorating pitch for four wickets to leave the visitors in early disarray at 6 for 134. Once again, Clingeleffer and the Casino-born Wright, acting as captain, displayed their tenacity in a 159-run stand for the seventh wicket in 175 minutes, setting New South Wales a target of 220 from 51 overs. Rain and early wickets caused the home side to settle for a draw. MacGill took four wickets in each innings while Jason Krejza enjoyed the rare distinction of twice dismissing Michael Bevan cheaply.

Man of Match: D. G. Wright.   *Attendance:* 2,327.

Close of play: First day, Tasmania (1) 7-266 (Wright 38, Doherty 13); Second day, New South Wales (1) 6-230 (Haddin 29, Nicholson 7); Third day, Tasmania (2) 6-167 (Clingeleffer 18, Wright 14).

asmania

.G. Dawson c Haddin b MacGill	65	– (2) b Nicholson	21
.R. Birt c Mail b Bracken	4	– (1) c Katich b MacGill	25
I.G. Bevan c MacGill b Krejza	21	– lbw b Krejza	12
.G. Dighton c Thornely b MacGill	23	– b Nicholson	42
.J.G. Lockyear c and b Bracken	0	– lbw b Nicholson	20
.J. Bailey c Nicholson b MacGill	70	– b Nicholson	0
S.G. Clingeleffer lbw b Krejza	20	– c Nicholson b Bollinger	68
D.G. Wright b Bracken	38	– c Nicholson b MacGill	83
.J. Doherty b MacGill	20	– c Mail b MacGill	5
A.R. Griffith b Bracken	0	– (11) not out	2
A.G. Downton not out	2	– (10) c Mail b MacGill	8
B 5, l-b 6, n-b 2	13	B 12, l-b 11, w 1, n-b 5	29

104 overs, 396 mins)   276   (101.4 overs, 409 mins)   315
'all: 8 55 109 110 122 199 240 266 274 276   Fall: 41 49 86 129 129 134 293 296
                                                    311 315

Bowling: *First Innings*—Nicholson 18–4–46–0; Bracken 18–7–32–4; Bollinger 16–4–34–0; Krejza 18–3–63–2; MacGill 34–9–90–4. *Second Innings*—Nicholson 26–6–77–4; Bracken 12–5–24–0; MacGill 38.4–7–98–4; Krejza 14–2–51–1; Bollinger 9–1–34–1; Thornely 2–0–8–0.

New South Wales

G.J. Mail c Doherty b Wright	3	– (5) not out	9
P.A. Jaques c Dawson b Griffith	18	– (1) c and b Griffith	14
*S.M. Katich c Bailey b Downton	30	– (2) lbw b Doherty	12
M.J. Phelps b Bevan	67	– (3) c Wright b Doherty	15
D.J. Thornely b Doherty	70	– (4) not out	44
†B.J. Haddin c Bailey b Doherty	114		
J.J. Krejza c Dawson b Bevan	0		
M.J. Nicholson lbw b Wright	17		
N.W. Bracken lbw b Doherty	31		
S.C.G. MacGill run out (Bailey)	4		
D. Bollinger not out	3		
B 1, l-b 10, w 1, n-b 3	15	L-b 4, n-b 2	6

(121.1 overs, 460 mins)   372   (44 overs, 175 mins)   (3 wkts) 100
Fall: 15 35 61 188 208 209 266 341 360 372   Fall: 22 29 57

Bowling: *First Innings* – Wright 22-5-66-2; Griffith 22-7-63-1; Downton 29-9-87-1; Doherty 41.1-5-126-3; Bevan 7-0-19-2. *Second Innings* – Wright 10-4-20-0; Griffith 12-7-21-1; Doherty 15-2-38-2; Bevan 2-0-3-0; Downton 4-1-14-0; Bailey 1-1-0-0.

Umpires: N.S.D. Fowler and D.J. Harper.

At Adelaide Oval, Adelaide, January 18, 19, 20, 21, 2005. NEW SOUTH WALES defeated SOUTH AUSTRALIA by 200 runs.

NEW SOUTH WALES v QUEENSLAND

At Bankstown Memorial Oval, Bankstown, January 28, 29, 30, 31, 2005. Match draw
Toss: New South Wales. New South Wales 2 pts. *First-class debut:* J. R. Packman.

Queensland's early misfortunes with Andy Bichel, Joe Dawes and Ashley Noffke a
troubling New South Wales' top-order batsmen was hardly reflected at 1 for 252 late c
the first day, Phil Jaques eventually driving, cutting and pulling his way to his secon
double-century of the season, a feat last achieved for New South Wales by Bob Simps
30 years before. Jaques hammered 33 boundaries in his 240 not out from 402 balls in 58
minutes for his third first-class hundred for the state and 11th overall and shared a 218
run partnership in 314 minutes with the more sedate Matthew Phelps, who was dropp
at the wicket at 32 from Noffke, before being dismissed by the same bowler for 90 wit
seven fours and a six from 258 balls. Although Bankstown's usually serene pitc
improved gradually, only Clinton Perren and the dashing James Hopes with a lat
contribution by Bichel capitalised on the conditions. Stuart Clark and Nathan Bracke
troubled Queensland's early batsmen before Perren found a punishing ally in Hopes fo
a 77-run partnership in 64 minutes and later 67 with Bichel. Otherwise resistance wa
mediocre. Brad Haddin surprised by deciding against enforcing the follow-on and wit
rain interrupting the game and hampered by a slow outfield, New South Wales extende
their lead to 425 runs before Haddin's declaration, allowing his bowlers 74 overs t
dismiss the Bulls. Though Stuart MacGill's leg-spinners threatened Queensland as seve
wickets fell in 22 overs, five to MacGill, their last batsmen, Nathan Hauritz and Dawes
defied New South Wales for 43 gripping minutes to avoid defeat.

Man of Match: P. A. Jaques. *Attendance:* 2,262.

Close of play: First day, New South Wales (1) 2-256 (Jaques 131, Cowan 1); Second
day, Queensland (1) 6-141 (Perren 62, Noffke 0); Third day, New South Wales (2) 2-
47 (Mail 16, Cowan 17).

New South Wales

G. J. Mail c Maher b Bichel	11	– c Seccombe b Dawes	18
P. A. Jaques not out	240	– c Seccombe b Dawes	0
M. J. Phelps c Seccombe b Noffke	90	– lbw b Bichel	9
E. J. M. Cowan c Love b Dawes	7	– c Nash b Hopes	66
D. J. Thornely c Seccombe b Noffke	10	– c Seccombe b Dawes	17
*†B. J. Haddin c Nash b Bichel	36	– not out	80
J. R. Packman st Seccombe b Hauritz	15	– st Seccombe b Hauritz	4
M. J. Nicholson c Seccombe b Bichel	6	– not out	15
N. W. Bracken not out	26		
L-b 11, w 10, n-b 4	25	B 2, l-b 7	9

(142 overs, 583 mins) (7 wkts dec) 466 (67.2 overs, 269 mins) (6 wkts dec) 218
Fall: 34 252 271 327 373 398 413 Fall: 2 19 59 83 156 167

S. R. Clark, S. C. G. MacGill (did not bat).

Bowling: *First Innings*—Bichel 33–6–80–3; Dawes 20–2–63–1; Noffke 30–9–88–2; Hopes
25–9–61–0; Hauritz 34–5–163–1. *Second Innings*—Bichel 15–5–37–1; Dawes 20–7–54–3; Noffke
12–3–25–0; Hopes 13.2–2–59–1; Hauritz 7–0–34–1.

Queensland

*J. P. Maher lbw b Clark	5	– c Phelps b MacGill	73
B. P. Nash lbw b Bracken	16	– c Haddin b Bracken	2
M. L. Love c Haddin b Clark	1	– c Jaques b MacGill	6
C. T. Perren c Haddin b Bracken	103	– lbw b Clark	18
C. A. Philipson c Nicholson b MacGill	3	– c Phelps b MacGill	26
J. R. Hopes b Nicholson	47	– st Haddin b MacGill	1
†W. A. Seccombe lbw b MacGill	2	– c Mail b MacGill	0
A. A. Noffke lbw b MacGill	19	– (9) c Haddin b Clark	2
A. J. Bichel not out	40	– (8) lbw b Clark	24
N. M. Hauritz b Clark	13	– not out	8
J. H. Dawes run out (Cowan/Bracken)	4	– not out	6
L-b 5, n-b 1	6	B 2, l-b 2	4

(88.4 overs, 357 mins)	259	(74 overs, 298 mins) (9 wkts)	170
Fall: 22 22 23 46 123 134 168 235 252 259		Fall: 6 29 93 123 125 125 138 151 156	

Bowling: *First Innings*—Bracken 27.4–7–64–2; Nicholson 13–3–41–1; MacGill 29–5–74–3; Clark 19–3–75–3. *Second Innings*—Nicholson 5.2–2–12–0; Bracken 15–8–28–1; Mail 0.4–0–0–0; MacGill 30–6–72–5; Clark 21–3–51–3; Phelps 2–0–3–0.

Umpires: B. N. J. Oxenford and P. R. Reiffel.

At WACA Ground, Perth, February 24, 25, 26, 27, 2005. NEW SOUTH WALES lost to WESTERN AUSTRALIA by eight wickets.

At Bellerive Oval, Hobart, March 3, 4, 5, 6, 2005. NEW SOUTH WALES defeated TASMANIA by 25 runs.

NEW SOUTH WALES v VICTORIA

At Sydney Cricket Ground, Sydney, March 10, 11, 12, 13, 2005. New South Wales won by five wickets. *Toss:* Victoria. New South Wales 6 pts.

New South Wales were third in the competition before this game with an outright win essential to reach the final. Victoria's batsmen failed to capitalise on this knowledge and the advantage of winning the toss, being dismissed in just over four hours with only Nick Jewell, returning to the side after a two-year absence, playing attractively for 80 from 144 balls in 218 minutes with 13 boundaries. New South Wales' trio of Nathan Bracken, Stuart Clark and Matthew Nicholson disconcerted Victoria with their pace assortment, each capturing two wickets, while leg-spinner Stuart MacGill harvested three late wickets. Matthew Phelps confirmed his standing as a slips fieldsman par excellence with a New South Wales record six catches for the match against Victoria although video evidence indicated Matthew Elliott should have held his ground. Phil Jaques continued his magnificent season with a 273-minute innings of 116 from 205 balls with 11 fours, sharing a 131-run opening stand with a revitalised Greg Mail in Mail's 50th match for New South Wales. Having comfortably passed Victoria's score at 2 for 226, eight New South Wales wickets fell for 66 runs in 21.3 overs with Michael Lewis aggressively taking four wickets with the new ball. Victoria displayed more resolve in their second innings, six batsmen reaching 30 or better, but a major century-maker failed to emerge as Nicholson dismissed four batsmen and with MacGill advantage of the wearing pitch. New South Wales faced an awkward run objective of 225, which they achieved for the loss of five wickets through tenacious half-centuries by opener Jaques, Dominic Thornely and James Packman.

Man of Match: P. A. Jaques.   *Attendance:* 2,725.

Close of play: First day, New South Wales (1) 1-132 (Jaques 73, Nicholson 0); Second day, Victoria (2) 4-170 (Rummans 3, White 5); Third day, New South Wales (2) 3-129 (Thornely 24, Packman 7).

Victoria

M. T. G. Elliott c Phelps b Bracken	10	– (2) c Mail b MacGill	3
J. L. Arnberger c Jaques b Bracken	1	– (1) lbw b Nicholson	5
D. J. Hussey b Nicholson	1	– b Clark	6
N. Jewell b Krejza	80	– c Phelps b MacGill	2
G. C. Rummans c Phelps b Nicholson	5	– c Phelps b Clark	17
*C. L. White st Haddin b MacGill	32	– c Phelps b Nicholson	4
†A. J. Crosthwaite c Jaques b MacGill	12	– lbw b Nicholson	24
I. J. Harvey lbw b Clark	0	– not out	30
M. L. Lewis c Jaques b Clark	4	– c MacGill b Nicholson	3
S. M. Harwood c Phelps b MacGill	10	– c Haddin b Bracken	35
M. W. H. Inness not out	0	– c Jaques b MacGill	6
B 6, w 2, n-b 6	14	B 17, l-b 9, n-b 3	29

(58.2 overs, 247 mins)	169
Fall: 5 9 20 34 86 118 119 126 169 169	

(103.2 overs, 423 mins) 347
Fall: 91 155 160 162 228 258 261 265 334 347

Bowling: *First Innings*—Nicholson 14–1–43–2; Bracken 13–3–20–2; Clark 15–2–48–2; MacGill 16–5–52–3; Krejza 0.2–0–0–1. *Second Innings*—Nicholson 22–5–48–4; Bracken 16–4–33–1; Krejza 8–1–34–0; Clark 24–1–88–2; MacGill 33.2–6–118–3.

New South Wales

G. J. Mail c Elliott b White	55	– lbw b Lewis	4
P. A. Jaques c Crosthwaite b Lewis	116	– c Crosthwaite b Lewis	78
M. J. Nicholson c Crosthwaite b Lewis	5		
M. J. Phelps c Crosthwaite b Lewis	43	– (3) run out (Hussey)	11
D. J. Thornely lbw b Lewis	0	– (4) b White	56
J. R. Packman b Harwood	25	– (5) b White	48
*†B. J. Haddin st Crosthwaite b Harvey	1	– (6) not out	18
J. J. Krejza b White	16	– (7) not out	2
N. W. Bracken c Jewell b Harwood	8		
S. R. Clark b Harwood	3		
S. C. G. MacGill not out	1		
B 9, l-b 6, n-b 4	19	N-b 11	11

(87 overs, 365 mins)	292
Fall: 131 138 226 226 239 254 271 287 291 292	

(61 overs, 259 mins) (5 wkts) 228
Fall: 17 82 117 197 222

Bowling: *First Innings*—Lewis 20–3–77–4; Inness 12–3–35–0; Harvey 14–0–55–1; Harwood 21–3–58–3; White 20–3–52–2. *Second Innings*—Lewis 15–1–57–2; Inness 13–3–37–0; Harwood 9–2–49–0; Harvey 5–0–12–0; White 16–3–55–2; Rummans 3–0–18–0.

Umpires: S. J. Davis and P. D. Parker.

FINAL

At Brisbane Cricket Ground, Brisbane, March 18, 19, 20, 2005. NEW SOUTH WALES defeated QUEENSLAND by one wicket. For details see page 412.

NSW DOMESTIC FIRST-CLASS RESULTS TABLE

	First Game	M	Won	Lost	Drawn	Tied
South Australia	Dec 16, 1892	201	111	54	36	0
Victoria	Dec 24, 1892	207	75	65	66	1
Queensland	Nov 26, 1926	152	60	38	54	0
Western Australia ...	Jan 30, 1948	108	44	32	32	0
Tasmania	Mar 4, 1978	52	20	12	20	0
Total		720	310	201	208	1

NSW DOMESTIC FIRST-CLASS RECORDS

Highest score for:	452*	D. G. Bradman v Queensland at Sydney	1929-30
Highest score against:	365*	C. Hill (South Australia) at Adelaide	1900-01
Best bowling for:	9-41	W. J. O'Reilly v South Australia at Adelaide	1937-38
Best bowling against:	10-36	T. W. Wall (South Australia) at Sydney	1932-33
Highest total for:	918	v South Australia at Sydney	1900-01
Highest total against:	1,107	by Victoria at Melbourne	1926-27
Lowest total for:	56	v Western Australia at Perth	1998-99
Lowest total against:	27	by South Australia at Sydney	1955-56

MOST RUNS

	M	I	NO	R	HS	100s	50s	Avge
M. G. Bevan	93	163	31	8,174	216	32	33	61.92
M. E. Waugh	93	158	18	7,232	229*	23	30	51.66
S. R. Waugh	85	147	14	6,609	216*	22	24	49.69
A. F. Kippax	61	95	9	6,096	315*	23	14	70.88
M. A. Taylor	85	147	3	6,090	199	15	34	42.29
J. Dyson	82	150	16	5,648	241	11	29	42.15
K. D. Walters	91	159	16	5,602	253	17	24	39.17
G. R. J. Matthews	116	177	27	5,567	184	8	28	37.11
R. B. McCosker	70	124	15	5,280	168	17	26	48.44
B. C. Booth	81	128	14	4,943	177	10	25	43.36
M. A. Noble	51	81	9	4,896	281	19	17	68.00
M. J. Slater	69	130	3	4,890	204	12	25	38.50
N. C. O'Neill	61	104	10	4,749	233	15	21	50.52
D. G. Bradman	31	52	9	4,633	452*	17	12	107.74
R. B. Simpson	57	99	15	4,399	359	12	17	52.37
W. Bardsley	47	77	8	4,171	235	15	14	60.45
P. M. Toohey	64	109	10	4,038	158	15	14	40.79
G. Thomas	59	93	7	3,992	229	13	14	46.42
S. M. Small	66	113	3	3,984	184	5	29	36.22
D. M. Wellham	59	97	11	3,812	166	9	23	44.33

HIGHEST PARTNERSHIP FOR EACH WICKET

319	for 1st	R. B. McCosker and J. Dyson v Western Australia at Sydney	1980-81
378	for 2nd	L. A. Marks and K. D. Walters v South Australia at Adelaide	1964-65
363	for 3rd	D. G. Bradman and A. F. Kippax v Queensland at Sydney	1933-34
325	for 4th	N. C. O'Neill and B. C. Booth v Victoria at Sydney	1957-58
464*	for 5th	M. E. Waugh and S. R. Waugh v Western Australia at Perth	1990-91
332	for 6th	N. G. Marks and G. Thomas v South Australia at Sydney	1958-59
255	for 7th	G. Thomas and R. Benaud v Victoria at Melbourne	1961-62
270	for 8th	E. P. Barbour and V. T. Trumper v Victoria at Sydney	1912-13
226	for 9th	C. Kelleway and W. A. S. Oldfield v Victoria at Melbourne	1925-26
307	for 10th	A. F. Kippax and J. E. H. Hooker v Victoria at Melbourne	1928-29

MOST WICKETS

	M	Balls	Mdns	R	W	BB	5W/i	10W/m	Avge	Balls/W
G. F. Lawson	103	20,933	873	8,673	367	6-31	12	0	23.63	57.03
G. R. J. Matthews	116	26,764	1,376	10,518	363	8-52	19	4	28.98	73.73
R. Benaud	73	18,106	474	7,172	266	7-32	12	3	26.96	68.07
J. W. Martin	70	15,890	239	7,949	263	8-97	12	0	30.22	60.42
S. C. G. MacGill	66	14,703	447	8,417	260	6-64	14	0	32.37	56.55
M. R. Whitney	77	14,983	562	7,314	251	7-75	10	0	29.14	59.69
A. K. Davidson	62	13,425	275	5,195	246	7-31	10	0	21.12	54.57
W. J. O'Reilly	33	10,740	363	3,472	203	9-41	18	7	17.10	52.91
R. G. Holland	60	15,435	806	6,250	193	9-83	7	1	32.38	79.97
K. J. O'Keeffe	58	11,971	315	5,065	187	6-49	11	1	27.08	64.02
L. S. Pascoe	49	9,560	279	4,895	183	8-41	8	2	26.75	52.24
A. A. Mailey	37	11,732	127	5,861	180	8-81	13	2	32.56	65.18
D. J. Colley	62	10,645	145	5,535	179	6-30	5	0	30.92	59.47
W. J. Holdsworth	52	9,204	269	5,518	164	7-41	9	1	33.65	56.12
D. A. Renneberg	46	9,759	145	4,925	161	7-33	6	1	30.59	60.61
M. A. Noble	51	8,887	430	3,587	159	7-44	7	1	22.56	55.89
W. P. Howell	36	9,548	482	3,742	157	9-52	9	1	23.83	60.82
D. W. Hourne	38	8,612	191	4,222	150	9-77	10	2	28.15	57.41
P. I. Philpott	46	9,112	137	4,235	143	7-53	7	2	29.62	63.72
R. R. Lindwall	34	7,098	97	2,904	139	7-45	5	1	20.89	51.06

MOST DISMISSALS

	M	Catches	Stumpings	Total
P. A. Emery	109	298	41	339
S. J. Rixon	94	218	43	261
H. B. Taber	64	179	32	211
W. A. S. Oldfield	51	109	70	179
B. J. Haddin	54	148	14	162

MOST CATCHES

M. A. Taylor	120 in 85 matches	S. R. Waugh .... 83 in 85 matches
M. E. Waugh	112 in 93 matches	J. W. Martin .... 78 in 70 matches
G. R. J. Matthews	102 in 116 matches	R. B. Simpson ...... 73 in 57 matches
R. Benaud	92 in 73 matches	S. M. Small .... 67 in 66 matches
R. B. McCosker	91 in 70 matches	J. Dyson .... 67 in 82 matches

MOST APPEARANCES

116	G. R. J. Matthews	1982-83 – 1997-98	93	M. E. Waugh	1985-86 – 2003-04
109	P. A. Emery	1987-88 – 1999-00	91	K. D. Walters	1962-63 – 1980-81
103	G. F. Lawson	1977-78 – 1991-92	85	M. A. Taylor	1985-86 – 1998-99
94	S. J. Rixon	1974-75 – 1987-88	85	S. R. Waugh	1984-85 – 2003-04
93	M. G. Bevan	1990-91 – 2003-04	82	J. Dyson	1975-76 – 1988-89

QUEENSLAND

Doubly the bridesmaids

by STEPHEN GRAY

Pura Cup: Runners-up
ING Cup: Runners-up
Captain: Jimmy Maher
Coach: Terry Oliver

Jimmy Maher

Always the most expressive and effervescent of characters, Queensland captain Jimmy Maher is enduring a masters course in how to mask disappointment and deliver noble concession speeches. His heart-on-his-sleeve response to the wrenching Pura Cup final loss shows that he is still capable of revealing his inner self without much trouble, but like the rest of the Queensland side, he is learning to live with the letdown.

On the surface, 2004-05 seemed nearly a carbon copy of the 2003-04 season – Queensland finishing as the silver medallists again after being in the position to win both domestic championships. However, it was beneath the surface, where the twin losses cut deepest, that the difference lay between the two seasons.

Previous Queensland teams had finished so close yet so far away in a series of stumbles before the moment of triumph in March 1995 when they won the Sheffield Shield for the first time. This time the heartbreak happened in their own backyard, leaving the Queenslanders nursing their wounds from the twin home invasions.

Their unexpected loss to Tasmania in the ING Cup final at the Gabba was highly disappointing, considering the Queenslanders had dominated the regular season. They had twice collected double bonus points, the only team to do so since that innovation was introduced, and had locked in the right to host the final with several games in hand. The Pura Cup final surged like a tidal flow, with New South Wales on top early before Queensland swept back in the

final climactic hour, only to be dashed on the rocks of a tail-end
partnership between Stuart MacGill and Nathan Bracken.

Despite the glaring gaps in the trophy cabinet, not everything
went pear-shaped for Queensland. A little number-crunching indicates that Queensland had claims as the best team of the season.
Playing their first season without their champion of the past decade,
Stuart Law, they finished with 42 points in the Pura Cup and 35
points in the ING Cup for a total of 77 overall. The next closest to
them was Western Australia, 20 points behind on 57. But you have
to win the matches that count.

The coach, Terry Oliver, has built Queensland into an adaptable
outfit able to switch between the four-day and one-day games relatively comfortably. The team did not lose a game outright away
from home, and defeated Tasmania, South Australia and Victoria
outright on their home turfs. The flip side is that the Gabba, where
Queensland had been all but impregnable in recent seasons, proved
more assailable for opposition as well – apart from the two finals,
Victoria continued their recent Brisbane winning streak to turn history on its head by becoming a hoodoo team for the Queenslanders
at the Gabba. Cricket can be a perverse old thing at times.

Individually, there were outstanding performances, some more obvious than others. Andy Bichel might be consigned to domestic duties
these days, but he still cut a swathe through batting line-ups across the
country. His haul of 60 wickets at 22.10 was a Queensland record
(eclipsing his former mentor Craig McDermott's record of 54 in
1989-90) and second only to Shaun Tait's 65. Bichel, who took the
fourth ten-wicket haul of his career against NSW, the most by a
Queenslander, carried the campaign to some extent, but Joe Dawes
provided the ideal accompaniment. The steadfast Dawes took 46
wickets at 21.93 to underline his value to Queensland once again. The
next best with the ball was Ashley Noffke (23 at 37.91), who continues to struggle with form and injury.

The story with the bat was similar. Maher led the way in both
first-class and one-day forms of the game, punching out 841 runs at
40.41 and 490 at 44.54 respectively. His most reliable foil was
Clinton Perren, who continues to make a solid fist of the opening
position in four-day cricket, producing 708 runs at 33.71 without
quite showing his best form. All-rounders James Hopes (609 at
40.60) and Shane Watson (588 at 42.00) did their bit. Martin Love,
after being one of the most dependable Pura Cup batsmen over

recent seasons and playing for Australia, lost form completely until his defiant century in the final.

The all-rounder usually occupies a solitary spot within a cricket team, but Queensland was the state to be if you aspired to do a bit with bat and ball. Watson, Hopes and Andrew Symonds happily co-existed in the Queensland line-up with each contributing something to the mix. Symonds was only in coloured clothes for half the season for Queensland but his 339 ING Cup runs at 84.75, including four half-centuries in six innings, was magnificent batting. He was complemented by Hopes, whose bubbling one-day form saw him win the national ING Cup Player of the Year award and achieve Australian selection when Watson was injured before the tour of New Zealand. Nathan Hauritz returned from India a Test player but achieved little with bat or ball and was dropped from the Pura Cup side, though he still contributed usefully to the ING Cup campaign. Life has seldom been easy for Queensland spinners.

Of the next generation, the Queenslanders like the way young batsman Craig Philipson is developing, and his 447 first-class runs at 37.25 and 208 one-day runs at 41.60 suggest he could be on the cusp of taking his game to the next level. Likewise, wicket-keeper Chris Hartley is mounting the same sort of pressure on Wade Seccombe that Seccombe used to produce when he was the deputy to Ian Healy. Lachlan Stevens showed considerable promise in his two matches as a fluent middle-order batsman. Finally, 23-year-old left-arm quick Mitchell Johnson, the tantalising pace bowler, completed his first full season of cricket since leaving the youth ranks. He threw in a few glimpses of his potential, bowling with the sort of pace that makes life awkward for batsmen.

A betting man would keep the Queenslanders safe for another season. And if proven performers like Love and Hauritz can regain their true form, and promising players like Lee Carseldine and Nick Kruger can recover from the injuries that kept them out of 2004-05, there is no reason why Queensland should not regain their status as the top team in the nation. Maher's speech writer certainly hopes so.

QUEENSLAND RESULTS, 2004-05

All first-class matches – Played 11: Won 6, Lost 2, Drawn 3.
Pura Cup matches – Played 11: Won 6, Lost 2, Drawn 3.
ING Cup matches – Played 11: Won 7, Lost 4.

Front row: Clinton Perren, Martin Love, Andrew Symonds, Jimmy Maher (*Captain*), Andrew Bichel, Michael Kasprowicz, Joe Dawes, Brendan Nash *Middle row:* Terry Oliver (*Coach*), Justin Sternes (*Technical Officer*), Nathan Rimmington, Craig Philipson, James Hopes, Nathan Hauritz, Aaron Nye, Lee Carseldine, Chris Hartley, John Hetherington (*Conditioner*), Tony Wilson (*Performance Co-ordinator*), *Back row:* Lachlan Stevens, Chris Simpson, Shane Watson, Scott Brant, Ashley Noffke, Mitchell Johnson, Shane Jurgensen, Ryan Le Loux, *Absent:* Matthew Hayden, Wade Seccombe, Brett McKenDan

PURA CUP AVERAGES, 2004-05

BATTING

	M	I	NO	R	HS	100s	50s	Avge	Ct/St	S-R
S. R. Watson	8	15	1	588	136	1	3	42.00	5	59.27
J. R. Hopes	9	16	1	609	107	1	3	40.60	3	71.23
J. P. Maher	11	21	0	841	170	2	4	40.05	16	51.79
A. Symonds	7	13	0	516	126	1	3	39.69	8	74.35
L. M. Stevens	2	4	0	158	67	0	1	39.50	2	58.09
C. A. Philipson	7	14	2	447	119	1	2	37.25	5	60.82
M. G. Johnson	3	4	1	108	51*	0	1	36.00	0	46.55
C. T. Perren	11	21	0	708	105	2	4	33.71	10	48.10
B. P. Nash	2	4	0	130	92	0	1	32.50	2	41.27
A. A. Noffke	9	15	3	273	53	0	1	22.75	4	54.60
A. J. Bichel	11	18	4	311	69	0	1	22.21	4	68.50
N. M. Hauritz	6	10	4	121	45*	0	0	20.17	2	35.80
W. A. Seccombe	8	16	2	255	84	0	2	18.21	38/2	46.53
M. L. Love	8	16	0	295	116	1	1	18.44	7	39.97
C. D. Hartley	3	4	0	71	50	0	1	17.75	19	37.57
A. J. Nye	3	5	0	74	31	0	0	14.80	5	34.91
J. H. Dawes	11	17	7	117	34*	0	0	11.70	4	45.51
R. N. Le Loux	1	1	0	5	5	0	0	5.00	0	35.71
C. P. Simpson	1	2	0	8	8	0	0	4.00	1	23.53

* Denotes not out.

BOWLING

	O	Mdns	R	W	BB	5W/I	10W/M	Avge	Balls/W
J. H. Dawes	347.5	84	1,009	46	6-49	3	0	21.93	45.37
A. J. Bichel	417.2	99	1,326	60	7-77	4	1	22.10	41.73
J. R. Hopes	179.2	60	476	18	4-39	0	0	26.44	59.78
S. R. Watson	137.4	32	499	16	4-25	0	0	31.19	51.63
M. G. Johnson	81	14	325	9	3-23	0	0	36.11	54.00
A. A. Noffke	282.1	56	872	23	4-58	0	0	37.91	73.61
A. Symonds	145.4	34	446	11	2-14	0	0	40.55	79.45
A. J. Nye	11	0	45	1	1-39	0	0	45.00	66.00
N. M. Hauritz	147	23	576	6	2-16	0	0	96.00	147.00
R. N. Le Loux	1	0	1	0	–	0	0	–	–
L. M. Stevens	19	3	69	0	–	0	0	–	–
C. P. Simpson	2	0	6	0	–	0	0	–	–

QUEENSLAND v NEW SOUTH WALES

At Brisbane Cricket Ground, Brisbane, October 15, 16, 17, 18, 2004. Queensland won by two wickets. *Toss:* New South Wales. Queensland 6 pts. *First-class debut:* J. J. Krejza.

Former Test batsman Martin Love broke his finger in the field but batted bravely to help Queensland steal a thrilling win as darkness set in over the Gabba. Needing 240 to win, Queensland had hoped they would not need Love to bat, but he had to be called on with the home side teetering at 6 for 182. He batted at No. 8 and scored only six runs, but he kept New South Wales at bay for 39 minutes while Andy Bichel did the damage at the other end. Bichel hit the winning runs, a fitting climax to a great all-round performance which included match figures of 10 for 127. He took career-best interstate figures of 7 for 77 in the second innings, getting the better of a running verbal battle with Brad Haddin, whose batting had been the most spirited in each of his team's innings.

Bichel dedicated his performance to his uncle Don, a former Queensland off-spinner, who had recently died. Left-arm swing merchant Nathan Bracken was the pick of the NSW bowlers and almost hoisted his side to a come-from-behind victory in the second innings. Earlier James Hopes had rescued the Queensland first innings single-handedly with an aggressive knock that took his side to a narrow first-innings lead. The final day of the match was marred by rain and murky conditions which made batting devilishly difficult. It finished under artificial light, Bichel later confessing that he had not seen the skied ball he hit to third man for the winning runs.

Match reports by BEN DORRIES.

Man of Match: A. J. Bichel.   *Attendance:* 1,796.

Close of play: First day, Queensland (1) 2-64 (Maher 23, Symonds 29); Second day, New South Wales (2) 2-110 (Phelps 43, Thornely 6); Third day, Queensland (2) 2-116 (Perren 39, Symonds 71).

New South Wales

G. J. Mail c Seccombe b Dawes	7	– (2) lbw b Noffke	38
P. A. Jaques lbw b Hopes	44	– (1) lbw b Bichel	12
M. J. Phelps c Nye b Bichel	20	– b Bichel	84
D. J. Thornely c Seccombe b Dawes	3	– c (sub) C. P. Philipson b Bichel	12
A. W. O'Brien c Perren b Bichel	0	– lbw b Bichel	7
*†B. J. Haddin c Simpson b Dawes	66	– c Seccombe b Noffke	64
J. J. Krejza c Seccombe b Dawes	11	– b Bichel	0
M. J. Nicholson b Bichel	2	– c Hopes b Bichel	3
N. W. Bracken c Seccombe b Dawes	16	– c Maher b Noffke	0
S. R. Clark c Noffke b Dawes	4	– not out	0
S. C. G. MacGill not out	0	– c Seccombe b Bichel	4
B 8, l-b 11, w 4, n-b 7	30	B 4, l-b 9, w 5, n-b 3	21

(73.5 overs, 293 mins)   203
Fall: 25 89 89 89 97 133 145 195 203 203

(88.5 overs, 345 mins)   245
Fall: 23 81 127 136 219 223 241 241 241 245

Bowling: *First Innings*—Bichel 20–8–50–3; Dawes 18.5–5–49–6; Noffke 14–3–30–0; Symonds 13–4–38–0; Hopes 8–4–17–1. *Second Innings*—Bichel 26.5–10–77–7; Dawes 17.5–8–32–0; Noffke 19–2–64–3; Hopes 19.1–9–35–0; Symonds 4–0–18–0; Simpson 2–0–6–0.

Queensland

*J. P. Maher c Haddin b Bracken	25	– (2) c Nicholson b Bracken	2
C. T. Perren c Haddin b Nicholson	1	– (3) lbw b Bracken	40
M. L. Love b Jaques b Nicholson	4	– (9) c Phelps b Bracken	6
A. Symonds lbw b Bracken	44	– b Bracken	79
A. J. Nye c Thornely b MacGill	13	– run out (Clark)	24
J. R. Hopes not out	82	– hit wicket b Nicholson	27
†W. A. Seccombe c Mail b Nicholson	0	– c Haddin b Nicholson	10
C. P. Simpson c Haddin b Bracken	8	– (1) lbw b Bracken	0
A. J. Bichel c Mail b Clark	10	– (8) not out	28
A. A. Noffke c Krejza b Nicholson	3	– not out	15
J. H. Dawes c Thornely b MacGill	4		
B 4, l-b 7, w 4	15	B 4, l-b 4, n-b 2	10

(65.4 overs, 263 mins)   209
Fall: 7 17 84 87 118 127 164 180 204 209

(65.2 overs, 292 mins)   (8 wkts) 241
Fall: 0 11 123 132 174 182 197 216

Bowling: *First Innings*—Nicholson 17–2–64–4; Bracken 18–6–43–3; MacGill 14.4–2–50–2; Clark 16–6–41–1. *Second Innings*—Bracken 18–4–49–5; Nicholson 16.2–1–54–2; Clark 22–5–63–0; MacGill 3–0–22–0; Thornely 5–1–27–0; Krejza 1–0–18–0.

Umpires: N. S. D. Fowler and D. L. Orchard.

At Adelaide Oval, Adelaide, November 9, 10, 11, 12 2004. QUEENSLAND defeated SOUTH AUSTRALIA by 53 runs.

At WACA Ground, Perth, November 21, 22, 23, 24, 2004. QUEENSLAND drew with WESTERN AUSTRALIA.

QUEENSLAND v TASMANIA

At Brisbane Cricket Ground, Brisbane, November 29, 30, December 1, 2, 2004. Queensland won by seven wickets. *Toss:* Tasmania. Queensland 6 pts. *First-class debut:* R. . Le Loux, R. J. G. Lockyear.

The match was one-way traffic from the moment Queensland skipper Jimmy Maher reached a century. His knock was the on-field highlight of the first day, but it was overshadowed by Queensland's surprise selection of 20-year-old leg-spinner Ryan Le Loux. The move to play two specialist spinners – Le Loux and Nathan Hauritz – was a break from more than a decade of Queensland tradition and a radical change in direction for a side which had relied heavily on its pace bowling depth. However, Le Loux was only called upon for one over in the match as Queensland delivered a traditional dose of fast-bowling venom. Tasmania were forced to follow-on, and despite four hours of classy resistance from Michael Bevan, they fared little better the second time around in the face of some fine bowling led by Andy Bichel. After losing three early wickets to the hard-working Tasmanian opening pair of Damien Wright and Adam Griffith, Queensland polished off the victory target in quick time. Maher praised young stand-in wicket-keeper Chris Hartley, who took nine catches. Maher, a one-eyed Queenslander, thinks the 22-year-old Hartley may time his run just right to be a ready replacement for Adam Gilchrist when the Test star retires. The match produced a quirky sidelight when celebrity poet Rupert McCall was sent onto the ground as a substitute fielder for Queensland.

Man of Match: A. J. Bichel. *Attendance:* 1,384.

Close of play: First day, Queensland (1) 6-310 (Hartley 3, Bichel 23); Second day, Tasmania (1) 8-190 (Wright 55, Doherty 6); Third day, Tasmania 253 all out.

Queensland

*J. P. Maher b Griffith	148	–	(2) b Griffith	15
C. T. Perren b Griffith	28	–	(1) c Clingeleffer b Wright	0
S. R. Watson lbw b Downton	22	–	not out	32
A. Symonds b Wright	3	–	lbw b Griffith	0
C. A. Philipson c Bevan b Wright	40	–	not out	39
J. R. Hopes c Marsh b Wright	26			
†C. D. Hartley c Marsh b Griffith	7			
A. J. Bichel c Wright b Doherty	69			
N. M. Hauritz lbw b Griffith	0			
R. N. Le Loux c Birt b Wright	5			
J. H. Dawes not out	17			
L-b 12, w 1, n-b 6	19		L-b 1	1
(117.4 overs, 474 mins)	384		(16.5 overs, 76 mins) (3 wkts)	87
Fall: 61 121 125 219 282 282 318 318 339 384			Fall: 0 26 30	

Bowling: *First Innings*—Wright 36.5–11–111–3; Griffith 37–9–109–5; Downton 15.1–3–57–1; Doherty 20.4–5–68–1; Marsh 7–0–22–0; Dighton 1–0–5–0. *Second Innings*—Wright 8.5–1–45–1; Griffith 5–1–24–2; Downton 3–0–17–0.

Tasmania

D. G. Dawson c Hartley b Watson	24	– (2) c Hopes b Dawes	0
T. R. Birt c Hartley b Bichel	5	– (1) b Hopes	48
M. G. Bevan c Hartley b Bichel	11	– c Hartley b Bichel	93
M. G. Dighton run out (Le Loux/Watson)	4	– c Symonds b Bichel	6
R. J. G. Lockyear lbw b Dawes	24	– c Maher b Bichel	2
*D. J. Marsh lbw b Dawes	13	– lbw b Symonds	21
†S. G. Clingeleffer b Symonds	22	– c Maher b Hauritz	4
D. G. Wright not out	71	– c Hartley b Bichel	5
A. R. Griffith c Perren b Hopes	9	– c Hartley b Bichel	37
X. J. Doherty c Hartley b Hopes	7	– c Hartley b Hopes	27
A. G. Downton c Hartley b Hopes	6	– not out	0
B 2, l-b 13, w 1, n-b 4	20	B 4, l-b 3, w 3	10

(80.5 overs, 323 mins)	216	(82.3 overs, 339 mins)	253

Fall: 5 23 44 68 87 103 137 168 200 216

Fall: 0 59 81 85 122 135 152 187 249 253

Bowling: *First Innings*—Bichel 15–7–23–2; Dawes 16–2–33–2; Symonds 16–5–34–1; Watson 14–2–64–1; Hopes 10.5–6–23–3; Hauritz 8–3–23–0; Le Loux 1–0–1–0. *Second Innings*—Bichel 21.3–5–70–5; Dawes 17–4–50–1; Watson 10–4–33–0; Hopes 12–4–23–2; Symonds 8–2–10–1; Hauritz 14–2–60–1.

Umpires: T. P. Laycock and P. D. Parker.

QUEENSLAND v VICTORIA

At Brisbane Cricket Ground, Brisbane, December 19, 20, 21, 22, 2004. Victoria won by 156 runs. *Toss:* Victoria. Victoria 6 pts, Queensland 2 pts.

Hostile interstate tensions, simmering for a decade, bubbled over after Victoria's back-from-the-dead win. On the back of second-innings centuries to Jason Arnberger and Cameron White, Victoria re-wrote history by recovering from a first-innings deficit of 183 to post an astounding victory. Only three other teams in the 1,729-game history of the domestic first-class competition had won after following on. Queensland dominated the first day and a half. Led by fluent innings from Clinton Perren and James Hopes, they posted a sound total in their first innings, before Andy Bichel and Joe Dawes ran through the Victorian batting. Jimmy Maher enforced the follow-on, but the plan backfired. Arnberger and Matthew Elliott began with a commanding opening partnership before determined bowling by Bichel and Shane Watson had the visitors 6 for 293, with an overall lead of only 110. Then Ian Harvey joined White in a three-hour seventh-wicket partnership that put Victoria on top. White brought up his maiden first-class century with a four and a six off Nathan Hauritz, and declared early on the last morning with a lead of 325. The Queenslanders, tired and dispirited after nearly two days in the field, were bowled out by the Victorian pacemen with a session to spare. The Victorian coach, Greg Shipperd, said Maher had shown a lack of respect for Victoria and underestimated them when he enforced the follow-on. Maher, who did not back away from his decision to enforce the follow-on, dismissed the comments. It was Queensland's first Pura Cup loss of the season and Maher blamed his batsmen for a sub-standard performance.

Man of Match: J. L. Arnberger.   *Attendance:* 4,480.

Close of play: First day, Queensland 371; Second day, Victoria (2) 1–171 (Arnberger 97, Roach 0); Third day, Victoria (2) 6–472 (White 105, Harvey 71).

Queensland

*J.P. Maher c (sub) G.C. Rummans b Wise	19	– (2) c Roach b Harvey	19
C.T. Perren c Roach b White	86	– (1) c Arnberger b Wise	52
M.L. Love c Hodge b Wise	0	– c Roach b Wise	7
S.R. Watson c White b Wise	49	– lbw b Lewis	0
A. Symonds c Roach b Wise	16	– lbw b Harvey	16
J.R. Hopes c Roach b Inness	107	– (10) c Hussey b Lewis	0
†C.D. Hartley lbw b White	50	– (6) c Moss b Inness	8
A.J. Bichel b White	6	– (7) c Lewis b Inness	2
A.A. Noffke b Harvey	21	– (8) not out	45
N.M. Hauritz not out	1	– (9) c Roach b Lewis	0
J.H. Dawes b Harvey	4	– b Harvey	8
L-b 9, w 1, n-b 2	12	L-b 12	12

(93.4 overs, 389 mins)   371   (59 overs, 243 mins)   169
Fall: 54 56 155 159 186 297 303 361 367 371   Fall: 34 51 58 92 108 108 111 142 142 169

Bowling: *First Innings*—Inness 15-3-68-1; Lewis 21-4-79-0; Harvey 14.4-4-40-2; Wise 16-4-63-4; Moss 10-2-36-0; White 17-4-76-3. *Second Innings*—Lewis 18-8-51-3; Inness 11-3-31-2; Harvey 12-4-29-3; Wise 15-8-27-2; White 3-0-19-0.

Victoria

M.T.G. Elliott c Love b Dawes	2	– (2) c Hartley b Watson	71
J.L. Arnberger lbw b Bichel	1	– (1) lbw b Bichel	152
B.J. Hodge c Maher b Symonds	61	– (4) c Hartley b Bichel	4
J. Moss c Love b Bichel	0	– (5) b Watson	20
D.J. Hussey b Dawes	3	– (6) c Hartley b Bichel	23
*C.L. White b Symonds	44	– (7) c Hartley b Bichel	119
I.J. Harvey c Maher b Noffke	16	– (8) not out	90
†P.J. Roach lbw b Dawes	14	– (3) c Perren b Bichel	11
M.L. Lewis lbw b Dawes	21	– b Bichel	2
M.W.H. Inness c Symonds b Dawes	15		
A.B. Wise not out	1		
L-b 2, w 5, n-b 3	10	B 1, l-b 10, w 3, n-b 2	16

(45.2 overs, 206 mins)   188   (150.5 overs, 576 mins) (8 wkts dec) 508
Fall: 3 7 16 23 110 131 149 149 168 188   Fall: 167 199 203 246 288 293 498 508

Bowling: *First Innings*—Bichel 11-2-50-2; Dawes 13.2-2-54-5; Noffke 11-2-35-1; Watson 4-0-33-0; Symonds 6-1-14-2. *Second Innings*—Bichel 30.5-6-108-6; Dawes 25-3-94-0; Watson 23-4-103-2; Symonds 26-7-66-0; Noffke 17-2-60-0; Hauritz 29-6-66-0.

Umpires: N.S. McNamara and B.N.J. Oxenford.

At Bellerive Oval, Hobart, January 18, 19, 20, 21, 2005. QUEENSLAND defeated TASMANIA by 168 runs.

At Bankstown Memorial Oval, Bankstown, January 28, 29, 30, 31, 2005. QUEENSLAND drew with NEW SOUTH WALES

QUEENSLAND v SOUTH AUSTRALIA

At Brisbane Cricket Ground, Brisbane, February 24, 25, 26, 2005. Queensland won by 165 runs. *Toss:* South Australia. Queensland 6 pts. *First-class debut:* L.M. Stevens.
    Darren Lehmann slammed the state of the green and cracking Gabba wicket after his side lost in less than three days. Chasing a victory target of 366, Lehmann belted 16 fours in making 104 off 85 balls as his side raced to 1 for 166 after 28 overs. But his dismissal exposed South Australia's soft underbelly to a tricky pitch and triggered a collapse of 9

for 34 in 13 overs, which Lehmann suggested was brought about more by the pitch than by bad shots. "Next time in Adelaide when Queensland come down, it might be turning square from about ten overs in," Lehmann fumed. As Joe Dawes took 5 for 49, some observers remarked that the scores of the last eight batsmen – 2, 5, 0, 4, 8, 1, 0, 0 – resembled a telephone number. Even though the result was disappointing for South Australia, there was some good news in the continuing good form of lean young off-spinner Dan Cullen, who took seven wickets for the match on a wicket custom-made for fast bowlers. His 5 for 78 in the second innings included a spree of 3 for 6 in ten balls as he single-handedly tried to bowl his side back into the match. Largely due to Cullen, Queensland were struggling at 7 for 161, but Craig Philipson and Mitchell Johnson rallied with some venturesome batting to take the game out of South Australia's reach. It was Queensland's first victory in more than a month in either domestic competition.

Man of Match: J. H. Dawes.   *Attendance:* 1,187.

Close of play: First day, South Australia (1) 5-68 (Blewett 34, Manou 1); Second day, Queensland (2) 8-257 (Philipson 64, Johnson 28).

Queensland

*J. P. Maher c Plant b Rofe	14	– (2) lbw b Cullen		34
C. T. Perren lbw b Tait	58	– (1) lbw b Tait		22
M. L. Love lbw b Rofe	0	– lbw b Cullen		35
S. R. Watson b Rofe	8	– c Manou b Tait		29
C. A. Philipson c Manou b R. J. Harris	2	– c Manou b Tait		73
L. M. Stevens c Adcock b Cullen	46	– c R. J. Harris b Cullen		8
†W. A. Seccombe c D. J. Harris b Tait	0	– st Manou b Cullen		5
A. J. Bichel not out	47	– c Plant b Cullen		0
A. A. Noffke c D. J. Harris b Tait	1	– c Lehmann b Rofe		14
M. G. Johnson c and b Tait	4	– not out		51
J. H. Dawes b Cullen	4	– b Tait		11
B 6, l-b 7, w 2	15	B 9, l-b 16, w 1, n-b 1		27

(63.3 overs, 262 mins) 199
Fall: 21 21 38 45 133 133 149 150 184 199

(78.5 overs, 321 mins) 309
Fall: 48 74 129 135 151 161 161 195 273 309

Bowling: *First Innings*—Tait 18–5–61–4; Rofe 17–1–44–3; R. J. Harris 11–3–36–1; Blewett 8–2–26–0; Cullen 9.3–3–19–2. *Second Innings*—Tait 22.5–2–97–4; Rofe 19–2–66–1; R.J. Harris 16–5–40–0; Cullen 20–3–79–5; Lehmann 1–0–2–0.

South Australia

G. S. Blewett b Bichel	41	– (2) c Seccombe b Dawes		54
T. C. Plant lbw b Dawes	6	– (1) c Watson b Dawes		3
*D. S. Lehmann c Watson b Bichel	13	– b Johnson		104
D. J. Harris lbw b Dawes	0	– c Stevens b Dawes		2
C. J. Ferguson c Watson b Dawes	0	– lbw b Johnson		5
N. T. Adcock c Seccombe b Johnson	2	– c Noffke b Johnson		0
†G. A. Manou c Seccombe b Noffke	27	– c Seccombe b Bichel		4
R. J. Harris c Bichel b Noffke	32	– c Maher b Bichel		8
D. J. Cullen c Philipson b Noffke	0	– c Philipson b Dawes		1
S. W. Tait not out	1	– not out		0
P. C. Rofe lbw b Bichel	0	– c Maher b Dawes		0
B 2, l-b 8, w 6, n-b 5	21	B 2, l-b 11, w 6		19

(52.1 overs, 224 mins) 143
Fall: 23 38 39 39 57 81 116 126 143 143

(41.3 overs, 188 mins) 200
Fall: 9 166 173 182 186 190 199 200 200 200

Bowling: *First Innings*—Bichel 15.1–2–52–3; Dawes 17–7–39–3; Noffke 12–6–22–3; Johnson 8–2–20–1. *Second Innings*—Bichel 12–0–76–2; Dawes 10.3–1–49–5; Noffke 10–0–39–0; Johnson 9–2–23–3.

Umpires: R. L. Parry and S. J. A. Taufel.

At Melbourne Cricket Ground, Melbourne, March 3, 4, 5, 6, 2005. QUEENSLAND defeated VICTORIA by 78 runs.

QUEENSLAND v WESTERN AUSTRALIA

At Brisbane Cricket Ground, Brisbane, March 10, 11, 12, 13, 2005. Match drawn. *Toss:* Western Australia. Queensland 2 pts.

The match started with each side knowing they could host the final, or miss it altogether, depending on the result here and the outcome of New South Wales's clash against Victoria. Queensland needed just first-innings points to book a spot in the final. Western Australia's cause was scarcely helped when promising speedster Brett Dorey broke down in his eighth over of the match with a side strain and did not return. At the beginning of day three, with Western Australia needing another 57 runs with four wickets in hand, the race for first-innings points was evenly poised, but Andy Bichel took five wickets in seven balls to give Queensland a lead of 31 and a final at the Gabba. After a fine century by Clinton Perren, the Western Australian bowlers fought back to give their side the advantage before Wade Seccombe and the tail added 174 for the last three wickets. Queensland, having gained the points they wanted, did not seek to set Western Australia a target, as a victory to the visitors would have meant a final at the WACA. Eventually Western Australia needed 441 off 56 overs to snatch a spot in the final, and not surprisingly their batsmen showed little interest, and the match was called off early. Queensland still had to endure one nervous moment when star all-rounder James Hopes clutched a hamstring after bending down in the field late on the final day. But the injury was minor and Hopes was quickly cleared to take his place in the final. Queensland headed into their seventh consecutive four-day final full of confidence, with Maher declaring his side had the strike-power to beat NSW.

Man of Match: W. A. Seccombe.   *Attendance:* 2,126.

Close of play: First day, Queensland (1) 8-302 (Seccombe 35, Johnson 12); Second day, Western Australia (1) 6-298 (North 71, Magoffin 1); Third day, Queensland (2) 8-289 (Seccombe 28, Johnson 0).

Queensland

*J. P. Maher lbw b Dorey	20	–	(2) c Campbell b Magoffin	34
C. T. Perren c Campbell b Dorey	8	–	(1) c and b Hussey	105
M. L. Love lbw b Edmondson	19	–	c Hussey b Williams	5
S. R. Watson c Voges b Dorey	60	–	c (sub) G. B. Hogg b Edmondson	34
A. Symonds c (sub) G. B. Hogg b Hussey	62	–	c Campbell b Hussey	24
C. A. Philipson lbw b Hussey	27	–	(7) c Campbell b Williams	0
J. R. Hopes c Rogers b Voges	41	–	(6) c Campbell b Magoffin	16
†W. A. Seccombe c Williams b Hussey	69	–	c and b Edmondson	84
A. J. Bichel lbw b Voges	0	–	c Magoffin b Voges	27
M. G. Johnson c Rogers b Edmondson	27	–	c Rogers b Hussey	26
J. H. Dawes not out	0	–	not out	34
B 6, l-b 8, w 2, n-b 5	21		B 8, l-b 3, w 1, n-b 8	20
(99.2 overs, 405 mins)	354		(115.3 overs, 466 mins)	409

Fall: 39 44 88 141 208 224 289 289 343 354

Fall: 96 111 168 208 217 218 235 288 347 409

Bowling: *First Innings*—Williams 25.1–5–89–0; Magoffin 23–10–57–0; Dorey 7.5–0–28–3; Edmondson 18–3–76–2; Hussey 14.2-2–49–3; North 6–0–25–0; Voges 5–1–16–2. *Second Innings*—Williams 26–5–81–2; Magoffin 30–4–105–2; Edmondson 24.3–0–134–2; Voges 19–6–41–1; Hussey 15–2–34–3; North 1–0–3–0.

Western Australia

*M. E. K. Hussey b Dawes	13	– (2) lbw b Hopes	54
C. J. L. Rogers c Seccombe b Hopes	83	– (1) c Perren b Johnson	45
M. W. Goodwin c Symonds b Hopes	57	– c Maher b Symonds	45
M. J. North b Watson	88	– lbw b Symonds	45
S. E. Marsh c Perren b Dawes	12	– not out	4
A. C. Voges c (sub) A. A. Noffke b Symonds	27	– not out	1
†R. J. Campbell lbw b Watson	24		
S. J. Magoffin c Symonds b Bichel	4		
B. A. Williams c Seccombe b Bichel	0		
B. R. Dorey c Seccombe b Bichel	0		
B. M. Edmondson not out	0		
B 1, l-b 7, w 5, n-b 2	15	B 1, l-b 2, w 2	5

(105.4 overs, 433 mins)   323   (48 overs, 173 mins)   (4 wkts) 199
Fall: 29 147 158 181 246 291 317 321 323   Fall: 96 117 190 198

Bowling: *First Innings*—Bichel 30–10–70–3; Dawes 17–3–47–2; Hopes 15–3–40–2; Johnson 16–1–71–0; Watson 19.4–5–51–2; Symonds 8–1–36–1. *Second Innings*—Bichel 7–2–19–0; Dawes 2–0–5–0; Johnson 14–2–61–1; Symonds 19–4–86–2; Hopes 6–2–25–1.

Umpires: B. N. J. Oxenford and R. L. Parry.

FINAL

At the Brisbane Cricket Ground, Brisbane, March 18, 19, 20, 2005. QUEENSLAND lost to NEW SOUTH WALES by one wicket. For details see page 412.

QUEENSLAND DOMESTIC FIRST-CLASS RESULTS TABLE

	First Game	M	Won	Lost	Drawn	Tied
New South Wales	Nov 26, 1926	152	38	60	54	0
Victoria	Dec 17, 1926	145	43	52	50	0
South Australia	Dec 25, 1926	145	48	51	45	1
Western Australia	Feb 6, 1948	110	26	36	48	0
Tasmania	Feb 25, 1978	52	20	8	24	0
Total		604	175	207	221	1

QUEENSLAND DOMESTIC FIRST-CLASS RECORDS

Highest score for:	300*	M. L. Love v Victoria at St Kilda	2003-04
Highest score against:	452*	D. G. Bradman (New South Wales) at Sydney	1929-30
Best bowling for:	10-61	P. J. Allan v Victoria at Melbourne	1965-66
Best bowling against:	9-67	A. N. Connolly (Victoria) at Brisbane	1964-65
Highest total for:	687	v New South Wales at Brisbane	1930-31
Highest total against:	7-821	decby South Australia at Adelaide	1939-40
Lowest total for:	49	v Victoria at Melbourne	1936-37
Lowest total against:	54	by Western Australia at Brisbane	1972-73

MOST RUNS

	M	I	NO	R	HS	100s	50s	Avge
S. G. Law	142	234	28	9,034	216	24	47	43.85
S. C. Trimble	123	230	13	8,647	252*	22	40	39.84
M. L. Love	110	192	16	7,963	300*	19	34	45.24
M. L. Hayden	83	150	17	7,332	234	24	30	55.13
J. P. Maher	112	200	20	7,271	209	13	37	40.39
P. J. P. Burge	83	138	12	7,084	283	22	31	56.22
A. R. Border	87	143	19	6,779	196	15	37	54.67
K. D. Mackay	100	162	22	6,341	223	14	32	45.29
G. M. Ritchie	94	154	14	6,096	213*	14	34	43.54
T. J. Barsby	100	181	7	6,052	165	13	28	34.78
G. S. Chappell	52	84	11	5,037	194	17	22	69.00
R. B. Kerr	79	135	7	5,036	201*	15	24	39.34
K. C. Wessels	53	91	3	4,779	249	15	19	54.31
A. Symonds	77	126	9	4,287	163	11	16	36.64
T. V. Hohns	105	170	30	3,965	103	2	25	28.32
P. H. Carlson	81	144	14	3,825	110*	5	18	29.42
D. Tallon	69	124	7	3,594	193	5	17	30.72
G. R. Reynolds	50	83	9	3,518	203*	12	13	47.54
W. A. Brown	37	65	3	3,493	215	9	17	56.34
J. A. MacLean	86	150	20	3,277	156	2	12	25.21

HIGHEST PARTNERSHIP FOR EACH WICKET

388	for 1st	K. C. Wessels and R. B. Kerr v Victoria at St Kilda	1982-83
368*	for 2nd	M. L. Hayden and M. L. Love v Tasmania at Hobart (Bel)	1995-96
326	for 3rd	M. L. Love and S. G. Law v Tasmania at Brisbane	1994-95
295	for 4th	P. J. P. Burge and T. R. Veivers v South Australia at Brisbane	1962-63
236	for 5th	M. L. Love and J. R. Hopes v Victoria at St Kilda	2003-04
211	for 6th	T. R. Veivers and J. D. Bratchford v South Australia at Brisbane	1959-60
335	for 7th	W. C. Andrews and E. C. Bensted v New South Wales at Sydney	1934-35
146	for 8th	T. V. Hohns and G. Dymock v Victoria at Melbourne	1978-79
152*	for 9th	A. T. W. Grout and W. T. Walmsley v New South Wales at Sydney	1956-57
105*	for 10th	W. T. Walmsley and J. E. Childe-Freeman v New South Wales at Brisbane	1957-58

MOST WICKETS

	M	Balls	Mdns	R	W	BB	5W/i	10W/m	Avge	Balls/W
M. S. Kasprowicz	89	19,599	843	9,409	387	6-47	24	2	24.31	50.64
C. G. Rackemann	102	22,400	920	10,079	383	7-43	12	1	26.32	58.48
A. J. Bichel	67	14,959	624	7,438	334	7-77	19	4	22.27	44.79
J. R. Thomson	77	15,172	410	7,927	328	7-27	17	3	24.17	46.26
C. J. McDermott	67	14,974	541	7,605	303	8-44	22	2	25.10	49.42
G. Dymock	75	17,110	449	7,032	266	6-79	6	0	26.44	64.35
D. Tazelaar	73	15,371	623	7,050	257	6-49	9	1	27.43	59.81
J. H. Dawes	63	12,274	543	5,850	238	7-67	9	2	24.58	51.57
T. V. Hohns	105	16,694	680	7,330	188	6-56	8	1	38.99	88.80
A. C. Dale	44	11,857	733	4,065	184	7-40	8	1	22.09	64.44
J. N. Maguire	64	12,945	438	5,893	176	6-62	7	1	33.11	72.72
P. J. Allan	47	9,840	153	4,603	176	10-61	11	3	26.15	55.91
J. R. F. Duncan	53	11,913	221	5,253	175	8-55	7	1	30.02	68.07
L. J. Johnson	43	11,774	235	4,171	171	7-43	12	1	24.39	68.85
V. N. Raymer	56	14,595	475	5,098	168	7-100	5	1	30.35	86.88
R. K. Oxenham	46	12,075	412	3,693	167	6-48	7	1	22.11	72.31
F. M. Francke	49	9,859	244	4,324	146	6-62	7	1	29.62	67.53
A. A. Noffke	40	8,025	294	4,069	134	6-24	5	0	30.37	59.89
P. W. Jackson	59	12,475	636	5,003	127	5-65	2	0	39.39	98.23
K. D. Mackay	100	12,757	269	4,574	123	5-15	5	0	37.19	103.72

MOST DISMISSALS

	M	Catches	Stumpings	Total
W. A. Seccombe	101	474	14	488
J. A. Maclean	86	289	24	313
A. T. W. Grout	84	213	63	276
R. B. Phillips	68	214	12	226
D. Tallon	67	145	61	206

MOST CATCHES

S. G. Law	126 in 142 matches	G. M. Ritchie	74 in 94 matches
J. P. Maher	126 in 142 matches	T. J. Barsby	73 in 100 matches
M. L. Love	124 in 110 matches	S. C. Trimble	72 in 123 matches
A. R. Border	99 in 87 matches	P. J. P. Burge	70 in 83 matches
M. L. Hayden	75 in 83 matches	R. B. Kerr	69 in 79 matches

MOST APPEARANCES

142	S. G. Law	1988-89 – 2003-04	102	C. G. Rackemann	1979-80 – 1995-96
123	S. C. Trimble	1959-60 – 1975-76	101	W. A. Seccombe	1993-94 – 2004-05
112	J. P. Maher	1993-94 – 2004-05	100	K. D. Mackay	1946-47 – 1963-64
110	M. L. Love	1991-92 – 2004-05	100	T. J. Barsby	1984-85 – 1996-97
105	T. V. Hohns	1972-73 – 1990-91	94	G. M. Ritchie	1980-81 – 1991-92

SOUTH AUSTRALIA

Case of the missing mid-season

by BERNARD WHIMPRESS

Pura Cup: Fifth
ING Cup: Fifth
Captain: Darren Lehmann
Coach: Wayne Phillips

Darren Lehmann

Just as you cannot judge a library by its bookends, nor can South Australia's Pura Cup season be judged by their win in the first match over the previous season's premiers Victoria, or their back-to-back victories in the last two games over Western Australia and Tasmania. These three outright wins have to be set against seven outright losses.

There was much excitement in the South Australian camp before the start of the season when chairman of selectors Paul Nobes spoke of South Australia's "magnificent seven" – wicket-keeper Graham Manou (who would captain the side ably most of the year), pace bowlers Shaun Tait, Paul Rofe and Mark Cleary, and batsmen Mark Cosgrove, Ben Cameron and Cameron Ferguson. Nobes stressed the trust in youth. The euphoria grew in mid-October after the state team – including first-class debutants Dan Cullen, Ferguson, Tom Plant and Jack Smith – inflicted a 118-run defeat on Victoria at Adelaide Oval. The trouble is that good sporting teams require a balance of youth and experience when times get tough, and only former Test batsman Greg Blewett represented an old head.

Losses against Queensland (at home) and Tasmania (away) darkened the mood. But the nadir came when they were bowled out for 29 in 14.4 overs at the SCG in December. No batsman reached double figures. It was South Australia's lowest score since Keith Miller blasted them out for 27 on the same ground in 1955. The second innings of the Sydney game brought further depression. Although Plant and Ferguson each made a maiden first-class century, and added 218 runs for the fourth wicket, eight of their team-mates again registered single-figure scores.

By the fourth game the obvious disappointment was Cameron, who had lost his place and would not regain it, while Cosgrove (the leading run-getter in 2003-04) would begin a series of scores – 0, 0, 0, 1, 8 and 1 – that cost him his position. Overall, the batting continued to let South Australia down, with only newcomer Ferguson and Blewett passing 600 runs, and only Shane Deitz and Darren Lehmann (who each played only two games) averaging more than 40. Smith, Manou, Daniel Harris and Ryan Harris all averaged in the low twenties, Cosgrove, Plant, Nathan Adcock and Luke Williams in the teens and Cameron less than ten.

The notable batting success was Ferguson, who bears the genetic strength of having parents who were both state tennis players, and whose powerful off-side driving was a feature of his play. His centuries against New South Wales and Western Australia and his 93 against Queensland exuded class. Blewett batted for long periods, but could not convert any of his four fifties into centuries. The state missed Lehmann, its long-time hero, who was on Australian duty most of the summer, but his second-innings century in Brisbane was a brilliant lone hand. Deitz played two gritty innings in the last two matches which helped to set up wins.

Without doubt, the player of the season was fast bowler Shaun Tait, who set a state record of 65 wickets at 20.16, with three five-wicket hauls. While his slinging action might offend aesthetes, his ability to dismiss top-order batsmen with fast outswingers delivered on a full length marked him as a leader of future Australian attacks. He took a wicket every six overs. Once again Paul Rofe offered great support with his accuracy and lift, but the team missed Mark Cleary for several matches because of injury.

The other major highlight was the bowling of young off-spinner Dan Cullen, whose loop, spin, aggression and accuracy won him plenty of admirers and suggested that he might be Australia's next finger-spinner. When fellow youngster, leg-spinner Cullen Bailey, was introduced into the side in the last game, long-time observers began to anticipate a spin combination in the style of Ashley Mallett and Terry Jenner.

South Australia's four wins in the ING Cup meant that they were competitive in that competition towards the end of the season, after four successive losses at the beginning had boded poorly. South Australia's best performances were the two wins over NSW, in Canberra and Adelaide, and the last-round victory over eventual champions Tasmania.

The Redbacks' recovery from 4 for 20 to make 167 at Manuka Oval owed much to Nathan Adcock's 62, after which Tait's 4 for 29 enabled South Australia to get a victory on the board. In the second game against Queensland at the Adelaide Oval, Greg Blewett was dominant, following his 125 opening the batting with 4 for 16. The side's other wins against Western Australia in Perth and Tasmania at home were marked by solid team contributions.

Blewett had a better one-day season than in the longer form of the game and led the run-getting with 472 runs at 59.00, with a second century in a losing cause at Hobart. Lehmann showed his immense value with 145 runs in two games. Of the other batsmen, Ferguson, Mark Higgs, Manou, Cosgrove and Adcock all scored solidly, the first three achieving strike-rates of more than 80. Tait again led the bowling aggregates and averages with 21 wickets at 19.90, while Cleary and Ryan Harris were the other bowlers to reach double figures.

Looking ahead, South Australia remains full of hope. Their youthful pace bowlers continue to deliver and Cullen has enormous potential. Some of the young batsmen faltered, but with the benefit of playing alongside Lehmann, Blewett, Deitz and Victorian recruit Matthew Elliott, supporters can look forward to Ferguson building on his excellent start, and players like Cosgrove, Cameron and Plant re-establishing their careers.

SOUTH AUSTRALIA RESULTS, 2004-05

All first-class matches – Played 10: Won 3, Lost 7.
Pura Cup matches – Played 10: Won 3, Lost 7.
ING Cup matches – Played 10: Won 4, Lost 6.

Front Row: Shane Deitz, Daniel Cullen, Jack Smith, Mark Higgs, Darren Lehmann (*Captain*), Wayne Phillips (*Coach*), Graham Manou (*Vice Captain*), Ben Cameron, Thomas Plant, Ryan Harris, Luke Williams *Back Row:* John Porter (*Physiotherapist*), Greg Blewett, Trent Kelly, Cullen Bailey, Matthew Weeks, Chris Duval, Paul Rofe, Jason Gillespie, Shaun Tait, Nathan Adcock, Mark Cleary, Mark Cosgrove, Jamie Siddons (*Assistant Coach*) Absent: C Ferguson, S Hurn, G Putland

SOUTH AUSTRALIA PURA CUP AVERAGES, 2004-05

BATTING

	M	I	NO	R	HS	100s	50s	Avge	Ct/St	S-R
S. A. Deitz	2	4	0	260	141	1	1	65.00	4	52.95
C. J. Borgas	1	1	0	53	53	0	1	53.00	0	34.64
D. S. Lehmann	2	4	0	169	104	1	0	42.25	2	109.03
C. J. Ferguson	10	19	0	733	114	2	4	38.58	2	51.69
G. S. Blewett	10	20	1	618	89	0	4	32.53	7	42.07
J. K. Smith	4	8	1	173	57	0	1	24.71	3	57.48
G. A. Manou	10	19	0	433	97	0	3	22.79	34/2	61.77
D. J. Harris	4	8	1	148	82	0	1	21.14	7	38.14
R. J. Harris	4	8	0	161	47	0	0	20.13	8	60.07
N. T. Adcock	7	13	0	247	67	0	1	19.00	8	33.07
M. F. Cleary	4	8	2	112	40	0	0	18.67	3	53.33
M. J. Cosgrove	6	12	0	223	82	0	3	18.58	6	41.07
T. C. Plant	8	16	0	286	125	1	0	17.88	3	39.45
S. W. Tait	10	18	7	190	58	0	1	17.27	3	57.93
D. J. Cullen	10	18	5	219	42	0	0	16.85	5	42.36
L. Williams	3	6	0	79	37	0	0	13.17	1	36.92
B. P. Cameron	3	6	0	53	31	0	0	8.83	4	36.81
P. C. Rofe	10	17	6	87	19*	0	0	7.91	3	57.62
T. P. Kelly	1	2	0	9	6	0	0	4.50	1	52.94
C. B. Bailey	1	1	0	0	0	0	0	0.00	0	0.00

Denotes not out.

BOWLING

	O	Mdns	R	W	BB	5W/I	10W/M	Avge	Balls/W
S. W. Tait	391.1	77	1,311	65	7-99	3	0	20.17	36.11
D. J. Cullen	409.4	76	1,306	43	5-38	2	0	30.37	57.16
P. C. Rofe	403.3	115	1,079	35	5-93	1	0	30.83	69.17
M. J. Cosgrove	28	9	98	3	1-26	0	0	32.67	56.00
T. P. Kelly	39	8	122	3	3-59	0	0	40.67	78.00
C. B. Bailey	19	2	82	2	2-82	0	0	41.00	57.00
R. J. Harris	113	23	395	9	4-92	0	0	43.89	75.33
M. F. Cleary	109.3	23	356	8	2-40	0	0	44.50	82.13
G. S. Blewett	76	17	249	4	2-64	0	0	62.25	114.00
D. S. Lehmann	5	0	20	0	–	0	0	–	–
N. T. Adcock	1	0	7	0	–	0	0	–	–

SOUTH AUSTRALIA v VICTORIA

At Adelaide Oval, Adelaide, October 16, 17, 18, 19, 2004. South Australia won by 118 runs. *Toss:* South Australia. South Australia 6 pts. *First-class debut:* D. J. Cullen, C. J. Ferguson, T. C. Plant, J. K. Smith.

A home side sporting four debutants and a new captain dodged Victoria's early blows and rumbled easily over the Pura Cup holders. Graham Manou's successful call gave his side first strike on an overcast morning, and after a useful opening stand was ended by Greg Blewett's unruly drive to point it appeared Victoria would continue their undefeated run from the previous season. However, Mark Cosgrove batted with authority and Manou showed a willingness to scrap. With Mark Cleary, they piloted South Australia to a defensible total. After a brief stint with Durham beset by run-up problems, Shaun Tait returned to somewhere near his best to blast out Matthew Elliot and nightwatchman Michael Lewis before Victoria reached double figures. The visitors still appeared to have first-innings points in hand on the second day until Cleary speared through the defences of Graeme Rummans and Jonathan Moss either side of tea. On his debut, Dan Cullen's hard-spun off-breaks were rewarded with a champagne first wicket – David Hussey bowled through the gate – and South Australia found themselves with a 31-run advantage. The home side's batsmen then worked hard to build a substantial lead. Blewett made South Australia's slowest-ever half-century (274 minutes), but it was less painful for the spectators than it was for the visitors. A crafty declaration left the Victorian openers with four overs before stumps on the third day, and when Cullen pinned Elliott on the back foot, South Australia had all the momentum. Tait was irresistible on the final morning, curling a perfect inswinger through Rummans, and though dropped catches allowed Moss a fifty, the result was never in doubt.

Match reports by DANIEL BRETTIG.

Man of Match: S. W. Tait. *Attendance:* 3,512.

Close of play: First day, Victoria (1) 2-14 (Joseland 5, Rummans 0); Second day, South Australia (2) 1-21 (Blewett 11, Cameron 7); Third day, Victoria (2) 1-7 (Joseland 0).

South Australia

T. C. Plant c Roach b Lewis		21	–	(2) c Moss b Harvey	1
G. S. Blewett c Rummans b Wise		32	–	(1) b Lewis	89
B. P. Cameron b Lewis		5	–	c Roach b Lewis	13
M. J. Cosgrove c Inness b Harvey		82	–	c Roach b Wise	57
C. J. Ferguson c Harvey b Lewis		2	–	c Roach b Inness	46
J. K. Smith c Roach b Moss		5	–	not out	47
*†G. A. Manou c Roach b Inness		50	–	c Harvey b McDonald	20
M. F. Cleary c Roach b Inness		40	–	not out	8
D. J. Cullen c McDonald b Wise		1			
S. W. Tait not out		7			
P. C. Rofe lbw b Inness		0			
L-b 3, n-b 6		9		L-b 4, n-b 4	8

(82.5 overs, 338 mins) 254
Fall: 47 59 66 68 101 174 238 245 249 254

(102 overs, 415 mins) (6 wkts dec) 289
Fall: 4 32 116 202 212 255

Bowling: *First Innings*—Inness 11.5–1–41–3; Harvey 11–5–42–1; Wise 15–2–51–2; Lewis 20–11–34–3; McDonald 12–4–41–0; Moss 10–2–34–1; Rummans 3–0–8–0. *Second Innings*—Inness 19–4–46–1; Harvey 14–4–47–1; McDonald 15–3–48–1; Lewis 21–9–48–2; Moss 10–2–24–0; Wise 21–8–59–1; Rummans 2–0–13–0.

Victoria

M. T. G. Elliott b Tait		6	–	lbw b Cullen	2
B. R. Joseland b Tait		51	–	c Manou b Tait	2
M. L. Lewis lbw b Tait		0	–	(9) c Rofe b Cullen	5
G. C. Rummans b Cleary		63	–	(3) b Tait	0
*J. Moss lbw b Cleary		44	–	(4) b Tait	50
D. J. Hussey b Cullen		11	–	(5) lbw b Rofe	7
A. B. McDonald c Cosgrove b Cullen		11	–	(6) b Rofe	36
I. J. Harvey c Manou b Rofe		2	–	(7) c Cameron b Blewett	32
†P. J. Roach not out		21	–	(8) b Rofe	29
M. W. H. Inness c Manou b Tait		0	–	lbw b Tait	19
A. B. Wise lbw b Tait		8	–	not out	2
L-b 5, w 3, n-b 2		10		B 5, l-b 13	18

(92.4 overs, 372 mins) 223
Fall: 9 9 95 164 175 188 191 210 211 223

(77 overs, 306 mins) 202
Fall: 7 8 17 34 102 110 163 178 184 202

Bowling: *First Innings*—Tait 19.4–5–39–5; Rofe 20–5–45–1; Cleary 22–8–47–2; Cullen 24–4–77–2; Blewett 7–3–10–0. *Second Innings*—Tait 15–3–34–4; Rofe 21–11–35–3; Cullen 22–7–53–2; Cleary 11–2–45–0; Blewett 8–1–17–1.

Umpires: S. J. Davis and I. H. Lock.

SOUTH AUSTRALIA v QUEENSLAND

At Adelaide Oval, Adelaide, November 9, 10, 11, 12 2004. Queensland won by 53 runs. *Toss:* South Australia. Queensland 6 pts.

South Australia showed great potential on the first and final days of this match, but lost their way in between to give an insurmountable advantage to the experienced Queenslanders. Graham Manou made the daring decision to send Queensland in on a flat but well-grassed pitch. The methodical Paul Rofe led a varied attack, and though James Hopes hustled his way to a fifty, South Australia appeared to hold all the aces at the end of the first day. Their subsequent collapse, after Greg Blewett and Tom Plant added 51 to get through the new ball, was baffling. In 32 overs South Australia lost all ten wickets for 99. Andy Bichel shared the spoils with Shane Watson, who claimed a wicket with his first ball for the state when he found the stumps via Blewett's inside edge. Queensland quickly built their lead through the authority of Jimmy Maher, the forcefulness of Watson and the brutality of Andrew Symonds. Shaun Tait persevered through cramp and illness to capture his best first-class figures and ensure South Australia did not have to chase 500. Bichel again deflated the South Australian top order, and despite Jack Smith's defiance the match looked over with a day remaining. Queensland did eventually win, but were pushed closer than comfort by a poised innings from Callum Ferguson, a punchy one from Manou, and an extraordinary hitting display by Tait. Not considered a batsman of any note, he stunned Queensland generally and Nathan Hauritz in particular with four sixes, one of which cleared the recently constructed Chappell Stands. Seemingly empowered by his fellow fast bowler, Rofe managed to scratch out his best first-class score, and while Queensland took the points, the post-match hubbub emanated from the South Australian rooms.

Man of Match: A.J. Bichel. *Attendance:* 1,440.

Close of play: First day, South Australia (1) 0-35 (Plant 18, Blewett 14); Second day, Queensland (2) 4-237 (Symonds 51, Hopes 25); Third day, South Australia (2) 5-185 (Ferguson 28, Manou 25).

Queensland

*J.P. Maher c Cleary b Rofe	8	–	c Cullen b Tait	80
C.T. Perren lbw b Tait	3	–	b Rofe	0
S.R. Watson b Cosgrove	17	–	c Cullen b Tait	61
A. Symonds c Manou b Cleary	44	–	c Cameron b Tait	52
A.J. Nye c Smith b Cullen	31	–	c Plant b Tait	0
J.R. Hopes c Cameron b Rofe	57	–	lbw b Rofe	26
†W.A. Seccombe lbw b Rofe	24	–	c Manou b Tait	12
A.J. Bichel c Manou b Rofe	1	–	b Tait	0
A.A. Noffke not out	44	–	b Cosgrove	26
N.M. Hauritz c Cleary b Cullen	13	–	c Manou b Tait	28
J.H. Dawes c Cullen b Rofe	15	–	not out	8
B 2, l-b 9, w 6, n-b 5	22		B 4, l-b 17, w 1, n-b 1	23

(82.2 overs, 326 mins)   279   (82.4 overs, 328 mins)   316

Fall: 11 17 76 80 164 190 196 209 244 279   Fall: 4 150 165 167 240 240 241
                                             258 298 316

Bowling: *First Innings*—Tait 15–5–38–1; Rofe 24.2–4–93–5; Cleary 19–3–45–1; Cosgrove 7–3–26–1; Cullen 17–2–66–2. *Second Innings*—Tait 29.4–5–99–7; Rofe 23–4–78–2; Cullen 12–3–49–0; Cleary 11–2–39–0; Cosgrove 7–1–30–1.

South Australia

T. C. Plant c Seccombe b Dawes	31	– (2) c Nye b Dawes	13
G. S. Blewett b Watson	37	– (1) lbw b Bichel	11
B. P. Cameron c Hauritz b Bichel	4	– lbw b Bichel	0
M. J. Cosgrove c Perren b Bichel	5	– c Seccombe b Bichel	0
C. J. Ferguson c Hopes b Noffke	27	– c Maher b Watson	93
J. K. Smith b Bichel	0	– c Nye b Watson	57
*†G. A. Manou c Nye b Bichel	0	– c Seccombe b Noffke	81
M. F. Cleary c Seccombe b Watson	14	– c Bichel b Watson	26
D. J. Cullen not out	15	– c Perren b Bichel	19
S. W. Tait c Maher b Watson	4	– c Symons b Bichel	58
P. C. Rofe b Watson	5	– not out	19
L-b 4, n-b 4	8	L-b 7, w 1, n-b 7	15

(49 overs, 218 mins)   150   (93.1 overs, 366 mins)   392

Fall: 51 64 74 97 100 104 120 126 137 150

Fall: 22 26 26 26 102 229 293 294 361 392

Bowling: *First Innings*—Bichel 19–4–71–4; Dawes 14–6–33–1; Hauritz 1–0–1–0; Watson 10–4–25–4; Noffke 5–1–16–1. *Second Innings*—Bichel 22.1–5–73–5; Dawes 19–3–68–1; Noffke 15–3–60–1; Hopes 3–1–15–0; Symonds 3–2–7–0; Watson 9–0–36–3; Hauritz 21–0–120–0; Nye 1–0–6–0.

Umpires: A. R. Craig and S. J. Davis.

At Bellerive Oval, Hobart, November 16, 17, 18, 19, 2004. SOUTH AUSTRALIA lost to TASMANIA by 195 runs.

At Sydney Cricket Ground, Sydney, December 2, 3, 4, 2004. SOUTH AUSTRALIA lost to NEW SOUTH WALES by an innings and 133 runs.

SOUTH AUSTRALIA v WESTERN AUSTRALIA

At Adelaide Oval, Adelaide, December 19, 20, 21, 2004. Western Australia won by 106 runs. *Toss:* Western Australia. Western Australia 6 pts.

Over in three days on a blameless pitch, this match played to a constant theme, with a busy left-hander as the hero. It was also a tale of two tails. Neither side's higher-order batting could exert its influence, each failing twice to keep out the opposition's bowlers. The difference came at the five-wicket mark – Western Australia were galvanised by the energetic strokeplay of Brad Hogg and the stubbornness of the rest of the tail, while South Australia's lower order, so dangerous with ball in hand, was unable to conjure a rescue act with the bat. On the first morning and second afternoon Western Australia's well-credentialled batsmen subsided in the face of Shaun Tait's pace and swing. Several fell to him without offering a shot, while others fenced indecisively at good-length balls. Allied to Paul Rofe's accuracy, Tait appeared irresistible, but in both innings Hogg returned fire with batting of urgency and great skill. The bowlers seemed to tire when he came to the crease, but his batting stood out like a beacon in a game where no other batsman dictated terms. South Australia's first reply was undone by paceman Steve Magoffin. After Greg Blewett and the impressively correct Callum Ferguson had added 89, a run-out allowed Magoffin to get amongst the tail. Bowling wicket-to-wicket, he took 4 for 0 in 27 balls. Set an unlikely 351 to win, South Australia were again given some hope by Blewett and Ferguson, but Hogg had the last word. He clutched a superlative one-handed return catch from Ferguson, spun through Blewett when he attempted a sweep, and ran out last batsman Nathan Adcock as he tried to keep the strike. The result meant South Australia spent Christmas at the foot of both domestic tables.

Man of Match: G. B. Hogg.   *Attendance:* 1,597.

Close of play: First day, South Australia (1) 3-53 (Blewett 21, Ferguson 28); Second day, South Australia (2) 2-27 (Cullen 1, Blewett 0).

Western Australia

*M. E. K. Hussey c Manou b Tait	5	–	(2) c Manou b Rofe		0
C. J. L. Rogers c Cleary b Tait	49	–	(1) b Tait		21
M. W. Goodwin c Manou b Rofe	1	–	b Tait		2
M. J. North b Tait	1	–	c Cosgrove b Cleary		67
S. E. Marsh c Cosgrove b Cleary	41	–	lbw b Tait		2
†R. J. Campbell b Tait	0	–	(8) c Manou b Cullen		38
K. M. Harvey lbw b Rofe	5	–	(6) c Adcock b Rofe		5
G. B. Hogg b Cleary	109	–	(7) lbw b Tait		61
B. R. Dorey b Cullen	14	–	c Williams b Cleary		22
S. J. Magoffin c Manou b Rofe	16	–	lbw b Cullen		0
B. M. Edmondson not out	2	–	not out		0
L-b 3, w 1, n-b 1	5		B 6, l-b 8, n-b 1		15

(74 overs, 298 mins) 248
Fall: 8 9 18 79 81 92 120 175 218 248

(56.3 overs, 241 mins) 233
Fall: 8 15 34 36 41 132 185 208
209 233

Bowling: *First Innings*—Tait 19–4–61–4; Rofe 20–6–69–3; Cleary 15–4–40–2; Blewett 6–2–21–0; Cullen 14–3–54–1. *Second Innings*—Tait 13–0–64–4; Rofe 16–8–39–2; Cleary 9.3–0–66–2; Cosgrove 2–1–4–0; Cullen 16–3–46–2.

South Australia

T. C. Plant lbw b Edmondson	2	–	(2) lbw b Edmondson		12
L. Williams c Marsh b Dorey	1	–	(1) lbw b Magoffin		12
G. S. Blewett lbw b Magoffin	42	–	(4) b Hogg		80
M. J. Cosgrove c Marsh b Edmondson	0	–	(5) lbw b Harvey		1
C. J. Ferguson run out (Marsh/Hussey)	54	–	(6) c and b Hogg		48
N. T. Adcock b Harvey	0	–	(7) run out (Hogg)		37
*†G. A. Manou c Marsh b Magoffin	0	–	(8) c and b Edmondson		5
M. F. Cleary not out	15	–	(9) c Edmondson b Hogg		7
D. J. Cullen c Hussey b Magoffin	0	–	(3) c (sub) B. Casson b Dorey		20
S. W. Tait b Magoffin	0	–	c Marsh b Magoffin		8
P. C. Rofe c North b Edmondson	14	–	not out		4
L-b 1, n-b 2	3		B 3, l-b 5, n-b 2		10

(45.2 overs, 192 mins) 131
Fall: 4 4 4 93 98 99 102 102 108 131

(86.4 overs, 351 mins) 244
Fall: 19 25 51 60 148 201 216
226 232 244

Bowling: *First Innings*—Magoffin 12–6–27–4; Dorey 12–5–25–1; Edmondson 11.2–1–45–3; Hogg 3–1–9–0; Harvey 7–2–24–1. *Second Innings*—Edmondson 22–7–68–2; Dorey 12–4–26–1; Magoffin 17.4–5–60–2; Harvey 15–7–36–1; Hogg 20–5–46–3.

Umpires: S. D. Fry and R. L. Parry.

SOUTH AUSTRALIA v NEW SOUTH WALES

At Adelaide Oval, Adelaide, January 18, 19, 20, 21, 2005. New South Wales won by 200 runs. *Toss*: New South Wales. New South Wales 6 pts. *Competition debut*: E. J. M. Cowan.

The scars opened by New South Wales's bowlers in the earlier match between these sides were again left raw as the visitors keenly exploited South Australia's lack of confidence and technique. Though Greg Mail and Matthew Phelps departed early to a pair of nice lifters, Dominic Thornely and Phil Jaques continued their exuberant form with a rollicking stand before the innings collapsed after tea. Matthew Nicholson squeezed out Tom Plant and Luke Williams by stumps then followed up with two more the next morning as South Australia fell apart. Greg Blewett applied himself until he was caught up in the tide of wickets, and Stuart MacGill flummoxed the tail with three victims in eight balls. Brad Haddin surprised some by not enforcing the follow-on, but the obdurate Phelps and arrogant Thornely took advantage with handsome strokes that conveyed the true demeanour of the pitch. Dan Cullen raised the ire of several of the NSW players with his verbal aggression. Haddin declared to leave South Australia with a day and a half to make 495. Early incisions by Stuart Clark and the run-out of Williams made a third-day finish a possibility until Callum Ferguson found a stubborn partner in Nathan Adcock. Ferguson looked as comfortable as Adcock seemed uncomfortable, and it was a surprise when Ferguson went first on the final morning. Manou also resisted, but the advent of the second new ball signalled the end.

Man of Match: D.J. Thornely. *Attendance:* 1,662.

Close of play: First day, South Australia (1) 2-23 (Blewett 4, Cullen 0); Second day, New South Wales (2) 2-150 (Phelps 61, Thornely 25); Third day, South Australia (2) 4-155 (Ferguson 70, Adcock 32).

New South Wales

G. J. Mail c Manou b Rofe	15	– c Manou b Rofe	1
P. A. Jaques run out (Harris/Manou)	82	– c Adcock b Cullen	41
M. J. Phelps c Manou b Tait	5	– not out	127
D. J. Thornely c Manou b Tait	74	– c Ferguson b Cullen	102
E. J. M. Cowan lbw b Harris	27	– lbw b Tait	4
*†B. J. Haddin c Rofe b Cullen	47	– c Cullen b Tait	22
J. J. Krejza c Adcock b Harris	6	– b Tait	4
M. J. Nicholson c Manou b Harris	7	– c Cosgrove b Tait	1
N. W. Bracken not out	15		
S. R. Clark c Manou b Cullen	0		
S. C. G. MacGill c Cullen b Rofe	13		
B 1, l-b 5, w 1	7	B 8, l-b 18, w 2, n-b 1	29
(83.1 overs, 338 mins)	298	(95 overs, 382 mins) (7 wkts dec)	331

Fall: 34 51 134 196 236 248 266 274 274 298

Fall: 15 83 269 289 313 329 331

Bowling: *First Innings*—Tait 20–3–83–2; Rofe 20.1–5–55–2; Harris 16–5–62–2; Blewett 3–0–10–0; Cullen 24–3–82–3. *Second Innings*—Tait 21–6–62–4; Rofe 26–6–79–1; Harris 17–4–43–0; Blewett 9–1–37–0; Cullen 21–1–77–2; Adcock 1–0–7–0.

South Australia

L. Williams c Krejza b Nicholson	14	– (2) run out	0
T. C. Plant b Nicholson	0	– (1) c Thornely b MacGill	33
G. S. Blewett c Mail b Nicholson	42	– lbw b Clark	3
D. J. Cullen b Nicholson	0	– (9) b Clark	3
M. J. Cosgrove c Haddin b Bracken	8	– (4) b Clark	1
C. J. Ferguson c Mail b Clark	7	– (5) c Haddin b Bracken	81
N. T. Adcock run out	21	– (6) lbw b Clark	67
*†G. A. Manou c Haddin b MacGill	13	– (7) c Krejza b Bracken	33
R. J. Harris b MacGill	12	– (8) c Phelps b Bracken	12
S. W. Tait c Mail b MacGill	4	– not out	16
P. C. Rofe not out	0	– c Jaques b Clark	17
L-b 9, w 1, n-b 4	14	B 5, l-b 21, n-b 2	28
(52.2 overs, 233 mins)	135	(96.4 overs, 399 mins)	294

Fall: 15 21 25 45 68 93 114 125 129 135

Fall: 16 19 29 71 178 244 244 255 269 294

Bowling: *First Innings*—Bracken 19–3–50–1; Nicholson 17–7–36–4; Clark 9–3–9–1; Thornely 3–0–14–0; MacGill 4.2–1–17–3. *Second Innings*—Nicholson 14–5–29–0; Bracken 28–9–62–3; Clark 25.4–5–91–5; MacGill 17–2–47–1; Krejza 12–3–39–0.

Umpires: S. D. Fry and G. T. D. Morrow.

At Melbourne Cricket Ground, Melbourne, January 28, 29, 30, 31, 2005. SOUTH AUSTRALIA lost to VICTORIA by an innings and 57 runs.

At Brisbane Cricket Ground, Brisbane, February 24, 25, 26, 2005. SOUTH AUSTRALIA lost to QUEENSLAND by 165 runs.

At WACA Ground, Perth, March 3, 4, 5, 6, 2005. SOUTH AUSTRALIA defeated WESTERN AUSTRALIA by 42 runs.

SOUTH AUSTRALIA v TASMANIA

At Adelaide Oval, Adelaide, March 10, 11, 12, 13, 2005. South Australia won by nine wickets. *Toss:* Tasmania. South Australia 6 pts. *First-class debut:* C.J. Bailey.

South Australia warmed up after a sluggish first day to best Tasmania comfortably and avoid finishing the season in last place. Wrist-spinner Cullen Bailey was given a state cap and he contributed on the first afternoon when a bouncing leg-break defeated Jamie Cox to end a 116-run stand with Michael Bevan. Bailey's exuberant celebration was overshadowed after tea as Bevan passed Matthew Elliot's domestic tally record in cantering to his eighth century of the summer, but Daniel Marsh and Bevan fell to Paul Rofe and Shaun Tait before the close to quell any Tasmanian momentum. Dan Cullen extracted turn and bounce to run through the tail the next morning, and the last eight wickets were mopped up for only 92 runs. South Australia had been inclined to collapse in reply to their opponents' first innings, but this time Shane Deitz, whose tenacity and shot selection were rewarded with his highest Pura Cup score, guided the young players expertly for six hours. Greg Blewett made a freewheeling fifty, Callum Ferguson strolled to 84 and Cameron Borgas, playing his first match since 2001 yet still only 21 years old, overcame a glacial start to compile his maiden fifty. Damien Wright was the only Tasmanian bowler to apply any pressure. Down by 152 runs, the visitors were squeezed by Cullen. Cox and Marsh were caught on the crease by sharp off-breaks, before Bevan's 1,464-run season was terminated when he deflected to first slip. Tait was down in pace after a long, fruitful summer, but still had enough left to collect the tail and the best season haul by a South Australian bowler.

Man of Match: S. A. Deitz. *Attendance:* 2,075.

Close of play: First day, Tasmania (1) 4-248 (Birt 8, Bailey 8); Second day, South Australia (1) 3-242 (Deitz 107, Ferguson 25); Third day, Tasmania (2) 3-35 (Bevan 12, Birt 1).

Tasmania

D.G. Dawson c Tait b Rofe	6	– lbw b Tait	7
J. Cox c Manou b Bailey	68	– c Deitz b Cullen	10
M.G. Bevan c Deitz b Tait	115	– c Adcock b Cullen	44
*D.J. Marsh c Adcock b Rofe	35	– lbw b Cullen	3
T.R. Birt st Manou b Cullen	38	– c and b Tait	2
G.J. Bailey c Harris b Cullen	13	– lbw b Tait	19
†S.G. Clingeleffer c Harris b Tait	5	– b Rofe	7
D.G. Wright c Rofe b Bailey	25	– b Tait	42
X.J. Doherty c Adcock b Cullen	0	– lbw b Cullen	3
A.R. Griffith c Harris b Cullen	0	– lbw b Tait	1
B. Geeves not out	3	– not out	16
B 2, l-b 5, w 1, n-b 3	11	B 7, l-b 5, w 2	14

(126 overs, 490 mins)	319	(63 overs, 244 mins)	168

Fall: 22 138 227 233 271 282 296 296 316 319   Fall: 13 21 31 42 80 99 99 112 117 168

Bowling: *First Innings*—Tait 24–7–54–2; Rofe 34–15–58–2; Blewett 10–4–22–0; Cullen 39–10–96–4; Bailey 19–2–82–2. *Second Innings*—Tait 21–4–71–5, Rofe 14 6–20–1; Cullen 28–6–65–4.

South Australia

D. J. Harris c Wright b Griffith	1	– (2) not out	
S. A. Deitz lbw b Wright	141	– (1) c Wright b Griffith	
G. S. Blewett c Clingeleffer b Wright	62	– not out	
N. T. Adcock c Marsh b Griffith	33		
C. J. Ferguson b Wright	84		
C. J. Borgas c Marsh b Wright	53		
*†G. A. Manou c Clingeleffer b Wright	11		
D. J. Cullen lbw b Marsh	28		
C. B. Bailey c Doherty b Marsh	0		
S. W. Tait c Griffith b Marsh	35		
P. C. Rofe not out	2		
B 4, l-b 10, n-b 7	21	L-b 2	2
(140.3 overs, 545 mins)	471	(4.4 overs, 19 mins) (1 wkt)	17
Fall: 13 125 189 327 340 352 405 405 441 471		Fall: 3	

Bowling: *First Innings*—Wright 43–15–108–5; Griffith 24–7–89–2; Doherty 30–8–98–0; Geeves 20–4–76–0; Marsh 21.3–2–72–3; Bevan 2–0–14–0. *Second Innings*—Wright 2.4–2–1–0; Griffith 2–0–14–1.

Umpires: I. H. Lock and D. L. Orchard.

SOUTH AUSTRALIA DOMESTIC FIRST-CLASS RESULTS TABLE

Opponent	First Game	M	Won	Lost	Drawn	Tied
New South Wales	Dec 16, 1892	201	54	111	36	0
Victoria	Dec 31, 1892	202	49	100	53	0
Queensland	Dec 25, 1926	145	51	48	45	1
Western Australia . . .	Nov 14, 1947	110	30	47	33	0
Tasmania	Feb 18, 1978	51	18	11	22	0
Total		709	202	317	189	1

SOUTH AUSTRALIA DOMESTIC FIRST-CLASS RECORDS

Highest score for:	365*	C. Hill v New South Wales at Adelaide	1900-91
Highest score against:	355*	G. R. Marsh (Western Australia) at Perth	1989-90
Best bowling for:	10-36	T. W. Wall v New South Wales at Sydney	1932-33
Best bowling against:	9-40	E. L. McCormick (Victoria) at Adelaide	1936-37
Highest total for:	7-821 dec	v Queensland at Adelaide	1939-40
Highest total against:	918	by New South Wales at Adelaide	1900-01
Lowest total for:	27	v New South Wales at Sydney	1955-56
Lowest total against:	41	by Western Australia at Adelaide	1990-91

MOST RUNS

	M	I	NO	R	HS	100s	50s	Avge
D.S. Lehmann	99	183	10	9,623	255	33	34	55.62
G.S. Blewett	110	210	11	9,412	268	23	47	47.30
D.W. Hookes	120	205	9	9,364	306*	26	44	47.78
L.E. Favell	121	220	4	8,269	164	20	43	38.28
I.M. Chappell	89	157	13	7,665	205*	22	45	53.23
H.N. Dansie	107	196	6	6,692	185	17	32	35.22
A.M.J. Hilditch	91	161	11	6,504	230	17	32	43.36
C. Hill	68	126	6	6,270	365*	18	27	52.25
P.R. Sleep	127	211	37	6,106	146*	12	29	35.09
V.Y. Richardson	77	146	7	6,027	203	18	27	43.36
J.D. Siddons	82	150	10	5,940	197	17	26	42.43
G.A. Bishop	84	152	6	4,871	224*	8	26	33.36
P.C. Nobes	63	114	4	4,608	141	10	31	41.89
P.L. Ridings	76	131	12	4,501	186*	9	21	37.82
K.G. Cunningham	76	133	10	4,330	203	6	24	35.20
D.G. Bradman	31	44	6	4,293	357	19	8	112.97
J.A. Brayshaw	52	96	11	3,969	146	9	24	46.69
D.A. Fitzgerald	61	118	2	3,943	202*	12	13	33.99
B.A. Johnson	65	123	14	3,884	168	9	16	35.63
A.J. Woodcock	68	124	2	3,793	141	4	26	31.09

HIGHEST PARTNERSHIP FOR EACH WICKET

281	for 1st	L.E. Favell and J.P. Causby v New South Wales at Adelaide	1967-68
386	for 2nd	G.S. Blewett and D.S. Lehmann v Tasmania at Hobart (Bel)	2001-02
286	for 3rd	G.S. Blewett and D.S. Lehmann v Tasmania at Adelaide	1993-94
462*	for 4th	D.W. Hookes and W.B. Phillips v Tasmania at Adelaide	1986-87
281	for 5th	C.L. Badcock and M.G. Waite v Queensland at Adelaide	1939-40
260	for 6th	D.S. Lehmann and T.J. Nielsen v Queensland at Adelaide	1996-97
198	for 7th	G.A. Bishop and T.B.A. May v Tasmania at Adelaide	1990-91
222	for 8th	M.C. Miller and B.E. Young v Queensland at Adelaide	2002-03
232	for 9th	C. Hill and E.A. Walkley v New South Wales at Adelaide	1900-01
104	for 10th	L. Michael and E.I. Pynor v Victoria at Adelaide	1949-50

MOST WICKETS

	M	Balls	Mdns	R	W	BB	5W/i	10W/m	Avge	Balls/W
C.V. Grimmett	78	28,144	445	12,878	504	9-180	47	13	25.55	55.84
A.A. Mallett	77	20,988	673	8,171	344	7-57	19	2	23.75	61.01
T.B.A. May	80	22,575	931	9,943	270	7-93	15	2	36.82	83.61
P.R. Sleep	127	19,482	671	9,883	252	8-133	7	0	39.22	77.31
P.E. McIntyre	61	17,419	576	8,974	215	6-64	8	2	41.74	81.07
E. Jones	39	12,145	501	5,516	208	8-157	19	3	26.52	58.39
T.J. Jenner	65	13,559	245	6,312	207	7-127	8	1	30.49	65.50
G. Giffen	38	11,682	402	5,676	192	9-147	18	7	29.56	60.90
G. Noblet	38	11,156	273	3,396	190	7-29	10	2	17.87	58.72
G.R. Attenborough	50	11,137	280	5,371	172	7-90	8	2	31.23	64.75
N.J.N. Hawke	50	11,712	210	5,026	169	8-61	9	4	29.74	69.30
M.A. Harrity	62	12,034	418	6,513	166	5-65	2	0	39.23	72.49
W.J. Whitty	38	10,681	298	5,012	154	7-66	7	1	32.55	69.36
T.W. Wall	42	9,299	118	4,242	150	10-36	2	1	28.28	61.99
J.W. Wilson	46	13,796	474	4,780	147	6-55	5	0	32.52	93.85
J.C. Scuderi	57	11,061	478	5,158	146	7-79	8	1	35.33	75.76
R.M. Hogg	34	6,705	183	3,182	144	7-53	9	2	22.10	46.56
S.P. George	51	9,962	315	5,617	143	6-51	2	0	39.28	69.66
P.C. Rofe	41	9,186	462	4,118	142	7-52	7	1	29.00	64.69
A.K. Zessers	40	10,131	550	3,808	136	7-67	4	0	28.00	74.49

MOST DISMISSALS

	M	Catches	Stumpings	Total
T. J. Nielsen	92	255	29	284
B. N. Jarman	77	193	57	250
C. W. Walker	57	103	87	190
G. A. Manou	51	160	14	174
G. R. A. Langley	46	111	24	135
K. J. Wright	36	102	9	111

MOST CATCHES

D. W. Hookes	123 in 120 matches	G. S. Blewett	67 in 110 matches
I. M. Chappell	113 in 89 matches	G. A. Bishop	60 in 84 matches
J. D. Siddons	113 in 82 matches	L. E. Favell	59 in 121 matches
V. Y. Richardson	99 in 77 matches	D. S. Lehmann	58 in 99 matches
P. R. Sleep	84 in 127 matches	A. M. J. Hilditch	57 in 91 matches

MOST APPEARANCES

127	P. R. Sleep	1976-77 – 1992-93	99	D. S. Lehmann	1987-88 – 2004-05
121	L. E. Favell	1951-52 – 1969-70	92	T. J. Nielsen	1990-91 – 1998-99
120	D. W. Hookes	1975-76 – 1991-92	91	A. M. J Hilditch	1982-83 – 1991-92
110	G. S. Blewett	1991-92 – 2004-05	89	I. M. Chappell	1961-62 – 1979-80
107	H. N. Dansie	1949-50 – 1966-67	84	G. A. Bishop	1982-83 – 1992-93

Bevan, boom and bust

by RIC FINLAY

Pura Cup: Sixth
ING Cup: First
Captain: Dan Marsh
Coach: Brian McFadyen

Dan Marsh

The Tasmanian squad learned the true place of cricket in the context of life when they lost one of their most popular team-mates, Scott Mason, to a heart condition shortly after the end of the season. Forced by his ailment to stand out of cricket for a year, Mason was making his first tentative steps back to the game when he collapsed at an indoor net session at Bellerive Oval on April 7 and died in hospital two days later, aged 28. A dedicated opening batsman who scored two quality centuries in his short 36-game career for Tasmania, Mason will be sadly missed.

Before this tragedy, Tasmania had experienced the elation of winning the limited-overs trophy for the first time since 1978-79, having only once (in 1986-87) even reached the final in the interim. The path to this success was unorthodox, for Tasmania won their first four home-and-away games, then only one of the next six. In the end, Tasmania had to rely on New South Wales defeating Victoria in the last round. The unattractive truth is that Tasmania won only two games of cricket in either competition after the third week of November; one of them happened to be the ING Cup final.

Tasmania's success was built upon the professionalism and indefatigability of Michael Bevan, the often spectacular big hitting of Travis Birt and Michael Dighton in the first 15 overs, and a stable and varied five-pronged attack that contained the run-rate of the opposition to less than five runs an over for the season. This formula seemed to work better when they batted first, as when they made a team record score of 5 for 340 against South Australia. The only time Tasmania seemed confident when batting second was in the final, when their execution of the chase was so clinical that it made one wonder what all the fuss had been previously.

It was fortunate for the Tasmanians that they won the ING Cup, for it defused criticism of their performance in the Pura Cup, in which they finished emphatically last, losing eight matches out of ten, a glum record in Sheffield Shield/Pura Cup history.

The outstanding domestic player of the season, and not just in Tasmania, was Bevan. Lured from Sydney by the offer of an assistant coach's role to go with his playing expertise, he crushed the previous records of runs and centuries in a season despite missing the first match through injury. Twice he scored three centuries in consecutive innings, each sequence including twin centuries in one match. He also scored more runs than anyone else in the ING Cup.

Yet the more Bevan dominated in the Pura Cup, the less his teammates seemed able to contribute. He scored an astonishing 28 per cent of his team's runs, and his average was almost three times that of the next highest, Michael Di Venuto, who scored 489 runs at 37.62 in seven matches. Di Venuto made a wonderful undefeated 157 against New South Wales in what turned out to be his last game of the season. Not for the first time in his career, injury twice took him away from the action just when he seemed to be at the peak of his form.

Only one other batsman could hold his head high. That was Damien Wright, who was selected mainly for his bowling. He became a dependable lower-order batsman, and for the first time made over 500 runs in a season, including his maiden century. He also took 36 wickets, and bowled more overs than anyone else in the land.

First-year player David Dawson could take some satisfaction from the season. He created a sensation in his first match, in Perth, not only making a hundred on debut, but carrying his bat through an innings. Despite this launching pad, he was able to total only 476 runs at 28.00 in nine matches, and his scoring rate of 30 runs per 100 balls tended to increase the pressure on those batting with and after him.

The pair who contributed so much to the one-day success, Birt and Dighton, had a lean year in the longer form of the game. Birt was prone to fall to catches behind the wicket, and the selectors lost patience with Dighton, discarding him with four matches to go, a disappointing fate for someone who had confidently blasted nearly

1,000 runs the summer before. The skipper, Dan Marsh, also had a mediocre season apart from one splendid century.

Another who was discarded was Jamie Cox, who was unable initially to force his way back into the team when an injured finger had healed. However, after strong performances in the 2nd XI, he was given Dawson's place for the last two matches, and his determination to play at the highest level possible was rewarded with two half-centuries, and a chance to claim the record for the most Sheffield Shield/Pura Cup appearances when the new season begins.

George Bailey played his first five matches in first-class cricket, after a couple of seasons of ING Cup experience, and like Dawson, started well before tapering off. He needs to tighten his technique against quality fast bowling. Sean Clingeleffer maintained his high standards behind the stumps, and also batted with pleasing authority in scoring 472 runs, mostly alongside Wright.

Wright was superbly supported by Adam Griffith when it was Tasmania's turn to bowl. In taking 45 wickets, Griffith enjoyed easily his best season, recovering from his "second-season blues" the year before. He bowled with consistent hostility throughout, even on the batsman-friendly wickets again produced by Bellerive curator Cameron Hodgkins.

The third seamer, Brett Geeves, could also be pleased with his development. Although sometimes expensive, he enjoyed a good strike-rate, and was able to take vital wickets at critical times in both competitions. A whole-hearted trier, he should continue to improve. The fourth pillar of the bowling attack, left-arm spinner Xavier Doherty, lacked penetration as the summer wore on. He will need to look for new ways to keep batsmen guessing.

Tasmania's coach for the past three years, Brian McFadyen, resigned at season's end to take up a position in the new Centre for Excellence in Brisbane. He can take away fond memories of his role in engineering a one-day cup win.

One long-shot that did not pay off was the recruitment of Zimbabwean all-rounder Andy Blignaut. Visa problems delayed his arrival, and he was rushed into the first Pura Cup match at Perth, where he failed to distinguish himself. Injury and poor form at grade level resulted in mutual disenchantment, and he returned to his native country.

Back row: Brian McFadyen (*Coach*), Jason Shelton, Kelby Pickering, Tim Paine, Luke Butterworth, Michael Dighton, Adam Griffith, Darren McNees, Rhett Lockyear, Scott Kremerskothen, George Bailey, Dane Anderson, Andy Blignaut, Dene Hills (*Assistant Coach*)
Front row: Sean Clingleffer, David Dawson, Michael Bevan, Brett Geeves, Damien Wright, Daniel Marsh, Michael Di Venuto, Travis Birt, Xavier Doherty, Andrew Downton, Jamie Cox

TASMANIA RESULTS, 2004-05

All first-class matches – Played 10: Won 1, Lost 6, Drawn 3.
Pura Cup matches – Played 10: Won 1, Lost 6, Drawn 3.
ING Cup matches – Played 11: Won 6, Lost 4, No Result 1.

TASMANIA PURA CUP AVERAGES, 2004-05

BATTING

Batsman	M	I	NO	R	HS	100s	50s	Avge	Ct/St	S-R
M. G. Bevan	9	18	3	1,464	190	8	2	97.60	3	54.08
M. J. Di Venuto	7	14	1	489	157*	1	2	37.62	9	54.21
D. G. Wright	10	19	2	534	111	1	2	31.41	7	59.33
J. Cox	5	10	0	302	84	0	3	30.20	5	46.53
D. G. Dawson	9	18	1	476	123*	1	2	28.00	8	30.71
S. G. Clingeleffer	10	18	0	472	92	0	3	26.22	27/2	51.93
D. J. Marsh	9	17	1	373	121	1	1	23.31	16	56.86
G. J. Bailey	5	9	1	185	70	0	1	23.13	3	50.14
T. R. Birt	8	16	0	331	57	0	2	20.69	3	41.43
B. Geeves	7	12	8	64	28	0	0	16.00	0	44.76
M. G. Dighton	6	12	0	166	42	0	0	13.83	4	39.90
R. J. G. Lockyear	2	4	0	46	24	0	0	11.50	0	39.32
X. J. Doherty	8	14	0	142	35	0	0	10.14	3	35.59
A. G. Downton	4	8	3	49	14	0	0	9.80	1	32.24
A. R. Griffith	9	16	3	119	37	0	0	9.15	4	32.34
A. M. Blignaut	1	2	0	9	9	0	0	4.50	1	45.00
D. A. McNees	1	2	0	0	0	0	0	0.00	0	0.00

* Denotes not out.

BOWLING

Bowler	O	Mdns	R	W	BB	5W/I	10W/M	Avge	Balls/W
A. R. Griffith	365.2	81	1,295	45	7-54	4	1	28.78	48.71
D. G. Wright	442	133	1,223	39	6-25	3	0	31.36	68.00
A. G. Downton	117.1	31	396	10	5-94	1	0	39.60	70.30
B. Geeves	218.3	28	928	23	4-94	0	0	40.35	57.00
M. G. Bevan	23	0	96	2	2-19	0	0	48.00	69.00
D. J. Marsh	96.3	14	340	6	3-72	0	0	56.67	96.50
X. J. Doherty	283.1	48	1,019	16	5-66	1	0	63.69	106.19
D. A. McNees	28	3	142	1	1-19	0	0	142.00	168.00
M. G. Dighton	15	3	52	0	–	0	0	–	–
A. M. Blignaut	12	0	79	0	–	0	0	–	–
J. Cox	2	0	20	0	–	0	0	–	–
G. J. Bailey	1	1	0	0	–	0	0	–	–

At WACA Ground, Perth, October 17, 18, 19, 20, 2004. TASMANIA lost to WESTERN AUSTRALIA by nine wickets.

TASMANIA v VICTORIA

At Bellerive Oval, Hobart, November 8, 9, 10, 11, 2004. Victoria won by 127 runs.
Toss: Tasmania. Victoria 6 pts.

In a match dominated first by the ball and then the bat, Victoria prevailed to break their 25-year drought in Hobart. Yet it looked set to continue on the opening day when Tasmania sent Victoria in on a green and lively wicket and bundled them out by tea. The destroyer was lanky basketballer-turned-paceman Adam Griffith with career-best figures. The only resistance came from Ian Harvey, who hit eight fours and a six while his team-mates struggled to lay bat on ball. Tasmania lacked even one decent innings and were skittled between tea and stumps, Michael Lewis and the irrepressible Harvey exploiting the conditions to good effect. After 20 wickets on the first day, the devil went out of the wicket and only five wickets fell on the second day. Graeme Rummans, filling in as opener, accumulated runs steadily, and shared valuable partnerships with Brad Hodge and David Hussey, who both took advantage of the improved conditions to play some fine strokes. Cameron White was able to declare just before lunch on the third day and set Tasmania an unlikely 494 for victory. In the face of some excellent pace bowling from Lewis and Mathew Inness, Tasmania crashed to 6 for 46 in the 16th over before Damien Wright joined Michael Bevan to add 215 in four hours in a sixth-wicket rearguard action. Wright, whose previous best first class score was 65, showed that he now had to be considered an all-rounder, while Bevan scored his first century for his new state in his usual relaxed, masterly fashion. Once Lewis finally broke the partnership on the fourth morning, however, it was just a matter of removing the stubborn tail-enders – Bevan was immovable – to give Victoria an easy victory.

Match reports by DAVID STOCKDALE.

Man of Match: I. J. Harvey.   *Attendance :* 1,172.

Close of play: First day, Tasmania all out 101; Second day, Victoria (2) 5-358 (Rummans 160*); Third day, Tasmania (2) 6-237 (Bevan 95, Wright 99).

Victoria

M. T. G. Elliott c Clingeleffer b Wright	6	–	(2) lbw b Griffith	8
G. C. Rummans c Marsh b Griffith	5	–	(1) c Cox b Downton	188
B. J. Hodge c Downton b Griffith	8	–	c Clingeleffer b Griffith	96
J. Moss b Griffith	2	–	lbw b Geeves	12
D. J. Hussey c Clingeleffer b Griffith	11	–	c Marsh b Griffith	67
*C. L. White lbw b Griffith	1	–	c Dighton b Downton	5
I. J. Harvey c Di Venuto b Wright	79	–	lbw b Downton	29
†P. J. Roach c Di Venuto b Griffith	11	–	c Dighton b Downton	6
M. L. Lewis lbw b Downton	8	–	c Clingeleffer b Downton	3
M. W. H. Inness c Marsh b Griffith	24	–	not out	1
A. B. Wise not out	2	–	not out	1
L-b 5	5		L-b 14, w 2	16

(57.1 overs, 240 mins)   162
Fall: 12 15 22 24 43 76 120 158 162

(120 overs, 497 mins) (9 wkts dec)   432
Fall: 16 182 207 342 358 409
421 426 429

Bowling: *First Innings*—Wright 20–8–33–2; Griffith 19.1–4–54–7; Geeves 9–0–35–0; Downton 9–1–35–1. *Second Innings*—Wright 38–11–84–0; Griffith 29–4–119–3; Downton 28–8–94–5; Geeves 15–2–56–1; Marsh 8–0–45–0; Bevan 2–0–20–0.

Tasmania

D. G. Dawson lbw b Lewis	11	–	(2) c Roach b Lewis		10
J. Cox c Moss b Inness	16	–	(1) c White b Lewis		5
M. G. Bevan lbw b Harvey	19	–	(4) not out		167
M. J. Di Venuto lbw b Wise	16	–	(3) lbw b Inness		4
M. G. Dighton c Roach b Wise	0	–	c Roach b Inness		2
*D. J. Marsh b Harvey	10	–	c Roach b Lewis		2
†S. G. Clingeleffer c Roach b Harvey	2	–	b Lewis		15
D. G. Wright b Lewis	5	–	c Elliott b Lewis		111
A. G. Downton not out	3	–	(10) lbw b White		10
A. R. Griffith c Roach b Lewis	8	–	(9) lbw b Moss		21
B. Geeves lbw b Moss	1	–	b Lewis		9
L-b 9, n-b 1	10		L-b 2, W 2, n-b 6		10

(37.2 overs, 165 mins) 101
Fall: 17 29 59 59 73 75 84 84 100 101

(118.3 overs, 481 mins) 366
Fall: 8 21 21 23 30 46 261 312 346 366

Bowling: First Innings – Inness 10-2-28-1; Lewis 10-5-13-3; Harvey 11-3-33-3; Wise 6-2-18-2; Moss 0.2-0-0-1. *Second Innings* – Lewis 31.2-6-84-6; Inness 15-1-62-2; Wise 22-2-82-0; Harvey 5.1-1-9-0; White 28-8-90-1; Moss 17-4-37-1.

Umpires: R. G. Patterson and J. H. Smeaton.

TASMANIA v SOUTH AUSTRALIA

At Bellerive Oval, Hobart, November 16, 17, 18, 19, 2004. Tasmania won by 195 runs. *Toss:* Tasmania. Tasmania 6 pts. *First-class debut:* T. P. Kelly.

Michael Bevan again led the way for Tasmania with a peerless century, and with the gritty support of opener David Dawson, who batted for over five hours, the home side looked set to cash in at 1 for 196. Then Shaun Tait and Paul Rofe took the second new ball and initiated a collapse in which Tasmania lost 7 for 49. But Michael Di Venuto restored the innings, batting fluently in partnership with a stubborn Xavier Doherty to put on a record Tasmanian ninth-wicket stand of 119. The paucity of South Australia's top order was ruthlessly exposed by the left-arm spin of Doherty. Only some cavalier hitting from Graham Manou, in a sparkling seventh-wicket stand of 133 with Daniel Cullen, gave the innings substance. Given his form, it surprised nobody when Bevan hit another graceful century in Tasmania's second innings. Daniel Marsh belted 58 off 47 balls to allow himself to declare and set South Australia a target of 366 off 84 overs. Before an hour was up they had lost four wickets to Damien Wright for 22 runs. Mark Cosgrove resisted for four hours, with stubborn support from Jack Smith and Cullen, but they could not defy the rampant Wright, who finished with his best figures, one week after making his highest score.

Man of Match: M. G. Bevan. *Attendance:* 1,260.

Close of play: First day, Tasmania (1) 7-240 (Di Venuto 13, Griffith 8); Second day, South Australia (1) 6-128 (Manou 16); Third day, Tasmania (2) 4-203 (Bevan 98, Marsh 22).

Tasmania

D. G. Dawson lbw b Tait	73	– (2) lbw b Kelly	1
J. Cox c Cosgrove b Tait	11	– (1) lbw b Tait	2
M. G. Bevan c Cameron b Cosgrove	106	– c Kelly b Tait	10
M. G. Dighton b Tait	12	– (5) c Cosgrove b Cullen	1
M. J. Di Venuto c Smith b Cullen	91	– (4) lbw b Cullen	22
*D. J. Marsh c Manou b Rofe	1	– not out	58
†S. G. Clingeleffer c Blewett b Rofe	0	– (8) b Kelly	22
D. G. Wright c Manou b Tait	0	– (7) b Tait	0
A. R. Griffith c Manou b Rofe	11	– c Smith b Kelly	2
X. J. Doherty c Blewett b Cullen	35	– run out	
B. Geeves not out	1	– not out	0
B 14, l-b 15, n-b 5	34	B 8, l-b 13, w 2	23

(141.2 overs, 538 mins)   375   (70 overs, 290 mins)   (9 wkts dec) 280
Fall: 17 196 217 222 223 223 224 245 364 375   Fall: 34 54 102 157 205 210 245
                                                 249 258

Bowling: *First Innings*—Tait 38–10–111–4; Rofe 38–19–50–3; Kelly 26–8–63–0; Cosgrove 10–4–29–1; Cullen 29.2–3–93–2. *Second Innings*—Tait 18–6–72–3; Rofe 17–5–42–0; Kelly 13–0–59–3; Cosgrove 2–0–9–0; Cullen 20.2–7–77–2.

South Australia

T. C. Plant run out	19	– (2) lbw b Wright	8
G. S. Blewett c Wright b Doherty	39	– (1) c Dawson b Wright	14
B. P. Cameron lbw b Doherty	31	– c Marsh b Wright	0
M. J. Cosgrove c Clingeleffer b Wright	11	– c Di Venuto b Geeves	58
C. J. Ferguson c Marsh b Geeves	3	– b Wright	0
J. K. Smith b Wright	12	– c Marsh b Wright	47
*†G. A. Manou st Clingeleffer b Doherty	97	– c Cox b Doherty	1
T. P. Kelly c Clingeleffer b Geeves	6	– c Clingeleffer b Wright	3
D. J. Cullen c Cox b Doherty	42	– not out	31
S. W. Tait not out	9	– c Clingeleffer b Geeves	0
P. C. Rofe b Doherty	12	– c Dighton b Griffith	0
L-b 2, n-b 7	9	B 2, l-b 4, w 1, n-b 1	8

(81.2 overs, 321 mins)   290   (79.3 overs, 314 mins)   170
Fall: 37 91 106 110 122 128 134 267 270 290   Fall: 17 17 22 22 109 110 119 150
                                                150 170

Bowling: *First Innings* – Wright 26–6–73–2; Griffith 17–4–55–0; Geeves 17–1–94–2; Doherty 21.2–4–66–5. *Second Innings* – Wright 23–11–25–6; Griffith 17.3–3–44–1; Geeves 11–4–21–2; Doherty 22–5–69–1; Dighton 3–2–3–0; Bevan 1–1–0–0; Marsh 1–1–0–0.

Umpires: B. W. Jackman and I. H. Lock.

At Brisbane Cricket Ground, Brisbane, November 29, 30, December 1, 2, 2004. TASMANIA lost to QUEENSLAND by seven wickets.

At Sydney Cricket Ground, Sydney, December 16, 17, 18, 19, 2004. TASMANIA drew with NEW SOUTH WALES.

TASMANIA v QUEENSLAND

At Bellerive Oval, Hobart, January 18, 19, 20, 21, 2005. Queensland won by 168 runs.
Toss: Queensland. Queensland 6 pts.

This game confirmed what Tasmania's brains trust already feared – the team which had been so good in the longer form of the game and so bad in the shorter form had done a 180-degree turnaround. After having Queensland reeling at 3 for 29, Tasmania lost the initiative and never regained it. Their bowlers were gored by the middle-order savagery of Craig Philipson's second first-class century (his first had come on his debut in the corresponding game in 2003-04) and James Hopes's 97 off 80 balls with 16 fours and one six. Brendan Nash had smoothed the way for that counter-attack. They say luck favours the brave and so it was with Nash, who often played and missed, was bowled not offering a shot to a Brett Geeves no-ball and next ball given out caught at short-leg, only to be recalled by the fieldsman, David Dawson, who said he had taken it on the half-volley. In reply Tasmania made a respectable score, thanks to Michael Di Venuto, Sean Clingeleffer and the tail. Adam Griffith followed up his fine bowling in the first innings to make Queensland struggle in the second, again with support from the energetic Geeves. But the failure of ten of the Queensland batsmen, who scored only 79 between them, was more than compensated for by Jimmy Maher's inspired 170 off 217 balls with 22 fours. That left Tasmania with a target of 340 for victory on the last day. Andy Bichel, Joe Dawes and Hopes never allowed the innings to settle, and the match was over before tea.

Man of Match: J. R. Hopes. *Attendance:* 1,335.

Close of play: First day, Queensland (1) 9-349 (Noffke 12, Dawes 0); Second day, Tasmania (1) 8-294 (Doherty 4); Third day, Queensland (2) 271.

Queensland

*J. P. Maher lbw b Wright	14	–	run out (Doherty)		170
B. P. Nash c Clingeleffer b Griffith	92	–	c Dawson b Griffith		20
M. L. Love c Clingeleffer b Griffith	0	–	c Di Venuto b Geeves		0
C. T. Perren c Dawson b Griffith	1	–	st Clingeleffer b Doherty		14
C. A. Philipson c Griffith b Geeves	119	–	c Clingeleffer b Geeves		4
J. R. Hopes c Dighton b Geeves	97	–	c Clingeleffer b Griffith		10
†W. A. Seccombe c Wright b Griffith	15	–	b Griffith		0
A. J. Bichel c Dawson b Wright	26	–	c Clingeleffer b Griffith		13
A. A. Noffke c Clingeleffer b Griffith	18	–	b Geeves		7
N. M. Hauritz b Geeves	2	–	not out		11
J. H. Dawes not out	1	–	b Geeves		0
L-b 6, w 1, n-b 9	16		B 4, l-b 7, w 1, n-b 10		22

(97.4 overs, 390 mins)	401	(70.3 overs, 311 mins)	271

Fall: 14 15 29 220 262 315 380 380 388 401

Fall: 65 65 147 188 206 206 227 257 263 271

Bowling: *First Innings*—Wright 23–4–75–2; Griffith 29.4–6–128–5; Geeves 19–2–104–3; Dighton 3–1–7–0; Doherty 19–3–66–0; Marsh 4–2–15–0. *Second Innings*—Wright 10–3–30–0; Griffith 30–6–85–4; Geeves 18.3–0–94–4; Dighton 5–0–23–0; Doherty 7–1–28–1.

Tasmania

D. G. Dawson c Seccombe b Noffke	6	– (2) c (sub) R. N. Le Loux b Hopes	38
T. R. Birt lbw b Bichel	2	– (1) c Maher b Dawes	4
M. G. Bevan c Love b Hopes	42	– c Maher b Bichel	4
M. J. Di Venuto c Love b Hauritz	79	– lbw b Bichel	1
M. G. Dighton lbw b Dawes	6	– lbw b Hopes	17
*D. J. Marsh c Seccombe b Dawes	20	– c Seccombe b Dawes	15
†S. G. Clingeleffer c Philipson b Bichel	73	– c Maher b Hopes	25
D. G. Wright c Seccombe b Bichel	41	– c (sub) A. J. Nye b Hopes	25
X. J. Doherty c Seccombe b Bichel	23	– lbw b Hauritz	8
A. R. Griffith c Bichel b Noffke	10	– c (sub) A. J. Nye b Hauritz	9
B. Geeves not out	0	– not out	3
B 8, l-b 14, w 3, n-b 6	31	B 4, l-b 4, w 11, n-b 3	22

(104.5 overs, 423 mins)	333
Fall: 8 29 96 135 163 179 277 294 329 333	

(66 overs, 274 mins)	171
Fall: 12 34 36 62 86 108 148 154 166 171	

Bowling: *First Innings*—Bichel 25–10–53–4; Dawes 23–5–83–2; Noffke 25.5–3–94–2; Hopes 15–7–41–1; Hauritz 16.5–40–1. *Second Innings*—Bichel 16–3–47–2; Dawes 10–3–25–2; Hopes 19–6–39–4; Noffke 17–2–36–0; Hauritz 4–1–16–2.

Umpires: B. N. J. Oxenford and R. L. Parry.

TASMANIA v WESTERN AUSTRALIA

At Bellerive Oval, Hobart, January 28, 29, 30, 31, 2005. Western Australia won by six wickets. *Toss:* Western Australia. Tasmania 2 and Western Australia 6 pts.

Michael Bevan's second set of twin centuries for the season and a third century from Dan Marsh were not enough for Tasmania to defeat Western Australia in a batsman's match. In the first innings, on a wicket which played like the Midlands Highway, Tasmania overcame an early stumble, as Bevan was ably supported by Marsh in a Tasmanian record fourth-wicket stand of 319 in four and a half hours. Sean Clingeleffer and the tail continued to bat brightly, raising an imposing total. Paceman Steve Magoffin reaped the rewards of hard work and a good line. Adam Griffith, Damien Wright and Brett Geeves followed his example and never allowed the Western Australian batsmen to dominate, though Murray Goodwin batted solidly and Ryan Campbell showed his customary flair. Mike Hussey declared 169 in arrears at tea on the third day, hoping to set the stage for a run-chase. Tasmania responded by looking for quick runs, especially during a partnership of 74 in 43 minutes between Bevan and George Bailey which allowed Bevan to reach his century and Marsh to declare. That set Western Australia the task of scoring 396 in less than a day. Hussey and Chris Rogers showed they were up to it by rattling on an opening stand of 133 in 112 minutes. When both fell to the left-arm spin of Marsh the home side looked back in the hunt. But Western Australia kept up the pace and Marcus North, who put on an unbroken 105 in 83 minutes with Adam Voges, hit a masterly innings to see his side home with nine balls to spare. "I just tried to keep the runs ticking over and when it got to 50 overs left we pretty much treated it like a one-day game," he said. The match yielded 1,454 runs for 28 wickets at a shade under four runs an over.

Man of Match: M. G. Bevan. *Attendance:* 1,443.

Close of play: First day, Tasmania (1) 3-301 (Bevan 161, Marsh 113); Second day, Western Australia (1) 2-177 (Goodwin 86, North 59); Third day, Tasmania (2) 5-183 (Bevan 91, Bailey 16).

Tasmania

D.G. Dawson lbw b Williams	0	–	(2) c North b Williams	16
T.R. Birt c Campbell b Magoffin	1	–	(1) c Hussey b Edmondson	20
M.G. Bevan lbw b Williams	190	–	not out	114
M.J. Di Venuto c Campbell b Magoffin	2	–	(5) c Rogers b Edmondson	5
*D.J. Marsh c Rogers b Magoffin	121	–	(6) run out	20
G.J. Bailey c Campbell b Casson	23	–	(7) not out	35
†S.G. Clingeleffer c and b Casson	92			
D.G. Wright b Magoffin	36	–	(4) c Voges b Casson	6
X.J. Doherty c Hussey b Casson	0			
A.R. Griffith c Goodwin b Magoffin	4			
B. Geeves not out	1			
B 8, l-b 9, w 7, n-b 6	30		L-b 5, w 1, n-b 4	10

(126.3 overs, 505 mins)   500   (53 overs, 217 mins)   (5 wkts dec) 226
Fall: 8 16 23 342 342 410 491 491 495 500   Fall: 31 63 70 93 152

Bowling: *First Innings*—Williams 30–8–104–2; Magoffin 26.3–4–76–5; Edmondson 22–4–138–0; Casson 29–4–89–3; Hussey 10–0–25–0; North 8–3–36–0; Voges 1–0–15–0. *Second Innings*—Williams 10–4–18–1; Magoffin 14–5–39–0; Edmondson 12–3–53–2; Casson 9–0–62–1; Voges 5–0–34–0; North 3–0–15–0.

Western Australia

*M.E.K. Hussey c Clingeleffer b Griffith	19	–	(2) lbw b Marsh	95
C.J.L. Rogers c Clingeleffer b Griffith	8	–	(1) lbw b Marsh	74
M.W. Goodwin c Clingeleffer b Geeves	138	–	c Clingeleffer b Griffith	31
M.J. North c Clingeleffer b Wright	59	–	not out	94
S.E. Marsh c Di Venuto b Wright	2	–	c Marsh b Geeves	41
A.C. Voges lbw b Wright	38	–	not out	55
†R.J. Campbell c Griffith b Wright	51			
B. Casson c Dawson b Geeves	1			
B.A. Williams b Geeves	0			
S.J. Magoffin not out	7			
B 3, l-b 2, n-b 3	8		B 2, l-b 3, n-b 2	7

(104.2 overs, 419 mins)   (9 wkts dec) 331   (85.3 overs, 337 mins)   (4 wkts) 397
Fall: 10 45 184 194 263 293 305 305 331   Fall: 133 185 212 292

B.M. Edmondson (did not bat).

Bowling: *First Innings*—Wright 29.2–9–61–4; Griffith 27–9–75–2; Geeves 24–4–86–3; Doherty 15–2–67–0; Marsh 6–0–24–0; Bevan 3–0–13–0. *Second Innings*—Wright 24.3–2–82–0; Griffith 11–1–65–1; Doherty 17–1–80–0; Geeves 15–0–88–1; Marsh 16–0–69–2; Bevan 2–0–8–0.

Umpires: S.D. Fry and D.L. Orchard.

At Melbourne Cricket Ground, Melbourne, February 24, 25, 26, 27, 2005. TASMANIA lost to VICTORIA by 114 runs.

TASMANIA v NEW SOUTH WALES

At Bellerive Oval, Hobart, March 3, 4, 5, 6, 2005. New South Wales won by 25 runs. *Toss*: New South Wales. New South Wales 6 pts, Tasmania by 2pts.

At 5 for 221 in quest of 259 to win and with plenty of time, it seemed to be the Pura Cup match Tasmania couldn't lose. But amazingly they did. As if mesmerised by the leg-spin of Stuart MacGill, they lost 5 for 12 and handed victory to NSW. MacGill admitted surprise at how tentative the batsmen were against him; Dan Marsh paid tribute to the batting of Jamie Cox, who had hit eight fours and three sixes, but added: "The rest of us have to take a good hard look at ourselves." The 35-year-old Cox had come back from a form slump and two severe hand injuries. When he was fifth out at 153, Sean

Clingeleffer and Michael Di Venuto looked set to take Tasmania over the line. Instead, they succumbed in the one over to young off-spinner Jason Krejza. On the first day Dominic Thornely had wrested the initiative from the Tasmanian bowlers, hitting 17 fours and two sixes in a fine unbeaten innings. Tasmania replied with an innings of total command, as Michael Bevan and Di Venuto added 277 in even time to enable Tasmania to cruise past NSW and take first-innings points. After rain delays on the third day, Marsh declared to give his bowlers a few overs at NSW before stumps. Far from intimidated, NSW batted with the urgency of a one-day match, starting briskly and accelerating until Krejza, Nathan Bracken and Matthew Nicholson hit 102 off 13 overs before Brad Haddin declared and tossed the ball to his leg-spinner.

Man of Match: S.C.G. MacGill. *Attendance:* 1,426.

Close of play: First day, New South Wales (1) 6-306 (Thornely 108, Nicholson 23); Second day, Tasmania (1) 2-252 (Bevan 104, Di Venuto 78); Third day, New South Wales (2) 0-14 (Mail 5, Jaques 9).

New South Wales

G.J. Mail c Clingeleffer b Wright	0	– lbw b Wright 40
P.A. Jaques c Di Venuto b Doherty	48	– c Bevan b Geeves 79
M.J. Phelps c Birt b Geeves	72	– (5) c Cox b Geeves 10
D.J. Thornely not out	135	– b Geeves 5
J.R. Packman c Clingeleffer b Griffith	1	– (6) c Bevan b Doherty 15
*†B.J. Haddin c Marsh b Geeves	30	– (3) lbw b Doherty 31
J.J. Krejza lbw b Wright	9	– not out 49
M.J. Nicholson c Doherty b Griffith	28	– (9) not out 21
N.W. Bracken c Di Venuto b Wright	22	– (8) c (sub) B.A. Lovell b Griffith .. 35
S.R. Clark not out	10	
L-b 3, n-b 9	12	L-b 3, n-b 4 7

(107 overs, 421 mins)   (8 wkts dec) 367
Fall: 0 85 155 183 238 255 312 353

(52 overs, 216 mins)   (7 wkts dec) 292
Fall: 92 139 153 155 179 190 253

S.C.G. MacGill (did not bat).

Bowling: *First Innings*—Wright 27–10–85–3; Griffith 26–4–101–2; Geeves 22–2–70–2; Doherty 31–6–104–1; Marsh 1–0–4–0. *Second Innings*—Wright 13–4–66–1; Griffith 13–1–73–1; Doherty 12–2–71–2; Geeves 13–0–70–3; Marsh 1–0–9–0.

Tasmania

J. Cox b Clark	19	– (2) b Bracken 84
T.R. Birt c Haddin b Clark	28	– (1) c Haddin b Nicholson 1
M.G. Bevan not out	170	– lbw b MacGill 26
M.J. Di Venuto not out	157	– (7) lbw b Krejza 35
*D.J. Marsh		– c Mail b MacGill 20
G.J. Bailey		– (4) c Haddin b MacGill 11
†S.G. Clingeleffer		– (6) c Nicholson b Krejza 39
D.G. Wright		– not out 8
X.J. Doherty		– c Clark b MacGill 4
A.R. Griffith		– c Krejza b MacGill 0
B. Geeves		– lbw b MacGill 0
B 9, l-b 6, w 6, n-b 6	27	B 2, l-b 3 5

(113 overs, 451 mins)   (2 wkts dec) 401
Fall: 40 124

(62 overs, 247 mins)   233
Fall: 8 63 89 135 153 221 222 233 233 233

Bowling: *First Innings*—Nicholson 20–5–84–0; Bracken 27–12–50–0; Clark 26–2–97–2; Krejza 14–2–47–0; MacGill 23–1–94–0; Mail 3–1–14–0. *Second Innings*—Nicholson 12–2–37–1; Bracken 9–1–38–1; Clark 10–2–33–0; MacGill 25–5–85–6; Krejza 6–0–35–2.

Umpires: S.J. Davis and B.N.J. Oxenford.

At Adelaide Oval, Adelaide, March 10, 11, 12, 13, 2005. TASMANIA lost to SOUTH AUSTRALIA by nine wickets.

TASMANIA DOMESTIC FIRST-CLASS RESULTS TABLE

	First Game	M	Won	Lost	Drawn	Tied
Western Australia ...	Oct 29, 1977	52	6	23	23	0
Victoria	Nov 18, 1977	51	10	16	25	0
South Australia	Feb 18, 1978	51	11	18	22	0
Queensland	Feb 25, 1978	52	8	20	24	0
New South Wales	Mar 4, 1978	52	12	20	20	0
Total		258	47	97	114	0

TASMANIA DOMESTIC FIRST-CLASS RECORDS

Highest score for:	265	D. F. Hills v South Australia at Hobart (Bellerive) ...	1997-98
Highest score against:	306*	D. W. Hookes (South Australia) at Adelaide	1986-97
Best bowling for:	8-95	P. M. Clough v Western Australia at Perth	1983-84
Best bowling against:	8-41	L. S. Pascoe (New South Wales) at Hobart (TCA) ...	1981-82
Highest total for:	592	v South Australia at Adelaide	1987-88
Highest total against:	673	by South Australia at Adelaide	1987-88
Lowest total for:	76	v New South Wales at Hobart (Bellerive)	1991-92
Lowest total against:	83	by Victoria at Melbourne	1981-82

MOST RUNS

	M	I	NO	R	HS	100s	50s	Avge
J. Cox	158	289	17	10,761	245	30	47	39.56
D. C. Boon	119	203	7	8,029	227	20	43	40.96
M. J. Di Venuto	111	196	8	7,532	189	12	54	40.06
D. F. Hills	100	187	8	6,887	265	18	36	38.47
S. Young	104	176	29	5,565	175*	10	35	37.86
R. T. Ponting	48	89	13	4,756	233	20	14	62.58
R. J. Tucker	90	153	24	4,611	165	7	24	35.74
D. J. Marsh	90	152	23	4,571	134	8	23	35.43
D. J. Buckingham	75	129	11	4,407	167	9	22	37.35
R. D. Woolley	68	114	13	4,120	144	7	25	40.79
B. F. Davison	41	75	7	3,062	173	5	13	45.03
M. N. Atkinson	84	124	43	2,350	76*	0	6	29.01
G. A. Hughes	35	62	3	2,244	147	2	16	38.03
M. G. Dighton	36	63	2	2,171	152	5	10	35.59
S. G. Clingeleffer	51	80	8	1,875	141*	2	9	26.04
S. R. Watson	26	46	4	1,802	157	5	10	42.90
S. L. Saunders	48	76	8	1,795	138*	4	10	26.40
D. G. Wright	57	90	16	1,722	111	1	8	23.27
M. Ray	38	67	2	1,682	94	0	8	25.88
D. M. Wellham	30	46	7	1,600	95	0	15	41.03

HIGHEST PARTNERSHIP FOR EACH WICKET

297	for 1st	D.F. Hills and J. Cox v Victoria at Hobart (Bellerive)	....	1997-98
294	for 2nd	J. Cox and M.J. Di Venuto v New South Wales at Hobart (Bellerive)	.....	1999-00
290	for 3rd	D.F. Hills and R.T. Ponting v South Australia at Adelaide	....	1993-94
258	for 4th	M.D. Taylor and D.J. Buckingham v South Australia at Adelaide	....	1987-88
319	for 5th	R.T. Ponting and R.J. Tucker v Western Australia at Hobart (Bellerive)	..	1994-95
213	for 6th	B.F. Davison and R.D. Woolley v South Australia at Adelaide	....	1980-81
215	for 7th	M.G. Bevan and D.G. Wright, v Victoria at Hobart (Bellerive)	....	2004-05
148	for 8th	B.F. Davison and P.I. Faulkner v South Australia at Adelaide	....	1983-84
119	for 9th	M.J. Di Venuto and X.J. Doherty, v South Australia at Hobart (Bellerive) .		2004-05
120	for 10th	S.L. Saunders and P.M. Clough v Western Australia at Perth	....	1981-82

MOST WICKETS

	M	Balls	Mdns	R	W	BB	5W/i	10W/m	Avge	Balls/W
C.R. Miller	54	13,846	556	6,657	210	7-49	8	2	31.70	65.93
S. Young	104	16,399	745	7,884	201	5-26	5	1	39.22	81.59
D.G. Wright	57	12,273	584	5,813	175	6-25	5	0	33.22	70.13
M.W. Ridgway	44	9,433	347	5,160	153	6-29	6	0	33.73	61.65
D.J. Marsh	90	10,970	421	5,521	125	7-57	1	0	44.17	87.76
C.D. Matthews	35	7,922	272	4,234	119	6-89	7	0	35.57	66.57
R.J. Tucker	90	9,139	316	4,561	112	4-56	0	0	40.72	81.60
D.R. Gilbert	36	7,345	247	3,513	110	7-127	5	0	31.94	66.67
P.M. Clough	28	6,142	226	2,913	102	8-95	5	0	28.56	60.22
A.G. Downton	31	5,830	228	3,338	94	6-56	3	0	35.51	62.02
P.T. McPhee	25	5,669	225	2,803	89	6-36	4	1	31.49	63.70
G.J. Denton	30	5,399	194	3,093	80	5-40	1	0	38.66	67.49
R.L. Brown	29	5,146	128	3,197	75	7-80	2	1	42.63	68.61
A.R. Griffith	20	4,316	163	2,461	74	7-54	5	1	33.26	58.32
G.D. Campbell	27	5,618	213	2,591	72	6-80	4	0	35.99	78.03
D.J. Saker	23	4,590	180	2,232	65	5-53	2	0	34.34	70.62
P.I. Faulkner	36	7,497	301	3,326	61	4-68	0	0	54.52	122.90
J.P. Marquet	21	4,159	132	2,446	59	5-94	1	0	41.46	70.49
S.L. Saunders	48	6,012	185	3,335	58	5-114	1	0	57.50	103.66
S.J. Jurgensen	17	3,441	155	1,551	54	6-65	4	2	28.72	63.72

MOST DISMISSALS

	M	Catches	Stumpings	Total
M.N. Atkinson	84	237	25	262
S.G. Clingeleffer	51	145	10	155
R.D. Woolley	43	97	13	110
R.E. Soule	51	103	4	107
J.M. Holyman	9	25	1	26

MOST CATCHES

M.J. Di Venuto	110 in 111 matches		S. Young	62 in 104 matches
D.J. Marsh	106 in 90 matches		R.J. Tucker	60 in 90 matches
D.C. Boon	93 in 119 matches		D.J. Buckingham	53 in 75 matches
J. Cox	77 in 158 matches		M. Ray	36 in 38 matches
D.F. Hills	67 in 100 matches		R.T. Ponting	32 in 48 matches

MOST APPEARANCES

158	J. Cox	1987-88 – 2004-05	90	R.J. Tucker	1988-89 – 1998-99
119	D.C. Boon	1978-79 – 1998-99	90	D.J. Marsh	1996-97 – 2004-05
111	M.J. Di Venuto	1991-92 – 2004-05	84	M.N. Atkinson	1991-92 – 1999-00
104	S. Young	1991-92 – 2001-02	75	D.J. Buckingham	1983-84 – 1993-94
100	D.F. Hills	1991-92 – 2001-02	68	R.D. Woolley	1977-78 – 1987-88

VICTORIA

One-year era comes to an end

by NABILA AHMED

Pura Cup: Fourth
ING Cup: Third
Captain: Cameron White
Coach: Greg Shipperd.

Cameron White

In the mad celebrations following Victoria's Pura Cup triumph in 2003-04, as captain Darren Berry announced his retirement and grandly foreshadowed a great era for the state's cricketers and long-suffering fans, it was easy to overlook Mathew Inness. But if you cared to look past the mayhem that followed the momentous win, the man Berry once described as the heart and soul of Victorian cricket was heartbroken. As players, wives and supporters converged on the MCG under sparkling sunshine, a tearful Inness stood clinging to his mother, who was sobbing openly. Inness was shattered to have been made 12th man for the final, and in the dressing-rooms as the party continued with beer and pizza, he was smiling but subdued. This was Victorian cricket's greatest moment in a long time, but looking at Inness while his team-mates celebrated with gusto, it was hard to fight off a sense of unease.

Something seemed not quite right again in Adelaide a few months later, when some Victorian players were observed out late drinking the night before their first match of 2004-05. The match was not due to not start until 11a.m., but you wondered whether the coach, Greg Shipperd, would not have preferred them asleep in bed. The players apparently promised themselves before that first match that they would do better than in the previous season, but they left Adelaide humiliated, having lost to the most inexperienced team in the country. That acting captain Jonathan Moss would not acknowledge properly the role in the match of South Australia's feisty young spinner Dan Cullen also struck an off note. Speaking the language of modern sportspeople, Moss blamed his team's inability to "execute our plans", while in the next dressing-room, a group of young South Australians sang their victory song off a whiteboard because most of them had not yet learnt the words.

Victoria won their next Pura Cup encounter in Hobart, but the performance was so unconvincing that the captain, Cameron White, fresh off the plane from India, wondered out loud about "cobwebs". They were slaughtered in their next match by New South Wales at St Kilda. In one match, White was seen to coax Ian Harvey to get up off the ground after a misfield. Another day, as another match slipped through the grasp of his team, White could do nothing but to call a mid-pitch meeting at 7.10 p.m. to try to work out what was going on and demand a better effort. After the impromptu chat, White had special words for Allan Wise, the towering left-armer who exploded onto the first-class arena the previous summer and whose last two overs of the day had just cost 22 runs, leaving his shoulders sagging and his arms hanging limply.

Matthew Elliott, who dazzled so brightly as the centrepiece of Victoria's win the previous summer, had clearly stopped enjoying the game – the quality he said sparked his record-breaking season. Once assessed by Steve Waugh as "up and down", Elliott, although vocal and leaderly in his criticism of past players who spoke ill of the team, was mostly down. Harvey interspersed moments of brilliance and determination with listlessness. Brad Hodge's results also suffered, although he rediscovered his best after Christmas. David Hussey never recovered the spectacular form of 2003-04 which had been such an important part of the team's success. Like Moss and Graeme Rummans, he contributed one impressive century but not much else.

Match after match, first-class and one-day alike, were continually filed under the "missed opportunity" category. And yet there were times when Victoria shone, if not always for an entire match. Their victory over Queensland at the Gabba was a good example. After a miserable first day-and-a-half, the entire team seemed to rally, enabling White to declare after following-on and let his pace quartet loose on the demoralised Queensland batting. It was an emphatic victory. It was followed by an innings defeat to Western Australia in Perth, and an innings victory over South Australia at the MCG which was led by Hodge's return to form with a double-century.

Peter Roach, who had been expected to make the most of his elevation to the role of leading wicket-keeper after so many often controversial years as Berry's deputy, lost form too, and yielded his position to Adam Crosthwaite. The pace bowling, which on paper seemed to offer an embarrassment of riches, never settled down to a fit and in-form combination. Only the stout-hearted Michael Lewis performed at his best. He bowled with pace and aggression in both competitions, and was the only Victorian player to emerge from the season with an enhanced reputation. The all-rounder Andrew McDonald, another key player of the 2003-04 success, lost form completely. Shane Warne's four first-class appearances did not make much difference to the side's fortunes.

Cameron White battled on determinedly, scoring useful runs and taking wickets in both competitions, but for a 21-year-old captain to handle the vicissitudes of Victoria's season and develop as a player was too much to expect. He could take some credit for Victoria's ING Cup campaign, which resulted in an even win-loss record and almost an appearance in the final. Going into the last match of the home-and-away series Victoria needed to win, but they were pummelled into the SCG by a NSW side at full strength. Hodge, Moss, Elliott and Hussey all batted consistently in the ING Cup, while in support of Lewis the young fast bowler Brad Knowles showed promise.

It was not an easy season, with the unsettling business of the committal hearing into David Hookes's violent death to contend with on top of the cricket. But with Elliott and Inness announcing moves interstate at the end of the season, Moss and Hodge considering going to NSW, and Harvey seeking new challenges in South Africa, Victoria seemed to be disintegrating. Berry questioned the modern player's love of his state, while calls for an all-Victorian Victoria could be heard once again. The brash talk of dynasty-building at the start of the season, which saw Shipperd's players scurrying to the library and into the sporting archives to learn about the likes of the Chicago Bulls, the Queensland Bulls and the AFL Kangaroos, seemed little more than a bad joke.

In the end, Hodge and Moss stayed on. Victoria, though, have a long way to go before they can even contemplate a return to the dizzy heights of 2003-04.

Matthew Elliott led the exodus of players from Victoria at the end of a troubled season.

VICTORIA RESULTS, 2004-05

All first-class matches – Played 10: Won 4, Lost 6.
Pura Cup matches – Played 10: Won 4, Lost 6.
ING Cup matches – Played 10: Won 5, Lost 5.

VICTORIA PURA CUP AVERAGES, 2004-05

BATTING

	M	I	NO	R	HS	100s	50s	Avge	Ct/St	S-R
B.J. Hodge	8	15	1	891	204*	3	4	63.64	5	67.14
J.L. Arnberger	6	11	0	639	152	3	4	58.09	2	56.40
N. Jewell	1	2	0	83	80	0	1	41.50	1	54.97
I.J. Harvey	9	15	3	434	90*	0	3	36.17	3	46.92
C.L. White	9	16	1	465	119	1	1	31.00	8	54.96
M.T.G. Elliott	10	19	0	585	120	1	5	30.79	5	49.41
G.C. Rummans	8	15	2	398	188	1	1	30.62	3	39.17
B.R. Joseland	1	2	0	53	51	0	1	26.50	0	36.05
J. Moss	9	17	1	401	114	1	2	25.06	5	56.72
D.J. Hussey	7	14	1	318	109*	1	2	24.46	3	63.98
S.K. Warne	4	5	0	113	75	0	1	22.60	6	68.48
B.A. Knowles	1	2	1	22	18	0	0	22.00	2	39.29
S.M. Harwood	5	5	1	64	35	0	0	16.00	1	45.39
A.J. Crosthwaite	3	4	0	60	24	0	0	15.00	10/2	55.05
A.B. McDonald	2	4	0	51	36	0	0	12.75	1	39.23
P.J. Roach	7	13	2	122	29	0	0	11.09	27/1	36.53
M.W.H. Inness	6	11	2	85	24	0	0	9.44	1	63.43
M.L. Lewis	8	13	2	72	21	0	0	6.55	2	34.43
A.B. Wise	6	11	7	25	8	0	0	6.25	0	34.20

* *Denotes not out.*

BOWLING

	O	Mdns	R	W	BB	5W/I	10W/M	Avge	Balls/W
M.L. Lewis	297.4	76	838	38	6-84	2	0	22.05	47.00
M.T.G. Elliott	17	1	68	3	3-68	0	0	22.67	34.00
I.J. Harvey	214.5	58	599	21	4-83	0	0	28.52	61.38
J. Moss	140.2	45	362	11	3-6	0	0	32.91	76.55
S.M. Harwood	144.2	37	442	13	3-47	0	0	34.00	66.62
A.B. Wise	162	41	513	15	4-63	0	0	34.20	64.80
S.K. Warne	155.3	30	403	11	3-50	0	0	36.64	84.82
B.J. Hodge	31	3	111	3	1-8	0	0	37.00	62.00
M.W.H. Inness	161.5	37	549	14	3-41	0	0	39.21	69.36
C.L. White	219.4	38	755	19	4-105	0	0	39.74	69.37
G.C. Rummans	22	2	106	2	1-1	0	0	53.00	66.00
B.A. Knowles	19	3	69	1	1-69	0	0	69.00	114.00
A.B. McDonald	44	12	129	1	1-48	0	0	129.00	264.00
J.L. Arnberger	3	0	12	0	–	0	0	–	–

At Adelaide Oval, Adelaide, October 16, 17, 18, 19, 2004. VICTORIA lost to SOUTH AUSTRALIA by 118 runs.

At Bellerive Oval, Hobart, November 8, 9, 10, 11, 2004. VICTORIA defeated TASMANIA by 127 runs.

VICTORIA v NEW SOUTH WALES

At Junction Oval, St Kilda, November 23, 24, 25, 2004. New South Wales won by an innings and 88 runs. *Toss:* Victoria. New South Wales 6 pts. *First-class debut:* B. A. Knowles.

It took just three matches for Victoria's Pura Cup triumph to fade into memory. By the time Victoria hosted their first match in Melbourne, Greg Shipperd's earnest post-final promise of building a cricketing dynasty appeared to have been little more than euphoric banter. It is easy to surmise that Victoria had no answers against Brad Haddin's furious onslaught and Simon Katich's measured calm, but the match was lost on the first day with the home team's poor batting performance. On a wicket that the Victorians had hoped would bring them at least 400, only a determined century by Jonathan Moss stood in the way of humiliation. He and Stuart MacGill had a great battle, which after some punishment the leg-spinner finally won. Good bowling by Allan Wise and Cameron White reduced New South Wales to 5 for 105, but when Haddin joined Katich NSW took over. Haddin, dropped early on by Matthew Elliott, pounded the Victorian attack around the Junction Oval for three and a half hours, hitting 22 fours and three sixes for his highest first-class score, putting on 131 for the seventh wicket with Jason Krejza in support. The confirmation of the Victorian decline in the eight months since Darren Berry raised the coveted trophy aloft came on the third day when they were skittled for just 91, the last nine wickets falling for 34 after lunch. Stuart Clark began with five maidens and appeared to mesmerise the Victorian middle order, while MacGill made merry at the other end. It was Victoria's greatest collapse in 78 years and their lowest total since the birth of the current captain.

Match reports by NABILA AHMED.

Man of Match: B. J. Haddin. *Attendance:* 1,764.

Close of play: First day, New South Wales (1) 2-42 (Katich 13, Bracken 1); Second day, New South Wales (1) 7-373 (Krejza 57, Nicholson 7).

Victoria

M. T. G. Elliott lbw b MacGill	58	– (2) b Krejza	12
G. C. Rummans c Haddin b Nicholson	0	– (1) c Clark b MacGill	22
B. J. Hodge c Haddin b Nicholson	17	– lbw b Clark	19
J. Moss c Phelps b MacGill	114	– b Clark	10
D. J. Hussey lbw b Bracken	8	– lbw b Clark	4
*C. L. White lbw b MacGill	0	– lbw b Clark	4
A. B. McDonald c Phelps b MacGill	4	– c Phelps b MacGill	0
†P. J. Roach c Mail b Nicholson	2	– c Phelps b MacGill	0
B. A. Knowles c Phelps b Krejza	18	– not out	4
M. W. H. Inness lbw b Krejza	0	– c (sub) A. W. O'Brien b MacGill	8
A. B. Wise not out	6	– b Clark	0
B 5, w 1, n-b 2	8	w 5, n-b 3	8

(79.3 overs, 323 mins)   235   (36.5 overs, 154 mins)   91
Fall: 1 33 125 145 146 161 164 213 213 235   Fall: 24 57 67 71 75 75 75 79 90 91

Bowling: *First Innings*—Bracken 17-7-38-1; Nicholson 17-5-47-3; MacGill 26.3-2-103-4; Clark 15-6-31-0; Krejza 4-1-11-2. *Second Innings*—Nicholson 5-1-12-0; Bracken 3-1-8-0; Krejza 4-1-20-1; Clark 13.5-8-10-5; MacGill 11-3-41-4.

New South Wales

G. J. Mail c Roach b Wise 6
P. A. Jaques lbw b Wise 22
*S. M. Katich lbw b Hodge 78
N. W. Bracken lbw b White 33
M. J. Phelps run out (McDonald/Knowles) 0
D. J. Thornely c and b White 4
†B. J. Haddin c Knowles b White 154
J. J. Krejza b Knowles 63

M. J. Nicholson run out
  (Knowles/Wise/Roach) 9
S. R. Clark not out 17
S. C. G. MacGill c Knowles b White . . 15
  B 5, l-b 3, n-b 5 13

(117.4 overs, 472 mins)   414
Fall: 8 36 98 99 105 209 340 379 383 414

Bowling: Inness 22–10–75–0; McDonald 17–5–40–0; Wise 19–4–66–2; Knowles 19–3–69–1; White 25.4–5–105–4; Moss 5–0–31–0; Hodge 9–2–20–1; Rummans 1–1–0–0.

Umpires: R. L. Parry and J. D. Ward.

VICTORIA v WESTERN AUSTRALIA

At Junction Oval, St Kilda, December 1, 2, 3, 4, 2004. Western Australia won by 46 runs. *Toss:* Western Australia. Western Australia 6 pts.

For the second time in a year, Victoria faced the greatest run-chase in their history. But the 455 for victory set by Western Australian captain Mike Hussey on the third day inspired rather than daunted the Victorians, whose successful pursuit of that exact number of runs against New South Wales the previous January had been the centrepiece of a brilliant season. Matthew Elliott set Victoria on the way to the target, and when he was out, the hero of that other chase, David Hussey, almost did it again with an unbeaten century. But with 87 runs needed from almost 20 overs, Victoria lost 6 for 40 and the only thing David Hussey had saved was his spot in the team, after entering the game with an average under 15. The difference between the two sides was Murray Goodwin's century in Western Australia's first innings. His masterly display of diligence was the only defiance of the pace bowling that dominated the first two days, when 20 wickets fell despite the loss of some play to rain. In Victoria's first innings Ben Edmondson claimed the wickets of Brad Hodge, Jonathan Moss and David Hussey in the space of four deliveries. On the third day Chris Rogers' commanding five-hour innings, against a Victorian attack lacking Shane Harwood, who had fractured a cheekbone, helped set up the final target.

Man of Match: M. W. Goodwin.   *Attendance:* 2,009.

Close of play: First day, Western Australia (1) 6-144 (Goodwin 64, Casson 7); Second day, Western Australia (2) 0-63 (Rogers 44, Hussey 19); Third day, Victoria (2) 1-89 (Elliott 52, Hodge 1).

Western Australia

*M. E. K. Hussey b Wise	24	– (2) c Roach b Harvey	36
C. J. L. Rogers c Hodge b Inness	0	– (1) b Harvey	153
M. W. Goodwin run out (Rummans/Roach)	130	– c (sub) J. L. Arnberger b White	14
M. J. North c Elliott b Inness	5	– b Moss	57
S. E. Marsh lbw b Harwood	34	– c Elliott b Harvey	7
†R. J. Campbell c Hussey b Harwood	0	– b Inness	31
K. M. Harvey c Roach b White	9	– not out	14
B. Casson c Roach b White	31		
B. R. Dorey c Roach b Inness	17	– (8) not out	6
S. J. Magoffin c Harvey b Harwood	16		
B. M. Edmondson not out	4		
L-b 6, n-b 1	7	B 7, l-b 4	11

(95.5 overs, 383 mins)   277   (93 overs, 350 mins)   (6 wkts dec) 329
Fall: 9 31 36 101 105 128 208 247 265 277   Fall: 113 144 253 267 273 319

Bowling: *First Innings*—Inness 21–6–68–3; Harwood 24.5–11–50–3; Wise 18–7–38–1; Harvey 11–5–25–0; White 14–1–56–2; Moss 3–1–11–0; Hodge 4–0–23–0. *Second Innings*—Inness 12–1–58–1; Wise 9–1–40–0; Harvey 17–3–53–3; White 20–4–71–1; Moss 23–7–58–1; Hodge 12–1–38–0.

Victoria

M. T. G. Elliott c Campbell b Casson	65	– (2) b Dorey	120
G. C. Rummans b Dorey	2	– (1) b Harvey	27
B. J. Hodge lbw b Edmondson	5	– lbw b Casson	55
J. Moss b Edmondson	0	– c Hussey b Edmondson	23
D. J. Hussey c Harvey b Edmondson	0	– not out	109
*C. L. White c Campbell b Dorey	39	– b Harvey	30
I. J. Harvey c Harvey b Dorey	2	– lbw b Harvey	8
†P. J. Roach not out	14	– lbw b Magoffin	1
S. M. Harwood retired hurt	15	– (10) b Magoffin	0
M. W. H. Inness lbw b Harvey	0	– (9) c Campbell b Magoffin	12
A. B. Wise lbw b Harvey	1	– lbw b Harvey	0
B 1, w 1, n-b 7	9	B 2, l-b 7, n-b 14	23

(57.2 overs, 241 mins)   (9 wkts dec) 152   (120 overs, 490 mins)   408
Fall: 13 23 23 23 113 117 122 149 152   Fall: 82 183 229 247 368 380 381
                                                              403 403 408

Bowling: *First Innings*—Magoffin 9–1–31–0; Dorey 15–5–26–3; Edmondson 13–2–42–3; Harvey 7.2–3–12–2; Casson 13–2–40–1. *Second Innings*—Magoffin 23–8–49–3; Dorey 25–7–79–1; Edmondson 20–4–82–1; Casson 26–5–84–1; Harvey 21–1–89–4; North 4–2–14–0; Hussey 1–0–2–0.

Umpires: R. L. Parry and P. R. Reiffel.

At Brisbane Cricket Ground, Brisbane, December 19, 20, 21, 22, 2004. VICTORIA defeated QUEENSLAND by 156 runs.

At WACA Ground, Perth, January 16, 17, 18, 2005. VICTORIA lost to WESTERN AUSTRALIA by an innings and 107 runs.

VICTORIA v SOUTH AUSTRALIA

At Melbourne Cricket Ground, Melbourne, January 28, 29, 30, 31, 2005. Victoria won by an innings and 57 runs. *Toss:* South Australia. Victoria 6 pts.

Two rain-interrupted, lacklustre days preceded a magnificent Brad Hodge double-century and a wicked spell of reverse swing bowling from Michael Lewis in a match where normality was restored for Victoria. Returning to the MCG for the first time since the 2003-04 Pura Cup final, they overcame their batting problems to post their highest first-innings total for the season as Hodge rediscovered his old, arrogant self. While the highlight of Hodge's eight-hour innings was a silky cut for four to reach three figures, what was most satisfying was his determination and concentration late on the second day, when he dropped anchor in treacherous, sultry conditions. Substantial innings from the mercurial Ian Harvey and Shane Warne in partnerships with Hodge also proved timely, as Victoria won their third match of the season and the inaugural David Hookes Trophy (which is determined by the results of the Pura Cup and ING Cup matches between the two sides each season). South Australian captain Graham Manou, whose team had conjured the upset of the season in the opening match against Victoria, feared for the psychological health of his battered young side after Lewis ripped through their batting on the last day, when South Australia lost their last nine wickets in two sessions. Victoria's victory gave them a chance of reaching the Pura Cup final to defend their title.

Man of Match: B.J. Hodge. *Attendance:* 2,561.

Close of play: First day, South Australia (1) 191; Second day, Victoria (1) 4-85 (Hodge 41, Harvey 4); Third day, South Australia (2) 1-41 (Williams 15, Blewett 6).

South Australia

L. Williams c White b Warne	37	– (2) c Warne b Lewis 15
T.C. Plant c White b Lewis	1	– (1) b Harvey 11
G.S. Blewett lbw b Lewis	1	– b Harwood 8
D.J. Harris st Roach b Warne	12	– c Roach b Harwood 12
C.J. Ferguson run out (Hodge/Roach)	33	– c Moss b Warne 24
N.T. Adcock c Arnberger b Moss	36	– lbw b Lewis 27
*†G.A. Manou c Hodge b Moss	43	– lbw b White 7
R.J. Harris lbw b Moss	6	– c Warne b Lewis 47
D.J. Cullen c and b Warne	5	– b Lewis 0
S.W. Tait not out	2	– b Lewis 13
P.C. Rofe c Lewis b Harwood	4	– not out 0
B 3, l-b 1, n-b 7	11	B 2, l-b 5, w 5, n-b 4 16

(86.4 overs, 327 mins)   191   (69.3 overs, 272 mins)   180
Fall: 1 11 48 57 102 163 173 178 186 191   Fall: 29 43 43 60 84 104 138 1
                                                 44 174 180

Bowling: *First Innings*—Lewis 17–8–35–2; Harwood 14.4–3–50–1; Harvey 11–6–23–0; Warne 30–9–50–3; White 7–1–19–0; Hodge 1–0–4–0; Moss 6–4–6–3. *Second Innings*—Lewis 19.3-3–46–5; Harwood 14–3–55–2; Warne 19–6–36–1; Harvey 7–2–17–1; White 8–3–19–1; Moss 2–2–0–0.

Victoria

G.C. Rummans c Manou b Rofe	6	†P.J. Roach lbw b Tait 8
J.L. Arnberger lbw b Rofe	8	S.K. Warne c Manou b R.J. Harris .. 75
B.J. Hodge not out	204	M.L. Lewis c Manou b Blewett 13
J. Moss c Blewett b Cullen	13	L-b 3, w 2, n-b 3 8
*C.L. White c Manou b Tait	12	
I.J. Harvey c Manou b Blewett	74	(128 overs, 515 mins) (9 wkts dec) 428
M.T.G. Elliott c R.J. Harris b Rofe	7	Fall: 12 15 41 71 217 236 257 407 428

S.M. Harwood (did not bat).

Bowling: Tait 27–5–69–2; Rofe 26–3–72–3; R.J. Harris 20–0–83–1; Cullen 41–10–137–1; Blewett 14–2–64–2.

Umpires: R.L. Parry and R.J. Tucker.

VICTORIA v TASMANIA

At Melbourne Cricket Ground, Melbourne, February 24, 25, 26, 27, 2005. Victoria won by 114 runs. *Toss:* Victoria. Victoria 6 pts. *First-class debut:* A.J. Crosthwaite, D.A. McNees.

If the Australian selectors were in any doubt as to how Brad Hodge felt to have been overlooked for Australia's one-day matches against New Zealand, they only had to watch him on the opening day. Hodge blasted a fiery century to set up another large first-innings total for Victoria. With Matthew Elliott and Jason Arnberger cementing their position as the state's best opening combination with another century stand, the struggling middle order was able to relax and construct a substantial contribution to a team effort. Adam Griffith maintained a threatening presence throughout, but lacked support. Tasmania responded at a rather measured gait, Michael Bevan taking seven and a quarter hours over his steadying innings, and David Dawson and Dan Marsh each batting an hour without reaching double figures. Arnberger and Hodge then scored quick runs from a lacklustre Tasmanian attack before Cameron White set a generous target of 313 from 88 overs. The Tasmanian batsmen signalled their intentions from the start when openers Travis Birt and Dawson took 14 overs to reach 20. Bevan nearly saved the match with another century, but Shane Warne and Jonathan Moss snared two wickets apiece to break budding partnerships, and Shane Harwood tore through the lower order as Tasmania lost their last six wickets for 52 runs and Victoria kept their slim finals chances simmering.

Man of Match: B.J. Hodge. *Attendance:* 3,096.

Close of play: First day, Victoria (1) 4-388 (Hodge 140, White 50); Second day, Tasmania (1) 3-158 (Bevan 51, Marsh 0); Third day, Victoria (2) 1-121 (Arnberger 67, Hodge 52).

Victoria

M. T. G. Elliott b Griffith	89	– (2) lbw b Wright	0
J. L. Arnberger lbw b Wright	60	– (1) c Marsh b Griffith	71
B. J. Hodge c Clingeleffer b Griffith	140	– c Bailey b McNees	88
G. C. Rummans c Clingeleffer b Wright	1	– not out	19
J. Moss c Marsh b Griffith	44	– not out	0
*C. L. White b Griffith	75		
I. J. Harvey not out	47		
†A. J. Crosthwaite lbw b Griffith	11		
S. K. Warne c Di Venuto b Griffith	0		
M. L. Lewis not out	4		
L-b 3, n-b 3	6	L-b 3	3

(126 overs, 482 mins)   (8 wkts dec) 477   (34 overs, 127 mins)   (3 wkts dec) 181
Fall: 148 160 169 261 391 426 440 445   Fall: 0 145 175

S. M. Harwood (did not bat).

Bowling: *First Innings*—Wright 36–15–100–2; Griffith 35–8–124–6; McNees 22–2–123–0; Doherty 26–4–97–0; Marsh 4–1–13–0; Bevan 3–0–17–0. *Second Innings*—Wright 11–2–57–1; Griffith 9–0–52–1; Doherty 6–0–41–0; McNees 6–1–19–1; Marsh 2–1–9–0.

Tasmania

D. G. Dawson lbw b Harvey	9	– (2) lbw b Moss	17
T. R. Birt c White b Moss	57	– (1) c Rummans b White	43
M. G. Bevan c Crosthwaite b Rummans	144	– c White b Warne	86
M. J. Di Venuto lbw b Moss	23	– lbw b Lewis	6
*D. J. Marsh b Lewis	7	– run out (Rummans)	7
G. J. Bailey c Crosthwaite b Lewis	8	– c White b Warne	6
†S. G. Clingeleffer c Harwood b Hodge	46	– lbw b Moss	8
D. G. Wright st Crosthwaite b Warne	24	– b Harwood	9
X. J. Doherty lbw b Warne	1	– c Crosthwaite b Harwood	8
D. A. McNees b Warne	0	– b Harwood	0
A. R. Griffith not out	4	– not out	1
B 1, l-b 6, w 3, n-b 13	23	B 1, l-b 3, w 2, n-b 1	7

(132.3 overs, 516 mins)	346	(65.5 overs, 262 mins)	198

Fall: 39 103 157 191 207 308 336 337 337 346

Fall: 62 62 81 112 146 161 185 193 197 198

Bowling: *First Innings*—Lewis 26–7–75–2; Harwood 20–7–42–0; Harvey 22–6–52–1; Warne 32.3–4–99–3; Moss 17–8–21–2; White 10–1–31–0; Hodge 4–0–18–1; Rummans 1–0–1–1. *Second Innings*—Lewis 12–2–35–1; Harwood 16.5–5–47–3; Harvey 9–3–23–0; White 9–1–25–1; Warne 11–1–37–2; Moss 8–2–27–2.

Umpires: D. L. Orchard and B. N. J. Oxenford.

VICTORIA v QUEENSLAND

At Melbourne Cricket Ground, Melbourne, March 3, 4, 5, 6, 2005. Queensland won by 78 runs. *Toss:* Queensland. Queensland 6 pts.

A fitting end to Victoria's season of missed opportunities, this match raised eyebrows across the Nullarbor, where Western Australian captain Justin Langer hinted at collusion. Victoria were pushed out of the match on the first day when Queensland, shaking off Victorian talk of a psychological edge, moved to a commanding position after choosing to bat on a lifeless pitch. They made unspectacular progress, the brightest contribution coming from Shane Watson, but perhaps most significant for Queensland was the return of Martin Love to some semblance of form. When they declared after lunch on the second day, the match appeared to be headed for a draw. After Jason Arnberger had made a century Victoria conceded first-innings points and waited for Queensland to set a total. Looking for action, Cameron White brought the very occasional bowlers Matthew Elliott and Graeme Rummans into the attack. The pair confounded expectations and reduced the Bulls to 4 for 55. Instead of going for the kill, as Victoria might have done under David Hookes, Victoria persisted with the pair in order to allow Queensland to set a target. They eventually did, and Victoria almost chased it down, thanks to sterling centuries from Jason Arnberger and Brad Hodge, who put on 266 in four hours. But Ashley Noffke took four wickets in four overs and Victoria lost their last nine wickets for 58. White was forced to admit he had "no idea" when it came to the batting performances of his team. Langer questioned the conduct of the match and the merits of the result. Both camps denied his allegations, White refusing even to comment.

Man of Match: J. L. Arnberger. *Attendance:* 2,050.

Close of play: First day, Queensland 3–270 (Watson 50, Philipson 4); Second day, Victoria (1) 2–167 (Arnberger 95, Rummans 26); Third day, Queensland (2) 4–129 (Philipson 27, Stevens 45).

Queensland

*J. P. Maher lbw b Harvey	79	–	(2) c Crosthwaite b Lewis	1
C. T. Perren c Warne b Lewis	68	–	(1) c Moss b Elliott	34
M. L. Love c Crosthwaite b Harwood	59	–	lbw b Rummans	13
S. R. Watson c Elliott b White	94	–	c Hodge b Elliott	7
C. A. Philipson c Rummans b Warne	27	–	not out	74
L. M. Stevens lbw b Lewis	37	–	c Crosthwaite b Elliott	67
†W. A. Seccombe not out	25	–	not out	2
B 6, l-b 12, n-b 9	27		L-b 2, n-b 1	3

(138.5 overs, 520 mins)	(6 wkts dec)	416
Fall: 116 173 263 318 343 416		

(45 overs, 129 mins)	(5 wkts dec)	201
Fall: 3 30 53 55 194		

A. J. Bichel, A. A. Noffke, M. G. Johnson, J. H. Dawes (did not bat).

Bowling: *First Innings*—Lewis 28.5–6–88–2; Harwood 21–3–79–1; Harvey 20–4–56–1; Warne 37–6–86–1; White 19–4–54–1; Moss 13–5–35–0. *Second Innings*—Lewis 3–0–8–1; Harwood 3–0–12–0; Elliott 17–1–68–3; Rummans 12–1–66–1; Arnberger 3–0–12–0; White 4–0–16–0; Warne 2–0–11–0; Moss 1–0–6–0.

Victoria

M. T. G. Elliott lbw b Johnson	35	–	(2) lbw b Bichel	0
J. L. Arnberger c Seccombe b Noffke	103	–	(1) c Philipson b Johnson	126
B. J. Hodge c Stevens b Dawes	5	–	c Philipson b Johnson	151
G. C. Rummans not out	43	–	c Seccombe b Noffke	0
J. Moss c Seccombe b Johnson	2	–	c Seccombe b Noffke	12
*C. L. White not out	6	–	b Noffke	1
I. J. Harvey		–	b Noffke	1
†A. J. Crosthwaite		–	c Noffke b Bichel	13
S. K. Warne		–	c Seccombe b Dawes	15
S. M. Harwood		–	c Seccombe b Dawes	4
M. L. Lewis		–	not out	0
B 2, l-b 2, n-b 6	10		L-b 8, n-b 4	12

(70 overs, 266 mins)	(4 wkts dec)	204
Fall: 69 85 182 194		

(78.5 overs, 330 mins)	335
Fall: 11 277 278 300 302 303 304	
327 331 335	

Bowling: *First Innings*—Bichel 12–0–51–0; Dawes 10–2–29–1; Johnson 13–3–45–2; Noffke 23–8–44–1; Stevens 12–3–31–0. *Second Innings*—Bichel 12.5–1–58–2; Dawes 16–1–48–2; Noffke 22–0–78–4; Johnson 21–4–105–2; Stevens 7–0–38–0.

Umpires: R. L. Parry and S. J. A. Taufel.

At Sydney Cricket Ground, Sydney, March 10, 11, 12, 13, 2005. VICTORIA lost to NEW SOUTH WALES by five wickets.

VICTORIA DOMESTIC FIRST-CLASS RESULTS TABLE

Opponent	First Game	M	Won	Lost	Drawn	Tied
New South Wales	Dec 24, 1892	207	65	75	66	1
South Australia	Dec 31, 1892	202	100	49	53	0
Queensland	Dec 17, 1926	145	52	43	50	0
Western Australia ...	Dec 5, 1947	107	33	31	43	0
Tasmania	Nov 18, 1977	51	16	10	25	0
Total		712	266	208	237	1

VICTORIA DOMESTIC FIRST-CLASS RECORDS

Highest score for:	437	W. H. Ponsford v Queensland at Melbourne	1927-28
Highest score against:	357	D. G. Bradman (South Australia) at Melbourne	1935-36
Best bowling for:	9-40	E. L. McCormick v South Australia at Adelaide	1936-37
Best bowling against:	10-44	I. J. Brayshaw (Western Australia) at Perth	1967-68
Highest total for:	1,107	v New South Wales at Melbourne	1926-27
Highest total against:	815	by New South Wales at Sydney	1908-09
Lowest total for:	31	v New South Wales at Melbourne	1906-07
Lowest total against:	49	by Queensland at Melbourne	1936-37

MOST RUNS

	M	I	NO	R	HS	100s	50s	Avge
D. M. Jones	110	194	16	9,622	324*	31	40	54.06
M. T. G. Elliott	103	197	16	9,470	203	32	43	52.32
B. J. Hodge	106	195	19	7,435	204*	21	33	42.24
W. M. Lawry	85	139	14	6,615	266	17	41	52.92
G. N. Yallop	76	137	9	5,881	246	18	31	46.67
A. L. Hassett	58	97	10	5,535	229	18	27	63.62
W. H. Ponsford	43	70	5	5,413	437	21	14	83.28
D. F. Whatmore	85	150	7	5,235	170	10	31	36.61
I. R. Redpath	76	132	11	5,222	261	11	28	43.16
W. W. Armstrong	59	106	7	4,997	250	17	17	50.47
J. L. Arnberger	66	125	10	4,783	214	11	26	41.59
J. D. Siddons	64	109	11	4,703	245	13	24	47.99
J. Ryder	60	104	12	4,613	295	12	22	50.14
J. Potter	73	120	14	4,608	221	12	24	43.47
P. A. Hibbert	71	121	9	4,321	163	8	23	38.58
R. N. Harvey	52	85	3	4,116	209	11	21	50.20
R. M. Cowper	56	85	13	4,040	195*	10	21	56.11
I. J. Harvey	78	133	14	4,065	136	4	29	34.16
K. E. Rigg	59	97	8	3,938	167*	11	20	44.25
D. S. Berry	129	198	29	3,816	166*	4	10	22.58

HIGHEST PARTNERSHIP FOR EACH WICKET

375	for 1st	W. M. Woodfull and W. H. Ponsford v New South Wales at Melbourne ...	1926-27
314	for 2nd	W. H. Ponsford and H. S. T. L. Hendry v Queensland at Melbourne	1927-28
390*	for 3rd	J. M. Wiener and J. K. Moss v Western Australia at St Kilda	1981-82
309*	for 4th	J. Moss and D. J. Hussey v Western Australia at Perth	2003-04
316*	for 5th	L. D. Harper and G. B. Gardener v South Australia at Carlton	1997-98
290	for 6th	M. T. G. Elliott and D. S. Berry v New South Wales at Sydney	1996-97
205	for 7th	C. L. White and I. J. Harvey v Queensland at Brisbane	2004-05
215	for 8th	R. L. Park and W. W. Armstrong v South Australia at Melbourne	1919-20
143	for 9th	G. R. Hazlitt and A. Kenny v South Australia at Melbourne	1910-11
211	for 10th	M. Ellis and T. J. Hastings v South Australia at Melbourne	1902-03

MOST WICKETS

	M	Balls	Mdns	R	W	BB	5W/i	10W/m	Avge	Balls/W
P. R. Reiffel	86	19,137	843	8,242	318	6-57	7	2	25.92	60.18
A. N. Connolly	71	17,973	365	7,745	297	9-67	12	4	26.08	60.52
A. I. C. Dodemaide ...	94	19,892	822	8,884	281	6-67	12	0	31.62	70.79
M. G. Hughes	76	16,762	582	8,169	267	7-81	10	2	30.60	62.78
R. J. Bright	101	22,899	1,013	8,821	252	6-61	10	0	35.00	90.87
L. O. Fleetwood-Smith	41	11,576	119	6,034	246	9-135	25	8	24.53	47.06
J. D. Higgs	75	14,961	376	7,202	240	8-66	12	2	30.01	62.34
D. W. Fleming	67	14,648	657	6,675	221	7-90	7	1	30.20	66.28
M. H. N. Walker	62	15,011	429	6,476	220	6-49	11	0	29.44	68.23
H. Ironmonger	44	14,594	432	5,290	215	7-13	16	4	24.60	67.87
M. W. H. Inness	59	11,027	522	5,099	199	7-19	5	2	25.62	55.41
J. V. Saunders	37	10,209	375	5,129	196	8-106	18	4	26.17	52.09
I. J. Harvey	78	12,262	521	5,973	182	7-44	3	0	32.82	67.37
I. W. Johnson	51	10,996	258	4,387	180	6-46	11	2	24.37	61.09
W. W. Armstrong	59	11,030	462	4,270	177	6-66	5	0	24.12	62.32
A. G. Hurst	44	9,717	159	4,687	177	8-84	6	1	26.48	54.90
D. T. Ring	50	11,614	190	5,277	172	6-41	4	1	30.69	67.52
D. J. Saker	45	10,551	482	4,888	166	7-32	2	1	29.45	63.56
H. Trumble	30	9,386	488	3,327	159	8-39	10	4	20.92	59.03
M. L. Lewis	45	8,584	320	4,518	158	6-59	6	0	28.59	54.33

MOST DISMISSALS

	M	Catches	Stumpings	Total
D. S. Berrry	129	468	44	512
R. D. Robinson	68	213	26	239
R. C. Jordan	70	199	31	230
M. G. D. Dimattina	60	149	19	168
J. L. Ellis	49	111	45	156

MOST CATCHES

M. T. G. Elliott	125 in 103 matches	G. N. Yallop	66 in 76 matches
D. F. Whatmore	110 in 85 matches	R. J. Bright	62 in 101 matches
D. M. Jones	96 in 110 matches	R. M. Cowper	61 in 56 matches
J. D. Siddons	76 in 64 matches	I. R. Redpath	61 in 76 matches
W. W. Armstrong	68 in 59 matches	J. Potter	60 in 73 matches

MOST APPEARANCES

129	D. S. Berry	1990-91 – 2003-04	94	A. I. C. Dodemaide	1983-84 – 1997-98
110	D. M. Jones	1981-82 – 1997-98	86	P. R. Reiffel	1987-88 – 2000-01
106	B. J. Hodge	1993-94 – 2004-05	85	W. M. Lawry	1955-56 – 1971-72
103	M. T. G. Elliott	1992-93 – 2004-05	85	D. F. Whatmore ...	1975-76 – 1988-89
101	R. J. Bright	1972-73 – 1987-88	78	I. J. Harvey	1993-94 – 2004-05

WESTERN AUSTRALIA

New broom, bit of stick

by KEN CASELLAS

Pura Cup: Third
ING Cup: Fourth
Captain: Justin Langer
Coach: Wayne Clark

Justin Langer

In the biggest revolution in the history of
Western Australian sport, former firebrand
fast bowler Dennis Lillee was swept into
power in spring 2004 as the supremo of the
state's cricket. Lillee, former Western
Australian Test players Graeme Wood and
Sam Gannon and lawyer David Williams were elected with an overwhelming majority. Lillee received about 90 per cent of the vote to
oust Brian Rakich from the presidency. Other notable casualties
in the most fiercely contested election in the WACA's 119-year
history included vice-presidents Bob Paulsen and Bill Bryant,
whose posts were filled by Wood and Gannon. Williams, a former
club cricketer and a hotel industry executive, took over from
Charles Fear as chairman.

Disgruntled members believed it was time for a change and they
quickly warmed to the Lillee team, who had expressed deep
concern over the WACA's direction and performance. Major areas
of concern included a poor relationship with the state government,
declining membership, the borrowing of $13 million to redevelop
the ground without the approval of members, and poor staff morale.

After the election, cost-cutting measures (after the WACA had
posted a $1.3 million loss in the 2003-04 financial year) were
immediately taken. The new board began to study the possibility of
creating a cricket centre of excellence, a gymnasium and crèche,
and even a golf driving range at the WACA and its surrounds.
The board was also considering a plan to sell other sections of the
WACA for residential apartments up to eight storeys high. The

profits (expected to be about $10 million) would not be used to retire the massive debt, but to pay for a new cricket administration centre and training facility elsewhere. The board was also considering playing international one-day cricket at football's Subiaco Oval where 40,000 could attend, compared with 25,000 at the WACA Ground. Also under consideration is the prospect of playing some Pura Cup fixtures in regional centres. On average only 300 members watch a day's play in Pura Cup matches in Perth.

While Lillee and his team were vowing to make the WACA a viable business, the side failed to qualify for the finals of the Pura Cup and ING Cup. It was the first time in nine seasons as a senior coach with WA and Yorkshire that a side under the control of Wayne Clark had failed to qualify for either a one-day or four-day final.

However, the side enjoyed a prosperous season, winning outright six of its ten Pura Cup matches and five of its ten ING Cup contests, finishing a close third in the four-day competition and fourth in the limited-overs series. It was the first time any state had gained six outright victories and had failed to qualify for the final.

There were many highlights during the season, including WA's outstanding effort in scoring 4 for 397 off 85.3 overs to beat Tasmania in a Pura Cup match at Bellerive Oval, deputy captain Mike Hussey's two double-centuries, Justin Langer's amazing assault on New South Wales leg-spinner Stuart MacGill in Perth, Adam Voges' record-breaking 62-ball ING Cup century at North Sydney Oval, and Kade Harvey's ING Cup hat-trick in Devonport.

Once again, even without international stars Adam Gilchrist and Damien Martyn for the entire season and Langer and Brad Hogg for much of it, WA's batting was of a generally high standard, with 12 Pura Cup centuries and 28 half-centuries, including eight from left-hander Marcus North. But the bowling told the same old story as in recent years: insufficient firepower, with only two five-wicket hauls in an innings throughout the season.

Not for the first time, injuries played havoc with the fast bowlers. Left-armer Michael Clark broke down again with back problems and appeared in only the opening Pura Cup match. He recovered to resume in grade cricket, but was not offered a contract for the 2005-06 season and sought to move interstate. A dislocated knee kept the side's main strike bowler Brad Williams on the sidelines for four successive

Pura Cup matches, while injuries also kept Ben Edmondson, Darren Wates and Brett Dorey out of action at various stages.

After WA failed to earn a point from their final two Pura Cup matches, Clark said that the inexperienced fast bowlers Steve Magoffin, Edmondson and Dorey were not sufficiently match-hardened. However, Magoffin, recruited from Queensland, and Dorey, plucked from club cricket, each enjoyed fine debut seasons in first-class ranks, Magoffin taking 32 wickets at 34.46 and Dorey 23 at 21.95. Neither can solve WA's problem of lacking a fiery speedster to assist Williams, as Magoffin and Dorey are essentially stout-hearted into-the-wind performers. Magoffin was exhausted towards the end of the season, yet he continued to bowl long spells for Melville in first-grade cricket. "We must learn to properly manage the bowlers," Clark said. "If they're fit, we encourage them to play in grade cricket. But in future, if a state bowler goes back to club cricket, he won't be bowling 25 overs in a day. By bowling ten to 15 overs they will keep fresher. We'll be looking for more control over that in future."

With the paucity of quality fast bowlers, it was no surprise that WA signed experienced Victorian new-ball bowler Mathew Inness for the coming season. After initial hesitation, Williams agreed to re-sign on a one-year contract. A close watch will be kept on emerging club fast bowlers, with Andrew James, Justin Coetzee, James Sprague and Chris Thompson among the youngsters with the potential to graduate to first-class ranks.

Former Zimbabwe Test all-rounder Sean Ervine took most of the summer to adjust to local conditions before revealing some of his class late in the season in club cricket. He will be one of the all-rounders anxious to press claims for Kade Harvey's spot in WA's limited-overs side. Harvey, a committed team man and the second most successful bowler in the history of the limited-overs competition, has retired.

Ryan Campbell had an excellent season in Pura Cup cricket that brought him 533 runs at 35.53 and 34 victims behind the stumps. The younger Luke Ronchi was preferred for ING Cup matches, but made only 140 runs (including a fine 75 in Adelaide) at 17.50. Ronchi, a highly competent wicket-keeper, is an explosive batsman who celebrated the first interstate Twenty20 match in Australia by blasting 67 off 24 deliveries against Victoria.

WA's immediate future appears rosy, even with limited appearances by Langer, Gilchrist and Martyn. A formidable list of batsmen includes Hussey, North, Murray Goodwin, Chris Rogers, the up-and-coming Shaun Marsh, Voges, Campbell, Hogg and Scott Meuleman. Much will depend on the fitness and form of the fast brigade.

WESTERN AUSTRALIA RESULTS, 2004-05

All first-class matches – Played 11: Won 7, Lost 2, Drawn 2.
Pura Cup matches – Played 10: Won 6, Lost 2, Drawn 2.
ING Cup matches – Played 10: Won 5, Lost 5.

WESTERN AUSTRALIA PURA CUP AVERAGES, 2004-05

BATTING

Batsman	M	I	NO	R	HS	100s	50s	Avge	Ct/St	S-R
P.C. Worthington	1	1	0	73	73	0	1	73.00	2	48.34
A.C. Voges	6	9	4	362	128	1	2	72.40	7	52.92
J.L. Langer	3	5	0	332	134	2	1	66.40	2	69.31
M.E.K. Hussey	8	15	2	721	223*	2	2	55.46	9	54.83
M.J. North	9	17	3	747	94*	0	8	53.36	4	51.70
M.W. Goodwin	10	19	2	840	138	2	5	49.41	3	55.05
C.J.L. Rogers	8	15	0	645	153	1	3	43.00	10	62.38
G.B. Hogg	4	6	0	243	109	1	1	40.50	1	83.51
R.J. Campbell	10	16	1	533	144	1	3	35.53	33/1	84.60
S.E. Marsh	10	17	2	530	103*	2	1	35.33	11	49.30
D.J. Wates	4	5	1	94	53	0	1	23.50	1	36.86
S.J. Magoffin	10	13	5	111	29*	0	0	13.88	4	42.53
B.R. Dorey	5	8	1	91	22	0	0	13.00	1	56.52
S.W. Meuleman	1	2	0	23	21	0	0	11.50	2	21.30
B. Casson	3	4	0	36	31	0	0	9.00	1	27.07
K.M. Harvey	4	7	1	47	14*	0	0	7.83	5	34.81
B.M. Edmondson	7	7	4	20	13	0	0	6.67	3	25.64
B.A. Williams	6	6	0	23	13	0	0	3.83	2	53.49
M.W. Clark	1	1	0	1	1	0	0	1.00	1	16.67

* Denotes not out.

BOWLING

Bowler	O	Mdns	R	W	BB	5W/I	10W/M	Avge	Balls/W
M.E.K. Hussey	49.2	5	137	7	3-34	0	0	19.57	42.29
G.B. Hogg	118.3	18	341	16	6-44	1	0	21.31	44.44
B.R. Dorey	146.5	38	426	15	4-53	0	0	28.40	58.73
D.J. Wates	106.5	21	384	13	3-59	0	0	29.54	49.31
K.M. Harvey	99.2	23	332	11	4-89	0	0	30.18	54.18
S.J. Magoffin	335.3	79	983	28	5-76	1	0	35.11	71.89
P.C. Worthington	26.2	3	107	3	2-37	0	0	35.67	52.67
B.M. Edmondson	241.5	45	1,056	29	3-42	0	0	36.41	50.03
A.C. Voges.........	69	18	223	6	2-16	0	0	37.17	69.00
B.A. Williams.......	223	53	678	18	4-53	0	0	37.67	74.33
B. Casson	102	16	363	9	3-88	0	0	40.33	68.00
M.J. North	86.1	15	300	6	3-93	0	0	50.00	86.17
M.W. Clark.........	36	10	94	1	1-50	0	0	94.00	216.00
S.E. Marsh	2	0	26	0	–	0	0	–	–
M.W. Goodwin......	1	0	2	0	–	0	0	–	–

WESTERN AUSTRALIA v TASMANIA

At WACA Ground, Perth, October 17, 18, 19, 20, 2004. Western Australia won by nine wickets. *Toss:* Tasmania. Western Australia 6 pts. *First-class debut:* T.R. Birt, D.G. Dawson, B. Geeves, S.J. Magoffin.

Records tumbled in a highly entertaining contest in which Western Australia flexed their muscles and showed they would be formidable opponents in the four-day competition. Five of the top six Tasmanian batsmen got a decent start, but not one was able to make a substantial score against a spirited attack in which debutant Steve Magoffin and Darren Wates (a late inclusion for the injured Ben Edmondson) stood out. In reply, Mike Hussey took full toll of the Tasmanian bowlers, who fell into the trap

Back row: Sam Howman, Peter Worthington, Aaron Heal, Chris Rogers, Darren Wates, Scott Meuleman, Kade Harvey, Mike Hussey, Marcus North, Brad Williams, Murray Goodwin, Ryan Campbell. *Middle row:* Shaun Marsh, Adam Voges, Steve Magoffin, Andrew James, Luke Ronchi, Justin Coetzee, Craig Simmons, Steve Jacques, Beau Casson, Michael Clark. *Front row:* Ben Edmondson, Liam Davis, Sean Ervine, Brad Hogg. *Absent:* Justin Langer, Alan Gabe, Ryan McLaren.

of pitching short far too often. Hussey and Shaun Marsh added 274 for the fourth wicket before Hussey miscued a pull at the hard-working Damien Wright and was caught at mid-wicket. After three triple-centuries for Northamptonshire, it was his first double-century for his state. The 21-year-old left-hander Marsh, revealing growing maturity, survived a torrid time from Brett Geeves and Wright before playing some delightful shots on both sides of the wicket. Tasmania folded up in their second innings and would have been humiliated had it not been for the determination and application of David Dawson, who became the first Australian in 146 years of first-class cricket to carry his bat as well as scoring a century on debut. His fellow debutant Geeves helped him to his century during their tenth-wicket stand of 59, the longest partnership of the innings. Brad Hogg was the wrecker, taking three wickets in one over and finishing with career-best figures and the best analysis by a WA wrist-spinner in an interstate match in Perth.

Match reports by KEN CASELLAS.

Man of Match: M. E. K. Hussey. *Attendance:* 2,223.

Close of play: First day, Western Australia (1) 0-2 (Hussey 1, Campbell 1); Second day, Western Australia (1) 3-365 (Hussey 195, Marsh 81); Third day, Tasmania (2) 8-159 (Dawson 81, Downton 6).

Tasmania

D. G. Dawson b Magoffin	40	–	(2) not out	123
J. Cox c Campbell b Williams	54	–	(1) c Campbell b Magoffin	12
M. J. Di Venuto c Hussey b Magoffin	36	–	c Campbell b Wates	12
M. G. Dighton lbw b Hogg	26	–	run out (Clark)	9
*D. J. Marsh lbw b Magoffin	0	–	c Goodwin b Hogg	20
T. R. Birt c Voges b Wates	52	–	lbw b Hogg	1
†S. G. Clingeleffer b Magoffin	24	–	st Campbell b Hogg	0
A. M. Blignaut c North b Wates	9	–	c Campbell b Hogg	0
D. G. Wright c Campbell b Wates	0	–	c Clark b Hogg	5
A. G. Downton c Hussey b Williams	6	–	lbw b Clark	14
B. Geeves not out	2	–	c Campbell b Hogg	28
L-b 3, w 2, n-b 4	9		B 9, l-b 5, w 1, n-b 5	20

(93 overs, 375 mins)	258	(90.1 overs, 356 mins)	244

Fall: 80 134 135 135 169 219 236 240 252 258

Fall: 33 68 80 122 132 132 132 145 185 244

Bowling: *First Innings*—Williams 20–7–48–2; Clark 18–5–44–0; Wates 20–3–59–3; Magoffin 23–4–70–4; Hogg 12–2–34–1. *Second Innings*—Williams 5–3–7–0; Wates 19–6–58–1; Clark 18–5–50–1; Magoffin 20–5–57–1; Hussey 3–0–9–0; Hogg 22.1–4–44–6; Voges 3–1–5–0.

Western Australia

*M. E. K. Hussey c Cox b Wright	210	– not out	7
†R. J. Campbell lbw b Geeves	25	– c Clingeleffer b Geeves	10
M. W. Goodwin c Dawson b Wright	34	– not out	4
M. J. North c and b Wright	8		
S. E. Marsh c Marsh b Wright	101		
A. C. Voges not out	52		
G. B. Hogg c Marsh b Wright	0		
D. J. Wates c Birt b Marsh	6		
M. W. Clark c Di Venuto b Downton	1		
B. A. Williams c Blignaut b Downton	0		
S. J. Magoffin not out	16		
L-b 7, w 2, n-b 16	25	L-b 1, n-b 6	7

(137.1 overs, 528 mins)   (9 wkts dec) 478   (6.4 overs, 27 mins)   (1 wkt) 28
Fall: 29 112 121 395 411 411 422 426 426   Fall: 20

Bowling: *First Innings*—Geeves 32–9–115–1; Wright 34.1–9–93–5; Downton 29–9–92–2; Blignaut 12–0–79–0; Marsh 25–7–58–1; Cox 2–0–20–0; Dighton 3–0–14–0. *Second Innings*—Wright 3.4–1–8–0; Geeves 3–0–19–1.

Umpires: J. K. Brookes and B. N. J. Oxenford.

At Sydney Cricket Ground, Sydney, November 2, 3, 4, 2004. WESTERN AUSTRALIA lost to NEW SOUTH WALES by an innings 134 runs.

WESTERN AUSTRALIA v QUEENSLAND

At WACA Ground, Perth, November 21, 22, 23, 24, 2004. Match drawn. *Toss:* Queensland. Queensland 2 pts. *First-class debut:* B. R. Dorey.

A memorable innings by Ryan Campbell was the highlight of a run glut in which only 24 wickets fell for 1,307 runs. On the final day, Mike Hussey's declaration enabled the umpires to call off the match 40 minutes early. Andrew Symonds later argued that matches should be ended much earlier when there was no possibility of a result. "Cricket needs to review why we are out there," he said. "As soon as the captains agree there is nothing to play for, they should call it off." A green pitch influenced Jimmy Maher to bowl first, but after early wickets Chris Rogers, having missed Western Australia's opening two Pura Cup matches while recovering from surgery, played a gritty innings of just under four hours. Marcus North gave solid support, and Brad Hogg hammered nine boundaries in 24 minutes. Campbell exploded into action on the second day when he blasted 112 runs in the pre-lunch session to equal the late Barry Shepherd's WA record of scoring a century in a session three times. Campbell, particularly severe on Shane Watson and Nathan Hauritz, faced only 143 deliveries and hit eight sixes and 11 fours. Facing the huge total, Queensland were undismayed, and after a brisk opening stand between Maher and Clinton Perren, Watson and Symonds punished the undermanned attack, adding 197 for the third wicket in 165 minutes. The pace slowed on the third afternoon as Ashley Noffke and Hauritz carefully added the runs that took Queensland to first-innings points. After early wickets on the fourth morning gave Queensland a faint hope of outright victory, North and Marsh held on comfortably and the match petered out.

Man of Match: R. J. Campbell. *Attendance:* 2,479.

Close of play: First day, Western Australia (1) 7-306 (Campbell 21, Wates 0); Second day, Queensland (1) 2-195 (Watson 33, Symonds 31); Third day, Queensland (1) 9-560 (Hauritz 44, Dawes 0).

Western Australia

*M. E. K. Hussey c Hartley b Dawes	16	– (2) c Noffke b Dawes	6
C. J. L. Rogers c Hauritz b Dawes	95	– (1) c Hartley b Dawes	0
M. W. Goodwin c Hartley b Watson	13	– b Bichel	21
M. J. North c Hartley b Bichel	70	– not out	78
S. E. Marsh c Hartley b Dawes	36	– c (sub) C. P. Simpson b Hopes	68
†R. J. Campbell c Perren b Symonds	144	– not out	53
K. M. Harvey c Hartley b Dawes	0		
G. B. Hogg c Nye b Watson	44		
D. J. Wates c Watson b Nye	53		
B. R. Dorey b Symonds	13		
S. J. Magoffin not out	10		
B 4, l-b 10, w 2, n-b 2	18	B 4, l-b 2, n-b 2	8

(143.2 overs, 553 mins)   512   (76.2 overs, 299 mins)   (4 wkts) 234
Fall: 43 86 160 230 250 252 303 487 493 512   Fall: 5 24 34 168

Bowling: First Innings—Bichel 25–1–109–1; Dawes 33–8–99–4; Watson 25–6–82–2; Noffke 19–4–69–0; Hauritz 13–1–53–0; Hopes 7–3–16–0; Symonds 11.2–2–31–2; Nye 10–0–39–1. *Second Innings*—Bichel 14–6–46–1; Dawes 14–9–19–2; Watson 8–5–16–0; Noffke 7–2–24–0; Symonds 17.2–3–76–0; Hopes 16–3–47–1.

Queensland

*J. P. Maher c Wates b Hogg	76	A. A. Noffke c Harvey b Hogg	53
C. T. Perren b Wates	41	N. M. Hauritz not out	45
S. R. Watson c and b Harvey	136	J. H. Dawes b Hogg	1
A. Symonds b Dorey	126		
A. J. Nye c Marsh b Wates	6	B 5, l-b 16, n-b 16	37
J. R. Hopes lbw b Hogg	33		
A. J. Bichel lbw b Hussey	1	(149.2 overs, 563 mins) 561
†C. D. Hartley c Campbell b Harvey	6	Fall: 112 151 348 391 425 426 446
		467 559 561

Bowling: Magoffin 8–1–35–0; Wates 26–3–107–2; Dorey 31–4–110–1; Harvey 28–5–104–2; Hogg 39.2–6–121–4; Marsh 1–0–13–0; North 11–1–33–0; Hussey 5–1–17–1.

Umpires: A. R. Craig and D. L. Orchard.

At Junction Oval, St Kilda, December 1, 2, 3, 4, 2004. WESTERN AUSTRALIA defeated VICTORIA by 46 runs.

At Adelaide Oval, Adelaide, December 19, 20, 21, 2004. WESTERN AUSTRALIA defeated SOUTH AUSTRALIA by 106 runs.

WESTERN AUSTRALIA v VICTORIA

At WACA Ground, Perth, January 16, 17, 18, 2005. Western Australia won by an innings and 107 runs. *Toss:* Victoria. Western Australia 6 pts.

Mike Hussey handed back the Western Australian captaincy to Justin Langer for the first time in the Pura Cup season, but he stole the limelight with another exceptional batting performance. The No. 7 strip was green and fast, but Cameron White decided to bat first against an attack led by Brad Williams, returning to action after a lengthy injury lay-off. The WA pace quartet exploited the conditions and the Victorians' faulty techniques, dismissing them by tea on the first day. Langer and Hussey calmly reached Victoria's total before the first wicket fell. Hussey, a model of concentration, stout defence and nimble footwork, and with a vast array of attacking shots, rarely looked bothered. He had a life on 131 when he edged a ball from Ian Harvey low and hard to first slip where Shane Warne failed to hold the catch. It was Hussey's eighth first-class double-century, taking ten hours and 407 balls, and the first time in the interstate competition a batsman had carried his bat while scoring a double-century. Victoria capitulated again to the speed of Williams and Ben Edmondson and the swing of Darren Wates, the lop-sided contest ending at 4.23 p.m. on the third day. The resounding victory took WA to the top of the competition table for the first time in six years.

Man of Match: M. E. K. Hussey. *Attendance:* 2,397.

Close of play: First day, Western Australia (1) 0-129 (Langer 59, Hussey 69); Second day, Western Australia (1) 6-414 (Hussey 202, Wates 7).

Victoria

M. T. G. Elliott lbw b Williams	4	– (2) b Edmondson	53
J. L. Arnberger c Voges b Edmondson	53	– (1) b Williams	6
B. J. Hodge c Campbell b Wates	37	– c Campbell b Williams	1
J. Moss lbw b Wates	0	– c Langer b Williams	55
D. J. Hussey b Magoffin	6	– lbw b Edmondson	12
*C. L. White c Campbell b Edmondson	17	– c Magoffin b Wates	35
I. J. Harvey c Rogers b Williams	9	– run out (Magoffin)	15
†P. J. Roach c Langer b Edmondson	0	– lbw b Wates	5
S. K. Warne c Rogers b Williams	8	– b Wates	15
M. L. Lewis c Hussey b Magoffin	9	– b Edmondson	0
A. B. Wise not out	4	– not out	0
B 4, l-b 4	8	B 4, l-b 1	5

(53.2 overs, 231 mins)   155
Fall: 18 66 66 75 111 134 134 136 147 155

(49.5 overs, 215 mins)   202
Fall: 12 16 104 122 135 156 161
189 198 202

Bowling: *First Innings*—Williams 14–2–41–3; Magoffin 13.2–5–26–2; Edmondson 14–2–61–3; Wates 11–4–19–2; Voges 1–1–0–0. *Second Innings*—Williams 14–1–45–3; Magoffin 13–4–22–0; Wates 14.5–2–70–3; Edmondson 7–1–52–3; Voges 1–0–8–0.

Western Australia

*J. L. Langer c Roach b Lewis	75	B. A. Williams b Harvey	13
M. E. K. Hussey not out	223	S. J. Magoffin c Hussey b Harvey	0
C. J. L. Rogers c Warne b Hodge	40	B. M. Edmondson b Harvey	0
M. W. Goodwin lbw b Warne	4		
S. E. Marsh c Roach b Lewis	13	L-b 9, n-b 4	13
A. C. Voges c Warne b Wise	16		
†R. J. Campbell c Hodge b White	46	(146 overs, 599 mins)	464
D. J. Wates lbw b Harvey	21	Fall: 155 219 224 259 308 396 434	
		464 464 464	

Bowling: Lewis 35–3–108–2; Wise 21–3–69–1; Harvey 31–8–83–4; Warne 24–4–84–1; Moss 15–6–36–0; White 19–0–67–1; Hodge 1–0–8–1.

Umpires: B. Bennett and A. R. Craig.

At Bellerive Oval, Hobart, January 28, 29, 30, 31, 2005. WESTERN AUSTRALIA defeated TASMANIA by six wickets. *Toss:* Western Australia. Western Australia 6 pts, Tasmania 2pts.

WESTERN AUSTRALIA v NEW SOUTH WALES

At WACA Ground, Perth, February 24, 25, 26, 27, 2005. Western Australia won by eight wickets. *Toss:* New South Wales. Western Australia 6 pts.

The highlight of a high-scoring match was Justin Langer's onslaught on leg-spinner Stuart MacGill in the pre-lunch session on the second day. MacGill, on his 34th birthday, was nonplussed as Langer launched into an amazing assault in which he plundered 60 runs from MacGill's first 22 deliveries – including six fours and five sixes. He hit three successive sixes in MacGill's fourth over to record his 68th first-class century. Langer went on to hit a hundred before he was dismissed for 134 off 114 deliveries just after lunch. It was a sensational innings that played a major role in the home side's easy victory. New South Wales had posted a competitive total, dominated by a sparkling century by Dominic Thornely, who faced only 142 balls. After Langer departed, a delightful maiden first-class century from Adam Voges and substantial contributions from Murray Goodwin, Ryan Campbell and Peter Worthington reduced the wearying NSW attack to mediocrity. Facing a deficit of 302, NSW batted with spirit. Phil Jaques and Greg Mail opened brightly, Mail defying a run of bad form to reach a century. James Packman, in only his second first-class appearance, brought up an impressive maiden century during a last-wicket stand of 49 in 22 minutes with Doug Bollinger, and batted just over two hours in all. But it was not quite enough, and WA had the last session in which to make 108 runs for victory.

Man of Match: J. L. Langer. *Attendance:* 3,755.

Close of play: First day, Western Australia (1) 0-38 (Langer 23, Rogers 13); Second day, Western Australia (1) 6-456 (Voges 74, Worthington 13); Third day, New South Wales (2) 4-184 (Mail 63, Haddin 18).

New South Wales

G. J. Mail c Campbell b Williams	8	– c North b Edmondson	101
P. A. Jaques c Voges b Edmondson	50	– c Magoffin b North	73
M. J. Phelps c Campbell b Worthington	40	– lbw b North	0
D. J. Thornely c Marsh b Williams	100	– lbw b Edmondson	5
E. J. M. Cowan run out (Worthington/Magoffin)	12	– lbw b North	16
*†B. J. Haddin run out (Worthington)	1	– c Marsh b Williams	52
J. R. Packman c Worthington b Voges	27	– c and b Worthington	107
N. W. Bracken c Rogers b Voges	16	– c Campbell b Worthington	4
S. R. Clark c Voges b Williams	14	– c Williams b Magoffin	13
S. C. G. MacGill c Rogers b Williams	11	– run out (Magoffin)	11
D. Bollinger not out	4	– not out	2
B 4, l-b 7, w 1, n-b 10	22	B 12, l-b 6, w 1, n-b 6	25

(84.3 overs, 344 mins) 305   (110.2 overs, 420 mins) 409
Fall: 16 97 103 146 154 222 259 289 290 305   Fall: 112 114 127 154 237 285 306 332 369 409

Bowling: *First Innings*—Williams 14.3–3–53–4; Magoffin 20–6–49–0; Edmondson 20–5–58–1; Worthington 18–2–70–1; Voges 9–1–43–2; North 3–0–21–0. *Second Innings*—Williams 29–7–93–1; Magoffin 18–3–53–1; Worthington 8.2–1–37–2; Edmondson 19–2–108–2; North 34–6–93–3; Voges 2–0–7–0.

Western Australia

*J. L. Langer lbw b Clark	134	– c Haddin b Clark	2
C. J. L. Rogers c Packman b Bracken	29	– c Haddin b Clark	7
M. W. Goodwin c Phelps b Clark	86	– not out	49
M. J. North b Bracken	1	– not out	44
S. E. Marsh c Haddin b Clark	26		
A. C. Voges c Mail b Clark	128		
†R. J. Campbell c MacGill b Bollinger	74		
P. C. Worthington c Haddin b Mail	73		
S. J. Magoffin not out	29		
B 7, l-b 11, n-b 9	27	L-b 2, n-b 4	6

(143.2 overs, 569 mins)	(8 wkts dec) 607	(28.5 overs, 122 mins) (2 wkts) 108
Fall: 98 194 207 280 289 414 550 607		Fall: 3 25

B. A. Williams, B. M. Edmondson (did not bat).

Bowling: *First Innings*—Bracken 34–10–89–2; Clark 38–5–167–4; Bollinger 23–6–97–1; MacGill 36–4–181–0; Thornely 7–2–23–0; Mail 5.2–0–32–1. *Second Innings*—Bollinger 10.5–0–39–0; Clark 8–2–35–2; Bracken 4–2–10–0; Mail 2–0–14–0; Thornely 4–0–8–0.

Umpires: S. J. Davis and P. D. Parker.

WESTERN AUSTRALIA v SOUTH AUSTRALIA

At WACA Ground, Perth, March 3, 4, 5, 6, 2005. South Australia won by 42 runs. *Toss:* Western Australia. South Australia 6 pts.

After five consecutive outright victories Western Australia faced the under-achieving South Australians in a match in which a victory would assure an appearance in the final. With four fast bowlers and no specialist spinner, Justin Langer decided to bowl first, but after three hours he had called on his seventh bowler. Shane Deitz and Daniel Harris got South Australia away to a splendid start, and Callum Ferguson played several superb cover drives as he held the middle and late order together, bringing up his century during an eighth-wicket stand of 102 in 26 overs with Dan Cullen. In reply, WA collapsed against the fiery pace of Shaun Tait. A fifth-wicket stand of 100 between Marcus North and Shaun Marsh provided the only bright spot of the innings before Cullen dealt with the tail. Darren Lehmann declined to enforce the follow-on, and after he blazed 47 off 36 balls he declared, leaving WA a target of 497 runs from a minimum of 126 overs. Langer had a life on 12 late on the third day, and the next morning Murray Goodwin was dropped on 15, and they made the most of their good fortune to put on 162 for the second wicket. Marsh and Adam Voges took the score to 4 for 309 at tea, leaving 188 runs to be scored off 46 overs in the final session. Rash shots and steady bowling ended WA's hopes of pulling off a remarkable victory with 14 overs still to be bowled. But Marsh scored a fine century, and WA made their highest-ever fourth-innings total and almost pulled off a remarkable win.

Man of Match: D. J. Cullen.   *Attendance*: 3,241.

Close of play: First day, South Australia (1) 6-295 (Ferguson 35, RJ Harris 8); Second day, Western Australia (1) 9-178 (Voges 15, Edmondson 13); Third day, Western Australia (2) 1-41 (Langer 22, Goodwin 0).

South Australia

D. J. Harris c Campbell b Edmondson	82	– (2) c Campbell b Dorey 32
S. A. Deitz c Campbell b Magoffin	90	– (1) c Campbell b Edmondson 29
G. S. Blewett c and b Voges	33	– c Magoffin b Edmondson 7
N. T. Adcock c Campbell b Edmondson	0	– c Campbell b Edmondson 12
C. J. Ferguson c Rogers b North	114	– c Campbell b Dorey 9
*D. S. Lehmann c Marsh b Dorey	5	– (7) b Dorey 47
†G. A. Manou c Dorey b Magoffin	23	– (6) c Campbell b Dorey 9
R. J. Harris c Campbell b Magoffin	37	– run out (Rogers) 7
D. J. Cullen run out (Magoffin)	34	– not out 13
S. W. Tait c Goodwin b North	4	– not out 23
P. C. Rofe not out	8	
B 18, l-b 6, w 1, n-b 2	27	B 17, l-b 9, w 1, n-b 2 29

(139.1 overs, 544 mins) 457 (60.2 overs, 261 mins) (8 wkts dec) 217
Fall: 165 214 216 228 234 277 338 442 447 457 Fall: 68 82 84 99 113 127 163 173

Bowling: First Innings—Williams 21–6–59–0; Magoffin 30–5–91–3; Dorey 28–8–79–1; Edmondson 25–8–85–2; North 13.1–3–53–2; Voges 20–6–51–1; Goodwin 1–0–2–0; Marsh 1–0–13–0. *Second Innings*—Williams 14.2–2–40–0; Magoffin 13–2–41–0; Edmondson 14–3–54–3; Dorey 16–3–53–4; Voges 3–2–3–0.

Western Australia

*J. L. Langer lbw b Tait	1	– c Deitz b Cullen 120
C. J. L. Rogers c D. J. Harris b Tait	25	– b Tait 16
M. W. Goodwin c R. J. Harris b Tait	3	– c Manou b R. J. Harris 95
M. J. North c Deitz b R. J. Harris	73	– c Manou b Rofe 30
S. E. Marsh b Blewett b Cullen	34	– not out 103
A. C. Voges not out	15	– c Manou b Rofe 30
†R. J. Campbell c Lehmann b Cullen	0	– c Adcock b Tait 9
B. R. Dorey c Manou b Cullen	4	– b R. J. Harris 15
S. J. Magoffin b Cullen	1	– c D. J. Harris b R. J. Harris 11
B. A. Williams b Tait	0	– c Ferguson b Cullen 10
B. M. Edmondson b Cullen	13	– b R. J. Harris 1
L-b 6, n-b 3	9	B 6, l-b 8 14

(50.5 overs, 212 mins) 178 (109 overs, 448 mins) 454
Fall: 6 12 43 143 147 147 155 161 162 178 Fall: 41 202 259 273 344 371 393
                                               421 434 454

Bowling: First Innings—Tait 13–0–50–4; Rofe 12–3–45–0; R. J. Harris 11–1–39–1; Cullen 14.5–3–38–5. *Second Innings*—Tait 23–4–109–2; Rofe 28–6–85–2; R. J. Harris 22–5–92–4; Cullen 26–2–107–2; Blewett 6–1–29–0; Lehmann 4–0–18–0.

Umpires: I. H. Lock and P. D. Parker.

At Brisbane Cricket Ground, Brisbane, March 10, 11, 12, 13, 2005. WESTERN AUSTRALIA drew with QUEENSLAND.

WESTERN AUSTRALIA DOMESTIC FIRST-CLASS RESULTS TABLE

Opponent	First Game	M	Won	Lost	Drawn	Tied
South Australia	Nov 14, 1947	110	47	30	33	0
Victoria	Dec 5, 1947	107	31	33	43	0
New South Wales	Jan 30, 1948	108	32	44	32	0
Queensland	Feb 6, 1948	110	36	26	48	0
Tasmania	Oct 29, 1977	52	23	6	23	0
Total		487	169	139	179	0

WESTERN AUSTRALIA DOMESTIC FIRST-CLASS RECORDS

Highest score for:	355*	G. R. Marsh v South Australia at Perth	1989-90
Highest score against:	356	B. A. Richards (South Australia) at Perth	1970-71
Best bowling for:	10-44	I. J. Brayshaw v Victoria at Perth	1967-68
Best bowling against:	8-66	J. D. Higgs (Victoria) at Melbourne	1974-75
Highest total for:	654	v Victoria at Perth	1986-87
Highest total against:	4-601 dec	by New South Wales at Perth	1990-91
Lowest total for:	41	v South Australia at Adelaide	1989-90
Lowest total against:	52	by Queensland at Perth	1982-83

MOST RUNS

	M	I	NO	R	HS	100s	50s	Avge
T. M. Moody	132	228	22	8,853	272	20	46	42.98
J. L. Langer	86	155	12	7,685	274*	24	27	53.74
M. R. J. Veletta	114	198	20	7,306	262	18	40	41.04
M. E. K. Hussey	99	181	10	7,192	223*	15	35	42.06
G. R. Marsh	100	175	12	7,009	355*	21	28	43.00
G. M. Wood	109	174	25	6,904	186*	20	32	46.34
R. J. Inverarity	108	188	18	6,888	187	20	29	40.52
D. R. Martyn	93	163	16	6,705	203*	20	33	45.61
R. J. Campbell	81	141	5	5,029	203	9	33	36.98
B. K. Shepherd	75	127	13	4,934	219	11	26	43.28
R. W. Marsh	86	139	9	4,412	168*	6	23	33.94
W. S. Andrews	82	126	12	4,292	139	5	29	37.65
T. J. Zoehrer	107	157	19	4,248	168	7	22	30.78
G. Shipperd	62	107	14	4,025	167*	9	21	43.28
M. W. Goodwin	56	103	8	4,013	201*	10	18	42.24
R. Edwards	64	110	14	3,939	158	10	19	41.03
K. J. Hughes	57	96	3	3,925	183	11	20	42.20
I. J. Brayshaw	91	145	20	3,771	104	1	24	30.17
D. Chadwick	59	106	8	3,651	137	9	13	37.26
M. T. Vernon	65	111	4	3,631	173	7	19	33.93

* Denotes not out.

HIGHEST PARTNERSHIP FOR EACH WICKET

431 for 1st M. R. J. Veletta and G. R. Marsh v South Australia at Perth 1989-90
254 for 2nd G. R. Marsh and M. R. J. Veletta v Queensland at Brisbane 1985-86
330 for 3rd G. M. Wood and G. R. Marsh v New South Wales at Sydney 1983-84
369 for 4th C. J. L. Rogers and M. J. North v New South Wales at Perth 2002-03
301* for 5th R. B. Simpson and K. D. Meuleman v New South Wales at Perth 1959-60
244 for 6th J. T. Irvine and R. Edwards v New South Wales at Sydney 1968-69
204 for 7th G. Shipperd and T. J. Zoehrer v New South Wales at Perth 1982-83
242* for 8th T. J. Zoehrer and K. H. MacLeay v New South Wales at Perth 1990-91
168* for 9th K. H. MacLeay and V. J. Marks v New South Wales at Perth 1986-87
91 for 10th I. J. Brayshaw and J. B. Gannon v Queensland at Brisbane 1969-70

MOST WICKETS

	M	Balls	Mdns	R	W	BB	5W/i	10W/m	Avge	Balls/W
J. Angel	105	22,351	1,033	10,418	419	6-35	13	0	24.86	53.34
T. M. Alderman	97	20,482	778	9,299	384	7-28	17	3	24.22	53.34
D. K. Lillee	70	16,617	439	7,544	323	7-36	18	4	23.36	51.45
G. A. R. Lock	66	20,107	544	7,210	302	7-53	16	2	23.87	66.58
B. P. Julian	87	16,143	612	8,573	292	7-39	15	2	29.36	55.28
G. D. McKenzie	73	16,566	287	7,322	232	6-100	7	0	31.56	71.40
K. H. MacLeay	90	17,761	836	7,033	229	6-93	5	0	30.71	77.56
T. M. Moody	132	14,431	673	6,297	220	7-38	5	1	28.62	65.60
C. D. Matthews	44	9,741	342	4,678	188	8-101	11	0	24.88	51.81
A. L. Mann	68	12,627	329	5,729	181	6-94	5	0	31.65	69.76
B. A. Reid	49	11,520	496	4,980	181	6-54	7	1	27.51	63.65
D. E. Hoare	49	9,834	182	4,637	176	8-98	9	1	26.35	55.88
I. J. Brayshaw	91	10,961	295	4,096	167	10-44	7	2	24.53	65.63
B. Yardley	52	9,698	387	4,131	159	7-44	11	2	25.98	60.99
M. F. Malone	37	8,283	288	3,422	139	6-33	7	0	24.62	59.59
T. G. Hogan	47	11,737	547	4,786	139	6-57	6	0	34.43	84.44
W. M. Clark	41	9,673	313	3,893	133	6-39	4	0	29.27	72.73
B. A. Williams	32	6,870	283	3,602	132	6-74	7	0	27.29	52.05
L. C. Mayne	29	7,206	103	3,672	118	7-75	5	0	31.12	61.07
P. A. Capes	37	7,527	273	3,670	115	5-69	3	1	31.91	65.45
M. J. Nicholson	35	7,138	259	3,651	115	5-49	2	0	31.75	62.07

MOST DISMISSALS

	M	Catches	Stumpings	Total
T. J. Zoehrer	107	331	28	359
R. W. Marsh	81	311	33	344
A. C. Gilchrist	51	250	8	258
R. J. Campbell	46	165	9	174
B. L. Buggins	57	131	18	149

MOST CATCHES

R. J. Inverarity	138 in 108 matches		M. E. K. Hussey	85 in 99 matches
M. R. J. Veletta	138 in 114 matches		G. A. R. Lock	80 in 66 matches
T. M. Moody	114 in 132 matches		T. M. Alderman	80 in 97 matches
I. J. Brayshaw	95 in 91 matches		G. M. Wood	80 in 66 matches
D. R. Martyn	89 in 93 matches		J. L. Langer	71 in 86 matches

MOST APPEARANCES

132	T. M. Moody	1985-86 – 2000-01	105	J. Angel	1991-92 – 2003-04
114	M. R. J. Veletta	1983-84 – 1994-95	100	G. R. Marsh	1977-78 – 1993-94
109	G. M. Wood	1977-78 – 1991-92	99	M. E. K. Hussey	1994-95 – 2004-05
108	R. J. Inverarity	1962-63 – 1978-79	97	T. M. Alderman	1974-75 – 1992-93
107	T. J. Zoehrer	1980-81 – 1993-94	93	D. R. Martyn	1990-91 – 2002-03

ING Cup, 2004-05

by PETER ENGLISH

Tasmania's ground-breaking ING Cup triumph wasn't quite an "I remember where I was" moment like Queensland's Sheffield Shield success in 1994-95. Whereas the Queenslanders almost drowned in XXXX-fuelled hysteria, the Tasmanians accepted cascades of applause as they lifted the Waterford crystal trophy in a ceremony almost as rare as their mascot. The seven-wicket victory at the Gabba was a romantic conclusion to a competition which is now anticipating the elbow of Twenty20, its fast-growing and unpredictable sibling.

It was the second time a trophy had crossed Bass Strait. However, the first prize, the Gillette Cup of 1978-79, came with a hefty discount of only one qualifying match before the final. Back then Tasmania were on half-rations in the Sheffield Shield and registered an 18-year-old David Boon alongside the two 37-year-old English professionals Jack Simmons and Jack Hampshire. A 47-run win over Western Australia made January 14, 1979, the state's proudest cricketing day, but it became more stark in its isolation over 26 succeeding years. The 2004-05 success, built around the prolific import Michael Bevan and a team of crunchy home-grown apples, was achieved more defiantly and deservedly with second place in the ten-match group phase, followed by a thorough demolition in the final of the competition leaders. February 20 was the new date for island cricket fans to be proud.

For Queensland it was a denouement of disappointment. A month later the defeat became the fourth bullet-point in a five-step sequence of finals losses. Consistent to the extreme, Queensland charged in the preliminary rounds before the barbs of the banderillas from their rivals and the national selectors set them up for collapse. Jimmy Maher's men raced to a nine-point lead in the home-and-away matches, including a whopping seven bonus points, before suffering a home-ground pounding. Maher did his best with an outstanding 104 in the decider, but the international absences of James Hopes and Andrew Symonds, and Shane Watson's side injury, meant too much blood had already flowed.

Led by Michael Dighton, Dan Marsh and Bevan, Tasmania easily mopped up the target of 247 with 17 balls to spare and began popping corks. "It's awesome," said Michael Di Venuto. "I've played for Tassie for a long time, been involved in three finals losses, so to come back with a trophy is just an unbelievable feeling." Marsh described it as relief combined with enjoyment. "We had our best game of the year in the final," he said. "You can't ask for much more than that."

However, spectators will soon request extra topping from a tournament that has held hands with the first-class competition since 1969-70 under different corporate names and formats. No tinkering has been as extreme as Twenty20, which the states will trial properly in January 2006 with a block of fixtures. The danger for the ING Cup, which has regular weekend television coverage, is of being knocked down by mothers, fathers, sons and daughters in their rush to imbibe the new craze.

Despite the approaching battle over public relevance, the Old Faithful showed its undisputed value as an assembly line producing players ready for internationals. Hopes, the Player of the Year, made his national debut on the tour of New Zealand and Mike Hussey quickly sealed a spot at his second opportunity, a place he held through the two one-day series in England. Brad Haddin was another important contributor as the on-call wicket-keeper who made sure Australia could spell Adam Gilchrist. No amount of biffing over 20 overs could replace such an important tool aimed towards global dominance. The upshot from 2004-05 was that the health of the competition remained high.

As in the Pura Cup, Bevan finished as the standout batsman, with 519 runs at 86.50, emphatically showing that his one-day powers had not evaporated with his Cricket Australia contract. Four not-outs re-confirmed his status as an innings closer and it was fitting that he was unbeaten as Marsh collected the trophy-winning single. Dighton and Travis Birt also made telling batting contributions as Marsh and Di Venuto struggled for consistency. An eye-catching display came from Brett Geeves, an incisive medium-fast seamer suited to the shorter game, who captured 20 wickets at 20, propelling him to second on the bowling list.

The season was an individual success for Queensland even if the group card trick wobbled near completion. During the pre-season Hopes, a golfing all-rounder tracked through the state and national under-age systems, was wondering how long he would last with the return home of Watson from Tasmania. The spur proved timely and earned Hopes a step up in class when he took the injured Watson's national place after collecting 293 runs at 32.55 and 11 wickets. In six matches Symonds belted runs at a strike-rate of 110, including a 31-ball half-century to share the Fastest Fifty award with Victoria's Shane Harwood and New South Wales's Phil Jaques. Maher was consistent at the top of the order and Andy Bichel returned regular wickets in his desperate grab at the fringe of the national team.

Another team celebrating player gongs without overall success was Western Australia. Finishing fourth, the Western Australians cheered Kade Harvey's 16 wickets, his hat-trick against Tasmania, and then his career as the all-rounder retired as the state's most successful limited-overs bowler. Adam Voges, 25, enjoyed a profitable summer as he broke the domestic record for the quickest century, taking seven deliveries off Stuart Law's 69-ball mark when he pounded 100 not out against NSW at North Sydney Oval. He also hit one of the sponsor's signs, improving his bank balance by $50,000, the only time a sign was struck throughout the season. For regular quality output Marcus North, one of four players to pass 400 runs for the summer, was WA's leading batsman, while Hussey's four half-centuries down the order justifiably impressed Trevor Hohns.

Victoria's campaign was halted on the final day of the regular season when they faced the state-scene irregulars Brett Lee and Glenn McGrath. The pair turned up to help the last-placed NSW and relegated their opponents to third for the second time in two seasons. The muscular batting of Brad Hodge, David Hussey, Matthew Elliott and Jonathan Moss launched most innings while the pace bowling was led by the improving Mick Lewis and the ageing Ian Harvey. Cameron White, the captain, made marks with leg-spin and lower-order batting, but the mystery is why his side was not tucked safely in the final before the Australian players returned.

In South Australia they again craved Darren Lehmann as the South Australians came fifth. In his two matches the captain showed how much his state relied on him, and it was left to Greg

Blewett to provide the glue as he hit two centuries and averaged one wicket in each of nine games. However, nothing the batsmen did could match the bowlers. Shaun Tait bustled through an impressive 21 victims at 19.90 to top the wicket list, Mark Cleary offered exceptional support and Dan Cullen scooped up a Cricket Australia contract to go alongside his Best New Talent award.

NSW's success in the four-day competition meant nothing in the limited-overs tournament and they propped up the field. Haddin collected an impressive highlights reel from his haul of 366 attractive runs and 12 dismissals, including four stumpings, and MacGill's rise ahead of Kade Harvey to the head of the domestic table with 109 wickets was another impressive milestone for the attacking legspinner. Shawn Bradstreet performed with his usual solidity with bat and ball, but the number of mediocre returns from the other players reflected the seven losses in ten games. Just as Tasmania feasted in one form and starved in the other, NSW balanced Pura Cup glory with the gloom of the one-day cellar.

2004-05 POINTS TABLE

	Played	Won	Lost	Abandoned	Bonus Points	Points	Net Run-Rate
Queensland	10	7	3	0	7	35	0.7280
Tasmania	9	5	4	1	2	24	−0.1851
Victoria	10	5	5	0	3	23	0.3040
Western Australia	10	5	5	0	1	21	−0.2192
South Australia	10	4	6	0	2	18	−0.3886
New South Wales	9	3	6	1	1	14.5	−0.2785

Net run-rate was calculated by subtracting runs conceded per over from runs scored per over.

ING CUP FINAL, 2004-05

QUEENSLAND v TASMANIA

At Brisbane Cricket Ground, Brisbane, February 20, 2005. Tasmania won by seven wickets. *Toss:* Queensland.

February 20, 2005, was the Tigers' perfect day. Tasmanian cricket usually measures success by individual achievements: David Boon's outstanding career or Ricky Ponting's elevation to the Australian captaincy. Before this season, the only token of team triumph in the trophy cabinet was the 1978-79 Gillette Cup, won at the old TCA ground when Boon was 18 and batting at No. 7.

To add to this solitary piece of silverware last season, the Tasmanians had to overcome many hoodoos and much bad form. After a blistering start to the year, in which they were undefeated after four games, their one-day form plummeted. They won only one of their last six matches, and another was washed out. In the final roster game, Tasmania knew that only victory over South Australia in Adelaide would guarantee them a place in the final against Queensland.

The build-up was hardly smooth. Captain Ricky Ponting chose to sit out the game, resting from a hectic international season, despite the fact that the Tasmanians were facing their most important one-day game in more than a decade. Ponting's decision to attend a Sting concert in Perth with Adam Gilchrist instead of playing for Tasmania attracted the ire of the Tasmanian cricketing public. They pointed out that the Tigers would need to have their best team available for the match, as the South Australian team was at full strength, with Darren Lehmann and Jason Gillespie.

Tasmania lost by a wide margin, but still progressed to the final after New South Wales, including Glenn McGrath, Simon Katich, Brett Lee and Michael Clarke, hammered Victoria in Sydney.

Match day saw the Tigers at the Gabba, where Tasmania had not won a domestic one-day game in 21 years. Their changing rooms were adorned with best wishes from Ponting, now in New Zealand with the Australian team, Boon, Tasmania's football coach Mathew Armstrong, Premier Paul Lennon, Victorian coach and former Tigers supremo Greg Shipperd and plenty from the Tasmanian public. On the whiteboard on the way from the rooms to the ground was written: "Trust your preparation", "Be yourself" and "Enjoy".

The travelling group included non-playing veteran Jamie Cox, who spent 17 seasons with the Tasmanians and was a member of three losing Pura Cup finals teams, and Scott Mason, the left-hand opener, who had been forced to take the season off with a heart complaint.

After building a game plan based on defending first-innings totals, Visiting captain Dan Marsh lost the toss, and Queensland chose to bat, forcing Tasmania to chase a target under finals pressure. The nerves were obvious early: straightforward fielding became fumbles and free runs. But the butterflies settled when Adam Griffith claimed the first two wickets, and the Queenslanders were restricted to a gettable 7 for 246. Captain Jimmy Maher made a century, but with inadequate support from the other batsmen it was somewhat wasted.

For the first time all season, the Tigers produced a clinical run-chase. They began brightly and always looked well on target, especially during the unbeaten 121-run fourth-wicket partnership between Marsh and the state's newest recruit, assistant coach and former one-day international star Michael Bevan.

The winning run, a push for a single by Marsh with 17 balls to spare, prompted jubilation from the players, coaching staff, TCA board members and the smattering of Taswegians in attendance. The celebrations included the mandatory beer spraying and arm-in-arm team-song shouting. The scenes put into perspective Tasmania's lack of success: for Bevan, this was his tenth domestic one-day final, and his sixth title.

The team's victory was front-page news in Tasmania's sole metropolitan and two regional newspapers and the Tigers were welcomed home with a state reception. The Tasmanian flag flew over the Gabba for a week as the happy result of a bet between Lennon and his Queensland counterpart, Peter Beattie.

But reality soon returned. The Tasmanians lost focus, losing their remaining three Pura Cup games outright and finishing last on the four-day table.

The season also had a tragic postscript. Mason endured more heart problems and operations before being given the all-clear. He was batting in the Bellerive nets in April when he felt dizzy and fainted. He was rushed to hospital but died on the operating table after a series of heart attacks, aged 28. Sombrely, players, coaches and friends recalled how much it had meant to Mason to have been at the Gabba on the Tigers' one perfect day.
– BRETT STUBBS.

Man of Match: J. P. Maher. *Man of the Series:* J. R. Hopes (Qld). *Attendance:* 12,357.

Queensland

*J. P. Maher b Wright	.............104 (122)	A. A. Noffke c and b Wright	...... 1 (3)
L. M. Stevens c Marsh b Griffith	..... 18 (30)	†W. A. Seccombe not out	.... 1 (2)
A. J. Bichel c Di Venuto b Griffith	... 1 (8)		
C. T. Perren c Bevan b Butterworth	... 22 (53)	B 2, l-b 3, w 5	 10
C. A. Philipson c Doherty b Geeves	.. 56 (51)		
A. J. Nye not out	.... 28 (22)	(50 overs, 209 mins) (7 wkts)	246
N. M. Hauritz c Doherty b Geeves	... 5 (9)	Fall: 46 50 98 207 209 239 243	

B. P. Nash, M. G. Johnson (did not bat).

Bowling: Griffith 10–1–37–2; Geeves 10–0–53–2; Wright 10–1–41–2; Butterworth 9–0–65–1; Doherty 10–0–41–0; Marsh 1–0–4–0.

Tasmania

T. R. Birt c Seccombe b Johnson	..... 36 (36)		
†M. G. Dighton run out			
(Noffke/Seccombe)	.... 57 (74)	L-b 2, w 6, n-b 4	 12
M. J. Di Venuto c Nye b Noffke	..... 28 (41)		
M. G. Bevan not out	.... 47 (52)	(47.1 overs, 196 mins) (3 wkts)	247
*D. J. Marsh not out	.... 67 (84)	Fall: 55 126 126	

G. J. Bailey, L. R. Butterworth, D. G. Wright, X. J. Doherty, B. Geeves, A. R. Griffith (did not bat).

Bowling: Johnson 10–0–57–1; Bichel 9–0–40–0; Nash 1–0–16–0; Noffke 9–1–47–1; Stevens 10–0–43–0; Hauritz 8.1–0–42–0.

Umpires: S. J. Davis and D. L. Orchard.
TV Umpire: P. D. Parker.

STATISTICS, 2004-05

	M	Batting			Bowling		
		Runs	Overs	Run-rate	Runs	Overs	Run-rate
Tasmania	10	2,318	467.3	4.95	2,303	469	4.91
Queensland	11	2,523	478	5.27	2,430	523.3	4.64
Victoria	10	2,149	433.5	4.95	2,114	450	4.69
Western Australia	10	2,171	453.2	4.78	2,228	450.2	4.94
South Australia	10	2,221	481.5	4.60	2,199	419.5	5.23
New South Wales	9	1,967	419	4.69	2,075	420.4	4.93

MOST RUNS, 2004-05

	M	I	NO	R	HS	100s	50s	Avge	S-R
M. G. Bevan (Tas)	10	10	4	519	118	1	2	86.50	76.78
J. P. Maher (Qld)	11	11	–	490	104	1	3	44.55	76.56
G. S. Blewett (S Aust)	9	9	1	472	125	2	1	59.00	75.52
M. J. North (W Aust)	10	10	1	412	134*	1	3	45.78	69.95
M. T. G. Elliott (Vic)	10	10	–	393	77	0	5	39.30	72.78
M. E. K. Hussey (W Aust)	10	10	–	383	79	0	4	38.30	69.89
B. J. Haddin (NSW)	7	7	1	366	120	1	2	61.00	100.00
B. J. Hodge (Vic)	9	9	1	344	108	1	3	43.00	88.21
M. G. Dighton (Tas)	10	10	–	343	72	0	3	34.30	77.78
A. Symonds (Qld)	6	6	2	339	77	0	4	84.75	110.42

* Denotes not out.

MOST WICKETS, 2004-05

Bowler	M	O	Mdns	R	W	BB	5W/i	Avge	RPO
S. W. Tait (S Aust)	10	87.1	1	418	21	4-29	0	19.90	4.80
B. Geeves (Tas)	9	78.2	4	400	20	5-45	1	20.00	5.11
M. L. Lewis (Vic)	10	82.3	6	321	18	3-30	0	17.83	3.89
S. C. G. MacGill (NSW) ..	8	70	1	381	16	4-37	0	23.81	5.44
K. M. Harvey (W Aust) ...	10	82	3	406	16	4-25	0	25.38	4.95
A. J. Bichel (Qld)	11	93	9	367	14	3-30	0	26.21	3.95
M. F. Cleary (S Aust)	7	63.4	3	324	14	3-33	0	23.14	5.09
C. L. White (Vic)	9	54.5	1	304	13	4-15	0	23.38	5.54
L. R. Butterworth (Tas) ...	9	75	5	382	12	3-38	0	31.83	5.09
D. J. Wates (W Aust)	7	68	6	301	11	3-32	0	27.36	4.43
D. G. Wright (Tas)	10	85.5	4	381	11	2-33	0	34.64	4.44
I. J. Harvey (Vic)	8	74	6	311	11	4-29	0	28.27	4.20
J. R. Hopes (Qld)	10	83.2	5	356	11	4-36	0	32.36	4.27

AUSTRALIAN DOMESTIC LIMITED-OVERS WINNERS

Australasian (V & G) Knock-Out Competition

Season	Winner	Runner-up	Season	Winner	Runner-up
1969-70	New Zealanders	Victoria	1970-71	Western Australia	Queensland

Australasian (Coca-Cola) Knock-Out Competition

1971-72	Victoria	South Australia	1972-73	New Zealanders	Queensland

Gillette Cup

1973-74	Western Australia	New Zealanders	1976-77	Western Australia	Victoria
1974-75	New Zealanders	Western Australia	1977-78	Western Australia	Tasmania
1975-76	Queensland	Western Australia	1978-79	Tasmania	Western Australia

McDonald's Cup

1979-80	Victoria	New South Wales	1984-85	New South Wales	South Australia
1980-81	Queensland	Western Australia	1985-86	Western Australia	Victoria
1981-82	Queensland	New South Wales	1986-87	South Australia	Tasmania
1982-83	Western Australia	New South Wales	1987-88	New South Wales	South Australia
1983-84	South Australia	Western Australia			

FAI Insurance Cup

1988-89	Queensland	Victoria	1990-91	Western Australia	New South Wales
1989-90	Western Australia	South Australia	1991-92	New South Wales	Western Australia

Mercantile Mutual Cup

1992-93	New South Wales	Victoria	1997-98	Queensland	New South Wales
1993-94	New South Wales	Western Australia	1998-99	Victoria	New South Wales
1994-95	Victoria	South Australia	1999-00	Western Australia	Queensland
1995-96	Queensland	Western Australia	2000-01	New South Wales	Western Australia
1996-97	Western Australia	Queensland			

ING Cup

2001-02	New South Wales	Queensland	2002-03	New South Wales	Western Australia
2003-04	Western Australia	Queensland	2004-05	Tasmania	Queensland

MATCH RESULTS, 1969-70 to 2004-05

	M	W	L	NR	T	Won Batting First	Won Batting Second
Australian Capital Territory . .	18	3	15	0	0	16.67%	16.67%
New South Wales	160	92	64	1	3	52.87%	66.67%
New Zealanders	10	7	3	0	0	60.00%	80.00%
Queensland	160	92	64	4	0	54.32%	64.00%
South Australia	153	60	91	0	1	42.67%	36.84%
Tasmania	140	41	95	3	1	30.16%	30.14%
Victoria	157	68	82	5	2	40.96%	50.75%
Western Australia	178	112	60	5	1	65.33%	64.95%
Total	488					48.00%	52.00%

RESULTS AT EACH VENUE

	First Game	M	NR	T	Won Batting First	Won Batting Second
Melbourne (MCG)	1969-70	61	1	1	42.37%	57.63%
Perth	1969-70	95	3	1	47.25%	52.75%
Sydney	1969-70	48	1	0	38.30%	61.70%
Adelaide (Adelaide Oval) . .	1970-71	79	0	1	47.44%	52.56%
Brisbane (Gabba)	1970-71	82	2	0	42.50%	58.23%
Launceston	1970-71	8	1	0	57.14%	42.86%
Hobart (TCA)	1973-74	12	0	0	66.67%	33.33%
Melbourne (Waverley)	1979-80	1	0	0	100.00%	–
Melbourne (St Kilda)	1981-82	4	0	0	50.00%	50.00%
Devonport	1984-85	7	0	1	50.00%	50.00%
Adelaide (Football Park) . . .	1986-87	2	0	0	50.00%	50.00%
Hobart (Bellerive)	1988-89	36	1	0	57.14%	42.86%
North Sydney	1989-90	18	0	0	66.67%	33.33%
Melbourne (Carlton)	1992-93	2	0	0	50.00%	50.00%
Canberra	1997-98	11	0	0	72.73%	27.27%
Bendigo	1997-98	1	0	0	100.00%	–
Melbourne (Richmond)	1999-00	5	0	0	20.00%	80.00%
Brisbane (Albion)	1999-00	2	0	0	50.00%	50.00%
Sydney (Bankstown)	2000-01	3	0	0	66.67%	33.33%
Coffs Harbour	2001-02	2	0	0	50.00%	50.00%
Ballarat	2002-03	2	0	0	50.00%	50.00%
Drummoyne	2002-03	2	0	0	100.00%	0.00%
Homebush	2002-03	3	0	0	66.67%	33.33%
Bowral	2003-04	1	0	0	0.00%	100.00%
Newcastle	2004-05	1	0	0	0.00%	100.00%

LAST TEN YEARS' PLACINGS

	95-96	96-97	97-98	98-99	99-00	00-01	01-02	02-03	03-04	04-05
Australian Capital Territory	–	–	6	6	6	–	–	–	–	–
New South Wales .	3	3	2	2	3	1	1	1	4	6
Queensland	1	2	1	3	2	4	2	3	2	2
South Australia . . .	4	6	4	4	4	3	3	6	5	5
Tasmania	5	5	5	7	6	5	6	4	6	1
Victoria	6	4	7	1	5	6	5	5	3	3
Western Australia .	2	1	3	5	1	2	4	2	1	4

HIGHEST INNINGS SCORES

187	J. P. Maher	Queensland v Western Australia at Brisbane	2003-04
167	M. W. Goodwin	Western Australia v New South Wales at Perth	2000-01
164	R. B. McCosker	New South Wales v South Australia at Sydney	1981-82
159	S. G. Law	Queensland v Tasmania at Brisbane	1993-94
152*	M. L. Hayden	Queensland v Victoria at Melbourne	1998-99
151	C. J. Richards	New South Wales v Western Australia at Perth	2001-02
146	J. L. Langer	Western Australia v South Australia at Perth	1999-00
145	T. R. Birt	Tasmania v South Australia at Hobart (Bellerive)	2004-05
142*	D. S. Lehmann	South Australia v Tasmania at Adelaide	1994-95
140*	P. C. Nobes	South Australia v Western Australia at Perth	1994-95
140	D. R. Martyn	Western Australia v Tasmania at Hobart (Bellerive)	1997-98

* Denotes not out.

FASTEST HALF-CENTURIES

21	D. W. Hookes	South Australia v Western Australia at Perth	1990-91
24	D. A. Nash	New South Wales v Western Australia at North Sydney	2000-01
26	S. G. Law	Queensland v Tasmania at Hobart (Bellerive)	2003-04
27	I. J. Harvey	Victoria v Tasmania at Hobart (Bellerive)	1998-99
28	D. S. Berry	Victoria v New South Wales at North Sydney	1997-98
29	G. A. Manou	South Australia v Tasmania at Adelaide	2002-03
30	M. G. Bevan	New South Wales v Victoria at Sydney	1992-93
31	R. W. Marsh	Western Australia v South Australia at Adelaide	1983-84
31	B. J. Hodge	Victoria v Tasmania at Hobart (Bellerive)	1998-99
31	M. A. Higgs	New South Wales v Queensland at Sydney	2001-02
31	P. A. Jaques	New South Wales v Tasmania at Sydney	2004-05
31	S. M. Harwood	Victoria v Tasmania at Hobart (Bellerive)	2004-05
31	A. Symonds	Queensland v Tasmania at Launceston	2004-05

FASTEST CENTURIES

62	A. C. Voges	Western Australia v New South Wales at North Sydney	2004-05
69	S. G. Law	Queensland v Tasmania at Hobart (Bellerive)	2003-04
74	S. G. Law	Queensland v Tasmania at Brisbane	1998-99
74	B. J. Haddin	New South Wales v Tasmania at Bankstown	2001-02
74	J. L. Langer	Western Australia v Queensland at Perth	2003-04
82	R. J. Campbell	Western Australia v Queensland at Perth	1999-00
83	D. S. Lehmann	South Australia v Victoria at Adelaide	2000-01
84	J. P. Maher	Queensland v Western Australia at Brisbane	2003-04
85	D. J. Marsh	Tasmania v Western Australia at Perth	2004-05
86	D. J. Marsh	Tasmania v New South Wales at Bankstown	2001-02
88	J. P. Maher	Queensland v Western Australia at Perth	1999-00
89	S. M. Katich	New South Wales v Tasmania at Hobart (Bellerive)	2003-04

MOST RUNS

	M	I	NO	R	HS	100s	50s	Avge	S-R
J. P. Maher (Qld)	84	84	9	3,627	187	8	20	48.36	77.57
D. S. Lehmann (S Aust/Vic)	77	76	10	3,240	142*	6	24	49.09	86.35
G. S. Blewett (S Aust)	88	86	8	3,212	125	5	18	41.18	67.94
M. G. Bevan (S Aust/NSW/Tas)	70	70	24	2,997	135*	2	24	65.15	73.67
B. J. Hodge (Vic)	84	82	9	2,987	118*	7	19	40.92	75.05
J. L. Langer (W Aust)	80	76	6	2,828	146	6	19	40.40	68.61

	M	I	NO	R	HS	100s	50s	Avge	S-R
M. T. G. Elliott (Vic)	78	76	6	2,640	118*	6	17	37.71	70.78
M. E. K. Hussey (W Aust)	75	71	10	2,603	106	3	21	42.67	75.01
S. G. Law (Qld)	85	78	7	2,534	159	6	10	35.69	93.06
M. L. Love (Qld)	82	79	11	2,412	127*	4	9	35.47	76.84
S. R. Waugh (NSW)	55	54	10	2,269	131	5	13	51.57	84.26
M. J. Di Venuto (Tas)	82	80	7	2,233	129*	3	10	30.59	78.05
M. L. Hayden (Qld)	51	51	9	2,231	152*	8	11	53.12	72.18
D. M. Jones (Vic)	55	52	10	2,122	139*	4	12	50.52	74.12
S. M. Katich (W Aust/NSW)	58	56	7	2,105	136*	4	13	42.96	75.21
T. M. Moody (W Aust)	75	71	12	2,004	102*	2	14	33.97	72.22
M. E. Waugh (NSW)	64	60	6	1,984	123	3	10	36.74	80.55
D. R. Martyn (W Aust)	53	50	7	1,880	140	3	13	43.72	74.07
J. Cox (Tas)	75	73	4	1,879	99	0	14	27.23	64.31
D. J. Marsh (S Aust/Tas)	82	75	16	1,831	106*	3	7	31.03	76.45

* Denotes not out.

HIGHEST PARTNERSHIP FOR EACH WICKET

253	for 1st	R. B. McCosker and J. Dyson, NSW v South Australia at Sydney	1981-82
260	for 2nd	M. L. Hayden and S. G. Law, Queensland v Tasmania at Brisbane	1993-94
257	for 3rd	M. W. Goodwin and M. E. K. Hussey, Western Australia v NSW at Perth	2000-01
180	for 4th	G. C. Rummans and S. Lee, NSW v Queensland at Brisbane	1999-00
180	for 5th	J. P. Maher and C. T. Perren, Queensland v South Australia at Brisbane	2003-04
173*	for 6th	M. E. K. Hussey and G. B. Hogg, Western Australia v Victoria at Melbourne	1999-00
124	for 7th	G. T. Cunningham and C. M. Smart, ACT v Victoria at Richmond	1999-00
106*	for 8th	A. C. Gilchrist and B. P. Julian, Western Australia v NSW at Sydney	1995-96
96*	for 9th	S. M. Thompson and S. D. Bradsteeet, NSW v Queensland at North Sydney	1998-99
54	for 10th	B. E. McNamara and G. R. Robertson, NSW v South Australia at Adelaide	1996-97

Denotes unbroken partnership.

HIGHEST INNINGS TOTALS

Batting First

4-405	Queensland defeated Western Australia at Brisbane	2003-04
4-397	New South Wales defeated Tasmania at Bankstown	2001-02
5-340	Tasmania defeated South Australia at Hobart (Bellerive)	2004-05
5-328	Western Australia defeated New South Wales at North Sydney	2004-05
6-325	South Australia defeated Tasmania at Hobart (TCA)	1986-87
5-325	Western Australia defeated New South Wales at Perth	2000-01
4-320	Queensland defeated Tasmania at Brisbane	1993-94
7-319	New South Wales defeated South Australia at North Sydney	1997-98
8-311	Tasmania defeated Victoria at Melbourne	2002-03
4-310	New South Wales defeated South Australia at Sydney	1981-82
5-310	New South Wales defeated Victoria at North Sydney	1991-92
6-310	Western Australia defeated Tasmania at Hobart (Bellerive)	1997-98

Batting Second

7-327	Tasmania lost to New South Wales at Bankstown	2001-02
6-325	New South Wales lost to Western Australia at North Sydney	2004-05
3-298	Western Australia defeated Queensland at Perth	2003-04
9-288	South Australia lost to New South Wales at Drummoyne	2003-04
8-287	South Australia lost to Victoria at Adelaide	2003-04
7-284	Western Australia defeated Victoria at Perth	1990-91
7-284	Queensland defeated Western Australia at Perth	1997-98
282	South Australia lost to New South Wales at North Sydney	1997-98
5-282	South Australia defeated Victoria at Adelaide	2000-01
6-281	South Australia defeated Western Australia at Perth	1994-95

LOWEST COMPLETED INNINGS TOTALS

Total	Overs		
51	(28)	South Australia v Tasmania at Hobart (Bellerive)	2002-03
59	(21.3)	Western Australia v Victoria at Melbourne	1969-70
62	(20.3)	Queensland v Western Australia at Perth	1976-77
65	(30.4)	Victoria v Queensland at Ballarat	2002-03
76	(26.1)	Western Australia v New Zealanders at Melbourne	1974-75
77	(22.5)	Western Australia v Queensland at Perth	1976-77
78	(42.1)	Victoria v Queensland at Brisbane	1989-90
79	(23.5)	Queensland v Western Australia at Melbourne	1970-71
80	(34.3)	Tasmania v New South Wales at Devonport	1984-85
83	(21)	South Australia v Queensland at Brisbane	2002-03

MOST WICKETS

	M	Overs	Mdns	R	W	BB	5Wfi	Avge	RPO
S. C. G. MacGill (NSW) ..	54	457.5	22	2,388	109	5-40	3	21.91	5.22
K. M. Harvey (W Aust) ...	80	581.2	33	2,794	103	4-8	0	27.13	4.81
J. Angel (W Aust)	74	614.2	52	2,525	94	5-16	2	26.86	4.11
M. S. Kasprowicz (Qld) ..	67	577.5	43	2,383	84	4-19	0	28.37	4.12
P. Wilson (S Aust/W Aust)	65	592.4	56	2,339	83	4-23	0	28.18	3.95
I. J. Harvey (Vic)	69	501.1	30	2,220	81	5-34	1	27.41	4.43
S. R. Clark (NSW)	60	533.3	42	2,143	72	4-24	0	29.76	4.02
T. M. Moody (W Aust) ...	75	534.1	41	2,131	70	4-30	0	30.44	3.99
S. A. Prestwidge (Qld) ...	45	364.5	18	1,755	67	5-59	1	26.19	4.81
J. R. Hopes (Qld)	47	388.5	29	1,705	66	5-29	1	25.83	4.38
M. L. Lewis (Vic)	47	377.3	35	1,663	64	4-41	0	25.98	4.41
D. G. Wright (Tas)	52	461.5	42	1,774	62	4-23	0	28.61	3.84
N. M. Hauritz (Qld)	42	325.4	4	1,467	61	4-39	0	24.05	4.50
A. J. Bichel (Qld)	57	486.4	36	2,077	61	4-45	0	34.05	4.27
G. S. Blewett (S Aust)	88	383	15	1,934	60	4-16	0	32.23	5.05
B. P. Julian (W Aust)	54	386.2	19	1,779	59	4-41	0	30.15	4.60
N. W. Bracken (NSW) ...	46	401.2	37	1,725	59	5-38	1	29.24	4.30
B. E. McNamara (NSW) ..	42	334.1	22	1,281	57	6-25	1	22.47	3.83
M. A. Harrity (S Aust) ...	40	338.2	26	1,551	57	5-42	1	27.21	4.58
S. Lee (NSW)	59	359.1	13	1,695	54	4-59	0	31.39	4.72

HAT-TRICKS

A. G. Hurst	Victoria v Western Australia at Perth	1978-79
R. M. Baker	Western Australia v Australian Capital Territory at Perth	1999-00
N. W. Bracken	New South Wales v Victoria at Melbourne	2001-02
D. Bollinger	New South Wales v South Australia at Canberra	2004-05
K. M. Harvey	Western Australia v Tasmania at Devonport	2004-05

BEST BOWLING FIGURES

8-43	S. W. Tait	South Australia v Tasmania at Adelaide	2003-04
7-34	C. G. Rackemann	Queensland v South Australia at Adelaide	1988-89
6-18	J. R. Thomson	Queensland v South Australia at Brisbane	1978-79
6-25	B. E. McNamara	New South Wales v Tasmania at Sydney	1996-97
5-15	D. L. Boyd	Western Australia v Victoria at Perth	1982-83
5-16	J. Angel	Western Australia v Victoria at Perth	2001-02
5-20	G. D. Watson	Victoria v Western Australia at Melbourne	1969-70
5-22	H. J. Howarth	New Zealanders v New South Wales at Sydney	1969-70
5-23	R. J. McCurdy	South Australia v Western Australia at Adelaide	1984-85
5-23	J. P. Marquet	Tasmania v Queensland at Hobart (Bellerive)	1995-96

MOST CATCHES IN A MATCH

5	B. E. Young	South Australia v Tasmania at Launceston	2001-02
4	J. W. Scholes	Victoria v New Zealanders at Melbourne	1971-72
4	I. M. Chappell	South Australia v New Zealanders at Adelaide	1972-73
4	M. A. Taylor	New South Wales v Queensland at Sydney	1998-99
4	J. D. Siddons	South Australia v ACT at Canberra	1999-00

MOST CATCHES

J. P. Maher (Qld)	43 in 84 matches	J. D. Siddons (Vic/S Aust) 31 in 62 matches
M. J. Di Venuto (Tas)	41 in 82 matches	S. Lee (NSW) 31 in 59 matches
J. L. Langer (W Aust)	35 in 80 matches	M. T. G. Elliott (Vic) 31 in 78 matches
B. J. Hodge (Vic)	34 in 85 matches	M. L. Love (Qld) 31 in 82 matches

MOST DISMISSALS IN A MATCH

6	(all ct)	K. J. Wadsworth	New Zealanders v NSW at Sydney	1969-70
6	(5ct, 1st)	B. J. Haddin	NSW v Western Australia at Perth	2001-02
6	(5ct, 1st)	R. J. Campbell	Western Australia v New South Wales at Perth	2000-01
6	(all ct)	R. J. Campbell	Western Australia v Tasmania at Perth	2000-01
5	(all ct)	R. Edwards	Western Australia v New Zealanders at Perth	1970-71
5	(all ct)	I. A. Healy	Queensland v Tasmania at Hobart (Bellerive)	1995-96
5	(all ct)	R. J. Campbell	Western Australia v NSW at Coffs Harbour	2002-03
5	(4ct, 1st)	S. G. Clingeleffer	Tasmania v Victoria at Hobart (Bellerive)	2002-03
5	(5ct)	N. S. Pilon	NSW v Victoria at Bowral	2003-04
5	(5ct)	A. C. Gilchrist	Western Australia v Victoria at Perth	2003-04
5	(5ct)	G. A. Manou	South Australia v Western Australia at Adelaide	2004-05

MOST DISMISSALS

	M	Catches	Stumpings	Total
D. S. Berry (S Aust/Vic)	87	105	29	134
W. A. Seccombe (Qld)	77	104	22	126
B. J. Haddin (ACT/NSW)	60	81	23	104
R. J. Campbell (W Aust)	47	82	6	88
P. A. Emery (NSW)	58	70	11	81
G. A. Manou (S Aust)	55	75	3	78
A. C. Gilchrist (NSW/W Aust)	38	64	6	70
T. J. Nielsen (S Aust)	45	54	3	57
I. A. Healy (Qld)	29	47	7	54
R. W. Marsh (W Aust)	33	50	1	51

MOST APPEARANCES

88	G. S. Blewett (S Aust)	1992-93 – 2004-05	82	M. J. Di Venuto (Tas) 1997-98 – 2004-05
87	D. S. Berry (S Aust/Vic)	1989-90 – 2003-04	80	J. L. Langer (W Aust) 1992-93 – 2004-05
85	S. G. Law (Qld)	1988-89 – 2003-04	80	K. M. Harvey (W Aust) 1994-95 – 2004-05
84	J. P. Maher (Qld)	1993-94 – 2004-05	75	T. M. Moody (W Aust) 1985-86 – 2000-01
84	B. J. Hodge (Vic)	1993-94 – 2004-05	75	J. Cox (Tas) 1988-89 – 2003-04
82	M. L. Love (Qld)	1993-94 – 2004-05	75	D. S. Lehmann (SA/Vic) 1988-89 – 2003-05
82	D. J. Marsh (S Aust/Tas)	1993-94 – 2004-05		

NEW SOUTH WALES ING CUP RESULTS, 2004-05

Played 9: Won 3, Lost 6, Abandoned 1. *Finished sixth.*

NEW SOUTH WALES RUN-SCORERS

Batsman	M	I	NO	R	HS	100s	50s	Avge	Ct/St	S-R
B. J. Haddin	7	7	1	366	120	1	2	61.00	8/4	100.00
S. M. Katich	3	3	0	254	92	0	3	84.67	2	75.15
P. A. Jaques	9	9	0	228	70	0	1	25.33	2	76.00
S. D. Bradstreet	8	8	3	206	53*	0	1	41.20	4	69.83
M. J. Phelps	9	9	0	195	66	0	2	21.67	4	87.05
D. J. Thornely	9	8	1	142	53*	0	1	20.29	3	65.44
G. J. Mail	4	4	0	86	58	0	1	21.50	2	55.84
E. J. M. Cowan	4	3	1	79	57	0	1	39.50	3	61.72
D. Smith	2	2	1	49	49*	0	0	49.00	0/1	80.33
A. W. O'Brien	4	4	0	43	22	0	0	10.75	0	52.44
J. R. Packman	2	2	0	35	33	0	0	17.50	1	58.33
M. J. Clarke	1	1	0	35	35	0	0	35.00	1	47.95
M. J. Nicholson	3	3	0	30	16	0	0	10.00	2	50.85
N. W. Bracken	8	6	2	27	15*	0	0	6.75	0	52.94
J. J. Krejza	4	3	1	26	19	0	0	13.00	0	68.42
B. Lee	3	3	2	18	9*	0	0	18.00	0	72.00
S. C. G. MacGill	8	5	2	16	8	0	0	5.33	2	69.57
S. R. Clark	7	3	0	12	7	0	0	4.00	3	63.16
D. Bollinger	3	2	1	1	1	0	0	1.00	2	20.00
G. D. McGrath	1	–	–	–	–	–	–	–	0	–

*Denotes not out.

NEW SOUTH WALES WICKET-TAKERS

Bowler	O	Mdns	R	W	BB	5W/i	Avge	RPO
S. C. G. MacGill	70	1	381	16	4-37	0	23.81	5.44
S. D. Bradstreet	50.5	2	297	9	3-43	0	33.00	5.84
S. R. Clark	66	5	269	7	4-24	0	38.43	4.08
N. W. Bracken	74	6	313	7	2-44	0	44.71	4.23
J. J. Krejza	28	0	173	5	3-45	0	34.60	6.18
D. Bollinger	28	5	112	4	4-24	0	28.00	4.00
G. D. McGrath	10	0	36	4	4-36	0	9.00	3.60
D. J. Thornely	31.4	1	157	4	1-7	0	39.25	4.96
B. Lee	26	1	114	2	1-24	0	57.00	4.38
M. J. Nicholson	24	0	119	1	1-52	0	119.00	4.96
A. W. O'Brien	12	0	67	1	1-38	0	67.00	5.58
G. J. Mail	0.1	0	4	0	–	0	–	24.00

At Brisbane Cricket Ground, Brisbane, October 10, 2004. NEW SOUTH WALES lost to QUEENSLAND by two wickets.

NEW SOUTH WALES v TASMANIA

At Newcastle Sports Ground, Newcastle, October 24, 2004. Tasmania won by three wickets. *Toss:* New South Wales. Tasmania 4 pts. *Competition debut:* J. J. Krejza.

New South Wales' batsmen failed to capitalise on sound starts, no player continuing on for a half-century whereas Tasmania refused to relinquish the stranglehold on a game initially applied by new-ball bowler Adam Griffith's three wickets. That the home side recovered from 6 for 111 to present Tasmania with a reasonably challenging target was due to wily allrounder Shawn Bradstreet, who scratched and scrambled 45 runs from

73 balls at No 7. Michael Dighton hammered two sixes and six fours in his 75-ball 58 in an opening stand of 77 with Michael Di Venuto and though New South Wales' bowlers exerted sufficient pressure to create twinges of panic in the Tasmanian camp at 6 for 160, George Bailey and Damien Wright added an invaluable 20 runs for the seventh wicket to put their side within sight of victory. Bailey coolly concluded the game for an unbeaten 30 from 48 balls to provide the win his bowlers deserved and set Tasmania securely on the path to a rare cup final victory.

Match reports by PHIL WILKINS.

Man of Match: A. R. Griffith.   *Attendance:* 3,816.

New South Wales

P. A. Jaques c Di Venuto b Griffith . . . 25 (28)	M. J. Nicholson c Dighton b Butterworth 4 (13)	
G. J. Mail c Marsh b Griffith 5 (14)	N. W. Bracken not out 15 (22)	
M. J. Phelps run out (Dighton) 25 (40)	S. C. G. MacGill not out 1 (1)	
*†B. J. Haddin c Dawson b Griffith . . 20 (28)		
D. J. Thornely c Dawson b Butterworth 14 (34)	L-b 5, w 6, n-b 1 12	
A. W. O'Brien run out (Bailey/Butterworth)8 (19)		
S. D. Bradstreet c Di Venuto b Geeves 45 (73)	(50 overs, 200 mins) (9 wkts) 193	
J. J. Krejza run out (Butterworth) 19 (29)	Fall: 27 40 66 97 107 111 145 160 190	

Bowling: Wright 7–1–36–0; Griffith 10–0–43–3; Geeves 10–2–33–1; Doherty 10–1–31–0; Butterworth 10–1–33–2; Marsh 3–0–12–0.

Tasmania

M. G. Dighton c Nicholson b MacGill 58 (75)	D. G. Wright b Krejza 10 (19)	
M. J. Di Venuto c Haddin b Thornely . 27 (35)	X. J. Doherty not out 4 (9)	
†D. G. Dawson c Mail b Bracken 20 (36)		
M. G. Bevan c Thornely b Krejza . . . 15 (34)	L-b 4, w 9 13	
*D. J. Marsh st Haddin b MacGill 12 (25)		
G. J. Bailey not out 30 (48)	(48.1 overs, 180 mins) (7 wkts) 197	
L. R. Butterworth c Phelps b Krejza . . 8 (8)	Fall: 77 97 118 130 149 160 180	

A. R. Griffith, B. Geeves (did not bat).

Bowling: Bracken 8–0–25–1; Nicholson 6–0–34–0; Thornely 10–0–32–1; O'Brien 4–0–29–0; MacGill 10–1–24–2; Krejza 10–0–45–3; Mail 0.1–0–4–0.

Umpires: N. S. D. Fowler and R. J. Tucker.
TV Umpire: S. A. Reed.

NEW SOUTH WALES v WESTERN AUSTRALIA

At North Sydney Oval, North Sydney, October 31, 2004. Western Australia won by three runs. *Toss:* New South Wales. Western Australia 4 pts.

A wonderful, last-ball game saw New South Wales lose their third successive ING Cup match. On a traditionally high-scoring ground, Western Australia's No. 3 Adam Voges became the fastest century scorer in interstate history, experiencing the exhilaration of a 62-ball hundred from the last delivery of the innings, and eclipsing Stuart Law's 69-ball Australian record by smashing seven sixes and six fours. Western Australia began with a brisk 151-run opening stand by Scott Meuleman and Marcus North in just under two hours and Voges increased the tempo, striking the sponsor's sign at mid-wicket for a $50,000 reward during a whirlwind performance which carried his side to its highest limited-over innings. With Brad Haddin thundering to his third limited-over century with seven sixes and nine fours in a 110-ball innings, New South Wales seemed in charge at 3 for 302 only for the previous season's final hero Kade Harvey to bowl the New South Wales captain and then run out Shawn Bradstreet. Dominic Thornely's unbeaten half-century was insufficient to gain his team a marvellous win.

Man of Match: A. C. Voges.   *Attendance:* 3,593.

Western Australia

S. W. Meuleman st Haddin b Krejza . .	59	(89)	
M. J. North c Haddin b Krejza	72	(95)	
A. C. Voges not out	100	(62)	
*M. E. K. Hussey c Haddin b Bradstreet	13	(18)	
M. W. Goodwin c Mail b MacGill	36	(23)	
K. M. Harvey st Haddin b MacGill . . .	17	(12)	

†L. Ronchi not out 1 (1)

B 1, l-b 8, w 21 30

(50 overs, 197 mins)   (5 wkts) 328

Fall: 151 170 219 287 326

G. B. Hogg, D. J. Wates, M. W. Clark, S. J. Magoffin (did not bat).

Bowling: Bracken 10–1–53–0; Clark 10–0–30–0; Thornely 4–0–39–0; Bradstreet 8–0–68–1; Krejza 9–0–63–2; MacGill 9–0–66–2.

New South Wales

P. A. Jaques c Meuleman b Wates	40	(43)	
G. J. Mail c Ronchi b Wates	23	(40)	
M. J. Phelps c Ronchi b Hogg	66	(58)	
*†B. J. Haddin b Harvey	120	(110)	
D. J. Thornely not out	53	(40)	
S. D. Bradstreet run out (Harvey)	0	(1)	

A. W. O'Brien lbw b Magoffin 9 (7)
J. J. Krejza not out 5 (2)

L-b 1, w 5, n-b 3 9

(50 overs, 194 mins)   (6 wkts) 325

Fall: 67 69 211 302 303 320

N. W. Bracken, S. R. Clark, S. C. G. MacGill (did not bat).

Bowling: Wates 10–0–56–2; Clark 5–1–27–0; Magoffin 10–2–62–1; Harvey 10–0–56–1; Voges 3–0–30–0; Hogg 7–0–59–1; North 10–0–34–0.

Umpires: G. T. D. Morrow and S. A. Reed.
TV Umpire: N. S. D. Fowler.

At Junction Oval, St Kilda, November 21, 2004. NEW SOUTH WALES defeated VICTORIA by five wickets.

NEW SOUTH WALES v SOUTH AUSTRALIA

At Manuka Oval, Canberra, December 11, 2004. South Australia won by 14 runs. *Toss:* New South Wales. South Australia 4 pts. *Competition debut:* D. J. Cullen.

In a game reduced to 40 overs a side due to the saturated outfield, South Australia won a low-scoring, fascinating game after being laid low at 4 for 20 by New South Wales' shaven-headed, left-arm new-ball bowler, Doug Bollinger. Bollinger claimed only the fourth hat-trick in the interstate competition, his predecessors being Alan Hurst (1978-79), Rob Baker (1999-00) and Nathan Bracken (2001-02). South Australia's No. 6 Nathan Adcock tenaciously overcame the aggressors in a two-hour defiance for an unbeaten 62, aided in the difficult conditions by opener Greg Blewett and skipper Graham Manou. With a comfortable win apparently assured, New South Wales' batsmen were unable to cope with the speed of Shaun Tait and off-spin subtleties of Daniel Cullen and it required all of Greg Mail's obstinacy and Shawn Bradstreet's predictably cussed batting to get within striking distance of the Redbacks.

Man of Match: N. T. Adcock. *Attendance:* 2,177.

South Australia

G. S. Blewett c Thornely b MacGill	..	18	(56)	R. J. Harris run out (O'Brien/Bracken)	2	(3)
M. J. Cosgrove b Bollinger	....	8	(20)	D. J. Cullen c and b Bradstreet	......	8	(6)
B. P. Cameron b Bollinger	....	0	(8)	S. W. Tait run out (Thornely)	......	1	(2)
J. K. Smith b Bollinger	....	0	(1)			
C. J. Ferguson lbw b Bollinger	......	0	(1)	L-b 2, w 9, n-b 3	....	14
N. T. Adcock not out	....	62	(84)			
*†G. A. Manou c Haddin b MacGill	..	39	(34)	(38 overs, 163 mins)		167
M. F. Cleary c Bollinger b Bradstreet	.	15	(15)	Fall: 14 17 20 20 64 127 152 156 165 167		

Bowling: Bracken 7–0–23–0; Bollinger 8–2–24–4; Nicholson 8–0–33–0; MacGill 8–0–42–2; Bradstreet 7–0–43–2.

New South Wales

P. A. Jaques c Cullen b Tait	....	15	(17)	N. W. Bracken c Manou b Tait	.....	3	(7)
G. J. Mail lbw b Cullen	....	58	(92)	S. C. G. MacGill b Tait	....	3	(7)
M. J. Phelps lbw b Tait	....	0	(2)	D. Bollinger not out	....	0	(2)
*†B. J. Haddin c Cosgrove b Harris	..	2	(7)			
D. J. Thornely run out (Smith/Manou)		17	(30)	B 1, l-b 3, w 6	....	10
S. D. Bradstreet b Blewett	....	31	(42)			
A. W. O'Brien c and b Cullen	....	4	(7)	(39.1 overs, 161 mins)		153
M. J. Nicholson b Cleary	....	10	(21)	Fall: 21 22 27 66 123 134 139 145 153 153		

Bowling: Tait 8–0–29–4; Harris 8–1–21–1; Blewett 8–0–29–1; Cleary 7.1–0–34–1; Cosgrove 1–0–9–0; Cullen 7–0–27–2.

Umpires: R. D. Goodger and P. D. Parker.
TV Umpire: S. A. Reed.

At WACA Ground, Perth, January 2, 2005. Day/night game. NEW SOUTH WALES defeated WESTERN AUSTRALIA by three wickets.

NEW SOUTH WALES v QUEENSLAND

At Telstra Stadium, Homebush, January 15, 2005. Day/night game. Queensland won by 121 runs. *Toss:* Queensland. Queensland 5 pts. *Competition debut:* J. R. Packman, D. Smith

Queensland never relinquished their grasp on this game from the time Jimmy Maher won the toss. The Bulls employed aggressive tactics by promoting allrounder James Hopes to opener and Andrew Bichel to No. 3, and the strategy worked. Hopes struck two sixes and two fours in a better than a run-a-minute 57-run opening stand with Maher, combining good fortune and daring strokeplay, after which Bichel savaged 62 from 67 balls for his highest limited-over score. Clinton Perren and Craig Philipson completed the domination of New South Wales' attack with a swift, unbeaten 94-run partnership in less than an hour only for the home side's batting to fail comprehensively in their pursuit. Bichel and Mitchell Johnson struck early and fast, leaving New South Wales stranded at 3 for 8 with only new recruits James Packman and Ed Cowan displaying fortitude in the face of adversity before their run outs, both falling victim to the hand of the nimble Brendan Nash. Conspicuously, it was New South Wales' lowest point of the ING Cup, their most inglorious performance of the season and fifth defeat in seven Cup games.

Man of Match: A. J. Bichel. *Attendance:* 13,751.

Queensland

J. R. Hopes b Thornely	32	(38)	C. A. Philipson not out	39	(42)	
*J. P. Maher b Bracken	26	(48)	L-b 2, w 7, n-b 1	10		
A. J. Bichel c Cowan b Clark	62	(67)				
M. L. Love c MacGill b Bradstreet	34	(41)	(50 overs, 196 mins) (4 wkts)	267		
C. T. Perren not out	64	(66)	Fall: 57 83 149 173			

B. P. Nash, †W. A. Seccombe, A. A. Noffke, N. M. Hauritz, M. G. Johnson (did not bat).

Bowling: Clark 10–0–53–1; Bracken 10–0–49–1; MacGill 10–0–66–0; Thornely 5–0–34–1; Krejza 5–0–32–0; Bradstreet 10–0–31–1.

New South Wales

M. J. Phelps lbw b Bichel	2	(10)	N. W. Bracken c Love b Nash	0	(2)	
†D. Smith lbw b Johnson	0	(1)	S. R. Clark c Bichel b Hauritz	7	(8)	
P. A. Jaques c Seccombe b Bichel	0	(8)	*S. C. G. MacGill c Seccombe b Hauritz	0	(2)	
D. J. Thornely c Seccombe b Noffke	27	(42)				
E. J. M. Cowan run out (Nash/Hauritz)	57	(88)	L-b 2, w 8	10		
J. R. Packman run out (Nash/Seccombe)	33	(47)				
S. D. Bradstreet not out	8	(18)	(38.5 overs, 159 mins)	146		
J. J. Krejza c Johnson b Nash	2	(7)	Fall: 0 3 8 72 128 129 138 138 145 146			

Bowling: Bichel 8–2–11–2; Johnson 7–1–26–1; Hopes 5–0–31–0; Noffke 7–0–27–1; Nash 7–0–31–2; Hauritz 4.5–0–18–2.

Umpires: B. N. J. Oxenford and S. A. Reed.

At Adelaide Oval, Adelaide, January 23, 2005. Day/night game. NEW SOUTH WALES lost to SOUTH AUSTRALIA by 87 runs.

At Bellerive Oval, Hobart, February 5, 2005. NEW SOUTH WALES and TASMANIA game abandoned due to rain.

NEW SOUTH WALES v VICTORIA

At Sydney Cricket Ground, Sydney, February 13, 2005. New South Wales won by 114 runs. *Toss:* New South Wales. New South Wales 5 pts.

The return of five internationals led to New South Wales depriving Victoria of an ING Cup final position while arriving too late to prevent acceptance of the competition wooden spoon. Simon Katich and Michael Clarke opened the game with a 106-run partnership from 25 overs, Clarke content to allow Katich to be the innings pacemaker with 78 from 100 balls after which Brad Haddin electrified the ground with an unbeaten 96 from 71 balls, striking three sixes and five fours with sublime power. Shane Warne's involvement made little difference despite his dismissal of Katich and the game was as good as finished when Glenn McGrath skimmed the cream of Victoria's batting with the first four wickets, reducing the visitors to 4 for 61 by the 16th over. Cameron White swung lustily for four sixes and two fours for 61 from 62 balls while players fell around him and the end came quickly in 36.4 overs.

Man of Match: B. J. Haddin. *Attendance:* 6,769.

New South Wales

M. J. Clarke st Crosthwaite b Moss ... 35 (73)
*S. M. Katich c Hodge b Warne 78 (100)
†B. J. Haddin not out 96 (71)
M. J. Phelps lbw b White 0 (2)
P. A. Jaques b Lewis 30 (47)

B. Lee not out 8 (8)
  B 2, l-b 4, w 12, n-b 1 19

(50 overs, 207 mins)   (4 wkts) 266
Fall: 106 146 147 234

D. J. Thornely, E. J. M. Cowan, S. R. Clark, G. D. McGrath, S. C. G. MacGill (did not bat).

Bowling: Lewis 10-0-48-1; Knowles 6-2-33-0; McDonald 6-1-30-0; Harvey 10-0-50-0; Moss 4-0-14-1; Warne 10-0-54-1; White 4-0-31-1.

Victoria

J. Moss lbw b McGrath 26 (39)
M. T. G. Elliott lbw b McGrath 6 (10)
B. J. Hodge c Phelps b McGrath 18 (29)
D. J. Hussey b McGrath 1 (8)
*C. L. White c Cowan b MacGill 61 (62)
A. B. McDonald lbw b MacGill 10 (18)
†A. J. Crosthwaite c MacGill b Lee .. 6 (17)
I. J. Harvey c Katich b MacGill 11 (22)

S. K. Warne c Clarke b MacGill 0 (2)
B. A. Knowles c Haddin b Thornely . 3 (10)
M. L. Lewis not out 2 (4)

  B 1, l-b 1, w 5, n-b 1 8

(36.4 overs, 156 mins)   152
Fall: 12 52 54 61 79 120 145 145 149 152

Bowling: Lee 6-0-24-1; McGrath 10-0-36-4; Clark 10-1-38-0; MacGill 8-0-45-4; Thornely 2.4-0-7-1.

Umpires: N. S. D. Fowler and S. A. Reed.
TV Umpire: R. D. Goodger.

NSW DOMESTIC LIMITED-OVERS RESULTS

Opponent	First Game	M	Won	Lost	No Result	Tied
v Queensland	Dec 6, 1969	35	19	16	0	0
v New Zealanders	Dec 30, 1969	1	0	1	0	0
v Western Australia	Nov 27, 1971	37	18	18	0	1
v Victoria	Dec 17, 1972	33	18	13	1	1
v Tasmania	Dec 17, 1973	26	21	4	0	1
v South Australia	Nov 23, 1975	25	13	12	0	0
v Australian Capital Territory	Dec 14, 1997	3	3	0	0	0
Total		160	92	64	1	3

NSW RECORDS

Highest score for:	164	R. B. McCosker v South Australia at Sydney	1981-82
Highest score against:	165	M. W. Goodwin (Western Australia) at Perth	2000-01
Best bowling for:	6-25	B. E. McNamara v Tasmania at Sydney	1996-97
Best bowling against:	5-22	H. J. Howarth (New Zealanders) at Sydney	1969-70
Highest total for:	4-397	v Tasmania at Bankstown	2001-02
Highest total against:	5-328	by Western Australia at North Sydney	2004-05
Lowest total for:	92	v Queensland at Brisbane	1972-73
Lowest total against:	80	by Tasmania at Devonport	1984-85

MOST RUNS

	M	I	NO	R	HS	100s	50s	Avge	S-R
M. G. Bevan	58	58	19	2,400	135*	1	21	61.54	73.24
S. R. Waugh	55	54	10	2,269	131	5	13	51.57	84.26
M. E. Waugh	64	60	6	1,984	123	3	10	36.74	80.55
S. Lee	59	53	6	1,412	115	2	7	30.04	87.11
B. J. Haddin	51	50	2	1,395	120	2	10	29.06	97.28

	M	I	NO	R	HS	100s	50s	Avge	S-R
M. A. Taylor	38	38	0	1,218	84	0	12	32.05	59.33
C. J. Richards	47	44	4	1,172	151	2	6	29.30	70.31
M. J. Slater	50	47	2	1,023	96	0	7	22.73	67.13
S. M. Katich	20	19	4	927	136*	2	5	61.80	80.82
R. Chee Quee	22	22	1	860	131	1	5	40.95	66.62

HIGHEST PARTNERSHIP FOR EACH WICKET

253	for 1st	R. B. McCosker and J. Dyson, v South Australia at Sydney	1981-82
199	for 2nd	R. Chee Quee and M. G. Bevan, v Western Australia at Sydney	1993-94
240	for 3rd	S. R. Waugh and M. E. Waugh, v Victoria at North Sydney	1991-92
180	for 4th	G. C. Rummans and S. Lee, v Queensland at Brisbane	1999-00
156	for 5th	K. J. Roberts and R. Chee Quee, v South Australia at Sydney	1995-96
105	for 6th	M. G. Bevan and G. R. J. Matthews, v Western Australia at Perth	1990-91
105*	for 6th	S. R. Waugh and M. A. Higgs, Queensland at Sydney	2001-02
116	for 7th	C. J. Richards and B. J. Haddin, v South Australia at North Sydney	2000-01
90	for 8th	B. E. McNamara and P. A. Emery, v Tasmania at Sydney	1992-93
96*	for 9th	S. M. Thompson and S. D. Bradstreet, v Victoria at North Sydney	1998-99
54	for 10th	B. E. McNamara and G. R. Robertson, v South Australia at Adelaide	1996-97

MOST WICKETS

	M	Balls	Mdns	R	W	BB	5W/i	Avge	RPO
S. C. G. MacGill	54	2,747	22	2,388	109	5-40	3	21.91	5.22
S. R. Clark	60	3,201	42	2,143	72	4-24	0	29.76	4.02
N. W. Bracken	46	2,408	37	1,725	59	5-38	1	29.24	4.30
B. E. McNamara	42	2,005	22	1,281	57	6-25	1	22.47	3.83
S. Lee	59	2,155	13	1,695	54	4-59	0	31.39	4.72
G. R. J. Matthews	50	2,302	25	1,500	49	3-29	0	30.61	3.91
S. D. Bradstreet	49	1,780	17	1,478	45	4-23	0	32.84	4.98
M. R. Whitney	36	1,926	36	1,188	41	4-30	0	28.98	3.70
G. F. Lawson	35	1,811	38	1,053	39	4-31	0	27.00	3.49
S. R. Waugh	55	1,104	18	853	34	4-32	0	25.09	4.64

MOST DISMISSALS

	M	Catches	Stumpings	Total
B. J. Haddin	51	72	23	95
P. A. Emery	58	70	11	81
S. J. Rixon	25	25	6	31
H. B. Taber	6	8	1	9
N. S. Pilon	4	6	3	9

MOST CATCHES

M. E. Waugh	37 in 64 matches	C. J. Richards	18 in 47 matches
S. Lee	31 in 59 matches	S. D. Bradstreet	17 in 49 matches
M. A. Taylor	24 in 38 matches	G. R. J. Matthews	15 in 50 matches
S. R. Waugh	19 in 55 matches	D. J. Thornely	15 in 33 matches

MOST APPEARANCES

64	M. E. Waugh	1985-86 – 2002-03	55	S. R. Waugh	1984-85 – 2002-03
60	S. R. Clark	1997-98 – 2004-05	54	S. C. G. MacGill	1997-98 – 2004-05
59	S. Lee	1992-93 – 2002-03	51	B. J. Haddin	1999-00 – 2004-05
58	P. A. Emery	1987-88 – 1998-99	50	G. R. J. Matthews	1982-83 – 1997-98
58	M. G. Bevan	1990-91 – 2002-03	50	M. J. Slater	1992-93 – 2002-03

QUEENSLAND ING CUP RESULTS, 2004-05

Played 11: Won 7, Lost 4. *Finished second.*

QUEENSLAND RUN-SCORERS

	M	I	NO	R	HS	100s	50s	Avge	Ct/St	S-R
J. P. Maher	11	11	0	490	104	1	3	44.55	7	76.56
A. Symonds	6	6	2	339	77	0	4	84.75	1	110.42
J. R. Hopes	10	10	1	293	73	0	2	32.56	3	95.44
C. T. Perren	11	10	1	268	117	1	1	29.78	1	74.86
C. A. Philipson	7	6	1	208	70	0	2	41.60	2	88.51
A. J. Bichel	11	11	0	170	62	0	1	15.45	3	85.86
A. J. Nye	6	6	2	113	35	0	0	28.25	3	77.40
M. L. Love	4	4	1	97	48	0	0	32.33	3	73.48
N. M. Hauritz	8	7	3	75	32*	0	0	18.75	1	93.75
S. R. Watson	3	3	0	73	71	0	1	24.33	1	82.95
W. A. Seccombe. . . .	8	5	1	63	43	0	0	15.75	12/2	55.26
B. P. Nash.	9	4	1	47	19	0	0	15.67	4	62.67
A. A. Noffke.	10	6	4	37	18	0	0	18.50	5	63.79
M. G. Johnson	4	2	0	35	27	0	0	17.50	1	44.87
L. M. Stevens	2	2	0	26	18	0	0	13.00	0	56.52
C. P. Simpson	3	2	0	5	3	0	0	2.50	2	38.46
C. D. Hartley	3	1	0	5	5	0	0	5.00	5/1	83.33
M. S. Kasprowicz . . .	1	1	1	3	3*	0	0	–	0	75.00
S. J. Jurgensen	4	2	1	1	1*	0	0	1.00	0	50.00

*Denotes not out.

QUEENSLAND WICKET-TAKERS

	O	Mdns	R	W	BB	5W/i	Avge	RPO
A. J. Bichel.	93	9	367	14	3-30	0	26.21	3.95
J. R. Hopes	83.2	5	356	11	4-36	0	32.36	4.27
A. A. Noffke.	90	5	435	10	2-54	0	43.50	4.83
A. Symonds	51	0	254	7	3-45	0	36.29	4.98
N. M. Hauritz	66	0	283	7	2-18	0	40.43	4.29
M. G. Johnson	37	2	200	6	4-45	0	33.33	5.41
C. P. Simpson	16.1	0	65	6	3-30	0	10.83	4.02
M. S. Kasprowicz.	10	1	37	4	4-37	0	9.25	3.70
S. J. Jurgensen	29	0	161	3	2-57	0	53.67	5.55
S. R. Watson.	27	0	122	3	1-22	0	40.67	4.52
B. P. Nash.	8	0	47	2	2-31	0	23.50	5.88
L. M. Stevens	13	0	57	0	–	0	–	4.38

QUEENSLAND v NEW SOUTH WALES

At Brisbane Cricket Ground, Brisbane, October 10, 2004. Queensland won by two wickets. *Toss:* New South Wales. Queensland 4 pts. *Competition debut:* A. J. Nye.

Queensland fans finally saw the best of Andrew Symonds as he played a mature innings to guide his side to victory. The nonchalant Symonds has been a match-winner for Australia many times, but all too rarely for his state. His controlled 71 off 66 balls – mixing sensible strokeplay with the odd "brain explosion" – was the difference between the two sides despite the best efforts of NSW leg-spinner Stuart MacGill, who bowled superbly. Chasing Queenslands' modest total, Symonds steadied the innings as wickets fell around him. His innings contained just six fours and one six – a much smaller proportion of boundaries than usual – as he toned down his attacking arsenal. The Bulls fell to 6 for 201 when Symonds departed, caught at slip off MacGill in the 43rd over, but James Hopes got them over the line with 13 balls to spare when he hit a six of Shawn Bradstreet. One of the highlights of the match was a catch engineered by Queensland rookie Aaron Nye to dismiss Brad Haddin. Nye, standing at deep mid-wicket, grabbed the catch with both hands and flicked it back to Martin Love just before stepping over the boundary rope. "We couldn't believe it: Lovey had his hands in the air like John Travolta," Symonds quipped. Symonds has still never hit a one-day century for Queensland, but fans left the ground sensing it would only be a matter of time.

Match reports by BEN DORRIES.

Man of Match: A. Symonds. *Attendance:* 4,369.

New South Wales

G. J. Mail c Maher b Bichel	0	(8)	
P. A. Jaques c Noffke b Jurgensen	11	(14)	
M. J. Phelps b Bichel	18	(21)	
*†B. J. Haddin c Love b Symonds	88	(88)	
D. J. Thornely c Love b Bichel	0	(2)	
A. W. O'Brien run out (Jurgensen/Bichel)	22	(49)	
S. D. Bradstreet not out	53	(74)	
M. J. Nicholson lbw b Simpson	16	(25)	

N. W. Bracken c and b Simpson	4	(6)
S. R. Clark st Seccombe b Simpson	1	(8)
S. C. G. MacGill not out	4	(5)
L-b 3, w 5	8	
(50 overs, 194 mins) (9 wkts)	225	
Fall: 5 23 36 36 106 152 182 190 198		

Bowling: Bichel 8–1–30–3; Jurgensen 8–0–43–1; Noffke 10–1–39–0; Hopes 7–0–19–0; Symonds 10–0–61–1; Simpson 7–0–30–3.

Queensland

*J. P. Maher c Nicholson b Bracken	28	(39)	
M. L. Love c Bradstreet b MacGill	48	(67)	
(Thornely/Bradstreet)	4	(2)	
A. J. Bichel c Bradstreet b MacGill	12	(18)	
A. Symonds c Bradstreet b MacGill	71	(66)	
C. T. Perren c Haddin b Nicholson	1	(6)	
A. J. Nye c Clark b O'Brien	19	(43)	
J. R. Hopes not out	30	(32)	

C. P. Simpson st Haddin b MacGill	3	(7)
†W. A. Seccombe run out		
A. A. Noffke not out	4	(7)
L-b 3, w 3	6	
(47.5 overs, 194 mins) (8 wkts)	226	
Fall: 55 81 102 105 153 201 205 210		

S. J. Jurgensen (did not bat).

Bowling: Clark 6–0–37–0; Bracken 10–3–32–1; O'Brien 8–0–38–1; Nicholson 10–0–52–1; MacGill 10–0–37–4; Bradstreet 3.5–0–27–0.

Umpires: T. P. Laycock and P. D. Parker.
TV Umpire: B. N. J. Oxenford.

QUEENSLAND v SOUTH AUSTRALIA

At Brisbane Cricket Ground, Brisbane, October 23, 2004. Queensland won by 69 runs. *Toss:* Queensland. Queensland 5 pts.

With Jimmy Maher in a punishing mood, Queensland raced to 1 for 129 after 25 overs against the young South Australians, but the Queenslanders then lost 8 for 92 and scored just 93 off the last 20 overs. The fact that the total was restrained to 9 for 264 was largely due to the cagey off-spin of John Davison, who slowed the scoring and made it easier for strike bowler Shaun Tait at the other end. The run-out of Maher for 92, caught millimetres short of his ground after a mix-up with Aaron Nye, was a setback, although Andrew Symonds took over the dominant role with 73 off 72 balls. When South Australia batted, Andy Bichel, who bowled an exceptionally miserly spell, and the rest of Queensland's pace brigade suffocated the life out of the opposition with impeccable line and length. After the dismissal of a patient Greg Blewett, the required run-rate ballooned to more than eight, and the South Australians tied themselves in knots trying to recover momentum. Young off-spinner Chris Simpson polished off the tail as Queensland grabbed a bonus point. The result continued South Australia's woeful record against Queensland, which stands at five wins from 27 games in 34 years of one-day cricket.

Man of Match: J.P. Maher. *Attendance:* 2,148.

Queensland

*J.P. Maher run out (Ferguson/Harris)	92	(123)	C.P. Simpson b Tait	2	(6)
J.R. Hopes b Tait	7	(8)	A.A. Noffke not out	2	(3)
A. Symonds c Blewett b Harris	73	(72)	S.J. Jurgensen not out	1	(1)
C.T. Perren c and b Davison	6	(11)			
A.J. Nye b Cleary	29	(39)	L-b 9, w 15, n-b 2	26	
B.P. Nash b Cleary	19	(23)			
A.J. Bichel b Cleary	2	(8)	(50 overs, 211 mins)	(9 wkts) 264	
†W.A. Seccombe lbw b Tait	5	(8)	Fall: 40 172 182 195 235 248 253 261 263		

Bowling: Harris 7–0–45–1; Tait 10–0–37–3; Miller 8–2–35–0; Cleary 10–0–59–3; Davison 10–1–42–1; Blewett 3–0–25–0; Higgs 2–0–12–0.

South Australia

G.S. Blewett b Hopes	39	(73)	J.M. Davison st Seccombe b Simpson	11	(9)
B.P. Cameron c Nye b Bichel	12	(20)	R.J. Harris c Nash b Hopes	6	(9)
C.J. Ferguson c Seccombe b Bichel	0	(2)	S.W. Tait c Hopes b Simpson	0	(1)
M.J. Cosgrove c Simpson b Noffke	26	(47)			
*†G.A. Manou c Seccombe b Symonds	29	(49)	L-b 9, w 6	15	
M.A. Higgs b Simpson	30	(38)			
M.C. Miller not out	22	(32)	(49.1 overs, 190 mins)	195	
M.F. Cleary run out (Noffke)	5	(15)	Fall: 28 36 84 92 148 152 161 176 189 195		

Bowling: Jurgensen 6–0–25–0; Bichel 7–0–16–2; Hopes 9–1–29–2; Noffke 8–0–36–1; Symonds 10–0–45–1; Simpson 9.1–0–35–3.

Umpires: N.S. McNamara and B.N.J. Oxenford.
TV Umpire: P.D. Parker.

At Adelaide Oval, Adelaide, November 7, 2004. QUEENSLAND defeated SOUTH AUSTRALIA by five wickets.

At WACA Ground, Perth, November 19, 2004. Day/night game. QUEENSLAND defeated WESTERN AUSTRALIA by 11 runs.

QUEENSLAND v TASMANIA

At Brisbane Cricket Ground, Brisbane, December 4, 2004. Day/night game. Queensland won by 94 runs. *Toss:* Queensland 5 pts.

The clash between the only unbeaten teams in the competition was a mismatch, with the Queensland juggernaut claiming its fifth successive one-day win in emphatic fashion. The 94-run demolition of Tasmania not only gave the home side their best ever start to a season in domestic one-day cricket, it also virtually sealed a spot in the final with more than two months remaining. Clinton Perren bankrolled the win by thumping four sixes in an entertaining hundred. Perren's first century in his 52nd one-day match clearly caught the operators of the electronic Gabba scoreboard by surprise. The board initially flashed up the message "Congratulations Luke Perrin" which was hastily changed to the still incorrect "Clinton Perrin". Perren combined well with up-and-comer Craig Philipson as they led their side to an imposing total. Tasmania lost regular wickets in reply and never recovered after wicket-keeper Chris Hartley stood up to the stumps to take a superb reflex catch to dismiss Michael Bevan. Queensland's thumping win, without national all-rounders Andrew Symonds and Shane Watson, was watched by a bumper crowd of 15,918 – the second-largest at the Gabba for an interstate one-dayer. Tasmania left the ground sore and sorry – especially rookie wicket-keeper David Dawson, who was struck a nasty blow in the face by an outfield throw.

Man of Match: C. T. Perren. *Attendance:* 15,918.

Queensland

*J. P. Maher c Dighton b Wright	12	(18)	N. M. Hauritz not out	17	(14)
J. R. Hopes c Griffith b Wright	21	(23)	A. A. Noffke not out	1	(1)
C. T. Perren lbw b Geeves	117	(118)	L-b 3, w 4, n-b 2	9	
C. A. Philipson c Geeves b Marsh	70	(82)			
A. J. Bichel c Doherty b Butterworth	7	(8)	(50 overs, 209 mins) (6 wkts)	289	
A. J. Nye c Dawson b Geeves	35	(38)	Fall: 25 50 203 218 253 284		

B. P. Nash, †C. D. Hartley, S. J. Jurgensen (did not bat).

Bowling: Wright 9–1–40–2; Griffith 9–1–61–0; Butterworth 10–1–60–1; Geeves 9–0–46–2; Doherty 6–1–39–0; Marsh 7–0–40–1.

Tasmania

M. G. Dighton b Jurgensen	20	(24)	X. J. Doherty st Hartley b Hauritz	11	(23)
T. R. Birt c Maher b Bichel	30	(24)	B. Geeves run out	2	(5)
M. G. Bevan c Hartley b Hopes	35	(41)	A. R. Griffith c Hartley b Hopes	0	(4)
†D. G. Dawson lbw b Jurgensen	3	(14)			
*D. J. Marsh c Hartley b Hopes	22	(24)	L-b 7, w 5	12	
G. J. Bailey not out	45	(53)			
L. R. Butterworth run out	1	(14)	(38.2 overs, 166 mins)	195	
D. G. Wright c Nash b Hopes	14	(14)	Fall: 56 63 81 120 124 125 154 183 194 195		

Bowling: Jurgensen 10–0–57–2; Bichel 8–1–42–1; Noffke 6–0–30–0; Hopes 9.2–1–36–4; Hauritz 5–0–23–1.

Umpires: N. S. McNamara and D. L. Orchard.

QUEENSLAND v VICTORIA

At Brisbane Cricket Ground, Brisbane, December 17, 2004. Day/night game. Victoria won by 11 runs. *Toss:* Victoria. Victoria 4 pts.

It took something special to snap Queensland's five-match winning streak and Cameron White provided it. The blond leg-spinner with the giant hands grasped two magnificent return catches in the 45th over to help steal an amazing victory for his side. Chasing 247 to win, Queensland were cruising at 4 for 199 before White dismissed top-scorer Shane Watson. White then caught-and-bowled Brendan Nash and Andy Bichel in the space of three balls. The second of the catches, off a full-blooded drive by Bichel, just seemed to stick in White's out-thrust left hand to send an incredulous Bichel on his way. Queensland needed 17 off the last over with the final two batsmen at the crease, and it proved too much for them. Queensland had lost 6 for 36 to fall to their first loss of the season in either competition. White's heroics represented the second time in the match Victoria had climbed off the canvas. The visitors would not have posted a competitive total if not for some late big hitting from 20-year-old Adam Crosthwaite, who cracked an unbeaten 54 off 38 balls. He and Brad Knowles came together with the Victorians 8 for 175 and added 71 in the last ten overs. The result continued Queensland's poor recent record against Victoria and was a portent for the thrilling Pura Cup match between the sides which followed a few days later.

Man of Match: A. J. Crosthwaite. *Attendance:* 8,669.

Victoria

J. Moss c Maher b Bichel	44 (39)	†A. J. Crosthwaite not out	54 (38)
M. T. G. Elliott c Maher b Noffke	19 (28)	I. S. L. Hewett c and b Hauritz	4 (10)
B. J. Hodge lbw b Noffke	0 (1)	B. A. Knowles run out (Hauritz/Hartley)	17 (34)
D. J. Hussey run out (Hopes)	52 (73)	L-b 2, w 11, n-b 1	14
G. C. Rummans c Hopes b Watson	12 (25)		
*C. L. White c Watson b Symonds	24 (43)	(50 overs, 209 mins)	(9 wkts) 246
I. J. Harvey c Noffke b Hauritz	6 (10)	Fall: 48 48 70 98 147 164 168 175 246	

M. L. Lewis (did not bat).

Bowling: Noffke 10–0–63–2; Bichel 10–0–60–1; Watson 8–0–22–1; Hopes 7–0–33–0; Symonds 5–0–24–1; Hauritz 10–0–42–2.

Queensland

J. R. Hopes c Elliott b Lewis	26 (32)	N. M. Hauritz c Crosthwaite b Knowles	0 (2)
*J. P. Maher c Hewett b Harvey	59 (90)	†C. D. Hartley run out (Hewett/Knowes)	5 (6)
A. Symonds c Moss b Harvey	12 (25)	A. A. Noffke not out	11 (12)
S. R. Watson c Hussey b White	71 (78)		
C. T. Perren c Hodge b White	8 (23)	L-b 9, w 3, n-b 3	15
C. A. Philipson run out (Moss/Crosthwaite)	26 (27)		
B. P. Nash c and b White	2 (4)	(49.4 overs, 223 mins)	235
A. J. Bichel c and b White	0 (2)	Fall: 36 85 162 180 199 207 207 210 220 235	

Bowling: Hewett 10–1–51–0; Lewis 10–1–29–1; Harvey 10–2–33–2; Knowles 8.4–0–58–1; White 9–0–42–4; Moss 2–0–13–0.

Umpires: T. P. Laycock and D. L. Orchard.

At NTCA Ground, Launceston, January 2, 2005. QUEENSLAND defeated TASMANIA by six wickets.

At Telstra Stadium, Homebush, January 15, 2005. Day/night game. QUEENSLAND defeated NEW SOUTH WALES by 121 runs.

At Eastern Oval, Ballarat, February 6, 2005. QUEENSLAND defeated VICTORIA by 138 runs.

QUEENSLAND v WESTERN AUSTRALIA

At Brisbane Cricket Ground, Brisbane, February 11, 2005. Day/night game. Western Australia won by 57 runs. *Toss:* Western Australia. Western Australia 5 pts.

The match started on a disappointing note for home fans, who arrived at the ground to discover Matthew Hayden had been ruled out with a viral infection and was home in bed. Queensland could have done with Hayden, as they capitulated when set a modest target. Ball dominated bat all match, with Michael Kasprowicz conjuring a magical spell of seam bowling to take 4 for 8 in 22 deliveries over two spells. Kasprowicz, recently overlooked for Brett Lee in Australia's VB Series final win over Pakistan, was simply too good for the Western Australian batsmen, who struggled to lay bat on ball. With left-armer Mitchell Johnson bowling with venom, Western Australian opener Marcus North was the only batsman to pass 50. Queensland fared even worse. Five batsmen reached double figures but no one bettered Jimmy Maher's score of 34. Western Australian paceman Steve Magoffin bowled well against his former state and was ably assisted by the unflappable Kade Harvey and Darren Wates. A season which had started so well for Queensland was starting to fall apart, and they limped into the final against Tasmania, not in winning form.

Man of Match: D. J. Wates. *Attendance:* 8,146.

Western Australia

M. J. North run out (Perren)	55 (76)	D. J. Wates not out	28 (24)
C. J. L. Rogers c Nash b Kasprowicz	43 (85)	B. A. Williams c Maher b Johnson	9 (7)
A. C. Voges c Seccombe b Kasprowicz	1 (8)	S. J. Magoffin not out	2 (3)
*M. E. K. Hussey c Nash b Kasprowicz	21 (43)		
M. W. Goodwin c Perren b Johnson	19 (27)	L-b 2, w 8, n-b 5	15
†L. Ronchi c Bichel b Johnson	1 (3)		
K. M. Harvey lbw b Kasprowicz	11 (18)	(50 overs, 212 mins) (9 wkts)	210
B. Casson c Philipson b Johnson	5 (11)	Fall: 102 107 107 144 146 163 163 180 193

Bowling: Johnson 10–1–45–4; Bichel 7–1–28–0; Hopes 10–0–35–0; Kasprowicz 10–1–37–4; Hauritz 10–0–49–0; Stevens 3–0–14–0.

Queensland

*J. P. Maher c Magoffin b Harvey	34 (52)	N. M. Hauritz lbw b Wates	7 (28)
L. M. Stevens b North b Magoffin	8 (16)	M. G. Johnson c Rogers b Wates	8 (29)
C. T. Perren c Rogers b Harvey	28 (33)	M. S. Kasprowicz not out	3 (4)
C. A. Philipson c Ronchi b Wates	1 (5)		
J. R. Hopes c Magoffin b Harvey	2 (8)	B 4, l-b 4, w 16, n-b 1	25
B. P. Nash lbw b Casson	15 (34)		
†W. A. Seccombe c Williams b Magoffin	10 (22)	(41 overs, 175 mins)	153
A. J. Bichel c and b Magoffin	12 (16)	Fall: 24 82 87 89 95 114 131 131 148 153

Bowling: Magoffin 10–0–40–3; Williams 8–2–20–0; Harvey 7–1–32–3; Wates 8–1–32–3; Casson 8–0–21–1.

Umpires: B. N. J. Oxenford and P. D. Parker.

FINAL

At Brisbane Cricket Ground, Brisbane, February 20, 2005. TASMANIA defeated QUEENSLAND by seven wickets. For details see page 512.

QUEENSLAND DOMESTIC LIMITED-OVERS RESULTS

	First Game	M	Won	Lost	No Result	Tied
New South Wales	Dec 7, 1969	35	16	19	0	0
South Australia	Dec 6, 1970	28	23	5	0	0
Western Australia	Feb 6, 1971	34	15	17	2	0
Victoria	Dec 5, 1971	28	14	13	1	0
Tasmania	Dec 31, 1972	31	21	9	1	0
New Zealanders	Jan 21, 1973	1	0	1	0	0
Australian Capital Territory	Jan 31, 1998	3	3	0	0	0
Total		160	92	64	4	0

QUEENSLAND RECORDS

Highest score for:	187	J. P. Maher v Western Australia at Brisbane	2003-04
Highest score against:	131	S. R. Waugh (New South Wales) at Brisbane	1992-93
Best bowling for:	7-34	C. G. Rackemann v South Australia at Adelaide	1988-89
Best bowling against:	5-23	J. P. Marquet (Tasmania) at Hobart (Bellerive)	1995-96
Highest total for:	4-405	v Western Australia at Brisbane	2003-04
Highest total against:	6-301	by Western Australia at Perth	1999-00
Lowest total for:	62	v Western Australia at Perth	1976-77
Lowest total against:	65	by Victoria at Ballarat	2002-03

MOST RUNS

	M	I	NO	R	HS	100s	50s	Avge	S-R
J. P. Maher	84	84	9	3,627	187	8	20	48.36	77.57
S. G. Law	85	78	7	2,534	159	6	10	35.69	93.06
M. L. Love	82	79	11	2,412	127*	4	9	35.47	76.84
M. L. Hayden	51	51	9	2,231	152*	8	11	53.12	72.18
C. T. Perren	58	51	11	1,659	117	1	13	41.48	67.85
A. Symonds	61	57	8	1,491	91	0	9	30.43	98.61
T. J. Barsby	42	41	2	1,145	101	1	10	29.36	61.10
A. R. Border	43	40	8	1,049	97	0	9	32.78	72.60
G. M. Ritchie	27	24	4	825	114	1	5	41.25	74.93
W. A. Seccombe	77	56	16	794	67*	0	3	19.85	78.15

HIGHEST PARTNERSHIP FOR EACH WICKET

250	for 1st	M. L. Hayden and J. P. Maher, v Australian Capital Territory at Canberra	1999-00
260	for 2nd	M. L. Hayden and S. G. Law, v Tasmania at Brisbane	1993-94
187	for 3rd	J. M. Thomas and S. G. Law, v Western Australia at Brisbane	1993-94
173	for 4th	M. L. Love and C. T. Perren, v Tasmania at Brisbane	2001-02
180	for 5th	J. P. Maher and C. T. Perren, v South Australia at Brisbane	2003-04
108	for 6th	A. Symonds and J. R. Hopes, v New South Wales at North Sydney	2002-03
91	for 7th	J. N. Langley and J. A. Maclean, v South Australia at Brisbane	1975-76
55	for 8th	S. A. Prestwidge and A. J. Bichel, v New South Wales at Sydney	1997-98
55*	for 8th	J. P. Maher and A. J. Bichel, v Tasmania at Brisbane	2001-02
62	for 9th	S. A. Prestwidge and M. S. Kasprowicz, v New South Wales at Brisbane	1997-98
33	for 10th	M. L. Love and C. G. Rackemann, v New South Wales at Brisbane	1993-94

MOST WICKETS

	M	Balls	Mdns	R	W	BB	5W/i	Avge	RPO
M. S. Kasprowicz	67	3,467	43	2,383	84	4-19	0	28.37	4.12
S. A. Prestwidge	45	2,189	18	1,755	67	5-59	1	26.19	4.81
J. R. Hopes	47	2,333	29	1,705	66	5-29	1	25.83	4.38
A. J. Bichel	57	2,920	36	2,077	61	4-45	0	34.05	4.27
N. M. Hauritz	42	1,954	4	1,467	61	4-39	0	24.05	4.50
C. G. Rackemann	36	1,975	38	1,249	48	7-34	1	26.02	3.79
A. A. Noffke	34	2,315	31	1,825	46	4-32	0	39.67	4.73
G. Dymock	23	1,300	20	749	39	5-27	1	19.21	3.46
A. C. Dale	27	1,451	20	842	36	4-26	0	23.39	3.48
J. R. Thomson	25	1,273	19	821	35	6-19	1	23.46	3.87

MOST DISMISSALS

	M	Catches	Stumpings	Total
W. A. Seccombe	77	104	22	126
I. A. Healy	29	47	7	54
J. A. Maclean	19	32	1	33
R. B. Phillips	18	22	0	22
C. D. Hartley	4	5	3	8

MOST CATCHES

J. P. Maher	43 in 84 matches	C. T. Perren	17 in 58 matches
S. G. Law	35 in 85 matches	A. J. Bichel	17 in 57 matches
M. L. Love	31 in 82 matches	M. L. Hayden	16 in 51 matches
A. Symonds	27 in 61 matches	M. S. Kasprowicz	14 in 67 matches
A. R. Border	26 in 43 matches		

MOST APPEARANCES

85	S. G. Law	1988-89 – 2003-04	61	A. Symonds	1993-94 – 2004-05
84	J. P. Maher	1993-94 – 2004-05	58	C. T. Perren	1997-98 – 2004-05
82	M. L. Love	1993-94 – 2004-05	57	A. J. Bichel	1992-93 – 2004-05
77	W. A. Seccombe	1994-95 – 2004-05	51	M. L. Hayden	1992-93 – 2001-02
67	M. S. Kasprowicz	1989-90 – 2004-05	47	J. R. Hopes	2000-01 – 2004-05

SOUTH AUSTRALIA ING CUP RESULTS, 2004-05

Played 10: Won 4, Lost 6. *Finished fifth.*

SOUTH AUSTRALIA RUN-SCORERS

	M	I	NO	R	HS	100s	50s	Avge	Ct/St	S-R
G. S. Blewett	9	9	1	472	125	2	1	59.00	3	75.52
C. J. Ferguson......	9	9	1	225	72*	0	2	28.13	1	82.72
M. J. Cosgrove	8	8	0	210	73	0	1	26.25	3	70.71
M. A. Higgs	7	7	0	182	48	0	0	26.00	0	87.50
N. T. Adcock	7	7	1	182	62*	0	2	30.33	2	60.07
G. A. Manou.......	10	10	1	176	43	0	0	19.56	16/0	88.00
D. S. Lehmann	2	2	0	145	92	0	2	72.50	0	84.30
B. P. Cameron	5	5	0	100	77	0	1	20.00	1	53.76
M. F. Cleary	7	7	1	95	34	0	0	15.83	3	71.97
R. J. Harris	8	7	1	80	26	0	0	13.33	3	59.70
M. C. Miller	2	2	1	50	28	0	0	50.00	0	64.94
J. M. Davison	4	4	0	45	19	0	0	11.25	1	84.91
J. K. Smith	4	4	0	36	23	0	0	9.00	1	62.07
D. J. Cullen.......	6	5	2	33	13*	0	0	11.00	2	64.71
S. B. Tubb.......	3	3	0	29	29	0	0	9.67	0	87.88
M. C. Weeks.......	2	2	1	17	11	0	0	17.00	0	62.96
T. C. Plant.......	1	1	0	9	9	0	0	9.00	0	29.03
D. J. Harris	1	1	0	5	5	0	0	5.00	1	83.33
S. W. Tait	10	6	4	4	2*	0	0	2.00	3	26.49
J. N. Gillespie......	1	1	0	4	4	0	0	4.00	0	19.05
C. J. Duval	2	1	1	1	1*	0	0	–	1	100.00
P. C. Rofe.........	2	0	0	0	–	0	0	–	0	–

*Denotes not out.

SOUTH AUSTRALIA WICKET-TAKERS

	O	Mdns	R	W	BB	5W/i	Avge	RPO
S. W. Tait	87.1	1	418	21	4-29	0	19.90	4.80
M. F. Cleary	63.4	3	324	14	3-33	0	23.14	5.09
R. J. Harris	72	7	330	10	2-31	0	33.00	4.58
D. J. Cullen...........	47.2	2	221	9	3-55	0	24.56	4.67
G. S. Blewett	34	3	151	9	4-16	0	16.78	4.44
P. C. Rofe	12.1	0	62	4	2-30	0	15.50	5.10
J. M. Davison	25.3	1	148	2	1-42	0	74.00	5.80
D. S. Lehmann	12	0	36	1	1-22	0	36.00	3.00
C. J. Duval	15	0	125	1	1-61	0	125.00	8.33
M. C. Weeks	9	0	69	1	1-25	0	69.00	7.67
J. N. Gillespie..........	10	0	46	1	1-46	0	46.00	4.60
M. A. Higgs	5	0	36	0	–	0	–	7.20
M. J. Cosgrove	12	0	88	0	–	0	–	7.33
M. C. Miller	15	2	70	0	–	0	–	4.67

At Brisbane Cricket Ground, Brisbane, October 23, 2004. QUEENSLAND defeated SOUTH AUSTRALIA by 69 runs.

SOUTH AUSTRALIA v VICTORIA

At Adelaide Oval, Adelaide, October 30, 2004. Victoria won by seven wickets. *Toss:* South Australia. Victoria 4 pts. *Competition debut:* M. C. Weeks.

An even display by Victoria's bowlers and dismissive innings by two of their batsmen brought the visitors a comfortable victory. On a sun-kissed morning, Greg Blewett started with a pair of smart cover drives from Ian Harvey, and pulled Shane Harwood over square leg for six before nicking an attempted cut from the same bowler. Mark Cosgrove played with his customary uncomplicated power but slowed markedly as partners came and went at the other end. Jonathan Moss struck once in his first over and twice in his third, finding a broad gap between Callum Ferguson's bat and pad. When Michael Lewis defeated Cosgrove, South Australia had lost 5 for 56 and there were few heroics from the tail. Ian Harvey gifted Shaun Tait the first wicket of Victoria's reply when he sliced to third man, and Brendan Joseland's demise to a horizontal lunge by Ben Cameron suggested South Australia might exert some pressure. But Matthew Elliott and David Hussey showed few signs of anxiety. In 138 balls they added 126 runs, severely punishing debutant medium-pacer Matthew Weeks and off-spinner John Davison.

Match reports by DANIEL BRETTIG.

Man of Match: D. J. Hussey. *Attendance:* 2,097.

South Australia

G. S. Blewett c Crosthwaite b Harwood	17	(23)	M. F. Cleary b Lewis	10	(25)
M. J. Cosgrove c Elliott b Lewis	73	(113)	M. C. Weeks b Lewis	11	(16)
B. P. Cameron c Hussey b Knowles	3	(11)	S. W. Tait not out	0	(5)
M. A. Higgs c Hussey b Moss	11	(21)			
C. J. Ferguson b Moss	4	(6)	L-b 6, w 6, n-b 2	14	
*†G. A. Manou c Crosthwaite b Moss	1	(3)			
M. C. Miller b Harvey	28	(45)	(47.1 overs, 192 mins)	185	
J. M. Davison b Harvey	13	(17)	Fall: 34 62 84 94 96 136 158 159 180 185		

Bowling: Harvey 8–1–33–2; Harwood 9–0–57–1; McDonald 7–1–11–0; Knowles 4–0–21–1; Moss 10–0–27–3; Lewis 9.1–0–30–3.

Victoria

M. T. G. Elliott c Tait b Davison	76	(94)			
I. J. Harvey c Cleary b Tait	8	(3)	L-b 3, w 2, n-b 2	7	
B. R. Joseland c Cameron b Cleary	7	(24)			
D. J. Hussey not out	81	(86)	(36.3 overs, 141 mins) (3 wkts)	189	
*J. Moss not out	10	(14)	Fall: 9 26 152		

G. C. Rummans, A. B. McDonald, †A. J. Crosthwaite, B. A. Knowles, S. M. Harwood, M. L. Lewis (did not bat).

Bowling: Tait 8–1–39–1; Cleary 9–3–21–1; Weeks 6–0–44–0; Miller 7–0–35–0; Davison 6.3–0–47–1.

Umpires: S. J. Davis and S. D. Fry.
TV Umpire: K. D. Perrin.

SOUTH AUSTRALIA v QUEENSLAND

At Adelaide Oval, Adelaide, November 7, 2004. Queensland won by five wickets. *Toss:* Queensland. Queensland 6 pts. *Competition debut:* C. J. Duval and J. K. Smith.

A brutal thrashing moved into the realm of the farcical when South Australia unwittingly allowed Queensland to snatch two bonus points. The inexperienced home side's profligacy in the field was disheartening after its batsmen worked hard to forge a playable total against a Queensland attack that was disciplined and deep. Ben Cameron was never convincing, but stuck vigilantly to his task until Andrew Symonds threw down the stumps while lying prostrate. Shaun Tait took it upon himself to remove Jimmy Maher, but after a good leg-before appeal was turned down and a blow to the ribs absorbed, Tait and his fellow bowlers were struck senseless. James Hopes was dropped at slip off Tait but otherwise struck the ball keenly, while Symonds and a promoted Andy Bichel were murderous in bringing the second bonus point within sight. Belatedly, word filtered out to Graham Manou that defeat inside half the overs would mean six points for his opponents, and though Shane Watson and Clinton Perren fell in the 25th over, Symonds was on hand to belt the final ball down the ground for four. Manou commented later, "We expected some lows this season, but probably not this low."

Man of Match: J. R. Hopes. *Attendance:* 2,675.

South Australia

J. M. Davison c Seccombe b Bichel	..	19 (24)
M. J. Cosgrove run out (Nye)	....	1 (3)
B. P. Cameron run out (Symonds)	....	77 (127)
N. T. Adcock c Seccombe b Hopes	...	9 (29)
C. J. Ferguson run out (Nash/Seccombe)		30 (44)
J. K. Smith c Noffke b Watson	......	23 (39)
*†G. A. Manou lbw b Noffke	....	1 (2)

M. F. Cleary b Symonds	....	16 (19)
M. C. Weeks not out	....	6 (11)
C. J. Duval not out	....	1 (1)
L-b 7, w 12	....	19

(50 overs, 209 mins) (8 wkts) 202

Fall: 6 26 60 138 165 167 184 199

S. W. Tait (did not bat).

Bowling: Bichel 10–2–25–1; Noffke 10–0–39–1; Watson 10–0–49–1; Hopes 10–1–38–1; Symonds 10–0–44–1.

Queensland

*J. P. Maher c Cosgrove b Cleary	....	29 (30)
J. R. Hopes c Cleary b Weeks	......	69 (68)
A. Symonds not out	....	44 (32)
A. J. Bichel c Cosgrove b Duval	....	23 (15)
S. R. Watson c Tait b Cleary	....	1 (3)
C. T. Perren b Cleary	....	2 (2)

A. J. Nye not out	....	1 (2)
B 4, l-b 14, w 10, n-b 7	......	35

(25 overs, 114 mins) (5 wkts) 204

Fall: 85 142 196 197 199

C. P. Simpson, B. P. Nash, †W. A. Seccombe, A. A. Noffke (did not bat).

Bowling: Tait 7-0-46-0; Cleary 8-0-54-3; Duval 7-0-61-1; Weeks 3-0-25-1.

Umpires: A. R. Craig and S. D. Fry.
TV Umpire: K. D. Perrin.

At Bellerive Oval, Hobart, November 21, 2004. TASMANIA defeated SOUTH AUSTRALIA by 114 runs.

At Manuka Oval, Canberra, December 11, 2004. SOUTH AUSTRALIA defeated NEW SOUTH WALES by 14 runs.

SOUTH AUSTRALIA v WESTERN AUSTRALIA

At Adelaide Oval, Adelaide, December 17, 2004. Day/night game. Western Australia won by seven runs. *Toss:* Western Australia. Western Australia 4 pts.

As they would do in the subsequent Pura Cup game between these sides, Western Australia lost their first five wickets for precious few runs before bounding to a winning total through a resilient middle order. A jumble of wides from Shaun Tait and Ryan Harris helped Western Australia's openers make a swift start, but Mark Cleary's appearance as first change messed with the visitors' rhythm. Graham Manou delightedly pouched the first four catches of the game in the space of six overs. Mike Hussey held firm among the wreckage, and turned the game in concert with an explosive Luke Ronchi. On a day of high temperatures, the pair sapped South Australia with hard running and four sixes, putting on 116 from 18 overs. Brad Hogg emerged after Ronchi's departure and hustled the total past 260. Helped by Brad Williams' injured exit after a single over, South Australia's reply was held together by Greg Blewett. Kade Harvey pegged things back, but it was part-time spinner Marcus North who landed the vital blow. On a pitch that had barely turned, North found a sharp, bouncing off-break to bemuse an advancing Blewett. A quick partnership between Manou and Cleary brought the sides close together, but after their dismissals the South Australian tail was unable to finish the task.

Man of Match: L. Ronchi. *Attendance:* 2,665.

Western Australia

C. J. L. Rogers c Manou b Harris	18	(16)	B. R. Dorey c Tait b Blewett	2	(9)
M. J. North c Manou b Cleary	10	(32)	B. A. Williams not out	2	(5)
A. C. Voges c Manou b Harris	3	(4)	S. J. Magoffin lbw b Cleary	1	(5)
*M. E. K. Hussey lbw b Cullen	69	(96)			
M. W. Goodwin c Manou b Cleary	10	(17)	L-b 10, w 25	35	
K. M. Harvey c Harris b Tait	2	(5)			
†L. Ronchi c Manou b Tait	75	(64)	(48.3 overs, 201 mins)	262	
G. B. Hogg c Harris b Blewett	35	(39)	Fall: 42 44 46 63 66 182 243 251 261 262		

Bowling: Tait 8–0–50–2; Harris 10–2–50–2; Cleary 9.3–0–33–3; Blewett 7–1–21–2; Cullen 10–0–54–1; Higgs 3–0–24–0; Cosgrove 1–0–20–0.

South Australia

M. J. Cosgrove c Dorey b Harvey	36	(33)	R. J. Harris b Harvey	2	(5)
G. S. Blewett st Ronchi b North	83	(102)	D. J. Cullen run out (Magoffin)	3	(8)
N. T. Adcock run out (North/Ronchi)	9	(29)	S. W. Tait not out	2	(3)
M. A. Higgs b Dorey	23	(26)			
C. J. Ferguson run out (Goodwin/North)	13	(16)	L-b 8, w 4, n-b 3	15	
J. K. Smith lbw b Harvey	5	(10)			
*†G. A. Manou b Dorey	30	(31)	(49.1 overs, 204 mins)	255	
M. F. Cleary b Hogg	34	(35)	Fall: 66 100 155 175 179 182 236 239 251 255		

Bowling: Williams 1–0–1–0; Magoffin 10–0–68–0; Dorey 9.1–1–38–2; Harvey 10–0–40–3; Hogg 10–0–44–1; Hussey 2–0–15–0; Voges 3–0–20–0; North 4–0–21–1.

Umpires: R. L. Parry and K. D. Perrin.

At Melbourne Cricket Ground, Melbourne, January 2, 2005. VICTORIA defeated SOUTH AUSTRALIA by five wickets.

SOUTH AUSTRALIA v NEW SOUTH WALES

At Adelaide Oval, Adelaide, January 23, 2005. Day/night game. South Australia won by 87 runs. *Toss:* New South Wales. South Australia 5 pts.

Greg Blewett, who glided to his highest limited-overs score, then followed up with his best bowling figures, turning Stuart MacGill's state captaincy into a disaster. MacGill's decision to field first looked justified when two wickets fell early, but former New South Welshman Mark Higgs instilled confidence in his team-mates in a breezy knock. Blewett bloomed when MacGill brought himself on, thrashing a pair of sixes, while at the other end Callum Ferguson waltzed to an easy, attractive 72. Matthew Phelps and Phil Jaques began the visitors' reply with aggression, racing to 78 in the 12th over, and it took a pair of good deliveries by Paul Rofe to dismiss them. The NSW batting line-up had arrived dotted with inexperienced practitioners, and their collapse to 5 for 93 was not hugely surprising as Ryan Harris, Shaun Tait and Daniel Cullen all bowled studiously. Shawn Bradstreet and Daniel Smith added 87 to avert the possibility of conceding double bonus points, but Blewett separated them before closing the innings with the sort of bowling that once persuaded the Australian selectors to pick him as an all-rounder.

Man of Match: G. S. Blewett. *Attendance:* 2,151.

South Australia

M. J. Cosgrove c Cowan b Clark	21	(23)	R. J. Harris st Smith b Bradstreet	9	(12)
G. S. Blewett c Packman b Bradstreet	.125	(145)	D. J. Cullen not out	1	(1)
N. T. Adcock lbw b Clark	0	(1)			
M. A. Higgs c Thornely b Bracken	48	(46)	L-b 3, w 1, n-b 4	8	
C. J. Ferguson not out	72	(70)			
*†G. A. Manou run out (Bradstreet/Smith)	2	(4)	(50 overs, 216 mins) (7 wkts)	286	
S. B. Tubb run out (Phelps)	0	(2)	Fall: 38 38 133 232 239 239 281		

P. C. Rofe, S. W. Tait (did not bat).

Bowling: Rofe 9–0–43–1; Clark 10–1–54–2; Bollinger 10–1–49–0; Bradstreet 9–1–62–2; Thornely 6–0–26–0; MacGill 6–0–49–0.

New South Wales

P. A. Jaques c Manou b Rofe	22	(23)	S. R. Clark c Manou b Blewett	4	(3)
M. J. Phelps b Rofe	55	(55)	*S. C. G. MacGill b Blewett	8	(8)
E. J. M. Cowan lbw b Harris	0	(3)	D. Bollinger b Blewett	1	(3)
D. J. Thornely b Tait	4	(12)			
J. R. Packman c Manou b Tait	2	(13)	L-b 4, w 9	13	
S. D. Bradstreet c Adcock b Blewett	41	(62)			
†D. Smith not out	49	(60)	(42 overs, 169 mins)	199	
N. W. Bracken c Ferguson b Cullen	0	(9)	Fall: 78 80 85 92 93 180 181 185 197 199		

Bowling: Tait 7–0–37–2; Rofe 7–0–32–2; Harris 8–0–36–1; Cullen 9–0–34–1; Cosgrove 7–0–40–0; Blewett 4–1–16–4.

Umpires: A. R. Collins and G. T. D. Morrow.

At WACA Ground, Perth, February 4, 2005. Day/night game. SOUTH AUSTRALIA defeated WESTERN AUSTRALIA by 98 runs.

SOUTH AUSTRALIA v TASMANIA

At Adelaide Oval, Adelaide, February 12, 2005. South Australia won by 20 runs. *Toss:* South Australia. South Australia 4 pts.

Tasmania suffered a surprise reverse at the hands of a resurgent South Australian side, whose bowlers were marshalled expertly by Darren Lehmann. The early overs suggested a fat local total and a high-scoring match, but they were misleading. Damien Wright found his outswinger in the tenth over to dislodge Graham Manou and Greg Blewett, and the remainder of the innings was a struggle. Lehmann, though incapacitated by a shoulder problem, bunted his way to an invaluable fifty. The team total of 218 appeared defensible, and the return of Jason Gillespie to partner Shaun Tait, Ryan Harris and Daniel Cullen gave South Australia's bowling attack a rare level of class, especially as Ricky Ponting was decided to rest before the tour to New Zealand. Michael Dighton and Michael Di Venuto succumbed to the new ball, before Cullen won a somewhat fortunate leg-before verdict to see off Travis Birt. There was no question about Michael Bevan's dismissal, edging behind, and it took an impish innings by Luke Butterworth to tighten the margin. The result left the Tasmanians with a nervous wait for the result of the match between NSW and Victoria to find out if they had made the final, while South Australia, buoyed by some good form at last, could not wait for the arrival of the new season.

Man of Match: G. A. Manou. *Attendance:* 2,888.

South Australia

†G. A. Manou c Butterworth b Wright	43	(36)	
G. S. Blewett c Dighton b Wright	19	(24)	
N. T. Adcock b Marsh b Geeves	19	(34)	
M. A. Higgs run out (Bailey/Dighton)	28	(33)	
C. J. Ferguson b Butterworth	9	(11)	
*D. S. Lehmann c Marsh b Geeves	53	(76)	
S. B. Tubb c Di Venuto b Butterworth	0	(1)	
R. J. Harris c Bevan b Doherty	22	(32)	
J. N. Gillespie st Dighton b Doherty	4	(21)	
D. J. Cullen c Bevan b Butterworth	8	(23)	
S. W. Tait not out	0	(0)	

L-b 4, w 7, n-b 2 13

(48.1 overs, 193 mins)   218

Fall: 65 66 113 115 134 134 185 197 214 218

Bowling: Griffith 9–1–55–0; Geeves 8.1–0–44–2; Wright 9–1–35–2; Butterworth 10–2–38–3; Marsh 5–0–24–0; Doherty 7–0–18–2.

Tasmania

†M. G. Dighton c Manou b Gillespie	1	(2)	
T. R. Birt lbw b Cullen	25	(48)	
M. J. Di Venuto b Tait	15	(19)	
M. G. Bevan c Manou b Harris	25	(38)	
*D. J. Marsh lbw b Harris	13	(29)	
G. J. Bailey b Lehmann	27	(61)	
D. G. Wright run out (Tubb)	0	(2)	
L. R. Butterworth run out (Harris)	44	(58)	
X. J. Doherty c Manou b Tait	10	(19)	
B. Geeves b Tait	6	(14)	
A. R. Griffith not out	5	(6)	

B 4, l-b 7, w 15, n-b 1 27

(49.1 overs, 196 mins)   198

Fall: 1 30 76 78 100 101 171 184 191 198

Bowling: Tait 9.1–0–39–3; Gillespie 10–0–46–1; Harris 10–1–31–2; Cullen 10–2–30–1; Lehmann 8–0–22–1; Blewett 2–0–19–0.

Umpires: S. D. Fry and D. J. Harper.
TV Umpire: A. R. Collins.

SA DOMESTIC LIMITED-OVERS RESULTS

Opponent	First Game	M	Won	Lost	No Result	Tied
Western Australia	Nov 30, 1969	37	13	24	0	0
Victoria	Oct 18, 1970	32	10	21	0	1
Queensland	Dec 6, 1970	28	5	22	0	0
Tasmania	Nov 14, 1971	26	17	9	0	0
New Zealanders	Jan 14, 1973	2	0	2	0	0
New South Wales	Nov 23, 1975	25	12	13	0	0
Australian Capital Territory	Nov 2, 1997	3	3	0	0	0
Total		152	60	91	0	1

SA RECORDS

Highest score for:	142	D. S. Lehmann v Tasmania at Adelaide	1994-95
Highest score against:	164	R. B. McCosker (New South Wales) at Sydney	1981-82
Best bowling for:	8-43	S. W. Tait v South Australia at Adelaide	2003-04
Best bowling against:	7-34	C. G. Rackemann (Queensland) at Adelaide	1988-89
Highest total for:	6-325	v Tasmania at Hobart (TCA)	1986-87
Highest total against:	5-340	by Tasmania, Hobart (Bellerive)	2004-05
Lowest total for:	51	v Tasmania, Hobart (Bellerive)	2002-03
Lowest total against:	119	by Queensland at Adelaide	1993-94

MOST RUNS

	M	I	NO	R	HS	100s	50s	Avge	S-R
G. S. Blewett	88	86	8	3,212	125	5	18	41.18	67.94
D. S. Lehmann	66	66	9	3,048	142*	6	23	53.47	87.69
J. D. Siddons	42	40	4	1,169	102	1	8	32.47	78.77
D. A. Fitzgerald	40	40	1	1,160	114	2	7	29.74	68.97
D. W. Hookes	38	38	1	1,149	101	1	6	31.05	80.07
B. A. Johnson	58	57	7	1,117	83	0	3	22.34	68.57
C. J. Davies	38	37	1	970	125	1	5	26.94	65.06
P. R. Sleep	30	28	4	846	90	0	4	35.25	65.58
P. C. Nobes	27	27	4	745	140*	1	4	32.39	58.43
G. A. Bishop	26	25	1	708	119*	2	2	29.50	66.48

HIGHEST PARTNERSHIP FOR EACH WICKET

217*	for 1st	D. S. Lehmann and P. C. Nobes, v Tasmania at Adelaide	1994-95
145	for 2nd	B. A. Richards and I. M. Chappell, v Queensland at Adelaide	1970-71
153	for 3rd	C. J. Davies and D. S. Lehmann, v Victoria at Adelaide	2000-01
125	for 4th	G. S. Chappell and K. G. Cunningham, v Western Australia at Perth	1972-73
133*	for 5th	A. M. J. Hilditch and M. D. Haysman, v Queensland at Brisbane	1984-85
130	for 6th	D. S. Lehmann and M. C. Miller, v Tasmania at Adelaide	2003-04
111	for 7th	G. A. Manou and M. F. Cleary, v New South Wales at Adelaide	2003-04
64*	for 8th	D. S. Lehmann and B. A. Swain, v ACT at Canberra	1999-00
61*	for 9th	M. Hendrick and A. A. Mallett, v Western Australia at Perth	1974-75
32	for 10th	T. B. A. May and C. J. Owen, v Tasmania at Adelaide	1991-92

MOST WICKETS

Bowler	M	Balls	Mdns	R	W	BB	5Wfi	Avge	RPO
P. Wilson	46	2,540	42	1,676	70	4-23	0	23.94	3.96
G. S. Blewett	88	2,298	15	1,934	60	4-16	0	32.33	5.05
M. A. Harrity	40	2,030	26	1,551	57	5-42	1	27.21	4.58
J. N. Gillespie	24	1,390	24	914	39	4-46	0	23.44	3.95
S. W. Tait	20	1,019	7	822	39	8-43	1	21.08	4.84
B. E. Young	42	1,671	6	1,390	38	4-24	0	36.58	4.99
J. C. Scuderi	37	1,759	13	1,357	32	3-36	0	42.41	4.63
M. F. Cleary	22	1,123	9	949	30	4-55	0	31.63	5.07
S. P. George	20	1,049	7	881	29	4-33	0	30.28	3.99
B. N. Wigney	26	1,318	23	876	29	3-24	0	30.21	5.04
R. J. Harris	25	1,128	11	942	29	4-43	0	32.48	5.01

MOST DISMISSALS

Wicket-keeper	M	Catches	Stumpings	Total
G. A. Manou	55	75	3	78
T. J. Nielsen	45	55	3	58
W. B. Phillips	13	18	0	18
K. J. Wright	14	15	3	18
D. S. Berry	4	5	2	7

MOST CATCHES

G. S. Blewett	28 in 88 matches		D. S. Lehmann	17 in 66 matches
B. E. Young	25 in 42 matches		D. A. Fitzgerald	15 in 40 matches
D. W. Hookes	22 in 38 matches		R. J. Harris	14 in 25 matches
B. A. Johnston	21 in 58 matches		C. J. Davies	12 in 38 matches
J. D. Siddons	20 in 42 matches		J. M. Vaughan	11 in 23 matches

MOST APPEARANCES

88	G. S. Blewett	1992-93 – 2004-05	45	T. J. Nielsen	1991-92 – 1989-99
66	D. S. Lehmann	1988-89 – 2004-05	42	J. D. Siddons	1991-92 – 1999-00
58	B. A. Johnson	1994-95 – 2003-04	42	B. E. Young	1996-97 – 2002-03
55	G. A. Manou	1999-00 – 2004-05	40	D. A. Fitzgerald	1997-98 – 2002-03
46	P. Wilson	1993-94 – 2001-02	40	M. A. Harrity	1995-96 – 2002-03

TASMANIA ING CUP RESULTS, 2004-05

Played 11: Won 6, Lost 4 No result 1. *Finished champions*

TASMANIA RUN-SCORERS

	M	I	NO	R	HS	100s	50s	Avge	Ct/St	S-R
M. G. Bevan	10	10	4	519	118	1	2	86.50	4	76.78
M. G. Dighton	10	10	0	343	72	0	3	34.30	5/1	77.78
T. R. Birt.	7	7	0	308	145	1	1	44.00	1	95.65
D. J. Marsh	10	10	2	257	106*	1	1	32.13	8	84.82
M. J. Di Venuto	7	7	0	213	84	0	1	30.43	6	82.56
G. J. Bailey	10	9	3	185	45*	0	0	30.83	6	70.61
D. G. Wright	10	6	0	96	52	0	1	16.00	3	72.18
L. R. Butterworth . . .	9	7	2	94	44	0	0	18.80	2	77.69
X. J. Doherty	9	6	1	63	28	0	0	12.60	5	51.64
D. G. Dawson	6	5	0	55	20	0	0	11.00	5	44.72
S. P. Kremerskothen.	3	2	1	13	9	0	0	13.00	0	68.42
B. Geeves.	9	5	2	10	6	0	0	3.33	3	40.00
A. R. Griffith	10	3	1	5	5*	0	0	2.50	5	35.71

*Denotes not out.

TASMANIA WICKET-TAKERS

	O	Mdns	R	W	BB	5W/i	Avge	RPO
B. Geeves.	78.2	4	400	20	5-45	1	20.00	5.11
L. R. Butterworth	75	5	382	12	3-38	0	31.83	5.09
D. G. Wright.	85.5	4	381	11	2-33	0	34.64	4.44
X. J. Doherty	75	3	334	10	4-41	0	33.40	4.45
A. R. Griffith	82	6	421	9	3-43	0	46.78	5.13
S. P. Kremerskothen.	24.5	0	114	5	3-50	0	22.80	4.59
D. J. Marsh	45	1	215	4	1-7	0	53.75	4.78
G. J. Bailey.	3	0	19	1	1-19	0	19.00	6.33

At WACA Ground, Perth, October 15, 2004. Day/night game. TASMANIA defeated WESTERN AUSTRALIA by 62 runs.

At Newcastle Sports Ground, Newcastle, October 24, 2004. TASMANIA defeated NEW SOUTH WALES by three wickets.

TASMANIA v VICTORIA

At Bellerive Oval, Hobart, November 5, 2004. Tasmania won by 43 runs. *Toss:* Victoria. Tasmania 4 pts.

A blistering 160-run opening partnership between Michael Di Venuto and Michael Dighton in just over 25 overs set up Tasmania's third consecutive win and their first at home for the season . Di Venuto was first man to fall, but only after hitting ten fours and two sixes. The solid foundation allowed Michael Bevan, with free-hitting support from George Bailey and Dan Marsh, to guide the Tasmanians to their highest one-day score on the ground. Victorian paceman Michael Lewis was the only visiting bowler to take a wicket; the other two dismissals were run-outs. The Victorians' run-chase never got going, although several players made useful starts, and they plummeted to 8 for 180 in the 40th over. Tasmanian left-arm orthodox spinner Xavier Doherty took the heart out of the middle-order. The only downside for the home side was the squandered opportunity to pick up a vital bonus point. It seemed a foregone conclusion until Shane Harwood slogged the Tasmanians for five fours and two sixes.

Match reports by BRETT STUBBS.

Man of Match: M. J. Di Venuto. *Attendance:* 815.

Tasmania

M. J. Di Venuto c McDonald b Lewis . 84 (77)	*D. J. Marsh c Harvey b Lewis 27 (22)
M. G. Dighton c Rummans b Lewis . . 72 (79)	B 1, l-b 4, w 9 14
M. G. Bevan not out 46 (56)	
†D. G. Dawson run out (White) 18 (38)	(50 overs, 192 mins) (5 wkts) 298
G. J. Bailey run out	
(McDonald/Crosthwaite) 3 (28)	Fall: 160 164 202 250 298

L. R. Butterworth, D. G. Wright, X. J. Doherty, B. Geeves, A. R. Griffith (did not bat).

Bowling: Harvey 10–0–61–0; Harwood 10–1–40–0; McDonald 3–0–38–0; Lewis 9–1–46–3; Moss 10–1–45–0; White 8–0–63–0.

Victoria

I. J. Harvey run out (Bailey/Griffith) . . 15 (25)	†A. J. Crosthwaite b Doherty 0 (3)
M. T. G. Elliott c Di Venuto b Griffith 3 (7)	A. B. McDonald not out 28 (46)
B. J. Hodge c Bailey b Geeves 51 (56)	S. M. Harwood not out 50 (31)
D. J. Hussey b Butterworth 29 (28)	L-b 3, w 1, n-b 3 7
J. Moss b Doherty 19 (32)	
*C. L. White c (sub) S. P. Kremerskothen	(50 overs, 195 mins) (8 wkts) 255
b Doherty 31 (50)	Fall: 8 37 99 103 130 165 165 180
G. C. Rummans c Dawson b Doherty . 22 (23)	

M. L. Lewis (did not bat).

Bowling: Wright 10–0–40–0; Griffith 7–0–36–1; Butterworth 10–0–44–1; Geeves 8–0–60–1; Doherty 10–0–41–4; Marsh 5–0–31–0.

Umpires: B. W. Jackman and R. G. Patterson.
TV Umpire: J. H. Smeaton.

TASMANIA v SOUTH AUSTRALIA

At Bellerive Oval, Hobart, November 21, 2004. Tasmania won by 114 runs. *Toss:* Tasmania. Tasmania 5 pts. *Competition debut:* T. C. Plant.

The late withdrawal of Michael Di Venuto with a finger injury led to the call-up of chunky left-handed opener Travis Birt, who proceeded to crash the South Australian attack to all parts of Bellerive Oval. Playing in his first game for the year and just the fourth of his career, the 23-year-old Birt smashed six sixes on his way to the highest one-day score by a Tasmanian. It was a day of records for the Tasmanians: Birt shared a 225-run second-wicket partnership in 30 overs with Michael Bevan, the highest Tasmanian partnership in a limited-overs game. Bevan also scored his first one-day century for Tasmania. The duo's brilliant batting performance enabled the locals to make their largest total in one-day matches. Needing a good start, South Australia never threatened the huge total after Mark Cosgrove was dismissed in the 11th over. Greg Blewett's 118 not out from 122 balls was a heroic solo effort. The win gave Tasmania a perfect start to the season, with four wins from four games and a bonus point from this game – their best-ever start to a domestic one-day season.

Man of Match: T. R. Birt. *Attendance:* 1,572.

Tasmania

T. R. Birt c Duval b Cleary	145 (143)	S. P. Kremerskothen not out	4	(3)
M. G. Dighton c Blewett b Harris	36 (47)			
M. G. Bevan b Tait	118 (97)	B 2, l-b 6, w 16, n-b 2	26	
G. J. Bailey not out	5 (5)			
*D. J. Marsh b Tait	1 (3)	(50 overs, 193 mins)	(5 wkts) 340	
L. R. Butterworth c Smith b Cleary	5 (3)	Fall: 88 313 321 327 332		

†D. G. Dawson, D. G. Wright, X. J. Doherty, A. R. Griffith (did not bat).

Bowling: Tait 10–0–51–2; Duval 8–0–64–0; Harris 10–2–66–1; Cleary 10–0–73–2; Davison 9–0–59–0; Cosgrove 3–0–19–0.

South Australia

J. M. Davison c Doherty b Griffith	2 (3)	M. F. Cleary b Marsh	15	(22)
M. J. Cosgrove c Bevan b Wright	38 (36)	R. J. Harris not out	13	(43)
G. S. Blewett not out	118 (122)			
B. P. Cameron c Griffith b Butterworth	8 (20)	L-b 3, w 3	6	
J. K. Smith c Marsh b Butterworth	8 (8)			
T. C. Plant b Doherty	9 (31)	(50 overs, 179 mins)	(7 wkts) 226	
*†G. A. Manou c Marsh b Doherty	9 (15)	Fall: 3 61 87 97 125 144 181		

C. J. Duval, S. W. Tait (did not bat).

Bowling: Wright 6–0–29–1; Griffith 8–1–44–1; Butterworth 10–1–29–2; Kremerskothen 7–0–28–0; Doherty 10–0–47–2; Marsh 9–0–46–1.

Umpires: I. H. Lock and B. J. Muir.

At Brisbane Cricket Ground, Brisbane, December 4, 2004. Day/night game. QUEENSLAND defeated TASMANIA by 94 runs.

At Junction Oval, St Kilda, December 12, 2004. VICTORIA defeated TASMANIA by 96 runs.

TASMANIA v QUEENSLAND

At NTCA Ground, Launceston, January 2, 2005. Queensland won by six wickets. *Toss:* Tasmania. Queensland 6 pts.

It was a humiliating day for Tasmania, who not only suffered their third consecutive loss, but also conceded two bonus points. Batting first on a good wicket, they slumped to 5 for 105 before Michael Bevan again rescued the side in an 84-run partnership with Damien Wright. They gave the innings some substance, but the eventual total was nothing like enough. After helping destroy Tasmania with the ball, all-rounders James Hopes and Andrew Symonds then set about destroying them with the bat. The inadequacy of Tasmania's score soon became all too apparent. In an amazing 24.1 overs, the visitors scorched past the paltry target to earn the two bonus points. The Tasmanian fielders and bowlers looked helpless against the onslaught. The ball clattered everywhere around the NTCA Ground, Hopes hitting 11 fours and Symonds seven fours and two sixes. Brett Geeves and Luke Butterworth were the only wicket-takers, but each conceded ten runs an over.

Man of Match: J. R. Hopes. *Attendance:* 2,596.

Tasmania

†M. G. Dighton c Maher b Noffke	... 27	(41)	L. R. Butterworth c and b Symonds ..	0	(1)
T. R. Birt c Seccombe b Bichel	0	(3)	X. J. Doherty b Symonds	2	(4)
M. J. Di Venuto c Seccombe b Bichel .	9	(11)	B. Geeves not out	2	(1)
M. G. Bevan not out	89	(124)	L-b 3, w 3	6	
*D. J. Marsh c Noffke b Hopes	1	(7)			
G. J. Bailey c Maher b Hopes	19	(36)	(50 overs, 184 mins) (8 wkts)	207	
D. G. Wright b Symonds	52	(72)	Fall: 6 17 65 69 105 189 189 205		

A. R. Griffith (did not bat).

Bowling: Noffke 10–1–48–1; Bichel 10–1–38–2; Hopes 10–1–49–2; Hauritz 10–0–24–0; Symonds 10–0–45–3.

Queensland

*J. P. Maher c Bailey b Geeves	28	(34)	N. M. Hauritz not out	11	(5)
J. R. Hopes b Geeves	73	(46)	L-b 2, w 2, n-b 5	9	
A. J. Bichel c Wright b Butterworth	16	(20)			
A. Symonds not out	62	(35)	(24.1 overs, 114 mins) (4 wkts)	209	
M. L. Love lbw b Butterworth	10	(10)	Fall: 80 104 161 175		

C. T. Perren, C. A. Philipson, B. P. Nash, †W. A. Seccombe, A. A. Noffke (did not bat).

Bowling: Griffith 4–0–26–0; Wright 6–0–37–0; Doherty 4–0–39–0; Geeves 6.1–0–62–2; Marsh 1–0–13–0; Butterworth 3–0–30–2.

Umpires: B. W. Jackman and J. H. Smeaton.

TASMANIA v WESTERN AUSTRALIA

At Devonport Oval, Devonport, January 23, 2005. Tasmania won by two wickets. *Toss:* Western Australia. Tasmania 4 pts.

In a low-scoring match on a wicket offering variable bounce, Michael Bevan saved the Tasmanians and kept their final chances alive. In the Western Australian innings Brett Geeves took the first three wickets, and although Adam Voges led a steady recovery, the Tasmanians restricted Western Australia to a modest total. All the action was in the Tasmanians run-chase. Travis Birt and Michael Di Venuto batted with more enterprise than the Western Australian batsmen, and the homeside appeared to be cruising to victory at 3 for 111 with Bevan and Dan Marsh at the crease. Then veteran medium-pacer Kade Harvey turned the game on its head. He bowled Marsh before removing George Bailey and Damien Wright leg-before with his next two balls to complete only the fifth hat-trick in the competition's history and leave Tasmania 6 for 111. Bevan found a firm ally in Xavier Doherty and the pair added 50 for the eighth wicket. Harvey returned to put the Tasmanians run-chase in jeopardy by removing Doherty with eight runs remaining. But Bevan, just as he had done so many times for Australia, was able to steer the Tigers over the line.

Man of Match: M. G. Bevan. *Attendance:* 1,919.

Western Australia

*J. L. Langer b Geeves	8	(22)	B. R. Dorey run out (Kremerskothen)	17	(24)
†L. Ronchi c Marsh b Geeves	4	(5)	B. A. Williams b Kremerskothen	9	(6)
M. J. North c Bailey b Geeves	21	(39)	B. M. Edmondson not out	0	(2)
A. C. Voges c Doherty b Griffith	52	(90)			
M. E. K. Hussey c Bailey b Doherty	26	(63)	B 3, l-b 4, w 15, n-b 1	23	
M. W. Goodwin lbw b Doherty	2	(7)			
K. M. Harvey b Kremerskothen	15	(33)	(49.5 overs, 191 mins)	182	
B. Casson b Marsh	5	(9)	Fall: 7 33 40 122 122 124 136 167 182 182		

Bowling: Griffith 10–1–26–1; Geeves 9–0–39–3; Wright 10–0–28–0; Kremerskothen 7.5–0–36–2; Doherty 10–0–39–2; Marsh 3–1–7–1.

Tasmania

T. R. Birt run out (Hussey)	32	(33)	X. J. Doherty b Harvey	28	(55)
†M. G. Dighton lbw b Williams	3	(10)	B. Geeves not out	0	(3)
M. J. Di Venuto c North b Edmondson	42	(58)			
M. G. Bevan not out	48	(94)	B 7, l-b 2, w 7, n-b 3	19	
*D. J. Marsh b Harvey	4	(7)			
G. J. Bailey lbw b Harvey	0	(1)	(45.5 overs, 199 mins)	(8 wkts) 185	
D. G. Wright lbw b Harvey	0	(1)	Fall: 14 66 99 111 111 111 127 177		
S. P. Kremerskothen c Langer b Casson	9	(16)			

A. R. Griffith (did not bat).

Bowling: Dorey 10–0–45–0; Williams 8.5–0–39–1; Harvey 9–2–25–4; North 2–0–13–0; Edmondson 10–2–24–1; Casson 6–1–30–1.

Umpires: B. J. Muir and J. H. Smeaton.

TASMANIA v NEW SOUTH WALES

At Bellerive Oval, Hobart, February 6, 2005. Match abandoned without a ball bowled due to rain. Tasmania 2 pts, New South Wales 2 pts.

Umpires: B. W. Jackman and J. H. Smeaton.

At Adelaide Oval, Adelaide, February 12, 2005. SOUTH AUSTRALIA defeated TASMANIA by 20 runs.

FINAL

At Brisbane Cricket Ground, Brisbane, February 20, 2005. TASMANIA defeated QUEENSLAND by seven wickets. For details see page 512.

TASMANIA DOMESTIC LIMITED-OVERS RESULTS

Opponent	First Game	M	Won	Lost	No Result	Tied
Victoria	Nov 22, 1969	24	10	13	1	0
Western Australia	Nov 4, 1970	29	7	21	1	0
South Australia	Nov 14, 1971	26	9	17	0	0
Queensland	Dec 31, 1972	31	9	21	1	0
New South Wales	Dec 17, 1973	26	4	21	0	1
New Zealanders	Jan 17, 1975	1	0	1	0	0
Australian Capital Territory	Nov 16, 1997	3	2	1	0	0
Total		140	41	95	3	1

TASMANIA RECORDS

Highest score for:	145	T. R. Birt v South Australia at Hobart (Bellerive)	2004-05
Highest score against:	159	S. G. Law (Queensland) at Brisbane	1993-94
Best bowling for:	5-23	J. P. Marquet v Queensland at Hobart (Bellerive)	1995-96
Best bowling against:	8-43	S. W. Tait (South Australia) at Adelaide	2003-04
Highest total for:	5-340	v South Australia at Hobart (Bellerive)	2004-05
Highest total against:	4-397	by New South Wales at Bankstown.	2001-02
Lowest total for:	80	v New South Wales at Devonport	1984-85
Lowest total against:	51	by South Australia at Hobart (Bellerive)	2002-03

MOST RUNS

	M	I	NO	R	HS	100s	50s	Avge	S-R
M. J. Di Venuto........	82	80	7	2,233	129*	3	10	30.59	78.05
J. Cox	75	73	4	1,879	99	0	14	27.23	64.33
D. C. Boon	55	52	4	1,725	116	1	16	35.94	66.22
D. J. Marsh	71	66	12	1,689	106*	3	6	31.28	76.01
S. Young.............	64	56	6	1,428	96	0	9	28.56	65.59
M. G. Dighton.........	36	35	0	1,148	113	1	8	32.80	70.91
D. F. Hills	42	39	3	1,137	81	0	8	31.58	56.40
R. T. Ponting..........	32	32	4	942	102	1	6	33.64	77.92
R. J. Tucker..........	39	38	2	869	75	0	6	24.14	76.56
S. R. Watson	26	35	0	805	113	1	6	32.20	68.34

HIGHEST PARTNERSHIP FOR EACH WICKET

210	for 1st	J. Cox and D. C. Boon, v New South Wales at Hobart (Bellerive)	1998-99
225	for 2nd	T. R. Birt and M. G. Bevan, v South Australia at Hobart (Bellerive)	2004-05
152	for 3rd	G. W. Goodman and J. H. Hampshire, v Queensland at Brisbane	1978-79
121	for 4th	M. G. Dighton and D. J. Marsh, v South Australia at Hobart (Bellerive) ...	2003-04
158	for 5th	J. Cox and D. J. Marsh, v Queensland at Hobart (Bellerive)	2002-03
95	for 6th	D. J. Marsh and G. T. Cunningham, v New South Wales at Bankstown ...	2001-02
96*	for 7th	T. W. Docking and J. Simmons, v Western Australia at Hobart (TCA)	1978-79
58	for 8th	J. Cox and S. P. Kremerskothen, v New South Wales at Devonport	2002-03
67	for 9th	G. T. Cunningham and D. J. Saker, v Western Australia at Perth	2000-01
28	for 10th	M. G. Farrell and M. W. Ridgway, v Western Australia at Hobart (Bellerive) .	1996-97
28	for 10th	S. G. Clingeleffer and S. B. Tubb, South Australia at Adelaide	2001-02

MOST WICKETS

	M	Balls	Mdns	R	W	BB	5W/i	Avge	RPO
D. G. Wright	52	2,771	42	1,774	62	4-23	0	28.61	3.84
S. Young	64	2,642	39	1,864	43	3-16	0	43.35	4.23
D. J. Marsh	71	2,011	5	1,624	40	3-33	0	40.60	4.85
B. Geeves	28	1,340	15	1,056	37	5-45	1	28.54	4.73
R. J. Tucker	39	1,461	4	1,263	34	4-31	0	37.15	5.19
C. R. Miller	33	1,843	31	1,267	34	4-48	0	37.26	4.12
A. R. Griffith	29	1,511	19	1,200	34	3-14	0	35.29	4.77
S. P. Kremerskothen	41	1,066	5	945	29	3-33	0	32.59	5.32
M. W. Ridgway	21	1,170	22	868	28	4-37	0	31.00	4.12
M. G. Farrell	28	1,224	3	885	27	4-51	0	32.78	4.34

MOST DISMISSALS

r	M	Catches	Stumpings	Total
M. N. Atkinson	35	43	7	50
S. G. Clingeleffer	40	39	3	42
R. D. Woolley	22	16	1	17
R. E. Soule	11	9	0	9
B. R. Doolan	7	6	1	7

MOST CATCHES

M. J. Di Venuto	41 in 82 matches		S. P. Kremerskothen	14 in 41 matches
D. J. Marsh	36 in 71 matches		M. G. Dighton	14 in 32 matches
S. Young	23 in 64 matches		R. J. Tucker	13 in 39 matches
J. Cox	19 in 75 matches		R. T. Ponting	13 in 32 matches
D. C. Boon	16 in 55 matches			

MOST APPEARANCES

82	M. J. Di Venuto	1992-93 – 2004-05	52	D. G. Wright	1997-98 – 2004-05
75	J. Cox	1988-89 – 2003-04	42	D. F. Hills	1992-93 – 2001-02
71	D. J. Marsh	1996-97 – 2004-05	41	S. P. Kremerskothen	1998-99 – 2004-05
64	S. Young	1990-91 – 2001-02	40	S. G. Clingeleffer	2000-01 – 2003-04
55	D. C. Boon	1978-79 – 1998-99	39	R. J. Tucker	1987-88 – 1998-99

VICTORIA ING CUP RESULTS, 2004-05

Played 10: Won 5, Lost 5. *Finished third.*

VICTORIA RUN-SCORERS

	M	I	NO	R	HS	100s	50s	Avge	Ct/St	S-R
M. T. G. Elliott	10	10	0	393	77	0	5	39.30	3	72.78
B. J. Hodge	9	9	1	344	108	1	3	43.00	4	88.21
J. Moss	10	10	1	333	77	0	3	37.00	4	81.82
D. J. Hussey	10	10	2	322	81*	0	3	40.25	6	79.70
C. L. White	9	8	1	195	61	0	1	27.86	3	74.71
G. C. Rummans	8	7	2	137	54*	0	1	27.40	1	84.57
I. J. Harvey	8	8	1	76	16	0	0	10.86	1	70.31
A. B. McDonald	6	4	3	66	28*	0	0	66.00	1	71.74
A. J. Crosthwaite . . .	10	5	2	65	54*	0	1	21.67	13/2	97.01
S. M. Harwood	2	1	1	50	50*	0	1	–	0	161.29
B. A. Knowles	9	4	1	35	17	0	0	11.67	1	50.00
I. S. L. Hewett	3	2	0	14	10	0	0	7.00	3	77.78
B. R. Joseland	1	1	0	7	7	0	0	7.00	0	29.17
M. L. Lewis	10	2	1	7	5	0	0	7.00	3	30.43
S. K. Warne	3	2	0	2	2	0	0	1.00	2	14.29
T. H. Welsford	1	0	0	0	–	0	0	–	0	–
G. J. Denton	1	0	0	0	–	0	0	–	0	–

*Denotes not out.

VICTORIA WICKET-TAKERS

	O	Mdns	R	W	BB	5W/i	Avge	RPO
M. L. Lewis	82.3	6	321	18	3-30	0	17.83	3.89
C. L. White	54.5	1	304	13	4-15	0	23.38	5.54
I. J. Harvey	74	6	311	11	4-29	0	28.27	4.20
B. A. Knowles	64.4	7	289	9	2-14	0	32.11	4.47
J. Moss	51	1	261	6	3-27	0	43.50	5.12
A. B. McDonald	36	3	154	5	2-23	0	30.80	4.28
S. K. Warne	27.2	0	125	4	2-20	0	31.25	4.57
S. M. Harwood	19	1	97	1	1-57	0	97.00	5.11
I. S. L. Hewett	25	2	130	0	–	0	–	5.20
D. J. Hussey	1	0	13	0	–	0	–	13.00
G. J. Denton	9.4	1	37	0	–	0	–	3.83
B. J. Hodge	5	1	16	0	–	0	–	3.20

At Adelaide Oval, Adelaide, October 30, 2004. VICTORIA defeated SOUTH AUSTRALIA by seven wickets.

At Bellerive Oval, Hobart, November 5, 2004. TASMANIA defeated VICTORIA by 43 runs.

VICTORIA v WESTERN AUSTRALIA

At Junction Oval, St Kilda, November 14, 2004. Western Australia won by four runs. *Toss:* Victoria. Western Australia 4 pts. *Competition debut:* T. H. Welsford, B. R. Dorey.

A rain-reduced farce ended in humiliation when Victoria's most experienced batsmen, Matthew Elliott and Brad Hodge, contrived to fall to Marcus North in the space of three balls in the dying stages of the game. Progressing towards the Duckworth/Lewis target of 108 at a run a ball after a bonus point had been within reach earlier, Victoria self-destructed. Graeme Rummans and David Hussey needed 11 runs off eight balls for victory but Hussey managed to swing twice without contact, leaving Victoria pondering what might have been. Western Australian captain Michael Hussey was named Man of the Match for the fighting half-century that lifted the total to semi-respectability. The visitors had slumped to 4 for 44 in the 11th over after play finally got under way at 2 p.m.

Match reports by NABILA AHMED.

Man of Match: M. E. K. Hussey.   *Attendance:* 1,318.

Western Australia

M. J. North c Hussey b McDonald	... 11	(18)		K. M. Harvey c Crosthwaite b Lewis	. 19	(19)
†L. Ronchi c Hodge b Lewis	... 24	(21)		P. C. Worthington not out	... 1	(2)
A. C. Voges c Moss b McDonald	 0	(8)		L-b 2, w 5	 7	
*M. E. K. Hussey c Lewis b White	... 60	(57)			—	
M. W. Goodwin c Crosthwaite b Knowles	3	(11)		(24 overs, 97 mins)	(7 wkts) 128	
S. W. Meuleman c Elliott b Knowles	. 3	(7)		Fall: 22 37 37 44 63 116 128		

G. B. Hogg, B. R. Dorey, S. J. Magoffin (did not bat).

Bowling: Lewis 5–0–23–2; McDonald 5–1–23–2; Knowles 5–0–14–2; Moss 4–0–31–0; White 5–0–35–1.

Victoria

M. T. G. Elliott b North	 54	(51)				
J. Moss c Ronchi b Harvey	 8	(10)		L-b 3, w 2, n-b 1	 6	
B. J. Hodge b North	 28	(46)			—	
D. J. Hussey not out	 3	(5)		(19 overs, 74 mins)	(3 wkts) 103	
G. C. Rummans not out	 4	(3)		Fall: 13 96 97		

*C. L. White, T. H. Welsford, †A. J. Crosthwaite, A. B. McDonald, B. A. Knowles, M. L. Lewis (did not bat).

Bowling: Harvey 4–0–19–1; Magoffin 3–1–10–0; Worthington 3–0–20–0; Dorey 3–0–16–0; Hogg 3–0–20–0; North 3–0–15–2.

Umpires: R. L. Parry and P. R. Reiffel.
TV Umpire: R. G. Patterson.

VICTORIA v NEW SOUTH WALES

At Junction Oval, St Kilda, November 21, 2004. New South Wales won by five wickets. *Toss:* Victoria. New South Wales 4 pts.

For the second time in a week, it was up to David Hussey to win the match for Victoria, and for the second time he failed. But the fault was not Hussey's for being unable to deliver at the death under pressure, but of his captain and team-mates that it should have been left to him. He had already done his part with the bat, striking a half-century to go along with the contributions of Jonathan Moss and Cameron White. Still, Victoria had fallen short of a commanding total, and Simon Katich combined with Phil Jaques to compose a promising start for NSW, who did not lose their first wicket until just 82 runs were required for victory. Injuries to Michael Lewis and Gerard Denton left White with little to choose from and the young captain opted to assign regular bowlers to the overs at hand, rather than plan who would bowl the final overs, because he did not believe the match would go that far. But three quick dismissals thwarted the progress of NSW, who needed until the final over from Hussey to secure a win. With two overs left 20 were still required, but when Shawn Bradstreet smacked two sixes and a run-out chance was botched, the Bushrangers had found yet another way to lose.

Man of Match: S. M. Katich.   *Attendance:* 2,618.

Victoria

J. Moss c Clark b Thornely	74 (106)	A. B. McDonald not out	9	(9)
M. T. G. Elliott run out (Thornely/Haddin)	27 (50)			
B. J. Hodge c Phelps b MacGill	0 (4)	L-b 3, w 7, n-b 1	11	
D. J. Hussey b Jaques b MacGill	67 (79)			
G. C. Rummans not out	54 (47)	(50 overs, 201 mins)	(5 wkts) 245	
*C. L. White c Katich b Bracken	3 (5)	Fall: 79 79 145 217 232		

†A. J. Crosthwaite, B. A. Knowles, M. L. Lewis, G. J. Denton (did not bat).

Bowling: Lee 10–1–38–0; Bracken 10–1–44–1; Bradstreet 3–0–23–0; Clark 10–1–33–0; MacGill 9–0–52–2; Thornely 4–1–19–1; Krejza 4–0–33–0.

New South Wales

P. A. Jaques c Crosthwaite b White	70 (96)	S. D. Bradstreet not out	26	(17)
*S. M. Katich b White	92 (119)			
M. J. Phelps c Hodge b McDonald	25 (27)	B 4, l-b 4, w 4	12	
†B. J. Haddin run out (Hussey/Crosthwaite)	17 (27)			
D. J. Thornely b McDonald	0 (2)	(50 overs, 204 mins)	(5 wkts) 251	
B. Lee not out	9 (12)	Fall: 164 178 213 214 217		

J. J. Krejza, N. W. Bracken, S. R. Clark, S. C. G. MacGill (did not bat).

Bowling: Lewis 1.2–0–5–0; Knowles 10–0–56–0; Denton 9.4–1–37–0; Moss 7–0–44–0; McDonald 10–0–27–2; White 10–1–58–2; Hodge 1–0–3–0; Hussey 1–0–13–0.

Umpires: G. T. D. Morrow and P. R. Reiffel.

VICTORIA v TASMANIA

At Junction Oval, St Kilda, December 12, 2004. Victoria won by 96 runs. *Toss:* Victoria. Victoria 5 pts.

Greg Shipperd's quest to locate the missing magic was halted briefly in this match, when for one day Victoria looked like their formidable selves of the previous season. It was evident in Brad Hodge's marauding century, in Cameron White's career-best bowling and in the way Victoria managed to maintain their hold on the match even after Tasmania's run-chase began with explosive pyrotechnics from openers Travis Birt and Michael Dighton. Batting on a hot, sunny morning, Victoria posted a respectable total with the help of Hodge, David Hussey and the sometimes unconvincing Jonathan Moss, who was dropped three times. Brett Geeves underlined his growing value to Tasmania with career-best figures, a reward for keeping a good line under pressure. Birt and Dighton raced to 82 in the 12th over, thrashing the bowling of Ian Hewett and Moss. But the introduction of Ian Harvey, White and Brad Knowles ruffled the Tasmanians, who lost 5 for 31 in just over 11 overs. With dark clouds creeping towards Junction Oval and rain imminent, Tasmania were forced to take risks as the Duckworth/Lewis par score increased steadily. Michael Bevan was dismissed with a sensational running, diving outfield catch by Hewett off White, and Tasmania's slim hopes of salvaging a victory went with him.

Man of Match: B. J. Hodge.   *Attendance:* 2,208.

Victoria

M. T. G. Elliott c Geeves b Wright	... 13	(23)	†A. J. Crosthwaite not out	 2	(3)
J. Moss c Birt b Geeves	 60	(61)	I. S. L. Hewett b Geeves	 10	(8)
B. J. Hodge c Griffith b Geeves	108	(111)	B. A. Knowles c Marsh b Geeves	... 2	(2)
D. J. Hussey c Griffith b Bailey	 34	(42)	L-b 1, w 3	 4	
G. C. Rummans run out (Wright)	 0	(1)			
*C. L. White b Wright	 28	(36)	(50 overs, 208 mins)　　　　(9 wkts) 277		
I. J. Harvey c Dighton b Geeves	 16	(13)	Fall: 37 97 151 151 231 263 263 275 277		

M. L. Lewis (did not bat).

Bowling: Wright 10–0–62–2; Griffith 8–0–46–0; Butterworth 10–0–54–0; Geeves 10–0–45–5; Doherty 8–1–39–0; Bailey 3–0–19–1; Marsh 1–0–11–0.

Tasmania

T. R. Birt c Moss b Lewis	 40	(35)	X. J. Doherty c Hewett b White	 8	(12)
M. G. Dighton c Moss b Harvey	 47	(46)	B. Geeves c Crosthwaite b White	... 0	(2)
M. G. Bevan c Hewett b White	 41	(58)	A. R. Griffith lbw b White	 0	(4)
†D. G. Dawson lbw b Knowles	 1	(3)			
*D. J. Marsh b Knowles	 4	(12)	L-b 1, w 4, n-b 7	 12	
G. J. Bailey run out (Hussey/Crosthwaite)	1	(13)			
D. G. Wright run out (Moss/Crosthwaite)	20	(25)	(38.5 overs, 166 mins)　　　　181		
L. R. Butterworth not out	 7	(27)	Fall: 82 92 96 108 113 158 167 177 181 181		

Bowling: Hewett 5–0–40–0; Lewis 8–1–39–1; Moss 3–0–32–0; Harvey 6–0–17–1; Knowles 6–1–24–2; White 6.5–0–15–4; Hodge 4–1–13–0.

Umpires: R. G. Patterson and J. D. Ward.
TV Umpire: R. L. Parry.

At Brisbane Cricket Ground, Brisbane, December 17, 2004. Day/night game. VICTORIA defeated QUEENSLAND by 11 runs.

VICTORIA v SOUTH AUSTRALIA

At Melbourne Cricket Ground, Melbourne, January 2, 2005. Victoria won by five wickets. *Toss:* Victoria. Victoria 4 pts.

A forceful innings from Darren Lehmann was the highlight of this match, though it was won comfortably by Victoria. As chairman of selectors Trevor Hohns looked on, the man he and his colleagues had left out of the third Test against Pakistan sent a strong message with ten powerfully struck boundaries, including three off an over from Cameron White. However, Lehmann was the first to admit his innings had been in vain as the South Australians slumped to their sixth consecutive one-day loss to Victoria. The Victorians stumbled in their first over, when Jonathan Moss played on to Shaun Tait. But a joyous partnership of 110 at five an over between an effortless Matthew Elliott and a brutal Brad Hodge laid the foundations for Victoria, although hopes of securing a bonus point by reeling in the target inside 40 overs diminished when Daniel Cullen extracted a faint edge from a driving Elliott, then lured Hodge down the pitch and bowled him through the gate. It fell to White to guide his team to victory, and he relished the opportunity to lift Cullen deep into the Southern Stand to end the match with 28 balls to spare. Lehmann made a point of criticising the pitch, which was expected to host two more one-day matches in the next week.

Man of Match: D. S. Lehmann. *Attendance:* 3,105.

South Australia

G. S. Blewett b Harvey	31	(56)	†G. A. Manou not out	5	(5)
M. J. Cosgrove c and b Lewis	7	(22)	M. F. Cleary not out	0	(1)
N. T. Adcock c Lewis b Moss	30	(44)	L-b 3, w 8	11	
*D. S. Lehmann c Crosthwaite b Lewis	92	(96)			
C. J. Ferguson c Crosthwaite b Knowles	33	(62)	(50 overs, 203 mins) (6 wkts)	227	
M. A. Higgs c Knowles b Lewis	18	(14)	Fall: 25 56 95 194 205 224		

R. J. Harris, D. J. Cullen, S. W. Tait (did not bat).

Bowling: Hewett 10–1–39–0; Lewis 10–1–40–3; Harvey 10–0–56–1; Knowles 8–0–25–1; Moss 7–0–30–1; White 5–0–34–0.

Victoria

M. T. G. Elliott c Manou b Cullen	62	(83)	I. J. Harvey not out	0	(0)
J. Moss b Tait	0	(2)			
B. J. Hodge b Cullen	52	(58)	B 1, l-b 2, w 6, n-b 1	10	
D. J. Hussey c Cleary b Cullen	38	(60)			
G. C. Rummans b Cleary	20	(25)	(45.2 overs, 181 mins) (5 wkts)	228	
*C. L. White not out	46	(46)	Fall: 4 114 125 158 222		

†A. J. Crosthwaite, I. S. L. Hewett, B. A. Knowles, M. L. Lewis (did not bat).

Bowling: Tait 10–0–44–1; Harris 9–0–43–0; Cleary 10–0–50–1; Blewett 4–0–19–0; Cullen 8.2–0–55–3; Lehmann 4–0–14–0.

Umpires: G. T. D. Morrow and P. R. Reiffel.

At WACA Ground, Perth, January 14, 2005. Day/night game. WESTERN AUSTRALIA defeated VICTORIA by 27 runs.

VICTORIA v QUEENSLAND

At Eastern Oval, Ballarat, February 6, 2005. Victoria won by 138 runs. *Toss:* Queensland. Victoria 5 pts.

The last time Victoria toured Ballarat for this fixture, an embarrassing collapse for just 65 runs raised the ire of David Hookes, the Victorian coach, who apologised to Queensland for his team's failure to provide a contest. This time around, the players, who in 2003 were housed in an old boys' home with no air-conditioning and resorted to sleeping naked on the floor in an effort to keep cool, first ensured their accommodation would be comfortable. Next, they set about conquering their country demons with a win over the best one-day team of the season, though they still left Ballarat dissatisfied, after messing up a chance to secure two bonus points and strengthen their finals hopes. In a dramatic finish in front of a good crowd, rookie wicket-keeper Adam Crosthwaite missed a catch and a stumping off the bowling of Shane Warne, allowing Queensland to avoid a double-bonus-point defeat by just one run. Still, Victoria took home one bonus point and the memory of a blistering start to the day by Matthew Elliott and Jonathan Moss, who pummelled the Queensland attack to post a first-wicket partnership of 145 at six an over, and a sensational overhead catch by Cameron White to plunge Queensland into early trouble.

Man of Match: B. J. Hodge.

Victoria

M. T. G. Elliott c Noffke b Hauritz ... 56	(71)	A. B. McDonald not out 19 (19)
J. Moss c Philipson b Hauritz 77	(88)	
B. J. Hodge not out 82	(78)	B 2, l-b 3, w 16 21
D. J. Hussey c (sub) Nash b Noffke ... 16	(21)	
*C. L. White c Seccombe b Noffke ... 0	(7)	(50 overs, 201 mins) (5 wkts) 277
I. J. Harvey c (sub) Nash b Hopes ... 6	(16)	Fall: 145 153 201 203 217

†A. J. Crosthwaite, S. K. Warne, B. A. Knowles, M. L. Lewis (did not bat).

Bowling: Johnson 10–0–72–0; Bichel 6–0–33–0; Jurgensen 5–0–36–0; Noffke 10–0–54–2; Hopes 9–0–44–1; Hauritz 10–0–33–2.

Queensland

*J. P. Maher c Warne b Lewis 6	(8)	M. G. Johnson c Crosthwaite b Warne 27 (49)
J. R. Hopes c White b Lewis 10	(14)	S. J. Jurgensen b Harvey 0 (1)
C. T. Perren c Crosthwaite b Knowles . 1	(10)	M. L. Love not out 5 (14)
C. A. Philipson c Hussey b Harvey ... 16	(28)	
†W. A. Seccombe b Harvey 43	(80)	B 4, l-b 2, w 4 10
A. J. Bichel c Crosthwaite b Harvey . 0	(3)	
A. A. Noffke c Crosthwaite b McDonald 18	(32)	(40.2 overs, 169 mins) 139
N. M. Hauritz lbw b Warne 3	(3)	Fall: 7 20 24 42 42 82 87 126 126 139

Bowling: Knowles 7–2–29–1; Lewis 10–2–30–2; Harvey 10–1–29–4; McDonald 5–0–25–1; Warne 8.2–0–20–2.

Umpires: R. L. Parry and A. P. Ward.

At Sydney Cricket Ground, Sydney, February 13, 2005. NEW SOUTH WALES defeated VICTORIA by 114 runs.

VICTORIA DOMESTIC LIMITED-OVERS RESULTS

Opponent	First Game	M	Won	Lost	No Result	Tied
Tasmania	Nov 22, 1969	24	13	10	1	0
Western Australia	Dec 30, 1969	35	6	27	2	0
New Zealanders	Jan 1, 1970	2	1	1	0	0
South Australia	Oct 18, 1970	32	21	10	0	1
Queensland	Dec 5, 1971	28	13	14	1	0
New South Wales	Dec 17, 1972	33	13	18	1	1
Australian Capital Territory	Nov 23, 1997	3	1	2	0	0
Total		157	68	82	5	2

VICTORIA RECORDS

Highest score for:	139*	D. M. Jones v New South Wales at Sydney	1986-87
Highest score against:	150*	M. L. Hayden (Queensland) at Melbourne	1998-99
Best bowling for:	5-20	G. D. Watson v Western Australia at Melbourne	1969-70
Best bowling against:	5-15	D. L. Boyd (Western Australia) at Perth	1982-83
Highest total for:	7-293	v South Australia at Adelaide	2003-04
Highest total against:	5-310	by New South Wales at North Sydney	1991-92
Lowest total for:	51	v Queensland at Ballarat	2002-03
Lowest total against:	59	by Western Australia at Melbourne	1969-70

MOST RUNS

	M	I	NO	R	HS	100s	50s	Avge	S-R
B. J. Hodge	84	82	9	2,987	118*	7	19	40.92	75.05
M. T. G. Elliott	78	76	6	2,640	118*	6	17	37.71	70.78
D. M. Jones	55	52	10	2,122	139*	4	12	50.52	74.07
I. J. Harvey	61	56	4	1,061	72	0	6	20.40	82.38
J. M. Wiener	20	20	2	1,003	108*	1	10	55.72	66.52
J. Moss	40	35	3	840	77	0	7	26.25	72.16
D. S. Berry	83	63	21	767	64*	0	1	18.26	68.36
D. J. Hussey	23	21	5	673	113	1	3	40.81	85.70
M. Klinger	25	25	4	591	80*	0	4	28.14	60.99
G. M. Watts	19	19	0	590	85	0	6	31.05	51.39

HIGHEST PARTNERSHIP FOR EACH WICKET

194	for 1st	M. T. G. Elliott and G. R. Vimpani, v New South Wales at North Sydney . .	1999-00
221	for 2nd	M. T. G. Elliott and B. J. Hodge, v Queensland at Brisbane	2003-04
227	for 3rd	B. J. Hodge and D. J. Hussey, v South Australia at Adelaide	2003-04
127	for 4th	G. N. Yallop and J. K. Moss, v Western Australia at Perth	1978-79
124*	for 5th	B. J. Hodge and S. A. J. Craig, v Australian Capital Territory at Canberra . .	1998-99
92	for 6th	B. J. Hodge and P. R. Reiffel, v New South Wales at North Sydney	1997-98
98*	for 7th	T. J. Laughlin and R. J. Bright, v New South Wales at Sydney	1976-77
73*	for 8th	A. M. Smith and A. I. C. Dodemaide, v Queensland at Melbourne	1996-97
75	for 9th	A. B. McDonald and S. M. Harwood, v Tasmania, Hobart (Bellerive)	2004-05
30	for 10th	D. W. Fleming and D. J. Saker, v Western Australia at Melbourne	1995-96

MOST WICKETS

Bowler	M	Balls	Mdns	R	W	BB	5Wi	Avge	RPO
I. J. Harvey	69	3,007	30	2,220	81	5-34	1	27.41	4.43
M. L. Lewis	47	2,265	35	1,663	64	4-41	0	25.98	4.41
D. W. Fleming	46	2,433	43	1,584	48	3-25	0	33.00	3.91
S. K. Warne	28	1,489	17	1,109	42	5-35	1	26.40	4.47
P. R. Reiffel	40	1,844	35	1,201	37	4-14	0	32.46	3.91
A. I. C. Dodemaide	38	2,019	34	1,268	35	3-11	0	36.23	3.77
M. G. Hughes	30	1,523	26	1,147	33	4-34	0	34.76	4.52
J. Moss	40	1,291	10	1,008	31	5-47	1	32.52	4.68
I. S. L. Hewett	25	1,135	14	893	29	4-22	0	30.79	4.72
C. L. White	30	1,135	7	992	28	4-15	0	35.43	5.24

MOST DISMISSALS

Wicket-keeper	M	Catches	Stumpings	Total
D. S. Berry	83	100	27	127
M. G. D. Dimattina	18	16	2	18
A. J. Crosthwaite	11	13	3	16
R. D. Robinson	17	11	4	15
P. G. Sacristani	4	8	0	8

MOST CATCHES

B. J. Hodge	34 in 84 matches	M. L. Lewis	13 in 47 matches
M. T. G. Elliott	31 in 78 matches	P. R. Reiffel	12 in 40 matches
D. M. Jones	29 in 55 matches	S. K. Warne	12 in 28 matches
I. J. Harvey	20 in 69 matches	J. D. Siddons	11 in 20 matches
D. J. Hussey	13 in 23 matches	J. Moss	11 in 40 matches

MOST APPEARANCES

84	B. J. Hodge	1993-94 – 2004-05
83	D. S. Berry	1990-91 – 2003-04
78	M. T. G. Elliott	1992-93 – 2004-05
69	I. J. Harvey	1993-94 – 2004-05
55	D. M. Jones	1981-82 – 1997-98
47	M. L. Lewis	1999-00 – 2004-05
46	D. W. Fleming	1988-89 – 2001-02
40	P. R. Reiffel	1987-88 – 2000-01
40	J. Moss	2000-01 – 2004-05
38	A. I. C. Dodemaide	1983-84 – 1997-98

WESTERN AUSTRALIA ING CUP RESULTS, 2004-05

Played 10: Won 5, Lost 5. *Finished fourth.*

WESTERN AUSTRALIA RUN-SCORERS

	M	I	NO	R	HS	100s	50s	Avge	Ct/St	S-R
M. J. North	10	10	1	412	134*	1	3	45.78	3	69.95
M. E. K. Hussey	10	10	0	383	79	0	4	38.30	0	69.89
A. C. Voges	10	10	1	287	100*	1	2	31.89	1	77.36
M. W. Goodwin	10	10	0	214	63	0	1	21.40	4	80.15
L. Ronchi	9	9	1	140	75	0	1	17.50	13/3	97.90
K. M. Harvey	10	10	0	129	28	0	0	12.90	1	64.15
G. B. Hogg	6	4	1	83	35	0	0	27.67	0	88.30
C. J. L. Rogers	4	4	0	68	43	0	0	17.00	3	51.91
S. W. Meuleman . . .	4	3	0	62	59	0	1	20.67	1	59.05
D. J. Wates	7	5	3	42	28*	0	0	21.00	0	76.36
B. A. Williams	5	4	1	37	17	0	0	12.33	1	108.82
B. Casson	4	4	1	31	18	0	0	10.33	0	63.27
B. R. Dorey	5	3	0	19	17	0	0	6.33	4	55.88
M. W. Clark	2	1	1	14	14*	0	0	–	0	116.67
J. L. Langer	2	2	0	13	8	0	0	6.50	1	27.66
R. J. Campbell	1	1	0	11	11	0	0	11.00	2	100.00
B. M. Edmondson. . .	4	3	2	6	3*	0	0	6.00	0	23.08
S. J. Magoffin	6	3	1	3	2*	0	0	1.50	4	30.00
P. C. Worthington. . .	1	1	1	1	1*	0	0	–	0	50.00

*Denotes not out.

WESTERN AUSTRALIA WICKET-TAKERS

	O	Mdns	R	W	BB	5W/i	Avge	RPO
K. M. Harvey	82	3	406	16	4-25	0	25.38	4.95
D. J. Wates	68	6	301	11	3-32	0	27.36	4.43
B. Casson.	34	1	142	8	3-34	0	17.75	4.18
B. M. Edmondson	40	4	161	7	2-34	0	23.00	4.03
S. J. Magoffin	52	6	272	6	3-40	0	45.33	5.23
G. B. Hogg	49	0	294	5	3-56	0	58.80	6.00
B. R. Dorey	42.1	6	151	4	2-27	0	37.75	3.58
M. J. North	20	0	134	4	2-15	0	33.50	6.70
B. A. Williams	36.1	3	135	4	2-45	0	33.75	3.73
M. W. Clark	15	2	59	2	2-32	0	29.50	3.93
A. C. Voges	6	0	50	0	–	0	–	8.33
M. E. K. Hussey	3	0	34	0	–	0	–	11.33
P. C. Worthington	3	0	20	0	–	0	–	6.67

WESTERN AUSTRALIA v TASMANIA

At WACA Ground, Perth, October 15, 2004. Day/night game. Tasmania won by 62 runs. *Toss:* Tasmania. Tasmania 5 pts. *Competition debut:* D. G. Dawson, S. J. Magoffin, A. C. Voges.

Steve Magoffin will long remember his first match in senior ranks. The tall right-armer, recruited from Queensland in a bid to boost West Australia's flagging fast bowling stocks, impressed in his opening spell of five overs which cost a mere ten runs. Michael Di Venuto failed to lay bat on ball to Magoffin's first 13 deliveries as he got the ball to seam dangerously. But in his second spell, Magoffin got both hands to a solid drive from Dan Marsh before spilling a return catch. Marsh was then on seven and his side 3 for 88, and he made the home side pay dearly for the error. He hammered the next delivery from Magoffin to the extra-cover boundary before flaying the attack in scoring an unbeaten century. Little went right for the home side after losing the toss. Opening batsman Scott Meuleman dislocated his left shoulder in the opening over of the contest when he landed awkwardly in the infield. Wicket-keeper Luke Ronchi, promoted to open in place of the injured Meuleman, lobbed a catch to mid-on off the first ball of the WA innings to repeat the first-ball duck of his only previous ING Cup innings, against Victoria 33 months earlier. Mike Hussey played a typically busy innings, but he lacked adequate support. Match reports by KEN CASELLAS

Man of Match: D.J. Marsh. *Attendance:* 4,582.

Tasmania

M. G. Dighton c North b Wates	22	(43)	L. R. Butterworth not out	29	(20)
M. J. Di Venuto c Voges b Wates	8	(17)			
†D. G. Dawson lbw b Clark	13	(32)	L-b 9, w 6, n-b 1	16	
M. G. Bevan c Ronchi b Clark	55	(82)			
*D. J. Marsh not out	106	(90)	(50 overs, 198 mins) (5 wkts)	270	
G. J. Bailey st Ronchi b North	21	(17)	Fall: 20 42 62 151 201		

D. G. Wright, B. Geeves, A. R. Griffith, S. P. Kremerskothen (did not bat).

Bowling: Wates 10–1–42–2; Magoffin 10–2–51–0; Clark 10–1–32–2; Harvey 9–0–57–0; Hogg 9–0–55–0; Hussey 1–0–19–0; North 1–0–5–1.

Western Australia

†L. Ronchi c Geeves b Wright	0	(1)	M. W. Clark not out	14	(12)
M. J. North c Di Venuto b Griffith	1	(6)	D. J. Wates c Dawson b Geeves	5	(12)
A. C. Voges c Butterworth b Geeves	25	(60)	S. J. Magoffin c Dighton b Wright	0	(2)
*M. E. K. Hussey c Bailey b Kremerskothen	79	(96)	L-b 4, w 18, n-b 3	25	
M. W. Goodwin c Bailey b Kremerskothen	21	(15)			
K. M. Harvey c Griffith b Kremerskothen	28	(61)	(46.5 overs, 195 mins) (9 wkts)	208	
G. B. Hogg c Wright b Marsh	10	(17)	Fall: 0 1 83 116 169 185 188 201 208		

S. W. Meuleman (did not bat).

Bowling: Wright 8.5–0–33–2; Griffith 7–1–47–1; Geeves 8–2–18–2; Butterworth 3–0–29–0; Kremerskothen 10–0–50–3; Marsh 10–0–27–1.

Umpires: B. Bennett and B. N. J. Oxenford.

At North Sydney Oval, North Sydney, October 31, 2004. WESTERN AUSTRALIA defeated NEW SOUTH WALES by three runs.

At Junction Oval, St Kilda, November 14, 2004. WESTERN AUSTRALIA defeated VICTORIA by four runs.

WESTERN AUSTRALIA v QUEENSLAND

At WACA Ground, Perth, November 19, 2004. Day/night game. Queensland won by 11 runs. *Toss:* Queensland.

A maiden domestic limited-overs century from Marcus North was not quite enough to give Western Australia victory. Visiting captain Jimmy Maher overcame the temptation to bowl first on a grassy strip, and his opening stand of 104 with James Hopes gave the Queenslanders the early impetus to push on to a big total. Maher took his tally against Western Australia in limited-overs cricket to 1,029 runs at 64.31, giving him the distinction of becoming the first batsman in the competition to score 1,000 runs against another state. Andrew Symonds hit three sixes in his bludgeoning innings, and Nathan Hauritz blazed 21 runs off the 50th over (sent down by North), which proved vital to the outcome. Brett Dorey gave further proof of his potential by dismissing both openers and, alone among the Western Australian bowlers, troubling all the batsmen. Andy Bichel removed Scott Meuleman and Adam Voges in his second over to leave the home side in trouble. Undeterred, North carried on in grand style, but Murray Goodwin departed in the 40th over after the pair had added 134 in 22 overs, and from there the target was always just out of Western Australia's grasp.

Man of Match: M. J. North.   *Attendance:* 7,138.

Queensland

J. R. Hopes b Dorey	23 (38)	B. P. Nash not out	11 (14)
*J. P. Maher c Goodwin b Dorey	72 (76)	N. M. Hauritz not out	32 (19)
A. J. Bichel c Campbell b Magoffin	35 (33)		
A. Symonds c Dorey b Hogg	77 (77)	B 2, l-b 9, w 7, n-b 2	20
S. R. Watson c Campbell b Magoffin	1 (7)		
C. T. Perren c Dorey b Hogg	19 (36)	(50 overs, 201 mins)	(7 wkts) 291
A. J. Nye c Magoffin b Hogg	1 (2)	Fall: 104 109 162 164 235 245 245	

†C. D. Hartley, A. A. Noffke (did not bat).

Bowling: Magoffin 9–1–41–2; Wates 10–1–49–0; Dorey 10–1–27–2; Harvey 6–0–61–0; Hogg 10–0–56–3; North 5–0–46–0.

Western Australia

S. W. Meuleman c Hartley b Bichel	0 (9)	K. M. Harvey run out	0 (0)
M. J. North not out	134 (153)	G. B. Hogg not out	25 (18)
A. C. Voges c Hartley b Bichel	2 (4)	B 1, l-b 3, w 19, n-b 1	24
*M. E. K. Hussey c and b Hopes	21 (40)		
M. W. Goodwin c Bichel b Noffke	63 (66)	(50 overs, 208 mins)	(6 wkts) 280
†R. J. Campbell c Nye b Watson	11 (11)	Fall: 9 11 76 210 233 236	

D. J. Wates, B. R. Dorey, S. J. Magoffin (did not bat).

Bowling: Noffke 10–2–52–1; Bichel 10–1–44–2; Watson 9–0–51–1; Hopes 7–1–42–1; Symonds 6–0–35–0; Hauritz 8–0–52–0.

Umpires: J. K. Brookes and D. L. Orchard.

At Adelaide Oval, Adelaide, December 17, 2004. Day/night game. WESTERN AUSTRALIA defeated SOUTH AUSTRALIA by seven runs.

WESTERN AUSTRALIA v NEW SOUTH WALES

At WACA Ground, Perth, January 2, 2005. Day/night game. New South Wales won by three wickets. *Toss:* Western Australia. New South Wales 4 pts. *Competition debut:* E. J. M. Cowan.

The hype preceding this match centred on the return to state cricket of Brett Lee, relieved for once of his Test 12th man duties to have some match practice. The prospect of watching the charismatic Lee at full tilt attracted a bumper crowd of 11,905. Lee did not disappoint them, as he generated ferocious pace and bounce from the WACA pitch. However, despite troubling all the batsmen, he did not earn the success he deserved and was upstaged by his team-mates – trundlers by comparison – Stuart Clark and Shawn Bradstreet. Yet it would be unfair to under-rate the performances of Clark, Bradstreet and Nathan Bracken, particularly the burly Clark, who was at his miserly best after his cheap dismissals of Marcus North and Chris Rogers. Fifties from Adam Voges and Mike Hussey helped the home side to recover, but NSW's eight maidens told their tale and the Western Australia total looked flimsy. Lee bowled some superb inswingers with the breeze and he frequently had the batsmen ducking for cover. Simon Katich, opening the innings, steered NSW towards victory with a composed, polished innings, and Ed Cowan saw them home with an over to spare. Once again Brett Dorey bowled with great economy. Playing without a spinner, NSW were penalised for a slow over-rate.

Man of Match: S. M. Katich.   *Attendance:* 11,905.

Western Australia

C.J.L. Rogers c Bollinger b Clark	5	(21)	D.J. Wates not out	3	(6)
M.J. North c and b Clark	2	(12)	B.R. Dorey b Bracken	0	(1)
A.C. Voges c Phelps b Bradstreet	52	(68)	B.M. Edmondson c Jaques b Clark	3	(9)
*M.E.K. Hussey c Haddin b Bradstreet	59	(92)			
M.W. Goodwin c Haddin b Lee	31	(44)	L-b 5, w 12	17	
†L. Ronchi lbw b Bradstreet	0	(1)			
G.B. Hogg b Clark	13	(20)	(50 overs, 221 mins)	207	
K.M. Harvey b Bracken	22	(26)	Fall: 7 111 99 133 133 168 201 201 201 207		

Bowling: Lee 10–0–52–1; Clark 10–2–24–4; Bollinger 10–2–39–0; Bracken 10–1–44–2; Bradstreet 10–1–43–3.

New South Wales

P.A. Jaques c Dorey b Wates	15	(24)	B. Lee b Harvey	1	(5)
*S.M. Katich c Ronchi b Harvey	84	(119)	N.W. Bracken not out	5	(5)
M.J. Phelps c Ronchi b Wates	4	(9)			
†B.J. Haddin c Ronchi b Edmondson	23	(35)	B 4, l-b 7, w 12, n-b 3	26	
D.J. Thornely c Ronchi b Edmondson	27	(55)			
E.J.M. Cowan not out	22	(43)	(49 overs, 204 mins) (7 wkts)	209	
S.D. Bradstreet lbw b Harvey	2	(8)	Fall: 26 33 92 165 181 191 196		

S. R. Clark, D. Bollinger (did not bat).

Bowling: Wates 10-0-45-2; Dorey 10-4-25-0; Edmondson 10-1-39-2; Harvey 9-0-29-3; Hogg 10-0-60-0.

Umpires: J. K. Brookes and A. R. Craig.

WESTERN AUSTRALIA v VICTORIA

At WACA Ground, Perth, January 14, 2005. Day/night game. Western Australia won by 27 runs. *Toss:* Western Australia. Western Australia 4 pts.

All 11 bowlers used took at least one wicket in a lacklustre contest on a flat and generally unhelpful pitch. The standard for painstaking play was set from the outset when openers Justin Langer and Luke Ronchi struggled and then failed. Langer poked five singles from 24 deliveries before cutting at Brad Knowles and being caught overhead by David Hussey at point. Then Ronchi departed for six off 25 balls when he had his off stump bent back by Ian Harvey. It was mainly thanks to a solid knock from Marcus North that the home side managed to reach 200. However, apart from Matthew Elliott, the Victorian batsmen failed against a spirited attack. Elliott, dropped at mid-off by Ben Edmondson off Brad Williams in the seventh over, held firm as wickets tumbled around him. The early breakthroughs were made by Darren Wates, who had Victoria struggling at 3 for 43 when he got a fingertip to an Elliott drive and watched the ball crash into the stumps to run out David Hussey. Beau Casson celebrated his first ING Cup appearance of the season with some sterling bowling which netted him three wickets.

Man of Match: B. Casson.   *Attendance:* 6,071.

Western Australia

*J. L. Langer c Hussey b Knowles	...	5	(25)	D. J. Wates not out	....	6	(10)
†L. Ronchi b Harvey	....	6	(25)	B. Casson not out	....	3	(1)
M. J. North b Lewis	....	71	(112)				
A. C. Voges c Warne b Moss	....	21	(28)	B 2, l-b 8, w 15	.....	25	
M. E. K. Hussey lbw b White	....	28	(29)				
M. W. Goodwin st Crosthwaite b Warne		24	(45)	(50 overs, 202 mins)	(7 wkts)	204	
K. M. Harvey b Lewis	....	15	(24)				

B. A. Williams, B. M. Edmondson (did not bat).

Fall: 16 19 56 105 155 189 201

Bowling: Knowles 10–2–29–1; Lewis 10–0–31–2; Harvey 10–2–32–1; Moss 4–0–25–1; Warne 9–0–51–1; White 7–0–26–1.

Victoria

J. Moss b Wates	....	15	(16)	S. K. Warne c Ronchi b Edmondson	.	2	(12)
M. T. G. Elliott c Goodwin b Casson	..	77	(123)	B. A. Knowles not out	....	13	(24)
B. J. Hodge b Wates	....	5	(7)	M. L. Lewis b Williams	....	5	(19)
D. J. Hussey run out (Wates)	....	1	(2)				
G. C. Rummans lbw b Casson	....	25	(38)	L-b 7, w 8	....	15	
*C. L. White st Ronchi b Casson	.....	2	(12)				
I. J. Harvey lbw b Harvey	....	14	(19)	(46.2 overs, 207 mins)		177	
†A. J. Crosthwaite lbw b Edmondson	.	3	(6)	Fall: 21 31 43 85 104 133 137 152 160 177			

Bowling: Williams 8.2–1–30–1; Wates 10–1–41–2; Edmondson 10–1–34–2; Casson 10–0–34–3; Harvey 8–0–31–1.

Umpires: B. Bennett and J. K. Brookes.

At Devonport Oval, Devonport, January 23, 2005. TASMANIA defeated WESTERN AUSTRALIA by two wickets.

WESTERN AUSTRALIA v SOUTH AUSTRALIA

At WACA Ground, Perth, February 4, 2005. Day/night game. South Australia won by 98 runs. *Toss:* South Australia. South Australia 5 pts. *Competition debut:* D. J. Harris.

Titleholders Western Australia bowed out of the competition with an inept display. They lasted only 34.1 overs as they were bundled out to lose by 98 runs, a margin that equalled their heaviest home defeat, against New South Wales in 1998. Most of the visiting batsmen made solid contributions, with Nathan Adcock and Callum Ferguson each bringing up a half-century with a six. However, neither went on to make a substantial score, each lofting catches to long-on off Beau Casson. The youthful Ferguson gave an impressive display of compact and well organised batting, and after he left, the tail added useful quick runs. With a place in the final at stake, most home fans felt that the big target was well within the capabilities of a strong batting line-up. However, after Chris Rogers fell to Paul Rofe for two, Western Australia never threatened against a vibrant attack, spearheaded by the volatile Shaun Tait, who again revealed his wonderful capacity of bowling fiery inswinging yorkers. Less ferocious, but equally efficient, was medium-pacer Ryan Harris, who struck vital blows by having both Mike Hussey and Murray Goodwin caught behind for low scores. It was a fine team effort by South Australia.

Man of Match: R. J. Harris. *Attendance:* 4,097.

South Australia

G. S. Blewett c Ronchi b Williams	... 22	(24)	......R. J. Harris run out (Harvey) 26
		(30)	
*†G. A. Manou c Goodwin b Williams	17	(21)	D. J. Cullen not out 13 (13)
N. T. Adcock c Harvey b Casson	 53	(82)	S. W. Tait not out 1 (4)
M. A. Higgs c Ronchi b Edmondson	... 24	(30)	L-b 2, w 4 6
C. J. Ferguson c Goodwin b Casson	64	(60)	—
D. J. Harris c Ronchi b Casson	 5	(6)	(50 overs, 206 mins) (8 wkts) 260
S. B. Tubb c Rogers b Edmondson	... 29	(30)	Fall: 33 44 80 161 168 201 236 255

P. C. Rofe (did not bat).

Bowling: Williams 10–0–45–2; Wates 10–2–36–0; Edmondson 10–0–64–2; Harvey 10–0–56–0; Casson 10–0–57–3.

Western Australia

C. J. L. Rogers c Blewett b Rofe	 2	(9)	D. J. Wates lbw b Tait 0 (3)
†L. Ronchi c Adcock b Tait	 29	(22)	B. A. Williams lbw b Cullen 17 (16)
M. J. North c Manou b Blewett	 35	(46)	B. M. Edmondson not out 3 (15)
*M. E. K. Hussey c Manou b R. J. Harris	7	(14)	
M. W. Goodwin c Manou b R. J. Harris	5	(12)	L-b 5, w 9, n-b 1 15
A. C. Voges c R. J. Harris b Rofe	 31	(39)	—
K. M. Harvey c D. J. Harris b Blewett	. 0	(3)	(34.1 overs, 150 mins) 162
B. Casson lbw b Tait	 18	(28)	Fall: 6 37 59 88 88 88 113 121 141 162

Bowling: Tait 10–0–46–3; Rofe 5.1–0–30–2; Harris 10–1–38–2; Blewett 6–1–22–2; Cullen 3–0–21–1.

Umpires: B. Bennett and J. K. Brookes.

At Brisbane Cricket Ground, Brisbane, February 11, 2005. Day/night game. WESTERN AUSTRALIA defeated QUEENSLAND by 57 runs.

WA DOMESTIC LIMITED-OVERS RESULTS

Opponent	First Game	M	Won	Lost	No Result	Tied
South Australia	Nov 22, 1969	37	24	13	0	0
Victoria	Dec 30, 1969	35	27	6	2	0
Tasmania	Nov 4, 1970	29	21	7	1	0
New Zealanders	Jan 31, 1971	3	2	1	0	0
Queensland	Feb 6, 1971	34	17	15	2	0
New South Wales	Nov 27, 1971	37	18	18	0	1
Australian Capital Territory	Jan 2, 1998	3	3	0	0	0
Total		178	112	60	5	1

WA RECORDS

Highest score for:	167	M. W. Goodwin v New South Wales at Perth	2000-01
Highest score against:	187	J. P. Maher (Queensland) at Brisbane	2003-04
Best bowling for:	5-15	D. L. Boyd v Victoria at Perth	1982-83
Best bowling against:	5-23	R. J. McCurdy (South Australia) at Adelaide	1984-85
Highest total for:	5-328	v New South Wales at North Sydney	2004-05
Highest total against:	4-405	by Queensland at Brisbane	2003-04
Lowest total for:	59	v Victoria at Melbourne	1969-70
Lowest total against:	62	by Queensland at Perth	1976-77

MOST RUNS

	M	I	NO	R	HS	100s	50s	Avge	S-R
J.L. Langer	80	76	6	2,828	146	6	19	40.40	68.61
M.E.K. Hussey	75	71	10	2,603	106	3	21	42.67	75.01
T.M. Moody	75	71	12	2,004	102*	2	14	33.97	72.22
D.R. Martyn	53	50	7	1,880	140	3	13	43.72	73.90
G.R. Marsh	38	37	7	1,596	110	3	12	53.20	62.30
R.J. Campbell	70	68	1	1,475	108	1	6	22.01	85.21
M.W. Goodwin	50	46	7	1,465	167	1	10	37.56	85.12
S.M. Katich	38	37	3	1,178	118	2	8	34.65	71.31
M.R.J. Veletta	42	39	8	1,077	105*	1	8	34.74	62.18
A.C. Gilchrist	36	33	3	980	115	1	7	32.67	87.34

HIGHEST PARTNERSHIP FOR EACH WICKET

171	for 1st	G.R. Marsh and M.W. McPhee, v Queensland at Perth	1990-91
188*	for 2nd	J.L. Langer and D.R. Martyn, v Victoria at Melbourne	1997-98
257	for 3rd	M.W. Goodwin and M.E.K. Hussey, v New South Wales at Perth	2000-01
167	for 4th	M.E.K. Hussey and S.M. Katich, v Victoria at Perth	2001-02
129	for 5th	J.L. Langer and W.S. Andrews, v Queensland at Brisbane	1992-93
173	for 6th	M.E. Hussey and G.B. Hogg, v Victoria at Melbourne	1999-00
111*	for 7th	R.W. Marsh and B. Yardley, v New South Wales at Sydney	1973-74
106*	for 8th	A.C. Gilchrist and B.P. Julian, v New South Wales at Sydney	1995-96
57	for 9th	D.R. Martyn and B.P. Julian, v Queensland at Brisbane	1997-98
43	for 10th	P.C. Worthington and M.W. Clark, v New South Wales at Perth	2002-03

MOST WICKETS

Bowler	M	Balls	Mdns	R	W	BB	5W/i	Avge	RPO
K.M. Harvey	80	3,487	33	2,794	103	4-8	0	27.13	4.81
J.Angel	74	3,686	52	2,525	94	5-16	2	26.46	4.11
T.M. Moody	75	3,205	41	2,131	70	4-30	0	30.40	3.99
B.P. Julian	54	2,318	19	1,779	59	4-41	0	30.15	4.60
K.H. MacLeay	38	1,896	32	1,165	53	5-30	1	21.98	3.69
D.K. Lillee	26	1,505	32	766	48	4-21	0	15.96	3.05
G.B. Hogg	65	1,704	4	1,461	48	4-50	0	30.44	5.14
B.A. Williams	31	1,536	17	1,105	47	4-29	0	23.51	4.32
T.M. Alderman	35	1,938	34	1,169	40	4-14	0	29.23	3.62
J. Stewart	32	1,564	9	1,117	36	4-34	0	31.03	4.29

MOST DISMISSALS

Wicket-keeper	M	Catches	Stumpings	Total
R.J. Campbell	47	82	6	88
A.C. Gilchrist	36	64	6	70
R.W. Marsh	33	50	1	51
T.J. Zoehrer	35	40	4	44
L. Ronchi	11	16	3	19

MOST CATCHES

M.E.K. Hussey	40 in 75 matches	M.R.J. Veletta	17 in 40 matches
J.L. Langer	35 in 80 matches	M.W. Goodwin	17 in 50 matches
G.B. Hogg	27 in 65 matches	B.P. Julian	16 in 54 matches
T.M. Moody	27 in 75 matches	D.R. Martyn	16 in 53 matches
G.R. Marsh	20 in 38 matches	R.J. Inverarity	14 in 19 matches

MOST APPEARANCES

80	J. L. Langer	1991-92 - 2004-05	
80	K. M. Harvey	1994-95 - 2004-05	
75	T. M. Moody	1985-86 - 2000-01	
75	M. E. K. Hussey	1996-97 - 2004-05	
74	J. Angel	1992-93 - 2003-04	
70	R. J. Campbell	1992-93 - 2004-05	
65	G. B. Hogg	1993-94 - 2004-05	
54	B. J. Julian	1991-92 - 2000-01	
53	D. R. Martyn	1991-92 - 2003-04	
50	M. W. Goodwin	1994-95 - 2004-05	

Commonwealth Bank Centre of Excellence, 2004-05

by STEPHEN GRAY

At one point, the 2004 year at the Commonwealth Bank Centre of Excellence (formerly the Commonwealth Bank Cricket Academy) resembled the result of an over-zealous building redevelopment. The Centre – now in the second year at Allan Border Field in Brisbane – was like a building façade remnant left by a demolition firm that couldn't quite get the necessary planning permission to deliver a clean site.

The 2004 scholarship year went smoothly enough, applying the finishing touches to a number of players who went on to make noteworthy contributions for their states during the season. But once the scholarship intake had returned to their homes, the Centre underwent a major clear-out in management, with the head coach, Bennett King, and a host of senior coaches moving on.

King, who had been headhunted by Cricket Australia as the man to transform the Academy into a wider-ranging centre of cricketing excellence, was finally enticed to accept the job as West Indies coach. He took with him the well-respected scholarship coach David Moore as his assistant. Others to depart included former Test paceman Damien Fleming, who returned to Melbourne, and senior coach John Harmer, who took on the job as Northern Territory Institute of Sport cricket coach. As one observer quipped, it was excellent that the Centre was helping to develop pathways for coaches, but it was a shame that they all led away from it.

However, by the time the 2005 scholarship intake arrived, the coaching staff had been extensively retooled, with former South Australian wicket-keeper Tim Nielsen as the new head coach, experienced first-class players Jamie Siddons and Dene Hills and ex-Tasmanian Tigers coach Brian McFadyen in senior roles, and up-and-coming coaches Richard McInnes and Mark Sorrell also in the group.

The appointment of retired Australian women's captain and experienced administrator Belinda Clark as the new general manager, replacing the foundation boss Trevor Robertson midway through 2005, completed the redevelopment. The impending delivery of new facilities at Queensland Cricket's Albion headquarters will further enhance this stage of the transformation.

On the playing front, the outstanding graduates from 2004 included South Australian off-spinner Daniel (later to become better known as Dan) Cullen and Western Australian duo Adam Voges and Ben Edmondson, who enjoyed his return home to Brisbane after the young man had opted to "go west" in 2003. The strike-rate for scholars who went on to play either first-class or domestic one-day cricket for their states was impressive. They included Tasmanian duo Travis Birt and George Bailey, New South Wales paceman Doug Bollinger (who took an ING Cup hat-trick), South Australian leg-spinner Cullen Bailey and batsmen Tom Plant and Ken Skewes, Queensland leg-spinner Ryan Le Loux, Victorian all-rounder Brad Knowles, Western Australian batsman Craig Simmons and New South Wales off-spinner Jason Krezja.

The 2004 scholarship year was: Cullen Bailey (S Aust), George Bailey (Tas), Travis Birt (Tas), Aiden Blizzard (Vic), Doug Bollinger (NSW), Ryan Broad (Qld), Daniel Cullen (S Aust), Brendan Drew (NSW), Ben Edmondson (W Aust), Matthew Harrison (Vic), Aaron Heal (W Aust), Cameron Huckett (Vic), Brad Knowles (Vic), Jason Krezja (NSW), Ryan Le Loux (Qld), Darren McNees (ACT), Tim Paine (Tas), Steve Paulsen (Qld), Jim Plant (S Aust), Tom Plant (S Aust), Adam Rhynehart (ACT), Peter Siddle (Vic), Craig Simmons (W Aust), Ken Skewes (S Aust), Grant Sullivan (Qld) and Adam Voges (W Aust).

Continuing the recent trend to expose as many of the next potential generation of Australian cricketers to the vagaries of playing on the sub-continent, a touring party was selected to tour India: Adam Voges (captain), Tom Plant, Craig Simmons, Travis Birt, Ryan Broad, Jason Krezja, Matthew Harrison, Tim Paine, Dan Cullen, Brad Knowles, Darren McNees, Doug Bollinger, Brendan Drew, Jim Plant and Brett Lee, who was at the MRF Pace Academy in India around the same time, also featured in games on tour.

The side played seven games in Bangalore and Chennai, a mixture of two-day and one-day fixtures, and there were some notable individual efforts. Tasmanian thrasher Travis Birt hit 101 from 104 balls in the opening game, alongside Tom Plant's 98. Plant and his brother Jim also produced good scores in the last game against an MRF XI, Tom scoring 59 and Jim 65 not out. Cullen's 5 for 19 from 10.2 overs against the National Cricket Academy Under-19s underscored his potential.

The 2005 residential scholarship holders are: Michael Shaw (ACT), Stewart Heaney (ACT), Aaron Bird (NSW), Murray Creed (NSW), James Packman (NSW), Nathan Rimmington (Qld), Greg Chiesa (Qld), Nathan Reardon (Qld), Gary Putland (SA), Ken Skewes (SA), Ryan Harris (SA), Chris Duval (SA), Jason Shelton (TAS), Dane Anderson (TAS), David Dawson (TAS), Aiden Blizzard (Vic), Clinton McKay (Vic), Peter Nevill (Vic), Carl Sandri (Vic), Liam Davis (WA), Clint Heron (WA), Justin Coetzee (WA) and Hayden Patrizi (WA).

Cricket Australia Cup, 2004-05

by KEN PIESSE

As an increasing number of Australia's most athletic teenagers prefer to specialise in the football codes, cricket was glad to win one back with Nick Jewell's re-emergence in Victoria's senior team in 2005. The ex-Caulfield Grammarian had always preferred the summer game, but the opportunity to play at Australian Football League level, albeit temporarily, with Richmond was irresistible and set his cricket advancement on hold. "The opportunity to be on a league [AFL] list was too good not to take up and I learned so much from the experience," he said. "Now with some places opening up in the first-class side, I hope to play more of a regular role with the No. 1 team."

Having previously promised much opening for Victoria in the ING Cup, Jewell, 27, finally showed he was ready for the step up to four-day cricket. He hit four centuries before Christmas, three for the Victorian 2nd XI in the Cricket Australia Cup and another for his powerful club team St Kilda. With 461 runs at an average of 65-plus, Jewell was the leading run-maker for the unbeaten Victorians, who won three of their four games outright. In Victoria's final Pura Cup fixture of the season, against eventual champions New South Wales in Sydney, Jewell made 80 and 3. He had been Victoria's 12th man in the three previous fixtures.

The season's leading run-maker, Luke Williams, 25, regained a place in the senior South Australian team with some big scores, including an eight-hour 221 against Tasmania at Adelaide Oval No. 2, and 172 against ACT on a benign Manuka Oval, a game in which he shared a 360-run third-wicket stand with Mark Higgs (221*).

There was another double-centurion, too, during the series: ACT left-hander Cade Brown, who made 223 batting at No. 3 against the Queensland Academy of Sport XI, which included Damien MacKenzie, Mitch Johnson and Scott Brant, at Allan Border Field.

Originally from Wodonga, Brown, 28, represented ACT in the interstate limited-overs competition in 1999-00, and has also played for the Australian Country XI. His team-mate Duncan Brede had a fine double of 42 and 151 against the South Australia 2nd XI in Canberra. Having tried Melbourne club cricket, he has been happy to return home, where his batting is as valuable as his polished work behind the stumps.

The competition's leading wicket-taker was South Australia's Chris Duval, who mixes baseball with his cricket. He produced the finest figures of the season with 7 for 24 against Western Australia 2nd XI at Fletcher Park, Perth. Four of the Western Australian batsmen fell for ducks to Duval, who bowled unchanged for almost two hours on the opening day. He was immediately selected in South Australia's one-day team. His 20-year-old team-mate Cullen Bailey, a leg-spinner, also showed good form.

Another promising paceman promoted to ING Cup ranks was athletic Victorian right-armer Brad Knowles, who had one game late in 2003-04 before playing nine of Victoria's ten one-day matches in 2004-05. He took ten wickets in three 2nd XI appearances, including 4 for 55 against Tasmania at Bellerive. His Victorian team-mate Tim Welsford, with 14 wickets and 100 runs, continued to press his claims as a bowling all-rounder. In his solitary appearance for Victoria in a one-day game against West Indies, he dismissed the great Brian Lara, much to the jubilation of a cohort of his mates down from Bendigo for the occasion.

Queensland's wicket-keeper/batsman Chris Hartley, with 77 and 68, had a fine double against the NSW 2nd XI at Drummoyne Oval. He hit five sixes in his first innings, and 17 fours for the match. The NSW teenage pace bowler Moises Henriques, winner of Cricket Australia's Rexona Scholarship and an Australian Under-19 World Cup representative in 2004, avoided Hartley's flashing blade to take 3 for 46 from 17 overs. Aaron Bird, another emerging young Blue, also claimed three wickets.

Tasmania's wicket-keeper/batsman Tim Paine, who captained the Australians at the 2004 Under-19 World Cup, continued to press his claims for senior selection with 15 dismissals in three matches. Best of the fieldsmen was Jewell, with eight catches in the slips. Zimbabwean Sean Ervine added an international touch by appearing several times for the Western Australia 2nd XI. His best return was 4 for 79 from 18 overs against the Victorians on a flat Princes Park No. 2 wicket.

The round-robin style of the competition will see every team play each other home and away over a three-year period. Western Australia and NSW, which played only two official games in 2004-05, will have more fixtures in 2005-06 and 2006-07. With the scheduling imbalance, no Cup was awarded in 2004-05. Some extra 2nd XI matches were played outside the competition, Victoria's match against NSW being ruined by rain.

CRICKET AUSTRALIA CUP POINTS TABLE, 2004-05

	Played	WO	WI	D	LI	LO	T	Points	Quotient
Victoria 2nd XI	4	3	1	–	–	–	–	20	1.394
New South Wales 2nd XI	4	1	1	–	1	1	–	10	1.267
Queensland Academy of Sport	4	1	2	–	–	1	–	10	1.021
South Australia 2nd XI	4	1	1	–	–	2	–	10	1.006
Tasmania 2nd XI	4	1	1	–	1	1	–	8	0.852
Western Australia 2nd XI	4	1	–	–	1	2	–	6	0.952
Australian Capital Territory	4	1	–	–	1	2	–	6	0.629

Quotient: Runs per wicket scored divided by runs per wicket conceded

MOST RUNS, 2004-05

	M	I	NO	R	HS	100s	50s	Avge	S-R
L. Williams (S Aust)	3	6	0	591	221	2	2	98.50	55.18
C. Brown (ACT)	4	7	0	479	223	1	3	68.43	78.01
N. Jewell (Vic)	4	8	1	461	138*	3	0	65.86	64.75
C. D. Hartley (Qld)	4	7	1	388	85	0	4	64.67	51.46
D. M. Payne (Qld)	4	8	0	372	123	1	1	46.50	63.81
D. J. Anderson (Tas)	4	8	1	349	122	1	3	49.86	78.78
C. J. Simmons (W Aust)	4	8	1	340	137	1	2	48.57	54.49
J. Cox (Tas)	2	4	0	312	162	2	0	78.00	63.41
D. J. Richards (ACT)	4	7	0	290	107	1	2	41.43	51.88
R. J. G. Lockyear (Tas)	4	8	0	277	73	0	3	34.63	51.11
M. G. Dighton (Tas)	2	3	0	276	163	1	1	92.00	62.59
A. C. Voges (W Aust)	3	5	0	254	111	1	1	50.80	59.07
S. W. Meuleman (W Aust)	4	8	1	252	93*	0	2	36.00	61.02
T. C. Plant (S Aust)	3	6	1	246	88*	0	2	49.20	64.91
L. M. Stevens (Qld)	2	4	1	242	105	1	1	80.67	78.32
S. P. Heaney (ACT)	4	7	1	241	72	0	3	40.17	57.38
R. A. Broad (Qld)	3	6	0	227	100	1	1	37.83	44.34
S. J. Paulsen (Qld)	3	6	1	224	102*	1	0	44.80	58.64
M. A. Higgs (S Aust)	1	1	0	221	221	1	0	221.00	77.82
B. J. Rohrer (NSW)	3	5	0	217	85	0	3	43.40	53.58

* Denotes not out.

MOST WICKETS, 2004-05

	M	O	Mdns	R	W	BB	5W/i	10W/m	Avge	Balls/W
C.J. Duval (S Aust) ..	4	132	28	389	16	7-24	1	0	24.31	49.50
T.H. Welsford (Vic) ..	4	92	27	277	14	3-18	0	0	19.79	39.43
M.A. Cameron (NSW)	3	72.3	22	211	13	5-34	1	0	16.23	33.46
B.W. Hilfenhaus (Tas)	3	120.5	32	391	13	4-83	0	0	30.08	55.77
J.L. Shelton (Tas)	4	83.2	11	401	13	4-91	0	0	30.85	38.46
B. Casson (W Aust)	4	112.5	16	406	13	4-114	0	0	31.23	52.08
A.C. Bird (NSW)	4	98	27	273	12	3-18	0	0	22.75	49.00
C.B. Bailey (S Aust) ..	4	139.3	25	472	12	4-94	0	0	39.33	69.75
T.P. Kelly (S Aust) ...	4	129.4	26	518	11	3-46	0	0	47.09	70.73
D.R. MacKenzie (Qld)	3	95	25	267	11	4-36	0	0	24.27	51.82
D. Bollinger (NSW) ..	3	72.3	16	228	11	4-17	0	0	20.73	39.55
R.N. Le Loux (Qld) ..	4	108.3	22	354	11	4-45	0	0	32.18	59.18
M.G. Johnson (Qld) ..	2	59.3	7	187	10	6-41	1	0	18.70	35.70
B.A. Knowles (Vic) ..	3	41	5	182	10	4-55	0	0	18.20	24.60
B.R. Dorey (W Aust) .	3	88	18	279	9	4-28	0	0	31.00	58.67
J.J. Krejza (NSW) ...	4	67.4	15	256	9	4-86	0	0	28.44	45.11
A.J. Heading (ACT) ..	3	71.1	11	298	8	3-45	0	0	37.25	53.38
K.S. Pickering (Tas) .	2	79	13	303	8	3-57	0	0	37.88	59.25

NEW SOUTH WALES 2nd XI v VICTORIA 2nd XI

At Bankstown Memorial Oval, Bankstown, September 27, 28, 29, 30, 2004. Victoria 2nd XI won by 20 runs. *Toss:* Victoria 2nd XI.

Close of play: First day, New South Wales 2nd XI (1) 8-109 (Bradstreet 4, Nash 4); 2nd day, Victoria 2nd XI (2); Third day, New South Wales 2nd XI (2) 7-103 (Bird 12, Nash 5).

Victoria 2nd XI

J.L. Arnberger c Smith b Nash	0	– c Zammit b Nash	3
B.R. Joseland b Bird	5	– c Bradstreet b Nash	4
N. Jewell lbw b Bollinger	19	– b Bird	0
A.C. Blizzard lbw b Nash	4	– c Bird b Bradstreet	25
G.C. Rummans b Bollinger	5	– b Nash	24
M. Klinger c Wallace b Bollinger	6	– lbw b Bollinger	10
*†P.J. Roach lbw b Bollinger	6	– c Krejza b Bird	56
T.H. Welsford b Bird	9	– c Mott b Nash	21
B.A. Knowles not out	4	– c Cowan b Krejza	0
S.M. Harwood b Bird	0	– c Cowan b Lambert	33
B.D. Harrop b Krejza	10	– not out	2
B 1, l-b 7, w 16, n-b 3	27	B 8, l-b 3, w 2, n-b 1	14

(38.2 overs, 176 mins) 95
Fall: 11 18 24 49 54 65 72 77 79 95

(58.4 overs, 258 mins) 192
Fall: 6 7 10 42 67 80 108 123 187 192

D.P. Nannes (did not bat).

Bowling: *First Innings*—Bird 11–6–18–3; Nash 12–4–25–2; Bollinger 8–1–17–4; Lambert 5–0–23–0; Bradstreet 2–1–4–0; Krejza 0.2–0–0–1. *Second Innings*—Bird 10.4–3–30–2; Nash 13–3–23–4; Bollinger 12–2–64–1; Lambert 5–0–21–1; Bradstreet 3.4–1–8–1; Krejza 11.2–3–30–1; Zammit 3–0–5–0.

New South Wales 2nd XI

D. P. Wallace c Roach b Welsford	38	– c Roach b Harrop	28
G. M. Lambert lbw b Harwood	0	– b Nannes	25
E. J. M. Cowan c Jewell b Knowles	18	– b Harrop	0
M. P. Mott b Knowles	3	– b Nannes	0
J. J. Krejza b Harwood	13	– b Welsford	6
D. T. Christian lbw b Harwood	6	– b Harwood	15
†D. Smith lbw b Nannes	9	– lbw b Harwood	2
*S. D. Bradstreet lbw b Harwood	9		
A. C. Bird lbw b Nannes	0	– (8) c Blizzard b Nannes	16
D. A. Nash c Roach b Nannes	15	– (9) not out	26
L. A. Zammit not out	0	– (10) c Roach b Harrop	8
D. Bollinger		– b Nannes	1
L-b 3, w 4, n-b 7	14	L-b 10, w 2, n-b 3	15

(41.2 overs, 177 mins)   125
Fall: 2 50 71 71 83 101 101 101 121 125

(42.3 overs, 194 mins)   142
Fall: 50 50 53 58 82 82 93 117 139 142

Bowling: *First Innings*—Harwood 13–6–26–4; Nannes 8.2–1–36–3; Welsford 9–1–20–1; Harrop 5–0–29–0; Knowles 6–1–11–2. *Second Innings*—Harwood 10–5–18–2; Knowles 8–0–51–0; Harrop 9–1–17–3; Nannes 9.3–1–27–4; Welsford 6–1–19–1.

Umpires: R. D. Goodger and R. J. Tucker.

QUEENSLAND ACADEMY OF SPORT v TASMANIA 2nd XI

At Allan Border Field, Albion, October 11, 12, 13, 14, 2004. Match drawn. *Toss:* Queensland Academy of Sport.

Close of play: First day, Queensland Academy of Sport (1) 8-368 (Le Loux 0); Second day, Tasmania 2nd XI (1) 9-241 (Downton 3); Third day, Tasmania 2nd XI (2) 0-38 (Paine 25, Harris 12).

Queensland Academy of Sport

R. A. Broad lbw b Downton	18	– (2) c Paine b Hilfenhaus	67
D. M. Payne lbw b Hilfenhaus	4	– (1) c Paine b Pickering	31
B. P. Nash lbw b Kremerskothen	46	– c Paine b Downton	23
C. A. Philipson c Kremerskothen b Pickering	30	– c Kremerskothen b Downton	1
S. J. Paulsen c Kremerskothen b Pickering	48	– not out	102
S. J. Farrell c Clingeleffer b Downton	5	– c Paine b Downton	7
*†C. D. Hartley c Lockyear b Downton	85	– c Clingeleffer b Harris	34
L. M. Stevens c Clingeleffer b Hilfenhaus	105	– not out	41
R. N. Le Loux b Hilfenhaus	1		
D. R. MacKenzie c Cunningham b Hilfenhaus	9		
B. P. Boardman not out	0		
L-b 12, w 1, n-b 14	27	B 3, n-b 3	6

(103.5 overs, 396 mins)   378
Fall: 8 44 106 117 150 184 362 368 369 378

(79 overs, 293 mins)   (6 wkts dec)   312
Fall: 42 94 104 152 159 240

G. S. Chiesa (did not bat).

Bowling: *First Innings*—Downton 24–7–83–3; Hilfenhaus 27.5–9–83–4; Pickering 21–5–76–2; Kremerskothen 12–3–26–1; Harris 13–2–57–0; Shelton 6–2–41–0. *Second Innings*—Hilfenhaus 20–2–66–1; Pickering 18–3–89–1; Downton 14–3–37–3; Kremerskothen 8–2–30–0; Shelton 5–1–30–0; Lockyear 4–0–16–0; Harris 10–1–41–1.

Tasmania Second XI

T. D. Paine c Hartley b MacKenzie	45	– c Hartley b Nash	92
B. L. Harris c Broad b Boardman	14	– c Hartley b Nash	13
T. R. Birt c Le Loux b Stevens	59	– run out (Paulsen)	54
*S. P. Kremerskothen st Hartley b Stevens	4		
R. J. G. Lockyear c Stevens b Le Loux	54	– (4) c and b Le Loux	73
†S. G. Clingeleffer lbw b Le Loux	2	– (5) c Le Loux b Stevens	2
G. T. Cunningham c Hartley b MacKenzie	34	– c Philipson b Nash	27
D. J. Anderson c and b Chiesa	2	– c Payne b Stevens	71
A. G. Downton not out	3	– (6) run out (Farrell)	3
J. L. Shelton lbw b MacKenzie	2	– (9) c Chiesa b Le Loux	9
K. S. Pickering b MacKenzie	0	– not out	3
B. W. Hilfenhaus		– (10) not out	40
B 1, l-b 7, w 3, n-b 11	22	B 7, l-b 6, w 1, n-b 1	15

(85.3 overs, 323 mins)   241   (118 overs, 408 mins)   (9 wkts) 402

Fall: 28 109 113 176 181 207 222 237 241 241   Fall: 48 138 207 212 222 273
273 296 375

Bowling: *First Innings*—MacKenzie 22.3–3–56–4; Boardman 12–2–42–1; Nash 13–4–25–0; Stevens 14–3–41–2; Chiesa 11–1–50–1; Le Loux 13–8–19–2. *Second Innings*—MacKenzie 13–7–26–0; Nash 32–6–86–3; Le Loux 31–7–111–2; Stevens 26–6–94–2; Chiesa 16–2–72–0.

Umpires: A. R. Curran and N. S. McNamara.

SOUTH AUSTRALIAN 2nd XI v NEW SOUTH WALES 2nd XI

At Adelaide Oval No 2, Adelaide, October 11, 12, 13, 14, 2004. New South Wales won by 187 runs. *Toss:* New South Wales 2nd XI.

Close of play: First day, South Australia 2nd XI (1) 2-45 (T. C. Plant 24); Second day, New South Wales 2nd XI (2) 0-62 (Smith 42, Wallace 19); Third day, South Australia 2nd XI (2) 2-67 (Miller 12, J. W. Plant 5).

New South Wales 2nd XI

†D. Smith c J. W. Plant b Kelly	2	– c J. W. Plant b Miller	88
D. P. Wallace c Smith b Duval	6	– run out	124
E. J. M. Cowan c T. C. Plant b Harris	2	– b Duval	77
B. J. Rohrer lbw b Duval	14	– lbw b Miller	5
J. J. Krejza c Harris b Kelly	75		
*M. P. Mott c J. W. Plant b Harris	43	– (8) not out	55
D. T. Christian c J. W. Plant b Bailey	2	– (6) lbw b Duval	3
S. N. J. O'Keefe c Littlewood b Kelly	19	– (7) c T. C. Plant b Duval	45
A. C. Bird c T. C. Plant b Weeks	5	– b Kelly	10
L. A. Zammit c Weeks b Bailey	26	– not out	6
D. Bollinger not out	12		
D. S. Wotherspoon		– (5) run out (Skewes)	1
L-b 13, w 2, n-b 7	22	L-b 12, n-b 9	21

(79.3 overs, 312 mins)   228   (95 overs, 367 mins)   (8 wkts dec) 435

Fall: 8 8 10 55 146 155 159 169 189 228   Fall: 129 284 293 296 299 314 402 417

M. A. Cameron (did not bat).

Bowling: *First Innings*—Kelly 21–9–46–3; Duval 15–3–37–2; Harris 17–8–49–2; Weeks 19–3–59–1; Bailey 7.3–2–24–2. *Second Innings*—Kelly 14–2–57–1; Weeks 11–4–37–0; Duval 20–4–88–3; Harris 15–3–57–0; Miller 22–2–95–2; Bailey 13–1–89–0.

South Australia 2nd XI

T. C. Plant lbw b Cameron	63	– c Cowan b Bollinger	3*
*J. K. Smith b Bollinger	0	– c Cowan b Bollinger	12
M. C. Miller c Cowan b Krejza	15	– c Cowan b O'Keefe	3*
W. D. Thomas c Christian b Zammit	20	– (5) b Bollinger	4(
K. J. Skewes c Cowan b O'Keefe	41	– (6) lbw b Cameron	24
M. C. Weeks c Rohrer b Cameron	11	– (7) b Cameron	(
M. Littlewood lbw b Zammit	55	– (8) c Smith b Cameron	(
R. J. Harris c Christian b Krejza	17	– (9) c Smith b Cameron	2
†J. W. Plant b Bollinger	20	– (4) c Mott b Bird	22
T. P. Kelly b Bollinger	4	– not out	22
C. J. Duval not out	0		
C. B. Bailey		– c Christian b Zammit	6
B 1, l-b 1, w 6, n-b 7	15	B 6, l-b 2, w 2, n-b 7	17
(94.3 overs, 351 mins)	261	(78.5 overs, 295 mins)	215

Fall: 1 45 96 123 152 160 192 256 258 261

Fall: 31 55 108 125 163 163 163 175 192 215

Bowling: *First Innings*—Bollinger 20.3–9–36–3; Bird 15–1–56–0; Krejza 14–3–46–2; Cameron 13–2–34–2; Zammit 17–4–38–2; O'Keefe 14.4–4–44–1; Mott 1–0–5–0. *Second Innings*—Bollinger 18–4–42–3; Bird 15.4–4–53–1; Cameron 16–6–52–4; Zammit 10.5–3–25–1; O'Keefe 19–9–35–1.

Umpires: A. R. Collins and K. D. Perrin.

WESTERN AUSTRALIA 2nd XI v SOUTH AUSTRALIA 2nd XI

At Fletcher Oval, Fletcher, October 25, 26, 27, 28, 2004. South Australia 2nd XI won by 132 runs. *Toss:* Western Australia 2nd XI.

Close of play: First day, South Australia 2nd XI (2) 0–47 (Williams 16, Deitz 20); Second day, South Australia 2nd XI (2) 7–351 (Kelly 26, Thomas 22); Third day, Western Australia 2nd XI (2) 7–246 (Ervine 25, Casson 3).

South Australia 2nd XI

†S. A. Deitz b Dorey	10	– (2) lbw b Casson	81
L. Williams b Dorey	19	– (1) lbw b Casson	80(
*N. T. Adcock c Ronchi b James	12	– c (sub) L. C. Swards b Ervine	53
W. D. Thomas c and b Worthington	0	– c Simmons b Casson	0
K. J. Skewes c Ronchi b Worthington	27	– c Ronchi b Worthington	46
M. Littlewood c Ronchi b Dorey	13	– (7) c Heal b Ervine	12
S. B. Tubb c Ronchi b Dorey	8	– c Ronchi b Howman	15
T. P. Kelly b Casson	28	– (8) c Ronchi b Worthington	33
O. C. Thomas c Simmons b Ervine	1	– (9) not out	55
C. B. Bailey lbw b Casson	4	– (10) lbw b Casson	4
C. J. Duval not out	1	– (11) c Casson b Worthington	28
B 5, l-b 4, w 2, n-b 2	13	B 4, l-b 10, w 5	19
(57.5 overs, 232 mins)	136	(128.5 overs, 496 mins)	426

Fall: 24 37 38 49 70 95 99 106 125 136

Fall: 170 185 187 243 280 298 304 362 367 426

G. D. Putland (did not bat).

Bowling: *First Innings*—Dorey 16–6–28–4; Ervine 12–2–40–1; Worthington 16–4–27–2; James 7–1–20–1; Casson 6.5–2–12–2. *Second Innings*—Dorey 3–0–16–0; Worthington 30.1–9–75–3; Ervine 22–7–54–2; James 1.4–0–6–0; Heal 14–3–56–0; Howman 22–6–73–1; Casson 32–4–114–4; Voges 4–0–18–0.

Western Australia 2nd XI

S. W. Meuleman c Bailey b Duval	0	– (2) c Adcock b O. C. Thomas	18
C. J. Simmons not out	24	– (1) c Deitz b Duval	96
L. M. Davis lbw b Putland	0	– c Deitz b Bailey	18
*A. C. Voges b Putland	5	– lbw b Bailey	25
C. J. Heron c Littlewood b Duval	1	– b Kelly	15
P. C. Worthington lbw b Duval	0	– c Putland b Bailey	14
†L. Ronchi c Williams b Duval	0	– c Putland b Bailey	20
S. M. Ervine c Deitz b Duval	12	– b Kelly	27
B. Casson lbw b O. C. Thomas	0	– not out	43
A. K. Heal b Duval	4	– c Littlewood b Putland	49
B. R. Dorey c Kelly b Duval	0		
S. G. Howman		– lbw b Kelly	34
L-b 4, n-b 3	7	B 5, l-b 7, w 5, n-b 1	18
(27 overs, 113 mins)	53	(112.1 overs, 428 mins)	377
Fall: 0 3 9 14 16 24 39 40 47 53		Fall: 56 121 151 169 193 199 223	
		248 307 377	

A. C. L. James (did not bat).

Bowling: *First Innings*—Duval 14–5–24–7; Putland 7–3–14–2; O. C. Thomas 6–3–11–1. *Second Innings*—Duval 26.5–5–62–1; Putland 13–0–54–1; O. C. Thomas 13.2–4–42–1; Kelly 24.5–5–112–3; Bailey 34–7–94–4; Tubb 1–0–1–0.

Umpires: B. Bennett and A. R. Craig.

QUEENSLAND ACADEMY OF SPORT v AUSTRALIAN CAPITAL TERRITORY

At Allan Border Field, Albion, November 15, 16, 17, 18, 2004. Queensland Academy of Sport won by six wickets. *Toss:* Queensland Academy of Sport.

Close of play: First day, Australian Capital Territory (1) 9-369 (Hatton 11, Bayly 3); Second day, Queensland Academy of Sport (1) 4-305 (Hartley 67, Paulsen 2); Third day, Queensland Academy of Sport (2) 2-92 (Philipson 22, Paulsen 8).

Australian Capital Territory

D. J. Richards c Stevens b MacKenzie	6	– (2) c Paulsen b MacKenzie	10
A. G. Rhynehart b Brant	19	– (1) b MacKenzie	4
C. Brown c Hartley b MacKenzie	223	– c Wallis b Johnson	62
S. P. Heaney c Nash b Le Loux	64	– (7) c Wallis b Rimmington	14
*C. R. A. McLeod c Payne b Le Loux	42	– (4) lbw b MacKenzie	0
M. A. Divin lbw b MacKenzie	0	– (5) c Rimmington b Le Loux	32
P. B. Radford c Paulsen b Le Loux	0	– (8) not out	23
†D. C. Brede b Johnson	8	– (6) c Payne b Le Loux	10
A. J. Heading b Le Loux	3	– b Rimmington	6
M. A. Hatton not out	24	– run out (Payne)	13
T. Bayly b Johnson	8	– b MacKenzie	0
L-b 2, w 7, n-b 9	18	L-b 11, n-b 2	13
(103.5 overs, 394 mins)	415	(47.3 overs, 191 mins)	187
Fall: 7 46 252 338 338 339 354 362 384 415		Fall: 4 21 21 113 115 134 148 162	
		180 187	

B. T. Anderton (did not bat).

Bowling: *First Innings*—MacKenzie 24–8–63–3; Johnson 23.5–3–76–2; Brant 9–0–60–1; Sullivan 8–1–44–0; Stevens 10–0–40–0; Rimmington 8–1–56–0; Le Loux 17–3–45–4; Nash 4–0–29–0. *Second Innings*—MacKenzie 9.3–2–36–4; Brant 6–0–34–0; Johnson 8–1–26–1; Sullivan 5–2–17–0; Le Loux 11–0–36–2; Rimmington 8–1–27–2.

Queensland Academy of Sport

D. M. Payne run out	123	– lbw b Anderton	23
L. M. Stevens lbw b Heading	58	– c Heading b Divin	38
B. P. Nash c Brede b Hatton	19		
*†C. D. Hartley retired	67		
C. A. Philipson c Brede b Heading	25	– (3) st Brede b Hatton	26
S. J. Paulsen b Anderton	11	– (4) c Brede b Bayly	33
S. J. Farrell lbw b Anderton	5	– (5) not out	35
R. N. Le Loux lbw b Divin	76		
M. G. Johnson c Anderton b Heading	3		
D. R. MacKenzie c Brede b Bayly	17		
N. J. Rimmington c Radford b Bayly	6		
S. A. Brant not out	16		
D. L. Wallis		– (6) not out	0
B 1, l-b 11, w 3, n-b 3	18	B 3, l-b 1, n-b 1	5

(114.3 overs, 432 mins)	444	(39.5 overs, 145 mins) (4 wkts)	160
Fall: 112 147 248 305 320 325 330 354 369 444		Fall: 48 71 100 152	

G. J. Sullivan (did not bat).

Bowling: *First Innings*—Bayly 25–1–113–2; Anderton 24–5–85–2; Hatton 21–3–79–1; Heading 29–7–108–3; Divin 15.3–4–47–1. *Second Innings*—Anderton 15–3–59–1; Heading 5–0–30–0; Divin 6–0–32–1; Bayly 5–2–4–1; Hatton 8.5–3–31–1.

Umpires: G. N. Cubit and T. P. Laycock.

VICTORIA 2nd XI v WESTERN AUSTRALIA 2nd XI

At Optus Oval, Carlton, November 15, 16, 17, 18, 2004. Match drawn. *Toss:* Victoria 2nd XI.

Close of play: First day, Western Australia 2nd XI (1) 2-18 (Rogers 9, Heal 2); Second day, Victoria 2nd XI (2) 1-134 (Arnberger 67, Jewell 42); Third day, Western Australia 2nd XI (2) 0-107 (Simmons 40, Meuleman 66).

Victoria 2nd XI

J. L. Arnberger c Patrizi b Wates	20	– retired	133
*N. Jewell c Rogers b Ervine	138	– (3) retired	112
B. R. Joseland b Dorey	4	– (4) not out	29
M. Klinger lbw b Wates	0	– (5) c Rogers b Heal	4
T. H. Welsford c Rogers b Ervine	2	– (6) not out	30
A. C. Blizzard c Heal b Ervine	0		
†A. J. Crosthwaite c Davis b Ervine	17		
N. S. Pilon c Patrizi b Heath	98	– (2) c and b Howman	24
C. J. McKay c Dorey b Heal	36		
G. J. Denton not out	13		
B. E. McGain not out	11		
B 6, l-b 4, w 6, n-b 17	33	B 8, l-b 3, w 1	12

(84 overs, 336 mins)	(9 wkts dec) 372	(91 overs, 334 mins) (4 wkts dec)	344
Fall: 43 49 61 70 70 94 287 321 349		Fall: 38 0 0 289	

S. R. Pietersz (did not bat).

Bowling: *First Innings*—Dorey 19–3–84–1; Wates 15.2–2–73–2; Heath 16.4–4–52–1; Ervine 18–2–79–4; Heal 10–2–43–1; Casson 5–0–29–0; Meuleman 1–0–2–0. *Second Innings*—Dorey 7–2–19–0; Howman 16–2–80–1; Heath 14–4–59–0; Heal 23–4–83–1; Ervine 13–1–45–0; Marsh 1–0–1–0; Casson 17–3–46–0.

Western Australia 2nd XI

S. W. Meuleman lbw b Denton	0	– (2) lbw b McGain	77
C. J. Simmons c Crosthwaite b Denton	7	– (1) c Klinger b Welsford	137
*C. J. L. Rogers c Blizzard b Welsford	37	– lbw b Welsford	66
A. K. Heal c Pilon b Pietersz	23	– (8) c Jewell b Denton	4
S. E. Marsh c Jewell b Denton	24	– (4) run out (Arnberger/Pilon)	49
L. M. Davis b Welsford	1	– (5) lbw b McGain	52
D. J. Wates b Welsford	4		
S. M. Ervine c Jewell b McKay	18	– (6) c Pilon b McKay	20
B. Casson c Pietersz b McGain	26	– (7) c Klinger b McKay	34
†H. P. Patrizi not out	16	– (9) not out	10
B. R. Dorey c Crosthwaite b McKay	12		
L-b 1, n-b 1	2	B 12, l-b 6, n-b 1	19

(70.2 overs, 282 mins)	170	(135 overs, 530 mins) (8 wkts)	479

Fall: 0 13 51 90 93 93 98 142 142 170

Fall: 137 241 329 366 396 454 454 458

J. M. Heath (did not bat).

Bowling: *First Innings*—Denton 14.4–3–35–3; Pietersz 20–10–36–1; McGain 11–1–51–1; Welsford 16–10–18–3; McKay 8.4–0–29–2. *Second Innings*—Denton 25–4–80–1; Pietersz 23–5–76–0; Welsford 27–6–99–2; McGain 35–7–123–3; McKay 16–5–60–1; Joseland 9–4–23–0.

Umpires: A. P. Ward and J. D. Ward.

TASMANIA 2nd XI v VICTORIA 2nd XI

At Bellerive Oval, Hobart, December 6, 7, 8, 2004. Victoria 2nd XI won by eight wickets. *Toss:* Tasmania.

Close of play: First day, Victoria 2nd XI (1) 4-119 (Jewell 82, Klinger 28); Second day, Victoria 2nd XI (2) 2-53 (Joseland 13, Buchanhan 15).

Tasmania 2nd XI

†T. D. Paine c Cassell b Huckett	7	– (2) c Crosthwaite b Cassell	13
S. P. Kremerskothen c Crosthwaite b Huckett	0	– (1) c Bailey b Cassell	0
R. J. G. Lockyear lbw b Knowles	12	– lbw b Huckett	26
*G. J. Bailey c Crosthwaite b Welsford	20	– c Jewell b Cassell	2
D. J. Anderson not out	77	– c Klinger b Welsford	13
L. R. Butterworth b Knowles	2	– b Welsford	8
A. M. Blignaut c Crosthwaite b Knowles	2	– c Jewell b Welsford	16
A. W. Polkinghorne c O'Brien b Huckett	28	– c Huckett b Knowles	24
D. A. McNees lbw b Knowles	17	– not out	18
B. W. Hilfenhaus b Welsford	2	– lbw b McGain	22
J. L. Shelton c Crosthwaite b Huckett	19	– lbw b Huckett	6
L-b 5, n-b 1	6	B 1, l-b 2, n-b 1	4

(56.1 overs, 224 mins)	192	(44.3 overs, 167 mins)	152

Fall: 0 13 42 42 50 56 95 145 150 192

Fall: 0 39 41 41 59 79 90 104 143 152

Bowling: *First Innings*—Cassell 14–6–32–0; Huckett 14.1–4–46–4; Knowles 14–2–55–4; Welsford 14–2–54–2. *Second Innings*—Cassell 14–2–42–3; Huckett 10.3–2–33–2; Welsford 9–4–23–3; Knowles 7–0–45–1; McGain 4–1–6–1.

Victoria 2nd XI

N. Jewell not out	138	– lbw b Hilfenhaus	16
N. O'Brien c McNees b Blignaut	2	– c Paine b Hilfenhaus	7
B. R. Joseland c Paine b McNees	0	– not out	33
L. G. L. Buchanan lbw b McNees	0	– not out	93
N. S. Pilon c Paine b Blignaut	2		
M. Klinger c Paine b Blignaut	30		
†A. J. Crosthwaite c Kremerskothen b Hilfenhaus	0		
*T. H. Welsford c Bailey b Shelton	14		
B. A. Knowles c Paine b Shelton	0		
B. E. McGain c Paine b Polkinghorne	3		
R. J. Cassell c and b Shelton	0		
L-b 4, w 1, n-b 2	7	L-b 3	3

(61.2 overs, 259 mins)   196   (38.5 overs, 142 mins)   (2 wkts) 152
Fall: 23 30 30 33 129 130 176 176 181 196   Fall: 24 35

C. Huckett (did not bat).

Bowling: *First Innings*—Blignaut 12–3–34–3; McNees 14–2–52–2; Butterworth 8–2–28–0; Hilfenhaus 14–5–49–1; Polkinghorne 9–3–16–1; Shelton 4.2–0–13–3. *Second Innings*—Polkinghorne 3–0–16–0; Hilfenhaus 10–3–30–2; McNees 10–4–33–0; Butterworth 8.5–4–28–0; Kremerskothen 1–1–0–0; Shelton 6–0–42–0.

Umpires: S. Maxwell and K. J. McGinniss.

AUSTRALIAN CAPITAL TERRITORY v SOUTH AUSTRALIA 2nd XI

At Manuka Oval, Canberra, December 13, 14, 15, 16, 2004. Australian Capital Territory won by seven wickets. *Toss:* Australian Capital Territory.

Close of play: First day, South Australia (1) 4-514 (Skewes 35, Tubb 41); Second day, South Australia (2) 0-68 (Williams 40, T.C. Plant 28); Third day, Australian Capital Territory (2) 3-332 (Heaney 68, McLeod 1).

South Australia 2nd XI

T. C. Plant c Heading b Anderton	5	– (2) not out	88
L. Williams c Starr b Hatton	172	– (1) b Hatton	87
W. D. Thomas lbw b Heading	21		
*M. A. Higgs b Gill	221		
K. J. Skewes not out	35		
S. B. Tubb not out	41		
C. J. Borgas		– (3) not out	3
B 9, l-b 2, w 2, n-b 6	19	L-b 2	2

(122 overs, 453 mins)   (4 wkts dec) 514   (30 overs, 105 mins)   (1 wkt dec) 180
Fall: 8 35 395 443   Fall: 148

M. C. Weeks, †J. W. Plant, T. P. Kelly, C. J. Duval, C. B. Bailey (did not bat).

Bowling: *First Innings*—Anderton 30–3–121–1; Gill 25–3–126–1; Heading 19–4–66–1; Divin 12–0–51–0; Shaw 14–3–53–0; Hatton 22–5–86–1. *Second Innings*—Anderton 4–0–10–0; Gill 8–1–62–0; Hatton 11–0–48–1; Divin 7–0–58–0.

Australian Capital Territory

†D. C. Brede c Thomas b Bailey	42	– lbw b Kelly	151
D. J. Richards c and b Kelly	68	– lbw b Thomas	84
C. Brown c (sub) B. P. Cameron b Weeks	88	– c J. W. Plant b Tubb	4
S. P. Heaney c J. W. Plant b Weeks	72	– not out	68
*C. R. A. McLeod c Borgas b Skewes	31	– not out	1
M. A. Divin c Williams b Bailey	23		
R. Starr not out	7		
A. J. Heading not out	5		
L-b 5, w 1, n-b 23	29	L-b 13, w 1, n-b 10	24

(93.3 overs, 360 mins)　　　　(6 wkts dec) 365	(76.5 overs, 294 mins)　　　(3 wkts) 332
Fall: 105 127 295 302 351 359	Fall: 179 194 323

M. A. Hatton, F. Gill, M. E. L. Shaw, B. T. Anderton (did not bat).

Bowling: *First Innings*—Duval 14–1–58–0; Kelly 21–3–100–1; Weeks 14–1–82–2; Skewes 13.3–5–23–1; Tubb 5–0–19–0; Bailey 26–2–78–2. *Second Innings*—Kelly 16.5–1–83–1; Duval 11–1–41–0; Weeks 10–0–56–0; Skewes 5–2–11–0; Bailey 21–1–78–0; Thomas 3–1–8–1; Tubb 10–1–42–1.

Umpires: A. Barrett and A. Shelley.

SOUTH AUSTRALIA 2nd XI v TASMANIA 2nd XI

At Adelaide Oval No 2, Adelaide, January 3, 4, 5, 6, 2005. Match drawn. *Toss:* South Australia 2nd XI.
　　Close of play: First day, Tasmania 2nd XI (1) 1-88 (Cox 52, Gloury 13); Second day, South Australia 2nd XI (2) 0-21 (Williams 4, Plant 16); Third day, South Australia 2nd XI (2) 3-337 (Williams 182, Borgas 60).

South Australia 2nd XI

T. C. Plant c McNees b Butterworth	7	– (2) c Anderson b Hilfenhaus	48
L. Williams lbw b Butterworth	12	– (1) c Shelton b Dighton	221
†S. A. Deitz lbw b McNees	0	– st Paine b Doherty	10
*B. P. Cameron c Paine b Butterworth	20	– lbw b Hilfenhaus	30
C. J. Borgas b Hilfenhaus	5	– lbw b Dighton	83
M. Littlewood c Paine b Hilfenhaus	54	– (7) st Paine b Shelton	9
M. C. Weeks c Bailey b Hilfenhaus	19	– (6) c Dighton b Shelton	7
J. P. Pratt b McNees	28	– b Doherty	6
T. P. Kelly c Dighton b McNees	0	– (10) c Bailey b Shelton	1
C. B. Bailey not out	18	– (9) b Doherty	15
C. J. Duval st Paine b Shelton	34	– not out	0
B 1, l-b 2, w 2, n-b 1	6	L-b 5, n-b 5	10

(73.2 overs, 272 mins)　　　　　203	(148.3 overs, 533 mins)　　　　440
Fall: 12 16 26 48 49 71 150 150 154 203	Fall: 92 113 192 397 402 414 419 431 440 440

G. D. Putland (did not bat).

Bowling: *First Innings*—McNees 17–4–42–3; Hilfenhaus 21–7–64–3; Butterworth 18–4–58–3; Doherty 11–4–20–0; Shelton 6.2–0–16–1. *Second Innings*—McNees 24–4–60–0; Hilfenhaus 28–6–99–2; Butterworth 25–9–58–0; Doherty 40–4–133–3; Shelton 17.3–4–70–3; Dighton 14–8–15–2.

Tasmania 2nd XI

†T. D. Paine c Deitz b Putland	21	– (7) lbw b Bailey	1
J. Cox lbw b Weeks	106	– (1) lbw b Duval	27
T. P. Gloury c and b Bailey	70	– c Deitz b Duval	6
R. J. G. Lockyear c Deitz b Putland	53	– lbw b Weeks	7
M. G. Dighton lbw b Putland	77	– (2) c Putland b Bailey	36
*G. J. Bailey lbw b Putland	0	– (5) lbw b Kelly	13
D. J. Anderson b Kelly	6	– (6) b Weeks	0
L. R. Butterworth c (sub) W. D. Thomas b Duval	14	– not out	26
D. A. McNees c Cameron b Weeks	14	– not out	15
P. N. Doherty not out	7		
J. L. Shelton lbw b Bailey	0		
L-b 6, w 3, n-b 7	16	L-b 13, n-b 6	19

(103 overs, 422 mins) 384   (54.3 overs, 225 mins) (7 wkts) 150
Fall: 41 196 239 325 325 334 358 362 383 384   Fall: 37 53 75 85 86 90 107

B. W. Hilfenhaus (did not bat).

Bowling: *First Innings*—Kelly 21–3–90–1; Putland 23–4–78–4; Duval 22–5–59–1; Weeks 15–2–60–2; Bailey 22–4–91–2. *Second Innings*—Kelly 11–3–30–1; Putland 8–0–47–0; Duval 10–4–20–2; Weeks 9–2–22–2; Bailey 16–8–18–2.

Umpires: A. R. Collins and K. D. Perrin.

QUEENSLAND ACADEMY OF SPORT v WESTERN AUSTRALIA 2nd XI

At WACA Ground, Perth, January 3, 4, 5, 2005. Western Australia 2nd XI won by nine wickets. *Toss:* Queensland Academy of Sport.

Close of play: First day, Western Australia 2nd XI (1) 6-115 (Voges 59, Worthington 0); Second day, Queensland Academy of Sport (2) 5-167 (Farrell 8).

Queensland Academy of Sport

D. M. Payne c Ronchi b Wates	46	– (2) c Heron b Worthington	89
R. A. Broad c Ronchi b Petrie	16	– (1) c Ronchi b Coetzee	15
*A. J. Nye c Heron b Petrie	9	– b Coetzee	0
S. J. Paulsen b Wates	10	– c Ronchi b Petrie	20
N. Reardon c Worthington b Wates	10	– b Casson	30
S. J. Farrell c Ronchi b Williams	1	– c Ronchi b Williams	8
†C. D. Hartley c Ronchi b Williams	36	– c Coetzee b Casson	21
R. N. Le Loux b Coetzee	10	– lbw b Wates	4
M. G. Johnson lbw b Coetzee	0	– not out	76
D. R. MacKenzie c Williams b Coetzee	4		
N. J. Rimmington not out	10	– (10) b Williams	5
S. A. Brant		– c Casson b Worthington	18
L-b 1, w 3, n-b 4	8	B 5, l-b 2, w 6, n-b 4	17

(55 overs, 236 mins) 160   (86.2 overs, 366 mins) 303
Fall: 33 55 86 88 91 101 114 114 122 160   Fall: 40 40 88 141 167 169 185
231 245 303

Bowling: *First Innings*—Williams 14–4–40–2; Wates 13–6–26–3; Petrie 13–3–39–2; Worthington 3–1–9–0; Coetzee 10–3–27–3; Casson 2–0–18–0. *Second Innings*—Williams 14–6–15–2; Wates 13–2–48–1; Coetzee 14–2–65–2; Petrie 16–5–46–1; Worthington 12.2–3–69–2; Casson 16–4–53–2; Voges 1–1–0–0.

Western Australia 2nd XI

S. W. Meuleman c Le Loux b Johnson	14	– (2) not out		93
C. J. Simmons c Le Loux b Johnson	1	– (1) c MacKenzie b Johnson		10
C. J. Heron c Hartley b Johnson	5	– not out		81
*A. C. Voges c Reardon b Le Loux	111			
D. C. Bandy c Reardon b Johnson	23			
†L. Ronchi c Hartley b Johnson	4			
J. P. Coetzee c Reardon b Johnson	1			
P. C. Worthington c Paulsen b Rimmington	76			
B. Casson b Nye b Brant	19			
D. J. Wates c Le Loux b Rimmington	10			
M. J. Petrie not out	1			
B 4, l-b 4, n-b 5	13	L-b 4		4

(86.1 overs, 359 mins)   278   (38.4 overs, 158 mins)   (1 wkt) 188
Fall: 2 23 24 101 107 110 207 250 265 278   Fall: 28

B. A. Williams (did not bat).

Bowling: *First Innings*—MacKenzie 17–4–43–0; Johnson 19–3–41–6; Rimmington 23.1–7–70–2; Brant 17–4–64–1; Le Loux 10–1–52–1. *Second Innings*—Johnson 8.4–0–44–1; MacKenzie 9–1–43–0; Brant 8–2–28–0; Rimmington 4–1–18–0; Nye 3–0–22–0; Paulsen 6–0–29–0.

Umpires: I. H. Lock and R. R. Pease.

AUSTRALIAN CAPITAL TERRITORY v NEW SOUTH WALES 2nd XI

At Manuka Oval, Canberra, January 31, February 1, 2, 3, 2005. Match drawn. *Toss:* Australian Capital Territory.

Close of play: First day, New South Wales 2nd XI (1) 4-285 (Rohrer 69, Krejza 5); Second day, Australian Capital Territory (1) 2-103 (Brown 37, Heaney 16).

New South Wales 2nd XI

C. J. Richards c Starr b Anderton	48	D. Smith c Cameron b Divin	35
M. W. Creed c Starr b Gill	90	†S. D. Stanton not out	1
*G. M. Lambert c Starr b Shaw	26	B 4, l-b 6, n-b 6	16
B. J. Rohrer lbw b Ritchard	85		
S. N. J. O'Keefe run out	36	(115 overs, 436 mins) (6 wkts dec)	395
J. J. Krejza not out	58	Fall: 85 141 189 255 322 389	

M. Henriques, A. C. Bird, D. Bollinger, M. A. Cameron (did not bat).

Bowling: Gill 17–3–59–1; Ritchard 26–9–79–1; Anderton 31–5–101–1; Divin 10–1–44–1; Shaw 16–2–52–1; Hatton 15–1–50–0.

Australian Capital Territory

D. J. Richards c Smith b Cameron	11	M. A. Hatton c Stanton b Bird	3
S. R. Cameron lbw b Cameron	21	M. E. L. Shaw b Bird	8
C. Brown st Stanton b Krejza	72	A. Ritchard not out	2
S. P. Heaney c and b Krejza	19	B 11, l-b 12, n-b 15	38
*C. R. A. McCleod c Lambert b Krejza	30		
M. A. Divin lbw b O'Keefe	5	(76.2 overs, 322 mins)	292
†R. Starr c Stanton b Lambert	47	Fall: 39 40 122 192 180 186 266	
F. Gill c Smith b Krejza	36	274 282 292	

B. T. Anderton (did not bat).

Bowling: Bollinger 14–0–69–0; Cameron 11–3–30–2; O'Keefe 7–1–19–1; Krejza 25–6–86–4; Bird 10.2–2–20–2; Henriques 4–0–25–0; Lambert 5–1–20–1.

Umpires: S. Balchin and A. Barrett.

VICTORIA 2nd XI v AUSTRALIAN CAPITAL TERRITORY

At Jubilee Park, Frankston, February 14, 15, 16, 2005. Victoria 2nd XI won by six wickets. *Toss:* Victoria 2nd XI.

Close of play: First day, Victoria 2nd XI (1) 5-213 (Welsford 23, Pilon 16); Second day, Australian Capital Territory (2) 9-319 (Gill 21, Anderton 1).

Australian Capital Territory

S. R. Cameron b Knowles	10	–	(2) c Denton b Welsford	29
D. J. Richards c Joseland b Cassell	4	–	(1) c Pilon b Cassell	107
C. Brown b Knowles	1	–	(4) b McDonald	29
S. P. Heaney c Buchanan b Knowles	3	–	(5) c Pilon b McDonald	1
*C. R. A. McLeod c Knowles b McDonald	27	–	(6) c Jewell b McDonald	0
M. A. Divin b Cassell	1	–	(3) b Cassell	33
A. J. Heading c Pilon b Denton	12	–	b McDonald	1
†R. Starr c Pilon b McDonald	4	–	lbw b Welsford	64
F. Gill b McKay	8	–	not out	38
M. A. Hatton not out	5	–	b Denton	7
A. Ritchard c Jewell b McKay	0			
B. T. Anderton		–	c Cassell b Denton	5
L-b 5, w 1, n-b 1	7		B 4, l-b 22	26

(30.3 overs, 135 mins)	82	(80.3 overs, 334 mins)	340

Fall: 12 16 16 30 31 56 68 68 78 82

Fall: 34 102 139 141 141 143 284 288 317 340

Bowling: *First Innings*—Cassell 9–4–23–2; Denton 7–0–16–1; Knowles 6–2–20–3; McDonald 5–3–10–2; Mangan 2–1–4–0; McKay 1.3–0–4–2. *Second Innings*—Denton 12.3–4–49–2; Cassell 20–5–65–2; McKay 18–3–60–0; Welsford 11–3–44–2; Mangan 8–0–52–0; McDonald 11–4–42–4.

Victoria 2nd XI

N. Jewell c Starr b Ritchard	24	–	b Anderton	14
M. N. Harrison c McLeod b Gill	19	–	c Gill b Divin	50
*A. B. McDonald lbw b Divin	57	–	c Starr b Hatton	6
B. R. Joseland b Gill	0	–	lbw b Heading	35
L. G. L. Buchanan c Ritchard b Heading	63	–	not out	39
T. H. Welsford c Starr b Gill	24	–	not out	0
†N. S. Pilon c Heaney b Heading	19			
B. A. Knowles c Gill b Heading	21			
C. J. McKay c Ritchard b Hatton	21			
G. J. Denton c Gill b Anderton	12			
R. J. Cassell not out	0			
B 2, l-b 6, n-b 3	11		L-b 3, w 1, n-b 4	8

(84 overs, 312 mins)	271	(35.1 overs, 138 mins)	(4 wkts)	152

Fall: 44 48 48 138 182 215 223 248 265 271

Fall: 33 42 99 148

J. P. Mangan (did not bat).

Bowling: *First Innings*—Anderton 20–8–45–1; Ritchard 15–3–39–1; Gill 13–4–44–3; Hatton 20–4–69–1; Heading 12–0–45–3; Divin 4–1–21–1. *Second Innings*—Anderton 9–2–31–1; Ritchard 6–0–19–0; Hatton 5–1–22–1; Gill 8–1–28–0; Heading 6.1–0–49–1; Divin 1–1–0–1.

Umpires: A. P. Ward and J. D. Ward.

TASMANIA 2nd XI v WESTERN AUSTRALIA 2nd XI

At Bellerive Oval, Hobart, February 14, 15, 16, 17, 2005. Tasmania won by 58 runs.
Toss: Tasmania 2nd XI.

Close of play: First day, Tasmania 2nd XI (1) 4-350 (Dighton 122, Anderson 34); Second day, Western Australia 2nd XI (1) 5-261 (Heron 9); Third day, Tasmania 2nd XI (2) 3-209 (Anderson 102, Wells 17).

Tasmania 2nd XI

*J. Cox c James b Wates	162	– (6) c Voges b James	17
†T. D. Paine c Marsh b Dorey	4	– (1) c Worthington b Dorey	21
T. P. Gloury c Marsh b Dorey	7		
G. T. Cunningham b James	10	– c and b Casson	21
M. G. Dighton c Meuleman b Casson	163		
D. J. Anderson c Meuleman b Dorey	58	– (3) c Simmons b James	122
R. J. G. Lockyear c Simmons b Casson	21	– (2) c and b James	31
P. N. Doherty c Ronchi b Coetzee	6	– c Heron b Casson	0
D. A. McNees not out	1	– (7) b James	7
J. L. Shelton not out	0	– (9) st Ronchi b Casson	8
L. C. Swards		– (10) not out	1
J. Wells	..	– (5) b James	39
B 1, l-b 5, w 3, n-b 4	13	B 4, l-b 4, w 1, n-b 8	17

(120.5 overs, 479 mins)   (8 wkts dec) 445   (82 overs, 334 mins)   (9 wkts dec) 284
Fall: 9 17 35 262 390 433 440 444   Fall: 33 65 131 251 252 262
265 275 284

K. S. Pickering (did not bat).

Bowling: *First Innings*—Dorey 25–4–80–3; Wates 17–5–57–1; James 20–3–92–1; Coetzee 17.5–3–76–1; Worthington 17–5–48–0; Casson 20–3–64–2; Voges 4–0–22–0. *Second Innings*—Dorey 18–3–52–1; Wates 5–2–14–0; Coetzee 12–3–44–0; James 12–3–37–5; Worthington 19–5–57–0; Casson 14–0–70–3; Voges 2–0–2–0.

Western Australia 2nd XI

C. J. Simmons c Paine b Pickering	3	– (2) c Wells b Shelton	62
S. W. Meuleman c Cox b McNees	41	– (1) c Shelton b Pickering	9
*A. C. Voges run out	92	– c Pickering b McNees	21
S. E. Marsh c Paine b Shelton	93	– c Cox b Swards	1
C. J. Heron not out	71	– c Lockyear b Doherty	15
†L. Ronchi b Paine	16	– c Cox b Shelton	50
P. C. Worthington b Pickering	0	– c Wells b Pickering	18
B. Casson c Anderson b Shelton	21	– (9) c McNees b Shelton	17
D. J. Wates not out	31	– (10) b Shelton	28
B. R. Dorey		– (8) b Pickering	24
J. P. Coetzee (did not bat).		– not out	44
B 1, l-b 7, n-b 2	10	B 1, l-b 1, n-b 2	4

(105 overs, 377 mins)   (7 wkts dec) 378   (65.1 overs, 255 mins)   293
Fall: 21 76 228 238 261 262 302   Fall: 17 52 55 88 156 163 200
206 229 293

A. C. L. James (did not bat).

Bowling: *First Innings*—McNees 18–5–58–1; Pickering 24–4–81–2; Swards 21–3–78–0; Doherty 17–1–43–0; Shelton 20–2–98–2; Paine 5–1–12–1. *Second Innings*—McNees 17–1–67–1; Pickering 16–1–57–3; Swards 7–0–32–1; Doherty 7–0–44–1; Shelton 18.1–2–91–4.

Umpires: K. J. McGinniss and B. J. Muir.

NEW SOUTH WALES 2nd XI v
QUEENSLAND ACADEMY OF SPORT

At Drummoyne Oval, Drummoyne, February 28, March 1, 2, 3, 2005. Match drawn.
Toss: Queensland Academy of Sport.

Close of play: First day, Queensland Academy of Sport (1) 6-261; Second day, New South Wales 2nd XI (1) 2-147 (O'Brien 36, Krejza 1); Third day, Queensland Academy of Sport (2) 4-42 (Reardon 0, Hartley 5).

Queensland Academy of Sport

D. M. Payne b O'Brien	47	–	(2) lbw b Cameron	9
R. A. Broad c O'Brien b Bird	100	–	(1) c Henriques b Roden	11
*A. J. Nye c Bird b Krejza	16	–	c O'Brien b Roden	7
C. P. Simpson lbw b O'Brien	23	–	lbw b Cameron	1
N. J. Reardon c O'Keefe b Henriques	26	–	c Smith b Bird	32
†C. D. Hartley lbw b Bird	77	–	c Smith b Cameron	68
N. M. Hauritz b Bird	3	–	c Roden b O'Keefe	33
D. J. Tate lbw b Henriques	86	–	b O'Keefe	2
R. N. Le Loux b Henriques	16	–	c Smith b Cameron	3
S. J. Jurgensen not out	6			
N. J. Rimmington		–	(10) c Roden b Cameron	11
G. J. Sullivan		–	not out	1
B 2, l-b 8, n-b 10	20		B 2, l-b 7, n-b 7	16

(129.1 overs, 496 mins)	(9 wkts dec) 420	(62.3 overs, 248 mins)	194

Fall: 85 120 160 216 220 223 353 401 420

Fall: 15 34 37 37 104 175 179 179 193 194

Bowling: *First Innings*—Bird 25–9–72–3; Cameron 19–5–61–0; Roden 23–2–80–0; Henriques 16.1–5–46–3; O'Brien 24–6–43–2; Krejza 17–3–94–1; O'Keefe 5–0–14–0. *Second Innings*—Roden 15–5–58–2; Cameron 13.3–6–34–5; O'Brien 13–2–37–0; Bird 11–2–24–1; O'Keefe 10–2–32–2.

New South Wales 2nd XI

C. J. Richards lbw b Jurgensen	17	–	c Payne b Sullivan	7
M. W. Creed b Jurgensen	86	–	(8) c Rimmington b Simpson	12
A. W. O'Brien run out (Hauritz)	83	–	(2) c Hauritz b Tate	30
J. J. Krejza retired	1			
E. J. M. Cowan c Hartley b Jurgensen	3	–	(4) run out	64
B. J. Rohrer c Nye b Sullivan	60	–	(5) c Broad b Simpson	53
S. N. J. O'Keefe b Tate	15	–	not out	18
B. J. Davis lbw b Sullivan	40	–	(3) c Nye b Tate	7
*†D. Smith c Hartley b Tate	6	–	(6) c Rimmington b Simpson	11
M. Henriques b Tate	3			
G. W. Roden c Payne b Jurgensen	9			
A. C. Bird not out	0	–	(9) not out	0
B 6, l-b 5, w 2, n-b 3	16		B 2, l-b 2	4

(121 overs, 469 mins)	339	(53.3 overs, 211 mins)	(7 wkts) 206

Fall: 34 143 154 245 278 282 292 310 336 339

Fall: 13 33 54 157 175 175 202

M. A. Cameron (did not bat).

Bowling: *First Innings*—Jurgensen 27–6–51–4; Rimmington 18–3–57–0; Sullivan 20–5–47–2; Le Loux 18–2–62–0; Simpson 21–7–57–0; Tate 12–3–30–3; Nye 1–0–3–0; Hauritz 4–0–21–0. *Second Innings*—Jurgensen 7–1–21–0; Sullivan 5–0–22–1; Tate 8–1–27–2; Rimmington 3–1–6–0; Le Loux 8.3–1–29–0; Hauritz 10–0–50–0; Simpson 12–0–47–3.

Umpires: W. Hendricks and T. J. Keel.

CRICKET AUSTRALIA CUP COMPETITION WINNERS

2000-01	Western Australia 2nd XI
2001-02	New South Wales 2nd XI
2002-03	Queensland Academy of Sport
2003-04	New South Wales 2nd XI
2004-05	Victoria 2nd XI

CRICKET AUSTRALIA CUP TEAM RESULTS

	First Game	M	W	L	D	% Won
Australian Cricket Academy	Sep 27 1999	26	9	13	4	34.61
Queensland Academy of Sport	Sep 27 1999	29	14	8	7	48.28
South Australia 2nd XI	Oct 5 1999	33	11	17	5	33.33
Australian Capital Territory	Oct 25 1999	30	8	19	3	26.67
Western Australia 2nd XI	Nov 1 1999	32	16	9	7	50.00
Victoria 2nd XI	Nov 8 1999	33	17	8	8	51.52
New South Wales 2nd XI	Nov 15 1999	29	16	7	6	55.17
Tasmania 2nd XI	Nov 15 1999	32	9	19	4	28.57

MOST RUNS

	M	I	NO	R	HS	100s	50s	Avge	S-R
L. Williams (ACA)	34	56	6	2,593	221	7	13	51.86	50.57
A. C. Voges (W Aust)	30	45	6	1,709	144	5	6	43.82	57.08
C. Brown (ACT)	21	39	1	1,565	223	3	9	41.18	56.36
C. J. L. Rogers (W Aust)	17	29	4	1,499	151*	3	11	59.96	62.85
M. Klinger (ACA)	23	37	3	1,357	138	1	12	39.91	56.00
N. Jewell (Vic)	15	26	1	1,165	138*	6	1	46.60	66.42
S. W. Meuleman (W Aust)	19	37	2	1,148	94	0	9	32.80	50.15
D. M. Payne (Qld)	15	29	1	1,114	123	1	8	39.79	61.71
G. C. Rummans (NSW)	16	26	3	1,109	210	2	6	48.22	80.19
G. T. Cunningham (ACT)	22	40	0	1,098	85	0	7	27.45	67.95
S. R. Mason (Tas)	18	31	0	1,088	153	2	6	35.10	44.50
S. P. Heaney (ACT)	20	37	4	1,034	160*	1	7	31.33	44.53
M. J. North (ACA)	18	31	2	1,030	101	2	8	35.52	56.91
S. E. Marsh (W Aust)	16	28	1	1,029	129	2	7	38.11	57.13

* Denotes not out.

MOST WICKETS

	M	O	Mdns	R	W	BB	5W/i	10W/m	Avge	Balls/W
A. G. Downton (ACA)	18	543	134	1,695	74	7-46	4	2	22.91	44.03
E. Kellar (ACT)	20	768.2	210	2,000	70	6-41	5	1	28.57	65.86
P. C. Rofe (ACA)	16	416.4	90	1,205	58	6-63	2	1	20.78	43.10
G. M. Lambert (NSW)	18	363.5	68	1,242	53	6-52	3	0	23.43	41.13
D. A. Nash (NSW)	9	278.5	83	715	53	6-61	3	1	13.49	31.57
S. J. Magoffin (ACA)	13	407.5	95	1,204	50	6-37	1	0	24.08	48.94
M. D. Pascoe (Qld)	14	399.5	108	1,094	49	5-31	3	0	22.33	48.96
S. J. Karppinen (W Aust)	16	433	110	1,321	46	5-44	1	0	28.72	56.48
A. B. McDonald (ACA)	22	411	116	1,325	45	4-26	0	0	29.44	54.80
A. C. L. James (ACT)	13	341.4	57	1,366	41	5-37	2	0	33.32	50.00
S. J. Jurgensen (Tas)	16	419	100	1,254	40	5-66	1	0	31.35	62.85

HIGHEST INDIVIDUAL SCORES

260	M. J. Cosgrove	South Australia v ACT at Adelaide	2003-04
239	B. P. Van Deinsen	New South Wales v Victoria at St Kilda	2001-02
233*	C. J. Davies	South Australia v ACT at Adelaide	2001-02
230*	L. A. Carseldine	Queensland v ACT at Canberra	2001-02
223	C. Brown	ACT v Queensland at Albion	2004-05
221	M. A. Higgs	South Australia v ACT at Canberra	2004-05
221	L. Williams	South Australia v Tasmania at Adelaide	2004-05
210	R. C. Rummans	Victoria v Queensland at Albion	2002-03
208	L. G. Buchanan	Victoria v ACT at St Kilda	2002-03
201*	L. Williams	Cricket Academy v South Australia at Adelaide	2000-01

BEST BOWLING IN AN INNINGS

9-67	J. M. Davison	Victoria v South Australia at Adelaide	2001-02
8-73	B. E. Young	South Australia v ACT at Canberra	2002-03
7-46	A. G. Downton	Cricket Academy v Victoria at South Melbourne	1999-00
7-24	C. J. Duval	South Australia v Western Australia at Fletcher	2004-05
6-29	A. G. Downton	Tasmania v Queensland at Albion	2002-03
6-31	M. A. Harrity	South Australia v Queensland at Adelaide	2000-01
6-35	J. Moss	Victoria v Queensland at Albion	2000-01
6-36	S. G. Howman	Western Australia v ACT at Perth	2003-04
6-37	S. J. Magoffin	Queensland v ACT at Albion	2002-03
6-41	S. M. Harwood	Victoria v Tasmania at Camberwell	2001-02
6-41	E. Kellar	ACT v Cricket Academy at Canberra	2000-01
6-41	M. G. Johnson	Queensland v Western Australia at Perth	2004-05

MOST WICKETS IN A MATCH

14-146	B. E. Young	South Australia v ACT at Canberra	2002-03
12-91	A. G. Downton	Cricket Academy v Tasmania at South Melbourne	1999-00
11-92	A. R. Griffith	Tasmania v New South Wales at Hobart	2003-04
11-149	G. J. Denton	Tasmania v Western Australia at Perth	2003-04
10-35	D. A. Nash	New South Wales v South Australia at Adelaide	2002-03
10-111	P. C. Rofe	Cricket Academy v Victoria at South Melbourne	2000-01
10-139	A. G. Downton	Tasmania v Queensland at Albion	2002-03
10-140	E. Kellar	ACT v Cricket Academy at Canberra	2000-01
10-163	M. A. Harrity	South Australia v Tasmania at Adelaide	2000-01

HIGHEST WICKET PARTNERSHIPS

1st	198	M. J. Phelps and N. J. Catalano	NSW v ACT at Canberra	2002-03
2nd	302	L. Williams and P. A. Jaques	ACA v S Aust at Adelaide	2000-01
3rd	277	L. G. Buchanan and C. J. Peake	Vic v ACT at St Kilda	2002-03
4th	371	C. J. Ferguson and M. J. Cosgrove	S Aust v ACT at Adelaide	2003-04
5th	221	A. J. Sainsbury and M. G. Betsey	NSW v ACT at Boomanulla	2000-01
6th	202	D. J. Thornely and G. M. Lambert	NSW v S Aust at Bankstown	2004-05
7th	242	D. J. Thornely and S. D. Bradstreet	NSW v ACT at Hurstville	2003-04
8th	157	R. J. Tucker and D. C. Brede	ACT v NSW at Bankstown	1999-00
9th	133	A. J. Heading and E. Kellar	ACT v ACA at Canberra	2000-01
10th	151	S. A. Holcolme and D. A. McNees	ACT v S Aust at Adelaide	2003-04

SYDNEY GREGORY CUP, 2004-05

NEW SOUTH WALES COLTS v QUEENSLAND COLTS

At Hurstville Oval, Hurstville, October 18 (no play), 19, 20, 21 (no play), 2004. Match drawn. *Toss:* New South Wales Colts.

Close of play: First day, no play; Second day, Queensland Colts (1) 3-48 (Paulsen 21, Nielsen 2); Third day, New South Wales Colts (1) 1-25 (Smith 21, O'Keefe 1).

Queensland Colts

*R. A. Broad lbw b O'Keefe	19	N. Rimmington c Allsopp b Daley	0
A. P. Maynard c and b Fleming	3	M. G. D. Turrich c Freeburn b O'Keefe	1
N. J. Reardon c Drew b Fleming	0	G. J. Sullivan c Allsopp b Drew	30
S. J. Paulsen c Allsopp b Drew	64		
J. C. Nielsen lbw b Daley	2	B 3, l-b 6	9
P. J. Reimers lbw b Fleming	14		—
R. N. Le Loux c Allsopp b Daley	30	(68.4 overs, 273 mins)	207
†B. G. W. Gledhill not out	35	Fall: 4 6 44 48 99 109 170 170 173 207	
G. S. Chiesa (did not bat).			

Bowling: Daley 20–6–30–3; Fleming 16–4–40–3; Drew 10.4–2–57–2; O'Keefe 11–2–23–2; Beadle 4–2–9–0; Cook 7–0–39–0.

New South Wales Colts

*D. Smith not out	21		
A. Jeffrey b Rimmington	2		
S. N. J. O'Keefe not out	1		
L-b 1	1		
	—		
13 overs, 49 mins	(1 wkt) 25		
Fall: 23			

P. Forrest, J. Dean, A. Beadle, J. B. Allsopp, A. L. Fleming, B. G. Drew, T. Freeburn, K. M. Daley, J. Cook (did not bat).

Bowling: Rimmington 7-2-12-1; Sullivan 5-2-12-0; Turrich 1-1-0-0.

Umpires: R. D. Goodger and G. L. Lill.

Australian Under-19s, 2004-05

by GREG McKIE

Poor weather marred the middle stages of the Australian Under-19s championship in Melbourne. Competition rules allow no points for drawn games, which gave a huge advantage to the sides who managed to achieve wins in the rain-affected rounds. However, New South Wales retained the Kookaburra Shield by being clearly the best side. To underline their superiority, they defeated their closest rivals, Victoria, in a hard-fought match in round six. Victoria were bowled out for 140, then had New South Wales 6 for 64. The New South Wales ninth-wicket pair of Daniel Rixon and Mitchell Cleary then equalled the competition best for this wicket, adding 121 – Cleary hitting 81 not out in just over an hour.

For New South Wales, this was a year of outstanding triumphs at all levels. They won every Australian under-age championship contested: male Under-17s and Under-19s as well as female Under-19s, Under-17s and Under-15s. The weather kept scores down, and only five players exceeded 250 runs in the seven rounds. Scoring rates in some games were abysmal, with wet outfields slowing things down. As the weather improved, so did the scores. In the last round, Australian Capital Territory successfully chased 342, whilst Victoria overhauled a target of 334. Queensland took the game away from Northern Territory, scoring 2 for 360.

Tasmania had a miraculous win in round one. With one ball to go against Western Australia, Tasmania needed two runs. No score was made, but a no-ball was called because of a fielding circle violation, bringing scores level. From the subsequent extra delivery the winning run was scored. Wade Irvine from the Australian Capital Territory scored an unbeaten 89 against Queensland, being well supported by Mark Hall in a competition record tenth-wicket partnership of 105. The Queensland openers Andrew Michael (101) and Daniel Pearce (89) then added 189 for the first wicket. The also put on 217 against Northern Territory in the last round, Pearce just missing a century yet again, while Michael hit a stroke-filled 190. South Australia medium-pacer Simon Weise took 7 for 64 against Victoria to almost bring his side victory. Victoria were 7 for 109 chasing 132 before Nick Lynch anchored the innings as the last three wickets more than doubled the score. Victorian keeper Peter Nevill took six catches and effected one stumping in the game.

John Hastings of NSW was the player of the series. He scored aggressively in the middle order or when opening the batting, as well as taking useful wickets with his medium-pacers. The four playing here who had represented Australia in the 2003-04 Under-19s World Cup in Bangladesh (Gary Putland, Josh Mangan, Moises Henriques and Matthew Harrison) performed below expectations.

New South Wales carried all before them for the first five rounds. Success against Victoria was followed by a batting rout against South Australia, where at one stage New South Wales lost eight wickets for less than 50. Usman Khawaja and Hastings were their main batsmen, but consistent lower-order resistance, especially from Rixon and Cleary, generally gave them enough runs. Jackson Bird was the bowler of the carnival with his 18 wickets and he was well supported by Hastings and Patrick Darwen. With six 17-year-olds in the team, New South Wales are poised for further success.

Victoria's batting let them down, although their main batsmen all recorded reasonable scores. Aaron Finch was their most consistent, although Matthew Harrison scored 137 against Western Australia. Leg-spinner Mangan was their leading wicket-taker for the third year in a row with 15, but he was over-bowled, wheeling down almost 80 overs in the last two games for figures of 3 for 219. Steven Seymour finished the carnival with the lowest bowling average and the best economy rate and could have been used more. Nevill was easily the best keeper on display and his 19 dismissals included eight stumpings.

Queensland had high-scoring opening bats in Pearce and Michael. Michael finished as the batsman of the carnival with his 390 runs at 55.86. Wade Townsend and Graeme Skennar provided good support, so runs were not usually the problem. The opening attack of Joshua Kemp and Nick Fitzpatrick was effective, but lacked support. Queensland were the big movers this year, rising three places.

South Australia slipped two places, because their batting almost started and finished with Shannon Hurn, who scored three fifties to finish with 244 runs at 48.80. No one else aggregated more than 130 and the team only reached 200 in the last round. However, the team's overall bowling efforts were the best on display, Putland, Weise, Andy Delmont, Carl Tietjens and Tim Delvins performing well in almost every game.

Australian Capital Territory achieved their highest-ever placing. They had three reasonably consistent bats in John Rogers, David Griffiths and Irvine, who were backed up in attack by medium-pacer Adam Ritchard and leg-spinner Sam Gaskin. An outright win over Northern Territory was followed by an even more meritorious run-chase against Tasmania in the last round. Most of their players will be available again in 2005-06.

Tasmania made more than 340 against Australian Capital Territory but even this was insufficient protection for their attack which paid far too much for its wickets. With the exception of Scott Nichols, their batting also struggled. Liam Reynolds took 5 for 13 against Northern Territory but bowled few overs in total.

Western Australia were the big losers, dropping four places to seventh. The loss of points from two rain-affected games did no help them, but the real problem was lack of depth. Matthew Johnston held their batting together in almost every game. His only real support came from Chris Wood and Drew Porter. Their bowling attack was mainly in the hands of Corry Verco, Chris Thompson and Porter.

After performing so well last year, Northern Territory did no gain any points, and suffered an outright defeat at the hands of ACT. None of their batsmen averaged over 23 and their bowlers were far too expensive. The batsmen seemed content at times to protect their wickets, regardless of whether runs were coming at a reasonable pace.

2004-05 AUSTRALIAN UNDER-19 TEAM

Peter Forrest, John Hastings, Jackson Bird, Usman Khawaja (NSW), Josh Manga, Peter Nevill (Vic), Matthew Johnston, Chris Thompson (WAust), Gary Putland (S Aust Andrew Michael, Graeme Skennar (Qld), Scott Nichols (Tas).

UNDER-19s CRICKET CHAMPIONSHIP, 2004-05

ROUND ONE

New South Wales 9 for 271 (U. Khawaja 89, S. Cazzulino 36, M. Henriques 22; N. Meyer 2-35, A. Dilley 2-43) defeated Northern Territory 7 for 132 (N. Akers 33, P. Brown 22; P. Darwen 2-15, J. Bird 2-21) by 139 runs.

Victoria 8 for 240 (P. Nevill 76, A. Finch 64, M. Harrison 25, S. Sanders 22*, T. Stray 21; A. Blacka 3-38) defeated Australian Capital Territory 152 (S. Rooney 47, W. Irvine 28; S. Seymour 4-16) by 88 runs.

Queensland 239 (A. Michael 54, A. Eden 50, G. Skennar 47, B. Gledhill 28; T. Delvins 4-42, G. Putland 2-34, A. Delmont 2-51) defeated South Australia 195 (S. Hurn 60, T. Davey 37, T. Delvins 22; J. Kemp 3-31, J. Hughes 2-41, S. Powell 2-47) by 44 runs.

Western Australia 7 for 206 (M. Johnston 48, D. Porter 35, B. Wright 26*, H. Patrizi 21, C. Claverley 20; C. Lindsay 2-22, C. Clemons 2-36) lost to Tasmania 9 for 207 (S. Nichols 36, M. Lister 35, B. Alistair 33, H. Fenton 28; D. Porter 3-30, C. Verco 3-40, C. Hansberry 2-58) by one wicket.

ROUND TWO

Northern Territory 157 (A. Dilley 41, N. Drummond 27; S. Sanders 4-29) lost to Victoria 6 for 162 (T. Stray 62*, M. Harrison 49; M. Hodson 2-29) by four wickets.

Queensland 8 for 205 (A. Greig 44, B. Gledhill 39, A. Eden 30, A. Michael 27; P. Wells 2-37) lost to New South Wales 6 for 206 (P. Forrest 83*, D. Warner 41, T. Cooper 33; N. Fitzpatrick 2-25, J. Kemp 2-42) by four wickets.

South Australia 178 (J. Pratt 51, S. Hurn 46*, S. Roberts 28; C. Clemons 3-36, L. Bateman 2-24, G. Kerr 2-32, S. Nichols 2-34) defeated Tasmania 134 (S. Nichols 48; G. Putland 4-18, T. Delvins 2-19) by 44 runs.

Australian Capital Territory and Western Australia abandoned due to rain.

ROUND THREE

Northern Territory 151 (R. McCard 40, N. Drummond 27; C. Verco 3-20, D. Porter 2-8, M. Johnston 2-26) lost to Western Australia 3 for 151 (M. Johnston 69*, C. Wood 33*, D. Porter 25) by seven wickets.

Tasmania 4 for 164 (M. Lister 67*, L. Reynolds 26, H. Fenton 22, A. Doolan 20; J. Bird 2-40) lost to New South Wales (target 187 from 31 overs) 3 for 187 (J. Hastings 67, U. Khawaja 39, P. Forrest 31*, T. Cooper 29; L. Reynolds 2-36) by seven wickets.

Queensland 215 (G. Skennar 62, W. Townsend 37, J. Kemp 23, A. Greig 22; J. Mangan 4-30, J. McNamara 2-31, J. Wild 2-47) played a no result game against Victoria 3 for 45 (J. Kemp 2-16).

Australian Capital Territory 8 for 175 (D. Griffith 63; L. Pastyn 2-27, G. Putland 33) played a no result game against South Australia 1 for 21.

ROUND FOUR

South Australia 9 for 166 (J. Pratt 32, G. Putland 25, T. Davey 23; S. Regan 2-11) defeated Northern Territory 84 (C. Tietjens 3-12, A. Delmont 3-16, S. Wiese 2-15) by 82 runs.

Australian Capital Territory 94 (W. Irvine 23; P. Forrest 3-10, J. Bird 2-20) lost to New South Wales 5 for 95 (J. Hastings 48; A. Ritchard 3-31) by five wickets.

Queensland 9 for 127 (S. Powell 35*; C. Thompson 4-26, D. Porter 2-12) defeated Western Australia 121 (S. Rakich 29, M. Johnston 21; D. Clark 3-31, S. Powell 2-24, N. Fitzpatrick 2-25) by six runs.

Victoria 7 for 250 (A. Finch 88, S. Dean 55, J. Wild 47, N. Lynch 37; C. Clemons 3-53, S. Nichols 2-39) defeated Tasmania (target 209) 112 (S. Nichols 23, M. Wade 20; S. Seymour 3-24, J. Mangan 3-36, J. Wild 2-13) by 96 runs.

ROUND FIVE

South Australia 132 (P. Allegretto 47, A. Carey 24; J. Mangan 4-57, S. Seymour 3-29, S. Sanders 2-13) and 4 for 135 (J. Harford 50, A. Carey 35*) lost to Victoria 238 (N. Lynch 93*A. Finch 27, J. Mangan 26, M. Harrison 20; S. Wiese 6-64, T. Delvins 2-19) on first innings.

Tasmania 212 (M. Wade 50, J. Wells 42, G. Kerr 40, C. Lindsay 22; A. Dilley 3-23, S. Regan 2-4, T. Pemble 2-21) and 4 for 79 (H. Fenton 31, L. Reynolds 21*; R. McCard 2-18) defeated Northern Territory (153 (R. Hodson 44*, N. Drummond 21, P. Brown 20; L. Reynolds 5-13, S. Nichols 2-28) on first innings.

Australian Capital Territory 200 (W. Irvine 91*, M. Hall 25; N. Fitzpatrick 4-43, J. Kemp 4-50) lost to Queensland 4 for 217 (A. Michael 101, D. Pearce 89; M. Bell 3-48) on first innings

New South Wales 288 (J. Hastings 85, U. Khawaja 66, D. Rixon 36, P. Forrest 26, S. Cazzulino 22; C. Verco 3-57, C. Thompson 3-67) and 2 for 47 (P. Darwen 39*) defeated Western Australia 193 (M. Johnston 79, B. Sutton 33, C. Wood 33; J. Bird 3-54, M. Hendriques 2-29, J. Hastings 2-35) on first innings.

ROUND SIX

Queensland 8 for 300 declared (W. Townsend 127, G. Skennar 85, A. Eden 24; L. Reynolds 3-37, G. Kerr 3-50) defeated Tasmania 178 (S. Nichols 80, L. Reynolds 31; N. Fitzpatrick 5-33, M. Salerno 4-63) and 2 for 75 (J. Wells 23, L. Reynolds 20) on first innings.

Victoria 140 (J. Wild 24, S. Dean 23; J. Hastings 3-20, J. Bird 3-36, M. Cleary 2-10, P. Wells 2-28) lost to New South Wales 288 (M. Cleary 81*, D. Rixon 51, D. Warner 48, M. Hendriques 26*, P. Darwen 21; S. Seymour 2-18, J. McNamara 2-79) on first innings

Northern Territory 82 (S. Gaskin 4-12, A. Ritchard 3-24, D. Poidevin 2-24) and 198 (N. Akers 52, R. McCard 39, A. Dilley 37; A. Ritchard 3-44, W. Irvine 2-34, S. Gaskin 2-37) lost to Australian Capital Territory 5 dec for 242 (J. Rogers 84, D. Griffith 78, P. O'Callaghan 25, W. Irvine 21*; N. Meyer 3-71) and 3 for 40 (S. Regan 2-18) on first innings.

Western Australia 189 (C. Claverley 48, D. Porter 42, B. Wright 40*, C. Hensberry 22; A. Delmont 3-21, G. Putland 3-53) lost to South Australia 7 for 196 (T. Delvins 69*, S. Hurn 64; C. Verco 3-40, C. Thompson 2-45) on first innings.

ROUND SEVEN

South Australia 234 (S. Hurn 56, L. Pastyn 41, A. Delmont 30, A. Carey 29, J. Harford 25; J. Bird 3-29, P. Darwen 3-45) and 2 for 37 (J. Bird 2-6) defeated New South Wales 169 (U. Khawaja 52, D. Rixon 31, T. Cooper 25; L. Pastyn 3-48, C. Tietjens 2-21, J. Harford 2-24, A. Delmont 2-25) on first innings.

Western Australia 9 for 333 declared (C. Wood 57, D. Porter 53, H. Patrizi 53, B. Wright 48, M. Johnston 42, C. Claverley 37, C. Thompson 22; S. Gilmour 2-47, J. McNamara 2-102, J. Mangan 2-140) lost to Victoria 5 dec for 338 (M. Harrison 137, A. Finch 48, E. Gulbis 41*) on first innings.

Tasmania 8 for 341 declared (A. Doolan 88, M. Wade 73, J. Wells 44, A. Biffin 35, S. Nichols 27, H. Fenton 26*; R. Van Aalst 2-46, A. Ritchard 2-55, S. Gaskin 2-65) lost to Australian Capital Territory 7 for 351 (J. Rogers 119, D. Poidevin 73*, D. Griffith 46, P. O'Callaghan 36, S. Gaskin 32; G. Kerr 3-60) on first innings.

Northern Territory 236 (A. Dilley 70, R. Hogson 45, N. Akers 34, S. Regan 25; J. Kemp 3-41, V. S. Powell 2-46) lost to Queensland 2 for 360 (M. Michael 190, D. Pearce 96, W. Townsend 50*) on first innings.

Rounds one to four were limited-over matches and Rounds six and seven were two-day fixtures.

UNDER-19s CHAMPIONSHIPS, 2004-05

POINTS TABLE, 2004-05

	P	W	L	No Result	Bonus Points	Points	Quotient
New South Wales	7	6	1	0	6	34	1.437
Victoria	7	5	1	1	3	27	1.343
Queensland	7	5	1	1	0	26	1.584
South Australia	7	4	2	1	2	22	1.137
Australian Capital Territory	7	2	3	2	0	16	0.929
Tasmania	7	2	5	0	0	10	0.717
Western Australia	7	1	5	1	2	6	0.955
Northern Territory	7	0	7	0	0	0	0.470

MOST RUNS, 2004-05

	I	NO	R	HS	Avge
A. Michael (Qld)	7	0	391	190	55.86
M. Johnston (WAust)	6	1	275	79	55.00
U. Khawaja (NSW)	7	0	271	89	38.71
W. Townsend (Qld)	7	2	260	127	52.00
M. Harrison (Vic)	7	1	256	137	42.67
A. Finch (Vic)	7	0	247	88	35.28
D. Pearce (Qld)	7	0	246	96	35.14
S. Hurn (SAust)	7	2	244	64	48.80

MOST WICKETS, 2004-05

	O	Mds	R	W	BB	5W/i	Avge
J. Bird (NSW)	74.1	12	238	18	3-29	0	13.22
J. Kemp (Qld)	80.2	18	241	15	4-50	0	16.06
J. Mangan (Vic)	136.3	25	402	15	4-30	0	26.80
N. Fitzpatrick (Qld)	61.4	13	145	14	5-33	1	10.35
C. Verco (WAust)	83	13	258	14	3-20	0	18.42
S. Seymour (Vic)	50.5	24	116	13	4-16	0	8.92
G. Putland (SAust)	74.2	15	183	12	4-18	0	15.25
C. Thompson (WAust)	56	9	195	12	4-26	0	16.25

UNDER-19s CRICKET CHAMPIONSHIPS RECORDS

CHAMPIONSHIP WINNERS

Series	Venue	Winner	Player of the Year
1969-70	Melbourne	Victoria	no award
1970-71	Sydney	Victoria	no award
1971-72	Adelaide	Victoria	R. Wallace (Qld)
1972-73	Canberra	New Zealand	G. C. Hughes (NSW)
1973-74	Melbourne	South Australia	D. W. Hookes (S Aust)
1974-75	Brisbane	Victoria	D. Brown (Qld)
1975-76	Perth	New South Wales	D. M. Wellham (NSW)
1976-77	Hobart	New Zealand	J. J. Crowe (NZ)
1977-78	Christchurch	New South Wales	P. S. Clifford (NSW)
1978-79	Sydney	Western Australia	R. J. Thomas (NZ)
1979-80	Adelaide	Western Australia/Victoria	M. D. Crowe (NZ)
1980-81	Brisbane	Victoria	D. Knox (NSW)
1981-82	Canberra	Victoria	M. R. J. Veletta (W Aust)
1982-83	Perth	Victoria	I. A. Healy (Qld)
1983-84	Melbourne	South Australia	S. R. Waugh (NSW)
1984-85	Hobart	Victoria	J. K. Pyke (ACT)
1985-86	Sydney	Queensland/New South Wales	J. C. Scuderi (Qld)
1986-87	Adelaide	New South Wales	G. R. Parker (Vic)
1987-88	Brisbane	Western Australia	R. C. Kelly (W Aust)
1988-89	Canberra	New South Wales	M. G. Bevan (ACT)
1989-90	Melbourne	New South Wales	J. E. R. Gallian (NSW)
1990-91	Sydney	South Australia	A. C. Gilchrist (NSW)
1991-92	Perth	Western Australia	A. D. McQuire (NSW)
1992-93	Brisbane	Victoria	J. P. Bray (NSW)
1993-94	Melbourne	Western Australia	J. L. Cassell (Qld)
1994-95	Sydney	Queensland/New South Wales	B. A. Clemow (NSW)
1995-96	Adelaide	Victoria	P. A. Sutherland (NSW)
1996-97	Canberra	New South Wales	D. J. McLauchlan (NSW)
1997-98	Melbourne	South Australia	G. A. Manou (S Aust)
1998-99	Adelaide	New South Wales	M. Klinger (Vic)
1999-00	Perth	Victoria/Queensland	L. Buchanan (Vic)
2000-01	Hobart	Queensland	B. Casson (W Aust)
2001-02	Newcastle	New South Wales	A. J. Crosthwaite (Vic)
2002-03	Canberra	South Australia	M. J. Cosgrove (S Aust)
2003-04	Brisbane	New South Wales	C. J. Ferguson (S Aust)
2004-05	Melbourne	New South Wales	J. Hastings (NSW)

LAST TEN YEARS' PLACINGS

	95-96	96-97	97-98	98-99	99-00	00-01	01-02	02-03	03-04	04-05
Australian Capital Territory	7	6	7	6	7	7	8	7	8	5
New South Wales .	2	1	2	1	3	4	1	3	1	1
Northern Territory .	8	8	8	8	8	8	7	8	5	8
Queensland	3	5	3	2	1	1	2	4	6	3
South Australia . . .	5	3	1	4	5	5	6	2	2	4
Tasmania	6	7	6	7	4	6	3	5	7	6
Victoria	1	2	5	3	1	2	4	1	4	2
Western Australia .	4	4	4	5	6	3	5	6	3	7

HIGHEST INDIVIDUAL SCORES

244	G. H. Armstrong, Australian Capital Territory v Queensland at Brisbane	1987-88
242	R. J. Davison, New South Wales v Northern Territory at Brisbane	1987-88
222*	M. P. Mott, Queensland v Northern Territory at Perth	1991-92
215*	G. S. Milliken, New South Wales v Tasmania at Perth	1982-83
214	D. A. Tuckwell, Queensland v Northern Territory at Sydney	1985-86
206*	M. L. Love, Queensland v South Australia at Brisbane	1992-93
205*	B. Zacny, ACT v Northern Territory at Melbourne	1997-98
202*	G. S. Blewett, South Australia v Tasmania at Melbourne	1989-90
201	R. Bowden, Northern Territory v Australian Capital Territory at Sydney	1990-91
200	J. J. Krejza, New South Wales v South Australia at Newcastle	2001-02

HIGHEST PARTNERSHIP FOR EACH WICKET

318	for 1st	V. W. Williams and D. S. Wotherspoon, NSW v South Australia at Canberra	1996-97
324	for 2nd	J. Allenby and S. E. Marsh, Western Australia v Northern Territory at Hobart	2000-01
239	for 3rd	M. Armstrong and S. P. Heaney, ACT v Northern Territory at Perth	1999-00
240	for 4th	A. I. C. Dodemaide and A. Grant, Victoria v South Australia at Perth	1982-83
231	for 5th	D. M. Wellham and M. Cox, NSW v Australian Capital Territory at Perth .	1975-76
		M. L. Love and A. Walduck, Queensland v Tasmania at Perth	1991-92
226	for 6th	K. J. Skewes and L. Mauger, Northern Territory v Tasmania at Newcastle .	2001-02
251	for 7th	C. Mason and K. M. Harvey, Western Australia v Queensland at Melbourne	1993-94
144	for 8th	A. J. Heading and A. C. L. James, ACT v Northern Territory at Hobart . . .	2000-01
121	for 9th	C. D. Hartley and N. J. Rimmington, Queensland v NSW at Hobart	2000-01
121	for 9th	D. Rixon and M. Cleary, New South Wales v Victoria at Camberwell	2004-05
103	for 10th	W. Irvine and M. Hall, ACT v Queensland at Melbourne	2004-05

BEST BOWLING IN AN INNINGS

8-11	D. J. McLauchlan, New South Wales v South Australia at Canberra	1996-97
8-70	M. C. Dolman, South Australia v Western Australia at Sydney	1978-79
7-13	C. P. Simpson, Queensland v Northern Territory at Melbourne	1997-98
7-25	M. Reidy-Crofts, Western Australia v ACT at Adelaide	1979-80
7-31	S. Hill, Western Australia v New Zealand at Sydney	1978-79
7-41	M. L. Clews, ACT v South Australia at Melbourne	1969-70
7-46	I. Woolf, Victoria v South Australia at Adelaide	1971-72
7-49	R. J. Thomas, New Zealand v ACT at Sydney	1978-79
7-58	P. Walker, ACT v Tasmania at Adelaide	1971-72
7-78	M. White, ACT v South Australia at Sydney	1978-79
7-84	S. P. Davis, Victoria v Tasmania at Christchurch	1977-78

BEST BOWLING IN A MATCH

14-15	D. J. McLauchlan, New South Wales v South Australia at Canberra	1996-
13-18	C. P. Simpson, Queensland v Northern Territory at Melbourne	1997-
11-54	M. J. Bright, New South Wales v Tasmania at Canberra	2002-
10-43	D. W. Fleming, Victoria v Northern Territory at Canberra	1988-
10-59	A. J. De Winter, Tasmania v Western Australia at Sydney	1985-

HAT-TRICKS

D. A. Johnston, South Australia v Tasmania at Canberra	1972-
R. Bucholz, Queensland v Victoria at Adelaide	1979-
H. V. Hammelman, Queensland v South Australia at Perth	1982-
A. J. De Winter, Tasmania v Western Australia at Sydney	1985-
M. G. Bevan, ACT v New South Wales at Adelaide	1986-
I. Connell, Tasmania v ACT at Brisbane	1992-
J. Southam, Northern Territory v South Australia at Adelaide	1995-
S. G. Busbridge, South Australia v ACT at Canberra	1996-
P. D. Waite, Western Australia v Queensland at Canberra	1996-
D. R. Mackenzie, Queensland v South Australia at Adelaide	1998-

Australian Under-17s, 2004-05

by GREG McKIE

ew South Wales deservedly won the Parish Cup at the Australian
Under-17s championship in Hobart. Having already comprehen-
vely defeated Victoria in an earlier round, they repeated the
erformance in the final. Although the final margin of victory of
74 runs was clear-cut, this does not completely portray the run of
lay. NSW were struggling at 6 for 86 before Ryan Beaven and
hris Small added 145 for the seventh wicket. Matthew Day,
oming in at No. 10, helped put on 84 for the ninth wicket and 49 for
e tenth, ending with an even 100 in only 106 balls. This was the
rst century recorded by a batsman coming in so low in the order in
ny Australian under-age championship.

Like the Under-19s, the Under-17s were plagued by rain. Poor
eather led to the abandonment of all games on the afternoon of the
cond day of round one. For NSW, this did not matter – they had
lready thrashed Victoria.

New South Wales deservedly had four players picked in the
ustralian Under-17s team. It could have been more, Dean Burns
nd Beaven having done enough to be picked in most years. Burns
nished with the equal top bowling aggregate as well as the lowest
verage. Beaven took 14 catches behind the stumps and his 66 in the
nal, batting at No. 8, was invaluable. Phillip Hughes scored two
enturies, and he and the consistent Small were NSW's leading
ats. Small virtually made the final safe for NSW with his deter-
ined 99, after NSW had been 4 for 51. Day complemented his
entury in the final by finishing equal second in the carnival bowling
ggregates. Simon Keen, in his third year in the team and captain
is time, took ten cheap wickets.

Victoria suffered from a lack of runs. No one aggregated 200 runs
r averaged over 40. Rees Thomas and Michael Hill were the lead-
ng bats but the team suffered some inexplicable batting collapses,

none worse than their first-round effort against NSW, when they were scuttled for 87 after being 7 for 39. Opening bowler Matthew Wilkie was tireless, claiming 13 wickets. The other opener, Dean Scheetz, gave Wilkie his best support. Andrew Brindley batted consistently in the lower order and also kept well. A young side, their prospects for next year are encouraging.

Western Australian Brian Shields showed remarkable consistency with consecutive scores of 68, 65 not out, 59, three and 60. Michael Innes and Michael Johnson both scored centuries, but neither reached an aggregate of 200. Jordan Uszko was the best all-rounder on show, taking ten wickets with his medium-pacers and scoring over 150 runs. The bowling had Tim Monteleone, Glen Stockden and Uszko as useful contributors, but little support.

South Australian captain Cory Knight was the carnival's leading batsman with 333 runs at 47.57. He also took handy wickets at low cost. Kirk Pascoe scored 140 against Northern Territory and aggregated almost 250 runs. Medium-pacer Trent Pascoe was their leading wicket-taker with 11, supported by Ryan Sawade with ten. Wicket-keeper Tim Davey scored useful runs down the order.

Tasmanian captain Jonathon Wells was the player of the series. Opening the batting, he often had to fight alone. He highlighted his effectiveness with eight cheap wickets. He won the Australian Cricketers' Association 2005 Development Award, which meant he toured with the Australian team for seven days as a full member of the side – team meetings, sitting in the rooms during all games, practice and all tactics sessions. Tasmania had little other batting apart from Brady Jones, but the attack of Wells, Ben Howard, Richard Howe and Matthew Woods generally kept the opposition in check. This was Matthew Wade's third time in the Under-17s. His 20 wickets this time (17 catches and three stumpings) put him six wickets clear of the next keeper and in second place in the all-time records.

Australian Capital Territory were best served by Nick Death and Adam Tett in batting, but runs were always hard to come by. No one reached an aggregate of 200 and only Tett reached 120 runs, courtesy of his century against the hapless Queensland. The varied attack of Death (slow left-arm), Jacob Taylor (left-arm medium-fast) and Ashley Vest (right-arm medium-fast) was effective but lacked support. At least eight of the side will be available again next year.

Northern Territory medium-pacer Michael Hanna took 13 wickets. Jamie Wyatt and Callan Richardson gave him a measure of support, but the rest of their attack was expensive. Trent Devereaux was their leading batsman, but he only scored 130 runs. Only one individual fifty was recorded.

Queensland slumped four places to finish at the bottom of the table for only the second time. The batting could not score enough runs and the bowlers paid too much for their wickets. Cameron Farrell and Chris Marshall were the best in attack whilst Alex Boukogiannis and Alex Machin were the only batsmen of note. They were saved from a terrible thrashing in the washed-out first round. Chasing WA's 6 for 337, Queensland slumped to 5 for 27 and only desperate defence from their captain, Brent Wilde, who scored 25 not out in more than two hours, enabled them to hang on.

The Australian Under-17s team, announced after the tournament, was: Matthew Day, Phillip Hughes, Simon Keen, Chris Small (NSW), Michael Hanna (NT), Cory Knight (S Aust), Jonathon Wells (Tas), Michael Hill, Dean Scheetz, Matthew Wilkie (Vic), Michael Johnson, Brian Shields, Jordan Uszko (W Aust).

ROUND ONE

New South Wales 9 for 278 (M. Singh 58, C. Ridley 55, S. Keen 54, M. Day 38, C. Small 31; M. Wilkie 3-30, B. Vance 2-60) defeated Victoria 87 (A. Brindly 23; M. Day 3-7, S. Keen 2-13, J. Lalor 2-18) and 0 for 7 on first innings.

Western Australia 6 for 337 (M. Johnson 134*, B. Shields 68, L. Towers 25, J. Uszko 24, T. Monteleone 24*, J. Newnham 23; C. Farrell 2-38, N. Fanning 2-71) and Queensland 6 for 71 (B. Wilde 25*; J. Uszko 3-11, G. Stockden 2-14); match abandoned.

South Australia 207 (T. Davey 81, C. Knight 37; J. Taylor 3-10, N. Death 2-21, L. Jorgensen 2-30, A. Tett 2-39) Australian Capital Territory 8 for 156 (T. Thornton 26, J. Williams 23, J. Taylor 21*, A. May 20; R. Sawarde 4-35, T. Pascoe 2-35); match abandoned.

Tasmania 8 for 293 (J. Philp 51*, M. Battle 47, T. Graham 43, M. Wade 37, R. Howe 36; M. Hanna 4-34, S. Compain 3-39) and Northern Territory 8 for 106 (C. Allen 33, T. Pemble 25; M. Battle 2-13, M. Woods 2-28); no result.

ROUND TWO

Victoria 6 for 267 (M. Crook 61*, R. Thomas 54, J. Davies 44, A. Brindly 28*, M. Hill 27, A. Barton 22; J. Uszko 2-42, T. Monteleone 2-58) defeated Western Australia 164 (B. Shields 65*, J. Uszko 25, J. Newnham 20; K. Clark 2-22, D. Scheetz 2-24, B. Vance 2-28, J. Davies 2-30) on first innings.

Queensland 7 for 186 (A. Boukogiannis 50, D. Michael 49, P. Dein 41; M. Day 2-38, S. Keen 240) lost to New South Wales 210 (C. Bennett 47, C. Small 36, M. Gowland 32, S. Keen 25, C. Ridley 22; C. Marshall 3-21, C. Farrell 2-30, J. Fenwick 2-31) on first innings.

Tasmania 7 for 212 declared (J. Wells 68, J. Philp 27, B. Jones 27, M. Battle 23; N. Death 3-42) defeated Australian Capital Territory 186 (A. Tett 41; T. West 2-27) on first innings.

Northern Territory 123 (J. Lamborn 34, T. Pemble 23; J. Draper 3-28, T. Pascoe 2-16, C. Knight 2-16) lost to South Australia 5 for 316 (K. Pascoe 140, P. Connelly 48, R. Porter 39, T. Davey 31*; C. Richardson 2-41) on first innings.

ROUND THREE

Queensland 8 for 200 declared (A. Boukogiannis 58, B. Wilde 45, P. Dein 44; M. Crook 2-14, D. Scheetz 2-25, M. Wilke 2-28) and 4 for 26 (A. McGuinness 2-6) lost to Victoria 9 for 281 declared (R. Thomas 66, M. Hill 57, J. Davies 56, A. Brindly 39, A. Barton 29; C. Farrell 2-29, C. Marshall 2-43, N. Fanning 2-43) on first innings.

New South Wales 9 for 291 declared (P. Hughes 114, C. Small 78, M. Day 27*; P. Donaldson 3-45, G. Stockden 3-53, J. Uszko 2-35) defeated Western Australia 177 (B. Shields 59, J. Uszko 35, J. Newnham 20; C. Small 3-16, D. Burns 3-39, S. Keen 2-24, M. Singh 2-43) on first innings.

Australian Capital Territory 203 (L. McCarthy 63*, J. Taylor 29; J. Wyatt 3-26, B. Reichstein 2-16, M. Hanna 2-35, T. Scollay 2-46) lost to Northern Territory 9 for 227 (N. Drummond 61, J. Lamborn 40, T. Pemble 25, T. Scollay 20; A. Twigg 4-32, A. Vest 3-33) on first innings.

Tasmania 159 (J. Wells 82, M. Battle 22; E. Laubscher 5-29, J. Draper 2-34) and 2 for 81 (C. Bury 35*, M. Wade 37*) lost to South Australia 214 (C. Knight 52, R. Bock 50, T. Pascoe 33, K. Pascoe 26; B. Howard 5-46, S. Nichols 2-27) on first innings.

POINTS TABLE

Section A	P	WO	W1	D	L1	LO	T	Points	Quotient
New South Wales	3	0	3	0	0	0	0	6	1.644
Victoria	3	0	2	0	1	0	0	4	1.192
Western Australia	3	0	0	1	2	0	0	0	0.871
Queensland	3	0	0	1	2	0	0	0	0.583
Section B	P	WO	W1	D	L1	LO	T	Points	Quotient
South Australia	3	0	2	1	0	0	0	4	1.704
Tasmania	3	0	1	1	1	0	0	2	1.527
Northern Territory	3	0	1	1	1	0	0	2	0.478
Australian Capital Territory	3	0	0	1	2	0	0	0	0.783

Quotient equals runs per wicket scored divided by runs per wicket conceded.

SEMI-FINALS

Australia Capital Territory 260 (A. Tett 108; A. Machin 3-14) defeated Queensland 253 (A. Kemp 62, A. Machin 52; R. Van Aalst 3-39) on first innings.

Northern Territory 155 (T. Devereaux 45; M. Woods 4-24) were defeated by Tasmania 8 for 219 (B. Jones 89, J. Wells 55; M. Hanna 4-55) on first innings.

Western Australia 141 (M. Innes 50; D. Scheetz 4-36, M. Wilkie 3-20) and 2 for 132 (L. Towers 63; J. Uszko 52*) were defeated by Victoria 288 (M. Hill 67; J. Uszko 3-65, G. Stockden 3-74) on first innings.

South Australia 101 (D. Burns 4-6, S. Keen 3-19, M. Day 3-21) and 5 for 236 (K. Pascoe 57) were defeated by New South Wales 7 for 328 dec (P. Hughes 160, M. Singh 91; C. Knight 4-35) on first innings.

CONSOLATION FINALS

Australian Capital Territory 162 (A. Tett 46, T. Thornton 34, A. May 27, N. Death 25; T. Monteleone 5-19, G. Stockden 2-27, K. Sanders 2-32) lost to Western Australia 286 (M. Innes 100, B. Shields 60, P. Donaldson 28*, L. Towers 21, A. Strijk 21; A. Vest 3-37) on first innings.

South Australia 173 (C. Knight 100, T. Davey 38; S. Nichols 4-9, J. Wells 3-24) and 9 for 251 (H. White 74*, C. Knight 64, R. Porter 41, P. Connelly 27; J. Wells 3-49, R. Howe 2-21) defeated Tasmania 99 (S. Nichols 27; T. Pascoe 4-10, R. Sawade 3-37, E. Laubscher 2-6) on first innings.

Queensland 90 (A. Boukogiannis 28; T. Pemble 3-25, C. Richardson 2-7, J. Wyatt 2-10, M. Hanna 2-18) and 2 for 144 (A. Machin 61*, B. Wilde 44, A. Kemp 28) lost to Northern Territory 213 (T. Devereaux 47, J. Lamborn 37, T. Pemble 32, N. Drummond 31, J. Wyatt 21*; J. Fenwick 4-23, B. Matheson 2-31, C. Marshall 2-41) on first innings.

FINAL

New South Wales 367 (M. Day 100, C. Small 99, R. Beaven 66, C. Bennett 32; M. Wilke 4-55, K. Clark 3-40) defeated Victoria 193 (R. Thomas 47, J. Davies 33, B. Vance 30*, K. Clark 29, A. McGuinness 22; D. Burns 4-23, M. Holmes 2-35, J. Lalor 2-43) on first innings.

FINAL STANDINGS

	Won	Lost	Draw
New South Wales	5	0	0
Victoria	3	2	0
Western Australia	1	3	1
South Australia	3	1	1
Tasmania	2	2	1
Australian Capital Territory	1	3	1
Northern Territory	1	3	1
Queensland	1	3	1

UNDER-17s CRICKET CHAMPIONSHIP, 2004-05

MOST RUNS, 2004-05

	M	I	NO	R	HS	100s	50s	Avge
C. Knight (S Aust)	5	7	0	333	100	1	2	47.57
P. Hughes (NSW)	5	5	0	290	160	2	0	58.00
C. Small (NSW)	5	5	1	264	99	0	2	66.00
B. Shields (W Aust)	5	5	1	255	68	0	4	63.75
K. Pascoe (S Aust)	5	7	0	249	140	1	0	35.57
J. Wells (Tas)	5	6	0	218	82	0	3	36.33

MOST WICKETS, 2004-05

	R	W	BB	Avge
D. Burns (NSW)	153	13	4-6	11.76
M. Wilkie (Vic)	156	13	4-55	12.00
M. Hanna (NT)	203	13	4-34	15.61
T. Pascoe (S Aust)	142	11	4-10	12.90
M. Day (NSW)	184	11	3-7	16.72
S. Keen (NSW)	124	10	3-16	12.40

MOST DISMISSALS, 2004-05

M. Wade (Tas) 20	(17 ct, 3 st)
R. Beaven (NSW) 14	(all ct)

UNDER-17s CRICKET CHAMPIONSHIPS RECORDS

CHAMPIONSHIP WINNERS

Series	Venue	Winner	Player of the Year
1977-78	Perth	Victoria	not awarded
1978-79	Rockhampton	Western Australia	S. P. O'Donnell (Vic)
1979-80	Melbourne	Victoria	I. A. Healy (Qld)
1980-81	Launceston	Victoria	D. Brown (Vic)
1981-82	Adelaide	Queensland	G. Hayden (Qld)
1982-83	Sydney	Queensland	G. R. Parker (Vic)
1983-84	Brisbane	Victoria	G. R. Parker (Vic)
1984-85	Canberra	Queensland	J. Smith (Tas)
1985-86	Perth	New South Wales	G. H. Armstrong (ACT)
1986-87	Melbourne	New South Wales	M. Galbraith (Vic)
1987-88	Launceston	New South Wales	J. C. Young (NSW)
1988-89	Sydney	South Australia	M. J. P. Minagall (SA)
1989-90	Adelaide	Victoria	T. F. Corbett (Vic)
1990-91	Brisbane	New South Wales	J. P. Maher (Qld)
1991-92	Canberra	New South Wales	B. J. Hodge (Vic)
1992-93	Hobart	New South Wales	B. A. Clemow (NSW)
1993-94	Adelaide	New South Wales	M. D. Pascoe (Qld)
1994-95	Perth	New South Wales	D. J. Thornely (NSW)
1995-96	Melb/Geelong	Queensland	M. J. North (WAust)
1996-97	Brisbane	New South Wales	L. Williams (SAust)
1997-98	Hobart	Victoria	A. J. Kent (Vic)
1998-99	Sydney	New South Wales	E. J. M. Cowan (NSW)
1999-00	Brisbane	Victoria	P. Boraston (Vic)
2000-01	Brisbane	South Australia	C. J. Borgas (S Aust)

eries	*Venue*	*Winner*	*Player of the Year*
001-02	Melbourne	New South Wales	C. J. Ferguson (S Aust)
002-03	Perth	New South Wales	D. N. Porter (W Aust)
003-04	Adelaide	Victoria	T. Cooper (NSW)
004-05	Hobart	New South Wales	J. Wells (Tas)

Note: No player of the championships awarded prior to 1978-79.

LAST TEN YEARS' PLACINGS

	95-96	96-97	97-98	98-99	99-00	00-01	01-02	02-03	03-04	04-05
Australian Capital Territory	7	7	7	5	7	7	8	7	6	6
New South Wales	6	1	6	1	2	2	1	1	2	1
Northern Territory	8	8	4	7	8	8	5	8	8	7
Queensland	1	2	8	2	4	4	3	4	4	8
South Australia	2	4	5	8	3	1	2	3	5	4
Tasmania	5	6	3	6	6	5	7	5	7	5
Victoria	3	5	1	4	1	3	4	2	1	2
Western Australia	4	3	2	3	5	6	6	6	3	3

HIGHEST INDIVIDUAL SCORES

.58*	C. J. Ferguson, South Australia v Queensland	2001-02
55*	A. J. Kent, Victoria v New South Wales	1997-98
25*	L. Williams, South Australia v Northern Territory	1996-97
.18*	E. J. M. Cowan, New South Wales v Australian Capital Territory	1998-99
.06	B. A. Clemow, New South Wales v Australian Capital Territory	1992-93
'04	A. Symonds, Queensland v South Australia	1991-92
02*	S. Dean, Victoria v South Australia	2003-04

HIGHEST PARTNERSHIP FOR EACH WICKET

st	324	E. J. M. Cowan and A. Alley New South Wales v Australian Capital Territory	1998-99
nd	208	R. Hadley and S. E. Marsh Western Australia v Australian Capital Territory	1998-99
rd	252	T. Cooper and G. Clarence New South Wales v South Australia	2003-04
th	282	M. Galbraith and D. Shinkfield Victoria v Western Australia	1985-86
5th	207	A. M. Rowe and S. R. Watson Queensland v South Australia	1996-97
5th	168	M. Labrizzi and G. Matthews Western Australia v Victoria	1987-88
7th	211	J. Lalich and K. M. Harvey Western Australia v Australian Capital Territory	1992-93
8th	219*	A. J. Kent and G. Turner Victoria v New South Wales	1997-98
9th	134	B. Deledio and J. McNamara Victoria v New South Wales	2003-04
0th	125	D. A. Nash and C. Davis New South Wales v Victoria	1994-95

BEST BOWLING IN AN INNINGS

0-28	D. Davidson, New South Wales v South Australia	1957-58
-20	A. A. Mallett, Western Australia v New South Wales	1957-58
-68	P. Ryan, Queensland v Victoria	1978-79
-33	M. Smith, Queensland v New South Wales	1956-57
-36	I. McMullen, Victoria v Western Australia	1964-65
-49	J. Reynolds, South Australia v Western Australia	1963-64

BEST BOWLING IN A MATCH

17-50	D. Davidson, New South Wales v South Australia	1957-5
13-36	S. Bell, New South Wales v Western Australia	1963-6
13-43	B. Walton, South Australia v New South Wales	1954-5
12-45	A. A. Mallett, Western Australia v New South Wales	1957-5
12-80	G. Crispe, Queensland v Western Australia	1964-6
11-47	P. Siddle, Victoria v South Australia	2001-0
11-72	W. J. Scholes, Victoria v Queensland	1964-6

HAT-TRICKS

F. Speare	Queensland v South Australia	1954-5
R. W. Bulger	Australian Capital Territory v Tasmania	1997-9
M. J. Cosgrove	South Australia v Western Australia	2000-0

ACT First-Grade, 2004-05

by ADAM MOREHOUSE

Eastlake won their first premiership since 1993-94 by defeating Tuggeranong Valley in the final. Tuggeranong Valley had been undefeated in 20 previous matches in the two-day competition, an ACT First Grade record. Eastlake's performance was built around the all-round brilliance of captain Mark Divin, who broke the ACT record for the most runs in a season, scoring 1,209 at the remarkable average of 120.90. He was also the leading wicket-taker for the season with 51, including 12 in the final. Divin's performance was complemented by opening batsmen Nigel Page, who scored 738 runs without a century, and Chris Lejsek, who made 531. Former Australian Under-19 fast bowler Brett Anderton assisted Divin in the pace bowling, taking 42 wickets, while spinners Matt Ramage, Michael Shaw and Mark Hatton proved a formidable trio, each taking more than 20 wickets.

Tuggeranong Valley were minor premiers for the second season in a row, but fell at the final hurdle. Their success was built around their captain, David Jeffrey, who scored 719 runs and took 35 wickets with his swing bowling. Bowling was their strength, the batting of Jeffrey and Stewart Heaney aside. Born in Canada but locally raised, Heaney scored 977 runs and was rewarded with selection in the Prime Minister's XI. The key bowlers were evergreen Evan Kellar and young paceman Adam Ritchard, who took 41 and 26 wickets respectively.

Weston Creek tasted success for the first time in two seasons, winning the Konica-Minolta limited-overs cup after hard-fought victories in both the semi-final and the final. The star of the Creek season was Victorian import Francis Gill, a swing bowler who took 54 wickets at an average of only 17. The side made the semi-finals for the fifth season in a row despite being hampered by rain early in the season. Their highlight in the two-day competition was the successful chase of a target of 408 in just over 80 overs against Wests, breaking a 60-year-old ACT record; their 18-year-old opening batsman John

Rogers made 170 off just 171 balls. Veterans Sean Maxwell and Ewan Mackenzie were a consistent force, Mackenzie taking up leadership responsibilities part-way through the season. Rogers, with Wade Irvine and Matthew Bell, showed great promise during the season, and all three won ACT Under-19 selection, while Daniel Mowbray and Nicholas Curran were consistent. Weston Creek were the ACT representatives in the NSW Country Cup Finals in Dubbo but lost a close fourth-round match against Cardiff with a weakened side, and then were well beaten by Wagga Wagga in the consolation match in Parkes.

Western District–University of Canberra returned to the semi finals, with captain Darren Richards leading the way. Richards made 644 runs, while all-rounder Danny Byrne took 42 wickets including a club record 8 for 28 against Ginninderra.

Queanbeyan were serious contenders for the finals for the first time in a couple of seasons, and made the semi-finals of the limited overs competition. Their best performances were from a fully fit Adam Heading, who scored 661 runs and took 21 wickets, and the pace duo of Dean Southwell and Nathan Madsen.

Sixth were Ginninderra–West Belconnen. A lack of runs meant that the bowlers had little to play with. Only two batsmen, Daniel Poidevin and Sam Gaskin, scored 300 runs for the season. Opening bowlers Andrew Jones and Josh Kentwell performed well, taking 28 and 26 wickets respectively.

Australian National University finished seventh, mainly thanks to their new captain, Randall Starr. Starr, a former NSW Country representative, made 686 runs at an average of 38. Other leading performers for the club were Stephen Sorbello with 338 runs and Achila Siriwardhane with 22 wickets.

North Canberra–Gungahlin were disappointing, finishing at the foot of the table after making the final the previous season. The main reason was a lack of batsmen to support the top-order effort of Scott Cameron, 453 runs, and Trevor Power, 338 runs, and a quality opening bowler to support the spin of the captain, Heath Axelby, who took 24 wickets.

ACT FIRST-GRADE TABLE, 2004-05

	M	WO	WI	D	TI	LI	LO	T	Points	Quotient
Tuggeranong Valley	10	1	8	1	0	0	0	0	58	1.5078
Eastlake	10	2	5	1	0	2	0	0	54	1.5559
Western District-Uni. of Canberra	10	1	5	3	0	1	0	0	40	1.1384
Weston Creek	10	0	5	2	0	3	0	0	30	1.1021
Queanbeyan	10	0	2	1	0	5	1	0	18	0.7597
Ginninderra West Belconnen	10	0	2	0	0	6	2	0	18	0.6716
Australian National University ..	10	1	0	1	0	6	2	0	12	0.7425
North Canberra-Gungahlin	10	0	2	3	0	5	0	0	12	1.0070

BATTING AVERAGES, 2004-05

(Qualification: 300 runs)

	M	I	NO	R	HS	100s	50s	Avge
M. A. Divin (Eastlake)	16	15	5	1,209	172*	5	5	120.90
S. P. Heaney (Tuggeranong Valley)	16	18	1	977	157	4	3	57.47
D. M. Jeffrey (Tuggeranong Valley)	16	17	4	719	132	2	4	55.31
D. J. Richards (Western District-UC)	14	16	1	644	101	2	4	42,93
A. J. Heading (Queanbeyan)	15	18	2	661	92	0	7	41.31
N. M. Page (Eastlake)	17	21	3	738	84	0	7	41.00
R. Starr (ANU)	13	20	2	686	122	1	5	38.11
S. L. Maxwell (Weston Creek)	16	15	4	401	81	0	3	36.45
S. R. Cameron (North Canberra-Gungahlin)	12	15	2	453	183	1	1	34.85
B. G. Phillips (Western District-UC)	14	14	0	483	84	0	4	34.50

* Denotes not out.

BOWLING AVERAGES, 2004-05

(Qualification: 20 wickets)

	M	O	Mdns	R	W	BB	5W/i	10W/m	Avge
D. M. Jeffrey (Tuggeranong Valley) ...	16	248.5	81	539	35	6-30	3	0	15.40
B. T. Anderton (Eastlake)	14	237.5	51	649	42	5-35	1	0	15.45
M. J. Clark (ANU)	12	109.2	13	311	20	6-33	1	0	15.55
D. Southwell (Queanbeyan)	14	211.5	42	613	39	7-31	2	0	15.72
M. A. Divin (Eastlake)	16	272.3	66	815	51	7-23	4	1	15.98
E. Kellar (Tuggeranong Valley)	16	301	76	667	41	7-69	2	0	16.27
B. A. Mikkelsen (North Canberra-Gungahlin)	5	101.2	18	333	20	7-46	1	0	16.65
H. R. Axelby (North Canberra-Gungahlin)	11	174.4	62	409	24	5-41	1	0	17.04
F. J. Gill (Weston Creek)	15	241	50	583	34	5-71	1	0	17.15
D. P. Byrne (Western District-UC)	14	236.5	32	802	42	8-28	3	0	19.10

ACT FIRST-GRADE SEMI-FINALS, 2004-05

TUGGERANONG VALLEY v WESTON CREEK

At Manuka Oval, Manuka, March 12, 13, 2005. *Toss:* Tuggeranong Valley. Tuggeranong Valley won on first innings. Weston Creek 156 (J.W. Rogers 31, S.L. Maxwell 30; E. Kellar 6-49, M. Wescombe 2-31, A.M. Ritchard 2-36) lost to Tuggeranong Valley 1-237 (S.P. Heaney 131*, C.J. Males 100*).

EASTLAKE v WESTERN DISTRICT-UNIVERSITY OF CANBERRA

At Chisholm No.1 Oval, Chisholm, March 12,13,14, 2005. *Toss:* Western District-University of Canberra. Eastlake won on first innings. Western District-University of Canberra 157 (B. Lyon 47, D.B. Hall 33; J. Shaw 3-18, M.H. Ramage 3-41, M.A. Divin 3-44) and 285 for 9 declared (D.P. Byrne 64, B. Lyon 49, D.B. Hall 44, D.J. Richards 28, B.G. Phillips 25, L.M. Funnell 25; M.A. Hatton 4-97, M.H. Ramage 3-49) lost to Eastlake 316 (M.A. Divin 172*, M.A. Kendall 25, J. Shaw 25; D.P. Byrne 4-88, B.M. Keens 4-90) and 2-127 (N.M. Page 45, M.A. Hatton 27*).

FINAL

TUGGERANONG VALLEY v EASTLAKE

At Manuka Oval on March 19, 20, 21, 2005. *Result:* Eastlake won on the first innings. *Toss:* Eastlake.

In overcast conditions and on a wicket with some life in it, Eastlake won the toss and sent Tuggeranong Valley in. Minor premiers Tuggeranong lost only one wicket in the first hour, but collapsed to be 7 for 66 at lunch. Eastlake mopped up the tail after the lunch break and Tuggeranong were out for a paltry 87. Mark Divin, who was almost unplayable, bowled unchanged throughout the innings.

Eastlake batted out the rest of the day and gained a first-innings lead, but suffered the vital loss of Divin just before stumps to give Tuggeranong a chance. Tuggeranong dominated the second day's play with both the bat and ball. Batting slowly to draw out their innings, Eastlake lost veteran Michael Kavanagh after he had batted nearly four hours for 58 runs. The last six Eastlake wickets fell for only 19 runs, most of them to David Jeffrey's swing bowling. He restricted Eastlake to a 99-run lead.

Eastlake struck back at Tuggeranong immediately, dismissing Matthew Armstrong with the first ball of the second innings. Soon it was 3 for 10 and the match looked likely to finish inside two days. Prime Minister's XI representative Stewart Heaney and Jeffrey set about a rescue mission, and their forthright partnership of 162 in 176 minutes put Tuggeranong in a winning position. At the start of the final day, any sort of result was possible. Divin mopped up the tail, to finish with 12 for 114 for the match.

Set 193 for an outright victory, Eastlake tucked their first-innings lead under their belts and batted dourly, taking 55 overs to reach 1 for 96 before gloomy skies and rain intervened, bringing the match to an end. Opener Nigel Page was the surprise choice as man of the match.

Greg Irvine Medal: N.M. Page (Eastlake).

Close of Play: Tuggeranong Valley (2) 5-217.

Tuggeranong Valley

M. A. Armstrong c Kavanagh b Divin	8	– lbw b Anderton	0
C. J. Males c M. E. L. Shaw b Anderton	12	– c Kavanagh b Divin	0
S. P. Heaney c Kendall b Divin	19	– (4) c Divin b M. E. L. Shaw	93
*D. M. Jeffrey c Kendall b Divin	6	– (5) c J. Shaw b Divin	131
J. M. Haywood lbw b Anderton	0	– (3) c Divin b Anderton	10
J. D. Evans b Anderton	1	– lbw b Lejsek	25
A. Blacka c M. E. L. Shaw b Divin	4	– b Divin	4
M. Wescombe c M. E. L. Shaw b Divin	5	– b Divin	0
†S. Osbourne b Divin	9	– c M. E. L. Shaw b Divin	6
E. Kellar c Divin b Lejsek	9	– b Divin	5
A. M. Ritchard not out	5	– not out	7
B 2, l-b 3, n-b 4	9	L-b 6, n-b 4	10

(33.3 overs, 139 mins)   87
Fall: 19 33 47 48 52 54 59 66 75 87

(73.3 overs, 338 mins)   291
Fall: 0 10 10 172 211 225 229
250 274 291

Bowling: *First Innings*—Anderton 15–4–31–3, Divin 16.3–5–38–6, Lejsek 2–0–13–1. *Second Innings*—Anderton 18–4–60–2, Divin 21.3–2–76–6, Hatton 14–2–46–0, Lejsek 5–0–20–1, Ramage 8–5–49–0, M. E. L. Shaw 9–3–33–1.

Eastlake

N. M. Page c Osbourne b Jeffrey	40	– not out	59
C. P. Lejsek lbw b Kellar	5	– lbw b Wescombe	30
M. J. Kavanagh c Evans b Males	58	– not out	3
*M. A. Divin c Osbourne b Wescombe	29		
T. M. McGrath b Kellar	2		
M. A. Hatton lbw b Jeffrey	25		
†M. A. Kendall not out	6		
M. E. L. Shaw c Osbourne b Jeffrey	4		
J. Shaw b Jeffrey	0		
B. T. Anderton c Osbourne b Jeffrey	2		
M. H. Ramage c Males b Kellar	1		
B 8, l-b 2, n-b 4	14	B 3, l-b 1	4

(78.1 overs, 329 mins,)   186
Fall: 14, 71, 127, 134, 167, 177, 183, 185, 186

(55 overs, 200 mins)   (1 wkt)   96
Fall: 77

Bowling: *First Innings*—Kellar 28.1–9–50–3, Ritchard 20–6–51–0, Jeffery 17–9–26–5, Males 14–6–27–1, Wescombe 6–1–17–1, Blacka 3–1–5–0. *Second Innings*—Kellar 17–9–26–0, Ritchard 8–1–27–0, Jeffery 7–3–10–0, Males 14–7–13–0, Wescombe 9–3–16–1.

Umpires: S. G. Balchin and A. I. Shelley.

ACT FIRST-GRADE RECORDS

ALL-TIME LEADING RUN-SCORERS

	Runs	Club
P. J. Solway	9,401	Queanbeyan, ANU, Eastlake
M. J. Kavanagh	7,868	South Canberra, Eastlake
M. J. Frost	7,132	Queanbeyan, Weston Creek
L. Maloney	6,766	Ainslie, Hall
G. R. Irvine	6,763	Weston Creek, ANU
S. L. Maxwell	6,207	Weston Creek
S. E. Frost	6,167	Queanbeyan
L. Lees	5,944	Northbourne, Ainslie
D. M. Jeffrey	5,943	Tuggeranong Valley
B. D. Bretland	5,832	South Woden, Woden Valley, South Canberra, Tuggeranong Valley

ALL-TIME LEADING BOWLERS

	Runs	Club
G. J. Smith	864	Turner, Ainslie, Northern Suburbs, Ginninderra
W. C. Tickner	775	Duntroon, Hall, Northbourne
D. A. Moore	626	East Canberra, Northern Suburbs, Western District
K. V. McCarty	556	Ainslie, Northbourne, Turner, City
G. J. Samuels	511	Turner, City, ANU, Queanbeyan
A. J. Macdonald	462	Ainslie, City, Western District
K. L. Bone	456	Woden, Weston Creek
L. Lees	454	Northbourne, Ainslie
F. Nash	414	Queanbeyan
M. J. Howell	409	ANU
D. B. Robin	404	Manuka, Kingston

Sydney First-Grade, 2004-05

by TERRY SMITH

University of NSW fell a wicket short of completing a remarkable double in the Sydney grade competition when Sydney University scraped home in the premiership final. As the Sydney University No. 11 watched from the bowler's end, former Test star Greg Matthews, 45 years old but as combative as ever, struck the ball to the boundary. Earlier in the summer, University of NSW had won the one-day series, beating their arch-rivals Sydney University in the final.

As their one-day final loss was one of only two defeats suffered by Sydney University all season, nobody could begrudge their second premiership in three years. They accumulated 100 points in the lead-up to the final series in which they disposed first of Manly–Warringah and then Fairfield–Liverpool, thus avenging an earlier defeat at the hands of the latter. When their big guns were on deck, Sydney University looked unbeatable. Led by Shane Stanton, a bright spark who graduated in pure maths, their ranks included Stuart MacGill, the evergreen Matthews and state trio Greg Mail, Ed Cowan and Matthew Phelps. Stanton's contribution of 865 runs at 45.43 and 51 victims as wicket-keeper was crucial, while Cowan managed 917 runs at 61.13 despite missing matches while on NSW duty. He posted three centuries, including a score of 160 against Blacktown. All-rounder Ian Moran, who opened both bowling and batting, was the leading wicket-taker with 48 at 17.70. On a dodgy pitch in a semi-final at University Oval, he whipped out five batsmen for 11 runs to spark the collapse of Fairfield–Liverpool for only 34 after University had fallen for 101. Praising his bowlers, Stanton pointed out that only five teams scored 250 against the students, who conceded only one century all season.

University of NSW had their finest season in years, following the arrival from Wagga of innovative coach Warren Smith, the man who was Michael Slater's mentor from the age of seven. A man who thinks outside the square, Smith goes to the gym to study the footwork of boxing champion Kostya Tszyu. Captained by David Carson, who Smith called "my Allan Border", the Bumble Bees produced the season's most prolific scorer in Murray Creed, a former South African Under-19 international who has played first-class cricket for Eastern Province. When he rang another club looking for a game, the secretary said his team was overloaded with batsmen and advised Creed to try University of NSW. A diligent practiser, the technically correct Creed scored 1,102 runs at 58 including four centuries and four fifties, with a top score of 166 against Mosman. Tim Lang, who came from St George seeking a chance, and Ian Salisbury, the former England leg-spinner, contributed 83 wickets to the cause, and took a week off from his county commitments with Surrey to fly in for the final. The rangy Lang finished third in the wicket-takers with 51 wickets at 18.08 including an eight-wicket haul in the final, which won him the Benaud Medal for the outstanding player. He had also taken 7 for 20 to rout Campbelltown–Camden at Raby. Playing only eleven matches, Salisbury snared 31 wickets at 12.28 to finish second in the first-grade averages. Another key man for University of NSW was Andrew Neilan, who was the top wicket-keeper with 5 victims. Dan Christian emphasised his talent by whipping up 126 to wipe out Northern Districts in a semi-final.

Fairfield–Liverpool finished in second place on the table, six points ahead of University of NSW, who made a slow start to the season. Doug Bollinger was the hero for the Fairfield Lions, topping the competition averages with 67 wickets at 12.53 with his left-arm quicks, including figures of 7 for 28 in the semi-final against Sydney University.

Boosted by the return of Brett van Deinsen and Jarrod Burke from stints with other clubs, Campbelltown–Camden finished in fourth spot, with each player scoring two centuries and Burke winning the O'Reilly Medal for his all-round effort of 780 runs at 41.05 and 37 wickets, including 7 for 31 against Gordon. Northern District were fifth, with Ben Davis and Mark Daykin each topping 800 runs, including an innings of 143 by Daykin to sink Fairfield–Liverpool in the qualifying final. Cameron Eve was the top wicket-taker with 38.

Manly–Warringah rounded out the final six, with Shawn Bradstreet, quick bowler Mark Cameron and wicket-keeper Mark Atkinson producing some strong performances. Cameron was the competition's second-highest wicket-taker with 55 at 15.44, and Bradstreet took a stunning 8 for 40 in a qualifying semi-final against Sydney University and hit an unbeaten 116 against Sutherland. Atkinson hit two centuries and claimed 33 victims behind the stumps.

The previous season's premiers Eastern Suburbs tied with Manly on 67 points but missed out because of their inferior quotient. Bankstown were next on 66, their bright spot an unbeaten 200 by former state opening bat Corey Richards against Gordon at Killara. Sutherland's Matthew O'Brien topped the competition's batting averages with 800 runs at 61.54.

In the one-day final at University Oval, Camperdown, on January 30, Sydney University were dismissed for 129, and University of NSW reached the target with the loss of five wickets. Dan Christian won the man of the match award for his 49 for University of NSW.

SYDNEY FIRST-GRADE TABLE, 2004-05

	M	WO	W1	D	L1	LO	T	Points	Quotient
ydney University	19	1	15	2	1	0	0	100	1.6348
airfield-Liverpool	19	0	13	3	3	0	0	78	1.4395
niversity of NSW	19	0	12	2	5	0	0	72	1.3583
ampbelltown-Camden	19	0	12	1	6	0	0	72	1.0152
orthern District	19	1	10	2	5	1	0	70	1.3166
anly-Warringah	19	1	9	2	6	0	1	67	1.2372
astern Suburbs	19	1	9	2	6	0	1	67	1.1685
ankstown	19	0	11	1	7	0	0	66	1.0818
osman	19	1	9	3	6	0	0	64	1.0967
andwick Petersham	19	0	8	3	7	1	0	48	0.9647
TS-Balmain	19	1	6	1	9	2	0	46	0.8437
utherland	19	0	7	3	8	1	0	42	1.0813
enrith	19	0	5	2	11	0	1	33	0.8024
arramatta	19	0	5	5	9	0	0	30	0.8851
acktown	19	0	5	2	12	0	0	30	0.7380
awkesbury	19	0	5	4	10	0	0	30	0.7177
George	19	0	4	4	10	0	1	27	0.8427
orth Sydney	19	0	4	2	13	0	0	24	0.8823
estern Suburbs	19	0	4	4	11	0	0	24	0.7980
ordon	19	0	4	2	12	1	0	24	0.7013

BATTING AVERAGES, 2004-05

(Qualification: 400 runs)

	M	I	NO	R	HS	100s	50s	Avge
M. D. O'Brien (Sutherland)	17	18	5	800	118*	2	6	61.54
E. J. M. Cowan (Sydney University)	17	18	3	917	160	3	4	61.13
R. C. Aitken (North Sydney)	17	17	3	820	107*	2	5	58.57
M. W. Creed (University of NSW)	21	25	6	1,102	169	4	4	58.00
B. J. Davis (Northern District)	20	21	5	863	178*	4	3	53.94
M. J. Bright (Western Suburbs)	15	14	0	754	122	1	7	53.86
J. R. Packman (Gordon)	14	16	2	710	110	2	6	50.71
R. M. Nelson (Northern District)	20	14	6	405	77	0	2	50.62
J. Vero (Mosman)	17	18	1	860	118	4	4	50.59
C. J. Richards (Bankstown)	18	21	3	884	200*	3	3	49.11

* Denotes not out.

BOWLING, 2004-05

(Qualification: 20 wickets)

	M	O	Mdns	R	W	BB	5W/i	10W/m	Avge
M. J. Nicholson (Gordon)	9	136.5	40	318	25	7-55	2	0	12.7.
S. R. Clark (Sutherland)	7	102.4	21	285	22	6-45	2	0	12.9'
D. A. Nash (Fairfield-Liverpool)	13	206.1	47	590	41	5-34	2	0	14.3'
J. Lewis (Randwick-Petersham)	19	338.3	93	795	52	7-35	3	0	15.2'
W. J. Adlam (Mosman)	21	333.2	83	946	57	7-41	3	1	16.5'
D. T. Johnston (Mosman)	18	188.1	41	551	33	6-17	2	0	16.6'
S. M. Thompson (Bankstown)	22	283.3	62	846	47	6-26	1	0	18.0'
M. Henriques (St George)	12	145.5	22	505	28	7-40	1	1	18.0.
T. Keirath (Sydney University)	12	120.3	18	406	22	3-23	0	0	18.4.
C. P. Eve (Northern District)	19	263.3	56	798	43	5-52	0	1	18.5'

SYDNEY FIRST-GRADE QUALIFYING FINALS, 2004-05

SYDNEY UNIVERSITY v MANLY-WARRINGAH

At University No.1 Oval, Camperdown, March 19, 20, 2005. Sydney University won o
first innings. Manly-Warringah 137 (I. Moran 5-28; M. Pascal 3-47) and 149 for
declared (J. N. Sullivan 55, T. W. R. Kierath 3-68) lost to Sydney University 140 ('
Moran 42, S. D. Bradstreet 8-40) and 6 for 112 (S. Whiteman 41; S. Cleary 3-20, S
D. Bradstreet 3-22).

FAIRFIELD-LIVERPOOL v NORTHERN DISTRICT

At Hurstville Oval, March 19, 20, 2005. Northern District won on first inning. Fairfiel
Liverpool 126 (C. P. Eve 5-39) and 3-87 lost to Northern District 300 (M. R. Daykin 14:
R. M. Nelson 44; D. Bollinger 7-111).

UNIVERSITY OF NEW SOUTH WALES v
CAMPBELLTOWN-CAMDEN

At Village Green, Kensington, March 19, 20, 2005. University of New South Wales wc
on first innings. Campbelltown-Camden 221 for 8 declared (D. G. Lonergan 84; E. J. W
Zehner 3-32, T. E. Lang 3-47) lost to University of New South Wales 8-223 (M. W
O'Connor 58, D. J. Carson 47; C. K. L. Nupier 3-41).

SEMI-FINALS

BANKSTOWN V EASTERN SUBURBS

At University No.1 Oval, Camperdown, March 26, 27, 2005. Sydney University won on first innings. Sydney University 101 (D. Bollinger 7-28, G. M. Lambert 3-46) and 8-100 (G. M. Lambert 4-31) defeated Fairfield-Liverpool 34 (I. Moran 5-11).

UNIVERSITY OF NEW SOUTH WALES v NORTHERN DISTRICT

At Village Green, Kensington, March 26,27, 2005. Match drawn. University of New South Wales 309 for 4 declared (D. T. Christian 136, D. J. Carson 81*) drew with Northern District did not bat.

FINAL

SYDNEY UNIVERSITY v UNIVERSITY OF NSW

At University No.1 Oval, Camperdown on April 1, 2, 3, 2005. Sydney University won by one wicket. *Toss:* Sydney University.

Sydney University's last two men were at the wicket with four runs needed to win the final for the second time in three years. The gap was cut to three when University of NSW pace bowler Eric Zehner bowled a wide to last man Marty Pascal. Dan Christian took the ball and thundered in to bowl to Greg Matthews, who slashed the ball to the boundary square of the wicket for the winning runs. University of NSW had given away eight wides and 15 no-balls as Sydney University chased 204 to win.

Sent in on a softish wicket, University of NSW were dismissed cheaply, but Sydney University did even worse in reply. University of NSW were in a solid position at 1 for 71 in their second innings when Stuart MacGill gained the decisive break by capturing three wickets in four balls, all of them leg-before.

The third day developed into a tense battle, with Sydney University struggling at 3 for 59 until a stand of 73 by Ed Cowan and Shane Stanton swung the game in their direction. Then four wickets tumbled for 20 runs. Despite MacGill's nine wickets, the Benaud Medal deservedly went to Tim Lang, whose windmill action gave him figures of 8 for 88 from 45.4 lion-hearted overs.

Benaud Medal: T. E. Lang

Close of play: First day, Sydney University (1) 7-87. Second day, Sydney University (2) 1-39.

University of NSW

M. W. O'Connor lbw b Paskal	2	–	b Paskal	12
M. W. Creed b Paskal	2	–	c Mail b Paskal	57
C. Brown c Stanton b Matthews	12	–	lbw b MacGill	26
D. T. Christian c Mail b Paskal	40	–	lbw b MacGill	0
*D. J. Carson c Phelps b Matthews	26	–	lbw b MacGill	1
T. L. W. Cooper st Stanton b MacGill	15	–	c Moran b Paskal	55
T. E. Lang st Stanton b MacGill	9	–	lbw b MacGill	8
I. D. K. Salisbury lbw b Matthews	12	–	lbw b Paskal	0
E. J. W. Zehner not out	8	–	c Stanton b MacGill	13
†A. M. Neilan run out (Cowan)	7	–	not out	0
T. D. Cox lbw b MacGill	0	–	c Stanton b MacGill	0
L-b 3, w 1	4		L-b 2	2

(61.3 overs, 238 mins) 137
Fall: 4 7 42 68 97 105 122 126 137 137

63.3 overs, 249 mins 174
Fall: 14 73 73 77 139 154 155 174 174 174

Bowling: *First Innings*—Paskal 14–5–28–3, Moran 8–4–20–0, Sanders 5–0–15–0, Matthews 23–12–35–3; MacGill 11.3–0–36–3. *Second Innings*—Paskal 14–3–34–4, Moran 8–3–20–0, MacGill 22.3–7–68–6, Matthews 14–2–35–0, Kierath 3–0–13–0, Sanders 2–0–2–0.

Sydney University

I. Moran lbw b Lang	0	–	(2) b Cox	21
G. J. Mail st Neilan b Salisbury	33	–	(1) lbw b Zehner	1
M. J. Phelps lbw b Cox	16	–	c Neilan b Lang	17
E. J. M. Cowan st Neilan b Salisbury	21	–	st Neilan b Salisbury	37
*†S. D. Stanton b Lang	13	–	b Lang	64
D. Butchart c Neilan b Lang	0	–	lbw b Zehner	15
P. Sanders lbw b Salisbury	1	–	c & b Zehner	7
T. W. R. Kierath c Carson b Lang	2	–	(9) lbw b Zehner	1
M. Paskal c Carson b Salisbury	7	–	(11) not out	0
G. R. J. Matthews not out	8	–	(8) not out	8
S. C. G. MacGill b Lang	3	–	(10) lbw b Lang	6
L-b 2, n-b 2	4		B 1, l-b 4, w 8, n-b 15	28

(44.4 overs, 190 mins) 108
Fall: 0 28 60 84 86 87 87 91 101 108

(85.3 overs, 400 mins)   (9 wkts) 205
Fall: 1 45 59 132 169 180 191 192 200

Bowling: *First Innings*—Lang 16.4–3–40–5, Cox 10–1–28–2, Zehner 6–2–16–0, Salisbury 12–2–22–4. *Second Innings*—Lang 29–11–46–3, Zehner 16–3–41–4, Salisbury 18–1–70–1, Cox 17–8–27–1, Christian 5.3–1–16–0.

Umpires: N. S. D. Fowler and R. J. Tucker.

SYDNEY FIRST-GRADE RECORDS

ALL-TIME LEADING RUN-SCORERS

	Runs	*Club*	*Duration*
W. Bardsley	12,119	Glebe, Western Suburbs	1898-1933
T. J. E. Andrews	11,672	Petersham	1909-43
S. J. Carroll	11,314	Gordon	1939-66
J. W. Burke	11,231	Manly, Northern District	1946-72
G. J. Hayne	11,220	UTS Balmain, Gordon	1987-
R. J. Bower	11,219	Bankstown, Penrith, Balmain	1977-98
A. Alderson	10,705	Cumberland, Sydney University	1941-68
B. C. Booth	10,674	St George	1952-77
J. W. Chegwyn	10,455	Randwick	1926-56
P. H. Marks	10,413	Balmain, Manly-Warringah, N Sydney	1979-2001

ALL-TIME LEADING BOWLERS

	Wickets	*Club*	*Duration*
H. C. Chilvers	1,153	Northern District	1925-52
K. C. Gulliver	1,028	Mosman	1930-63
W. J. O'Reilly	962	North Sydney, St George	1926-49
O. P. Asher	861	Sydney, Paddington	1910-33
R. Aitken	774	Parramatta, Sydney	1960-88
R. M. Pearce	771	Balmain	1937-57
D. M. Chardon	762	Petersham-Marrickville, Sydney	1967-90
K. Hall	752	Bankstown, Hawkesbury, Penrith	1975-2002
R. H. Guy	717	Gordon	1953-75
W. A. Wellham	684	Western Suburbs	1950-78

Brisbane First-Grade, 2004-05

by STEPHEN GRAY

It might well be a coincidence, but Shane Warne's legacy to world cricket appears to have had a manifestation in the ranks of the Brisbane first-grade premiership. At any stage in the 2004-05 season, there were as many as eight leg-spinners ripping, flipping and googlying their way around. Most of them were in their early twenties, so their formative years had been spent watching Warne bamboozle and befuddle batsmen around the world. The healthy crop of leggies looks set to provide a future harvest for the Queensland selectors. While young spinners tend to be like olive trees – it takes plenty of pruning and some patience before a crop is returned – there is reason to hope that the state's slow-bowling options might soon be richer.

Redlands' 21-year-old Ryan Le Loux became the first wrist-spinner to be picked for Queensland since Bruce Oxenford in 1992-93. While he saw limited time in the interstate arena, he is near the top of the pecking order. Norths leggie Greg Chiesa, 23, and Beenleigh-Logan's 21-year-old Luke Davis have both appeared at Queensland youth level and in the colours of the Queensland Academy of Sport, with Chiesa selected as a Cricket Academy scholar in 2005 before injury intervened. But it was a newcomer, former Victorian Daniel Doran, who provided much of the excitement in his debut season. Playing for Gold Coast, the 24-year-old Doran finished as the leading wicket-taker in the competition, taking 46 scalps at 17.84, and was invited to Queensland training for the final few weeks of the season. The last time a leg-spinner dominated the competition in this fashion is beyond memory. Doran had five hauls of five wickets or better, but had to take a back seat when it came to the best individual bowling performances, with his club captain, Chris Swan, taking 9 for 40 against Toombul and Redlands seamer Brad Eathorne routing Wynnum-Manly with 8 for 14.

Doran's ascendancy was matched by the feats of 26-year-old Valley left-hander Trevor Irvine, who topped the run-scoring list with 780 runs at a muscular 97.50. Amazingly, that was not enough to lead the averages, with University of Queensland all-rounder Duncan Betts claiming the mark with 421 runs at 105.25. Irvine, a former Queensland Colts player who has developed into a solid, if unspectacular first-grader, was better known before last season for having been dismissed for 99 on three occasions. However, his breakthrough came early in the season when he scored 131 against Beenleigh-Logan. Having knocked down that barrier, a few rounds later he hit 170 not out, the second-highest score of the season. Not far behind Irvine was former NSW opener Rod Davison (714 runs at 44.90), who has stiffened the once fragile Beenleigh-Logan batting.

The highest score came from robust Souths all-rounder Michael Buchanan, who slammed 186 against Wynnum-Manly only to see his side lose by one run. Buchanan, a former Queensland Under-19s rugby centre and the son of the Australian cricket coach, belted 19 fours and seven sixes in his 229-ball innings. There were seven scores in excess of 150 with another three of 148 or 149, two of those to Toombul's Kieran Murphy, who scored three centuries, equal with the veteran Sandgate-Redcliffe wicket-keeper Gavin Fitness, who passed 7,000 runs for his club to set a new benchmark.

Despite these impressive individual feats, the Peter Burge Medal was claimed by Toombul all-rounder Derek Tate, who took out the award by one point from his former Beenleigh-Logan and Toombul team-mate Alan Rowe. Tate was runner-up to Nathan Rimmington in 2003-04 and produced dependable form across what was a wildly inconsistent summer for wooden-spooners Toombul. The 24-year-old right-hand middle-order bat and right-arm seamer hit 566 runs at 37.73 and took 24 wickets at 27.54 on the way to making his Cricket Australia Cup debut for the QAS.

In the other major individual award, Wynnum-Manly all-rounder Trish Brown claimed her third consecutive Kath Smith Medal as the best and fairest player in the Katherine Raymont Shield women's premiership. Brown, a former Australian squad member who has also represented her country at Gaelic football, has won the only three medals named in honour of the late Kath Smith, a pioneer of women's cricket in Queensland and vice-captain of Australia in the 1930s. Brown also tasted premiership success, with Wynnum-Manly (213) overcoming Beenleigh-Logan (118) in the final.

University of Queensland took out the first-grade minor premie ship, club championship and Spirit of Cricket award – but save their worst for the semi-final. Batting first, they were dismissed fe 148 and then saw fourth-placed Sandgate-Redcliffe reach 7 for 25 with opener Glen Batticciotto scoring 103. Second-placed Wes took the other route, batting the better part of two days again third-placed Sunshine Coast to score 382 and draw the game witho the Scorchers having the chance to mount a run-chase.

The one-day competition was won by Northern Suburbs, wi left-arm quick Scott Brant claiming 5 for 36 as Sunshine Coast we dismissed for 123 in reply to the Vikings' total of 223, which w underpinned by a classy 90 from Clinton Perren.

BRISBANE FIRST-GRADE TABLE, 2004-05

	M	WO	WI	D	T	Ll	LO	Match Points	Bonus Points	Tota Poir
University of Queensland	11	1	6	3	0	1	0	90.00	68.59	158.
Western Suburbs	11	1	6	2	0	2	0	88.00	53.88	141.
Sunshine Coast	11	0	6	0	0	5	0	60.00	79.38	138.
Sandgate-Redcliffe	11	0	5	1	0	5	0	58.00	72.21	130.
Gold Coast	11	2	3	0	0	5	1	64.00	62.22	126.
Beenleigh/Logan	11	0	5	2	1	3	0	64.00	58.96	122.
Northern Suburbs	11	0	5	2	0	4	0	64.00	57.73	121.
Valley	11	0	5	1	0	5	0	62.00	57.75	119.
Wynnum-Manly	11	0	4	0	1	5	1	52.00	63.41	115.
South Brisbane	11	0	4	1	0	6	0	50.00	61.85	111.
Redlands	11	1	2	0	0	9	0	24.00	63.72	87.7
Toombul	11	0	4	0	0	5	3	36.00	47.22	83.2

(Redlands defeated Toombul outright after trailing on first innings.)

BATTING AVERAGES, 2004-05

(Qualification: 200 runs)

	M	I	NO	R	HS	Av
D. M. Betts (University)	11	10	6	421	125*	105.
G. T. Irvine (Valley)	10	11	3	780	170*	97.
L. M. Stevens (University)	10	11	2	606	153	67.
R. J. Davison (Beenleigh/Logan)	11	12	1	714	149*	64.
G. A. J. Fitness (Sandgate-Redcliffe)	11	12	1	649	160	59.
C. D. Hartley (Norths)	9	9	0	520	153	57.
M. Johnson (Norths)	9	8	3	283	113	56.
M. Buchanan (Souths)	8	11	0	485	186	44.
N. J. Reardon (University)	11	13	1	529	106	44.
C. A. Philipson (University)	8	9	1	343	151	42.

BOWLING AVERAGES, 2004-05

(Qualification: 20 wickets)

	M	O	Mdns	R	W	Avge
Swan (Gold Coast)	9	158	44	378	26	14.53
J. Jurgensen (Sandgate-Redcliffe)	10	210	61	506	30	16.86
Glass (Wests)	10	166	41	526	31	16.96
Doran (Gold Coast)	10	233	32	821	46	17.84
J. Rowell (Wests)	10	169.1	46	383	21	18.23
M. Schossow (Wests)	11	219.5	47	696	38	18.31
Boardman (University)	8	148.5	45	368	20	18.40
Cash (Sunshine Coast)	11	203	60	488	26	18.76
Dever (University)	10	191	48	524	26	20.15
James (Souths)	11	171	41	506	25	20.24

BRISBANE FIRST-GRADE SEMI-FINALS, 2004-05

WESTERN SUBURBS v SUNSHINE COAST

Graceville No. 1. Match drawn. Western Suburbs proceeded to the final as the higher-
placed team. Western Suburbs 382.

UNIVERSITY OF QUEENSLAND v SANDGATE-REDCLIFFE

W.E.P. Harris Oval. Sandgate-Redcliffe won on first innings. University of
Queensland 148 (S.J. Jurgensen 5-46, N.J Rimmington 4-74); Sandgate-Redcliffe 7
for 258 (G. Batticciotto 103, G. A.J. Fitness 60; D. M. Betts 5-76).

FINAL

WESTERN SUBURBS v SANDGATE-REDCLIFFE

Allan Border Field, Albion, March 12, 13, 19, 20, 2005. Western Suburbs won by 435
runs. *Toss:* Sandgate-Redcliffe.

The first day of the four-day final saw pacemen dominate. Sandgate-Redcliffe took
early ascendancy, thanks to the bowling of Shane Jurgensen. But Western Suburbs
quickly consigned their past catastrophes to the history books, stunning their opponents
with a pace barrage by Greg Rowell and the late-blooming Greg Schossow. Sandgate
slumped to 7 for 97 at stumps on the first day but by the end of the weekend were in a dire
position.

When Wests batted a second time Steve Paulsen peeled off a dashing century to lead
the batting charge. Paulsen, who had twice been dismissed in the nineties in finals, raced
to 104 from 99 balls. With half-centuries to opener Julian Nielsen and Aaron Nye already
in the scorebook, Paulsen's older brother Geoff, a former Queensland Country batsman,
followed up his first-innings top score as he and Matt Lane pushed the eventual tally to
483. Rookie Sandgate paceman John Loader took five wickets but they came at a cost.
Nathan Rimmington, one of the destroyers in 2003-04, also found the Border Field
wickets more often than he would have liked. The Gators' attack was flayed at a rate of
almost a run a ball.

Sandgate-Redcliffe had five working days to ponder how they might make 484 to
again snatch an improbable premiership title. In 2003-04, having been able to set
Western Suburbs a target of only 84, they had dismissed them for 31. But any hopes they
had of a batting miracle this time were quickly dashed when play began, as they were

summarily dispatched by Rowell and Schossow. The ginger-headed Schossow, a forme Queensland Country representative, bowled hooping outswingers at a more tha respectable clip to befuddle his rivals.

After their humiliating loss in 2003-04, success for Western Suburbs this time wa especially sweet. The 38-year-old Rowell, who had changed his mind about retiremen after the previous season's shemozzle, delivered his second retirement speech in happie circumstances.

Close of play. First day; Sandgate-Redcliffe (1) 7-97; Second day, Western Suburb (2) 423.

Western Suburbs

J. C. c Nielsen lbw b Rimmington	13	– lbw b Jurgensen	
S. J. Paulsen c McLauchlan b Jurgensen	5	– c Batticciotto b Rimmington	1
*A. J. Nye c Hughes b Loader	15	– c Fitness b Loader	
G. Paulsen c Francey b Summerfeldt	65	– b Rimmington	
M. Lane c Francey b Rimmington	4	– c Fitness b Loader	
D. Tuckwell b Jurgensen	28	– b Loader	
†A. Cavanough c Batticciotto b Summerfeldt	12	– c Francey b Rimmington	
G. J. Rowell c Summerfeldt b Jurgensen	8	– c Rimmington b Loader	
C. Glass lbw b Jurgensen	7	– c Summerfeldt b Loader	
A. Murnane not out	4	– c Summerfeldt b Rimmington	
G. M. Schossow c McLauchlan b Jurgensen	6	– not out	
B 1, l-b 4, w 1, n-b 8	14	B 1, l-b 5, w 2, n-b 13	

(67.2 overs)	181	(74.4 overs)	4
Fall: 5 24 50 55 115 143 158 165 171 181		Fall: 134 214 224 360 370 393	
		393 395 396 423	

Bowling: *First Innings*—Jurgensen 26.2–11–55–5; Rimmington 25–3–69–2; Loader 5–0–22–Summerfeldt 7–2–17–2; Pink 4–1–13–0. *Second Innings*—Jurgensen 18–4–79–1; Rimmingt 23.4–3–141–4; Loader 19–3–101–5; Summerfeldt 8–1–52–0; Pink 4–1–25–0; Batticciotto 1–0–8–Pearce 1–0–11–0.

Sandgate-Redcliffe

*A. Francey c Cavanough b Rowell	14	– b Rowell	
G. Batticciotto lbw b Rowell	3	– lbw b Schossow	
D. Pearce lbw b Schossow	0	– c Cavanough b Rowell	
†G. A. J. Fitness c Cavanough b Schossow	35	– c Lane b Schossow	
L. McLauchlan c Nielsen b Schossow	5	– c Nye b Rowell	
G. Hughes c Cavanough b Schossow	15	– c and b Rowell	
A. Summerfeldt lbw b Paulsen	0	– c Nye b Schossow	
N. J. Rimmington lbw b Schossow	13	– (10) not out	
P. D. Pink b Glass	4	– (8) c Nielsen b Schossow	
S. J. Jurgensen not out	9	– (9) c Glass b Rowell	
J. Loader c Lane b Schossow	4	– c Cavanough b Schossow	
B 5, l-b 1, w 4, n-b 9	19		

(33.4 overs)	121	(19.4 overs)	
Fall: 23 24 24 34 80 89 97 107 115 121		Fall: 0 9 12 12 12 12 20 29 38 49	

Bowling: *First Innings*—Rowell 10–0–42–2; Schossow 16.4–5–55–6; Murnane 2–0–14–0; Gl 4–3–4–1; S. J. Paulsen 1–1–0–1. *Second Innings*—Rowell 10–4–12–5; Schossow 9.4–2–37–5.

Umpires: N. S. McNamara and T. P. Laycock.

Adelaide A-Grade, 2004-05

by LAURIE COLLIVER

In a summer in which ball dominated bat, Northern Districts clinched their first premiership after eight years in the competition. The club was formed when Salisbury, which had won nine premierships, combined with Elizabeth, which was promoted to A-Grade in 1993-94. For much of the season, the team was carried by all-rounder Ryan Harris, who had a brilliant season. Damian Brandy made useful runs before heading back to England before the final, when state keeper Graham Manou returned to make his most important contribution.

Adelaide's batting failed to fire when it was needed most in the final. Their playing coach, Chris Davies, had a respectable season before announcing his retirement, Ben Johnson continued to be worth two players as he batted and bowled superbly, while the Williams brothers, Sam and Luke, continued to provide the backbone for most innings. When he was not on state duty, Daniel Cullen continued his outstanding bowling form of the previous season.

Despite their talented line-up, West Torrens failed in the preliminary final, extending their premiership drought to 43 seasons. Veteran David Ritossa was valuable with the bat, while young paceman Trent Kelly (46 wickets) was unlucky not to play more cricket for the state team. Mark Harrity emerged from retirement to be a dominant force with the ball.

Kensington had a woeful year with the bat but still made the final four. Jake Brown looks to be a good batting prospect, while Jamie Panelli, with 37 wickets, and Ben Johnswood carried the attack. Despite having some of the biggest names in the competition, Glenelg failed to make the finals. Most of their work was left to Ben Hook, who has been a sterling player for more than a decade. Neither David Fitzgerald nor Tom Plant produced the volume of runs that might have been expected. Glenelg's bowler's, particularly Hook, Neil Rowe and leg-spinner Ryan Bulger (36 wickets at 21.53), were much more reliable.

Sturt was possibly the best side to miss the top four. Cameron Borgas batted superbly, earning a first-class recall, while Ben Higgins crossed from West Torrens and made useful runs. Young leg-spinner Cullen Bailey (44 wickets at 20.36) was rewarded for his excellent season with a state game against Tasmania, while paceman Oliver Thomas was a solid performer. Despite the batting efforts of Shane Deitz and Rowan Brewster, Southern Districts again failed to make the finals. No one else averaged more than 25. Brett Bevan (30 wickets at 18.70) continues to provide yeoman service, while left-armer Gary Putland (28 at 19.61) played in the South Australia 2nd XI. Like most clubs, Southern Districts simply need more runs.

University was another club that struggled to make respectable totals during the season. Brent Hutchison (621 runs at 36.53) batted and kept well, while Nathan Adcock batted soundly when available. Liam Plunkett proved to be a very useful bowler. Prospect finished badly after a promising start. They unearthed a good all-rounder in Tim Delvins, while Joel Southam (28 wickets at 22.39) and Mike Harden (23 at 23.57) continue to serve the club well with the ball.

Woodville captain Daniel Harris's batting was one of the highlights of the grade season, and earned him a recall to the state side. But the team missed all-rounder Mick Miller after he retired from first-class cricket to return to Darwin after Christmas to start a fishing charter service. Ken Skewes's all-round ability (499 runs at 33.27, 23 wickets at 18.35) will come under the state selectors' scrutiny in the coming season. Port Adelaide made little progress. Matthew Weeks had a stellar summer, with solid support from Andrew Staunton (32 wickets at 24.72) but batting was again the club's weak point.

Tea Tree Gully fell from second to 12th. New skipper Wes Thomas (585 runs at 39.00, 30 wickets at 17.73) carried the team, while Travis Borlace (41 wickets at 17.73) did well with the ball. Numerous off-field problems will ensure that the team has a new look to it in 2005-06. East Torrens finished a long last despite the best efforts of veteran Craig Bradbrook (558 runs at 32.82). Spinner Ash Bourne had a good year after a lengthy absence, while paceman Andrew Watherston performed admirably at his fifth club.

The summer included the innovation of a number of Twenty20 matches. Most of these fixtures were well attended, with some games drawing around 500 patrons, which helped clubs make a few extra dollars in bar trade. Floodlights were used in some of the games and celebrities were drafted in. Port Adelaide AFL captain Warren Tredrea played one match for West Torrens: he took a catch and made one run.

ADELAIDE A-GRADE TABLE, 2004-05

	M	WO	WI	D	T	LI	LO	Match Points	Bonus Points	O/rate Pen Pts	Total Points
Adelaide	12	1	8	0	1	2	0	147.50	76.25	0	223.75
Northern Districts	12	0	10	0	0	2	0	150.00	72.65	0.5	222.15
Kensington	12	1	7	0	0	4	0	115.00	82.53	0	197.53
West Torrens	12	0	7	0	0	3	2	115.00	76.15	0	191.15
Glenelg	12	1	6	0	0	5	0	110.00	74.56	0	184.56
Stuart	12	1	5	0	0	6	0	95.00	77.26	0	172.26
Southern District	12	1	5	0	1	5	0	102.50	69.62	0	172.12
Woodville	12	0	6	0	0	6	0	90.00	78.15	0.25	167.90
University	12	2	4	0	0	4	2	90.00	76.05	0	166.05
Prospect	12	1	3	0	0	8	0	65.00	69.12	0	134.12
Port Adelaide	12	0	3	0	0	8	1	55.00	72.89	1.25	126.64
Tea Tree Gully	12	0	3	0	0	7	2	55.00	69.20	0	124.20
East Torrens	12	1	1	0	0	8	2	25.00	65.08	0	90.08

BATTING AVERAGES, 2004-05

(Qualification: 400 runs)

	M	I	NO	R	HS	100s	50s	Avge
C. J. Borgas (Sturt)	11	14	3	666	176	2	4	60.55
D. J. Harris (Woodville)	11	17	0	882	177	3	3	51.88
S. A. Deitz (Southern District)	12	15	2	646	113	2	5	49.69
T. Delvins (Prospect)	11	12	3	421	119*	1	3	46.78
R. J. Brewster (Southern District)	12	15	0	677	126	1	5	45.13
D. J. Ritossa (West Torrens)	14	16	6	430	57*	0	3	43.00
M. J. Weeks (Port Adelaide)	11	14	2	504	145	1	4	42.00
D. Brandy (Northern Districts)	11	13	3	414	64	0	4	41.40
R. J. Harris (Northern Districts)	11	13	3	412	107*	1	2	41.20
C. J. Davies (Adelaide)	12	15	0	588	120	1	3	39.20

* Denotes not out.

BOWLING AVERAGES, 2004-05

(Qualification: 25 wickets)

	M	O	Mds	R	W	BB	5W/i	10W/m	Avge
L. E. Plunkett (Adelaide University)	7	166	59	312	29	5-29	1	0	10.76
R. J. Harris (Northern Districts)	11	203.1	61	454	42	6-45	2	1	10.81
B. A. Johnson (Adelaide)	14	223.2	83	493	40	7-14	3	1	12.33
C. J. Slattery (Adelaide University)	10	164.4	42	377	30	5-28	1	0	12.57
B. M. Johnswood (Kensington)	9	170	35	483	36	5-25	2	0	13.42
M. A. Harrity (West Torrens)	9	166.2	43	438	31	4-11	0	0	14.13
D. J. Cullen (Adelaide)	6	132.2	30	361	25	6-37	2	0	14.44
B. J. Hook (Glenelg)	12	246.1	84	576	35	6-23	0	0	16.46
O. C. Thomas (Sturt)	10	194.5	47	562	34	6-57	2	0	16.53
N. M. Rowe (Glenelg)	11	278.5	107	557	32	6-48	1	0	17.41

ADELAIDE A-GRADE FINALS SERIES, 2004-05

MAJOR SEMI-FINAL
NORTHERN DISTRICTS v ADELAIDE

At Adelaide Oval, March 5, 6 2005. *Toss:* Northern Districts. Adelaide won on first innings. Northern Districts 138 (G. Tume 38; N. Job 4-23, E. Bernhardt 3-17); Adelaide 2 for 139 (J. K. Smith 64*).

KNOCKOUT SEMI-FINAL
WEST TORRENS v KENSINGTON

At Adelaide Oval No. 2, March 5 (no play-rain), 6, 2005. *Toss:* West Torrens. West Torrens won on first innings. West Torrens 8 for 235 (C. Knight 48, D. J. Ritossa 57*, J. Panelli 3-49); Kensington 91 (J. Lee 38; M. A. Harrity 3-23, D. Bourn 3-19, T. P. Kelly 4-9).

PRELIMINARY FINAL
NORTHERN DISTRICTS v WEST TORRENS

At Salisbury Oval, March 12, 13, 2005. *Toss:* Northern Districts. Northern Districts won on first innings. Northern Districts 235 (A. Costello 75, M. A. Harrity 4-70, T. P. Kelly 4-41); West Torrens 199 (D. J. Ritossa 57*; R. J. Harris 4-47, S. Busbridge 3-54).

FINAL
NORTHERN DISTRICTS v ADELAIDE

At Adelaide Oval, March 19, 20, 2005. Northern Districts by seven wickets. *Toss:* Northern Districts.

Northern Districts won their first A-Grade premiership in a low-scoring final which proceeded at fast-forward speed. The match was a triumph for two players who had risen from the Jets' junior ranks, Graham Manou and Ryan Harris.

Adelaide went into the final as warm favourites after their eight-wicket victory in the major semi-final, but the Northern Districts fast bowlers shot out the Buffalos' batting line-up by just after lunch. After Harris knocked over Luke Williams, left-arm quick Steven Busbridge quickly reduced Adelaide to 4 for 38. With some solid strokeplay Sam Williams and Chris Davies tried to resurrect the innings, but when Harris returned after lunch, he swung the ball too sharply for the Adelaide batsmen.

The Jets got off to a flying start before losing three wickets for no runs, the last of them Mark Higgs, shouldering arms to Daniel Cullen. In strode Manou, who played a bold hand lasting just 73 balls as he took the attack to the Adelaide bowlers. He cut and pulled beautifully, and wasn't scared to loft the medium-pacers back over their heads. He did, though, show the utmost respect for the off-spin of Cullen, who was always a threat. Manou received excellent support from Redback rookie-listed player Shannon Hurn, who helped him add a vital 79 for the sixth wicket. Amazingly, Ben Johnson didn't return for his second spell with the ball until well after tea, when the first-innings result had been decided. When he did come back, he and Cullen disposed of the lower order, keeping the deficit to just 67.

Adelaide went in search of quick runs on the second day in an attempt to keep their faint chances of an outright victory alive. They were well on the way to setting a target of around 150 when Dale Agars and Davies fell to Mark Cosgrove, and the rest of the atting collapsed. Harris again showed that his good late-season form with the state eam was no fluke, and he finished the match with 11 for 94.

This left Northern Districts just 85 to win, and they knocked off the runs in an hour when Higgs hit the winning six off Cullen. Ryan Harris was a good choice as Man of he Match, but without Manou's outstanding display in the first innings the Jets may well ave floundered.

David Hookes Medal: R. J. Harris
Close of play: First day, Adelaide (2) 0-7 (L. D. Williams 5, Agars 2).

Adelaide

. Agars c Cosgrove b Busbridge	8	– (2) c Manou b Cosgrove	37
.D. Williams lbw b Harris	0	– (1) c Manou b Harris	25
.K. Smith c Cosgrove b Busbridge	7	– c Hall b Harris	4
. Williams c Manou b Busbridge	52	– (6) c Costello b Busbridge	5
.A. Johnson c Manou b Busbridge	0	– (5) c Cosgrove b Busbridge	13
.J. Davies c Cosgrove b Harris	30	– (4) b Cosgrove	45
J.K. McLean c Manou b Harris	0	– b Harris	0
.J. Cullen b Harris	2	– hit wicket b Harris	6
. Bernhardt lbw b Harris	2	– c Hall b Busbridge	3
. Bradley b Harris	6	– b Harris	2
. Job not out	0	– not out	0
B 8, l-b 2, n-b 1	11	N-b 1	1

45.1 overs, 189 mins) 118   (37 overs, 151 mins) 151
all: 5, 21, 30, 38, 86, 90, 92, 98, 104, 118   Fall: 38, 45, 90, 117, 125, 130, 130, 134, 140, 151

owling: *First Innings*—Harris 18–5–45–6; Duval 7–3–12–0; Busbridge 17.1–6–42–4; Cosgrove
-0–9–0; Higgs 1–1–0–0. *Second Innings*—Harris 13–3–49–5; Duval 6–0–31–0; Busbridge
2–1–54–3; Cosgrove 6–0–17–2.

Northern Districts

.J. Cosgrove c McLean b Johnson	24	– (2) c Johnson b Cullen	26
. Tume c McLean b Bradley	13	– (1) c Bernhardt b Cullen	22
. Costello lbw b Cullen	13	– c S. Williams b Cullen	6
‡.A. Higgs b Cullen	0	– not out	24
†G. A. Manou c and b Cullen	99	– not out	7
.J. Harris c McLean b Cullen	0		
. Hurn c Davies b Johnson	17		
. Hall c S. Williams b Cullen	6		
. Duncan c Agars b Johnson	5		
.J. Duval c Smith b Johnson	1		
. Busbridge not out	4		
L-b 1, n-b 2	3	L-b 1	1

44.5 overs, 174 mins) 185   (17.4 overs, 64 mins) (3 wkts) 86
all: 38, 38, 38, 86, 90, 169, 169, 178, 180, 185   Fall: 34, 48, 63

owling: *First Innings*—Bradley 8–2–39–1; Johnson 12.5–3–39–4; Cullen 17–4–46–5; Bernhardt
-0–23–0; Job 4–0–37–0. *Second Innings*—Johnson 9–2–45–0; Cullen 8.4–0–40–3.

Umpires: S. D. Fry and A. Collins

ADELAIDE A-GRADE RECORDS

ALL-TIME LEADING RUN-SCORERS

Wayne Bradbrook	9,619	J. C. Reedman	7,346
R. J. Zadow	9,318	V. Y. Richardson	7,326
M. P. Faull	9,093	Craig Bradbrook	7,214
B. J. Hook	7,748	C. E. Pellew	7,154
N. R. Fielke	7,616	A. P. Kimber	6,610

ALL-TIME LEADING BOWLERS

N. L. Williams	894	D. J. Lambert	636
J. P. F. Travers	819	R. J. Stratfold	624
A. T. W. Sincock	762	R. M. O'Shannassy	621
G. Giffen	744	B. M. Hurn	615
G. C. Clarke	724	R. M. Sharpe	587

Hobart First-Grade, 2004-05

By BRETT STUBBS

n a season in which many past players questioned the standard of TCA cricket, Clarence's quest for a premiership hat-trick fell short as the North Hobart team finally realised its potential.

At the start of the season, Glenorchy coach and former Tasmanian batsman Glen Hughes publicly challenged former players and district players to have a crack at TCA cricket, such was his concern over the lack of experienced cricketers in the competition. He believed the standard had slipped in recent years, across all grades. Hughes's sentiments were shared by rival clubs, retired players and by TCA chairman Brent Palfreyman.

Again the TCA pledged to make the roster more player-friendly, with the one-day Kookaburra Cup incorporated into the premiership roster for the second season and a reduction of Sunday play. Whether these changes create the desired effect is too early to tell.

The first-grade season soon developed a split, with Lindisfarne, Kingborough and New Town dropping off the pace quickly, while North Hobart, Clarence, University, South Hobart–Sandy Bay and Glenorchy contested for the final four.

After a pre-season recruiting drive, South Hobart–Sandy Bay led the ladder early but once they lost Xavier Doherty, Travis Birt and George Bailey to state duties, and Andrew Downton because of injury, their depth was found wanting and their season fizzled out in a one-sided semi-final loss to North Hobart at Bellerive.

It was a similar story for Glenorchy. After making the grand final the previous two seasons, the Magpies had a woeful time after the Christmas break and failed to make the top four. Without paceman Brett Geeves and all-rounder Luke Butterworth, who were playing for the state, they lacked fire power. Their new recruit Dane Anderson provided the highlight. Transferring from NTCA club Westbury, Anderson scored 957 runs to set a club first-grade record.

Glenorchy did not finish the season empty-handed, winning the Kookaburra Cup final over South Hobart–Sandy Bay.

Perhaps the biggest disappointment was University. Boasting many state 2nd XI players, plus former state duo Brad Thomas and Josh Marquet, once again University failed to make it past the semi-finals. Playing the semi-final on their home ground against Clarence, University had Clarence reeling at 9 for 129 in humid conditions. But Roos veteran and former state batsman Andrew Dykes found a willing partner in fellow stalwart Mark Colegrave. The pair added 76, taking the score to 205 before Dykes was last man out for 74. University's top order faltered in the chase, and dismissal for 189 was a disappointing end for such a talented squad.

South Hobart–Sandy Bay missed a grand final berth, but only after another remarkable individual season for their captain, Adam Polkinghorne. The aggressive left-hand batsman and right-arm fast-medium bowler dominated the TCA Medal vote count, missing votes in only three rounds. His 626 runs at 44.71 and 59 wickets at 10.61 won Polkinghorne his fourth medal – equalling the record of Ian "Snowy" Beven – by nine votes ahead of Anderson and Colegrave.

TCA FIRST-GRADE TABLE, 2004-05

	Played	Won	Draw	Lost	Match Points	Bonus Points
North Hobart	13	8	1	4	60	107.98
University	13	8	0	5	56	102.49
Clarence	13	7	1	5	54	101.10
South Hobart–Sandy Bay	13	8	1	4	48	93.48
Kingborough	13	6	1	6	36	77.26
Glenorchy	13	5	1	7	34	77.73
New Town	13	3	0	10	22	58.59
Lindisfarne	13	3	1	9	18	56.91

BATTING AVERAGES, 2004-05

(Qualification: 300 runs)

	M	I	NO	R	HS	100s	50s	Avg
A. J. Dykes (Clarence)	12	13	6	551	171*	1	4	78.7
S. G. Clingeleffer (North Hobart)	8	7	1	434	145	1	4	72.3
D. J. Anderson (Glenorchy)	13	17	1	957	116*	2	9	59.8
L. R. Butterworth (Glenorchy)	7	8	1	341	99*	0	3	48.7
A. W. Polkinghorne (Sth Hobart–Sandy Bay)	13	14	0	626	194	2	4	44.7
R. J. G. Lockyear (University)	12	16	3	573	103	1	5	44.0
B. Teece (Lindisfarne)	5	7	0	306	83	0	3	43.7
T. D. Paine (University)	13	17	4	468	71	0	4	36.0
R. A. Allanby (Lindisfarne)	12	15	1	480	109	2	4	34.2
W. Quarrell (Clarence)	13	16	1	422	109	1	3	28.1

*Denotes not out.

BOWLING AVERAGES, 2004-05

(Qualification: 20 wickets)

	M	O	Mds	R	W	BB	5W/inn	10W/m	Avrge
A. W. Polkinghorne (Sth Hobart–Sandy Bay)	13	245.5	69	626	59	6-36	5	0	10.61
J. M. Dakin (North Hobart)	12	129.2	30	324	30	6-20	2	0	10.80
M. D. Colegrave (Clarence)	11	224.5	77	533	49	8-27	5	1	10.88
S. Stewart (North Hobart)	9	183.1	50	490	43	8-48	2	1	11.40
B. W. Hilfenhaus (University) ..	10	142.3	31	365	29	5-58	1	0	12.59
L. Swards (Kingborough)	12	220.4	39	684	44	6-63	2	0	15.55
J. T. Knott (Kingborough)	10	134.0	26	459	27	5-39	1	0	17.00
R. A. O'Connell (Kingborough) .	12	127.3	30	421	24	4-35	0	0	17.54
D. A. McNees (University)	11	195.4	44	478	27	5-28	1	0	17.70
H. Griggs (Sth Hobart–Sandy Bay)	13	199.5	50	599	33	4-22	0	0	18.15

TCA FIRST-GRADE SEMI-FINALS, 2004-05

NORTH HOBART v SOUTH HOBART–SANDY BAY

At Bellerive Oval, Bellerive, March 12, 13, 2005. North Hobart won on first innings. *Toss:* South Hobart–Sandy Bay. North Hobart 349 (J. M. Dakin 114*; M. W. Stewart 3-74); South Hobart–Sandy Bay 138 (H. Griggs 48; M. Harry 4-42).

UNIVERSITY v CLARENCE

At University Oval, Hobart, March 12, 13, 2005. Clarence won on first innings. *Toss:* Clarence. Clarence 205 (A. J. Dykes 74, W. Quarrell 45; B. J. Thomas 6-64) and 0 for 61 (B. L. Harris 31*); University 189 (S. N. B. Bakes 54; M. D. Colegrave 6-64, S. P. Kremerskothen 3-56).

TCA FIRST-GRADE GRAND FINAL, 2004-05

NORTH HOBART v CLARENCE

At Bellerive Oval, Bellerive, March 18, 19, 20, 2005. North Hobart won on first innings. *Toss:* Clarence.

The TCA got the grand final it wanted: the star-studded North Hobart line-up against the reigning two-time premiers Clarence, and it lived up to its billing. Grant Costelloe won the toss and inserted the Demons on a wicket offering some early life. But few expected to see the top order crumble the way it did, including the three big guns – Michael Dighton, Sean Clingeleffer and Dan Marsh – to have North 5 for 28. But a series of determined partnerships from the last six batsmen helped North wriggle out of trouble twice. Former Essex and Leicestershire all-rounder Jon Dakin followed his semi-final century with the only half-century of the innings, but the Demons were again in difficulty at 8 for 149. Then the captain, Adam Griffith, found support from Chris Free and Patrick Doherty, and the trio swung lustily to take North to 225.

Clarence's innings was almost a mirror image of the Demons', with the top order crumbling only for the tail to wag. Clarence's reign looked all but over at 5 for 37 and again at 8 for 137 but the lower order refused to concede. In his first season as captain, Costelloe had endured a horror year with the bat, going into the game with 76 runs at 8.44 and only one run in three innings since Christmas. But he recaptured his best in the grand final, and appeared set to guide the Roos to a first-innings victory. He and Matthew Clingeleffer – brother of the opposition's Sean – had taken the score to 8 for 200 when the second new ball fell due. Adam Griffith made the vital breakthrough when he had Costelloe caught at first slip by Marsh, and Clingeleffer scooped an attempted on-drive from Dakin straight to mid-on to end the fightback 14 runs short.

However, there appeared to be one last twist on the final day. Needing only to bat out time to win the flag, North's top order again faltered under a sustained, aggressive bowling spell from Damien Wright. With support from veteran swing bowler Mark Colegrave, Wright had the Demons 5 for 65, only for the lower order once again to come to the rescue. Dakin maintained his excellent form, while David Collins – batting with a runner due to a strained quadriceps – batted for 100 minutes to see North safely to 8 for 178, when the game was called off.

Man of the Match: J. M. Dakin.

Close of play: First day, North Hobart (1) 225. Second day, North Hobart (2) 0-18.

North Hobart

D. G. Mizzen b Colegrave	6	– (2) b Wright	10
P. Guinane c Quarrell b Colegrave	3	– (1) lbw b Colegrave	11
†S. G Clingeleffer b Wright	1	– b Wright	23
M. G. Dighton lbw b Wright	3	– b Wright	8
D. J. Marsh c Wade b Colegrave	5	– lbw b Colegrave	2
J. M. Dakin c and b Kremerskothen	51	– c Dykes b Wright	48
M. Harry lbw b Stirling	33	– c Wright b Kremerskothen	26
D. Collins lbw b Stirling	20	– (9) not out	17
C. T. Free lbw b Colegrave	35	– (8) c Wade b Wright	8
*A. R. Griffith not out	35	– not out	7
P. Doherty c Clingeleffer b Colegrave	13		
B 1, l-b 11, n-b 8	20	B 5, l-b 6, w 1, n-b 6	18
(94.2 overs, 357 mins)	225	(94 overs, 354 mins) (8 wkts)	178

Fall: 5 10 14 22 28 105 122 149 183 225

Fall: 23 32 45 48 65 131 145 154

J. Pregnell did not bat

Bowling: *First Innings*—Colegrave 28.2–10–63–5, Wright 28–5–72–2, Dykes 4–2–6–0, Harris 5–1–9–0, Kremerskothen 15–5–38–1, Stirling 14–8–25–2. *Second Innings*—Colegrave 28–12–42–2 Wright 32–11–64–5, Kremerskothen 13–5–28–1, Stirling 11–2–29–0, Harris 3–2–1–0, Dykes 7–5–3–0.

Clarence

J. Wells c Clingeleffer b Griffith	0	B. Bannister c Clingeleffer b Pregnell	16
B. L. Harris c Collins b Dakin	0	M. J. Clingeleffer c Mizzen b Dakin	30
S. P. Kremerskothen c Dakin b Griffith	6	M. D. Colegrave not out	2
M. Wade c Marsh b Dakin	7		
W. Quarrell b lbw b Dakin	18	L-b 9, n-b 1	10
A. J. Dykes c Clingeleffer b Harry	11		
D. G. Wright c Harry b Griffith	38	(85.4 overs, 320 mins)	211
*G. Costelloe c Marsh b Griffith	73	Fall: 0 2 17 21 37 59 96 137 205 211

M. J. Stirling did not bat

Bowling: Griffith 24–6–57–4; Dakin 18.4–5–45–4; Harry 11–3–29–1; Pregnell 6–0–26–1; Marsh 18–7–30–0; Doherty 8–2–15–0.

Umpires: J. H. Smeaton and B. W. Jackman.

Victorian Premier Cricket, 2004-05

by KEN WILLIAMS

St Kilda continued to dominate Victorian Premier Cricket, comfortably defeating Melbourne in the final to secure their third consecutive premiership and their fourth in five years. They have now won 17 premierships, one short of Melbourne's record.

Batsmen generally did well. There were three double-centuries: St Kilda's Graeme Rummans made 233 not out, Northcote's English import Jamie Dalrymple, the Crusaders/Sir Ron Brierley Scholarship holder, made 226 not out, while Matthew Elliott, in probably his last Premier innings, made 201 for Camberwell Magpies in the semi-final. Michael Klinger of St Kilda and Hawthorn-Monash University's Simon Dart exceeded 1,000 runs. The 39-year-old Warren Ayres became the most prolific batsman in the history of the competition, as he successively overhauled the three previous top run-scorers, Jack Ryder, John Scholes and Gary Watts, to end the season with 13,209 runs at 43.88. He also equalled Ryder's record of 37 centuries.

The outstanding bowler was Essendon's Mathew Inness, who headed both the averages and aggregate with 50 wickets at 10.68. He took 14 for 84 (7 for 37 and 7 for 47) against South Melbourne, the best match figures since the introduction of covered wickets in 1981-82. The next highest wicket-takers were Clinton McKay, Inness's new-ball partner at Essendon, who won the Robert Rose/Crusaders Scholarship as Best Young Cricketer of the Year, and promising Prahran speedster Cameron Huckett, who each took 47.

St Kilda were clearly the best side. They lost only two matches for the season and easily accounted for Dandenong and Melbourne University in the first two weeks of the finals. They faced tougher opposition from Melbourne in the final. Klinger, Rummans, Nick Jewell (747 at 41.50) and Shawn Craig (612 at 40.80) formed a powerful quartet at the top of the batting order and were backed up by Robert Quiney and Tim O'Sullivan, the captain, who for the second year in a row played a crucial innings in the final. The attack was headed by the consistent Adrian Jones, whose 39 wickets at 18.64 took his career tally past 400, and Adam Warren, 35 at 19.54. Damon Rowan (44 dismissals) was the season's leading keeper. For Melbourne, Liam Buchanan made 891 runs at 46.89, new skipper Andrew McDonald 591 at 84.42, and Andrew Kent 783 at 41.21. Rob Cassell (29 wickets at 20.41) was the leading wicket-taker, and his absence through injury late in the season was a major loss.

Melbourne University, for whom skipper Brendan Joseland made 782 runs at 52.13 and coach Shawn Flegler 625 at 32.89, failed to reach the final after being dismissed for under 200 in both the qualifying and semi-finals. The other semi-finalists were Camberwell Magpies, who were in second-last place at Christmas. Matthew Hayward, who has since returned to Queensland, made 938 runs at 42.63, which included consecutive scores of 180. Sean Pietersz (40 wickets at 20.75) and Brad Knowles (32 at 14.75) headed the attack.

Northcote finished the home-and-away season in fourth place. Their best players were skipper Rob Bartlett (691 runs at 36.36), Dalrymple (527 runs at 40.53 and 22 wickets at 15.27) and Tim Welsford (410 runs and 25 wickets). The other finalists, Dandenong, reached the finals for the first time since 1993-94. Ayres made 602 runs and the strong attack was led by Peter Siddle (42 wickets at 21.73) and David Pattinson (34 at 21.64).

Last season's runners-up, Hawthorn-Monash University, slipped to 11th, despite the outstanding form of Dart. They gained consolation, however, by winning the inaugural Twenty20 title and reaching the final of the 50-over competition. North Melbourne fell from fifth to 16th, although Darren Dempsey made 723 runs at 51.64. Fitzroy-Doncaster, premiers in 2001-02, fell from 11th to last. South Melbourne moved one rung off the bottom, thanks to Steven Spoljaric (753 runs at 41.83 and 30 wickets at 24.70). The club, to be known in future as Casey-South Melbourne, will move to a new ground at Cranbourne, in Melbourne's outer south-east, from 2006-07.

St Kilda and Hawthorn-Monash University played off for the one-day premiership. The Hawks' total of 4 for 209, which included an unbeaten 95 from Dart, was not enough to trouble the Saints, for whom Klinger made 119 not out. In the inaugural Twenty20 competition, in which 12 of the 18 clubs took part, Hawthorn-Monash University defeated Melbourne in an exciting final by nine runs. Dart top-scored for the winners with 39 not out and took 3 for 18.

The following 12 players were named as the team of the season: Matthew Hayward, Michael Klinger, Simon Dart, Brendan Joseland, Darren Dempsey, Liam Buchanan, Steven Spoljaric, Andre Borovec, Clinton McKay, Bryce McGain (captain), Cameron Huckett and Matthew Inness. Dart capped off a wonderful season by winning the Ryder Medal. He polled 43 votes to win narrowly from Spoljaric, whose tally of 41 was the highest ever recorded by a runner-up. The consistent Joseland (35 votes) finished third.

VICTORIAN PREMIER CRICKET FIRST XI TABLE, 2004-05

	M	WO	WI	TI	LO	LI	D	A	Points
Melbourne University	18	1	11	1	0	3	2	1	79
St Kilda	18	0	13	0	0	2	3	1	78
Melbourne	18	1	9	1	0	3	4	1	67
Northcote	18	1	8	0	1	6	2	1	58
Dandenong	19	1	8	0	0	6	4	–	58
Camberwell Magpies	18	1	6	1	1	6	3	1	49
Geelong	18	0	8	0	0	6	4	1	48
Richmond	18	0	8	0	0	8	2	1	48
Essendon	18	1	6	0	1	8	2	1	46
Ringwood	18	1	6	0	0	6	5	1	46
Hawthorn-Monash University	18	0	7	0	0	8	3	1	42
Prahran	18	0	6	0	2†	7	3	1	40
Carlton	18	0	6	1	0	6	5	1	39
Footscray Edgewater	17	0	6	0	0	9	2	2	36
Frankston Peninsula	18	0	6	0	1	9	2	1	36
North Melbourne	18	1*	4	0	0	9	4	1	30
South Melbourne	19	0	5	0	2	8	4	0	30
Fitzroy-Doncaster	19	0	1	0	0	14	4	0	6

* North Melbourne won one match outright after trailing on the first innings (6 points).

† Prahran obtained 4 points for leading on the first innings in a match lost outright.

BATTING AVERAGES, 2004-05

(Qualification: 500 runs)

	M	I	NO	R	HS	100s	50s	Avge
S. P. Dart (Hawthorn-Monash U)	19	19	6	1,098	135	3	7	84.46
A. B. McDonald (Melbourne)	11	9	2	591	154	3	2	84.42
G. C. Rummans (St Kilda)	12	12	2	820	233*	3	3	82.00
M. Klinger (St Kilda)	22	23	6	1,105	166	5	3	65.00
B. R. Joseland (Melbourne Uni)	18	18	3	782	93*	0	6	52.13
D. M. Dempsey (North Melbourne)	18	18	4	723	183*	2	3	51.64
L. G. L. Buchanan (Melbourne)	21	21	2	891	129	3	4	46.89
L. Walker (Frankston Peninsula)	18	17	5	522	74	0	6	43.50
M. R. Hayward (Camberwell Mag)	20	23	1	938	180	2	5	42.63
S. Spoljaric (South Melbourne)	19	20	2	753	138*	2	4	41.83

* Denotes not out.

BOWLING AVERAGES, 2004-05

(Qualification: 25 wickets)

	M	O	Mds	R	W	BB	5Wi	10W/m	Avge
M. W. H. Inness (Essendon)	16	248	68	534	50	7-14	3	1	10.68
B. A. Knowles (Camberwell Mag)	12	170.3	44	472	32	6-30	2	0	14.75
D. J. Groves (Frankston Peninsula)	16	213.3	54	516	30	4-13	0	0	17.20
C. J. McKay (Essendon)	18	345.4	78	849	47	6-76	1	0	18.06
A. P. Jones (St Kilda)	22	254.3	61	727	39	5-72	1	0	18.64
M. G. Gale (Ringwood)	17	273.4	56	754	39	5-17	3	1	19.33
B. E. McGain (Prahran)	18	195.5	42	600	31	4-22	0	0	19.35
A. C. Warren (St Kilda)	21	242.1	47	684	35	4-24	0	0	19.54
C. S. Huckett (Prahran)	18	274.4	46	956	47	8-71	2	0	20.34
R. J. Cassell (Melbourne)	17	193.2	37	592	29	4-13	0	0	20.41

VICTORIAN PREMIER CRICKET TWENTY20 FINAL

HAWTHORN-MONASH UNIVERSITY v MELBOURNE

At St Kilda Cricket Ground, St Kilda, January 26, 2005 (20-over match). Hawthorn-Monash University won by seven runs. Hawthorn-Monash University 8 for 123; Melbourne 114 (S. P. Dart 3-18).

VICTORIAN PREMIER CRICKET ONE-DAY FINAL

ST KILDA v HAWTHORN-MONASH UNIVERSITY

At St Kilda Cricket Ground, St Kilda, March 14, 2005 (50-over match). St Kilda won by eight wickets. Hawthorn-Monash University 4 for 209 (S. P. Dart 95*, M. J. Cox 41); St Kilda 2 for 210 (M. Klinger 119*, G. C. Rummans 51).\

VICTORIAN PREMIER CRICKET QUALIFYING FINALS

MELBOURNE v NORTHCOTE

At Albert Ground, March 19, 20, 2005. Melbourne won on first innings. Melbourne 8 for 446 declared (A. J. Kent 173, A. B. Mcdonald 121, R. J. Cooper 79; W. C. Hanser 3-59, M. L. Lewis 3-89); Northcote 284 (I. J. Harvey 79, R. A. Bartlett 44).

MELBOURNE UNIVERSITY v CAMBERWELL MAGPIES

At University Oval, Parkville, March 19, 20, 2005. Camberwell Magpies won on first innings. Melbourne University 199 (S. L. Flegler 90; A. D. Kellett 4-27, B. A. Knowles 3-32); Camberwell Magpies 6 for 200 (S. F. Hill 65*, J. G. Weinstock 45).

ST KILDA v DANDENONG

At St Kilda Cricket Ground, St Kilda, March 19, 20, 2005. St Kilda won on first innings. St Kilda 9 for 429 dec. (M. Klinger 166, G. C. Rummans 146; C. L. White 7-132) Dandenong 128 (A. C. Warren 4-24, A. P. Jones 3-29).

SEMI-FINALS

MELBOURNE v CAMBERWELL MAGPIES

At Albert Ground, Melbourne, March 26, 27, 2005. Drawn. Melbourne qualified for the final. Camberwell Magpies 6 for 387 dec (M. T. G. Elliott 201, D. J. Davies 63, M. R. Hayward 54, D. R. Shanahan 47); Melbourne 8 for 333 (L. G. L. Buchanan 105, A. J. Kent 59*, A. B. Mcdonald 59; B. A. Knowles 5-77).

ST KILDA v MELBOURNE UNIVERSITY

At St Kilda Cricket Ground, St Kilda, March 26, 27, 2005. St Kilda won on first innings. Melbourne University 196 (A. P. Jones 4-38, A. C. Warren 4-64); St Kilda 3 for 197 (N. Jewell 83*, M. Klinger 78*).

FINAL

ST KILDA v MELBOURNE

Played at St Kilda Cricket Ground, St Kilda, April 1, 2, 3, 2005. St Kilda won on first innings. *Toss:* St Kilda.

St Kilda included ten members of their 2003-04 premiership side, the only newcomer being well-performed paceman Adam Warren. For Melbourne only Matthew Pinniger remained from their last premiership side, in 1997-98. On the four previous occasions the clubs had met in a final, most recently in 1958-59, Melbourne had won each time.

Batting first in good conditions, St Kilda suffered early setbacks when Graeme Rummans, Michael Klinger and Shawn Craig, who had scored nearly 2,500 runs between them during the season, fell to Shane Harwood and Phil Halbish within five balls with the score on 24. Nick Jewell and Rob Quiney steadied the innings with a fourth-wicket stand of 106, but both fell to left-armer Aaron Edrich shortly after reaching half-centuries. At 6 for 153 St Kilda's chances of building a competitive score rested on their last recognised batsman, the captain, Tim O'Sullivan. Picking the right ball to hit, he put on 47 for the seventh wicket with Damon Rowan and a crucial 82 for the eighth with the defiant Warren, who fell to the last ball of the first day. When the innings closed early next morning, O'Sullivan was left unbeaten after a fine rearguard display in which he faced 177 balls and hit 15 fours. As in 2003-04, he reserved his best innings of the season for the final.

Melbourne began poorly in reply, losing both openers cheaply. Liam Buchanan and Andrew McDonald then added 64 in a bright third-wicket stand, but both fell in quick succession to Jewell, bowling an accurate spell of left-arm medium-pace which changed the course of the match. Thereafter Melbourne's batsmen were unable to regain the initiative against St Kilda's persistent pace attack of Adrian Jones, Warren, Jewell and Oliver Oostermeyer, although Robert Cooper batted with determination until he was ninth out.

Trailing by 111, Melbourne needed to capture early wickets in St Kilda's second innings to have any chance of forcing an outright win. Openers Rummans and Craig did not look like getting out, however, and the match was called off after just under an hour's play on the third morning. Tim O'Sullivan deservedly won the John Scholes Medal for Player of the Final, and he and his team-mates celebrated St Kilda's fourth premiership in five years.

Close of play: First day – St Kilda (1) 8-282 (O'Sullivan 84); Second day – St Kilda (2) 0-1 (Rummans 1, Craig 0).

St Kilda

G. C. Rummans b Harwood	16	– not out	42
S. A. J. Craig c Nevill b Halbish	8	– not out	16
M. Klinger c Kent b Harwood	0		
N. Jewell c Nevill b Edrich	54		
R. J. Quiney c Nevill b Edrich	52		
G. A. Lalor c Buchanan b Halbish	12		
*T. D. B. O'Sullivan not out	90		
†D. N. Rowan c Harwood b Mangan	14		
A. C. Warren lbw b Mangan	34		
A. P. Jones c Nevill b Harwood	8		
O. V. Oostermeyer b Mangan	0		
L-b 7, n-b 1	8	L-b 5	5

(110 overs, 409 mins) 296   (17 overs, 61 mins) (0 wkt) 63
Fall: 24 24 24 130 137 153 200 282 295 296

Bowling: *First Innings*—Harwood 28–11–58–3; Edrich 17–3–70–2; Halbish 21–6–57–2; McDonald 22–7–62–0; Mangan 22–6–42–3. *Second Innings*—Harwood 8–2–18–0; Edrich 2–1–10–0; McDonald 3–0–12–0; Halbish 2–0–10–0; Mangan 2–1–8–0.

Melbourne

M. S. Pinniger c Rowan b Jones	15	†P. M. Nevill c Klinger b Warren	4
P. J. Dickson c O'Sullivan b Warren	1	J. P. Mangan not out	0
L. G. L. Buchanan c Rowan b Jewell	29	A. K. Edrich c Craig b Warren	0
*A. B. McDonald b Jewell	39		
A. J. Kent lbw b Warren	24	L-b 4, nb 4	8
R. J. Cooper c Rummans b Jones	45		
S. M. Harwood c Klinger b Oostermeyer	17	(81.3 overs, 302 mins)	185
P. J. Halbish c Rowan b Oostermeyer	3	Fall: 16 18 82 97 126 155 166 181 185 185	

Bowling: Jones 18–6–35–2; Warren 19.3–5–40–4; Lalor 6–3–19–0; Jewell 18–6–34–2; Oostermeyer 12–3–42–2; Rummans 8–4–11–0.

Umpires: G. T. D. Morrow and R. L Parry.

Perth First-Grade, 2004-05

by KEN CASELLAS

The vexed question of whether club cricket finals should be played over two or four days continues to be debated after a return to a four-day contest in 2004-05. The strong argument against a four-day match is that the players have performed in two-day fixtures to qualify for the finals and therefore this format should be continued. Advocates of the longer fixture maintain that tough four-day matches prepare players for elevation to the interstate four-day competition. No decision regarding the duration of the final in 2005-06 had been made by a review committee by the start of July. The return to the four-day final in 2004-05 came after widespread dissatisfaction at the conditions for two-day finals in previous years when, with no compulsory declaration, the side that had finished higher on the premiership table could simply bat for the entire match and take the title.

The trend of batsmen dominating in club cricket continued, with 72 centuries posted, which smashed the previous record of 58 in 2003-04. On the first day in round 11 in February, 2,561 runs were scored and only 59 wickets fell in eight matches. There were five centuries that day and 14 fifties, and only one bowler, Fremantle's former Zimbabwe international Sean Ervine (5 for 42 off 26 overs against Willetton), managed a five-wicket haul.

Flat, batsman-friendly pitches continued to make life tough for new-ball bowlers. The WA selectors continue to bemoan the fact that very few promising fast bowlers are being produced in the competition. Reflecting this is the recruitment for the 2005-06 season of Victorian left-arm fast bowler Mathew Inness, who will become the tenth interstate recruit to take the new ball for WA in eight years, following Shane Jurgensen, Steve Nikitaras, Brad Williams, Stuart Karppinen, Matthew Nicholson, Paul Wilson, John Taylor, Ben Edmondson and Steve Magoffin. This is remarkable for a state that has produced such outstanding fast men as

Graham McKenzie, Dennis Lillee, Terry Alderman, Bruce Reid, Brendon Julian and Jo Angel, to name just a few.

There were few devastating fast bowling performances in club cricket and the top three in the first-grade averages (all new-ball men) were from the eastern states. Queenslander Matt Petrie, playing for Willetton, finished on top with 46 wickets at 15.28. He was followed by University's Andrew James, originally from Canberra, and Queenslander Steve Magoffin. For good measure, former Sydney grade fast bowler Jamie Heath finished sixth in the averages, with 49 wickets at 17.69 for Fremantle. James, who missed several matches through injury, finished the summer in fine style for University, and in round 12 took 9 for 93 against Midland-Guildford. Perhaps the most encouraging sign was the emergence of right-arm fast bowler James Sprague and Joondalup teenager Chris Thompson.

Hampshire fast bowler Chris Tremlett appeared in three matches with Melville and his figures of 2 for 68, 5 for 34, 0 for 3 and 1 for 48 showed that he didn't have things all his own way. A couple of months later he was bowling for England in one-day internationals. Most sides contained an Englishman, with Essex's Ravi Bopara and Warwickshire's Jim Troughton each scoring three centuries. Bopara scored 568 runs at 63.11 for Rockingham-Mandurah and Troughton 442 at 40.18 for Claremont-Nedlands. An interesting newcomer to Perth club cricket was 42-year-old former South African limited-overs international all-rounder Mike Rindel, who scored 543 runs at 45.25 and took 25 wickets at 18.76 for Joondalup.

Perth seam bowler Paul Keenan was one of 13 players to notch 100 first-grade appearances, and the 30-year-old capped a splendid season by winning the Olly Cooley Medal for the fairest-and-best player in the competition. In qualifying-round matches Keenan took 52 wickets and scored 267 runs at 29.66. He polled 20 votes to finish one ahead of Subiaco-Floreat swing bowler Sam Howman (47 wickets) and two ahead of Petrie. Scarborough all-rounder David Bandy enjoyed another bountiful season, scoring a club record of 1,012 runs at 63.25 and taking 26 wickets at 22.65. He just failed to equal the performance of his grandfather Laurie Bandy, who scored 1,070 runs at 62.94 for North Perth in 1943-44. Dashing opener Hugh Brown enhanced his reputation with 919 runs at 57.44 for South Perth, who failed to reach the finals. Former Western Australian and Tasmanian new ball bowler Dennis Baker will take over from Rod Redmond as South Perth's coach.

PERTH FIRST-GRADE TABLE, 2004-05

	M	WO	W1	D	L1	LO	T	Points
Scarborough	13	0	11	1	1	0	0	179.84
Melville	13	1	8	0	4	0	0	160.65
Subiaco-Floreat	13	0	9	1	3	0	0	156.57
Fremantle	13	0	7	1	5	0	0	139.89
Wanneroo	13	1	6	3	3	0	0	139.73
Perth	13	1	6	1	5	0	0	137.16
Joondalup	13	0	6	1	6	0	0	126.43
Mount Lawley	13	0	6	1	6	0	0	118.31
University	13	0	5	0	8	0	0	112.43
Midland-Guildford	13	0	5	1	7	0	0	111.05
Willetton	13	0	5	0	8	0	0	109.14
Claremont-Nedlands	13	0	5	0	8	0	0	108.84
South Perth	13	1	3	0	9	0	0	103.65
Bayswater-Morley	13	0	4	1	7	1	0	99.35
Rockingham-Mandurah	13	0	4	1	7	1	0	94.62
Gosnells	13	0	4	0	7	2	0	93.31

BATTING AVERAGES, 2004-05

(Qualification: 300 runs)

	M	I	NO	R	HS	100s	50s	Avge
S. E. Marsh (Fremantle)	11	11	2	722	142*	3	3	80.22
D. C. Bandy (Scarborough)	16	18	2	1,012	181	4	5	63.25
R. S. Bopara (Rockingham-Mandurah)	8	9	0	568	171	3	1	63.11
P. C. Worthington (Midland-Guildford)	13	13	3	603	133*	2	2	60.30
H. F. Brown (South Perth)	12	16	0	919	174	4	2	57.44
S. M. Rakich (Mount Lawley)	12	11	2	499	116	1	5	55.44
T. P. Doropoulos (Scarborough)	13	15	2	714	216*	2	2	54.92
A. C. Voges (Melville)	12	11	0	598	130	3	2	54.36
W. S. Gillies (Melville)	16	18	3	809	162*	2	4	53.93
C. A. King (Wanneroo)	14	16	0	799	130	3	2	53.27

* Denotes not out.

BOWLING AVERAGES, 2004-05

(Qualification: 25 wickets)

	M	O	Mds	R	W	BB	5W/i	10W/m	Avge
M. J. Petrie (Willetton)	13	310.5	97	703	46	7-23	1	0	15.28
A. C. James (University)	7	125.5	21	451	29	9-93	3	0	15.55
S. J. Magoffin (Melville)	9	183.4	44	516	33	6-52	2	0	15.64
L. K. Platel (Melville)	11	169.1	43	488	31	5-15	1	0	15.74
P. Keenan (Perth)	14	386.2	130	957	55	6-30	6	1	17.40
J. M. Heath (Fremantle)	15	297.4	76	867	49	6-29	3	0	17.69
K. M. Harvey (Scarborough)	14	197	45	557	32	5-49	2	0	17.40
M. J. R. Rindel (Joondalup)	13	181.4	45	474	25	4-43	0	0	18.96
P. C. Worthington (Midland-Guildford)	13	187	46	570	30	5-20	2	0	19.00
M. R. Healey (University)	12	272.4	73	704	37	5-47	1	0	19.02

PERTH FIRST-GRADE ELIMINATION FINALS, 2004-05

SUBIACO-FLOREAT v FREMANTLE

At WACA Ground, Perth, March 12, 13, 2005. Fremantle won on first innings. Fremantle 8 for 327 dec. (S. M. Ervine 119, R. T. Shuttleworth 70; D. J. Bolton 3-40, S. G. Howman 3-85); Subiaco-Floreat 183 (D. J. Bolton 44, M. P. Simpson 35, K. Kapinkoff 30; S. A. Miller 4-38, J. M. Heath 4-42).

SCARBOROUGH v PERTH

At Abbett Park, Scarborough, March 12, 13, 2005. Scarborough won on first innings. Perth 284 (F. Grobler 81, G. A. Nottle 47; K. M. Harvey 5-79); Scarborough 9 for 286 (G. M. Cavanagh 104, K. M. Harvey 58; R. F. Scali 3-61, P. Keenan 3-76).

MELVILLE v WANNEROO

At Tompkins Park, Melville, March 12, 13, 2005. Melville won on first innings. Melville 387 (B. J. Lillis 148, S. W. Meuleman 87, D. N. Porter 54, S. R. Russell 35*; V. Clarke 4-141); Wanneroo 297 (W. M. Robinson 120*; L. K. Platel 3-31).

SEMI-FINALS

SCARBOROUGH v FREMANTLE

At WACA Ground, Perth, March 19, 20, 2005. Scarborough won on first innings. Scarborough 5 for 459 dec. (T. P. Doropoulos 216*, D. C. Bandy 102, B. Casson 83; J. M. Heath 3-105); Fremantle 241 (S. E. Marsh 131*, J. M. Ifould 45; K. M. Harvey 4-57, D. C. Bandy 3-16).

MELVILLE v SUBIACO-FLOREAT

At Kingsway Reserve, Wanneroo, March 19, 20, 2005. Melville won on first innings. Subiaco-Floreat 68 (L. K. Platel 4-15, A. D. Mascarenhas 4-34) and 154 (S. A. Glew 68, A. S. Malcolm 42*; A. C. Voges 6-68); Melville 193 (D. J. Weston 43, S. W. Meuleman 42, B. J. Lillis 39; C. J. Hansberry 5-50, M. W. Clark 3-43).

FINAL

SCARBOROUGH v MELVILLE

At WACA Ground, Perth, March 25, 26, 27, 28, 2005. Melville won by eight wickets. *Toss:* Melville.

When Scarborough were coasting at 2 for 201 shortly after tea on the first day of the four-day final, many Melville supporters were questioning the wisdom of Adam Voges, who had sent the opposition in to bat. Scarborough defied the swing and seam of the Melville attack during a sultry first session and appeared on the path to a massive total, but immediately after tea lanky fast-medium bowler Steve Magoffin changed the course of the contest. He removed teenage opener Liam Davis for 105 and Beau Casson for a duck, and Voges, bowling his left-arm finger-spin, got rid of the dangerous Theo Doropoulos as three wickets crashed in the space of two overs. Davis, a stocky right-hander, had given Scarborough a wonderful start with his century that was posted off 184 deliveries and included 15 fours and a six. Normally a dasher, Davis modified his game, and after taking 16 deliveries to get off the mark he delighted the crowd with a series of spanking drives straight down the ground. Kade Harvey received spirited support early on the second day from tailender Brett Hugo. Medium-pacer Dimitri Mascarenhas, making light of a damaged right shoulder, gave a tremendous display of accuracy and stamina.

Melville quickly assumed control, and after their aggressive opener Scott Meuleman fell for 70, they were well placed when bad light ended the second day. Centuries to Voges and Ben Lillis strengthened Melville's grip on the third day. They added 228 for the second wicket, a club record, and the second-highest partnership in a WACA final, behind the 281 for the fourth wicket by North Perth's Neil Hawke and Peter Wishart against Nedlands in 1959. Melville's last nine wickets fell for 99 runs, but not before they had secured a clear lead.

It was a forlorn hope for Scarborough on the final day as they set out to score quick runs and then attempt to bowl the opposition out cheaply. Magoffin, generating lively pace, swinging the ball and getting plenty of bounce, revelled in the Scarborough run-chase and was chiefly responsible for Scarborough's dismissal for 149. Clint Heron played a sheet-anchor role and Harvey hit out boldly, caught at long-off attempting a third successive six. Melville then lost two wickets as they strolled to victory to record successive premierships.

Close of play: First day, Scarborough 7-291 (K. M. Harvey 53, B. Hugo 3); second day, Melville 1-135 (B. J. Lillis 44, A. C. Voges 18); third day, Melville 9-429 (S. J. Magoffin 0, L. K. Platel 0).

Scarborough

L. M. Davis c Weston b Magoffin	105	–	(2)c Porter b Magoffin	12
C. J. Heron c Voges b Mascarenhas		–	(1)c Weston b Magoffin	43
D. C. Bandy c Lillis b Mascarenhas	41	–	c Porter b Magoffin	7
T. P. Doropoulos c Russell b Voges	46	–	c Meuleman b Russell	11
B. Casson c Weston b Magoffin	0	–	(6)lbw b Magoffin	0
*K. M. Harvey c Magoffin b Russell	77	–	(7)c sub (Anderson) b Platel	30
G. M. Cavanagh b Mascarenhas	7	–	(8)c Mascarenhas b Magoffin	0
J. P. Coetzee c Lillis b Gillies	16	–	(5)c Porter b Russell	10
B. Hugo c Lillis b Voges	40	–	c Russell b Magoffin	0
†M. A. Johnson lbw b Platel	0	–	not out	20
R. Slowey not out	1	–	c Mascarenhas b Voges	6
B 5, l-b 8, n-b 7	20		B 8, l-b 1, n-b 1	10

(121.2 overs)	353	(38.1 overs)	149

Fall: 0 117 201 203 208 239 288 328 341 353

Fall: 13 20 50 65 75 106 118
118 135 149

Bowling: *First Innings*—Magoffin 25–5–76–2; Mascarenhas 22–10–38–3; Russell 27–2–102–1; Platel 20–6–55–1; Gillies 11–2–33–1; Voges 16.2–3–36–2. *Second Innings*—Magoffin 18–7–52–6; Russell 17–2–69–2; Platel 2–0–19–1; Voges 1.1–1–0–1.

Melville

S. W. Meuleman lbw b Bandy	70	–	(2)not out	25
B. J. Lillis b Casson	137	–	(1)c Davis b Bandy	12
*A. C. Voges lbw b Harvey	130	–	c Johnson b Slowey	28
W. S. Gillies lbw b Harvey	0	–	not out	4
D. N. Porter c Johnson b Bandy	36			
C. N. Wood lbw b Casson	3			
A. D. Mascarenhas c Johnson b Hugo	16			
S. R. Russell lbw b Bandy	9			
†D. J. Weston c Harvey b Slowey	4			
S. J. Magoffin not out	4			
L. K. Platel c Johnson b Harvey	0			
B 1, l-b 4, w 5, n-b 5	15			

(136.2 overs)	434	(11.1 overs)	(2 wkts) 69
Fall: 107 335 343 351 379 401 419 429 429 434		Fall: 19 64	

Bowling: *First Innings*—Harvey 27.2–9–55–3; Slowey 24–6–103–1; Bandy 26–12–72–3; Coetzee 13–2–77–0; Casson 26–4–78–2; Hugo 17–4–38–1; Doropoulos 3–2–6–0. *Second Innings*—Harvey 5–0–33–0; Bandy 5.1–0–32–1; Slowey 1–0–4–1.

Umpires: I. H. Lock and J. Brookes.

PERTH FIRST-GRADE RECORDS

ALL-TIME LEADING RUN-SCORERS

S. H. D. Rowe	12,035	H. C. Howard	9,448
J. P. McGuire	10,003	A. R. Edwards	9,106
D. C. McKenzie	9,792	H. W. H. Rigg	9,095
L. H. Bandy	9,458	I. R. Dick	9,054
G. J. Ireland	9,453	M. T. Vernon	9,050

ALL-TIME LEADING BOWLERS

A. H. Christian	1,002	R. B. Strauss	724
R. A. Selk	959	W. A. Evans	718
A. L. Mann	933	C. W. Puckett	668
H. G. Bevan	805	A. G. Zimbulis	663
E. G. Bishop	735	J. S. Everett	632

Newcastle First-Grade, 2003-04

by JACK BROWN

For the first time since 1997-98, when Wallsend defeated Belmont, neither Hamilton-Wickham nor Merewether made the final. Stockton, appearing in their first final since 1994-95, claimed the trophy with a comfortable win over Wallsend for their eighth title.

Hamilton-Wickham and Merewether still made the top four. Stockton defeated Hamilton-Wickham in their low-scoring semi-final, thanks to opening bowler Terry Crittenden's 5 for 26. In the other semi-final Wallsend had Merewether in deep trouble at 8 for 61, but David Hall and Michael Hogan restored the innings. Wallsend were 3 for 83 before Rhys Soper and teenager Brett Jackson took them towards victory.

The competition was more even this season, with just three points separating the top five teams. After lingering in the depths of the table for four seasons, Wallsend shot up to equal first. An off-season recruitment drive added experience to their talented young list and made their side more competitive. Stockton moved from fifth to equal first. Waratah, third last season, slipped down to ninth, while University, with the aid of two outright wins, moved from wooden spooners to sixth.

Rain affected play less than in previous years. There were 17 scores over 300, four each by Wallsend and Hamilton-Wickham, who twice scored over 400. There were 28 centuries, three in succession by Hamilton-Wickham's Andrew Mullard. The highest score was 243 by Stockton's Hassan Khan against Cardiff, the equal second-highest score in the competition's history. Brett Jackson had a highest score of 109 not out, and three scores in the nineties, two of them not out.

The best bowling figures went to University's spinner James Hillery, who took 8 for 74 against Newcastle City, and 37 wickets for the season. The best district average was from Wallsend's skipper and left-arm spinner Gavin Wilson, who took 29 wickets at 14, including 7 for 66 against West. The leading wicket-keeper in the competition was Hamilton-Wickham's Michael Jordan, with 33 dismissals.

The winner of both one-day competition finals was Hamilton-Wickham, defeating arch-rivals Merewether in the 50-over final (the Tom Locker Cup) and Albion Park in the State Wide Country Cup in Wollongong. It was their third win in the four seasons of that competition.

The Newcastle representative side, coached by former District great Greg Geise, won the State Wide Challenge Final at the SCG, defeating Sydney University. They also won the Country Championship Final, defeating Illawarra in Wollongong, after losing the last three finals in a row. Newcastle Under-21s performed well in the Country Colts Programme, with six Newcastle players gaining selection for Northern NSW in the final against their southern counterparts in a washed-out game at Bathurst. Northern scored 355, with Luke Penfold scoring 135, before rain stopped play. Penfold won the Junior Representative Player of the Season award.

Newcastle hosted an ING Cup match this season. Tasmania defeated the NSW Blues side at Newcastle's No. 1 sports ground, where Pura Cup matches are expected to be played in 2005-06.

At the District presentation evening, Terry Crittenden won the Players' Player Award, while Brett Jackson collected two more awards for a total of four: the best batsman under 21 and the Umpires' Player of the Season award. Wallsend were voted the Umpires' Club of the Season. Charlestown's leg-spinner, Ben Woolmer, won the Senior Representative Player of the Season award.

NEWCASTLE FIRST-GRADE TABLE, 2004-05

	M	WI	WO	LI	LO	D	Points	Quotient
Stockton	12	7	1	3	0	1	43	1.650
Wallsend	13	10	0	3	0	0	43	1.340
Merewether	11	7	1	3	0	0	41	1.326
Hamilton-Wickham	13	9	0	3	0	1	41	1.320
Belmont	12	6	1	4	0	1	40	1.107
University	12	3	2	5	1	1	37	0.895
Cardiff-Boolaroo	13	5	1	6	0	1	36	0.984
Charlestown	12	5	0	6	0	1	30	0.907
Waratah	12	4	0	7	0	1	27	0.975
Newcastle City	12	3	0	8	0	1	24	0.716
West	12	2	1	8	0	1	21	0.616
Southern Lakes	12	2	0	6	4	0	17	0.672

Note: Results are based only on matches that actually commenced. Matches washed out were recorded as drawn.

BATTING AVERAGES, 2004-05

(Qualification: 300 runs)

	M	I	NO	R	HS	100s	50s	Avge
B. Jackson (Wallsend)	12	14	7	612	109*	1	5	87.43
R. Wilson (Stockton)	8	8	1	409	108	1	3	58.43
A. Weekes (Waratah)	10	10	1	441	121*	1	3	49.00
H. Khan (Stockton)	12	12	1	512	243	2	0	46.55
M. Dries (Belmont)	10	10	2	379	125*	1	2	47.38
M. Gerits (Belmont)	7	7	2	233	70*	0	1	46.60
D. Hall (Merewether)	8	8	2	276	76	0	2	46.00
A. Mullard (Ham-Wick)	14	15	–	592	144	3	1	39.47
S. Mace (Charlestown)	10	12	2	401	112	1	1	40.10
T. Bush (West)	11	12	2	394	114	1	1	39.40

* Denotes not out.

BOWLING AVERAGES, 2004-05

(Qualification: 20 wickets)

	M	O	Mdns	R	W	BB	5Wi	Avge
T. Crittenden (Stockton)	13	176	40	455	34	6-29	3	13.38
P. Coleman (Cardiff)	12	178	38	539	35	5-45	2	15.40
S. Webber (Ham-Wick)	12	185	47	447	29	5-46	1	15.41
G. Wilson (Wallsend)	13	207	64	526	34	7-66	1	15.47
H. Quinlivan (University)	8	130	30	430	25	5-41	2	17.20
S. Threadgold (Charlestown)	10	144	28	449	26	7-60	2	17.27
J. Lawson (Belmont)	9	153	29	398	23	6-31	1	17.30
J. Kneller (Cardiff)	13	157	27	502	29	5-63	2	17.31
B. Bannister (Belmont)	9	195	56	463	26	4-60	0	17.81
M. Dries (Belmont)	11	164	33	373	20	6-30	2	18.65

NEWCASTLE FIRST-GRADE SEMI-FINALS, 2004-05

MEREWETHER v WALLSEND

At Lynn Oval, Stockton, March 12, 13, 2005. Wallsend won on first innings. Merewether 224 (M. Hogan 79*, D. Hall 76; C. Sutton 6-72); Wallsend 4 for 226 (B. Jackson 63*, R. Soper 60).

STOCKTON v HAMILTON-WICKHAM

At Cahill Oval, Belmont, March 12, 13, 2005. Stockton won on first innings. Hamilton-Wickham 125 (A. Mullard 56; T. Crittenden 5-26, M. Cooper 3-20) and 8 for 136 (H. Khan 4-75); Stockton 153 (A. Williams 46; S. Hughes 3-25, S. Webber 3-50).

FINAL

STOCKTON V WALLSEND

At Newcastle No. 1 Sports Ground, March 19, 20, 26, 2005. Stockton won on first innings. *Toss:* Wallsend.

Although heavy rain during the week prevented play on the scheduled first day, the ground staff managed to restore the surface to an excellent standard by the time play commenced on the Sunday. After wickets fell early, Shaun Hassall and Hassan Khan added 61 for the fourth wicket, but Wallsend's four-pronged attack took wickets regularly, and Stockton slipped to 9 for 222 in the 76th over. Then Simon Middleton joined Shane Burley and the pair put on 42 valuable runs for the last wicket off just 32 balls.

In the nine remaining overs of the day, Wallsend batted cautiously to finish at 0 for 15. On resumption six days later, the openers lost their wickets early, in successive overs, and when the rising batting stars Luke Penfold and Brett Jackson were both out leg-before to Khan, the score was 4 for 54 in the 19th over. Rhys Soper was the only batsman to withstand the attack of Khan and Terry Crittenden for long, but after a fighting knock of two hours he was finally dismissed and Wallsend were soon all out. This was Stockton's eighth title.

Stockton

T. Crittenden b Soper	16	S. O'Sullivan c Bunt b Price	6
A. Williams c Bunt b Price	17	S. Burley lbw b Sutton	9
S. Hassall c Bunt b Sutton	54	S. Middleton not out	33
J. Whitehead c Penfold b Price	16		
H. Khan c Elkovich b Wilson	35	L-b 3, w 1, n-b 13	17
R. Drage c Jackson b Wilson	33		
N. Foster c and b Wilson	22	(80.5 overs, 279 mins)	264
M. Cooper c Sutton b Wilson	6	Fall: 32 42 76 137 172 191 204 222 222 264

Bowling: Soper 20–2–74–1; Sutton 18.5–4–73–2; Price 16–5–33–3; Jackson 2–1–5–0; Wilson 24–7–76–4.

Wallsend

J. Woweries c Hassall b Khan	23	C. Sutton c Whitehead b Cooper	8
S. Beveridge c O'Sullivan b Crittenden	14	G. Wilson not out	3
L. Penfold lbw b Khan	3	A. Chad lbw b Cooper	0
R. Soper c Middleton b Khan	49		
B. Jackson lbw b Khan	5	B 8, l-b 4, w 2	14
S. Elkovich c Burley b Crittenden	14		
J. Bunt lbw b Khan	3	(52.5 overs, 227 mins)	143
N. Price c Williams b Khan	7	Fall: 39 41 46 54 100 113 118 137 143 143

Bowling: Crittenden 21–6–45–2; Khan 25.4–6–62–6; Middleton 4–2–20–0; Foster 1–0–1–0; Cooper 1.5–0–3–2.

Umpires: M. Jones and R. Aurelius.

NEWCASTLE FIRST-GRADE RECORDS

ALL-TIME LEADING RUN-SCORERS

Jack Mayes (Waratah)	14,028	Jack Anderson (Hamilton)	9,023
Reg Beatty (various)	11,064	Ken Hill (Lambton)	8,988
Greg Geise (Wallsend)	10,228	Mick Hill (various)	8,496
Ron Camps (Wickham)	9,500	Wal Moy (various)	8,200
Jim De Courcy (Lambton)	9,424	Greg Arms (Waratah)	8,041
Mark Curry (Charlestown)	9,326		

ALL-TIME LEADING BOWLERS

Ken Hill (Lambton)	1,128	Mick Hill (various)	650
Bob Holland (Southern Lakes)	799	Percy Lee (Hamilton)	632
Reg Woolston (Wickham, Waratah)	772	Ernie O'Brien (Merewether)	626
Harry Hodges (Stockton)	731	Jack Bull (Wickham)	505
Wal Moy (various)	724	Neil Budden (Waratah)	451
Arch Frazer (Waratah)	667		

Darwin A-Grade, 2004

by ANDREW HYDE

Darwin is an outdoor town like almost no other. With an average age of around 29 and glorious, warm conditions for much of the year, the city of 100,000-plus is a Mecca for all things sporting. And yet cricket has always had an unusual position here. While the local competition is healthy, the number of participants (according to the Northern Territory Cricket Association) has remained relatively static for at least a decade, with junior numbers declining. For many years cricket was a game for the southern blow-ins – today it remains one of the lesser sports in the Territory.

The "Top End Tours" of 2003 and 2004 have proved that cricket in the Territory continues to require widespread promotion and development. As Adam Gilchrist put it during the build-up to the July 2004 Test against Sri Lanka: "Darwin still has the feel of a neutral venue." Better to be neutral than altogether foreign, but to many Top Enders, particularly those in the indigenous communities, cricket remains strangely distant.

The 2004 season brought big-time cricket back to Darwin and potentially offered inspiration to young local cricketers. One of the challenges now is to stop the decline in junior numbers. Cricket in Darwin is facing a major threat from traditional wet-season sports such as Australian rules and rugby union, which are planning to move over into the middle of the year in line with the rest of the country. The game's administrators need to find a way to overcome the absence in Darwin of a summer cricket culture.

Despite this, the 2004 season of the Darwin & Districts Cricket Association kicked off with much anticipation amongst the converted for the forthcoming Test match. The chance to be one of the locals in the Chief Minister's XI to play Sri Lanka in the warm-up game again offered considerable incentive to the players.

Chasing a fourth consecutive premiership, Palmerston got off to a sound start. Perennial finalists Pint, with a batting line-up boosted by Port Adelaide recruit Simon Lavers and the consistent wicket-keeper/batsman Martin Brown, showed signs of being the team to beat. Southern Districts started poorly and were languishing in seventh position after ten rounds despite the makings of a bumper season from batsman Dwaine Richards. Darwin, while generally considered premiership contenders, were proving inconsistent with the bat and relied heavily on a balanced attack led by seamer Gary Hancock and skipper Greg Brautigam. At Nightcliff, the Tigers were also proving inconsistent and things might have been considerably worse without experienced swing bowler and captain Brad Hatton. Utilising his considerable height and the strong dry-season breezes, Hatton's out-swing ultimately collected 42 wickets at less than 13 runs apiece, making him the leading wicket-taker for the season.

As Pint firmed as premiership favourites, Southern Districts were beginning to turn their season around. Richards, who hadn't scored a century since his debut in 2000, somehow found the appetite for long innings and struck three centuries on his way to 600 runs for the season. His efforts were almost matched by Ian Redpath, whose 513 runs and 24 wickets contributed to a remarkable form reversal. Waratahs' Shane Piercy was also enjoying outstanding all-round form in an otherwise disappointing season for the club. Simon Lavers provided one of the individual highlights of the season when he broke Pint's club record with an outstanding 222 not out against Tracy Village, only to smash it again during the finals series.

Pint sealed the minor premiership, losing just five games, but reigning premiers Palmerston lost two of their last three matches despite consistent form from left-handed all-rounder Anthony Dent and young paceman Bayly. Piercy produced a brilliant 6 for 53 and 100 for Waratahs against Pint in the final round. However, the game was marred by an incident which left the wicket unplayable on the first day. A fault with a recently installed irrigation system caused flooding of the centre square and left Waratahs insufficient time to chase outright victory and a place in the final four.

In the first semi-final Palmerston's inconsistent batting maintained form, reaching 257 only thanks to a 94-run stand for the tenth wicket. That stand proved decisive after Bayly ripped through Darwin with 6 for 34. In the second semi-final Pint produced a massive 7 for 475, featuring a 273-ball 260 from Simon Lavers. This broke the record for the highest individual score in the 45-year history of the competition, which had been held by the New Zealand wicket-keeper Brendon McCullum, who scored 250 not out for Palmerston in 2002. Going into the final, Palmerston appeared short of the hunger required for a fourth consecutive flag, while Pint were confronting a 20-year finals hoodoo.

DARWIN A-GRADE TABLE, 2004

	M	Won	Lost	Draw	Match Points	Bonus Points	Batting Points	Bowling Points	Total Points
Pint	14	9	5	0	52.00	5	19.18	17.80	93.98
Palmerston	14	9	5	0	47.75	3	19.45	19.60	88.80
Darwin	14	8	6	0	38.00	4	20.08	15.60	77.68
Southern Districts	14	7	7	0	36.00	4	18.38	17.60	75.98
N.T.I.S.	14	8	5	1	41.00	2	15.89	14.80	73.69
Nightcliffe	14	6	7	1	31.00	5	16.99	15.40	68.39
Waratah	14	6	8	0	28.75	4	15.95	19.20	67.90
Tracy Village	14	2	12	0	11.25	2	19.83	12.80	45.88

BATTING AVERAGES, 2004

(Qualification: 300 runs)

	M	I	NO	R	HS	Avge
B. T. Wilson (Darwin)	11	9	4	259	143*	51.80
D. K. Richards (Sthn Dist.)	12	13	0	600	140	46.15
M. Redpath (Sthn Dist.)	12	13	0	513	163	39.46
S. V. Piercy (Waratahs)	14	16	1	580	100	38.67
S. Lavers (Pint)	14	17	1	582	222*	36.38
R. M. Bowden (Waratahs)	10	11	1	363	75	36.30
M. M. Brown (Pint)	12	14	2	435	113	36.25
S. Compain (Sthn Dist.)	12	11	4	250	66	35.71
R. C. Weckert (Darwin)	9	11	1	349	117	34.90
D. L. Treumer (Tracy Vill.)	11	13	2	377	118*	34.27

* Denotes not out.

BOWLING AVERAGES, 2004

(Qualification: 20 wickets)

	M	O	Mdns	R	W	BB	Avge
K. Gibbs (Nightcliff)	11	95.3	20	274	22	4-51	12.45
B. J. Hatton (Nightcliff)	13	181.5	49	530	42	7-48	12.62
J. Akers (Sthn Dist.)	14	173.2	48	391	29	4-9	13.48
C. E. Scollay (Nightcliff)	14	97.3	16	289	20	5-34	14.45
M. Redpath (Sthn Dist.)	12	131.2	30	388	25	6-55	15.52
T. G. Bayly (Palmerston)	12	177.5	37	498	32	6-41	15.56
S. V. Piercy (Waratahs)	14	164.2	35	540	33	6-50	16.36
R. Hodgson (Pint)	13	150.5	21	487	28	4-21	17.39
A. C. Dent (Palmerston)	12	184.5	44	482	27	5-53	17.85
G. M. Hancock (Darwin)	14	185.0	38	572	32	7-34	17.88

SEMI-FINALS

DARWIN v PALMERSTON

At Power Park, September 11, 2004. Palmerston won on first innings. *Toss:* Darwin. Palmerston 257 (A. N. Williams 76, N. J. Drummond 56, R. R. McCard 50*, T. G. Bayly 22; G. Brautigam 5-47, A. D. Nicholson 2-46) and 1-36; Darwin 147 (B. T. Wilson 23; T. G. Bayly 6-34, A. C. Dent 2-71).

SOUTHERN DISTRICTS v PINT

At Marrara No. Ground, September 11, 2004. Pint won on first innings. *Toss:* Pint. Pint 7 for 475 (S. Lavers 260, A. F. Reeves 95, M. M. Brown 50, A. G. Dilley 18; R. W. Street 2-48, I. M. Redpath 2-59); Southern Districts 189 (J. P. Bell 36, S, H, Regan 33, M. R. Wright 32, S. Moon 20; N. L. Berry 3-4, A. G. Dilley 3-30; A. F. Reeves 2-16).

FINAL

PINT v PALMERSTON

At Marrara No. 1 Ground, Darwin, September 18, 19, 2004. Pint won on first innings. *Toss:* Palmerston.

Two decades of finals frustration finally ended for Pint when Alan Reeves clung on to a spectacular diving catch to remove Palmerston tail-ender Rod McCard. Pint claimed their first flag since 1984, despite competing in 17 final series and six finals during the 20-year drought.

Stifling early wet-season conditions met the players. Despite a lifeless track and some promising starts, Pint struggled to establish any early partnerships of note. Palmerston fast bowler Terry Bayly and left-arm seamer Anthony Dent produced sustained spells in the tropical heat, maintaining pressure on the Pint top order. Pint' finals curse appeared to be alive and well when it was discovered that Reeves had been dismissed by the seventh legal delivery from medium-pacer Ken Vowles's fifth over. After Pint slumped to 6 for 109 their veteran captain, David King, came in. Suffering from severe finals thirst, having spent most of his career in premiership drought, he rallied the side in an engrossing last-wicket stand with Matt Ryan. Their 86-minute partnership contributed 67 vital runs and only ended when Ryan ran himself out looking for a sharp single.

Palmerston's experienced batting line-up would have considered the target of 223 to be achievable. However, Glen Patrick was quickly caught behind off Ritchie Hodgson and Brett Sinclair was well held by Nick Berry in the gully, leaving Palmerston 2 for 1 at stumps. Wickets continued to fall the following morning, Palmerston slumping to for 47. Despite a patient innings from Darren Treumer and some lower-order resistance Palmerston's chase for a fourth consecutive flag failed to gain momentum.

Pint

S. Lavers c Sinclair b Bayly 19	R. A. Edis c Williams b Vowles 3
N. L. Berry c Sinclair b Dent 18	R. Hodgson lbw b Vowles 5
R. J. Kensey lbw b Dent 10	M. C. Ryan run out (Bayly/Dent) . . . 16
N. J. Rosser c Patrick b Bayly 39	
†M. M. Brown lbw b Vowles 13	B 3, l-b 7, w 3, n-b 1 14
A. F. Reeves b Vowles 0	—
A. G. Dilley c Treumer b Dent 28	(87.1 overs) 222
*D. J. King not out 57	Fall: 29 45 53 101 101 109 138 141 155 222

Bowling: Bayly 30–7–62–2; Dent 25.1–5–68–3; McCard 10–1–38–0; Cook 2–0–2–0; Vowles 20–5–42–4.

Palmerston

G. Patrick c Berry b Rosser 5	A. C. Dent lbw b Edis 17
B. Sinclair c Brown b Hodgson 2	T. G. Bayly not out 22
A. N. Williams lbw b Berry 25	R. R. McCard c Reeves b Edis 0
P. A. Cook lbw b Berry 0	
S. J. Chatto lbw b Ryan 26	L-b 4 w 4 n-b 5 13
N. J. Drummond b Berry 1	—
*†D. L. Treumer c Kensey b Berry . . . 40	(70.3 overs) 170
K. E. Vowles c Kensey b Ryan 19	Fall: 3 13 19 40 47 94 120 134 165 170

Bowling: Hodgson 18–5–45–1; Ryan 10–4–21–2; Rosser 5–3–10–1; Berry 28–9–52–4; Edis 7.3–1–19–2; Dilley 2–0–19–0.

Umpires: P. Creek and A. McGovern

National Country Cricket Championships, 2004-05

by WARWICK TORRENS

Success for a player in the National Country Championships usually attracts an offer from a capital city grade club. For a successful team, this can mean several changes in the stock of available players for the following season. Failure in one season can also prompt change for the next. This has been the way since the championships began.

Lack of success in 2003-04 drove changes to the Queensland team for 2004-05, with the result that it went through the five-match series undefeated. The Queenslanders were threatened only in one match against Western Australia. In the opening round, Queensland fell away badly after passing the South Australian score with only five batsmen out and finished with a lead of just 44. In round two, WA lacked the bowling depth to capitalise when Queensland were 6 for 106 chasing 170, and Queensland gained the lead without further loss. In the remaining rounds, Queensland outplayed reigning champions Victoria, fell only slightly short of an outright result against East Asia-Pacific and finally crushed New South Wales. There was little doubt Queensland were the best team at the championships, and this was reflected when six of their players were named in the honorary Australian Country team.

The Queenslanders were capably led by Brian May, still the only player to record 2,000 runs in all championships matches, and now well within sight of 3,000. New pace bowler Ben Cust from Cairns also had a successful series and against East Asia-Pacific joined Jason Stein as the only bowlers to capture ten wickets in a championship match. Wicket-keeper and vice-captain Steven Baker was also successful, with 17 dismissals, advancing to second on the all-time wicket-keeping tally.

East Asia-Pacific, in their second series, again failed to win a match. Jamie Brazier had a good series and was one of only three batsmen to pass 300 runs. Other batsmen performed usefully, but there were too many failures. The bowling lacked depth and penetration.

New South Wales retain top spot with eight victories out of 21 championships. Customarily, NSW provide strong opposition but in this series their early batsmen collapsed against Victoria, and in the final round faltered badly against Queensland. Against Victoria there was a middle-order revival, but it was not enough. Against Queensland, NSW lost their eighth wicket at 58 and seemed destined to record their lowest total before Ian Gregory and Daniel Hughes joined the adventurous Brad Bannister in two useful partnerships. Queensland passed the target of 118 with only one wicket down.

South Australia finished fourth. Perhaps they were fortunate that their last game had to be abandoned as a draw, as they looked to be on the way to defeat, and the other two games in the round reached a conclusion. Their outstanding player was left-arm medium-pacer Andy Paltridge, who took 17 wickets in his debut series. The captain, Michael Johnston, proved consistent with the bat without making a big score and was also a worthy workhorse with the ball.

Despite losing several players, Victoria still seemed strong. They managed a narrow first-innings lead over New South Wales in the opening round, but it was the lower-order batting that raised a winning total. Their outstanding player was opening batsman Sam Ahmet, who made at least a useful score every time he went to the crease. Many of the top order performed below expectations, and it was too often left to the tail to provide the runs. Against Queensland, everybody was found wanting and Victoria suffered the indignity of following on.

Western Australia had another disappointing series. Their best batting effort was the opening partnership of 124 in the second innings against Victoria, when Ben Drummond and Blake Reynolds each recorded half-centuries. The side's only other half-century for the series was made by the captain, Brendon King, in the final match. With the ball, Craig Tonkin continued to take regular wickets and Chris Waddingham also chipped in, but there was little else.

The 12-day championship was arranged by the Far North Coast Cricket Council of New South Wales and the Lismore Cricket Association. It was well supported by the Lismore City Council and other local authorities. Unfortunately, rain interrupted many of the matches.

It was also unfortunate that no match could be arranged for the Australian Country team selected from the championships. The honorary Australian Country team for 2005, announced at the end of the championships, in batting order, was: Brian May (captain, Qld), David Else (Qld), Sam Ahmet (Vic), Wade Frazer (Qld), Steve Mudford (NSW), Jamie Brazier (EAP), Ben Woolmer (NSW), Steven Baker (Qld), Brad Hauenstein (Vic), Andy Paltridge (SAust), Ben Cust (Qld), Jason Stein (Qld).

Player of the Series: Brian May (Qld) and Ben Woolmer (NSW) (joint)
Don Bradman Batting Trophy: Brian May (Qld)
Bill O'Reilly Bowling Trophy: Ben Woolmer (NSW)
Fieldsman of the Series: Stephen Baker (Qld)

ROUND ONE

At Queen Elizabeth Park, Casino, January 4, 5, 2005. East Asia-Pacific 115 (A. Uda 29; C. G. R. Tonkin 3-23, C. R. Phelps 3-25, C. A. Waddingham 2-24) and 4 for 198 (J. L. Brazier 101*, M. Ahmed 53, A. Uda 23) lost to Western Australia 143 (C. D'Mello 45, B. M. Drummond 23, L. Sounness 22; C. Amini 2-4, D. Eliaba 2-25, H. Areni 2-33) on first innings.

At Oakes Oval, Lismore, January 4, 5, 2005. Victoria 248 (P. Bradley 46, D. A. Petersen 32, J. P. Mathers 31, S. Ahmet 30, C. F. Hopper 27, B. G. Hauenstein 26, R. X. Hassett 24; B. A. Woolmer 7-93, D. A. Hughes 2-25) and 2 for 59 (S. Ahmet 34) defeated New South Wales 231 (M. D. Walters 83, B. G. Bannister 53, B. Nott, 29; B. G. Hauenstein 5-58, C. T. Owen 3-54) on first innings.

At Heaps Oval, Lismore, January 4, 5, 2005. South Australia 185 (R. R. Reid 51, M. S. Johnston 30, A. W. Paltridge 29; B. S. Cust 3-29, M. D. Brennan 3-54, K. W. Charles 2-20) and 2 for 87 (M. S. Johnston 29, A. Willis 29*; M. D. Brennan 2-37) lost to Queensland 229 (W. A. Frazer 60, D. B. Frakes 43, B. K. D. May 34, M. Sippel 24; A. W. Paltridge 5-41, T. K. Bahr 2-31, R. J. Hunter 2-38) on first innings.

ROUND TWO

At Oakes Oval, Lismore, January 6, 7, 2005. East Asia-Pacific 156 (R. Dikana 37, K. Vagi 26, I. Morea 26; B. A. Woolmer 6-49, D. A. Hughes 2-20, D. McIlveen 2-37) and 4 for 132 (J. L. Brazier 58*, J. Ovia 32*; B. A. Woolmer 2-49) lost to New South Wales 4 dec for 220 (S. D. Mudford 89, A. E. Alley 62, B. A. Woolmer 32) on first innings.

At Heaps Oval, Lismore, January 6, 7, 2005. Western Australia 9 dec for 170 (B. S. Reynolds 41, C. G. R. Tonkin 29; J. C. Stein 3-49, M. D. Brennan 2-54) and 1 for 3 lost to Queensland 6 for 227 (B. K. D. May 78*, K. W. Charles 70, D. R. Else 24; C. G. R. Tonkin 3-60) on first innings.

At Stan Thompson Oval, Brunswick Heads, January 6, 7, 2005. South Australia 125 (B. K. Vince 24; P. Bradley 3-30, C. F. Hopper 3-32) and 1 for 21 lost to Victoria 258 (P. Bradley 65, B. J. Glenn 51, J. P. Mathers 39, S. Ahmet 33; M. S. Johnston 4-53, R. J. Hunter 3-81, A. W. Paltridge 2-50) on first innings.

ROUND THREE

At Richards Oval, Lismore, January 9, 10, 2005. South Australia 274 (R. J. Hunter 84, B. K. Vince 74, A. Pitt 26, B. J. Cleaver 21; R. Dikana 2-33, J. L. Brazier 2-39, M. Ahmed 2-42) defeated East Asia-Pacific 225 (M. Ahmed 48, J. Ovia 35, K. Vagi 33, A. Uda 26, A. Mansale 26, J. L. Brazier 22; B. K. Vince 3-35, M. S. Johnston 2-23) on first innings.

At Fripp Oval, Ballina, January 9, 10, 2005. New South Wales 7 dec for 318 (S. D. Mudford 100, T. L. W. Cooper 69, B. A. Woolmer 53*, S. G. Moore 32; C. A. Waddingham 3-73, C. D'Mello 2-62) defeated Western Australia 71 (B. A. Woolmer 4-20, I. J. Gregory 3-20) and 4 for 92 (B. M. Drummond 29, C. G. R. Tonkin 25*; D. McIlveen 2-10, B. A. Woolmer 2-28) on first innings.

At Oakes Oval, Lismore, January 9, 10, 2005. Queensland 7 dec for 352 (B. K. D. May 138, M. Sippel 66, W. A. Frazer 64, D. B. Frakes 33; B. G. Hauenstein 5-88) defeated Victoria 160 (B. J. Glenn 54, S. Ahmet 47, B. G. Hauenstein 24; M. Salerno 2-23, B. S. Cust 2-27, K. W. Charles 2-33, J. C. Stein 2-36) and 0 for 67 (S. Ahmet 43*, J. P. Mathers 22*) on first innings.

ROUND FOUR

At Nielson Park, East Lismore, January 11, 12, 2005. Western Australia 162 (L. Sounness 42, B. M. Drummond 37, B. S. Reynolds 31; P. Bradley 5-66, C. F. Hopper 4-45) and 3 for 151 (B. S. Reynolds 78, B. M. Drummond 55*; C. F. Hopper 2-37) lost to Victoria 7 dec for 275 (S. Ahmet 129*, B. G. Hauenstein 54*, B. Major 39, B. J. Glenn 20; C. G. R. Tonkin 3-66, C. R. Phelps 2-50, C. A. Waddingham 2-53) on first innings.

At Kingsford Smith Park, Ballina, January 11, 12, 2005. East Asia-Pacific 143 (J. L. Brazier 72, C. Amini 20; B. S. Cust 5-26) and 184 (R. Dikana 54*, J. Ovia 43, J. L. Brazier 36; B. S. Cust 5-49, M. D. Brennan 2-28) lost to Queensland 5 dec for 179 (D. R. Else 70, B. K. D. May 62; R. Dikana 2-30) and 4 for 70 (W. F. Frazer 39*; T. Gaudi 2-24, D. Eliaba 2-44) on first innings.

At Stan Thompson Oval, Brunswick Heads, January 11, 12, 2005. New South Wales 276 (S. G. Moore 85, A. E Alley 48, T. L. W. Cooper 44, T. Kensall 21, S. D. Mudford 20, B. G. Bannister 20; M. S. Johnston 4-76, A. W. Paltridge 4-83) defeated South Australia 106 (T. Williamson 33*, B. J. Cleaver 25; I. J. Gregory 5-21, D. McIlveen 2-18, B. A. Woolmer 2-45) and 3 for 148 (B. J. Cleaver 62, B. K. Vince 39, C. Woolford 21) on first innings.

ROUND FIVE

At Oakes Oval, Lismore, January 14, 15, 2005. Western Australia 233 (B. P. King 72, C. R. Phelps 36, C. D'Mello 35, M. Oxford 34; C. A. Waddingham 22; A. W. Paltridge 5-50) drew with South Australia 6 for 134 (B. K. Vince 42; C. G. R. Tonkin 3-32, C. A. Waddingham 2-29).

At Richards Oval, Lismore, January 14, 15, 2005. East Asia-Pacific 179 (D. Eliaba 38*, M. Ahmed 29, J. Ovia 26, J. L. Brazier 23; C. F. Hopper 3-41, C. T Owen 2-24, B. G. Hauenstein 2-52) lost to Victoria 4 for 180 (A. S. Blackwell 74*, S. Ahmet 46, B. Major 28; H. Areni 2-20).

At Heaps Oval, Lismore, January 14, 15, 2005. New South Wales 118 (B. G. Bannister 50*; J. C. Stein 6-22, B. S. Cust 2-32) lost to Queensland 6 for 214 (D. R. Else 104*, B. K. D. May 73; D. McIlveen 3-39, B. G. Bannister 2-67.

POINTS TABLE, 2004-05

	P	WO	WI	D	LI	LO	T	Points
Queensland	5	0	5	0	0	0	0	61.31
Victoria	5	0	4	0	1	0	0	51.77
New South Wales ...	5	0	3	0	2	0	0	47.33
South Australia	5	0	1	1	3	0	0	34.80
Western Australia ...	5	0	1	1	3	0	0	31.25
East Asia-Pacific ...	5	0	0	0	5	0	0	24.42

MOST RUNS, 2004-05

	M	I	NO	R	HS	100s	50s	Avge
B. K. D. May (Qld)	5	6	1	387	138	1	3	77.40
S. Ahmet (Vic)	5	7	2	362	129*	1	0	72.40
J. L. Brazier (EAP)	5	8	2	323	101*	1	2	53.83
D. R. Else (Qld)	5	6	2	215	104*	1	1	53.75
S. D. Mudford (NSW)	5	5	0	209	100	1	1	41.80
W. A. Frazer (Qld)	5	6	1	197	64	0	2	39.40
B. Drummond (W Aust)	5	8	3	189	55*	0	1	37.80
B. K. Vince (S Aust)	5	7	2	186	74	0	1	37.20
M. Ahmed (EAP)	5	8	0	182	53	0	1	22.75
J. Ovia (EAP)	5	8	2	171	43	0	0	28.50

MOST WICKETS, 2004-05

	M	O	Mdns	R	W	BB	5/Wi	10/Wm	Avge
B. A. Woolmer (NSW)	5	121.3	33	354	24	7-93	2	0	14.75
B. S. Cust (Qld)	4	72.1	17	173	17	5-26	2	1	10.17
A. W. Paltridge (S Aust) ...	5	83.3	13	252	17	5-41	2	0	14.82
J. C. Stein (Qld)	5	136.1	41	273	17	6-22	2	0	16.05
C. F. Hopper (Vic)	5	132.3	52	303	14	4-45	0	0	21.64
B. G. Hauenstein (Vic)	5	84	22	250	13	5-58	2	0	19.23
C. G. R. Tonkin (W Aust)	5	93.1	13	234	12	3-23	0	0	19.50
I. J. Gregory (NSW)	5	69	16	168	11	5-21	1	0	15.27
P. Bradley (Vic)	5	136	44	303	11	5-66	1	0	27.54
M. D. Brennan (Qld)	5	80.3	18	219	10	3-54	0	0	21.90
M. S. Johnston (S Aust)	5	81.3	27	171	10	4-53	0	0	17.10
C. A. Waddingham (W Aust)	5	84	24	216	10	3-73	0	0	21.60
D. McIlveen (NSW)	5	88	19	209	10	3-39	0	0	20.90

CHAMPIONSHIP WINNERS

Season	Venue	Winner	Player of the Series
1984-85	Beenleigh, Qld	New South Wales	R. T. Staff (Qld)
1985-86	Riverland, S Aust	New South Wales	S. J. Scuderi (Qld)
1986-87	Dubbo, NSW	ACT	G. R. Irvine (ACT)
1987-88	Canberra, ACT	Queensland	L. D. Mason (Qld)
1988-89	Bunbury, W Aust	New South Wales	A. M. Fort (NSW)
1989-90	Bendigo, Vic	New South Wales	M. S. Curry (NSW)
1990-91	Townsville, Qld	Victoria	M. S. Curry (NSW)
1991-92	Riverland, S Aust	New South Wales	M. S. Curry (NSW)
1992-93	Newcastle, NSW	New South Wales	A. M. Stuart (NSW)

Season	Venue	Winner	Player of the Series
1993-94	Canberra, ACT	ACT	P. L. Evans (ACT)
1994-95	Albany-Mt Barker, W Aust	Queensland	I. F. Sartori (Vic)
1995-96	Sale-Maffra, Vic	New South Wales	M. J. Warden (Qld)
1996-97	Toowoomba, Qld	Queensland	M. J. Warden (Qld)
1997-98	Mount Gambier, S Aust	Western Australia	M. J. Warden (Qld)
1998-99	Barooga, NSW	Queensland	B. J. Smith (Qld)
1999-00	Canberra, ACT	Queensland	B. K. D. May (Qld)
2000-01	Albany-Mt Barker, W Aust	New South Wales	B. K. D. May (Qld)
2001-02	Warrnambool, Vic	Queensland	D. R. Else (Qld)
2002-03	Bundaberg, Qld	Western Australia	D. A. Burns (W Aust)
2003-04	Mount Gambier, S Aust	Victoria	B. L. Campbell (Vic) & C. F. Hooper (Vic)
2004-05	Lismore, NSW	Queensland	B. K. D. May (Qld) & B. A. Woolmer (NSW)

PLAYER TROPHY WINNERS

Season	Player of Series	Batting	Bowling	Fielding
1984-85	R. T. Staff (Qld)	–	–	–
1985-86	S. J. Scuderi (Qld)	S. J. Scuderi (Qld)	M. A. Polzin (Qld)	–
1986-87	G. R. Irvine (ACT)	G. R. Irvine (ACT)	D. J. Francis (W A)	–
1987-88	L. D. Mason (Qld)	L. D. Mason (Qld)	D. F. Benson (Vic)	–
1988-89	A. M. Fort (NSW)	A. M. Fort (NSW)	G. P. Williams (S A)	–
1989-90	M. S. Curry (NSW)	S. J. Scuderi (Qld)	E. L. Nix (ACT)	–
1990-91	M. S. Curry (NSW)	B. P. Inwood (NSW)	M. J. Warden (Qld)	–
1991-92	M. S. Curry (NSW)	P. J. Solway (ACT)	G. A. Bush (ACT)	–
1992-93	A. M. Stuart (NSW)	D. R. W. Temple (Qld)	A. M. Stuart (NSW) R. H. Menasse (W A)	–
1993-94	P. L. Evans (ACT)	P. L. Evans (ACT)	P. S. Nemes (ACT) M. J. Warden (Qld)	–
1994-95	I. F. Sartori (Vic)	G. R. O'Sullivan (NSW)	M. J. Warden (Qld)	A. K. D. Gray (W A)
1995-96	M. J. Warden (Qld)	N. D. Tatterson (Vic)	M. J. Warden (Qld)	M. T. Hegarty (ACT)
1996-97	M. J. Warden (Qld)	J. R. Mosey (S Aust)	M. J. Warden (Qld)	K. N. Spencer (WA)
1997-98	M. J. Warden (Qld)	G. J. Dehring (W Aust)	M. J. Warden (Qld)	B. K. D. May (Qld)
1998-99	B. J. Smith (Qld)	G. A. Grimmond (NSW)	D. K. Wrixon (NSW)	S. A. Sweet (S A)
1999-00	B. K. D. May (Qld)	B. K. D. May (Qld)	M. J. Warden (Qld)	S. A. Baker (Qld)
2000-01	B. K. D. May (Qld)	A. D. McQuire (ACT)	D. A. Ellis (W A)	R. Starr (NSW) B. D. Ward (WA)
2001-02	D. R. Else (Qld)	B. K. D. May (Qld)	D. A. Hughes (NSW)	S. A. Baker (Qld)
2002-03	D. A. Burns (W Aust)	M. J. Gerits (NSW)	P. J. Toohey (Qld)	S. A. Baker (Qld)
2003-04	B. L. Campbell (Vic) C. F. Hopper (Vic)	B. L. Campbell (Vic)	C. F. Hopper (Vic)	R. Starr (NSW)
2004-05	B. K. D. May (Qld) B. A. Woolmer (NSW)	B. K. D. May (Qld)	B. A. Woolmer (NSW)	S. A. Baker (Qld)

HIGHEST PARTNERSHIP FOR EACH WICKET

152	for 1st	T. G. Wilson and S. T. Catchpole, WAust v SAust at Narrabundah	....	1993-94
135	for 2nd	M. P. O'Rourke and D. M. Jeffrey, ACT v WAust at Narrabundah	....	1999-00
26*	for 3rd	D. M. Jeffrey and I. A. Garrity, ACT v Vic at Tocumwal	....	1998-99
152	for 4th	M. S. Curry and P. Dyson, NSW v Qld at Loxton North	....	1991-92
155	for 5th	G. K. John and R. Bedford, Vic v SAust at Merewether	....	1992-93
112	for 6th	B. L. Campbell and B. J. Glenn, Vic v SAust at Albany North	......	2000-01
42*	for 7th	R. Starr and S. J. Lockhart, NSW v SAust at Albany West	....	2000-01
71	for 8th	G. R. O'Sullivan and D. B. Marshall, NSW v Qld at Albany North	......	1994-95
38	for 9th	S. A. Sweet and D. M. Stratford, SAust v Vic at Albany North	....	2000-01
103	for 10th	S. A. Bannerman and M. W. Radcliffe, ACT v Qld at Penola	....	1997-98

MOST RUNS

	M	I	NO	R	HS	100s	50s	Avge
B. K. D. May (Qld)	48	56	11	2,806	171*	11	12	62.35
P. J. Solway (NSW/ACT)	48	51	5	1,984	169*	3	11	43.13
M. S. Curry (NSW)	39	39	10	1,916	138	5	13	66.02
R. Bedford (Vic)	38	43	1	1,746	127	2	14	41.57
G. J. Dehring (WAust)	40	42	4	1,626	194	2	13	42.78
G. K. John (Vic)	40	43	4	1,617	157	3	5	41.46

MOST WICKETS

	M	Overs	Mdns	R	W	BB	5Wfi	Avge
M. J. Warden (Qld)	35	808.3	219	1,913	125	8/69	12	15.30
D. F. Benson (Vic)	29	518.1	133	1,265	67	5/19	2	18.88
G. R. Irvine (NSW/ACT) .	42	611.2	178	1,284	63	6/61	3	20.38
M. S. Curry (NSW)	39	515.0	143	1,224	61	6/55	2	20.06
D. J. Francis (WAust)	30	545.3	166	1,221	61	6/50	2	20.01
P. J. Toohey (Qld)	27	541.3	133	1,518	55	5/65	1	27.60
G. A. Bush (ACT)	28	517.4	82	1,537	53	5/61	2	29.00

MOST DISMISSALS

	Catches	Stumpings	Total
B. P. King (WAust)	73	6	79
S. A. Baker (Qld)	74	2	76
T. K. Waldron (WAust)	63	1	64
G. W. Vivian (SAust)	52	6	58

Imparja Cup, 2004-05

by BARRY NICHOLLS

The Imparja Cup is one of the lesser-known jewels of Cricket Australia's calendar. Played in Alice Springs for the last decade, the national indigenous cricket carnival provides the perfect platform for the promotion of cricket and for the identification of Aboriginal talent around the country.

This year's championship saw each state and the Northern Territory represented. Several formats including Twenty20, 30-over, and Super Eight cricket were contested during the five-day tournament. Queensland, with six representatives at first-grade level in Brisbane, again proved their potency, taking the honours for the second year in a row without being seriously challenged. They trounced New South Wales by eight wickets in the final.

The championship was not without controversy. While there is little doubt in the minds of NT cricket officials that Alice Springs is the spiritual home of the national indigenous cricket carnival, a question remains as to whether a town of only 25,000 and with only two turf wickets can continue to host a national carnival that is growing in size and stature. The 2004-05 Imparja Cup highlighted the need for more and better-prepared turf wickets in Alice Springs to ensure that teams are not forced to play back-to-back matches on the same day in the Central Australian summer heat.

Leading the call for a shift in venue and an extension of the games from a 30-over format was the Queensland captain Barry Weare: 'For the tournament to be considered a national one it must be played in other states and territories. I appreciate that Alice Springs is where the championship began and they've done a great job, but it is important for indigenous talent to be showcased outside of Alice Springs.

"The timing this year was also poor, because it coincided with local grade finals, which stopped some of the senior players taking part. Players on the whole will choose to play for their grade team in the finals because a strong performance there has more weight than in the Imparja Cup. Also, playing conditions left a little to be desired. When you're trying to boost the profile of indigenous cricket, you need the best conditions and the best players."

NT CEO cricket, Neil Dalrymple acknowledged that a third turf wicket and sightscreens are essential if Alice Springs is to continue to host the carnival, but he rejects calls for the Imparja Cup to be shifted. "It is a festival of indigenous cricket involving not just states and territories but also communities, and Alice Springs is the home for indigenous cricket. The states have the opportunity to host other national tournaments."

The pitch at Traeger Park, the premier cricket ground in Alice Springs, was slow and green, and the lush outfield limited scoring. The centre square and outfield were prepared so that within a week the ground would be suitably soft for a pre-season AFL game.

Cricket Australia's desire for greater diversity within the overall cricket community can only be achieved with continued encouragement of a championship such as the Imparja Cup. And participation rates, particularly in the NT, are a cause for optimism. In the NT alone cricket has considerable impetus in indigenous communities with thriving club competitions in Darwin and Alice Springs supplemented by the five teams in the Katherine competition. The biggest breakthrough is with indigenous women's cricket, with three women's sides in a new Alice Springs competition and four in Darwin. Cricket in the Tiwi Islands is also booming, with a permanent wicket being installed at Milikipati on Melville Island and new practice nets for Nguiu on Bathurst Island.

This year Queensland marked their early dominance by brushing aside South Australia without losing a wicket. Key championship contenders NSW, who warmed up for the championship with matches against their state's Colts side and a Fijian team, were easily accounted for when Queensland cruised to victory by five wickets with almost ten overs to spare. Despite a four-wicket haul from NT medium-pacer Lincoln Burke, the Queenslanders finished their match against the home side 32 runs ahead. Last year's browbeaten finalists Tasmania provided Queensland with the greatest challenge of the tournament, the eventual champions reaching the required total with just three overs remaining.

NSW's path to the final was impressive, although less assured. They trounced Victoria before defeating NT and South Australia. A loss to Queensland by five wickets provided an ominous grand final preview. Western Australia, who through a quirk of scheduling did not play Queensland, just missed out on a final berth after a single loss against NT. The Territorians finished with two wins from four games, missing a final berth after losing to Queensland and NSW. South Australia and Tasmania each had only one win, against Victoria, which lost all four matches.

The highest run-scorer of the tournament was Matt Abrahamson of WA, with 213 runs at 53.25. In his top score of 88 off 39 balls he hit eight fours and six sixes. Former AFL player Adrian McAdam made the highest score with an undefeated 99 for NT against WA, hitting six fours and eight sixes off 56 balls. Many bowlers took cheap wickets in the helpful conditions. Kerrin Ugle of WA was the leading wicket-taker with 11 at 10.45.

In the Imparja Shield division one final, Alice Springs beat Darwin by three wickets. The division two final saw Alkupitija beat Melville Island by 25 runs. In the women's competition, Darwin completed their undefeated record by beating Alice Springs by six runs.

The Imparja Cup 2005 team, selected after the tournament, was: Matt Abrahamson (WAust), Lincoln Burke (NT), Keith Charles (Qld), Tim Croft (NSW), Ron Cox (WAust), John Duckett (NSW), Barry Firebrace (Vic), Tim Hardingham (Qld), Peter Lake (NT), Colin Lamont (Tas), Adrian McAdam (NT), Kerrin Ugle (WAust), Damien Watts (Qld), Barry Weare (Qld). Abrahamson and Hardingham shared the Player of the Series trophy.

IMPARJA CUP

At Traeger Park, February 23, 2005. South Australia 124 (R. Johncock 32; T. Croft 4-17, P Rosser 3-16) lost to New South Wales 2 for 125 (J. Duckett 46, D. Donnelly 27, P. Rosser 21; M. Austin 2-48) by eight wickets.

At Traeger Park, February 24, 2005. Northern Territory 89 (G. Lewis 19; A. Shepherd 3-13, G. Wellington 3-17, P. Rosser 2-30) lost to New South Wales 7 for 90 (P. Rosser 33; L. Burke 2-14, G. Smith 2-20, I. Redpath 2-20) by three wickets.

At Albrecht Oval, February 24, 2005. Western Australia 6 for 213 (M. Abrahamson 76, R. Cox 40, M. Davis jr 21, G. Flanagan 21*; B. Firebrace 2-24) defeated Victoria 143 (B. Firebrace 61, S. Collins 25; K. Ugle 4-14, T. Ugle 3-27, P. Cooper 2-25) by 70 runs.

At Albrecht Oval, February 24, 2005. Queensland 0 for 98 (D. Budd 42*, K. Charles 41*) defeated South Australia 96 (V. Coulthard 39; B. Wearne 3-3, T. Hardingham 3-21, K. Gibbs 2-19) by two runs.

At Traeger Park, February 24, 2005. Tasmania 113 (C. Lamont 27, B. Stevenson 24; L. Burke 3-18, K. Vowles 2-18, J. Wyatt 2-25) lost to Northern Territory 4 for 114 (B. Manning 50*, M. Tippett 20; B. Lamont 2-18) by six wickets.

At Traeger Park, February 25, 2005. New South Wales 8 for 88 (T. Croft 26*; M. Rush 3-16, T. Hardingham 2-5, D. Watts 2-20) lost to Queensland 5 for 89 (B. Weare 20; T. Croft 3-25, A. Gordon 2-16) by five wickets.

At Albrecht Oval, February 25, 2005. Victoria 9 for 133 (H. Button 34; N. Kopper 5-37) lost to Tasmania 3 for 135 (C. Lamont 47, B. Lamont 34, D. Harris 30; D. Nelson 2-4) by seven wickets.

At Albrecht Oval, February 25, 2005. Western Australia 7 for 193 (M. Abrahamson 37, J. Davis 36, G. Ugle 35*; V. Coulthard 2-39, L. Thomas 2-45) defeated South Australia 186 (K. Thomas 56, R. Johncock 48, N. Hartman 30; K. Ugle 3-35, G. Ugle 3-43, J. Davis 2-33) by seven runs.

At Traeger Park, February 25, 2005. Queensland 7 for 156 (K. Charles 52*, K. Gibbs 26, W. Williams 21*; L. Burke 4-23, K. Vowles 2-30) defeated Northern Territory 124 (L. Burke 25, I. Redpath 23; W. Williams 3-16, B. Weare 3-31) by 32 runs.

At Traeger Park, February 26, 2005. Victoria 6 for 164 (D. Nelson 32*, J. Coltman 31, B. Firebrace 29, H. Button 24; V. Coulthard 2-37) lost to South Australia 8 for 166 (K. Thomas 38, N. Hartman 37*, V. Coulthard 33*; M. Hoye 3-27, B. Firebrace 2-31) by two wickets.

At Albrecht Oval, February 26, 2005. Northern Territory 4 for 208 (A. McAdam 99*, G. Lewis 36*, M. Tippett 24, K. Vowles 21; T. Ugle 3-34) defeated Western Australia 8 for 170 (R. Cox 55, P. Cooper 26, T. Ugle 20; A. McAdam 2-19, I. Redpath 2-32, J. Wyatt 2-40) by 38 runs.

At Albrecht Oval, February 26, 2005. Tasmania 6 for 147 (S. Gower 45*, J. Wells 26, B. Lamont 25; K. Gibbs 3-18) lost to Queensland 3 for 149 (J. Marsh 57*, B. Wearne 35*) by seven wickets.

At Traeger Park, February 26, 2005. New South Wales 6 for 176 (J. Duckett 57, P. Rosser 28, A. Gordon 27; D. Nelson 3-35) defeated Victoria 5 for 99 (D. Nelson 24*; S. Phillis 3-16) by 77 runs.

At Albrecht Oval, February 27, 2005. Western Australia 8 for 193 (M. Abrahamson 88, T. Ugle 27, J. Davis 23; W. Lee 2-16, S. Gower 2-19) defeated Tasmania 184 (C. Lamont 67, G. Grey 30, S. Gower 23; K. Ugle 4-36, P. Cooper 3-35) by nine runs.

IMPARJA CUP FINAL, 2004-05

QUEENSLAND v NEW SOUTH WALES

At Traeger Park, February 27, 2005. Queensland won by eight wickets. *Toss:* New South Wales.

On a parched evening under the lights, a reddish glow reflecting from the McDonnell Ranges helped provide what must be one of the world's most picturesque cricket grounds. Spectators looking closely recognised the familiar gait of Paul Reiffel, the former Test bowler turned umpire, who gained experience by officiating in the five-day tournament.

Having elected to bat, New South Wales quickly lost John Duckett, one of a handful of players to have hit a century in an Imparja Cup match. The batsmen struggled with the pace of Keith Charles, Craig Trindall and Damian Watts before off-spinner Kieran Gibbs completed the rout. NSW all-rounder Andrew Gordon was the only batsman to stand out, before succumbing to the wiles of Queensland captain Barry Weare.

Queensland were largely unchanged from the previous year, when they thrashed Tasmania in the final. The sense of inevitability about their second successive win was confirmed when openers Damien Budd and wicket-keeper Brett Smith hit 50 runs off the first ten overs. Both soon fell, but the momentum of the game had been set, and veteran left-hander Joe Marsh and Weare had no trouble reaching the meagre target with several overs to spare.

New South Wales

D. Donnelly c Williams b Watts	9	(59)	T. Croft st Weare b Gibbs	2	(9)
J. Duckett c Smith b Charles	5	(5)	G. Wellington lbw b Williams	8	(16)
P. Rosser b Trindall	9	(14)	A. Shepherd not out	0	(2)
A. Gordon lbw b Wearne	55	(51)			
*M. Parkins c Watts b Gibbs	10	(19)	B 1, l-b 3, w 6, n-b 5	15	
B. Champion c Charles b Gibbs	4	(17)			
J. Manning-Bancroft c Weare b Watts	1	(3)	(36.2 overs, 156 mins)	118	
†R. Donovan c Williams b Gibbs	0	(6)	Fall: 8 24 40 63 72 91 94 105 118 118		

Bowling: Charles 5–2–14–1, Trindall 8–2–16–1, Hardingham 0.1–0–0–0, Watts 7.5–2–31–2, Rush 5–0–21–0, Gibbs 8–0–28–4, Weare 2–0–4–1, Williams 0.2–0–0–1.

Queensland

B. Smith c Parkins b Rosser	20	(34)	L-b 4, w 6	10	
D. Budd b Shepherd	28	(24)			
J. Marsh not out	38	(44)	(22.1 overs, 90 mins)	(2 wkts) 119	
†B. Weare not out	23	(30)	Fall: 50 54		

K. Charles, K. Gibbs, W. Williams, T. Hardingham, C. Trindall, M. Rush, D. Watts (did not bat).

Bowling: Shepherd 8–0–37–1, Croft 4–0–28–0, Rosser 7–0–39–1, Gordon 3.1–0–11–0.

Umpires: P. R. Reiffel and J. Ward.

IMPARJA SHIELD – Division One

Alice Springs defeated Tennant Creek by 4 wkts
Darwin defeated Katherine by 6 wkts
Katherine defeated Tennant Creek by 60 runs
Alice Springs defeated Darwin by 40 runs
Alice Springs defeated Katherine by 3 wkts
Tennant Creek tied Darwin

Playoff 3rd-4th

Tennant Creek defeated Katherine by 17 runs

Final

At Traeger Park, February 27, 2005. Darwin 9 for 94 (R. Walters 29, M. McGregor 14, S. Sutton 13, J. Mortimer 11; B. Rowse 2-13) lost to Alice Springs 7 for 96 (T. Bruce 19, B. Rowse 12, R. Kennedy 10*; K. Solien 2-17, R. Walters 2-19) by three wickets.

SMEC IMPARJA SHIELD – Division Two

Tangentyere defeated Mt Allen by 120 runs
Alkupitija defeated Borroloola by 33 runs
Melville Island defeated Timber Creek by 4 wickets
CAT defeated Bathurst Island by 42 runs
Melville Island defeated Mt Allen by 9 wickets
Alkupitija defeated Bathurst Island by 8 wickets
Timber Creek defeated Tangentyere by 37 runs
Borroloola defeated CAT by 9 runs
Timber Creek defeated Mt Allen by 70 runs
Alkupitija defeated CAT by 10 wkts
Melville Island defeated Tangentyere by 6 wickets
Borroloola defeated Bathurst Island by 69 runs

Playoff for 7th-8th Place

Mt Allen defeated Bathurst Island by 6 wickets

Playoff for 5th-6th Place

CAT defeated Alkupitija by 66 runs

Playoff for 3rd-4th Place

Borroloola defeated Timber Creek by 24 runs

Final

At Traeger Park, February 27, 2005. Alkupitija 4 for 108 (T. Presley 41*, K. Braun 18, W. Braun 12*, D. Talbot 10; L. Kerinuia 2-21) defeated Melville Island 7 for 83 (G. Dunn 40*, M. Wilson 12, A. Clayton 12; D. Talbot 3-14, A. Satour 2-13) by 25 runs.

LORD'S TAVERNERS WOMEN

Darwin defeated Alice Springs Team 1 by 19 runs
Alice Springs Team 2 defeated Tennant Creek by 9 wickets
Darwin defeated Tennant Creek by 49 runs
Tennant Creek defeated Alice Springs Team 1 by 34 runs
Darwin defeated Alice Springs Team 2 by 46 runs
Alice Springs Team 1 defeated Alice Springs Team 2 by 7 wickets

Playoff for 3rd-4th Place

Tennant Creek defeated Alice Springs Team 2 by 28 runs

Final

At Traeger Park, February 27, 2005. Darwin 1 for 102 (T. Harrod 38*, A. Heath 29*) defeated Alice Springs Team 1 6 for 96 (M. Liddle 35, S. Trindle-Price 16*, G. Smith 11; F. White 3-19, A. Heath 2-16) by six runs.

IMPARJA CUP

MOST RUNS, 2004-05

	M	I	NO	R	HS	100s	50s	Avrge
M. Abrahamson (W Aust)	4	4	0	213	88	0	2	53.25
C. Lamont (Tas)	4	4	0	158	67	0	1	39.50
J. Marsh (Qld)	5	4	2	118	57*	0	1	59.00
R. Cox (W Aust)	4	4	0	116	55	0	1	29.00
A. McAdam (N.T)	4	4	1	116	99*	0	0	38.67
B. Firebrace (Vic)	4	4	0	115	61	0	1	28.75
K. Thomas (S Aust)	4	4	0	115	56	0	1	28.75
J. Duckett (NSW)	5	5	0	113	57	0	1	22.60

MOST WICKETS, 2004-05

	M	O	Mds	R	W	BB	5W/i	10W/M	Avge
K. Ugle (W Aust)	4	16	0	115	11	4-14	0	0	10.45
L. Burke (NT)	4	20	1	95	10	4-23	0	0	9.50
K. Gibbs (Qld)	5	23	2	88	9	4-28	0	0	9.78
B. Weare (Qld)	5	11.1	0	59	7	3-3	0	0	8.43
T. Croft (NSW)	4	22	0	83	7	4-17	0	0	11.86
D. Nelson (Vic)	4	18	0	96	7	3-35	0	0	13.71
T. Ugle (W Aust)	4	21.5	1	133	7	3-27	0	0	19.00

Women's Cricket, 2004-05

by ERICA SAINSBURY

A four-year strategic plan and rebuilding process reached a successful culmination in April 2005, when Australia dominated the eighth Women's Cricket World Cup to regain the title lost so narrowly four years before to New Zealand. Competing for the first time in South Africa, Australia remained undefeated throughout the tournament and comprehensively outplayed first-time finalists India to take their fifth world championship trophy.

Series victories earlier in the season against India and New Zealand proved the ideal preparation, and the youth development program continued to bear fruit with the inclusion of Kate Blackwell in the senior national team alongside her twin sister Alex Indeed it was a very busy year for Kate, who was the vice-captain of the national youth side which enjoyed success on a first-ever tour of Sri Lanka. Another debutante, South Australian Shelley Nitschke, proved the value of her left-arm spinners by leading the wicket-taking for Australia at the World Cup and returning the most economical figures of any bowler at the championship.

On the domestic scene, the national title changed hands again with Victoria running out victors over traditional rivals New South Wales in the National League finals series, although NSW dominated all other competitions from Under-15s to 2nd XI. Karen Rolton and Cathryn Fitzpatrick confirmed their pre-eminence with bat and ball respectively, and continued to provide the foundations around which Australian performances were built.

The winter tour of England and Ireland, held in conjunction with the men's tour, proved a dramatic contrast to the successful summer. Australia had not lost a Test series to England since 1963, nor a one-day international since 1993, but England had demonstrated at the World Cup and in their own domestic season that they were a team on the rise, and they confirmed this emphatically. They won the

Test series 1-0, claiming the women's version of the Ashes for the first time they were contested twenty-one years previously. Australia took the one-day series 3-2 and were victorious in the Twenty20 match, but their aura of invincibility was convincingly shattered. Considerable speculation surrounds the playing intentions of a number of the longest-serving members of the Australian team following this tour, so there may be a new-look combination to take on the challenges of the 2005-2006 international commitments which will see clashes with New Zealand and India.

On the broader international scene, the trend towards amalgamating men's and women's cricket organisations continued with the merger between the International Cricket Council and its counterpart the International Women's Cricket Council. The ICC will now be responsible for the overall development of women's cricket, with the ICC Women's Cricket Committee making recommendations to the ICC Development Committee. The negotiations preceding the merger were substantially driven by the now retired president of IWCC, Australia's Christine Brierley; Australia is now represented internationally by Belinda Clark.

AUSTRALIAN PLAYER PROFILES

BELINDA CLARK *Right-hand batter, right-arm off-spin bowler* **NSW**
By her own high standards, the 2004-05 season was not one which Belinda Clark will rank amongst her best, as the world record one-day run-scorer managed only two half-centuries over three international series. However, Clark oversaw her side's success in those three tournaments, capped by the unbeaten run which saw Australia regain the World Cup they had lost so narrowly to New Zealand four years previously. Her form in domestic competition remained solid, and it was not clear why she was unable to score runs as consistently at international level. After 15 years at the highest level, Clark's experience and shrewd understanding of the game make her a fierce competitor and feared opposition captain with an unrivalled record. She has officially announced her departure from international competition and takes up her appointment as the Director of the Commonwealth Bank Centre of Excellence in Brisbane in September.

	M	I	NO	Runs	HS	100s	50s	Avge	Ct	St	W	Avge	BB
Test Cricket	15	25	5	919	136	2	6	45.95	4	0	1	28.00	1-10
Int'l. limited-overs	118	114	12	4,844	229*	5	30	47.49	45	0	3	17.00	1-7
Int'l. Twenty20	1	1	0	4	4	0	0	4.00	1	0	–	–	–

KAREN ROLTON *Left-hand batter, left-arm medium bowler* **SA**
It is no overstatement to suggest that Karen Rolton is the major reason for Australia's current dominance on the international scene. Once again she took out numerous awards and accolades in both domestic and international competition, but the pinnacle of her achievements was undoubtedly her brilliant match-winning century in the World Cup final. Occasionally criticised as a little scratchy early in an innings, Rolton is unsurpassed at applying the accelerator as an innings moves towards its final stages, and her ability to place shots through almost imperceptible gaps makes her the most dangerous batter

in the world game. On top of that, her left-arm medium-pace seamers often provide the critical breakthrough for her captain, and she is difficult to put away. Possessed of a highly developed cricket brain, and having served under Belinda Clark for many years, Rolton is the heir apparent as Australian captain when Clark finally puts away her bat.

	M	I	NO	Runs	HS	100s	50s	Avge	Ct	St	W	Avge	BB
Test Cricket	11	17	4	870	209*	2	4	66.92	8	0	11	28.63	2-6
Int'l. limited-overs	96	88	24	3,624	154*	7	26	56.62	18	0	77	22.11	3-9
Int'l. Twenty20	1	1	1	96	96*	0	1	–	0	0	2	13.00	2-26

ALEX BLACKWELL *Right-hand batter, right-arm medium bowler*   **NSW**
Alex Blackwell continued to make use of her opportunities to consolidate her position in the middle order. Her maiden half-century against New Zealand in the World Cup confirmed her potential and her fighting ability with the bat, and she adds an element of brilliance to the fielding of the Australian team. Although rarely called upon to bowl, her medium-pace is a useful string to her bow, and she is clearly being groomed to take on roles of greater responsibility in the future.

	M	I	NO	Runs	HS	100s	50s	Avge	Ct	St	W	Avge	BB
Test Cricket	4	8	1	132	58	0	1	18.85	2	0	0	–	–
Int'l. limited-overs	28	21	8	313	53	0	1	24.07	2	0	6	10.50	2-8
Int'l. Twenty20	1	–	–	–	–	–	–	–	0	0	–	–	–

KATE BLACKWELL *Right-hand batter*   **NSW**
Widely tipped in recent years to join her twin sister in the Australian team, Kate Blackwell made this step after solid performances in the National League and Australian youth team over the last two seasons. Although she had only limited opportunities, Kate showed her ability and levelheadedness in helping to steer Australia home in a number of close run-chases, and she equalled her sister for excellence in the field. At only 21 Kate will grow in confidence as she gains more experience at the top level, and her all-round ability and knowledge of the game are likely to make her one of the leaders of the next generation of Australian stars.

	M	I	NO	Runs	HS	100s	50s	Avge	Ct	St	W	Avge	BB
Test Cricket	2	4	0	102	72	0	1	26.63	4	0	–	–	–
Int'l. limited-overs	14	10	2	132	50	0	1	16.50	7	0	–	–	–
Int'l. Twenty20	1	1	1	43	43*	0	0	–	0	0	–	–	–

LOUISE BROADFOOT *Right-hand batter, right-arm leg-break-googly bowler*
Victoria
Louise Broadfoot returned to the Australian squad for the Rosebowl and World Cup campaigns after several years out of the team. Her ability to bat anywhere in the order together with her deceptive leg-spin, made her a valuable member of the side, and they given match time, she fulfilled the roles she was assigned. The success of Shelley Nitschke as Australia's front-line spinner made it difficult for Broadfoot to force her way into the first team, however, and the future of her international career remains in some doubt.

	M	I	NO	Runs	HS	100s	50s	Avge	Ct	St	W	Avge	BB
Test Cricket	2	2	0	95	71	0	1	47.50	2	0	–	–	–
Int'l. limited-overs	10	6	1	52	21	0	0	10.40	1	0	4	19.25	1-4

LEONIE COLEMAN *Right-hand batter, wicket-keeper*   **NSW**
After a successful debut season, Leonie Coleman was keen to consolidate her place as the premier wicket-keeper in Australia, and her performances on the tour of India were of a very high standard. Unfortunately, the serious facial injury she sustained during the tour appeared to undermine her confidence, and her form fell away a little in the second

half of the National League season, opening the way for the return of Julia Price. She is determined to regain her place, and she remains in strong contention should Price falter in performance or choose to retire.

	M	I	NO	Runs	HS	100s	50s	Avge	Ct	St	W	Avge	BB
Int'l. limited-overs	10	3	2	21	11*	0	0	21.00	5	3	–	–	–

CATHRYN FITZPATRICK *Right-hand batter, right-arm fast bowler* **Victoria**

What Karen Rolton is to batting, Cathryn Fitzpatrick is to bowling, and it is no coincidence that the period of Australia's dominance in world cricket has paralleled Fitzpatrick's playing career. Still acknowledged as the fastest bowler in women's cricket, Fitzpatrick does not rely solely on pace for her penetration, and she rarely fails to make an early breakthrough. She holds numerous wicket-taking records for one-day internationals, and was the first to pass 150 scalps, a milestone she reached this season. Over recent seasons, she has also worked on her batting, and is now acknowledged as an all-rounder who can be relied on for quick runs or solid defence depending on the situation. Having been a major factor in Australia's successful quest for the World Cup, Fitzpatrick's playing future is also the subject of speculation, particularly since the 37-year-old has been awarded a coaching scholarship at the Commonwealth Bank Centre of Excellence in Brisbane for 2005-06.

	M	I	NO	Runs	HS	100s	50s	Avge	Ct	St	W	Avge	BB
Test Cricket	12	8	0	149	53	0	1	18.62	5	0	55	19.01	5-29
Int'l. limited-overs	96	50	17	470	43	0	0	14.24	22	0	160	15.89	5-14
Int'l. Twenty20	1	–	–	–	–	–	–	–	1	0	0	–	–

JULIE HAYES *Right-hand batter, right-arm medium bowler* **NSW**

Julie Hayes continued to add variety and versatility to the Australian team through her nagging medium-pace bowling and speed and accuracy in the field. Although her role was rarely spectacular, she was a central member of the team and almost always made a useful contribution. She is adept at containing the run-rate and is often called upon to apply the brakes when an opposing team is threatening to wrest the initiative. In a strong batting line-up, she bats in a position which belies her abilities, and in 2004-05 she had few chances to play a significant role, although she did top-score in Australia's disastrous innings of 77 in the final match in India.

	M	I	NO	Runs	HS	100s	50s	Avge	Ct	St	W	Avge	BB
Test Cricket	5	8	1	112	57	0	1	16.00	4	0	8	28.50	3-9
Int'l. limited-overs	52	24	11	175	44	0	0	13.46	10	0	58	23.15	4-31
Int'l. Twenty20	1	–	–	–	–	–	–	–	1	0	0	–	–

MELANIE JONES *Right-hand batter, right-arm medium bowler* **Victoria**

Melanie Jones' performances at the international level in 2004-05 were patchy, with a single half-century to show for her efforts. While maintaining an aggressive approach, she showed a tendency to throw her wicket away after making a start, although she was a contributor to a number of important partnerships throughout the season. She has lost little of her flair in the field, or her ability to pick up extraordinary catches. It is clear, however, that to maintain her place in the side she will need more than her fielding brilliance, and the selectors will be keen for her to regain the consistency she showed with the bat in 2003-04.

	M	I	NO	Runs	HS	100s	50s	Avge	Ct	St	W	Avge	BB
Test Cricket	5	8	1	251	131	1	1	35.85	3	0	0	–	–
Int'l. limited-overs	61	54	6	1,028	58	0	4	21.41	15	0	0	–	–
Int'l. Twenty20	1	1	–	4	4	0	0	4.00	1	0	–	–	–

LISA KEIGHTLEY *Right-hand batter, right-arm bowler* **NSW**
Lisa Keightley continued to open Australia's innings with distinction, although like her opening partner Belinda Clark, she would have preferred to perform with a little more consistency. She excelled in an all-round capacity on the tour of India, where she was a surprise performer with the ball, taking eight wickets in four games with her gentle out-swing. She also deputised as wicket-keeper when Leonie Coleman was injured, and she proved her versatility with more than competent glove work. Although not subsequently called upon to bowl, she scored an elegant century against South Africa in what is likely to have been her final World Cup. Keightley has announced that she will retire from first-class cricket after the Ashes tour of England and Ireland, but her contribution to the game will continue as she takes up the position of full-time coach of the NSW women's team from 2005-06.

	M	I	NO	Runs	HS	100s	50s	Avge	Ct	St	W	Avge	BB
Test Cricket	9	14	0	378	90	3	0	27.00	5	0	–	–	–
Int'l. limited-overs	82	78	12	2,630	156*	4	21	39.84	27	2	8	10.87	4-19
Int'l. Twenty20	1	1	–	1	1	0	0	1.00	0	1	–	–	–

EMMA LIDDELL (nee Twining) *Right-hand batter, left-arm medium bowler* **NSW**
Emma Liddell enjoyed a more productive season in 2004-05 than in the previous year when her form and confidence fell away and she struggled to maintain a regular place in the team. In 2004-05 she played in most games, although on occasion she was in competition with Clea Smith for the position as Cathryn Fitzpatrick's opening partner. Her determination was rewarded with career-best figures in the final Rosebowl match, and she may have been unlucky to miss a place in the World Cup final. The experience of the past two seasons has toughened Liddell mentally, and this is likely to stand her in good stead.

	M	I	NO	Runs	HS	100s	50s	Avge	Ct	St	W	Avge	BB
Test Cricket	3	4	2	24	24	0	0	12.00	0	0	12	13.00	4-57
Int'l. limited-overs	33	5	3	3	2*	0	0	1.50	1	0	32	29.40	4-17

SHELLEY NITSCHKE *Left-hand batter, slow left-arm bowler* **SA**
Regarded by some as a surprise replacement for Kris Britt on the tour of India, Shelley Nitschke rapidly developed into an integral part of the Australian side, and was rewarded for a series of consistent performances with the thrill of capturing the wicket which ensured her country's victory in the World Cup final. Nitschke's forte is her left-arm orthodox spin, and her success was built around subtle variations in flight and pace. She proved the perfect foil for Lisa Sthalekar, and by the end of the World Cup could rightly be regarded as the No. 1 spinner. Like Julie Hayes, she suffered from the strength of the batting line-up, and received few chances to show her considerable ability with the bat at Australian level, but she performed consistently for South Australia and would be capable of batting higher in the order. She appears to have a bright future with the Australian side.

	M	I	NO	Runs	HS	100s	50s	Avge	Ct	St	W	Avge	BB
Test Cricket	2	4	2	175	88*	0	2	87.50	0	0	4	32.75	3-59
Int'l. limited-overs	17	8	4	17	8*	0	0	4.25	7	0	25	13.28	7-24
Int'l. Twenty20	1	–	–	–	–	–	–	–	0	0	1	23.00	1-23

JULIA PRICE *Right-hand batter* **Queensland**
Replaced last season behind the stumps by Leonie Coleman, Julia Price believed that she still had much to offer Australian cricket, and a Player of the Year performance with gloves and bat for Queensland took her back into the national side for the Rosebowl and World Cup campaigns. Price is a fierce competitor and her on-field ebullience is a significant factor in Australia's success. She performed to her usual level of excellence throughout the two series, and contributed quick runs when needed during the World

Cup. She has not shown any indication of wanting to retire, and the competition between Price and Coleman for the Australian wicket-keeping spot may continue for some time.

	M	I	NO	Runs	HS	100s	50s	Avge	Ct	St	W	Avge	BB
Test Cricket	10	11	5	114	80*	0	1	19.00	20	2	–	–	–
Int'l. limited-overs	84	37	14	365	38	0	0	15.86	70	30	–	–	–

CLEA SMITH *Right-hand batter, right-arm medium bowler* **SA**

2004-05 was a pivotal year for Clea Smith, who realised the potential she had displayed over previous years. Experienced and highly effective as the opening partner of Cathryn Fitzpatrick for Victoria, Smith extended this partnership into the international arena, and added the ability to make early breakthroughs to her proven expertise in containing run-scoring. She further developed her skills in batting and fielding, and was instrumental in achieving a victory for her state against South Australia as part of an unbeaten half-century ninth-wicket partnership. Smith appeared to be more confident and comfortable in her role in the team in 2004-05, and looks likely to be a central member of the Australian team in future.

	M	I	NO	Runs	HS	100s	50s	Avge	Ct	St	W	Avge	BB
Test Cricket	1	2	0	46	42	0	0	23.00	0	0	1	25.00	1-25
Int'l. limited-overs	27	6	3	29	11	0	0	9.66	6	0	24	21.95	3-17

LISA STHALEKAR *Right-hand batter, right-arm off-spin bowler* **NSW**

Lisa Sthalekar added consistent batting in 2004-05 to her regular contribution to Australia's bowling and fielding effort, culminating in her second place in the Australian batting averages at the World Cup. Her half-century in the final of that competition was the ideal support for Karen Rolton's century, and she has continued to grow in stature in all aspects of her game. Her off-spin bowling rarely failed to reap rewards and her agility in the field led to some outstanding catches and run-outs. In the past she has perhaps suffered somewhat from uncertainty about her place in the batting order, but having settled now at either four or five she has had the confidence to develop.

	M	I	NO	Runs	HS	100s	50s	Avge	Ct	St	W	Avge	BB
Test Cricket	4	8	1	221	120*	1	0	31.57	2	0	10	21.80	3-44
Int'l. limited-overs	46	43	9	925	100*	1	5	21.80	15	0	45	25.53	2-16
Int'l. Twenty20	1	1	0	0	0	0	0	0.00	0	0	1	37.00	1-37

WOMEN'S NATIONAL CRICKET LEAGUE, 2004-05

Victoria took out their third National League and 38th interstate championship title following a hard-fought three-match finals series at Bankstown Oval in Sydney. NSW had the title in their sights after a comfortable victory in the first match, but their batting fell away dramatically in the remaining two matches in a disappointing conclusion to an otherwise evenly fought season. South Australia finished in their perennial position of third, and it is unlikely that they will become serious contenders until they find a number of players to support the world's best all-rounder – and once again Player of the National League – Karen Rolton. Queensland and Western Australia exchanged places from 2003-04, with the former achieving their only victories over the latter, who remained without any points for the season. The major highlights for Queensland were the form of wicket-keeper Julia Price and youngster Jodie Purves with the bat, and Australian youth team member Kirsten Pike with the ball. Price was rewarded with a recall to the Australian team for the World Cup, and both Purves and Pike continue to make strong claims for national honours.

State Players of the Year for the 2004-05 WNCL

New South Wales (Belinda Clark Medal)	Julie Hayes
Queensland	Julia Price
South Australia	Karen Rolton
Victoria (Sharon Tredrea Award)	Belinda Clark
Western Australia	Zoe Goss

PRELIMINARY GAMES

At Raby Oval, Campbelltown, October 30, 2004. New South Wales won by 77 runs. *Toss:* New South Wales. New South Wales 5 for 220 (K. A. Blackwell 59*, A. J. Blackwell 54; P. Berthold 3-33); Western Australia 143 (Z. J. Goss 71; S. E. Aley 3-24, L. C. Sthalekar 2-28).

At North Sydney Oval No. 2, North Sydney, October 31, 2004. New South Wales won by 107 runs. *Toss:* New South Wales. New South Wales 2 for 285 (M. A. Winch 101*, L.C. Sthalekar 96*, L.M. Keightley 44); Western Australia 7 for 178 (J. Burnett 55, E.P. Campbell 48; J. Hayes 4-30, L.M. Keightley 2-14).

At Allan Border Field, Albion, November 6, 2004. South Australia won by six wickets. *Toss:* Queensland. Queensland 9 for 191 (J. M. Purves 44, J. C. Price 39, A. Murnane 35; L. K. Ebsary 3-32); South Australia 4 for 192 (K. L. Rolton 70, K. L. Britt 33).

At Allan Border Field, Albion, November 7, 2004. Match between Queensland and South Australia abandoned.

At Settlers Hill, Baldivis, November 13, 2004. Victoria won by 74 runs. *Toss:* Western Australia. Victoria 7 for 236 (S. J. Edwards 90, B. J. Clark 48, M. Jones 43; D. Holden 2-50); Western Australia 162 (Z. J. Goss 57; C. L. Fitzpatrick 2-13, L. C. Broadfoot 2-30).

At Settlers Hill, Baldivis, November 13, 2004. Victoria won by nine wickets. *Toss:* Western Australia. Western Australia 6 for 196; Victoria 1 for 197 (B. J. Clark 75*, M. Jones 66*, S. J. Edwards 35).

At Harry Trott Oval, Melbourne, November 20, 2004. Victoria won two wickets. *Toss:* Queensland. Queensland 142 (K. Marxsen 53, J. C. Price 32; C. R. Smith 2-9, C. L. Fitzpatrick 2-23, J. Franklin 2-34); Victoria 8 for 143 (C. L. Fitzpatrick 37; B. Matheson 4-12, K. E. Pike 2-25).

At Henley Oval, Adelaide, November 20, 2004. New South Wales won by one wicket. *Toss:* South Australia. South Australia 7 for 162 (S. Nitschke 55; S. E. Aley 2-30, E. Twining 2-33); New South Wales 9 for 163 (K. A. Blackwell 53*; K. L. Rolton 5-13).

At Harry Trott Oval, Melbourne, November 20, 2004. Victoria won by 66 runs. *Toss:* Victoria. Victoria 5 for 240 (B. J. Clark 107*, M. Jones 48; K. E. Pike 2-48); Queensland 9 for 174 (J. C. Price 46; C. L. Fitzpatrick 2-27, L. C. Broadfoot 2-29, C. R. Smith 2-41).

At Henley Oval, Adelaide, November 20, 2004. New South Wales won by seven wickets. *Toss:* South Australia. South Australia 144 (E. Twining 2-17); New South Wales 3 for 145 (S. B. Cunneen 55, L. M. Keightley 35).

At Drummoyne Oval, Sydney, January 15, 2005. New South Wales won by three wickets. *Toss:* Victoria. Victoria 114 (S. J. Edwards 40; L. C. Sthalekar 4-32, E. Twining 2-12); New South Wales 7 for 115 (A. J. Blackwell 34; C. L. Fitzpatrick 3-21, J. Hunter 2-19).

At Adelaide Oval No. 2, Adelaide, January 15, 2005. South Australia won by 29 runs. *Toss:* Western Australia. South Australia 4 for 226 (K. L. Rolton 125, K. L. Britt 36; L. Shave 2-33); Western Australia 197 (L. N. Stammers 41, Z. J. Goss 37; S. Nitschke 4-37, L. Ebsary 2-26).

At Sydney Olympic Stadium, Homebush, January 16, 2005. Victoria won by four wickets. *Toss:* Victoria. New South Wales 142 (L. M. Keightley 34, S. B. Cunneen 32; M. Pauwels 3-13, J. Dean 2-23, L. C. Broadfoot 2-29); Victoria 6 for 145 (M. Jones 43; S. J. Andrews 2-29).

At Adelaide Oval No. 2, Adelaide, January 16, 2005. South Australia won by ten wickets. *Toss:* Western Australia. Western Australia 64 (K. L. Rolton 5-7, S. Nitschke 2-13, N. Iles 2-15); South Australia 0 for 68 (L. Ebsary 36*).

At Hale School, Perth, January 22, 2005. Queensland won by five wickets. *Toss:* Western Australia. Western Australia 9 for 208 (A. Gray 57, E. P. Campbell 41; T. E. Brown 3-17, K. E. Pike 3-36); Queensland 5 for 209 (J. M. Purves 77, B. Matheson 72; J. Burnett 2-51).

At Hale School, Perth, January 23, 2005. Queensland won by nine wickets. *Toss:* Western Australia. Western Australia 183 (L. N. Stammers 51; A. Murnane 2-36, T. E. Brown 2-37, B. Matheson 2-41); Queensland 1 for 187 (M. J. Bulow 108, J. M. Purves 60*).

At Harry Trott Oval, Melbourne, January 29, 2005. Victoria won by 12 runs. Match reduced to 25 overs. *Toss:* South Australia. Victoria 8 for 111 (S. Nitschke 3-19, K. L. Rolton 3-22); South Australia 8 for 99 (C. Atkins 35, S. Nitschke 33; J. Hunter 2-19).

At Allan Border Field, Albion, January 29, 2005. New South Wales won by three wickets. *Toss:* Queensland. Queensland 8 for 178 (J. C. Price 34, M. J. Bulow 31; L. C. Sthalekar 3-33, J. Hayes 2-38); New South Wales 7 for 179 (M. A. J. Goszko 44; T. E. Brown 2-30).

At Harry Trott Oval, Melbourne, January 30, 2005. Victoria won by seven wickets. *Toss:* Victoria. South Australia 6 for 171 (K. L. Rolton 96*, C. Atkins 38; K. M. Applebee 3-18, L. C. Broadfoot 2-29); Victoria 3 for 172 (M. Jones 79*, B. J. Clark 78; N. Iles 2-22).

At Allan Border Field, Albion, January 30, 2005. New South Wales won by six wickets. *Toss:* Queensland. Queensland 6 for 216 (T. E. Brown 86*, J. C. Price 79; L. M. Keightley 2-25, J. Hayes 2-49); New South Wales 5 for 217 (M. A. J. Goszko 51*, A. J. Blackwell 48, S. B. Cunneen 46; K. E. Pike 2-21, T. E. Brown 2-29).

POINTS TABLE, 2004-05

	Played	Won	Lost	No Result	Bonus	Points	Net Run Rate
New South Wales	8	7	1	0	4	32	0.728
Victoria	8	7	1	0	4	32	0.643
South Australia	8	3	4	1	2	16	0.275
Queensland	8	2	5	1	1	11	−0.091
Western Australia	8	0	8	0	0	0	−1.621

(Net run-rate was calculated by subtracting runs conceded per over from runs scored per over. One bonus point was awarded for scoring at a rate in excess of 25 per cent faster than the opposition. A second bonus point was awarded for scoring at a rate in excess of twice that of the opposition.)

FIRST FINAL

NEW SOUTH WALES v VICTORIA

At Bankstown Oval, Bankstown, February 11, 2005. New South Wales won by 21 runs. *Toss*: Victoria.

A steady but unspectacular batting effort by NSW had Belinda Clark regretting her decision to field first, as the home team's top order all made solid contributions to a respectable total. A century opening partnership was only broken by good fielding, and none of the seven Victorian bowlers looked particularly threatening. Michelle Goszko and Martha Winch finished the innings with a brisk unbroken half-century partnership peppered with some skilful running. The Victorian reply faltered when Clark and Melanie Jones were dismissed cheaply. Sarah Edwards and Kelly Applebee consolidated but Victoria fell further and further behind the target run-rate. Victoria compounded their difficulties with some injudicious calling which resulted in three run-outs, and veteran Julie Hayes combined with newcomer Sarah Aley to clean up the innings and leave the visitors well short.

New South Wales Women

L. M. Keightley st Lavery b Franklin	.	49
S. B. Cunneen run out		56
L. C. Sthalekar b Hunter		16
M. A. J. Goszko not out		43
M. A. Winch not out		21

B 2, l-b 4, w 7, n-b 2 15
—
(50 overs) (3 wkts) 200
Fall: 103 127 149

K. A. Blackwell, A. J. Blackwell, †L. A. Coleman, *J. Hayes, S. E. Aley, S. J. Andrews, E. Twining (did not bat).

Bowling: Fitzpatrick 10-2-31-0; Smith 7-1-24-0; Dean 4-0-11-0; Hunter 9-0-58-1; Pauwels 7-0-22-0; Franklin 9-1-31-1; Broadfoot 4-0-17-0.

Victoria Women

S. Edwards b Hayes	64
*B. J. Clark lbw b Twining	6
M. Jones c Cunneen b Hayes	2
K. M. Applebee c Cunneen b Aley	30
L. C. Broadfoot run out (K. A. Blackwell)	30
C. L. Fitzpatrick run out (Goszko)	5
C. R. Smith run out (K. A. Blackwell-Hayes)	0
J. Dean st Coleman b Hayes	1

M. Pauwels c K. A. Blackwell b Hayes	3
J. A. Franklin c and b Aley	5
J. Hunter not out	4

B 1, l-b 7, w 18, n-b 3 29
—
(49.1 overs) 179
Fall: 13 23 94 135 157 159 165 168 171 179

†C. Lavery (did not bat).

Bowling: Twining 10-3-33-1; Andrews 9-1-30-0; Hayes 10-1-31-4; Sthalekar 7-1-27-0; Aley 8.1-1-26-2; Blackwell 1-0-6-0; Keightley 4-1-18-0.

Umpires: T. M. Donahoo and W. D. Hendricks.

SECOND FINAL

NEW SOUTH WALES v VICTORIA

At Bankstown Oval, Bankstown, February 12, 2005. Victoria won by five wickets.
Toss: New South Wales.

It was difficult to recognise the NSW team as the same outfit from the previous day as they slumped to their lowest-ever National League total. The pitch had not changed significantly, nor had the composition of the two teams, and while Victoria's bowling was noticeably tighter in line and length, even they must have been surprised at the ease with which they dominated the home team's batting. Within an hour, NSW had slumped to 5 for 22, and only a late contribution from Sarah Andrews lifted them above the half-century. Clea Smith finished with career-best figures of 4 for 10, and was well-supported by Cathryn Fitzpatrick, whose eight overs cost only nine runs. Victoria were not without their own worries however, losing five wickets as the NSW bowlers took up the challenge. The target was eventually too difficult for NSW to defend, and Kelly Applebee and Fitzpatrick saw the Victorians safely home to level the series.

New South Wales Women

S. B. Cunneen lbw b Pauwels 2	†L. A. Coleman c Lavery b Smith ... 4
L. M. Keightley run out 13	S. J. Andrews not out 19
L. C. Sthalekar lbw b Smith 4	S. E. Aley run out 2
M. A. J. Goszko c Dean b Smith 1	
M. A. Winch c Clark b Dean 0	L-b 1, w 3 4
A. J. Blackwell run out 13	....
K. A. Blackwell run out 3	(43.4 overs) 71
*J. Hayes c Broadfoot b Smith 6	Fall: 2 16 19 20 22 33 41 48 65 71

E. Twining (did not bat).

Bowling: Pauwels 8-1-22-1; Fitzpatrick 8-2-9-0; Smith 10-3-10-4; Dean 10-4-10-1; Broadfoot 4-0-10-0; Franklin 3.4-0-9-0.

Victoria Women

*B. J. Clark run out (Hayes) 20	C. L. Fitzpatrick not out 12
S. Edwards c Winch b Andrews 3	
M. Jones c Coleman b Twining 0	L-b 1, w 7, n-b 2 10
K. M. Applebee not out 27	
L. C. Broadfoot c Sthalekar b Hayes .. 0	(39.1 overs) (5 wkts) 72
E. McIntyre c Coleman b Hayes 0	Fall: 4 6 42 44 48

C. R. Smith, J. A. Franklin, M. Pauwels, J. Dean, †C. Lavery (did not bat).

Bowling: Twining 7-1-12-1; Andrews 6-3-10-1; Sthalekar 10-3-18-0; Hayes 10-3-18-2; Keightley 3.1-1-4-0; Aley 3-0-9-0.

Umpires: T. M. Donahoo and W. D. Hendricks.

THIRD FINAL

NEW SOUTH WALES v VICTORIA

At Bankstown Oval, Bankstown, February 13, 2005. Victoria won by 50 runs. *Toss:* New South Wales.

A solid bowling effort gave NSW a hope of defending their title, but again the batting proved unequal to the task as the home side capitulated. The Victorian innings never achieved any great heights, with four players making 20 but none reaching 30. Louise Broadfoot and Cathryn Fitzpatrick shared a quick partnership for the sixth wicket, but the total of 159 looked to be well within NSW's reach, notwithstanding the poor batting display of the previous day. The home side began very cautiously, but this approach backfired as wickets continued to fall regularly with only modest run accumulation. The Blackwell twins and Sarah Aley tried to increase the momentum but the damage had been done and NSW limped to the unflattering total of 109 to give Victoria a comprehensive victory and the national title.

Victoria Women

J. Hunter b Hayes	15	C. L. Fitzpatrick run out	20
*B. J. Clark c Aley b Hayes	26	C. R. Smith not out	8
M. Jones lbw b Sthalekar	28	B 3, l-b 3, w 6, n-b 1	18
K. M. Applebee st Coleman b Sthalekar	0		
S. Edwards b Aley	15	(50 overs) (6 wkts)	159
L. C. Broadfoot not out	29	Fall: 30 60 70 91 106 143	

J. Dean, M. Pauwels, J. A. Franklin, †C. Lavery (did not bat).

Bowling: Twining 9-2-35-0; Andrews 6-0-11-0; Keightley 6-3-10-0; Hayes 9-2-37-2; Sthalekar 10-1-26-2; Aley 10-1-29-1.

New South Wales Women

L. M. Keightley run out (Jones)	11	*J. Hayes st Lavery b Franklin	1
S. B. Cunneen run out	5	†L. A. Coleman c Smith b Franklin	3
L. C. Sthalekar b Franklin	5	S. J. Andrews run out	1
M. A. J. Goszko c and b Dean	2		
M. A. Winch c (sub) b Hunter	7	B 1, l-b 5, w 13, n-b 2	21
A. J. Blackwell c Hunter b Broadfoot	24		
S. E. Aley b Hunter	12	(43.4 overs)	109
K. A. Blackwell not out	17	Fall: 12 23 29 35 58 79 98 94 107 109	

E. Twining (did not bat).

Bowling: Fitzpatrick 8-2-15-0; Pauwels 6-2-10-0; Smith 7-3-9-0; Franklin 8.4-0-25-3; Dean 6-2-9-1; Broadfoot 4-0-22-1; Hunter 4-0-13-2.

Umpires: T. M. Donahoo and W. D. Hendricks.

AUSTRALIAN WOMEN'S TOUR OF INDIA

Although Australia visited India in 1997 for the World Cup, more than twenty years had elapsed since the previous dedicated Australian tour, so the December 2004 series was eagerly anticipated by both nations. Australia took the opportunity to make some final adjustments to the team which would later seek to regain the World Cup, and brought in Kate Blackwell and Shelley Nitschke at the expense of Shannon Cunneen and Kris Britt. Blackwell joined her sister Alex as a middle-order batter and outstanding fielder, while Nitschke provided both useful bowling variation through her left-arm spin and a solid lower-order batting contribution. In what was perhaps a glimpse of the future, India proved to be highly competitive, and it was no surprise that they later reached the World Cup final.

Overall the ball dominated the bat, although Karen Rolton and Mithali Raj stood tall for their respective teams in the middle order. For Australia, Lisa Keightley demonstrated previously hidden all-round talent in adding wicket-taking and wicket-keeping to her role in opening the batting. Although the series was decided with two matches remaining, India showed considerable fight to reduce the margin to a single game, and inflict Australia's first defeats on Indian soil. It was not an easy tour for the Australians, who suffered a number of injuries, and experienced the aftermath of the Boxing Day tsunami on their arrival in Chennai for the final match, but the experience was invaluable as preparation for the even more gruelling World Cup campaign.

B. J. Clark (*captain*), K. L. Rolton (*vice-captain*), A. J. Blackwell, K. A. Blackwell, L. A. Coleman, C. L. Fitzpatrick, J. Hayes, M. Jones, L. M. Keightley, S. Nitschke, C. R. Smith, L. C. Sthalekar, E. Twining.

INDIA A v AUSTRALIANS

At Infosys Ground, Mysore, December 9, 2004. Match tied. *Toss:* Australian XI. Australian XI 134 (B. J. Clark 39; P. Dimri 4-26, R. Dhar 3-25); India A 8 for 134 (J. Hayes 2-16, C. R. Smith 2-23).

INDIA v AUSTRALIA

First Limited-Overs International

At Infosys Ground, Mysore, December 11, 2004. Australia won by 14 runs. *Toss:* India.

After a cautious start by the openers, the tourists compiled what turned out to be their highest total of the series. The innings was built around a 97-run third-wicket partnership between top-scorer Karen Rolton and Indian-born Lisa Sthalekar. Rolton showed the benefit of her previous experience of Indian conditions, both as part of the World Cup team in 1997 and on previous youth tours, and was quickly at home at the wicket. Medium-pace bowler Amita Sharma was the most successful bowler, although spinners Nooshin Al Khader and Neetu David gave notice that they would be a force. The Indians replied cautiously, treating fast bowler Cathryn Fitzpatrick with the utmost respect. The initial breakthrough came through a direct-hit run-out of Anju Jain by Belinda Clark. Two solid partnerships put the home side in a great position at 2 for 118, before Clark and Sthalekar combined to run through the middle order. Although Mithali Raj stood firm and added runs fluently, her partners were no match for the varied Australian attack, and the innings folded with India comfortably short of their target.

Australian Women

L. M. Keightley lbw b David	13	
*B. J. Clark lbw b A. Sharma	20	
K. L. Rolton c and b A. Sharma	82	
L. C. Sthalekar st Jain b David	34	
M. Jones c Marathe b Al Khader	10	
A. J. Blackwell c Jain b A. Sharma	2	

C. L. Fitzpatrick not out	11
J. Hayes not out	4
B 4, l-b 5, w 8, n-b 2	19
	—
(50 overs) (6 wkts)	195

Fall: 30 59 156 166 175 181

†L. A. Coleman, S. Nitschke, E. Twining (did not bat).

Bowling: A. Sharma 10-1-37-3; Goswami 10-2-29-0; Al Khader 10-0-46-1; Marathe 10-0-33-0; David 10-2-41-2.

India Women

†A. Jain run out (Clark)	14	
J. Sharma b Rolton	58	
A. Chopra b Hayes	18	
M. Raj not out	60	
H. Kala c Keightley b Sthalekar	13	
*M. Maben c Clark b Sthalekar	0	
A. Sharma run out (Clark)	0	

D. M. Marathe c Coleman b Twining	5
N. Al Khader b Fitzpatrick	0
J. Goswami b Twining	2
L-b 3, w 8	11
	—
(50 overs) (9 wkts)	181

Fall: 33 76 118 143 143 143 173 174 181

N. David (did not bat).

Bowling: Fitzpatrick 10-1-32-1; Twining 9-1-35-2; Hayes 10-3-37-1; Sthalekar 10-1-31-2; Nitschke 6-0-19-0; Rolton 5-0-24-1.

Umpires: V. Balendu Mouli and S. Muralidhara.

INDIA v AUSTRALIA

Second Limited-Overs International

At Infosys Ground, Mysore, December 13, 2004. Australia won by three wickets. *Toss:* Australia.

Australia followed the lead in inviting their opponents to bat, and were reasonably happy in restricting a strong line-up to 171 from their full 50 overs. Cathryn Fitzpatrick again applied early pressure without taking wickets, conceding a miserly single run from her first five overs, and her aggressive approach was well complemented by the naggingly accurate Clea Smith. India's top order again proved resilient, and the score reached 127 with only two wickets down. The combination of Kate Blackwell (on debut) and Lisa Sthalekar removed both Anju Jain and the dangerous Mithali Raj, while Julie Hayes and Leonie Coleman accounted for Hemlata Kala and Mamatha Maben as the Indian innings lost its way. In reply, Belinda Clark began aggressively, clubbing five fours in her run-a-ball 31, and the Indian attack made little impression on the top order. Only a series of run-outs gave the Indians a glimmer of hope, but the solidity of Karen Rolton steered Australia home in useful partnerships with Fitzpatrick and Hayes.

India Women

†A. Jain c Blackwell b Sthalekar	51	D. M. Marathe not out	3
J. Sharma c Jones b Smith	0	N. Al Khader not out	2
A. Chopra c Rolton b Nitschke	43		
M. Raj c Blackwell b Sthalekar	22	B 7, l-b 7, w 6	20
H. Kala run out (Hayes)	7		
*M. Maben run out (Hayes)	18	(50 overs) (7 wkts)	171
V. Raphael b Fitzpatrick	5	Fall: 0 101 127 138 143 158 168	

J. Goswami, N. David (did not bat).

Bowling: Fitzpatrick 10-5-20-1; Smith 7-2-21-1; Hayes 10-1-30-0; Sthalekar 10-1-36-2; Rolton 9-0-26-0; Nitschke 4-0-24-1.

Australian Women

*B. J. Clark run out (Goswami)	31	J. Hayes b Goswami	12
L. M. Keightley run out (Goswami/Jain)	10	S. Nitschke not out	1
K. L. Rolton not out	62		
L. C. Sthalekar run out	30	L-b 4, w 5	9
M. Jones c Maben b Marathe	6		
K. A. Blackwell c Raj b David	0	(49.2 overs) (7 wkts)	172
C. L. Fitzpatrick c Maben b David	11	Fall: 42 47 108 124 129 147 170	

†L. A. Coleman, C. R. Smith (did not bat).

Bowling: Goswami 5-1-18-1; Maben 4.2-0-15-0; Marathe 10-0-27-1; Al Khader 10-1-22-0; Raphael 10-0-47-0; David 10-1-39-2.

Umpires: V. Balendu Mouli and M. Sreenivasa Murthy.

INDIA v AUSTRALIA

Third Limited-Overs International

At Gymkhana Ground, Mumbai, December 16, 2004. India won by six wickets. *Toss:* India.

India fought back in the series to win in a dominant display of all-round cricket. Australia's top three batters put their side in a strong position to make a score in excess of 200, but the loss of Lisa Sthalekar at 128 triggered a collapse which saw eight wickets all for 19 runs. Wickets were shared between spinner Neetu David and medium-pacers Jhulan Goswami and Amita Sharma, but poor running resulted in three run-outs which the Australians could ill afford. The Indian reply was disciplined and confident, and built around an unbeaten half-century by Mithali Raj, whose fluent strokeplay saw her reach the boundary on numerous occasions. Jaya Sharma provided solid support, and the total was easily overhauled with almost six overs in hand.

Australian Women

L. M. Keightley run out (A. Sharma) . .	56	S. Nitschke c Jain b A. Sharma	0
B. J. Clark c and b David	32	†L. A. Coleman not out	2
L. L. Rolton c Jain b David	40	E. Twining lbw b Goswami	0
K. C. Sthalekar run out (Raj)	2		
M. Jones b David	1	L-b 3, w 6, n-b 1	10
A. J. Blackwell run out (J. Sharma) . .	0		
J. L. Fitzpatrick lbw b Goswami	4	(47.1 overs)	147
J. Hayes run out (A. Sharma)	0	Fall: 63 120 128 137 137 142 142 142 146 147

Bowling: Chopra 9-3-20-1; A. Sharma 9-3-20-1; Goswami 5.1-1-22-2; Al Khader 10-0-39-0; David 10-2-27-3; Marathe 10-2-24-0.

India Women

A. Jain lbw b Hayes	12	A. Kirkire not out	0
J. Sharma c Coleman b Keightley	47	W 3, n-b 2	5
A. Chopra lbw b Rolton	10		
M. Raj not out	62	(44.1 overs) (4 wkts)	151
S. M. Maben c Keightley b Sthalekar . .	15	Fall: 30 45 105 147	

N. David, D. M. Marathe, N. Al Khader, A. Sharma, J. Goswami (did not bat).

Bowling: Fitzpatrick 10-3-32-0; Twining 6.1-1-27-0; Hayes 9-0-24-1; Rolton 7-1-23-1; Sthalekar 6-1-19-1; Nitschke 2-0-13-0.

Umpires: Ajit Datar and Marcus Couto.

INDIA v AUSTRALIA

Fourth Limited-Overs International

At Bilakhiya Stadium, Vapi, December 19, 2004. Australia won by eight wickets. *Toss: Australia.*

A more consistent all-round performance saw Australia take a commanding series lead. Fielding first, the tourists managed to break the Indian partnerships with more regularity than in previous matches, and never allowed the innings to build up momentum despite the fact that most of the Indian batters made something of a start. Cathryn Fitzpatrick was again miserly and threatening, while Lisa Keightley provided unexpected difficulties with her gentle medium-pace out-swing. Keightley completed a dominant double with a solid half-century, and her 96-run partnership with Karen Rolton all but secured victory. For once, India's bowlers lacked penetration, and the target was reached with more than five overs to spare. In what may turn out to be a significant milestone, the Blackwell twins represented Australia together for the first time.

India Women

†A. Jain b Twining	8	J. Goswami not out	16
J. Sharma c Fitzpatrick b Keightley	43	N. David not out	3
A. Chopra c Fitzpatrick b Sthalekar	26		
M. Raj c Sthalekar b Keightley	22	B 1, l-b 1, w 7, n-b 1	10
*M. Maben c Clark b Keightley	8		
A. Kirkire b Fitzpatrick	21	(50 overs) (7 wkts)	170
A. Sharma c Coleman b Fitzpatrick	13	Fall: 17 84 84 112 125 149 156	

D. M. Marathe, N. Al Khader (did not bat).

Bowling: Fitzpatrick 10-4-21-2; Twining 9-3-47-1; Hayes 10-0-30-0; Rolton 2-0-23-0; Sthalekar 9-0-30-1; Keightley 10-3-17-3.

Australian Women

L. M. Keightley st Jain b David	80	L-b 3, w 1, n-b 2	6
*B. J. Clark b Goswami	23		
K. L. Rolton not out	52	(44.5 overs) (2 wkts)	173
L. C. Sthalekar not out	12	Fall: 61 157	

M. Jones, A.J. Blackwell, C.L. Fitzpatrick, J. Hayes, S. Nitschke, †L.A. Coleman, E. Twining (did not bat).

Bowling: A. Sharma 6-0-26-0; Goswami 9-0-32-1; Maben 1-0-12-0; Al Khader 10-1-22-0; Marathe 9-1-33-0; David 9.5-1-45-1.

INDIA v AUSTRALIA

Fifth Limited-Overs International

At Pithwala Stadium, Surat, December 22, 2004. Australia won by 32 runs. *Toss: Australia.*

Australia took an unbeatable 4-1 series lead in an eventful fifth match. Having been required to field first, India were well satisfied in restricting Australia to a disappointing 160 runs, with all of the top six batters contained after solid starts. The key to their success was maintaining good line, and tempting the Australians into taking risks in order to accelerate their scoring. The run-rate hovered around three runs an over throughout the innings, and the middle and lower order had only limited opportunities to attempt to increase it. For an unknown reason the umpires permitted Neetu David to bowl 11 overs, but no obvious advantage accrued to India as a result. The Indian reply was punctuated by a serious injury to diminutive wicket-keeper Leonie Coleman, whose cheekbone was fractured as a result of a return from the outfield by Alex Blackwell, and the keeping duties were subsequently shared by Lisa Keightley and Blackwell. Cathryn Fitzpatrick and Clea Smith mesmerised the Indian batters in the early stages, and Julie Hayes was similarly miserly, but it was the introduction of Keightley which turned the tide in Australia's favour as she snared four quick wickets to race through the middle order.

Australian Women

B. J. Clark lbw b David	26
C. M. Keightley b Chopra	10
L. L. Rolton b Raphael	32
C. Sthalekar b Goswami	26
M. Jones b Goswami	25
A. J. Blackwell run out (Marathe)	13
L. L. Fitzpatrick b Raphael	3
J. Hayes c Sharma b Al Khader	0
†L. A. Coleman b Marathe	8
S. Nitschke not out	1
L-b 4, w 11, n-b 1	16

C. R. Smith (did not bat).

(50 overs)   (9 wkts) 160

Fall: 19 59 81 129 134 143 144 159 160

Bowling: Goswami 10-3-25-2; Chopra 6-1-23-1; Al Khader 9-2-23-1; David 11-3-39-1; Marathe 4-0-15-1; Raphael 10-0-31-2.

India Women

A. Jain run out (Rolton)	20
R. Sharma b Smith	4
A. Chopra c Keightley b Hayes	4
M. Raj c Clark b Hayes	36
M. Maben b Keightley	28
S. Kirkire c Nitschke b Keightley	4
A. Raphael c Rolton b Keightley	7
M. Marathe c Jones b Keightley	1
J. Goswami run out (Clark)	7
N. Al Khader b Fitzpatrick	6
N. David not out	2
W 8, n-b 1	9

(47.1 overs) 128

Fall: 7 23 46 84 89 103 109 118 123 128

Bowling: Fitzpatrick 8.1-1-19-1; Smith 10-5-17-1; Hayes 10-3-16-2; Nitschke 2-0-17-0; Sthalekar 6-2-22-0; Keightley 7-2-22-4; Rolton 4-0-15-0.

Umpires: K. D. Doodhwala and Ravi Deshmukh.

INDIA v AUSTRALIA

Sixth Limited-Overs International

At IPCL Ground, Baroda, December 24, 2004. India won by six wickets. *Toss:* India.

If Australia had been hoping for a repeat of their 1997 Christmas Eve victory ove India in the sixth World Cup, they were sadly disappointed as they slipped to a close bu decisive six-wicket loss. New Indian captain Mithali Raj stamped her presence on th match with clever use of her bowlers to restrict the Australian top order to a modest rur rate on a good pitch. Only Lisa Sthalekar was able to break the shackles to some degree and a late partnership between the Blackwell twins of better than a run a ball pushed th innings towards respectability. Raj led from the front with an unbeaten and elegant 92 and she was well supported by Hemlata Kala, and Anju Jain batting in an unfamilia middle-order spot. Clea Smith made early breakthroughs and kept the reins tight for he ten-over spell, but none of the other bowlers could ruffle Raj as she steered her team t a well-crafted victory with ten balls to spare.

Australian Women

†L. M. Keightley b Goswami	23
*B. J. Clark st Jain b David	35
K. L. Rolton c and b Marathe	17
L. C. Sthalekar st Jain b Al Khader	43
M. Jones c Jain b David	9
K. A. Blackwell run out (Goswami)	15
A. J. Blackwell c A. Sharma b Goswami	19
C. L. Fitzpatrick not out	6
J. Hayes not out	2
B 4, l-b 2, w 9	15
(50 overs) (7 wkts)	184

C. R. Smith, E. Twining (did not bat).

Fall: 70 70 96 137 155 156 181

Bowling: Goswami 10-3-29-2; A. Sharma 10-1-36-0; Al Khader 10-1-25-1; Marathe 10-0-52-1; Dav 10-2-36-2.

India Women

M. Sumra c Keightley b Smith	0
J. Sharma b Smith	9
*M. Raj not out	92
H. Kala run out (Rolton)	41
†A. Jain st Keightley b Clark	27
A. Kirkire not out	2
B 4, l-b 2, w 8	14
(47.4 overs) (4 wkts)	185

D. M. Marathe, J. Goswami, N. David, A. Sharma, N. Al Khader (did not bat).

Fall: 3 20 129 176

Bowling: Fitzpatrick 10-2-30-0; Smith 10-5-13-2; Twining 6-0-27-0; Sthalekar 6-1-24-0; Hayes 8-42-0; Keightley 2-0-17-0; Rolton 4-0-17-0; Clark 1.4-0-9-1.

Umpires: V. Dongra and K. D. Doodhwala.

INDIA v AUSTRALIA

Seventh Limited-Overs International

At Mayajaal Sports Village, Chennai, December 28, 2004. India won by 88 runs. *Toss:* India.

India gained a great deal of pride as they comprehensively defeated a tired Australian side. Arriving in Chennai in the aftermath of the Boxing Day tsunami, the Australians appeared to struggle in maintaining focus, and their batting let them down after a sound performance in the field. Anju Jain and Mithali Raj again provided the Indian backbone, but after both were dismissed, Cathryn Fitzpatrick and Lisa Sthalekar stormed through the middle order to bring the innings to a close. The target appeared eminently gettable, but the Australian innings collapsed after Lisa Keightley's first-ball duck. At 7 for 31, the possibility of succumbing for under 50 looked to be a real prospect. Some semblance of respectability was restored by Julie Hayes, who combined with the lower order to add 46 for the last three wickets, but the final result was never really in doubt. The 4-3 series result was probably a good reflection of the relative strengths of the two sides, although India undoubtedly enjoyed their home ground advantage.

India Women

†A. Jain c Jones b Smith	39	D. M. Marathe not out		8
M. Sumra run out (Blackwell)	25	N. David c Clark b Fitzpatrick		0
*M. Raj run out (Rolton)	1	N. Al Khader not out		5
H. Kala lbw b Fitzpatrick	33			
A. Chopra c Keightley b Sthalekar	0	B 6, l-b 3, w 11, n-b 5		25
A. Kirkire st Keightley b Sthalekar	6			
A. Sharma b Fitzpatrick	20	(50 overs)	(9 wkts)	165
V. Raphael b Fitzpatrick	3	Fall: 74 76 79 80 98 140 146 155 155		

Bowling: Fitzpatrick 10-2-25-4; Smith 4-0-17-1; Twining 7-2-27-0; Nitschke 7-0-26-0; Hayes 10-3-23-0; Sthalekar 9-2-27-2; Rolton 3-0-11-0.

Australian Women

*B. J. Clark c and b Al Khader	12	S. Nitschke b Raphael	8
†L. M. Keightley b Sharma	0	C. R. Smith run out (Raj)	11
K. L. Rolton lbw b Sharma	1	E. Twining not out	0
L. C. Sthalekar b Al Khader	5		
M. Jones c Marathe b Raphael	6	L-b 2, w 6	8
K. A. Blackwell b Sharma	0		
C. L. Fitzpatrick b David	4	(36.4 overs)	77
J. Hayes st Jain b Al Khader	22	Fall: 2 4 19 20 22 29 31 49 75 77	

Bowling: Sharma 8-0-21-3; Al Khader 7.4-2-14-3; David 7-3-14-1; Raphael 8-3-14-2; Marathe 6-2-12-0.

Umpires: S. M. Raju and S. Ramji.

AUSTRALIA v NEW ZEALAND

ROSEBOWL SERIES

The selectors made only one change to the team which toured India, as veteran wicket-keeper Julia Price replaced Leonie Coleman. Coleman had recovered from the fractured cheekbone sustained in India, but her keeping exhibited signs of a decrease in confidence, and Price's excellent season with both gloves and bat tipped the odds in her favour. Louise Broadfoot was added to make up an expanded 14-player squad to take on New Zealand in the annual Rosebowl series and then to travel directly to South Africa for the World Cup.

The absence of veteran Emily Drumm from the New Zealand line-up meant that the burden of scoring runs fell onto too few shoulders, and this lack of depth exposed an all-too-familiar vulnerability to the now seasoned Australian side. Although the middle match of the series was close, Australia's dominance was never significantly challenged as the home side completed a clean sweep. While both teams used the series as a means of ensuring all squad members had some match practice, this aspect certainly did not overshadow the annual trans-Tasman rivalry. Australia clearly showed evidence of the lessons learned in India, particularly in their batting, and confirmed their status as favourites for the World Cup.

B.J. Clark (*captain*), K.L. Rolton (*vice-captain*), A.J. Blackwell, K.A. Blackwell, L. C. Broadfoot, C.L. Fitzpatrick, J. Hayes, M. Jones, L.M. Keightley, E. Liddell (nee Twining), S. Nitschke, J.C. Price, C.R. Smith, L.C. Sthalekar.

AUSTRALIA v NEW ZEALAND

First Limited-Overs International

At Lilac Hill, Perth, March 10, 2005. Australia won by 87 runs. *Toss:* Australia.

After an unusually quiet – by her standards – tour of India, Australian captain Belinda Clark returned to form as she dominated the first match of the Rosebowl series. Although the innings began sedately, Clark remained in control to compile a hard-fought 86 and lead the acceleration which pushed the Australian total over the 200 mark. She was ably supported by the aggressive Melanie Jones after Karen Rolton had been contained by the tight spin of Rebecca Steele. A late flurry, particularly by Cathryn Fitzpatrick, saw the loss of wickets to run-outs, but the final total was defensible. Fitzpatrick and Clea Smith seriously dented New Zealand's chances as they removed Maia Lewis and the talented Haidee Tiffen with only three runs on the board, and the innings failed to gain momentum at any stage. Six Australian bowlers enjoyed success, and all returned economical figures as the home side completed a comfortable victory over their traditional rivals.

Australian Women

*B. J. Clark lbw b Browne	86	†J. C. Price run out (Tiffen) 3
L. M. Keightley c Lewis b Browne	5	L. C. Broadfoot not out 1
K. L. Rolton b Steele	16	
M. Jones run out (Milliken)	55	L-b 8, w 13 21
A. J. Blackwell c Rolls b Milliken	6	
L. C. Sthalekar run out (Pullar)	3	(50 overs) (8 wkts) 207
C. L. Fitzpatrick run out (McGlashan)	11	Fall: 28 79 176 188 189 195 206 207

J. Hayes, C. R. Smith (did not bat).

Bowling: Milliken 9-2-36-1; Pullar 10-0-42-0; Browne 8-0-37-2; Steele 10-2-24-1; Corbin 8-0-40-0; Watson 5-0-20-0.

New Zealand Women

*M. A. M. Lewis b Smith	1	A. M. Corbin c Broadfoot b Hayes	7
M. F. Fahey run out (Smith)	21	L. E. Milliken c Price b Rolton	5
H. M. Tiffen b Fitzpatrick	0	R. J. Steele b Rolton	2
†R. J. Rolls c Fitzpatrick b Broadfoot	20	
S. J. McGlashan run out (Keightley)	5	L-b 3, w 5 8
R. J. Pullar c Sthalekar b Smith	10	
H. M. Watson lbw b Blackwell	12	(46 overs) 120
N. J. Browne not out	29	Fall: 1 3 36 50 55 68 82 95 112 120

Bowling: Fitzpatrick 9-0-26-1; Smith 10-2-29-2; Hayes 10-2-24-1; Rolton 6-1-16-2; Broadfoot 6-2-12-1; Blackwell 4-0-8-1; Sthalekar 1-0-2-0.

Umpires: B. Bennett and A. R. Craig.

AUSTRALIA v NEW ZEALAND

Second Limited-Overs International

At WACA Ground, Perth, March 12, 2005. Australia won by seven runs. *Toss:* Australia.

Australia held their nerve in the face of sustained pressure to take out the Rosebowl series with a hard-fought victory in the second match. A more determined effort by the New Zealand bowlers saw no Australian batter pass 40, but the runs were more evenly shared. As is becoming common, Cathryn Fitzpatrick provided a late run-spree which proved critical to the final outcome after Karen Rolton was fifth out with the score on 137. New Zealand's quest to reach the target of 203 started disastrously with Maia Lewis falling victim to the fire of Fitzpatrick in the first over, but Haidee Tiffen set about building a series of partnerships which allowed the Kiwis to mount a serious challenge. Tiffen played a measured innings and steered her side into a winning position at 5 for 187 before falling to the medium-pace of Emma Liddell. Following her dismissal, Nicola Browne continued to push for victory, but Australia rose to the challenge with both Belinda Clark and Rolton bringing about critical run-outs to deny New Zealand in a close finish.

Australian Women

*B. J. Clark c Rolls b Steele	38	†J. C. Price not out	9
L. M. Keightley c Rolls b Browne	29	J. Hayes not out	9
K. L. Rolton c Lewis b Scripps	31		
M. Jones c McGlashan b Milliken	11	L-b 9, w 14, n-b 1	24
L. C. Broadfoot b Watson	1		
A. J. Blackwell run out	27	(50 overs) (7 wkts)	202
C. L. Fitzpatrick run out	23	Fall: 67 81 105 109 137 174 180	

C. R. Smith, E. Twining (did not bat).

Bowling: Milliken 7-1-28-1; Scripps 10-1-37-1; Browne 10-0-41-1; Burke 6-1-34-0; Steele 10-3-26-1; Watson 7-1-27-1.

New Zealand Women

*M. A. M. Lewis c Price b Fitzpatrick	0	L. E. Milliken run out	4
M. F. Fahey b Hayes	7	S. K. Burke run out	0
H. M. Tiffen c Fitzpatrick b Twining	92	N. Scripps not out	0
†R. J. Rolls c Smith b Hayes	16	B 5, l-b 6, w 5, n-b 1	17
S. J. McGlashan lbw b Smith	23		
H. M. Watson b Rolton	12	(50 overs) (8 wkts)	196
N. J. Browne not out	25	Fall: 0 43 67 106 137 188 195 195	

R. J. Steele (did not bat).

Bowling: Fitzpatrick 10-2-40-1; Smith 8-3-22-1; Twining 10-0-41-1; Hayes 10-3-24-2; Broadfoot 6-0-29-0; Rolton 6-0-28-1.

Umpires: J. K. Brookes and A. R. Craig.

AUSTRALIA v NEW ZEALAND

Third Limited-Overs International

At WACA Ground, Perth, March 13, 2005. Australia won by three wickets. *Toss: Australia.*

Australia completed a clean sweep of the Rosebowl series, and finalised their preparation for the World Cup, in a low-scoring encounter under lights. Originally scheduled as a day game, the match was changed at short notice to a day-night fixture because of difficulties with the sprinklers. After Australia chose to bowl first, New Zealand's start was disastrous as Cathryn Fitzpatrick and Emma Liddell had them reeling at three wickets for a single run. Liddell went on to record her best figures, including the vital wickets of Haidee Tiffen and Rebecca Rolls. After the sixth wicket fell for only 31 runs, Nicola Browne completed a solid series with the bat in compiling the top score and steadying the innings, but the total of 114 always looked inadequate. Australia made heavy work of their reply however, losing seven wickets, with only Karen Rolton really subduing the New Zealand bowling. Rolton showed why she is regarded as the world's best woman cricketer as she combined solid defence and punishing attack, and after her dismissal sufficient overs remained for Kate Blackwell to guide Australia cautiously but inexorably towards the target.

New Zealand Women

*M. A. M. Lewis c Blackwell b Sthalekar	11	A. M. Corbin b Twining	5
M. F. Fahey c Price b Fitzpatrick	0	N. Scripps not out	9
H. M. Tiffen b Twining	0	R. J. Steele not out	5
†R. J. Rolls b Twining	0		
S. J. McGlashan c Blackwell b Fitzpatrick	1	B 1, l-b 5, w 9, n-b 1	16
R. J. Pullar c Keightley b Hayes	14		
H. M. Watson b Nitschke	23	(50 overs) (9 wkts)	114
N. J. Browne b Twining	30	Fall: 0 1 1 11 31 31 89 98 100	

Bowling: Fitzpatrick 10-2-28-2; Twining 9-2-17-4; Hayes 8-2-16-1; Sthalekar 10-4-27-1; Nitschke 9-0-16-1; Rolton 4-1-4-0.

Australian Women

*B. J. Clark c Corbin b Steele	3	M. Jones run out (Watson)	4
L. M. Keightley run out (McGlashan)	13	J. Hayes not out	4
K. L. Rolton c Tiffen b Watson	43		
L. C. Sthalekar c Tiffen b Watson	9	L-b 3, w 15, n-b 1	19
K. A. Blackwell not out	17		
C. L. Fitzpatrick c and b Watson	1	(45.3 overs) (7 wkts)	118
†J. C. Price c Fahey b Corbin	5	Fall: 9 41 81 82 91 101 109	

S. Nitschke, E. Twining (did not bat).

Bowling: Pullar 10-2-21-0; Steele 10-4-21-1; Scripps 7.3-1-24-0; Browne 4-1-11-0; Corbin 7-2-24-1; Watson 7-1-14-3.

Umpires: J. K. Brookes and A. R. Craig.

WOMEN'S CRICKET WORLD CUP
IN SOUTH AFRICA, 2004-05

After two close series against India and New Zealand, the Australian team was match-seasoned and confident of their ability to hold off all challenges and wrest back the World Cup they lost to New Zealand in 2000. Playing in South Africa was a new experience for most of the team, as Australia had never previously sent a side to Africa, although individual players had visited. The competition was expected to be closer than had been the case in the previous World Cup, which was dominated by Australia and New Zealand, and this expectation was borne out as both England and India performed strongly.

The Australians remained undefeated and managed to garner bonus points in four of the five completed matches to finish at the top of the table, followed by India, New Zealand and England. West Indies overcame tremendous difficulties, both logistic and financial, to finish an extremely commendable fifth, while Sri Lanka scraped into sixth position and automatic qualification for the next World Cup by a single point. The major disappointment was the form of the hosts South Africa, who slipped from semi-finalists to seventh despite a victory over Sri Lanka, although they were unlucky to have their match against tournament wooden-spooners Ireland abandoned because of rain.

The semi-finals were decided in favour of the two most highly placed teams, and resulted in India becoming only the fourth team to make an appearance in a World Cup final. Australia, celebrating their fifth such appearance, showed the advantage of experience – both in World Cup finals and in recent clashes with India – to take out their fifth title with a comfortable 98-run victory.

Karen Rolton underlined her premier status in women's cricket in being named Player of the Series (and Player of the Final) with 265 runs at an average of 61.5, and ten wickets at 11.2. England's Charlotte Edwards topped the run-scoring with 280, while veteran Indian spinner Neetu David finished top of the wicket-takers with 20. For Australia, Rolton, Lisa Keightley and Lisa Sthalekar dominated the batting, while Shelley Nitschke took the bowling honours with 11 wickets at an average of 8.27 and an economy rate of 2.06 runs per over. She was well supported by both Rolton and Cathryn Fitzpatrick with ten wickets apiece, and Clea Smith, who conceded a miserly 1.86 runs per over.

B. J. Clark (*captain*), K. L. Rolton(*vice-captain*), A. J. Blackwell, K. A. Blackwell , L. C. Broadfoot, C. L. Fitzpatrick, J. Hayes, M. Jones, L. M. Keightley, E. Liddell (nee Twining), S. Nitschke, J. C. Price, C. R. Smith, L. C. Sthalekar.

AUSTRALIA v ENGLAND

ROUND 1

At Technikon Oval, Pretoria, March 22, 2005. Match drawn. *Toss:* England.

No results were possible in a disappointing first round as rain wiped out play halfway through all matches. In a much-anticipated clash against a resurgent England, Australia were well on top after restricting England to 169 runs from their full 50 overs. The total could have been considerably smaller had it not been for a fighting lower-order innings by Jenny Gunn, who was willing to play her shots in an unbeaten eighth-wicket partnership with Jane Smit. Julie Hayes was the only multiple wicket-taker for Australia, but all bowlers played their part to contain England to a manageable total. Unfortunately rain intervened before the second innings started, and the points for the match were shared.

Player of the match: K. L. Rolton.

England Women

C. M. Edwards lbw b Hayes	26	J. L. Gunn not out	40
L. K. Newton c Liddell b Hayes	31	†J. Smit not out	7
S. C. Taylor c Hayes b Rolton	24		
*C. J. Connor b Liddell	0	B 1, l-b 1, w 3	5
L. Greenway c Smith b Sthalekar	11		
R. A. Birch run out (Hayes/Price)	8	(50 overs) (7 wkts)	169
N. J. Shaw b Fitzpatrick	17	Fall: 44 63 63 94 95 102 128	

K. H. Brunt, L. C. Pearson (did not bat).

Bowling: Fitzpatrick 10-4-30-1; Smith 4-0-24-0; Hayes 10-2-32-2; Liddell 9-1-38-1; Rolton 7-3-17-1; Sthalekar 10-1-26-1.

Umpires: Z. Ndamane and B. M. White.

Australia Women

*B. J. Clarke, K. L. Rolton, L. M. Keightley, L. C. Sthalekar, M. Jones, A. J. Blackwell, C. L. Fitzpatrick, J. Hayes, †J. C. Price, E. Liddell, C. R. Smith.

Umpires: Z. Ndamane and B. M. White.

Other first-round results

South Africa 7 for 204 (S. A. Fritz 48, C. S. Terblanche 41, M. Terblanche 36; B. M. McDonald 2-26, J. A. Whelan 2-38) from 48 overs against Ireland.

New Zealand 8 for 178 (M. A. M. Lewis 77; P. Thomas 2-19, N. Williams 2-32) against West Indies.

Sri Lanka 116 (N. David 3-17, N. Al Khader 2-28); India 0 for 4.

AUSTRALIA v NEW ZEALAND

ROUND 2

At L. C. de Villiers Oval, Pretoria, March 24, 2005. Australia won by 32 runs. *Toss:* Australia.

Australia continued their successful season against New Zealand, although they were forced to fight back from the precarious position of 5 for 50 at the halfway stage of their innings. Alex Blackwell and Cathryn Fitzpatrick both surpassed their previous highest scores in putting together a match-saving partnership of 85 in only 70 minutes, and after Fitzpatrick's departure, Blackwell continued to build a respectable score together with wicket-keeper Julia Price. The total of 174 looked precarious, but New Zealand proved unequal to the challenge despite the strengthening of their batting line-up with the return of Emily Drumm. The experienced opening pair of Fitzpatrick and Clea Smith made early inroads into the New Zealand top order, and it was not until Drumm joined Rebecca Rolls that the innings gained any momentum. New Zealand's most experienced pair took the total to 100 before Rolls was caught from a lofted stroke, and her dismissal precipitated a second collapse as the final seven wickets fell for only 42. Drumm remained defiant throughout to be the last batter dismissed. Karen Rolton compensated for her relative failure with the bat to take the bowling honours and the player of the match award.

Player of the Match: K. L. Rolton.

Australian Women

L. M. Keightley lbw b Pullar	7		†J. C. Price not out	19
*B. J. Clark c Tiffen b Milliken	4		C. R. Smith not out	0
K. L. Rolton c Rolls b Steele	10			
M. Jones c Watson b Browne	3		L-b 6, w 16	22
L. C. Sthalekar lbw b Watson	13			
A. J. Blackwell lbw b Browne	53		(50 overs) (7 wkts)	174
C. L. Fitzpatrick c Rolls b Pullar	43		Fall: 16 16 30 35 50 135 167	

J. Hayes, E. Liddell (did not bat).

Bowling: Milliken 10-1-44-1; Pullar 10-3-30-2; Browne 9-1-37-2; Steele 10-5-15-1; Watson 8-2-30-1; Corbin 3-0-12-0.

New Zealand Women

M. F. Fahey b Fitzpatrick	0		A. M. Corbin run out (Clark)	2
*M. A. M. Lewis c Keightley b Liddell	6		L. E. Milliken b Rolton	3
H. M. Tiffen c Price b Smith	3		R. J. Steele not out	5
†R. J. Rolls c Clark b Rolton	60			
E. C. Drumm run out (Blackwell/Price)	42		L-b 7, w 3	10
H. M. Watson b Rolton	0			
N. J. Browne run out (Hayes/Rolton)	3		(49.3 overs)	142
R. J. Pullar st Price b Hayes	8		Fall: 1 6 23 100 102 108 118 124 132 142	

Bowling: Fitzpatrick 10-1-24-1; Smith 7-3-5-1; Liddell 6.3-0-20-1; Hayes 10-1-30-1; Sthalekar 4-0-23-0; Keightley 2-0-11-0; Rolton 10-2-22-3.

Umpires: B. N. Harrison and G. Pienaar.

Other second-round results

South Africa 169 (C. Z. Brits 72; P. Thomas 4-42, D. A. Lewis 2-24, V. Felician 2-31) defeated West Indies 168 (J. Nero 41; C. Z. Brits 4-37) by one run.

England 4 for 284 (S. C. Taylor 136, C. M. Edwards 63, C. J. Connor 54; P. M. Udawatte 3-38) defeated Sri Lanka 70 (L. C. Pearson 3-23, J. L. Gunn 3-28, R. A. Birch 2-14) by 214 runs.

India 1 for 68 (A. Jain 32*) defeated Ireland 65 (M. E. Grealey 38; A. Sharma 3-12, J. Goswami 2-15, N. Al Khader 2-19) by nine wickets.

AUSTRALIA v WEST INDIES

ROUND 3

At Olympia Park, Rustenburg, March 26, 2005. Australia won by 79 runs. *Toss:* West Indies.

The absence of captain Belinda Clark, sidelined through illness, proved no handicap as the Australians completed a comfortable 79-run win over a rebuilding West Indies side. Stand-in captain Karen Rolton revelled in her responsibilities to anchor the innings after Australia were sent in to bat, well supported by Lisa Keightley. The innings fell away after Rolton's departure, but the platform of 180 runs for the first three partnerships was sufficiently solid and the final few overs saw the additional of useful but not critical runs. West Indies performed creditably in their reply to compile their highest score against Australia, but they were no real match for the experienced and varied bowling attack. Juliana Nero stood firm and Shane de Silva hit out towards the end, but the damage was done by then. Most successful for Australia were the medium-pacers and spinners, Rolton wrapping up a second player of the match award with a good double.

Player of the Match: K. L. Rolton.

Australian Women

L. M. Keightley c Nero b Goordial	56	J. Hayes c Nero b Lewis	5
L. C. Sthalekar lbw b E. Williams	17	S. Nitschke run out (Nero)	1
*K. L. Rolton c (sub) K. Alexander b E. Williams	69	C. R. Smith not out	3
M. Jones st Power b de Silva	27		
A. J. Blackwell run out (sub) K. Alexander)	0		
L. C. Broadfoot c (sub) K. Alexader b E. Williams	19	B 2, l-b 1, w 20, n-b 2	25
C. L. Fitzpatrick b Lavine	0		
†J. C. Price c Power b Lavine	8	(49.2 overs)	230

Fall: 53 107 180 180 189 191 210 223 224 230

Bowler: Lewis 8-1-28-1; Thomas 10-1-37-0; E. Williams 8.2-0-38-3; Lavine 10-0-45-2; Goordial 7-0-37-1; Felician 4-0-30-0; de Silva 2-0-12-1.

West Indies Women

N. Williams c Rolton b Sthalekar	 24		D. A. Lewis run out (Hayes/Price)	... 3
I. Goordial c and b Nitschke	 8		P. Thomas not out	 9
J. Nero st Price b Hayes	 40		E. Williams run out (Sthalekar/Rolton)	8
N. George st Price b Sthalekar	 6			
P. Lavine c Rolton b Broadfoot	 10		B 2, l-b 5, w 3	 10
S. de Silva c Jones b Rolton	 29			
*†S. Power run out (Jones/Price)	 0		(48.3 overs)	151
V. Felician c Hayes b Rolton	 4		Fall: 29 39 47 78 105 105 118 126 142 151	

Bowling: Fitzpatrick 9-0-32-0; Smith 7-2-11-0; Hayes 10-1-31-1; Nitschke 8-3-15-1; Broadfoot 5-0-16-1; Rolton 5.3-1-23-2; Sthalekar 4-0-16-2.

Umpires: Z. Ndamane and D. J. Smith.

Other third-round results

India 6 for 81 (R. Dhar 33*; A. E. Smith 4-19) defeated South Africa 80 (D. M. Marathe 4-1, A. Sharma 3-23, N. David 2-8) by four wickets.

England 6 for 221 (C. J. Connor 82*, A. Brindle 51) defeated Ireland 8 for 93 (C. E. Taylor 2-13, C. J. Connor 2-14) by 128 runs.

New Zealand 3 for 59 (P. M. Udawatte 2-27) defeated Sri Lanka 58 (H. M. Watson 2-0, R. J. Pullar 2-6, A. M. Corbin 2-15) by seven wickets.

SOUTH AFRICA v AUSTRALIA

ROUND 4

At L. C. de Villiers Oval, Pretoria, March 28, 2005. Australia won by 97 runs. *Toss:* South Africa.

Belinda Clark returned to the side for the fourth round, which again produced a comfortable victory for the Cup front-runners. Sent in by Alison Hodgkinson, Australia pushed to their highest total of the tournament on the back of Lisa Keightley's fourth century for her country in one-day internationals. She was well supported by Karen Rolton, with whom she shared a 96-run partnership, and Lisa Sthalekar chipped in to take the score past 250. Australia's total was somewhat flattered by the large number of extras – 43, including 33 wides – contributed by the fielding side, which led to a one-over penalty for a slow over-rate. The loss of an over was not critical as the South African reply never threatened the target, although Cri-Zelda Brits showed plenty of aggression in top-scoring with 49. All six Australian bowlers were successful, and Cathryn Fitzpatrick and Julie Hayes proved highly economical as South Africa could manage only 159.

Player of the Match: L. M. Keightley.

Australia Women

*B. J. Clark c van der Westhuizen b Logtenberg	15	C. L. Fitzpatrick not out 6
L. M. Keightley c and b van der Westhuizen	103	
K. L. Rolton c Pillay b Brits	46	L-b 7, w 33, n-b 3 43
M. Jones c Fritz b Logtenberg	16	
L. C. Sthalekar not out	22	(50 overs) (5 wkts) 256
K. A. Blackwell run out (Fritz/Pillay)	5	Fall: 61 157 202 230 242

†J. C. Price, S. Nitschke, E. Liddell, J. Hayes (did not bat).

Bowling: Brits 6-0-54-1; Smith 10-1-32-0; Kilowan 8-0-49-0; van der Westhuizen 10-1-38-1; Logtenberg 8-0-38-2; de Beer 5-0-25-0; Fritz 3-1-13-0.

South Africa Women

M. Terblanche b Hayes	15	†S. Pillay not out 11
C. Z. Brits run out (Clark/Price)	49	A. P. C. Kilowan c Nitxchke b Liddell 16
J. Logtenberg run out (Blackwell/Price)	3	L. de Beer not out 3
A. E. Smith b Rolton	3	
S. A. Fritz b Nitschke	20	B 1, l-b 3, w 2 6
*A. L. Hodgkinson lbw b Sthalekar	27	
C. S. Terblanche c Blackwell b Nitschke	1	(49 overs) (9 wkts) 159
C. van der Westhauizen lbw b Fitzpatrick	5	Fall: 44 51 54 84 106 115 118 126 153

Bowling: Fitzpatrick 10-0-26-1; Liddell 8-0-34-1; Sthalekar 7-1-26-1; Hayes 10-1-28-1; Rolton 6-1-9-1; Nitschke 8-0-32-2.

Umpires: L. M. Englebrecht and J. E. P. Ostrom.

Other fourth-round results

India 3 for 141 (A. Chopra 64*, R. Dhar 42*) defeated England 139 (C. M. Edwards 58, A. Brindle 51*; J. Goswami 4-27, N. David 3-23) by seven wickets.

West Indies 2 for 256 (N. Williams 70*, J. Nero 44) defeated Sri Lanka 152 (H. A. S. D. Siriwardene 52, S. P. de Alwis 32; V. Felician 2-13) by 104 runs.

New Zealand 1 for 95 (A. L. Mason 49*, M. A. M. Lewis 39*) defeated Ireland 91 (C. M. Beggs 30; H. M Watson 3-19, L. E. Milliken 2-16, N. Scripps 2-17) by nine wickets.

AUSTRALIA v SRI LANKA

ROUND 5

At L. C. de Villiers Oval, Pretoria, March 30, 2005. Australia won by eight wickets. *Toss:* Australia.

Australia's outing against Sri Lanka was somewhat of a mismatch, which had been predicted following the comprehensive series of defeats inflicted on the Sri Lankans by Australia's youth team earlier in the season. Fewer than 40 overs were needed to wrap up the Sri Lankan innings, with only captain Shashi Siriwardene able to reach double figures. Cathryn Fitzpatrick was rested for the match, but this proved to be no respite for Sri Lanka as they fell to the left-arm spin of Shelley Nitschke, who finished with career-best figures and the player of the match award. Julie Hayes and Emma Liddell each captured two wickets, but bowling figures were flattered to some extent by the unwillingness of the batters to play attacking shots. Australia's reply needed only 17 overs, although both openers were dismissed with only six runs required.

Player of the match: S. Nitschke.

Sri Lanka Women

P. R. C. S. Kumarihami b Hayes 6	L. D. V. V. Silva c Nitschke b Liddell 5
P. M. Udawatte lbw b Liddell 0	A. D. Jakanthymala b Nitschke 4
W. H. D. Fernando c and b Smith 7	†E. M. T. P. Ekanayake not out 0
S. P. de Alwis c Hayes b Sthalekar ... 2	
H. A. S. D. Siriwardene	
c K. A. Blackwell b Nitschke ... 14	W 11, n-b 1 12
*S. K. Dolawatte c Price b A. J. Blackwell 3	
L. E. Kaushalya b Hayes 2	(38.2 overs)　　　　　　　57
S. I. Galagedara c Clark b Nitschke ... 2	Fall: 1 14 17 23 36 40 45 47 57 57

Bowler: Liddell 7.2-2-11-2; Smith 7-3-8-1; Hayes 10-4-14-2; Sthalekar 6-2-11-1; A.J. Blackwell 2-0-8-1; Nitschke 6-3-5-3.

Australia Women

L. M. Keightley b Siriwardene 23	B 1, w 7, n-b 1 9
*B. J. Clark run out	
(Udawatte/Kaushalya/Ekanayake) . 21	
M. Jones not out 4	(16.4 overs)　　　　(2 wkts) 58
L. C. Sthalekar not out 1	Fall: 52 52

A. J. Blackwell, J. Hayes, †J. C. Price, S. Nitschke, E. Liddell, C. R. Smith, K. A. Blackwell (did not bat).

Bowling: Udawatte 6-1-14-0; Jakanthymala 5-0-20-0; Siriwardene 3-0-10-1; Kaushalya 2.4-0-13-0.

Umpires: A. Crafford and D. J. Smith.

Other fifth-round results

England 2 for 180 (C. M. Edwards 99, S. C. Taylor 55*; A. E. Smith 2-35) defeated South Africa 6 for 174 (C. Z. Brits 46, A. E. Smith 31; L. C. Pearson 2-23, I. T. Guha 2-36) by eight wickets.

New Zealand 9 for 184 (S. J. McGlashan 57, A. L. Mason 36; N. David 5-32, N. Al Khader 3-44) defeated India 9 for 168 (M. Raj 52, A. Chopra 48; L. E. Milliken 5-25, N. J. Browne 2-33) by 16 runs.

West Indies 2 for 162 (J. Nero 71*, P. Lavine 66*) defeated Ireland 6 for 159 (C. N. Joyce 37, C. M Beggs 31*; V. Felician 2-22) by eight wickets.

AUSTRALIA v IRELAND

ROUND 6

At Eesterust Cricket Club Ground, Pretoria, April 1, 2005. Australia won by ten wickets. *Toss:* Ireland.

Australia's match against Ireland was almost a carbon copy of the previous round, although the winning total was achieved without the loss of a wicket. Having chosen to bat first, the Irish held out the attack for over half an hour, but once Cathryn Fitzpatrick made the initial breakthrough, wickets tumbled regularly. Once again all of the Australian bowlers took wickets, with Fitzpatrick, Louise Broadfoot and Shelley Nitschke all giving up less than one run per over. Ireland managed to bat through the full 50 overs, but their total of 66 was not a challenge to Australia, who only needed 14 overs for victory. With Lisa Keightley rested, Lisa Sthalekar joined Belinda Clark for some batting practice against a disheartened Ireland attack.

Player of the Match: C. L. Fitzpatrick.

Ireland Women

E. A. Beamish lbw b Fitzpatrick 10	H. Whelan not out 8
†C. N. Joyce lbw b Smith 8	B. M. McDonald c Nitschke b Rolton 1
C. M. Beggs lbw b Liddell 2	J. A. Whelan not out 1
M. E. Grealey c Rolton b Broadfoot .. 21	B 2, w 4 6
*C. M. A. Shillington b Sthalekar 9	
N. J. Coffey c Price b Nitschke 0	(50 overs) (8 wkts) 66
U. G. Budd b Fitzpatrick 0	Fall: 19 21 27 48 55 55 55 62

M.T. Herbert (did not bat).

Bowling: Fitzpatrick 10-5-9-2; Smith 10-3-16-1; Liddell 9-1-13-1; Sthalekar 6-1-15-1, Nitschke 6-3-3-1; Broadfoot 6-4-4-1; Rolton 3-1-4-1.

Australian Women

*B. J. Clark not out 35	
L. C. Sthalekar not out 28	
W 4, n-b 1	5
(14 overs) (0 wkt) 68	

K. L. Rolton, A. J. Blackwell, C. L. Fitzpatrick, †J. C. Price, S. Nitschke, E. Liddell, K. A. Blackwell, L. C. Broadfoot, C. R. Smith (did not bat).

Bowling: H. Whelan 3-0-11-0; McDonald 4-0-18-0; Herbert 4-0-22-0; Grealey 3-0-17-0.

Umpires: D. Ntuli and B. M. White.

Other sixth-round results

India 2 for 139 (A. Jain 68*, J. Sharma 47; V. Felician 2-31) defeated West Indies 135 (P. Lavine 43, N. George 33; J. Goswami 4-16, N. David 3-11) by eight wickets.

Sri Lanka 158 (W. H. D. Fernando 78*, S. P. de Alwis 32; C. van der Westhuizen 2-26, A. E. Smith 2-32) defeated South Africa 126 (J. Logtenburg 39; S. P. de Alwis 3-19, A. D. Jakanthymala 2-18) by 32 runs.

New Zealand 5 for 180 (H. M. Tiffen 43, S. J. McGlashan 35, M. A. M. Lewis 30; N. J. Shaw 2-22) defeated England 6 for 179 (S. C. Taylor 46, A. Brindle 42, L. K. Newton 30) by five wickets.

AUSTRALIA v INDIA

ROUND 7

At Laudium Oval, Tshwane, Pretoria, April 3, 2005. Match abandoned.

All other seven matches were washed out without a ball being bowled.

POINTS TABLE

	Played	Won	Lost	No-Result	Bonus	Points	Net Run-Rate
Australia	7	5	0	2	4	35	2.041
India	7	4	1	2	3	30	1.059
New Zealand	7	4	1	2	2	29	0.872
England	7	3	2	2	3	26	1.493
West Indies	7	2	3	2	2	19	−0.221
Sri Lanka	7	1	4	2	1	12	−1.930
South Africa	7	1	4	2	0	11	−1.065
Ireland	7	0	5	2	0	6	−2.621

(Net run-rate was calculated by subtracting runs conceded per over from runs scored per over. One bonus point was awarded for scoring at a rate in excess of 25 per cent faster than the opposition.)

AUSTRALIA v ENGLAND

First Semi-Final

At Sedgars Park, Potchefstroom, April 5, 2005. Australia won by five wickets. *Toss:* Australia.

Having missed their opportunity to complete a match against England in the first round, Australia relished the chance to test themselves in the semi-final. After being invited to bat by Belinda Clark, the English were quickly in trouble at 3 for 21 in the seventh over, all three wickets falling to a rampant Cathryn Fitzpatrick. Clare Connor and Arran Brindle stabilised the innings with a partnership of 59 before a middle-order collapse saw five wickets fall for only 26 runs. The final three batters added respectability to the total before the innings concluded in the 50th over. For the fourth consecutive match, all Australia's bowlers were successful in taking at least one wicket. The Australian reply was well paced, and based on a patient half-century by Clark, who shared a series of partnerships which gradually wore down the England bowlers. Lisa Sthalekar took over after Clark was dismissed by Isa Guha, and the finishing touches were added by Fitzpatrick and Alex Blackwell as the target was reached with three overs in hand. England were disappointed not to reach their fourth World Cup final, but were at least glad to have bettered their 2000 position of fifth.

Player of the match: B. J. Clark

England Women

C. M. Edwards c Price b Fitzpatrick	13		C. E. Taylor b Rolton	13
L. K. Newton b Fitzpatrick	4		I. T. Guha b Rolton	13
S. C. Taylor c Price b Fitzpatrick	0		K. H. Brunt not out	8
*C. J. Connor lbw b Hayes	35			
A. Brindle st Price b Nitschke	32		L-b 5, w 7, n-b 1	13
N. J. Shaw c Price b Nitschke	3			
J. L. Gunn b Sthalekar	4		(49.4 overs)	158
†J. Smit lbw b Rolton	4		Fall: 16 20 21 80 91 96 96 106 131 158	

Bowling: Fitzpatrick 10-2-27-3; Liddell 8.4-3-28-1; Hayes 10-3-27-1; Rolton 9-3-28-2; Nitschke 7-0-22-2; Sthalekar 5-0-21-1.

Australia Women

L. M. Keightley run out (Brindle)	4		C. L. Fitzpatrick not out	13
*B. J. Clark c and b Guha	62			
K. L. Rolton run out (Brindle)	14		L-b 2, w 10	12
M. Jones b Connor	15			
L. C. Sthalekar run out (Gunn)	29		(47 overs) (5 wkts)	159
A. J. Blackwell not out	10		Fall: 12 47 92 123 143	

†J. C. Price, J. Hayes, S. Nitschke, E. Liddell (did not bat)

Bowling: Brunt 9-2-28-0; Gunn 6-1-31-0; Guha 10-1-33-1; Connor 10-3-24-1; C. E. Taylor 10-1-31-0; Shaw 1-0-6-0; Brindle 1-0-4-0.

Umpires: Z. Ndamane and G. Pienaar.

INDIA v NEW ZEALAND

Second Semi-Final

At Sedgars Park, Potchefstroom, April 7, 2005. India won by 40 runs. *Toss:* New Zealand. India 6 for 204 (M. Raj 91*, A. Chopra 44; R. J. Pullar 4-39); New Zealand 164 (M. Fahey 73*, S. J. McGlashan 23; A. Sharma 3-24, N. Al Khader 3-39, N. David 2-28).

AUSTRALIA v INDIA

FINAL

At Supersport Park, Centurion, April 10, 2005. Australia won by 98 runs. *Toss:* Australia.

Having finished top of the table, Australia enjoyed the luxury of a four-day break before taking on first-time finalists India in the battle for supremacy in women's cricket. Australia were at top strength, while India were hampered by an injury to captain and star batter Mithali Raj, who had injured her knee while fielding in the semi-final. Raj took the field but was clearly not fully fit. Australia had no hesitation in batting first on a good, firm pitch. Belinda Clark, in her third and probably last World Cup final, was keen to get on with the job of compiling an unreachable total, but she feathered a catch to wicket-keeper Anju Jain from the bowling of Amita Sharma when the score was only

24. She was soon joined in the pavilion by Lisa Keightley, who edged a low catch to Rumeli Dhar from Jhulan Goswami. A cautious Karen Rolton was joined by Melanie Jones, and together they took the score to 71 before Jones attempted a sweep shot and was trapped in front by veteran spinner Neetu David. This brought Lisa Sthalekar to the crease, and she proved the perfect foil for Rolton, who grew in confidence and aggression as the innings progressed. Rolton's shot-making was complemented by Sthalekar's deft placement for singles and twos. When Sthalekar was finally dismissed, the pair had added 139 – a record against India – and Rolton had reached a well-deserved century – the first ever in a formal World Cup final. The Australians were aided by some sloppy fielding by India, who showed the effects of both nervousness and fatigue at the end of a long tournament. India's reply was cautious, and nerves showed again when Jaya Sharma and Anju Jain found themselves at the same end after Jain did not respond to a call from her partner. The easy run-out seemed to demoralise the Indians, and they fell further and further behind the required run-rate. Jain chipped a simple catch to mid-wicket, leaving India's hopes resting with Anjum Chopra and the injured Raj. Neither was able to take control of the experienced Australian attack, and the frustration of not being able to pierce the field took its toll in rash shots and poor running between the wickets. Clark and Julie Hayes hit the stumps to run out Chopra and Dhar, while Rolton brilliantly fielded a throw from Sthalekar to break the stumps with Hemlata Kala short of her crease. With little hope remaining, Amita Sharma and Goswami shared in the highest partnership of the innings, but when Shelley Nitschke bowled Nooshin Al Khader, the final total was almost 100 runs short of the target. Australia were justifiably jubilant at their achievement, and their victory was doubly sweet for the seven players who had been on the losing side in the 2000 final.

Player of the Match: K. L. Rolton. *Player of the Tournament:* K. L. Rolton.

Australian Women

*B. J. Clark c Jain b A. Sharma	19
L. M. Keightley c Dhar b Goswami	5
K. L. Rolton not out	107
M. Jones lbw b David	17
L. C. Sthalekar c and b Dhar	55
A. J. Blackwell not out	4
L-b 2, w 2, n-b 4	8
(50 overs) (4 wkts)	215
Fall: 24 31 71 210	

C. L. Fitzpatrick, †J. C. Price, J. Hayes, S. Nitschke, C. R. Smith (did not bat).

Bowling: Goswami 9-2-45-1; A. Sharma 10-2-39-1; Dhar 6-0-34-1; Al Khader 10-1-35-0; David 10-1-39-1; Marathe 5-0-21-0.

India Women

†A. Jain c Sthalekar b Smith	29
J. Sharma run out (Sthalekar/Price)	5
A. Chopra run out (Hayes)	10
*M. Raj lbw b Nitschke	6
R. Dhar run out (Clark)	6
H. Kala run out (Sthalekar/Rolton)	3
A. Sharma lbw b Sthalekar	22
J. Goswami c (sub) K. A. Blackwell b Fitzpatrick	18
D. M. Marathe not out	7
N. David b Fitzpatrick	0
N. Al Khader b Nitschke	0
B 2, l-b 3, w 5, n-b 1	11
(46 overs)	117
Fall: 14 39 54 59 63 64 93 115 116 117	

Bowling: Fitzpatrick 8-1-23-2; Smith 10-4-20-1; Hayes 10-1-28-0; Nitschke 9-2-14-2; Rolton 5-1-9-0; Sthalekar 4-1-18-1.

Umpires: S. George and Z. Ndamane.

AUSTRALIA UNDER-23s TOUR OF SRI LANKA

L. Poulton (NSW) (captain), K. A. Blackwell (NSW) (vice-captain), S. J. Andrews (NSW), K. M. Applebee (Vic), S. E. Aley (NSW), L. Bates (Qld), S. J. Edwards (Vic), J. Hunter (Vic), K. E. Pike (Qld), J. M. Purves (Qld), L. N. Stammers (W Aust), J. L. Woerner (S Aust), L. Wright (NSW).

In an innovative move for the two countries, the first tour of Sri Lanka by an Australian side was undertaken by the Under-23s team, a proven breeding ground for the senior Australian side. Led by the New South Wales pair of Leah Poulton and Kate Blackwell, the young Australians remained undefeated throughout, with one match drawn because of rain. The visitors dominated in all areas, with strong batting performances from Julie Woerner, Sarah Edwards and Poulton complemented by the fine bowling of Kirsten Pike, Sarah Andrews and Julie Hunter and an accomplished fielding display by all members of the team. Blackwell, who contributed valuably with both bat and ball, was rewarded for her versatility with selection in the senior side for the remainder of the summer, and it is likely that a number of members of this talented group will join her before too long.

At Kettarama International Ground, Colombo, September 1, 2004. Australia Under-23s won by nine wickets. *Toss:* Australia Under-23s. Sri Lanka 102 (J. Hunter 5-30, S. J. Andrews 2-21); Australia Under-23s 1 for 105 (J. L. Woerner 58*).

At Kettarama International Ground, Colombo, September 4, 2004. Australia Under-23s won by 60 runs. *Toss:* Australia Under-23s. Australia Under-23s 9 for 215 (J. L. Woerner 50, K. M. Applebee 35, J. M. Purves 30; S. K. Dolewatte 3-39, H. A. S. D. Siriwardene 2-30, S. P. de Alwis 2-45); Sri Lanka 9 for 155 (N. M. Kaushalya 41; S. J. Andrews 3-44, K. E. Pike 2-25).

At Moratuwa International Ground, Colombo, September 6, 2004. Match drawn. *Toss:* Sri Lanka. Australia Under-23s 5 for 133 (S. J. Edwards 51, L. Poulton 48; S. P. de Alwis 2-18); Sri Lanka 1 for 5.

At Moratuwa International Ground, Colombo, September 8, 2004. Australia Under-23s won by 157 runs. *Toss:* Australia Under-23s. Australia Under-23s 9 for 244 (J. L. Woerner 39, L. Poulton 33, S. J. Andrews 31*, S. E. Aley 30; R. A. I. Dilrukshi 4-37, S. Fernando 2-38); Sri Lanka A 87 (K. A. Blackwell 4-8, K. E. Pike 3-15, L. Poulton 2-10).

At Kettarama International Ground, Colombo, September 10, 11, 12, 2004. Australia Under-23s won by 140 runs. *Toss:* Australia Under-23s. Australia Under-23s 234 (S. J. Edwards 97, J. Hunter 44; H. A. S. D. Siriwardene 4-47, S. P. de Alwis 2-32) and 8 for 150 dec (J. L Woerner 47, L. Poulton 40; S. P. de Alwis 6-36); Sri Lanka 132 (H. A. S. D. Siriwardene 49; S. E. Aley 3-20, S. J. Andrews 3-24) and 112 (S. K. Dolewatte 32; K. E. Pike 3-0, K. A. Blackwell 2-11, L. Bates 2-29).

BOUNDARIES: TOO MUCH REWARD?

There are various factors behind the increasing success of bat over ball, but certainly improving bats and smaller fields (due to boundary ropes) must be having an effect. These are difficult to analyse statistically, but one measurable factor is the increasing proportion of boundary hits. Apart from a brief spell at the peak of the Golden Age (1895 to 1905) where the incidence was over 50%, for most of Test history, about 46-48% of runs were scored as boundaries. In the late 1980s, this proportion began to rise, slowly at first, but passing 52% in the late 1990s, recently reaching 56%.

The change can be illustrated anecdotally. When Chris Gayle hit 317 at St. John's (tiny ground , fast outfield) against South Africa, he hit 37 fours and only 2 threes. When Bob Cowper hit 307 at the MCG in 1966 (big ground, very slow outfield, no boundary ropes), he hit 20 fours and 26 threes. Overall the conditions probably lost Cowper over 50 runs. The ratio of fours to threes at St John's is almost 8 to 1, whereas in Australia it is closer to 4 to 1. Another recent report tells how Hershelle Gibbs used at least 47 different bats in a single year. These bats were needed for no more than 47 innings in senior cricket in 2004, scoring just 1547 runs. Apparently the bats are not rolled or hardened, thus offering more spring and power, but wearing out incredibly quickly.

Cricket has become more entertaining, so perhaps we shouldn't complain, but if scoring levels change permanently, the game loses contact with its traditional standards, and that would be a real loss. The place in history of our leading players will become uncertain.

– CHARLES DAVIS

BOWLERS CELEBRATING A WICKET THAT DIDN'T FALL:
Glenn McGrath and Brett Lee after holding out
for an Ashes draw in Manchester.
Picture by Hamish Blair, Getty Images.

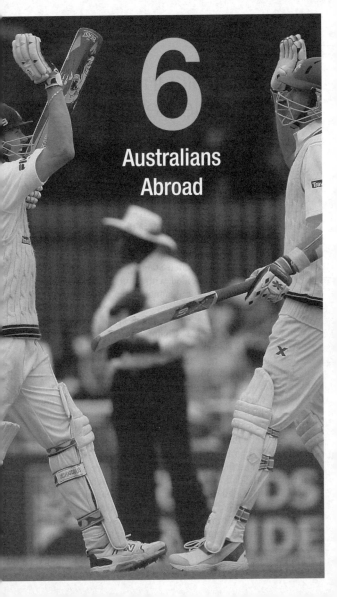

6
Australians
Abroad

Australia in England and the Netherlands, 2004

by GREG BAUM

Somewhere in Australia's bulging trophy cabinet sits the Videocon Cup and an award for the NatWest International, but not the ICC Champions Trophy. These were the obscure spoils of an off-season month spent wandering aimlessly around England and the Netherlands, achieving nothing more than to harden the suspicions that cricket will grow rotten from over-playing. Australia kitted up for seven matches in a month, but the first two were washed out and another was against the United States of America and lasted barely 30 overs. The tour coincided with football finals in all codes in Australia and passed virtually unnoticed in this country.

The Videocon Cup, a triangular series staged in Holland, and the NatWest International, a single match against Pakistan at Lord's, were warm-ups for the ICC Champions Trophy, itself a subsidiary tournament. It was conceived honourably, to create focus between World Cups and to raise funds for the game's development, but at its fourth staging it looked already to have run its race. Australia have never won it, and did not this time, falling in a semi-final to England, who in turn surprisingly succumbed to West Indies in the final – which meant that at least one team went home happy. Officials were pleased enough with an experiment whereby no-balls were called by the third umpire.

But the tournament suffered from poor timing: this was September, and the few worthwhile matches began in the dew and finished in the dark. Weak sides led to mismatches – none of Kenya, the USA, Bangladesh and Zimbabwe managed a win – and the muddle was compounded by botched logistics and marketing, with games played in front of some modest crowds, which managed to create disturbances anyway. Because of television, the tournament was restricted to three grounds. Lord's was not one, but Hampshire's new Rose Bowl was; there, a spectator might take two hours to get to the entrance, whereupon he or she was liable – as at Birmingham and The Oval – to be searched for non-official soft drinks and chips.

The Videocon Cup was just as ill-starred. In Amsterdam's wettest August for more than 90 years, Australia made the final without winning either of the preliminary matches, which were both washed out. The Australians beat Pakistan by a narrow margin in the final, and again a week later in the NatWest International at Lord's. But it is doubtful that Australia's heart was ever in these events: within ten months the side was due back in England for an authentic championship.

AUSTRALIAN TOURING SQUAD

R. T. Ponting (*captain*), D. S. Lehmann (*vice-captain*), M. J. Clarke, J. N. Gillespie, B. J. Haddin, I. J. Harvey, M. L. Hayden, B. J. Hogg, M. S. Kasprowicz, B. Lee, D. R. Martyn, G. D. McGrath, A. Symonds and S. R. Watson.

A. C. Gilchrist (W Aust) did not tour the Netherlands but joined the touring party for the ICC Champions Trophy in England.

Manager: S. R. Bernard. *Coach*: J. M. Buchanan. *Performance Analyst/Assistant coach*: T. J. Nielsen. *Physiotherapist*: E. L. Alcott. *Physical Performance Manager*: J. A. Campbell. *Specialist Fielding and Throwing Consultant*: M. Young. *Media Manager*: J. Rose.

LIMITED-OVERS INTERNATIONAL RUN-SCORERS

	M	I	NO	R	HS	100s	50s	Avge	Ct/St	S-R
M. L. Hayden	6	6	0	227	59	0	2	37.83	4	63.94
A. Symonds	6	5	2	223	104*	1	1	74.33	0	108.78
D. R. Martyn	6	5	2	169	65	0	2	56.33	1	74.45
M. J. Clarke	6	4	0	116	42	0	0	29.00	2	122.11
R. T. Ponting	6	4	1	106	29	0	0	21.20	0	68.39
D. S. Lehmann	6	4	0	106	40	0	0	26.50	2	67.09
A. C. Gilchrist	3	3	1	65	37	0	0	32.50	2/0	81.25
B. J. Haddin	3	3	0	28	13	0	0	9.33	5/0	50.00
G. B. Hogg	2	2	1	17	17*	0	0	17.00	0	120.57
B. Lee.............	5	2	1	16	15	0	0	16.00	1	88.89
S. R. Watson.......	2	1	1	7	7*	0	0	–	2	116.67
J. N. Gillespie	5	1	0	0	0	0	0	0.00	1	0.00
M. S. Kasprowicz...	5	1	1	0	0*	0	0	–	3	0.00
G. D. McGrath	5	1	1	0	0*	0	0	–	0	0.00

* Denotes not out.

LIMITED-OVERS INTERNATIONAL WICKET-TAKERS

	O	Mdns	R	W	BB	5Wi	Avge	RPO
M. S. Kasprowicz.......	36.2	3	145	12	5-47	1	12.08	3.99
J. N. Gillespie.........	40	4	141	9	4-15	0	15.67	3.53
B. Lee...............	30.3	1	182	5	2-65	0	36.40	5.97
G. D. McGrath	31.1	2	110	4	3-39	0	27.50	3.53
A. Symonds	28	4	119	4	2-25	0	29.75	4.25
D. S. Lehmann	26	0	104	3	2-36	0	34.67	4.00
G. B. Hogg...........	7	0	43	1	1-43	0	43.00	6.14
M. J. Clarke	2	0	13	0	–	0	–	6.50
S. R. Watson..........	15	0	79	0	–	0	–	5.27

Note: Matches in this section were official limited-over internationals.

VIDEOCON TROPHY

INDIA v PAKISTAN

At VRA Ground, Amstelveen, August 21, 2004. Pakistan won by 66 runs. Pakistan 6 for 192 (Shoaib Malik 68, Abdul Razzaq 35*; L. Balaji 3-27); India 127 (V. V. S. Laxman 37; Shahid Afridi 4-20, Shoaib Malik 3-18).
  Man of Match: Shoaib Malik (Pakistan).

AUSTRALIA v INDIA

At VRA Ground, Amstelveen, August 23, 2004. No result. *Toss:* Australia.
  Rain reduced Australia's innings to 32 overs, then stopped it two balls short anyway, after which no further play was possible. Balaji used the conditions to move the ball and put Australia off balance until Clarke thumped 42 from 28 balls before he was caught at long-on. None of it mattered.
  Man of Match: No award.

Australia

M. L. Hayden c Ganguly b Balaji	 29	(49)	G. B. Hogg not out 17	(14)
†B. J. Haddin c Balaji b Nehra	 5	(13)	B. Lee not out 1	(1)
*R. T. Ponting lbw b Balaji	 26	(28)		
D. R. Martyn b Sehwag	 12	(17)	B 1, l-b 4, w 6, n-b 1 12	
A. Symonds c Dravid b Kumble	 12	(12)		
D. S. Lehmann c Gavaskar b Kumble	. 19	(29)	(31.4 overs, 141 mins) (7 wkts) 175	
M. J. Clarke c Sehwag b Balaji	 42	(28)	Fall: 23 69 70 83 101 138 169	

M. S. Kasprowicz, G. D. McGrath (did not bat).

Bowling: Pathan 6.4–0–34–0; Nehra 6–0–44–1; Sehwag 6–0–35–1; Balaji 6–0–20–3; Kumble 7–0–37–2.

India

V Sehwag, *S. C. Ganguly, V. V. S. Laxman, †R. S. Dravid, Yuvraj Singh, M. Kaif, R. S. Gavaskar, I. K. Pathan, L. Balaji, A. R. Kumble and A. Nehra.

Umpires: S. A. Bucknor (West Indies) and J. W. Lloyds (England).
TV Umpire: D. R. Shepherd (England).
Referee: B. C. Broad (England).

AUSTRALIA v PAKISTAN

At VRA Ground, Amstelveen, August 25, 2004. Match abandoned without a ball bowled.

Australia made the final without bowling a ball. The organisers proposed to reschedule the two washed-out games and postpone the final by a day, but Australia baulked; there was the Champions Trophy to play in England, after all.

Umpires: S. A. Bucknor (West Indies) and J. W. Lloyds (England).
TV Umpire: D. R. Shepherd (England).
Referee: B. C. Broad (England).

FINAL

AUSTRALIA v PAKISTAN

At VRA Ground, Amstelveen, August 28, 2004. Australia won by 17 runs. *Toss:* Australia.

Australia won their fifth successive one-day tournament in a final that was delayed 90 minutes by drizzle and never really got going after that. Mohammad Sami contained Australia at the beginning, but a partnership of 61 between Hayden and Lehmann liberated Symonds to swing lustily at the end of the innings. Hayden's 59 was out of character in its circumspection, but Lehmann and Symonds were their usual enterprising selves. The Pakistanis began steadily, then true to type turned on themselves, Yousuf Youhana running out Shoaib Malik and Shahid Afridi in consecutive balls – generosity that Australia would not reciprocate. Pakistan protested at umpire Shepherd's decisions against Youhana and Inzamam-ul-Haq, chairman of selectors Wasim Bari calling them "target killings".

Man of Match: A. Symonds.

Australia

M. L. Hayden c Yasir Hameed b Shoaib Akhtar	59 (114)	M. J. Clarke c Inzamam-ul-Haq b Shoaib Akhtar	1	(2)
†B. J. Haddin b Mohammad Sami	10 (30)	G. B. Hogg run out (Moin Khan)	0	(0)
*R. T. Ponting c Imran Farhat b Abdul Razzaq	25 (45)	B 2, l-b 4, w 5, n-b 4	15	
D. S. Lehmann c Moin Khan b Shabbir Ahmed	40 (66)			
A. Symonds b Shoaib Akhtar	36 (41)	(50 overs, 196 mins) (7 wkts)	192	
D. R. Martyn not out	6 (5)	Fall: 21 65 126 183 189 192 192		

B. Lee, J. N. Gillespie, G. D. McGrath (did not bat).

Bowling: Mohammad Sami 10–1–26–1; Shabbir Ahmed 8–1–25–1; Shoaib Akhtar 10–0–40–3; Abdul Razzaq 8–1–30–1; Shahid Afridi 6–0–20–0; Shoaib Malik 8–0–45–0.

Pakistan

Yasir Hameed b Lee	17	(43)		Mohammad Sami b Lehmann	5	(12)
Imran Farhat c Hayden b Symonds	17	(49)		Shoaib Akhtar c Haddin b McGrath	2	(5)
Shoaib Malik run out				Shabbir Ahmed not out	0	(2)
(Symonds/Lehmann)	36	(58)				
*Inzamam-ul-Haq c Haddin b Symonds	7	(14)		B 6, l-b 2, w 8	16	
Yousuf Youhana c Haddin b Hogg	43	(57)				
Shahid Afridi run out						
(Symonds/Haddin)	0	(0)				
Abdul Razzaq c Clarke b Lehmann	26	(33)		(47.1 overs, 196 mins)	175	
†Moin Khan c Haddin b Gillespie	6	(12)		Fall: 24 47 65 93 93 154 161 171 175 175		

Bowling: McGrath 7.1–1–12–1; Gillespie 9–0–22–1; Lee 7–1–29–1; Hogg 7–0–43–1; Symonds 7–1–25–2; Lehmann 10–0–36–2.

Umpires: S. A. Bucknor (West Indies) and D. R. Shepherd (England).
TV Umpire: M. R. Benson (England).
Referee: B. C. Broad (England).

AUSTRALIA v PAKISTAN

At Lord's Cricket Ground, London, September 4, 2004. Australia won by ten runs. *Toss:* Pakistan.

This match was an addendum to a series between England and India, staged to give Australia and Pakistan practice before the Champions Trophy, but also with an eye on the gate. It was a rematch of the 1999 World Cup final between these sides on this ground. Pakistan fielded five players from that match, but Australia only two (Ponting and Lehmann); they were looking ahead. Australia strained in their traces as the white ball moved around early, until Symonds clubbed a typical century, featuring two chances, much hard hitting and 17 from mercurial Shoaib Akhtar's last over. Kasprowicz's art reduced Pakistan to 4 for 66, but a polished stand of 162 between Inzamam-ul-Haq and Yousuf Youhana brought victory into view. Then Symonds, bowling off-spin, had Inzamam caught, triggering a characteristic and fatal crash.

Man of Match: A. Symonds.

Australia

M. L. Hayden b Shahid Afridi	52	(80)		M. J. Clarke c Shoaib Malik		
				b Shoaib Akhtar	31	(31)
†B. J. Haddin c Shoaib Malik				S. R. Watson not out	7	(6)
b Mohammad Sami	13	(13)		L-b 9, w 12, n-b 2	23	
*R. T. Ponting lbw b Mohammad Sami	4	(5)				
D. R. Martyn c Imran Farhat						
b Shoaib Malik	26	(43)		(50 overs, 205 mins) (6 wkts)	269	
A. Symonds not out	104	(103)		Fall: 19 30 99 109 148 236		
D. S. Lehmann run out (Shoaib Malik)	9	(21)				

B. Lee, M. S. Kasprowicz, J. N. Gillespie (did not bat).

Bowling: Mohammad Sami 10–1–56–2; Naved–ul–Hasan 9–0–46–0; Shoaib Akhtar 8–0–70–1; Abdul Razzaq 4–0–12–0; Shoaib Malik 10–0–36–1; Shahid Afridi 9–0–40–1.

Pakistan

Yasir Hameed c Hayden b Kasprowicz	47	(61)	Naved-ul-Hasan run out (Ponting)	. .	2	(2)
Imran Farhat c Haddin b Lee	11	(16)	Mohammad Sami b Kasprowicz	. . . .	10	(6)
Shahid Afridi lbw b Gillespie	0	(7)	Shoaib Akhtar not out	. . . .	2	(1)
Shoaib Malik c Lee b Kasprowicz	2	(9)				
Inzamam-ul-Haq c Watson b Symonds	72	(84)	L-b 4, w 2, n-b 4		10	
Yousuf Youhana c Watson b Kasprowicz	88	(98)				
Abdul Razzaq c and b Kasprowicz	15	(8)	(48.2 overs, 216 mins)		259	
Moin Khan c Martyn b Gillespie	0	(1)	Fall: 30 45 50 66 228 239 245 247 250 259			

Bowling: Gillespie 8–2–26–2; Lee 10–0–67–1; Kasprowicz 9.2–1–47–5; Lehmann 5–0–24–0; Symonds 5–0–31–1; Watson 9–0–47–0; Clarke 2–0–13–0.

Umpires: S. A. Bucknor (West Indies) and D. R. Shepherd (England).
TV Umpire: J. W. Lloyds (England).
Referee: B. C. Broad (England).

ICC CHAMPIONS TROPHY

NEW ZEALAND v UNITED STATES OF AMERICA

Game 1 – Pool A: At Kennington Oval, London, September 10, 2004. New Zealand won by 210 runs. New Zealand 4 for 347 (N. J. Astle 145*, S. B. Styris 75, C. D. McMillan 64*; R. W. Staple 2-76). United States of America 137 (C. B. Lambert 39; J. D. P. Oram 5-36, D. L. Vettori 3-14).
Man of Match: N. J. Astle (New Zealand).

ENGLAND v ZIMBABWE

Game 1 – Pool D: At Edgbaston, Birmingham, September 10, 11, 2004. England won by 152 runs. England 7 for 299 (V. S. Solanki 62, P. D. Collingwood 80*, G. O. Jones 38; D. T. Hondo 2-66, E. C. Rainsford 2-43); Zimbabwe 147 (T. Taibu 40, E. Chigumbura 42*; D. Gough 2-24, S. J. Harmison 3-29, A. Flintoff 3-11, A. F. Giles 2-35).
Man of Match: P. D. Collingwood (England).

INDIA v KENYA

Game 1 – Pool C: At The Rose Bowl, Southampton, September 11, 2004. India won by 98 runs. India 4 for 290 (S. C. Ganguly 90, V. V. S. Laxman 79, M. Kaif 49*, R. S. Dravid 30*; T. M. Odoyo 2-43); Kenya 7 for 192 (R. D. Shah 33, M. A. Ouma 49, B. J. Patel 40*; I. K. Pathan 2-11, Harbhajan Singh 3-33).
Man of Match: S. C. Ganguly (India).

BANGLADESH v SOUTH AFRICA

Game 1 – Pool B: At Edgbaston, Birmingham, September 12, 2004. South Africa won by nine wickets. Bangladesh 93 (Nafees Iqbal 40; C. K. Langeveldt 3-17, M. Ntini 3-19, N. Boje 3-23). South Africa 1 for 94 (G. C. Smith 42*, J. H. Kallis 40*).
Man of Match: C. K. Langeveldt (South Africa).

AUSTRALIA v UNITED STATES OF AMERICA

Game 2 – Pool A: At The Rose Bowl, Southampton, September 13, 2004. Australia won
by nine wickets. *Toss:* Australia.

Ponting planned a swift kill here, in case of accident or rain when playing New
Zealand, the other team in this group. The outcome was that the USA – in truth a
gathering of ageing Caribbean ex-pats – were bowled out for 65 and Australia picked
off the runs in 7.5 overs, the third-shortest run chase in one-day internationals. The
whole match lasted two hours and 44 minutes. The USA's score, the third-lowest in
Champions Trophy history, included just 26 runs made in front of square, and 14 extras.
Lee struck with his second ball and Kasprowicz and Gillespie helped themselves to four
wickets each. Australia's innings was a series of contemptuously premeditated shots.
Ponting later asked aloud if this tournament was appropriate for a team like the USA;
the crowd of about 500 did not think so.

Man of Match: M. S. Kasprowicz.

United States of America

R. P. Alexander c Gilchrist b Kasprowicz	8	(28)	Nasir Javed not out	2	(19)
†M. R. Johnson b Lee	0	(1)	D. L. Blake lbw b Gillespie	0	(2)
L. C. Romero run out (Martyn)	1	(5)	H. R. Johnson b Gillespie	9	(15)
S. J. Massiah c Lehmann b Kasprowicz	23	(42)			
*R. W. Staple lbw b Kasprowicz	4	(10)	L-b 2, w 7, n-b 5	14	
C. A. Reid lbw b Kasprowicz	2	(6)			
Rashid Zia lbw b Gillespie	1	(16)	(24 overs, 116 mins)	65	
Aijaz Ali c Gilchrist b Gillespie	1	(6)	Fall: 1 2 32 38 46 46 49 53 53 65		

Bowling: Lee 5–0–21–1; McGrath 6–1–13–0; Kasprowicz 7–1–14–4; Gillespie 6–1–15–4.

Australia

†A. C. Gilchrist not out	24	(25)
M. L. Hayden c M. R. Johnson b H. R. Johnson	23	(17)
*R. T. Ponting not out	8	(8)
L-b 1, w 6, n-b 4	11	

(7.5 overs, 33 mins)   (1 wkt) 66
Fall: 41

D. S. Lehmann, A. Symonds, D. R. Martyn, M. J. Clarke, M. S. Kasprowicz, B. Lee, J. N. Gillespie,
G. D. McGrath (did not bat).

Bowling: H. R. Johnson 3–0–26–1; Reid 3–0–26–0; Blake 1–0–7–0; Rashid Zia 0.5–0–6–0.

Umpires: Aleem Dar (Pakistan) and B. F. Bowden (New Zealand).
TV Umpire: S. A. Bucknor (West Indies).
Referee: R. S. Madugalle (Sri Lanka).

SRI LANKA v ZIMBABWE

Game 2 – Pool D: At Kennington Oval, London, September 14, 2004. Sri Lanka won
by four wickets. Zimbabwe 191 (E. Chigumbura 57, P. Utseya 31; D. N. T. Zoysa 3–19,
M. F. Maharoof 3-38, U. D. U. Chandana 2-39); Sri Lanka 6 for 195 (M. S. Atapattu 43,
W. S. Jayantha 36; E. Chigumbura 3-37).

Man of Match: E. Chigumbura (Zimbabwe).

KENYA v PAKISTAN

Game 2 – Pool C: At Edgbaston, Birmingham, September 14, 15, 2004. Pakistan won by seven wickets. Kenya 94 (K. O. Obuya 33; Shoaib Malik 3-15, Shahid Afridi 5-11). Pakistan 3 for 95 (Yasir Hameed 41, Imran Farhat 38*; R. G. Aga 2-17).

Man of Match: Shahid Afridi (Pakistan).

BANGLADESH v WEST INDIES

Game 2 – Pool B: At The Rose Bowl, Southampton, September 15, 2004. West Indies won by 138 runs. West Indies 3 for 269 (C. H. Gayle 99, W. W. Hinds 82, R. R. Sarwan 80*; Tapash Baisya 2-58); Bangladesh 131 (Khaled Mahmud 34*; M. Dillon 5-29, C. H. Gayle 2-12).

Man of Match: C. H. Gayle (West Indies).

AUSTRALIA v NEW ZEALAND

Game 3 – Pool A: At Kennington Oval, London, September 16, 2004. Australia won by seven wickets. *Toss:* Australia.

Symonds' thunderous 71 not out from 47 balls made this victory appear easier than it was. New Zealand's innings was gutted by McGrath's spell of 3 for 3 in 19 balls, but wicket-keeper McCullum's initiative and some stout lower-order resistance allowed the Kiwis to reach nearly 200, a respectable total on a sluggish pitch. McCullum and the always redoubtable Vettori put on 68 for the ninth wicket, a national record. Gilchrist did not last an over, but Hayden, Ponting and Martyn steadily accelerated the innings towards Symonds' crescendo, which included seven fours and four sixes. Sadly, ntemperate Antipodeans invaded the pitch at the end, injuring six security guards.

Man of Match: A. Symonds.

New Zealand

*S. P. Fleming c Gillespie b Kasprowicz	29	(51)	†B. B. McCullum c Kasprowicz		
N. J. Astle lbw b McGrath	18	(19)	b Gillespie	47	(68)
H. J. H. Marshall lbw b McGrath	0	(2)	D. L. Vettori not out	29	(42)
S. B. Styris c Clarke b McGrath	0	(11)	K. D. Mills not out	3	(3)
C. D. McMillan run out					
(Symonds/Kasprowicz)	18	(27)			
J. D. P. Oram c and b Kasprowicz	15	(27)	L-b 4, w 7, n-b 2	13	
C. L. Cairns lbw b Kasprowicz	0	(1)			
C. Z. Harris c and b Lehmann	26	(51)	(50 overs, 204 mins) (9 wkts)	198	
			Fall: 30 36 49 49 79 79 89 124 192		

Bowling: McGrath 10–0–39–3; Gillespie 9–1–46–1; Kasprowicz 10–1–32–3; Watson 6–0–32–0; Symonds 10–2–29–0; Lehmann 5–0–16–1.

Australia

†A. C. Gilchrist b Oram	4	(5)
M. L. Hayden c Cairns b Harris	47	(74)
*R. T. Ponting b Styris	14	(28)
D. R. Martyn not out	60	(71)
A. Symonds not out	71	(47)

L-b 1, w 1, n-b 1 3

(37.2 overs, 132 mins)   (3 wkts) 199

Fall: 4 49 99

D. S. Lehmann, M. J. Clarke, M. S. Kasprowicz, S. R. Watson, J. N. Gillespie, G. D. McGrath (did not bat).

Bowling: Oram 9–2–34–1; Mills 5.2–0–34–0; Vettori 10–0–52–0; Styris 2–0–9–1; Cairns 3–0–17–0; Harris 7–1–36–1; McMillan 1–0–16–0.

Umpires: S. A. Bucknor (West Indies) and R. E. Koertzen (South Africa).
TV Umpire: D. R. Shepherd (England).
Referee: R. S. Madugalle (Sri Lanka).

ENGLAND v SRI LANKA

Game 3 – Pool D: At The Rose Bowl, Southampton, September 17, 18, 2004. England won by 49 runs (D-L Method). England 7 for 251 (M. E. Trescothick 66, A. Flintoff 104, P. D. Collingwood 39; W. P. U. J. C. Vaas 2-51); Sri Lanka 5 for 95 (S. J. Harmison 2-21, A. Flintoff 2-21).
Man of Match: A. Flintoff (England).

SOUTH AFRICA v WEST INDIES

Game 3 – Pool B: At Kennington, London, September 18, 19, 2004. West Indies won by five wickets. South Africa 6 for 246 (G. C. Smith 45, H. H. Gibbs 101, J. A. Rudolph 46; I. D. R. Bradshaw 2-40, C. H. Gayle 3-50); West Indies 5 for 249 (R. R. Sarwan 75, B. C. Lara 49, S. Chanderpaul 51*; S. M. Pollock 2-56, M. Ntini 2-26).
Man of Match: R. R. Sarwan (West Indies).

INDIA v PAKISTAN

Game 3 – Pool C: At Edgbaston, Birmingham, September 19, 2004. Pakistan won by three wickets. India 200 (R. S. Dravid 67, A. B. Agarkar 47; Naved-ul-Hasan 4-25, Shoaib Akhtar 4-36); Pakistan 7 for 201 (Inzamam-ul-Haq 41, Yousuf Youhana 81*; I. K. Pathan 3-34).
Man of Match: Yousuf Youhana (Pakistan).

QUALIFYING POINTS TABLES

Pool A	Played	Won	Lost	Points	Net Run-rate
Australia	2	2	0	4	+3.237
New Zealand	2	1	1	2	+1.603
United States of America	2	0	2	0	−5.121

Pool B	Played	Won	Lost	Points	Net Run-rate
West Indies	2	2	0	4	+1.471
South Africa	2	1	1	2	+1.552
Bangladesh	2	0	2	0	−3.111

Pool C	Played	Won	Lost	Points	Net Run-rate
Pakistan	2	2	0	4	+1.413
India	2	1	1	2	+0.944
Kenya	2	0	2	0	−2.747

Pool D	Played	Won	Lost	Points	Net Run-rate
England	2	2	0	4	+2.716
Sri Lanka	2	1	1	2	−0.252
Zimbabwe	2	0	2	0	−1.885

FIRST SEMI-FINAL

ENGLAND v AUSTRALIA

At Edgbaston, Birmingham, September 21, 2004. England won by six wickets. *Toss:* England.

England beat Australia for the first time in 15 one-dayers, spanning more than five years, and hoped then that it was a presentiment of good times to come. The match was a personal triumph for Vaughan, the captain, who on a sleepy pitch was able to bowl his full quota of off-spinners as Australia made struggling progress to 9 for 259. Vaughan then put on 140 for England's second wicket with Trescothick, who hit McGrath for four fours in an over, after which it was left only for Strauss to make an impressive introduction to the Australians. Both teams were careful publicly not to read too much into this result for the Ashes. The day was cold, but the crowd of just 8,700 was a bitter disappointment; for the fans, this was at best a forerunner.

Man of Match: M. P. Vaughan.

Australia

A. C. Gilchrist c Trescothick b Gough	37	(50)
M. L. Hayden c Trescothick b Harmison	17	(21)
R. T. Ponting c Gough b Giles	29	(41)
D. R. Martyn c Trescothick b Vaughan	65	(91)
D. S. Lehmann b Vaughan	38	(42)
A. Symonds run out (Vaughan)	0	(2)
M. J. Clarke b Flintoff	42	(34)
B. Lee b Gough	15	(17)
J. N. Gillespie b Gough	0	(1)
M. S. Kasprowicz not out	0	(2)
G. D. McGrath not out	0	(1)
B 3, l-b 4, w 7, n-b 2	16	
(50 overs, 209 mins) (9 wkts)	259	

Fall: 44 69 114 189 190 210 249 249 258

Bowling: Gough 7–1–48–3; Harmison 10–0–53–1; Flintoff 10–0–56–1; Giles 10–0–40–1; Wharf 3–0–13–0; Vaughan 10–0–42–2.

England

M. E. Trescothick b Symonds	.... 81 (88)	P. D. Collingwood not out	.... 6 (4
V. S. Solanki lbw b Gillespie	.... 7 (18)	L-b 5, w 5, n-b 4	 14
*M. P. Vaughan c Hayden b Lee	..... 86 (122)		
A. J. Strauss not out	.... 52 (42)	(46.3 overs, 194 mins) (4 wkts) 262	
A. Flintoff c Hayden b Lee	.... 16 (9)	Fall: 21 161 227 249	

†G. O. Jones, A. G. Wharf, A. F. Giles, D. Gough, S. J. Harmison (did not bat).

Bowling: McGrath 8–0–46–0; Gillespie 8–0–32–1; Kasprowicz 10–0–52–0; Lee 8.3–0–65–2
Lehmann 6–0–28–0; Symonds 6–1–34–1.

Umpires: B. F. Bowden (New Zealand) and R. E. Koertzen (South Africa).
TV Umpire: Aleem Dar (Pakistan).
Referee: M. J. Procter (South Africa).

SECOND SEMI-FINAL

WEST INDIES v PAKISTAN

At The Rose Bowl, Southampton, September 22, 2004. West Indies won by seve
wickets. Pakistan 131 (Yasir Hameed 39; C. D. Collymore 2-24, D. J. J. Bravo 2-4
W. W. Hinds 2-27); West Indies 3 for 132 (R. R. Sarwan 56*, B. C. Lara 31; Shoai
Akhtar 2-18).

Man of Match: R. R. Sarwan (West Indies).

FINAL

ENGLAND v WEST INDIES

At Kennington Oval, London, September 25, 2004. West Indies won by two wickets
England 217 (M. E. Trescothick 104, A. F. Giles 31; I. D. R. Bradshaw 2-54
W. W. Hinds 3-24). West Indies 8 for 218 (S. Chanderpaul 47, C. O. Browne 35*
I. D. R. Bradshaw 34*; S. J. Harmison 2-34, A. Flintoff 3-38, P. D. Collingwood 2-22
Man of Match: I. D. R. Bradshaw. *Man of the Series*: R. R. Sarwan (West Indies).

Australia in India,
2004-05

by SAMBIT BAL

n time, the story of Australia's fulfilment in India in 2004-05 will cquire its own legends. It didn't quite turn out to be the titanic truggle that was anticipated. In a sense, the series was doomed by xpectations: after the miracle-filled contest in 2000-01 and the grand spectacle of 2003-04, anything short of a celestial showdown vould have seemed a letdown.

But Australia, seeking their first series victory in India for 35 years and the validation of their status as the pre-eminent team of heir era, would let nothing distract them from their goal. In the end t was as much a triumph of Australia's ambition and their will as it vas of their skill.

They would not be denied this time because they left nothing to chance. Sanjay Manjrekar, who commentated on the series, tells an anecdote that speaks volumes about Australia's resolve. One look at he playing surface at Mumbai, the venue for the last Test, was enough to persuade anyone not to bother buying a ticket for the ourth day. Before the game, Manjrekar asked Glenn McGrath what he made of the pitch. 'Maybe it's a cross-seam pitch again,' McGrath responded nonchalantly, implying that the fast bowlers vould have to hold the seam at right angles to the fingers to let the ball grip on an abrasive pitch, as they had done at Bangalore and Chennai.

Australia went on to lose the Test, which lasted barely two days and yielded 29 wickets to spinners – six of those for nine runs to Michael Clarke – but McGrath's refusal to be concerned by the state of the wicket underlined the essence of Australia's campaign. Many visiting sides have lost Tests in India even before they began playing, by allowing themselves to be daunted by the look of the pitch, by the weather or by the crowds. Australia would let nothing deter or distract them this time – not even their own impetuosity.

If there was any consolation for India, who had been beaten in a home Test series only once since 1986-87, and who went into the series with the genuine hope of installing themselves as the second ranking Test side in the world, it was that they had forced Australia to change their game. Adam Gilchrist, who captained Australia in the first three Tests in the absence of Ricky Ponting – who was nursing a broken thumb – paid India a high compliment by saying that Australia had learnt from India's performances against them. " didn't know what losing a Test felt like then," he said about his pre vious tour to India. "This time we have come knowing what it is to win and what it is to lose."

There were lessons from Adelaide 2003, too, where Australia had watched India retrieve a hopeless situation and then walk away to a famous win. India won that Test because they refused to be hustled and in Rahul Dravid and V.V.S. Laxman they had two players will ing to bat for a long time. Australia lost because they could not when the situation demanded, practise the art of withdrawal.

Great teams don't repeat their mistakes. On this tour, Australia refused to be hostage to their own aura; instead, they waited India out. No one exemplified this better than Gilchrist. The first sign came in Australia's opening tour match against Mumbai where he studiously played down the ground to the spinners. In the first Test at Bangalore, he walked out to bat when the match was still in the balance at 5 for 256, and India promptly set up the sweep trap with men back at square leg and mid-wicket, and a short fine leg for the top edge. Gilchrist's first sweep didn't come until he had scored 87 By his standards, it was a measured and patient innings. And by the time he was out at 6 for 423, Australia had reached an unassailable position.

Intimidation was forsaken in favour of caution on the field, too where Australia chose to strangle rather than decimate their oppo nents. It wasn't a conservative approach – rather, it was realistic born of respect for the conditions and for the opponents. Gone was the arrogant slip cordon. On pitches where edges were hardly likely to carry, the Australians set deep fields and homed in on the stumps

Straight off, there was a point halfway to the fence for Virender Sehwag and two men on the leg for Laxman. No Indian batsman was given room to free his hand. Dravid, who had been in resplen dent form during India's tour of Australia, was pinned down by relentless in-cutters pitching just outside the off stump. There was ardly a full ball from McGrath or Jason Gillespie, and Shane Warne didn't let his desperation to succeed in India distract him from team tactics. To all the top-order batsmen, he bowled quicker and flatter; only Sehwag, who had the form and the courage, managed to collar him.

Two balls in the first Test put in perspective the success of the Indian batsmen in Australia. The first, from McGrath, pitched on a length 15 centimetres outside Dravid's off stump, cut in sharply and found its way between bat and pad on to the stumps. The second, from Warne, pitched 15 centimetres outside Laxman's leg stump, spun past his groping bat and took off. Two magic balls and India's miracle workers were gone. Dravid ended the series with 162 runs, scored off 612 balls at a strike-rate of 27.28, while Laxman managed just 123 at an average of 17.57.

Warne's return of 14 wickets from three Tests was far from spectacular, but unlike Stuart MacGill, who was a perennial source of boundary balls in the previous series, he gave no leeway to the Indian top order. McGrath, who had also been missing during India's tour of Australia, made the biggest difference. India's batting success in the previous series was built on solid opening partnerships provided by the flamboyant Sehwag and the obdurate Aakash Chopra. McGrath allowed no such luxuries here, stamping his mark at the start of the series with two wickets in his first two overs and another wicket in the third over of the second innings. India's opening partnerships in the series read: 0, 1, 28, 31, 1, 11 and 5.

Australia were also helped by the presence of batsmen who didn't freeze in their tracks at the sight of a turning ball. Although Matthew Hayden could not quite repeat his success of 2000-01, Michael Clarke, Simon Katich and Damien Martyn responded magnificently. Ponting's absence became a blessing as it gave Clarke his debut in Bangalore. Light on his feet and supple with his wrists, he made a stunning entry into Test cricket. The Indian spinners expected the Australian batsmen to sweep, but Clarke and Katich met them down the pitch and adjusted their strokes at the last instant. Although India had seen a bit of Katich at Sydney in 2004 and flashes of Clarke in one-day cricket, these two were peripheral to India's game-plan before the series started. Once they assumed central roles, India ran out of ideas.

Australia wouldn't have won the series without Martyn. With contrasting hundreds at Chennai and Nagpur, he first denied India certain victory and then placed Australia on the road to a win Martyn has always been a beautiful batsman to watch, and he is a worthy successor to Mark Waugh whose No. 4 position he has come to occupy. Surprisingly, perhaps, having spent his learning years on the hard, lightning-fast pitches of Perth, he has emerged as Australia's most consummate player of spin bowling in the subcontinent. His hundreds against Muttiah Muralidaran were vital to Australia breaking their 12-year drought in Sri Lanka, and his second-innings century at Chennai against Anil Kumble and Harbhajan Singh was a masterful effort in diligent defence and sublime strokeplay. He got off to a dreadful start in the series, jabbing a catch to short leg after advancing down the track to Kumble, but he learned his lesson quickly. Unlike Clarke and Katich, he stayed back in the crease, watched every ball on to his bat and dropped them dead at his feet with soft hands. But he was forever alert to any lapse in line and length, cutting and driving off the back foot with relish. Unseasonal rain scuppered what could have been a classic in Chennai, but while India held the reins for much of the Test Martyn, it must be said, had given Australia a fair shot at a win Luck, Indian supporters would argue, deserted the home team for most of the series. They got the rough end of umpiring decisions in Bangalore, were denied a shot at equalling the series by the weather, and at Nagpur were caught in the middle of a political battle between the local cricket association and the powers-that-be at the Board of Control for Cricket in India which ensured a lively pitch that – to put in mildly – suited the Australians infinitely more than it did the Indians.

To be honest, it was the best pitch of the series: there was carry and there was movement off the pitch, but the bounce was true and the pace even, and batsmen, if they got into their groove, got full value for their strokes. But the Indians, smarting from being denied in Chennai, allowed themselves to be consumed by negativity at the sight of grass on the pitch. They were not helped by the mysterious withdrawal at the eleventh hour of Sourav Ganguly, who after failing to persuade the curator to shave off the grass, went home citing a muscle tear which was diagnosed, uncharitably, as "green-wickets" by a member of the Indian think-tank.

The 2-1 scoreline and the rained-out draw could be advanced to suggest a close contest. Indeed, the series could have been 2-2. Bu t could very well have been 3-1 to Australia. India were crushed at Bangalore and Nagpur, and won on a pitch unfit for Test cricket in Mumbai.

India were outsmarted and outplayed by a team that conceived and executed a plan to perfection. Thirty-five years was a long wait, and Australia made sure they were not denied. Gilchrist couldn't hold back his tears after his side had sealed the series in Nagpur – it meant that much to Australia. It would not be remembered as a great series, but as one where a great team overcame its final challenge.

AUSTRALIAN TOURING SQUAD

R. T. Ponting (*captain*), A. C. Gilchrist (*vice-captain*), M. J. Clarke, J. N. Gillespie, M. L. Hayden, N. M. Hauritz, S. M. Katich, M. S. Kasprowicz, D. R. Martyn, G. D. McGrath, J. L. Langer, B. Lee, D. S. Lehmann, S. K. Warne, S. R. Watson, C. L. White.
B. J. Hodge – added September 23rd to cover for injured Ponting.
Manager: S. R. Bernard. *Coach*: J. M. Buchanan. *Assistant coach*: T. J. Nielsen. *Physiotherapist*: E. Alcott. *Masseur*: Ms L. Frostick. *Physical performance manager*: J. A. Campbell. *Yoga and massage consultant*: K. Turner. *Performance manager*: B. Romalus. *Media Manager*: J. Rose.

AUSTRALIAN TOUR RESULTS

Test matches – Played 3: Won 2, Lost 1, Drawn 1.
First-class matches – Played 4, Won 2, Lost 1, Drawn 2.
Wins – India (2). Losses – India (1), Draws – Mumbai (1).

TEST BATTING AVERAGES

	M	I	NO	R	HS	100s	50s	Avge	Ct/St	S-R
A. B. Agarkar (India)	1	2	1	59	44*	0	0	59.00	1	72.84
M. J. Clarke (Aust). .	4	8	1	400	151	1	2	57.14	7	55.25
D. R. Martyn (Aust) .	4	8	0	444	114	2	2	55.50	2	50.40
V. Sehwag (India) . .	4	8	1	299	155	1	1	42.71	0	68.89
S. M. Katich (Aust) .	4	8	1	276	99	0	2	39.43	1	46.94
I. K. Pathan (India). .	2	3	0	100	55	0	1	33.33	0	33.33
P. A. Patel (India). . .	3	5	0	156	54	0	1	31.20	7/1	41.38
A. C. Gilchrist (Aust)	4	8	1	218	104	1	0	31.14	16/0	78.14
M. Kaif (India)	3	5	0	153	64	0	2	30.60	7	40.26
M. L. Hayden (Aust)	4	8	0	244	58	0	1	30.50	3	55.58
J. L. Langer (Aust) . .	4	8	0	228	71	0	2	28.50	1	44.19
R. S. Dravid (India) .	4	7	1	167	60	0	1	27.83	13	27.29
D. S. Lehmann (Aust)	3	5	0	132	70	0	1	26.40	1	72.93
S. C. Ganguly (India)	2	3	0	59	45	0	0	19.67	0	49.58
V. V. S. Laxman (India)	4	7	0	123	69	0	1	17.57	6	48.43
S. R. Tendulkar (India)	2	4	0	70	55	0	1	17.50	1	41.92
A. R. Kumble (India)	4	7	2	86	26	0	0	17.20	2	40.57
Yuvraj Singh (India)	2	4	1	47	27	0	0	15.67	6	34.31
Harbhajan Singh (India)	3	5	0	69	42	0	0	13.80	5	55.20
J. N. Gillespie (Aust)	4	7	2	66	26	0	0	13.20	0	18.23

	M	I	NO	R	HS	100s	50s	Avge	Ct/St	S-R
Zaheer Khan (India).	4	7	3	47	25	0	0	11.75	0	82.46
R. T. Ponting (Aust).	1	2	0	23	12	0	0	11.50	2	67.65
S. K. Warne (Aust)..	3	5	0	38	31	0	0	7.60	4	51.35
N. M. Hauritz (Aust)	1	2	0	15	15	0	0	7.50	1	62.50
G. D. McGrath (Aust)	4	7	3	27	11*	0	0	6.75	2	47.37
M. Kartik (India) ...	2	4	0	27	22	0	0	6.75	1	56.25
M. S. Kasprowicz (Aust)	4	7	0	46	19	0	0	6.57	0	46.94
A. Chopra (India)...	2	4	0	15	9	0	0	3.75	5	20.55
G. Gambhir (India)..	1	2	0	4	3	0	0	2.00	0	19.05
K. K. D. Karthik (India)	1	2	0	14	10	0	0	7.00	1/1	40.00

TEST BOWLING AVERAGES

	O	Mdns	R	W	BB	5Wi	10W/m	Avge	S-R
M. J. Clarke (Aust)	7.2	0	13	6	6-9	1	0	2.17	7.33
J. N. Gillespie (Aust)...	132.5	33	323	20	5-56	1	0	16.15	39.85
M. Kartik (India)......	73.3	10	207	12	4-44	0	0	17.25	36.75
N. M. Hauritz (Aust)...	27	4	103	5	3-16	0	0	20.60	32.40
Harbhajan Singh (India)	178.5	32	504	21	6-78	3	1	24.00	51.10
A. R. Kumble (India)..	197.3	29	685	27	7-48	3	1	25.37	43.89
G. D. McGrath (Aust)..	141	51	356	14	4-55	0	0	25.43	60.43
M. S. Kasprowicz (Aust)	108.3	29	255	9	2-11	0	0	28.33	72.33
S. K. Warne (Aust)	140	27	421	14	6-125	1	0	30.07	60.00
Zaheer Khan (India) ...	123.3	22	368	10	4-95	0	0	36.80	74.10
I. K. Pathan (India)	57	14	168	2	1-38	0	0	84.00	171.00
A. B. Agarkar (India) ..	44	9	167	1	1-99	0	0	167.00	264.00
S. R. Tendulkar (India) .	14	2	41	0	–	0	0	–	–
V. Sehwag (India).....	9	1	45	0	–	0	0	–	–
S. M. Katich (Aust)	2	0	7	0	–	0	0	–	–
D. S. Lehmann (Aust) ..	11	3	40	0	–	0	0	–	–
Yuvraj Singh (India)...	4	0	10	0	–	0	0	–	–
S. C. Ganguly (India) ..	3	1	2	0	–	0	0	–	–

*Denotes not out.

MUMBAI v AUSTRALIANS

At Brabourne Stadium, Mumbai, September 30, October 1, 2, 2004. Match drawn
Australians 7 dec 302 (M. L. Hayden 67, S. M. Katich 30, D. R. Martyn 71, B. J. Hodg
30, A. C. Gilchrist 42*; R. R. Powar 2-104, N. M. Kulkarni 2-65). Mumbai 25
(W. Jaffer 48, A. A. Muzumdar 52, A. B. Agarkar 37; G. D. McGrath 4-25, B. Lee 2-53
S. R. Watson 2-23). Australians 2 for 207 (J. L. Langer 108, M. J. Clarke 52.

INDIA v AUSTRALIA

First Test Match

by PETER LALOR

At M. Chinnaswamy Stadium, Bangalore, October 6, 7, 8, 9, 10, 2004. Australia wo
by 217 runs. *Toss:* Australia. Test debut: M. J. Clarke.

Stephen Waugh's final frontier was a tour too far for the flinty former captain, but thi
well-drilled outfit arrived in India still bearing his standard and determined to clair
this last unconquered territory. The team had not won a tour on Indian soil since 1969
70 and many of the squad still bore the mental scars from India's follow-on defyin

ictory at Eden Gardens in 2001. Australia's new captain Ricky Ponting was absent
ith a broken thumb, but the competitive scales were balanced by the absence of Sachin
endulkar who was ruled out by a bout of tennis elbow apparently caused by excessive
et sessions in the lead-up to the series.

Ponting's absence gave the chance to blood New South Wales batsman Michael
larke. The 23-year-old's parents and grandparents flew in from Sydney on the
nnouncement of his inclusion, taking their seats in the colourful Chinnaswamy Stadium
time to see Shane Warne present the youngster with his baggy green. Five hours later,
e player his team-mates call 'Pup' joined Simon Katich at the crease with the score at
for 149. Both used their feet well to counter the spin of Anil Kumble and Harbhajan
ingh, but the debutant was particularly fearless, coming out of his crease and hitting the
all with confidence and power. Katich became Kumble's 400th test wicket with his
core on 81 and the innings steadied at 5 for 256. The first day ended with Clarke on 76
nd acting captain Adam Gilchrist on 35.

The next day all eyes were on Clarke as he moved quickly towards his maiden
entury. Fulfilling a promise he had made to his father, he called for the baggy green as
ree figures approached, but the moment seemed to overpower his natural instinct; like
any before him, he was almost paralysed by indecision and anxiety in the nineties. A
lose lbw was turned down on 92, but 42 painful balls later – after much coaxing and
ounselling from Gilchrist – he had navigated his way to a debut century. His crisp
itting and footwork returned with the hundred and it wasn't long before he had moved
151. The innings came to an end after 341 minutes, but will long be remembered for
s drama and joy. In the meantime, Gilchrist had slipped under the radar, picking up his
wn century from only 103 balls. Harbhajan's belligerent spin brought him five lower-
rder wickets and the Australian innings ended before tea with the score at 474.

India entered the third day two wickets down and 450 runs in arrears. Unfortunately
or the home side, Glenn McGrath had rediscovered the rhythm and form which some
uspected injury and age had robbed him of. His miserly line and length tested the
esolve of the impatient Indian batsmen and was matched by fellow pacemen Jason
illespie and Michael Kasprowicz who stuck tenaciously to a defensive game plan that
aw even Warne abandon his usual attacking style. India folded for 246 with none of the
atsmen making a half-century and only young wicket-keeper Parthiv Patel (46)
isplaying any determination to occupy the crease. The Indian bowlers performed better
Australia's second innings as the baked clay surface began to show some wear and
ear. The completely grass-free strip in the middle of the lush oval had raised the
yebrows of the Australian cricketers and press pack who dubbed it a "Kumble
rumbler", suspecting it had been specially prepared for the local spinner. However, it

HUNDRED ON DEBUT FOR AUSTRALIA

C. Bannerman (165†) v Eng at Melb	1876-77		G. J. Cosier (109) v WI at Melb	1975-76
J. Graham (107) v Eng at Lord's	1893		D. M. Wellham (103) v Eng at	
R. A. Duff (104) v Eng at Melb	1901-02		The Oval	1981
H. J. Hartigan (116) v Eng at Adel	1907-08		K. C. Wessels (162) v Eng at Brisb	1982-83
H. L. Collins (104) v Eng at Syd	1920-21		W. B. Phillips (159) v Pak at Perth	1983-84
W. H. Ponsford (110) v Eng at Syd	1924-25		M. E. Waugh (138) v Eng at Adelaide	1990-91
A. Jackson (164) v Eng at Adel	1928-29		G. S. Blewett (102*) v Eng at Adel	1994-95
J. W. Burke (101*) v Eng at Adel	1950-51		M. J. Clarke (151) v India at	
K.D. Walters (155) v Eng at Brisb	1965-66		Bangalore	2004-05
G. S. Chappell (108) v Eng at Perth	1970-71		*† Retired Hurt*	

was Harbhajan who made the most of the bounce and turn, picking up six wickets
make a match tally of 11 as the Australians stumbled to 228 – an underwhelming effo
but enough to give them a commanding lead.

The Indians again began badly, the relentless line of Australia's fast bowlers in sta
contrast to the ill-disciplined efforts of the home team's top order which never recover
from losing Virender Sehwag in the third over to McGrath and Aakash Chopra in the fif
to Gillespie. Captain Sourav Ganguly ran himself out in the seventh and Warne trappe
V.V.S. Laxman in front of his stumps in the 12th over. Only Rahul Dravid and bowl
Irfan Pathan showed any resistance, but with a day left to play the game was lost.

The Indians were all out for 239, falling 217 runs short of the Australians, whos
focus and ruthless determination had sought out and exploited every minor crack in th
home team's character. The Indians had real problems, with neither of the pace bowle
showing any penetration during the match and few batsmen displaying the concentratio
needed to counter the tourists' defensive fielding and bowling. Gilchrist ably fille
Ponting's shoes and managed to juggle the job of keeper, batsman and leader in th
trying conditions.

Clarke was voted man of the match by officials and the good-natured crowd wh
were enchanted by his sparkling eyes and dancing feet. One of the lighter moments
the Test was played out in the traffic jam outside the ground on day two. Australian fan
had arrived with a long banner which celebrated Clarke's 150 on debut, but local fan
hijacked it and staged a riotous celebration on the street in front of Clarke's family. H
71-year-old grandfather Les had never left Australia before but had been confident o
his grandson's chances of a century when a bird defecated on his shirt during the fir
day's play. Believing it to be a lucky omen, he was still wearing the shirt the next da
when Clarke reached his 150th run. "If I died tonight I'd still be ahead," he said in th
midst of the chaos.

Man of Match: M. J. Clarke.

Close of play: First day, Australia (1) 5-316 (Clarke 76, Gilchrist 35); Second da
India (1) 6-150 (Patel 18, Pathan 1); Third day, Australia (2) 4-127 (Martyn 29, Clark
11); Fourth day, India (2) 6-105 (Dravid 47, Pathan 7).

Australia

	R	B	4/6		R	B	4/6
J.L. Langer b Pathan	52	126	5	– lbw b Pathan	0	4	0
M.L. Hayden c Yuvraj Singh							
b Harbhajan Singh	26	53	2	– run out (Harbhajan Singh)	30	53	4
S.M. Katich b Kumble	81	168	8	– c Dravid b Kumble	39	69	5
D.R. Martyn c Chopra b Kumble	3	12	0	– c (sub) Kaif b Harbhajan Singh	45	138	6
D.S. Lehmann c Dravid b Kumble	17	23	3	– c Chopra b Harbhajan Singh	14	18	2
M.J. Clarke c Patel b Zaheer Khan	151	249	18	4 – c Chopra b Harbhajan Singh	17	55	2
*†A.C. Gilchrist c and b Harbhajan Singh	104	109	13	3 – c Chopra b Kumble	26	39	2
S.K. Warne c Dravid b Harbhajan Singh	1	9	0	– c Yuvraj b Harbhajan Singh	31	49	5
J.N. Gillespie not out	7	31	1	– c Yuvraj b Harbhajan Singh	8	23	1
M.S. Kasprowicz c Yuvraj Singh b H. Singh	4	4	0	– c Dravid b Harbhajan Singh	8	13	1
G.D. McGrath lbw b Harbhajan Singh	0	4	0	– not out	3	11	0
B 5, l-b 15, w 1, n-b 8	29			B 2, l-b 1, w 1, n-b 3	7		

(130 overs, 564 mins)   474   (78.1 overs, 336 mins)   228

Fall: 50 124 129 149 256 423 427 471 474 474   Fall: 0 65 86 104 146 167 204 216 217 228

Bowling: *First Innings*—Pathan 21–6–62–1; Zaheer Khan 22–2–60–1; Harbhajan Singh 41–7–146–
Kumble 39–4–157–3; Sehwag 5–0–26–0; Yuvraj Singh 2–0–3–0. *Second Innings*—Pathan 12–2–38–
Zaheer Khan 13–1–45–0; Harbhajan Singh 30.1–5–78–6; Kumble 23–4–64–2.

Michael Clarke leaps, and so does a nation's heart, after a spectacular debut century.

India

	R	B	4/6			R	B	4/6
A. Chopra lbw b McGrath	0	4	0	– lbw b Gillespie		5	11	0
V. Sehwag c Langer b Kasprowicz	39	57	6	– lbw b McGrath		0	7	0
R. S. Dravid b McGrath	0	5	0	– lbw b Kasprowicz		60	187	11
*S. C. Ganguly c Gilchrist b Kasprowicz	45	85	5	– run out (Kasprowicz/Gilchrist)	5	5	1
V. V. S. Laxman b Warne	31	50	5	– lbw b Warne		3	14	0
Yuvraj Singh c Gilchrist b McGrath	5	22	0	– c Gilchrist b McGrath		27	67	4
†P. A. Patel b Gillespie	46	125	5	– lbw b Warne		4	6	1
I. K. Pathan c Gilchrist b Warne	31	96	3	– c Gilchrist b Gillespie		55	141	8
A. R. Kumble b Gillespie	26	79	3	– b Kasprowicz		2	4	0
Harbhajan Singh c Lehmann b McGrath	8	15	0	– c McGrath b Gillespie		42	67	7
Zaheer Khan not out	0	1	0	– not out		22	20	4
B 5, l-b 2, w 5, n-b 3	15			B 6, l-b 5, n-b 3		14		

(89.2 overs, 396 mins) 246   (87.4 overs, 383 mins) 239

Fall: 0 4 87 98 124 136 196 227 244 246

Fall: 1 7 12 19 81 86 118 125 214 239

Bowling: *First Innings*—McGrath 25–8–55–4; Gillespie 16.2–3–63–2; Warne 28–4–78–2; Kasprowicz 20–4–43–2. *Second Innings*—McGrath 20–10–39–2; Gillespie 14.4–4–33–3; Kasprowicz 14–7–23–2; Warne 32–8–115–2; Lehmann 6–3–14–0; Clarke 1–0–4–0.

Umpires: B. F. Bowden (New Zealand) and S. A. Bucknor (West Indies).
TV Umpire: A. V. Jayaprakash.
Referee: R. S. Madugalle (Sri Lanka).

INDIA v AUSTRALIA

Second Test Match

by BERNARD WHIMPRESS

At M. A. Chidambaram Stadium (Chepauk), Chennai, October 14, 15, 16, 17, 18 (n play), 2004. Match drawn. *Toss*: Australia.

This was a game that had everything except an ending, or as Nobel prize-winning first-class cricketer Samuel Beckett might have put it, an endgame. Locals suggested tha scheduling cricket at Chennai in October was crazy as there was a 70 per cent likelihoo of interruptions. When the monsoon rains come – and there hadn't been a good monsoo for four years – they come in October. Hence, four days of superb cricket instead of five

The pendulum swung wildly. On the first day, Australia dominated the first two and-a-half hours before India snatched control. India consolidated on the secon morning and Virender Sehwag's brilliant batting gave the home team the ascendancy but the Australians fought back before India recovered again to forge ahead. By lunc on the third day, India had a first innings lead of 141 and appeared to be in a match winning position. However, the Australians then opened solidly before four wicket fell in the final session to return a slight advantage to India. Damien Martyn and Jaso Gillespie's great partnership on day four put the odds back in Australia's favour, but b stumps, with the Indians taking 19 runs off three overs, the home team was favoured But instead of a grandstand finish, there was only rain.

Coming just four days after their win in Bangalore the Australian side wa understandably unchanged, and the Indian selectors did not panic. Only opener Aakas Chopra went out of the side, replaced by Yuvraj Singh as opener, with Mohammed Kai coming into the middle-order after a three-year absence.

Adam Gilchrist won the toss for the second successive match and in high humidit Matthew Hayden and Justin Langer were so much in charge after the morning session in reaching 111 from a sluggish 25 overs, that 400 by the end of the day looked likely However, at 136 Harbhajan Singh made a double strike. Hayden was caught at long-of (154 minutes, 91 balls, 6 fours, 2 sixes) from a miscued drive when seeking to impos himself on the attack and then Langer (158 minutes, 113 balls, 8 fours) was surprised by a turning delivery that took the edge of his bat for a low catch to Rahul Dravid at slip. A touch of arrogance brought about the first dismissal and a genuine disguise the second.

Sourav Ganguly made a tactical error by maintaining pace at one end and allowing new batsmen Simon Katich and Martyn to settle in. After 45 overs (2 for 171) Anil Kumble had only bowled four overs but then re-entered the attack. After helping to add 53 runs in serene comfort, Martyn failed to read Kumble's top-spinner and was caught at short leg, right on tea. But while India had come back into the game, Australia were still comfortably placed.

All that would change as Kumble operated like a demon from the Wallajah Road end. Darren Lehmann cut hard and bottom-edged Kumble to wicket-keeper Parthiv Patel without scoring, Michael Clarke was trapped lbw playing back, Gilchrist was bamboozled by a ball turning on to his pads to give a short-leg catch, and Shane Warne was caught and bowled from an attempted drive. When Gillespie and Michael Kasprowicz were caught in the close-in cordon Kumble had taken seven wickets, and he had a hand in the eighth when he ran out Glenn McGrath. Kumble's 7 for 48 from 17.3 overs gave him his best figures at the Chepauk ground. The last eight Australian wickets collapsed for just 46 runs and the last seven batsmen failed to reach double figures. Katich remained unconquered, but in his laborious innings failed to take any initiative when batting with the tail. At the end of the day India negotiated 13 overs in reaching 1 for 28. Yuvraj Singh failed to convince as an opener: dropped by Clarke at second slip in McGrath's first over, he was caught by Gilchrist off Warne.

On the second day, the Australians were offered chances and half-chances they didn't take. There was a vociferous welcome for a record by an Australian, and some wonderfully entertaining batting. The Australians dropped Sehwag twice after he had reached his century, Kaif twice before he had scored, and Ganguly and Patel once each. The record fell to Warne when he removed nightwatchman Irfan Pathan for a patient 14 – for the only wicket in the morning session – to surpass Muttiah Muralidaran's world mark of 532 Test wickets. Sehwag was cautious early but opened out after reaching his fifty, and he had an exhilarating battle with Warne, hitting many boundaries from the leg-spinner with well-timed sweeps and on-drives, and bringing up his century with a push through the covers for four off Kasprowicz.

It was just as well that Sehwag was in control of his game because the other leading batsmen faltered. Dravid battled for nearly two hours before getting an inside edge to Kasprowicz, and after the 200 had been raised Gillespie made a double breakthrough, inducing Ganguly to give an edge to Gilchrist and bowling Laxman with a shooter. At 5 for 213, and 6 for 233 when Sehwag (356 minutes, 221 balls, 20 fours) was caught at deep mid-wicket off Warne, the Australians must have had hopes of restricting the Indians to 250. However, two of Kaif's nervous edges off Warne evaded Gilchrist's gloves and he subsequently looked more in command against McGrath with the second new ball as he and the gritty Patel maintained their wickets at the close.

India advanced to 7 for 360 on the third morning when the ground temperature was 43 degrees, losing only Patel (169 minutes, 121 balls, 8 fours) in the morning session after a partnership of 102 with Kaif. However, the slimline Kaif suffered dehydration at the break and only resumed with a runner at the fall of the ninth wicket. In farcical circumstances he lofted Warne for a four off the first ball and then was run out off the next (247 minutes, 158 balls, 6 fours) after he reverse-swept the leg-spinner, collapsed with cramp after setting off for a run and was unable to regain his ground. Warne polished off the innings to finish with 6 for 125, his first five-wicket haul on the sub-continent, but two further missed catches (by Warne) off Gillespie marred that bowler's figures, while Kasprowicz's solitary wicket did him no justice. India's lead of 141 was handy, although if Kaif had not wilted it might have been greater. In simmering heat, umpires David Shepherd and Rudi Koertzen kept their ties fully knotted; mad dogs and Englishmen were only part of the story.

Australia needed a good start but could have been 2 for 0 if Patel had not missed a snick from Hayden in Zaheer Khan's first over and a confident appeal for lbw against Langer been upheld. Instead, a further dropped chance by Patel from Hayden allowed the visitors to reach 0 for 53 at tea, the game moving back towards the Australians. Kumble had Langer picked up first ball after the interval, at which point Gilchrist made a series-winning move by promoting himself to No. 3 to show leadership from the front. He struggled at first, but the employment of the sweep shot against Kumble and Harbhajan – and Ganguly's strange fields, with a few close catchers (slip, short leg, silly point) and the rest of the fielders protecting boundaries – meant that easy singles were available.

Hayden eventually fell to Kumble from a skied sweep at 2 for 76 but Gilchrist moved sweetly into the forties, kept company by Katich, playing a defensive role. The return of Zaheer Khan brought the removal of Katich, lbw on the back foot, but luck ran with the Australians. Martyn was twice almost bowled by Harbhajan before the deficit was passed, and had play ended then, the Australians would have been on top. However, a magnificent over of wrong'uns by Kumble saw Gilchrist missed by Patel and bowled round his legs next ball (137 minutes, 81 balls, 3 fours). Kumble, who almost bowled nightwatchman Gillespie, appeared to have swung the advantage back to India: at day's end, Australia led by nine runs with six wickets intact.

Gillespie is a disciplined cricketer, an aggressive fast bowler who bowls a tight line and a batsman who sells his wicket dearly. Several times in Test cricket he has batted for a couple of hours, but in this swelter, against quality spin, his rock-like resistance in support of Martyn for almost two sessions in a partnership of 139 enabled Australia to make a remarkable recovery. Martyn, of course, was the main batting hero, and as against Sri Lanka earlier in the year, he extricated his side when it trailed on the first innings. Martyn's strengths were his shots square of the wicket, but he raised his century in the grandest manner with a lofted drive from Kumble over long-off for six. Shortly afterwards, Martyn (280 minutes, 210 balls, 11 fours, one six) edged Harbhajan to Dravid, and when Gillespie (242 minutes, 165 balls, 1 four) went the same way in the same over at 6 for 284, the game was in the balance. Clarke and Lehmann played in such a carefree fashion in adding 67 runs in 17 overs that the question of a Gilchrist declaration began to arise. Then Kumble again turned up the heat. The Karnataka leg-spinner's dismissal of Lehmann to a top edge, Warne caught and bowled, and Kasprowicz lbw, quickly wound up the innings and gave him 6 for 133, and 13 for 181 for the match. The Australian total of 369 produced a competitive lead of 228, but such was the ominous touch of Sehwag in cracking three fours in three overs before stumps that he seemed likely to win the game by himself. Some further questions might be posed. Would Warne be able to dig deep and manufacture his own brand of spin magic? Would Gillespie be able to raise much of a gallop after his energy-draining stay at the crease? Would the Australians rue the absence of a second quality spin bowler?

We would never know. A great contest edging towards a superb climax was cut off by rain. The covers were on and a veritable army of attendants with mops, buckets and towels tried to soak up the water, unavailingly. The scene had a particularly Indian feel about it – touching the void. French philosopher Jacques Derrida, whose recent death had been widely reported in Indian papers, would no doubt have been able to deconstruct some extra meaning. I couldn't.

Man of Match: A. R. Kumble.

Close of play: First day, India (1) 1-28 (Sehwag 20, Pathan 0); Second day, India (1) 6-291 (Kaif 34, Patel 27); Third day, Australia (2) 4-150 (Martyn 19, Gillespie 0); Fourth day, India (2) 0-19 (Yuvraj Singh 7, Sehwag 12).

Australia

	R	B	4/6			R	B	4/6
J. L. Langer c Dravid b Harbhajan Singh	71	113	8	– c Dravid b Kumble		19	56	2
M. L. Hayden c Laxman b Harbhajan Singh	58	91	6 [2]	– c Laxman b Kumble		39	72	3
S. M. Katich not out	36	106	2	– (4) lbw b Zaheer Khan		9	47	0
D. R. Martyn c Yuvraj Singh b Kumble	26	53	5	– (5) c Dravid				
				b Harbhajan Singh		104	210	11 [1]
D. S. Lehmann c Patel b Kumble	0	6	0	– (8) c Patel b Kumble		31	51	3
M. J. Clarke lbw b Kumble	5	28	0	– (7) not out		39	98	4
*†A. C. Gilchrist c Yuvraj Singh b Kumble	3	9	0	– (3) b Kumble		49	81	3
S. K. Warne c and b Kumble	4	7	1	– (9) c Kaif b Kumble		0	2	0
J. N. Gillespie c Kaif b Kumble	5	12	1	– (6) c Dravid				
				b Harbhajan Singh		26	165	1
M. S. Kasprowicz c Laxman b Kumble	4	3	1	– lbw b Kumble		5	19	0
G. D. McGrath run out (Khan/Patel/Kumble)	2	5	0	– b Harbhajan Singh		2	6	0
B 7, l-b 4, w 1, n-b 4	21			B 19, l-b 15, w 3, n-b 4	46			

(71.3 overs, 319 mins)	235	(133.5 overs, 602 mins)	369

Fall: 136 136 189 191 204 210 216 224 228 235   Fall: 53 76 121 145 284 285 347 347 364 369

Bowling: *First Innings*—Pathan 12–3–29–0; Zaheer Khan 11–2–44–0; Harbhajan Singh 29–2–90–2; Kumble 17.3–4–48–7; Sehwag 2–1–8–0. *Second Innings*—Pathan 12–3–39–0; Zaheer Khan 22–6–36–1; Harbhajan Singh 46.5–12–108–3; Kumble 47–7–133–6; Sehwag 1–0–5–0; Yuvraj Singh 2–0–7–0; Ganguly 3–1–2–0.

India

	R	B	4/6			R	B	4/6
Yuvraj Singh c Gilchrist b Warne	8	40	1	– not out		7	8	1
V. Sehwag c Clarke b Warne	155	221	20	– not out		12	10	3
I. K. Pathan c Hayden b Warne	14	63	0 [1]					
R. S. Dravid b Kasprowicz	26	95	3					
*S. C. Ganguly c Gilchrist b Gillespie	9	29	1					
V. V. S. Laxman b Gillespie	4	19	1					
M. Kaif run out (Martyn/Gillespie)	64	158	6					
†P. A. Patel c Gilchrist b Warne	54	121	8					
A. R. Kumble b Warne	20	47	2					
Harbhajan Singh c and b Warne	5	15	0					
Zaheer Khan not out	0	5	0					
B 6, l-b 3, w 2, n-b 6	17				0			

(134.3 overs, 592 mins)	376	(3 overs, 12 mins) (0 wkt)	19

Fall: 28 83 178 203 213 233 335 369 372 37

Bowling: *First Innings*—McGrath 25–4–74–0; Gillespie 35–8–70–2; Warne 42.3–5–125–6; Kasprowicz 25–5–65–1; Lehmann 5–0–26–0; Katich 2–0–7–0. *Second Innings*—McGrath 2–0–18–0; Gillespie 1–0–1–0.

Umpires: R. E. Koertzen (South Africa) and D. R. Shepherd (England).
TV Umpire: A. V. Jayaprakash.
Referee: R. S. Madugalle (Sri Lanka).

INDIA v AUSTRALIA

Third Test Match

by ROBERT CRADDOCK

At Vidarbha CA Ground, Nagpur, October 26, 27, 28, 29, 2004. Australia won by 342 runs. *Toss:* Australia.

India officially surrendered the Border-Gavaskar Trophy after being beaten by Australia in a home series for the first time in 35 years. Australia won the Test by 342 runs and were as upbeat all week as India were downcast. Both teams stayed at the same small 75-room hotel and cut vastly contrasting figures as they sat each side of the breakfast buffet.

The downcast expression carried by Indian coach John Wright as he left the Pride Hotel breakfast room 90 minutes before the toss embodied the mood of a nervous team and a fatalistic nation. He had just been told ace spinner Harbhajan Singh would not be leaving his room that day due to a gastric complaint and that captain Sourav Ganguly was hobbling his way through a fitness test on a mysterious hip complaint and was unlikely to be fit. Both subsequently withdrew.

Wright shook his head and looked at the floor with the painfully arched eyebrows of a man who sensed those floorboards were about to give way beneath him. He looked a beaten man, and so did his team without two of its biggest stars. When Wright got to the ground, batting-great-turned-commentator Barry Richards said to him: "I bet you could write a good book about your experiences here" – and Wright nodded with the wry grin of a man who knew much more than he could ever commit to print. In the end, despite a series of caustic rumours, India could do nothing more than take the word of its two absent stars that their reasons for withdrawal were genuine.

From the moment a stubborn curator announced he would not bow to the wishes of Ganguly and shave the considerable grass cover off the pitch, the vibes for India were all bad. Harbhajan spent 20 agonising minutes looking at the pitch the day before he withdrew and told groundstaff he feared for his prospects on such an unusual wicket. The Australians, by contrast, could not believe their good fortune. Captain Adam Gilchrist described the pitch as "almost Australian-looking", and while it was no nightmare deck it had generous bounce and occasional seam, and that was all the Australian bowlers needed to give them a match-winning edge over India's out-of-form top order.

There was sense of destiny about the game from the moment Australia won the toss. Damien Martyn, combining patience and flair in equal measure, crafted his fourth century on the subcontinent for the year. Martyn and Darren Lehmann bankrolled a competitive total of 398 with a fourth-wicket stand of 148 off 181 balls. Lehmann pulled a hamstring late in his innings and speculation mounted that the innings could have been his last in Tests. He looked a forlorn figure after stumps on day one. Michael Clarke's jaunty 91 was just the tonic Australia were looking for after Lehmann's exit as the youngster profited from two missed chances by keeper Parthiv Patel.

It was clear India's philosophy in the match was to eek out a draw which would enable them to regroup for a fresh assault on the raging turner of Mumbai a week later. But Australia rarely lose wars of attrition and they relished India's go-slow tactics. Virender Sehwag smashed four boundaries off Jason Gillespie's first over, but the powderkeg start soon fizzled out. Aakash Chopra made nine off 42 balls, Rahul Dravid 21 off 140 and Sachin Tendulkar eight off 36 in his first match of the series after recovering from a tennis elbow injury. The Australian attack bowled with suffocating precision. Glenn McGrath, in his 100th Test, conceded 18 runs in his first 20 overs, and Gillespie (5 for 56) probed a ruthless channel just on off-stump and his venomous lift often made keeper Gilchrist take the ball with fingers pointing skywards. India were bowled out for 185 and Australia's lead of 213 was always likely to prove the match-winner.

After declining to enforce the follow-on, Australia accepted that recklessness rather than Indian resolve was their greatest enemy in the second innings. The first seven overs of the post-lunch session on day three were maidens and just 16 runs trickled off 15 overs as Australia presented broad defensive shields before fastening their bayonets later in the innings. Simon Katich, again a cool head under pressure, quashed any chance of an Indian revival with a polished knock that showcased his skills as a fighter and a flair player. At one stage he smacked Anil Kumble out of the attack and took 38 off the 31 balls he faced from him; clearly this grass-knoll was not Kumble's strip. Katich played the spinners with consummate ease and his footwork was swift and decisive. One of his few misjudgments came on 99 when he tried to work Murali Kartik to leg but was beaten by the pace of a quicker ball and was palpably lbw.

Once Katich had laid the platform for a decent total on day three, Martyn and Clarke provided the fancy interior decorating on day four with some of the most swashbuckling strokeplay of the series. Clarke unleashed some blistering back-foot drives that reminded old-timers of Doug Walters, although some of his cross-batted swipes looked as much baseball as cricket. But with his head kept conspicuously still and his balance nigh perfect, he normally made sweet contact. Martyn edged towards the cherished feat of three consecutive Test centuries but, after being dropped cutting on 85 by Sehwag at point, he was caught behind off the relentless Zaheer Khan for 97 just before lunch.

Chasing an impossible 543 for victory, India emerged a side bereft of confidence and fight. Australia's pace attack, with five and six vultures in the slips sensing an edge any ball, simply swarmed their crestfallen rivals in the second innings as mercilessly as a Bengal Tiger swooping on a hobbling prey. Chopra played the wrong line and was bowled by Gillespie, Dravid once again left a gap between bat and pad and edged on to his stumps, Tendulkar fended a sharp lifter to gully to provide McGrath with his 450th Test victim, and V.V.S. Laxman's fighting instincts were so scrambled he pulled Michael Kasprowicz's first ball down fine leg's throat. At 5 for 37 the game was gone.

Sehwag provided the main resistance with a feisty 58. As always, he was interesting to watch. Even the Australians enjoyed his flair, to the point where Matthew Hayden at one stage walked up to him and said: "I love the way you bat, mate." Heckled about his aggressive shot-selection by the Australian slips, he nonchalantly spun on his heel and retorted: "I am here to entertain."

India finally fell for 200, sparking jubilant scenes among the Australians. The final frontier had fallen. Gilchrist, who looked close to breaking point earlier in the series, claimed it was the most satisfying moment of his cricketing life. Former captain Steve Waugh, who desperately wanted to make the tour, somehow managed to be the first phone caller through to the Australian dressing-room in the minutes after the win.

The Australians celebrated long into the night. Some of the younger players in the squad went to bed at 11 p.m., but the old hard-heads were having none of that. A 35-year drought had been broken; it was time to salute it in style.

Man of Match: D. R. Martyn.

Close of play: First day, Australia (1) 7-362 (Clarke 73, Gillespie 4); Second day, India (1) 5-146 (Kaif 47, Patel 20); Third day, Australia (2) 3-202 (Martyn 41, Clarke 10).

Australia

	R	B	4/6			R	B	4/6
J. L. Langer c Dravid b Zaheer Khan	44	73	8	– c Laxman b Kartik		30	119	2
M. L. Hayden c Patel b Zaheer Khan	23	39	2	– b Zaheer Khan		9	28	2
S. M. Katich c Chopra b Kumble	4	14	0	– lbw b Kartik		99	157	14
D. R. Martyn c Agarkar b Kumble	114	165	16 [1]	– c Patel b Zaheer Khan		97	184	8
D. S. Lehmann c Dravid b Kartik	70	83	10					
M. J. Clarke c Patel b Zaheer Khan	91	160	13	– (5) c Kaif b Kumble		73	95	11 [1]
*†A. C. Gilchrist c and b Kartik	2	6	0	– (6) not out		3	6	0
S. K. Warne st Patel b Kartik	2	7	0					
J. N. Gillespie lbw b Zaheer Khan	9	48	2					
M. S. Kasprowicz c Patel b Agarkar	0	3	0					
G. D. McGrath not out	11	12	2					
B 6, l-b 13, w 1, n-b 8	28			B 1, l-b 15, w 2		18		

(100.2 overs, 436 mins)   398

Fall: 67 79 86 234 314 323 337 376 377 398

(98.1 overs, 410 mins) (5 wkts dec)   329

Fall: 19 99 171 319 329

Bowling: *First Innings*—Agarkar 23–2–99–1; Zaheer Khan 26.2–6–95–4; Kumble 25–6–99–2; Kartik 20–1–57–3; Tendulkar 6–1–29–0. *Second Innings*—Zaheer Khan 21.1–5–64–2; Agarkar 21–7–68–0 Kumble 21–1–89–1; Tendulkar 8–1–12–0; Kartik 26–5–74–2; Sehwag 1–0–6–0

India

	R	B	4/6			R	B	4/6
A. Chopra c Warne b Gillespie	9	42	2	– b Gillespie		1	16	0
V. Sehwag c Gilchrist b McGrath	22	20	4	– c Clarke b Warne		58	94	8
*R. S. Dravid c Warne b McGrath	21	140	2	– b Gillespie		2	6	0
S. R. Tendulkar lbw b Gillespie	8	36	0	– c Martyn b McGrath		2	14	0
V. V. S. Laxman c Clarke b Warne	13	26	3	– c McGrath b Kasprowicz		2	9	0
M. Kaif c Warne b McGrath	55	151	7 [1]	– c Gilchrist b Kasprowicz		7	8	1
†P. A. Patel c Hayden b Warne	20	72	2	– c Gilchrist b Gillespie		32	53	6
A. B. Agarkar c Clarke b Gillespie	15	20	3	– not out		44	61	8
A. R. Kumble not out	7	25	1	– b Gillespie		2	17	0
M. Kartik c Clarke b Gillespie	3	13	0	– c Gilchrist b McGrath		22	27	4
Zaheer Khan b Gillespie	0	7	0	– c Martyn b Warne		25	17	2 [2]
L-b 10, w 1, n-b 1	12			L-b 2, n-b 1		3		

(91.5 overs, 379 mins)   185

Fall: 31 34 49 75 103 150 173 178 181 185

(53.3 overs, 237 mins)   200

Fall: 1 9 20 29 37 102 114 122 148 200

Bowling: *First Innings*—McGrath 25–13–27–3; Gillespie 22.5–8–56–5; Kasprowicz 21–4–45–0; Warne 23–8–47–2. *Second Innings*—McGrath 16–1–79–2; Gillespie 16–7–24–4; Kasprowicz 7–1–39–2; Warne 14.3–2–56–2.

Umpires: Aleem Dar (Pakistan) and D. R. Shepherd (England).
TV Umpire: K. Hariharan.
Referee: R. S. Madugalle (Sri Lanka).

INDIA v AUSTRALIA

Fourth Test Match

by MIKE COWARD

At Wankhede Stadium, Mumbai, November 3, 4, 5, 2004. India won by 13 runs. *Toss:* India. Test debut: G. Gambhir, K. K. D. Karthik, N. M. Hauritz.

This was one of the shortest and most controversial of Test matches. From the moment the trophy-toting Australians and the vanquished Indians reached the metropolis, there was intense discussion about the quality of the pitch. While conjecture about pitches is commonplace in India, there was an edge to this speculation which drove the combatants to something harder than chai or lassi. Legendary 78-year-old Pahlanji 'Polly' Umrigar, the former Indian captain and overseer of pitch preparation at the ground since its inception as a Test venue in 1975, was unusually defensive. Two days before the match Umrigar was feted at the opening of a bar named in his honour at the imposing Cricket Club of India at Brabourne Stadium, but the social chitchat was not so much of Polly's distinguished record but the latest on the Test pitch.

Compounding matters was the decision by Indian captain Sourav Ganguly to forgo a fitness Test that had been semaphored by team officials. Furthermore, rather than staying in Mumbai to help supervise the induction of four new players to the squad, Ganguly returned home to Calcutta, and by doing so gave the impression he had abandoned his men at a time of great need. Naturally enough his decision to leave his crestfallen team in the hands of the capable but confused vice-captain, Rahul Dravid, led to more whispers and tittle-tattle. Former Indian captain Ravi Shastri joined the debate in his column in *The Times of India*. He wrote: "Finally, there has been profuse speculation about whether it was groin or grass that kept the Indian captain out of the Nagpur Test match. I do hope it was the former because otherwise it sends the wrong signals about Indian cricket." Tongues had been wagging since Ganguly withdrew at the 11th hour from the Nagpur Test after publicly admonishing officials for refusing to take grass off the pitch, thereby handing the Australian pace bowlers a significant advantage.

If this was not dramatic enough, the world's most prolific wicket-taker, Shane Warne, cracked his right thumb at practice and was hastily despatched to Australia for treatment and rest to ensure he could play in the first Test against New Zealand a fortnight later. But rather than introduce Warne's protege, Victorian captain Cameron White, to the Test arena, on-duty selector Allan Border and his colleagues opted for 23-year-old off-spinner Nathan Hauritz.

As it happened, the pitch was so bad that proceedings lasted to the end of the third day only because unseasonable rain restricted India to 2 for 22 in just 11 overs on the first day. Dravid, who won the toss – the first for India in seven home Tests with Australia – had no option but to bat after choosing orthodox left-armer Murali Kartik to complement the guiles of Anil Kumble and Harbhajan Singh. The cynics and the critics who had been so conspicuous in advance of the match were proved correct. The reddish pitch was diabolical and made a mockery of Test cricket. On the second day 18 wickets tumbled, equalling the record for the greatest number of wickets to fall in a day in a Test match in India. (At Delhi in 1987-88, India were dismissed for 75 and by stumps West Indies had replied with 8 for 118.) Unbelievably, a new mark was established just 24 hours later when India sagged from 0 for 5 to 205 all out and Australia were routed for 93 – an avalanche of 20 wickets tumbling for 293 on what proved to be the last day of the series. As bad as it was, the pitch could not excuse the batting of the Australians who were in the grip of what is known in dressing-room vernacular as "departure-lounge" or "dead-rubber" syndrome. And while this condition may make nonsense of the players' solemn pledge to an "unconditional professionalism", it is bound to recur if such intense playing schedules are maintained. This was the fourth match in a sequence that demanded the Australians play six Tests in eight weeks and an unprecedented nine Tests in 13 weeks.

Be that as it may, neither the schedule nor the woeful condition of the pitch excused an Australian team of such calibre batting for just 30.5 overs when offered the priceless opportunity to win the series 3-0. That there were only three half-centuries and five scores of more than 30 provided ample evidence of the poor conditions and encouraged some critics to press for an inquiry. To the unbridled delight of his myriad devotees, Sachin Tendulkar made light of the discomfort in his left elbow to construct a handsome 55 with some trademark offerings off the front foot through extra cover. And to the undisguised relief of his many admirers, V.V.S. Laxman regained some confidence and touch when wisely promoted to No. 3. He responded with 69 – the highest score in the match – after his previous six innings in the series had netted him a paltry 54 runs. That Damien Martyn was the third half-century maker surprised no one who had witnessed his imperious centuries in Chennai and Nagpur. Matthew Hayden managed 35 and if nothing else celebrated the fact that he and Justin Langer had eclipsed the record of Mark Taylor and Michael Slater (aggregate 3,887 runs) to become Australia's most prolific opening pair. In addition to the satisfaction of engineering success, Dravid with an admirable unbeaten 31 and 27 passed 7,000 Test runs and also overtook Sunil Gavaskar's record of 108 catches in Tests for India.

Inevitably, given the circumstances, the slow men dominated proceedings, with 29 wickets falling to their wiles. While the redoubtable Anil Kumble claimed five wickets in an innings for the 27th time – and the ninth against Australia – Hauritz took a wicket with his third ball in Test cricket and in the second innings claimed both Tendulkar and Laxman. It was, however, the extraordinary analysis of Michael Clarke that stunned all. A part-time left-arm finger-spinner, Clarke, who had previously bowled just one over in three Test appearances, took six wickets for nine runs from 38 balls as India tumbled from 3 for 153 to 205 all out. But not even Clarke's freakish performance was enough to inspire the distracted Australians, and in the end it mattered nothing to India that their first-innings score of 104 in 42 overs was their lowest at home against Australia.

Man of Match: M. Kartik. *Man of the Series:* D. R. Martyn.

Close of play: First day, India (1) 2-22 (Dravid 9, Tendulkar 2); Second day, India (2) 0-5 (Gambhir 1, Sehwag 4).

India

	R	B	4/6		R	B	4/6
G. Gambhir lbw b Gillespie	3	8	0	– c Clarke b McGrath	1	13	0
V. Sehwag b McGrath	8	11	1	– lbw b McGrath	5	14	1
*R. S. Dravid not out	31	104	3	– (5) c Gilchrist b Clarke	27	75	3
S. R. Tendulkar c Gilchrist b Kasprowicz	5	35	0	– c Clarke b Hauritz	55	82	6
V. V. S. Laxman c Gilchrist b Gillespie	1	10	0	– (3) c and b Hauritz	69	126	12
M. Kaif lbw b Gillespie	2	3	0	– lbw b Clarke	25	60	3
†K. K. D. Karthik b Kasprowicz	10	28	2	– c Ponting b Clarke	4	7	1
A. R. Kumble c Ponting b Hauritz	16	19	4	– not out	13	21	1
Harbhajan Singh c Katich b Hauritz	14	26	3	– c Hayden b Clarke	0	2	0
M. Kartik c Gilchrist b Hauritz	0	3	0	– b Clarke	2	5	0
Zaheer Khan b Kasprowicz	0	3	0	– lbw b Clarke	0	4	0
B 6, l-b 7, n-b 1	14			B 4	4		
	104				205		

(41.3 overs, 190 mins) 104

Fall: 11 11 29 31 33 46 68 100 102 104

(68.2 overs, 300 mins) 205

Fall: 5 14 105 153 182 188 195 195 199 205

Bowling: *First Innings*—McGrath 16–9–35–1; Gillespie 12–2–29–4; Kasprowicz 8.3–3–11–2; Hauritz 5–0–16–3. *Second Innings*—Gillespie 15–1–47–0; Hauritz 22–4–87–2; McGrath 12–6–29–2; Kasprowicz 13–5–29–0; Clarke 6.2–0–9–6.

Australia

	R	B	4/6			R	B	4/6
J. L. Langer c Dravid b Zaheer Khan	12	23	2	– c Kartik b Zaheer Khan	0	2	0
M. L. Hayden c Kaif b Kartik	35	73	1 3	– b Harbhajan Singh	24	30	4
*R. T. Ponting lbw b Kumble	11	19	1	– c Laxman b Kartik	12	15	2
D. R. Martyn b Kartik	55	114	3	– lbw b Kartik	0	5	0
S. M. Katich c Kaif b Kumble	7	15	0	– c Dravid b Harbhajan Singh	1	12	0
M. J. Clarke st Kartik b Kumble	17	28	0 2	– b Kartik	7	11	1
†A. C. Gilchrist c Kaif b Kartik	26	18	3 1	– c Tendulkar b Harbhajan Singh	5	11	0
J. N. Gillespie c Kaif b Kumble	2	32	0	– not out	9	51	1
N. M. Hauritz c Harbhajan Singh b Kumble	0	6	0	– lbw b Kumble	15	18	2
M. S. Kasprowicz c Kumble b Kartik	19	28	2	– c Dravid b Harbhajan Singh	7	28	0
G. D. McGrath not out	9	17	2	– c Laxman b Harbhajan Singh	0	2	0
B 2, l-b 4, n-b 4	10			B 8, l-b 5	13		

(61.3 overs, 258 mins) 203   (30.5 overs, 136 mins) 93
Fall: 17 37 81 101 121 157 167 171 184 203   Fall: 0 24 24 33 48 48 58 78 93 93

Bowling: *First Innings*—Zaheer Khan 6–0–10–1; Harbhajan Singh 21–4–53–0; Kumble 19–0–90–5; Kartik 15.3–1–44–4. *Second Innings*—Zaheer Khan 2–0–14–1; Harbhajan Singh 10.5–2–29–5; Kartik 12–3–32–3; Kumble 6–3–5–1.

Umpires: Aleem Dar (Pakistan) and R. E. Koertzen (South Africa).
TV Umpire: K. Hariharan.
Referee: R. S. Madugalle (Sri Lanka).

Australia in New Zealand, 2004-05

by ANDREW RAMSEY

There was much to generate enthusiasm prior to Australia's six-week skirmish across the Tasman. Initially, there was a five-match limited-overs series between the two top-rated teams according to the official international rankings. Then followed three Tests, and although New Zealand had been found sadly wanting several months earlier in Australia, a belief existed that they would prove far sterner opponents on home pitches.

Or so the predictions went. By the time Ricky Ponting's team packed their kit for the trip home and the two-month break that awaited most of them before their Ashes campaign, they had humiliated the Black Caps in the Test arena, made a clean sweep of the one-dayers and even triumphed in the historic first Twenty20 international. The appetite-whetting prospect of mixing it with the world champions, of which New Zealand captain Stephen Fleming spoke at the tour's outset, tasted increasingly sour for the home team's fans.

And no player suffered more than Fleming himself. Found wanting by the sheer speed of Brett Lee in the limited-overs matches, Fleming – by then bereft of confidence – was hunted and bagged by Glenn McGrath during a Test series which netted New Zealand's most accomplished batsman just 104 runs from six completed innings at a meagre 17.33. So successful were the Australians in targeting their most potent rival that, after the second Test in Wellington – the one match in which New Zealand escaped defeat, by dint of the capital's famously bleak weather – Fleming announced he would surrender his recently-instituted role as an opener and revert to the relative sanctuary of his traditional berth in the middle order.

By then it was too late to stem the Australians' momentum, built largely on the bowling deeds of the remarkable McGrath. Having turned 35 in the week before the team landed in Auckland, McGrath insisted that the successful ankle surgery he endured in 2003 had enabled him to bowl as well or better than at any time in his career. His results in New Zealand and the fact that he finished the tour on the cusp of 500 Test wickets certainly added credibility to his claim. His efforts on the opening day of the final Test at Eden Park, in which he delivered 24 overs at a cost of a mere 20 runs, provided one of the more enduring memories of a lopsided series.

Most of the other highlights were delivered by the blazing bat of Adam Gilchrist. The sublimely-gifted left-hander effectively altered the course of the first two Tests with brilliant centuries. His run-a-ball 121 in Christchurch not only allowed Australia to snatch the initiative after New Zealand had wrested the advantage for much of the first two days, but its breathtaking brutality and audacity put paid to the Black Caps' morale and self-belief for the remaining Tests.

It was entirely appropriate that during another whirlwind hundred in the Wellington Test, Gilchrist overtook his predecessor, Ian Healy, to become the most prolific run-scorer among Australia's rich tradition of influential wicket-keeper/batsmen. The fact that in that innings he went on to achieve his second-highest Test score also underlined his unflappable temperament, for less than an hour before the third day's play unexpectedly resumed thanks to a break in the weather, Gilchrist was blissfully entertaining his three-year-old son in the team's hotel pool. Not even a rushed trip to the Basin Reserve or the absence of any preparation could help the New Zealand bowlers find a way past his bludgeoning bat.

While Gilchrist and McGrath were the undisputed stars of the series, the depth of Australia's playing resources, and the other players' willingness and ability to chime in with meaningful contributions on cue, provided a stark contrast to an undermanned and overwhelmed New Zealand line-up. With the bat, it was Simon Katich (in Christchurch), Damien Martyn (Wellington) and Ponting (Auckland) who produced standout innings when they were needed. On the bowling side, Shane Warne came up with some vintage gems in the first Test, Michael Kasprowicz reached a deserved milestone of 100 Test wickets with clever bowling in the second and Jason Gillespie finally had luck go his way in the third.

But perhaps the most instructive contribution came from the Australian selectors, who opted not to play Lee even though he equalled the fastest recorded delivery of his career during a one-dayer in Napier and frightened the life out of New Zealand's top order in all five limited-overs encounters. Had the blond speedster been born on the opposite side of the Tasman, he would have been the first picked in their team. As it was, he spent the Test series delivering drinks instead of scorching bouncers and inswinging yorkers.

Australia's complete supremacy must be viewed in the light of the difficulties New Zealand faced in the absence of key personnel. The best strike bowler, Shane Bond, took his first tentative steps to a comeback from back surgery during the tour, but only at domestic level, and was not prepared to risk rushing an international return. Key all-rounder Jacob Oram, the success story of New Zealand's tour of Australia in late 2004, was also sidelined because of a back complaint, as was promising fast bowler Ian Butler. To compound these woes, batting all-rounder Scott Styris suffered a recurrence of a knee injury during the one-day matches and did not appear in the Test arena, which robbed the Black Caps of some crucial top-order stability.

Throw in the retirement of reliable opener Mark Richardson after the Australian tour, and the complete mental disintegration of new-ball bowler Daryl Tuffey during a disastrous one-day hit-out, and the burden of tackling the world's most formidable opposition fell squarely on the shoulders of the few proven Test players who remained fit and able – up to a point. Fleming was one of the few whose physical fitness did not desert him although, as noted, his confidence was left badly beaten.

Left-arm spinner Daniel Vettori was far and away New Zealand's most accomplished bowler, but his ability to deliver lengthy and repeated spells was compromised by a nagging lower-back injury. And experienced batsmen Nathan Astle and Craig McMillan struggled against the relentless Australian attack; McMillan eventually was dropped for the final Test. The Black Caps' one bright spot came in the form of impressive No. 3 batsman Hamish Marshall, whose century in the opening Test was just his second in a lengthy first-class career, and his team's only three-figure score of the Test series. That – along with the fact that No. 8 batsman Vettori was New Zealand's second-highest run-scorer in the Tests – succinctly summed up a lamentable month-and-a-half for Fleming's demoralised band.

AUSTRALIAN TOUR RESULTS

Test matches – Played 3: Won 2, Drawn 1.
First-class matches – Played 3, Won 2, Drawn 1.
Wins – New Zealand (2).
International limited-overs matches – Played 5: Won 5.
Other non first-class matches: Played 1: Won 1. *Wins*: New Zealand.

AUSTRALIAN LIMITED-OVERS SQUAD

R. T. Ponting (*captain*), A. C. Gilchrist (*vice-captain*), M. J. Clarke, J. N. Gillespie, M. L. Hayden, G. B. Hogg, J. R. Hopes, M. E. K. Hussey, M. S. Kasprowicz, S. M. Katich, B. Lee, D. R. Martyn, G. D. McGrath and A. Symonds.

Manager: S. R. Bernard. *Coach*: J. M. Buchanan. *Performance analyst/assistant coaches*: D. Holder, J. D. Siddons and D. F Hills. *Physiotherapist*: A. Kountouri. *Masseur*: Ms L. Frostick. *Physical performance manager*: J. A. Campbell. *Media manager*: J. Rose.

Note: *Matches in this section that were not first-class are signified by a dagger.*

LIMITED-OVERS INTERNATIONAL RUN SCORERS

	M	I	NO	R	HS	100s	50s	Avge	Ct/St	S-R
R. T. Ponting	4	4	1	266	141*	1	2	88.67	1	93.01
H. J. H. Marshall. . . .	5	5	0	198	76	0	2	39.60	1	76.45
M. L. Hayden	2	2	0	185	114	1	1	92.50	2	79.40
C. D. McMillan	5	5	0	173	63	0	1	34.60	1	86.50
D. R. Martyn	5	5	1	171	65*	0	2	42.75	1	80.28
A. C. Gilchrist	5	5	0	167	91	0	2	33.40	11/1	117.61
A. Symonds	5	5	0	152	53	0	1	30.40	1	113.43
M. J. Clarke	5	5	2	147	71*	0	1	49.00	2	100.68
N. J. Astle	4	4	0	132	65	0	1	33.00	1	59.19
S. M. Katich	4	4	0	106	58	0	1	26.50	2	76.26
B. B. McCullum	5	5	0	104	36	0	0	20.80	5	65.82
D. L. Vettori	4	4	1	99	83	0	1	33.00	1	101.02
M. E. K. Hussey . . .	4	3	3	97	65*	0	1	–	3	104.19
S. P. Fleming	5	5	0	79	37	0	0	15.80	1	66.95
C. L. Cairns	5	4	0	70	36	0	0	17.50	0	94.59
G. B. Hogg	4	2	2	34	25*	0	0	–	1	80.95
J. W. Wilson	2	2	0	23	22	0	0	11.50	3	79.31
C. D. Cumming	2	2	0	23	13	0	0	11.50	2	50.00
J. A. H. Marshall . . .	3	3	0	23	14	0	0	7.67	0	60.53
K. D. Mills	5	5	1	20	10	0	0	5.00	0	60.61
T. K. Canning	1	1	0	16	16	0	0	16.00	0	64.00
M. S. Sinclair	2	2	0	15	15	0	0	7.50	1	42.86
S. B. Styris	1	1	0	14	14	0	0	14.00	0	29.79
B. Lee	5	1	1	4	4*	0	0	–	1	133.33
L. J. Hamilton	2	2	2	3	2*	0	0	–	0	50.00
M. H. W. Papps. . . .	1	1	1	3	3†	0	0	–	1	30.00
D. R. Tuffey	3	3	2	1	1	0	0	1.00	0	45.45
J. N. Gillespie	3	–	–	–	–	–	–	–	0	–
J. R. Hopes	1	–	–	–	–	–	–	–	0	–
G. D. McGrath	4	–	–	–	–	–	–	–	1	–
M. S. Kasprowicz . . .	4	–	–	–	–	–	–	–	2	–

* *Denotes not out; † Denotes retired hurt.*

LIMITED-OVERS INTERNATIONAL WICKET-TAKERS

	O	Mdns	R	W	BB	5Wi	Avge	RPO
B. Lee	43	4	169	10	3-41	0	16.90	3.93
G. D. McGrath	36.3	4	151	9	4-16	0	16.78	4.14
A. Symonds	31	1	154	7	3-41	0	22.00	4.97
K. D. Mills	45	3	271	5	2-62	0	54.20	6.02
C. L. Cairns	36	1	203	5	2-56	0	40.60	5.64
M. S. Kasprowicz	36	6	160	5	3-36	0	32.00	4.44
S. B. Styris	10	1	40	4	4-40	0	10.00	4.00
G. B. Hogg	36.4	0	191	4	3-45	0	47.75	5.21
J. N. Gillespie	25.4	1	105	4	2-45	0	26.25	4.09
D. L. Vettori	40	0	132	2	2-31	0	66.00	3.30
C. D. McMillan	21.2	0	141	2	1-31	0	70.50	6.61
J. W. Wilson	15	0	125	1	1-68	0	125.00	8.33
M. J. Clarke	9	0	48	1	1-13	0	48.00	5.33
J. R. Hopes	10	1	38	1	1-38	0	38.00	3.80
L. J. Hamilton	18	0	143	1	1-76	0	143.00	7.94
D. R. Tuffey	18	1	145	1	1-73	0	145.00	8.06
T. K. Canning	10	0	80	1	1-80	0	80.00	8.00
N. J. Astle	18	0	85	0	–	0	–	4.72
M. E. K. Hussey	3	0	22	0	–	0	–	7.33
C. D. Cumming	3	0	17	0	–	0	–	5.67

†NEW ZEALAND V AUSTRALIA

TWENTY20 International

At Eden Park, Auckland, February 17, 2005. Day/night game. Australia won by 44 runs. *Toss:* Australia. All players Twenty20 International debuts.

Australia trumped New Zealand in the first-ever international Twenty20 – not that anyone seemed to care that much. For this was more fancy dress party than legitimate cricket contest; an event where the New Zealand players sported afro hairstyles and handlebar moustaches, and the 30,000-strong crowd saved their loudest cheers for the retro soundtrack blasted from the PA system. Sadly for the New Zealanders, facial hair, beige uniforms and Dexy's Midnight Runners couldn't help them reproduce the form of their mid-80s forebears. After Ricky Ponting bludgeoned 98 not out from just 55 deliveries, the New Zealanders never appeared in the chase, losing four quick wickets to Michael Kasprowicz and unwittingly setting the tone for the remainder of Australia's tour. Ponting hammered Daryl Tuffey for 6, 2, 6, 6, 4, 6 off a single over, while Andrew Symonds (32 off 13 balls), Mike Hussey (31 off 15) and Simon Katich (30 off 25) provided able support. The win ensured Australia a unique place in cricketing history, having triumphed in the inaugural Test (in 1876-77), limited-overs international (in 1970-71) and now the Twenty20 international. But fun, rather than history, remained the over-riding theme for the evening, summed up by Glenn McGrath's feigned underarm ball to Kyle Mills to end the match.

Match reports by ALEX BROWN.

Man of Match: R. T. Ponting. *Attendance:* 29,500.

Australia

†A. C. Gilchrist c McMillan b Mills ..	1	(3)	M. E. K. Hussey not out 31	(15)
M. J. Clarke c McMillan b Tuffey	7	(4)		
A. Symonds c McCullum b Mills ...	32	(13)	L-b 9, w 3 12	
*R. T. Ponting not out	98	(55)		
D. R. Martyn b Mills	3	(5)	(20 overs, 71 mins) (5 wkts) 214	
S. M. Katich b Cairns	30	(25)	Fall: 10 21 46 54 135	

J. R. Hopes, B. Lee, M. S. Kasprowicz, G. D. McGrath (did not bat).

Bowling: Tuffey 4–0–50–1; Mills 4–0–44–3; Cairns 4–0–28–1; Wilson 4–0–43–0; Adams 4–0–40–0.

New Zealand

†B. B. McCullum c Ponting b Kasprowicz 36		(24)	J. W. Wilson b McGrath 18	(14)
*S. P. Fleming b Kasprowicz 18		(13)	K. D. Mills c Kasprowicz b McGrath 0	(1)
M. S. Sinclair c Katich b Kasprowicz . 0		(1)	D. R. Tuffey not out 5	(2)
S. B. Styris b Lee 66		(39)		
C. D. McMillan c Hussey b Hopes ... 9		(8)	W 2 2	
C. L. Cairns c McGrath b Kasprowicz . 1		(4)		
H. J. H. Marshall b Symonds 8		(7)	(20 overs, 73 mins) 170	
A. R. Adams run out (McGrath/Symonds) 7		(7)	Fall: 49 49 67 93 95 105 121 161 165 170	

Bowling: Lee 4–0–26–1; McGrath 4–0–48–2; Kasprowicz 4–0–29–4; Hopes 3–0–23–1; Symonds 3–0–33–1; Clarke 2–0–11–0.

Umpires: B. F. Bowden and A. L. Hill.
TV Umpire: D. B. Cowie.

†NEW ZEALAND v AUSTRALIA
First Limited-Overs International

At WestpacTrust Stadium, Wellington, February 19, 2005. Day/night game. Australia won by 10 runs. *Toss:* Australia.

If the Twenty20 game was a light-hearted arm-wrestle, the first one-dayer in Wellington was an all-out cage match. The Australians eventually emerged with a gripping victory, but not before Glenn McGrath was involved in a verbal altercation with a stadium security guard, Matthew Hayden was spat on by a spectator and Simon Katich was pelted with bottles. McGrath, who claimed 4 for 16, later said the hostile environment at Wellington's "Cake Tin" had provided added motivation to turn the match back in Australia's favour, after Hamish Marshall's dashing 76 from 69 deliveries had steered the Black Caps to within sight of victory. The New Zealanders were eventually dismissed for 226 in the 49th over – an innings highlighted by the free hitting of Marshall and the quick thinking of Adam Gilchrist, who orchestrated McGrath's first-ever stumping dismissal. Earlier, Matthew Hayden enjoyed a welcome return to form, hitting an occasionally charmed 71. His second-wicket stand with Ricky Ponting largely negated Australia's middle-order collapse during which four wickets fell for the addition of just five runs in 23 deliveries.

Man of Match: G. D. McGrath.

Australia

†A. C. Gilchrist c Sinclair b Mills	....	4	(5)	G. B. Hogg not out	25 (33)
M. L. Hayden b Styris	....	71	(109)	B. Lee not out	4 (3)
*R. T. Ponting c Vettori b Styris	.....	61	(84)		
D. R. Martyn b Styris	....	7	(16)	B 1, l-b 1, w 4, n-b 5	11
A. Symonds b Cairns	....	53	(44)		
M. J. Clarke c Marshall b Styris	....	0	(5)	(50 overs, 197 mins) (7 wkts)	236
S. M. Katich c McCullum b Cairns	...	0	(5)	Fall: 7 140 153 158 158 160 229	

M. S. Kasprowicz, G. D. McGrath (did not bat).

Bowling: Tuffey 8–0–47–0; Mills 9–1–48–1; Cairns 10–0–56–2; Styris 10–1–40–4; Vettori 10–0–33–0; Astle 3–0–10–0.

New Zealand

*S. P. Fleming lbw b Lee	....	5	(10)	D.L. Vettori b Lee	0 (1)
N. J. Astle b Hogg	....	65	(112)	K.D. Mills not out	1 (1)
M. S. Sinclair c Gilchrist b McGrath	..	0	(8)	D. R. Tuffey b McGrath	1 (2)
S. B. Styris c Hayden b Symonds	..	14	(47)		
C. L. Cairns run out (Clarke/Gilchrist)		0	(3)	L-b 6, w 8, n-b 5	19
H. J. H. Marshall b McGrath	....	76	(69)		—
C. D. McMillan st Gilchrist b McGrath	37	(30)	(48.4 overs, 213 mins)	226	
†B. B. McCullum c Katich b Lee	....	8	(13)	Fall: 13 16 72 73 113 179 218 224 224 226	

Bowling: Lee 9–1–41–3; McGrath 9.4–3–16–4; Kasprowicz 10–1–62–0; Symonds 10–0–52–1; Hogg 9–0–44–1; Clarke 1–0–5–0.

Umpires: Aleem Dar (Pakistan) and B. F. Bowden.
TV Umpire: E. A. Watkin.
Referee: C. H. Lloyd (West Indies).

†NEW ZEALAND v AUSTRALIA

Second Limited-Overs International

At Lancaster Park, Christchurch, February 22, 2005. Day/night game. Australia won by 106 runs. *Toss:* New Zealand.

The fallout from Australia's spiteful victory over New Zealand in Wellington dominated headlines and, in the case of Black Caps captain Stephen Fleming, provoked a stinging response ahead of this next clash. Agitated by the media's "obsession" with the world champions, Fleming declared he would not discuss any positive aspect of the Australians' play for the remainder of the tour. As it turned out, he didn't need to. For all that was good about Australia's one-day side was clearly on display at Jade Stadium, with Matthew Hayden scoring a powerful century and the tourists claiming a devastating victory. After Fleming made the curious decision to send the Australians in to bat on the kind of hard, fast wicket they generally relish, Hayden posted 114 from 124 deliveries as Australia swept to a commanding total. The innings concluded on a controversial note, with home umpire Billy Bowden docking the visitors one run for running on the pitch. But it hardly mattered. The second half was notable only for the late heroics of Daniel Vettori – who almost tripled his previous highest one-day score with a brisk 83 – and a shoulder injury sustained by Hayden while taking a spectacular outfield catch. This was hardly the comeback Jeff Wilson had envisaged, making his return to international cricket after a celebrated 12-year rugby career.

Man of Match: M. L. Hayden.

Australia

†A. C. Gilchrist c McCullum b Tuffey	0	(2)
M. L. Hayden c Wilson b Mills	114	(124)
*R. T. Ponting run out (Marshall)	 53	(57)
D. R. Martyn run out (McMillan)	 58	(70)
A. Symonds c Wilson b Mills	 13	(10)
M. J. Clarke c McCullum b Cairns	... 23	(13)

M. E. K. Hussey not out	 32	(20)
G. B. Hogg not out	 9	(9)
L-b 1, w 6, n-b 5	....	12
(50 overs, 207 mins) (6 wkts)		314

Fall: 0 99 232 237 254 283

B. Lee, J. N. Gillespie, G. D. McGrath (did not bat).

Bowling: Tuffey 8–1–73–1; Mills 10–0–62–2; Cairns 10–0–62–1; Vettori 10–0–31–0; Wilson 6–0–57–0; Astle 6–0–28–0.

New Zealand

*S. P. Fleming c Gilchrist b Lee	.....	1	(4)
N. J. Astle c Gilchrist b McGrath	....	3	(8)
M. S. Sinclair c Gilchrist b Lee	......	15	(27)
H. J. H. Marshall c Gilchrist b McGrath	16	(20)
C. D. McMillan c Gilchrist b Symonds	12	(20)
C. L. Cairns c Hayden b Symonds	....	22	(16)
†B. B. McCullum c and b Symonds	..	20	(41)
D. L. Vettori c (sub) Katich b Gillespie	83	(77)

J. W. Wilson c Ponting b Gillespie	..	22	(27)
K. D. Mills run out (Clarke)	....	4	(7)
D. R. Tuffey not out	....	0	(0)
L-b 3, w 4, n-b 3	....	10
(40.4 overs, 166 mins)		208

Fall: 4 12 28 49 72 73 135 197 208 208

Bowling: Lee 8–2–28–2; McGrath 7–0–42–2; Gillespie 9.4–1–45–2; Symonds 6–0–41–3; Hogg 10–0–49–0.

Umpires: Aleem Dar (Pakistan) and B. F. Bowden.
TV Umpire: A. L. Hill.
Referee: C. H. Lloyd (West Indies).

†NEW ZEALAND v AUSTRALIA

Third Limited-Overs International

At Eden Park, Auckland, February 26, 2005. Day/night game. Australia won by 86 runs. *Toss:* Australia. *Limited-overs international debut:* J. A. H. Marshall.

It was bizarre, occasionally violent and again controversial, but the result remained the same. In a match noted for Daryl Tuffey's horrendous first over and Brett Lee's beam-ball to Brendon McCullum, the Australians clinched the series, thus completing New Zealand's first home one-day series defeat in four years. Kiwi coach John Bracewell had called in sports psychologist Gilbert Enoka ahead of the match to work with several of his players, but clearly Tuffey needed more time on the couch. The right-arm quick began with a sequence of four no-balls (one of which was cut to the boundary by Adam Gilchrist), two wides, another Gilchrist boundary and a leg-side wide; he bowled just two overs for 25 runs. Michael Clarke (71 not out from 75 balls) and Michael Hussey (65 not out from 73) compounded New Zealand's misery late in the innings, combining for a record sixth-wicket partnership of 136 that propelled the tourists to their highest-ever total at Eden Park. The Black Caps' run-chase appeared doomed from the start when Lee dismissed Stephen Fleming for the third game in succession and then sent Michael Papps to hospital after a searing bouncer thudded into the batsman's helmet. Lee later struck McCullum with a beam-ball that would prove a contentious topic of conversation throughout the week. It had little impact on the result, however.

Man of Match: M. J. Clarke.

Australia

†A. C. Gilchrist c Astle b Cairns	18	(36)	M. E. K. Hussey not out	65	(73)
S. M. Katich lbw b Vettori	58	(78)			
*R. T. Ponting run out (Papps/McCullum)	11	(18)	L-b 2, w 7, n-b 10	19	
D. R. Martyn lbw b Vettori	1	(3)			
A. Symonds c Papps b Mills	21	(27)	(50 overs, 197 mins) (5 wkts)	264	
M. J. Clarke not out	71	(75)	Fall: 68 85 90 117 128		

G. B. Hogg, B. Lee, J. N. Gillespie, M. S. Kasprowicz (did not bat).

Bowling: Tuffey 2–0–25–0; Mills 9–0–57–1; Cairns 10–1–55–1; Astle 9–0–47–0; Vettori 10–0–31–2; McMillan 10–0–47–0.

New Zealand

*S. P. Fleming b Lee	1	(6)	D. L. Vettori c Gilchrist b Hogg	0	(1)
N. J. Astle c Gilchrist b Kasprowicz	27	(43)	K. D. Mills c Kasprowicz b Hogg	1	(6)
M. H. W. Papps retired hurt	3	(10)	D. R. Tuffey not out	0	(0)
H. J. H. Marshall run out (Symonds)	55	(87)			
C. D. McMillan c Hussey b Symonds	26	(43)	L-b 8, w 4, n-b 4	16	
J. A. H. Marshall run out (Symonds)	14	(16)			
C. L. Cairns c Hussey b Lee	12	(20)	(41.4 overs, 182 mins) (9 wkts)	178	
†B. B. McCullum c Hussey b Hogg	23	(22)	Fall: 7 45 114 135 136 161 162 172 178		

Bowling: Lee 7-0-25-2; Gillespie 6-0-14-0; Kasprowicz 8-1-28-1; Symonds 10-1-36-1; Hussey 3-0-22-0; Hogg 7.4-0-45-3.

Umpires: Aleem Dar (Pakistan) and D. B. Cowie.
TV Umpire: A. L. Hill.
Referee: C. H. Lloyd (West Indies).

†NEW ZEALAND v AUSTRALIA
Fourth Limited-overs International

At Basin Reserve, Wellington, March 1, 2005. Australia won by seven wickets. *Toss:* Australia. Limited-overs International debut: L. J. Hamilton, J. R. Hopes.

Another day, another loss, another injury for the New Zealanders. In assessing his side's seven-wicket defeat to Australia, during which key batsman Nathan Astle was admitted to the Black Caps' ever-expanding infirmary, Stephen Fleming made the downtrodden concession that "anyone who has a little bit of talent is going to get thrown in a black uniform at the moment". It was tough to argue otherwise. Without one-day mainstays Daniel Vettori, Jacob Oram and Scott Styris, the Kiwis were forced to call up the 31-year-old real estate agent Lance Hamilton to make his international debut, joining other inexperienced players such as Jeff Wilson and Craig Cumming. None made a substantial impact. The match began promisingly for the New Zealanders, with Fleming and Astle combining for an opening stand of 84. Australia's pace attack, however, stymied the remainder of the home side's batting line-up, Brett Lee again leading the charge with 2 for 41. Debutant James Hopes also claimed a wicket with his medium-pacers and Michael Clarke completed one of the plays of the year, diving full stretch off his own bowling to catch Hamish Marshall, as the Black Caps set Australia 234 to win. Even without the injured duo of Ricky Ponting and Matthew Hayden, the Australians made short work of hauling in the modest target. Stand-in captain Adam Gilchrist,

Damien Martyn, Andrew Symonds and Simon Katich propelled the tourists to victory in just 34.2 overs to claim a 4–0 series lead. "We're trialling players out to see how they'll go at international level," Fleming said after the match. "To do that against the best side in the world … well, you've seen the results."

Man of Match: A. C. Gilchrist.

New Zealand

*S. P. Fleming c Lee b Gillespie	37	(53)	J. W. Wilson lbw b McGrath	1	(2)
N. J. Astle c Gilchrist b Kasprowicz	37	(60)	K. D. Mills run out		
			(K'wicz/Hussey/G'christ)	4	(7)
C. D. Cumming c Clarke b McGrath	10	(22)	L. J. Hamilton not out	2	(4)
H. J. H. Marshall c and b Clarke	23	(42)			
C. D. McMillan lbw b Hopes	35	(36)	B 1, l-b 12, w 5, n-b 4	22	
J. A. H. Marshall c Gilchrist b Gillespie	9	(21)			
C. L. Cairns c Martyn b Lee	36	(35)	(49.5 overs, 211 mins)	233	
†B. B. McCullum c Katich b Lee	17	(21)	Fall: 84 90 104 145 163 173 214 220 226 233		

Bowling: Lee 9–1–41–2; McGrath 9.5–1–48–2; Gillespie 10–0–46–2; Kasprowicz 8–2–34–1; Hopes 10–1–38–1; Clarke 3–0–31–1.

Australia

*†A. C. Gilchrist c McMillan b Wilson	54	(37)			
S. M. Katich c McCullum b Cairns	43	(41)	L-b 3, w 8, n-b 5	16	
D. R. Martyn not out	65	(78)			
A. Symonds c Wilson b McMillan	48	(37)	(34.2 overs, 146 mins) (3 wkts)	236	
M. J. Clarke not out	10	(17)	Fall: 78 113 212		

J. R. Hopes, M. E. K. Hussey, B. Lee, J. N. Gillespie, M. S. Kasprowicz, G. D. McGrath (did not bat).

Bowling: Mills 7–1–37–0; Hamilton 8–0–67–0; Wilson 9–0–68–1; Cairns 6–0–30–1; McMillan 4.2–0–31–1.

Umpires: Aleem Dar (Pakistan) and A. L. Hill.
TV Umpire: D. B. Cowie.
Referee: C. H. Lloyd (West Indies).

†NEW ZEALAND v AUSTRALIA

Fifth Limited-Overs International

At McLean Park, Napier, March 5, 2005. Australia won by 122 runs. *Toss:* New Zealand.

The Australians continued to rewrite cricket's record books, completing the first-ever 5–0 one-day series sweep by a touring team in New Zealand and attaining the highest limited-overs rating ever recorded. Australia's victory also relegated the Black Caps to third place in the International Cricket Council's one-day table, while Ricky Ponting recorded the highest one-day total by an Australian against New Zealand and Brett Lee broke the 160 km/h barrier twice in an over. The match began in the worst possible fashion for New Zealand as they lost Jeff Wilson before play with an ankle injury and Chris Cairns after four overs to a hamstring strain. Without two of their strike bowlers, the already injury-ravaged New Zealand attack was destroyed first by Adam Gilchrist (91 off 62 balls) and then Ponting (141 not out from 127). Ponting's second-highest one-day innings led Australia to their second-highest one-day total against the Black Caps. Given the way the series had evolved to this point, New Zealand had no chance of scoring the near seven runs an over required from the outset. Lee's lightning pace – topping out at 160.8 kph – and Michael Kasprowicz's quick dismissals of Stephen Fleming and James Marshall confirmed as much, and the Australians entered the Test component of the tour brimming with confidence; New Zealand's, in stark contrast, can hardly ever have been lower.

Man of Match: R. T. Ponting.

Australia

†A. C. Gilchrist c Cumming b Canning 91 (62)	M. E. K. Hussey not out 0 (0)	
S. M. Katich c McCullum b Hamilton . 5 (15)		
*R. T. Ponting not out . . . . .141(127)	L-b 7, w 2, n-b 1 10	
D. R. Martyn c Fleming b Mills 40 (46)		
A. Symonds run out (Vettori/McMillan)17 (16)	(50 overs, 196 mins) (5 wkts) 347	
M. J. Clarke c Cumming b McMillan . 43 (36)	Fall: 37 129 204 241 335	

B. Lee, G. B. Hogg, M. S. Kasprowicz, G. D. McGrath (did not bat).

Bowling: Mills 10–1–67–1; Hamilton 10–0–76–1; Canning 10–0–80–1; Vettori 10–0–37–0; McMillan 7–0–63–1; Cumming 3–0–17–0.

New Zealand

C. D. Cumming lbw b Lee 13 (24)	D. L. Vettori not out 16 (19)	
*S. P. Fleming c Gilchrist b Kasprowicz 35 (45)	K. D. Mills c Kasprowicz b McGrath 10 (12)	
H. J. H. Marshall run out (Clarke) 28 (41)	L. J. Hamilton not out 1 (2)	
J. A. H. Marshall b Kasprowicz 0 (1)	B 1, l-b 1, w 3, n-b 2 7	
C. D. McMillan c Hogg b Symonds . . 63 (71)		
†B. B. McCullum c McGrath b Symonds 36 (61)	(50 overs, 192 mins) (8 wkts) 225	
T. K. Canning b Kasprowicz 16 (25)	Fall: 39 60 60 103 167 196 199 223	

C. L. Cairns (did not bat).

Bowling: Lee 10–0–34–1; McGrath 10–0–45–1; Kasprowicz 10–2–36–3; Hogg 10–0–53–0; Clarke 5–0–30–0; Symonds 5–0–25–2.

Umpires: A. L. Hill and D. R. Shepherd (England).
TV Umpire: D. B. Cowie.
Referee: C. H. Lloyd (West Indies).

AUSTRALIAN TEST SQUAD

R. T. Ponting (*captain*), A. C. Gilchrist (*vice-captain*), M. J. Clarke, M. L. Hayden, J. N. Gillespie, B. J. Hodge, M. E. K. Hussey, M. S. Kasprowicz, S. M. Katich, J. L. Langer, B. Lee, D. R. Martyn, G. D. McGrathand S. K. Warne.

TEST BATTING AVERAGES

	M	I	NO	R	HS	100s	50s	Avge	Ct/St	S-R
A. C. Gilchrist	3	3	1	343	162	2	1	171.50	7/0	102.69
R. T. Ponting	3	5	2	293	105	1	1	97.67	2	72.70
D. R. Martyn	3	3	0	235	165	1	0	78.33	1	48.35
J. L. Langer.	3	5	2	206	72*	0	2	68.67	3	68.67
D. L. Vettori	3	5	2	198	65	0	1	66.00	0	68.99
S. M. Katich	3	3	0	188	118	1	0	62.67	3	50.40
H. J. H. Marshall. . . .	3	6	0	269	146	1	1	44.83	0	43.25
N. J. Astle.	3	6	1	196	74	0	2	39.20	2	49.87
M. S. Kasprowicz. . .	3	3	2	38	23	0	0	38.00	0	61.29
M. L. Hayden	3	5	0	158	61	0	1	31.60	1	49.69
L. Vincent	3	6	0	160	63	0	1	26.67	2	50.16
C. D. Cumming	3	6	1	133	74	0	1	26.60	2	33.33
S. K. Warne	3	3	1	53	50*	0	1	26.50	1	79.10
S. P. Fleming	3	6	0	104	65	0	1	17.33	2	35.74

	M	I	NO	R	HS	100s	50s	Avge	Ct/St	S-R
.N. Gillespie......	3	3	0	49	35	0	0	16.33	4	21.68
3.B. McCullum....	3	5	0	81	29	0	0	16.20	8/0	57.04
.A.H. Marshall....	1	2	0	32	29	0	0	16.00	0	50.79
?.J. Wiseman......	1	2	0	31	23	0	0	15.50	1	72.09
.E.C. Franklin....	3	5	1	57	26	0	0	14.25	1	35.63
C.D. McMillan	2	3	0	38	20	0	0	12.67	0	48.10
M.J. Clarke	3	3	0	38	22	0	0	12.67	2	34.23
.E. O'Brien.......	2	3	0	10	5	0	0	3.33	1	35.71
C.S. Martin	3	5	2	5	4*	0	0	1.67	0	13.16
3.D. McGrath	3	2	0	0	0	0	0	0.00	1	0.00

TEST BOWLING AVERAGES

	O	Mdns	R	W	BB	5Wi	10W/m	Avge	S-R
M.J. Clarke..........	8	1	24	2	1-8	0	0	12.00	24.00
3.D. McGrath........	126.2	47	283	18	6-115	1	0	15.72	42.11
S.K. Warne.........	131.3	25	374	17	5-39	1	0	22.00	46.41
.E.C. Franklin......	92.1	13	415	12	6-119	1	0	34.58	46.08
M.S. Kasprowicz.....	98.2	20	319	8	3-42	0	0	39.88	73.75
.N. Gillespie	107	25	320	7	3-38	0	0	45.71	91.71
D.L. Vettori	123.5	22	397	8	5-106	1	0	49.63	92.88
N.J. Astle	55	15	155	3	1-32	0	0	51.67	110.00
?.J. Wiseman	34.3	7	77	1	1-64	0	0	77.00	207.00
.E. O'Brien	43	7	197	2	1-73	0	0	98.50	129.00
C.S. Martin..........	94	17	397	2	1-92	0	0	198.50	282.00
R.T. Ponting	4	1	10	0	–	0	0	–	–

*Denotes not out

NEW ZEALAND v AUSTRALIA

First Test Match

by MICHAEL CRUTCHER

At Lancaster Park, Christchurch, March 10, 11, 12, 13, 2005. Australia won by nine wickets. *Toss:* Australia. Test debut: C.D. Cumming, I.E. O'Brien.

The Australian team had to wait until late on the eve of the match before learning the answer to the most discussed question leading into the series – would Brett Lee play in the first Test? Lee had mounted an almost irresistible case to end his 14-month Test absence by tormenting the New Zealand batsmen in the one-day series. He bowled the equal fastest delivery of his career in the final one-day match in Napier and his control had impressed captain Ricky Ponting. But Lee was told before he slept on a Wednesday night in central Christchurch that selectors had retained the proven pace combination of Glenn McGrath, Jason Gillespie and Michael Kasprowicz.

Ponting never publicly revealed whether he wanted Lee to play, but New Zealand's batsmen privately admitted they preferred not to face him. And their batting on the first day at Jade Stadium had a relaxed feel as they jolted a below-par Australia. Hamish Marshall posted his maiden Test century in the final overs before stumps as New Zealand edged to 3 for 265 in their first innings. Marshall had finally proved that he could build innings of substance at the highest level after waiting five years for his maiden first-class century. He batted with maturity and certainty, scoring his 146 from 256 balls. Debutant Craig Cumming supplied a gritty 74 before falling to a leg-side trap against Kasprowicz, while Stephen Fleming was unconvincing. The New Zealand captain had volunteered to fill the opening role vacated by the retired Mark Richardson, but he struggled against McGrath's accuracy. His dismissal for a scratchy 18 from 60 balls was one of the few joys on the opening day for Ponting, who had sent a team in for the first time in his Test captaincy. He had expected some early assistance from a wicket that played remarkably well considering that a Super 12 rugby union match had been played on it five days earlier

Ponting was regretting his decision on the second day when Marshall and Nathan Astle (74 in 216 minutes) guided the Black Caps to 3 for 330. McGrath then intervened in outstanding fashion, proving again that he was not faltering despite reaching his 35th birthday four weeks earlier. He had become the first Australian fast bowler since Ray Lindwall in 1960 to start a Test after turning 35. He overcame a minor stomach muscle strain on the first day to charge through the New Zealand batting order with sharp reverse swing, claiming 6 for 40 in nine overs. The Kiwis were dismissed for 433.

Justin Langer and Matthew Hayden made a brutal start to the Australian innings. The left-handers thumped 15 runs from the first over bowled by Chris Martin, adding to the doubts about New Zealand's ability to bowl out Australia twice without injured players Shane Bond and Jacob Oram. But the cheeky Black Caps again proved they should not be under-estimated on their own soil when they had Australia floundering at 6 for 201 early on the third morning.

Daniel Vettori played a key role in unhinging the Australian top order after Langer, Hayden, Ponting and Damien Martyn had made promising starts. But the New Zealanders' hopes of a significant first-innings lead were blown away by Adam Gilchrist and Simon Katich when the pair thrashed 212 runs in a three-hour partnership. Gilchrist was devastating against Vettori's left-arm spin; Fleming placed three men on the leg-side boundary but Gilchrist took them on, lofting three balls from Vettori deep into the western grandstand. He scored 121 from 126 deliveries, with six sixes and 12 fours. Katich did not use the same force in his classy 118, which lasted 229 balls and contained 20 fours and one six, but his innings was just as valuable. He took a large step toward nailing down his middle-order position after taking over from Darren Lehmann. He maintained his concentration despite a bizarre sight while celebrating his century. As he raised his bat to the crowd, a streaker sprinted past him, only to be tackled heavily by a security guard; the streaker was taken to hospital with rib injuries.

The New Zealanders gathered themselves up after the Gilchrist-Katich partnership to claim the last four wickets for 19 runs, including McGrath's national record 30th Test duck. They took a one-run lead into the second innings and reached 0 for 9 at stumps on the third day, setting up an intriguing final two days.

But the hopes of a tense finish were blown away as Australia restored order to the cricketing world, winning the match with almost 10 overs remaining on the fourth day. Warne took his 1,000th first-class wicket as the New Zealanders suffered another fourth-day meltdown, collapsing for 131 in 50 overs. Fleming and coach John Bracewell were clueless later that day when quizzed about New Zealand's record of fourth-day collapses. Fleming had been the first batsman to fall in the second innings, out lbw to a McGrath delivery which bent towards leg stump. Jason Gillespie claimed three deserved wickets but Warne was the most dangerous bowler as he targeted the footmarks. He dismissed Marshall for the second time when the right-hander was bowled around his legs, not playing a shot. The only question was whether Australia's batsmen would try for a quick kill or tempt fate and the Christchurch weather by delaying until the fifth day. Langer answered that with slick 72 not out from 85 balls while Ponting supplied an unbeaten 47 from 75 balls.

Ponting was delighted with the win, less than 30 hours after Australia had been trailing New Zealand by 232 runs in their first innings with only four wickets in hand. It was Australia's sixth consecutive win – a feat achieved by only 15 teams in Test history. But such was Australia's winning habit that this streak barely rated a mention in the match reviews.

Man of Match: A. C. Gilchrist.

Close of play: First day, New Zealand (1) 3-265 (Marshall 103, Astle 29); Second day, Australia (1) 3-141 (Ponting 41, Gillespie 0); Third day, New Zealand (2) 0-9 (Cumming 2, Fleming 7).

New Zealand

	R	B	4/6		R	B	4/6
C. D. Cumming c Gillespie b Kasprowicz	74	206	10	– lbw b Gillespie	7	38	1
*S. P. Fleming lbw b Warne	18	60	1	– lbw b McGrath	17	41	3
H. J. H. Marshall b Warne	146	256	23 1	– b Warne	22	77	2
L. Vincent lbw b Clarke	27	50	5	– lbw b Gillespie	4	9	1
N. J. Astle lbw b McGrath	74	148	10	– b Kasprowicz	21	34	4
C. D. McMillan c Gilchrist b McGrath	13	38	2	– c Katich b Warne	5	7	1
B. B. McCullum c Langer b McGrath	29	35	6	– lbw b Gillespie	24	37	4
D. L. Vettori not out	24	32	4	– lbw b Warne	23	34	3
E. C. Franklin lbw b McGrath	0	3	0	– not out	5	16	1
I. E. O'Brien c Gilchrist b McGrath	5	13	1	– lbw b Warne	0	7	0
C. S. Martin c Gilchrist b McGrath	1	7	0	– lbw b Warne	0	1	0
B 4, l-b 14, w 2, n-b 2	22			B 1, l-b 1, n-b 1	3		

(141 overs, 560 mins)   433   (50 overs, 225 mins)   131

Fall: 56 153 199 330 355 388 403 403 415 433   Fall: 20 30 34 71 78 87 121 127 131 131

Bowling: *First Innings*—McGrath 42–9–115–6; Gillespie 29–5–87–0; Kasprowicz 25–6–85–1; Warne 40–6–112–2; Clarke 5–0–16–1. *Second Innings*—McGrath 14–7–19–1; Gillespie 12–2–38–3; Kasprowicz 10–3–33–1; Warne 14–3–39–5.

Australia

	R	B	4/6		R	B	4/6
J. L. Langer b Franklin	23	28	4	– not out	72	85	12 1
M. L. Hayden c Astle b O'Brien	35	74	6	– c Cumming b Vettori	15	30	2
*R. T. Ponting c McCullum b Martin	46	104	6 1	– not out	47	75	7 1
D. R. Martyn lbw b Vettori	32	62	4				
A. N. Gillespie c Cumming b Vettori	12	73	2				
M. J. Clarke c McCullum b Franklin	8	8	2				
S. M. Katich c Vincent b Astle	118	229	20 1				
†A. C. Gilchrist c O'Brien b Vettori	121	126	12 6				
S. K. Warne c Astle b Vettori	2	20	0				
M. S. Kasprowicz not out	13	16	2				
G. D. McGrath lbw b Vettori	0	4	0				
B 2, l-b 13, w 3, n-b 4	22			N-b 1	1		

(123.2 overs, 497 mins)   432   (31.3 overs, 125 mins)(1 wkt) 135

Fall: 48 75 140 147 160 201 413 418 426 432   Fall: 25

Bowling: *First Innings*—Martin 29–6–104–1; Franklin 26–5–102–2; O'Brien 14–3–73–1; Vettori 40.2–13–106–5; Astle 14–6–32–1. *Second Innings*—Martin 8–0–27–0; Franklin 5–1–26–0; Vettori 13.3–0–55–1; O'Brien 5–0–27–0.

Umpires: Aleem Dar (Pakistan) and D.R. Shepherd (England).
TV Umpire: A. L. Hill.
Referee: C. H. Lloyd (West Indies).

NEW ZEALAND v AUSTRALIA

Second Test Match

by RICHARD BOOCK

At Basin Reserve, Wellington, March 18 (no play), 19, 20, 21, 22 2005. Match drawn
Toss: New Zealand.

Although fog and drizzle saved New Zealand's bacon in this Test, there was still
enough time for Damien Martyn and Adam Gilchrist to strut their stuff with the bat, for
Michael Kasprowicz to claim his 100th Test wicket with the ball, and for Glenn McGrath
to maintain his stranglehold over opposition captains. On this occasion his unfortunate
victim was Stephen Fleming who – after being trapped in front by McGrath for 17 in the
second innings of the previous Test, fell lbw here for 0 and 1. By the time the match was
abandoned on the fifth afternoon, Fleming had been dismissed eight times by McGrath
in 25 innings against Australia, in which he had averaged just 24.48, against his career
average of 38.50.

Australia had headed into the Test expecting a stern challenge from Wellington's
notorious gales, but instead found themselves becalmed in a pea-souper that wiped out
the first day and most of the last. But when finally presented with the opportunity they
played some compelling cricket, putting the New Zealand attack to the sword despite the
fact that conditions were initially stacked in favour of the bowlers, and Fleming had won
the toss.

Adam Gilchrist goes to work one day in Wellington. This ball went through a window of the Members' Stand.

Matthew Hayden and Justin Langer had a couple of initial frights, but countered in such belligerent fashion that Fleming had to call left-arm spinner Daniel Vettori into the attack after just 15 overs in an effort to slow the scoring. It worked for a while. Vettori removed Langer for 46 and Ricky Ponting for 9, Franklin chipped out Hayden for 61, and when Nathan Astle sent Michael Clarke packing, Australia were looking less certain at 4 for 163. But Martyn and Gilchrist immediately went about redressing the balance, Martyn reaching his century off 173 balls following a third-session blitzkrieg.

When play eventually resumed on a damp third day, it was more of the same, the pair snuffing out any chance of a New Zealand comeback, extending their partnership to 256 – an Australian sixth-wicket record against New Zealand, and also for the Basin Reserve.

Martyn was finally caught behind for 165 – the highest of his 12 Test centuries and the seventh time he had raised three figures in just over a year when his tally was 1,570 runs.

Gilchrist made an even bigger impact, his 162 coming from just 146 balls and propelling him into the record books as the highest-scoring Australian wicket-keeper in history, his total of 4,392 pipping Ian Healy's mark of 4,356. To make his effort even more noteworthy, Gilchrist was caught short after match officials brought forward the start time on the third morning, leaving the Aussie gloveman swimming with his son at the hotel pool, blissfully unaware of the impending start. When flustered Australian officials finally located their missing man, the clock was ticking, and Gilchrist eventually arrived at the ground just 15 minutes before the first ball was to be bowled. Gilchrist was joined in another flurry of run-scoring at the end of the innings by Warne, who smashed 50 off just 37 balls before Ponting declared the innings closed at 8 for 570.

Already 1–0 down in the series, New Zealand made another pig's ear of their batting effort, losing Fleming to the first ball he faced, Hamish Marshall and Craig Cumming to attempted hook shots, and Nathan Astle to an ambitious drive. By the time more fog forced play to be abandoned they were teetering at 4 for 122, with Lou Vincent unbeaten on 38, but only one recognised batsman, Craig McMillan, up their sleeve.

The only periods of consolation for the home side on the fourth day – when the morning and final sessions were washed out – were the work of Vincent, who played gamely to push his overnight score through to 63, and from Daniel Vettori, who raised brief hopes of averting the follow-on during an inventive last-wicket partnership of 32 with Chris Martin. Vettori struck eight fours in his 45 but eventually perished while attempting to put Warne over the mid-wicket fence, leaving New Zealand adrift by 326 on the first innings.

Asked to follow-on, New Zealand were saved from any further embarrassment by the Wellington weather, which wiped out most of the last day. There was time only for Fleming to be further humiliated by McGrath – a setback that was exacerbated when Hamish Marshall perished in a similar manner two balls later – and for Vincent to depart as Kasprowicz's 100th Test victim, before the umpires led the players from the field for the final time.

Man of Match: A. C. Gilchrist.

Close of play: First day, no play (rain); Second day, Australia (1) 5-337 (Martyn 106, Gilchrist 45); Third day, New Zealand (1) 4-122 (Vincent 38, Franklin 6); Fourth day, New Zealand 244 all out.

Australia

	R	B	4/6		R	B	4/6
J. L. Langer c McCullum b Vettori	46	100	6	S. K. Warne not out	50	37	5 [2]
M. L. Hayden c Vincent b Franklin	61	147	6	J. N. Gillespie b Franklin	2	8	0
*R. T. Ponting lbw b Vettori	9	30		M. S. Kasprowicz not out	2	6	0
D. R. Martyn c McCullum b O'Brien	165	287	24	B 4, l-b 8, w 2, n-b 16	30		
M. J. Clarke c Fleming b Astle	8	32	0			—	
S. M. Katich c McCullum b Franklin	35	63	6	(140 overs, 561 mins)			
†A. C. Gilchrist c and b Franklin	162	146	22 [5]	(8 wkts dec)	570		

G. D. McGrath (did not bat).

Fall: 82 100 146 163 247 503 557 559

Bowling: Martin 28–6–123–0; Franklin 28–4–128–4; O'Brien 24–4–97–1; Vettori 47–5–170–2; Astle 13–2–40–1.

New Zealand

	R	B	4/6		R	B	4/6
C. D. Cumming b Kasprowicz	37	69	5	– not out	10	53	2
*S. P. Fleming lbw b McGrath	0	1	0	– lbw b McGrath	1	7	0
H. J. H. Marshall c Gillespie b McGrath	18	29	4	– lbw b McGrath	0	2	0
L. Vincent c Gilchrist b Kasprowicz	63	164	6	– b Kasprowicz	24	33	2
N. J. Astle c Warne b Clarke	9	34		– not out	4	10	0
J. E. C. Franklin c Gilchrist b Kasprowicz	26	71	3				
C. D. McMillan b Warne	20	34	2 [1]				
†B. B. McCullum c Clarke b Warne	3	3	0				
D. L. Vettori c Martyn b Warne	45	63	8				
I. E. O'Brien b Gillespie	5	8	0				
C. S. Martin not out	0	16	0				
B 4, l-b 8, w 1, n-b 5	18			B 3, l-b 5, n-b 1	9		

(81.1 overs, 330 mins) 244

Fall: 9 55 78 108 166 180 184 201 212 244

(17.2 overs, 74 mins)(3 wkts) 48

Fall: 3 3 37

Bowling: *First Innings*—McGrath 14–3–50–2; Gillespie 20–4–63–1; Kasprowicz 16–2–42–3; Warne 28.1–7–69–3; Clarke 3–1–8–1. *Second Innings*—McGrath 6–3–10–2; Gillespie 5–2–5–0; Warne 3.2–0–14–0; Kasprowicz 3–0–11–1.

Umpires: R. E. Koertzen (South Africa) and D. R. Shepherd (England).
TV Umpire: E. A. Watkin.
Referee: C. H. Lloyd (West Indies).

NEW ZEALAND v AUSTRALIA

Third Test Match

by GLENN MITCHELL

At Eden Park, Auckland, March 26, 27, 28, 29, 2005. Australia won by nine wickets. *Toss:* New Zealand. Test debut: J. A. H. Marshall.

After floating the possibility of a four-man pace attack in the lead-up to the Test, the Australian selectors maintained faith in a tried and trusted line-up, with Brett Lee once again designated as the game's highest-profile drinks waiter. The Black Caps made two changes. Veteran Craig McMillan's form had been modest (38 at 12.7) and he was replaced by James Marshall, identical twin brother of First Test century-maker Hamish, while medium-pacer Iain O'Brien gave way to off-spinner Paul Wiseman.

The opening day started beneath leaden skies, and the scoreboard mirrored the gloomy conditions. Stephen Fleming won the toss and elected to bat, opting himself to return to his more familiar position at No. 4. By stumps, after a full 90 overs, the Kiwis had lost just five wickets, on the face of it a respectable performance against the Australian attack. The problem was they had made just 199. Discounting the 14 sundries, the New Zealand batsmen scored a mere 185 runs in a full day. It was a throwback to Test cricket as it was played in the late-1950s.

The batting side's intention was obvious – don't lose wickets. But while they steadfastly defended their position, they failed to budge the scoreboard. Fleming was one of the main offenders, scoring just a solitary run from the first 30 deliveries he received from Glenn McGrath. He eventually fell for 65 from 169 balls. In his defence was the fact that McGrath had claimed him lbw in three of his four previous innings in the series and the skipper was intent on resurrecting his standing as his team's premier batsman. The metronomic Australian paceman's first spell of seven overs cost just seven runs, and by stumps he had rolled out 17 maidens from his 24 overs, conceding just 20 runs and taking the wicket of James Marshall.

New Zealand displayed more intent on the second day, but the innings ended on 292, eight minutes before lunch. By stumps, the Australians had moved to 4 for 219, with Ricky Ponting having completed a glorious century. He signalled his intentions early, getting off the mark by hitting Chris Martin for six; his innings absorbed just 110 balls and included 13 fours and four sixes. He shared a 103-run third-wicket partnership with Damien Martyn, who contributed a mere 28, as Ponting changed the complexion of the match by himself.

Day three was punctuated by a series of rain stoppages, but the momentum remained with Australia. Nightwatchman Jason Gillespie and Simon Katich shared a 71-run partnership for the sixth wicket before Adam Gilchrist's unbeaten 60 from 62 balls swelled Australia total to 383. McGrath's dismissal for a duck left Gilchrist's ambition to make it four centuries in as many Tests out of reach. James Franklin finished with a career-best 6 for 119, while the two spinners, Wiseman and Daniel Vettori, claimed just one wicket from their joint 50 overs. By stumps on the third day the Black Caps had further unravelled, as McGrath snapped up both openers, leaving the home side teetering at 2 for 11 by stumps.

Once again, the top order failed to impress as the slide continued on the fourth day. Jason Gillespie's superb effort to catch Fleming off his own bowling put him level with Richie Benaud's career tally of 248 Test wickets and left New Zealand imperilled at 3 for 15. When Brendon McCullum was dismissed by Shane Warne for a duck, the score was a sick and sorry 6 for 93. It was left to Nathan Astle (69) and the tail to try to provide some respectability. Astle added 81 with the typically plucky Vettori, who made 65 to finish the series with 198 runs at an average of 66. Franklin and Wiseman each contributed 23, the latter's dismissal signalling the end of the innings. It was also McGrath's 499th Test scalp. While McGrath would have to wait for the Lord's Ashes Test in July to achieve the 500-wicket milestone, the Australian team only had to wait a little over two hours to achieve victory.

Needing just 164 for a 2-0 series scoreline, Australia lost Matthew Hayden, whose lean run continued when he was run out by a Vettori direct hit. The burly Queenslander finished the series with an average of 31.60, and had not made a century for 12 Tests and 22 innings. As the late afternoon gloom began to gather, Fleming and his charges did all they could to slow down the game and force it into a fifth day, in the hope that rain would be their saviour. The stalling tactics clearly annoyed the Australian skipper, who launched a brazen attack on the bowling in an endeavour to end the game. His physical assault became a verbal one in the post-match media conference as he condemned the Kiwis' approach. Midway through the 30th over, Justin Langer (59 not out) launched into a cover drive that completed a nine-wicket victory. Ponting's unconquered 86 from 84 balls sealed his man of the match award.

For the Australians, it was the end of a flawless tour. Only the Wellington weather prevented a clean sweep, following a 5-0 whitewash in the one-day series. Australia left New Zealand contemplating their readiness for another Ashes defence, while the Black Caps had just a week to regroup ahead of the rescheduled two-Test series against Sri Lanka.

Man of Match: R. T. Ponting. *Man of the Series:* A. C. Gilchrist.

Close of play: First day, New Zealand (1) 5-199 (Astle 7, McCullum 1); Second day, Australia (1) 4-219 (Clarke 18, Gillespie 1); Third day, New Zealand (2) 2-11 (H. J. H. Marshall 3, Fleming 1).

New Zealand

	R	B	4/6		R	B	4/6
C. D. Cumming lbw b Gillespie	5	31	0	– lbw b McGrath	0	2	0
J. A. H. Marshall c Hayden b McGrath	29	56	3	– c Langer b McGrath	3	7	0
H. J. H. Marshall c Ponting b Warne	76	208	9	– c Gilchrist b McGrath	7	50	0
*S. P. Fleming b Kasprowicz	65	169	8 [1]	– c and b Gillespie	3	13	0
N. J. Astle c Langer b McGrath	19	60	2	– c Katich b Warne	69	107	11 [1]
L. Vincent b Gillespie	2	30	0	– run out (Clarke)	40	33	4 [2]
†B. B. McCullum c Gilchrist b McGrath	25	63	5	– lbw b Warne	0	4	0
D. L. Vettori not out	41	50	8	– c McGrath b Warne	65	108	8
J. E. C. Franklin c Katich b Warne	3	11	0	– c Ponting b Warne	23	59	1 1
P. J. Wiseman c Gillespie b Warne	8	20	1	– b McGrath	23	23	3 1
C. S. Martin c Clarke b Kasprowicz	0	2	0	– not out	4	12	1
B 4, l-b 13, n-b 2	19			B 1, l-b 14, n-b 2	17		

(116.2 overs, 479 mins)   292   (69.2 overs, 298 mins)   254

Fall: 15 53 179 183 194 228 247 262 288 292   Fall: 0 9 15 23 93 93 174 220 227 254

Bowling: *First Innings*—McGrath 34–20–49–3; Gillespie 25–8–64–2; Kasprowicz 30.2–7–89–2; Warne 23–4–63–3; Ponting 4–1–10–0. *Second Innings*—McGrath 16.2–5–40–4; Gillespie 16–4–63–1; Kasprowicz 14–2–59–0; Warne 23.5–5–77–4.

Australia

	R	B	4/6		R	B	4/6
J. L. Langer b Franklin	6	11	1	– not out	59	76	10
M. L. Hayden lbw b Franklin	38	49	7	– run out (Vettori)	9	18	1
*R. T. Ponting c McCullum b Astle	105	110	13 4	– not out	86	84	12 2
D. R. Martyn b Wiseman	38	137	4				
M. J. Clarke run out (J. A. H..Marshall)	22	71	1				
J. N. Gillespie c McCullum b Martin	35	145	6				
S. M. Katich c Wiseman b Franklin	35	81	4				
†A. C. Gilchrist not out	60	62	10 1				
S. K. Warne c Fleming b Franklin	1	10	0				
M. S. Kasprowicz b Franklin	23	40	3				
G. D. McGrath c McCullum b Franklin	0	2	0				
B 4, l-b 7, n-b 9	20			L-b 10, n-b 2	12		
(118.1 overs, 459 mins)	383			(29.3 overs, 137 mins) (1 wkt)	166		

Fall: 8 84 187 215 226 297 297 303 377 383

Fall: 18

Bowling: *First Innings*—Martin 21–4–92–1; Franklin 26.1–3–119–6; Astle 21–7–50–1; Vettori 19–4–47–0; Wiseman 31–7–64–1. *Second Innings*—Martin 8–1–51–0; Franklin 7–0–40–0; Vettori 4–0–19–0; Astle 7–0–33–0; Wiseman 3.3–0–13–0.

Umpires: R. E. Koertzen (South Africa) and J. W. Lloyds (England).
TV Umpire: D. B. Cowie.
Referee: C. H. Lloyd (West Indies).

Australia in England, 2005

by GIDEON HAIGH

In the year of the bicentenary of the battle of Trafalgar, England cricket fans expected that every player in the team would do his duty – but not, perhaps, quite so well. The 2-1 victory of Michael Vaughan's XI turned cricket on its head, ending a 16-year Australian hegemony and reflating the currency of Anglo-Australian cricket. They did it, moreover, by borrowing some of the techniques that had made Australia cricket's market leader for a decade.

The Ashes summer of 2005 will go down as one of history's most extraordinary and effervescent. The middle three Tests went to the wire; the first and last contained passages of play that made them minor classics. The games unfolded at breakneck pace, yet also had time for moments of decency and sportsmanship one had almost ceased to associate with the game. Even Ricky Ponting called the series "the best I have played in". It was certainly the best that almost everyone had watched.

The rubber contained two titanic performances. Andrew Flintoff, winner of the inaugural Compton-Miller Medal for player of the series, had come back from his tour of South Africa injured and in need of an operation. He played almost no first-class cricket before the First Test at Lord's and scored only three rusty runs. From that point, however, he towered over almost every exchange in which he was involved, with his power-packed batting and strength-through-joy bowling.

Flintoff's batting matured during the series. He was sound in defence and judicious in attack. In the Second Test at Edgbaston, he hit brutally, dishing out as many as nine sixes; by the Fourth at Trent Bridge, he was capable of a century as serene and poised as any seen in recent years. With the ball he was a revelation, regularly achieving pace in excess of 90mph, and mastery of reverse as well as orthodox swing. Above all, he impressed with his physical prowess, at the Oval bowling 18 consecutive overs in which the last was as fast as the first. On the field he was a joy to watch, infectiously enthusiastic, hugging his team-mates not as a footballer might but with unfeigned warmth and affection.

In any other summer, Shane Warne's 40 wickets at 19 and 249 runs at 27 would have guaranteed some individual award. It carried, indeed, its own badge of distinction. Warne, for long a great player in a grand side, was here seen in a new guise: Australia's best, last and sometimes only hope. Time and again he redeemed Australia's cause on his own, apparently by sheer force of will. In the only Test in which he did not clean up with the ball, at Old Trafford, he hefted 90 and 32. Warne's lead-up to the series had been what might euphemistically be called less than ideal; in particular, publicity about a new round of sexual peccadilloes finally drove off his long-suffering wife. Yet once on the field, he sunk himself entirely in his task. The crowd at The Oval paid him warm tribute with a chant of "we only wish you were English" – taking the words, as it were, from the tabloid newspapermen's mouth.

Warne's workload, however, was itself a confession of Australian weakness. With Glenn McGrath absent from two Tests, and at impaired effectiveness in two others, shortcomings in Australian bowling glimpsed during the Border-Gavaskar Trophy of 2003-04 became clear as day. Brett Lee toiled manfully, and sometimes bowled very fast indeed, but without the variety or finesse of his great contemporaries. Without the pressure exerted by their stars, the auxiliary members of the attack, Jason Gillespie, Michael Kasprowicz and Shaun Tait, were markedly less effective.

Watching the Australians bat, meanwhile, was sometimes a little like watching a club side. There was always, somehow, the hint of wickets in the offing, with only three century partnerships achieved. The captain enjoyed only one major innings, a brave 156 to save Australia's bacon in Manchester. The obstinate Justin Langer appeared to enjoy the fight and Michael Clarke had his moments; but Matthew Hayden, Damien Martyn, Simon Katich and even Adam Gilchrist were barely more conspicuous than the Bradleys Haddin and Hodge. Gilchrist, hemmed in from round the wicket and confronted by Flintoff's brazen aggression, could not decide whether to play with or against his own attacking grain. As a result he did neither, not lasting long enough for a single half-century.

Where the Australians impressed least, however, was in the leadership. Ponting off the field said many of the right things, but on the field was depressingly stereotyped in his thinking. His bowling changes seemed at times to be being made by rote – witness his decision to spell Lee with 5-2-6-1 at Old Trafford when the out-of-form Vaughan came to the crease – and his field settings were defensive, bordering on defeatist. His long consultations with bowlers suggested a man who took too much counsel. Coach John Buchanan, so impressive in maintaining Australia's motivation in his six years extracting from the excellent the better yet, suddenly found the team failing in matters of detail, which he seemed either unwilling or unable to remedy.

In hindsight, the period that mattered was when almost no one was watching: immediately after the First Test, when England somehow convinced themselves they could still compete, and Australia persuaded themselves that England could not. The Australians dispersed, playing barely any cricket before the Second Test; the English wrote the First off to experience and came back twice as hard. They were none for 60 after an hour, 1 for 130 at lunch, and a lickety-split 407 all out in a day. It was the kind of aggression that has been Australia's hallmark for the last five years, and here it was being turned against them.

England would have won comfortably at Old Trafford but for rain's exactions, and only won narrowly at Trent Bridge because of Warne's unearthly genius. Deprived again of McGrath's services at Nottingham by injury, Australia seemed simply to be trying to hold the line. There was no coherent plan for victory, merely progressive formations of defence. When Warne was not bowling, England seemed to bat under no pressure at all. As Flintoff and Geraint Jones put on 177 in 235 balls in the first innings, it was like watching the middle overs of a one-day international, with the field devoid of catchers as deep fielders prowled the boundaries.

Vaughan looked a better captain for the dilatory nature of his rival. He also made mistakes – probably taking his foot off Australia's throat on the third day at Old Trafford – and his bat was muted aside from his 166 at Manchester. But he was firm, decisive, canny, clearly popular, and enjoyed an excellent rapport with his coach Duncan Fletcher. Moreover, England kept taking leaves from the Australian playbook, resisting discretionary changes to their starting XI even when there seemed logic to them, because of the value inherent in an unchanged unit. The decision to include a fifth bowler and promote Flintoff to No. 6 was an inspired piece of selection, for Simon Jones turned out to be as effective as any of the other four. His and Flintoff's mastery of reverse swing made the middle overs of each Australian innings compulsive viewing.

Australia faced some soul searching in the aftermath of this tour. The age of the present team is not nearly so concerning as the ages of those considered its next generation: Simon Katich (30), Martin Love (31), Matthew Elliott (33), Michael Hussey (30), Andrew Symonds (30), Phil Jaques (26), Dominic Thornely (26) and Chris Rogers (28). The best-performed quick bowler outside this touring squad, Brad Williams, is 30 – likewise the bowling cover that Australia called up after Edgbaston, Stuart Clark. Some players face hard decisions. Others face having hard decisions made for them. As for England, they would face the same dilemma as Australia has: that England would expect as much, if not more, again.

AUSTRALIAN LIMITED-OVERS SQUAD

R. T. Ponting (*captain*), A. C. Gilchrist (*vice-captain*), M. J. Clarke, J. N. Gillespie, B. J. Haddin, M. L. Hayden, G. B. Hogg, M. E. K. Hussey, M. S. Kasprowicz, S. M. Katich, B. Lee, D. R. Martyn, G. D. McGrath, A. Symonds and S. R. Watson.

AUSTRALIAN TEST SQUAD

R. T. Ponting (*captain*), A. C. Gilchrist (*vice-captain*), M. J. Clarke, J. N. Gillespie, B. J. Haddin, M. L. Hayden, B. J. Hodge, J. L. Langer, M. S. Kasprowicz, S. M. Katich, B. Lee, S. C. G. MacGill, D. R. Martyn, G. D. McGrath, S. W. Tait, and S. K. Warne.

S. R. Clark (NSW) added to the squad in early August to cover Glenn McGrath.

Manager: S. R. Bernard. *Coach:* J. M. Buchanan. *Assistant coach/performance analyst:* J. D. Siddons. *Physiotherapist:* E. L. Alcott. *Masseur:* Ms L. Frostick. *Physical performance manager:* J. A. Campbell. *Media managers:* B. J. Dennett and J. D. Rose.

AUSTRALIAN TOUR RESULTS

Test matches – Played 5: Won 1, Lost 2, Drawn 2.
First-class matches – Played 7, Won 1, Losses 2, Drawn 4.
Wins – England (1); *Losses* – England (2); Draws – England (2), Leicestershire (1), Worcestershire (1).
International limited-overs – Played 10, Won 5, Lost 3, Tied 1, No result 1.
Wins – Bangladesh (2), England 3; *Losses* – Bangladesh (1), England 1; *Ties* – England (1); No results – England (1).
Other non-first-class matches: Played 6, Won 2, Lost 2, Drawn 2.

INTERNATIONAL LIMITED-OVERS RUN-SCORERS

	M	I	NO	R	HS	100s	50s	Avge	Ct/St	S-R
A.J. Strauss (Eng) ..	10	10	1	466	152	1	2	51.78	3	87.92
A.C. Gilchrist (Aus)	10	10	2	393	121*	1	1	49.13	15/1	102.61
M.E. Trescothick (Eng)	10	10	3	379	104*	2	1	54.14	3	85.55
D.R. Martyn (Aus). .	10	9	3	307	77	0	2	51.17	2	66.88
R.T. Ponting (Aus) .	10	9	0	303	111	1	1	33.67	4	75.94
M.E.K. Hussey (Aus)	10	6	3	273	84	0	1	91.00	3	94.46
Mohammad Ashraful (Ban)....	6	6	0	259	100	1	2	43.17	0	105.71
M.L. Hayden (Aus) .	9	9	1	253	66*	0	1	31.63	3	73.33
P.D. Collingwood (Eng)	10	7	2	230	112*	1	1	46.00	4	73.25
A. Symonds (Aus) ..	8	6	2	229	74	0	2	57.25	3	81.79
K.P. Pietersen (Eng)	10	6	1	228	91*	0	2	45.60	8	96.61
A. Flintoff (Eng) ...	10	7	0	202	87	0	1	28.86	1	75.09
M.J. Clarke (Aus) ..	8	6	1	186	80*	0	1	37.20	6	63.48
Javed Omar (Ban) ..	6	6	0	175	81	0	2	29.17	0	49.16
Nafees Iqbal (Ban)..	6	6	0	170	75	0	1	28.33	2	64.15
M.P. Vaughan (Eng)	8	7	2	132	59*	0	2	26.40	0	64.36
Khaled Mashud (Ban)	6	5	2	126	71*	0	1	42.00	2/1	69.23
G.O. Jones (Eng). ...	10	7	2	126	71	0	1	25.20	24/1	68.48
Habibul Bashar (Ban)	6	6	0	122	47	0	0	20.33	1	70.93
V.S. Solanki (Eng). .	6	4	1	108	53*	0	1	36.00	0	63.16
Aftab Ahmed (Ban) .	6	6	1	99	51	0	1	19.80	0	80.49
Mohammad Rafique (Ban)	6	6	2	75	30	0	0	18.75	1	61.98
Tushar Imran (Ban) .	6	6	0	70	32	0	0	11.67	1	63.64
S.M. Katich (Aus) ..	3	2	1	66	36*	0	0	66.00	2	77.65
D. Gough (Eng)	9	3	2	63	46*	0	0	63.00	0	96.92
A.F. Giles (Eng) ...	8	4	2	51	25*	0	0	25.50	2	104.08
B. Lee (Aus).......	8	3	2	39	21*	0	0	39.00	0	92.86
S.R. Watson (Aus)..	5	3	1	39	25	0	0	19.50	0	69.64
Mashrafe Mortaza (Ban)	6	4	1	30	29*	0	0	10.00	1	78.95
G.B. Hogg (Aus)	7	3	1	28	16	0	0	14.00	1	68.29
Khaled Mahmud (Ban)	2	2	0	22	22	0	0	11.00	2	95.65
S.J. Harmison (Eng)	9	3	3	17	11*	0	0	–	2	84.58
J.N. Gillespie (Aus).	10	3	0	15	14	0	0	5.00	2	71.43
C.T. Tremlett (Eng).	3	1	0	8	8	0	0	8.00	0	44.44
Nazmul Hossain (Ban)	5	3	2	8	6	0	0	8.00	0	26.67
J. Lewis (Eng)	3	1	1	7	7*	0	0	–	0	46.67
Tapash Baisya (Ban)	3	1	0	3	3	0	0	3.00	0	50.00
G.D. McGrath (Aus)	9	3	2	2	2*	0	0	2.00	0	20.00
Manjural Islam Rana (Ban)	2	1	0	2	2	0	0	2.00	0	40.00
M.S. Kasprowicz (Aus)	5	1	0	1	1	0	0	1.00	3	33.33
S.P... Jones (Eng) ..	6	1	0	1	1	0	0	1.00	0	50.00
B.J. Haddin (Aus) ..	1	0	0	0	–	0	0	–	0/0	–

  * *Denotes not out*

INTERNATIONAL LIMITED-OVERS WICKET-TAKERS

	M	O	Mdns	R	W	BB	5Wfi	Avge	RPO
S. J. Harmison (Eng)	9	86.5	6	404	17	5-33	1	23.76	4.65
A. Flintoff (Eng)	10	87	6	392	14	4-29	0	28.00	4.51
B. Lee (Aus)	8	68	6	309	14	5-41	1	22.07	4.54
P. D. Collingwood (Eng) .	10	54	1	207	11	6-31	1	18.82	3.83
G. B. Hogg (Aus)	7	46	2	197	11	3-29	0	17.91	4.28
D. Gough (Eng)	9	73.3	2	416	10	3-70	0	41.60	5.66
G. D. McGrath (Aus)	9	76	15	279	9	3-25	0	31.00	3.67
J. N. Gillespie (Aus)	10	77.2	4	403	8	3-44	0	50.38	5.21
M. S. Kasprowicz (Aus) . .	5	48	3	240	7	2-40	0	34.29	5.00
A. Symonds (Aus)	8	57.2	4	203	6	5-18	1	33.83	3.54
C. T. Tremlett (Eng)	3	24.2	5	111	5	4-32	0	22.20	4.56
Nazmul Hossain (Ban) . . .	5	37	3	281	4	3-83	0	70.25	7.59
J. Lewis (Eng)	3	25	1	124	4	3-32	0	31.00	4.96
S. P. Jones (Eng)	6	42	5	199	4	2-53	0	49.75	4.74
Tapash Baisya (Ban)	3	26	1	213	4	3-69	0	53.25	8.19
S. R. Watson (Aus)	5	34.3	0	166	4	3-43	0	41.50	4.81
A. F. Giles (Eng)	8	67	2	300	3	1-28	0	100.00	4.48
Manjural Islam Rana (Ban)	2	13.5	0	83	3	3-57	0	27.67	6.00
Mashrafe Mortaza (Ban) . .	6	50	3	261	3	2-44	0	87.00	5.22
Mohammad Rafique (Ban) .	6	52	1	266	2	2-44	0	133.00	5.12
Aftab Ahmed (Ban)	6	35.5	0	188	1	1-65	0	188.00	5.25
Khaled Mahmud (Ban) . . .	2	13	0	93	1	1-54	0	93.00	7.15
M. E. K. Hussey (Aus) . . .	10	9	0	55	1	1-31	0	55.00	6.11
Mohammad Ashraful (Ban)	1	0.1	0	4	0	–	0	–	24.00
M. J. Clarke (Aus)	8	18	1	97	0	–	0	–	5.39
M. P. Vaughan (Eng)	8	7	0	46	0	–	0	–	6.57
Tushar Imran (Ban)	6	3	0	26	0	–	0	–	8.67
V. S. Solanki (Eng)	6	2	0	14	0	–	0	–	7.00

TEST MATCH BATTING AVERAGES

	M	I	NO	R	HS	100s	50s	Avge	Ct/St	S-R
K. P. Pietersen (Eng)	5	10	1	473	158	1	3	52.56	0	71.45
J. L. Langer (Aus) . . .	5	10	1	394	105	1	2	43.78	2	58.63
M. E. Trescothick (Eng)	5	10	0	431	90	0	3	43.10	3	60.28
A. Flintoff (Eng)	5	10	0	402	102	1	3	40.20	3	74.17
R. T. Ponting (Aus) .	5	9	0	359	156	1	1	39.89	4	59.63
A. J. Strauss (Eng) . .	5	10	0	393	129	2	0	39.30	6	57.79
M. J. Clarke (Aus) . .	5	9	0	335	91	0	2	37.22	2	54.38
G. D. McGrath (Aus)	3	5	4	36	20*	0	0	36.00	1	63.16
M. L. Hayden (Aus) .	5	10	1	318	138	1	0	35.33	10	46.97
S. P. Jones (Eng)	4	6	4	66	20*	0	0	33.00	1	67.35
M. P. Vaughan (Eng)	5	10	0	326	166	1	1	32.60	2	60.82
S. K. Warne (Aus) . .	5	9	0	249	90	0	1	27.67	5	70.54
S. M. Katich (Aus) . .	5	9	0	248	67	0	2	27.56	4	46.79
B. Lee (Aus)	5	9	3	158	47	0	0	26.33	2	65.02
G. O. Jones (Eng) . . .	5	10	1	229	85	0	1	25.44	15/1	57.97
A. C. Gilchrist (Aus)	5	9	1	181	49*	0	0	22.63	18/1	71.83
D. R. Martyn (Aus) . .	5	9	0	178	65	0	1	19.78	4	53.13
A. F. Giles (Eng) . . .	5	10	2	155	59	0	1	19.38	5	50.64
I. R. Bell (Eng)	5	10	0	171	65	0	2	17.10	8	45.36
M. S. Kasprowicz (Aus)	2	4	0	44	20	0	0	11.00	3	67.69
S. J. Harmison (Eng)	5	8	2	60	20*	0	0	10.00	1	84.51
P. D. Collingwood (Eng)	1	2	0	17	10	0	0	8.50	1	22.08
S. W. Tait (Aus)	2	3	2	8	4	0	0	8.00	0	29.63
J. N. Gillespie (Aus) .	3	6	0	47	26	0	0	7.83	1	21.56
M. J. Hoggard (Eng) .	5	9	2	45	16	0	0	6.43	0	19.65

* Denotes not out

TEST MATCH BOWLING AVERAGES

	M	O	Mdns	R	W	BB	5W/i	10W/m	Avge	RPO
R. T. Ponting (Aus)	5	6	2	9	1	1-9	0	0	9.00	1.50
S. K. Warne (Aus)	5	252.5	37	797	40	6-46	3	2	19.93	3.15
S. P. Jones (Eng)	4	102	17	378	18	6-53	2	0	21.00	3.71
G. D. McGrath (Aus)	3	134	22	440	19	5-53	2	0	23.16	3.28
A. Flintoff (Eng)	5	194	32	655	24	5-78	1	0	27.29	3.38
M. J. Hoggard (Eng)	5	122.1	15	473	16	4-97	0	0	29.56	3.87
S. J. Harmison (Eng)	5	161.1	22	549	17	5-43	1	0	32.29	3.41
B. Lee (Aus)	5	191.1	25	822	20	4-82	0	0	41.10	4.30
S. W. Tait (Aus)	2	48	5	210	5	3-97	0	0	42.00	4.38
S. M. Katich (Aus)	5	12	1	50	1	1-36	0	0	50.00	4.17
A. F. Giles (Eng)	5	160	18	578	10	3-78	0	0	57.80	3.61
M. S. Kasprowicz (Aus)	2	52	6	250	4	3-80	0	0	62.50	4.81
J. N. Gillespie (Aus)	3	67	6	300	3	2-91	0	0	100.00	4.48
I. R. Bell (Eng)	5	7	2	20	0	–	0	0	–	2.86
M. J. Clarke (Aus)	5	2	0	6	0	–	0	0	–	3.00
P. D. Collingwood (Eng) ...	1	4	0	17	0	–	0	0	–	4.25
M. P. Vaughan (Eng)	5	5	0	21	0	–	0	0	–	4.20

FIRST-CLASS BATTING AVERAGES

	M	I	NO	R	HS	100s	50s	Avge	Ct/St	S-R
B. J. Haddin	1	1	0	94	94	0	1	94.00	2	97.92
J. L. Langer	7	13	2	574	115	2	3	52.18	3	59.11
R. T. Ponting	7	12	1	557	156	2	2	50.64	5	61.21
M. L. Hayden	7	12	1	472	138	1	2	42.91	14	56.05
D. R. Martyn	6	10	1	332	154*	1	1	36.89	4	61.14
G. D. McGrath	3	5	4	36	20*	0	0	36.00	1	63.16
M. J. Clarke	7	12	0	412	91	0	3	34.33	3	58.11
B. J. Hodge	1	2	0	59	38	0	0	29.50	1	45.38
S. K. Warne	5	9	0	249	90	0	1	27.67	5	70.54
J. N. Gillespie	5	8	2	149	53*	0	1	24.83	1	40.60
S. M. Katich	7	11	0	266	67	0	2	24.18	5	46.34
B. Lee	6	10	3	164	47	0	0	23.43	2	64.31
A. C. Gilchrist	6	10	1	207	49*	0	0	23.00	20/1	72.13
S. W. Tait	3	4	2	30	22	0	0	15.00	0	65.22
M. S. Kasprowicz ...	4	5	0	52	20	0	0	10.40	5	69.33
S. C. G. MacGill	2			0		0	0	–	1	–

* Denotes not out

FIRST-CLASS BOWLING AVERAGES

	M	O	Mdns	R	W	BB	5W/i	10W/m	Avge	RPO
R. T. Ponting	7	6	2	9	1	1-9	0	0	9.00	1.50
S. K. Warne	5	252.5	37	797	40	6-46	3	2	19.93	3.15
G. D. McGrath	3	134	22	440	19	5-53	2	0	23.16	3.28
S. C. G. MacGill	2	44	6	207	7	4-122	0	0	29.57	4.70
S. W. Tait	3	61	9	261	7	3-97	0	0	37.29	4.28
B. Lee	6	218.1	30	953	25	4-53	0	0	38.12	4.37
M. S. Kasprowicz	4	99	15	417	10	5-67	1	0	41.70	4.21
S. M. Katich	7	12	1	50	1	1-36	0	0	50.00	4.17
J. N. Gillespie	5	110	16	445	7	2-40	0	0	63.57	4.05
M. J. Clarke	7	7	0	42	0	–	0	0	–	6.00

†PCA MASTERS XI v AUSTRALIANS

At Arundel Castle, Arundel, June 9, 2005. Australians won by eight wickets. PCA Masters XI 6 for 167 (D. L. Maddy 70*, P. D. Collingwood 38, M. A. Ealham 39; M. J. Clarke 3-36). Australians 2 for 170 (A. C. Gilchrist 53, M. L. Hayden 79, R. T. Ponting 31*).

The Australians opened their tour with a competent win in a Twenty20 fixture against an invitation XI assembled by the Professional Cricketers' Association. Ricky Ponting inserted the Masters and pouched Kiwi skipper Stephen Fleming first ball at slip. The individual highlight came in an unlikely hat-trick by the mercurial Michael Clarke, one of his victims being Kevin Pietersen. Expecting to meet some sledging on his first encounter with the Australians, Pietersen was greeted with silence; discomfited, he made a rash swipe after five deliveries. A 57-ball 70 from Leicestershire's Darren Maddy set a teasing target that the visitors only reached from the penultimate ball of their innings; Chris Tremlett, Hampshire's tall paceman, was responsible for some mean overs. Gilchrist's 53 took 50 deliveries, Hayden's 79 just 46. A buoyant crowd basked in warm sunlight around this picturesque ground as the most traditional of tours made its decidedly non-traditional beginning. Almost two thirds of the runs in the game accrued in boundaries: 42 fours and seven sixes.

†LEICESTERSHIRE v AUSTRALIANS

At Grace Road, Leicester, June 11, 2005. Australians won by 95 runs. Australians 4 for 321 (M. L. Hayden 107, D. R. Martyn 85, A. Symonds 92*; O. D. Gibson 2/65). Leicestershire 8 for 226 (H. D. Ackerman 38, P. A. Nixon 43, O. D. Gibson 50; G. D. McGrath 2-33, G. B. Hogg 3-56).

Australia flexed their batting pectorals over 50 overs, with Matthew Hayden's 92-ball hundred (13 fours and two sixes) and Andrew Symonds' 59-ball 92 (ten fours and three sixes) the highlights. In the later stages, however, they let the game drift, permitting Ottis Gibson (50, 49 balls) and Phil Nixon (43, 53 balls) to add a sprightly 94, and donating ten wides. In the game's aftermath, Michael Kasprowicz and Michael Clarke had kit stolen as it awaited loading on to the team coach. Kasprowicz had his one-day shirts and pads lifted, while Clarke lost his entire supply of gear: five bats, seven pairs of gloves, three pairs of spiked shoes, his yellow pads for the one-day series, two pairs of rubber-soled shoes – and even his box.

†ENGLAND v AUSTRALIA

Twenty20 International

At The Rose Bowl, Southampton, June 13, 2005. England won by 100 runs. *Toss:* England.

The first Twenty20 international in England was fast, funny, farcical – and an embarrassment for Australia when they lost seven wickets for eight runs, including the cream of their batting, in 20 deliveries. The power of Marcus Trescothick (41, 37 balls), Kevin Pietersen (34, 18 balls) and Paul Collingwood (46, 26 balls) had already nonplussed Australia's attack, which conceded 100 in 11 overs. Both captains had reason to be dismissive of the game. Ricky Ponting, who drove his first ball straight to cover, described it as "a bit of a laugh"; Michael Vaughan, who chipped his first ball to mid-wicket, saw it as "a bit of a lottery" and thought nobody should "read too much into a Twenty20 victory". The English press agreed to differ. David Hopps opined in the broadsheet *Guardian*: "Australia will forever insist it was just a bit of fun, but it was nothing of the sort. The moment Australian green and gold splashed on to the outfield for the inaugural Twenty20 international in England, the scent of an Ashes kill was unmistakable." John Etheridge of the tabloid *Sun* was a little more tongue in cheek: "The Aussies – are they Bangladesh in disguise?" he asked, echoing the crowd's mockery. "Is this the worst Twenty20 side ever to visit these shores? Go on, have some fun and enjoy the moment. It might not happen too often."

Man of Match: K. P. Pietersen.

England

M. E. Trescothick c Hussey b Symonds	41	(37)	V. S. Solanki c Hussey b McGrath	9	(5)
†G. O. Jones c Kasprowicz b McGrath	19	(14)	J. Lewis not out	0	(0)
A. Flintoff c Symonds b Kasprowicz	6	(5)			
K. P. Pietersen c Hayden b Clarke	34	(18)	L-b 1, w 3, n-b 2	6	
*M. P. Vaughan c Ponting b Symonds	0	(1)			
P. D. Collingwood c Ponting b McGrath	46	(26)	(20 overs, 79 mins) (8 wkts)	179	
A. J. Strauss b Gillespie	18	(16)	Fall: 28 49 100 102 109 158 175 179		

D. Gough, S. J. Harmison (did not bat).

Bowling: Lee 3–0–31–0; McGrath 4–0–31–3; Kasprowicz 3–0–28–1; Gillespie 4–0–49–1; Clarke 3–0–25–1; Symonds 3–0–14–2.

Australia

†A. C. Gilchrist c Pietersen b Gough	15	(14)	J. N. Gillespie c Trescothick b Collingwood	24	(18)
M. L. Hayden c Pietersen b Gough	6	(4)	M. S. Kasprowicz not out	3	(5)
A. Symonds c Pietersen b Lewis	0	(2)	G. D. McGrath b Harmison	5	(12)
M. J. Clarke c Jones b Lewis	0	(1)			
M. E. K. Hussey c Flintoff b Gough	1	(6)	B 1, l-b 2, w 1, n-b 2	6	
*R. T. Ponting c Solanki b Lewis	0	(3)			
D. R. Martyn c Trescothick b Lewis	4	(4)	(14.3 overs, 64 mins)	79	
B. Lee c Harmison b Collingwood	15	(20)	Fall: 23 23 23 24 24 28 31 67 72 79		

Bowling: Gough 3–0–16–3; Lewis 4–0–24–4; Harmison 2.3–0–13–1; Flintoff 3–0–15–0; Collingwood 2–0–8–2.

Umpires: N. J. Llong and J. W. Lloyds.
TV Umpire: M. R. Benson.
Referee: J. J. Crowe (New Zealand).

†SOMERSET v AUSTRALIANS

At County Ground, Taunton, June 15, 2005. Somerset won by four wickets. Australian XI 5 for 342 (M. L. Hayden 76, R. T. Ponting 80, D. R. Martyn 44, M. J. Clarke 63*, M. E. K. Hussey 51). Somerset 6 for 345 (G. C. Smith 108, S. T. Jayasuriya 101, J. C. Hildreth 38*; G. D. McGrath 2-49, M. E. K. Hussey 2-41).

Having suffered a batting malfunction at Rose Bowl, the Australians lost their way in the field at Somerset's home. Every batsman got a start on Phil Frost's excellent pitch, Ricky Ponting and Matthew Hayden choosing to retire after stays of 86 and 53 deliveries respectively, in a 50-over total studded with 31 fours and five sixes. Somerset countered with 35 fours and five sixes of their own, as South African captain Graeme Smith took only 68 balls over his ton and former Sri Lankan captain Sanath Jayasuriya 77. There could be few opening partnerships so destructive in international cricket, let alone on the county scene, but Australia's attack, once Brett Lee decided against further stress on a shoulder struck by an Andrew Flintoff bouncer during the Twenty20, came disturbingly alike to their opponents, who prevailed with 19 surplus deliveries.

NATWEST SERIES

†ENGLAND v BANGLADESH

At The Oval, London, June 16, 2005. England won by ten wickets. *Toss:* England. Points: England 6. *International limited-overs debut*: J. Lewis.

England made short work of Bangladesh, winning in less than half their allotted batting time without the loss of a wicket. Only the promising Aftab Ahmed looked at home on the bouncy Oval pitch, hitting four fours and two sixes in his 58-ball stay, after Bangladesh had lost their first three wickets to the debutant Jon Lewis. Steve Harmison also worked up a good head of steam. Marcus Trescothick and Andrew Strauss then made hay on a fast, freshly-mown outfield, requiring not an hour and three-quarters to do the needful: England's first 100 runs took only a few balls more than in the Twenty20 international.

Man of Match: M. E. Trescothick.

Bangladesh

Javed Omar lbw b Lewis	13	(19)	Mashrafe Mortaza not out	29	(24)
Nafees Iqbal c Jones b Lewis	19	(28)	Khaled Mahmud c Pietersen		
			b Harmison	0	(1)
Mohammad Ashraful c Flintoff b Lewis	0	(1)	Nazmul Hossain c Jones b Gough	6	(23)
Tushar Imran b Harmison	10	(27)			
*Habibul Bashar c Jones b Harmison	19	(28)	L-b 4, w 4, n-b 4	12	
Aftab Ahmed run out (Pietersen/Jones)	51	(58)			
†Khaled Mashud c Jones b Harmison	1	(10)	(45.2 overs, 189 mins)	190	
Mohammad Rafique c Harmison					
b Gough	30	(57)	Fall: 19 19 39 57 72 76 152 159 159 190		

Bowling: Gough 8.2–0–33–2; Lewis 10–0–32–3; Harmison 10–0–39–4; Collingwood 8–0–36–0; Flintoff 9–2–46–0.

England

M. E. Trescothick not out	100	(76)
A. J. Strauss not out	82	(77)
L-b 5, w 1, n-b 4	10	
(24.5 overs, 103 mins) (0 wkt)	192	
Fall:		

*M. P. Vaughan, P. D. Collingwood, A. Flintoff, K. P. Pietersen, †G. O. Jones, V. S. Solanki, J. Lewis, D. Gough, S. J. Harmison (did not bat).

Bowling: Mashrafe Mortaza 6–1–33–0; Nazmul Hossain 7–0–61–0; Khaled Mahmud 3–0–39–0; Mohammad Rafique 6–0–40–0; Aftab Ahmed 2.5–0–14–0.

Umpires: Aleem Dar (Pakistan) and M. R. Benson.
TV Umpire: N. J. Llong.
Referee: J. J. Crowe (New Zealand).

†AUSTRALIA v BANGLADESH

At Sophia Gardens, Cardiff, June 18, 2005. Bangladesh won by five wickets. *Toss:* Australia. Points: Bangladesh 5, Australia 1.

Australia rather coasted to their third consecutive defeat and the first over any distance to Bangladesh. When Adam Gilchrist and Ricky Ponting succumbed to early movement, the Australians took their time consolidating, Mohammad Rafique bowling his left-arm slows with impunity. Damien Martyn and Michael Clarke also undermined their efforts by holing out when set. Mike Hussey and Simon Katich heartened their fellows by plundering 93 runs from the last ten overs, and Bangladesh were 3 for 72 in the 21st over needing more than a run a ball. But the 20-year-old Mohammad Ashraful played a perfectly-paced innings whose 11 boundaries each seemed to be struck just when needed. Aftab Ahmed launched the first ball of the final over from Jason Gillespie for a massive six over mid-on, and the contest was clinched with a scuttled bye. The Australians were inconvenienced – and annoyed – by the absence of Andrew Symonds, who was omitted at the last minute when he presented at the warm-up under the influence of alcohol, an indiscretion for which team management penalised him two match fees and imposed a two-match suspension.

Man of Match: Mohammad Ashraful.

Australia

†A. C. Gilchrist lbw b Mashrafe Mortaza	0	(2)	S. M. Katich not out	36 (23)
M. L. Hayden b Nazmul Hossain	37	(50)		
*R. T. Ponting lbw b Tapash Baisya	1	(16)	L-b 3, w 2, n-b 8	13
D. R. Martyn c Nafees Iqbal b Tapash Baisya	77	(112)		—
M. J. Clarke c Mashrafe Mortaza b Tapash Baisya	54	(84)	(50 overs, 205 mins) (5 wkts)	249
M. E. K. Hussey not out	31	(21)	Fall: 0 9 57 165 183	

G. B. Hogg, J. N. Gillespie, M. S. Kasprowicz, G. D. McGrath did not bat.

Bowling: Mashrafe Mortaza 10–2–33–1; Tapash Baisya 10–1–69–3; Nazmul Hossain 10–2–65–1; Mohammad Rafique 10–0–31–0; Aftab Ahmed 10–0–48–0.

Bangladesh

Javed Omar c Hayden b Kasprowicz	19	(51)	Mohammad Rafique not out	9 (7)
Nafees Iqbal c Gilchrist b Gillespie	8	(21)		
Tushar Imran c Katich b Hogg	6	(30)	B 1, l-b 11, w 6, n-b 4	22
Mohammad Ashraful c Hogg b Gillespie	100	(101)		
*Habibul Bashar run out (Gillespie)	47	(72)	(49.2 overs, 199 mins) (5 wkts)	250
Aftab Ahmed not out	21	(13)	Fall: 17 51 72 202 227	

†Khaled Mashud, Mashrafe Mortaza, Tapash Baisya, Nazmul Hossain did not bat.

Bowling: McGrath 10–1–43–0; Gillespie 9.2–1–41–2; Kasprowicz 10–0–40–1; Hogg 9–0–52–1; Clarke 6–0–38–0; Hussey 5–0–24–0.

Umpires: B. F. Bowden (New Zealand) and D. R. Shepherd.
TV Umpire: M. R. Benson.
Referee: J. J. Crowe (New Zealand).

†ENGLAND v AUSTRALIA

At County Ground, Bristol, June 19, 2005. England won by three wickets. *Toss:* Australia. Points: England 5, Australia 1.

Australia's tour ran a little further off the rails when, after a promising start here, they lost four wickets for six runs in 27 deliveries, Ricky Ponting lasting only one of these, stepping into a full delivery as he had the previous day. Mike Hussey's industrious innings repaired the damage, Michael Clarke and Shane Watson offering handy support, but Steve Harmison's best one-day figures checked the Australians' final thrust and Jason Gillespie next vouchsafed England an 11-ball first over as the reply began. Marcus Trescothick was yorked, and Andrew Strauss and Paul Collingwood played on, but Michael Vaughan kept his team in the game with a poised half-century. Then Kevin Pietersen took 18 off the 42nd over (from Michael Kasprowicz) and 17 off the 46th (from Gillespie) to ensure the Australians' fourth defeat in a week; "almost genius-like", decided his captain. Umpires

Aleem Dar and Jeremy Lloyds had excellent games; third umpire Nigel Llong, correctly, granted Pietersen a crucial reprieve when Ponting threw the stumps down.

Man of Match: K. P. Pietersen.

Australia

†A. C. Gilchrist c Jones b Harmison	26	(32)	J. N. Gillespie c Jones b Flintoff	14	(18)
M. L. Hayden c Collingwood b Harmison	31	(44)	M. S. Kasprowicz b Gough	1	(3)
*R. T. Ponting lbw b Harmison	0	(1)	G. D. McGrath not out	0	(1)
D. R. Martyn c Pietersen b Harmison	0	(2)			
M. J. Clarke b Lewis	45	(71)	L-b 6, w 6, n-b 4	16	
M. E. K. Hussey b Harmison	84	(83)			
S. R. Watson b Flintoff	25	(36)	(50 overs, 216 mins)	(9 wkts)	252
G. B. Hogg not out	10	(13)	Fall: 57 57 57 63 168 220 220 244 248		

Bowling: Gough 10–0–47–1; Lewis 10–0–69–1; Harmison 10–0–33–5; Flintoff 10–1–39–2; Collingwood 2–0–11–0; Vaughan 6–0–33–0; Solanki 2–0–14–0.

England

M. E. Trescothick b McGrath	16	(32)	V. S. Solanki run out (Gilchrist)	13	(14)
A. J. Strauss b McGrath	16	(23)	J. Lewis not out	7	(15)
*M. P. Vaughan lbw b Hogg	57	(92)			
P. D. Collingwood b Kasprowicz	14	(28)	L-b 1, w 7, n-b 10	18	
A. Flintoff c Kasprowicz b Hogg	19	(22)			
K. P. Pietersen not out	91	(65)	(47.3 overs, 217 mins)	(7 wkts)	253
†G. O. Jones c Martyn b Hogg	2	(5)	Fall: 39 42 82 119 150 160 214		

D. Gough, S. J. Harmison (did not bat).

Bowling: McGrath 9–1–34–2; Gillespie 10–1–66–0; Kasprowicz 9–0–68–1; Watson 9.3–0–42–0; Hogg 10–1–42–3.

Umpires: Aleem Dar (Pakistan) and J. W. Lloyds.
TV Umpire: N. J. Llong.
Referee: J. J. Crowe (New Zealand).

†ENGLAND v BANGLADESH

At Trent Bridge, Nottingham, June 21, 2005. Day/night game. England won by 168 runs. *Toss:* England. Points: England 6. International limited-overs debut: C. T. Tremlett, Nafees Iqbal.

An all-round performance by Paul Collingwood was the highlight of another catchweight contest begun by a 141-run opening partnership between Marcus Trescothick and Andrew Strauss in 99 balls; Strauss fell to the penultimate ball of the innings for his best one-day score. Collingwood saw the day through with an unconquered 112, including ten fours and five sixes, before taking up the ball to end a dangerous partnership between Mohammad Ashraful and Javed Omar with the first of six wickets. Ashraful's delectable 94 took only 52 deliveries, but Bangladesh shed their last seven wickets in the space of 42 runs over barely a dozen overs.

Man of Match: P. D. Collingwood.

England

M. E. Trescothick c Nafees Iqbal b Nazmul Hossain	85 (65)	†G. O. Jones not out	2 (1)
A. J. Strauss lbw b Nazmul Hossain	152 (128)	B 1, l-b 4, w 9, n-b 9	23
*M. P. Vaughan b Nazmul Hossain	0 (8)		
A. Flintoff c Habibul Bashar b Aftab Ahmed	17 (21)	(50 overs, 211 mins) (4 wkts)	391
P. D. Collingwood not out	112 (86)	Fall: 141 148 179 389	

K. P. Pietersen, A. F. Giles, J. Lewis, C. T. Tremlett, S. J. Harmison (did not bat).

Bowling: Mashrafe Mortaza 10–0–71–0; Tapash Baisya 7–0–87–0; Nazmul Hossain 10–0–83–3; Mohammad Rafique 10–0–54–0; Aftab Ahmed 10–0–65–1; Tushar Imran 3–0–26–0.

Bangladesh

Javed Omar b Collingwood	59 (106)	Mashrafe Mortaza b Collingwood	0 (8)
Nafees Iqbal b Tremlett	10 (28)	Tapash Baisya b Tremlett	3 (6)
Tushar Imran c Jones b Tremlett	0 (1)	Nazmul Hossain not out	2 (6)
Mohammad Ashraful b Collingwood	94 (52)		
*Habibul Bashar c Strauss b Collingwood	16 (23)	W 6, n-b 6	12
Aftab Ahmed c and b Collingwood	0 (1)		
†Khaled Mashud c Jones b Collingwood	8 (12)	(45.2 overs, 187 mins)	223
Mohammad Rafique b Tremlett	19 (33)	Fall: 30 30 155 181 181 196 201 201 205 223	

Bowling: Lewis 5–1–23–0; Tremlett 8.2–1–32–4; Harmison 8–1–55–0; Flintoff 4–0–30–0; Giles 10–0–52–0; Collingwood 10–1–31–6.

Umpires: B. F. Bowden (New Zealand) and D. R. Shepherd.
TV Umpire: M. R. Benson.
Referee: J. J. Crowe (New Zealand).

†ENGLAND v AUSTRALIA

At Riverside, Chester-le-Street, June 23, 2005. Day/night game. Australia won by 57 runs. *Toss:* England. Points: Australia 6.

Australia made a tentative start and a slow finish in this game after being surprisingly sent in by Marcus Trescothick, who was deputising for the injured Michael Vaughan, yet so dominated proceedings between times as to silence the growing group of doubters, at least for the moment. Andrew Symonds and Damien Martyn added 142 in 145 deliveries for the fourth wicket with a few hearty strokes but mostly through excellent running, and England never recovered from being 3 for 6 after 33 deliveries. Brett Lee added a keen edge to Australia's bowling, while Glenn McGrath and Brad Hogg continued their handy early-season form. Darren Gough and Steve Harmison made a mockery of their predecessors' work by adding 64 in the last 12 overs of England's innings with barely a false shot, but by then it was far too late.

Man of Match: A. Symonds.

Australia

†A. C. Gilchrist c Jones b Tremlett	... 18	(31)
M. L. Hayden c Jones b Flintoff	 39	(56)
*R. T. Ponting c Giles b Harmison	... 27	(40)
D. R. Martyn not out	 68	(81)
A. Symonds run out (Trescothick)	... 73	(81)
M. E. K. Hussey c Collingwood b Flintoff	5	(10)

S. R. Watson not out 11   (7)

L-b 12, w 7, n-b 6 25
                                   ——
(50 overs, 211 mins)   (5 wkts) 266
Fall: 44 95 96 238 247

G. B. Hogg, J. N. Gillespie, B. Lee, G. D. McGrath (did not bat).

Bowling: Gough 10–0–41–0; Tremlett 9–0–53–1; Harmison 9–2–44–1; Flintoff 10–0–55–2; Giles 9–1–44–0; Collingwood 3–0–17–0.

England

*M. E. Trescothick c Gilchrist b McGrath	0	(15)
A. J. Strauss b Lee	 3	(13)
V. S. Solanki c Ponting b Hogg	 34	(69)
P. D. Collingwood b McGrath	 0	(2)
A. Flintoff c Gillespie b Hogg	 44	(61)
K. P. Pietersen c Hussey b Symonds	.. 19	(28)
†G. O. Jones c Hayden b Watson	 23	(31)
A. F. Giles c Symonds b Lee	 4	(3)

C. T. Tremlett c Hussey b Gillespie . . 8 (18)
D. Gough not out 46 (47)
S. J. Harmison not out 11 (17)

L-b 8, w 6, n-b 3 17
                                 ——
(50 overs, 217 mins)   (9 wkts) 209
Fall: 4 6 6 85 94 123 133 145 159

Bowling: Lee 10–2–27–2; McGrath 10–1–31–2; Gillespie 9–0–36–1; Watson 8–0–51–1; Hogg 6–0–19–2; Symonds 7–0–37–1.

Umpires: Aleem Dar (Pakistan) and M. R. Benson.
TV Umpire: J. W. Lloyds.
Referee: J. J. Crowe (New Zealand).

†AUSTRALIA v BANGLADESH

At Old Trafford, Manchester, June 25, 2005. Australia won by ten wickets. *Toss:* Australia. Points: Australia 6.

Played under a grey sky and ended in barely half the time allocated, this was a no-contest after a third-wicket partnership of 90 at a run a ball between Mohammad Ashraful and Nafees Iqbal was broken by the first of five wickets to Andrew Symonds. Bangladesh lost their last eight wickets for 26 in 70 deliveries, and Adam Gilchrist and Matthew Hayden made light of their target with 82 in boundaries. Mohammad Rafique, so economical at Cardiff, was here treated roughly; when Manjural Islam Rana's first over, the innings' 13th, was called after only five balls, he did not look disappointed.

Man of Match: A. Symonds.

Bangladesh

Javed Omar lbw b Lee	 3	(20)
Nafees Iqbal b Symonds	 47	(57)
Tushar Imran c Gilchrist b Lee	 4	(12)
Mohammad Ashraful c and b Symonds	58	(86)
*Habibul Bashar c Gilchrist b Symonds	0	(1)
Aftab Ahmed b Symonds	 5	(13)
†Khaled Mashud b Hogg	 4	(12)
Manjural Islam Rana st Gilchrist b Hogg	2	(5)

Mohammad Rafique b Symonds 0 (6)
Mashrafe Mortaza c Martyn b Hogg . 0 (3)
Nazmul Hossain not out 0 (1)

L-b 6, w 6, n-b 4 16
                                 ——
(35.2 overs, 154 mins)   139
Fall: 13 23 113 113 124 137 139 139 139 139

Bowling: Lee 6–1–36–2; McGrath 6–1–19–0; Gillespie 3–0–17–0; Watson 4–0–14–0; Hogg 9–1–29–3; Symonds 7.2–1–18–5.

Australia

†A. C. Gilchrist not out 66 (60)
M. L. Hayden not out 66 (54)
     W 7, n-b 1 8
                     —

  (19 overs, 73 mins)   (0 wkt) 140

*R. T. Ponting, D. R. Martyn, A. Symonds, M. E. K. Hussey, S. R. Watson, G. B. Hogg, J. N. Gillespie, B. Lee, G. D. McGrath (did not bat).

Bowling: Mashrafe Mortaza 6–0–32–0; Nazmul Hossain 3–0–29–0; Mohammad Rafique 6–0–53–0; Manjural Islam Rana 4–0–26–0.

Umpires: B. F. Bowden (New Zealand) and J. W. Lloyds.
TV Umpire: N. J. Llong.
Referee: J. J. Crowe (New Zealand).

†ENGLAND v BANGLADESH

At Headingley, Leeds, June 26, 2005. England won by five wickets. *Toss:* Bangladesh. Points: England 6.

A patient innings of more than three hours by Javed Omar and some brisk hitting by Khaled Mashud did not show England's attack to its best advantage, but hopes of a target that might stretch England ended when Mohammad Ashraful was caught at slip first ball. Despite losing wickets at inconvenient intervals, England's batsmen were seldom troubled, Andrew Strauss making the most of two and a half hours in the middle, but falling with the scores level as he tried to negotiate a century.

Man of Match: A. J. Strauss.

Bangladesh

Javed Omar b Flintoff 81 (150)
Nafees Iqbal c Trescothick b S. P. Jones 11 (15)
Tushar Imran b Flintoff 32 (34)
Mohammad Ashraful c Trescothick
  b Flintoff 0 (1)
*Habibul Bashar run out (Collingwood) 10 (24)
Aftab Ahmed b Giles 15 (27)
†Khaled Mashud not out 42 (43)

Mashrafe Mortaza b Flintoff 1 (3)
Mohammad Rafique not out 2 (5)

    L-b 1, w 11, n-b 2 14
                     —
(50 overs, 205 mins)   (7 wkts) 208
Fall: 22 92 92 112 138 183 189

Manjural Islam Rana, Nazmul Hossain (did not bat).

Bowling: Gough 9–0–59–0; S. P. Jones 9–0–44–1; Tremlett 7–0–26–0; Flintoff 9–1–29–4; Collingwood 6–0–21–0; Giles 10–0–28–1.

England

*M. E. Trescothick c Khaled Mashud
  b M. I. Rana 43 (38)
A. J. Strauss b Manjural Islam Rana .. 98 (104)
A. Flintoff lbw b Mohammad Rafique 22 (29)
V. S. Solanki lbw b Mohammad Rafique 8 (25)
K. P. Pietersen c Mohammad Rafique
  b M. I. Rana 23 (26)
P. D. Collingwood not out 8 (8)

†G. O. Jones not out 0 (3)

    L-b 4, w 3 7
                   —
(38.5 overs, 153 mins) (5 wkts) 209
Fall: 99 134 151 182 208

A. F. Giles, D. Gough, C. T. Tremlett, S. P. Jones (did not bat).

Bowling: Nazmul Hossain 7–1–43–0; Mashrafe Mortaza 9–0–48–0; Manjural Islam Rana 9.5–0–57–3; Mohammad Rafique 10–1–44–2; Aftab Ahmed 3–0–13–0.

Umpires: Aleem Dar (Pakistan) and M. R. Benson.
TV Umpire: N. J. Llong.
Referee: J. J. Crowe (New Zealand).

†ENGLAND v AUSTRALIA

At Edgbaston, Birmingham, June 28, 2005. Day/night game. No result. *Toss:* Australia. Points: England 3, Australia 3

A match brimming with potential, with England needing 164 to win in 27 overs after rain adjustments, ended up brimming with water after a series of showers. Some tempers needed cooling, too, after a throw from bowler Simon Jones early in Australia's innings hit Matthew Hayden on the arm, eliciting a verbal volley from the batsman and some gratuitous advice from fielders. Andrew Symonds and Mike Hussey, fast becoming the most reliable components of Australia's batting, added a sprightly 101 in 15 overs to wrest the initiative, but the innings faltered in its final overs, and England were well-placed after Andrew Strauss's four fours in a Glenn McGrath over, when the heavens descended.

Man of Match: No award.

Australia

†A. C. Gilchrist c G. O. Jones b S. P. Jones	19	(18)	B. Lee not out	21	(18)
M. L. Hayden lbw b S. P. Jones	14	(24)	J. N. Gillespie c Pietersen b Gough	1	(2)
*R. T. Ponting c G. O. Jones b Flintoff	34	(40)	G. D. McGrath not out	2	(5)
D. R. Martyn c Pietersen b Harmison	36	(65)			
A. Symonds run out (Collingwood)	74	(75)	B 1, l-b 4, w 4, n-b 1	10	
M. E. K. Hussey c G. O. Jones					
b Harmison	45	(42)			
M. J. Clarke c G. O. Jones b Gough	3	(6)	(50 overs, 209 mins)	(9 wkts) 261	
G. B. Hogg c G. O. Jones b Gough	2	(6)	Fall: 34 46 95 123 224 234 236 242 254		

Bowling: Gough 9–0–70–3; S. P. Jones 10–2–53–2; Harmison 10–1–38–2; Flintoff 10–0–38–1; Giles 10–1–44–0; Vaughan 1–0–13–0.

England

M. E. Trescothick not out	11	(19)
A. J. Strauss c Gillespie b McGrath	25	(18)
*M. P. Vaughan not out	0	(0)
N-b 1	1	

(6 overs, 25 mins)   (1 wkt) 37
Fall: 37

A. Flintoff, K. P. Pietersen, P. D. Collingwood, †G. O. Jones, A. F. Giles, D. Gough, S. J. Harmison, S. P. Jones (did not bat).

Bowling: Lee 3–0–13–0; McGrath 3–0–24–1.

Umpires: B. F. Bowden (New Zealand) and D. R. Shepherd.
TV Umpire: J. W. Lloyds.
Referee: J. J. Crowe (New Zealand).

†AUSTRALIA v BANGLADESH

At St Lawrence Ground, Canterbury, June 30, 2005. Australia won by six wickets. *Toss:* Australia. Points: Australia 5, Bangladesh 1.

In their last appearance of summer, Bangladesh again gave Australia a workout. Although Mohammad Ashraful was yorked by Brett Lee after pulling him for six, the 19-year-old left-hander Nafees Iqbal made Australia work for his wicket, and keeper Khaled Mashud again showed an effective array of strokes. Bangladesh's score was also bulked by the donation of 23 extras. Australia were 3 for 83 in the 15th over, and it needed a timely return to form for Michael Clarke and some meaty blows from Andrew Symonds before their team could feel safe. Adam Gilchrist was dismissed in bizarre fashion when a ball exploded from a footmark and ended up at first slip. Under the impression he had nicked the ball, yet clearly puzzled that he had not felt it, Gilchrist "walked"; replays showed he had been nowhere near it.

Man of Match: Nafees Iqbal.

Bangladesh

Javed Omar c Gilchrist b Gillespie	0	(10)	Mohammad Rafique c Gilchrist	
			b Watson	15 (13)
Nafees Iqbal c Gilchrist b Watson	75	(116)	Khaled Mahmud c Ponting b Gillespie	22 (22)
Tushar Imran b Lee	0	(1)		
Mohammad Ashraful b Lee	7	(4)	L-b 9, w 8, n-b 6	23
*Habibul Bashar c Gilchrist b Watson	30	(24)		
Aftab Ahmed c Gilchrist b Kasprowicz	7	(11)	(50 overs, 210 mins) (8 wkts)	250
†Khaled Mashud not out	71	(105)	Fall: 8 9 19 57 75 169 193 250	

Tapash Baisya, Mashrafe Mortaza (did not bat).

Bowling: Lee 10–0–62–2; Gillespie 9–0–49–2; Watson 10–0–43–3; Kasprowicz 9–0–46–1; Symonds 10–0–36–0; Clarke 2–1–5–0.

Australia

†A. C. Gilchrist c Khaled Mahmud				
b Tapash Baisya	45	(36)	A. Symonds not out	42 (37)
M. L. Hayden c Khaled Mahmud				
b Mashrafe Mortaza	1	(4)	L-b 3, w 5, n-b 3	11
*R. T. Ponting c Tushar Imran				
b Mashrafe Mortaza	66	(95)		
D. R. Martyn c Khaled Mashud				
b Khaled Mahmud	9	(16)	(48.1 overs, 187 mins) (4 wkts)	254
M. J. Clarke not out	80	(104)	Fall: 15 63 83 168	

M. E. K. Hussey, S. R. Watson, B. Lee, J. N. Gillespie, M. S. Kasprowicz (did not bat).

Bowling: Mashrafe Mortaza 9–0–44–2; Tapash Baisya 9–0–57–1; Khaled Mahmud 10–0–54–1; Aftab Ahmed 10–0–48–0; Mohammad Rafique 10–0–44–0; Mohammad Ashraful 0.1–0–4–0.

Umpires: Aleem Dar (Pakistan) and J. W. Lloyds.
TV Umpire: M. R. Benson.
Referee: J. J. Crowe (New Zealand).

FINAL

†ENGLAND v AUSTRALIA

At Lord's Cricket Ground, London, July 2, 2005. Match tied. *Toss:* England.

A remarkable match on a sporting pitch under overcast skies ended when a last-ball misfield at third man by Brett Lee permitted the running of a second leg-bye, levelling the scores. England exulted; Australia were dejected, as well they might have been, having earlier reduced the hosts to 5 for 33 after 56 deliveries. Australia struggled after being inserted, despite Adam Gilchrist's four consecutive fours in Simon Jones' second over, with Steve Harmison again achieving alarming lift and Andrew Flintoff allowing no liberties. Mike Hussey was marooned by the tail after another crisp innings of 81 deliveries with six fours. England found batting conditions no easier, and fighting against the pitch with a series of aggressive shots seemed likely to cost them the match. Where previous England teams might at this point have capitulated, however, this one rallied. Paul Collingwood and Geraint Jones added 116 from 205 deliveries with patience and common sense. Both fell to full tosses – Collingwood hitting his to cover and running, Jones being hit on the boot missing a sweep – but Darren Gough and Ashley Giles were not to be denied. Although Gough was caught short of his ground by bowler McGrath's direct hit from the penultimate delivery, the towering figures of Giles and Harmison galumphed England to parity.

Man of Match: G.O. Jones. *Man of the Series*: A. Symonds.

Australia

†A.C. Gilchrist c Pietersen b Flintoff	27	(32)	B. Lee c G.O. Jones b Flintoff 3 (5)
M.L. Hayden c Giles b Gough	17	(19)	J.N. Gillespie c G.O. Jones b Flintoff 0 (1)
*R.T. Ponting c G.O. Jones b Harmison	7	(18)	G.D. McGrath c Collingwood b Gough 0 (4)
D.R. Martyn c G.O. Jones b Harmison	11	(24)	
A. Symonds c Strauss b Collingwood	29	(71)	B 4, l-b 5, w 7, n-b 6 22
M.J. Clarke lbw b S.P. Jones	2	(19)	
M.E.K. Hussey not out	62	(81)	(48.5 overs, 208 mins) 196
G.B. Hogg c G.O. Jones b Harmison	16	(22)	Fall: 50 54 71 90 93 147 169 179 179 196

Bowling: Gough 6.5–1–36–2; S.P. Jones 8–2–45–1; Flintoff 8–2–23–3; Harmison 10–2–27–3; Collingwood 8–0–26–1; Giles 8–0–30–0.

England

M.E. Trescothick c Ponting b McGrath	6	(16)	S.P. Jones b Hussey 1 (2)
A.J. Strauss b Lee	2	(8)	D. Gough run out (McGrath) 12 (13)
*M.P. Vaughan b McGrath	0	(7)	
K.P. Pietersen c Gilchrist b Lee	6	(10)	S.J. Harmison not out 0 (0)
A. Flintoff c Hayden b McGrath	8	(9)	B 2, l-b 12, w 3, n-b 2 19
P.D. Collingwood run out (Symonds/Gilchrist)	53	(116)	
†G.O. Jones lbw b Hogg	71	(100)	(50 overs, 232 mins) (9 wkts) 196
A.F. Giles not out	18	(21)	Fall: 11 13 19 19 33 149 161 162 194

Bowling: Lee 10–1–36–2; McGrath 10–4–25–3; Gillespie 10–1–42–0; Symonds 10–2–23–0; Hogg 6–0–25–1; Hussey 4–0–31–1.

Umpires: B.F. Bowden (New Zealand) and D.R. Shepherd.
TV Umpire: J.W. Lloyds.
Referee: J.J. Crowe (New Zealand).

NATWEST CHALLENGE

†ENGLAND v AUSTRALIA

At Headingley, Leeds, July 7, 2005. England won by nine wickets. *Toss:* England.

On the day that London was rocked by a chain of terrorist bombs, England's top order finally clicked, enjoying the warm afternoon sun denied the visitors. After Adam Gilchrist had hit five fours and two sixes in his brief stay, Australia's run-rate dwindled steadily, and it was only the reliable Mike Hussey who rallied them, managing an unbeaten eighth-wicket partnership of 51 from the last 31 deliveries of the innings with Brett Lee. The first of four useful wickets for Paul Collingwood was obtained by a finely judged ankle-high catch by Kevin Pietersen at deep mid-wicket, ending Ricky Ponting's uneasy stay. The pitch flattened after lunch, and Australia failed to grasp such advantages as they were offered. Andrew Strauss got off the mark when he was dropped behind off Glenn McGrath; the second of seven no-balls from Lee was uppercut by Marcus Trescothick to third man. Their opening partnership was only broken by a needless reverse sweep, 20 years after Peter May's famous ban on the shot. Trescothick proceeded unmolested to his first hundred against Australia in any form of cricket, with eight fours and a soaring straight six off Brad Hogg. With his best form of the summer, Michael Vaughan helped him add 120 in 129 balls. This was the first one-day international in which "super substitutes" were permitted, Simon Jones giving way to

Vikram Solanki after the former finished his spell at the 31-over mark of Australia's innings, and Brad Hogg replacing Hayden after 22 overs of England's reply. Also, fielding captains were allowed to designate "powerplays": both chose to get them out of the way in the first 20 overs. No one seemed to care much. Vaughan said afterwards that the television was on in England's dressing room all day as news of events in London flowed in.

Man of Match: M. E. Trescothick.

Australia

†A. C. Gilchrist c G. O. Jones b Harmison	42	(51)	S. R. Watson c Strauss b Harmison	3	(13)
M. L. Hayden c Pietersen b Flintoff	17	(47)	B. Lee not out	15	(19)
*R. T. Ponting c Pietersen b Collingwood	14	(30)			
D. R. Martyn c G. O. Jones b Collingwood	43	(71)	B 2, l-b 12, w 15, n-b 2	31	
A. Symonds c Trescothick b Collingwood	6	(10)			
M. J. Clarke b Collingwood	2	(9)	(50 overs, 218 mins) (7 wkts)	218	
M. E. K. Hussey not out	46	(52)	Fall: 62 68 107 116 120 159 168		

J. N. Gillespie, G. D. McGrath, G. B. Hogg (did not bat).

Bowling: Gough 10–1–50–0; S. P. Jones 10–1–28–0; Harmison 10–0–39–2; Flintoff 10–0–54–1; Collingwood 10–0–34–4.

England

M. E. Trescothick not out	104	(134)
A. J. Strauss c Gilchrist b Hogg	41	(84)
*M. P. Vaughan not out	59	(65)
B 1, l-b 2, w 3, n-b 11	17	
(46 overs, 197 mins) (1 wkt)	221	
Fall: 101		

K. P. Pietersen, A. Flintoff, P. D. Collingwood, †G. O. Jones, A. F. Giles, D. Gough, S. J. Harmison, S. P. Jones, V. S. Solanki (did not bat).

Bowling: Lee 9–0–48–0; McGrath 8–1–26–0; Gillespie 10–0–66–0; Watson 3–0–16–0; Symonds 10–0–32–0; Hogg 6–0–30–1.

Umpires: M. R. Benson and R. E. Koertzen (South Africa).
TV Umpire: N. J. Llong.
Referee: R. S. Mahanama (Sri Lanka).

NATWEST CHALLENGE

†ENGLAND v AUSTRALIA

At Lord's Cricket Ground, London, July 10, 2005. Australia won by seven wickets. *Toss:* Australia.

Ricky Ponting had his best day of an indifferent tour so far with a punishing 111 from 115 balls containing 14 fours and a six amid the kind of win that his team and its supporters have been rather more used to in recent years. The captain also took an astounding catch, diving across and backwards at mid-off to arrest a flat drive from Ashley Giles in one outstretched hand. The match winner, however, was Brett Lee, whose figures were the best by an Australian in a one-day match at Lord's. His first wicket, that of Kevin Pietersen, left England 4 for 45 after 16 overs, and he claimed Andrew Flintoff, Paul Collingwood and Geraint Jones as each loomed as a threat to

Australia's hold on the game. Flintoff's restrained innings – his first half-century against Australia – again made Jason Gillespie look ordinary, but it was England's turn to seem sloppy in the field, beginning when Darren Gough removed Adam Gilchrist's off-stump with his third ball as umpire Lloyds was extending his arm. Ponting feasted on a healthy ration of short bowling in a 135-ball partnership of 120 with Damien Martyn as they cruised to victory. The day began with a minute's silence in memory of the terrorist bombing victims; later, patriotic applause greeted the flight of a Lancaster bomber, Spitfire and Hurricane that were taking part in London's official commemorations to mark 60 years since the end of World War II.

Man of Match: B. Lee.

England

M. E. Trescothick c Gilchrist			A. F. Giles c Ponting b Lee	....	4	(6)
b Kasprowicz	14	(36)	D. Gough not out	....	5	(5)
A. J. Strauss b Kasprowicz	11	(25)	S. J. Harmison not out	....	6	(3)
*M. P. Vaughan lbw b McGrath	1	(3)	L-b 3, w 14, n-b 2	....	19	
K. P. Pietersen b Lee	15	(23)				
A. Flintoff c Hussey b Lee	87	(112)	(50 overs, 207 mins)	(8 wkts)	223	
P. D. Collingwood c Gilchrist b Lee	34	(56)				
†G. O. Jones c Katich b Lee	27	(33)	Fall: 25 28 28 45 148 193 210 214			

S. P. Jones (did not bat).

Bowling: Lee 10–2–41–5; McGrath 10–2–37–1; Kasprowicz 10–2–40–2; Gillespie 7–0–42–0; Symonds 7–0–31–0; Clarke 6–0–29–0.

Australia

†A. C. Gilchrist c G. O. Jones b Flintoff	29	(20)			
S. M. Katich c Harmison b Giles	30	(62)	L-b 2, w 4, n-b 4	....	10
*R. T. Ponting c Pietersen b Gough	11	(115)			
D. R. Martyn not out	39	(67)	(44.2 overs, 190 mins)	(3 wkts)	224
A. Symonds not out	5	(6)	Fall: 36 96 216		

M. J. Clarke, M. E. K. Hussey, B. Lee, J. N. Gillespie, M. S. Kasprowicz, G. D. McGrath, B. J. Haddin (did not bat).

Bowling: Gough 6.2–0–43–1; S. P. Jones 5–0–29–0; Harmison 10–0–48–0; Flintoff 8–0–44–1; Giles 10–0–38–1; Collingwood 5–0–20–0.

Umpires: R. E. Koertzen (South Africa) and J. W. Lloyds.
TV Umpire: M. R. Benson.
Referee: R. S. Mahanama (Sri Lanka).

NATWEST CHALLENGE

†ENGLAND v AUSTRALIA

At The Oval, London, July 12, 2005. Australia won by eight wickets. *Toss:* Australia.

Ricky Ponting's 100th game as Australia's one-day captain, and David Shepherd's last as an umpire after 92 Tests and 172 one-day internationals, was an emphatic reassertion of Australian purpose. There remained room for improvement – Michael Vaughan and Andrew Strauss were both dropped from mishooks, the former by the hapless Jason Gillespie, the latter by a circling Adam Gilchrist – but the captain looked an altogether happier man, even running out his rival with a direct hit. Brett Lee claimed his 200th one-day international wicket when he removed the dangerous Marcus Trescothick, making him the second swiftest to the milestone, and Glenn McGrath began with a parsimonious spell including four consecutive maidens. When one Jones (Geraint) fell in the 28th over, England "super-substituted" the other Jones (Simon) with extra batsman Vikram Solanki, who helped Kevin Pietersen add 93 from 95 deliveries for the seventh wicket. Pietersen played some extraordinary strokes, taking 15 from Gillespie's penultimate over including a flat-batted six over mid-on from a ball dropped in short as he advanced. But the bowler removed him in the next over with a slower delivery, and achieved his best rhythm and speed of the tour. Although Solanki and Ashley Giles added a useful 42 from the last 39 deliveries of England's innings, Gilchrist and Matthew Hayden immediately hefted 45 from the first 30 balls of Australia's reply. Steve Harmison was tamed by Gilchrist's four boundaries in his third over, and Darren Gough was seemingly consigned to oblivion. Gilchrist's 81-ball hundred, his first in one-day matches in England and his first since January 2004, was an ominous portent for the hosts – who had been so confident just three weeks earlier – with the first Test only nine days away.

Man of Match: A. C. Gilchrist. *Man of the Series*: R. T. Ponting.

England

M. E. Trescothick c Kasprowicz b Lee	0	(12)	V. S. Solanki not out 53	(63)
A. J. Strauss c Gilchrist b Kasprowicz .	36	(50)	A. F. Giles not out 25	(19)
*M. P. Vaughan run out (Ponting)	15	(30)		
K. P. Pietersen b Gillespie	74	(84)	L-b 1, w 7, n-b 2 10	
A. Flintoff c Gilchrist b Kasprowicz ..	5	(15)	—	
P. D. Collingwood c Symonds b Gillespie	9	(18)	(50 overs, 218 mins) (7 wkts) 228	
†G. O. Jones c Kasprowicz b Gillespie	1	(11)	Fall: 4 44 61 74 87 93 186	

S. J. Harmison, D. Gough, S. P. Jones (did not bat).

Bowling: Lee 10–0–46–1; McGrath 10–4–40–0; Kasprowicz 10–1–46–2; Gillespie 10–1–44–3; Symonds 6–1–26–0; Clarke 4–0–25–0.

Australia

†A. C. Gilchrist not out 121	(101)	L-b 2, w 4, n-b 4 10	
M. L. Hayden c G. O. Jones b Gough .	31	(47)	—	
*R. T. Ponting st G. O. Jones b Giles ..	43	(44)	(34.5 overs, 160 mins) (2 wkts) 229	
D. R. Martyn not out	24	(21)	Fall: 91 185	

A. Symonds, M. J. Clarke, M. E. K. Hussey, B. Lee, J. N. Gillespie, M. S. Kasprowicz, G. D. McGrath, S. M. Katich (did not bat).

Bowling: Harmison 9.5–0–81–0; Gough 4–0–37–1; Flintoff 9–0–34–0; Giles 10–0–64–1; Collingwood 2–0–11–0.

Umpires: R. E. Koertzen (South Africa) and D. R. Shepherd.
TV Umpire: J. W. Lloyds.
Referee: R. S. Mahanama (Sri Lanka).

LEICESTERSHIRE v AUSTRALIANS

At Grace Road, Leicester, July 15, 16, 17, 2005. Match drawn. *Toss:* Leicestershire.

After some early fireworks from Brett Lee, who trapped Darren Robinson with the first ball of the match and put John Sadler in hospital with a blow on the shoulder, Australia's only first-class match before the first Test proceeded at a languid pace. The outstanding player on the home team was West Australian left-hander Chris Rogers, who batted almost seven hours for 56 and 219, hitting a total of 40 fours and three sixes, and was deaf to Matthew Hayden's urgings that he should throw his wicket away for the sake of Australian cricket. Justin Langer and Hayden blasted 131 in the 90 minutes of Australia's reply, the former proceeding to 115 from 169 balls in his first tour innings. Ricky Ponting (119 in 172 balls, nine fours, two sixes) and Damien Martyn (154 in 208 balls, 14 fours) added 201 for Australia's fourth wicket, whereupon Jason Gillespie enjoyed a fruitful hour's batting. But Leicestershire rose to the challenge with spirit, Rogers and Robinson commencing with an opening partnership of 247 in 219 minutes that largely secured a stalemate.

Close of play: First day, Australians (1) 2-169 (Langer 71, Ponting 6); Second day, Australians (1) 7-582 (Martyn 154, Gillespie 49).

Leicestershire

D. D. J. Robinson lbw b Lee	0	– b Lee	81
C. J. L. Rogers c Kasprowicz b Lee	56	– c Ponting b MacGill	209
J. K. Maunders c Hayden b Lee	17	– c Hayden b MacGill	33
J. L. Sadler retired hurt	4		
*H. D. Ackerman lbw b Kasprowicz	12	– (4) c and b MacGill	1
J. J. Krejza b MacGill	38	– (5) lbw b MacGill	19
†T. J. New c Hayden b Lee	18	– (6) not out	1
O. D. Gibson lbw b MacGill	30		
D. D. Masters c Gilchrist b Gillespie	15		
S. C. J. Broad c Gilchrist b Gillespie	0		
C. M. Willoughby not out	0		
B 10, l-b 7, n-b 10	27	L-b 10, n-b 9	19

(55.2 overs)	(9 wkts dec) 217	(79.4 overs) (5 wkts) 363

Fall: 0 36 83 119 143 157 215 217 217

Fall: 247 332 339 348 363

Bowling: *First Innings*—Lee 14–2–53–4; Gillespie 11–1–40–2; Kasprowicz 12–1–43–1; MacGill 18.2–4–64–2. *Second Innings*—Lee 13–3–78–1; Gillespie 20–7–60–0; Kasprowicz 20–4–57–0; MacGill 21.4–1–122–4; Clarke 5–0–36–0.

Australia

J. L. Langer c (sub) M. A. G. Boyce b Maunders	115	B. Lee c Robinson b Broad	6	
M. L. Hayden c New b Maunders	75	J. N. Gillespie not out	49	
M. J. Clarke lbw b Maunders	9			
*R. T. Ponting b Gibson	119	B 15, l-b 8, n-b 2	25	
D. R. Martyn not out	154			
S. M. Katich b Masters	4	(125 overs) (7 wkts dec) 582		
†A. C. Gilchrist b Broad	26	Fall: 131 159 245 446 451 495 509		

M. S. Kasprowicz, S. C. G. MacGill (did not bat).

Bowling: Gibson 18–1–77–1; Willoughby 17–1–77–0; Broad 22–1–77–2; Krejza 25–0–136–0; Maunders 21–1–89–3; Masters 20–0–98–1; Rogers 2–0–5–0.

Umpires: S. A. Garratt and R. Palmer.

ENGLAND v AUSTRALIA

First Test Match

At Lord's Cricket Ground, London, July 21, 22, 23, 24, 2005. Australia won by 239 runs. *Toss:* Australia. Test debut: K. P. Pietersen.

The Lord's crowd rose as one just before tea on the first day to acclaim England's feat of routing the visiting Australians in a heady, hectic 40 overs. It was another false dawn. Only rain delayed Australia's victory until as late as 5 p.m. on the fourth day, after some frail English batting and lenient fielding, featuring seven dropped catches.

Thirteen of 17 wickets fell from the Pavilion End on the first day. Five fell to Steve Harmison, who was unendingly hostile. His second ball hit Justin Langer's unprotected upper arm, his 16th struck Matthew Hayden's helmeted head, and his 34th opened a cut under Ricky Ponting's eye from which blood flowed vividly. The Australians batted at breakneck pace, both Langer and Simon Katich top-edging misconceived hook shots, and Damien Martyn and Adam Gilchrist fanning at balls they need not have played. As though Harmison had stung them into attempted retaliation, Australia played their briefest first innings for more than eight years.

The other bag-of-five obtained from the Pavilion End belonged to Glenn McGrath, his third in a Lord's Test and his 27th in all. He struck with the first ball after tea which went away down the slope to Marcus Trescothick – his 500th Test victim – then did the same four balls later to Andrew Strauss. The right-handers quickly encountered the opposite problem, deliveries hurrying back which whisked away Michael Vaughan, Ian Bell and Andrew Flintoff in successive overs. The only resistance came from the debutant Kevin Pietersen, who played extremely straight and made the most of some tentative overs from Jason Gillespie. Ashley Giles fell to the last delivery of the day's play, caught behind as he trod on his stumps. England were 98 runs adrift of Australia's first innings at the close, but with only three wickets in reserve.

The last three, in fact, made a fair fist of closing the gap. Pietersen pilfered 14 from three McGrath deliveries the next morning, including a six over mid-off into the Pavilion, and it took an outstanding outfield catch by Damien Martyn, on the run in front of the Grand Stand, to thwart him. Harmison and Simon Jones added a bold 33 for the last wicket, narrowing the arrears to 35. With both openers gone before Australia's second innings reached 50, the match was delicately poised. Patient and determined batting, first from Ponting, who passed 7,000 Test runs, then from Martyn, who passed 4,000, closed the door on England; ebullient and powerful strokeplay from Clarke, who made his first Test half-century since the Brisbane Test against New Zealand, slammed the shutters on England's fingers.

Ponting lasted an hour and 40 minutes, Martyn more than three and a half hours, while Clarke skated to his 91 in just two and a half hours with 15 fours, his stand with Martyn worth 155 in 208 deliveries. England's capacity for self-harm had now reappeared. Pietersen blotted his copybook by putting Clarke down at short cover on 21 – his third and most costly miss of the match. Geraint Jones the next morning offered two reprieves, while Flintoff spared McGrath with the worst of the lot, fumbling a lame steer to second slip. The last two Australian wickets added 95, with Simon Katich carving out a phlegmatic 67 in three hours.

England needed 420 to win, or cleansing and prolonged rain to draw. They set off as if in pursuit of victory, Trescothick and Strauss calmly negotiating the opening burst of McGrath and Brett Lee. The breach was opened when Strauss aborted a pull and Lee intercepted the bunt by diving forward at short cover, whereupon Shane Warne induced catatonia among the batsmen. Trescothick was handily snared at slip, Bell baffled by a straight ball, Flintoff snaffled behind, and Lee finished off Vaughan's strokeless three-quarters of an hour with a ball that held its line and flattened off stump.

Incessant rain washed away two sessions on Monday, but England's last vestiges of resistance lasted only 61 deliveries, defeat postponed only by some hearty blows from Pietersen, who became the eighth English representative to begin his Test career with two fifties in a match.

Man of Match: G. D. McGrath.

Close of play: First day, England (1) 7-97 (Pietersen 29); Second day, Australia (2) 7-279 (Katich 10); Third day, England (2) 5-156 (Pietersen 42, G. O. Jones 6).

Australia

	R	B	4/6		R	B	4/6
J. L. Langer c Harmison b Flintoff	40	44	5	– run out (Pietersen)	6	15	1
M. L. Hayden b Hoggard	12	25	2	– b Flintoff	34	54	5
*R. T. Ponting c Strauss b Harmison	9	18	1	– c (sub) J. C. Hildreth b Hoggard	42	65	3
D. R. Martyn c G. O. Jones b S. P. Jones	2	4	0	– lbw b Harmison	65	138	8
M. J. Clarke lbw b S. P. Jones	11	22	2	– b Hoggard	91	106	15
S. M. Katich c G. O. Jones b Harmison	27	67	5	– c S. P. Jones b Harmison	67	113	8
†A. C. Gilchrist c G. O. Jones b Flintoff	26	19	6	– b Flintoff	10	14	1
S. K. Warne b Harmison	28	29	5	– c Giles b Harmison	2	7	0
B. Lee c G. O. Jones b Harmison	3	8	0	– run out (Giles)	8	16	1
J. N. Gillespie lbw b Harmison	1	11	0	– b S. P. Jones	13	52	3
G. D. McGrath not out	10	6	2	– not out	20	32	3
B 5, l-b 4, w 1, n-b 11	21			B 10, l-b 8, n-b 8	26		

(40.2 overs, 209 mins) **190**
Fall: 35 55 66 66 87 126 175 178 178 190

(100.4 overs, 457 mins) **384**
Fall: 18 54 100 255 255 274 279
289 341 384

Bowling: *First Innings*—Harmison 11.2–0–43–5; Hoggard 8–0–40–1; Flintoff 11–2–50–2; S. P. Jones 10–0–48–2. *Second Innings*—Harmison 27.4–6–54–3; Hoggard 16–1–56–2; Flintoff 27–4–123–2; S. P. Jones 18–1–69–1; Giles 11–1–56–0; Bell 1–0–8–0.

England

	R	B	4/6		R	B	4/6
M. E. Trescothick c Langer b McGrath	4	17	1	– c Hayden b Warne	44	103	8
A. J. Strauss c Warne b McGrath	2	21	0	– c and b Lee	37	67	6
*M. P. Vaughan b McGrath	3	20	0	– b Lee	4	26	1
I. R. Bell b McGrath	6	25	1	– lbw b Warne	8	15	0
K. P. Pietersen c Martyn b Warne	57	89	8 2	– not out	64	79	6 2
A. Flintoff b McGrath	0	4	0	– c Gilchrist b Warne	3	11	0
†G. O. Jones c Gilchrist b Lee	30	56	6	– c Gillespie b McGrath	6	27	1
A. F. Giles c Gilchrist b Lee	11	13	2	– c Hayden b McGrath	0	2	0
M. J. Hoggard c Hayden b Warne	0	16	0	– lbw b McGrath	0	15	0
S. J. Harmison c Martyn b Lee	11	19	1	– lbw b Warne	0	1	0
S. P. Jones not out	20	14	3	– c Warne b McGrath	0	6	0
B 1, l-b 5, n-b 5	11			B 6, l-b 5, n-b 3	14		

(48.1 overs, 227 mins) **155**
Fall: 10 11 18 19 21 79 92 101 122 155

(58.1 overs, 268 mins) **180**
Fall: 80 96 104 112 119 158 158
164 167 180

Bowling: *First Innings*—McGrath 18–5–53–5; Lee 15.1–5–47–3; Gillespie 8–1–30–0; Warne 7–2–19–2. *Second Innings*—McGrath 17.1–2–29–4; Lee 15–3–58–2; Gillespie 6–0–18–0; Warne 20–2–64–4.

Umpires: Aleem Dar (Pakistan) and R. E. Koertzen (South Africa).
TV Umpire: M. R. Benson.
Referee: R. S. Madugalle (Sri Lanka).

WORCESTERSHIRE v AUSTRALIANS

At County Ground, Worcester, July 30, 31, August 1, 2005. Match drawn. *Toss:* Worcestershire.

Once a showpiece opener on Ashes tours, the Australians' visit to New Road was on this occasion a damp squib. The first day was reduced by rain to a single over. The second featured a painstaking opening partnership of 110 in three and three-quarter hours between Matthew Hayden and Justin Langer, some absent-minded middle-order batting redeemed by a barnstorming innings from deputy keeper Brad Haddin, whose

94 from 96 deliveries included 16 4s and a six, and Jason Gillespie's patient half-century in 149 minutes. Gillespie also made the most of the third day, giving some encouraging signs of form, while Michael Kasprowicz collected a bag of five before the inevitable batting practice.

Close of play: First day, Australians (1) 0-4 (Langer 4, Hayden 0); Second day, Australians (1) 9-406 (Gillespie 53).

Australia

J. L. Langer c Pipe b Mason	54	– (4) not out	11
M. L. Hayden c Peters b Mason	79		
B. J. Hodge c Smith b Malik	38	– b De Bruyn	21
M. J. Clarke lbw b Malik	9	– (1) run out (Peters-Price)	59
S. M. Katich b Price	14		
*R. T. Ponting c Hick b Kabir Ali	20	– (2) not out	59
†B. J. Haddin c Moore b Malik	94		
J. N. Gillespie not out	53		
M. S. Kasprowicz c Pipe b De Bruyn	8		
S. W. Tait b Price	22		
B 5, l-b 8, w 2	15	B 6, l-b 5	11

(98 overs, 414 mins)   (9 wkts dec) 406   (38 overs, 156 mins)   (2 wkts) 161
Fall: 110 149 162 197 223 227 350 373 406   Fall: 80 120

S. C. G. MacGill (did not bat).

Bowling: *First Innings*—Kabir Ali 20-2-124-1; Mason 22-5-65-2; Malik 22-6-78-3; De Bruyn 15-3-58-1; Price 19-2-68-2. *Second Innings*—Kabir Ali 6-2-34-0; Mason 7-2-34-0; Malik 7-1-30-0; Price 12-2-26-0; De Bruyn 6-1-26-1.

Worcestershire

S. D. Peters lbw b Tait	0	R. W. Price b Kasprowicz	0
S. C. Moore c Hayden b Tait	69	M. S. Mason c Langer b MacGill	3
G. A. Hick c Haddin b Gillespie	21	M. N. Malik c and b Kasprowicz	16
B. F. Smith c Hodge b Gillespie	1		
*V. S. Solanki c Haddin b Kasprowicz	36	L-b 3, n-b 8	11
Z. De Bruyn c Katich b Kasprowicz	4		
Kabir Ali c Clarke b Kasprowicz	4	(44 overs, 187 mins)	187
†D. J. Pipe not out	22	Fall: 9 44 48 133 140 144 144 148 151 187	

Bowling: Gillespie 12-2-45-2; Tait 13-4-51-2; Kasprowicz 15-4-67-5; MacGill 4-1-21-1.

Umpires: D. J. Constant and D. B. Hair.

ENGLAND v AUSTRALIA

Second Test Match

At Edgbaston, Birmingham, August 4, 5, 6, 7, 2005. England won by two runs. *Toss:* Australia.

The closest result in 309 Tests between England and Australia was a fitting result for a titanic struggle, in which the visitors threatened to wrest victory at the very last, having been outplayed for most of the three preceding days. It was a match, like the First Test, played at a hectic pace, featuring more than 700 runs in boundaries, despite the superiority that bowlers enjoyed for a good deal of the time. There were three principal dramatis personae. After an inconsequential Lord's Test, all-rounder Andrew Flintoff was man of the match with scores of 68 and 73, seven wickets for 131 and two catches. Shane Warne obtained the best Australian bowling figures at Edgbaston, 6 for 46, in his match bag of 10 for 162. Arguably the most significant figure, however, was Glenn

McGrath, who at 9.15 a.m. on the first morning sustained a ligament strain in his right ankle after he trod on a stray cricket ball during a warm-up game of touch rugby. Ricky Ponting, who at the time was looking at the pitch with a suspicion of early moisture, decided to insert England regardless. In fact, apart from roughening up from the first day, which made life awkward for left-handed batsmen, Steve Rouse's surface was slow and easy-paced, despite a tornado in Birmingham the previous week having limited its preparation time.

The Australian bowlers were slow to work out that the pitch would not do the work for them, and provided plenty of width for England's openers to exploit. Warne turned a ball out of the rough to bowl Andrew Strauss through his back stroke, but England went to lunch on the first day at 1 for 132, an amazing turnabout given the frailty of their batting at Lord's; Marcus Trescothick finished the session by plundering 18 from a wayward Brett Lee over, including a six over third man. Although McGrath's proxy Michael Kasprowicz had Trescothick and Ian Bell caught at the wicket in four balls soon afterwards, and Michael Vaughan holed out to long leg after a promising cameo, Kevin Pietersen and Flintoff thought valour the better part of discretion and plundered 103 from 105 balls, an English record for the fifth wicket at Edgbaston. Pietersen was largely orthodox in his 76-ball 71; Flintoff swung his bat in brutal arcs during his 62-ball 68, which included six fours and five sixes. The last four English wickets, in further contrast to Lord's, sold themselves for 114 in 133 deliveries; the overall scoring rate of 5.13 left a big and boisterous crowd happily entertained.

The frenetic pace continued the next morning after the early loss of Matthew Hayden, Ponting hitting a dozen scintillating boundaries in his 61 from 76 deliveries. But the loss of Damien Martyn, thrown out at the non-striker's end by a direct hit from Vaughan at mid-wicket in the last over before lunch, meant that England enjoyed the better of the session. Despite 276 minutes of patient application by Justin Langer, England worked steadily through the Australian batting thanks to a subtle and patient spell into the rough by the much-maligned Ashley Giles and some intelligent reverse swing from Flintoff and Simon Jones. Michael Clarke achieved the greatest fluency, hitting seven boundaries before falling to a clever quicker ball. Even Adam Gilchrist was subdued, spending two hours over his unbeaten 49, and Australia barely avoided a three-figure deficit. Australian solace for the day was an extraordinary delivery from Warne, pitching in the rough and veering at almost right angles to bowl Strauss behind his legs – an appropriate way for Warne to become the first foreign bowler to take 100 Test wickets in England.

Australia bounced back into the game the next morning when Lee struck thrice in 15 balls to remove Trescothick, Vaughan and nightwatchman Matthew Hoggard; England's lead at this stage was only 130. Pietersen, sweeping two enormous sixes from Warne, added a calm 41 in 69 balls with Bell. But when umpire Rudi Koertzen adjudged both batsmen caught behind, Australia achieved a brief favourite's status, perhaps prematurely. The acceptance of a return catch from Geraint Jones would have left England 7 for 84 just before lunch. Instead, the luckless Jason Gillespie fluffed it, and Flintoff, after a reconnaissance, surged into action, being last out for 73 off 86 deliveries. He was incommoded by a left-shoulder twinge suffered during one vigorous follow-through, but after lunch he lashed six fours and four sixes. The only bowler to whom he showed respect was Warne, who bowled with superb control and variation. But again, England's last four made an invaluable contribution to the addition of 107 in 158 deliveries.

On their fourth-innings chase for 282, Australia made an affirmative beginning. Then came Flintoff, who failed to secure a carry-over hat-trick from the first innings, but who charged in from the pavilion end to hit Langer's inside edge and Ponting's outside edge in six deliveries. As England attacked with the crowd at their back, the Australians even seemed intimidated. Simon Katich was undone by an effective arm ball, but Hayden, Martyn and Gilchrist all perished carelessly. Clarke and Warne batted attractively when

England took an extra half-hour, as they were entitled to, before Steve Harmison made England's day complete by bowling Clarke with a full-pitched slower ball.

Australia began the fourth day needing 107 to win with two wickets remaining. While the sun shone and the beer flowed, England supporters would have been content with a day lasting two deliveries. In fact, it lasted 133, amid increasing and at times almost unbearable tension. The ball beat the bat countless times, the batsmen absorbed numberless body blows, but Lee added 45 in 59 balls with Warne, and 59 in 77 balls with Kasprowicz. Runs came easily with attacking formations in favour and a fast outfield repaying aggression. When a hard-handed Simon Jones dropped Kasprowicz with ten runs needed, it seemed England had blown their opportunity. When the fallible Geraint Jones dived for a looping touch down the leg side off Kasprowicz's glove with three needed, he seemed only an even-money chance of gloving it. But, amid scenes of ecstasy, he made sure of only the second English win in a 'live' Ashes Test since 1986.

Man of Match: A. Flintoff.

Close of play: First day, England (1) 407; Second day, England (2) 1-25 (Trescothick, 19, Hoggard 0); Third day, Australia (2) 8-175 (Warne 20).

England

	R	B	4/6		R	B	4/6
M.E. Trescothick c Gilchrist b Kasprowicz	90	102	15 2	– c Gilchrist b Lee	21	38	4
A.J. Strauss b Warne	48	76	10	– b Warne	6	12	1
*M.P. Vaughan c Lee b Gillespie	24	41	3	– (4) b Lee	1	2	0
I.R. Bell c Gilchrist b Kasprowicz	6	3	1	– (5) c Gilchrist b Warne	21	43	2
K.P. Pietersen c Katich b Lee	71	76	10 1	– (6) c Gilchrist b Warne	20	35	0 2
A. Flintoff c Gilchrist b Gillespie	68	62	6 5	– (7) b Warne	73	86	6 4
†G.O. Jones c Gilchrist b Kasprowicz	1	15	0	– (8) c Ponting b Lee	9	19	1
A.F. Giles lbw b Warne	23	30	4	– (9) c Hayden b Warne	8	36	0
M.J. Hoggard lbw b Warne	16	49	2	– (3) c Hayden b Lee	1	27	0
S.J. Harmison b Warne	17	11	2 1	– c Ponting b Warne	0	1	0
S.P. Jones not out	19	24	1 1	– not out	12	23	3
L-b 9, w 1, n-b 14	24			L-b 1, n-b 9	10		

(79.2 overs, 356 mins) 407   (52.1 overs, 249 mins) 182

Fall: 112 164 170 187 290 293 342 348 375 407   Fall: 25 27 29 31 72 75 101 131 131 182

Bowling: *First Innings*—Lee 17–1–111–1; Gillespie 22–3–91–2; Kasprowicz 15–3–80–3; Warne 25.2–4–116–4. *Second Innings*—Lee 18–1–82–4; Gillespie 8–0–24–0; Kasprowicz 3–0–29–0; Warne 23.1–7–46–6.

Australia

	R	B	4/6			R	B	4/6
J.L. Langer lbw b S.P. Jones	82	154	7	– b Flintoff		28	47	4
M.L. Hayden c Strauss b Hoggard	0	1	0	– c Trescothick b S.P. Jones		31	64	4
*R.T. Ponting c Vaughan b Giles	61	76	12	– c G.O. Jones b Flintoff		0	5	0
D.R. Martyn run out (Vaughan)	20	18	4	– c Bell b Hoggard		28	36	5
M.J. Clarke c G.O. Jones b Giles	40	68	7	– b Harmison		30	57	5
S.M. Katich c G.O. Jones b Flintoff	4	18	1	– c Trescothick b Giles		16	21	3
†A.C. Gilchrist not out	49	69	4	– c Flintoff b Giles		1	4	0
S.K. Warne c Giles	8	14	2	– (9) hit wicket b Flintoff		42	59	4²
B. Lee c Flintoff b S.P. Jones	6	10	1	– (10) not out		43	75	5
J.N. Gillespie lbw b Flintoff	7	37	1	– (8) lbw b Flintoff		0	2	0
M.S. Kasprowicz lbw b Flintoff	0	1	0	– c G.O. Jones b Harmison		20	31	3
B 13, l-b 7, w 1, n-b 10	31			B 13, l-b 8, w 1, n-b 18	40			

(76 overs, 346 mins) 308
Fall: 0 88 118 194 208 262 273 282 308 308

(64.3 overs, 301 mins) 279
Fall: 47 48 82 107 134 136 137 175 220 279

Bowling: *First Innings*—Harmison 11–1–48–0; Hoggard 8–0–41–1; S.P. Jones 16–2–69–2; Flintoff 15–1–52–3; Giles 26–2–78–3. *Second Innings*—Harmison 17.3–3–62–2; Hoggard 5–0–26–1; Giles 15–3–68–2; Flintoff 22–3–79–4; S.P. Jones 5–1–23–1.

Umpires: B.F. Bowden (New Zealand) and R.E. Koertzen (South Africa).
TV Umpire: J.W. Lloyds.
Referee: R.S. Madugalle (Sri Lanka).

ENGLAND v AUSTRALIA

Third Test Match

At Old Trafford, Manchester, August 11, 12, 13, 14, 15, 2005. Match drawn. *Toss:* England.

England outplayed Australia more convincingly than in any Test match for eight years, yet rain and an exemplary captain's innings by Ricky Ponting prevented it counting where it mattered. The hosts had to be content with orchestrating one of the most fascinating Tests of modern times – and the most exciting in a week – as Brett Lee and Glenn McGrath fended off the last four overs from Andrew Flintoff and Steve Harmison in dying light before a crowd that had been gripped for the whole of the final day.

For McGrath, it was a surprising conclusion to a startling inclusion. Having bounced back from the ankle injury sustained before the Edgbaston Test, he was the only change to either side, and found himself in the action at once when Michael Vaughan took first innings on a bouncy but otherwise blameless pitch. Vaughan's rehabilitation after a miserable beginning to the series was even more profound. He was aided in the compilation of his 15th Test century by some unaccountable captaincy from his opposite number, who spelled Lee when he was bowling very fast, and introduced the struggling Jason Gillespie from whose errors of length all batsmen profited. Meanwhile, Shane Warne, on the trail of his 600th wicket, did not enter the attack until the 34th over. Vaughan, on 41, also had two slices of fortune during McGrath's tenth over shortly after lunch: an edge eluded Adam Gilchrist as the keeper trespassed on first slip, and the extraction of his off stump was invalidated by the bowler's foot fault. Otherwise it was one-way traffic, with Vaughan in increasingly sumptuous form off back and front foot, and even rediscovering his long-lost swivel pull shot, hitting 20 fours and a six from 215 balls in 281 minutes, while his partners Marcus Trescothick and Ian Bell lent dedicated support.

Warne's long-awaited landmark accrued in nondescript fashion, Gilchrist pouching an alert catch from a miscued sweep. Otherwise, he had a frustrating day, bowling well but without luck; his luck seemed to flow to Simon Katich, who finally removed England's captain with a full toss, shovelled to long-on.

The second new ball and over-ambition spelt the end for Kevin Pietersen and Bell late on Thursday and early the next, but the innings was then prolonged by a partnership of 87 in 103 balls by Flintoff and Geraint Jones. England's fair total looked increasingly imposing as the second day unfolded. Australia were 1 for 73 at tea, but the sense of a foundation well laid was upset by Simon Jones' first delivery after the break, which took the shoulder of Ponting's bat on the way to gully, was further undermined by a lovely ball from Ashley Giles taking the top of Damien Martyn's off stump, and then mangled by further inroads from Simon Jones and Flintoff. The phenomenon of reverse swing again played a crucial role, aided by some naïve shots. Michael Clarke, unable to field for most of the match and thus unable to bat higher than No. 7 because of an irritated disc, looked particularly uncomfortable.

Ponting's team had much to thank Warne for that afternoon, and more by Saturday evening when he stopped what the rain didn't on a bleak day of only 14 overs. After he reached 50 in 70 balls, Geraint Jones reprieved him twice, fluffing a stumping off Giles and dropping a straightforward chance off Flintoff. Otherwise, with the barely moving bat of Gillespie at the other end, he compiled his second Test ninety in characteristically hearty and homespun fashion, saving Australia from the indignity of the follow-on and the pressure of huge arrears.

The significance of the innings was underlined when Warne holed out on Sunday morning, and England moved quickly to secure and then enlarge their 142-run lead. The afternoon belonged to Andrew Strauss, whose sixth Test century, from 158 deliveries and spanning just over four hours, was well-organised and well-paced, and culminated in a dominant flourish. Regardless of his recent lack of runs, he was always enterprising; regardless of a dressing on his right ear from a wound inflicted in the first innings by Lee, he pulled fearlessly. Lee might have had him early again: at 1, a waist-high edge bisected an unmoving Warne and Ponting at first and second slip. Such consolations, though, were out of the old English excuse book, for which the newly assertive hosts had no time. Virile strokes from Bell and Geraint Jones sped them towards a declaration that left Australia 423 to win.

Dismissing Australia was always likely to take some doing. The pitch was by now benign, and England's thrust was stemmed that evening by Vaughan's need to bowl himself and Giles because of the poor light. England quickly made inroads on the final morning, when Matthew Hoggard had Justin Langer caught behind with the eighth ball of the day, and Matthew Hayden was baffled and bowled by Flintoff's smooth changes of direction. When reverse swing then accounted for Martyn, Katich and Gilchrist after lunch, the Australian effort condensed around the captain, whose form came flooding back to him after an uneasy first half-hour. Ponting has compiled many bold and brazen Test hundreds; his 23rd was a flawless rearguard with sufficient strokes to tax bowlers but so much discretion that he barely played a false shot let alone offered a catch.

This remarkable Test had twists in it yet. Clarke, now recovered, then Warne, never dismayed, offered such stalwart support either side of tea as to nourish fantasies of a startling rally. Clarke helped his captain add 81 in 106 balls, Warne 76 in 123 balls. Vaughan looked momentarily bereft when Pietersen dropped his fifth consecutive Test catch in spilling Warne behind square leg, and might have been plunged into despair when in the next over a Warne snick escaped Strauss's grasp at slip; Geraint Jones, however, interposed a glove between the ball and the ground, and five overs later moved well to his left to accept a leg-side nick from Ponting. His best Test score against England had lasted 411 minutes and absorbed 275 deliveries, 16 of which were hit for four and one hooked for six. Lee could find nothing but air when he came in, and the appearance of McGrath seldom occasions confidence. When they survived, Australia were as cock-a-hoop about the final over as England had been about any of the preceding 367.

Man of Match: R. T. Ponting.

Close of play: First day, England (1) 5-341 (Bell 59); Second day, Australia (1) 7-214 (Warne 45, Gillespie 4); Third day, Australia (1) 7-264 (Warne 78, Gillespie 7); Fourth day, Australia (2) 0-24 (Langer 14, Hayden 5).

England

	R	B	4/6		R	B	4/6
M. E. Trescothick c Gilchrist b Warne ..	63	117	9	– b McGrath	41	56	6
A. J. Strauss b Lee	6	28	0	– c Martyn b McGrath	106	158	9 2
*M. P. Vaughan c McGrath b Katich ...	166	215	20 1	– c (sub) B. J. Hodge b Lee ...	14	37	2
I. R. Bell c Gilchrist b Lee	59	155	8	– c Katich b McGrath	65	103	4 1
K. P. Pietersen c (sub) B. J. Hodge b Lee	21	28	1	– lbw b McGrath	0	1	0
M. J. Hoggard b Lee	4	10	1				
A. Flintoff c Langer b Warne	46	67	7	– (6) b McGrath	4	18	0
†G. O. Jones b Gillespie	42	51	6	– (7) not out	27	12	2 2
A. F. Giles c Hayden b Warne	0	6	0	– (8) not out	0	0	0
S. J. Harmison not out	10	11	1				
S. P. Jones b Warne	0	4	0				
B 4, l-b 5, w 3, n-b 15	27			B 5, l-b 3, w 1, n-b 14 ..	23		

(113.2 overs, 503 mins)   444

Fall: 26 163 290 333 341 346 433 434 438 444

(61.5 overs, 288 mins)

(6 wkts dec) 280

Fall: 64 97 224 225 248 264

Bowling: *First Innings*—McGrath 25-6-86-0; Lee 27-6-100-4; Gillespie 19-2-114-1; Warne 33.2-5-99-4; Katich 9-1-36-1. *Second Innings*—McGrath 20.5-1-115-5; Lee 12-0-60-1; Warne 25-3-74-0; Gillespie 4-0-23-0.

Australia

	R	B	4/6		R	B	4/6
J. L. Langer c Bell b Giles	31	50	4	– c G. O. Jones b Hoggard ...	14	41	3
M. L. Hayden lbw b Giles	34	71	5	– b Flintoff	36	91	5 1
*R. T. Ponting c Bell b S. P. Jones	7	12	1	– c G. O. Jones b Harmison .	156	275	16 1
D. R. Martyn b Giles	20	41	2	– lbw b Harmison	19	36	3
S. M. Katich b Flintoff	17	28	1	– c Giles b Flintoff	12	23	2
†A. C. Gilchrist c G. O. Jones b S. P. Jones	30	49	4	– c Bell b Flintoff	4	30	0
S. K. Warne c Giles b S. P. Jones	90	122	11 1	– (9) c G. O. Jones b Flintoff .	34	69	5
M. J. Clarke c Flintoff b S. P. Jones	7	18	0	– (7) b S. P. Jones	39	63	7
J. N. Gillespie lbw b S. P. Jones	26	111	1 1	– (8) lbw b Hoggard	0	5	0
B. Lee c Trescothick b S. P. Jones	1	16	0	– not out	18	25	4
G. D. McGrath not out	1	4	0	– not out	5	9	1
B 8, l-b 7, w 8, n-b 15	38			B 5, l-b 8, W 1, n-b 20 ..	34		

(84.5 overs, 393 mins)   302

Fall: 58 73 86 119 133 186 201 287 293 302

(108 overs, 474 mins)

(9 wkts) 371

Fall: 25 96 129 165 182 263 264 340 354

Bowling: *First Innings*—Harmison 10-0-47-0; Hoggard 6-2-22-0; Flintoff 20-1-65-1; S. P. Jones 17.5-6-53-6; Giles 31-4-100-3. *Second Innings*—Harmison 22-4-67-2; Hoggard 13-0-49-2; Giles 26-4-93-0; Vaughan 5-0-21-0; Flintoff 25-6-71-4; S. P. Jones 17-3-57-1.

Umpires: B. F. Bowden (New Zealand) and S. A. Bucknor (West Indies).
TV Umpire: N. J. Llong.
Referee: R. S. Madugalle (Sri Lanka).

†SCOTLAND v AUSTRALIANS

At The Grange, Edinburgh, August 18, 2005. (50-over match.) Match abandoned without a ball bowled.

†NORTHAMPTONSHIRE v AUSTRALIANS

At County Ground, Northampton, August 20, 21, 2005. Match drawn. Australian XI 6 dec 374 (M. L. Hayden 136, M. J. Clarke 121, B. J. Hodge 34, B. J. Haddin 32*; B. J. Phillips 2-50, P. S. Jones 2/70). Northamptonshire 169 (B. J. Phillips 37*; G. D. McGrath 3-24, B. Lee 2-30, S. W. Tait 2-52). Australian XI 2 for 226 (S. M. Katich 63, J. L. Langer 86*, D. R. Martyn 43*) .

Matthew Hayden, whose 136 from 205 balls included 104 in boundaries, and Michael Clarke, whose 121 from 177 deliveries featured 90 in boundaries, made the most of this otherwise unremarkable match. Shaun Tait also showed a good turn of pace, sending Tim Roberts to hospital and dismissing former Test batsman Usman Afzaal and local captain David Sales in three balls, to stake a claim for Jason Gillespie's place in the Nottingham Test.

ENGLAND v AUSTRALIA

Fourth Test Match

At Trent Bridge, Nottingham, August 25, 26, 27, 28, 2005. England won by three wickets. *Toss:* England. Test debut: S. W. Tait.

Shane Warne predicted "something special" from Australia in the Fourth Test to break the deadlock in the series: it duly came, but too late to redirect what had been three and a half days of mostly one-way traffic. Australia followed on for the first time against England since the Bicentenary Test, and for the first time in an Ashes series for 20 years. From there it was too far to come back, hard as Warne tried.

Michael Vaughan won an important toss, and his alacrity in batting was all the greater for the last-minute withdrawal of Glenn McGrath with an injured elbow. The young Shaun Tait had already come in for his out-of-form state team-mate Jason Gillespie, so this readmitted the struggling Michael Kasprowicz and deepened the responsibility on Brett Lee.

Lee strove so strenuously to discharge his obligation that he overstepped six times in a total of 18 transgressions in the 20 overs of pre-lunch pace. The seventh hundred partnership between Marcus Trescothick and Andrew Strauss accumulated in better than even time and was only broken by a strange dismissal involving the third umpire: an under-edged sweep by Strauss travelled to slip and only video could establish whether boot or ground had interposed.

Rain and bad light intervened at lunch, eventually cutting the day's overs by a third, and batting became rather more difficult. Tait was less diffident in his second spell, and removed Trescothick and Ian Bell in nine deliveries from the Radcliffe Road end, requiring some conscientious application from Vaughan and Kevin Pietersen. Ricky Ponting eventually removed his opposite number with a ball that need not have been played, and Australia were in good heart when Pietersen edged a full delivery in the fifth over of the second day.

That, however, was as good as it got. Aided by some ordinary bowling and unimaginative captaincy, Andrew Flintoff and Geraint Jones accumulated the biggest partnership of the series – 177 in 235 deliveries – without a ghost of a chance. Flintoff's maiden Ashes hundred lasted 132 balls with 14 fours and a swept six from Warne; Jones was an energetic escort, his 85 taking 149 balls including eight fours. Though a tired shot and a good return catch saw them off, England passed 450 for only the third time against Australia in 15 years with the help of a dedicated tail, and a no-ball tally of 25.

Thirty-four overs of the second day remained when Australia began their reply; within 20, their top four had been removed for 58, three of them by Matthew Hoggard, who before this innings had bowled only 65 overs in the series. Ponting and Damien Martyn both had grounds for complaint – replays suggesting the slightest of inside edges – but the losses were irrecoverable. Michael Clarke was trapped by the day's last ball, and 5 for 99 would have been worse but for Bell missing Simon Katich at short-leg first ball. As it was, Australia remained 378 in arrears when the day's encircling gloom prevented further cricket.

Adam Gilchrist and Katich began the third day in a blaze of strokes, raising a partnership of 58 at a run-a-ball as they belted Hoggard out of the attack. This, however, simply introduced Flintoff and Simon Jones. Flintoff removed Gilchrist for the fourth time in the series through the agency of a stunning, perhaps freakish, catch by Strauss going wide to his left, while Jones took 4 for 22 from his last 32 deliveries. The only resistance came from Lee, who hefted 47 of 45 deliveries including three gargantuan sixes before being caught on the boundary at third man. The follow-on after Australia's first innings had lasted less than 50 overs was almost inevitable.

Justin Langer and Matthew Hayden made a positive start in Australia's second innings, raising 50 in an hour before Ashley Giles caught Hayden in the gully from Flintoff. Anterior cruciate impingement cost Vaughan the services of Jones, and Langer pooled his resources with his captain for the next 21 overs, adding 79. After tea came the breaks: Langer bat-pad, Ponting run out, Martyn caught at the wicket. The most of these was the most significant, not only because of the Australian captain's prestigious wicket, but the circumstances – thrown out by a substitute, Gary Pratt of Durham, from cover in response to a poor call from Martyn. Irked all tour by England's free use of substitute fielders, Ponting was furious; he clashed verbally with several England players and, in the pavilion, their coach, which cost him three-quarters of his match fee and some of his admirers.

England got no further for a while, for Clarke and Katich joined forces to achieve Australia's first hundred partnership since Lord's in a painstaking 295 balls. Clarke had his moments of good fortune against Giles: Geraint Jones should have stumped him at 35, Bell should have caught him at 43. But Katich was resolute, showing the kind of determination for which Australia had wanted all tour, guiding his team into credit just after noon on the fourth day. Ten minutes before lunch, however, Clarke followed a ball from Hoggard, who also trapped Gilchrist shortly after the interval. Warne hit effectively, twice hoicking Giles well beyond the leg-side rope. But Katich's 262-minute vigil was ended by judges Steve Harmison and Aleem Dar, with the batsman a dissenting verdict – a view shared too freely and costing him, like his captain, a portion of his match fee.

Only some more intelligent application by Lee enlarged Australia's credit balance to as much as 128 runs, although some jeremiahs now pointed to the parallels with Headingley '81 where Australia enforced the follow-on, ended up chasing 130 and failed. Some crisp strokes by Trescothick sped England to 32 from the first five overs and put supporters in good heart. But then came Warne with 3 for 7 in his first 29 balls, spinning the ball prodigiously to batsmen hemmed in by close fielders and apprehensive about the leg-stump rough. Nerves also got the better of Bell, who helped Lee down fine-leg's throat. Pietersen and Flintoff added 46 from 61 balls by blocking out Warne and attacking Tait, but Pietersen edged the first ball of Lee's second spell, and Flintoff was beaten by the reverse swing of the fourth ball of Lee's next over. Geraint Jones tried to break the tension by advancing on Warne, but hit him high rather than long to leave his team 13 runs from victory with only three wickets remaining. It was left to Giles and Hoggard to add the necessary runs from the match's last 23 balls amid unbearable tension. The bowling and fielding were probably Australia's best for the tour, but their arrival was too late.

Man of Match: A. Flintoff.

Close of play: First day, England (1) 4-229 (Pietersen 33, Flintoff 8); Second day, Australia (1) 5-99 (Katich 20); Third day, Australia (2) 4-222 (Clarke 39, Katich 24).

England

	R	B	4/6			R	B	4/6
M. E. Trescothick b Tait	65	111	8 1	– c Ponting b Warne		27	22	4
A. J. Strauss c Hayden b Warne	35	64	4	– c Clarke b Warne		23	37	3
*M. P. Vaughan c Gilchrist b Ponting	58	99	4	– c Hayden b Warne		0	6	0
I. R. Bell c Gilchrist b Tait	3	5	0	– c Kasprowicz b Lee		3	20	0
K. P. Pietersen c Gilchrist b Lee	45	108	6	– c Gilchrist b Lee		23	34	3
A. Flintoff lbw b Tait	102	132	14 1	– b Lee		26	34	3
†G. O. Jones c and b Kasprowicz	85	149	8	– c Kasprowicz b Warne		3	13	0
A. F. Giles lbw b Warne	15	35	4	– not out		7	17	0
M. J. Hoggard c Gilchrist b Warne	10	28	1	– not out		8	13	1
S. J. Harmison st Gilchrist b Warne	2	6	0					
S. P. Jones not out	15	27	3					
B 1, l-b 15, w 1, n-b 25	42			L-b 4, n-b 5		9		

(123.1 overs, 537 mins)	477
Fall: 105 137 146 213 241 418 450 450 454 477	

(31.5 overs, 168 mins)
(7 wkts) 129
Fall: 32 36 57 57 103 111 116

Bowling: *First Innings*—Lee 32-2-131-1; Kasprowicz 32-3-122-1; Tait 24.4-4-97-3; Warne 29.1-4-102-4; Ponting 6-2-9-1. *Second Innings*—Lee 12-0-51-3; Kasprowicz 2-0-19-0; Warne 13.5-2-31-4; Tait 4-0-24-0.

Australia

	R	B	4/6			R	B	4/6
J. L. Langer b Hoggard	27	59	5	– c Bell b Giles		61	112	8
M. L. Hayden lbw b Hoggard	7	27	1	– c Giles b Flintoff		26	41	4
*R. T. Ponting lbw b S. P. Jones	1	6	0	– run out ((sub) G. J. Pratt)		48	89	3 1
D. R. Martyn lbw b Hoggard	1	3	0	– c G. O. Jones b Flintoff		13	30	1
M. J. Clarke lbw b Harmison	36	53	5	– c G. O. Jones b Hoggard		56	170	6
S. M. Katich c Strauss b S. P. Jones	45	66	7	– lbw b Harmison		59	183	4
†A. C. Gilchrist c Strauss b Flintoff	27	36	3 1	– lbw b Hoggard		11	11	2
S. K. Warne c Bell b S. P. Jones	0	1	0	– st G. O. Jones b Giles		45	42	5 2
B. Lee c Bell b S. P. Jones	47	44	5	– not out		26	39	3
M. S. Kasprowicz b S. P. Jones	5	7	1	– c G. O. Jones b Harmison		19	26	1
S. W. Tait not out	3	9	0	– b Harmison		4	16	1
L-b 2, w 1, n-b 16	19			B 1, l-b 4, n-b 14		19		

(49.1 overs, 247 mins)	218
Fall: 20 21 22 58 99 157 157 163 175 218	

(124 overs, 548 mins)   387
Fall: 50 129 155 161 261 277 314
        342 373 387

Bowling: *First Innings*—Harmison 9-1-48-1; Hoggard 15-3-70-3; S. P. Jones 14.1-4-44-5; Flintoff 11-1-54-1. *Second Innings*—Hoggard 27-7-72-2; S. P. Jones 4-0-15-0; Harmison 30-5-93-3; Flintoff 29-4-83-2; Giles 28-3-107-2; Bell 6-2-12-0.

Umpires: Aleem Dar (Pakistan) and S. A. Bucknor (West Indies).
TV Umpire: M. R. Benson.
Referee: R. S. Madugalle (Sri Lanka).

†ESSEX v AUSTRALIANS

At County Ground, Chelmsford, September 3, 4, 2005. Match drawn. Essex 4 dec 502 (W. I. Jefferson 64, A. N. Cook 214, R. S. Bopara 135, J. S. Foster 38*; S. W. Tait 2-72, M. S. Kasprowicz 2-85). Australian XI 6 for 561 (J. L. Langer 87, M. L. Hayden 150, S. M. Katich 72, B. J. Hodge 166, B. J. Haddin 59; J. D. Middlebrook 2-110, T. J. Phillips 2-137).

The Australians added another unwanted distinction to their tour record by becoming the first team from Australia to concede 500 runs in a day, before themselves putting on a similar batting exhibition on the second day. Left-hander Alistair Cook (20), who the previous evening had accepted the Cricket Writers' Club Young Cricketer of the Year Award, showed why in an innings of 335 minutes, 238 balls, 33 fours and a six. His fifth hundred of the summer included a second-wicket partnership of 270 with another 20-year-old, Ravi Bopara. Ricky Ponting, having been so voluble on the subject, made a cameo appearance as a substitute fielder before Essex's overnight declaration. Australia's stocks recovered from there, Matthew Hayden enjoying the same conditions for his own 90-ball hundred, which included 18 fours and seven sixes; he retired at lunch with the score on 244. After the break, Brad Hodge finally reminded onlookers that he was the reserve batsman for the tour with his maiden hundred in Australian colours, in 119 balls. By this time, as much interest attended the net form of Glenn McGrath, eager to recover from his elbow injury in time for the final Test.

ENGLAND v AUSTRALIA

Fifth Test Match

At The Oval, London, September 8, 9, 10, 11, 12, 2005. Match drawn. *Toss:* England.

England recovered the Ashes after 16 years by holding Australia to a draw in the final Test: without the time lost to rain and bad light, they might even have won a third victory. In what Shane Warne had indicated would be his farewell appearance on an English Test ground, he took ten wickets in a Test for the tenth time: 12 for 246. He also, in a cruel twist, dropped a catch at slip that might have brought about a surprise Australian win: Kevin Pietersen was a skittish 15 when an outside edge travelled head-high to him at first slip and went down. Pietersen, like his South African countryman Basil d'Oliveira on the same ground 37 years earlier, went on to a power-packed 158 – his maiden Test hundred, including 14 fours and seven sixes.

The other decisive factor in the match was the weather, with rain and bad light taking a third of the second and fourth days plus almost half of the third. On the announcement of the itinerary, wise heads had observed that Test cricket played this late in the season would run foul of the elements, and warned that England might have cause to regret it. They were right about the former and wrong about the latter.

The signs were auspicious for Australia on the eve of the Test. Glenn McGrath returned to the colours after the elbow injury that had kept him from selection at Trent Bridge, while Simon Jones – heading England's bowling averages – did not pass a fitness test, and was replaced by the batsman Paul Collingwood. After a smooth start by the openers, Warne struck tellingly, thrice before lunch and once after to reduce England to 4 for 131. England were revived by an intelligent and well-paced fifth-wicket partnership of 143 from 220 deliveries between the Andrews Strauss and Flintoff. Warne had a hand in both their dismissals, taking Flintoff at first slip and having Strauss caught at silly point to end the century-maker's controlled innings.

Further inroads by the second new ball left England on 8 for 325 after nine deliveries of the second day. While some husky blows by Ashley Giles and Steve Harmison and some defensive captaincy by Ricky Ponting extended the innings another 15 overs and

48 runs, a return to form by Justin Langer and Matthew Hayden had at tea taken Australia's response to 112: their 14th hundred partnership for the first wicket in Tests, four years from the corresponding fixture in which they had first done the job for Australia.

Then the elements took a hand. Australia's openers came out after tea only to accept an offer of bad light which did not permit a resumption. Play then started half an hour late on Saturday and finished six overs early as the visitors pressed for a decisive lead. Langer reached a 22nd Test century in which he passed his 7,000th Test run, Hayden a 21st Test century in which he passed his 6,000th, but both had to work hard for their runs against an eager attack and some excellent ground fielding, while enjoying some good fortune with umpiring decisions. Umpiring may have contributed indirectly to Langer's dismissal, Rudi Koertzen's decision to call two vertiginous wides and a no-ball for persistent short-pitched bowling stirring Harmison to a very fast over in which he finally smashed through the batsman's defences. Late in the day, too, Flintoff began the decisive spell of the match, producing a delivery that reared to remove Ponting and encouraging the acceptance of another light offer.

Sunday's play began beneath a thick duvet of cloud, and Flintoff and Matthew Hoggard also soon enjoyed the incentive of a new ball. They bowled superbly, Flintoff with unflagging aggression, Hoggard with persistent accuracy, while Australia's batsmen tried unsuccessfully to accelerate. With the last seven Australian wickets subsiding for 44 in 90 balls, England even eked out a six-run first-innings lead. Warne quickly saw to Strauss, but after another brief period of play the light closed in patriotically at 3.42 p.m. and play was finally abandoned for the day at 6.15 p.m. There were some good-humoured exchanges between English and Australian supporters, the former opening their umbrellas as though to invite rain, the latter stripping off their shirts to bask in imaginary sunshine. The Australian fielders entered into the spirit by appearing in their sunglasses.

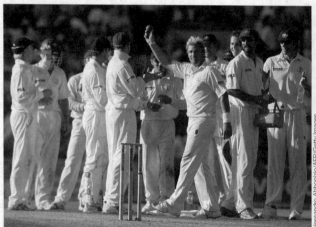

One man and his team: Shane Warne after taking five wickets on the first day of the fifth Ashes Test at The Oval.

Alessandro Abbonizio/AFP/Getty Images

They actually needed them on the last morning, which dawned bright and balmy, and McGrath warmed to his task, inducing edges from Michael Vaughan and Ian Bell off consecutive deliveries after 40 minutes. Warne by this time had commenced a 31-over entrenchment at the Vauxhall End, and saw off Marcus Trescothick with a huge turning delivery and Flintoff with a nimble caught and bowled. England at lunch were 5 for 127 from 39 overs with a lot of cricket left. By this time, however, Warne had already missed Pietersen, and the batsman had also survived a chance to Hayden at slip steered down by the influence of Adam Gilchrist's glove. Pietersen now drove expansively and hooked fearlessly, scattering spectators at long-leg as Brett Lee gave away 37 in three overs, and racing to 50 in 70 balls and a maiden Test hundred from 124 shortly before tea which he celebrated exultantly by throwing his arms around his partner Giles and gesturing to each corner of the ground. At tea, England were 7 for 221, with Australia still not out of the game, but the next hour lowered the boom. Giles proved a valiant partner for his mercurial team-mate, and they broke an eighth-wicket record at The Oval that had stood since 1886 with their partnership of 109 in 156 balls. McGrath finally bowled Pietersen when the second new ball was taken as soon as it was due, but Giles reached his fifty with two driven boundaries through the covers and straight.

Warne finished with Test wickets from his first and last deliveries in England when the innings finally concluded at 5.45 p.m. Australia needed 342 from 18 overs, but faced only four deliveries in their second innings before the openers accepted an offer of the light. Amid scenes of noisy rapture, Vaughan and his team visited each corner of the ground reciprocating the crowd's good wishes. The next morning, after a long night of celebrations, some bleary-eyed English cricketers were driven in an open-top bus through the packed streets of London to Trafalgar Square where they faced Admiral Nelson and a cheering audience of tens of thousands. The Australians headed home for a rather different reception.

Man of Match: K. P. Pietersen. Compton-Miller Medal for Player of the Series: A. Flintoff.

Close of play: First day, England (1) 7-319 (Jones 21, Giles 5); Second day, Australia (1) 0-112 (Langer 75, Hayden 32); Third day, Australia (1) 2-277 (Hayden 110, Martyn 9); Fourth day, England (2) 1-34 (Trescothick, 14, Vaughan, 19).

England

	R	B	4/6		R	B	4/6
M. E. Trescothick c Hayden b Warne	43	65	8	– lbw b Warne	33	84	1
A. J. Strauss c Katich b Warne	129	210	17	– c Katich b Warne	1	7	0
*M. P. Vaughan c Clarke b Warne	11	25	2	– c Gilchrist b McGrath	45	65	6
I. R. Bell lbw b Warne	0	7	0	– c Warne b McGrath	0	1	0
K. P. Pietersen b Warne	14	25	2	– b McGrath	158	187	15 7
A. Flintoff c Warne b McGrath	72	115	12 1	– c and b Warne	8	13	1
P. D. Collingwood lbw b Tait	7	26	1	– c Ponting b Warne	10	51	1
†G. O. Jones b Lee	25	41	5	– b Tait	1	12	0
A. F. Giles lbw b Warne	32	70	1	– b Warne	59	97	7
M. J. Hoggard c Martyn b McGrath	2	36	0	– not out	4	35	0
S. J. Harmison not out	20	20	4	– c Hayden b Warne	0	2	0
B 4, l-b 6, w 1, n-b 7	18			B 4, w 7, n-b 5	16		

(105.3 overs, 471 mins) 373

Fall: 82 102 104 131 274 289 297 325 345 373

(91.3 overs, 432 mins) 335

Fall: 2 67 67 109 126 186 199
308 333 335

Bowling: *First Innings*—McGrath 27–5–72–2; Lee 23–3–94–1; Tait 15–1–61–1; Warne 37.3–5–122–6; Katich 3–0–14–0. *Second Innings*—McGrath 26–3–85–3; Lee 20–4–88–0; Warne 38.3–3–124–6; Clarke 2–0–6–0; Tait 5–0–28–1.

Australia

	R	B	4/6			R	B	4/6
J. L. Langer b Harmison	105	146	11	2 – not out		0	4	0
M. L. Hayden lbw b Flintoff	138	303	18	– not out		0	0	0
*R. T. Ponting c Strauss b Flintoff	35	56	3					
D. R. Martyn c Collingwood b Flintoff	10	29	1					
M. J. Clarke lbw b Hoggard	25	59	2					
S. M. Katich lbw b Flintoff	1	11	0					
†A. C. Gilchrist lbw b Hoggard	23	20	4					
S. K. Warne c Vaughan b Flintoff	0	10	0					
B. Lee c Giles b Hoggard	6	10	0					
G. D. McGrath c Strauss b Hoggard	0	6	0					
S. W. Tait not out	1	2	0					
B 4, l-b 8, w 2, n-b 9	23					0		

(107.1 overs, 494 mins)   367   (0.4 overs, 3 mins) (0 wkt) 0
Fall: 185 264 281 323 329 356 359 363 363 367   Fall:

Bowling: *First Innings*—Harmison 22–2–87–1; Hoggard 24.1–2–97–4; Flintoff 34–10–78–5; Giles 23–1–76–0; Collingwood 4–0–17–0. *Second Innings*—Harmison 0.4–0–0–0.

Umpires: B. F. Bowden (New Zealand) and R. E. Koertzen (South Africa).
TV Umpire: J. W. Lloyds.
Referee: R. S. Madugalle (Sri Lanka)

Australians in County Cricket, 2004

by CATHERINE HANLEY

In 2004, county cricket's overseas player situation finally became a farce. It had been threatening for years as the rules gradually slackened: first, counties were allowed two players instead of one, then they were permitted replacements for international call-ups, and then for any reason. A number of counties fielded as many as five official overseas players during the season.

Many Australians took advantage of the opportunities to sign up for stints, although only three managed a full complement of county championship games. It was noted during the season that there were probably enough Australians around to play a game against each other; in fact the 34 who eventually appeared could easily have held their own three-way tournament. Add these to the number of non-England-qualified players holding British passports or signed under the Kolpak ruling – who are not included here – and some counties managed to turn out sides in which barely half the players were eligible for England. Rumblings of discontent were heard around the counties, suggesting that changes to the regulations may be expected in future years.

But 2004 was fruitful for some Australians – mainly those who managed to escape the worst of the rain – and less successful for others. The two principal competitions were the first-class Frizzell County Championship, involving four-day games, and the one-day totesport League (TSL), both split into two divisions with three sides promoted and three relegated at the end of the season. For the League only, the second division was expanded to ten teams by including a side representing Scotland. Other competitions were the knockout one-day Cheltenham & Gloucester (C&G) Trophy, and – following its success in 2003 – the Twenty20 Cup. Once again this proved popular both with spectators and players, although the statistics suggest that batsmen (typical strike rate: 130) may have enjoyed it more than bowlers, for whom an economy rate of 7.5 runs per over was honourable.

ANDY BICHEL (Worcestershire)
Perenially popular at Worcester, Andy Bichel's exploits with the bat during 2004 endeared him further to supporters: he scored 717 first-class runs at a very respectable 42.17, including three swashbuckling centuries in consecutive Championship games. However, Worcestershire had hired him primarily for his bowling, and here he under-achieved, managing just 33 Championship wickets at over 46, which was not enough to help his county avoid relegation to the second division. His one-day form was much more respectable, and his economical wickets ensured that Worcestershire was promoted in the totesport League, but he was released by the county after three seasons.

	M	I	NO	Runs	HS	100s	50s	Avge	Ct	St	W	Avge	BB
First-class	14	18	1	717	142	3	2	42.17	3	0	33	46.93	5-87
County Championship	14	18	1	717	142	3	2	42.17	3	0	33	46.93	5-87
C&G	5	5	2	68	38*	0	0	22.66	1	0	10	16.00	4-17
TSL	12	12	1	161	42	0	0	14.63	2	0	15	24.60	4-60
Twenty20	6	6	3	180	58*	0	1	60.00	5	0	8	20.25	3-36

MICHAEL CLARKE (Hampshire)
Michael Clarke's first Championship match for Hampshire served as a metaphor for his whole season: he scored a superb 75 in the first innings and a duck in the second. Throughout the year he seemed to have trouble coming to terms with the bowler-friendly pitches at the Rose Bowl, Hampshire's home ground, and he saved his best performances for away matches. During one particular phase towards the end of July he scored his maiden county century against Nottinghamshire, followed it up with another hundred in the second innings, and then travelled to Cardiff three days later to record a third successive century. His travails at home continued, though, and he will be disappointed with a season's tally of 709 first-class runs at a moderate 35.45.

	M	I	NO	R	HS	100s	50s	Avge	Ct	St	W	Avge	BB
First-class	12	20	0	709	140	3	2	35.45	20	0	1	160.00	1-52
County Championship	12	20	0	709	140	3	2	35.45	20	0	1	160.00	1-52
C&G	1	1	0	13	13	0	0	13.00	0	0	1	30.00	1-30
TSL	11	10	0	285	68	0	3	28.50	6	0	5	19.80	2-17
Twenty20	6	6	0	151	46	0	0	25.16	4	0	1	76.00	1-27

JAMIE COX (Somerset)
Jamie Cox managed fewer matches for Somerset in 2004 than was customary for him, due to the arrival of Ricky Ponting for a short stint. There were some who might say that the part he played in bringing the Australian captain over was his most meaningful contribution to Somerset's season, but this would be to under-estimate his role. He scored over 1,000 first-class runs in a batting line-up which often looked weak, playing with his old fluency. Cox recorded a one-day career-best 131 in Somerset's first C&G game of the season, and ended the year on an even bigger high: in his last first-class innings for the club, he scored a superb 250 against Nottinghamshire, an innings which he later described as the purest he had ever played. Drained by six years of continuous cricket, he elected not to return for a seventh season with Somerset in 2005, and departed to plaudits from players and supporters alike.

	M	I	NO	R	HS	100s	50s	Avge	Ct	St	W	Avge	BB
First-class	13	20	1	1,013	250	3	4	53.31	7	0	0	–	–
County Championship	12	19	1	841	250	2	4	46.72	6	0	–	–	–
C&G	2	2	0	136	131	1	0	68.00	0	0	–	–	–
TSL	12	12	0	356	71	0	4	29.66	3	0	–	–	–
Twenty20	3	3	1	11	8*	0	0	5.50	0	0	–	–	–

MATTHEW ELLIOTT (Glamorgan)
Despite the rain which affected nearly all of Glamorgan's home games in 2004, the Welsh county had a very successful season, winning promotion in the Championship and the cup in the totesport League's first division. Nobody made a greater impact than Matthew Elliott: he was the top scorer in the League, his 686 runs coming at an average of 98 and including two centuries and four fifties. At one point in May he averaged an incredible 359 in one-day cricket in 2004. His first-class form was no less prolific, as he easily sailed past the 1,000-run mark to end the season as the county's highest scorer. Particular highlights were his 157 and 87 against Somerset, and his 77 not out against Hampshire at Cardiff, where he carried his bat while all around him were falling to the wiles of Shane Warne. One claim to fame eluded him, though – he was missing from Glamorgan's record-breaking game against Essex when his side conceded 642 in the first innings and still won.

	M	I	NO	R	HS	100s	50s	Avge	Ct	St	W	Avge	BB
First-class	15	26	1	1,346	157	4	6	53.84	15	0	0	–	–
County Championship	14	24	1	1,245	157	4	5	54.13	15	0	0	–	–
C&G	2	2	0	172	87	0	2	86.00	0	0	–	–	–
TSL	12	12	5	66	112*	2	4	98.00	6	0	0	–	–
Twenty20	2	2	0	63	48	0	0	31.50	0	0	–	–	–

MURRAY GOODWIN (Sussex)
The 2004 season was always going to be something of a comedown for Murray Goodwin after the excitement of helping Sussex to their first Championship title in 2003. This time around the county managed only mid-table positions – in the Championship first division and the League's second tier – and Goodwin failed to reach the 1,000-run mark for the first time in four years. However, it is to his credit that the fall was not too severe: he managed over 1,600 runs in all cricket, and helped to drag his county from the bottom of the first-division table where they were in danger of relegation most of the season. Perhaps unexpectedly for such an accomplished batsman, he did not seem able to adapt his style of play to the Twenty20, where he struggled.

	M	I	NO	R	HS	100s	50s	Avge	Ct	St	W	Avge	BB
First-class	17	27	2	875	119	3	4	35.00	9	0	–	–	–
County Championship	16	25	2	756	119	2	4	32.86	9	0	–	–	–
C&G	2	2	0	47	47	0	0	23.50	1	0	–	–	–
TSL	18	18	1	600	91	0	5	35.29	7	0	–	–	–
Twenty20	4	3	0	26	17	0	0	8.66	1	0	–	–	–

BRAD HODGE (Leicestershire)
Runs, runs and more runs: Brad Hodge started his season for Leicestershire with two hundreds in his first game and never looked back. Of the five first-class hundreds he blasted, three were double-centuries – a club record for a single season – and he has now scored five in total for the county, another record. Yet another record fell as he blazed 154 not out in a League game against Sussex, the highest one-day score for the county. Add this to his 77 from 53 balls in the final of the Twenty20 Cup, which Leicestershire won, and the supporters could not get enough of him. However, his team-mates were unable to live up to his example, and Leicestershire finished the season in the bottom half of both second divisions. Partly, this was due to a falling away in the second half of the season under Hodge's captaincy. He took over when Phillip DeFreitas stood down in early July, but his leadership was not as inspirational as it might have been. In an off-season recruiting coup, Hodge was lured away by Lancashire.

	M	I	NO	R	HS	100s	50s	Avge	Ct	St	W	Avge	BB
First-class	15	25	0	1,548	262	5	4	61.92	6	0	10	36.50	2-18
County Championship	15	25	0	1,548	262	5	4	61.92	6	0	10	36.50	2-18
C&G	1	1	0	20	20	0	0	20.00	2	0	–	–	–
TSL	17	15	2	454	154*	1	0	34.92	8	0	5	37.40	2-11
Twenty20	7	7	1	223	78	0	2	37.16	4	0	0	–	–

BRAD HOGG (Warwickshire)
Warwickshire were the county champions in 2004, despite playing in a fashion that was efficient but rarely exciting. Success – the side was unbeaten in the Championship but won only five games, a record low – was built around strong team performances rather than starring roles, and Brad Hogg was one who made a solid, if not spectacular, showing. He was very successful with the bat, scoring a 50 in his debut innings and adding six more during the season, as well as one century – his first for eight years. His form with the ball was weaker, as he managed only 14 Championship wickets at an average of over 60. Somewhat perversely, he bowled with greater rhythm and success in the League, but had less of an impact; Warwickshire were relegated to the second division.

	M	I	NO	R	HS	100s	50s	Avge	Ct	St	W	Avge	BB
First-class	12	13	3	706	158	1	7	70.60	6	0	18	53.11	4-90
County Championship	11	12	2	662	158	1	7	66.20	4	0	14	62.92	4-90
C&G	3	2	1	112	94*	0	1	112.00	2	0	4	27.75	2-14
TSL	15	14	3	355	74	0	1	32.27	4	0	19	24.00	5-23
Twenty20	6	6	0	118	54	0	1	19.66	2	0	13	10.92	4-9

DAVID HUSSEY (Nottinghamshire)
When David Hussey was first signed by Nottinghamshire as cover for Damien Martyn, there were some supporters who thought that the first name was a misprint, such has his career been overshadowed by his brother's. But he soon put paid to any doubts about his own talent. Playing a full season – Martyn being unable to appear at all due to injury – he rocketed to 1,315 first-class runs, including seven centuries, three of which came in successive innings, and finished third in the national first-class averages. A particular highlight was his 166 not out against Durham, where he shared in a last-wicket partnership of 120 with his fellow Australian Stuart MacGill, and swatted seven sixes. His contribution to Nottinghamshire did not stop with the bat; although his bowling average is perhaps best ignored, he pouched an outstanding 24 catches at slip which helped turn the tide of a number of games. His commitment to the club could not be faulted, even his reprimand for dissent following a dismissal against Hampshire being attributed to his disappointment at himself. So impressed were Nottinghamshire that they re-appointed him for 2005 and 2006; next time nobody will get his name wrong.

	M	I	NO	R	HS	100s	50s	Avge	Ct	St	W	Avge	BB
First-class	17	33	4	1,315	170	7	2	69.21	24	0	2	145.00	1-6
County Championship	16	22	3	1,208	170	6	2	63.57	24	0	1	284.00	1-7
C&G	2	2	0	2	2	0	0	1.00	0	0	0	–	–
TSL	16	16	4	444	87*	0	2	37.00	2	0	2	38.50	1-5
Twenty20	5	5	0	59	33	0	0	11.80	5	0	–	–	–

PHIL JAQUES (Yorkshire)
Confusion reigned over the status of Phil Jaques at the beginning of the 2004 season. In 2003 he had turned out for Northamptonshire as a non-overseas player by virtue of a British passport, but when he appeared for New South Wales during the Australian season, also as a non-overseas player, his status was revoked. Northamptonshire already had a full quota of overseas players, so it looked as though Jaques would miss the season, until Yorkshire invited him north as a replacement for Darren Lehmann's international absences. In the event this proved beneficial both for Yorkshire and for Jaques, who in just 19 innings compiled 1,118 first-class runs. His crowning glory came on the bowler-friendly pitch at Hampshire in June, when he stroked his way to 243 – the highest score ever recorded at the Rose Bowl – while everyone else remained confounded. His one-day form was slightly less prolific, but an impressive 105 from only 87 balls against Sussex helped him to average over 50 in the League. Jaques was re-signed by Yorkshire for 2005.

	M	I	NO	R	HS	100s	50s	Avge	Ct	St	W	Avge	BB
First-class	11	19	0	1,118	243	3	5	58.84	11	0	0	–	–
County Championship	11	19	0	1,118	243	3	5	58.84	11	0	0	–	–
C&G	2	2	0	60	55	0	1	30.00	0	0	–	–	–
TSL	9	8	1	366	105	1	3	52.28	5	0	–	–	–
Twenty20	5	5	1	180	92	0	1	45.00	1	0	–	–	–

STUART LAW (Lancashire)

So towering have been Stuart Law's performances on the English stage in recent years
that it seems scarcely possible for him to have had – by his own standards at least – a
mediocre season, without reaching 1,000 runs. A back injury that kept him out for seven
weeks was the main problem: he managed only 12 first-class games. His season started
brightly with 108 in the first Championship match, and 171 not out in the second as
Lancashire walloped the previous year's champions, Sussex, by ten wickets. The county
was unable to keep up the momentum, however, and under-achieved in the absence of
its brightest star. Pre-season, Lancashire had been title favourites, but ended up suffering
the indignity of being relegated. Law therefore reappeared in 2005 in the second
division, but with a new status: having been granted British citizenship early in the year,
he now resumed with Lancashire as an England-qualified player.

	M	I	NO	R	HS	100s	50s	Avge	Ct	St	W	Avge	BB
First-class	12	18	1	867	171*	3	1	51.00	17	0	0	–	–
County Championship	12	18	1	867	171*	3	1	51.00	17	0	0	–	–
C&G	3	3	0	87	48	0	0	29.00	2	0	–	–	–
TSL	9	9	0	275	83	0	3	30.55	2	0	–	–	–
Twenty20	3	3	0	63	31	0	0	21.00	1	0	–	–	–

STUART MacGILL (Nottinghamshire)

Without being spectacular, Stuart MacGill made a very useful contribution to
Nottinghamshire's successful season. One of the reasons for this was that the other
bowlers in the side also managed good performances, so he was not obliged to carry the
entire attack, as might have been the case previously. His haul of 39 Championship
wickets was not among the most prolific in the country, but it helped Nottinghamshire
to five consecutive wins in the middle part of the season, a major factor in the club
winning the second-division title, and he bowled with penetration when it was most
needed. MacGill also played his part in the League, with 25 wickets at less than 20, and
the county was promoted here as well. Despite his success and popularity at the club, he
was not retained for 2005, mainly due to fears surrounding his availability should he be
selected for the Ashes squad.

	M	I	NO	R	HS	100s	50s	Avge	Ct	St	W	Avge	BB
First-class	15	12	2	126	28	0	0	12.60	3	0	40	35.20	7-109
County Championship	14	12	2	126	28	0	0	12.60	2	0	39	35.76	7-109
C&G	2	1	1	7	7*	0	0	–	0	0	0	–	–
TSL	13	1	0	26	26	0	0	26.00	1	0	25	19.72	4-18
Twenty20	–	–	–	–	–	–	–	–	–	–	–	–	–

MARCUS NORTH (Durham)

It was another miserable season for Durham: not only the wettest for many years, but one
full of poor performances. The county failed to win one home game and came rock
bottom of the Championship second division. It was also unlucky with some overseas
players: one, South African Herschelle Gibbs, was forced out by injury, and this led to
the call-up of Marcus North from a local league. As a stand-in, he did the county proud.
His 969 runs came at an average of only 32.20 (although this was enough to place him
second in the county's averages), but included some sparkling performances which

served as an example to his team-mates. His career-best 219 against Glamorgan, when only two of his colleagues passed 30 in the match, was a particular example. North also contributed handily in the League, his 121 not out from 114 balls against Nottinghamshire staying long in the memory, but here again he was unable to drag the club up the table by himself, and it finished sixth in the second division.

	M	I	NO	R	HS	100s	50s	Avge	Ct	St	W	Avge	BB
First-class	17	31	1	969	219	2	4	32.20	8	0	7	15.57	4-16
County Championship	16	29	1	879	219	2	3	31.39	8	0	3	31.00	2-45
C&G	1	1	0	30	30	0	0	30.00	2	0	2	22.50	2-45
TSL	16	16	1	511	121*	2	2	34.06	2	0	4	29.50	2-10
Twenty20	2	2	0	25	21	0	0	12.50	1	0	0	–	–

SHANE WARNE (Hampshire)

Outstanding bowler, adventurous captain, shining example – all were terms used to describe Shane Warne during his season at Hampshire, and the plaudits were richly deserved. Although his 51 wickets did not add up to an outstanding haul, he frequently bamboozled batsmen on the county circuit until they hardly knew which way to turn. He instigated some spectacular collapses, none more so than in an away match at Somerset in August: chasing 351, the hosts were 3 for 300 before he took centre stage to bowl them out for 340 (Warne 6 for 127). He took on the role of county captain with gusto, and his excellent tactical awareness coupled with his determination to win every game, no matter what the situation, encouraged some of his less positive team-mates. While not entirely a one-man band, Warne was the decisive factor in Hampshire gaining promotion to the first division of the Championship for 2005.

	M	I	NO	R	HS	100s	50s	Avge	Ct	St	W	Avge	BB
First-class	12	16	2	381	57	0	1	27.21	9	0	51	24.13	6-65
County Championship	12	16	2	381	57	0	1	27.21	9	0	51	24.13	6-65
C&G	2	2	0	1	1	0	0	0.50	0	0	4	11.75	4-23
TSL	12	10	0	116	48	0	0	11.60	4	0	18	25.00	4-27
Twenty20	1	1	0	0	0	0	0	0.00	0	0	0	–	–

A number of other players managed seasons of a reasonable length. **Mike Hussey** made seven first-class appearances for Gloucestershire, where he batted well but not as outstandingly as county fans have come to expect. He also played a bit-part role in the C&G final, making 20 as Gloucestershire raced to their second successive victory in the competition. He joined Durham in 2005 as captain. **Darren Lehmann** scored his 20th century for Yorkshire in only his 70th appearance for the club, during a shortened season where he topped both the county's first-class batting averages (592 runs at 59.20) and their bowling averages, snaring 15 wickets at a parsimonious 17.40. Ian Harvey moved from Gloucestershire to Yorkshire to join Lehmann, but was less successful at his new county, averaging 24.81 with the bat and 61.42 with the ball, figures he would probably like to see reversed. His batting in the Twenty20 was more impressive: an average of 122 with a strike-rate of 182.

Andrew Symonds batted with his customary gusto for Kent. He averaged 72.28 in his five Championship games, scored 146 in 110 balls in a League match – a county record – and had the phenomenal strike-rate of 217 in the Twenty20, including a 34-ball century of extreme savagery. A less savoury aspect of the season was his part in the dressing-room unrest at Kent which led to the undermining of the vice-captain, Ed Smith, and the resignation of the chairman of cricket, former England captain Mike Denness.

Of those who were less known around the counties before the season started, **Chris Rogers** deputised at Derbyshire for its long-time overseas player Michael Di Venuto, who was unable to play in 2004. He made an instant impact, averaging over 55 with the bat, but managed only six first-class matches before a shoulder injury cut short his season. **Jonathan Moss** was another whose season was curtailed by injury – a neck problem caused when taking a catch early in the season. He played 11 first-class games for Derbyshire, averaging 35.76, and returned in 2005.

Other batsmen made more fleeting appearances. **Martin Love** scored 394 first-class runs in only two games for Northamptonshire, including twin unbeaten centuries at Worcester; he was re-signed by the club for 2005. **Ricky Ponting** enjoyed a brief but highly successful stay at Somerset, his enthusiasm and encouragement firing the imagination, as well as scoring 297 runs at 99.00 in just four innings. However, **Michael Bevan** will probably want to forget about his brief spell at Kent, his fourth county, after averaging 12.85 with the bat. **Simon Katich** scored 183 first-class runs at 36.60 in four matches for Hampshire, a county who employed two more Australians on blink-or-you'll-miss-it contracts: **Shane Watson** had a very short but eventful period there, playing in one Championship game to score a chanceless 112 not out when batting with a runner for the first time, while **Michael Dighton** appeared in a solitary one-day game, making 74.

Most Australian bowlers playing county cricket in 2004 made few appearances, and met with mixed success. **Shaun Tait's** season at Durham might charitably be described as a nightmare: the highly-rated young bowler appeared in only two games before being dropped, taking 0 for 176 in 18 overs and registering 26 no-balls. **Scott Brant** also endured a wretched season: injury and poor form restricted him to six matches for Essex, where his bowling figures were a less-than-impressive 9 for 597. In contrast, **Michael Kasprowicz** had his season cut short for the altogether more pleasant reason of selection for the national side; he managed seven Championship matches for Glamorgan, taking 21 wickets, but at a costly average of 42.52.

Nathan Bracken slipped in for two matches with Gloucestershire, taking five wickets at just over 20; **Paul Rofe** took 12 wickets at 42.08 in five Championship games for Northamptonshire; and **Mark Cleary** took a first-class career-best 7 for 80 during his spell at Leicestershire, while impressing in the Twenty20 with an amazing strike rate of a wicket every ten balls. Stuart Clark took ten wickets in a three-match stint at Middlesex, while **Glenn McGrath** had his four-match contract at the same county cut to two games on the orders of Cricket Australia, but showed what might have been with nine Championship wickets at 23.88. Finally, **Mick Lewis** played in three first-class games for Glamorgan, during which time he took six wickets and got a duck in his only innings.

FOLLOW-ON NO LONGER FOLLOWED

An interesting new fashion in Tests has seen captains turning away from enforcing the follow-on. Once a rarity, batting again when leading by over 200 is fast becoming normal. Stats tell the story: from 1975 to 2000, the follow-on was enforced 93% of the time. In the Tests since then this figure has dropped to 77%, and in 2004 it was below 50% (six out of thirteen). How successful is the change in strategy? Overall, since 1975, teams enforcing the follow-on have won 81% of the time, while teams in similar positions, but choosing not to enforce, have won over 93%. There have been two losses by teams enforcing the follow-on, both well known to Australian supporters - Leeds 1981 and Kolkata 2001. The last time a team lost after choosing not to enforce the follow-on was in 1950.

With Tests being played so frequently, captains are probably becoming more aware that "burn-out" of bowlers by enforcing the follow-on can not only affect teams within matches, but in subsequent matches also.

– CHARLES DAVIS

NO BALL, NO GOOD.
Picture by Hamish Blair, Getty Images.

7

History
and Law

History of Cricket

What is cricket?

Cricket is a game played between two teams, generally of 11 members each. In essence, it is single combat, in which an individual batsman does battle against an individual bowler, who has helpers known as fielders. The bowler propels the ball with a straight arm from one end of the 22-yard pitch in an attempt to dismiss the batsman by hitting a target known as the wicket at the other end, or by causing the batsman to hit the ball into the air into a fielder's grasp, or by inducing one of a number of other indiscretions. The batsman attempts to defend the wicket with the bat and to score runs – the currency of the game – by striking the ball to the field boundary, or far enough from the fielders to allow the batsman to run to the other end of the pitch before the ball can be returned. At least two bowlers must take turns, from alternating ends; also, there are always two batsmen on the field, each to take a turn as required. When all but one of the batting team have been dismissed – or after an agreed period – the teams' roles are reversed. After all the players required to bat on both sides have done so either once or twice (which can take from a few hours to five days) the total number of runs accumulated determines the winner. But sometimes there isn't one.

Origins of the game

The origins of cricket lie somewhere in the Dark Ages – probably after the Roman Empire, almost certainly before the Normans invaded England, and almost certainly somewhere in Northern Europe. All research concedes that the game derived from a very old, widespread and uncomplicated pastime by which one player served up an object, be it a small piece of wood or a ball, and another hit it with a suitably fashioned club.

How and when this club-ball game developed into one where the hitter defended a target against the thrower is simply not known. Nor is there any evidence as to when points were awarded dependent upon how far the hitter was able to despatch the missile; nor when helpers joined the two-player contest, thus beginning the evolution into a team game; nor when the defining concept of placing wickets at either end of the pitch was adopted.

Etymological scholarship has variously placed the game in the Celtic, Scandinavian, Anglo-Saxon, Dutch and Norman-French traditions; sociological historians have variously attributed its mediaeval development to high-born country landowners, emigré Flemish cloth-workers, shepherds on the close-cropped downland of south-east England and the close-knit communities of iron- and glass-workers deep in the Kentish Weald. Most of these theories have a solid academic basis, but none is backed with enough evidence to establish a watertight case. The research goes on.

What is agreed is that by Tudor times cricket had evolved far enough from club-ball to be recognisable as the game played today; that it was well established in many parts of Kent, Sussex and Surrey; that within a few years it had become a feature of leisure time at a significant number of schools; and – a sure sign of the wide acceptance of any game – that it had become popular enough among young men to earn the disapproval of local magistrates.

Dates in cricket history

*c.*1550	Evidence of cricket being played in Guildford, Surrey.
1598	Cricket mentioned in Florio's Italian-English dictionary.
1611	Randle Cotgrave's French-English dictionary translates the French word "crosse" as a cricket staff.
	Two youths fined for playing cricket in Sidlesham, Sussex.
1624	Jasper Vinall becomes first man known to be killed playing cricket: hit by a bat while trying to catch the ball, at Horsted Green, Sussex.
1676	First reference to cricket being played outside Britain, by British residents in Aleppo, Syria.
1709	First recorded inter-county match: Kent v Surrey.
1729	Date of earliest surviving bat, belonging to John Chitty, now in the pavilion at The Oval, London.
1771	Width of bat limited to 4¼ inches, where it has remained ever since.
1774	LBW law devised.
1776	Earliest known scorecards, at the Vine Club, Sevenoaks, Kent.
1780	The first six-seamed cricket ball, manufactured by Dukes of Penshurst, Kent.
1788	First revision of the Laws of Cricket by Marylebone Cricket Club (MCC).
1795	First recorded case of a dismissal "leg before wicket".
1804	First cricket match in Australia by officers and crew of HMS *Calcutta* at Hyde Park, Sydney.
1807	First mention of "straight-armed" (i.e. round-arm) bowling: by John Willes of Kent.
1814	Lord's ground opened on its present site, in St John's Wood, London.
*c.*1836	Batting pads invented.
1838	Melbourne Cricket Club formed. Oldest surviving cricket club in Australia.
1844	First official international match: Canada v United States.
*c.*1850	Wicket-keeping gloves first used.
1851	Initial first-class match in Australia: Tasmania v Victoria at Launceston Racecourse.
1854	First match at MCG: Melbourne Cricket Club v Geelong.
1856	First Victoria v NSW match at MCG. NSW won by three wickets.
1857	First first-class match in Sydney at The Domain.
1858	First recorded instance of a hat being awarded to a bowler taking three wickets with consecutive balls.
1861	First touring team to visit Australia, captained by Heathfield Stephenson, all matches against odds.
1864	"Overhand bowling" authorised by MCC.
	John Wisden's *The Cricketer's Almanack* first published.
1868	Team of Australian Aborigines tour England.
1877	First Test match: Australia beat England by 45 runs in Melbourne.
1880	First Test match in England: England beat Australia by five wickets at The Oval.
1882	First Test match at SCG: Australia beat England by five wickets.

Following England's first defeat by Australia in England, an "obituary notice" to English cricket in the *Sporting Times* leads to the tradition of The Ashes.

1884   First Test match at Adelaide Oval: England defeat Australia by eight wickets.

1887-88   Charles Turner the only bowler to take 100 wickets in an Australian first-class season: 106 in 12 matches.

1889   Declarations first authorised, but only on the third day, or in a one-day match.

1891   George Giffen scores 271 and takes 16 for 166 versus Victoria at Adelaide Oval, the greatest all-round performance in first-class cricket.

1892-93   Sheffield Shield competition begins with three competing colonies: NSW, Victoria and South Australia. Won by Victoria.

1894-95   George Giffen scores 902 runs and captures 93 wickets in 11-game season.

1899   A. E. J. Collins scores 628 not out in a junior house match at Clifton College, England, the highest individual score in any match.

            Green and gold colours first worn by Australian Test team on English tour.

            George Beldam takes his photograph of Victor Trumper stepping out to drive.

1900   Bernard Bosanquet, an English leg-spinner, invents the googly.

1905   Australian Board of Control for International Cricket, now called Cricket Australia, is formed.

1909   Imperial Cricket Conference (now the International Cricket Council) set up, with England, Australia and South Africa the original members.

1910   Six runs given for any hit over the boundary, instead of only for a hit out of the ground.

1911   Adelaide Oval scoreboard opened. Oldest functioning mechanical board.

1912   The "Big Six" – Clem Hill, Victor Trumper, Warwick Armstrong, Tibby Cotter, Hanson Carter and Vernon Ransford – refuse to tour England because of a dispute over player rights.

1915   Victor Trumper dies, aged 37.

            W. G. Grace dies, aged 67.

1920-21   Warwick Armstrong's team defeat England 5–0: remains the only whitewash in Ashes history.

1926-27   Queensland becomes the fourth state to enter the Sheffield Shield.

            Victoria score 1,107 v NSW in Melbourne, the record total for a first-class innings.

1928-29   First Test match at Brisbane Exhibition Ground: England defeat Australia by 675 runs.

            Don Bradman scores 1,690 runs in a season, still a record for an Australian season.

1930   Bradman scores 452 not out for NSW v Queensland at the SCG, which remains the highest first-class innings by an Australian.

            Bradman's first tour of England: he scores 974 runs in the five Ashes Tests, still a record for any Test series.

1931   First Test match at the Gabba: Australia defeat South Africa by an innings and 163 runs.

1932-33   The Bodyline tour of Australia in which England bowl at batsmen's bodies with a packed leg-side field to neutralise Bradman's scoring.

Tim Wall captures 10 for 36 for SA v NSW at the SCG, the best figures in first-class cricket in Australia.

1934   Jack Hobbs retires with 197 centuries and 61,237 first-class runs, both records.

First women's Test: Australia v England in Brisbane.

1935   MCC condemn and outlaw Bodyline.

1935-36 Clarrie Grimmett takes 44 wickets at 14.59 against South Africa, the highest number of wickets in a Test series for Australia. He is never selected again.

1936-37 A total of 954,290 spectators, the most for any series, watch Australia come back from 2–0 down to beat England 3–2.

1938   A Test is broadcast on TV for the first time: England v Australia at Lord's.

1947-48 Western Australia enters the Sheffield Shield on a restricted basis and wins the trophy.

1948   Bradman concludes Test career with a second-ball duck at The Oval and a batting average of 99.94 — four runs short of 100. His team go through England undefeated and become known as The Invincibles.

1953   England regain the Ashes after a 19-year gap, the longest ever.

1956   Jim Laker of England takes 19 for 90 v Australia in Manchester, the best match analysis in first-class cricket.

1957   Declarations authorised at any time.

1960   First tied Test, Australia v West Indies in Brisbane.

1962-63 Garry Sobers becomes the first player to achieve the double of 1,000 runs and 50 wickets in an Australian season.

1963   Distinction between amateur and professional cricketers abolished in English cricket.

Ian Meckiff called for throwing four times in one over against South Africa at the Gabba. He retires instantly.

1963-64 Sobers repeats the double and remains the only player to do so.

1969-70 Domestic one-day cricket begins in Australia.

1970   South Africa excluded from international cricket because of their government's apartheid policies.

First Test match at the WACA: Australia draws match against England.

1971   First one-day international: Australia v England in Melbourne, won by Australia.

1972   Bob Massie takes 16 for 137 on his Test debut at Lord's, the best match figures by an Australian.

1975   First World Cup: West Indies beat Australia in final at Lord's.

1977   Centenary Test in Melbourne, with identical result to the first match: Australia beat England by 45 runs.

Australian media tycoon Kerry Packer signs 51 of the world's leading players in defiance of the cricketing authorities.

1977-78 Tasmania enters the Sheffield Shield on a restricted basis.

1978   Graham Yallop wears a protective helmet to bat in a Test match, the first player to do so.

1979   Packer and official cricket agree on a peace deal. Channel Nine broadcasts a Test match for the first time.

1980	Eight-ball over abolished in Australia, making the six-ball over universal.
1981	Trevor Chappell, under instruction from his brother Greg, bowls an underarm delivery to the New Zealand tailender Brian McKechnie.
	England beat Australia in Leeds Test after following on, with bookmakers offering odds of 500 to 1 against them winning.
1982	The first electronic scoreboard, complete with TV replays and ads, makes its Test debut at the MCG.
1984	Dennis Lillee, Greg Chappell and Rod Marsh play their farewell Test against Pakistan at the SCG.
1986	Second tied Test, India v Australia in Chennai.
1987	Australia win the World Cup for the first time, defeating England in the final at Eden Gardens, Kolkata.
1988	The Cricket Academy opens in Adelaide.
1991	South Africa return to international cricket, with a one-day series in India.
1993	The ICC ceases to be administered by MCC, becoming an independent organisation with its own chief executive.
	Shane Warne bowls his first delivery in England. A huge leg-break, it bowls Mike Gatting and is proclaimed the ball of the century.
1994	Allan Border retires after setting world Test record of 11,174 runs and captaining Australia in 93 Test matches.
	Brian Lara becomes the only player to pass 500 in a first-class innings: 501 not out for Warwickshire v Durham.
1999-2000	Pura Milk sponsors interstate cricket, signifying the end of the Sheffield Shield as the major domestic competition.
2000	South Africa's captain Hansie Cronje banned from cricket for life after admitting receiving bribes from bookmakers in match-fixing scandal.
2001	Don Bradman dies, aged 92.
	Steve Waugh's Australian side ends 16-Test winning streak when defeated by India at Eden Gardens, Kolkata.
2003	First Test match at Marrara Cricket Ground, Darwin: Australia defeat Bangladesh by an innings and 132 runs.
	First Test match at Cazaly's Stadium, Cairns: Australia defeat Bangladesh by an innings and 98 runs.
	Matthew Hayden hits 380 against Zimbabwe at the WACA, the highest Test score by an Australian.
2004	Steve Waugh retires after world-record 168 Test appearances.
	Brian Lara of West Indies becomes the only player to reach 400 in a Test innings: 400 not out v England.
	Richie Benaud attends his 500th Test, more than any living person.
2005	Shane Warne becomes the first man to take 600 Test wickets.
	International Cricket Council moves from Lord's to new headquarters in Dubai.
	England re-takes Ashes from Australia after 16 years.

Cricket Organisations

INTERNATIONAL CRICKET COUNCIL

On June 15, 1909, representatives of cricket in England, Australia and South Africa met at Lord's and founded the Imperial Cricket Conference. Membership was confined to the governing bodies of cricket in countries within the British Commonwealth where Test cricket was played. India, New Zealand and West Indies were elected as members on May 31, 1926, Pakistan on July 28, 1952, Sri Lanka on July 21, 1981, Zimbabwe on July 8, 1992 and Bangladesh on June 26, 2000. South Africa ceased to be a member of ICC on leaving the British Commonwealth in May, 1961, but was elected as a Full Member on July 10, 1991.

On July 15, 1965, the Conference was renamed the International Cricket Conference and new rules were adopted to permit the election of countries from outside the British Commonwealth. This led to the growth of the Conference, with the admission of Associate Members, who were each entitled to one vote, while the Foundation and Full Members were each entitled to two votes, on ICC resolutions. On July 12, 13, 1989, the Conference was renamed the International Cricket Council and revised rules were adopted.

On July 7, 1993, ICC ceased to be administered by MCC and became an independent organisation with its own chief executive, the headquarters remaining at Lord's. The category of Foundation Member, with its special rights, was abolished. On October 1, 1993, Sir Clyde Walcott became the first non-British chairman of ICC. On June 16, 1997, ICC became an incorporated body, with an executive board and a president instead of a chairman.

Officers

President: Ehsan Mani (2003–05). *Vice-President:* P. H. F. Sonn *Chief Executive:* M. W. Speed.
Chairmen of Committees: Chief Executives' Committee: M. W. Speed; *Cricket:* S. M. Gavaskar;
Development: M. W. Speed; *Audit Committee:* Sir John Anderson.

Executive Board: The president, vice-president and chief executive sit on the board and all committees *ex officio*. They are joined by Ali Asghar (Bangladesh), Sir John Anderson (New Zealand), P. F. Chingoka (Zimbabwe), J. Dalmiya (India), E. H. C. Griffith (West Indies), R. Mali (South Africa), R. F. Merriman (Australia), F. D. Morgan (England), S. Perlman (Israel), J. Rayani (Kenya), Shaharyar Khan (Pakistan), T. Sumathipala (Sri Lanka), HGH Tunku Imran (Malaysia).

General Manager – Cricket: D. J. Richardson. *Cricket Operations Manager:* C. D. Hitchcock. *Umpires and Referees Manager:* C. S. Kelly. *Umpires' High Performance Manager:* K. T. Medlycott. *Global Development Manager:* M. R. Kennedy. *General Manager – Corporate Affairs:* B. F. McClements. *Chief Financial Officer:* F. Hasnain. *Commercial Manager:* D. C. Jamieson. *Human Resources and Administration Manager:* J. Moore. *In-house Lawyer:* U. Naidoo.

Constitution

President: Each Full Member has the right, by rotation, to appoint ICC's president. In 1997, India named J. Dalmiya to serve until June 2000, when M. A. Gray of Australia took over. Ehsan Mani of Pakistan succeeded Gray in June 2003; he and subsequent presidents will serve for two years. P. H. F. Sonn, elected vice-president in July 2004, is due to take over.

Chief Executive: Appointed by the Council. M. W. Speed was appointed in June 2001.

Membership

Full Members: Australia, Bangladesh, England, India, New Zealand, Pakistan, South Africa, Sri Lanka, West Indies and Zimbabwe.

Associate Members*: Argentina (1974), Bermuda (1966), Canada (1968), Cayman Islands (2002), Denmark (1966), Fiji (1965), France (1998), Germany (1999), Gibraltar (1969), Hong Kong (1969), Ireland (1993), Israel (1974), Italy (1995), Kenya (1981), Malaysia (1967), Namibia (1992), Nepal (1996), Netherlands (1966), Nigeria (2002), Papua New Guinea (1973), Scotland (1994), Singapore (1974), Tanzania (2001), Uganda (1998), United Arab Emirates (1990), USA (1965), Zambia (2003).

Affiliate Members*: Afghanistan (2001), Austria (1992), Bahamas (1987), Bahrain (2001), Belgium (1991), Belize (1997), Bhutan (2001), Botswana (2001), Brazil (2002), Brunei (1992), Chile (2002), China (2004), Cook Islands (2000), Costa Rica (2002), Croatia (2001), Cuba (2002), Cyprus (1999), Czech Republic (2000), Finland (2000), Gambia (2002), Ghana (2002), Greece (1995), Indonesia (2001), Iran (2003), Isle of Man (2004), Japan (1989), Kuwait (1998), Lesotho (2001), Luxembourg (1998), Malawi (2001), Maldives (2001), Malta (1998), Mexico (2004), Morocco (1999), Mozambique (2003), Norway (2000), Oman (2000), Panama (2002), Philippines (2002), Portugal (1996), Qatar (1999), Rwanda (2003), St Helena (2001), Samoa (2000), Saudi Arabia (2003), Sierra Leone (2002), South Korea (2001), Spain (1992), Suriname (2002), Sweden (1997), Switzerland (1985), Thailand (1995), Tonga (2000), Turks & Caicos Islands (2002) and Vanuatu (1995).

* *Year of election shown in parentheses.*

The following governing bodies for cricket shall be eligible for election.

Full Members: The governing body for cricket recognised by the ICC of a country, or countries associated for cricket purposes, or a geographical area, from which representative teams are qualified to play official Test matches.

Associate Members: The governing body for cricket recognised by the ICC of a country, or countries associated for cricket purposes, or a geographical area, which does not qualify as a Full Member but where cricket is firmly established and organised.

Affiliate Members: The governing body for cricket recognised by the ICC of a country, or countries associated for cricket purposes, or a geographical area (which is not part of one of those already constituted as a Full or Associate Member) where the ICC recognises that cricket is played in accordance with the Laws of Cricket. Affiliate Members have no right to vote or to propose or second resolutions at ICC meetings.

CRICKET AUSTRALIA

Officers

Chairman: R. Merriman AM.   *Chief Executive:* J. Sutherland.

Board of Directors: R. Merriman (*chairman*), A. Border AO, J. Clarke, B. Collins QC, W. Edwards, D. Foster OAM, H Harinath, T. Harrison, D. G. Mullins SC, I. McLachlan AO, F. C. O'Connor, T. Steele, G. L. Tamblyn, M. Taylor AO.

AUSTRALIAN CRICKETERS' ASSOCIATION

The Australian Cricketers' Association was incorporated in February 1997. It represents the collective voice of all first-class cricketers in Australia. The ACA has recently completed negotiating a Memorandum of Understanding with Cricket Australia, which formalises remuneration and welfare issues between the players and their respective cricket boards within Australia. The ACA is actively involved in protecting and providing benefits to all members, particularly in the area of professional advice and secular career training.

President: I. Healy.   *Chief Executive Officer:* Paul Marsh.

ADDRESSES

INTERNATIONAL CRICKET COUNCIL

M. W. Speed, The Clock Tower, Lord's Ground, London NW8 8QN (44 20 7266 1818; fax 44 20 7266 1777; website www.icc-cricket.com; email enquiry@icc-cricket.com).

Full Members

AUSTRALIA: Cricket Australia, J. Sutherland, 60 Jolimont Street, Jolimont, Victoria 3002 (03 9653 9999; fax 03 9653 9900; website www.cricket.com.au).

BANGLADESH: Bangladesh Cricket Board, Tehsin, Navana Tower (5th floor), 45 Gulshan Avenue, Dhaka 10 (880 2 966 6805; fax 880 2 956 3844; email tehsin@banglacricket.com).

ENGLAND: England and Wales Cricket Board, D. G. Collier, Lord's Ground, London NW8 8QZ (44 20 7432 1200; fax 44 20 7289 5619; website www.ecb.co.uk).

INDIA: Board of Control for Cricket in India, Kairali, GHS Lane, Manacaud, Trivandrum 695009 (91 471 245 3307; fax 91 471 246 4620; email secbcci@sify.com).

NEW ZEALAND: New Zealand Cricket Inc., M. C. Snedden, PO Box 958, Christchurch (64 3 366 2964; fax 64 3 365 7491; website www.nzcricket.org.nz).

PAKISTAN: Pakistan Cricket Board, C. Mujahid, Gaddafi Stadium, Ferozepur Road, Lahore 54600 (92 42 571 7231; fax 92 42 571 1860; website www.pcboard.com.pk; email pcboard@paknet4.ptc.pk).

SOUTH AFRICA: United Cricket Board of South Africa, M. G. Majola, PO Box 55009, North Street, Illovo, Northlands 2116 (27 11 880 2810; fax 27 11 880 6578; website www.cricket.co.za; email ucbsa@ucb.co.za).

SRI LANKA: Cricket Board Sri Lanka, L. R. D. Mendis, 35 Maitland Place, Colombo 7 (94 1 1267 9568; fax 94 1 1289 7405; email: info@srilankacricket.ik).

WEST INDIES: West Indies Cricket Board, R. Braithwaite, Factory Road, PO Box 616 W, Woods Centre, St John's, Antigua (1 268 481 2450; fax 1 268 481 2498; www.windiescricket.com; email wicb@candw.ag).

ZIMBABWE: Zimbabwe Cricket Union, V. Hogg, PO Box 2739, Josiah Tongogara Avenue, Harare (263 4 704616; fax 263 4 729370; website www.zcu.cricket.org; email zcu@mweb.co.zw).

Associate and Affiliate Members

Afghanistan: taj_afghancricket@hotmail.com
Argentina: cricarg@fibertel.com.ar
Austria: chairman@austrian-cricket.info
Bahamas: firstslip@hotmail.com
Bahrain: richard@batelco.com.bh
Belgium: moyson_david@mine.be
Belize: juniorbest@btl.net
Bermuda: bcbc@ibl.bm
Bhutan: bccb@druknet.bt
Botswana: chico@botsnet.bw
Brazil: john.landers@apis.com.br
Brunei: mirbash@brunet.bn
Canada: canada@cricamericas.com
Cayman Islands: cicaadmin@candw.ky
Chile: clive.marriott@outokumpu.com
China: cui203@tom.com
Cook Islands: ghosking@oyster.net.ck
Costa Rica: trillingworth@yahoo.co.uk
Croatia: croatia@cricinfo.com
Cuba: cubacricket_98@yahoo.es
Cyprus: carrs@globalsoftmail.com.cy
Czech Republic: talacko@vol.cz
Denmark: dcf@cricket.dk
Fiji: osaberi@fea.com.fj
Finland: fcachairman@cricketfinland.com
France: francecricket@ffbsc.org
Gambia: jon_gomez@hotmail.com
Germany: brimarfell@t-online.de
Ghana: whackman@africaonline.co.gh
Gibraltar: poplar@gibnyex.gi
Greece: crickadm@otenet.gr
Guernsey: david.piesing@pkfguernsey.com
Hong Kong: hkca@hkabc.net

Indonesia: suresh@rencapasia.com
Iran: mbzbaseballir@hotmail.com
Ireland: peterthompson@irishcricket.org
Isle of Man: iomca@mcb.net
Israel: israel@cricket.org
Italy: segreteria@crickitalia.org
Japan: info@jca-cricket.ne.jp
Jersey: kd_laforge@jerseymail.co.uk
Kenya: kcricket@iconnect.co.ke
Kuwait: h_farman@hotmail.com
South Korea: haksu@mac.com
Lesotho: assumption@leo.co.ls
Luxembourg: lcf@cricket.lu
Malawi: shiraz.yusuf@mw.ey.com
Malaysia: crikmal@tm.net.my
Maldives: ccbm@avasmail.com.mv
Mali: femacrik@yahoo.fr
Malta: maltacricket@yahoo.co.uk
Mexico: mexicocricketassociation@yahoo.co.uk
Morocco: marocricket@caramail.com
Mozambique: debala.group@teledata.mz
Namibia: cricket@iway.na
Nepal: can@cricketnepal.org
Netherlands: cricket@kncb.nl
Nigeria: segun_adeuk@yahoo.co.uk
Norway: afsar@online.no
Oman: omancric@omantel.net.om
Panama: manvelr@hotmail.com
Papua New Guinea: cricketpng@daltron.com.pg
Philippines: william.d.bailey@ph.pwc.com
Portugal: mail@portugalcricket.org
Qatar: qatarca@hotmail.com
Rwanda: rwandacricketassociation@yahoo.com
St Helena: ye.olde.yarde@helanta.sh
Samoa: laki@samoa.ws
Saudi Arabia: saudicricket@sps.net.sa
Scotland: admin@cricketscotland.com
Sierra Leone: cyrilpanda2002@yahoo.com
Singapore: cricket@singnet.com.sg
Slovenia: mark.oman@hotmail.com
Spain: sainsbury@ctv.es
St Helena: ye.olde.yarde@helanta.sh
Suriname: scb@surimail.sr
Sweden: mohan_Sweden@hotmail.com
Switzerland: alex.mackay@swisscricket.ch
Tanzania: wizards@cats-net.com
Thailand: ravisehgal1@hotmail.com
Tonga: sportedu@kalianet.to
Turks and Caicos Islands: min_finance@gov.tc
Uganda: azuba@dwd.co.ug
United Arab Emirates: cricket@emirates.net.ae
USA: gadainty@aol.com
Vanuatu: bdomail@bdo.com.vu
Zambia: moffatmbewe@yahoo.com

Note: Full contact details for all Associate and Affiliate Members are available from the ICC.

UK ADDRESSES

ENGLAND AND WALES CRICKET BOARD: T. M. Lamb, Lord's Ground, London NW8 8QZ (44 20 7432 1200; fax 44 06 5583; website www.ecb.co.uk).

MARYLEBONE CRICKET CLUB: R. D. V. Knight, Lord's Ground, London NW8 8QN (44 20 7289 1611; fax 44 20 7289 9100. Tickets 44 20 7432 1066; fax 44 20 7432 1061).

AUSTRALIAN STATE CRICKET ASSOCIATION ADDRESSES

AUSTRALIAN CAPITAL TERRITORY: ACT Cricket, PO Box 3379, Manuka, Australian Capital Territory 2603 (02 6239 6002; fax 02 6295 7135).

NEW SOUTH WALES: Cricket NSW, PO Box 333, Paddington, New South Wales 2021 (02 9339 0999; fax 02 9360 6877). *Chief Executive:* D. R. Gilbert. *Chairman:* R. E. Horsell.

QUEENSLAND: Queensland Cricket, PO Box 575, Albion, Queensland 4010 (07 3292 3100; fax 07 3262 9160). *Chief Executive:* G. J. Dixon. *Chairman:* D. G. Mullins SC. *Coach:* T. G. Oliver.

SOUTH AUSTRALIA: South Australian Cricket Association, Adelaide Oval, North Adelaide, South Australia 5006 (08 8300 3800; fax 08 8231 4346). *Chief Executive:* M. J. Deare. *President:* I. M. McLachlan AO. *State Manager of Cricket:* W. Phillips.

TASMANIA: Tasmanian Cricket Association, PO Box 495, Rosny Park, Tasmania 7018 (03 6211 4000; fax 03 6244 3924). *Chief Executive:* D. A. Johnston. *Chairman:* B. Palfreyman.

VICTORIA: Cricket Victoria, VCA House, 86 Jolimont Street, Jolimont, Victoria 3002 (03 9653 1100; fax 03 9653 1196). *Chief Executive Officer:* K. W. Jacobs. *Chairman:* R. F. Merriman.

WESTERN AUSTRALIA: Western Australian Cricket Association, PO Box 6045, East Perth, Western Australia 6892 (08 9265 7222; fax 08 9221 1823). *Chief Executive Officer:* T. Dodemaide. *President:* D.K. Lillee.

Other Bodies

ASSOCIATION OF CRICKET UMPIRES AND SCORERS: G. J. Bullock, PO Box 399, Camberley, Surrey, GU153JZ, UK (44 1276 27962; fax 44 1276 62277; website www.acus.org.uk; email admin@acus.org.uk).

AUSTRALIAN CRICKETERS' ASSOCIATION: Suite 41, Level 4, 424 St Kilda Road, Melbourne, Victoria 3004 (03 9828 0700).

AUSTRALIAN SCHOOLS' CRICKET COUNCIL INC: A. A. K.Gifford, 29 George Street, Avalon, New South Wales 2107 (02 9918 3103; fax 02 9918 7211).

BRADMAN MUSEUM: R. Mulvaney, PO Box 9994, Bowral, NSW 2576 (02 4862 1247; fax 02 4861 2536).

CRUSADERS, THE: Swan Richards, 69 Victoria Parade, Collingwood, Victoria, 3066 (03 9415 6924; fax 03 9417 6911; website www.crusaderscricket.com.au; email cricket@vegas.com.au).

CRICKET ASSOCIATIONS AND SOCIETIES

AUSTRALIAN CRICKET SOCIETY INC., Mr Ken Penaluna (secretary), Suite 15, 47 Bourke Street, Melbourne, Victoria 3000 (03 9639 6530). There are branches of the Society in each state.

The Laws of Cricket

As updated in 2003. World copyright of MCC and reprinted by permission of MCC. Copies of the "Laws of Cricket" may be obtained from Lord's Cricket Ground or from the MCC website at www.lords.org

INDEX TO THE LAWS

THE PREAMBLE – THE SPIRIT OF CRICKET

Cricket is a game that owes much of its unique appeal to the fact that it should be played not only within its Laws but also within the Spirit of the game. Any action which is seen to abuse this spirit causes injury to the game itself. The major responsibility for ensuring the spirit of fair play rests with the captains.

1.   There are two Laws which place the responsibility for the team's conduct firmly on the captain.

   Responsibility of captains
   The captains are responsible at all times for ensuring that play is conducted within the Spirit of the game as well as within the Laws.

   Player's conduct
   In the event of a player failing to comply with instructions by an umpire, or criticising by word or action the decisions of an umpire, or showing dissent, or generally behaving in a manner which might bring the game into disrepute, the umpire concerned shall in the first place report the matter to the other umpire and to the player's captain, and instruct the latter to take action.

2.   Fair and unfair play
   According to the Laws the umpires are the sole judges of fair and unfair play.
   The umpires may intervene at any time and it is the responsibility of the captain to take action where required.

3.   The umpires are authorised to intervene in cases of:
   • time wasting
   • damaging the pitch
   • dangerous or unfair bowling
   • tampering with the ball
   • any other action that they consider to be unfair

4.   The spirit of the game involves respect for:
   • your opponents
   • your own captain and team
   • the role of the umpires
   • the game's traditional values

5.   It is against the spirit of the game:
   • to dispute an umpire's decision by word, action or gesture
   • to direct abusive language towards an opponent or umpire
   • to indulge in cheating or any sharp practice, for instance:
       a) to appeal knowing that the batsman is not out
       b) to advance towards an umpire in an aggressive manner when appealing
       c) to seek to distract an opponent either verbally or by harassment with persistent clapping or unnecessary noise under the guise of enthusiasm and motivation of one's own side

6.   Violence
   There is no place for any act of violence on the field of play.

7.   Players
   Captains and umpires together set the tone for the conduct of a cricket match.
   Every player is expected to make an important contribution to this.

The players, umpires and scorers in a game of cricket may be of either gender and the Laws apply equally to both. The use, throughout the text, of pronouns indicating the male gender is purely for brevity. Except where specifically stated otherwise, every provision of the Laws is to be read as applying to women and girls equally as to men and boys.

LAW 1.   THE PLAYERS

1. Number of Players

A match is played between two sides, each of 11 players, one of whom shall be captain. By agreement a match may be played between sides of more or less than 11 players, but not more than 11 players may field at any time.

2. Nomination of Players

Each captain shall nominate his players in writing to one of the umpires before the toss. No player may be changed after the nomination without the consent of the opposing captain.

3. Captain

If at any time the captain is not available, a deputy shall act for him.

- (a) If a captain is not available during the period in which the toss is to take place, then the deputy must be responsible for the nomination of the players, if this has not already been done, and for the toss. See 2 above and Law 12.4 (The Toss).

- (b) At any time after the toss, the deputy must be one of the nominated players.

4. Responsibilities of Captains

The captains are responsible at all times for ensuring that play is conducted within the spirit and traditions of the game as well as within the Laws. See The Preamble – The Spirit of Cricket and Law 42.1 (Fair and Unfair Play – Responsibility of Captains).

LAW 2. SUBSTITUTES AND RUNNERS; BATSMAN OR FIELDER LEAVING THE FIELD; BATSMAN RETIRING; BATSMAN COMMENCING INNINGS

1. Substitutes and Runners

(a) If the umpires are satisfied that a player has been injured or become ill after the nomination of the players, they shall allow that player to have:

    (i) a substitute acting instead of him in the field

    (ii) a runner when batting.

Any injury or illness that occurs at any time after the nomination of the players until the conclusion of the match shall be allowable, irrespective of whether play is in progress or not.

(b) The umpires shall have discretion, for other wholly acceptable reasons, to allow a substitute for a fielder, or a runner for a batsman, at the start of the match or at any subsequent time.

(c) A player wishing to change his shirt, boots, etc. must leave the field to do so. No substitute shall be allowed for him.

2. Objection to Substitutes

The opposing captain shall have no right of objection to any player acting as substitute on the field, nor as to where the substitute shall field. However no substitute shall act as wicket-keeper. See 3 following.

3. Restrictions on the Role of Substitutes

A substitute shall not be allowed to bat or bowl nor to act as wicket-keeper or as captain on the field of play.

4. A Player for Whom a Substitute Has Acted

A player is allowed to bat, bowl or field even though a substitute has previously acted for him.

5. Fielder Absent or Leaving the Field

If a fielder fails to take the field with his side at the start of the match or at any later time, or leaves the field during a session of play:

- (a) The umpire shall be informed of the reason for his absence.

- (b) He shall not thereafter come on to the field during a session of play without the consent of the umpire. See 6 following. The umpire shall give such consent as soon as is practicable.

- (c) If he is absent for 15 minutes or longer, he shall not be permitted to bowl thereafter, subject to (i), (ii) or (iii) below, until he has been on the field for at least that length of playing time for which he was absent.

(i) Absence or penalty for time absent shall not be carried over into a new day's play.

(ii) If, in the case of a follow-on or forfeiture, a side fields for two consecutive innings, this restriction shall, subject to (i) above, continue as necessary into the second innings but shall not otherwise be carried over into a new innings.

(iii) The time lost for an unscheduled break in play shall be counted as time on the field for any fielder who comes onto the field at the resumption of play. See Law 15.1 (An Interval).

6. Player Returning Without Permission

If a player comes onto the field of play in contravention of 5(b) above and comes into contact with the ball while it is in play:

(i) the ball shall immediately become dead and the umpire shall award five penalty runs to the batting side. See Law 42.17 (Penalty Runs). The ball shall not count as one of the over.

(ii) the umpire shall inform the other umpire, the captain of the fielding side, the batsmen and, as soon as practicable, the captain of the batting side of the reason for this action.

(iii) the umpires together shall report the occurrence as soon as possible to the Executive of the fielding side and any Governing Body responsible for the match, who shall take such action as is considered appropriate against the captain and player concerned.

7. Runner

The player acting as a runner for a batsman shall be a member of the batting side and shall, if possible, have already batted in that innings. The runner shall wear external protective equipment equivalent to that worn by the batsman for whom he runs and shall carry a bat.

8. Transgression of the Laws by a Batsman Who Has a Runner

(a) A batsman's runner is subject to the Laws. He will be regarded as a batsman except where there are specific provisions for his role as a runner. See 7 above and Law 29.2 (Which is a Batsman's Ground).

(b) A batsman with a runner will suffer a penalty for any infringement of the Laws by his runner as though he himself had been responsible for the infringement. In particular he will be out if his runner is out under any of Laws 33 (Handled the Ball), 37 (Obstructing the Field) or 38 (Run Out).

(c) When a batsman with a runner is striker he remains himself subject to the Laws and will be liable to the penalties that any infringement of them demands. Additionally if he is out of his ground when the wicket is put down at the wicket-keeper's end he will be out in the circumstancs of Law 38 (Run Out) or Law 39 (Stumped) irrespective of the position of the non-striker or the runner. If he is thus dismissed, runs completed by the runner and the other batsman before the dismissal shall not be scored. However, the penalty for a No Ball or a Wide shall stand, together with any penalties to either side that may be awarded when the ball is dead. See Law 42.17 (Penalty Runs).

(d) When a batsman with a runner is not the striker:

(i) he remains subject to Laws 33 (Handled the Ball) and 37 (Obstructing the Field) but is otherwise out of the game.

(ii) he shall stand where directed by the striker's end umpire so as not to interfere with play.

(iii) he will be liable, notwithstanding (i) above, to the penalty demanded by the Laws should he commit any act of unfair play.

9. Batsman Leaving the Field or Retiring

A batsman may retire at any time during his innings. The umpires, before allowing play to proceed, shall be informed of the reason for a batsman retiring.

(a) If a batsman retires because of illness, injury or any other unavoidable cause, he is entitled to resume his innings subject to (c) below. If for any reason he does not do so, his innings is to be recorded as "Retired – not out".

(b) If a batsman retires for any reason other than as in (a) above, he may only resume his innings with the consent of the opposing captain. If for any reason he does not resume his innings it is to be recorded as "Retired – out".

(c) If after retiring a batsman resumes his innings, it shall only be at the fall of a wicket or the retirementr of another batsman.

10. Commencement of a Batsman's Innings

Except at the start of a side's innings, a batsman shall be considered to have commenced his innings when he first steps onto the field of play, provided "Time" has not been called. The innings of the opening batsmen, and that of any new batsman at the resumption of play after a call of "Time", shall commence at the call of "Play".

LAW 3.   THE UMPIRES

1. Appointment and Attendance

Before the match, two umpires shall be appointed, one for each end, to control the game as required by the Laws, with absolute impartiality. The umpires shall be present on the ground and report to the Executive of the ground at least 45 minutes before the scheduled start of each day's play.

2. Change of Umpires

An umpire shall not be changed during the match, other than in exceptional circumstances, unless he is injured or ill. If there has to be a change of umpire, the replacement shall act only as the striker's end umpire unless the captains agree that he should take full responsibility as an umpire.

3. Agreement with Captains

Before the toss the umpires shall:

    (a) ascertain the hours of play and agree with the captains:

        (i) the balls to be used during the match. See Law 5 (The Ball).

        (ii) times and durations of intervals for meals and times for drinks intervals. See Law 15 (Intervals).

        (iii) the boundary of the field of play and allowances for boundaries. See Law 19 (Boundaries).

        (iv) any special conditions of play affecting the conduct of the match.

    (b) inform the scorers of the agreements in (ii), (iii) and (iv) above.

4. To Inform Captains and Scorers

Before the toss the umpires shall agree between themselves and inform both captains and both scorers:

    (i) which clock or watch and back-up time piece is to be used during the match.

    (ii) whether or not any obstacle within the field of play is to be regarded as a boundary. See Law 19 (Boundaries).

5. The Wickets, Creases and Boundaries

Before the toss and during the match, the umpires shall satisfy themselves that:

    (i) the wickets are properly pitched. See Law 8 (The Wickets).

    (ii) the creases are correctly marked. See Law 9 (The Bowling, Popping and Return Creases).

    (iii) the boundary of the field of play complies with the requirements of Law 19.2 (Defining the Boundary – Boundary Marking).

6. Conduct of the Game, Implements and Equipment

Before the toss and during the match, the umpires shall satisfy themselves that:

    (a) the conduct of the game is strictly in accordance with the Laws.

    (b) the implements of the game conform to the requirements of Laws 5 (The Ball) and 6 (The Bat), together with either Laws 8.2 (Size of Stumps) and 8.3 (The Bails) or, if appropriate, Law 8.4 (Junior Cricket).

(c) (i) no player uses equipment other than that permitted. See Appendix D.

    (ii) the wicket-keeper's gloves comply with the requirements of Law 40.2 (Gloves).

7. Fair and Unfair Play

The umpires shall be the sole judges of fair and unfair play.

8. Fitness of Ground, Weather and Light

The umpires shall be the final judges of the fitness of the ground, weather and light for play. See 9 below and Law 7.2 (Fitness of the Pitch for Play).

9. Suspension of Play for Adverse Conditions of Ground, Weather or Light

(a) (i) All references to ground include the pitch. See Law 7.1 (Area of Pitch).

    (ii) For the purpose of this Law and Law 15.9 (b)(ii) (Intervals for Drinks) only the batsmen at the wicket may deputise for their captain at any appropriate time.

(b) If at any time the umpires together agree that the condition of the ground, weather or light is not suitable for play, they shall inform the captains and, unless:

    (i) in unsuitable ground or weather conditions both captains agree to continue, or to commence, or to restart play, or

    (ii) in unsuitable light the batting side wish to continue, or to commence, or to restart play, they shall suspend play, or not allow play to commence or to restart.

(c) (i) After agreeing to play in unsuitable ground or weather conditions, either captain may appeal against the conditions to the umpires before the next call of Time. The umpires shall uphold the appeal only if, in their opinion, the factors taken into account when making their previous decision are the same or the conditions have further deteriorated.

    (ii) After deciding to play in unsuitable light, the captain of the batting side may appeal against the light to the umpires before the next call of Time. The umpires shall uphold the appeal only if, in their opinion, the factors taken into account when making their previous decision are the same or the condition of the light has further deteriorated.

(d) If at any time the umpires together agree that the conditions of ground, weather or light are so bad that there is obvious and foreseeable risk to the safety of any player or umpire, so that it would be unreasonable or dangerous for play to take place, then notwithstanding the provisions of (b)(i) and (b)(ii) above, they shall immediately suspend play, or not allow play to commence or to restart. The decision as to whether conditions are so bad as to warrant such action is one for the umpires alone to make. The fact that the grass and the ball are wet and slippery does not warrant the ground conditions being regarded as unreasonable or dangerous. If the umpires consider the ground is so wet or slippery as to deprive the bowler of a reasonable foothold, the fielders of the power of free movement, or the batsmen of the ability to play their strokes or to run between the wickets, then these conditions shall be regarded as so bad that it would be unreasonable for play to take place.

(e) When there is a suspension of play it is the responsibility of the umpires to monitor the conditions. They shall make inspections as often as appropriate, unaccompanied by any of the players or officials. Immediately the umpires together agree that conditions are suitable for play they shall call upon the players to resume the game.

(f) If play is in progress up to the start of an agreed interval then it will resume after the interval unless the umpires together agree that conditions are or have become unsuitable or dangerous. If they do so agree, then they shall implement the procedure in (b) or (d) above, as appropriate, whether or not there had been any decision by the captains to continue, or any appeal against the conditions by either captain, prior to the commencement of the interval.

10. Exceptional Circumstances

The umpires shall have the discretion to implement the procedures of 9 above for reasons other than ground, weather or light if they consider that exceptional circumstances warrant it.

11. Position of Umpires

The umpires shall stand where they can best see any act upon which their decision may be required.

Subject to this over-riding consideration the umpire at the bowler's end shall stand where he does not interfere with either the bowler's run up or the striker's view.

The umpire at the striker's end may elect to stand on the off side instead of the on side of the pitch, provided he informs the captain of the fielding side, the striker and the other umpire of his intention to do so.

12. Umpires Changing Ends

The umpires shall change ends after each side has had one completed innings. See Law 14.2 (Forfeiture of an Innings).

13. Consultation between Umpires

All disputes shall be determined by the umpires. The umpires shall consult with each other whenever necessary. See also Law 27.6 (Consultation by Umpires).

14. Signals

(a) The following code of signals shall be used by umpires.

    (i) Signals made while the ball is in play:

Dead Ball	– by crossing and re-crossing the wrists below the waist.
No-ball	– by extending one arm horizontally.
Out	– by raising the index finger above the head. If not out, the umpire shall call "Not out".
Wide	– by extending both arms horizontally.

    (ii) When the ball is dead, the signals above, with the exception of the signal for Out, shall be repeated to the scorers. The signals listed below shall be made to the scorers only when the ball is dead.

Boundary 4	– by waving an arm from side to side finishing with the arm across the chest.
Boundary 6	– by raising both arms above the head.
Bye	– by raising an open hand above the head.
Commencement of Last Hour	– by pointing to a raised wrist with the other hand.
Five Penalty Runs to be Awarded to the batting side	– by repeated tapping of one shoulder with the opposite hand.
Five Penalty Runs to be Awarded to the fielding side	– by placing one hand on the opposite shoulder.
Leg-bye	– by touching a raised knee with the hand.
New Ball	– by holding the ball above the head.
Revoke last signal	– by touching both shoulders, each with the opposite hand.
Short Run	– by bending one arm upwards and touching the nearer shoulder with the tips of the fingers.

(b) The umpires shall wait until each signal to the scorers has been separately acknowledged by a scorer before allowing play to proceed.

15. Correctness of Scores

Consultation between umpires and scorers on doubtful points is essential. The umpires shall satisfy themselves as to the correctness of the number of runs scored, the wickets that have fallen and, where appropriate, the number of overs bowled. They shall agree these with the scorers at least at every interval, other than a drinks interval, and at the conclusion of the match. See Laws 4.2 (Correctness of Scores), 21.8 (Correctness of Result) and 21.10 (Result not to be Changed).

LAW 4. THE SCORERS

1. Appointment of Scorers

Two scorers shall be appointed to record all runs scored, all wickets taken and, where appropriate, number of overs bowled.

2. Correctness of Scores

The scorers shall frequently check to ensure that their records agree. They shall agree with the umpires, at least at every interval, other than a drinks interval, and at the conclusion of the match, the runs scored, the wickets that have fallen and, where appropriate, the number of overs bowled. See Law 3.15 (Correctness of Scores).

3. Acknowledging Signals

The scorers shall accept all instructions and signals given to them by the umpires. They shall immediately acknowledge each separate signal.

LAW 5. THE BALL

1. Weight and Size

The ball, when new, shall weigh not less than 5½ oz/155.9g, nor more than 5¾ oz/163g; and shall measure not less than 81⁄₁₆ in/22.4cm, nor more than 9 in/22.9cm in circumference.

2. Approval and Control of Balls

(a) All balls to be used in the match, having been approved by the umpires and captains, shall be in the possession of the umpires before the toss and shall remain under their control throughout the match.

(b) The umpire shall take possession of the ball in use at the fall of each wicket, at the start of any interval and at any interruption of play.

3. New Ball

Unless an agreement to the contrary has been made before the match, either captain may demand a new ball at the start of each innings.

4. New Ball in Match of More than One Day's Duration

In a match of more than one day's duration, the captain of the fielding side may demand a new ball after the prescribed number of overs has been bowled with the old one. The Governing Body for cricket in the country concerned shall decide the number of overs applicable in that country, which shall not be less than 75 overs.

The umpires shall indicate to the batsmen and the scorers whenever a new ball is taken into play.

5. Ball Lost or Becoming Unfit for Play

If, during play, the ball cannot be found or recovered or the umpires agree that it has become unfit for play through normal use, the umpires shall replace it with a ball which has had wear comparable with that which the previous ball had received before the need for its replacement. When the ball is replaced the umpires shall inform the batsmen and the fielding captain.

6. Specifications

The specifications, as described in 1 above, shall apply to men's cricket only. The following specifications will apply to

    (i)   *Women's cricket*
        Weight: from 4⁵⁄₁₆ oz/140g to 55/16 oz/151g.
        Circumference: from 8¼ in/21.0cm to 8⅞ in/22.5cm.

    (iii) *Junior cricket*
        Weight: from 4¹⁄₁₆ oz/133g to 5¹⁄₁₆ oz/144g.
        Circumference: 8¹⁄₁₆ in/20.5cm to 8¹¹⁄₁₆ in/22.0cm.

LAW 6.   THE BAT

1. Width and Length

The bat overall shall not be more than 38 in/96.5cm in length. The blade of the bat shall be made solely of wood and shall not exceed 4 ¼ in/10.8cm at the widest part.

2. Covering the Blade

The blade of the bat may be covered with material for protection, strengthening or repair. Such material shall not exceed ⅟₁₆ in/1.56mm in thickness, and shall not be likely to cause unacceptable damage to the ball.

3. Hand or Glove to Count as Part of Bat

In these Laws,

(a) reference to the bat shall imply that the bat is held by the batsman.

(b) contact between the ball and either

(i) the striker's bat itself, or

(ii) the striker's hand holding the bat, or

(iii) any part of a glove worn on the striker's hand holding the bat

shall be regarded as the ball striking or touching the bat, or being struck by the bat.

LAW 7.   THE PITCH

1. Area of Pitch

The pitch is a rectangular area of the ground 22 yds/20.12m in length and 10ft/3.05m in width. It is bounded at either end by the bowling creases and on either side by imaginary lines, one each side of the imaginary line joining the centres of the two middle stumps, each parallel to it and 5ft/1.52m from it. See Laws 8.1 (Width and Pitching) and 9.2 (The Bowling Crease).

2. Fitness of the Pitch for Play

The umpires shall be the final judges of the fitness of the pitch for play. See Laws 3.8 (Fitness of Ground, Weather and Light) and 3.9 (Suspension of Play for Adverse Conditions of Ground, Weather or Light).

3. Selection and Preparation

Before the match, the Ground Authority shall be responsible for the selection and preparation of the pitch. During the match, the umpires shall control its use and maintenance.

4. Changing the Pitch

The pitch shall not be changed during the match unless the umpires decide that it is unreasonable or dangerous for play to continue on it and then only with the consent of both captains.

5. Non-Turf Pitches

In the event of a non-turf pitch being used, the artificial surface shall conform to the following measurements:

Length: a minimum of 58 ft/17.68m.

Width: a minimum of 6 ft/1.83m.

See Law 10.8 (Non-turf Pitches).

LAW 8.   THE WICKETS

1. Width and Pitching

Two sets of wickets shall be pitched opposite and parallel to each other at a distance of 22 yds/20.12m between the centres of the two middle stumps. Each set shall be 9 in/ 22.86cm wide and shall consist of three wooden stumps with two wooden bails on top.

2. Size of Stumps

The tops of the stumps shall be 28 in/71.1cm above the playing surface and shall be dome shaped except for the bail grooves. The portion of a stump above the playing surface shall be cylindrical, apart from the domed top, with circular section of diameter not less than 1⅜ in/3.49cm nor more than 1½ in/3.81cm.

3. The Bails

(a) The bails, when in position on top of the stumps,

   (i) shall not project more than ½ in/1.27cm above them.

   (ii) shall fit between the stumps without forcing them out of the vertical.

(b)   Each bail shall conform to the following specifications

Overall length:	4⁹⁄₁₆ in/10.95cm
Length of barrel:	2⅛ in/5.40cm
Longer spigot:	1⅜ in/3.49cm
Shorter spigot:	1³⁄₁₆ in/2.06cm

4. Junior Cricket

In junior cricket, the same definitions of the wickets shall apply subject to the following measurements being used.

Width:	8 in/20.32cm
Pitched for Under-13:	21 yds/19.20m
Pitched for Under-11:	20 yds/18.29m
Height above playing surface:	27 in/68.58cm

Each stump

Diameter:	not less than 1¼ in/3.18cm
	nor more than 1⅜ in/3.49cm

Each bail

Overall length:	31¹³⁄₁₆ in/9.68cm
Length of barrel:	1¹³⁄₁₆ in/4.60cm
Longer spigot:	1¼ in/3.18cm
Shorter spigot:	¾ in/1.91cm

5. Dispensing with Bails

The umpires may agree to dispense with the use of bails, if necessary. If they so agree then no bails shall beused at either end. The use of bails shall be resumed as soon as conditions permit.

See Law 28.4 (Dispensing with Bails).

LAW 9.   THE BOWLING, POPPING AND RETURN CREASES

1. The Creases

A bowling crease, a popping crease and two return creases shall be marked in white, as set out in 2, 3 and 4, at each end of the pitch.

2. The Bowling Crease

The bowling crease, which is the back edge of the crease marking, shall be the line through the centres of the three stumps at that end. It shall be 8ft 8 in/2.64m in length, with the stumps in the centre.

3. The Popping Crease

The popping crease, which is the back edge of the crease marking, shall be in front of and parallel to the bowling crease and shall be 4ft/1.22m from it. The popping crease shall be marked to a minimum of 6ft/1.83m on either side of the imaginary line joining the centres of the middle stumps and shall be considered to be unlimited in length.

4. The Return Creases

The return creases, which are the inside edges of the crease markings, shall be at right angles to the popping crease at a distance of 4ft 4 in/1.32m either side of the imaginary line joining the centres of the two middle stumps. Each return crease shall be marked from the popping crease to a minimum of 8ft/2.44m behind it and shall be considered to be unlimited in length.

LAW 10. PREPARATION AND MAINTENANCE OF THE PLAYING AREA

1. Rolling

The pitch shall not be rolled during the match except as permitted in (a) and (b) below.

    (a) Frequency and Duration of Rolling
    During the match the pitch may be rolled at the request of the captain of the batting side, for a period of not more than seven minutes, before the start of each innings, other than the first innings of the match, and before the start of each subsequent day's play. See (d) below.

    (b) Rolling After a Delayed Start
    In addition to the rolling permitted above, if, after the toss and before the first innings of the match, the start is delayed, the captain of the batting side may request to have the pitch rolled for not more than seven minutes. However, if the umpires together agree that the delay has had no significant effect on the state of the pitch, they shall refuse the request for the rolling of the pitch.

    (c) Choice of Rollers
    If there is more than one roller available the captain of the batting side shall have the choice.

    (d) Timing of Permitted Rolling
    The rolling permitted (maximum seven minutes) before play begins on any day shall be started not more than 30 minutes before the time scheduled or rescheduled for play to begin. The captain of the batting side may, however, delay the start of such rolling until not less than ten minutes before the time scheduled or rescheduled for play to begin, should he so desire.

    (e) Insufficient Time to Complete Rolling
    If a captain declares an innings closed, or forfeits an innings, or enforces the follow-on, and the other captain is prevented thereby from exercising his option of the rolling permitted (maximum seven minutes), or if he is so prevented for any other reason, the extra time required to complete the rolling shall be taken out of the normal playing time.

2. Sweeping

    (a) If rolling is to take place the pitch shall first be swept to avoid any possible damage by rolling in debris. This sweeping shall be done so that the 7 minutes allowed for rolling is not affected.

    (b) The pitch shall be cleared of any debris at all intervals for meals, between innings and at the beginning of each day, not earlier than 30 minutes nor later than 10 minutes before the time scheduled or rescheduled for play to begin. See Law 15.1 (An Interval).

    (c) Notwithstanding the provisions of (a) and (b) above, the umpires shall not allow sweeping to take place where they consider it may be detrimental to the surface of the pitch.

3. Mowing

    (a) The Pitch
    The pitch shall be mown on each day of the match on which play is expected to take place, if ground and weather conditions allow.

    (b) The Outfield
    In order to ensure that conditions are as similar as possible for both sides, the outfield shall be mown on each day of the match on which play is expected to take place, if ground and weather conditions allow.

    If, for reasons other than ground and weather conditions, complete mowing of the outfield is not possible, the ground authority shall notify the captains and umpires of the procedure to be adopted for such mowing during the match.

(c) Responsibility for Mowing

All mowings which are carried out before the match shall be the responsibility of the ground authority.

All subsequent mowings shall be carried out under the supervision of the umpires.

(d) Timing of Mowing

(i) Mowing of the pitch on any day of the match shall be completed not later than 30 minutes before the time scheduled or rescheduled for play to begin on that day.

(ii) Mowing of the outfield on any day of the match shall be completed not later than 15 minutes before the time scheduled or rescheduled for play to begin on that day.

4. Watering

The pitch shall not be watered during the match.

5. Re-marking Creases

The creases shall be re-marked whenever either umpire considers it necessary.

6. Maintenance of Footholes

The umpires shall ensure that the holes made by the bowlers and batsmen are cleaned out and dried whenever necessary to facilitate play. In matches of more than one day's duration, the umpires shall allow, if necessary, the re-turfing of footholes made by the bowler in his delivery stride, or the use of quick-setting fillings for the same purpose.

7. Securing of Footholds and Maintenance of Pitch

During play, the umpires shall allow the players to secure their footholds by the use of sawdust provided that no damage to the pitch is caused and that Law 42 (Fair and Unfair Play) is not contravened.

8. Non-Turf Pitches

Wherever appropriate, the provisions set out in 1 to 7 above shall apply.

LAW 11. COVERING THE PITCH

1. Before the Match

The use of covers before the match is the responsibility of the Ground Authority and may include full covering if required. However, the Ground Authority shall grant suitable facility to the captains to inspect the pitch before the nomination of their players and to the umpires to discharge their duties as laid down in Laws 3 (The Umpires), 7 (The Pitch), 8 (The Wickets), 9 (The Bowling, Popping and Return Creases) and 10 (Preparation and Maintenance of the Playing Area).

2. During the Match

The pitch shall not be completely covered during the match unless provided otherwise by regulations or by agreement before the toss.

3. Covering Bowlers' Run-ups

Whenever possible, the bowlers' run ups shall be covered in inclement weather, in order to keep them dry. Unless there is agreement for full covering under 2 above the covers so used shall not extend further than 5ft/1.52m in front of each popping crease.

4. Removal of Covers

(a) If after the toss the pitch is covered overnight, the covers shall be removed in the morning at the earliest possible moment on each day that play is expected to take place.

(b) If covers are used during the day as protection from inclement weather, or if inclement weather delays the removal of overnight covers, they shall be removed promptly as soon as conditions allow.

LAW 12.   INNINGS

1. Number of Innings

(a) A match shall be one or two innings of each side according to agreement reached before the match.

(b) It may be agreed to limit any innings to a number of overs or by a period of time. If such an agreement is made then:

  (i) in a one-innings match it shall apply to both innings.

  (ii) in a two-innings match it shall apply to either the first innings of each side or the second innings of each side or both innings of each side.

2. Alternate Innings

In a two-innings match each side shall take their innings alternately except in the case provided for in Law 13 (The Follow-on) or Law 14.2 (Forfeiture of an Innings).

3. Completed Innings

A side's innings is to be considered as completed if:

  (a) the side is all out, or

  (b) at the fall of a wicket, further balls remain to be bowled, but no further batsman is available to come in, or

  (c) the captain declares the innings closed, or

  (d) the captain forfeits the innings, or

  (e) in the case of an agreement under 1(b) above, either

  (i) the prescribed number of overs has been bowled or

  (ii) the prescribed time has expired.

4. The Toss

The captains shall toss for the choice of innings on the field of play not earlier than 30 minutes, nor later than 15 minutes, before the scheduled or any rescheduled time for the match to start. Note, however, the provisions of Law 1.3 (Captain).

5. Decision to be Notified

The captain of the side winning the toss shall notify the opposing captain of his decision to bat or to field, not later than 10 minutes before the scheduled or any rescheduled time for the match to start. Once notified the decision may not be altered.

LAW 13.   THE FOLLOW-ON

1. Lead on First Innings

(a) In a two innings match of 5 days or more, the side which bats first and leads by at least 200 runs shall have the option of requiring the other side to follow their innings.

(b) The same option shall be available in two innings matches of shorter duration with the minimum required leads as follows:

  (i) 150 runs in a match of three or four days;

  (ii) 100 runs in a two-day match;

  (iii) 75 runs in a one-day match.

2. Notification

A captain shall notify the opposing captain and the umpires of his intention to take up this option. Law 10.1(e) (Insufficient Time to Complete Rolling) shall apply.

3. First Day's Play Lost

If no play takes place on the first day of a match of more than one day's duration, 1 above shall apply in accordance with the number of days remaining from the actual start of the match. The day on which play first commences shall count as a whole day for this purpose, irrespective of the time at which play starts.

Play will have taken place as soon as, after the call of "Play", the first over has started. See Law 22.2 (Start of an Over).

LAW 14.   DECLARATION AND FORFEITURE

1. Time of Declaration

The captain of the batting side may declare an innings closed, when the ball is dead, at any time during a match.

2. Forfeiture of an Innings

A captain may forfeit either of his side's innings. A forfeited innings shall be considered as a completed innings.

3. Notification

A captain shall notify the opposing captain and the umpires of his decision to declare or to forfeit an innings. Law 10.1(e) (Insufficient Time to Complete Rolling) shall apply.

LAW 15.   INTERVALS

1. An Interval

The following shall be classed as intervals.

    (i) The period between close of play on one day and the start of the next day's play.

    (ii) Intervals between innings.

    (iii) Intervals for meals.

    (iv) Intervals for drinks.

    (v) Any other agreed interval.

All these intervals shall be considered as scheduled breaks for the purposes of Law 2.5 (Fielder Absent or Leaving the Field).

2. Agreement of Intervals

    (a) Before the Toss:

        (i)   the hours of play shall be established.

        (ii) except as in (b) below, the timing and duration of intervals for meals shall be agreed.

        (iii) the timing and duration of any other interval under 1(v) above shall be agreed.

    (b) In a one-day match no specific time need be agreed for the tea interval. It may be agreed instead to take this interval between the innings.

    (c) Intervals for drinks may not be taken during the last hour of the match, as defined in Law 16.6 (Last hour of match – number of overs). Subject to this limitation the captains and umpires shall agree the times for such intervals, if any, before the toss and on each subsequent day not later than 10 minutes before play is scheduled to start. See also Law 3.3 (Agreement with Captains).

3. Duration of Intervals

    (a) An interval for lunch or for tea shall be of the duration agreed under 2(a) above, taken from the call of "Time" before the interval until the call of "Play" on resumption after the interval.

    (b) An interval between innings shall be ten minutes from the close of an innings to the call of "Play" for the start of the next innings, except as in 4, 6 and 7 below.

4. No Allowance for Interval Between Innings

In addition to the provisions of 6 and 7 below:

(a) if an innings ends when ten minutes or less remain before the time agreed for close of play on any day, there will be no further play on that day. No change will be made to the time for the start of play on the following day on account of the ten minutes between innings.

(b) if a captain declares an innings closed during an interruption in play of more than ten minutes duration, no adjustment shall be made to the time for resumption of play on account of the ten minutes between innings, which shall be considered as included in the interruption. Law 10.1(e) (Insufficient Time to Complete Rolling) shall apply.

(c) if a captain declares an innings closed during any interval other than an interval for drinks, the interval shall be of the agreed duration and shall be considered to include the ten minutes between innings. Law 10.1(e) (Insufficient Time to Complete Rolling) shall apply.

5. Changing Agreed Time for Intervals

If for adverse conditions of ground, weather or light, or for any other reason, playing time is lost, the umpires and captains together may alter the time of the lunch interval or of the tea interval. See also 6, 7 and 9(c) below.

6. Changing Agreed Time for Lunch Interval

(a) If an innings ends when ten minutes or less remain before the agreed time for lunch, the interval shall be taken immediately. It shall be of the agreed length and shall be considered to include the ten minutes between innings.

(b) If, because of adverse conditions of ground, weather or light, or in exceptional circumstances, a stoppage occurs when ten minutes or less remain before the agreed time for lunch then, notwithstanding 5 above, the interval shall be taken immediately. It shall be of the agreed length. Play shall resume at the end of this interval or as soon after as conditions permit.

(c) If the players have occasion to leave the field for any reason when more than ten minutes remain before the agreed time for lunch then, unless the umpires and captains together agree to alter it, lunch will be taken at the agreed time.

7. Changing Agreed Time for Tea Interval

(a)   (i)   If an innings ends when 30 minutes or less remain before the agreed time for tea, then the interval shall be taken immediately. It shall be of the agreed length and shall be considered to include the ten minutes between innings.

(ii) If, when 30 minutes remain before the agreed time for tea, an interval between innings is already in progress, play will resume at the end of the ten-minute interval.

(b)   (i) If, because of adverse conditions of ground, weather or light, or in exceptional circumstances, a stoppage occurs when 30 minutes or less remain before the agreed time for tea, then unless either there is an agreement to change the time for tea, as permitted in 5 above, or the captains agree to forgo the tea interval, as permitted in 10 below, the interval shall be taken immediately. The interval shall be of the agreed length. Play shall resume at the end of this interval or as soon after as conditions permit.

(ii) If a stoppage is already in progress when 30 minutes remain before the time agreed for tea, 5 above will apply.

8. Tea Interval – Nine Wickets Down

If either nine wickets are already down when two minutes remain to the agreed time for tea, or the ninth wicket falls within these two minutes or at any later time up to and including the final ball of the over in progress at the agreed time for tea, then not withstanding the provisions of Law 16.5 (b) (Completion of an over) tea will not be taken until the end of the over in progress 30 minutes after the originally agreed time for tea, unless the players have cause to leave the field of play or the innings is completed earlier.

9. Intervals for Drinks

(a) If on any day the captains agree that there shall be intervals for drinks, the option to take such intervals shall be available to either side. Each interval shall be kept as short as possible and in any case shall not exceed five minutes.

(b)   (i) Unless both captains agree to forgo any drinks interval, it shall be taken at the end of the over in progress when the agreed time is reached. If, however, a wicket falls within five minutes of the agreed time then drinks shall be taken immediately. No other variation in the timing of drinks intervals shall be permitted except as provided for in (c) below.

   (ii) For the purpose of (i) above and Law 3.9(a)(ii) (Suspension of Play for Adverse Conditions of Ground, Weather or Light) only, the batsmen at the wicket may deputise for their captain.

(c)   If an innings ends or the players have to leave the field of play for any other reason within 30 minutes of the agreed time for a drinks interval, the umpires and captains together may rearrange the timing of drinks intervals in that session.

10. Agreement to Forgo Intervals

At any time during the match, the captains may agree to forgo the tea interval or any of the drinks intervals. The umpires shall be informed of the decision.

11. Scorers to be Informed

The umpires shall ensure that the scorers are informed of all agreements about hours of play and intervals, and of any changes made thereto as permitted under this Law.

LAW 16. START OF PLAY; CESSATION OF PLAY

1. Call of "Play"

The umpire at the bowler's end shall call "Play" at the start of the match and on the resumption of play after any interval or interruption.

2. Call of "Time"

The umpire at the bowler's end shall call "Time" on the cessation of play before any interval or interruption of play and at the conclusion of the match. See Law 27 (Appeals).

3. Removal of Bails

After the call of "Time", the bails shall be removed from both wickets.

4. Starting a New Over

Another over shall always be started at any time during the match, unless an interval is to be taken in the circumstances set out in 5 below, if the umpire, after walking at his normal pace, has arrived at his position behind the stumps at the bowler's end before the time agreed for the next interval, or for the close of play, has been reached.

5. Completion of an Over

Other than at the end of the match:

(a) if the agreed time for an interval is reached during an over, the over shall be completed before the interval is taken except as provided for in (b) below.

(b) when less than two minutes remain before the time agreed for the next interval, the interval will be taken immediately if either

   (i) a batsman is out or retires, or

   (ii) the players have occasion to leave the field

whether this occurs during an over or at the end of an over. Except at the end of an innings, if an over is thus interrupted it shall be completed on resumption of play.

6. Last Hour of Match – Number of Overs

When one hour of playing time of the match remains, according to the agreed hours of play, the over in progress shall be completed. The next over shall be the first of a minimum of 20 overs which must be bowled, provided that a result is not reached earlier and provided that there is no interval or interruption in play. The umpire at the bowler's end shall indicate the commencement of this 20 overs to the players and the scorers. The period of play thereafter shall be referred to as the last hour, whatever its actual duration.

7. Last Hour of Match – Interruptions of Play

If there is an interruption in play during the last hour of the match, the minimum number of overs to be bowled shall be reduced from 20 as follows.

(a) The time lost for an interruption is counted from the call of "Time" until the time for resumption of play as decided by the umpires.

(b) One over shall be deducted for every complete three minutes of time lost.

(c) In the case of more than one such interruption, the minutes lost shall not be aggregated; the calculation shall be made for each interruption separately.

(d) If, when one hour of playing time remains, an interruption is already in progress:

    (i) only the time lost after this moment shall be counted in the calculation.

    (ii) the over in progress at the start of the interruption shall be completed on resumption of play and shall not count as one of the minimum number of overs to be bowled.

(e) If, after the start of the last hour, an interruption occurs during an over, the over shall be completed on resumption of play. The two part-overs shall between them count as one over of the minimum number to be bowled.

8. Last Hour of Match – Intervals Between Innings

If an innings ends so that a new innings is to be started during the last hour of the match, the interval starts with the end of the innings and is to end ten minutes later.

(a) If this interval is already in progress at the start of the last hour, then to determine the number of overs to be bowled in the new innings, calculations are to be made as set out in 7 above.

(b) If the innings ends after the last hour has started, two calculations are to be made, as set out in (c) and (d) below. The greater of the numbers yielded by these two calculations is to be the minimum number of overs to be bowled in the new innings.

(c) Calculation based on overs remaining:

    (i) At the conclusion of the innings, the number of overs that remain to be bowled, of the minimum in the last hour, to be noted.

    (ii) If this is not a whole number it is to be rounded up to the next whole number.

    (iii) Three overs to be deducted from the result for the interval.

(d) Calculation based on time remaining:

    (i) At the conclusion of the innings, the time remaining until the agreed time for close of play to be noted.

    (ii) Ten minutes to be deducted from this time, for the interval, to determine the playing time remaining.

    (iii) A calculation to be made of one over for every complete three minutes of the playing time remaining, plus one more over for any further part of three minutes remaining.

9. Conclusion of Match

The match is concluded:

(a) as soon as a result, as defined in sections 1, 2, 3 or 4 of Law 21 (The Result), is reached.

(b) as soon as both

    (i) the minimum number of overs for the last hour are completed, and

(ii) the agreed time for close of play is reached unless a result has been reached earlier.

(c) if, without the match being concluded either as in (a) or in (b) above, the players leave the field, either for adverse conditions of ground, weather or light, or in exceptional circumstances, and no further play is possible thereafter.

10. Completion of Last Over of Match

The over in progress at the close of play on the final day shall be completed unless either

(i) a result has been reached, or

(ii) the players have occasion to leave the field. In this case there shall be no resumption of play, except in the circumstances of Law 21.9 (Mistakes in Scoring), and the match shall be at an end.

11. Bowler Unable to Complete an Over During Last Hour of Match

If, for any reason, a bowler is unable to complete an over during the last hour, Law 22.8 (Bowler Incapacitated or Suspended During an Over) shall apply.

LAW 17.   PRACTICE ON THE FIELD

1. Practice on the Field

(a) There shall be no bowling or batting practice on the pitch, or on the area parallel and immediately adjacent to the pitch, at any time on any day of the match.

(b) There shall be no bowling or batting practice on any other part of the square on any day of the match, except before the start of play or after the close of play on that day. Practice before the start of play:

    (i) must not continue later than 30 minutes before the scheduled time or any rescheduled time for play to start on that day.

    (ii) shall not be allowed if the umpires consider that, in the prevailing conditions of ground and weather, it will be detrimental to the surface of the square.

(c) There shall be no practice on the field of play between the call of "Play" and the call of "Time", if the umpire considers that it could result in a waste of time. See Law 42.9 (Time-Wasting by the Fielding Side).

(d) If a player contravenes (a) or (b) above he shall not be allowed to bowl until either at least one hour later than the contravention or until there has been at least 30 minutes of playing time since the contravention, whichever is sooner. If an over is in progress at the contravention he shall not be allowed to complete that over.

2. Trial Run-Up

No bowler shall have a trial run-up between the call of "Play" and the call of "Time" unless the umpire is satisfied that it will not cause any waste of time.

LAW 18.   SCORING RUNS

1. A Run

The score shall be reckoned by runs. A run is scored:

(a) so often as the batsmen, at any time while the ball is in play, have crossed and made good their ground from end to end.

(b) when a boundary is scored. See Law 19 (Boundaries).

(c) when penalty runs are awarded. See 6 below.

(d) when "Lost ball" is called. See Law 20 (Lost Ball).

2. Runs Disallowed

Notwithstanding 1 above, or any other provisions elsewhere in the Laws, the scoring of runs or awarding of penalties will be subject to any disallowance of runs provided for within the Laws that may be applicable.

3. Short Runs

(a) A run is short if a batsman fails to make good his ground on turning for a further run.

(b) Although a short run shortens the succeeding one, the latter if completed shall not be regarded as short. A striker taking stance in front of his popping crease may run from that point also without penalty.

4. Unintentional Short Runs

Except in the circumstances of 5 below:

(a) if either batsman runs a short run, unless a boundary is scored the umpire concerned shall call and signal "Short run" as soon as the ball becomes dead and that run shall not be scored.

(b) if, after either or both batsmen run short, a boundary is scored, the umpire concerned shall disregard the short running and shall not call or signal "Short run".

(c) if both batsmen run short in one and the same run, this shall be regarded as only one short run.

(d) if more than one run is short then, subject to (b) and (c) above, all runs so called shall not be scored.

If there has been more than one short run the umpire shall inform the scorers as to the number of runs scored.

5. Deliberate Short Runs

(a) Notwithstanding 4 above, if either umpire considers that either or both batsmen deliberately run short at his end, the following procedure shall be adopted:

   (i) The umpire concerned shall, when the ball is dead, warn the batsmen that the practice is unfair, indicate that this is a first and final warning and inform the other umpire of what has occurred. This warning shall continue to apply throughout the innings. The umpire shall so inform each incoming batsman

   (ii) The batsmen shall return to their original ends.

   (iii) Whether a batsman is dismissed or not, the umpire at the bowler's end shall disallow all runs to the batting side from that delivery other than the penalty for a No ball or Wide, or penalties under Laws 42.5 (Deliberate Distraction or Obstruction of Batsman) and 42.13 (Fielders Damaging the Pitch), if applicable.

   (iv) The umpire at the bowler's end shall inform the scorers as to the number of runs scored.

(b) If there is any further instance of deliberate short running by any batsman in that innings, when the ball is dead the umpire concerned shall inform the other umpire of what has occurred and the procedure set out in (a)(ii) and (iii) above shall be repeated. Additionally, the umpire at the bowler's end shall:

   (i) award five penalty runs to the fielding side. See Law 42.17 (Penalty Runs).

   (ii) inform the scorers as to the number of runs scored.

   (iii) inform the batsmen, the captain of the fielding side and, as soon as practicable, the captain of the batting side of the reason for this action.

   (iv) report the occurrence, with the other umpire, to the Executive of the batting side and any governing body responsible for the match, who shall take such action as is considered appropriate against the captain and player or players concerned.

6. Runs Scored for Penalties

Runs shall be scored for penalties under 5 above and Laws 2.6 (Player Returning Without Permission), 24 (No-ball), 25 (Wide Ball), 41.2 (Fielding the Ball), 41.3 (Protective Helmets Belonging to the Fielding Side) and 42 (Fair and Unfair Play).

7. Runs Scored for Boundaries

Runs shall be scored for boundary allowances under Law 19 (Boundaries).

8. Runs Scored for Lost Ball

Runs shall be scored when "Lost ball" is called under Law 20 (Lost Ball).

9. Batsman Dismissed

When either batsman is dismissed:

(a) any penalties to either side that may be applicable shall stand but no other runs shall be scored, except as stated in 10 below.

(b) 12(a) below will apply if the method of dismissal is Caught, Handled the Ball or Obstructing the Field. 12(a) will also apply if a batsman is Run Out, except in the circumstances of Law 2.8 (Transgression of the Laws by a Batsman Who Has a Runner) where 12(b) below will apply.

(c) the not out batsman shall return to his original end except as stated in (b) above.

10. Runs Scored When a Batsman is Dismissed

In addition to any penalties to either side that may be applicable, if a batsman is

(a) dismissed Handled the Ball, the batting side shall score the runs completed before the offence.

(b) dismissed Obstructing the Field, the batting side shall score the runs completed before the offence.

If, however, the obstruction prevents a catch from being made, no runs other than penalties shall be scored.

(c) dismissed Run Out, the batting side shall score the runs completed before the dismissal.

If, however, a striker with a runner is himself dismissed Run Out, no runs other than penalties shall be scored. See Law 2.8 (Transgression of the Laws by a Batsman Who Has a Runner).

11. Runs Scored When a Ball Becomes Dead

(a) When the ball becomes dead on the fall of a wicket, runs shall be scored as laid down in 9 and 10 above.

(b) When the ball becomes dead for any reason other than the fall of a wicket, or is called dead by an umpire, unless there is specific provision otherwise in the Laws, the batting side shall be credited with:

  (i) all runs completed by the batsmen before the incident or call, and

  (ii) the run in progress if the batsmen have crossed at the instant of the incident or call. Note specifically, however, the provisions of Laws 34.4(c) (Runs Permitted From Ball Lawfully Struck More Than Once) and 42.5(b)(iii) (Deliberate Distraction or Obstruction of Batsman), and

  (iii) any penalties that are applicable.

12. Batsman Returning to Wicket he has Left

(a) If, while the ball is in play, the batsmen have crossed in running, neither shall return to the wicket he has left, except as in (b) below.

(b) The batsmen shall return to the wickets they originally left in the cases of, and only in the cases of:

  (i) a boundary.

  (ii) disallowance of runs for any reason.

  (iii) the dismissal of a batsman, except as in 9(b) above.

LAW 19.   BOUNDARIES

1. The Boundary of the Field of Play

(a) Before the toss, the umpires shall agree the boundary of the field of play with both captains. The boundary shall if possible be marked along its whole length.

(b) The boundary shall be agreed so that no part of any sight-screen is within the field of play.

(c) An obstacle or person within the field of play shall not be regarded as a boundary unless so decided by the umpires before the toss. See Law 3.4(ii) (To Inform Captains and Scorers).

2. Defining the Boundary – Boundary Marking

(a) Wherever practicable the boundary shall be marked by means of a white line or a rope laid along the ground.

(b) If the boundary is marked by a white line:

    (i) the inside edge of the line shall be the boundary edge.

    (ii) a flag, post or board used merely to highlight the position of a line marked on the ground must be placed outside the boundary edge and is not itself to be regarded as defining or marking the boundary. Note, however, the provisions of (c) below.

(c) If a solid object is used to mark the boundary, it must have an edge or a line to constitute the boundary edge.

    (i) For a rope, which includes any similar object of curved cross section lying on the ground, the boundary edge will be the line formed by the innermost points of the rope along its length.

    (ii) For a fence, which includes any similar object in contact with the ground, but with a flat surface projecting above the ground, the boundary edge will be the base line of the fence.

(d) If the boundary edge is not defined as in (b) or (c) above, the umpires and captains must agree, before the toss, what line will be the boundary edge. Where there is no physical marker for a section of boundary, the boundary edge shall be the imaginary straight line joining the two nearest marked points of the boundary edge.

(e) If a solid object used to mark the boundary is disturbed for any reason during play, then if possible it shall be restored to its original position as soon as the ball is dead. If this is not possible, then:

    (i) if some part of the fence or other marker has come within the field of play, that portion is to be removed from the field of play as soon as the ball is dead.

    (ii) the line where the base of the fence or marker originally stood shall define the boundary edge.

3. Scoring a Boundary

(a) A boundary shall be scored and signalled by the umpire at the bowler's end whenever, while the ball is in play, in his opinion:

    (i) the ball touches the boundary, or is grounded beyond the boundary.

    (ii) a fielder, with some part of his person in contact with the ball, touches the boundary or has some part of his person grounded beyond the boundary.

(b) The phrases "touches the boundary" and "touching the boundary" shall mean contact with either

    (i) the boundary edge as defined in 2 above, or

    (ii) any person or obstacle within the field of play which has been designated a boundary by the umpires before the toss.

(c) The phrase "grounded beyond the boundary" shall mean contact with either

    (i) any part of a line or a solid object marking the boundary, except its boundary edge, or

    (ii) the ground outside the boundary edge, or

    (iii) any object in contact with the ground outside the boundary edge.

4. Runs Allowed for Boundaries

(a) Before the toss, the umpires shall agree with both captains the runs to be allowed for boundaries. In deciding the allowances, the umpires and captains shall be guided by the prevailing custom of the ground.

(b) Unless agreed differently under (a) above, the allowances for boundaries shall be six runs if the ball having been struck by the bat pitches beyond the boundary, but otherwise four runs. These allowances shall still apply even though the ball has previously touched a fielder. See also (c) below.

(c) The ball shall be regarded as pitching beyond the boundary and six runs shall be scored if a fielder:

> (i) has any part of his person touching the boundary or grounded beyond the boundary when he catches the ball.

> (ii) catches the ball and subsequently touches the boundary or grounds some part of his person beyond the boundary while carrying the ball but before completing the catch. See Law 32 (Caught).

5. Runs Scored

When a boundary is scored:

(a) the penalty for a No Ball or a Wide, if applicable, shall stand together with any penalties under any of Laws 2.6 (Player Returning Without Permission), 18.5(b) (Deliberate Short Runs) or 42 (Fair and Unfair Play) that apply before the boundary is scored.

(b) the batting side, except in the circumstances of 6 below, shall additionally be awarded whichever is the greater of:

> (i) the allowance for the boundary.

> (ii) the runs completed by the batsmen, together with the run in progress if they have crossed at the instant the boundary is scored. When these runs exceed the boundary allowance, they shall replace the boundary for the purposes of Law 18.12 (Batsman Returning to Wicket He Has Left).

6. Overthrow or Wilful Act of Fielder

If the boundary results either from an overthrow or from the wilful act of a fielder the runs scored shall be:

> (i) the penalty for a No-ball or a Wide, if applicable, and penalties under any of Laws 2.6 (Player Returning Without Permission), 18.5(b) (Deliberate Short Runs) or 42 (Fair and Unfair Play) that are applicable before the boundary is scored, and

> (ii) the allowance for the boundary, and

> (iii) the runs completed by the batsmen, together with the run in progress if they have crossed at the instant of the throw or act.

Law 18.12(a) (Batsman Returning to Wicket He Has Left) shall apply as from the instant of the throw or act.

LAW 20.   LOST BALL

1. Fielder to Call "Lost Ball"

If a ball in play cannot be found or recovered, any fielder may call "Lost ball". The ball shall then become dead. See Law 23.1 (Ball is Dead). Law 18.12(a) (Batsman Returning to Wicket He Has Left) shall apply as from the instant of the call.

2. Ball to Be Replaced

The umpires shall replace the ball with one which has had wear comparable with that which the previous ball had received before it was lost or became irrecoverable. See Law 5.5 (Ball Lost or Becoming Unfit for Play).

3. Runs Scored

(a) The penalty for a no-ball or a wide, if applicable, shall stand, together with any penalties under any of Laws 2.6 (Player Returning Without Permission), 18.5(b) (Deliberate Short Runs) or 42 (Fair and Unfair Play) that are applicable before the call of "Lost ball".

(b) The batting side shall additionally be awarded, either

> (i) the runs completed by the batsmen, together with the run in progress if they have crossed at the instant of the call, or

> (ii) six runs,

whichever is the greater.

4. How Scored

If there is a one-run penalty for a no-ball or for a wide, it shall be scored as a no-ball extra or as a wide as appropriate. See Laws 24.13 (Runs Resulting from a No-ball – How Scored) and 25.6 (Runs Resulting from a Wide – How Scored). If any other penalties have been awarded to either side, they shall be scored as penalty extras. See Law 42.17 (Penalty Runs).

Runs to the batting side in 3(b) above shall be credited to the striker if the ball has been struck by the bat, but otherwise to the total of byes, leg byes, no-balls or wides as the case may be.

LAW 21.   THE RESULT

1. A Win – Two-Innings Match

The side which has scored a total of runs in excess of that scored in the two completed innings of the opposing side shall win the match. Note also 6 below. A forfeited innings is to count as a completed innings. See Law 14 (Declaration and Forfeiture).

2. A Win – One-Innings Match

The side which has scored in its one innings a total of runs in excess of that scored by the opposing side in its one completed innings shall win the match. Note also 6 below.

3. Umpires Awarding a Match

(a) A match shall be lost by a side which either

    (i) concedes defeat, or

    (ii) in the opinion of the umpires refuses to play and the umpires shall award the match to the other side.

(b) If an umpire considers that an action by any player or players might constitute a refusal by either side to play then the umpires together shall ascertain the cause of the action. If they then decide together that this action does constitute a refusal to play by one side, they shall so inform the captain of that side. If the captain persists in the action the umpires shall award the match in accordance with (a)(ii) above.

(c) If action as in (b) above takes place after play has started and does not constitute a refusal to play

    (i) playing time lost shall be counted from the start of the action until play commences, subject to Law 15.5 (Changing Agreed Times for Intervals).

    (ii) the time for close of play on that day shall be extended by this length of time, subject to Law 3.9 (Suspension of Play for Adverse Conditions of Ground, Weather or Light).

    (iii) if applicable, no overs shall be deducted during the last hour of the match solely on account of this time.

4. A Tie

The result of a match shall be a tie when the scores are equal at the conclusion of play, but only if the side batting last has completed its innings.

5. A Draw

A match which is concluded, as defined in Law 16.9 (Conclusion of a Match), without being determined in any of the ways stated in 1, 2, 3 or 4 above, shall count as a draw.

6. Winning Hit or Extras

(a) As soon as a result is reached, as defined in 1, 2, 3 or 4 above, the match is at an end. Nothing that happens thereafter, except as in Law 42.17 (b), shall be regarded as part of it. Note also 9 below.

(b) The side batting last will have scored enough runs to win only if its total of runs is sufficient without including any runs completed before the dismissal of the striker by the completion of a catch or by the obstruction of a catch.

(c) If a boundary is scored before the batsmen have completed sufficient runs to win the match, then the whole of the boundary allowance shall be credited to the side's total and, in the case of a hit by the bat, to the striker's score.

7. Statement of Result

If the side batting last wins the match without losing all its wickets, the result shall be stated as a win by the number of wickets still then to fall. If the side batting last has lost all its wickets but, as the result of an award of five penalty runs at the end of the match, has scored a total of runs in excess of the total scored by the opposing side, the result shall be stated as a win to that side by penalty runs. If the side fielding last wins the match, the result shall be stated as a win by runs.

If the match is decided by one side conceding defeat or refusing to play, the result shall be stated as "Match conceded" or "Match awarded" as the case may be.

8. Correctness of Result

Any decision as to the correctness of the scores shall be the responsibility of the umpires. See Law 3.15 (Correctness of Scores).

9. Mistakes in Scoring

If, after the umpires and players have left the field in the belief that the match has been concluded, the umpires discover that a mistake in scoring has occurred which affects the result, then, subject to 10 below, they shall adopt the following procedure.

(a) If, when the players leave the field, the side batting last has not completed its innings, and either

(i) the number of overs to be bowled in the last hour has not been completed, or

(ii) the agreed finishing time has not been reached,

then unless one side concedes defeat the umpires shall order play to resume.

If conditions permit, play will then continue until the prescribed number of overs has been completed and the time remaining has elapsed, unless a result is reached earlier. The number of overs and/or the time remaining shall be taken as they were when the players left the field; no account shall be taken of the time between that moment and the resumption of play.

(b) If, when the players leave the field, the overs have been completed and time has been reached, or if the side batting last has completed its innings, the umpires shall immediately inform both captains of the necessary corrections to the scores and to the result.

10. Result Not to Be Changed

Once the umpires have agreed with the scorers the correctness of the scores at the conclusion of the match – see Laws 3.15 (Correctness of Scores) and 4.2 (Correctness of Scores) – the result cannot thereafter be changed.

LAW 22. THE OVER

1. Number of Balls

The ball shall be bowled from each wicket alternately in overs of six balls.

2. Start of an Over

An over has started when the bowler starts his run-up or, if he has no-run up, his delivery action for the first delivery of that over.

3. Call of "Over"

When six balls have been bowled other than those which are not to count in the over and as the ball becomes dead – see Law 23 (Dead Ball) – the umpire shall call "Over" before leaving the wicket.

4. Balls Not to Count in the Over

(a) A ball shall not count as one of the six balls of the over unless it is delivered, even though a batsman may be dismissed or some other incident occurs before the ball is delivered.

(b) A ball which is delivered by the bowler shall not count as one of the six balls of the over:

(i) if it is called dead, or is to be considered dead, before the striker has had an opportunity to play it. See Law 23 (Dead Ball).

(ii) if it is a no-ball. See Law 24 (No-Ball).

(iii) if it is a wide. See Law 25 (Wide Ball).

(iv) if it is called dead in the circumstances of Laws 23.3(b)(vi) (Umpire Calling and Signalling "Dead ball")

(v) When five penalty runs are awarded to the batting side under any of Laws 2.6 (Player Returning Without Permission), 41.2 (Fielding the Ball), 42.4 (Deliberate Attempt to Distract Striker) or 42.5 (Deliberate Distraction or Obstruction of Batsman).

5. Umpire Miscounting

If an umpire miscounts the number of balls, the over as counted by the umpire shall stand.

6. Bowler Changing Ends

A bowler shall be allowed to change ends as often as desired, provided only that he does not bowl two overs, or parts thereof, consecutively in the same innings.

7. Finishing an Over

(a) Other than at the end of an innings, a bowler shall finish an over in progress unless he is incapacitated, or he is suspended under any of Laws 17.1 (Practice on the Field), 42.7 (Dangerous and Unfair Bowling – Action By the Umpire), 42.9 (Time-Wasting by the Fielding Side), or 42.12 (Bowler Running on the Protected Area After Delivering the Ball).

(b) If for any reason, other than the end of an innings, an over is left uncompleted at the start of an interval or interruption of play, it shall be completed on resumption of play.

8. Bowler Incapacitated or Suspended During an Over

If for any reason a bowler is incapacitated while running up to bowl the first ball of an over, or is incapacitated or suspended during an over, the umpire shall call and signal "Dead ball". Another bowler shall complete the over from the same end, provided that he does not bowl two overs, or parts thereof, consecutively in one innings.

LAW 23.   DEAD BALL

1. Ball is Dead

(a) The ball becomes dead when:

(i) it is finally settled in the hands of the wicket-keeper or the bowler.

(ii) a boundary is scored. See Law 19.3 (Scoring a Boundary).

(iii) a batsman is dismissed.

(iv) whether played or not it becomes trapped between the bat and person of a batsman or between items of his clothing or equipment.

(v) whether played or not it lodges in the clothing or equipment of a batsman or the clothing of an umpire.

(vi) it lodges in a protective helmet worn by a member of the fielding side.

(vii) there is a contravention of either of Laws 41.2 (Fielding the Ball) or 41.3 (Protective Helmets Belonging to the Fielding Side).

(viii) there is an award of penalty runs under Law 2.6 (Player Returning Without Permission).

(ix) "Lost ball" is called. See Law 20 (Lost Ball).

(x) the umpire calls "Over" or "Time".

(b) The ball shall be considered to be dead when it is clear to the umpire at the bowler's end that the fielding side and both batsmen at the wicket have ceased to regard it as in play.

2. Ball Finally Settled

Whether the ball is finally settled or not is a matter for the umpire alone to decide.

3. Umpire Calling and Signalling "Dead Ball"

(a) When the ball has become dead under 1 above, the bowler's end umpire may call "Dead ball", if it is necessary to inform the players.

(b) Either umpire shall call and signal "Dead ball" when:

(i) he intervenes in a case of unfair play.

(ii) a serious injury to a player or umpire occurs.

(iii) he leaves his normal position for consultation.

(iv) one or both bails fall from the striker's wicket before he has the opportunity of playing the ball.

(v) he is satisfied that for an adequate reason the striker is not ready for the delivery of the ball and, if the ball is delivered, makes no attempt to play it.

(vi) the striker is distracted by any noise or movement or in any other way while he is preparing to receive or receiving a delivery. This shall apply whether the source of the distraction is within the game or outside it. Note, however, the provisions of Law 42.4 (Deliberate Attempt to Distract the Striker). The ball shall not count as one of the over.

(vii) the bowler drops the ball accidentally before delivery.

(viii) the ball does not leave the bowler's hand for any reason other than an attempt to run out the non-striker before entering his delivery stride. See Law 42.15 (Bowler Attempting to Run out Non-striker Before Delivery).

(ix) he is required to do so under any of the Laws.

4. Ball Ceases to Be Dead

The ball ceases to be dead – that is, it comes into play – when the bowler starts his run up or, if he has no run up, his bowling action.

5. Action on Call of "Dead Ball"

(a) A ball is not to count as one of the over if it becomes dead or is to be considered dead before the striker has had an opportunity to play it.

(b) If the ball becomes dead or is to be considered dead after the striker has had an opportunity to play the ball, except in the circumstances of 3(vi) above and Law 42.4 (Deliberate Attempt to Distract Striker), no additional delivery shall be allowed unless "No-ball" or "Wide" has been called.

LAW 24.   NO-BALL

1. Mode of Delivery

(a) The umpire shall ascertain whether the bowler intends to bowl right-handed or left-handed, and whether over or round the wicket, and shall so inform the striker. It is unfair if the bowler fails to notify the umpire of a change in his mode of delivery. In this case the umpire shall call and signal "No-ball".

(b) Underarm bowling shall not be permitted except by special agreement before the match.

2. Fair Delivery – The Arm

For a delivery to be fair in respect of the arm the ball must not be thrown. See 3 below.

Although it is the primary responsibility of the striker's end umpire to ensure the fairness of a delivery in this respect, there is nothing in this Law to debar the bowler's end umpire from calling and signalling "No-ball" if he considers that the ball has been thrown.

(a) If, in the opinion of either umpire, the ball has been thrown, he shall

(i) call and signal "No-ball".

(ii) caution the bowler, when the ball is dead. This caution shall apply throughout the innings.

(iii) inform the other umpire, the batsmen at the wicket, the captain of the fielding side and, as soon as practicable, the captain of the batting side of what has occurred.

(b) If either umpire considers that after such caution a further delivery by the same bowler in that innings is thrown, the umpire concerned shall repeat the procedure set out in (a) above, indicating to the bowler that this is a final warning. This warning shall also apply throughout the innings.

(c) If either umpire considers that a further delivery by the same bowler in that innings is thrown:

    (i) the umpire concerned shall call and signal "No-ball". When the ball is dead he shall inform the other umpire, the batsmen at the wicket and, assoon as practicable, the captain of the batting side of what has occurred.

    (ii) the umpire at the bowler's end shall direct the captain of the fielding side   to take the bowler off forthwith. The over shall be completed by another bowler, who shall neither have bowled the previous over nor be allowed to bowl the next over. The bowler thus taken off shall not bowl again in that innings.

    (iii) the umpires together shall report the occurrence as soon as possible to the Executive of the fielding side and any governing body responsible for the match, who shall take such action as is considered appropriate against the captain and bowler concerned.

3. Definition of Fair Delivery – The Arm

A ball is fairly delivered in respect of the arm if, once the bowler's arm has reached the level of the shoulder in the delivery swing, the elbow joint is not straightened partially or completely from that point until the ball has left the hand. This definition shall not debar a bowler from flexing or rotating the wrist in the delivery swing.

4. Bowler Throwing Towards Striker's End Before Delivery

If the bowler throws the ball towards the striker's end before entering his delivery stride, either umpire shall call and signal "No-ball". See Law 42.16 (Batsmen Stealing a Run). However, the procedure stated in 2 above of caution, informing, final warning, action against the bowler and reporting shall not apply.

5. Fair Delivery – The Feet

For a delivery to be fair in respect of the feet, in the delivery stride:

    (i) the bowler's back foot must land within and not touching the return crease.

    (ii) the bowler's front foot must land with some part of the foot, whether grounded or raised, behind the popping crease.

If the umpire at the bowler's end is not satisfied that both these conditions have been met, he shall call and signal "No-ball".

6. Ball Bouncing More Than Twice or Rolling Along the Ground

The umpire at the bowler's end shall call and signal "No-ball" if a ball which he considers to have been delivered, without having previously touched the bat or person of the striker, either

    (i) bounces more than twice, or

    (ii) rolls along the ground

before it reaches the popping crease.

7. Ball Coming to Rest in Front of Striker's Wicket

If a ball delivered by the bowler comes to rest in front of the line of the striker's wicket, without having touched the bat or person of the striker, the umpire shall call and signal "No-ball" and immediately call and signal "Dead ball".

8. Call of "No-Ball" for Infringement of Other Laws

In addition to the instances above, an umpire shall call and signal "No-ball" as required by the following Laws.

        Law 40.3 – Position of wicket-keeper,
        Law 41.5 – Limitation of on-side fielders,
        Law 41.6 – Fielders not to encroach on the pitch,

Law 42.6 – Dangerous and unfair bowling,
Law 42.7 – Dangerous and unfair bowling – action by the umpire,
Law 42.8 – Deliberate bowling of high full pitched balls.

9. Revoking a Call of "No-Ball"

An umpire shall revoke the call of "No-ball" if the ball does not leave the bowler's hand for any reason.

10. No-Ball to Override Wide

A call of "No-ball" shall over-ride the call of "Wide ball" at any time. See Law 25.1 (Judging a Wide) and 25.3 (Call and Signal of "Wide Ball").

11. Ball Not Dead

The ball does not become dead on the call of "No-ball".

12. Penalty for a No-Ball

A penalty of one run shall be awarded instantly on the call of "No-ball". Unless the call is revoked, this penalty shall stand even if a batsman is dismissed. It shall be in addition to any other runs scored, any boundary allowance and any other penalties awarded.

13. Runs Resulting from a No Ball – How Scored

The one run penalty for a no-ball shall be scored as a no-ball extra. If other penalty runs have been awarded to either side, these shall be scored as in Law 42.17 (Penalty Runs). Any runs completed by the batsmen or a boundary allowance shall be credited to the striker if the ball has been struck by the bat; otherwise they also shall be scored as no-ball extras. Apart from any award of a five-run penalty, all runs resulting from a no-ball, whether as no-ball extras or credited to the striker, shall be debited against the bowler.

14. No-Ball Not to Count

A no-ball shall not count as one of the over. See Law 22.4 (Balls Not to Count in the Over).

15. Out from a No-Ball

When "No-ball" has been called, neither batsman shall be out under any of the Laws except 33 (Handled the Ball), 34 (Hit the Ball Twice), 37 (Obstructing the Field) or 38 (Run Out).

LAW 25.   WIDE BALL

1. Judging a Wide

(a) If the bowler bowls a ball, not being a no-ball, the umpire shall adjudge it a wide if according to the definition in (b) below, in his opinion, the ball passes wide of the striker where he is standing and would also have passed wide of him standing in a normal guard position.

(b) The ball will be considered as passing wide of the striker unless it is sufficiently within his reach for him to be able to hit it with his bat by means of a normal cricket stroke.

2. Delivery Not a Wide

The umpire shall not adjudge a delivery as being a wide

(a) if the striker, by moving, either

(i) causes the ball to pass wide of him, as defined in 1(b) above, or

(ii) brings the ball sufficiently within his reach to be able to hit it with his bat by means of a normal cricket stroke.

(b) if the ball touches the striker's bat or person.

3. Call and Signal of "Wide Ball"

(a) If the umpire adjudges a delivery to be a wide he shall call and signal "Wide ball" as soon as the ball passes the striker's wicket. It shall, however, be considered to have been a wide from the instant of delivery, even though it cannot be called wide until it passes the striker's wicket.

(b) The umpire shall revoke the call of "Wide ball" if there is then any contact between the ball and the striker's bat or person.

(c) The umpire shall revoke the call of "Wide ball" if a delivery is called a "No-ball". See Law 24.10 (No-Ball to Over-ride Wide).

4. Ball Not Dead

The ball does not become dead on the call of "Wide ball".

5. Penalty For a Wide

A penalty of one run shall be awarded instantly on the call of "Wide ball". Unless the call is revoked (see 3 above), this penalty shall stand even if a batsman is dismissed, and shall be in addition to any other runs scored, any boundary allowance and any other penalties awarded.

6. Runs Resulting From a Wide – How Scored

All runs completed by the batsmen or a boundary allowance, together with the penalty for the wide, shall be scored as wide balls. Apart from any award of a five-run penalty, all runs resulting from a wide ball shall be debited against the bowler.

7. Wide Not to Count

A wide shall not count as one of the over. See Law 22.4 (Balls Not to Count in the Over).

8. Out From a Wide

When "Wide ball" has been called, neither batsman shall be out under any of the Laws except 33 (Handled the Ball), 35 (Hit Wicket), 37 (Obstructing the Field), 38 (Run Out) or 39 (Stumped).

LAW 26.   BYE AND LEG-BYE

1. Byes

If the ball, not being a no-ball or a wide, passes the striker without touching his bat or person, any runs completed by the batsmen or a boundary allowance shall be credited as byes to the batting side.

2. Leg-Byes

(a) If the ball delivered by the bowler first strikes the person of the striker, runs shall be scored only if the umpire is satisfied that the striker has either

(i) attempted to play the ball with his bat, or

(ii) tried to avoid being hit by the ball.

If the umpire is satisfied that either of these conditions has been met, and the ball makes no subsequent contact with the bat, runs completed by the batsmen or a boundary allowance shall be credited to the batting side as in (b). Note, however, the provisions of Laws 34.3 (Ball Lawfully Struck More Than Once) and 34.4 (Runs Permitted From Ball Lawfully Struck More Than Once).

(b) The runs in (a) above shall

(i) if the delivery is not a no-ball, be scored as leg-byes.

(ii) if no-ball has been called, be scored together with the penalty for the no-ball as no-ball extras.

3. Leg-Byes Not to Be Awarded

If in the circumstances of 2(a) above, the umpire considers that neither of the conditions (i) and (ii) has been met, then leg-byes will not be awarded. The batting side shall not be credited with any runs from that delivery apart from the one-run penalty for a no-ball if applicable. Moreover, no other penalties shall be awarded to the batting side when the ball is dead. See Law 42.17 (Penalty Runs).

The following procedure shall be adopted.

(a) If no run is attempted but the ball reaches the boundary, the umpire shall call and signal "Dead ball", and disallow the boundary.

(b) If runs are attempted and if:

(i) neither batsman is dismissed and the ball does not become dead for any other reason, the umpire shall call and signal "Dead ball" as soon as one run is completed or the ball reaches the boundary. The batsmen shall return to their original ends. The run or boundary shall be disallowed.

(ii) before one run is completed or the ball reaches the boundary, a batsman is dismissed, or the ball becomes dead for any other reason, all the provisions of the Laws will apply, except that no runs and no penalties shall be credited to the batting side, other than the penalty for a no-ball if applicable.

LAW 27.   APPEALS

1. Umpire Not to Give Batsman Out Without an Appeal

Neither umpire shall give a batsman out, even though he may be out under the Laws, unless appealed to by the fielding side. This shall not debar a batsman who is out under any of the Laws from leaving his wicket without an appeal having been made. Note, however, the provisions of 7 below.

2. Batsman Dismissed

A batsman is dismissed if either

(a) he is given out by an umpire, on appeal, or

(b) he is out under any of the Laws and leaves his wicket as in 1 above.

3. Timing of Appeals

For an appeal to be valid it must be made before the bowler begins his run-up or, if he has no run-up, his bowling action to deliver the next ball, and before "Time" has been called.

The call of "Over" does not invalidate an appeal made prior to the start of the following over provided "Time" has not been called. See Laws 16.2 (Call of Time) and 22.2 (Start of an Over).

4. Appeal "How's That?"

An appeal "How's That?" covers all ways of being out.

5. Answering Appeals

The umpire at the bowler's end shall answer all appeals except those arising out of any of Laws 35 (Hit Wicket), 39 (Stumped) or 38 (Run Out) when this occurs at the striker's wicket. A decision "Not out" by one umpire shall not prevent the other umpire from giving a decision, provided that each is considering only matters within his jurisdiction.

When a batsman has been given not out, either umpire may, within his jurisdiction, answer a further appeal provided that it is made in accordance with 3 above.

6. Consultation by Umpires

Each umpire shall answer appeals on matters within his own jurisdiction. If an umpire is doubtful about any point that the other umpire may have been in a better position to see, he shall consult the latter on this point of fact and shall then give his decision. If, after consultation, there is still doubt remaining the decision shall be "Not out".

7. Batsman Leaving his Wicket Under a Misapprehension

An umpire shall intervene if satisfied that a batsman, not having been given out, has left his wicket under a misapprehension that he is out. The umpire intervening shall call and signal "Dead ball" to prevent any further action by the fielding side and shall recall the batsman.

8. Withdrawal of an Appeal

The captain of the fielding side may withdraw an appeal only with the consent of the umpire within whose jurisdiction the appeal falls and before the outgoing batsman has left the field of play. If such consent is given the umpire concerned shall, if applicable, revoke his decision and recall the batsman.

9. Umpire's Decision

An umpire may alter his decision provided that such alteration is made promptly. This apart, an umpire's decision, once made, is final.

LAW 28.   THE WICKET IS DOWN

1. Wicket Put Down

(a) The wicket is put down if a bail is completely removed from the top of the stumps, or a stump is struck out of the ground by:

      (i)   the ball.

      (ii) the striker's bat, whether he is holding it or has let go of it.

      (iii) the striker's person or by any part of his clothing or equipment becoming detached from his person.

      (iii) a fielder, with his hand or arm, providing that the ball is held in the hand or hands so used, or in the hand of the arm so used.

The wicket is also put down if a fielder pulls a stump out of the ground in the same manner.

(b) The disturbance of a bail, whether temporary or not, shall not constitute its complete removal from the top of the stumps, but if a bail in falling lodges between two of the stumps this shall be regarded as complete removal.

2. One Bail Off

If one bail is off, it shall be sufficient for the purpose of putting the wicket down to remove the remaining bail, or to strike or pull any of the three stumps out of the ground, in any of the ways stated in 1 above.

3. Remaking the Wicket

If the wicket is broken or put down while the ball is in play, the umpire shall not remake the wicket until the ball is dead. See Law 23 (Dead Ball). Any fielder, however, may

      (i) replace a bail or bails on top of the stumps.

      (ii) put back one or more stumps into the ground where the wicket originally stood.

4. Dispensing with Bails

If the umpires have agreed to dispense with bails, in accordance with Law 8.5 (Dispensing with Bails), the decision as to whether the wicket has been put down is one for the umpire concerned to decide.

(a) After a decision to play without bails, the wicket has been put down if the umpire concerned is satisfied that the wicket has been struck by the ball, by the striker's bat, person, or items of his clothing or equipment separated from his person as described in 1(a)(ii) or 1(a)(iii) above, or by a fielder with the hand holding the ball or with the arm of the hand holding the ball.

(b) If the wicket has already been broken or put down, (a) above shall apply to any stump or stumps still in the ground. Any fielder may replace a stump or stumps, in accordance with 3 above, in order to have an opportunity of putting the wicket down.

LAW 29.   BATSMAN OUT OF HIS GROUND

1. When Out of His Ground

A batsman shall be considered to be out of his ground unless his bat or some part of his person is grounded behind the popping crease at that end.

2. Which is a Batsman's Ground?

(a) If only one batsman is within a ground:

      (i) it is his ground.

      (ii) it remains his ground even if he is later joined there by the other batsman.

(b) If both batsmen are in the same ground and one of them subsequently leaves it, (a)(i) above applies.

(c) If there is no batsman in either ground, then each ground belongs to whichever of the batsmen is nearer to it, or, if the batsmen are level, to whichever was nearer to it immediately prior to their drawing level.

(d) If a ground belongs to one batsman, then, unless there is a striker with a runner, the other ground belongs to the other batsman irrespective of his position.

(e) When a batsman with a runner is striker, his ground is always that at the wicket-keeper's end. However, (a), (b), (c) and (d) above will still apply, but only to the runner and the non-striker, so that that ground will also belong to either the non-striker or the runner, as the case may be.

3. Position of Non-Striker

The batsman at the bowler's end should be positioned on the opposite side of the wicket to that from which the ball is being delivered, unless a request to do otherwise is granted by the umpire.

LAW 30. BOWLED

1. Out Bowled

(a) The striker is out *Bowled* if his wicket is put down by a ball delivered by the bowler, not being a no-ball, even if it first touches his bat or person.

(b) Notwithstanding (a) above he shall not be out Bowled if before striking the wicket the ball has been in contact with any other player or with an umpire. He will, however, be subject to Laws 33 (Handled the Ball), 37 (Obstructing the Field), 38 (Run Out) and 39 (Stumped).

2. Bowled to Take Precedence

The striker is out *Bowled* if his wicket is put down as in 1 above, even though a decision against him for any other method of dismissal would be justified.

LAW 31. TIMED OUT

1. Out Timed Out

(a) Unless "Time" has been called, the incoming batsman must be in position to take guard or for his partner to be ready to receive the next ball within three minutes of the fall of the previous wicket. If this requirement is not met, the incoming batsman will be out, *Timed Out*.

(b) In the event of protracted delay in which no batsman comes to the wicket, the umpires shall adopt the procedure of Law 21.3 (Umpires awarding a match). For the purposes of that Law the start of the action shall be taken as the expiry of the three minutes referred to above.

2. Bowler Does Not Get Credit

The bowler does not get credit for the wicket.

LAW 32. CAUGHT

1. Out Caught

The striker is out *Caught* if a ball delivered by the bowler, not being a no-ball, touches his bat without having previously been in contact with any member of the fielding side and is subsequently held by a fielder as a fair catch before it touches the ground.

2. Caught to Take Precedence

If the criteria of 1 above are met and the striker is not out Bowled, then he is out Caught, even though a decision against either batsman for another method of dismissal would be justified. Runs completed by the batsmen before the completion of the catch will not be scored. Note also Laws 21.6 (Winning Hit or Extras) and 42.17(b) (Penalty Runs).

3. A Fair Catch

A catch shall be considered to have been fairly made if:

(a) throughout the act of making the catch:

(i) any fielder in contact with the ball is within the field of play. See 4 below.

(ii) the ball is at no time in contact with any object grounded beyond the boundary.

The act of making the catch shall start from the time when a fielder first handles the ball and shall end when a fielder obtains complete control over the ball and over his own movements.

(b) the ball is hugged to the body of the catcher or accidentally lodges in his clothing or, in the case of the wicket-keeper, in his pads. However, it is not a fair catch if the ball lodges in a protective helmet worn by a fielder. See Law 23 (Dead Ball).

(c) The ball does not touch the ground, even though the hand holding it does so in effecting the catch.

(d) a fielder catches the ball after it has been lawfully struck more than once by the striker, but only if the ball has not touched the ground since first being struck.

(e) a fielder catches the ball after it has touched an umpire, another fielder or the other batsman. However, it is not a fair catch if the ball has touched a protective helmet worn by a fielder, although the ball remains in play.

(f) a fielder catches the ball in the air after it has crossed the boundary provided that:

(i) he has no part of his person touching, or grounded beyond, the boundary at any time when he is in contact with the ball.

(ii) the ball has not been grounded beyond the boundary. See Law 19.3 (Scoring a Boundary).

(g) the ball is caught off an obstruction within the boundary, provided it has not previously been decided to regard the obstruction as a boundary.

4. Fielder Within the Field of Play

(a) A fielder is not within the field of play if he touches the boundary or has any part of his person grounded beyond the boundary. See Law 19.3 (Scoring a Boundary).

(b) six runs shall be scored if a fielder:

(i) has any part of his person touching, or grounded beyond, the boundary when he catches the ball.

(ii) catches the ball and subsequently touches the boundary or grounds some part of his person over the boundary while carrying the ball but before completing the catch.

See Laws 19.3 (Scoring a Boundary) and 19.4 (Runs Allowed for Boundaries).

5. No Runs to Be Scored

If the striker is dismissed Caught, runs from that delivery completed by the batsmen before the completion of the catch shall not be scored, but any penalties awarded to either side when the ball is dead, if applicable, will stand. Law 18.12(a) (Batsman Returning to Wicket He Has Left) shall apply from the instant of the catch.

LAW 33.   HANDLED THE BALL

1. Out Handled the Ball

Either batsman is out *Handled the Ball* if he wilfully touches the ball while in play with a hand or hands not holding the bat unless he does so with the consent of the opposing side.

2. Not Out Handled the Ball

Notwithstanding 1 above, a batsman will not be out under this Law if:

(i) he handles the ball in order to avoid injury.

(ii) he uses his hand or hands to return the ball to any member of the fielding side without the consent of that side. Note, however, the provisions of Law 37.4 (Returning the Ball To a Member of the Fielding Side).

3. Runs Scored

If either batsman is dismissed under this Law, any runs completed before the offence, together with any penalty extras and the penalty for a no-ball or wide, if applicable, shall be scored. See Laws 18.10 (Runs Scored When a Batsman is Dismissed) and 42.17 (Penalty runs).

4. Bowler Does Not Get Credit

The bowler does not get credit for the wicket.

LAW 34.   HIT THE BALL TWICE

1. Out Hit the Ball Twice

(a) The striker is out *Hit The Ball Twice* if, while the ball is in play, it strikes any part of his person or is struck by his bat and, before the ball has been touched by a fielder, he wilfully strikes it again with his bat or person, other than a hand not holding the bat, except for the sole purpose of guarding his wicket. See 3 below and Laws 33 (Handled the Ball) and 37 (Obstructing the Field).

(b) For the purpose of this Law, "struck" or "strike" shall include contact with the person of the striker.

2. Not Out Hit the Ball Twice

Notwithstanding 1(a) above, the striker will not be out under this Law if:

(i) he makes a second or subsequent stroke in order to return the ball to any member of the fielding side. Note, however, the provisions of Law 37.4 (Returning the Ball to a Member of the Fielding Side).

(ii) he wilfully strikes the ball after it has touched a fielder. Note, however, the provisions of Law 37.1 (Out Obstructing the Field).

3. Ball Lawfully Struck More Than Once

Solely in order to guard his wicket and before the ball has been touched by a fielder, the striker may lawfully strike the ball more than once with his bat or with any part of his person other than a hand not holding the bat.

Notwithstanding this provision, the striker may not prevent the ball from being caught by making more than one stroke in defence of his wicket. See Law 37.3 (Obstructing a Ball from Being Caught).

4. Runs Permitted from Ball Lawfully Struck More Than Once

When the ball is lawfully struck more than once, as permitted in 3 above, only the first strike is to be considered in determining whether runs are to be allowed and how they are to be scored.

(a) If on the first strike the umpire is satisfied that either

(i) the ball first struck the bat, or

(ii) the striker attempted to play the ball with his bat, or

(iii) the striker tried to avoid being hit by the ball

then any penalties to the batting side that are applicable shall be allowed.

(b) If the conditions in (a) above are met then, if they result from overthrows, and only if they result from overthrows, runs completed by the batsmen or a boundary will be allowed in addition to any penalties that are applicable. They shall be credited to the striker if the first strike was with the bat. If the first strike was on the person of the striker they shall be scored as leg-byes or no-ball extras, as appropriate. See Law 26.2 (Leg-Byes).

(c) If the conditions of (a) above are met and there is no overthrow until after the batsmen have started to run, but before one run is completed:

(i) only subsequent completed runs or a boundary shall be allowed. The first run shall count as a completed run for this purpose only if the batsmen have not crossed at the instant of the throw.

(ii) if in these circumstances the ball goes to the boundary from the throw then, notwithstanding the provisions of Law 19.6 (Overthrow or Wilful Act of Fielder), only the boundary allowance shall be scored.

(iii) if the ball goes to the boundary as the result of a further overthrow, then runs completed by the batsmen after the first throw and before this final throw shall be added to the boundary allowance. The run in progress at the first throw will count only if they have not crossed at that moment; the run in progress at the final throw shall count only if they have crossed at that moment. Law 18.12 (Batsman Returning to Wicket He Has Left) shall apply as from the moment of the final throw.

(d) If, in the opinion of the umpire, none of the conditions in (a) above have been met then, whether there is an overthrow or not, the batting side shall not be credited with any runs from that delivery apart from the penalty for a no-ball if applicable. Moreover, no other penalties shall be awarded to the batting side when the ball is dead. See Law 42.17 (Penalty Runs).

5. Ball Lawfully Struck More Than Once – Action By The Umpire

If no runs are to be allowed, either in the circumstances of 4(d) above, or because there has been no overthrow and:

(a) if no run is attempted but the ball reaches the boundary, the umpire shall call and signal "Dead ball" and disallow the boundary.

(b) if the batsmen run and:

    (i) neither batsman is dismissed and the ball does not become dead for any other reason, the umpire shall call and signal Dead Ball as soon as one run is completed or the ball reaches the boundary. The batsmen shall return to their original ends. The run or boundary shall be disallowed.

    (ii) a batsman is dismissed, or if for any other reason the ball becomes dead before one run is completed or the ball reaches the boundary, all the provisions of the Laws will apply except that the award of penalties to the batting side shall be as laid down in 4(a) or 4(d) above as appropriate.

6. Bowler Does Not Get Credit

The bowler does not get credit for the wicket.

LAW 35.   HIT WICKET

1. Out Hit Wicket

(a) The striker is out *Hit Wicket* if, after the bowler has entered his delivery stride and while the ball is in play, his wicket is put down either by the striker's bat or person as described in Law 28.1(a)(ii) and (iii) (Wicket Put Down) either:

    (i) in the course of any action taken by him in preparing to receive or in receiving a delivery, or

    (ii) in setting off for his first run immediately after playing, or playing at, the ball, or

    (iii) if he makes no attempt to play the ball, in setting off for his first run, providing that in the opinion of the umpire this is immediately after he has had the opportunity of playing the ball, or

    (iv) in lawfully making a second or further stroke for the purpose of guarding his wicket within the provisions of Law 34.3 (Ball Lawfully Struck More Than Once).

(b) If the striker puts his wicket down in any of the ways described in Law 28.1(a)(ii) and (iii) (Wicket Put Down) before the bowler has entered his delivery stride, either umpire shall call and signal "Dead ball".

2. Not Out Hit Wicket

Notwithstanding 1 above, the batsman is not out under this Law should his wicket be put down in any of the ways referred to in 1 above if:

(a) it occurs after he has completed any action in receiving the delivery, other than as in 1(a)(ii), (iii) or (iv) above.

(b) it occurs when he is in the act of running, other than in setting off immediately for his first run.

(c) it occurs when he is trying to avoid being run out or stumped.

(d) it occurs while he is trying to avoid a throw-in at any time.

(e) the bowler, after entering his delivery stride, does not deliver the ball. In this case either umpire shall immediately call and signal "Dead ball". See Law 23.3 (Umpire Calling and Signalling "Dead ball").

(f) the delivery is a no-ball.

LAW 36.   LEG BEFORE WICKET

1. Out LBW

The striker is out *LBW* in the circumstances set out below.

(a) The bowler delivers a ball, not being a no-ball and

(b) the ball, if it is not intercepted full pitch, pitches in line between wicket and wicket or on the off side of the striker's wicket, and

(c) the ball not having previously touched his bat, the striker intercepts the ball, either full-pitch or after pitching, with any part of his person, and

(d) the point of impact, even if above the level of the bails, either

(i) between wicket and wicket, or

(ii) is either between wicket and wicket or outside the line of the off stump, if the striker has made no genuine attempt to play the ball with his bat, and

(e) but for the interception, the ball would have hit the wicket.

2. Interception of the Ball

(a) In assessing points (c), (d) and (e) in 1 above, only the first interception is to be considered.

(b) In assessing point (e) in 1 above, it is to be assumed that the path of the ball before interception would have continued after interception, irrespective of whether the ball might have pitched subsequently or not.

3. Off Side of Wicket

The off side of the striker's wicket shall be determined by the striker's stance at the moment the ball comes into play for that delivery.

LAW 37.   OBSTRUCTING THE FIELD

1. Out Obstructing the Field

Either batsman is out *Obstructing the Field* if he wilfully obstructs or distracts the opposing side by word or action. It shall be regarded as obstruction if either batsman wilfully, and without the consent of the fielding side, strikes the ball with his bat or person, other than a hand not holding the bat, after the ball has touched a fielder. See 4 below.

2. Accidental Obstruction

It is for either umpire to decide whether any obstruction or distraction is wilful or not. He shall consult the other umpire if he has any doubt.

3. Obstructing a Ball from Being Caught

The striker is out should wilful obstruction or distraction by either batsman prevent a catch being made.

This shall apply even though the striker causes the obstruction in lawfully guarding his wicket under the provisions of Law 34.3 (Ball lawfully struck more than once).

4. Returning the Ball to a Member of the Fielding Side

Either batsman is out under this Law if, without the consent of the fielding side and while the ball is in play, he uses his bat or person to return the ball to any member of that side.

5. Runs Scored

If a batsman is dismissed under this Law, runs completed by the batsmen before the offence shall be scored, together with the penalty for a no-ball or a wide, if applicable. Other penalties that may be awarded to either side when the ball is dead shall also stand. See Law 42.17(b) (Penalty Runs).

If, however, the obstruction prevents a catch from being made, runs completed by the batsmen before the offence shall not be scored, but other penalties that may be awarded to either side when the ball is dead shall stand. See Law 42.17(b) (Penalty Runs).

6. Bowler Does Not Get Credit

The bowler does not get credit for the wicket.

LAW 38.   RUN OUT

1. Out Run Out

(a) Either batsman is out *Run Out*, except as in 2 below, if at any time while the ball is in play

   (i) he is out of his ground and

   (ii) his wicket is fairly put down by the opposing side.

(b) (a) above shall apply even though "No-ball" has been called and whether or not a run is being attempted, except in the circumstances of Law 39.3(b) (Not Out Stumped).

2. Batsman Not Run Out

Notwithstanding 1 above, a batsman is not out Run out if:

(a) he has been within his ground and has subsequently left it to avoid injury, when the wicket is put down.

(b) the ball has not subsequently been touched again by a fielder, after the bowler has entered his delivery stride, before the wicket is put down.

(c) the ball, having been played by the striker, or having come off his person, directly strikes a helmet worn by a fielder and without further contact with him or any other fielder rebounds directly on to the wicket. However, the ball remains in play and either batsman may be Run out in the circumstances of 1 above if a wicket is subsequently put down.

(d) he is out Stumped. See Law 39.1(b) (Out Stumped).

(e) he is out of his ground, not attempting a run and his wicket is fairly put down by the wicket-keeper without the intervention of another member of the fielding side, if "No-ball" has been called. See Law 39.3(b) (Not Out Stumped).

3. Which Batsman is Out

The batsman out in the circumstances of 1 above is the one whose ground is at the end where the wicket is put down. See Laws 2.8 (Transgression of the Laws by a Batsman Who Has a Runner) and 29.2 (Which is a Batsman's Ground).

4. Runs Scored

If a batsman is dismissed Run Out, the batting side shall score the runs completed before the dismissal, together with the penalty for a no-ball or a wide, if applicable. Other penalties to either side that may be awarded when the ball is dead shall also stand. See Law 42.17 (Penalty Runs).

If, however, a striker with a runner is himself dismissed Run Out, runs completed by the runner and the other batsman before the dismissal shall not be scored. The penalty for a no-ball or a wide and any other penalties to either side that may be awarded when the ball is dead shall stand. See Laws 2.8 (Transgression of the Laws by a Batsman Who Has a Runner) and 42.17(b) (Penalty Runs).

5. Bowler Does Not Get Credit

The bowler does not get credit for the wicket.

LAW 39. STUMPED

1. Out Stumped

(a) The striker is out *Stumped* if

(i) he is out of his ground, and

(ii) he is receiving a ball which is not a no-ball, and

(iii) he is not attempting a run, and

(iv) his wicket is put down by the wicket-keeper without the intervention of another member of the fielding side. Note Law 40.3 (Position of Wicket-Keeper).

(b) The striker is out Stumped if all the conditions of (a) above are satisfied, even though a decision of Run Out would be justified.

2. Ball Rebounding from Wicket-Keeper's Person

(a) If the wicket is put down by the ball, it shall be regarded as having been put down by the wicket-keeper if the ball

(i) rebounds on to the stumps from any part of his person or equipment, other than a protective helmet, or

(ii) has been kicked or thrown on to the stumps by the wicket-keeper.

(b) If the ball touches a helmet worn by the wicket-keeper, the ball is still in play but the striker shall not be out Stumped. He will, however, be liable to be Run Out in these circumstances if there is subsequent contact between the ball and any member of the fielding side. Note, however, 3 below.

3. Not Out Stumped

(a) If the striker is not out Stumped, he is liable to be out Run Out if the conditions of Law 38 (Run Out) apply, except as set out in (b) below.

(b) The striker shall not be out Run Out if he is out of his ground, not attempting a run, and his wicket is fairly put down by the wicket-keeper without the intervention of another member of the fielding side, if "No-ball" has been called.

LAW 40. THE WICKET-KEEPER

1. Protective Equipment

The wicket-keeper is the only member of the fielding side permitted to wear gloves and external leg guards. If he does so, these are to be regarded as part of his person for the purposes of Law 41.2 (Fielding the Ball). If by his actions and positioning it is apparent to the umpires that he will not be able to discharge his duties as a wicket-keeper, he shall forfeit this right and also the right to be recognised as a wicket-keeper for the purposes of Laws 32.3 (A Fair Catch), 39 (Stumped), 41.1 (Protective Equipment), 41.5 (Limitation of On Side Fielders) and 41.6 (Fielders Not to Encroach on the Pitch).

2. Gloves

If, as permitted under 1 above, the wicket-keeper wears gloves, they shall have no webbing between fingers except joining index finger and thumb, where webbing may be inserted as a means of support. If used, the webbing shall be:

(a) a single piece of non-stretch material which, although it may have facing material attached, shall have no reinforcement or tucks.

(b) such that the top edge of the webbing:

(i) does not protrude beyond the straight line joining the top of the index finger to the top of the thumb.

(ii) is taut when a hand wearing the glove has the thumb fully extended.

3. Position of Wicket-Keeper

The wicket-keeper shall remain wholly behind the wicket at the striker's end from the moment the ball comes into play until

(a) a ball delivered by the bowler either:

(i) touches the bat or person of the striker, or

(ii) passes the wicket at the striker's end

or

(b) the striker attempts a run.

In the event of the wicket-keeper contravening this Law, the umpire at the striker's end shall call and signal "No-ball" as soon as possible after the delivery of the ball.

4. Movement By the Wicket-Keeper

It is unfair if a wicket-keeper standing back makes a significant movement towards the wicket after the ball comes into play and before it reaches the striker. In the event of such unfair movement by the wicket-keeper, either umpire shall call and signal "Dead ball". It will not be considered a significant movement if the wicket-keeper moves a few paces forward for a slower delivery.

5. Restriction on Actions of Wicket-Keeper

If in the opinion of either umpire the wicket-keeper interferes with the striker's right to play the ball and to guard his wicket, Law 23.3(b)(vi) (Umpire Calling and Signalling "Dead ball") shall apply. If, however, the umpire concerned considers that the interference by the wicket-keeper was wilful, then Law 42.4 (Deliberate Attempt to Distract Striker) shall apply.

6. Interference with Wicket-Keeper by Striker

If, in playing at the ball or in the legitimate defence of his wicket, the striker interferes with the wicket-keeper, he shall not be out, except as provided for in Law 37.3 (Obstructing a Ball from Being Caught).

LAW 41. THE FIELDER

1. Protective Equipment

No member of the fielding side other than the wicket-keeper shall be permitted to wear gloves or external leg guards. In addition, protection for the hand or fingers may be worn only with the consent of the umpires.

2. Fielding the Ball

A fielder may field the ball with any part of his person but if, while the ball is in play he wilfully fields it otherwise:

(a) the ball shall become dead and 5 penalty runs shall be awarded to the batting side. See Law 42.17 (Penalty Runs). The ball shall not count as one of the over.

(b) the umpire shall inform the other umpire, the captain of the fielding side, the batsmen and, as soon as practicable, the captain of the batting side of what has occurred.

(c) the umpires together shall report the occurrence as soon as possible to the Executive of the fielding side and any governing body responsible for the match who shall take such action as is considered appropriate against the captain and player concerned.

3. Protective Helmets Belonging to the Fielding Side

Protective helmets, when not in use by fielders, shall only be placed, if above the surface, on the ground behind the wicket-keeper and in line with both sets of stumps. If a helmet belonging to the fielding side is on the ground within the field of play, and the ball while in play strikes it, the ball shall become dead. Five penalty runs shall then be awarded to the batting side. See Laws 18.11 (Runs Scored When Ball Becomes Dead) and 42.17 (Penalty Runs).

4. Penalty Runs Not Being Awarded

Notwithstanding 2 and 3 above, if from the delivery by the bowler the ball first struck the person of the striker and if, in the opinion of the umpire, the striker neither

    (i) attempted to play the ball with his bat, nor

    (ii) tried to avoid being hit by the ball,

then no award of five penalty runs shall be made and no other runs or penalties shall be credited to the batting side except the penalty for a "No-ball" if applicable. See Law 26.3 (Leg-Byes Not to Be Awarded).

5. Limitation of On-Side Fielders

At the instant of the bowler's delivery there shall not be more than two fielders, other than the wicket-keeper, behind the popping crease on the on side. A fielder will be considered to be behind the popping crease unless the whole of his person, whether grounded or in the air, is in front of this line. In the event of infringement of this Law by the fielding side, the umpire at the striker's end shall call and signal "No-ball".

6. Fielders Not to Encroach on the Pitch

While the ball is in play and until the ball has made contact with the bat or person of the striker, or has passed the striker's bat, no fielder, other than the bowler, may have any part of his person grounded on or extended over the pitch. In the event of infringement of this Law by any fielder other than the wicket-keeper, the umpire at the bowler's end shall call and signal "No-ball" as soon as possible after the delivery of the ball. Note, however, Law 40.3 (Position of Wicket-Keeper).

7. Movement by Fielders

Any significant movement by any fielder after the ball comes into play and before the ball reaches the striker is unfair. In the event of such unfair movement, either umpire shall call and signal "Dead ball". Note also the provisions of Law 42.4 (Deliberate Attempt to Distract Striker).

8. Definition of Significant Movement

    (a) For close fielders anything other than minor adjustments to stance or position in relation to the striker is significant.

    (b) In the outfield, fielders are permitted to move in towards the striker or striker's wicket, provided that 5 above is not contravened. Anything other than slight movement off line or away from the striker is to be considered significant.

    (c) For restrictions on movement by the wicket-keeper see Law 40.4 (Movement By Wicket-Keeper).

LAW 42.   FAIR AND UNFAIR PLAY

1. Fair and Unfair Play – Responsibility of Captains

The responsibility lies with the captains for ensuring that play is conducted within the spirit and traditions of the game, as described in The Preamble – The Spirit of Cricket, as well as within the Laws.

2. Fair and Unfair Play – Responsibility of Umpires

The umpires shall be the sole judges of fair and unfair play. If either umpire considers an action, not covered by the Laws, to be unfair, he shall intervene without appeal and, if the ball is in play, shall call and signal "Dead-ball" and implement the procedure as set out in 18 below. Otherwise the umpires shall not interfere with the progress of play, except as required to do so by the Laws.

3. The Match Ball – Changing Its Condition

    (a) Any fielder may:

        (i) polish the ball provided that no artificial substance is used and that such polishing wastes no time.

        (ii) remove mud from the ball under the supervision of the umpire.

        (iii) dry a wet ball on a towel.

(b) It is unfair for anyone to rub the ball on the ground for any reason, interfere with any of the seams or the surface of the ball, use any implement, or take any other action whatsoever which is likely to alter the condition of the ball, except as permitted in (a) above.

(c) The umpires shall make frequent and irregular inspections of the ball.

(d) In the event of any fielder changing the condition of the ball unfairly, as set out in (b) above, the umpires after consultation shall:

    (i) change the ball forthwith. It shall be for the umpires to decide on the replacement ball, which shall, in their opinion, have had wear comparable with that which the previous ball had received immediately prior to the contravention.

    (ii) inform the batsmen that the ball has been changed.

    (iii) award five penalty runs to the batting side. See 17 below.

    (iv) inform the captain of the fielding side that the reason for the action was the unfair interference with the ball.

    (v) inform the captain of the batting side as soon as practicable of what has occurred.

    (vi) report the occurrence as soon as possible to the executive of the fielding side and any governing body responsible for the match, who shall take such action as is considered appropriate against the captain and team concerned.

(e) If there is any further instance of unfairly changing the condition of the ball in that innings, the umpires after consultation shall:

    (i) repeat the procedure in (d)(i), (ii) and (iii) above.

    (ii) inform the captain of the fielding side of the reason for the action taken and direct him to take off forthwith the bowler who delivered the immediately preceding ball. The bowler thus taken off shall not be allowed to bowl again in that innings.

    (iii) inform the captain of the batting side as soon as practicable of what has occurred.

    (iv) report the occurrence as soon as possible to the executive of the fielding side and any governing body responsible for the match, who shall take such action as is considered appropriate against the captain and team concerned.

4. Deliberate Attempt to Distract Striker

It is unfair for any member of the fielding side deliberately to attempt to distract the striker while he is preparing to receive or receiving a delivery.

(a) If either umpire considers that any action by a member of the fielding side is such an attempt, at the first instance he shall:

    (i) immediately call and signal "Dead ball".

    (ii) warn the captain of the fielding side that the action is unfair and indicate that this is a first and final warning.

    (iii) inform the other umpire and the batsmen of what has occurred. Neither batsman shall be dismissed from that delivery and the ball shall not count as one of the over.

(b) If there is any further such deliberate attempt in that innings, by any member of the fielding side, the procedures, other than warning, as set out in (a) above shall apply. Additionally, the umpire at the bowler's end shall:

    (i) award five penalty runs to the batting side. See 17 below.

    (ii) inform the captain of the fielding side of the reason for this action and, as soon as practicable, inform the captain of the batting side.

    (iii) report the occurrence, together with the other umpire, as soon as possible to the executive of the fielding side and any governing body responsible for the match, who shall take such action as is considered appropriate against the captain and player or players concerned.

5. Deliberate Distraction or Obstruction of Batsman

In addition to 4 above, it is unfair for any member of the fielding side, by word or action, wilfully to attempt to distract or to obstruct either batsman after the striker has received the ball.

(a) It is for either one of the umpires to decide whether any distraction or obstruction is wilful or not.

(b) If either umpire considers that a member of the fielding side has wilfully caused or attempted to cause such a distraction or obstruction he shall

    (i) immediately call and signal "Dead ball".

    (ii) inform the captain of the fielding side and the other umpire of the reason for the call.

Additionally,

    (iii) neither batsman shall be dismissed from that delivery.

    (iv) five penalty runs shall be awarded to the batting side. See 17 below. In this instance, the run in progress shall be scored, whether or not the batsmen had crossed at the instant of the call. See Law 18.11 (Runs Scored When Ball Becomes Dead).

    (v) the umpire at the bowler's end shall inform the captain of the fielding side of the reason for this action and, as soon as practicable, inform the captain of the batting side.

    (vi) the ball shall not count as one of the over.

    (vii) the batsmen at the wicket shall decide which of them is to face the next delivery.

    (viii) the umpires shall report the occurrence as soon as possible to the executive of the fielding side and any governing body responsible for the match, who shall take such action as is considered appropriate against the captain and player or players concerned.

6. Dangerous and Unfair Bowling

(a) Bowling of Fast Short-Pitched Balls

    (i) The bowling of fast short-pitched balls is dangerous and unfair if the umpire at the bowler's end considers that by their repetition and taking into account their length, height and direction they are likely to inflict physical injury on the striker, irrespective of the protective equipment he may be wearing. The relative skill of the striker shall be taken into consideration.

    (ii) Any delivery which, after pitching, passes or would have passed over head height of the striker standing upright at the crease, although not threatening physical injury, shall be included with bowling under (i) both when the umpire is considering whether the bowling of fast short-pitched balls has become dangerous and unfair and after he has so decided. The umpire shall call and signal "No-ball" for each such delivery.

(b) Bowling of High Full-Pitched Balls

    (i) Any delivery, other than a slow paced one, which passes or would have passed on the full above waist height of the striker standing upright at the crease is to be deemed dangerous and unfair, whether or not it is likely to inflict physical injury on the striker.

    (ii) a slow delivery which passes or would have passed on the full above shoulder height of the striker standing upright at the crease is to be deemed dangerous and unfair, whether or not it is likely to inflict physical injury on the striker.

7. Dangerous and Unfair Bowling – Action by the Umpire

(a) As soon as the umpire at the bowler's end decides under 6(a) above that the bowling of fast short-pitched balls has become dangerous and unfair, or, except as in 8 below, there is an instance of dangerous and unfair bowling as defined in 6(b) above, he shall call and signal "No-ball" and, when the ball is dead, caution the bowler, inform the other umpire, the captain of the fielding side and the batsmen of what has occurred. This caution shall continue to apply throughout the innings.

(b) If there is any further instance of such dangerous and unfair bowling by the same bowler in the same innings, the umpire at the bowler's end shall repeat the above procedure and indicate to the bowler that this is a final warning. Both the above caution and final warning shall continue to apply even though the bowler may later change ends.

(c) Should there be any further repetition by the same bowler in that innings, the umpire shall:

    (i) call and signal "No-ball".

    (ii) direct the captain, when the ball is dead, to take the bowler off forthwith. The over shall be completed by another bowler, who shall neither have bowled the previous over nor be allowed to bowl the next over. The bowler thus taken off shall not be allowed to bowl again in that innings.

    (iii) report the occurrence to the other umpire, the batsmen and, as soon as practicable, the captain of the batting side.

    (iv) report the occurrence, with the other umpire, as soon as possible to the Executive of the fielding side and to any governing body responsible for the match, who shall take such action as is considered appropriate against the captain and bowler concerned.

8. Deliberate Bowling of High Full-Pitched Balls

If the umpire considers that a high full pitch which is deemed to be dangerous and unfair, as defined in 6(b) above, was deliberately bowled, then the caution and warning prescribed in 7 above shall be dispensed with. The umpire shall:

(a) call and signal "No-ball".

(b) direct the captain, when the ball is dead, to take the bowler off forthwith.

(c) implement the remainder of the procedure as laid down in 7(c) above.

9. Time-Wasting by the Fielding Side

It is unfair for any member of the fielding side to waste time.

(a) If the captain of the fielding side wastes time, or allows any member of his side to waste time, or if the progress of an over is unnecessarily slow, at the first instance the umpire shall call and signal "Dead ball" if necessary and

    (i) warn the captain, and indicate that this is a first and final warning.

    (ii) inform the other umpire and the batsmen of what has occurred.

(b) If there is any further waste of time in that innings, by any member of the fielding side, the umpire shall either

    (i) if the waste of time is not during the course of an over, award five penalty runs to the batting side. See 17 below, or

    (ii) if the waste of time is during the course of an over, when the ball is dead, direct the captain to take the bowler off forthwith. If applicable, the over shall be completed by another bowler, who shall neither have bowled the previous over nor be allowed to bowl the next over. The bowler thus taken off shall not be allowed to bowl again in that innings.

    (iii) inform the other umpire, the batsmen and, as soon as practicable, the captain of the batting side of what has occurred.

    (iv) report the occurrence, with the other umpire, as soon as possible to the executive of the fielding side and to any governing body responsible for the match, who shall take such action as is considered appropriate against the captain and team concerned.

10. Batsman Wasting Time

It is unfair for a batsman to waste time. In normal circumstances the striker should always be ready to take strike when the bowler is ready to start his run-up.

(a) Should either batsman waste time by failing to meet this requirement, or in any other way, the following procedure shall be adopted. At the first instance, either before the bowler starts his run-up or when the ball is dead, as appropriate, the umpire shall:

    (i) warn the batsman and indicate that this is a first and final warning. This warning shall continue to apply throughout the innings. The umpire shall so inform each incoming batsman.

    (ii) inform the other umpire, the other batsman and the captain of the fielding side of what has occurred.

    (iii) inform the captain of the batting side as soon as practicable.

(b) if there is any further time wasting by any batsman in that innings, the umpire shall, at the appropriate time while the ball is dead:

    (i) award five penalty runs to the fielding side. See 17 below.

    (ii) inform the other umpire, the other batsman, the captain of the fielding side and, as soon as practicable, the captain of the batting side of what has occurred.

    (iii) report the occurrence, with the other umpire, as soon as possible to the executive of the batting side and to any governing body responsible for the match, who shall take such action as is considered appropriate against the captain and player or players and, if appropriate, the team concerned.

11. Damaging the Pitch – Area to be Protected

(a) It is incumbent on all players to avoid unnecessary damage to the pitch. It is unfair for any player to cause deliberate damage to the pitch.

(b) An area of the pitch, to be referred to as "the protected area", is defined as that area contained within a rectangle bounded at each end by imaginary lines parallel to the popping creases and 5ft/1.52m in front of each and on the sides by imaginary lines, one each side of the imaginary line joining the centres of the two middle stumps, each parallel to it and 1ft/30.48cm from it.

12. Bowler Running on the Protected Area After Delivering the Ball

(a) If the bowler, after delivering the ball, runs on the protected area as defined in 11(b) above, the umpire shall at the first instance, and when the ball is dead:

    (i) caution the bowler. This caution shall continue to apply throughout the innings.

    (ii) inform the other umpire, the captain of the fielding side and the batsmen of what has occurred.

(b) If, in that innings, the same bowler runs on the protected area again after delivering the ball, the umpire shall repeat the above procedure, indicating that this is a final warning.

(c) If, in that innings, the same bowler runs on the protected area a third time after delivering the ball, when the ball is dead the umpire shall:

    (i) direct the captain of the fielding side to take the bowler off forthwith. If applicable, the over shall be completed by another bowler, who shall neither have bowled the previous over nor be allowed to bowl the next over. The bowler thus taken off shall not be allowed to bowl again in that innings.

    (ii) inform the other umpire, the batsmen and, as soon as practicable, the captain of the batting side of what has occurred.

    (iii) report the occurrence, with the other umpire, as soon as possible to the executive of the fielding side and to any governing body responsible for the match, who shall take such action as is considered appropriate against the captain and bowler concerned.

13. Fielder Damaging the Pitch

(a) If any fielder causes avoidable damage to the pitch, other than as in 12(a) above, at the first instance the umpire shall, when the ball is dead:

    (i) caution the captain of the fielding side, indicating that this is a first and final warning. This caution shall continue to apply throughout the innings.

    (ii) inform the other umpire and the batsmen.

(b) If there is any further avoidable damage to the pitch by any fielder in that innings, the umpire shall, when the ball is dead:

      (i) award five penalty runs to the batting side. See 17 below.

      (ii) inform the other umpire, the batsmen, the captain of the fielding side and, as soon as practicable, the captain of the batting side of what has occurred.

      (iii) report the occurrence, with the other umpire, as soon as possible to the executive of the fielding side and any governing body responsible for the match, who shall take such action as is considered appropriate against the captain and player or players concerned.

14. Batsman Damaging the Pitch

(a) If either batsman causes avoidable damage to the pitch, at the first instance the umpire shall, when the ball is dead:

      (i) caution the batsman. This caution shall continue to apply throughout the innings. The umpire shall so inform each incoming batsman.

      (ii) inform the other umpire, the other batsman, the captain of the fielding side and, as soon as practicable, the captain of the batting side.

(b) If there is a second instance of avoidable damage to the pitch by any batsman in that innings:

      (i) the umpire shall repeat the above procedure, indicating that this is a final warning.

      (ii) additionally he shall disallow all runs to the batting side from that delivery other than the penalty for a no-ball or a wide, if applicable. The batsmen shall return to their original ends.

(c) If there is any further avoidable damage to the pitch by any batsman in that innings, the umpire shall, when the ball is dead:

      (i) disallow all runs to the batting side from that delivery other than the penalty for a no-ball or a wide, if applicable.

      (ii) additionally award five penalty runs to the fielding side. See 17 below.

      (iii) inform the other umpire, the other batsman, the captain of the fielding side and, as soon as practicable, the captain of the batting side of what has occurred.

      (iv) report the occurrence, with the other umpire, as soon as possible to the executive of the batting side and any governing body responsible for the match, who shall take such action as is considered appropriate against the captain and player or players concerned.

15. Bowler Attempting to Run Out Non-Striker Before Delivery

The bowler is permitted, before entering his delivery stride, to attempt to run out the non-striker. The ball shall not count in the over. The umpire shall call and signal "Dead ball" as soon as possible if the bowler fails in the attempt to run out the non-striker.

16. Batsmen Stealing a Run

It is unfair for the batsmen to attempt to steal a run during the bowler's run up. Unless the bowler attempts to run out either batsman – see 15 above and Law 24.4 (Bowler Throwing Towards Striker's End Before Delivery) – the umpire shall:

      (i) call and signal "Dead ball" as soon as the batsmen cross in any such attempt.

      (ii) return the batsmen to their original ends.

      (iii) award five penalty runs to the fielding side. See 17 below.

      (iv) inform the other umpire, the batsmen, the captain of the fielding side and, as soon as practicable, the captain of the batting side of the reason for the action taken.

      (v) report the occurrence, with the other umpire, as soon as possible to the executive of the batting side and any governing body responsible for the match, who shall take such action as is considered appropriate against the captain and player or players concerned.

17. Penalty Runs

(a) When penalty runs are awarded to either side, when the ball is dead the umpire shall signal the penalty runs to the scorers as laid down in Law 3.14 (Signals).

(b) Notwithstanding the provisions of Law 21.6 (Winning Hit or Extras), penalty runs shall be awarded in each case where the Laws require the award. Note, however, that restrictions on awarding penalty runs in Laws 26.3 (Leg-Byes Not to Be Awarded), 34.4(d) (Runs Permitted From Ball Struck Lawfully More Than Once) and Law 41.4 (Penalty Runs Not to Be Awarded) will apply.

(c) When five penalty runs are awarded to the batting side, under either Law 2.6 (Player Returning Without Permission) or Law 41 (The Fielder) or under 3, 4, 5, 9 or 13 above, then:

   (i) they shall be scored as penalty extras and shall be in addition to any other penalties.

   (ii) they shall not be regarded as runs scored from either the immediately preceding delivery or the following delivery, and shall be in addition to any runs from those deliveries.

   (iii) the batsmen shall not change ends solely by reason of the five-run penalty.

(d) When five penalty runs are awarded to the fielding side, under Law 18.5(b) (Deliberate Short Runs), or under 10, 14 or 16 above, they shall be added as penalty extras to that side's total of runs in its most recently completed innings. If the fielding side has not completed an innings, the five penalty extras shall be added to its next innings.

18. Players' Conduct

If there is any breach of the Spirit of the Game by a player failing to comply with the instructions of an umpire, or criticising his decisions by word or action, or showing dissent, or generally behaving in a manner which might bring the game into disrepute, the umpire concerned shall immediately report the matter to the other umpire.

The umpires together shall:

   (i) inform the player's captain of the occurrence, instructing the latter to take action.

   (ii) warn him of the gravity of the offence, and tell him that it will be reported to higher authority.

   (iii) report the occurrence as soon as possible to the executive of the player's team and any governing body responsible for the match, who shall take such action as is considered appropriate against the captain and player or players, and, if appropriate, the team concerned.

REGULATIONS OF THE INTERNATIONAL CRICKET COUNCIL

Extracts

1. Standard Playing Conditions

In 2001, the ICC Cricket Committee amended its standard playing conditions for all Tests and one-day internationals to include the new Laws of Cricket. The following playing conditions were in force from October 1, 2004:

Duration of Test Matches

Test matches shall be of five days' scheduled duration and of two innings per side. The two participating countries may:

(a) Provide for a rest day during the match, and/or a reserve day after the scheduled days of play.

(b) Play on any scheduled rest day, conditions and circumstances permitting, should a full day's play be lost on any day prior to the rest day.

(c) Play on any scheduled reserve day, conditions and circumstances permitting, should a full day's play be lost on any day. Play shall not take place on more than five days.

(d) Make up time lost in excess of five minutes in each day's play due to circumstances outside the game, other than acts of God.

Hours of Play, Intervals and Minimum Overs in the Day

Start and Cessation times shall be determined by the home board, subject to there being six hours' scheduled for play per day (Pakistan a minimum of five and a half hours).

Minimum Overs in a Day

On days other than the last day, play shall continue on each day until the completion of a minimum target of 90 overs (or a minimum of 15 overs per hour) or the completion of the scheduled or rescheduled cessation time, which ever is the later but provided that play shall not continue for more than 30 minutes beyond the scheduled or rescheduled cessation time (permitted overtime). For the sake of clarity, if any of the minimum target number of overs have not been bowled at the completion of the permitted overtime, play shall cease upon completion of the over in progress. The overs not bowled shall not be made up on any subsequent day.

On the last day, a minimum of 75 overs (or 15 overs per hour) shall be bowled during the playing time other than the last hour of the match where a minimum of 15 overs shall be bowled. All calculations with regard to suspensions of play or the start of a new innings shall be based on one over for each full four minutes. If however, at any time after 30 minutes of the last hour have elapsed, both captains (the batsmen at the wicket may act for their captain) accept that there is no prospect of a result to the match, they may agree to cease play at that time. If any of the minimum of 75 overs, or as recalculated, have not been bowled when one hour of the scheduled playing time remains, the last hour of the match shall be regarded as the hour immediately following the completion of these overs.

Reduction in minimum overs: except in the last hour of the match, if play is suspended due to adverse weather or light or any other reason (other than normal intervals) for more than one hour on any day, the minimum number of overs shall be reduced by one over for each full four minutes of the aggregate playing time lost. For the avoidance of doubt, the aggregate of one hour shall be inclusive of any time that may have been brought forward from previous days due to playing time lost on such previous days..

Making Up Lost Time

On the day: subject to weather and light, except in the last hour of the match, in the event of play being suspended for any reason other than normal intervals, the playing time on that day shall be extended by the amount of time lost up to a maximum of one hour. For the avoidance of doubt, the maximum of one hour shall be inclusive of any time that may have been added to the scheduled playing time due to playing time having been lost on previous days.

On subsequent days: if any time is lost and cannot be made up, additional time of up to a maximum of 30 minutes per day shall be added to the scheduled playing hours for the next day, and subsequent day(s) as required (to make up as much lost time as possible).Where appropriate this additional time shall be added prior to the scheduled start of the first session. In circumstances where this is not possible, the additional time may be added to the second and/or the third sessions. When such additional time is added, the minimum overs for that day shall be increased by one over for each four minutes of additional time or part thereof.

On the last day only: the definition of playing time shall be the time up to the most recently scheduled time for the start of the last hour. Should an interruption in play commence prior to the most recently scheduled time for the last hour and continue past this time:

(a) Only the playing time lost prior to this last hour start time will be made up (subject to the maximum of one hour described in (a) above) with the start time for the last hour being rescheduled accordingly

(b) The period of time between the scheduled last hour start time at the start of the interruption and the time of the resumption of play will not be made up. The minimum number of overs to be bowled prior to the last hour at the start of the interruption will therefore be reduced by one for each full four minutes of aggregate time lost.

(c) The start time for the last hour will be the later of the rescheduled time as defined at the end of (i) above and the time at which the minimum overs prior to the last hour have been completed or reduced to zero.

(d) No time is made up in respect of any interruptions that commence after the start of the last hour.

Extra time: The umpires may decide to play 30 minutes (a minimum of eight overs) extra time at the end of any day (other than the last day) if requested by either captain if, in the umpire's opinion, it would bring about a definite result on that day. If the umpires do not believe a result can be achieved no extra time shall be allowed. If it is decided to play such extra time, the whole period shall be played out even though the possibility of finishing the match may have disappeared before the full period has expired. Only the actual amount of playing time up to the maximum 30 minutes' extra time by which play is extended on any day shall be deducted from the total number of hours of play remaining, and the match shall end earlier on the final day by that amount of time.

Use of Lights

If, in the opinion of the umpires, natural light is deteriorating to an unfit level, they shall authorise the ground authorities to use the available artificial lighting so that the match can continue in acceptable conditions. The lights are only to be used to enable a full day's play to be completed as provided for in Clause A. In the event of power failure or lights malfunction, the existing provisions of Clause A shall apply.

Dangerous and Unfair Bowling: The Bowling of Fast, Short-Pitched Balls: Law 42.6

1.   (a) A bowler shall be limited to two fast, short-pitched deliveries per over.

(b) A fast, short-pitched ball is defined as a ball which passes or would have passed above the shoulder height of the batsman standing upright at the crease.

(c) The umpire at the bowler's end shall advise the bowler and the batsman on strike when each fast short-pitched ball has been bowled.

(d) For the purpose of this regulation, a ball that passes above head height, that prevents the batsman from being able to hit it with his bat by means of a normal cricket stroke shall be called a wide.

(e) Any fast, short-pitched delivery called wide under this condition shall count as one of the allowable short-pitched deliveries in that over.

(f) In the event of a bowler bowling more than two fast, short-pitched deliveries in an over, the umpire at the bowler's end shall call and signal "no-ball" on each occasion. The umpire shall call and signal "no-ball" and then tap the head with the other hand.

(g) If a bowler delivers a third fast, short-pitched ball in one over, the umpire must call no-ball and then invoke the procedures of caution, final warning, action against the bowler and reporting as set out in Law 42.7. The umpires will report the matter to the ICC referee who shall take such action as is considered appropriate against the captain and bowler concerned

The above Regulation is not a substitute for Law 42.6 (as amended below), which umpires are able to apply at any time:

The bowling of fast, short-pitched balls is unfair if the umpire at the bowler's end considers that, by their repetition and taking into account their length, height and direction, they are likely to inflict physical injury on the striker, irrespective of the protective clothing and equipment he may be wearing. The relative skill of the striker shall also be taken into consideration.

The umpire at the bowler's end shall adopt the procedures of caution, final warning, action against the bowler and reporting as set out in Law 42.7. The ICC referee shall take any further action considered appropriate against the captain and bowler concerned.

New Ball: Law 5.4
The captain of the fielding side shall have the choice of taking a new ball any time after 80 overs have been bowled with the previous ball. The umpires shall indicate to the batsmen and the scorers whenever a new ball is taken into play.

Ball Lost or Becoming Unfit for Play: Law 5.5
The following shall apply in addition to Law 5.5:

> However, if the ball needs to be replaced after 110 overs for any of the reasons above, it shall be replaced by a new ball. If the ball is to be replaced, the umpires shall inform the batsmen.

Judging a Wide: Law 25.1
Law 25.1 will apply, but in addition:

> For bowlers attempting to utilise the rough outside a batsman's leg stump, not necessarily as a negative tactic, the strict limited-overs wide interpretation shall be applied.

Practice on the Field: Law 17
In addition to Law 17.1:

> The use of the square for practice on any day of any match will be restricted to any netted practice area on the square set aside for that purpose.

Fieldsman Leaving the Field: Law 2.5
If a fielder fails to take the field with his side at the start of the match or at any later time, or leaves the field during a session of play, the umpire shall be informed of the reason for his absence, and he shall not thereafter come on to the field during a session without the consent of the umpire. The umpire shall give such consent as soon as practicable. If the player is absent from the field longer than eight minutes, he shall not be permitted to bowl in that innings after his return until he has been on the field for at least that length of playing time for which he was absent. This restriction will, if necessary, be carried over into a new day's play, and in the event of a follow-on will continue into the second innings. Nor shall he be permitted to bat unless or until, in the aggregate, he has returned to the field and/or his side's innings has been in progress for at least that length of playing time for which he has been absent or, if earlier, when his side has lost five wickets. The restrictions shall not apply if he has suffered an external blow (as opposed to an internal injury such as a pulled muscle) while participating earlier in the match and consequently been forced to leave the field, nor if he has been absent for exceptional and acceptable reasons (other than injury or illness).

ICC CODE OF CONDUCT

1. Players and/or team officials shall at all times conduct play within the spirit of the game as well as within the Laws of Cricket, and the captains are responsible at all times for ensuring that this is adhered to.

2. Players and/or team officials shall at no time engage in conduct unbecoming to their status which could bring them or the game of cricket into disrepute.

3. Players and/or team officials shall be required to report to the captain and/or team manager or to a senior board official or to the Anti-Corruption and Security Unit any approach made to them by a bookmaker or any other corrupt approach or knowledge of such approach made to any other player or team official.

4. Players and/or team officials shall not bet on matches nor otherwise engage in any conduct of the nature described in the paragraphs below. For conduct in breach of this rule, the penalties to be considered are set out below, for individuals who have:

i. Bet on any match or series of matches, or on any connected event, in which such player, umpire, referee, team official or administrator took part or in which the Member country or any such individual was represented (penalty (a));

ii. Induced or encouraged any other person to bet on any match or series of matches or on any connected event or to offer the facility for such bets to be placed (penalty (b));

iii. Gambled or entered into any other form of financial speculation on any match or on any connected event (penalty (a));

iv. Induced or encouraged any other person to gamble or enter into any other form of financial speculation on any match or any connected event (penalty (b));

v. Was a party to contriving or attempting to contrive the result of any match or the occurrence of any connected event (penalty (c));

vi. Failed to perform on his merits in any match owing to an arrangement relating to betting on the outcome of any match or on the occurrence of any connected event (penalty (c));

vii. Induced or encouraged any other player not to perform on his merits in any match owing to any such arrangement (penalty (c));

viii. Received from another person any money, benefit or other reward (whether financial or otherwise) for the provision of any information concerning the weather, the teams, the state of the ground, the status of, or the outcome of, any match or the occurrence of any connected event unless such information has been provided to a newspaper or other form of media in accordance with an obligation entered into in the normal course and disclosed in advance to the cricket authority of the relevant Member country (penalty (b));

ix. Received any money, benefit or other reward (whether financial or otherwise) which could bring him or the game of cricket into disrepute (penalty (d));

x. Provided any money, benefit or other reward (whether financial or otherwise) which could bring the game of cricket into disrepute (penalty (d));

xi. Received any approaches from another person to engage in conduct such as that described above, and has failed to disclose the same to his captain or team manager, or to a senior board official or to the Anti-Corruption and Security Unit (penalty (e)); or

xii. Is aware that any other player or individual has engaged in conduct, or received approaches, such as described above, and has failed to disclose the same to his captain or team manager, or to a senior board official or to the Anti-Corruption and Security Unit (penalty (e));

xiii. Has received or is aware that any other person has received threats of any nature which might induce him to engage in conduct, or acquiesce in any proposal made by an approach, such as described above, and has failed to disclose the same to his captain or team manager, or to a senior board official or to the Anti-Corruption and Security Unit (penalty (e));.

xiv. Has engaged in any conduct which, in the opinion of the Executive Board, relates directly or indirectly to any of the above paragraphs (i to xiii) and is prejudicial to the interests of the game of cricket (penalty (e)).

Penalties:

(a) Ban for a minimum of two years and a maximum of five years. In addition, a fine may be imposed, the amount to be assessed in the circumstances.

(b) Ban for a minimum of two years and a maximum of five years if a bet was placed directly or indirectly for the benefit of the individual; otherwise, a ban for a minimum of 12 months. In addition, a fine may be imposed, the amount to be assessed in the circumstances.

(c) Ban for life (a minimum of 20 years).

(d) Ban for a minimum of two years and a maximum of life. In addition, a fine may be imposed, the amount to be assessed in the circumstances.

(e) Ban for a minimum of one year and a maximum of five years. In addition, a fine may be imposed, the amount to be assessed in the circumstances.

5. A valid defence may be made to a charge in respect of any prohibited conduct in paragraphs 4 (xi) to (xiii) above if a person proves that this conduct was the result of an honest and reasonable belief that there was a serious threat to the life or safety of himself or any member of his family.

History and Law

6. Players and/or team officials shall not use or in any way be concerned in the use or distribution of illegal drugs. Illegal drugs shall mean those drugs which are classified as unlawful in the player's or team official's home country or in the country in which he is touring. Any such conduct shall constitute behaviour prohibited under paragraph 2 and shall be dealt with as such. Players and team officials shall also be subject to any doping policy which is applied by their home board and such policies which are introduced for ICC events. Any breach of such doping policy shall be dealt with under the terms of such policy itself and not under this code.

CRICKET AUSTRALIA
PLAYING CONDITIONS, 2004-05

CRICKET
AUSTRALIA

Note: This section is an abridged version of the full Playing Conditions Booklet of Cricket Australia. Some parts have been omitted.

TEST MATCH PLAYING CONDITIONS

Except as modified for one-day international and in the sections on other tour matches, these playing conditions shall apply to all tour matches.

1. Laws of Cricket

The Laws of Cricket (2000 Code 2nd Edition - 2003) as modified by ICC Test Match Playing Conditions (2003-2004) shall apply to all Test Matches and Tour Matches except as modified in clause 3.2.

2. Duration of Matches

Test Matches shall be of five days scheduled duration, and of two innings per side. The two participating countries may:

(a) Provide for a rest day during the match, and/or a reserve day after the scheduled days of play.

(b) Play on any scheduled rest day, conditions and circumstances permitting, should a full day's play be lost on any day prior to the rest day.

(c) Play on any scheduled reserve day, conditions and circumstances permitting, should a full day's play be lost on any day. Play shall not take place on more than 5 days.

(d) Make up time lost in excess of 5 minutes in each day's play due to circumstances outside the game other than acts of God.

Other tour matches shall be as scheduled as in the tour program authorised by Cricket Australia.

3. Hours of Play and Intervals

3.1 Start and Cessation Times

Australia vs New Zealand

QLD
10.00 a.m. - 12.00 p.m.	Session 1
12.00 p.m. - 12.40 p.m.	Lunch
12.40 p.m. - 2.40 p.m.	Session 2
2.40 p.m. - 3.00 p.m.	Tea
3.00 p.m. - 5.00 p.m.	Session 3

SA
11.00 a.m. - 1.00 p.m.	Session 1
1.00 p.m. - 1.40 p.m.	Lunch
1.40 p.m. - 3.40 p.m.	Session 2
3.40 p.m. - 4.00 p.m.	Tea
4.00 p.m. - 6.00 p.m.	Session 3

AUSTRALIA vs PAKISTAN

WA, VIC, NSW

10.30 a.m. - 12.30 p.m.	Session 1
12.30 p.m. - 1.10 p.m.	Lunch
1.10 p.m. - 3.10 p.m.	Session 2
3.10 p.m. - 3.30 p.m.	Tea
3.30 p.m. - 5.30 p.m.	Session 3

3.2   Other Tour Matches

Wherever possible, the above conditions shall apply to all matches. However, the home board with the agreement of the visiting country's board may provide for local variations for matches other than Test and One Day International matches. In the case of one-day matches, starting and finishing times (and interval times) may be altered on any scheduled playing day with the prior approval of the State authority, Cricket Australia and the touring team Manager.

State players shall be bound by the terms of the Cricket Australia Code of Behaviour. Touring team players shall be bound by Law 42.18 and/or the terms of the ICC Code of Conduct for Players and Team Officials.

The local State Association shall appoint a representative to meet with the umpires and captains prior to the commencement of the match to secure uniform interpretation of these playing conditions and to adjudicate, if necessary, should there be any dispute.

The following playing times for tour matches will apply for the 2004-05 season:

11-14 November	**New South Wales vs New Zealand**	**Sydney**
11.00 a.m. - 1.00 p.m.	Session 1	
1.00 p.m. - 1.40 p.m.	Lunch	
1.40 p.m. - 3.40 p.m.	Session 2	
3.40 p.m. - 4.00 p.m.	Tea	
4.00 p.m. - 6.00 p.m.	Session 3	

7 December	**Chairman's XI vs Pakistan**	**Lilac Hill**
10.30 a.m. - 2.00 p.m.	Session 1	
2.00 p.m. - 2.45pm	Interval	
2.45pm - 6.15pm	Session 2	

9-12 December	**Western Australia vs Pakistan**	**Perth**
11.00 a.m. - 1.00 p.m.	Session 1	
1.00 p.m. - 1.40 p.m.	Lunch	
1.40 p.m. - 3.40 p.m.	Session 2	
3.40 p.m. - 4.00 p.m.	Tea	
4.00 p.m. - 6.00 p.m.	Session 3	

5 January	**Victoria vs West Indies**	**Melbourne**
2.30 p.m. - 6.00 p.m.	Session 1	
6.00 p.m. - 6.45pm	Interval	
6.45pm - 10.15pm	Session 2	

8 January	**Australia A vs West Indies**	**Hobart**
10.00 a.m. - 1.30 p.m.	Session 1	
1.30 p.m. - 2.15pm	Interval	
2.15pm - 5.45pm	Session 2	

9 January	**Australia A vs West Indies**	**Hobart**
10.00 a.m. - 1.30 p.m.	Session 1	
1.30 p.m. - 2.15pm	Interval	
2.15pm - 5.45pm	Session 2	

12 January	**Australia A vs Pakistan**	**Adelaide**
9.30 a.m. - 1.00 p.m.	Session 1	
1.00 p.m. - 1.45pm	Interval	
1.45pm - 5.15pm	Session 2	

25 January   **Prime Minister's XI vs Pakistan**   **Canberra**
Day match
Hours of Play and Interval to be advised

4 Law 5 - The Ball

ICC regulations shall apply as regards to the ball. The Kookaburra "Turf" brand red ball has been
approved by Cricket Australia.

VB SERIES
PLAYING CONDITIONS

1. Laws of Cricket

ICC Test Match Playing Conditions and Laws of Cricket (2000 Code 2nd Edition - 2003) - shall apply
in addition to ICC One Day International Match Playing Conditions (2003-2004).

2. Duration of Matches

One-day International Matches shall be of one day's scheduled duration. The participating countries
in a series may provide for a reserve day on which an incomplete match may be replayed (but not
continued from the scheduled day). The matches will consist of one innings per side and each innings
will be limited to 50 six-ball overs. A minimum of 25 overs per team shall constitute a match.

3. Hours of Play and Intervals

3.1   Start and Cessation Times

Day Matches

Queensland
9.00 a.m. - 12.30 p.m.   Session 1
12.30 p.m. - 1.15pm   Interval
1.15pm - 4.45pm   Session 2

South Australia
9.30 a.m. - 1.00 p.m.   Session 1
1.00 p.m. - 1.45pm   Interval
1.45pm - 5.15pm   Session 2

Tasmania
10.00 a.m. - 1.30 p.m.   Session 1
1.30 p.m. - 2.15pm   Interval
2.15pm - 5.45pm   Session 2

Western Australia
10.30 a.m. - 2.00 p.m.   Session 1
2.00 p.m. - 2.45pm   Interval
2.45pm - 6.15pm   Session 2

Day/Night Matches

Queensland
1.15pm - 4.45pm   Session 1
4.45pm - 5.30 p.m.   Interval
5.30 p.m. - 9.00 p.m.   Session 2

New South Wales, Victoria
2.15pm - 5.45pm   Session 1
5.45pm - 6.30 p.m.   Interval
6.30 p.m. - 10.00 p.m.   Session 2

South Australia

1.45pm - 5.15pm	Session 1
5.15pm - 6.00 p.m.	Interval
6.00 p.m. - 9.30 p.m.	Session 2

Western Australia

1.30 p.m. - 5.00 p.m.	Session 1
5.00 p.m. - 5.45pm	Interval
5.45pm - 9.15pm	Session 2

3.2 Extra Time

Subject to agreement by the participating countries, provision has been made for up to 15 minutes of extra playing time in day matches and up to 45 minutes in day/night matches.

4. The Ball

Cricket Australia shall provide cricket balls of an approved standard for One Day International cricket and spare used balls for changing during a match, which shall also be of the same brand. Kookaburra "Turf" brand white balls as approved by Cricket Australia will be used in all matches.

5. Finals Series – Australia vs West Indies vs Pakistan

The two teams with highest number of points at the completion of the preliminary matches shall play in the finals series.

In the event of a drawn final, the prizemoney will be shared equally between the two competing teams.

In the best of three final series, a third match will always be played where neither team has a clear two match advantage after the scheduled completion of the second match.

For the determination of the final series no reference will be made to preliminary match results, wins or run rates. In the event of a tied final series, the prizemoney will be shared equally between the two competing teams.

PURA CUP
PLAYING CONDITIONS

1. Laws of Cricket

Except as varied hereunder, the Laws of Cricket (2000 Code 2nd Edition - 2003) shall apply.

All references under the Laws of Cricket to 'Governing Body' shall be replaced with Cricket Australia for the purposes of these Playing Conditions.

2. Duration of Matches

Matches shall be four days scheduled duration.

3. Hours of Play and Intervals

3.1 Start and Cessation Times

Queensland

10.00 a.m. - 12.00 p.m.	Session 1
12.00 p.m. - 12.40 p.m.	Lunch
12.40 p.m. - 2.40 p.m.	Session 2
2.40 p.m. - 3.00 p.m.	Tea
3.00 p.m. - 5.00 p.m.	Session 3

New South Wales, South Australia, Tasmania, Victoria, Western Australia

11.00 a.m. - 1.00 p.m.	Session 1
1.00 p.m. - 1.40 p.m.	Lunch
1.40 p.m. - 3.40 p.m.	Session 2
3.40 p.m. - 4.00 p.m.	Tea
4.00 p.m. - 6.00 p.m.	Session 3

The following playing times shall apply to the specific matches below.

10.30 a.m. - 12.30 p.m.	Session 1
12.30 p.m. - 1.10 p.m.	Lunch
1.10 p.m. - 3.10 p.m.	Session 2
3.10 p.m. - 3.30 p.m.	Tea
3.30 p.m. - 5.30 p.m.	Session 3

16 – 19 October	South Australia vs Victoria
16 – 19 October	Western Australia vs Tasmania
3 – 6 March	Western Australia vs South Australia

3.2   Hours of Play

Any State Association wishing to change the hours of play must first obtain approval from Cricket Australia.

4. Minimum Overs in the Day

(a) Play shall continue on each day until the completion of a minimum number of overs or until the scheduled or rescheduled cessation time, whichever is the later.

The minimum number of overs to be completed, unless an innings ends or an interruption occurs, shall be:

   (i) On days other than the last day - a minimum of 96 overs (or a minimum of 16 overs per hour).

   (ii) On the last day – a minimum of 80 overs (or a minimum of 16 overs per hour) for playing time other than the last hour of the match when clause (e) below shall apply.

   (iii) Additional Hour: Subject to ground weather and light, except in the last hour of the match, in the event of play being suspended for any reason other than normal intervals, the playing time on that day shall be extended by the amount of time lost up to a maximum of one hour. In these circumstances, the minimum number of overs to be bowled shall be in accordance with the provisions of this clause i.e. a minimum of 16 overs per hour and the cessation time shall be rescheduled accordingly.

   (iv) If play has been suspended for 30 minutes or more prior to the commencement of the scheduled or rescheduled tea interval, the tea interval shall be delayed for 30 minutes.

   (v) If any time and overs are lost and cannot be made up under (iii) above, additional time and overs of up to a maximum of one hour per day (16 overs) shall be added to the scheduled playing hours for the next day, and subsequent day(s) as required (to make up as much lost time as possible). Where appropriate the first 30 minutes (or less) of this additional time shall be added prior to the scheduled start of the first session, and the remainder shall be added to the last session.

In circumstances where it is not possible to add this additional time prior to the scheduled start of the first session, the timing of the lunch and tea intervals will be adjusted to provide for a scheduled 2? hour session and not affect the start time.

On any day's play, except the last day, when the scheduled hours of play have been completed, but the required number of overs has not been bowled and adverse ground, weather or light causes play for that day to be abandoned, the overs which have not been bowled on that day shall be made up on the next or subsequent days (refer (v) above for timings). On any one day, a maximum of 16 additional overs shall be permitted.

When additional time is added to subsequent day(s), no scheduled days play shall exceed 7 hours. The length of each session of play is subject to the provisions of Law 15.

Under Law 15.5 timings can be altered at any time on any day if playing time is lost, not necessarily on that day. The captains, umpires and the local State Association can agree different timings under those circumstances before play starts on any day.

(b) When an innings ends a minimum number of overs shall be bowled from the start of the new innings. The last hour of the match shall be excluded from this calculation when clause (e) shall apply. Where there is a change of innings during a day's play (except at lunch or tea or when play is suspended due to adverse ground, weather or light conditions or for exceptional circumstances), 2 overs will be deducted from the minimum number of overs to be bowled.

(c) Except in the last hour of the match, for which clause (e) makes provision, if play is suspended due to adverse ground, weather or light for more than one hour in aggregate on any day, the minimum number of overs shall be reduced by one over for each full 3.75 minutes of the aggregate playing time lost on that day.

(d) On the last day, if any of the minimum of 80 overs, or as recalculated, have not been bowled when one hour of scheduled playing time remains, the last hour of the match for the purposes of clause (e) shall be the hour immediately following the completion of those overs.

(e) Laws 16.6, 16.7 and 16.8 will apply except that a minimum of 16 overs shall be bowled in the last hour and all calculations with regard to suspensions of play or the start of a new innings shall be based on one over for each full 3.75 minutes (refer (i) below). If, however, at any time after 30 minutes of the last hour have elapsed both captains (the batsmen at the wicket may act for their captain) accept that there is no prospect of a result to the match, they may agree to cease play at that time.

(f) Notwithstanding any other provision, there shall be no further play on any day, other than the last day, if a wicket falls or a batsman retires or if the players have occasion to leave the field during the last minimum over within 2 minutes of the scheduled or re-scheduled cessation time or thereafter.

(g) An over completed on resumption of a new day's play shall be disregarded in calculating minimum overs for that day.

(h) Except on the final day, if in the event of adverse ground, weather or light conditions causing a suspension of play and/or if the players are already off the field at the rescheduled cessation time or any time thereafter, stumps shall be drawn.

(i) Fractions are to be ignored in all final calculations regarding the number of overs, except where there is a change of innings in the day's play, when the over in progress at the conclusion of the innings shall be rounded up.

(j) The scoreboard shall show:

• The total number of overs bowled with the ball currently in use and

• The minimum number of overs remaining to be bowled in the day's play and

• The number of overs above or below the target overs for the match.

(k) Penalties shall apply for not achieving target overs.

Subject to the provisions of this clause, over rates shall be assessed on 16 overs per hour, i.e. a minimum of 96 overs in a six hour day, subject to the following deductions:

2 minutes	for every wicket taken
4 minutes	for each drinks break taken in any session
Actual time	where treatment by authorised medical personnel is required on the ground and/or for a player leaving the field due to serious injury.

Overs will be calculated at the end of the match. For each over short of the target number, 0.5 shall be deducted from the team's match points.

For the purpose of calculation of penalties.

(a) The scheduled last hour of the match, as defined in clause 4 (e) shall be excluded.

(b) A maximum allowance of 20 overs in any hour shall apply.

In the event of a match finishing within 3 scheduled playing days, penalties for not achieving the required over rates shall not apply, regardless of the hours played on those days.

A Commissioner appointed by Cricket Australia will hear and determine all appeals against penalties imposed. For the purpose of determining whether the fielding side has fallen short of the target number of overs, umpires may take into account any factor they consider relevant, including whether inclement weather has adversely affected the ability of the fielding side to comply with the required over rate.

Appeals shall be lodged within 14 days of the completion of the match. The onus shall be on the appellant to prove that the umpires have erred in their assessment of time allowances. Video evidence where available may be produced by the appellant in support of the appeal. Umpires will be required to record all delays and stoppages on the appropriate form.

5. Extra Time

The umpires may decide to play 30 minutes (a minimum of eight overs) extra time at the end of any day (other than the last day) if requested by either captain if, in the umpires opinion, it would bring about an outright result on that day (this is in addition to the maximum one hour's extra time provided for in 4(a) (iii) above). If the umpires do not believe an outright result can be achieved, no extra time shall be allowed.

If it is decided to play such extra time on one or more of these days, the whole period (30 minutes or a minimum of 8 overs) shall be played out even though the possibility of finishing the match may have disappeared before the full period has expired.

Only the actual amount of playing time up to the maximum 30 minutes extra time by which play is extended on any day shall be deducted from the total number of hours of play remaining, and the match shall end earlier on the final day by the amount of time by which play was previously extended under this clause.

6. Use of Lights

If in the opinion of the umpires, natural light is deteriorating to an unfit level, they shall authorize the ground authorities to use the available artificial lighting so that the match can continue in acceptable conditions. If natural light improves, the artificial lights may be turned off.

The lights are only to be used to enable a full day's play to be completed as provided in clauses 3, 4 and 5.

7. Lunch Interval

Law 15.6 shall apply and the lunch interval shall be of 40 minutes duration.

8. Tea Interval

A Tea interval of 20 minutes duration will be taken from or at the conclusion of the over in progress at the agreed time for the tea interval subject to the provisions of Law 15.

9. Intervals for Drinks

The provisions of Law 15.9 shall be strictly observed except that under conditions of extreme heat the umpires may permit extra intervals for drinks.

An individual player may be given a drink either on the boundary edge or at the fall of a wicket, on the field, provided that no playing time is wasted. If individual drinks have been brought onto the field at the fall of a wicket, the fielding side must be ready to continue play as soon as the new batsman reaches the wicket. No other drinks shall be taken onto the field without the permission of the umpires.

Any player taking drinks onto the field shall be dressed in approved clothing and equipment as described in Cricket Australia Rule 11- Wearing Apparel of Players and Umpires.

10. Time Keeping

The umpires must notify the local State Association which clock is to be followed, so that the spectators and representatives of the media may be informed. If the clock on the ground is out of order, the watches of the umpires shall determine the time.

11. Law 1.3 – Captain

The following shall apply in addition to Law 1.3 (a):
The deputy must be one of the nominated players.

12. Appointment of Umpires

Cricket Australia shall appoint all umpires from its panel of umpires. The umpires for the final shall be appointed by Cricket Australia and must be members of the ICC Elite or Cricket Australia National Panels.

Cricket Australia shall appoint a third umpire from its panel of umpires who shall act as the emergency umpire and officiate in regard to TV replays in all televised matches where the technology is available. The third umpire will officiate in regard to TV replays only when the umpires on the field have referred a decision to him in regard to hit wicket, run out and stumping appeals.

Either the on-field or third umpire shall be entitled to call for a TV replay to assist him in making a decision about whether the fieldsman had any part of his person in contact with the ball when he touched or crossed the boundary edge or whether a four or six had been scored (refer to Regulation 3.2.4(a) Boundary Decisions of ICC Standard Test Match Playing Conditions (2003-04)). Whether TV cameras are in use or not, the following applies. A decision is to be made immediately and cannot be changed thereafter. Immediately is taken to mean prior to the next delivery. In addition, no changes shall be made after the call of 'Time'.

13. Nomination of Players

Law 1.2 shall apply except that the players nominated shall include the selected emergency fieldsman.

Subject to advice being given by the home State to the visiting State or its Team Manager, the emergency fieldsman of the home State may be released to play with his Club team, in which case the home State shall supply another emergency fieldsman to act in his stead if required.

13.1 Replacement Player

Should any player during a match be required by Cricket Australia for playing duties elsewhere, that requirement shall take precedence.

(a) The player's State Association will then be able to select a like player as the replacement for the remainder of the match concerned.

(b) The player's State Association will submit nominations for the replacement player to the opposing team captain for approval that must not be unreasonably withheld.

(c) If after a replacement player has been chosen, the replaced player's services are no longer required by Cricket Australia, the player may resume his place in the team only if his replacement has not either batted or bowled in his absence. Otherwise the player may take no further part in the match and the replacement player must continue in his stead.

14. Substitutes

14.1 Law 2.5 – Fielder Absent or Leaving the Field - shall apply as modified:

(a) If a fielder fails to take the field with his side at the start of the match or at any later time, or leaves the field during a session of play, the umpire shall be informed of the reason for his absence, and he shall not thereafter come onto the field during a session of play without the consent of the umpire (See Law 2.6 as modified). The umpire shall give such consent as soon as practicable. If the player is absent from the field for longer than 8 minutes:

    (i)   The player shall not be permitted to bowl in that innings after his return until he has been on the field for at least that length of playing time for which he was absent. In the event of a follow-on, this restriction will, if necessary, continue into the second innings.

    (ii)   The player shall not be permitted to bat unless or until, in the aggregate, he has returned to the field and/or his side's innings has been in progress for at least that length of playing time for which he has been absent or, if earlier, when his side has lost five wickets.

(b) The restriction in (i) and (ii) above shall not apply if the player has suffered an external blow (as opposed to an internal injury such as a pulled muscle) whilst participating earlier in the match and consequently been forced to leave the field. Nor shall it apply if the player has been absent for very exceptional and wholly acceptable reasons (other than injury or illness).

(c) This restriction shall not apply at the commencement of a new day's play.

(d) In the event of a fieldsman already being off the field at the commencement of an interruption in play through adverse conditions of ground, weather or light, he shall be allowed to count any such stoppage time as playing time, provided that he personally informs the umpires that he is fit enough to take the field had play been in progress and then takes the field on resumption of play.

14.2 Injury to Player or Umpire

(a) An injured batsman who has temporarily retired, and is unable to return after the fall of the ninth wicket shall be recorded in the scorebooks as "Retired – not out" and the innings shall be deemed closed.

(b) Where an injury occurs to a batsman involved in a tenth wicket partnership, a maximum of five minutes will be allowed in order for the batsman to obtain treatment. If the injury occurs within 30 minutes of a scheduled interval, the interval shall be taken immediately if the batsman is unable to resume after the five minutes. If the batsman is unable to resume after the five minutes or after the early interval, he shall be recorded in the scorebooks as "Retired – not out", as described above.

(c) Where an injury occurs to an umpire, and he must leave the field for treatment, the other umpire shall officiate at the bowler's end. The local State Association shall provide a competent person to stand at the striker's end until the injured umpire is able to resume or a suitable replacement has been appointed.

15. Law 3.8 - Fitness of Ground, Weather and Light and Law 3.9 - Suspension of Play for Adverse Conditions of Ground, Weather or Light

15.1 Add the following to Law 3.8:

If conditions during a rain stoppage improve and the rain is reduced to drizzle, the umpires must consider if they would have suspended play in the first place under similar conditions. If the on-field umpires agree that the current drizzle would not have caused a stoppage, then play shall resume immediately. In these circumstances the provisions of Laws 3.9 (b) (i) and 3.9 (c) (i) shall not apply. However, should the umpires be of the opinion that a resumption of play under these circumstances would contribute to worsening ground conditions, they will resume play only with the approval of both captains.

15.2 In addition, attention is drawn to Law 3.9(d) with regards to application of clause 15.1.

"The fact that the grass and ball are wet and slippery does not warrant the ground conditions being regarded as unreasonable or dangerous. If the umpires consider the ground is so wet or slippery as to deprive the bowler of a reasonable foothold, the fielders the power of free movement, or the batsmen the ability to play their shots and run between the wickets, then these conditions shall be regarded as so bad that it would be unreasonable for play to take place."

15.3 The umpires shall disregard any shadow on the pitch from the stadium or from any permanent object on the ground.

If a shadow from the fielder falls across the strikers half of the pitch, the fielder must remain stationary from the time the bowler commences his run up until the striker has received the ball. In the event of a fielder moving before the striker receives the ball, the umpire shall call and signal 'Dead ball' if he considers the striker has been disadvantaged by the action. The provisions of Laws 23.5(a) and (b) shall apply as to whether any additional delivery is to be allowed.

15.4 Extreme Heat

All references to adverse weather shall include extreme heat (refer Cricket Australia guidelines on extreme heat). On days of extreme heat, play shall only take place during the scheduled hours of play. All provisions of Law 3.9 and clause 4 still apply.

16. The Ball

16.1 First quality balls approved by Cricket Australia shall be used in Pura Cup matches.

Note: The Kookaburra "Turf" brand red ball has been approved. Law 5.4 shall apply except that the fielding captain may demand a new ball after 80 overs have been bowled with the old one.

16.2 The umpires shall retain possession of the match ball(s) throughout the duration of the match when play is not actually taking place. During play, umpires shall periodically and irregularly inspect the condition of the ball and shall retain possession of it at the fall of a wicket, a drinks interval or any other disruption in play.

16.3 In the event of a ball becoming wet and soggy as a result of play continuing in inclement weather or it being affected by dew, and in the opinion of the umpires being unfit for play, the ball shall be replaced for a ball that has had a similar amount of wear. Either bowler or batsmen may raise the matter with the umpires and the umpires' decision as to a replacement or otherwise will be final.

16.4 Ball Lost or Becoming Unfit for Play

The following shall apply in addition to Law 5.5. However, if the ball needs to be replaced after 110 overs for any of the reasons above, it shall be replaced by a new ball. If the ball is to be replaced, the umpires shall inform the batsmen.

16.5 Law 5.6 Specifications, shall not apply.

17. Law 6 – The Bat

In addition to Law 6.1, the blade of the bat shall have a conventional flat face.

18. Law 7 – The Pitch

18.1 In addition to Law 7.3, the following will apply:

Captains, umpires and ground staff shall co-operate to ensure that, prior to the start of any day's play, no one bounces a ball on the pitch or strikes it with a bat to assess its condition or for any other reason, or causes damage to the pitch in any other way.

18.2 Prior to the start of play on any day, only the captain and team coach may walk on the pitch to assess its condition. Spiked footwear is not permitted.

18.3 Prior to the commencement of a day's play and during the lunch and tea intervals, one TV commentator and camera crew of the official licensed TV broadcaster/s (but not news crew) may be permitted to inspect the pitch and surrounds (without walking on the pitch or interfering with pitch preparation) subject to the following:
   – a ball must not be bounced on the pitch
   – a key or knife may only be inserted in the pitch in the area between the popping and bowling creases

18.4 In the event of any dispute, the local State Association will rule and their ruling will be final.

19. Law 7.4 – Changing the Pitch

19.1 Law 7.4 will not apply. In the event of a match being abandoned because of inadequate pitch and/or ground preparation it is considered that the match be awarded to the visiting team.

19.2 For the purposes of this clause, the pitch and/or ground preparation will be deemed to have been inadequate if the match is abandoned as a direct or indirect result of the local State Association (or any of its employees, contractors or agents) failing to take proper precautions in the circumstances to ensure that:

   (a) The pitch was properly prepared; or

   (b) The pitch was properly protected against the elements or other acts of God, vandalism or foul play, machinery or equipment failure or other reasonably foreseeable events.

   A groundsman who is responsible for the preparation of the pitch and who is employed by a body other than the local State Association, is deemed to be a contractor or agent of that Association.

19.3 The Cricket Australia Cricket Operations Department shall arrange and ensure that a thorough investigation of the circumstances into the abandonment of the match is conducted and that a report is presented to a forum (to be determined) for decision and penalty if appropriate.

19.4 Law 7.5 Non-Turf Pitches shall not apply.

20. Law 8 – The Wickets

The following shall apply in addition to Law 8.2:

For televised matches, the local State Association may provide a slightly larger stump to accommodate the stump camera. When the larger stump is used, all three stumps must be exactly the same size.

21. Law 9.3 – The Popping Crease

Law 9.3 shall apply, except that the reference to "a minimum of 6 ft" shall be replaced by "a minimum of 15 yards".

22. Law 10 – Preparation and Maintenance of the Playing Area

22.1 Mowing the Outfield – The outfield shall be mown daily before play begins.

22.2 Maintenance of Footholds - Law 10.6 will apply but add:

The umpires shall see that wherever possible and whenever it is considered necessary, action is taken during all intervals in play to do whatever is practicable to improve the bowler's footholds. As soon as possible after the conclusion of each day's play, bowler's footholds will be repaired.

22.3 Watering the Outfield

In order that the condition of the outfield can be maintained throughout the duration of a match, oval managers/curators must first be granted approval by both captains and umpires to water the outfield after any days play. Similarly, the oval manager/curator may wish to lightly water a pitch under preparation for an upcoming match. Agreement must be reached prior to the commencement of the match before any such watering will be permitted.

23. Law 11 – Covering the Pitch

In place of Laws 11.2, 11.3 and 11.4, the following shall apply:

23.1 In all matches, the pitch shall be entirely protected against rain up to the commencement of play and for the duration of the period of the match. It shall be wholly covered at the termination of each day's play or providing the weather is fine, within a period of two hours thereafter.

23.2 The covers shall be removed no earlier than 5.00 a.m. and no later than 7.00 a.m. on each morning of the match provided it is not raining at the time, but they will be replaced if rain falls prior to the commencement of play.

Note: The covers must totally protect the pitch and also the pitch surroundings to a minimum of five metres either side of the pitch and any worn or soft areas in the outfield, as well as the bowlers' run-ups to a distance of at least 10 x 10 metres.

Attention is drawn to clause 15.

24. Drying of Pitch and Ground

24.1 Prior to tossing for choice of innings, the artificial drying of the pitch and outfield shall be at the discretion of the groundsman. Thereafter and throughout the match the drying of the outfield may be undertaken at any time by the groundsman, but the drying of the affected area of the pitch shall be carried out only on the instructions and under the supervision of the umpires. The umpires shall be empowered to have the pitch dried without reference to the captains at any time they are of the opinion that it is unfit for play.

24.2 The umpires may instruct the groundsman to use any available equipment, including any roller for the purpose of drying the pitch and making it fit for play.

Note: an absorbent roller may be used to remove water from the covers including the cover on the match pitch.

25. Law 12 – Innings

Law 12.1 (a) shall apply as modified:

(a) A match shall be two innings per side subject to the provisions of Law 13.1.

Laws 12.1 (b) and 12.3 (e) shall not apply.

26. Law 13 – The Follow-On

Add the following to Law 13.1:

If the provision of clause 4 (a) (v) is applied, the additional time is regarded as part of that day's play for the purpose of Law 13.3, i.e. it is the number of days remaining and not the total number of hours available.

27. Law 17 – Practice on the Field

Add the following to Law 17.1:

The use of the square for practice on any day of any match will be restricted to any netted practice area on the square set aside for that purpose.

28. Law 19 – Boundaries

Add the following to Law 19.1:

28.1 All boundaries must be designated by a rope or similar object of a minimum standard as authorised by Cricket Australia from time to time. Where appropriate, the rope should be a required minimum distance (three yards) inside the perimeter fencing or advertising signs. For grounds with a large playing area, the maximum length of boundary should be used before applying the minimum three yards between the boundary and the fence.

28.2 If an unauthorized person enters the playing arena and handles the ball, the umpire at the bowler's end shall be the sole judge of whether the boundary allowance should be scored, or the ball be treated as still in play, or called Dead ball if a batsman is liable to be out as a result of the unauthorized person handling the ball. See Law 19.1 (c).

28.3 Sightscreens shall be provided at both ends of all grounds. Advertising shall be permitted on the sightscreen behind the striker, providing it is removed for the subsequent over from that end.

28.4 Attention is drawn to Law 19.2(e). Should a rope or similar object used to mark the boundary be disturbed during play, umpires, players and ground staff should cooperate to ensure that it is restored to its original position as soon as the ball is dead.

29. The Result

29.1 Match Points

(i)	For an outright win after leading on the first innings	6 points
(ii)	For an outright win after a tie in the first innings	6 points
(iii)	For an outright win after being behind on the first innings	6 points
(iv)	For a tie where both teams have completed two innings (irrespective of the first innings result)	3 points
(v)	For a first innings lead (to be retained even if beaten outright)	2 points
(vi)	For an outright loss after leading on the first innings	2 points
(vii)	For a tie on the first innings(and no outright result)	1 point each
(viii)	For an outright loss after a tie in the first innings	1point
(ix)	For a loss on the first innings	NIL
(x)	For an outright loss after being behind on the first innings	NIL
(xi)	Abandoned or drawn matches with no first innings result	NIL
(xii)	Abandoned match due to inadequate pitch and/or ground preparation. (see clause 19)	

29.2 Law 21 shall apply with the addition of the following:

Any query on the result of the match as defined in Laws 21.1, 21.3, 21.4, 21.5, 21.8, and 21.10 shall be resolved as soon as possible and a final decision made by the umpires.

29.3 *Note:* It is possible for a team to record a negative points tally on the Pura Cup table as a result of penalties incurred under the provisions of clause 4.

29.4   Qualifying for the Final

The two teams that have the highest aggregate of points at the end of a season shall play off in a final for the Pura Cup for that season (refer clause 46). In the event of an equality of points, the higher number of outright wins will determine the positions on the Pura Cup table. Should there be equality in both points and outright wins, the positions shall be determined by quotient calculated thus:

(i)   Divide the total number of runs scored by a team by the total number of wickets lost by it.

(ii)   Divide the total number of runs scored against a team by the total number of wickets taken by it.

(iii)   Divide the former (i) by the latter (ii).

The team having the higher quotient shall be considered to have the better performance.

For the purpose of the calculations and for individual averages a team forfeiting or declaring its innings closed shall be deemed to have lost only the number of wickets that have actually fallen.

29.5   Contrived Result

(a) Cricket Australia shall have the power to investigate a game or the actions of the captains of the teams or any player involved in a match, if it suspects reasonably that the competing States with or without the assistance of any other person or club have colluded to contrive the result of a match. If Cricket Australia decides to carry out an investigation, it will conduct such inquiries as it sees fit and invite submissions about the match or the conduct of either captain or any player, and will give the opportunity to be heard to interested parties, including representatives of both teams involved.

(b) If Cricket Australia finds that the teams, officials, captains or players have colluded unfairly to contrive the outcome of a match, to the detriment of any other team in the competition, it may in its absolute discretion do one or more of the following:

(i)   fine a team, captain or player;

(ii)   suspend a captain from playing in any match or matches;

(iii)   disallow any points earned by a team in respect of the match;

(iv)   amend any points earned by a team in the match; or

(v)   take such other action as is deemed appropriate.

(c) For the purpose of this playing condition, 'colluded unfairly to contrive the outcome of a match' means an agreement designed to contrive the outcome of a match in favour of a particular team or to achieve a result that is unfair to any of the other teams in the same competition. The operation of this playing condition is not intended to prevent competing captains from making aggressive declarations with a view to giving either side the chance of achieving an outright win.

30.   Law 22 – The Over

30.1 Law 22.5 shall apply with the following:

Whenever possible the third umpire or TV umpire shall liaise with the scorers and if possible inform the on-field umpires by the use of two way radio if the over has been or is likely to be miscounted.

30.2 Maximum Overs for Medium and Pace Bowlers

(a) Definitions

(i)   Bowling Type: Bowlers of medium pace or faster (as determined by the umpires and broadly defined as one to whom the wicket-keeper would normally stand back, or one who is not considered a slow bowler). The umpires shall immediately notify the captains of both sides of each bowler who they determine should be treated differently to this broad definition.

(ii) Players Age: The player's age shall be determined as their age on 1st September preceding each cricket season (ie. Under-19 players will be 17 or 18 on 1st September; Under-17 players will be 15 or 16 on 1st September etc.) and the appropriate bowling limitations shall apply for the entire season.

(b) Notification

The team captain must indicate to the umpires on the team sheet each player to whom this playing condition applies and indicate their age.

(c) Bowling Limitations

Bowling limitations apply at the following ages:

(i) Under-19:
A maximum spell of eight (8) consecutive overs.
A maximum daily allocation of twenty (20) overs.

(ii) Under-17:
A maximum spell of six (6) consecutive overs.
A maximum daily allocation of sixteen (16) overs.

(iii) Under-15:
A maximum spell of five (5) consecutive overs.
A maximum daily allocation of ten (10) overs.

(iv) Under-14:
A maximum spell of four (4) consecutive overs.
A maximum daily allocation of eight (8) overs.

(d) Length of Break

(i) The break between spells is to be a minimum of 60 minutes (including the lunch and tea interval and any unscheduled breaks in play).

(ii) A bowler who has bowled a spell of less than the maximum spell permitted for their age (defined in 30.2 (a) (ii) above) may resume bowling prior to the completion of the necessary break, but this will be considered an extension of the same spell and the maximum spell limit for that age of player shall still apply. Following the completion of the extended spell, the normal break of 60 minutes between spells will apply and the break within the spell is disregarded.

(iii) If a change of innings occurs, and a bowler commences bowling in the new innings within 60 minutes of bowling in the previous innings, this will be considered an extension of the same spell and the maximum spell limit and daily limits for that age of player shall still apply.

(iv) If any interval or interruption in play results in an over not being completed, then that part of the over bowled after the break shall constitute one over for the purposes of calculating the bowler's spell and daily limits. If this over is completed at the start of a new day's play, the over shall be considered the first over of a new spell for that bowler and the first over of the new daily limits.

(e) Change of Bowling Type

Where a bowler changes between medium pace (or faster) and slow bowling during a day's play:

(i) if the bowler begins with medium pace (or faster), the bowler is subject to the playing condition throughout the day.

(ii) if the bowler begins with slow bowling and changes to medium pace (or faster), the playing condition applies from the time of the change, and all overs of slow bowling bowled prior to the change shall not be taken into account in either the current spell or the daily limit.

(f) Management

(i) It is the responsibility of the fielding captain to ensure that this playing condition is upheld.

(ii) If the umpires become aware of breaches of this playing condition, when the ball is dead, they shall direct the captain to take the bowler off forthwith. If applicable, the over shall be completed by another bowler who shall have neither bowled the previous over nor be allowed to bowl the next over.

(iii) Should a dispute or uncertainty regarding the application of this playing condition occur during play, the umpires shall make the final decision on its application based on information available from the scorers or other sources.

31. Law 24 – No Ball

Law 24.1 (b) shall be replaced by the following:

The bowler may not deliver the ball underarm. If a bowler bowls a ball underarm, the umpire shall call and signal No ball.

32. Law 25.1 – Judging a Wide

Law 25.1 will apply with the addition of the following:

If in the umpires opinion the bowler is attempting to utilize the rough outside a batsman's leg stump, or is bowling down the leg side as a negative tactic, the umpire will call and signal Wide ball unless the ball passes sufficiently within the reach of the striker for him to be able to hit it with his bat by means of a normal cricket stroke. Refer to Law 25.1 Judging a Wide.

33. Batsmen

The following will apply to the batsman:

A batsman may call for a helmet to be brought out to him at any time. He must then wear or carry it personally all the time while play is in progress, or can have it taken off the field at the fall of a wicket, or at the end of an over, or at any drinks interval. In all cases, no actions involving helmets are to waste playing time. Umpires are not to hold helmets.

A batsman may only change other items of protective equipment (e.g. batting gloves, etc.) provided that there is no waste of playing time.

34. Law 41 – The Fielder

Law 41 shall apply with the following:

The exchanging of protective equipment between members of the fielding side on the field shall be permitted provided that the umpires do not consider that it constitutes a waste of playing time.

35. Law 42.3 – The Match Ball – Changing its Condition

Law 42.3 shall apply as modified below.

Delete Law 42.3 (e) (ii) and replace with the following:

Inform the captain of the fielding side of the reason for the action taken.

In addition to Law 42.3:

In the event that a ball has been interfered with and requires replacement, the batsmen at the wicket shall choose the replacement ball from a selection of six (6) other balls of various degrees of usage (including a new ball) and of the same brand as the ball in use prior to the contravention.

36. Law 42.6 (a) – Bowling of Fast Short Pitched Balls

Law 42.6 (a) (i) and (ii) shall be replaced by the following:

36.1　(a)　A bowler shall be limited to two fast short pitched deliveries per over.

(b)　A fast short pitched ball is defined as a ball, which after pitching, passes or would have passed above shoulder height of the batsman standing upright in his normal guard position at the crease (also see 36.1 (d)).

(c)　The umpire at the bowler's end shall advise the bowler and the batsman on strike when each fast short pitched delivery has been bowled.

(d)　In addition, for the purpose of this regulation, a ball that passes clearly above head height of the batsman, other than a fast short pitched ball as defined in 36.1 (b) above, that prevents him from being able to hit it with his bat by means of a normal cricket stroke shall be called a Wide and will also count as one of the allowable balls above shoulder height for that over.

36.2   (a) In the event of a bowler bowling more than two fast short pitched deliveries in an over as defined in 36.1 (b) above, the umpire at the bowler's end shall call and signal No ball on each occasion. A differential signal shall be used to signify a No ball for a fast short pitched delivery. The umpire shall call and signal No ball and then tap the head with the other hand.

      (b) If a bowler delivers a third fast short pitched ball in an over, the umpire, after the call of No ball and when the ball is dead, shall caution the bowler, inform the other umpire, the captain of the fielding side and the batsmen at the wicket of what has occurred. This caution shall apply throughout the innings. See 36.2 (d).

      (c) If there is a second instance of the bowler being no balled in the innings for bowling more than two fast short pitched deliveries in an over, the umpire shall advise the bowler that this is his final warning for the innings. The umpire will also inform the other umpire, the captain of the fielding side and the batsmen at the wicket of what has occurred.

      (d) Should there be any further instance by the same bowler in that innings, the umpire shall call and signal No ball and when the ball is dead direct the captain to take the bowler off forthwith. If necessary, the over shall be completed by another bowler, who shall neither have bowled the previous over nor be allowed to bowl the next over.

      (e) The bowler thus taken off shall not be allowed to bowl again in that innings.

      (f) The umpire will report the occurrence to the other umpire, the batsmen at the wicket and as soon as possible to the captain of the batting side.

      (g) The umpires will then report the matter to Cricket Australia which shall take such action as is considered appropriate against the captain and the bowler concerned. (Refer also to Law 42.1 Fair and Unfair Play – Responsibility of Captains.)

The above is not a substitute for Cricket Australia Playing Condition 37 below which umpires are able to apply at any time.

37. Law 42.7 – Dangerous and Unfair Bowling – Action by the Umpire

Law 42.7 shall be replaced by the following:

Regardless of any action taken by the umpire as a result of a breach of clauses 36, 38 or 39, the following shall apply at any time during the match.

    The bowling of fast short pitched balls is unfair if the umpire at the bowler's end considers that by their repetition and taking into account their length, height and direction, they are likely to inflict physical injury on the striker, irrespective of the protective clothing and equipment he may be wearing. The relative skill of the striker shall also be taken into consideration.

    In the event of such unfair bowling, the umpire at the bowler's end shall adopt the following procedure:

      (a) In the first instance the umpire shall call and signal No ball, and when the ball is dead, caution the bowler and inform the other umpire, the captain of the fielding side and the batsmen of what has occurred.

      (b) If there is a second instance by the same bowler in that innings, he shall repeat the above procedure and indicate to the bowler that this is a final warning.

      (c) Both the above caution and final warning shall continue to apply throughout the innings even though the bowler may later change ends.

Should there be a further instance by the same bowler in that innings, the umpire at the bowler's end shall:

    (i)   Call and signal No ball and when the ball is dead direct the captain to take the bowler off forthwith and to complete the over with another bowler, provided that the bowler does not bowl two overs or part thereof consecutively. See Law 22.8. (Bowler Incapacitated or Suspended during an Over).

    (ii)   Not allow the bowler, thus taken off, to bowl again in the same innings.

    (iii) Report the occurrence to the captain of the batting side as soon as the players leave the field for an interval.

    (iv) Report the occurrence to the Executive of the fielding side and to Cricket Australia, which shall take any further action which is considered to be appropriate against the captain and the bowler concerned. (Refer also to Law 42.1 Fair and Unfair Play – Responsibility of Captains.)

38. Law 42.6 (b) - Bowling of High Full Pitched Balls

Law 42.6 (b) shall apply as modified:

(a) Any delivery, other than a slow paced one, which passes or would have passed on the full above waist height of the bowler standing upright at the crease is deemed dangerous and unfair, whether or not is it likely to inflict physical injury on the striker.

(b) A slow delivery that passes or would have passed on the full above shoulder height of the striker standing upright at the crease is to be deemed dangerous and unfair, whether or not it is likely to inflict physical injury on the striker.

(c) In the event of a bowler bowling a high full pitched ball as defined in (a) and (b) above (i.e. a beamer), the umpire at the bowler's end shall adopt the following procedure:

(i)   In the first instance the umpire shall call and signal No ball and when the ball is dead, caution the bowler and issue a first and final warning. The umpire shall inform the other umpire, captain of the fielding side and the batsman of what has occurred.

(ii)   At the first repetition call and signal No ball and when the ball is dead, direct the captain of the fielding side to take the bowler off forthwith and to complete the over with another bowler, provided that the bowler does not bowl two overs or part thereof consecutively.

(iii)   Not allow the bowler, thus taken off, to bowl again in the same innings.

(iv)   At the first opportunity report the occurrence, with the other umpire, to the captain of the batting side and Cricket Australia which shall take any further action that is considered to be appropriate against the captain and the bowler concerned. (Refer also to Law 42.1 Fair and Unfair Play – Responsibility of Captains.)

39. Deliberate Bowling of High Full Pitched Balls

Law 42.8 shall be replaced with the following:

If the umpire considers that a high full pitch which is deemed dangerous and unfair as defined in clause 38 (a) and (b) was deliberately bowled, then the first and final warning process shall be dispensed with. The umpire at the bowlers end shall:

(a) Call and signal No ball.

(b) When the ball is dead, direct the captain to take the bowler off forthwith.

(c) Not allow the bowler to bowl again in that innings.

(d) Complete the over with another bowler provided that the bowler does not bowl two overs or part thereof consecutively.

(e) At the first opportunity, the umpires will report the occurrence to the captain of the batting side and Cricket Australia which shall take any further action which is considered appropriate against the captain and bowler concerned. (Refer also to Law 42.1 Fair and Unfair Play – Responsibility of Captains.)

40. Dangerous and Unfair Bowling - Action by the Umpires

The Bowling of Fast Short Pitched Deliveries, Dangerous and Unfair Bowling, The Bowling of High Full Pitched Balls and Deliberate Bowling of High Full Pitched Balls.

Cumulative cautions and warnings will not apply and each different form of dangerous and unfair bowling will be treated separately in the caution and warning process as defined in clauses 36, 37, 38 and 39.

41. Law 42.9 – Time Wasting by the Fielding Side

Law 42.9 shall apply, subject to Law 42.9 (b) being replaced by the following:

If there is any further waste of time in that innings, by any member of the fielding side the umpire shall:

(i)   Call and signal Dead ball if necessary, and

(ii)   Award five (5) penalty runs to the batting side (see Law 42.17).

(iii)   Inform the other umpire, the batsmen at the wicket and as soon as possible the captain of the batting side of what has occurred.

(iv)   Report the occurrence to Cricket Australia which shall take such action as deemed appropriate against the captain and the team concerned.

42. Law 42.18 – Players' Conduct

All players shall be bound by the terms of the Cricket Australia Code of Behaviour, Cricket Australia Racial and Religious Vilification Code, Cricket Australia Anti Harassment Policy and Cricket Australia Anti Doping Policy.

43. Hitting-up

Teams are required to observe ground authority regulations and to exercise the utmost care and caution when engaging in practice and pre-match warm-up and "hitting-up" activities so as to avoid the risk of injury to members of the public, damage to the centre wicket region and to perimeter fencing.

44. Interpretation of Playing Conditions

Uniform Interpretation

The local State Association shall be responsible to ensure uniform interpretation of these playing conditions and to adjudicate, if necessary, should there be any dispute.

45. Clothing, Equipment and Footwear

45.1 Commercial Logos and Advertising

Only approved logos and identification, as authorised by ICC policy and/or Cricket Australia/State Associations, are permitted to be worn in international and interstate matches.

45.2 Footwear

The use of non-spiked footwear by players is not permitted.

45.3 Ice Vests

Ice vests may be worn provided that they are white, display no branding and are worn under the shirt.

46. Pura Cup Final

Except as varied hereunder, Pura Cup playing conditions shall apply.

46.1 Duration of Match and Hours of Play

If the Final is played in Queensland, play will commence at 10.00 a.m., in New South Wales, Victoria, Tasmania or South Australia at 11.00 a.m., in Western Australia at 10.30 a.m..

(a)   The Final shall be of five days scheduled duration with scheduled hours of play to be advised on announcement of the venue.

(b)   If immediately prior to the commencement of the scheduled last hour of the match, a cumulative total of at least six hours scheduled play has been lost on account of weather, light, pitch or ground, then one extra day shall be added.

(c)   If the match has not commenced by the midway between lunch and tea on the fourth day (i.e. 2.40 p.m. assuming playing hours of 11.00 a.m. to 6.00 p.m.), then the match shall revert to a first innings match played under ordinary conditions. With make up time, the total playing time remaining will be 17? hours at this point.

46.2 Over Rates

As per Test Match Playing Conditions clause 16.1. That is, the initial minimum of overs shall be 90 per day calculated at one over for each full four minutes.

46.3 Penalties for not Achieving Over Rates

Overs will be calculated at the end of the match. For each over the team is short of the target number, 5%, of each players match fee (excluding twelfth man) is to be deducted for the first five overs and 10% per over thereafter.

46.4 Venue

The team that finished first on the points table at the conclusion of the preliminary matches shall have the choice of venue, provided that this venue is acceptable to Cricket Australia. Should the team waive this right, the choice shall be offered to the team that finished second. Otherwise the decision shall be made by Cricket Australia.

46.5 Umpires

The Umpires for the Final shall be appointed by Cricket Australia and must be members of the National Umpires Panel or ICC Elite Umpires Panel.

46.6 Match Referee

Cricket Australia will appoint a Match Referee for the Final.

46.7 Result

The team that finished second must defeat the team that finished first outright to win except where 46.1(c) above applies, whereby the match shall revert to a first innings result.

Note: If the Final is drawn or tied, the team that finished on top of the points table shall be declared the winner of the Pura Cup.

CRICKET AUSTRALIA
CODE OF BEHAVIOUR

PREAMBLE

Cricket is a game that owes much of its unique appeal to the fact that it is to be played not only within its Laws, but also within the spirit of the game. Any action seen as abusing this spirit causes injury to the game itself.

Embracing the spirit of the game means playing fairly and exhibiting respect for opponents, fellow team members, the umpires and the game's traditional values such as graciousness in defeat and humility in victory.

Cricket has a distinct place in Australian society and history. As an element in Australia's national identity, cricket plays a significant role. This status brings with it particular responsibilities for players and officials to conform to high standards of fair play and personal behaviour on and off the field.

This Code of Behaviour is intended to protect and enshrine such important qualities and standards so that all may continue to enjoy the game of cricket now and in the future.

SECTION 1: RULES FOR BEHAVIOUR – OFFENCES

Each of the rules for behaviour has a guideline. The guidelines are intended as an illustrative guide only and in the case of any doubt as to the interpretation of the Rule, the provisions of the Rule itself shall take precedence over the provisions of the guidelines. The guidelines should not be read as an exhaustive list of offences or prohibited conduct.

1. Level 1 Offences

The Offences set out at 1.1 to 1.6 below are Level 1 Offences. The range of penalties which shall be imposed for a Level 1 Offence is set out in Section 5 of this Code. Players and, where applicable, officials must not:

1.1 Abuse cricket equipment or clothing, ground equipment or fixtures and fittings

- Includes actions outside the course of normal cricket actions such as hitting or kicking the wickets and actions which intentionally or negligently result in damage to the advertising boards, boundary fences, dressing room doors, mirrors, windows and other fixtures and fittings.

1.2 Show dissent at an umpire's decision by action or verbal abuse

- Includes excessive, obvious disappointment with an umpire's decision or with an umpire making the decision and obvious delay in resuming play or leaving the wicket.
- This Rule does not prohibit the bowler involved in the decision or a team captain from asking an umpire to provide an explanation for a decision or a Team official from making a formal complaint.

1.3 Use language that is obscene, offensive or insulting and/or the making of an obscene gesture

- This includes swearing and offensive gestures which are not directed at another person such as swearing in frustration at one's own poor play or fortune.
- This offence is not intended to penalise trivial behaviour. The extent to which such behaviour is likely to give offence shall be taken into account when assessing the seriousness of the breach.

1.4 Engage in excessive appealing

- Excessive shall mean repeated appealing when the bowler/fielder knows the batsman is not out with the intention of placing the umpire under pressure. It is not intended to prevent loud or enthusiastic appealing. However, the practice of celebrating or assuming a dismissal before the decision has been given may also come within this Rule.

1.5 Point or gesture towards the pavilion in an aggressive manner upon the dismissal of a batsman

- Self explanatory.

1.6 Breach any regulation regarding approved clothing or equipment

- This includes regulations regarding bat logos and regulations regarding other logos or advertising which may be worn or displayed.

2. Level 2 Offences

The Offences set out at 2.1 to 2.9 below are Level 2 Offences. The range of penalties which shall be imposed for a Level 2 Offence is set out in Section 5 of this Code. Players and, where applicable, officials must not:

2.1 Show serious dissent at an umpire's decision by action or verbal abuse
- Dissent should be classified as serious dissent where the dissent is expressed by a specific action such as the shaking of the head, snatching cap from umpire, pointing at pad or inside edge, other displays of anger or abusive language directed at the umpire or excessive delay in resuming play or leaving the wicket.
- This Rule does not prohibit the bowler involved in the decision or a team captain from asking an umpire to provide an explanation for a decision or a Team official from making a formal complaint.

2.2 Engage in inappropriate and deliberate physical contact with other players or officials in the course of play
- Without limitation, players will breach this regulation if they deliberately walk or run into or shoulder another player, official or match official.

2.3 Charge or advance towards the umpire in an aggressive manner when appealing
- Self explanatory.

2.4 Deliberately distract or maliciously distract or obstruct another player or official on the field of play
- This does not replace clauses 39 and 40 of the Pura Cup Playing Conditions.
- Without limitation, players will breach this rule if they deliberately attempt to distract a striker by words or gestures or deliberately shepherd a batsman while running or attempting to run between wickets.

2.5 Throw the ball at or near a player or official in an inappropriate and/or dangerous manner
- This Rule will not prohibit a fielder or bowler from returning the ball to the stumps in the normal fashion.

2.6 Use language that is obscene, offensive or of a seriously insulting nature to another player, official or spectator.
- This is language of gestures which are directed at another person. See comments under Rule 1.3 above in relation to the seriousness of the breach.

2.7 Change the condition of the ball in breach of Law 42.3
- Prohibited behaviour includes picking the seam or deliberately throwing the ball into ground for the purpose of roughening it up and the application of moisture to the ball, save for perspiration and saliva.

2.8 Without limiting Rule 8, attempt to manipulate a Match in regard to the result, net run rate, bonus points or otherwise. The captain of any team guilty of such conduct shall be held responsible.
- Prohibited conduct under this rule will include incidents where a team bats in such a way as to either adversely affect its own, or improve its opponent's, bonus points, net run rate or quotient.

2.9 Seriously breach any regulation regarding approved clothing or equipment
- See guideline for Rule 1.6 above. Without limitation, a breach will be considered serious if it is done in bad faith or where it has serious commercial consequences (eg display of logo of competing CA or State sponsor)

3. Level 3 Offences

The Offences set out at 3.1 to 3.3 below are Level 3 Offences. The range of penalties which shall be imposed for a Level 3 Offence is set out in Section 5 of this Code. Players and, where applicable, officials must not:

3.1 Intimidate an umpire or referee whether by language or conduct
- Includes appealing in an aggressive or threatening manner.

3.2 Threaten to assault another player, Team official or spectator.
- Self explanatory.

3.3 Use language or gestures that offend, insult, humiliate, threaten, disparage or vilify another person on the basis of that person's race, religion, colour, descent or national or ethnic origin

- Self explanatory.

4. Level 4 Offences

The Offences set out at 4.1 to 4.4 below are Level 4 Offences. The range of penalties which shall be imposed for a Level 4 Offence is set out in Section 5 of this Code. Players and, where applicable, officials must not:

4.1 Threaten to assault an umpire or referee

- Self explanatory.

4.2 Physically assault another player, umpire, referee, official or spectator

- Self explanatory.

4.3 Engage in any act of violence on the field of play

- Self explanatory.

4.4 Use language or gestures that seriously offends, insults, humiliates, threatens, disparages or vilifies another person on the basis of that person's race, religion, colour, descent or national or ethnic origin

- Self explanatory.

5. Laws of Cricket and Spirit of the Game

Players must obey the Laws of Cricket and play within the spirit of the game. The captain and Team coach must use their best efforts to ensure that their Team and individual members of the Team complies with this rule

- This is meant as a general Rule to deal with situations where the facts or of the gravity or seriousness of the alleged incident are not adequately or clearly covered by the offences set out in Rules 1–4 (inclusive) of the Code.
- Conduct which will be prohibited under the clause includes using an illegal bat, time wasting and any conduct which is considered "unfair play" under Law 42 of the Laws of Cricket.
- This Rule is not intended to punish unintentional breaches of the Laws of Cricket.
- Reference may be made to any statement or explanation of the Spirit of Cricket published in conjunction with the Laws of Cricket.
- Nothing in this Rule or the Code alters the onus on the captain to ensure that the Spirit of the Game is adhered to as stated and defined in the preamble to the Laws of Cricket.

6. Unbecoming Behaviour

Without limiting any other rule, players and officials must not at any time engage in behaviour unbecoming to a representative player or official that could bring the game of cricket into disrepute or be harmful to the interests of cricket

- This is also meant as a general Rule to deal with situations where the facts or of the gravity or seriousness of the alleged incident are not adequately or clearly covered by the offences set out in Rules 1–4 (inclusive) of the Code.
- It is intended to include serious or repeated criminal conduct, public acts of misconduct, unruly public behaviour and cheating during play.
- This Rule applies in the following circumstances only (whichever is the longer):

  (a) subject to paragraph (b), participation in any Match, tour or training camp in Australia or overseas – from the time of departure from the player's or official's usual private residence prior to the tour or camp until return to that residence after the tour or camp;

  (b) participation in a Home Match or series of Matches – from the commencement of the day before the first day of the Match or series of Matches until the end of the day following the conclusion of the Match or series of Matches.

(c) participation in a home training session – from the time of arrival at the venue until departure; and

(d) attendance at an official cricket function or performance of obligations under a contract with Cricket Australia or a state or territory cricket association – from the time of departure from the player's or official's usual private residence prior to the function or performance of the obligation until return to that residence afterwards.

Notwithstanding the foregoing, this Rule applies at all times where the unbecoming behaviour involves:

(i) serious or repeated criminal conduct; or

(ii) public comment or comment to or in the media.

7. Anti-Doping Policy

Players and officials must obey Cricket Australia's Anti-Doping Policy (as amended from time to time).

Any behaviour prohibited by this Rule will be dealt with under the Anti-Doping Policy and not under the Code of Behaviour.

8. Betting, Match-fixing and Corruption

Players and officials must not, directly or indirectly, engage in the following conduct:

(a) bet, gamble or enter into any other form of financial speculation on any cricket match or on any event connected with any cricket match (for the purposes of this Rule, an Event);

(b) induce or encourage any other person to bet, gamble or enter into any other form of financial speculation on any cricket match or on any Event or to offer the facility for such bets to be placed;

(c) be a party to contriving or attempting to contrive the result of any cricket match or the occurrence of any Event in exchange for any benefit or reward (other than a benefit or reward received from his home Board);

(d) fail to attempt to perform to the best of his ability in any cricket match for any reason whatsoever (including, in particular, owing to an arrangement relating to betting on the outcome of any cricket match or on the occurrence of any Event) other than for legitimate tactical reasons in relation to that cricket match;

(e) induce or encourage any player not to attempt to perform to the best of the player's ability in any cricket match for any reason whatsoever (including, in particular, owing to an arrangement relating to betting on the outcome of any cricket match or on the occurrence of any Event) other than for legitimate tactical reasons in relation to that cricket match;

For the purpose of this Rule:

(a) a reference to a "cricket match" includes any cricket match whatsoever played anywhere in the world and is not restricted to a cricket match in which the player took part; and

(b) a reference to an "attempt" shall include an offer or an invitation.

(f) for benefit or reward (whether for the player him or herself or any other person), provide any information concerning the weather, the state of the ground, a Team or its members (including, without limitation, the Team's actual or likely composition, the form or individual players or tactics) the status or possible outcome of any cricket match or the possible occurrence of any Event other than in connection with bona fide media interviews and commitments;

(g) engage in any other form of corrupt conduct in relation to any cricket match or Event;

(h) fail to promptly disclose to the Chief Executive Officer of Cricket Australia that he or she has received an approach from another person to engage in conduct such as that described in paragraphs (a) – (g) above (such disclosure to be in writing and include full particulars of any such approach);

(i) fail to promptly disclose to the Chief Executive Officer of Cricket Australia that he or she knows or reasonably suspects that any current or former player or official or any other person has received, or been approached to engage in conduct, such as that described in paragraphs (a) – (g) above (such disclosure to be in writing and include full particulars of any such knowledge or suspicion):

(j) fail to promptly disclose to the Chief Executive Officer of Cricket Australia that he or she has received, or is aware or reasonably suspects that another player or official or any other person has received, actual or implied threats of any nature in relation to past or of proposed conduct such as that described in paragraphs (a) – (g) above (such disclosure to be in writing and include full particulars of any such knowledge or suspicion); or

(k) engage in conduct that relates directly or indirectly to any of the conduct described in paragraphs (a) – (j) above and is prejudicial to the interests of the game of cricket.

A valid defence may be made to a charge in respect of any prohibited conduct set out in this Rules 8(h), (i) and (j) if the person charged proves that the conduct was the result of an honest and reasonable belief that there was a serious threat to the life or safety of the person charged or any member of the person's family.

9. Detrimental Public Comment

Without limiting any other rule, players and officials must not make public or media comment which is detrimental to the interests of the game

Without limitation, players and officials will breach this if by making any public or media comment they:

- publicly denigrate another player or publicly denigrate or criticise an official, umpire, referee or team against which they have played or will play, whether in relation to incidents which occurred in a match or otherwise;
- denigrate a country in which they are or are likely to be touring or officiating;
- denigrate the home country of a touring team against which they are or are likely to be playing or in respect of which they are or are likely to be officiating;
- denigrate another player or official by inappropriately commenting on any aspect of his or her performance, abilities or characteristics;
- comment on the likely outcome of a hearing or a report or an appeal;
- criticise the outcome of a hearing or an appeal;
- criticise any evidence, submission or other comment made by any person at the hearing of a report or any appeal.

10. Racial and Religious Vilification Code

Without limiting Rules 3.3 and 4.4, players and officials must obey Cricket Australia's Racial and Religious Vilification Code (as amended from time to time).

Any behaviour prohibited by this Rule will be dealt with under the Racial and Religious Vilification Code and not under the Code of Behaviour, save where a report is made under another rule of the Code of Behaviour (in which case a player or official may also lodge a complaint under the Racial and Religious Vilification Code).

11. Anti-Harassment Policy

Players and officials must obey Cricket Australia's Anti-Harassment Policy (as amended from time to time).

Any behaviour prohibited by this Rule will be dealt with under the Anti-Harassment Policy and not under the Code of Behaviour, save where a report is made under another rule of the Code of Behaviour (in which case a player or official may also lodge a complaint under the Anti-Harassment Policy).

SECTION 5: PENALTIES

1. In the event the Commission decides that any person has breached any of Rules 1 – 4 (inclusive) of Section 1 of this Code and this Code of Behaviour, it will apply a penalty within the range of penalties for each level of offence set out in the table below and may also apply any or all of the penalties set out in Rule 2 of this Section (with the exception of Match bans and fines contemplated under Rules 2(a) and 2(c)).

The following rules of interpretation apply to any penalty imposed under this Rule:

(a) A "multi-day Match" means a Match of more than one days' scheduled duration and a "one-day Match" means a Match on one day's scheduled duration.

(b) The Commission must specify the type of Match or Matches in which the ban is to be served. The Commission must specify a different ban (within the applicable range) for each type of Match in respect of which the ban is to apply. For example, a player found guilty of a Level 3 offence may be banned for 4 Pura Cup Matches, 2 Test Matches, 6 ING Cup Matches and 5 One Day International Matches.

(c) In addition to any ban imposed under this Rule (and without limiting the Commission's powers with respect to Level 4 bans), the Commission may, if it deems appropriate, ban the person from participation in any club match or matches for a specified period of time.

(d) In the event that a player receives an ICC imposed international Match ban for a breach of any of the offences set out in either Level 3 or Level 4 of the ICC Code of Conduct (or their equivalent from time to time) other than a Level 3 offence under the ICC Code of Conduct for a repeat of a Level 2 offence within a twelve month period, the Senior Commissioner or the Deputy Senior Commissioner (or another Commissioner nominated by the Chief Executive Officer of Cricket Australia) will conduct a hearing to determine whether the player should receive a domestic Match ban during the period commencing on the first day of the ICC imposed ban and the last day of the ICC imposed ban, and if so, the type of Match or Matches in which the ban is to be served. As far as appropriate, the provisions of Section 4 of this Code will apply to any hearing under this paragraph (d) except that:

(i) the hearing will be a hearing as to penalty only (and will not be a review of the guilt or innocence of the player under the ICC Code of Conduct or a rule of this Code); and

(ii) the hearing must be convened within 10 business days of the relevant decision (or an appeal from that decision under the ICC Code of Conduct.

When imposing any penalty under this paragraph (d) the following principles will apply:

(i) the Commission may not impose a ban in relation to Test Matches or One Day International Matches;

(ii) the Commission may not impose a ban which extends beyond the last day of the ICC imposed match ban;

(iii) the number of domestic matches in a ban imposed by the Commission must not exceed the number of matches forming part of the ICC imposed match ban (for example, a player who receives a three Test Match ban may not receive a ban of more than three Pura Cup Matches); and

(iv) the Commission may take into account any circumstance it considers relevant, including those listed in Rule 3 of this Section 5.

(e) If a player or official repeats an offence within a particular Level (excluding Level 4) within a twelve month period, the Commission will impose a penalty in line with the next highest Level. For example, if a player is found to have committed a Level 2.3 offence and six months later is found to have committed a Level 2.6 offence, the player will be penalised as if he or she had committed a Level 3 offence.

(f) In relation to a fine which is determined by reference to a 'match fee' (as referred to in the table above), the relevant match will be the match in which the offence occurred.

2. Without limiting Rule 1 of this Section, in the event the Commission decides that any person has breached any of Rules 5, 6 or 9 of Section 1 of this Code of Behaviour, it will apply one or more of the following penalties:

(a) Ban the person from participating in any Match.

(b) Ban the person from holding (or continuing to hold) any position within Cricket Australia or a State or Territory Cricket Association (including as an employee, official or officer);

(c) Fine the person an amount that accords with Rule 11 of this Section;

(d) Direct that the person make reparation for damage caused by that person to any property;

(e) Require the person to undergo counselling for a specified time;

(f) Require the person to perform voluntary service to cricket or the community; and/or

(g) Reprimand the person.

3. Without limiting Rule 1 of this Section, when imposing any penalty upon a person who has breached this Code of Behaviour, the Commission may take into account any circumstance it considers relevant, including the following:

(a) the seriousness of the breach;

(b) the harm caused by the breach to the interests of cricket;

(c) the person's seniority and standing in the game;

(d) remorse shown by the person and the prospect of further breaches;

(e) the prior record of the person in abiding by this Code, the ICC Code of Conduct and any similar code of behaviour; and

(f) the impact of the penalty on the person, including the person's capacity to pay a fine as evidenced by the proportion of the person's annual income from Cricket Australia or a state or territory cricket association that the proposed fine represents.

4. In the event the Commission decides that a person is guilty of an offence under any of Rules 1 – 4 of Section 1 of this Code and the person is not described in the table under Rule 1 above, the Commission will impose one or more of the penalties set out in Rule 2 of this Section, taking into account any circumstance which it considers relevant including those set out in Rule 3 of this Section.

5. Penalties for behaviour which contravenes the codes and policies described in Rules 7, 10 and 11 of Section 1 will be determined in accordance with the relevant code or policy.

6. Any player or official required to pay a fine or to make reparation must so do within thirty (30) days or as otherwise decided by the Commission. Any failure to meet this requirement will render the player or official ineligible for selection or official duties in any Team or Match.

7. If the Commission finds a person reported for separate incidents within a match to be guilty of more than one offence, it should impose separate penalties in respect of each offence. Penalties in such cases are cumulative and not concurrent.

8. Plea bargaining is not permitted. It is open to the Commission to find a person guilty of an offence in a level lower than that in which he or she is charged where the constituent elements of the lesser offence are the same. For example, if a player is charged with serious dissent under Rule 2.1 of Section 1, it is open to the Commission to find the player guilty of dissent under Rule 1.2 of Section 1 rather than serious dissent.

9. In the event the Commission decides that any person has breached a provision of Rule 8 of Section 1, the Commission:

(a) may impose any or all of the penalties under Rules 2(c) to (g) inclusive; and

(b) will impose the penalties under Rules 2 (a) and (b) of this Section, and will ban the person from (in the case of a player) being selected in a Team or (in the case of an official) being involved in any Team or Match, for the following periods of time:

Rule 8(a)	–	Between 1 and 5 years
Rule 8(b)	–	Between 2 and 5 years if the player or official directly benefited (or intended to directly benefit) from his or her actions; otherwise, a minimum of 1 year
Rule 8(c)	–	life
Rule 8(d)	–	life
Rule 8(e)	–	life
Rule 8(f)	–	Between 2 and 5 years if the player or official directly benefited (or intended to directly benefit) from his or her actions; otherwise, a minimum of 1 year
Rule 8(g)	–	Between 2 years and life
Rule 8(h)	–	Between 1 and 5 years
Rule 8(i)	–	Between 1 and 5 years
Rule 8(j)	–	Between 1 and 5 years
Rule 8(k)	–	Between 1 and 5 years

10. Nothing in this Section limits the Commission's ability to impose a ban and a fine in respect of a breach of Rule 8 of Section 1.

11. When the Commission imposes a fine for a breach of Rules 5, 6, 8 or 9 of Section 1, it will not exceed the amounts listed in the following table, provided that no fines will be imposed on players or officials who do not receive remuneration as a result of their playing or officiating duties:

Rule Number	Description of Offence	First Breach	Further Breach
Rule 5	Laws of Cricket and Spirit of the Game	$5,750	$11,500
Rule 6	Unbecoming Behaviour	$5,750	$11,500
Rule 8	Betting, Match Fixing and Corruption	unlimited	unlimited
Rule 9	Detrimental Public Comment	$5,750	$11,500

Tuckered Out?

You would think from reading about the game that today's international cricketers are playing more than ever, and that the workload is getting too much for some senior players. But how does the amount of cricket played by today's players compare to earlier eras?

Here is a selection of Australian players from different eras, at the peaks of their careers, and the number of days of senior cricket (first-class and "List A" one-dayers) they played:

	days per year			days per year
C. Hill 1899-05	54		M.L. Hayden 2001-04	101
D.G. Bradman 1929-33	60		J.L. Langer 2001-04	96
R.N. Harvey 1953-57	80		A.C. Gilchrist 2001-04	100
W.M. Lawry 1961-66	75		R.T. Ponting 2001-04	100
G.S. Chappell 1972-77	98		G.D. McGrath 2001-04	79
A.R. Border 1986-91	108		J.N. Gillespie 2001-04	83
M.E. Waugh 1995-99	114			

In short, cricket workload has increased, but only over the long term, and not as much as you might think. None of today's senior players play quite as much cricket as Mark Waugh ten years ago, or Allan Border almost 20 years ago.

Mark Waugh actually played 173 days of cricket in one calendar year, 1995. He was able to combine his international duties with a full season of county cricket for Essex. The fact that, even in recent years, Australian players have chosen to play county cricket whenever there was a break in the international program, tends to undermine their claims that they are being overloaded.

The workloads today are only about 20% higher than they were 50 years ago (Harvey). And note that players like Harvey, Hill and even Bradman, probably played a lot more minor cricket than today's stars.

If you look at the English professional game, high workloads extend even further back. As early as the 1890s, Tom Hayward of Surrey was playing more than 100 days a year, while in the 1940s, Dennis Compton averaged almost 120 days per year. In Hayward and Compton's time, a day's cricket in England usually meant more than 130 or 140 overs. Today, 90 overs is a typical output.

– CHARLES DAVIS

KEITH MILLER shows the easy grace that made him such a popular figure with team-mates and fans.

Obituaries

by WARWICK FRANKS

ALLEY, WILLIAM EDWARD, died in Taunton, England on 26 November, 2004. Bill Alley was one of the large group of Australian cricketers who looked at the strength of the competition for places in state and national teams after World War II and decided to go to England. There, at the age of 38, he began more than a decade with Somerset during which he never ceased to be the archetypal Australian: tough, practical, resourceful and laconic. These qualities were emphasised in the portrait of Alley as one of Wisden's Five Cricketers of the Year in 1962: "Nothing daunts him and he breathes a spirit of confidence among his colleagues." A prime example of this was his performance against Middlesex at Lord's in 1957 when he opened both the batting and bowling and took the gloves when the regular keeper was indisposed.

Born in the northern Sydney suburb of Hornsby on 3 February, 1919, the red-haired Alley was raised by his grandmother in nearby Brooklyn. He joined the Northern District club in 1938-39, making an immediate impression with his aggressive batting and his wicket keeping. As a boilermaker on the New South Wales railways, he was in a reserved occupation and able to play grade cricket throughout the war. Moving to Petersham, he hammered 1,413 runs at 70.65 in 1943-44, still a Sydney record, and took 57 wickets with his developing medium-pacers at 15.12. Against University, he took 6 for 52 and then took the students' attack apart to the tune of 230 in 142 minutes, peppered with 12 sixes and 21 fours. He was called into the state team in 1945-46 and, while his bowling was little used, he made three rapid centuries to be placed fifth in the national aggregates. Alley always emphasised his lack of coaching but a good eye, strong arms and aggressive instincts were tempered by a respect for the orthodoxies. So swiftly did he score that in his second match, against South Australia at Adelaide, he raced to 111 in 130 minutes before a strained leg muscle forced him to retire hurt. He also took 119 off the Australian Services attack in only 127 minutes while in the return match against South Australia, he was more restrained, his undefeated 129 in 211 minutes holding the innings of 271 together.

At this stage, he was told by Don Bradman that he was a certainty for the forthcoming tour of New Zealand; to celebrate, he bought 12 top-quality cricket shirts, but then missed selection. The shirts were later snapped up by Ernie Toshack, who told Alley's wife: "He won't be needing them now." He did have an alternative: as Battling Bill Alley, he had gone from sparring partner and dance hall bouncer to 28 undefeated professional fights and the title of Australian welter-weight champion, with the possibility of bouts in the United States in the offing.

But the next year Alley had to deal with a succession of traumas: his first wife died in childbirth; his mother died; and he himself was seriously injured in practice at the Adelaide Oval when a shot from Jock Livingston struck him while he was bending to pick up a ball in an adjacent net. He spent two days in a coma and his broken jaw had to be reconstructed with the aid of 60 stitches. Not only did the injury put him out of first-class cricket for the rest of the year, but it also abruptly terminated his boxing career.

So Alley left Australia at Christmas 1947 to spend the next nine English summers in the leagues: five with Colne, four with Blackpool. He was both successful and popular: in his first season with Blackpool he pounded 1,345 runs at 149.44, besides adding 41 wickets at 16.05. In 1949-50 he was a member of the Commonwealth team which toured India, Pakistan and Ceylon. He was second in the aggregates, converting two of his three centuries into doubles, though he was more muted in the unofficial Tests.

It was when Alley joined Somerset in 1957 that he transformed his cricketing career into the stuff of legend. The county had finished 17th and bottom from 1953 to 1955. The arrival of Colin McCool in 1956 helped to promote a more determined approach and the advent of Alley turned it into a real team: in 1958 Somerset were third. Such was his impact that he received his county cap after only four matches, a tribute to the gusto and impact of his personality as well as his cricket.

In 12 seasons he reached 1,000 runs on 10 occasions, and took 50 wickets the same number of times. 1961 was his year of wonders with the bat: at the age of 42 he reached 3,000 runs, a feat never achieved since in an English season. Included in his 11 centuries was his highest first-class score of 221 not out against Warwickshire at Nuneaton, a remarkable innings played at  number four where his runs were made out of 318 inside four hours in an unavailing run chase. The touring Australians also felt the power of Alley's bat when he took their attack apart with innings of 134 and 95. For good measure, he took 62 wickets, showing how he relished English conditions in extracting maximum value in swinging and cutting his medium-pacers.

To emphasise his durability and consistency, he performed the 1,000 run-100 wicket double the next season: with 1,915 runs and 112 wickets which included his best first-class figures of 8 for 65 against Surrey at The Oval. Right through the 1960s, he continued to be a force in county cricket: aged 49, he rattled up another 1,000 runs and took useful wickets, even if Wisden noted some falling-off in his aggressive fielding in the

The archetypal Aussie: Bill Alley

gully. He claimed that by the time he finished his career most people were turning up to see if he was still alive and that players young enough to be his sons habitually asked him what it had been like to play with W.G. Grace. But he still took umbrage at being offered only a one-year contract for 1969, which added insult to the injury of never having been offered the captaincy. His loquacity and his toughness made him into the perfect stereotype of an Australian cricketer for English crowds and players. He trained on pints and found the ideal opponent in fast bowler Fred Trueman. Alley told of the occasion when he drove and hooked successive Trueman deliveries to the boundary, which were followed by a short volley of bouncers to which the Taunton crowd took vociferous exception. At the end of the over, batsman met bowler in mid-pitch with his bat raised, only for Trueman to promise: "First pint's on me tonight, Bill."

In 1969 he was appointed to the list of first-class umpires, remaining there for 15 years. Typically, he was alleged to have started his first season in the white coat by promising to have 100 wickets by the end of May. Alley was on the Test panel from 1974 to 1981 (excluding 1979) and umpired 10 Tests, including four involving Australia, plus nine one-day internationals. Despite their shared national background, at the Lord's Test in 1975, the Australian captain, Ian Chappell, gave him what Alley called "a rough and unpleasant ride". He married again in England, choosing to stay in the Taunton area where he became, at various times, a cider brewer, a bailiff for the County Court and a poultry farmer. Alley published two autobiographical volumes: *My Incredible Innings* (1969) and *Standing the Test of Time* (1999) in which he continued his campaign for positive, uninhibited cricket.

	M	I	NO	Runs	HS	100s	50s	Avge	Ct	St	W	Avge	BB
First-class	400	682	67	19,612	221*	31	92	31.88	293	0	788	22.68	8-65
Domestic first-class	3	6	0	69	36	0	0	11.50	0	0	3	15.00	2-1

ANDERSON, DAVID JOHN, died on 17 June, 2005, in Sydney, after a year's battle with cancer. Originally an opener, Anderson was a quick-footed left-hander who later batted in the middle order and had a wide array of strokes that he was prepared to play from the outset, sometimes to his own cost. Of medium height and slimly-built (173cm and 67kg), he was particularly rousing square of the wicket and his cuts and pulls had an echo of Neil Harvey about them. An athletic fieldsman with a strong arm, he was often a mobile presence in the covers. Until he switched to contact lenses, his black-rimmed glasses gave him a pensive air which belied the energy of his cricket.

Born in Warrnambool, Victoria, on 26 January, 1940, Anderson was educated at the local high school before moving to Melbourne and the Fitzroy club for the 1956-57 season. His 625 runs in 1960-61, his initial full season in the Firsts, saw him included in the state squad for the next season. After making a dashing 72 in a Colts game against New South Wales, he made an impressive first-class debut against South Australia at Melbourne by scoring 37 and 69. His second effort was a rousing affair which contributed to an opening partnership of 124 with Bill Lawry. Shortly afterwards, however, against New South Wales at Sydney, Anderson made a pair in which he was removed by Alan Davidson in the opening over of each innings.

Next season, he was replaced by Ian Redpath in the middle order and, when he returned towards the end of the season, it was in the middle order where it was felt that his approach would leave him more comfortable. In 1963-64, he made a well-organised 101 not out against the touring South Africans, and the next season he played several innings that demonstrated his capacity to bat over the long haul, including 136 at Perth to save the opening match. Against South Australia that year he recorded his best bowling figures in first-class cricket when he took 3 for 21. Anderson was one of several part-time Victorian spinners in the 1960s whose ability to turn the ball was more apparent than real, yet who were effective enough to conjure up the occasional wicket.

In 1965-66, he found his spot being challenged for by the young Paul Sheahan, and, though he was tried again as opener the next season, he was dropped for the seemingly-forgotten Ken Eastwood despite having scored two fifties, and finished his first-class career in the next season by filling in when Sheahan was away on Test duty. For Fitzroy, Anderson scored 4,044 runs at 30.87 with just one century and took 30 wickets at 27.86. He captained the side for the last two seasons before he retired in 1969-70 and was appointed captain-coach of Dandenong in the Sub-District competition. In 1980, he played in the Victorian side which won the masters' cricket championship in Sydney, scoring 43 not out in the final. Anderson worked for the Commonwealth Bank for over 40 years, living in Sydney after the mid-1970s, where he occupied senior management positions, including 10 years as secretary of the bank.

	M	I	NO	Runs	HS	100s	50s	Avge	Ct	St	W	Avge	BB
First-class	37	59	6	1,829	136	2	11	34.50	12	0	9	28.22	3-21
Domestic first-class	34	54	5	1,602	136	1	10	32.69	7	0	9	28.86	3-21

BEVAN, HUBERT GEORGE, died on 15 June, 2005, at East Fremantle.

In the early sixties, Hugh Bevan would periodically give visiting batsmen to Perth a sharp reminder of his skills as a bustling left-arm opening bowler. Later, he was a thoughtful and long-serving selector in the time at which the state became the dominant force in Australian domestic cricket. Born at the inner Perth suburb of Mount Lawley, Bevan completed his education at Perth Boys' High School. Soon after, he was playing baseball as a pitcher for Perth, using the game, like many cricketers of the time, to maintain winter fitness and skills. He first appeared for North Perth at the age of 16 but came to prominence in 1952-53 when he took 51 Pennant wickets at 13.76 to gain inclusion in the state squad. It was too strong, however, to allow him quick promotion.

Early in the 1956-57 season, Bevan took 7 for 18 against University and then turned 0 for 21 into 0 for 22 against Perth, so that when Ray Strauss was injured Bevan played the last games of the season, all at home. In the last of these matches, against Victoria, he took 6 for 106, impressing observers with his ability to make the ball get up steeply at an uncomfortable pace. It was 1960-61 before he gained a regular place and the following year he took 33 wickets at 25.24, which included 5 for 55 against New Zealand at Perth, 5 for 44 against Victoria at Melbourne and 6 for 65 against a Test-strength New South Wales at Perth. Tall (180cm) and well-built, Bevan was no classicist in style with his bustling approach and hurried action, but he could bowl a lethal in-swinger which he varied with angled deliveries: an approach that had echoes of Alan Davidson. His batting presence was usually only transitory.

Bustling bowler: Hugh Bevan

In 1961-62, he unhinged the Queensland first innings at Perth with his best first-class figures of 6 for 22 before he had to leave the field with persistent cramps. He began the next season with a pair of fine returns against the touring South Africans at Perth: 6 for 93 in the the state game and 5 for 65 for a Combined XI. Selected for the Australian XI match in Melbourne, Bevan may have been seen as an ideal replacement for the recently-retired Davidson but went into the match with a severe side strain which hampered his bowling and he contributed just 18 wicketless overs. The rest of the season was an anti-climax, his last 13 wickets for the season costing over 70 each. Always prone to bowl no-balls under the back-foot rule because of his long drag, Bevan, with his long delivery stride, found the front-foot rule introduced in 1963-64 to be a trial and, not counting the deliveries which were scored from, he was no-balled 80 times during the season.

Having announced his retirement from first-class cricket, Bevan continued on his productive way for North Perth for another decade, finishing with 257 games in which he took 805 wickets at 16.38 to be fifth in the all-time Perth bowling aggregates. He took five or more wickets in an innings 53 times, his best figures being 8 for 20, including a hat-trick, against Subiaco in 1956-57, the game in which he scored his only fifty. He captained the side in two successive seasons from 1964-65 and was still dangerous enough to head the Perth aggregates with 50 wickets in 1968-69.

Bevan was appointed to the state selection panel in 1971-72, joining Allan Edwards and Lawrie Sawle in what many regard as the most successful panel in the state's history. The trio remained intact until Sawle departed in 1980, and Bevan continued until 1992-93 to bring his service to a record 22 years, the last four as chairman. Western Australia won the Sheffield Shield 11 times during his tenure. The Western Australian Cricket Association recognised his outstanding service by awarding him life membership in 1989.

Joining the Commonwealth Bank as a junior clerk in 1948, Bevan spent his final 15 years prior to retirement in 1992 as the manager of the suburban branches at Karrinyup and Booragoon.

	M	I	NO	Runs	HS	100s	50s	Avge	Ct	St	W	Avge	BB
First-class	43	68	27	333	26	0	0	8.12	14	0	121	34.99	6-22
Domestic first-class	34	54	19	290	26	0	0	8.29	9	0	16	36.87	6-22

BICHEL, DONALD ALAN, died on 11 October, 2004, at the Wesley Hospital at the inner-Brisbane suburb of Auchenflower. Don Bichel was a capable off-spinner with enough batting ability to be considered as an all-rounder. His opportunities for a more permanent place in the Queensland team were limited by the selectors' preference for fellow off-spinner Tom Veivers, and two of Bichel's three Sheffield Shield appearances came when Veivers was away on Test duty. He was a big spinner of the ball and cultivated his variety by developing the art of bowling from well behind the crease. No great stylist with the bat, he was an effective striker who could drive with a power which belied his wiry frame (178 cm and 70 kg).

Bichel was born at Lowood, near Ipswich, on 4 May 1935. His grandparents had emigrated from Germany in 1886. They and their 12 children became the core of a large community of farmers of German descent in and around the Lockyer Valley. Bichel himself was the fifth of seven children, the family quickly providing the backbone of sporting teams in the district. In 1949, he equalled Ron Archer's achievement by being selected three years running for the Queensland State Primary Schools team. He completed his schooling at Brisbane State High School.

His early senior cricket was played with Prenzlau in the Lockyer competition and Booval in the Ipswich and West Moreton Association, whence he was selected as captain of the Country Colts team in 1953-54. Next season, he appeared in the Sydney Gregory Cup match without achieving much, but in the 1957-58 match, at the Gabba, he found enough control to take 3 for 63 in the New South Wales first innings.

Beginning against the MCC at Rockhampton in 1954-55, Bichel made seven appearances over the next 16 years for various Queensland Country combinations against touring sides, which brought him 24 wickets at 24.45. At Ipswich, in 1963-64, he captained the side against the South Africans, and took 7 for 52, his victims including Graeme Pollock for a duck.

His performance against the South Africans, together with 6 for 37 a fortnight earlier for South Queensland Country against Queensland at Bundaberg, earned him state selection at Sydney, when Veivers was on Test duty. Bichel took no wickets and only scored a single in each innings, but was more successful next season at the Gabba against New South Wales, when he made a thoughtful 46 and then took three wickets in the final over of the second day's play, finishing with 4 for 80 from 30 overs. Despite this, he was passed over for the southern tour, but was recalled for the home match against South Australia to partner Veivers in a twin-pronged off-spin attack.

From 1966-67, Bichel spent two seasons with Western Suburbs in the Q.C.A. competition, capturing 53 wickets at 20.81, while scoring 203 runs at 13.53. In 1970-71, he played for South Queensland against North Queensland, capturing 8 for 91 from 33 overs. He continued his involvement in cricket by coaching the Lockyer Association Under-16 teams over a number of years, and he played A grade tennis in both Lockyer and Ipswich. Don Bichel's older brothers, Clifford and Doug, were both good enough as cricketers to attend the Country Colts trials in 1949-50. His nephew, Andy, has been a key player for both Queensland and Australia, and his three daughters each played softball at both state and national level. Bichel continued the family tradition of mixed farming and involvement in the affairs of the local Lockrose Lutheran Church, where he was both secretary and treasurer from 1968 until his death.

	M	I	NO	Runs	HS	100s	50s	Avge	Ct	St	W	Avge	BB
First-class	3	6	0	63	46	0	0	10.50	2	0	6	47.67	4-80
Domestic first-class	3	6	0	63	46	0	0	10.50	2	0	6	47.67	4-80

BROWNLOW, BERTIE, died in Hobart on 22 October, 2004. A genuine sporting all-rounder, Bert Brownlow played both cricket and hockey for Tasmania and then gave decades of service to both sports as an administrator. He was an outstanding example of the tradition of amateur service to Australian sport, and was a warm and gregarious man who carried out his duties with both care and charm. He was born on 20 May, 1920, in Portland, New South Wales. Having played some grade cricket in Newcastle, Brownlow worked for the Electrolytic Zinc Corporation and, in 1941, moved to the company's plant in Hobart, where he made his debut for North-West Hobart in the 1941-42 season. An energetic left-hand batsman who relished going onto the front foot, he was also a wicketkeeper who was adept at covering ground to the quicker bowlers but equally at home as an aggressive presence over the stumps to the spinners.

His path to state selection was initially blocked by the selectors' preference for the capable Len Alexander and the younger Rex Davidson. Brownlow's moment finally came in the 1952-53 season when, aged 33, he was selected for both the state and the Combined XI games against the Australian team on its way to England. In the first of these matches, he allowed no byes in the visitors' total of 510 and cracked a hearty 40 in 55 minutes. Next season, against Victoria at the MCG, he reined in his customary aggression, with 46 in 168 minutes to help push Tasmania past 300. In general, though, he did not reproduce his grade consistency at the first-class level, his other 13 innings producing only 49 runs. His best match with the gloves came in his last game, when, against Victoria, at St Kilda in 1956-57, he held five first-innings catches. He continued with his club, which dropped the West from its name in 1947-48, until 1960-61. His 196 games produced 4,413 runs at 25.21, including 24 fifties and a highest score of 82, plus 248 catches and 75 stumpings. In the intra-island games, he represented South from 1944-45 to 1956-57, scoring 102 against North-West in 1954-55. After the war, Brownlow worked in a Hobart sports store before joining the state government the Lands Department until his retirement.

Brownlow had joined his club committee as soon as he arrived in Hobart and remained active in cricket administration until 1985. After eight years as its secretary, he became club delegate to the Tasmanian Cricket Association, becoming chairman in 1977. Always willing to pass on his skills, he was an astute coach who, in 1958, began an after-school coaching program at the T.C.A. ground in Hobart. In 1962 he became a state selector, later chairing the panel.

Also a skilful hockey player, Brownlow represented Tasmania at four Australian carnivals, and served various Tasmanian hockey organisations in just about every capacity over many years, including 28 years as a delegate to the national body. In 1984, he was awarded the Medal of the Order of Australia (OAM) for "service to sport, particularly cricket and hockey." A son, David, played cricket for North Hobart.

Brownlow also ensured that the Tasmanian Cricket Association's archive of historic photographs was properly preserved until it found a new home at Bellerive Oval.

	M	I	NO	Runs	HS	100s	50s	Avge	Ct	St	W	Avge	BB
First-class	8	15	2	135	46	0	0	10.38	13	1	–	–	

CARTLEDGE, BRIAN LEWIS, died on 22 October, 2004 at Burnie, Tasmania. Born 100 kilometres further west at Smithton on 3 March, 1941, "Bunny" Cartledge's approach to batting was to pay no great heed to science but to use a good eye and a powerful frame (188 cm and 85 kg) to transform his bat into a blunderbuss. Educated at Burnie High School, he played for South Burnie from 1958-59 and ran into good form with the Burnie club when he moved there four years later. During a solid season in 1963-64, he appeared for a Tasmanian Country XI in a one-day game against the touring South Africans at Devonport, in which he made 13.

After a prolonged run drought over the next few seasons, in 1967-68 he repaid the selectors' faith by making a spectacular 107 in 139 minutes for North-West against North, which he followed up with 73 a month later against South. Having surprisingly missed a place against the touring Indians, he made his first appearance for Tasmania in a non-first-class game against Western Australia, scoring 69 on an unpredictable Devonport pitch.

A knee operation restricted his appearances the next year and he only appeared in four first-class matches spread over three seasons from 1970-71, reaching double figures just once, scoring 29 on debut against the MCC at Hobart. That saw the season in which he set up his side for an unlikely victory in the V&G one-day match against Western Australia at Launceston. He clouted 56, the inaugural fifty by a Tasmanian in the one-day competition, of a third-wicket partnership of 68 with "Billy" Ibadulla, hoisting Tony Lock for three huge sixes in one over. When he was dismissed, Tasmania only needed 67 with plenty of overs to spare but the rest of the batting crumbled. 1972-73 saw his last appearance in both first-class and one-day cricket, but he had his best club season, hitting 435 runs at 29.00 in what was also to be his last full-time year as an A-grade cricketer. He continued as an active committeeman.

Better known as a hockey player, Cartledge was a robust and skilful full-back who played for Tasmania at both junior and senior levels. After spending 20 years in the motor industry, he served as a fireman for a further two decades.

	M	I	NO	Runs	HS	100s	50s	Avge	Ct	St	W	Avge	BB
First-class	4	7	0	53	29	0	0	7.57	1	0	–	–	–
Domestic limited-overs	3	3	0	100	56	0	1	33.33	0	0	–	–	–

CLINGLY, MICHAEL THOMAS, died in Adelaide on 16 August, 2004. An effervescent, larger-than-life presence, Mick Clingly exuded the sheer enjoyment of applying his many skills on both the cricket and the football fields. Born on 18 April, 1932, in the Adelaide suburb of Prospect, he was educated at the Christian Brothers' College in the city. Clingly's batting was based on a desire to use his burly frame (187cm and 95kg) to find the shortest way to the boundary, while his left-arm orthodox spinners were delivered at such a brisk pace that they were virtually medium-pace cutters, which meant that he often used the new ball in District cricket. More dangerous when there was something in the pitch, on good surfaces his consistent line and length gave batsmen no latitude.

Having made his first-grade debut with the Woodville club in 1953-54, he spent a single season with the Senior Colts side before returning to his old club. He performed consistently and caught the state selectors' attention in 1957-58 with a counter-attacking 103 not out in 80 minutes after Woodville were struggling at 7 for 131 against Glenelg. He also took 37 wickets at 15.27 for the season but was called twice for throwing against Senior Colts, which seems to have been the result of a prank on Clingly's part rather than any fundamental suspicion. He played in South Australia's last match of the season and then appeared in another four seasons later without reproducing his District form. His best effort with the bat was 20 at Melbourne while in the previous match he had taken 3 for 15 from 10 overs, supporting Brian Quigley as Queensland were hurried out for 127.

He then spent four seasons as captain-coach of Edwardstown in the Adelaide Turf competition before returning to Woodville for another 12 seasons, until he was 43. Age simply increased his guile and effectiveness, the best season of his career coming in 1971-72 when he took 40 wickets at 12.40. In all, Clingly made 4241 runs at 18.12 and totalled 445 wickets at 19.01. His son Michael, also played first-grade cricket for Woodville.

An imposing figure on the football field, Clingly was an outstanding player for the West Torrens club between 1951 and 1960. Agile and fearless, he was a prodigious and accurate kicker from centre half-forward, landing 219 goals for his club, the most remarkable of which was the ninth of his 12.3 against Glenelg in 1956 because it was the last to be scored in the SANFL competition from a place kick. He represented South Australia in 1954 and 1955 and only missed the next year because of injury.

	M	I	NO	Runs	HS	100s	50s	Avge	Ct	St	W	Avge	BB
First-class	5	9	0	79	20	0	0	8.78	5	0	9	54.33	3-15
Domestic first-class	5	9	0	79	20	0	0	8.78	5	0	9	54.33	3-15

COCKBURN, WILLIAM FREDERICK, died on 16 July, 2004, at Corowa, New South Wales. Although he played only once for Victoria, Bill Cockburn's lively left-arm fast-medium deliveries were good enough for E.H.M. Baillie of *The Sporting Globe* to declare in February 1940 that he "is developing into Richmond's Bill Voce". Born at the inner-Melbourne suburb of Richmond on 28 November, 1916, he played his initial first-grade game for the local club in 1937-38, but began to make his presence felt two seasons later. In successive matches, he took 5 for 65 and 3 for 71 against University and then 7 for 43 against Prahran. Possessed of an easy, fluent action, his accuracy was complemented by his ability to move the ball late in the air. Next season, he had to decline selection against Queensland at the Gabba because of work commitments. Cricket then was subsumed by his service with 51 Anti-Aircraft Regiment from 1942 to 1945.

Cockburn's state turn came in Victoria's opening match of the 1945-46 season, against Queensland at Melbourne. Opening the bowling with fellow debutant Bill Johnston, he trapped Geoff Cook in front in the early overs, but thereafter was relegated to a back seat in the attack. He was dropped forthwith and never earned a recall, although his best form against Richmond was still ahead of him and his batting also developed. When he finished with Richmond in 1955-56, he had played 95 games for 1606 runs at 20.07 and taken 186 wickets at 21.56.

He missed several seasons, however, after becoming a prolific performer in the Central Lancashire League. He had three seasons at Milnrow, where he began with 91 wickets at 9.12, and three with Littleborough, where in his first year, he took 9 for 16 against Heywood in less than an hour. In 1955-56, he replaced former state all-rounder Des Fitzmaurice as captain-coach of Yarraville in the Sub-District competition, a post which he held for five seasons. Age only increased his canniness, and in 1959-60 he showed the benefit of his years in England when he took 7 for 14 against Camberwell on an under-prepared pitch.

	M	I	NO	Runs	HS	100s	50s	Avge	Ct	St	W	Avge	BB
First-class	1	1	0	0	0	0	0	0.00	0	0	1	54.00	1-30

COLLEY, CLAUDE ARNOLD, died at Royal Brisbane Hospital, Herston, on 2 June, 2005, aged 98. Claude Colley had an extraordinary career, starting as a competent country player and making his debut in Brisbane A-grade aged 55. He was forced to retire aged 84 after a mild heart attack while dressing for yet another competition game. Born at the Sydney suburb of Redfern on 3 July, 1906, his family moved to farm by the Maroochy River in Queensland after the First World War. He appeared at Country week three times between 1929 and 1938 and was part of a Queensland Country team which played a two-day match at Lismore in 1934, in which he took 8 for 67 and 5 for 105 with his leg-breaks.

In 1948-49, he began his association with the Sandgate club and when the club became Sandgate-Redcliffe in 1961-62, he defied the years by making three A-grade appearances. When he finished with the club in 1976-77, he had taken at least 435 wickets and made 2,735 runs, figures which do not include seven seasons for which no records are available. In 1969-70, aged 62, he took 89 wickets at 10.76. Even after leaving Sandgate-Redcliffe, he still had 15 more years of cricket which he enjoyed to the hilt. Claude's brother Frank, played cricket in Mackay until he was almost 70, while his son Lindsay played cricket in the lower grades for Northern Suburbs.

DUNN, WALLACE PETER, died on 1 February, 2004, at the Perth suburb of Nedlands. In another time and place, Peter Dunn might have come under close scrutiny for Australian selection. He was a left-arm quick bowler with a smooth action, whose best weapon, according to his team mate, Allan Edwards, was the "left-armer's most precious asset – the ability to bowl late inswingers to right-hand batsmen". With his sartorial elegance, affability and habitual politeness, Dunn was a conspicuous departure from the stereotype of the quick bowler.

Born on 8 August, 1921, at Westonia, in the state's eastern wheat belt, he was educated at Perth Modern School before joining the Commonwealth Bank in 1937. He subsequently took a degree in economics at the University of Western Australia, graduating in 1948, having received a full Blue for cricket in 1940. He first appeared for Claremont in 1941-42, but his appearances over the next few seasons were necessarily restricted by his war service, mainly with anti-aircraft units.

Dunn began to make an impression from 1945-46 and, the next season, three wickets in one over in a state trial game saw him selected for the state Colts team against the MCC. But he had to wait three seasons before being called into the state side, against New South Wales at the WACA. He had Arthur Morris dropped in the gully from the second ball of the match, Morris then going on to make 163 of his side's 507. But against Queensland, Dunn took 4 for 38 and finished the season with 5 for 71 in Victoria's second innings at Melbourne.

Next season, he had figures of 6 for 26 and 3 for 29 against South Australia at Perth, his first innings figures including three in four balls. He also did well against touring teams, taking 4 for 105 against the MCC in 1950-51 and dismissing Reg Simpson from the seventh first-class ball that he faced in Australia, and 4 for 44 against the West Indians during the next season.

Dunn finished his first-class career while at his peak as a grade wicket-taker. From 1951-52, he headed the competition aggregates with 77, 60 and 63 wickets respectively, while from 1953-54, he captained his club for three seasons. He finished his grade career in 1959-60 having played 151 matches for his club, now called Claremont-Cottesloe, in which he scored 1146 runs at 11.58, with a lone 50 in his 128 innings. His 561 wickets at 13.26 included two hat-tricks taken when he was in his mid-thirties, and 35 returns of five wickets or more in an innings. He was president of the club between 1966 and 1971. From the mid-sixties, he spent a decade providing expert commentary on cricket on both radio and television, while his observance of and belief in the spirit of cricket were recognised when he was appointed by the Australian Cricket Board as Western Australia's first commissioner for the code of player behaviour.

He played hockey with the Old Modernians club, achieving state selection twice, and later became an accomplished golfer. Having transferred from the Commonwealth to the Reserve Bank, he retired in 1982 as Deputy State Manager. His son Rick played first-grade for University in the early 1970s.

	M	I	NO	Runs	HS	100s	50s	Avge	Ct	St	W	Avge	BB
First-class	18	32	12	169	33*	0	0	8.45	16	0	48	31.39	6-26
Domestic first-class	15	28	11	138	33*	0	0	8.12	15	0	37	32.62	6-26

EDWARDS, JOHN ERNEST, died on 23 May, 2005, in the Melbourne suburb of Elsternwick. Jack Edwards, like his older namesake who died in 2002, had a long association with the St Kilda club, both on and off the field, and as an administrator of Victorian cricket. Their linked paths had begun when they both attended Caulfield Central School. To clear up any confusion caused by their team mates who shared the nickname of "Coogan", John Ernest became Jack, while John Neild, four years older, remained John, or more commonly "Darky". Later in life, one of his family companies was named Nagooc Holdings Pty Ltd, revealing a wry streak of humour hidden under his official exterior.

Born in Melbourne on 29 August, 1930, Edwards completed his education at Wesley College, representing the school at cricket, tennis and football and gaining a place in the St Kilda First XI in 1949-50 as an opening batsman and occasional slow left-armer. His performances never reached spectacular heights; by the time he finished in first grade in 1960-61, he had made 2,800 runs at 18.54 and taken 20 wickets at 41.65. In 1964, he joined his club committee and became a delegate to the Victorian Cricket Association in 1972. In 1973, he was elected president of St Kilda, a post he held for 20 years.

From 1985 until 1997, he was a Victorian director of the Australian Cricket Board, serving as chair of the Program Committee. He was manager of the Australian team to Sharjah in 1994 and the successful team to the West Indies a year later. In 1992 he was elected president of the Victorian Cricket Association, a position he held for five years. Edwards spent his working life in the steel industry, the last decade as general manager of Surdex Industries.

EMERY, VICTOR RUPERT, died on 14 February, 2005, at Narrabeen, on Sydney's northern beaches. Although his first-class career was limited to five matches, Emery was a dominating presence on the Sydney first-grade scene over nearly three decades. Over 600 wickets and 4,000 runs make him one of the most significant all-rounders in Sydney cricket.

Born at St Leonard's on 24 December, 1920. Emery was educated at Mosman Boys' Intermediate High School. As a youth, he was a promising rugby league player, but a serious knee injury when he was 18 forced him out of the game and also destroyed his hopes of being a pace bowler. He re-fashioned himself as an off-spinner whose style carried the echo of his early ambitions with the new ball; bowling off almost a dozen paces, he pinned batsmen to the crease at virtually medium pace. Emery developed a complete repertoire, using his speed to drift the ball both ways and employing effective slower and straight balls, together with subtle variations in spin. He practised assiduously; long after other players had left the club nets, he would bowl with a handkerchief spread on the pitch at a good length as darkness fell. As a young man, he rode his bike to the city via Gladesville, both to save the Sydney Harbour Bridge toll and to keep fit. One legacy of this effort was that even in his forties, he could bowl 25 overs in an afternoon without any strain. Emery was an effective batsman who never sold his wicket cheaply. Originally capable of great power, and often used as an opener, his batting later became a canny collection of nudges and deflections.

Emery's initial appearance in the North Sydney first grade side came in 1941-42 during his war service at the headquarters of Eastern Command in Sydney. He slowly began to make a significant impression after the war and, in 1948-49, after his early grade figures included returns of 8 for 84 and 6 for 94, he was selected in a strong state side which included five Test players. In his first match, against Queensland at the Gabba, he was both accurate and effective throughout his 41 overs which produced 4 for 77. His next four matches only produced another two wickets and, although he was at his peak through the 1950s, he was never chosen again. His single-minded approach and direct manner may not have appealed to the selectors.

He lasted in the first-grade side until 1965-66 and was recalled, aged 49, four years later, claiming 37 wickets at 17.89, before returning to the lower grades for a final three seasons. He finished with 654 wickets in first grade at 20.35, including five in an innings 29 times. Bevyn White, a spinning partner over many seasons, said he was the best Australian off-spinner he ever saw.

Having served an apprenticeship as a motor mechanic, Emery subsequently plied his trade at the Neutral Bay tram depot. He then spent nearly 20 years as an electroplater in the printing trade, before technology rendered the skill redundant and he moved to clerical jobs. Emery played 52 games of first grade rugby league for North Sydney; his younger brother Vin was an attractive middle-order batsman for North Sydney and Balmain.

	M	I	NO	Runs	HS	100s	50s	Avge	Ct	St	W	Avge	BB
First-class	5	5	2	42	17	0	0	14.00	5	0	6	54.50	4-77
Domestic first-class	5	5	2	42	17	0	0	14.00	5	0	6	54.50	4-77

EYRES, GORDON, died on 21 August, 2004, at the Perth suburb of Peppermint Grove, at the age of 91. Born in Kalgoorlie on 20 December, 1912, Gordon Eyres was a tall, slim opening bowler who could deliver inswingers which moved wickedly late and who had the stamina to retain his lively pace over long spells. He was talented enough to impress commentators both at home and in the east, *The West Australian* proclaiming in March 1938 that he was "undoubtedly one of the finest bowlers this state has produced".

Educated at Christ Church Grammar School in Perth, he made his first grade debut with Claremont in 1930-31. He led the Perth bowling averages in successive seasons from 1936-37, and was particularly harsh on Fremantle, taking 28 wickets in four innings in none of which they reached three figures.

He was thus selected for Western Australia's eastern states' tour in 1937-38. Initially, however, he tended to waste the ball down the leg side too much at the higher level, but remedied the fault so well that he took 5 for 58 against South Australia at Adelaide.

In December, 1938, he was selected in the Melbourne Cricket Club's centenary match where, even though he only took 1 for 81, E. H. M. Baillie in the *Sporting Globe* noted that "he was able to keep all the batsmen, Bradman included, very quiet". Later in the season, he took 5 for 47 against Victoria. With no real pretensions as a batsman. Eyres only reached double figures twice in his 13 first-class innings, but on each of these occasions unleashed a brief hurricane of hitting. Against the Australians on their way through Perth to the 1938 Ashes series, he crashed 41 in 17 minutes, including 24 in an over off Frank Ward.

Eyres was given a place in the state trial match in September, 1946, and took 4 for 53, but failed to gain a recall. He retired from club cricket in 1950-51, his 105 games having produced 1,261 runs at 13.27 and 379 wickets at 12.72. During the war, he served with the RAAF, finishing his time as Wing Commander, 22 Squadron, having been an instructor at a number of training schools.

	M	I	NO	Runs	HS	100s	50s	Avge	Ct	St	W	Avge	BB
First-class	8	13	2	110	41	0	0	10.00	4	0	23	31.13	5-47

GOFFET, GORDON, died on 29 July, 2004, at the Mater Hospital, in the Newcastle suburb of Waratah. Gordon Goffet's approach as an opener was underlined in two responses to his innings of 89 for New South Wales at Melbourne in December 1968. Barry Gibbs, in *The Sporting Globe*, called him "the batting ugly duckling of first-class cricket, who is anything but a stylist", while Kevin Hogan, in *The Sun*, emphasised his "courage and determination" and commented that "Goffet's natural ability is limited, but he fights every inch of the way and does not panic under pressure". While there were no frills about his batting, he was strong square of the wicket, but above all, he was valued for his unflustered reliability, whose approach was as solid as his build (183cm and 83kg).

Born on 4 March, 1941, at Speers Point, New South Wales. He represented the three successive seasons from 1953-54 at the Australian State Schools' Carnival, and also excelled at tennis until his coach asked him to concentrate on one sport. He began his Newcastle grade career with Western Lakes and, having completed his education at Newcastle Boys' High School, joined the Rural Bank in 1958. He made 63 for the New South Wales Colts side at the Gabba in November, 1961. Over the next three years, he made another six such appearances, being seen at that stage as a middle-order batsman and supporting off-spinner.

After a work transfer to Sydney, Goffet joined the Waverley club in 1961-62, where he made sound, if unspectacular, progress until the 1965-66 season, when he made 734 runs at 61.17. His consistency gained him state selection against the MCC when Norm O'Neill withdrew, but Goffet scored only 2 and 0. Next season, when the Australian team was in South Africa, he was entrusted with the opener's role and responded with 576 runs at 41.14, which placed him sixth in the national aggregates. He began with 53 and 122 not out against Western Australia in the only first-class match ever played at the SCG No. 2, which was used when the main ground's surface was being regraded. The first effort was a gratifying affair after his side were 3 for 31; the century was far livelier, helped by six missed chances, three of them in four balls from an exasperated Bill Playle. In the event, his match total of 175 left Goffet with the arcane distinction of being the highest run scorer on the now-defunct ground. A month later, at Adelaide, he showed his resilience when he had to retire hurt after deflecting a delivery from Eric Freeman into his temple. After a day's rest, he returned and carried his score from 6 to 47.

Next season, an early injury, combined with the return of Bob Simpson, kept him out of the state side. He returned in 1968-69 after an injury to Lynn Marks, and had another consistent season, scoring 79 against the West Indian tourists and 89 against Victoria. In 1969-70, Bruce Francis, his opening partner at Waverley, and Alan Turner were the preferred openers and Goffet finished his first-grade career in Sydney, having had three seasons with Western Suburbs from 1967-68. For his two clubs, he made a total of 3,837 runs at 33.65 and took 144 wickets at 17.56, his bowling at that level being effective enough for him to have headed the Waverley aggregates in 1966-67 with 29 wickets at 16.31. Goffet captained Waverley in his final two seasons with the club. He returned to Newcastle and played for Cardiff-Boolaroo. In January, 1972, he was selected for Northern New South Wales against the World XI and in a rain-ruined match, scored an unusually cavalier 84 not out before proceedings came to a premature end.

In 1973, he left the bank and worked for solicitors' firms in Newcastle. Known as "Rin" from the comic character Rin Tin Tin, he was a relaxed, friendly man, forming a club called BOFTA, the Boring Old Farts Association, which would undertake mystery tours that often involved major sporting events. His son, Neil, played for the New South Wales Country Under-19 team.

	M	I	NO	Runs	HS	100s	50s	Avge	Ct	St	W	Avge	BB
First-class	17	32	1	1,036	122	1	7	33.41	6	0	9	38.00	1-1
Domestic first-class	15	28	1	927	122	1	6	34.33	9	0	2	13.00	1-1

HACKETT, JAMES VICTOR, died on 13 November, 2004, at his home in the Brisbane suburb of Wavell Heights. Born in Perth on 8 October, 1917, Jim Hackett moved to Townsville as a small child. Educated at Mount Carmel College in nearby Charters Towers, he played cricket in the Townsville competition with the Commercial Cricket Club, quickly establishing a reputation as a capable and consistent batsman and earning selection three times for the Northern side in the annual Country trials in Brisbane. He achieved little in the tournament until 1937-38, when he achieved a succession of decent scores to be picked for the Queensland Colts against their New South Wales counterparts at the Gabba, where he made a pair. Nevertheless, he was promoted to the state side for the home match against South Australia in January, becoming one of that small group of players to have represented their state without having played competition cricket in the capital city. He was run out for a duck by a direct hit from Don Bradman, though he did catch Bradman later – for 113. In the second innings, Hackett made 10, but in the next match, against Victoria, rain closed in on the third morning and stopped play before he had batted. He last appeared in the Country trials in October, 1946, playing on for a few further seasons in the Townsville competition where he continued to score heavily.

In March, 1941, Hackett joined the RAAF and, after training, served as a fighter pilot with 77 Squadron in the Pacific, rising to the rank of flight-lieutenant. He subsequently became an accountant, and was secretary, and then manager, of the Brisbane Stock Exchange, until his retirement to concentrate on golf in 1967.

	M	I	NO	Runs	HS	100s	50s	Avge	Ct	St	W	Avge	BB
First-class	2	1	0	10	10	0	0	5.00	0	1	0	–	–
Domestic first-class	2	1	0	10	10	0	0	5.00	0	1	0	–	–

JUNOR, LEONARD JOHN, died on 6 April, 2005, at Frankston, in Melbourne's south-east, just over three weeks before his ninety-first birthday. There is one Australian cricket record which will remain as Len Junor's for the foreseeable future: when he played for Victoria against Western Australia in January, 1930, at 15 years and 265 days old, he became, and remains, Australia's youngest first-class cricketer. The contemporary system of pathways development, whatever its virtues, effectively locks out any repetition of Junor's remarkable achievement. But he did not develop. Eight matches spread over the same number of years underlined the way in which his impetuosity limited his achievement at the first-class level. Junor himself admitted this: in 1996, making his first visit to the Melbourne Cricket Ground in 40 years, he said ruefully: "I didn't have enough brains to realise that the bowler up the other end was a pretty smart fellow." Yet, on his day, he was a thrilling stroke player capable of shredding the best District attacks, the suppleness of his wristwork and the power of his driving belying his slight build (163 cm and 75 kg).

Born in the Melbourne suburb of Northcote on 27 April, 1914, Junor was educated at Swinburne Technical College where he captained the school cricket team. He joined the Camberwell sub-District team in 1929-30 and began with a century in second grade. His sense of promise saw him offered the chance of coaching with the Colts side and in a game against the Country Colts at the Albert Ground in late October, he cracked an undefeated 134. His performance awakened Richmond's interest in him and he was quickly promoted to their first grade side. Possibly goaded by criticism of an ageing Victorian side, the state selectors made a spectacular riposte by picking Junor for the non-Shield match at the MCG. He made an attractive 41 in the first innings at number six and was immediately given a 2nd XI game against New South Wales in which he made 11.

But then nothing happened. After two seasons with the Colts side in District cricket, Junor returned to full-time appearances with Richmond but his form was too sporadic for the selectors to retain their interest in him. Yet he continued to show flashes of exuberance and was often included for the non-competitive state matches against Tasmania. At Launceston, in 1931-32, he top-scored with 42 in the second innings. Junor had an outstanding season for Richmond in 1937-38 which brought him 669 runs at 39.35 and three of his five District centuries. His form saw him selected for his last two state matches, so that he finished having played six times against Tasmania and twice against Western Australia. He played with Richmond until 1941-42, making 4,170 District runs at 28.75, which included a then club record second wicket partnership of 282 with Leo O'Brien against University in 1933-34 to which Junor contributed 125. He also played baseball for Richmond and Victoria.

From 1943 to 1945, he served with the 33 Australian Anti-Aircraft Battery. He worked in a number of clerical positions, including a long term as the secretary of the Rosebud Foreshore Committee on the Mornington Peninsula.

	M	I	NO	Runs	HS	100s	50s	Avge	Ct	St	W	Avge	BB
First-class	8	15	2	295	57	0	1	22.69	3	0	0	–	–

KILDEY, EDWARD KEITH. died on 12 February, 2005, in Melbourne. Keith Kildey was born at Leeton, New South Wales, on 30 April, 1919, but moved to Tasmania soon afterwards when his parents bought a farm. Educated at Devonport High School, he did well enough in local cricket to feel he should test himself in Melbourne District cricket. His father, by now the Tasmanian manager of the Produce Distribution Company, was able to secure him a clerical job at head office and he joined the strong South Melbourne club alongside such players as Lindsay Hassett, Ian Johnson and a young Keith Miller. Originally fancying himself as a batsman, Kildey was persuaded to become an opening bowler. Such was his potential that he topped the averages in both the 3rd and 2nd XIs in 1937-38, performances which saw him become a first-grader in 1938-39.

His first ball created a stir when he clean bowled Melbourne and Australian opener Keith Rigg, doing the same to Percy Beames in his second over. Fifteen hostile overs produced 6 for 36 and continued good performances during the season produced instant respect. Tall (183cm) and robust (82kg), he hit the bat hard after an energetic 15-pace approach and a high delivery which allowed him to vary his inswingers with the occasional ball which moved the other way. His start to the 1939-40 season was just as sensational, his 6 for 19 routing University for 45, and he then repeated the consistency of the previous seasons. The two seasons produced 54 wickets at 17.29, with four returns of five wickets or more in an innings, but 44 runs at 5.50 underlined the extent to which his batting had become marginal.

In November, 1940, he enlisted for training as a fighter pilot and, was posted to Number 3 Squadron in Syria, whence he flew Kittyhawks in the western desert campaign, winning a Distinguished Flying Medal. Later, he became a squadron leader and was appointed as commanding officer of the Air Defence headquarters at Port Moresby in New Guinea.

After the war, he returned to the family property but travelled to play with North Launceston each weekend, hoping the stronger competition there might help him attract the selectors' attention. He was right: having taken

5 for 118 for North against South at Hobart just after Christmas, 1946, Kildey was a late inclusion in the state side which met the MCC at Launceston a fortnight later. Kildey's sole wicket cost 93 runs but it was that of Len Hutton, who mistimed a hook and was caught at square-leg. With the bat, he was one of only three Tasmanians to reach double figures, with 12. During the match, he enjoyed the company of his fellow-pilot Bill Edrich.

He rejoined the RAAF in 1950 and served until 1972, retiring as a group captain, having worked mainly in air traffic control. Kildey spent the rest of his working life as Personnel Manager with Imperial Chemical Industries in Melbourne. During the 1956 Melbourne Olympics, the clay pigeon shooting events were held at Point Cook air base, where he was stationed at the time. Additional shooters were needed to meet Olympic regulations and Kildey, having won an RAAF preliminary event, was drafted in as a non-scoring competitor; it was later whispered to him that his score would have won him a bronze medal.

	M	I	NO	Runs	HS	100s	50s	Avge	Ct	St	W	Avge	BB
First-class	12	1	0	12	12	0	0	12.00	1	0	1	93.00	1-93

MASON, SCOTT ROBERT, died at the Royal Hobart Hospital on 9 April, 2005, at the age of 28. After complaining of lethargy in August, 2004, Mason was told he needed heart surgery to replace an aortic valve. Following the operation two months later, in which he chose to have a human valve inserted so he could continue to play elite sport, he missed the 2004-05 season and had hoped to resume his first-class career. Having faced a few balls at a net session at Bellerive Oval, Mason collapsed, and died in hospital two days later. Tasmanian Cricket Association doctor Peter Sexton later said that Mason's collapse was caused by a clogging of his heart's main arteries and was unrelated to the operation.

Born at Launceston on 27 July, 1976, Mason grew up 60 kilometres away at George Town. Educated at the local high school, he joined Old Scotch Cricket Club in Launceston at the age of 12, moving to David Boon's Launceston club in the 1996-97 season. A diminutive (170cm) left-hand opening batsman, he developed an ability to play long, methodical innings which saw him progress with equal steadiness through the state under-age teams into the Tasmanian Colts and 2nd XI. He made his initial first-class appearance against the touring South Africans at Devonport in 1997-98, but suffered the frustration of only making single appearances in each of the next three seasons when Jamie Cox and Dene Hills were the resident openers. He did give glimpses of what he might achieve. In 1999-2000 he moved to the New Town club in Hobart and in 2001-02, as the form of Hills declined, was given an extended run in the state side, but 187 runs at 20.77 was a disappointing return. Even so, his fighting qualities were still evident, even if productiveness was not. Against New South Wales, Mason made 41 of an opening stand of 106 with Cox which set their side on the path to victory. In the subsequent disappointment of being overwhelmed by Queensland in the Pura Cup Final, Mason adhered to the crease for long periods in making 17 and 39.

In Tasmania's miserable 2002-03, Mason topped the averages with 417 runs at only 37.91. Having made two fifties at number four, he rejoined Cox at the top of the order for the second half of the season. Against Victoria at Hobart, he finally played his long-awaited big innings. After a first innings duck, he made 174, his sound defence being enlivened by his ability to deal with anything loose, an innings that transformed a first innings deficit into the platform for a comfortable win. In 2003-04, he again struggled to find consistency but played another remarkable innings: with Tasmania needing 448 to win on the last day against Western Australia at Hobart, Mason gave rein to a full array of attractive strokes in making 126 from only 194 balls, which helped Tasmania to 8 for 396.

Mason's illness sapped the energy which had made him such a vibrant presence on the field, but during his convalescence he used his experience to help others. He became part of the "Life's a Ball" program, visiting schools to talk to students about dealing with adversity and setbacks. He also undertook a fitness training and leadership course and intended to become a coach – after he had regained his place in the Tasmanian side. Cox, who saw Mason as a possible future Tasmanian captain, said: "It is just tragic and ironic that a guy whose heart was metaphorically so big, and a man who was so courageous that it was the thing that cost him his life."

	M	I	NO	Runs	HS	Avge	100s	50s	Ct	St	W	Avge	BB
First-class	28	48	2	1,252	174	27.22	2	5	15	0	–	–	–
Domestic first-class	27	46	2	1,213	174	27.53	2	5	15	0	–	–	–
Domestic limited-overs	8	7	0	66	16	9.43	0	0	3	0	–	–	–

MUELEMAN, KENNETH DONALD, died on 10 September, 2004, at Nedlands, in Perth. A Test career of one scoreless innings might consign Ken Mueleman to a trivia question. This would obscure the fact that Mueleman was one of Australia's best batsmen in the 15 seasons after World War II. But having tried him once, the selectors lost interest in him: in the late 1940s Mueleman was unable to produce that crucial big innings at the right moment, and thereafter he was hampered by eastern states' bias.

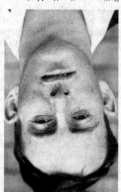

Batting sensation: Ken Mueleman

His batting was occasionally criticised for being too defensive, but the statistics of his more substantial innings do not lend credence to this. With a first-class average in the high forties, he made runs against all kinds of attacks in all kinds of conditions. He had few peers as a player of spin bowling; Hec de Lacy, of *Melbourne's Sporting Globe*, pointed to the nimbleness of Mueleman's footwork and called him "The Dancing Master of the Popping Crease" in 1945; Arthur Mailey nicknamed him Paylova. Never a flamboyant presence, his calm approach, technique and placement made him much appreciated by connoisseurs. Both his batting and his captaincy played a huge role in laying the foundations of Western Australia's rise as a power in the game.

Meuleman was born in Melbourne on 5 September, 1923, and educated at Essendon High School. Sported batting for Footscray, in the Sub-District competition, he played first-grade with Essendon in 1940-41. Despite army service in Darwin between 1942 and 1945, he was able to make intermittent appearances for his club, and began the 1944-45 season with two centuries separated by an innings of 98. The next year he continued with five centuries in nine innings, which made his selection for Victoria a formality. He stepped up with two centuries: 150 in 208 minutes against South Australia at St Kilda and 109 in 179 minutes against Queensland at the Gabba, which earned him a trip to New Zealand as the Australian side's youngest member. Three fifties in successive matches, and two century opening partnerships with skipper Bill Brown resulted in his selection for what was to become the Test match, at Wellington, where he was bowled by Jack Cowie for a duck.

Shut out of the Test opener's role for the 1946-47 Ashes series by Sid Barnes, Meuleman was twelfth man for the first two Tests and then only managed one fifty for the rest of the season. Despite 711 runs at 54.69 the next season, there was no recall against India and in 1948-49, with a trip to South Africa in the offing, he averaged only just over 30, including a century in the relaxed atmosphere of the Bradman Testimonial match at Melbourne. Late in the season he did get a place in the Kippax-Oldfield Testimonial match, at Sydney, which doubled as a selection trial, but Jack Moroney's double century compared to his 36 and 13 snuffed out his claims. In 1949-50, Meuleman was second in the national aggregates, his 612 runs including 150 against South Australia at Adelaide as he and Colin McDonald shared an opening stand of 337. At the end of the season he made a second trip to New Zealand under Bill Brown with the so-called B side.

It was about this time that, as captain of Essendon, he decided that batting at number four would best serve the interests of his team. This decision is rumoured to have brought him into conflict with the state selectors who are said to have decreed that if he did not open the innings in club cricket, there would be no place for him in the Victorian side. Meuleman refused to yield and spent 1951-52 playing District cricket and then headed west. In 85 matches for Essendon, he had made 3,486 runs at 42.15, including 11 centuries, and taken 17 wickets at 26.58 with his occasional leg-breaks.

His first innings for Western Australia was against the touring South Africans in 1952-53 and his 103 announced that Perth had a major new presence. Having missed the Ashes tour of 1953, Meuleman was subsequently part of the Commonwealth team to India in 1953-54. His ability to adapt to the differing conditions of the sub-continent was reflected by the fact that, with 1,158 runs at 52.63, he topped the tour aggregates. He was equally consistent in the five unofficial Tests, scoring a batting 124 against the spinners at Madras and a much freer 131 at Lucknow.

He opened the 1954-55 season by scoring 109 in 385 minutes against the MCC, causing Austin Robertson to report that ''he is now being nominated as an Australian Test possibility". No such nomination came. But two years later, in Western Australia's initial season as a full competitor in the Sheffield Shield, he became state captain, and Meuleman spent the rest of his career leading by a mixture of thoughtful strategy and batting example; in his four full seasons as captain, his lowest aggregate was 530 and his lowest average was 58.63. In 1956-57, he made 234 not out against South Australia at Perth, leading a recovery from 5 for 97 to 412. In what was to be his farewell season, he hit another three centuries in 1959-60. The next season, Meuleman was persuaded out of retirement for the eastern tour but a leg injury forced him to drop out after only one match.

Meuleman continued in Perth grade cricket, where he represented Midland-Guildford, Nedlands and Scarborough. He helped lift Nedlands from the weakest side in the competition to successive premierships. In all, he played 161 A grade games which produced 6,763 runs at 41.24, including 15 centuries, and 175 wickets at 21.99. He subsequently gave countless unpaid hours to coaching junior teams and was a constant source of wise advice. He was also a forthright commentator, advocating better facilities, conditions and pay.

Meuleman operated a successful sports store for many years in South Perth. Always an advocate of physical fitness, Meuleman umpired in the Western Australian National Football League during winter and when he opened a squash centre, he became one of its most skilled players. He later operated his business in partnership with his son, Bob, who also played for Western Australia. His grandson, Scott, made his debut for the state in 2000-01, the Meulemans becoming the third example, after the Raysons and the MacGills, of three succeeding generations from the one family appearing in Australian first-class cricket, and the first in which each member has scored a century. His elder brother, Ron, played District cricket in Melbourne, and was later a journalist with a special interest in harness racing.

To commemorate Ken's memory, in January, 2005 it was decided to institute the Meuleman Shield to be contested in all future first-class matches between Victorian and Western Australia. The Western Australian Cricket Association has named a room in his honour at the WACA museum. and has been considering his proposal for a Hall of Fame.

	M	I	NO	Runs	HS	100s	50s	Avge	Ct	St	W	Avge	BB
First-class	117	184	19	7,855	234*	22	41	47.60	35	0	19	50.31	3-7
Domestic first-class	70	114	13	4,916	234*	13	25	48.67	19	0	11	52.82	2-58
Tests	1	1	0	0	0	0	0	0.00	0	0	–	–	–

MILLER, KEITH ROSS, died on 11 October, 2004, at a nursing home at Mornington, near Melbourne. Denzil Batchelor, in The Book of Cricket, begins his sketch of Keith Miller: "If anybody wants to erect a statue of Australia Triumphant above the barrackers' hq on the Sydney Hill, Keith Ross Miller is the model for his money. Six feet tall, with a fiercely handsome face and a shock of hair streamlined like the tail of a comet, he is made to defy lightnings, blaze trails, and gloriously overthrow naked aggression."

This goes to the heart of Miller's appeal both as a cricketer and a man. There was the sheer physicality of his presence: strong, good-looking, his hair

Legendary all-rounder: Keith Miller

defying the cropped convention of the post-war short back and sides. He could hit effortless sixes, uncoil a casual hand in the slips to hold a fleeting chance or launch a bumper at a pace that made Ray Lindwall look, for just a moment, military medium. He was handsome enough to make Errol Flynn look faintly dowdy, yet there was no hint of foppishness about him: his Australian openness could well have made him a model for Max Dupain's famous photograph, 'The Sunbaker'. While the crowds in the outer respected him, they still saw him as one of their own. Miller might have made an unauthorised detour in his fighter-bomber over wartime Germany just to sneak a look at Bonn, the birthplace of Beethoven, but he would give you a tip for the Melbourne Cup if you caught him at the right moment.

After his death, there were a number of attempts to incorporate Miller into the mainstream of the Australian larrikin tradition. There was plenty of superficial evidence for such a view: the laconic understatement in his reply to the post-war question of whether he had ever been to Germany: "Only at night." There was, too, his fondness for living hard and defying authority, as when he took half the Australian team to Godfrey Evans' houseboat on the Thames the night before the 1956 tour of England, and the match against Hampshire on the remaining few players were given the job of not getting out until the party returned.

But Miller was much more subtle and complex, both as a cricketer and a man. Many of his best Test innings were circumspect and thoughtful, dedicated to the tactical needs of the team, and some of his best displays as a bowler came on that last Ashes tour when he performed wonders of guile and strategy even though the exuberant pace had gone. This sense of him is caught to perfection in Ross Freeman's beautiful photograph taken when Miller was batting in the state match at the SCG in 1950-51, which hung for so long in the prime ministerial office of Sir Robert Menzies. We see Miller playing a characteristic cut-drive in which body, head and bat have the easy elegance of a classical piece of sculpture. As a bowler, he seemed willing to extemporise on a whim; he might occasionally forget his marker, wheel round, duck his head and deliver an off-break or a thunderbolt. Yet, in his maturity, he was a bowler of infinite subtlety, able to plan a batsman's downfall through the mastery of making the ball work both in the air and off the pitch.

Miller was born, appropriately, at Sunshine, in Melbourne, on 28 November, 1919, and named after the Smith brothers, who were in the midst of the first flight from England to Australia. Educated at Melbourne High School, where Bill Woodfull taught him mathematics, and whence he was chosen for the Victorian schools' team, he entertained notions of becoming a jockey until rapid growth took him to 188cm, after which his passion for horses had to express itself in the betting ring. South Melbourne raised some cricketing eyebrows when the club took former state player Hughie Carroll's recommendation and drafted him into the first grade side as a fifteen year-old straight from local cricket, but his batting was remarkably mature already.

He made some impressive runs during some games with the Colts XI in District cricket in 1937-38 which resulted in his selection against Tasmania at the MCG at the age of 18 years, 166 days. Going in at 4 for 112, he was ninth out at 468, having made 181 in 289 minutes, but with only five fours. Two seasons later, Miller was given a spot in the Victorian Sheffield Shield side, making his mark with 108 in 169 minutes against South Australia, adding 161 for the second wicket with Lindsay Hassett, playing both Clarrie Grimmett and Frank Ward with easy aplomb. At this stage of his career, Miller was a specialist batsman; he did not bowl a first-class over until 1940-41.

Miller joined the Royal Australian Air Force and became part of 169 Squadron flying Beaufighter and Mosquito fighter-bombers out of Norfolk. A crash landing after a raid over Germany left him with chronic back pain which intermittently hampered his cricket in later years. Like many other service personnel, the experience of having survived intense danger left him with the determination to squeeze all that he could out of the rest of his life, an attitude which left him with a distaste for those who wanted to turn sport into war or debase sport's meaning by using the imagery of war.

The cricket played in the English summer of 1945 was a symbol of returning peace; and Miller's part in it signalled that he would be a significant presence in the post-war game. Two centuries in the five Victory Tests were followed by his dazzling 185 in 165 minutes including seven sixes for Dominions at Lord's, the final 124 of which came in only 90 minutes on the third morning. The magnificence of Miller's innings lay in the effortlessness of his strokes; he did not slog, he merely lifted the intensity of his normal technique. During the series, the pace and potential of his bowling was suddenly revealed. Denis Compton asked wicket-keeper Stan Sismey about this new bowler. Sismey said he didn't know but thought he was a change bowler who might be a bit quick. Launching himself off a short run, Miller was more than a bit quick. And he not merely took wickets, he intimidated the batsman both physically and psychologically.

He was part of the Australian team to New Zealand in 1945-46, where he made his Test debut. But it was his performances against England during the next season that announced his arrival as a Test cricketer. He began with 79 in the First Test, at the Gabba, and showed his bowling adaptability by taking 7 for 60 with medium-pace off-cutters as England were caught on a Brisbane sticky wicket. His first Test century, 141 not out at Adelaide, was a deliberate affair, enabling him to finish the series with 384 runs at 76.80 and 16 wickets at 21.31. During the Sheffield Shield matches, he had twice scalded the New South Wales attack with innings of unrestrained vigour. Having made 153 in just over three hours at Melbourne, he turned up the heat at Sydney with an unbeaten 206 in four hours, with one six landing in the top deck of the Members' Stand.

He was still combining his cricket with Australian Rules football, starring for St Kilda and turning out for Victoria in 1946. But Miller then moved to Sydney, after being offered a job as a liquor salesman. Naturally, he was selected for the 1948 side to England, where pace would be at a premium due to the 55 over new ball rule. Miller took wing at once: a double century in the second match, against Leicestershire, 163 against the MCC at Lord's, nine wickets in the gloomy dampness against Yorkshire; before the first Test, he had under his belt half of his runs and wickets for the tour. If the rest of the trip was a little more muted, he still made some important contributions to the Test series. He took seven wickets in the opening game, at Trent Bridge, including 3 for 38 in England's miserable first innings. He had to accept extra work second time around when Lindwall was absent with an injured groin: his 44 overs produced 4 for 125 and displeasure from the crowd when he hammered Len Hutton with five bouncers in eight balls. In the fourth Test, at Headingley, he shielded Neil Harvey at a crucial time when the youngster arrived with the score at 3 for 68 for his first Test innings in England. Miller's advice was: "Just get up the other end and get yourself organised. I'll take the bowling for a while." He promptly hit Jim Laker for two sixes and the pair added 121 in 90 minutes for the fourth wicket, Miller's 58 helping Harvey towards his century.

One result of the tour was a coolness in the relationship between Miller and Bradman. Even though neither of them discussed the issue in public, there is enough circumstantial evidence to suggest that Bradman saw Miller as too much of a dilettante, lacking in the dedication and seriousness that would make a Test captain. There was the (possibly apocryphal) story of Miller refusing to take part in the ritual slaughter of Essex by deliberately allowing Trevor Bailey to bowl him for a golden duck during as Australia gorged itself for 721. There was the issue of Miller throwing the ball back to Bradman and refusing to bowl during the Lord's Test because of a bad back. For his part, Miller seems to have been underwhelmed by what he saw as his captain's obsession with turning cricket into a kind of war, particularly when it was Miller who had experienced the real thing. Against Lancashire, Jack Ikin was bowled by Lindwall for 99 as the game dwindled to a draw and Miller having tested him with a few sharp bouncers.

These issues are worth remembering in the light of Miller's shock omission from the 1949-50 team to South Africa. Even though he had a quiet domestic season in 1948-49, there is no rational explanation for the decision. Subsequent comments from Bradman and "Chappie" Dwyer excusing themselves from any responsibility led Miller to speculate ironically that Jack Ryder must have had all three votes on the selection panel. Fortunately, the selectors were saved from their blunder by Bill Johnston's misfortune in being injured in a car accident after the first match so that Miller found himself sent as a successful replacement.

He began the 1950-51 season in commanding touch which brought him 616 runs in his first four innings of the season, including a bravura 138 not out against Queensland, and a vintage 214 against MCC. In the Third Test, at Sydney, Miller showed both his versatility and his all-round value. With England progressing steadily at 1 for 128 in its first innings, he improvised with a slower ball which undid Hutton, the first of three wickets which reduced England to 4 for 137. Miller then scored a sober 145 not out in nearly six hours, designed to maximise Australia's lead and grind down an injury-weakened attack.

After a century and two five wicket hauls in the Tests against the West Indies in 1951-52, Miller was appointed state captain for the 1952-53 season, replacing Arthur Morris who had led the side to the Shield in the previous year. Miller was apparently seen as more enterprising and more likely to provide the brighter cricket which was a contemporary concern. The stories continued to collect around him: placing a field by simply calling "Scatter" and solving the problem of having 12 men on the field by ordering, "One of you *** off, then."

While it is tempting to see this as typical of his cavalier attitude, it is also possible that he was simply treating his team as adults who could accept responsibility. The old back injury flared during the fourth Test against South Africa but he was fit again for the 1953 Ashes tour. Again, Miller began an English tour with a flourish: an unbeaten 220 at Worcester was followed two matches later by 159 not out against Yorkshire. In the Tests, he made a restrained 109 at Lord's as Australia built a formidable lead, while at Headingley, he got through 47 overs in taking 4 for 63 as the home side laboured. The 1954 Wisden chose this season to make him one of its five cricketers of the year.

With Hassett retiring at the end of the tour, Miller appeared to be his logical successor as captain, but Ian Johnson was appointed even though he was not a certainty for the side. The selectors' reasoning never became clear, but it was a choice of respectable mediocrity ahead of creative panache. Still, Miller made two memorable contributions to Australia's losing cause in the

1954-55 Ashes series. At Melbourne, in the third Test, he bowled throughout the first session of the match to have the lunchtime figures of 9-8-5-3, while in the next, at Adelaide, he reduced England to 4 for 49, briefly giving them palpitations, as they set out to gather the 94 needed to win the match. On the subsequent tour of the West Indies, Miller scored three Test centuries in the series.

He began his final Sheffield Shield season with 164 against Queensland and then in the next match, against South Australia at Sydney, delivered a performance which was quintessential Miller. He arrived in the nick of time for the start of the second day's play following hearty celebrations for the birth of another son, having forgotten to pick up one of his players and been forced to backtrack. Miller used a cross breeze to produce late swing and take 7 for 12 from 7.3 overs, five of his victims being clean bowled, as the visitors descended to 27 all out, the lowest-ever Sheffield Shield total.

Miller began the 1956 Ashes tour by scoring 281 not out, his highest first-class score, against Leicestershire. He did not bowl, however, until late May because of back trouble. It was a facet of Miller's Test career, that despite his earlier diffidence about bowling, he was both willing and able to bowl more as time went on, and did so without losing his edge. On an unhappy tour for Australia, he had an outstanding series with the ball, topping both the Test aggregates and averages for his team, even though he was unable to bowl in the Third Test because of an injured knee. At Lord's, he was integral to Australia's only victory in the series, with 10 for 152 in the match from 70.1 overs. After appearing in Australia's inaugural Test against Pakistan on the way back to Australia, Miller retired from first-class cricket, though he made a brief, improbable return in England in 1959, scoring 62 and an unbeaten 102 in two hours for Nottinghamshire against Cambridge University. Nine days later, he pulled a calf muscle and had to retire hurt while batting at Lord's for the MCC against Oxford.

Miller had switched to journalism soon after arriving in Sydney and had a long career with *The Sun*, as well as spending many years writing for the *London Daily Express*. In addition, he became well known as a commentator on both radio and television until his retirement in 1984, after which he continued to travel extensively and maintain his wide circle of friends from all walks of life. He was honoured in England, Lord's commissioning a portrait for the Long Room and a Miller Room being named at The Oval. Melbourne, too, was generous in remembering its long-departed son. A room was named after him in the Great Southern Stand in 1992, while he was an early inductee into the MCG's Hall of Fame in 1996. Melbourne High School named its school cricket ground the Woodfull-Miller Oval in 1999 and Miller's last public outing was to the unveiling of a Louis Laumen statue of him at the MCG in February, 2004. On that occasion, his ability to remember people from all walks of life remained as undimmed and spontaneous as ever. His latter years saw the ravages of time and illness take their toll on him and his departure from Sydney and his American-born wife, Peggy, brought its share of strains. There was, however, a fitting formal farewell to him at the state funeral held at Melbourne's St Paul's Cathedral when eulogies were delivered by Richie Benaud, Ian Chappell and John Bradman. In the Australia Day Honours of 2005, Miller was posthumously made a member of the General Division of the Order of Australia (AM) to complement the MBE he had received in 1955.

	M	I	NO	Runs	HS	100s	50s	Avge	Ct	St	W	Avge	BB
First-class	226	326	36	14,183	281*	41	63	48.90	136	0	497	22.30	7-12
Domestic first-class	52	74	8	3,803	206*	13	15	57.62	34	0	109	26.03	7-12
Tests	55	87	7	2,958	147	13	13	36.97	38	0	170	22.97	7-60

MURPHY, DOUGLAS GORDON MURTAGH, died at the Brisbane riverside suburb of Hamilton on 20 March, 2005. As an administrator in Queensland, he gave many years of service, and was president of the country division of the Queensland Cricket Association from 1969 to 1978. Douglas Murphy was born on 17 August, 1914, at the Melbourne suburb of Elsternwick. After war service, in which he rose to the rank of major, he became a stockbroker and was active in a wide range of community organisations such as the Asthma Foundation and the Bush Children's Association. He became a member of the Order of Australia (AM).

PARISH, ROBERT JAMES, died on 11 May, 2005, in the outer northern Melbourne suburb of Roxburgh Park. Ron Reed of the Melbourne Herald Sun, summed up Bob Parish as "one of the game's most respected, influential and hardest-working administrators". He was so firmly in the Australian tradition of amateur officialdom that he greeted the question of "administrative income" from an Australian Taxation Office with raucous laughter and the response that he could not submit a return for something which did not exist.

Born at the Melbourne suburb of Armadale on 7 May, 1916, Parish was educated at Melbourne Grammar School, following which he joined his father in the timber importing business; from 1946 to 1968 he was secretary of the Melbourne Timber Importers' Association.

An accurate bowler of just above medium pace, he joined the Prahran club, making his initial first-grade appearance in 1935-36. Between then and 1949-50 his 131 matches yielded him 200 wickets at 26.23, while his unprepossessing batting produced 812 runs at 8.92. Parish captained the side for four years, from 1942-43 until his regular playing days ended. These were his seasons of greatest productivity, and his 5 for 20 in 1944-45 against St Kilda was his best innings performance.

He was involved in club administration from the outset, joining the committee in 1936 and acting as chairman of selectors, vice-president from 1948 to 1955 and president for the succeeding 27 years. He was one of the club's two delegates to the Victorian Cricket Association from 1950 to 1992. this span of service falling just two years short of Jack Ryder's record 44 years for Collingwood. But his service to the club was not confined to white-collar work; rather, he simply did what had to be done, whether it was sweeping floors, serving drinks or working the scoreboard.

In 1954, Parish began his long administrative association with the Victorian Cricket Association by joining its executive, of which he was chairman from 1963 until 1992, besides serving as vice-president of the association for 22 years from 1970. It was a natural progression for him to become involved in the Australian Cricket Board, which he joined as a Victorian delegate in 1958, serving two terms as its chairman from 1966 to 1969 and again from 1975 to 1980. During the latter term he had the pleasure of the success of the Centenary Test in Melbourne, but was then immediately faced with the trauma of World Series Cricket. Parish did a competent job of salvaging something from the dramatically-changed world of cricket after 1979. In institutional terms, he was able to preserve the Board's administrative pre-eminence in the new order, even if ceding control in other areas, while in personal terms his good faith saw him well regarded by all parties.

He managed the 1965 team to the West Indies and the 1968 team to England. Parish and his close friend and colleague Ray Steele took leave of cricket on 31 August, 1992 at the annual meeting of the Victorian Cricket Association. Perhaps symbolic of their approach to administration was the fact that their farewell came without glitter and pomp at a regular meeting attended by the regular delegates and officials. For his service to cricket, he was appointed as a Commander of the Order of St Michael and St George (CMG) in 1981, having been awarded the OBE in 1975. His son, Rob (born 1941), also played for Prahran as an opening bowler, and was club secretary from 1963 until 1971.

POWER, JOHN FRANCIS, died on 6 April, 2005, at the Calvary Hospital, in the St George district of Sydney, after a long battle with cancer. In January, 1948, one of his friends persuaded Power to watch a day's play of the Test against India. The effect on a teenager previously lukewarm about cricket was instant: the sight of Ray Lindwall gliding into and unleashing red thunderbolts made him leave the ground fired with the desire to become a pace bowler. Nine years later, Power joined Lindwall in opening the bowling in a trial match for the 1956 Ashes tour and, even though he did not make the trip, was for ever warmed by the memory of bowling with his boyhood idol. Known widely as "Strawberry" because of the colour of his hair, his gregarious personality radiated warmth and wit. On one occasion, when an umpire had forgotten his bowling marker in a District match, an unperturbed Power told him: "It's all right; I'll use my false teeth."

Power was born at Port Melbourne on 23 March, 1932, and educated at St Ignatius' School, Richmond. His first club cricket was with South Yarra in the Victorian Junior Cricket Association, after which he joined the Prahran club in 1949-50. He was given a long apprenticeship but made his mark in the Firsts in 1952-53, beginning the season with Colin McDonald's wicket and ending it with 29 scalps at 19.86. By this stage, he had grown to 186cm and filled out to 86kg and was generating real pace from his Lindwallesque approach. He differed from his model, however, at the moment of delivery, with two large final strides and a pronounced drop in his left shoulder.

A destructive 7 for 45 against Essendon early in 1953-54 saw Power selected for Victoria. He made a sound start with figures of 2 for 48 and 3 for 46 against Queensland, at Melbourne, and made an immediate impact on such observers as Bill O'Reilly and Keith Miller. Over the next three seasons, however, his best innings figures were 4 for 54 against Queensland, at the Gabba. Despite his capacity to make the early breakthrough, Power tended to bowl too short and too wide, too often squandering his effectiveness. He was selected in the Taylor-Malley Testimonial match at Sydney in January, 1956, but his 4 for 110 in the first innings failed to gain him a trip to England. After 1955-56, Power spent three seasons out of the Victorian side, despite continuing to be highly effective for Prahran. Keith Miller, writing in *The Sporting Globe* in November, 1959, asserted that Power had fallen out with club captain Sammy Loxton who was a state selector. "It never pays to fall out with those who count in sport," Miller proclaimed, echoing his own experience. But Loxton was away managing the Australian side in Pakistan and India. So Power returned to the side a more mature bowler who had acquired control and the arts of cut and swing. He had his best first-class season, his 35 wickets at 24.68 placing him second in the national aggregates, his figures revealing consistency rather than one or two prolific performances: his best innings figures were 5 for 66 against Queensland at Melbourne. However, the next year, the selectors preferred Alan Connolly and Ron Gaunt as new-ball partners to Ian Meckiff.

Power left Prahran after 1961-62 and spent a season as captain-coach with Sub-District side Elsternwick before having a final season with Essendon. In District cricket he made 646 runs at 8.38 and took 314 wickets at 17.72. A left-hand batsman of decidedly more intent, he occasionally hit to good effect. A useful Australian Rules footballer, Power played with Port Melbourne in the Victorian Football Association and later was captain-coach of Ferntree Gully in the Mountain District League, leading the club to premierships in all three grades in the one season. A company representative in the textile industry, he moved to Sydney in the 1980s.

	M	I	NO	Runs	HS	100s	50s	Avge	Ct	St	W	Avge	BB
First-class	26	33	10	218	43	0	0	9.47	17	0	69	33.81	5-66
Domestic first-class	23	29	6	173	43	0	0	8.65	16	0	62	32.61	5-66

RAWLE, KEITH TREVILLIAN, died in Queensland on 6 March, 2005. An Essendon man to the core, Keith Rawle was born there on 29 October, 1924, educated at the local high school, and played both cricket and Australian Rules football for the black and reds. He made his cricket debut for Essendon as a 16-year-old and made an immediate impression as a free-stroking batsman whose devil-may-care driving was a strong feature of his game, despite his slight physique (171 cm and 63 kg). He was a member of the RAAF's 1 Aircraft Performance Unit between 1942 and 1946 and, even though he saw service in New Guinea, was able to maintain some continuity in club cricket. Appearing for Combined Services in a three-day non-first-class match against Victoria at Fitzroy in December, 1943, he hit an exuberant 101.

His best club season was 1947-48, when he made 599 runs at 54.45. Continued good form next season saw him selected for the state trip to Tasmania where he made his only first-class appearance, scoring 10 in his only innings at Hobart. Rawle finished at Essendon after the 1949-50 season, his 113 matches producing 3,217 runs at 27.97, while his change bowling netted him 47 wickets at 28.82, his best innings figures of 4 for 28 coming in his final season. Having moved to Ballarat, he played with and coached the Redan club until the mid-1970s, representing Ballarat at Country Week between 1951 and 1969. Rawle appeared for Victorian Country in a rain-ruined match against the MCC at Geelong in 1950-51, when he made 16, while a decade later, he bagged a pair at Ballarat against the West Indians, although he did dismiss Rohan Kanhai.

Rawle played 111 games for Essendon as second rover in the 1940s, his 98 goals being testament to his kicking skills and flair. Having been an emergency in the 1942 grand final, he played in the premiership sides of both 1946 and 1949. A chartered accountant, he spent some time as a partner in Lindsay Hassett's sports store in Melbourne before making a career in television sales in Ballarat, and finally becoming as sales manager of television station SEQ 8 at Maryborough in Queensland.

	M	I	NO	Runs	HS	100s	50s	Avge	Ct	St	W	Avge	BB
First-class	1	1	0	10	10	0	0	10.00	0	0	0	–	–

REWALD, DENNIS GRAHAM, died at Wondai, Queensland on 12 November, 2004. He made two appearances for Combined South Queensland teams against international touring sides as a middle-order batsman and right-arm off-spinner. In 1962-63, against the MCC at Toowoomba, he made 9 not out and took 2 for 64, while on his home ground at Murgon, he captained the side against the West Indian tourists of 1968-69. Rewald top-scored with 44 of his side's 121 and dismissed Roy Fredericks. Rewald was born at Murgon on 22 October, 1936, and was a dominating presence in local cricket for over 30 years, regularly representing the association at Country week. A farmer at Cloyna, he was a councillor on the Murgon Shire Council for 23 years.

SANDERS, LEYLAND ARTHUR, died on 3 January, 2005, at the northern Sydney suburb of Forestville. A member of one of Queensland's best-known sporting families, Ley Sanders was a talented cricketer whose potential was enough for the Queensland selectors to remain interested in him over five seasons, even if he carried the drinks as he played. Born at the Brisbane bayside suburb of Sandgate on 17 October, 1927, he was an outstanding sportsman at Yeronga State School, where he captained both the cricket and the Australian Rules sides, and was selected in the Queensland state schoolboys' side.

During the war, the young team was given the chance to play in the QCA's C-grade competition, where Sanders began to develop as a wicket-keeper/batsman, becoming captain of the Queensland Colts side for three successive seasons from 1948-49. In his final innings in these matches against

New South Wales colts, at the Gabba in November 1950, he made a composed 71, and was called up to the state side, but his experience in the final two matches of the season set a pattern. He made a useful 27 and 14 not out against South Australia and then was twelfth man against Victoria.

The presence of Don Tallon and Wally Grout blocked his future as a wicket-keeper. And he was unable to make enough runs to protect his place as a specialist batsman, although his sound defence and tenacity were never in doubt. His highest score came against Victoria at the Gabba in 1951-52, when he opened the innings and made 49 in 155 minutes without finding the boundary. Next season, at Sydney, he resisted the home side's Test-strength attack for 104 minutes in making 34, again with no fours, when he batted at number seven in the second innings. His state career came to an end after Jack Treanor, making his first-class debut, bowled him for a duck in each innings of the match against New South Wales which opened the 1954-55 Sheffield Shield season. In the second innings, Sanders was the middle dismissal in Treanor's hat-trick. After he traded in the gloves, he became an athletic outfield, with safe hands, swift feet and a strong arm. He took a spectacular catch against Western Australia at Brisbane in 1951-52, when his soaring leap pulled in a skied hit from Charlie Puckett off Colin McCool.

A gifted Australian Rules player, Sanders played with the Yeronga club from 1941, becoming captain at the age of 19. He then transferred to Coorparoo in the 1950s and represented Queensland at each Australian carnival from 1946 to 1959, where he was often picked out by Melbourne commentators as a potential VFL player. By this time, Sanders had moved into a career as an electrical sales representative, before becoming Sales Director and ultimately CEO in Australia for a British firm, which meant a move to Sydney, where he played cricket for Mosman in the City and Suburban competition.

Sanders was the product of a sporting family. His mother, then Linda Johnson, was the Queensland diving champion in 1920, while his father, "Big Bill", was president of the Australian Amateur Anglers' Association. His brothers, Alister and Darryl, both played high-standard cricket.

	M	I	NO	Runs	HS	100s	50s	Avge	Ct	St	W	Avge	BB
First-class	10	18	1	255	49	0	0	15.00	9	6	0	–	–
Domestic first-class	6	17	1	140	49	0	0	15.00	7	0	0	–	–

SMITH, LLOYD HAROLD JAMES, died on 26 August, 2004, in Hobart, where he had been born on 5 August, 1928. A stockily-built left-hand opening batsman, Lloyd Smith was a prolific scorer for Glenorchy in the Tasmanian Cricket Association competition in Hobart for nearly three decades from 1942-43 until 1970-71, having joined the club while still at Hobart High School. Third Man, writing in *The Mercury* of his 167 against Clarence in 1957-58, said of Smith: "His defence was sound, he got it right behind the ball, and when in aggressive mood, stroked crisply and forcibly." Yet, despite the basic soundness of his methods, he was unable to reproduce his club form at the first-class level.

He was first selected against Victoria, at Hobart, in 1950-51, a match which saw him make a careful 19 in the second innings. But over the next eight seasons, he played another seven games for a highest score of 31 against Victoria, at Hobart in 1953-54. He did show his capabilities, however, in a two-day non-first-class game against the South Africans at Hobart in 1952-53, when he made a long and stubborn 51 in the second innings. Smith was a fixture for South in intra-island matches for 15 years. In a club match against North Hobart in 1954-55, he recorded an eight, when, after driving Ted Richardson through long-on for an all-run four, the bowler shied the ball at the batsman's end only for it to race to the boundary. To complete Richardson's frustration, Smith hit his next delivery for another four.

Smith was a conscientious administrator, being a board member of the Tasmanian Cricket Association and the state Cricket Council from 1958 until 1976, and was treasurer of both bodies from 1962 until his retirement 14 years later. In addition, he was a state selector from 1967 until 1975. An accountant, he spent the last 25 years of his working life in both financial and managerial positions at Hobart's Cascade Brewery. His father, Harold ("Nip"), had been a prominent Australian Rules footballer in Tasmania in the 1920s.

	M	I	NO	Runs	HS	100s	50s	Avge	Ct	St	W	Avge	BB
First-class	8	15	0	165	31	0	0	11.00	–	–	0	0	– –

STARR, CECIL LEONARD BERRY, died on 25 January, 2005, in Adelaide, at the age of 96. Despite a prolific career of 27 years in Adelaide District cricket, Cec Starr only played seven games for South Australia, spread over 19 years. Born at the railway town of Quorn on 20 July, 1907, he was educated at Jamestown High School. Having moved to Adelaide, he joined the Colts side in 1925-26 and was selected for the state side in Perth a year later

Then he began his long association with the Adelaide club. Despite his small stature (169 cm and 65 kg), his sweet timing allowed him to produce real power, particularly when unfolding his signature cut shot. A chanceless and challenging 161 against Kensington and its trump card of Clarrie Grimmett in 1929-30 got him another game against Western Australia, this time at Adelaide, when he made a brisk 72.

The next two seasons brought him several more state games, his best innings being 33 against a strong New South Wales attack at Adelaide in 1931-32. Starr then had to wait a further 15 years for another call, which came in 1945-46 after he had scored successive District centuries. Even then, misfortune intervened: against New South Wales at Adelaide, he was struck on the hand by Ray Lindwall on the first morning; even though no bones were broken, he could take no further part in the match. Starr then batted well against Queensland at the Gabba, making a determined 43.

When he finished his District career in 1952-53, he had made 8,285 runs at 36.49, with 20 centuries, to be the fifth-highest scorer in Adelaide first-grade cricket. Starr's spells as an occasional off-spinner yielded 119 wickets at 29.95. With a short break in the late 1950s, he was a state selector from

1948-49 to 1965-66, mostly in the company of Sir Donald Bradman and Phil Ridings. In addition, he served on the Ground and Finance Committee from 1952 to 1978.

An accomplished tennis player in his youth, Starr played golf until he was 93 and played competition bowls at a high level. Starr had a long career in the retail clothing industry, managing the men's department of the Myer store in Adelaide and spending the last 15 years of his working life as the South Australian state manager for the Speedo sportswear company. His civic involvement included acting as the inaugural South Australian president of the Father's Day Council.

His family shared his love of and skill at sport: his wife, Jean, was prominent in women's golf in Adelaide, while his son, Barry, played for South Australian Schoolboys in 1952 and first-grade for both University and Glenelg, while his daughter, Jillian was South Australian state tennis champion for six consecutive years in the 1960s.

	M	I	NO	Runs	HS	100s	50s	Avge	Ct	St	W	Avge	BB
First-class	11	2	1	236	72	1	23.60	5	0	2	30.00	2-3	
Domestic first-class	1	2	-	54	33	0	27.00	0	0	0	-	-	

THOLLAR, DOUGLAS HUGH, died on 14 June, 2005, at the Sydney suburb of Kyeemagh. Born at George Town on 13 February, 1919, Doug Thollar was educated at Launceston High School and became a teenage sensation as a leg-spinner with the South Launceston club. With remarkable dexterity and ease, he developed into an attacking leg-spinner who was still accurate and controlled. He was so effective in his first season, 1936-37, that he was picked for the Launceston match against the MCC tourists as a 17-year-old and dismissed both Bob Wyatt and Les Ames.

Next season, he was even more prolific and took 80 wickets at 14.23, the highest aggregate ever in Launceston cricket. He took all 10 North Launceston wickets for 67 and wrecked Easts twice with 8 for 25 and 8 for 34. Towards the end of the season, Thollar played in Tasmania's Launceston match against the 1938 Australian tourists. With the visitors in a festive mood, he went for 116 runs from his 13 overs but picked up five wickets in the process, including those of Jack Fingleton and Stan McCabe. In 1938-39, he took another 65 club wickets and made his final state appearance, in which he went wicketless against Victoria at Launceston.

The advent of war meant that 1939-40 was his last season of cricket, so that he finished with 207 wickets from his 42 games in four seasons; his 309 runs attest to the modesty of his batting skills. Remarkably, in his short career, he took six wickets or more in an innings on 12 occasions for South Launceston. He also took 24 wickets in five intra-state matches. He spent much of the war in the Merchant Navy, before switching to aircraft; he spent 22 years as a radio operator for Qantas, a job that travel and hours that spelt an end to his cricket.

	M	I	NO	Runs	HS	100s	50s	Avge	Ct	St	W	Avge	BB
First-class	3	5	3	19	10*	0	0	9.50	1	0	8	33.50	5-116

WALKER, ALAN KEITH, died on 19 June, 2005, in Sydney. An outstanding cricketer and footballer, Walker played rugby union for Australia and toured with the Australian cricket team to South Africa in 1949-50 as a fast left-arm bowler. Having burst into first-class cricket in 1948-49, the speed triumvirate of Lindwall, Miller and Johnston made Test selection difficult and then a chronic shoulder injury put paid to his chances. Neville Cardus, in previewing the Australian side to South Africa, wrote evocatively of Walker: "He hurls himself at the batsman – from over the wicket; propels the ball dead towards the leg stump, and it rises viciously at the left or near the gloves. Compared to Lindwall, he is as the battering-ram to the flash of lightning. Still, the battering-rams can batter."

Outstanding: Alan Walker

Born at the Sydney beach suburb of Manly on 4 October, 1925, Walker was educated at Sydney Grammar School where he was a successful all-round sportsman. On leaving school in 1943, he joined the RAAF as a trainee pilot. He had been playing grade cricket with Manly since 1941-42 and turned in some startling performances in the immediate post-war period: 8 for 68 against Western Suburbs in 1945-46 was followed at the end of next season by 7 for 8 and 7 for 6 in his rout of Cumberland for 42 and 31, for him to finish 1946-47 with 53 wickets at 11.04.

His Wallaby tour of 1947-48 delayed his entry to state cricket but he made up for the lost time the next season, when his 39 wickets at 15.30 included 26 in the three Shield matches on the then-pacy Sydney pitch. He left the Queenslanders shattered: after finishing the first innings with wickets from successive deliveries, he took 6 for 20 in the second, including a hat-trick, without help from the field. Two matches later, against South Australia, he took 6 for 22 and 3 for 39 in enervating heat. At this stage of his career, there were some suspicions about a kinked arm as he delivered his faster ball, but he was never called for throwing and the muttering died away.

Walker's selection for South Africa was a formality but he never really hit his straps on tour, his 25 tour wickets falling short of expectations. Back in Australia, he had two satisfactory seasons; in 1950-51, he took 5 for 60 for an Australian XI against the MCC at Sydney, while next year, he again gave the Queenslanders more grievous nightmares with 9 for 72 in the match. Compactly built (175cm and 70kg), he generated disconcerting pace (almost that of Lindwall's, according to wicket-keeper Ossie Lambert) and late in-swing from a run-up of about a dozen paces.

With the Ashes tour of 1953 in sight, Walker missed most of the 1952-53 season with a shoulder injury sustained during a rugby game and he was never the same bowler again. He took the chance to switch to English league cricket, with two seasons at Rawtenstall where he became an all-round presence, so much so that when he moved to Norton in the Staffordshire and District League in 1955, he set a new competition record with an innings of 171.

During this time, he qualified for Nottinghamshire and cracked 61 in 45 minutes on his county debut against the touring Pakistanis. In his first full season of 1956, he had one real highlight, at Leicester, during an otherwise muted summer as a bowler, he became the first Australian in more than 27 years to take four wickets in four balls: one in the first innings and three to start the second. Two matches later, against Somerset at Trent Bridge, Walker made 62 of a last-wicket partnership of 123 with fellow Australian Bruce Dooland. In 1957, having opened the season with 7 for 56 against Middlesex at Lord's, Walker missed a month's cricket with a severe bout of mumps which again took the sting out of his bowling, although later in the season, he made his highest first-class score of 73 against Glamorgan at Trent Bridge. Early next season, his contract was terminated so that he and his family could return to Australia.

A speedy and elusive rugby union centre, Walker had a rapid rise to the state side in 1947, and was selected for the First in Test against New Zealand at Brisbane. A member of the 1947-48 Wallaby side to Europe, he was kept out of the early Tests but took his chance against England at Twickenham when he produced one of the most sublime moments in any code of Australian football. Receiving a chest-high pass on the Australian 25-yard line, Walker kicked over the heads of oncoming tacklers, regathered the ball and used all of his speed and elusiveness to evade the opposition and score in the corner to set up Australia's historic 11-0 victory. His feat entered the folklore of rugby union and has been reproduced in both diagrammatic and pictorial form on numerous occasions. A Test in France and two more against Great Britain in Australia completed his national career. During his subsequent time in England, he played rugby league with Leigh.

After his return from England, he became a finance officer with Custom Credit and from 1978 until his retirement in 1987 was general manager of Mercantile Credits Ltd. Walker was an alderman on Manly Municipal Council from 1969 until 1978.

	M	I	NO	Runs	HS	100s	50s	Avge	Ct	St	W	Avge	BB
First-class	94	118	26	1,603	73	8	0	17.42	37	0	221	27.47	7-56
Domestic first-class	23	26	6	281	42	0	0	14.05	7	0	93	21.17	6-20

Warwick Franks was the editor of Wisden Cricketers' Almanack Australia from 2001-02 to 2003-04.

Saint or sledger?

by MATT BUCHANAN

> "Even a leisurely game like cricket, demanding grace rather than strength, can cause much ill-will ... as we saw in the controversy over body-line bowling and over the rough tactics of the Australian team that visited England in 1921!"
>
> – George Orwell, *The Sporting Spirit* (1945)

Martin Amis wrote that a writer's greatness is decided by time, and that the assessment begins with the obituaries. For a cricketer it starts with retirement. The runs have been scored, the wickets taken, games won and lost, and conduct noted. Steve Waugh had a dream send-off in 2003-04. It is true that his retirement announcement before the first Test against India irked some, but the huge crowds that came to see him off – at Sydney it was the largest attendance since Bradman versus India in 1946-47 – cared little as to whether Waugh had placed his departure above the series in order to better harvest their adulation, and any commercial opportunities it might entrain. If some sniped about an apparent selfishness, surely it was mere cavilling. Here was a survivor, a man who had on countless occasions pulled Australia's chestnuts out of the fire, but had done it so very successfully that it no longer seemed possible they could be singed again.

The day after Waugh's triumphal exit, chaired around the SCG on the shoulders of his most devoted team-mates Justin Langer and Matthew Hayden, Mike Coward perhaps best summarised the general feeling in *The Australian*. "He has been much more than an exceptional cricketer," he wrote. "He has been a leader of distinction, a reformer, an innovator, an educator, and even added to the lexicon of the game. Cricket has given him his identity and he has given the game his heart and soul, along with vision and knowledge."

In the 18 months since, the opportunity has been taken to establish the longer view about Waugh and his legacy. Peter FitzSimons, Jack Egan and Greg Baum have jostled for posterity's ear. Waugh's autobiography, another collaboration with Geoff Armstrong for which he is said to have received a $1.6m advance, is also soon to be published. FitzSimons has written a popular celebration, Egan an unauthorised biography and Baum a critical analysis of Waugh and his times. Different in tone – breathless, earnest, and forensic, respectively – each offers an appreciation of what made Waugh tick, and with varying rigour tries to establish, given that Waugh captained such mighty players, the degree to which his leadership and example was responsible for Australia's unprecedented success and influence.

Each book also examines the manifestly aggressive spirit in which Australia played under Waugh, and questions whether the "mental disintegration" or sledging pushed so firmly was worth the victory if the aftertaste was a little sour. Egan's and Baum's books also dabble with the flipside to that issue: without his no-holds attitude and the hell-bent desire for victory that allowed sledging, could Waugh have been the man a nation so enormously admired? Could we have had one without the other? Can we live with the idea of a saint who swore?

FitzSimons' **Steve Waugh** (HarperCollins, $45) does not look for that answer. A large-format, coffee-table hagiography, it is endorsed by Waugh, who acknowledges that some of the proceeds will be gratefully received by the Steve Waugh Foundation. Between its hard covers are glossy pictures of big moments in Waugh's career – his clash with Curtly Ambrose in the 1995 West Indies series; shaking his brother Mark's hand during their series-defining partnership at Kingston. Elsewhere, should you want to read it, there is the story of Waugh's life in cricket as narrated by FitzSimons, the popular biographer, former Wallaby and awed fan. Written as only FitzSimons can write, it is EXCLAMATORY!, reverts to needless emphases, is sprinkled with Aussie-isms such as "fair dinkum", and features references to Tobruk and *The Man from Snowy River*. Quite dottily, the epilogue compares Waugh to Phar Lap. Indeed for much of his book FitzSimons writes as if his inkpot was a jar of Vegemite. "Play for Australia ... since time immemorial, that phrase has had a particular resonance for young Australian males of a sporting bent, and in the dreamtime of the young Waugh boys' lives the thought of one day pulling on the baggy green cap could put a bolt right through them." Time immemorial? Dreamtime? It is his newspaper style and more readers like it than do not – on the weekends at any rate – and he has his moments. When discussing Steve's reputation for reticence with Mark's apparent conviviality he writes: "Steve never really was one of the boys, and often retired to his room to work into the night, doing such things as writing the latest in his series of tour diaries. While Steve, thus, wrote a book a year, the public would have been surprised if Mark read, and staggered if it had been Steve's."

The only time FitzSimons engages in a critical way with his subject is in regard to sledging. After regaling us with the chucklesome quips of the modern era – including a reference to some bloke named "Bill Lawrie" (whoever he is, he also turns up in Egan's book on p.158) – FitzSimons quotes Waugh excusing mental disintegration as "being part of the game". FitzSimons suddenly breaks form and wags a finger. "Where Waugh and we critics parted company, however, was firstly in his assertion that that kind of sledging had always been around ... secondly that sledging was rarely straight at a player." Then ... blasphemy. FitzSimons makes the strongest accusation imaginable: he values the baggy green more than Waugh. "Ultimately it was an area of Waugh's career where he and many of his supporters agreed to differ. He thought it part of the game. We thought the game should be well above that, and that men who wore the baggy green doubly so."

> "Quite dottily, the epilogue compares Waugh to Phar Lap"

Egan's **One Who Will** (Allen & Unwin, $40.90) is a far more ambivalent portrait. Egan argues that Waugh's desire to get the best out of his own ability, and of those around him, combined to give Australian cricket unprecedented bounty, but at a cost. To Egan, the "vicious and obscene sledging" – the mental disintegration – is instead evidence of the moral disintegration of its practitioners, which taints the Waugh legacy. He compares Waugh to John McEnroe, someone whose behaviour was reprehensible but whose ability made him irresistible. "[He was] so hell bent on winning he didn't always respect the spirit of the game ... he was entertaining to watch because he played attacking cricket. He led by example."

Egan displays the obscenity and its personal nature by quoting a 2002 South Africa *Sports Illustrated* interview with the current captain Graeme Smith. "All [Shane] Warne does is call you a c***. When he walked past me, he said: 'You f***ing c***, what are you doing here?'" There are also reams of blue from Glenn McGrath. To his credit, Egan asks why it was so. One answer comes from an unexpected source: the New South Wales Labor Senator John Faulkner, a Noble Stand regular of 25 years. Egan remarked to Faulkner that he could not reconcile claims of Waugh's leadership qualities with instructions, tacit or explicit, to "attack" another team. Faulkner replied: "I've never seen a good leader who is weak ... I think you've got to accept that with these leadership qualities comes a pretty hard edge."

One Who Will is unapologetically anecdotal, as it must be. When it came to interviews, Waugh was One Who Would Not. Egan tells us Waugh's management opposed the book, asking Waugh's mother Bev, and at least one "senior player" to decline Egan's requests. "It is hard to write a book about someone who will not talk to you," he notes. Consequently, secondary sources abound. There is evidence of hundreds of hours of formidably scrutinised video footage and after making a comment about Waugh's technique, Egan mentions in passing his ownership on tape of nearly all Waugh's innings. He also judiciously cross-references cricket journalism and player biographies.

Waugh is presented as someone who was shaped not only by the oft-acknowledged inspiration and mentorship of Allan Border and Bob Simpson, and the humiliation of being flogged by just about anybody who felt like it in the mid-1980s, but also by the grassroots culture at Bankstown and NSW. "The Australian captain and coach's greatest assets are a climate and culture that encourage people to play cricket, and an infrastructure from club cricket to Cricket Australia." Egan recalls Waugh had a reputation as a young player for gracelessness upon getting bad news from the umpire. Umpires amused themselves by making up teams of the surliest dismissed: Waugh was their captain. They also made up a side of bowlers most disbelieving when their appeals were turned down. It was the first time Waugh captained two sides at once.

Egan doesn't leave it there and was wise to quote Coward's tender appreciation of Waugh in 1987. "He presents an unhappy and unsmiling soul," he wrote. "And this is a pity, for in so many ways he is such a special cricket person ... unfortunately he boils over at times and it is not a pretty sight. Because he is so proud, so single-minded, so intense, so committed, so ordered, so prepared, so poised, he does not believe he is ever out – save perhaps when he is bowled – or that any of his appeals when he is bowling should be refused. This trait has irritated his contemporaries ... and alienated umpires."

So how could we have been surprised that Waugh would be reluctant to accept the decisions of rather more powerful officials later in his career? Baum's **The Waugh Era** (ABC Books, $19.95) is an intelligent two-part analysis of the way Waugh and his times enjoyed a mutual influence. The first section summarises the achievement and sets the context. Waugh is appointed as captain of Australia in 1999, but is expected to fail rather than thrive. At 33, he had little experience as a leader and as a player his reflexes are expected to dull. Mark Taylor's Australia were already the best in the world, played attacking cricket, and were very popular with the fans. Baum provides a highly readable commentary along the route to Waugh's twin peaks – the 1999 World Cup and the 16-Test winning streak – and the gathering energy with which they were scaled. In 1999 Waugh's captaincy is described as "unenterprising". By 2003 Peter Roebuck is writing: "Waugh remains the most daring of captains."

In part two Baum examines in ten short chapters Waugh the man, player, captain, his tactics, the media and sledging. He likens the emergence of the Waugh-era team from the mighty shadows of Border and Taylor to the rise of the new MCG grandstand, an edifice built "tier by tier, layer by layer, player by player". Waugh's reign was "no celestial star but built upon hard-won foundations". There was not one Waugh era, but several. "Waugh the cricketer, Waugh the twin, Waugh the one-day captain, and Waugh the Test captain were all self-contained eras, each distinct and distinguished." And all of them, he notes dryly, "began inauspiciously".

Baum also advances a thesis that the increasing commercialism of the game, and the Waugh team's eyes-on-the-prize ruthlessness, are of a piece with cricket in the age of globalisation. When Waugh started in the 1980s, no one had heard of globalisation. By his retirement, its values were embedded in cricket, as everywhere. "When Waugh began under Border, there was no cricket academy, no third umpire and the MCG floodlights were new. James Sutherland was a 20-year-old fast bowler at Melbourne University. Australia had won three of 20 Test matches. They had no coach. No one did. The ACB had a staff of six, now it is 60. Everything except the Australian cap became available to the highest bidder. Even sentimentality – such a cricket sort of phenomenon – was discovered to turn a dollar and memorabilia became a hot commodity. Support staff of the national team burgeoned to include not just a manager but coach, assistant, psychologist ... Waugh swore by them all, especially the psychologist because he saw that a cricketer's ambition was confined only by the limits of his mind."

Waugh's era saw the maturation of corporate cricket, and Baum gives us a defining moment. "In Monaco in 2002, the Australians were named as International Team of the Year and won a Laureus award – a self-styled sporting Oscar. But it was hard to escape the feeling that this was not so much sportspeople getting a Laureus award as Laureus awarding itself sportspeople. That is what corporations do."

Things also altered on the field. "The big change was that batting reclaimed the game. Averages bloomed, fourth-innings score limits increased. Double-hundreds proliferated. Run-rates went through the roof. An average of 50 was once considered cricket's sound barrier but now there was a sonic boom every day." And Baum says it's not just because the batsmen are better, it's the age in which we live. Grounds are smaller because security measures demand the ropes be brought in. Curators prepare flat pitches to entertain. Increased scrutiny from improved technology has made umpires timid. The massive money-driven fixture list ensures fast bowlers break down more often. And, interestingly, pay television allows batsmen on different sides of the world an unprecedented inspiration to study and better their rivals' achievements.

As to the problem of the contradictory Waugh, Baum is humble enough to use another's words if they fit. "Roebuck, who knew Waugh from a very young age, saw how his apparent contradiction might be reconciled: 'International sport can be a terrifying business and it takes the worst as well the best to succeed at it.' Roebuck said Waugh knew the darkness in him that made him such a formidable cricketer and sought in the rest of his life to balance it with ennobling enterprises."

Baum admires Waugh's attachment to the baggy green, reports the ugliness of sledging, and acknowledges that he was not universally loved. He also suggests that cricket, partly because it is currently a micro-managed commodity, is in thrall to a "new puritanism". Like Egan, he reminds us that Waugh grew up playing for Bankstown, the home of Len Pascoe and Jeff Thomson, men "who did not stand on niceties". In other words, had Waugh behaved like Gandhi on the field we wouldn't still be talking about him. In that vein, Baum quotes Richie Benaud at the presentation of Australian Media Association Award for its best young player of 1987: "What I like best about Steve Waugh is that he's got a bit of shit in him."

Benaud could use a bit of it in himself. His **My Spin on Cricket** (Hodder & Stoughton, £18.99) is what Kerry O'Keeffe would call a straight-breaker. Little energy on the ball, no bite, no rip – no spin. Could it be that Benaud is trapped by his own standing in the game? With more than 500 Test matches as player and commentator, Benaud's experience has made him a verdict machine. By the end of his book you will never again want to read or hear any variation of the phrase "just about one of the best performances/matches/ catches/balls/innings/series I ever saw/have ever seen".

A little faith is lost when he describes Keith Miller as "the greatest all-rounder I ever played with or against", but rates Garry Sobers, who was "more of my time", as "the greatest all-around cricketer the world has ever seen". His concluding chapter on the virtues of Michael Clarke ("the best young batsman since Ricky Ponting"), and Andrew Flintoff ("best all-rounder produced by England since Ian Botham") ahead of their Ashes performances is reassuringly oracular, but the real problem is dull writing.

Mediocre sportswriting is characterised by mere retelling – stating not showing. Even when the author is an admired former player and commentator, a fresh or first-hand view must be offered. A verdict lacking either quality lacks all. Great sportswriting adds insight to recollection. It's said of Orwell that he saw himself as an honest man at the typewriter, someone able to face ugly truths, unafraid to say unpopular things, be unpopular. He also had a jealous appreciation of the English language, and was forever searching for a fresh phrase. In the world of cricket writing Roebuck comes as close as anyone to fitting this description. Broadcaster, columnist, author and, of late, memoirist, his is the dominant voice in Australian cricket commentary. He is respected by followers, players and peers, indeed he is quoted at one point or another by all but two books reviewed here (Lehmann and Benaud). He is also a dedicated coach and mentor. Much like Waugh, his former Somerset team-mate, he is pleased to be his own man.

Roebuck released two books this term; a memoir, **Sometimes I Forgot to Laugh** (Allen & Unwin, $35) and **It Takes All Sorts** (Allen & Unwin, $27), a stocking-filler collection of miniature profiles, or as Roebuck has it, "character studies in the form of reports of men in action". The former volume is new writing about his life, the latter contains material edited from his journalism, as well as fresh comment. They are both concerned with one thing above all: character, and its revelation through cricket.

The talent of the great might not be so different from that of the merely gifted, suggests Roebuck in *It Takes All Sorts*, but "it is what the player does with the gift that reveals character. Greatness is achievable only through great character, which is to say courage to learn from failure, and determination to keep chasing the end of the rainbow". Roebuck doesn't account for how a player can be a pillar of character on the ground yet be a flapping windsock the moment he steps off it. But even if it has more to do with concentration than any more permanent virtue, a valid point stands: success in sport is in the mind. A favourite exemplar for Roebuck is Waugh, a man still so much in everybody's thoughts. "With Waugh his determination is not God-given but forged in his mind, a choice he took never to take a backward step, never to think a cause lost."

Roebuck's own cause looked lost in 1999 when, as he reports in *Sometimes I Forgot to Laugh*, two 19-year-old men (two of many to receive board and coaching from Roebuck in England), brought assault charges against him. "A few whacks with a stick" is how Roebuck describes a similar "correction" meted out to another under his roof, one who apparently accepted that Roebuck's disciplinary regime was there to improve outlook and fitness. "My house provided an alternative to the feebleness of the prevailing youth culture. Youngsters could take it or leave it. Those who left early regretted and said so, in writing." Unflattering portraits of his regimen were leaked to friends of Botham, who had been openly hostile to Roebuck since falling out with him in their playing days at Somerset.

"Eventually those involved, or rather those around them, took their story to Botham's newspaper ... As soon as I found out Botham was involved I knew that any chance of the matter being dealt with quietly had gone. Journalists confirmed that he was gleeful." Roebuck was reporting Australia's tour of Sri Lanka when the *Daily Mirror* broke the news about the charges. The following April he was arrested at his home by three detectives. Interpol interviewed past visitors, some of whom "had been offered money by the newspapers". Serious charges were drawn up but a deal was struck whereby "I would plead guilty to the lowest form of assault". As part of the deal Roebuck "had to pretend consent was absent". "Of course it was nonsense ... I was sentenced to three months in prison suspended for two years ... But at least, and at last, it was over. After 28 months of investigation ... I could resume my life." The resumption would be in South Africa and Australia. He had finished with England.

Roebuck also reports a strained relationship with his father from which he eventually withdrew, but without bitterness. Things were hard. But 35 years later he appreciates his life as rich and rewarding. ("If someone is to blame might not they also deserve some credit?") There's a First in law at Cambridge, initial encounters with Botham and Viv Richards at Somerset as young men in 1974, and the feud that followed Somerset's "trophy" years. He offers a sane account of the infamous defeat captaining England A in Holland, and speaks warmly of the satisfaction he found playing – and winning – with the minor county Devon. Self-analysis, however, is persistently absent, noticeably so for someone whose stock-in-trade is the dissection of others. It is perhaps a Roebuckian trait to believe assessments of our characters should be made by anyone but oneself. At the close Roebuck quotes his father's assessment. "In ortho-dox spheres, Peter might be regarded as odd, whereas he is merely obscure and oblique. He is an unconventional loner, with an independent outlook on life, an ir-reverent sense of humour and sometimes a withering tongue ... His toughness on himself can, though, make him harsh in his judgment of others, especially the self-indulgent."

> "Roebuck's writing is not for everyone ... the lanes of Roebuckshire resound to an epi-grammatic clip-clop"

Doubtless. Hitherto. Hereabouts. Durst. Roebuck's writing is not for everyone. It is mannered. Often the lanes of Roebuckshire re-sound to an epigrammatic clip-clop. "All sport is boxing in another form." "A man must address his weaknesses: for only a fool does not." "Cricket is not a game of bat and ball. It is an internal struggle, a war waged between a man and himself. The opposition is merely a convenience." Yet he nails it more than not. Beside his much quoted observation of Waugh – "He looks like a man whose lawnmower won't start" – we can set this about McGrath. "He looks like a monk, periodically behaves like an enraged chook and bowls like a Swiss clock. On paper he is a basket case. On the field he is the best pace bower of his generation. He averages 16 on the subcontinent and in this age of batting averages 22 overall."

A character briefly touched upon in *Sometimes I Forgot to Laugh* wrote a foreword to it, and O'Keeffe is a friend for whom Roebuck reserves warm affection. Roebuck first encountered O'Keeffe during an Oxbridge match in 1977 and he was sledging. "Throughout O'Keeffe was calling the odds from short leg, giving quotes on this bloke reaching 50 or not. He had an irreverent sense of humour." Roebuck might have found it a laugh, but O'Keeffe surely could not. "I don't remember a single funny sledge from my era," he writes on p.161 of **According to Skull** (ABC Books, $29.95). O'Keeffe is dead against sledging, but so is everybody this year.

O'Keeffe is known to cricket audiences as a popular and amusing broadcaster, and as a veteran of the Chappell era, which is to say he is a potential publishing gold mine. Anecdotes of boozy larrikinism among hairy-chested cricket superstars of yesteryear play well in the Australian market. Readers just can't seem to get enough of how much Doug Walters could put away. Much gold has been spun from such accounts, and we might have expected a title such as *Kerry has the Last Laugh*.

Instead O'Keeffe gives a beer-flecked survivor's tale, with many references to benders with Walters and ten of the first 14 chapters ending in exclamation marks! But it's an affecting story, the confidential monologue of a good-humoured, intense man who after his retirement in 1981 came undone. He had no real mates from his playing days, he drank heavily – with people who like himself preferred drink to company – he was in and out of work, he gambled and was all but lost, slumped in a job as a security guard, before he met his wife Veronica. With her support he dropped the grog, or lowered the dosage, and with the occasional media gig putting a gust in his sails, navigated a way back. O'Keeffe redux: broadcaster, panellist, after-dinner speaker, "the bloke with the laugh". Enormously grateful to have found the shore after two decades he tells us with tap-running candour what filled his mind in the lonely dark of his absence – regret, mostly.

O'Keeffe wishes he'd made more of his opportunity as a cricketer. He was too "addicted" to the game; he wishes he'd sought a mentor, that he'd left the game with real friends. Two brief chapters report his reuniting with Dennis Lillee and David Hookes, abrasive characters who in their playing days overwhelmed the shy O'Keeffe. Their friendliness now was bittersweet. Where had it been back then? What did it mean now? And he regrets spending so much time drinking, even if it provides the anecdote about going with Walters and Rod Marsh on a brewery tour on the eve of his recall against Pakistan in 1976-77. "The brew is outstanding, all 24 pots of it. I'm assisted to the taxi at 11pm – I can't scratch myself, my return to Test match cricket is hours away and I'm lapsing into a yeast-induced coma. I wake up in the same clothes I visited the brewery in. At 9am, with no breakfast, I rush to the Adelaide Oval."

A few hours after waking, O'Keeffe is standing in a daze at gully when a cut from Zaheer Abbas crashes into him. He drops it. "I was lucky to get a chest on it." Self-deprecation can be overdone. The best reading comes when he's not looking to crack us up with his sheer uselessness. We believe O'Keeffe when he speaks of the "the fun years" playing third grade as a 15-year-old for St George and we feel him absorb the words of Bill O'Reilly: "If they tell you that you're bowling too quickly thank them for their advice and forget it immediately." If he winces at the memory of his obsessive bowling at a stump, in the dark, his account also reverberates with quiet admiration for how it paid off.

O'Keeffe's retelling of his performance for NSW against Ray Illingworth's tourists, in the lead-up to his Test debut at the MCG against England in 1970-71, is gripping. "The third day of the match was my day. Heavy cloud cover and a wearing surface are two valuable assets to a slow bowler who relies on sleight of hand. Almost at once the great Colin Cowdrey misread my off-break. Shoulders ... arms ... and the ball snapped back to remove the off-bail. I was euphoric."

Glory days, recalled with restrained pride – he was good enough. So too was Darren Lehmann, although it took long enough to prove it to the world. As Dean Jones (*One-Day Magic*), Michael Bevan (*The Best of Bevan*) and now Lehmann could tell you, the one thing you don't want to do upon finally establishing camp atop the cricketing mountain is to publish a book about the view. No sooner had Lehmann written "I finally felt I belonged in the Australian cricket team" on the final page of **Worth The Wait** (Hardie Grant, $35) than he was dropped.

Lehmann did it tough. An extraordinary talent, he was spotted early, cast aside, and returned a decade later to twinkle in his twilight. He played in two World Cup-winning teams and took a vital role in Australia's "last frontier" victory in India. He batted as if he enjoyed his talent and at his best he appeared as thrilled by it as the rest of us. In a team heavy with strokeplayers, he proved his value in other ways, not just by bowling tight darts when it counted, and he was worth his weight on and off the field. "No nonsense ... common sense ... a good one-liner ... every team could do with Darren in its line-up," wrote Ricky Ponting in his introduction. "One of the funniest, most enjoyable team-mates I've played with," said Adam Gilchrist in his. It's not hard to imagine and the Lehmann of *Worth the Wait* is easy to warm to. He was endearingly stoked to discover being a member of the Australian team opened doors: well, it allowed him to jump a nightclub queue with Merv

> "No sooner had Lehmann written 'I finally felt I belonged in the Australian cricket team' than he was dropped"

Hughes, or drink beer with Russell Crowe. It seems enough for Lehmann to forget being so long on the outer.

Elsewhere there are the scandals. His love for and pain over the loss of David Hookes; Warne weeping when addressing his team-mates in South Africa about the banned diuretics tablet; and the one big blot on the Lehmann landscape – the "two words" that almost cost him his career. Lehmann is still grumpy about his public chastisement for yelling out "black c****" upon leaving the field after his run-out against Sri Lanka in a one-dayer in January 2003. He admits he was wrong, but – given he admitted it, apologised in person, and took his bollocking from Clive Lloyd, the match referee – he's still scratching his scalp about why the ICC stepped in and suspended him. Lehmann is convinced an emotional situation was poorly handled, which seems a bit rich. Cricket pushes players to the edges and sometimes over them. Even so, the battle is best fought to its limits. There are signs that deep down, and not too deep, we probably like it that way. Baum quotes Waugh: "I don't think anyone – players, officials or spectators – wants the sport at the highest level to be placid or friendly ... No one needs abuse, but the game is about two sides confronting each other in a test of skill, courage and will."

Cricket has never been only a crucible of goodwill. Animosity will, indeed must, arise. As Orwell asks in *The Sporting Spirit*: "How could it be otherwise? I am always amazed when I hear people saying that sport creates goodwill between the nations, and that if only the common peoples of the world could meet one another at football or cricket, they would have no inclination to meet on the battlefield. You play to win, and the game has little meaning unless you do your utmost to win. On the village green, where you pick up sides and no feeling of local patriotism is involved, it is possible to play simply for the fun and exercise: but as soon as the question of prestige arises, as soon as you feel that you and some larger unit will be disgraced if you lose, the most savage combative instincts are aroused ... At the international level sport is frankly mimic warfare." As for Waugh? A cactus needs its prickles.

Matt Buchanan is a journalist at the Sydney Morning Herald.

Lights, camera, action

by JOHN COOMBER

Not so long ago, playing cricket for Australia served as a decent preparation for a career as a cigarette company representative or serving behind the counter of a sporting goods shop. Time spent beneath the baggy green was a precious diversion from the rigours of real life. But it didn't make you much money and when the bones began to creak and the selectors decided enough was too much, a bleak future beckoned. Cricketers whose ambitions reached beyond the dressing-room door found themselves having to get out of the game early so they could get on with the rest of their lives and build a career for themselves outside cricket. Others bumbled along for as long as they could and either became coaches or disappeared from view and had to cope with what former Foreign Minister Gareth Evans called "relevance deprivation syndrome".

These days the career path is much clearer – play as many Tests and one-day internationals as you can and then join the media. And many do, not as fumbling amateurs, but as ready-made presenters with polished communication skills to complement the cricketing knowledge and insight they bring to the job. This doesn't happen by accident, for throughout their playing days, media coaching has gone hand in hand with net practice and fielding drills. They will have attended regular briefings and media training sessions as a condition of their contracts with Cricket Australia.

If a player has scored a century or taken a bagful of wickets in a match, he knows his job is only half done. Success on the field also means he has to front up and be the "talent" at post-match media conferences. Before he faces the cameras and microphones, a professional media coach will have sat down with him, gone through the questions he might be asked, and discussed the type of things he might say. Mostly this will be fairly informal, but if there are other issues in the air, the coaching will be quite specific. He will be warned of likely questions on subjects such as politics (do you think it is morally defensible to be touring Zimbabwe?) or his personal life (how has your marriage break-up affected your ability to concentrate on bowling?). Long-time team members become very skilled at it. Senior players like Ricky Ponting, Adam Gilchrist, Glenn McGrath and Shane Warne are all at ease in front of the camera. Indeed Warne was being groomed for a television career until his serial off-field transgressions became too much for Kerry Packer's Channel Nine, which terminated his contract.

"Australian Test cricketers end up with so much media experience they would be qualified to set themselves up in a media consulting business," says Peter Young, Cricket Australia's general manager of public affairs. CA recognises that a great part of its responsibility in administering Australia's favourite game is in smoothing the wrinkles between what happens on the field and how people watch it, listen to it and read about it. Although Australia remains one of the few cricketing countries that can fill grounds for Test matches, gate receipts are an increasingly small part of the business. The financial strength of the game lies in its marketability in newspapers, magazines, on radio, on websites and mobile phones, and, most crucially, on television. This is reflected in Cricket Australia's balance sheet, which shows that 86 per cent of its revenue comes from the sale of media rights and the endorsements and sponsorship which hang from it.

"Public interest in the game, which is fuelled by media coverage, is one of Australian cricket's strongest assets," says CA chief executive James Sutherland. "It helps attract kids into the game and it encourages many to stay on as players. It also keeps our fans informed and excited. Cricket Australia recognises the public as the game's ultimate owner, and the role Australian and visiting international media play in helping to satisfy and stimulate the public's appetite for cricket."

CA, however, finds itself needing to strike a balance between promoting the game and safeguarding the intellectual property which is its primary asset. More than 1,000 people are accredited to cover cricket matches in Australia each season, and all are required to sign complex legalistic documents setting out what they can and can't do in the course of carrying out their duties. Most of the accreditations are for the myriad of people required to produce the live television pictures that are the game's lifeblood.

Television is also the lifeblood of the retired players who now have almost exclusive domain over the commentary boxes. You could have made a couple of handy teams from the ex-players who described the 2005 Ashes series for SBS and Fox Sports, among them Paul Allott, Greg Blewett, Ian Botham, Geoff Boycott, Mark Waugh, Brendon Julian, Michael Holding, Bob Willis, Nasser Hussain, David Lloyd, Allan Border, Richie Benaud, Mike Atherton, Tony Greig, Darren Lehmann, Greg Matthews and Dean Jones.

Cricket Australia's balance sheet shows that 86% of its revenue comes from the sale of media rights and the endorsements and sponsorship which hang from it.

Most are pretty good at what they do. The Godfather, Richie Benaud, has been outstanding for 40 years but cannot go on for much longer. Like Brian Lara's batting and Shane Warne's bowling, Benaud's commentary should be treasured for as long as we have it, because it will soon be gone, and in Australia there is no heir apparent.

The English seem far better at it. Boycott, a byword for dreariness as a willow-wielder, brings the same acuteness and professionalism to the microphone but adds a puckishness that was seldom evident in his batting. Botham has almost gone the other way. The larrikin all-rounder has become rather headmasterly in his analysis. And it is always a delight to listen to the rich Jamaican tones of Michael Holding. Like his bowling, the delivery is smooth and deadly.

The Ashes series of 2005, which by the third Test had stamped itself as one of the great contests in the game's history, proved a nice little earner for SBS television. The multicultural channel normally attracts a minuscule viewing audience, but serendipitously picked up free-to-air rights when Channel Nine decided rugby league was more important than the Ashes. Even then it took a little arm-twisting from the federal government. However the decision was arrived at, SBS head of sport Les Murray could scarcely contain his glee as the series unfolded and his battling network recorded unheard-of ratings in prime time. Advertisers jumped happily aboard and viewers without cable television found SBS's coverage from Channel Four in England a welcome change from the Channel Nine formula with its relentless plugging of tacky memorabilia.

The only blot on the SBS coverage was missing Glenn McGrath's 500th Test wicket at Lord's – SBS was showing the Tour de France at the time. It wasn't the first to botch a live television coverage. The previous year Nine copped flak from just about everyone including the Prime Minister for missing Warne's world wicket-taking record against Sri Lanka in Cairns, having switched to a mindless game show called *The Price is Right*. Thirty-five years ago, when tele-vised cricket was in its infancy, Aunty ABC fluffed the chance of showing a peachy-faced youth called Greg Chappell score a hun-dred in his Test debut against England in Perth. When he was in the late nineties they switched in at least one state to a pre-news pro-gramme about the price of fruit and vegetables.

One of cricket's enduring charms is live radio commentary. You have to be of a certain age to know the joy of lying awake at night with the ear pressed to the transistor secretly listening to John Arlott and Alan McGilvray when that was the only way you could follow an Ashes series in England. Radio pictures rely on the skill of the broadcaster to fill the blank spots in your mind, and good ones can bring the game alive in your imagination so that sometimes it is better to listen than to watch. The format has not changed much – ball-by-ball commentator to give you the basic information and "expert" to interpret it for you.

In Australia we are well served by the ABC radio team, led by the estimable Jim Maxwell, who never played first-class cricket but is getting on towards becoming an institution. Jim's voice doesn't have the treacly warmth of his mentor McGilvray (which is a mercy, as McGilvray's vocal cords were lubricated by lots of Scotch whisky and the residue of countless unfiltered cigarettes) but he is accurate and insightful. He also knows how to play straight man to Kerry O'Keeffe, who is the best thing to happen to sports radio commentary in a long while.

If there are rules about broadcasting cricket on the radio, O'Keeffe probably breaks all of them. None of which matters a fig. His store of material appears bottomless. He's even worth listening to when the game is there in front of you. It's a treat to sit in the Noble Stand at the Sydney Cricket Ground and become part of the live studio audience for O'Keeffe's radio gigs. This is the meeting place for serious cricket geeks who queue from dawn to secure favoured seats behind the bowler's arm. The whole stand rocks with laughter to O'Keeffe's gags, and the feeling of community is infectious. O'Keeffe gets away with it because he also has a deep knowledge of the game and a gift for picking trends in play before anyone else.

O'Keeffe finds himself thrust into the role of celebrity, which puzzles and delights him in equal measure. That is part of his charm. He's a star who is constantly in demand for sporting dinners, breakfasts and panel discussions, but he doesn't take himself seriously. In a studio discussion during the recent Ashes series O'Keeffe found himself on a panel with Johanna Griggs, the former swimmer and Channel Seven personality. O'Keeffe was clearly mesmerised by the strikingly attractive Griggs, and when she asked him a slightly complex question he found his mind had wandered from the subject. Rather than try to bluster his way through, O'Keeffe simply stated the truth. "I'm sorry, I lost you there," he said. "I was perving on you." Griggs blushed deeply and for the remainder of the show no one could finish a sentence without giggling. It brought to mind Brian Johnston's classic "The bowler's Holding, the batsman's Willey", after which no one could speak for the better part of an hour.

O'Keeffe's erstwhile team-mate Kim Hughes is cutting a niche for himself as an expert commentator who is not afraid to speak his mind. At one stage he found himself getting tetchy with the ABC's exhaustively pedantic Glenn Mitchell, who questioned the former Test captain's interpretation of a passage of play. "Well, I'm the expert, and I'm giving my expert opinion. That's what I'm paid to do," he snapped. It would have made great television.

John Coomber has been writing about Australian and international cricket for more than 30 years. He is a senior sports writer with AAP.

CRICKET PEOPLE, 2004-05

After stumps are drawn

by ASHLEY MALLETT

Like the great Don Tallon before him, **Ian Healy** was simply the best of his time as his country's keeper. Healy has gone on to a diverse range of activities since he hung up his gloves. Outside his role as a key Channel Nine commentator, Healy is a partner in the Greg Chappell Cricket Centre chain in Australia. The centre has six retail outlets. He is also a partner in a series of Handwash Cafes (car-washing, that is) and is patron for three charities: Retina Australia, Save the Children and Arthritis Australia.

The great Test all-rounder **Alan Davidson** was the New South Wales Cricket Association president for 33 years, but his involvement outside cricket has always been with the Sport of Kings. Davidson used to help out with Colin Hayes's horses long before Hayes became a champion trainer. Now Davidson is a member of the Integrity and Assurance Committee of Racing NSW, a board responsible for all integrity issues: stewards, swabbing, laboratory and drug agencies. He is also a member of a three-man committee of the Country Racing Development Board, which decides where money is spent on every racetrack in NSW.

Tim May has maintained a high profile since his retirement as a South Australian and Test off-spinner. Since 1997 he has been the chief executive of the Australian Cricketers' Association and in 2001 he became the joint chief executive of the Federation of International Cricketers' Associations. In 2003, he became sole chief executive of that body. In July 2005, May resigned from the ACA, but he intends to continue as a consultant "from time to time". May and his family now live in Austin, Texas.

Former Victorian and Test left-arm spinner **Ray Bright**, who recently threw his hat into the ring for a Test selector's job after Allan Border stepped down, works as a storeman and packer for South-Eastern Office Supplies in Melbourne. Bright, a Victorian selector, also coaches with the Bushrangers, and is a national youth team selector looking forward to the Under-19 World Cup in Malaysia in 2006.

Peter Sleep, South Australian and Test all-rounder, follows the sun these days. Sleep and his wife Hazel run The Wickets Inn, a pub in Lancashire. He spends the northern summer there, then flies to his Australian summer home near Yahl in the south-east of South Australia. Champion Aussie Rules footballer and Western Australian opening batsman **Derek Chadwick** continues to coach the summer term at Tonbridge School in Kent.

Former WA and SA wicket-keeper **Dennis Yagmich**, who grew up in WA's wine-growing region of Swan Valley, is an accountant by profession, but lately he has been producing good reds and whites under the Yagmich label. It is little wonder wine has come into the Yagmich equation, for years ago he used to keep to the leg-breaks and wrong'uns of **Tony Mann** on the verandah of his parents' home in Middle Swan. Tony's father Jack was the driving force at Houghton Wines for 51 years and the wine-maker who created the famous Houghton White Burgundy in 1937. Jack's eldest son Dorham has carried on the family's wine tradition; the Mann family believes in good wine, leg-spin, good fielding and big hitting. Dorham Mann, a good club cricketer with Midland-Guildford back in the days of Keith Slater, Kevin Gartrell, Barry Richards and Norm O'Neill, gave the ball an almighty thump.

Former WA and Test opening batsman **Graeme Wood** has been with Carlton & United Beverages since 1989. He is now in sales and marketing with GM Multi Beverage Sales, based in Perth. Wood is a member of the WACA Board and is one of four vice-presidents. He has been a member of the State Cricket Committee for the past four years and he is a WA representative on the Cricket Australia Game Development Committee.

Jim Higgs, the best Australian leg-spinner between Richie Benaud and Shane Warne, is Richmond's representative with Cricket Victoria and he co-runs what he calls a "boutique transport engineering consulting practice", supplying transport planning, traffic engineering and urban planning design services to government and private sector land developers. He has offices in Melbourne, Sydney, Brisbane and the Gold Coast. Higgs took 66 wickets in 23 Tests, and holds the record for not scoring a run on an Australian tour of England. Higgs faced only one ball on the 1975 tour, from Ray Illingworth, which hit the middle of his bat and spun back to hit the stumps. Higgs was outdone by **Sundown**, a member of the 1868 Australian tour of England (our first international sporting tour), who scored one run on that tour. It turned out that Sundown's run tally was a personal best – he never before (or since) scored a run in his life. Surely he was the hero of the legend: "He scored only one run in the first innings, but wasn't quite so successful in the second."

Troy Cooley, a fast bowler for Tasmania in the 1980s and 1990s, left the Australian Cricket Academy to take on a coaching role with the ECB National Academy, and for the past couple of seasons has been the England cricket team's bowling coach. Cooley worked hard to get paceman Steve Harmison to his peak after a poor Ashes series in 2002-03. Champion Test wicket-keeper **Rod Marsh** has ended his association with the Academy in England. He is now settling down to a more sedate lifestyle in Adelaide, where he can relax and play golf. No doubt state cricket officials will be seeking his coaching expertise in a consulting role.

Former Cricket Australia administrator **Richard Watson** spends his time painting these days; not Dulux on the walls and ceiling, but landscapes on canvas in watercolours and oils.

SACA president **Ian McLachlan**, who played for SA and was 12th man in one Test in the early 1960s, has been embroiled in an international battle with the People for Ethical Treatment

Rod Marsh, now a hero in England, too, with Adam Gilchrist.

Hamish Blair/Getty Images

of Animals (PETA). McLachlan, who as National Farmers' Federation president fought a successful battle for farmers against meat-worker picketers over live sheep exports in the late 1970s, is now the chairman of the Australian Wool Innovation group. PETA is against the practice of mulesing, the clearing of crinkly-skinned sheep rumps to guard against fly-strike. PETA considers mulesing to be a cruel practice, and threatens to boycott retail sales of woollen products in Australia unless mulesing is stopped.

Former SA fast bowler **Wayne Prior**, a more laid-back character than Graham McKenzie, runs a farm near Mount Pleasant in SA, not far from Yalumba Winery where he works as a storeman. Prior is also a dab hand at shearing, and does the odd small mob around the sheds in the Barossa Valley.

SA batsman **Chris Davies**, who has battled cystic fibrosis all his life and was forced to retire from cricket last summer due to a recurring arm injury, now works with BankWest, making money for his employer instead of runs for his state. Davies scored two first-class centuries for SA in a total of 1,266 runs at an average of 28.13. He was in the Australian Under-19s in 1997-98. Davies, 26, embodies all the good attributes of a professional sportsperson: dedicated, enthusiastic, polite, determined.

Cricket is full of unsung heroes. One is **Dr Donald Beard**, former fast bowler with Sturt in Adelaide and the SACA's medical officer for more years than the locusts have eaten. The Doc served in field hospitals in Korea and Vietnam. He was just about to turn 80 when he put away his scalpel and took up lawn bowls at Adelaide Oval. He was awarded the Order of Australia (Military) in 1986 and has been a great and valued friend of cricket.

Barry Curtin, a middle-order batsman for SA in the 1970s, sells cars and in his spare time promotes the Port Adelaide Football Club, as a frontman on the microphone at home game functions.

The effervescent Greg Matthews, at 45, still straps on his pads in Sydney grade cricket, and scored the winning run in this year's final. As Sydney University's high performance manager for men and women cricketers, Matthews continues to give back to the game he loves with a passion. He can be heard on Saturday mornings on "Dead-Set Legends" with Ray Warren on Triple M and is still a front man for Advance Hair, "yeah, yeah". His promotional work takes him to Vietnam and India. The opportunity to comment on the Ashes series with SBS TV was a highlight of Matthews' media life, and he continues to fit in work with Australian Financial Investments Group, among whose affiliates are Wizard Home Loans. The indefatigable old off-spinner also does the odd speaking gig. Matthews yearns for a return to the Australian Cricketers' Association executive.

Ian Craig, the NSW batsman who made the first of his two England tours at the age of 17 in 1953 and subsequently captained Australia at the age of 22, was on the SCG Trust in two stints over 18 years, then spent three years on the NSW Cricket Board in the late 1990s. He has been chairman of the Bradman Museum in Bowral for the past four years.

International umpire **Steve Davis** divides his time between umpiring Tests and first-class cricket and as a human resource consultant with Mercer, a component of Marsh & McLennan companies. Davis advises companies on what they should be paying employees.

Former Perth cricketer and Oxford University left-arm spinner **Rod Eddington** has been a man of flight since the days when he played first-class cricket in England. Once chief executive of Cathay Pacific, then Ansett Airlines, Eddington is the boss of British Airways. He has had a tough job, with the crash of the Concorde in France, the terrorist threat and the SARS epidemic. A highlight of his first-class career was to clean bowl Tony Greig. Also playing for Oxford against Sussex that day in 1975 were Imran Khan, Vic Marks and Chris Tavare. In Melbourne in 1993 Eddington convened a seminar on the state of spin bowling in Australia.

Every two years, cricket identity **Swan Richards** takes his Crusaders team to England. This year, Peter Sleep and Ian Frazer were the captains of a team which included a lot of old hands, among them business guru and cricket lover **Sir Ron Brierley**, a great benefactor of cricket in Australia and New Zealand and a leading contributor to the funding of the Bradman Museum. It was Sir Ron and another high-profile businessman, **Basil Sellers**, brother of ex-SA and Test spinner Rex Sellers, who ploughed in the lion's share of funding for the Museum. This was Swan Richards's ninth Crusaders tour of England, and the highlight of the trip was again a black-tie dinner with Queen Elizabeth II at Windsor Castle.

Former fiery Victorian fast bowler **Nigel Murch**, now 61, has finally called it a day as marketing manager for Puma in Melbourne. The unstinting Queensland opening batsman **Sam Trimble**, at the age of 71, is still head groundsman at Souths Cricket Club in Brisbane.

Ashley Mallett, an off-spinner, played 39 Tests for Australia between 1968 and 1980. He now coaches young spinners and has written a biography of Ian Chappell.

CRICKET MEMORABILIA, 2004-05

Making the cap fit

by STEPHEN W. GIBBS

All the talk was about provenance and ownership of Steve Waugh's baggy green Australia Test cap, and the saga that ensued. The vendor said it was his, and Waugh said it wasn't the vendor's to sell. The vendor said Waugh had given him this baggy green in the WACA dressing room. It ended with the item being withdrawn from the Charles Leski auction in May 2005. But second and third prize, Waugh's 1994-95 Test batting helmet and his "baggy yellow" ODI cap, were sold for $5,500 and $4,250 respectively.

Other baggy greens came tumbling out of wardrobes and bottoms of drawers. Caps belonging to Neil Harvey ($18,000), Ray Lindwall ($23,000), Kim Hughes ($7,000) and Richie Benaud's 1953 version ($22,000) were well received. Another Benaud cap, from 1963-64, together with his 1963-64 Test blazer and the 1963-64 Test cap and blazer of South African Eddie Barlow, realised $42,000. Charles Leski said it was the first time that rival players' gear had been sold as one item.

Some predictably high prices were paid at auctions conducted by Lawson-Menzies. Bradman's 1946-47 cap sold for $95,000 and Trumper's 1907 cap made $83,000. As a comparison in value, Berkelouw Books of Berrima in NSW in April 2005 offered the *Wisden Cricketers' Almanack* editions 1864 to 1996 uniformly bound in quarter calf with original wrappers for $35,000.

An emerging area of niche collecting is items relating to the conduct of the game. Victorian Ben Barnett's signed contract for the 1934 tour of England sold, with three lesser value items, for $1,250. Barnett went as reserve keeper on this tour; it would be interesting to compare his contract to some of those for the 2005 Ashes tour.

Modern limited editions need to be approached cautiously if the primary motivation is capital appreciation. A proven modern collecting icon is Steve Waugh. A revealing example promoted by Legends Genuine Memorabilia was the release of "Recollections of Waugh" – an edition of 168 bats, each a faithful replica of the one used by Steve in the corresponding Test match. From the Symonds Power Deluxe (Test No. 1) to the MRF Conqueror (Test 168) and everything in between, including the famous blank blades, the bats were reproduced right down to the detail of correct stickers and grip colour. Waugh wrote his personal recollections of each Test and these words accompanied the signed bats, essentially making each numbered edition unique. At $3,500 per bat, all were sold within five weeks of their release, grossing $588,000!

TOP 10 SELLERS OF 2004-05

1	Don Bradman's 1946-47 cap	$95,000
2	Victor Trumper's 1907 cap	$83,000
3	Don Bradman's 1946-47 bat	$67,500
4	Richie Benaud's 1963-64 cap, 1963-64 Test blazer and Eddie Barlow's blazer	$42,000
5	*Wisden Cricketers' Almanack* editions 1864 to 1996 in original wrappers	$35,000
6	Victor Trumper's 1909 Test bat	$35,000
7	Victor Trumper's 1907 cricket bat	$26,000
8	Ray Lindwall's cap	$23,000
9	Richie Benaud's 1953 cap	$22,000
10	Neil Harvey's cap	$18,000

Note: all auction prices quoted are before the payment of the buyer's premium and any GST.

Several new cricket collectables were introduced by Legends Genuine Memorabilia during the 2004-05 season, including Champs – a range of limited edition caricature figurines (Steve Waugh and Shane Warne the first two) – and a limited edition ceramic cricket ball with the facsimile signatures of the Australian Test team. Through the medium of television promotion, they represented an attainable entry level for new collectors and proved very popular.

Non-print cricket items are always attractive, providing a feel of the style and fashion of past eras. A Royal Worcester plate featuring the 1938 Australian team sold at Charles Leski in September 2004 for $1,150 and a similar plate celebrating the 1953 team to England sold for $750 through the same auction house. A modern Bradman caricature Bendigo pottery piece represented value at $320. An original painting, of the Don by Alan Fearnley, commissioned in 1986 and signed by artist and subject, realised $7,250.

Bats and balls, the essential implements of the game, regularly appeared during the auction year. Trumper's Test bat from 1909 fetched $35,000 and Bradman's bat used during his fifth-wicket Test partnership of 405 with Sid Barnes in 1946-47 realised $67,500 at the du Plessis auction in Adelaide in May 2005. At the same auction, the ball with which Clarrie Grimmett achieved his 100th Test wicket against England at The Oval in 1934 went for $8,000.

Lawson-Menzies auctions during the year saw $5,400 accepted for Ray Lindwall's trophy cricket ball with which he took 6 for 20 in the 1948 Test at The Oval; Bill Whitty's bat signed by the 1909 Australians made $5,200; a Bodyline series bat owned by Bert Oldfield realised $5,200; and Victor Trumper's 1907 match-used cricket bat sold for $26,000 in December 2004. Charles Leski offered a Benson & Hedges limited edition, one of 250, full-sized bat celebrating the 1977 Centenary Test in Melbourne with 30 signatures. It sold for $850.

The eyes of phillumenists attending the Cromwell's auction in Sydney in November 2004 lit up when two Bradman matchbox labels were offered. The G.F. Duncan & Co labels, produced in Melbourne in 1938, made $55 and $60. Is there no end to Bradmania? A very nice set of Griffith Brothers metal cricket badges, a part-set of ten of 14 issued during the 1929-30 season, featuring the Australian team, made $1,350. Four of the badges were additions to the 14 previously described as comprising the complete set.

Autograph material is always an anticipated feature of auctions. Charles Leski at auction in June 2005 offered a Jack Marsh (pencil) signature. It sold for $575. The signatures of 13 Australian players of the 1912 team realised $1,550. The autographs of 12 Australians who played in the 1910-11 series against the South Africans made $2,800 and a 1930 Australian group of sepia head-and-shoulder signed photographs reached $6,000. The perennially popular and highly prized Trumper signature, on a panel photograph by Bolland taken during the 1909 tour to England, made $3,700. A more modern offering related to the 1956-57 Australian team to New Zealand captained by Ian Craig. A photograph of the players in civilian clothes fully signed was sold by Lawson-Menzies for $1,400 in June 2005.

Collector cards are an accessible and appreciating part of the cricket memorabilia market. A set of the 1986 Scanlan "Clashes for the Ashes" cards offered by Charles Leski reached $200. Australian cricketers, including Bradman, featured in trade cards produced by Griffith Brothers in 1938, realised $425 in an almost complete (nine of 11 cards) set of the Black Crow Cough Drops brand; and ten of the set of 11 cards of the Cruising Coffee brand issued by the same company made $340.

Some items of special interest that went beyond their estimate included the 24-page match program for the Scotland v Australia game at the end of the 1948 tour, estimate $800 to $1,000, selling for $1,450; the program for the "Test Match: England (RAF) v Australia (RAAF)" played at New Delhi on November 25 and 26, 1944, estimate $100 to $150, sold for $240; and an invitation to Don Bradman's wedding on April 30, 1932, at Burwood in Sydney, after a fevered battle between two collectors, reached $5,000 on an estimate of $500 to $600.

The cricket memorabilia market in Australia is healthy and collectors are enjoying a wide variety of venues and opportunities to acquire pieces. The achievements of the current Australian team seem certain to acquire a collecting attraction to rival the 1921 and 1948 teams, and the heroes of the Trumper era – so astute purchases are now in order.

Stephen W. Gibbs is a cricket bibliographer, an indexer of cricket references and a player in the over-40s competition in Sydney.

Fixtures, 2005-06

CRICKET
AUSTRALIA

WEST INDIES, SOUTH AFRICA AND
SRI LANKA IN AUSTRALIA

2005-06 INTERNATIONAL SEASON

TOUR MATCHES

October 5	Australia v Rest of the World (day/night)	Melbourne TD
October 7	Australia v Rest of the World (day/night)	Melbourne TD
October 9	Australia v Rest of the World (day/night)	Melbourne TD
October 14-19	Australia v Rest of World	Sydney
October 27-30	Queensland v West Indians	Brisbane

3 MOBILE TESTS

November 3-7	Australia v West Indies (1st Test)	Brisbane
November 11-13	Victoria v West Indians	Melbourne MCG
November 17-21	Australia v West Indies (2nd Test)	Hobart
November 25-29	Australia v West Indies (3rd Test)	Adelaide
December 11-14	Western Australia v South Africans	Perth
December 16-20	Australia v South Africa (1st Test)	Perth
December 26-30	Australia v South Africa (2nd Test)	Melbourne MCG
January 2-6	Australia v South Africa (3rd Test)	Sydney

| **January 9** | Australia v South Africa (Twenty20) | Brisbane |

| **January 10** | Queensland v South Africans | Brisbane |
| **January 11** | Victoria v Sri Lankans | Melbourne |

VB SERIES

January 13	Australia v Sri Lanka (day/night)	Melbourne TD
January 13	Queensland Academy of Sport v South Africans	Albion
January 15	Australia v South Africa (day/night)	Brisbane
January 17	South Africa v Sri Lanka (day/night)	Brisbane
January 20	Australia v South Africa (day/night)	Melbourne TD
January 22	Australia v Sri Lanka (day/night)	Sydney
January 24	South Africa v Sri Lanka (day/night)	Adelaide
January 26	Australia v Sri Lanka (day/night)	Adelaide
January 27	Prime Minister's XI v South Africans	Canberra
January 29	Australia v Sri Lanka	Perth
January 31	South Africa v Sri Lanka (day/night)	Perth
February 3	Australia v South Africa (day/night)	Melbourne TD
February 5	Australia v South Africa (day/night)	Sydney
February 7	South Africa v Sri Lanka	Hobart
February 10	First Final (day/night)	Adelaide
February 12	Second Final (day/night)	Sydney
February 14	Third Final (day/night) (if required)	Brisbane

AUSTRALIA IN SOUTH AFRICA, 2005-06

February, March   Dates to be confirmed.

AUSTRALIA IN BANGLADESH, 2005-06

April   Dates to be confirmed.

PURA CUP

October 17-20	Queensland v Tasmania	Brisbane
October 18-21	Western Australia v Victoria	Perth
October 25-28	New South Wales v South Australia	Sydney
November 4-7	Tasmania v Victoria	Hobart
November 6-9	South Australia v Queensland	Adelaide
November 6-9	Western Australia v New South Wales	Perth
November 14-17	South Australia v Western Australia	Adelaide
November 18-21	Queensland v Victoria	Brisbane
November 18-21	New South Wales v Tasmania	Sydney
November 26-29	New South Wales v Queensland	Sydney
November 26-29	Victoria v South Australia	St Kilda
November 27-30	Western Australia v Tasmania	Perth
December 6-9	Victoria v New South Wales	St Kilda
December 12-15	Tasmania v South Australia	Hobart
December 17-20	Queensland v Western Australia	Brisbane
January 15-18	Western Australia v Queensland	Perth
January 16-19	New South Wales v Victoria	Lismore
January 16-19	South Australia v Tasmania	Adelaide
February 1-4	Tasmania v Western Australia	Hobart
February 2-5	Queensland v New South Wales	Brisbane
February 2- 5	South Australia v Victoria	Adelaide
February 13-16	Victoria v Tasmania	St Kilda
February 14-17	New South Wales v Western Australia	Sydney
February 19-22	Queensland v South Australia	Brisbane
March 2-5	Victoria v Queensland	St Kilda
March 2-5	Tasmania v New South Wales	Hobart
March 2-5	Western Australia v South Australia	Perth
March 10-13	Victoria v Western Australia	St Kilda
March 10-13	Tasmania v Queensland	Hobart
March 10-13	South Australia v New South Wales	Adelaide
March 24-28	Final	T.B.A.

ING CUP

October 14	Queensland v New South Wales (day/night)	Brisbane
October 22	Queensland v Tasmania (day/night)	Brisbane
October 23	New South Wales v Tasmania	North Sydney
October 23	Western Australia v Victoria	Perth
October 29	Victoria v Western Australia	St Kilda
October 30	New South Wales v Tasmania	Sydney
November 4	South Australia v Queensland (day/night)	Adelaide
November 4	Western Australia v New South Wales (day/night)	Perth
November 12	South Australia v Western Australia	Adelaide
November 13	New South Wales v Queensland	Sydney
November 25	Western Australia v Tasmania (day/night)	Perth
December 3	Victoria v South Australia	St Kilda
December 10	Tasmania v South Australia	Hobart
December 11	Victoria v Queensland	St Kilda
December 18	South Australia v New South Wales (day/night)	Adelaide
December 18	Tasmania v Victoria	T.B.A.
December 22	Queensland v Western Australia (day/night)	Brisbane
January 2	Victoria v New South Wales	Wangaratta
January 2	Tasmania v Queensland	Hobart
January 13	Western Australia v Queensland (day/night)	Perth
January 14	New South Wales v Victoria	Coffs Harbour
January 14	South Australia v Tasmania (day/night)	Adelaide
January 25	Queensland v Victoria (day/night)	Brisbane
January 25	Western Australia v South Australia (day/night)	Perth
January 25	Tasmania v New South Wales	Hobart
January 29	South Australia v Victoria (day/night)	Adelaide
January 29	Tasmania v Western Australia	T.B.A.
February 17	Queensland v South Australia (day/night)	Gabba
February 18	Victoria v Tasmania	St Kilda
February 19	New South Wales v Western Australia	Drummoyne
February 26	Final	T.B.A.

TWENTY20

January 6	Western Australia v Victoria (Pool A)	T.B.A.
January 6	Queensland v Tasmania (Pool B)	T.B.A.
January 8	Victoria v South Australia (Pool A)	T.B.A.
January 8	New South Wales v Queensland (Pool B)	T.B.A.
January 10	South Australia v Western Australia (Pool A)	T.B.A.
January 10	Tasmania v New South Wales (Pool B)	T.B.A.
January 21	Final - Winner Pool A v Winner Pool B	T.B.A.

CRICKET AUSTRALIA CUP, 2005-06

September 26-29	Qld Academy of Sport v Victoria 2nd XI	Albion
October 10-13	South Australia 2nd XI v A.C.T.	Adelaide Oval #2
October 10-13	Western Australia 2nd XI v NSW 2nd XI	Perth
November 21-24	Qld Academy of Sport v Western Australia 2nd XI	Albion
November 21-24	Tasmania 2nd XI v A.C.T.	Hobart (TCA)
December 5-8	Victoria 2nd XI v South Australia 2nd XI	Carlton
December 5-Thu 8	NSW 2nd XI v Tasmania 2nd XI	T.B.A
December 19-22	Tasmania 2nd XI v Qld Academy of Sport	Newtown
January 9-12	A.C.T. v Victoria 2nd XI	Canberra
January 9-12	NSW 2nd XI v South Australia 2nd XI	T.B.A.
January 23-26	Western Australia 2nd XI v Tasmania 2nd XI	T.B.A.
February 6-9	Victoria 2nd XI v NSW 2nd XI	T.B.A.
February 6-9	A.C.T. v Western Australia 2nd XI	Canberra
February 13-16	South Australia 2nd XI v Qld Academy of Sport	Adelaide

COMMONWEALTH BANK WOMEN'S NATIONAL CRICKET LEAGUE

November 5-6	South Australia v Queensland	Adelaide
November 19-20	Western Australia v New South Wales	WACA
November 19-20	South Australia v Victoria	Adelaide
December 3-4	New South Wales v Queensland	SCG
December 3-4	Victoria v Western Australia	Glen Waverley
December 17-18	New South Wales v South Australia	Newcastle
December 17-18	Queensland v Western Australia	AB Field
January 7-8	Victoria v New South Wales	Glen Waverley
January 21-22	Queensland v Victoria	AB Field
January 21-22	Westen Australia v South Australia	Perth
February 3	Finals Series Match 1	TBA
February 4	Finals Series Match 2	TBA
February 5	Finals Series Match 3 - If required	TBA

Note: At the time of publication all fixtures were correct. They are subject to change without notice.

Contributors

Nabila Ahmed writes on cricket for *The Age*, Melbourne.

Sambit Bal is editor of *Wisden Asia Cricket* and editor of Cricinfo in India.

John Benaud is a former Australian player, selector, journalist, editor and brother of Richie.

Martin Blake writes on sport for *The Age*, Melbourne.

Max Bonnell is the author of *How Many More Are Coming? The Short Life of Jack Marsh*.

Daniel Brettig is a journalist with AAP in Adelaide.

Alex Brown is a journalist with the *Sydney Morning Herald*.

Matt Buchanan is a journalist with the *Sydney Morning Herald*.

Jack Brown is secretary of the Wallsend Cricket Club in Newcastle.

Richard Boock is chief cricket writer for the *New Zealand Herald*.

Ken Casellas was chief cricket writer for *The West Australian* for 27 years.

Tony Charlton is a respected sports broadcaster.

Belinda Clark is the retired Australian women's cricket captain.

Lawrie Colliver is a sports reporter with 5AA in Adelaide.

Malcolm Conn is a cricket correspondent of *The Australian* newspaper.

John Coomber is a senior sports writer with Australian Associated Press (AAP).

Mike Coward is a freelance cricket journalist based in Sydney.

Robert Craddock is chief cricket writer for News Limited.

Michael Crutcher is cricket writer with *The Courier-Mail* in Brisbane.

Charles Davis is a Melbourne-based cricket writer and scientist. He writes a cricket statistics blog at www.sportstats.com.au/bloghome.html

Ben Dorries writes on cricket for *The Courier-Mail* Brisbane.

Ross Dundas is Australia's only full-time cricket statistician.

Peter English is a former assistant editor of *Inside Edge* and *Wisden Cricket Monthly*.

Ric Finlay is a Hobart statistician and that author of *Island Summers*.

Warwick Franks edited *Wisden Cricketers' Almanack Australia* from 2001-02 to 2003-04.

David Frith has written 26 books on cricket. His latest is *The Ross Gregory Story*.

Stephen W. Gibbs is a cricket bibliographer and indexer of cricket references.

Stephen Gray is media manager for Queensland Cricket.

Gideon Haigh edited *Wisden Cricketers' Almanack Australia* from 1999 to 2000-01.

Catherine Hanley is a Somerset supporter and a contributor to *Wisden* CricInfo.

Phil Wilkins is a Melbourne-based writer and the author of *Confessions of a Tragic Cricket Tragic*.

Andrew Hyde is a Darwin-based television producer.

Peter Lalor is sports writer with *The Australian*.

Tim Lane is a long-time cricket and Australian Rules commentator, now with Channel 10.

Geoff Lawson took 180 wickets in 46 Tests for Australia between 1980 and 1989.

Ashley Mallett took 132 wickets in 39 Tests for Australia between 1968 and 1980.

Trevor Marshallsea is cricket correspondent of the *Sydney Morning Herald*.

Adrian McGregor is a freelance writer and a regular commentator on news and politics with ABC radio in Brisbane.

Greg McKie is a long-time writer and statistician on Australia under-age cricket.

Glenn Mitchell is a football and cricket commentator with the ABC.

Adam Morehouse is a Canberra statistician and the author of *From Country to Comets*.

Barry Nicholls is an ABC radio presenter in Alice Springs.

Ken Piesse is the author of 28 cricket books and a former editor of *Cricketer* magazine.

Matt Price is a journalist in the Canberra press gallery who writes for *The Australian*.

Andrew Ramsey is a cricket writer with *The Australian*.

Ron Reed is senior sports writer for the *Herald Sun*, Melbourne.

Erica Sainsbury is a long-time scorer, statistician and writer about women's cricket.

Chloe Saltau is a cricket correspondent for *The Age*, Melbourne.

Terry Smith is a sports journalist with *Sunday Telegraph* in Sydney.

David Stockdale is a senior sports journalist with Hobart's *Mercury* newspaper.

Brett Stubbs is a Tasmanian cricket writer.

Warwick Torrens is a Queensland cricket historian and statistician.

John Townsend writes on cricket for *The West Australian*.

Andrew Webster, a Sydney journalist, was formerly staff feature writer of *Inside Sport*.

Phil Wilkins is a much-respected long time cricket writer, now retired.

Bernard Whimpress is curator of the SACA museum and the author of *Passport to Nowhere*.

Ken Williams is a Melbourne-based cricket writer and statistician.

PICTURE CREDITS